MOTOWN ENCYCLOPEDIA

GRAHAM BETTS

First Published by AC Publishing 2014

The moral right of Graham Betts to be identified as the author of this work has been asserted in accordance with the Copyright, Designs and Patents Act, 1988.

All rights reserved. No part of this publication may be reproduced or transmitted in any form or by any means, electronic or mechanical, including photocopy, recordings, or any information storage retrieval system, without permission in writing from the publisher.

ISBN-13: 978-1500471699
ISBN-10: 1500471690

Text copyright © Graham Betts
Cover design © Joanna Betts

INTRODUCTION

Motown means different things to different people. The mere mention of perhaps the most iconic record label in history is often enough to invoke memories and mental images of Marvin Gaye, Diana Ross, Stevie Wonder, The Temptations, The Jackson 5, The Supremes and numerous others. With each group recalled, there is an accompanying piece of music of the mind, from *Baby Love, My Girl, Signed Sealed Delivered, I Heard It Through The Grapevine, ABC* and *Tears Of A Clown* and countless more. Quite often, you can ask people what kind of music they like and they will simply answer 'Motown', and both they, and you, know exactly what is meant.

Or rather, what is implied. The Motown they are invariably thinking of is the label that dominated the charts in the mid 1960s with a succession of radio friendly, dance orientated hits, most of which were written and produced by the trio of Brian Holland, Lamont Dozier and Eddie Holland. This period is referred to, naturally enough, as the Golden Era, when Motown was not only the dominant force in its home city of Detroit but carried The Sound of Young America all around the world. The kind of music that had them Dancing In the Street from Los Angeles to London, Miami to Munich and San Francisco to Sydney. It was the kind of music that attracted scores of imitators; some good, some not so good. The kind of music that appealed to the public and presidents alike, and still does.

When I first thought up the idea of writing a Motown Encyclopedia, it was that Motown that I envisaged writing about. However, when you start digging deeper into the Motown story, you realise that throughout its life (which, for the purposes of this book, is its formation in 1959 through to its sale in 1988) it was constantly trying other musical genres, looking to grab hits out of jazz, country, pop, rock, middle of the road and whatever else might be happening at the time. Of course it wasn't particularly successful at some of the other genres, although those who claim Motown never did much in the rock market conveniently overlook the healthy sales figures achieved by Rare Earth, the group, and focus instead on the total sales achieved on Rare Earth, the label.

The same is true across the whole of Motown. For every Marvin Gaye that made it, there was a Leon Ware left by the wayside (and I don't mean to belittle Leon, an artist whose work I much admire, but who has never received the accolade his undoubted talents fully deserve). For every Little Stevie Wonder turned from a child performer into an adult star, there was a Stacie Johnson who released little. Every celebrated promotional campaign put behind The Supremes meant less in the proverbial coffers to push Celebration. A list of key Motown artists during the thirty or so years it was most active would probably run to a hundred or hundred and fifty names, yet there were nearly six hundred artists who recorded for Motown and its numerous imprints during that period. And speaking of imprints, as well as the obvious Tamla and Motown labels, there were homes for just about every conceivable musical style, including Workshop Jazz and Soul, and others intended to have an eclectic policy, such as MoWest and Miracle.

As the list of artists and labels to be featured grew, so did the realisation that you can't write about Motown's history and legacy without mentioning the executives, musicians, writers and producers who, in many cases, made it all possible. Without Holland-Dozier-Holland, there would have been no Supremes. Without Norman Whitfield, The Temptations story might have ended around about the mid 1960s, and without The Funk Brothers, there would have been no Motown Sound; they all played their part in ensuring that the Golden Era extended into the following decade and beyond. I will make no apologies for adopting a total inclusion policy when it comes to the artists or labels; if they had a record released or scheduled by Motown or its labels, then they are featured. That includes plenty who owe their appearance in this book to that fact that they had a single track on a soundtrack or compilation or were named performers on a cast recording. I've also included those labels that were distributed by Motown in America during the same period, since those records on Gull, Manticore, CTI and others would have been similarly promoted by Motown, with varying degrees of success. Also featured are several artists who had records released in Europe only, ranging from those who were signed to the British arm of MoWest and Rare Earth to those whose releases were designed to test the water, so to speak, into which category falls Lynda Carter, better known as Wonder Woman.

In addition to the who's who of Motown, I've included the hits; every single or album that reached the Top Ten in America or Britain has its own entry. The reason for selecting both is so that the respective national differences can be highlighted; *I'm Still Waiting* (Diana Ross), *It Should Have Been Me* (Yvonne Fair) and *The Onion Song* (Tammi Terrell & Marvin Gaye) made the Top Ten in the UK but stalled some way short in the US. Why is that? I have absolutely no idea, although several of the hits you will encounter owed their revived fortunes to the British phenomenon of Northern Soul.

To the who and what I've added numerous other entries that I hope will be of interest, including the singles that have received the highest airplay, the stars who have their own stars on the Hollywood Walk of Fame, the various films Motown produced and details of the very first Motortown Revues in America and Britain. In short, I hope, just about anything and everything you would want to know about Motown.

One of the problems with writing a book such as this is verifying the information contained within. Although several of the major artists have either written their own autobiographies or collaborated with others on biographies, infinitely more have not. Even those who have written their own books sometimes contradict one other. As an example, it is well known that Berry Gordy and Smokey Robinson first met when Smokey took his group, The Matadors, to audition for Jackie Wilson's manager Nat Tarnapol, with Berry in attendance as a regular writer for Jackie. Smokey and Berry both agree that Nat Tarnapol turned The Matadors down, but they disagree over the reason given, with Smokey claiming they were told they looked and sounded too much like The Platters and Berry claiming they were told to go and fashion themselves on The Platters! At least the mention of The Platters is consistent! And since logic would tend to dictate that The Matadors were too similar to The Platters, I have chosen to go with that version of the story. Similarly, several artist biographies, autobiographies and interviews contain the right facts but the wrong dates, or have forgotten that well known events actually happened to them. If only 'those who cannot remember the past are condemned to repeat it'!

So much for what is in the book; I feel I should also mention what has been left out, which for the most part is two thirds of the 'Sex And Drugs And Rock & Roll' cliché (or, if you are of an older generation, 'Wine, Women & Song'). Motown was not unlike any other record company (or probably any other American workplace for that matter, if 'Mad Men' is to be believed), with the staff and artists engaging in all manner of relationships with each other. I have chosen to only mention these where they are key to the Motown story, so Mickey Stevenson marrying Kim Weston and Mary Wells marrying Herman Griffin are mentioned, but who slept with who for the most part is not – if you want to find out more, several artists mention them in their own books. The two main exceptions to this rule are the relationships between Berry Gordy and Diana Ross, which obviously impacted on The Supremes, and David Ruffin and Tammi Terrell, which impacted on just about everyone else. During the course of research, there were numerous rumours about the sexuality of several of the artists, but for the most part, that is all they were – rumours – and so I've omitted them too. It is similar with the various tales about drug taking; Rick James made a virtual career out of his affection for marijuana, whilst David Ruffin (him again!) ruined his career (and his life) with his addictions, but whatever the rest of them got up to is not really a matter of my concern. After all, 'It's What's In The Grooves That Counts'.

Speaking of Berry Gordy and Diana Ross, both have suffered from adverse publicity of one sort or another over the years. In the case of Berry Gordy, he is invariably criticised personally by former artists for issues they may have had with Motown collectively. There have been numerous legal challenges over the years, many of which Berry ignored or dealt with outside the courts. That the majority of these centred on royalties should be of no surprise, for during the three decades plus I've been involved with the record industry, I have yet to meet an artist who didn't believe that any of their records should have gone higher in the chart or sold more than they actually did. Even when the legal challenges were at their greatest, Berry chose to remain silent. It was not until 1994 that Berry Gordy wrote his autobiography 'To Be Loved', a book that answered many of the questions that had arisen over the years but left countless more hanging in limbo. It is also far easier for sections of the media to report that Marvin Gaye criticised Berry at almost every opportunity (which they deem newsworthy), yet not print even one of Smokey Robinson or Deke Richards' utterances in Berry's support (which they don't). So let me state that if there is an implied criticism of Berry Gordy anywhere in this book, it is not intentional.

In the case of Diana Ross, many of the problems that have arisen are not of her making nor, it should said, attributable to any of the other ladies who at one time or another made up The Supremes. Instead, groups of fans have divided themselves in to camps supporting one member or another and snipe at each other across the worldwide web, despite frequent requests to cease from the very ladies they purport to back.

Over the years there have been numerous attempts at analysing Motown's success. Even during that Golden Era, other record companies would get hold of the latest Motown release and try and work out who was playing, what they were playing and then try to replicate the sound, as though it was a recipe to success. Berry Gordy merely said the Motown Sound was 'rats, roaches, soul, guts and love.' It was more than that, of course, a whole lot more. You had to have the right song, sung by the right artist, played by the right musicians and with the right producer calling the shots. Even having all of that was still not enough, for you needed the right salesmen to get the record into stores, pluggers to get it onto the radio and publicists to get the media writing or talking about the record or artist. Only when you had a synergy between all of these did you stand a chance of a hit. Fortunately, Motown had the right people in the right place at the right time to register more than fifty chart toppers on the Billboard pop chart and nearly three hundred Top Twenty hits.

We all know of the efforts the artists, writers, producers and musicians went through in order to turn those three minutes of magic into a major hit, and many of their stories are told in this book. One of the greatest stories, however, isn't; how Bob Dylan came to effusively praise Smokey Robinson, which was the creation of Motown's publicist extraordinaire Al Abrams. "One morning I received a memo from Berry reminding me that Smokey Robinson is one of our nation's greatest songwriters and I should really do something in a hurry to promote him as such in the media because he wasn't getting all the recognition he really deserved. I mentioned it to Al Aronowitz, a music writer who was also Dylan's biographer and very close friend. Al said that he had heard Dylan praise some of Smokey's lyrics as being poetical. I asked Al if he would let me get a quote from Dylan about Smokey. Al asked me what I had in mind and I suggested Smokey Robinson is America's Greatest Living Poet. Al thought about it for a minute and said, 'Why bother even telling Bob? That sounds just like something he'd say anyway. Go ahead and do it. If Bob sees it in print he'll think he said it. He's certainly never going to deny it.'"

The story has appeared in virtually *every* Smokey Robinson biography ever since and Bob Dylan has never denied it; perhaps he really did think Smokey was the greatest living poet.

If there was anyone better, then the chances are they worked at Motown; you can read all of their stories and more in the Motown Encyclopedia.

ACKNOWLEDGEMENTS

The list of people that I have to thank for helping me put together this book is almost as long as the list of entries that appear on the following pages, but simply put, this book would not have been possible without their assistance and advice along the way.

I'm especially grateful to those artists (or at least those I was able to contact) who took the time and trouble to read through their entries and suggest amendments and corrections.

There were also numerous fellow Motown writers and aficionados who read through various entries and sections and made helpful suggestions. In all, I have received an inordinate amount of assistance, all of which has made the book much better than it would have been left to my own devices! Of course, it goes without saying that any mistakes are all my own work (Speaking of which I feel I should point out that there are some differences in spelling used throughout the book - for example, the legendary venue in New York is the Apollo Theater, whilst here in London we have the Apollo Theatre, and I have used the spelling relevant to each respective territory, so 'theater' is used for American performances and 'theatre' for British ones).

Thanks therefore are due to Al Abrams, Peter Anders, Gary Anthony, Peter Benjaminson, Richard Blavaard, Janie Bradford, Trevor Churchill, Stephen Cohn, LeRoy Durbin, Guy Fletcher, Susaye Greene, Billy Griffin, Jim Honeycutt, Peter Hoorelbeke, Stacie Johnson, Frank Kavelin, Mike Konopka, Eric Le Blanc, Chris Lussier, Sherlie Matthews, Jon Miller, Lars Nilsson, Doug Payne, Steve Reed, Deke Richards, Leon Sylvers, Ralph Terrana, Greg Walker, Leon Ware, Kent Washburn and Kim Weston.

I am also extremely grateful to Steve Devereux, Paul Nixon and Karen Spreadbury for reading through the manuscript, checking for spelling and factual errors.

In addition to the numerous books mentioned in the bibliography found towards the end of the book, I should also thank the music magazines Blues & Soul, Black Music, Black Echoes, Melody Maker, Music Week, Record Mirror, Billboard, Cashbox and Record World, all of which I have referred to at some time or another in creating this book.

Finally, thank you to my daughter Joanna for the cover, and my son (Stevie) and wife (Caroline) for their assistance and support throughout.

Graham Betts
June 2014

THE ABBEY TAVERN SINGERS

In 1962 Minnie Scott-Lennon, owner of the Abbey Tavern in Howth, near Dublin in Ireland, reasoned that a group of musicians and balladeers performing at the tavern might prove popular with the punters. And so it proved, enough for The Abbey Tavern Singers to draw capacity crowds to the tavern and eventually the attention of record companies. Their first album was **The Rafters Ring At The Abbey Tavern**, issued on Pye Records in 1965, but it was the following year's **We're Off To Dublin In The Green** on ARC that broke big, with the title track appearing in a television beer commercial for Carling Breweries.

The success of this prompted a North American tour, with Motown picking up the album for release on their V.I.P. subsidiary and issuing it in February 1967. The Abbey Tavern Singers at this point consisted of Michael O'Connell (vocals), Margaret Monks (vocals), Tess Nolan (vocals), Michael Brookes (guitar and vocals), Bill Powers (banjo and mandolin), Tommy Rick (uilleann pipes), Seamus Gallagher (fiddle), Joe O'Leary (fiddle) and Paddy Joseph Downes (spoons).

Whilst this is the only album issued by the group by Motown (the title track, about the I.R.A. uprising in Dublin in 1916, was scheduled as a single in the summer of 1968 but remained unissued), the Abbey Tavern Singers continued releasing material through ARC and then their own label into the 1970s. They continue to perform at the Abbey Tavern, which is still owned by the Scott-Lennon's.

ALBUM: WE'RE OFF TO DUBLIN IN THE GREEN (1967)

ABC – THE JACKSON 5 [SINGLE]

After *I Want You Back* became a massive international hit, Berry Gordy was keen to maintain the momentum on his newest charges. To this end, Freddie Perren, Fonce Mizell and Deke Richards were instructed to come up with something equally as catchy as the Jackson 5's debut hit. Whilst this might be construed as formulaic writing, it had been a policy that had served Holland-Dozier-Holland well during their time at Motown. Thus Deke Richards looked at the chorus to *I Want You Back* and constructed a new song around it, with simplistic lyrics that were as easy as ABC to follow. Aimed at the same market as its predecessor, *ABC* took just six weeks to rise to the top of the Billboard singles chart and knock none other than The Beatles' *Let It Be* off the number one spot for the first of two weeks at the top of the pile.

Whilst Motown might have been targeting the youth market with The Jackson 5, the group and their hit retained enough of a soul feel to top the R&B charts for four weeks. In the UK the single made it into the Top Ten, peaking at #8 in June 1970. It became a hit all over again in 2009 following the death of Michael Jackson, hitting #50 in July.

ABC – THE JACKSON 5 [ALBUM]

Work on The Jackson 5's second album, **ABC** begun immediately after the session wrap-up for their first long player **Diana Ross Presents**. Indeed, so keen was Berry Gordy to get enough material in the can, Motown didn't even bother waiting to see how the singles performed, assembling material and booking recording dates confident that what they had got on tape for the first album would prove successful. This time the entire album was produced by The Corporation, the writing team of Freddie Perren, Deke Richards and Fonce Mizell with input from Hal Davis. As well as four Corporation originals (*ABC, The Love You Save, One More Chance* and *Found That Girl*), the album featured material plucked from the Jobete songbook, a favourite ploy of Motown's to ensure even more revenue flowing into the company. To this end, there were versions of *2-4-6-8, (Come 'Round Here) I'm The One You Need, Don't Know Why I Love You, Never Had A Dream Come True, True Love Can Be Beautiful* and *The Young Folks*.

To these were added cover versions of The Delfonics' hit *La-La (Means I Love You)* and Funkadelic's *I'll Bet You*. Whilst it would obviously be the potential success of any singles lifted (which, in the event proved to be *The Love You Save* and *ABC*) that would drive sales of the album, by the time **ABC** appeared on the market America had been hit with Jackson 5-mania, indicating that Motown's timing had been spot on. An R&B chart topper upon its release on 8 May 1970 (it would spend twelve weeks at the summit), the album would also crossover to the pop charts and hit #4, bettering the performance of the debut album by one place. It was also an international success, even if its final chart place of #22 in the UK was rather more modest. All told the album would go on to sell five and a half million copies around the world, making it one of the most popular of all Jackson 5 albums.

ABDULLAH

Joseph McLean was born in Brooklyn, New York and became a follower of Elijah Muhammad whilst in prison, converting to Islam and taking the name Abdullah. After arriving in Detroit (he supposedly walked carrying just his acoustic guitar) and becoming friendly with Frank Wilson and Hank Cosby, Abdullah got a deal with the Soul imprint, releasing the single *I Comma Zimba Zio (Here I Stand The Mighty One)* backed with *Why Them, Why Me* in October 1968.

When it didn't sell, Abdullah blamed the white staff of Motown for frustrating the promotional effort on his single and got into a heated argument with executive Ralph Seltzer over the matter. The argument ended with Abdullah pulling a machete, knife or letter opener (depending on who's telling the story) on Seltzer and being booted out of the building and off the label in double quick time.

EWART ABNER

A career record executive, Ewart was born Edward Gladstone Abner in Chicago, Illinois on 11 May 1923 and graduated from college as an accountant. At the time Ewart left college, Art Sheridan had launched the Chance record label in Chicago and offered him a job as accountant within the distribution and record plant, then running the pressing plant until this was closed down. Then Ewart became more involved in the record label, virtually serving as Sheridan's right hand man for the next four years. Despite some success with the likes of The Flamingos and The Moonglows, Sheridan shut down the company in December 1954 and invested money into Vee-Jay Records, with Ewart joining that company as General Manager in early 1955 and becoming President in 1961.

Whilst Ewart had grand plans to make Vee-Jay a major force in the industry, signing a number of potentially lucrative deals, the owners Vivian and Jimmy Bracken preferred a slow growth policy. There were also rumours that Ewart had siphoned off company funds in order to cover personal gambling debts (Ewart not only denied this but claimed that he had become a one-third owner of the company and thus money he gambled was his own), but irrespective of whether he had or not, the fact was that despite selling 2.6 million Beatles records in a single month in early 1964 as the British Invasion hit full swing, Vee-Jay was strapped for cash. By then Ewart had been forced out of the company and, with financial assistance from Art Sheridan, launched the Constellation Records label in 1963 (he had previously created the Falcon label in 1957 whilst at Vee-Jay, which changed its name to Abner upon the discovery of another label with the same name).

The new label had some success, especially with former Vee-Jay artists Dee Clark and Gene Chandler, but three years later, the Bracken's were staring bankruptcy in the face and asked Ewart to return to Vee-Jay. Despite his best efforts, Vee-Jay was effectively dissolved in 1967.

Ewart's abilities at running a company had brought admiring glances from many in the industry, not least Berry Gordy, who upon learning Abner had just re-entered the job market, hired him to head up ITM International, the company's talent management division. He proved a success in this role, so much so that when Berry Gordy decided to relinquish control of the record side in 1973 in order to concentrate on films, he promoted Ewart to the position of President. Whilst the company enjoyed some success, including five #1 hits that year, it did not last and Berry fired Ewart in 1975. To soften the blow he agreed a three year consultancy contract. This was eventually coupled with helping set up the Black Music Foundation, ten years as personal and business manager for Stevie Wonder (1975 to 1985) and executive assistant for Berry Gordy's Gordy Company from 1986 until his death from pneumonia on 27 December 1997.

ABRAHAM MARTIN AND JOHN – MARVIN GAYE [SINGLE]

Singer, songwriter and pianist Dick Holler wrote *Abraham, Martin & John* as a tribute following the assassinations of Martin Luther King (April 1968) and Bobby Kennedy (June 1968), working with Dion on the first version to feature on the charts. Dion's folk-rock version hit #4 towards the end of 1968, with the success of the song being noted by Smokey Robinson in particular. He and The Miracles recorded a cover version that was a Top 40 success the following year (it peaked at #33), whilst Marvin Gaye also recorded a version with producer Norman Whitfield in August 1969 that would appear on his **That's The Way Love Is** album.

By the time the album surfaced, Marvin had retreated from the music business, devastated by the death of his one-time singing partner Tammi Terrell. To all intents and purposes, Marvin had all but retired, refusing to tour or record as he came to terms with the loss of such a talented singer. Whilst there was to be no new material for the foreseeable future, Tamla Motown in the UK felt *Abraham Martin & John* would keep the hits coming, following closely on the Top Ten success of *Too Busy Thinking About My Baby* and *The Onion Song*. Released in April 1970 *Abraham Martin & John* would make #9 in June of that year and herald something of a switch to more politically aware material over the next few years. Despite the UK success of the single it was not released stateside.

AL ABRAMS

Eighteen year old Al Abrams (born in Detroit, Michigan on 19 February 1941) accompanied a friend on a job interview in May 1959 at 1719 Gladstone in Detroit, the then home address of Berry Gordy and Raynoma Liles (later to become Berry's second wife). The friend, Sanford Freed, was being interviewed for the job of driver for Berry, but didn't really want the job. Al, however, had been impressed with the music Berry and Raynoma played the pair during the course of the interview, much of which were tracks that others had paid $100 to have the Rayber Music Writing Company record, and pushed Berry into giving him a job as a promoter. Berry pulled one of the records from the pile, a track called *Teenage Sweetheart* on the Zelman label by a Yugoslavian singer who had changed his name to Mike Powers; if Al could get a play on that, he could have a job as a plugger. The next day Al took the record to WCHB Radio in Detroit, badgered the DJ Larry Dixon for three hours and got him to play the record on air, which Berry happened to be listening to at the time! Al therefore become not only the National Promotion Director for Tamla Records and Jobete Music Company, he became the first white employee on a salary of $15 a week.

Al was not afraid to use his colour to his advantage in order to get publicity for Motown artists. Later, by which time he was Director of Public Relations and confronted with one particular newspaper group that would not put any of Motown's (black) artists on the cover of its publications, Al discussed the matter with the features editor.

"Well, let me tell you the truth. You know how these black people like to play dice? Well, I really started Motown Records, and one night I got into a craps game with Berry Gordy, and I lost the whole thing, but they let me stay on and do the publicity anyway."

After exclaiming the story to be one of the saddest he'd ever heard, the features editor instructed the newspaper group to do all they could to help the poor, unfortunate Al; The Supremes appeared on the cover of the next edition of the TV magazine.

Al remained in Motown's employ through to December 1966 when he left, subsequently to form his own publicity company, Al Abrams Associates. Al has maintained his connection to Motown, co-writing the musical 'Memories Of Motown' with Mickey Stevenson in 2009 that was performed as a tribute to Motown's fiftieth anniversary celebrations and writing an autobiography that provided an insight into the early Motown days from the perspective of someone who was there.

FURTHER READING: HYPE & SOUL: BEHIND THE SCENES AT MOTOWN (2011)

JOHNNY ACE

Born John Marshall Alexander in Memphis, Tennessee on 9 June 1929, Johnny Ace was one of R&B biggest stars at the start of the 1950s, racking up a string of hits. He achieved greater notoriety, however, for shooting himself in the head backstage at the City Auditorium in Houston on Christmas Day 1954. Popularly reported that he shot himself whilst playing Russian roulette, it is more likely the result of attempting to prove the gun was not loaded. His biggest hit, *Pledging My Love*, was a posthumous R&B chart topper for ten weeks commencing February 1955. The track was featured on the soundtrack to 'Christine', released by Motown in November 1983.

ARTHUR ADAMS

Born Arthur Lee Reeves in Mecon, Tennessee on Christmas Day 1940, Arthur was already a seasoned professional by the time he joined Motown, via the Chisa label, in 1969. Inspired by the likes of B.B. King and Elmore James, guitarist Arthur toured with Gene Allison before getting stranded in Dallas in 1959. He remained in Dallas for the next five years, becoming a key musician in the area before a Vee-Jay contract prompted a move to Los Angeles in 1964, but lack of promotion on the single (*I Feel Alright*) saw him turn to session work, most notably for former Motown stalwart Mickey Stevenson's Venture label, and record under his own name for Modern.

In 1969 he got a contract with Chisa Records, recording three singles for the label, *It's Private Tonight*, *My Baby's Love* and *Can't Wait To See You*, with a fourth single *Uncle Tom* unreleased.

Arthur then returned to session work, including the soundtrack to 'Bonnie And Clyde', which saw him working with Wayne Henderson of The Crusaders (The Crusaders having also been signed to Chisa). Arthur got a contract with Fantasy thanks to Wayne, with the former Crusader producing his debut album in 1975. Arthur also fleetingly hit the UK chart, scoring a #38 pop placing with the club hit *You Got The Floor* on RCA in 1981.

PEPPER ADAMS

Born in Highland Park, Michigan on 8 October 1930, Park Frederick 'Pepper' Adams III was still a child when he learned to play the tenor saxophone and clarinet after his family moved to New York. Pepper then moved to Detroit when he was 16 and switched to baritone saxophone, getting a permanent gig with Lucky Thompson's band the following year. He later returned to New York, where he would play with the likes of Benny Goodman, John Coltrane, Donald Byrd and, from 1958 onwards, Charlie Mingus.

His only Motown album came with **Pepper Adams Plays The Compositions Of Charlie Mingus**, released on the Workshop Jazz label in August 1964, with Pepper leading a band that included Bob Cranshaw and Paul Chambers (bass), Danny Richman (drums), Hank Jones (piano), Zoot Sims (tenor saxophone), Bennie Powell (trombone) and Thad Jones (trumpet). Pepper, who would go on to garner three Grammy award nominations, died from lung cancer on 10 September 1986.

ALBUM: COMPOSITIONS OF CHARLIE MINGUS (1964)

CANNONBALL ADDERLEY

Julian Edwin Adderley was born in Tampa, Florida on 15 September 1928 and acquired the nickname Cannonball as a derivative of 'cannibal', a name bestowed upon him at high school in deference to his habit of fast eating. It is as a saxophonist, however, that he achieved lasting notoriety, both fronting his own combos and performing with Miles Davis. His only Motown involvement came on the soundtrack to 'Save The Children' released in 1974, with Cannonball performing *Country Preacher* during the live show. He died from a stroke on 8 August 1975.

WENDEL ADKINS

A protégé of Willie Nelson, country singer and guitarist Wendel Adkins (born in Louisville, Kentucky on 20 September 1946) was originally signed by the Hitsville label and released his debut album **The Sundowners** in January 1977. Although Wendel would score two minor country hit singles in *I Will* (#80) and *Laid Back Country Picker* (#91), the album failed to sell in sufficient quantities (although it did register on the country album chart at #46) so was re-released on the MC imprint in October the same year.

Two months later the album was repackaged and reissued again, this time as **Wendel Adkins** on MC, with a non-album single *Julieanne (Where Are You Tonight)* scraping into the very lower reaches of the country chart at #98. In between the first two releases, the UK branch of Hitsville issued *Texas Moon* as a single, the failure of which resulted in the album never making the release schedule. Adkins would later play at Willie Nelson's Whiskey River club in Dallas and tour with the likes of David Allan Coe and George Jones.

ALBUMS: SUNDOWNERS (1977), WENDEL ADKINS (1977)

THE AGENTS

According to some sources, The Agents was a Philadelphia vocal quintet formed by Nat Williams, Kenneth Davis, Warren Lundy, Jimmy Downs and Norman Bowen. Other sources, however, claim The Agents were effectively Junior Walker's All Stars recording without their erstwhile leader. There is a case for plumping for the second option, since the only Agents track that has surfaced, *Hey Girl, Come On Do The Pearl*, which was finally released in 2010 on the fourth volume of **A Cellarful Of Motown** was originally recorded in 1967 on sessions produced by Harvey Fuqua and Johnny Bristol (Junior Walker's regular producers at the time) and was co-written by Harvey, Johnny and All Stars members Vic Thomas and James Graves with Willie Brown and Raymond Freeman.

AIN'T NO MOUNTAIN HIGH ENOUGH – DIANA ROSS [SINGLE]

One of the first songs Ashford & Simpson wrote after being signed as songwriters by Motown and Jobete (although it may well have been written earlier, since it was later revealed that Dusty Springfield heard the song and wanted to record it, only to be turned down by Ashford & Simpson as they wanted to use the song as an entry into Motown), *Ain't No Mountain High Enough* was inspired by the Ike & Tina Turner hit *River Deep Mountain High*. At the time producers Johnny Bristol and Harvey Fuqua were working on material with Tammi Terrell and thought the song might be ideal for her. Tammi duly recorded a version, even though she had not completely learned the lyrics and sang from a lyric sheet partway through the session. Upon hearing a playback, it was suggested that the song might make a good duet for Tammi and Marvin Gaye, whose career was in need of a boost. With some of Tammi's vocals wiped off the master tape, Marvin added his vocals to make a seamless version of the song.

It was released as a single in April 1967 and made #19 pop and #3 R&B (as well as picking up a Grammy nomination for Best R&B Performance by a Duo), although it failed to register in the UK. The following year Diana Ross, The Supremes and The Temptations recorded a version for their album **Diana Ross & The Supremes Join The Temptations**. In 1970 Ashford & Simpson were working with Diana on her debut solo album and suggested doing an update on the song. Although Diana was reluctant, reasoning it was renowned as a Tammi & Marvin song, the producers convinced her that they could come up with an arrangement that would make the song hers, utilising the backing vocal abilities of Billie Rae Calvin and Brenda Joyce Evans of The Delicates (the pair would later be pinched by Norman Whitfield and placed in The Undisputed Truth) as well as Ashford and Simpson themselves.

The Diana Ross version was not universally popular within Motown, with even Berry Gordy reluctant to release it as anything other than an album track, but it was soon noticed that radio stations were doing their own edits (the album version runs to 6 minutes 18 seconds) in order to add the song to their playlists, and so an official edit was hastily called for. The final version, at 3 minutes 32 seconds, kept the key elements from the original recording and proved irresistible, helping the single power up the charts at a rapid rate. It would eventually top the Billboard pop charts for three weeks, the R&B chart for one week and hit #6 in the UK. It was also good enough to earn Diana a Grammy nomination for Best Female Pop Vocal Performance, although she lost out to Dionne Warwick's *I'll Never Fall In Love Again*. The song, however, has retained its popularity, becoming a Top 40 hit in the UK for Jocelyn Brown in 1998 (it peaked at #35), a #60 hit for Whitehouse the same year and was one half of a hi-nrg medley with *Remember Me* by Boystown Gang that hit #46 in 1981.

AIN'T NO SUNSHINE – MICHAEL JACKSON [SINGLE]

Written by Bill Withers and inspired by the film 'Days Of Wine And Roses', *Ain't No Sunshine* was originally released as the B-side to Bill's single *Harlem*, but after many DJ's began flipping the single, Sussex Records took to promoting *Ain't No Sunshine* as the lead side and were rewarded with a Top Ten hit on both the pop and R&B charts in 1971. At about the time Bill Withers was rising up the chart, work had started on Michael Jackson's debut solo album **Got To Be There**. A wide variety of material was chosen for the album, ranging from the ballad title track through to the more uplifting revival of *Rockin' Robin*, with both singles making the UK Top Ten.

As Bill Withers' original version of *Ain't No Sunshine* had missed out altogether on UK chart honours, Tamla Motown decided to go with a third single from the debut album and released Michael's version in July 1972. An instant success at both radio and retail, *Ain't No Sunshine* would make it three top ten hits in a row as it powered its way to #8 on the singles chart. Bill Withers received more than adequate compensation when the song won the 1971 Grammy Award for Best Rhythm & Blues Song.

AIN'T NOTHING LIKE THE REAL THING – MARVIN GAYE & TAMMI TERRELL [SINGLE]

Marvin Gaye and Tammi Terrell's album **United**, largely produced by Harvey Fuqua and Johnny Bristol, yielded three major R&B hits in *Ain't No Mountain High Enough, Your Precious Love* and *If I Could Build My Whole World Around You*. Two of these had been written by Nickolas Ashford and Valerie Simpson, who would write material at their New York home and then journey to Detroit for a week to ten days in order to have their material reviewed. At one such meeting, to which they presented the song *Ain't Nothing Like The Real Thing*, they expressed an interest in producing the song themselves. Berry Gordy gave them the go ahead, but for security instructed Harvey Fuqua and Johnny Bristol to produce a version too, opting to let Quality Control decide the fate of the respective tracks.

Ashford and Simpson took their place at Hitsville in October 1967 for their first Marvin and Tammi session, and couldn't help but let their nerves show. "Norman Whitfield and Smokey were watching us," said Nick Ashford. "The studio was so small, and you could just see their faces while we were trying to deal with the musicians and arrangers. They were standing up there like it was a party and didn't realise how nervous we were."

They managed to get through the session without too much trouble, but then came the Quality Control meeting, with Nick attending on his own.

"I'd never been to a Quality Control meeting before. Berry was right there at the middle of the table. Beads of sweat must have been popping out of my head! So there was a silence after our record was played, and then Berry said, 'I don't think we need to vote on this one. Let's just send it out right away.'"

In actual fact the single wasn't released until March 1968, but as soon as it hit the airwaves and shops, it was obvious it was a hit, going on to top the R&B chart and make #8 on the pop chart, although it made a rather modest #34 in the UK. In 1994 Marcella Detroit and Elton John took an update to #24 on the UK chart.

AIN'T THAT PECULIAR – MARVIN GAYE [SINGLE]

The Miracles' guitarist Marv Tarplin came up with the initial melody for *Ain't That Peculiar* whilst the group was touring Europe as part of the 1965 Motown Revue, with the rest of the group quickly catching on to the riff and fleshing it out in to a full-blown song. At the time The Miracles were one of the top writing teams at Motown, penning hits for themselves and The Temptations and decided that this song would be ideal for Marvin Gaye, who had recently recorded *I'll Be Doggone* by the same writing team of Smokey Robinson and assorted Miracles' members, and by giving it a new slant had taken it into the pop and R&B Top Ten.

"That's what was so great about working with Marvin. I'd show him a song one time and I knew he would sing it even better than the way I envisaged it. He'd always do something unexpected and wonderful. He sounded like he knew it before I even showed it to him."

Indeed, Marvin's ability to make a song his own showed itself to perfection on *Ain't That Peculiar*, resulting in an R&B chart topper and pop #8 following release in September 1965.

AIRPLAY

Berry Gordy placed such importance on radio airplay he had two mini speakers, equivalent to the sound that would be heard on a car radio, installed in the studio at Hitsville, reasoning that if a record sounded good on them it would sound good on any radio and could therefore be released. And Berry was careful to ensure Motown did not get involved in payola.

"I did not believe in payola for Motown when people were fighting for my records. Once a disc jockey played *Shop Around*, the phones lit up; that's how potent it was."

Indeed, Motown wouldn't have had to pay a single dollar in order to ensure plays on Marvin Gaye's *I Heard It Through The Grapevine*, which has received more than ten million plays on radio since its release! The top Motown songs according to the BMI (Broadcast Music Inc, the collecting agency) are as follows:

The Four Tops – *Baby I Need Your Lovin'* (10.9 million)
Marvin Gaye – *I Heard It Through The Grapevine* (10 million)
The Supremes – *You Can't Hurry Love* (9.5 million)
The Four Tops – *I Can't Help Myself* (6.8 million)
Martha Reeves – *Dancing In The Street* (6.6 million)
Stevie Wonder – *My Cherie Amour* (6.5 million)
The Isley Brothers – *This Old Heart Of Mine* (6.4 million)
The Four Tops – *Reach Out, I'll Be There* (6.4 million)
The Supremes – *You Keep Me Hangin' On* (6.2 million)
Stevie Wonder – *For Once In My Life* (6.1 million)
The Supremes – *Where Did Our Love Go?* (6.1 million)

AIRTO

Brazilian percussionist Airto Moreira was born in Itaiopolis on 5 August 1941 and first studied guitar and piano before switching to percussion. After playing locally throughout Brazil, during which time he was said to have collected some 120 different percussion instruments he moved to New York in 1968 with his wife, singer Flora Purim. His reputation alone ensured regular work, commencing with a spell with Miles Davis and Lee Morgan before becoming a member of Weather Report and later Chick Corea's Return To Forever.

By 1972 his standing was such that he was signed by CTI as a soloist, although it was Billy Cobham that produced his **Virgin Land** album, issued on the subsidiary Salvation label, as well as becoming the main label's in-house percussionist. Airto would continue to record both solo and with his wife over the decades, most notably in the group Fourth World and on **Life After That** from 2003 which also featured their daughter Diana.
ALBUM: VIRGIN LAND (1974)

LEE ALAN

Lee Alan Reicheld was born in Clinton, Iowa on 5 November 1934 and worked as a disc jockey at Detroit station WXYZ with his own show 'Lee Alan On The Horn' and a trademark klaxon horn he would blast between records. He was also a former school friend of Barney Ales and asked a favour of putting together a record in aid of the YMCA Camp Fund. The song was written by Lee, produced by Clarence Paul and recorded at Hitsville in 1964 with assistance from Marvin Gaye, Stevie Wonder, Smokey Robinson and The Vandellas (albeit misspelt on the label as The Vendellas). The single, *Set Me Free*, was only available to callers to the radio station, with WXYZ later claiming that over 50,000 copies had been sold in aid of the charity. After leaving the radio industry in 1972, Lee set up the Reicheld Corporation, a full service advertising agency and in house creative production source.
FURTHER READING: TURN YOUR RADIO ON – LIVE FROM MOTOWN (2004)

BARNEY ALES

A former stockman and promotion manager for Capitol and branch manager for Warner Brothers, Baldassare 'Barney' Ales (born on 13 May 1934) was lured to Motown from Aurora Distributors to head up the sales department. The appointment was seen as controversial by many, for whilst Motown was predominantly a black organisation, Barney Ales and the staff he brought in were white. However, it was observed by Gordy that it would be easier for a white head of sales to get payment from the predominantly white retailers and wholesalers, thus ensuring a steady cash flow for the burgeoning company. Barney was to remain with the company until 1972, subsequently going on to form Prodigal Records but eventually returned to Motown, along with his label, before replacing Ewart Abner as President in 1975. He remained as head of the company until 1979. He is also credited as a songwriter on several Motown cuts, including *Buttered Popcorn* by The Supremes.

DAVID ALEXANDER

Born in Blackwood, Monmouthshire in 1939, David Alexander Ebdon left Bedwelty Grammar School in Gwent at the age of sixteen and followed his father and eldest brother down the mines at Oakdale Colliery. After a few years of back breaking work, he left the mines and studied as a machine engineer before becoming foreman at a brake company. There he also joined singing company the Trenewdd Singers that appeared on 'Opportunity Knocks', with his performance being singled out as worthy of pursuing a singing career.
Acting on that advice and adopting the name Ricky Mason, he went out on the road performing across the country. It was, however, under the name David Alexander that he got his first recording contract with Columbia, releasing *If I Could See The Rhondda One More Time*. Several singles and years later, he was one of the artists briefly signed to Rare Earth in the UK, with Phil Cordell writing and producing *Love Love Love* that was released in February 1974. It was not released in the US and David went back to the Columbia label thereafter. He died from a heart attack on 4 February 1995.

ALL DIRECTIONS – THE TEMPTATIONS [ALBUM]

By the time The Temptations came to record **All Directions**, their relationship with producer and songwriter Norman Whitfield was fraught, to say the least. The group had embraced Norman's switch to psychedelic soul back in 1969, but three years later it seemed as though that was all Norman wanted them to record, with wistful ballads like *Just My Imagination* a rarity. Their other problem with the material was that much of it was not fresh, with Norman trying out his songs on a variety of artists, trying to coax something different out of each one.
This had already proven to be a problem for Gladys Knight & The Pips, who saw their showcase song *I Heard It Through The Grapevine* become Marvin Gaye's signature song barely a year later. Indeed, of the songs presented to The Temptations that would

go on to form **All Directions**, *Funky Music Sho' Nuff Turns Me On* had been a hit for Edwin Starr in April 1971 and *Papa Was A Rollin' Stone* recorded and due for release by The Undisputed Truth. Since the lyricist on both these songs, Barrett Strong, had already parted company with the producer (on amicable terms since he wished to revive his own recording career), Norman had no new songs.

Instead, alongside the two revivals of his earlier work he offered covers of *The First Time Ever (I Saw Your Face)* made famous by Roberta Flack, *Do Your Thing* (Isaac Hayes) and *Love Woke Me Up This Morning* (Marvin Gaye & Tammi Terrell), with the album rounded out with *Mother Nature*, *I Ain't Got Nothin'* and another controversial track in *Run Charlie Run*. Norman had recorded all of the music whilst The Temptations were out on the road, utilising The Funk Brothers and the likes of Melvin 'Wah Wah' Ragin, with much of it sounding as though it would not be out of place on a film soundtrack. Despite their hesitancy (and Otis Williams would later state he was sure the album and singles were going to flop), The Temptations excelled on the album, especially the full length near on twelve minute *Papa Was A Rollin' Stone*. And therein lay the other problem between Norman Whitfield and The Temptations; it seemed to the group that these extra long cuts had the effect of making them little more than backing singers on their own albums, a problem that would reach its peak with the next album **Masterpiece**.

In the meantime, **All Directions** was released in July 1972 and became one of their biggest sellers and most popular albums, shifting more than half a million copies and reached #1 R&B, #2 pop and #19 in the UK. Of course, much of this success was down to *Papa Was A Rollin' Stone,* which would go on to claim three Grammy Awards in 1973.

ALL I NEED – THE TEMPTATIONS [SINGLE]

Although Smokey Robinson and Norman Whitfield were still engaged in an almost head-to-head battle to try and get an exclusive on producing The Temptations, there were still occasions when other's within Motown got a chance to show their abilities. Frank Wilson, who had been one of the company's earliest employees in Los Angeles had proved his worth to The Temptations with his production on **In A Mellow Mood**, an album of standards, and came up with the basic idea for *All I Need*. He took the idea to Eddie Holland and R. Dean Taylor and between the three of them completed the song ready for recording in February 1967. Rather than come up with exactly the same kind of arrangement and feel that Norman was producing, Frank sought a different interpretation to the song, utilising The Andantes on backing vocals (something Holland-Dozier-Holland were doing extensively on their recordings with The Four Tops), which served to perfectly compliment David Ruffin's lead vocals. Released in the US in April 1967 it represented something of a musical departure for The Temptations but still found its mark, hitting #2 R&B and #8 pop before the month was out.

ALL NIGHT LONG (ALL NIGHT) – LIONEL RICHIE [SINGLE]

Lionel Richie's reputation during his latter days as a member of The Commodores had highlighted his abilities as a ballad writer. It was a reputation that was enforced by his debut solo album, giving rise to two massive hits in *You Are* and *Truly* at much the same time *Endless Love*, a Richie composition recorded as a duet with Diana Ross was also tearing up the charts. There would have been those expecting more of the same for the follow-up album **Can't Slow Down**, but when the first single appeared in September 1983, a couple of weeks ahead of the album, it was to be the Caribbean influenced *All Night Long (All Night)*. Indeed, the final version features a mix of Jamaican, African and Swahili phrasing, with Lionel having asked a knowledgeable friend how Bob Marley might have worded the song!

Aided by a promotional video directed by former Monkees member Michael Nesmith, something of a pioneer in the then relatively new promotional medium, *All Night Long* became an international hit, topping the US pop charts for four weeks, the R&B charts for seven and hit #2 in the UK, only held off the top spot by Culture Club's *Karma Chameleon* and then Billy Joel's *Uptown Girl* during its three week residency at number two. And it wasn't only the public who took to the song, as Lionel would recall.

"Stevie Wonder was performing in Radio City and in the middle of his show, he stopped everything. He told the audience that he wanted to play his current favourite song – and he played *All Night Long* on tape! Right in the middle of his show! That is the greatest honour anyone can give me. It's the ultimate compliment. It was the compliment of my life!"

All Night Long would garner two Grammy nominations, for Record of the Year and Song of the Year, although failed to win in either category.

ALL OF MY LIFE – DIANA ROSS [SINGLE]

Touch Me In The Morning had been a big hit for Diana Ross from the album of the same name but Motown in the US had decided there was little else on the album likely to generate interest or sales to the same extent. Besides, the priority in America had already switched to the forthcoming album of duets with Marvin Gaye, with *You're A Special Part Of Me* being selected for single release in September 1973. In the UK that single was delayed until November, but there were already concerns the track was not particularly strong enough for the UK market. This would have been embarrassing for Tamla Motown, even more so as Diana Ross was touring the country at the time.

Thus a decision was made to return to the **Touch Me In The Morning** album and release *All Of My Life*, a ballad in a similar vein to the title track. Written and produced by in-house writer Michael Randall, *All Of My Life* was something of a slow burner, being released on 30 November 1973 and finally hitting the UK chart on 5 January 1974. It would take another month to finally reach the Top Ten, peaking at #9, by which time Diana's UK tour was over.

SUSIE ALLANSON

A country music singer and later actress, Susie was born in Minneapolis, Minnesota on 17 March 1952 and began her singing career in 1970 as part of the touring company for 'Hair' and later 'Jesus Christ Superstar', also appearing the film version of the latter. After her 1976 debut album for ABC Susie was signed by Mike Curb for MC Records the following year and recorded one album, **A Little Love**, produced by Ray Huff but seemingly unissued apart from promotional copies.

Susie followed Mike Curb out of the company the same year, subsequently signing with his new imprint at Warner Brothers (where a reissue of her 1977 MC single *Without You* made #79 on the country charts in 1979) and later Elektra before finishing her country career with United Artists and Liberty/Curb.

ALBUM: A LITTLE LOVE (1977)

RICHARD 'PISTOL' ALLEN

Born Howard Richard Allen in Memphis, Tennessee on 12 August 1932 he moved to Michigan to work at AC Delco in the mid 1950s but found greater satisfaction playing drums in the jazz nightclubs around Detroit. Spotted by fellow drummer and future mentor Benny Benjamin, Richard was hired by Berry Gordy to become a member of the Funk Brothers, the legendary musical backing group for just about every Motown hit recorded between 1963 and 1972. Whilst this meant having to adapt his jazz style 'Pistol' Allen became a mainstay at Motown, appearing on such hits as *Heat Wave*, *How Sweet It Is* and *Baby Love*, among countless others. He died after a long battle with cancer on 30 June 2002, some six months before the release of the documentary film 'Standing In The Shadows Of Motown'.

THE ALLENS

Family group The Allens consisted of five of the eleven Allen siblings in Mitzi (born on 20 June 1959, vocals), Larry (born on 2 November 1957, keyboards), Gary (born on 23 November 1953, bass), Ronny (born on 10 November 1955, drums) and Tony Allen (born on 7 December 1952, guitar), with Motown insisting that the group had the ability to become the next generation of The Osmonds. That they had one of that number, Alan Osmond, as their writer and producer as well as a production and management deal with Mike Curb Productions accounted for Motown's confidence, but despite this *High Tide* (written and produced by Alan as Allen Osmond), scheduled for September 1974 was pulled from release. The following February, *A Bird In The Hand (Is Worth Two In The Bush)* did make the streets, prompting *High Tide* with Ronny on lead vocal to be rescheduled and released in May 1975. Thanks to Motown's initial promotional push, *High Tide* began to make some headway, both on radio and television, with the group appearing on 'American Bandstand' promoting the release.

"The song was playing on AM and FM stations and Billboard had it as pick of the week and it started to take off," remembered Gary. "However, we were told by our management company that there were problems with many record companies that were being investigated by the government cracking down on the practice of payola. This meant our record had to be introduced to new programme directors every week which in essence caused the freeze of monies to promote the record, resulting in it falling off playlists."

In the UK *High Tide* was issued in July 1975 on the MoWest label, but despite the company's best efforts failed to make any headway. The Allens would release one further single on Mercury in 1977 but never quite managed to attain the same level of success as The

Osmonds. The group eventually disintegrated, with Gary settling in Las Vegas where he regularly performs under the name Gary Anthony in Frank Sinatra and The Rat Pack tribute shows.

MICHELLE ALLER

Michelle Aller was born in Los Angeles, California on 26 October 1949 and recorded one single for MoWest, *The Morning After,* backed with *Spend Some Time Together*, both of which were written and produced by Michael Randall and scheduled for release in August 1972. Shortly before release, the A-side got pulled and replaced with another Randall song, *Just Not Gonna Make It,* with the title proving prophetic. Michelle also appeared on the soundtrack to 'Lady Sings The Blues', performing *Had You Been Around.*

She next appeared as a songwriter, linking with producer Bob Esty and co-writing four of the tracks from Cher's Casablanca album **Take Me Home**, including the Top Ten hit single title track. The same pair then co-wrote four tracks on her follow-up album **Prisoner**, with *Hell On Wheels* another hit single and also turning up in the film 'Roller Boogie.'

Michelle later sang with Cerrone, appearing on the album **Angelina** and also acted and sang under the name Mavis Vegas Davis, her monicker for her role as stage manager on 'American Idol'.

GENE ALLISON

Versie Eugene Allison was born in Pegram, Tennessee on 29 August 1934 and raised in Nashville, where he and his brother Leevert sang in the church choir. Despite being offered the opportunity of joining The Fairfield Four and The Skylarks, Gene opted to try his hand at secular music, eventually landing a recording contract with Vee-Jay after brief spells with Calvert, Champion and Cherokee Records. His debut single became a big success, with *You Can Make It If You Try* hitting #3 R&B and #36 pop in 1958, with Gene registering two more Top Twenty R&B hits before the year was out. *You Can Make It If You Try* later appeared on the compilation album **Hits From The Legendary Vee-Jay Records**, issued on CD by Motown in November 1986. Gene died of renal failure on 28 February 2004.

LUTHER ALLISON

Motown signed artists in virtually every possible genre and had varying degrees of success, although it would appear the one that eluded them at least as far as success was concerned was the blues. Among the first artists signed was Luther Allison, who would spend four years at the company and release three albums, none of which troubled the charts.

Born Luther Sylvester Allison in Benedict Township, Arkansas on 18 August 1939, he moved to Chicago with his family at the age of twelve and taught himself to play the guitar by listening to blues records of the time. When he felt he was proficient enough, he began hanging around nightclubs in the hope he'd be asked to perform.

In 1957 he got his chance, with Howlin' Wolf inviting him onstage, Luther's performance being such that fellow guitarist Freddy King took him under his wing. Luther would play clubs in and around Chicago for the next ten years, finally getting a recording deal with Delmark Records in 1967. A triumphant appearance at the Ann Arbor Blues Festival led to repeat performances at the festival and eventually to his signing by Motown's Gordy imprint in 1972.

Whilst the three albums he recorded were well received critically and enabled him to tour nationwide, sales were well below expectations and after leaving the label Luther moved to live in France, later recording for a number of European labels. He died from lung and brain cancer on 12 August 1997.

ALBUMS: BAD NEWS IS COMING (1972), LUTHER'S BLUES (1974), NIGHT LIFE (1976)

ALMOST SUMMER (1978 FILM)

The 1978 release 'Almost Summer' was produced by Motown Productions for Universal Pictures, written by Judith Berg, Sandra Berg, Martin Davidson and Marc Reid Rubel and directed by Martin Davidson, his second such directorial assignment. The best known actor in the film was Tim Matheson, who appeared in 'National Lampoon's Animal House' the same year. Although largely unsuccessful at the box office at the time of release, it has since gone on to acquire a degree of notoriety as one of the earliest youth genre films along with the presence of three professional skateboarders. Its notoriety has been achieved on word of mouth alone, for the film has never been issued on video or DVD since its initial release. The accompanying soundtrack was released by MCA; it features a group called Celebration that was assembled for the occasion, but this group has no connection to an earlier Motown group by the same name.

GERALD ALSTON

The nephew of former gospel singer Johnny Fields and Shirelles lead singer Shirley Alston Reeves, Gerald Alston (born in Henderson, North Carolina on 8 November 1951) learned to sing thanks to his preacher father. He formed a vocal group whilst still in his teens, going under the name The Gospel Jubilee when they performed in church and The New Imperials when in clubs. It was at the latter that Gerald was first spotted by members of The Manhattans in 1970, who were so impressed with his abilities they invited him to join them, although Gerald turned down their initial request. The group tried again in December 1970 following the illness and eventual death of founder member George Smith and this time found Gerald receptive to the switch.

He would become lead singer of The Manhattans in 1971 and scored major hits with *Kiss And Say Goodbye* (1976), *Shining Star* (1980) and *Crazy* (1983), among others. He left the group for a solo career in 1988, signing with Motown and scoring three Top Ten R&B hits (*Take Me Where You Want To*, *Slow Motion* and *Getting Back Into Love*) from the three albums he recorded for the label. After one further album for Scotti Brothers/Street Life, Gerald reunited with The Manhattans, initially for their thirtieth anniversary but subsequently on a permanent basis.

SHIRLEY ALSTON

The former lead singer with The Shirelles, Shirley Alston (born Shirley Owens in Henderson, North Carolina on 10 June 1941) formed the group in 1957 with classmates Doris Coley, Addi Harris and Beverley Lee as The Pequellos. After winning a school talent contest with their own composition *I Met Him On A Sunday*, they were recommended to Florence Greenberg, owner of Tiara Records, eventually signing up as The Shirelles and scored locally with their song thanks to national distribution by Decca. Both the Tiara label and The Shirelles contract were then bought by Decca for $4,000, but after two singles that did nothing, the group was dropped and handed back to Greenberg as Decca considered them a one-hit wonder.

Florence subsequently formed Scepter Records and re-signed The Shirelles, teaming them with Luther Dixon and seeing the group score numerous pop and R&B hits as the decade progressed. The departure of Dixon to start his own label saw The Shirelles become less of a feature on the charts, with the group also unhappy over their dealings with Scepter Records and the disappearance of a trust fund that the members were supposed to receive when they reached the age of 21. After seeing out their contract they would go on to sign for Bell, RCA and United Artists, without success, but the burgeoning oldies circuit kept them in work for another decade.

Shirley, who through marriages had acquired the surnames Alston and then Reeves, launched a solo career in 1975, signing with Barney Ales' Prodigal label and enlisting the help of The Flamingos, The Drifters, The 5 Satins, Danny & The Juniors, Herman's Hermits and others for her only album **With A Little Help From My Friends**, a collection of doo-wop and R&B classics. Two singles were released, *I Hear Those Church Bells Ringing-Chapel Of Love* with Dolores 'LaLa' Brooks (formerly a member of The Crystals) and *I'd Rather Not Be Loving You*.

ALBUM: WITH A LITTLE HELP FROM MY FRIENDS (1975)

AMERICAN MUSIC AWARDS

Created by television presenter Dick Clark in 1973 to compete with the Grammy Awards, the American Music Awards (now commonly known as the AMAs) first aired in February 1974, with Michael Jackson and Donny Osmond co-hosting the show. Whilst Grammy nominations and awards are based on votes cast by members of the recording industry, the AMAs are voted on by record buyers and are therefore seen as more representative of public opinion. Here are Motown's winners since the awards were inaugurated.

1974:
Favourite Pop/Rock Album – **Lady Sings The Blues** – Diana Ross
Favourite Soul/R&B Male Artist – Stevie Wonder
Favourite Soul/R&B Group – The Temptations
Favourite Soul/R&B Single – *Superstition* – Stevie Wonder

1975:
Favourite Soul/R&B Male Artist – Stevie Wonder
Favourite Soul/R&B Female Artist – Diana Ross

1976:
Favourite Soul/R&B Album – **A Song For You** – The Temptations

1977:
Favourite Soul/R&B Male Artist – Stevie Wonder
Favourite Soul/R&B Album – **Songs In The Key Of Life** – Stevie Wonder

1978:
Favourite Soul/R&B Male Artist – Stevie Wonder
Favourite Soul/R&B Album – **Songs In The Key Of Life** – Stevie Wonder

1979:
Favourite Pop/Rock Single – *Three Times A Lady* – The Commodores

1980:
Favourite Soul/R&B Group – The Commodores

1981:
Favourite Soul/R&B Female Artist – Diana Ross
Favourite Soul/R&B Single – *Upside Down* – Diana Ross

1982:
Favourite Pop/Rock Single – *Endless Love* – Lionel Richie & Diana Ross
Favourite Soul/R&B Male Artist – Stevie Wonder
Favourite Soul/R&B Album – **Street Songs** – Rick James
Favourite Soul/R&B Single – *Endless Love* – Lionel Richie & Diana Ross
Award of Merit – Stevie Wonder

1983:
Favourite Pop/Rock Single – *Truly* – Lionel Richie
Favourite Soul/R&B Male Artist – Lionel Richie
Favourite Soul/R&B Female Artist – Diana Ross

1984:
Favourite Soul/R&B Single – *All Night Long (All Night)* – Lionel Richie

1985:
Favourite Pop/Rock Male Artist – Lionel Richie
Favourite Pop/Rock Video – *Hello* – Lionel Richie
Favourite Soul/R&B Male Artist – Lionel Richie
Favourite Soul/R&B Video – *Hello* – Lionel Richie

1986:
Favourite Soul/R&B Male Artist – Stevie Wonder
Favourite Soul/R&B Video Artist – Stevie Wonder

1987:
Favourite Pop/Rock Male Artist – Lionel Richie
Favourite Pop/Rock Video – *Dancing On The Ceiling* – Lionel Richie
Favourite Soul/R&B Male Artist – Lionel Richie
Favourite Soul/R&B Male Video Artist – Lionel Richie

THE ANDANTES

Despite never registering a single hit in their own name, The Andantes remain an integral part of Motown history, recording, so it is said, some 20,000 tracks and appearing on more hit records than any other artist in history. Louvain Demps (born in New York on 7 April 1938) had been the first paying customer to turn up at Berry and Raynoma's Rayber Music Writing Company in 1959 and was subsequently used on various recording sessions as a backing vocalist, eventually linking up with Jackie Hicks (born on 4 November 1939) and Marlene Barrow (born on 25 September 1939) to form The Andantes.

After guesting on several recordings (they were credited with Billy Kent for his MAH's Records' release *Take All Of Me* in 1960) they were taken to Motown in 1960 by Richard 'Popcorn' Wylie and became the in-house vocal backing group following the disbanding of The Rayber Voices in 1962. They appeared on recordings by Martha Reeves & The Vandellas (on many recordings they were effectively The Vandellas), Stevie Wonder, The Supremes (Marlene substituted for Florence Ballard at several concert appearances, whilst The Andantes substituted for Mary Wilson and Cindy Birdsong on recordings between 1968 and 1969), The Four Tops, Marvin Gaye, Jimmy Ruffin, Edwin Starr, The Temptations, Mary Wells and The Marvelettes (becoming The Marvelettes on their final Motown album).

Despite their obvious vocal talents, Berry Gordy refused to allow them to either record or tour under their own name. This was largely because the Motown recording studio was working around the clock from 1963 to the end of the decade, requiring The Andantes to be on hand on an almost permanent basis, although one single in *Like A Nightmare* featuring Ann Bogan, later of The Marvelettes, was recorded (it was assigned a number on V.I.P. Records – 25006 – but copies were recalled soon after its March 1964 release, even if it did eventually turn up on the Northern Soul scene, where it is currently valued at £3,000!) and the group linked with Gladys Horton (also of The Marvelettes) to record *Too Hurt To*

Cry, Too Much In Love To Say Goodbye as The Darnells. The group, like many of the musicians in The Funk Brothers, undertook recordings for artists outside of Motown and sometimes Detroit, unbeknown to Berry Gordy, including Jackie Wilson's *Whispers (Gettin' Louder)* and *Higher And Higher*.

Like many former Motown artists, The Andantes resurfaced in the late 1980s thanks to Ian Levine's Motorcity label, once again providing backing vocals to many of the artists on the label but finally being given an opportunity to record themselves.

FURTHER READING: MOTOWN FROM THE BACKGROUND (2007)

THE ANGELS

Female vocal group The Angels formed in Orange, New Jersey in 1961 by Phyllis 'Jiggs' Allbut (born in Orange on 24 September 1942), her sister Barbara 'Bibs' Allbut (born in Orange on 24 September 1940), Barbara Carroll and Linda Malzone as The Starlets. Carroll left for a solo career before they recorded any material, and Linda Malzone was replaced by Linda Jansen. They originally recorded for the Caprice label towards the end of 1961, by which time they had become The Angels. Jansen left in 1962 and was replaced by Peggy Santiglia (born in New Jersey on 4 May 1944), and in 1963 the group signed with Smash Records. Their biggest hit was *My Boyfriend's Back*, which they originally recorded as a demo for The Shirelles but performed so well the publishers opted to release it by The Angels, resulting in a US #1 hit for three weeks (it spent a solitary week at #50 in the UK). *My Boyfriend's Back* was featured on the soundtrack to the documentary film 'Girl Groups: The Story Of A Sound' released in November 1983.

ANNA RECORDS

Formed in Detroit, Michigan in 1959 by Anna Gordy, Gwen Gordy and Billy Roquel Davis and named after the elder Gordy sister, Anna Records released 26 singles during its eighteen month existence. Aside from early releases by Joe Tex, David Ruffin, Johnny Bristol (as one half of Johnny & Jackie) and Lamont Anthony (later to become better known as writer Lamont Dozier), Anna Records main claim to fame was its involvement with Barrett Strong's *Money (That's What I Want)*, which was originally released on Tamla (T-54027) and subsequently licensed to Anna as A-1111. With national distribution by Chess Records, *Money* became a #2 R&B and #23 pop hit in 1960, Motown's first major hit, although the label was unable to do anything with the follow up *Yes, No, Maybe So* backed with *You Knows What To Do*.

Anna Records released its last record in January 1961 (Joe Tex' *Baby You're Right*) before closing up shop, with most of the artists, musicians (including drummer Marvin Gaye, then romantically linked with Anna Gordy), writers and producers throwing their lot in with Berry Gordy and his burgeoning company. One noticeable absentee was Paul Gayten, whose *The Hunch* backed with *Hot Cross Buns* was a minor US hit and was issued in the UK on the London American label (and appears on several Motown discographies, even if the connection is somewhat tenuous); Paul opted to take up an offer from Phil and Leonard Chess to move out to Los Angeles where he headed up Chess Records' West Coast operations before setting up his own Pzazz label.

ANONYMOUS CHILDREN OF TODAY

A group who pretty much lived up to their name, releasing one single on Chisa Records in 1969, *Can We Talk To You (For A Little While)* backed with *Love And Peace*. The A-side was written by two other artists on the Chisa stable, Wilton Felder (of The Jazz Crusaders) and Arthur Adams, with Adams linking with Larry Perrault for the flip. According to Arthur, the group really were anonymous children, friends of Wilton's from the local neighbourhood.

RICHARD ANTHONY

Richard Anthony had already achieved a certain degree of notoriety, becoming the first French artist to record a rock and roll number (*Peggy Sue* in 1959) before he became the first French artist to release a record on Motown, through its V.I.P. imprint in 1965.

Born Ricardo Btesh in Cairo on 13 January 1938, his career took off when he began taking popular songs and recording them in French and by 1962 had racked up 21 number one hits in France.

His only V.I.P. outing came with *I Don't Know What To Do*, ironically a song he wrote (misspelt on the single as 'Anthony') with Sylvano Santorio and which had originally been the B-side to his European release *Crying In The Rain*. In the US the single was coupled with *What Now My Love*, the Gilbert Becaud and Carl

Sigman standard. Whilst the single didn't do much in the US, it has become something of a favourite with the Northern Soul crowd.

APOLLO

Formed by Berry Gordy's son Kerry (born in Detroit, Michigan on 25 June 1959, keyboards), Benny Medina (vocals), Larry Robinson (guitar), Cliff Liles (bass) and Lenny Greene (drums) as Kryptonite, the group was forced to change their name owing to legal problems with the owners of the Superman trademark.
They signed with Gordy in 1979, where their debut album was produced by Raynoma Singleton (Berry Gordy's ex-wife and the mother of Kerry and Cliff Liles of the band), with *Astro Disco* attracting considerable club play. However, Motown's interest in the group soon waned, with a second album cancelled before the group could begin work on it. Cliff Liles later resurfaced in Kagny & The Dirty Rats who also recorded one album for Motown.
ALBUM: APOLLO (1977)

ARGO RECORDS

Launched by Chess Records in 1955 as Marterry Records, it switched name to Argo soon after following an objection by bandleader Ralph Marterie. Initially the label was home to Chess' growing jazz catalogue, although it soon developed an eclectic roster of pop and blues artists.
In October 1959 it signed a one-off distribution deal with Berry Gordy for Ron & Bill's single *It* backed with *Don't Say Bye Bye*, only the sixth single released by the fledgling Detroit label. Ron and Bill were better known as Ronnie White and Smokey Robinson of The Miracles, with *It* being too radical a departure from the trademark sound that would later captivate the record buying public. The single did little, bringing an abrupt halt to the deal soon after.

BILLY BOY ARNOLD

Born in Chicago, Illinois on 16 September 1935, Billy Boy Arnold took up the harmonica whilst still a child and received some informal training from Sonny Boy Williamson. Billy Boy made his recording debut in 1952 with *Hello Stranger* appearing on the Cool label, but it is with his body of work for Vee-Jay that he established his reputation. *I Wish You Would*, originally intended for Bo Diddley and which later attracted cover versions by The Yardbirds and David Bowie, appeared on the compilation album **Hits From The Legendary Vee-Jay Records** released on CD in November 1986.

ART & HONEY

Originally signed to MoWest, Art Posey and Honey Sessions' debut single *Let's Make Love Now* backed with *(I've Given You) The Best Years Of My Life* was scheduled for release in February 1973 and subsequently cancelled, only to appear on the main Motown label in September the same year. Both Art and Honey found a degree of success at Motown as writers or backing singers, with Art also releasing a number of singles on other labels that have attracted Northern Soul interest.

ARTIST DEVELOPMENT DEPARTMENT

Located at 2657 West Grand Boulevard, just across the road from the famed Hitsville USA studio, was the Artist Development Department. According to legend, Berry Gordy instigated the department after noticing that the artists he signed were being overshadowed by those brought in by Harvey Fuqua whenever the Motown Revue went out on the road, with Harvey's acts giving a much more polished presentation. Harvey was put in charge of the department and brought in choreographer Cholly Atkins, musical director Maurice King, pianist and arranger Johnny Allen and Maxine Powell, who was described as a 'charm school queen.' Harvey Fuqua was proud of the department and its work.
"Whenever a Motown act played they were always well polished. That came from my department. We had a regular schedule; we would start at ten in the morning. We drilled the whole thing into any and every artist before they'd made any kind of appearance anywhere."
Whilst Cholly and Maurice worked with the artists on how to present themselves on stage, it was Maxine's job to tutor the artists on how to conduct themselves off it, as Mary Wilson of The Supremes would later comment.
"Artist Development was preparation for the kind of work we were doing. The personal grooming, the work

ethic, all of that was just as important as the music, in some ways. Providing young people with the training they need for the work they choose to do, whatever it is – that was what Artist Development did for us, and it is still so important."

Her views were reinforced by Diana Ross, who also spent many an hour working at every aspect.

"The time in between, when we weren't popular yet was a real learning experience. They groomed us, helped us decide where we wanted to go and what kind of image we wanted. It was during this time that the style of The Supremes was developed. They assisted us in every manner possible – not just professionally, but personally, because if you're from a poor background, you don't know anything about clothes, dressings, hair, make-up and things like that. It was real artist development."

A minimum of two hours a day was spent with each artist grooming them in choreography, etiquette and vocal development, with the three disciplines complimenting each other. Whilst many of the artists were already well versed in how to perform at such venues as The Apollo, Maxine's lessons in particular were aimed at just two venues – The White House and Buckingham Palace. Thus the artists were taught how to walk and talk properly and, in the case of the female singers, even how to sit down gracefully! Fortunately, her pupils learnt their lessons well, eventually performing at The White House and in front of British royalty, although not at Buckingham Palace itself!

JACK ASHFORD

A native of Philadelphia, Pennsylvania, where he was born on 18 May 1934, Jack Ashford was spotted playing vibes with a trio in Boston in 1963 by Marvin Gaye. Accepting an offer to move to Detroit the same year, Jack Ashford became the in-house percussionist of The Funk Brothers, performing on at least a dozen traditional percussion instruments such as vibes, shakers, wood block and marimba as well as a few of his own creation, including knee slaps, foot stomps, the cowbell (which he stole directly from a cow spotted in a field during the Motown Revue of Britain in 1965!) and one called 'the hotel sheet.'

It is with the tambourine that he made his reputation, prompting the then EMI chairman Sir Joseph Lockwood (Tamla Motown's UK distributors) to remark that Motown's records wouldn't make it in the UK as the tambourine was mixed too hot!

Although Motown moved to Los Angeles in 1972, thus signalling an end to original Funk Brothers, Jack still found himself in great demand for session work, recording with Barry White, Bill Withers, Parliament, Johnny Mathis, Bob Seger and New Edition, among countless others. He also tried his hand at production and released a single on the Blaze label, owned by Barney Ales and distributed by Motown (*Do The Choo Choo*, issued in September 1975), but it is as a session musician that his legend remains. With the revival of interest in The Funk Brothers thanks to the documentary 'Standing In The Shadows Of Motown', Jack became part of an international touring group recreating the legendary Motown sound.

FURTHER READING: MOTOWN – THE VIEW FROM THE BOTTOM (2005)

ASHFORD & SIMPSON

The husband and wife team of Nickolas Ashford (born in Fairfield, South Carolina on 4 May 1941) and Valerie Simpson (born in New York City on 26 August 1946) had first recorded together as Valerie & Nick in 1964 for Glover Records, but after two singles left in order to concentrate on writing. Initially working at Scepter Records for The Shirelles, it was a successful Ray Charles cover of their song *Let's Get Stoned* that got them wider notice. Eventually they were lured to Motown as songwriters and producers in 1966.

"It was a dream come true. I mean, we were just writers, and Motown was Motown. It was the best thing that could have happened to us, it really was," was Valerie's recollection, as Nick would later confirm. "To us, Motown was it. And when they called us, we didn't hesitate. With a whole slew of artists our songs would get the chance to be recorded."

Among the recorded songs were *Ain't Nothing Like The Real Thing, You're All I Need To Get By, You Ain't Livin' Til Your Lovin', Good Lovin' Ain't Easy To Come By, The Onion Song* (all of which were hits by Marvin Gaye & Tammi Terrell), *Some Things You Never Get Used To* (Diana Ross & The Supremes), *Ain't No Mountain High Enough, Remember Me, Surrender, The Boss, It's My House, No One Gets The Prize* (Diana Ross) and *Request Line* (Zhane) among countless others. Many of these Nick and Val also produced, although like many at Motown, their contribution was often cloaked in secrecy, as Nick explained.

"That's just how Motown were. I thought it was really strange because they wanted to keep you in the dark. Everything was Motown. That was all that was supposed to be there. At least we got our names on records; they couldn't stop that but you never knew who was playing or anything. I think Motown were afraid, because of those contracts, that outsiders would get to you, talk to you, and perhaps wisen you up."

That uncertainty about who appeared on what song is exemplified by the confusion over the female vocalist on a couple of the tracks; it was alleged for many years that it was in fact Valerie's voice that featured on the Marvin Gaye & Tammi Terrell hits *Good Lovin'* and *The Onion Song* as Tammi was too ill to record, but this claim has been challenged in recent years, most notably by Tammi's own sister.

Whilst they were retained by Motown as producers and songwriters, Valerie did revive her own singing career in 1970 with Quincy Jones, performing on the albums **Gula Matari** and **Smackwater Jack.** This in turn prompted a brief Motown recording career of two albums, **Valerie Simpson Exposed** (1971) and **Valerie Simpson** (1972), but aside from a minor R&B hit with *Silly Wasn't I* in 1972 neither sold in sufficient quantities to suggest Motown was putting real marketing muscle behind the albums.

"We were considering this thing about being artists and realised that Motown maybe didn't see us as artists. My albums hadn't done very much so they weren't excited about the idea of doing anything on us. So it seemed the right thing to do. The contracts were up, so we left."

Motown's refusal to release an album of the pair recording a collection of their greatest songs was the tipping point, after which they left the label. Married in 1974, Ashford & Simpson subsequently signed with Warner Brothers and resumed their joint recording career, scoring international hits with *It Seems To Hang On, Don't Cost You Nothin'* and *Found A Cure* (which prompted Motown selecting the best tracks from Valerie's two albums which were issued as the compilation album **Keep It Comin'** in 1977) and later hits such as *Solid* and *Street Corner* for Capitol. They did return to Motown, however, writing and producing **The Boss** on Diana Ross in 1979. Nick died on 22 August 2011 after a lengthy battle with throat cancer.

ALBUMS: EXPOSED (1971), VALERIE SIMPSON (1972)
COMPILATION: KEEP IT COMIN' (1977)

STEVE ASHLEY

British folksinger and songwriter Steve Frank Ashley was born in London on 9 March 1946 and began his musical career at the age of fifteen, performing in the folk clubs of West London. He moved to Maidstone in 1964 to study graphic design but soon established a successful folk club in the town and would combine his studies with performing with The Tea Set and forming Tinderbox.

After a spell with Albion Country Band and Ragged Robin, he launched a solo career, recording **Stroll On** for Gull Records in 1974 (it would be issued in the US the following year as part of the Motown deal) and following it a year later with **Speedy Returns** (also issued by Motown in 1976). Despite critical acclaim at home and several successful tours of the US in support of both albums he remained largely unknown to American audiences. Although Gull's Motown deal came to an abrupt end on 1976, Steve Ashley continued to record into the following century, regarded by many as Britain's best ever folk artist.

ALBUMS: STROLL ON (1975), SPEEDY RETURNS (1976)

GIL ASKEY

After discharge from the US Army Air Corps in 1944, trumpet player Gil Askey (born Gilbert Alexander Askey in Austin, Texas on 9 March 1925) enrolled at the Boston Conservatory of Music and thereafter the Harnett National Music Studios in Manhattan. He got his first big break as arranger and trumpet player with Buddy Johnson's band and spent three years out on the road before rock and roll took over the music environment, leading to Gil becoming part of the house band that toured with the likes of Frankie Lymon & The Teenagers, The Platters, The Clovers, Jackie Wilson and Lloyd Price. In 1965 Berry Gordy invited him to produce six tracks on Billy Eckstine's **Prime Of My Life**, although Gil ended up doing the entire album and thus began an association with Motown that would see him work as a composer, producer and musical director for the likes of Diana Ross, The Supremes, The Four Tops, The Temptations and The Jackson 5, among others.

It was his work on the soundtrack to 'Lady Sings The Blues' that earned him an Oscar nomination for Best Music, Original Song Score and Adaptation, although he lost out to 'Cabaret', with a single from the soundtrack album, entitled *Don't Explain* backed with *C.C. Rider* released credited to the Gil Askey Orchestra. Having married an Australian woman, Gil relocated to Melbourne in 1980, although he was lured back to Motown in 1982 for the 'Motown 25' television special, eventually going back out on the road with The Temptations and The Four Tops for a further three years as well as co-producing the Regal Funkharmonic

Orchestra and the **Strung Out On Motown** album. He retired from touring in 1985 but continued to perform with a jazz combo on a weekly basis in Australia up until his death on 9 April 2014.

CHOLLY ATKINS

Formerly a member of a tap-dancing duo with Charles 'Honi' Coles, Cholly Atkins (born Charles Sylvan Atkinson in Pratt City, Alabama on 13 September 1913) worked as a freelance choreographer for the likes of The Cadillacs and The Miracles before being hired on a more permanent basis by Berry Gordy in 1964. At Motown his brief was to choreograph the likes of The Temptations (although group member Paul Williams had previously been responsible for all of the group's dance steps), Marvin Gaye, The Supremes, The Four Tops and Gladys Knight & The Pips and anyone else who came through the doors of Motown.

Cholly's work was not only confined to Motown, for he also choreographed The O'Jays and The Sylvers during the 1970s. He would collect a Tony Award (Broadway's equivalent of the Oscar and Grammy) for his work on the 1989 Broadway stage production 'Black And Blue'. After being diagnosed with pancreatic cancer in March 2003, Cholly died on 19 April in Las Vegas aged 89 years.

KAY AUSTIN

Country singer Kenne Jeanne Austin was born in Long Beach, California on 31 January 1944 and was known as KJ among her family. In time the 'J' got dropped and it was as Kay Austin that she would make her name in the record industry, touring coast to coast from the early 1970s. In 1974 she was one of the nominees for Most Promising Female Vocalist by the Academy of Country Music and four years later was one of the early artists signed to Mike Curb and Berry Gordy's joint MC Records label. Only one single appeared, *Try Me* before the venture came to an abrupt end.

For some reason Kay never quite managed to attain the heights many believed she was destined for, although she has established a sizeable reputation within country music circles for her live performances, earning the moniker The Country Fox. In 1983 she switched musical style to gospel and later became involved in real estate.

AUTOMATICALLY SUNSHINE – THE SUPREMES [SINGLE]

The success enjoyed by *Floy Joy* and its follow-up *Automatically Sunshine* provided The Supremes with something of an Indian summer, at least as far as their British fans were concerned. Whilst their American fan base had swiftly moved on after Diana Ross' departure, with only *Up The Ladder To The Roof* and *Stoned Love* returning them to the Top Ten, in Britain the hits kept coming. The **Floy Joy** album had indeed been a joy for both the group and their producer Smokey Robinson to record, among the last sessions the group was to record in Detroit. Once again Smokey allowed Jean and Mary to alternate the lead vocals, with The Andantes and Cindy Birdsong providing backing vocals.

Since the recording was pretty much done under the same kind of conditions that had been prevalent during the 1960s it was no surprise the final sound should invoke similar memories. Whilst *Automatically Sunshine* had too much of a 1960s feel for America, having to settle for a #37 pop and #21 R&B chart placing, it once again hit the mark in the UK. A final position of #10, the fifth post-Diana single to hit the Top Ten, confirmed The Supremes as still the girl group all the others looked up to. *Automatically Sunshine* hit the Top Ten on 5 August 1972; unfortunately they have yet to return.

B

BOB BABBITT

Born Robert Andrew Kreinar in Pittsburgh, Pennsylvania on 26 November 1937 to Hungarian parents, Bob was classically trained to play the upright bass but switched to the more modern electric bass after hearing it at a local nightclub. After turning down a music scholarship Bob moved to Detroit and worked in the construction industry during the day and played clubs at night. By the mid 1960s his reputation had grown to such an extent he was invited along to Golden World studio to perform on a number of recording sessions, usually alongside moonlighting Funk Brothers members.

Although Bob had tried to move to Motown officially in 1965 (he wanted to join The Supremes road band but was talked out of it by Ed Wingate), he found himself part of Motown in 1967 after Berry Gordy bought Golden World in order to eliminate the Detroit competition! Bob was often asked to stand in for the increasingly unreliable James Jamerson, whose drinking impacted on just about every aspect of his working and personal life, but as popular as James undoubtedly was, the rest of The Funk Brothers took to Bob Babbitt too.

Reportedly Bob had at one point been promised the opportunity of recording a solo album, although it failed to materialise (even a single, *Gospel Truth* was scheduled but then shelved), and as Motown began moving operations to the West Coast, work in and around Detroit began to diminish. After a brief period performing as a wrestler, Bob moved to New York in 1973 and went back to music, working with Barry Manilow and Bette Midler. He also got to work regularly in Philadelphia with Thom Bell and The Spinners, then Nashville with a host of country artists. Along with the rest of The Funk Brothers, Bob Babbitt's part in the Motown legacy was finally recognised with the release of the documentary 'Standing In The Shadows Of Motown'. He died from brain cancer on 16 July 2012.

BABY, BABY DON'T CRY – SMOKEY ROBINSON & THE MIRACLES [SINGLE]

As 1968 came to a close, Smokey Robinson had a troubled mind. There was a growing rift between him and other members of The Miracles, most notably Warren Moore, with finance the root of their disagreement. Smokey had pretty much made up his mind to leave the group and record solo; the only question that remained was when to bow out. In the meantime, a relative lack of recording success made it a difficult decision to make, for Smokey realised that whenever he did leave, it would severely impact on his former group's abilities to generate revenue on their own.

Whilst he continued to put off making the ultimate decision, he tried to smooth the working relationship with the group by bringing in other parties with which to work. To this end staff writers Al Cleveland and Terry Johnson (a former member of The Flamingos) co-wrote *Baby, Baby Don't Cry* and Smokey, Warren and Terry co-produced. If there was a frosty atmosphere in the studio then it didn't show, for the single returned The Miracles to the Top Ten on both the charts, peaking at #3 R&B and #8 pop.

BABY LOVE – THE SUPREMES [SINGLE]

Having finally broken into the upper echelons of the charts thanks to *Where Did Our Love Go*, it was imperative The Supremes returned with another hit as quickly as possible lest their new found fans and fame deserted them. Berry Gordy instructed Brian and Eddie Holland and Lamont Dozier to come up with something similar, with the result the trio constructed rather than wrote *Baby Love* with The Supremes in mind. Like its predecessor, *Baby Love* was not a song The Supremes were particularly keen on, but the success of *Where Did Our Love Go* dictated that whilst the production trio were hot, the singing trio would record what was placed in front of them.

All of the elements from *Where Did Our Love Go* were reincorporated into *Baby Love*, including instrumentation from the Funk Brothers and the foot stomps from Mike Valvano. However, one subtle change was the decision to allow Mary Wilson and Flo Ballard solo ad-libs towards the end of the song, virtually the only time they would get to do any solos on record for the rest of the decade. Recorded on 13 August 1964, *Baby Love* was hastily scheduled for US release on 17 September with the catalogue number M1066 and less than four weeks later had made its first appearance on the chart. A further four weeks was all the single took to arrive at the chart summit, displacing Manfred Mann's *Do Wah Diddy Diddy* and spending a further four weeks at #1. In the UK the release was scheduled for October, timed to coincide with an impending promotional visit by The Supremes. The timing proved advantageous, for the single entered the chart at much the same time the trio descended the steps at Heathrow Airport and, helped by an appearance on 'Top Of The Pops', *Baby Love* vaulted the UK chart almost as quickly as it had the American one. By 19 November it had reached #1, giving The Supremes the satisfaction of topping the charts on both sides of the Atlantic simultaneously, eventually ruling the UK charts for two weeks.

In the US the single would eventually be awarded a gold single to signify sales of over one million units; sales in the UK exceeded a quarter of a million copies, for which the group received a silver disc award from 'Disc' magazine. Whilst *Baby Love* may have been a simplistic song, its instant appeal went beyond the record-buying public, for at the end of the year it was nominated for a Grammy Award for Best Rhythm & Blues Recording, although losing out to Nancy Wilson's *How Glad I Am*. The single would become a British hit all over again in 1974 when it peaked at #12, whilst a later cover version by post-punk singer Honey Bane made #53 in 1981.

BACK IN MY ARMS AGAIN – THE SUPREMES [SINGLE]

The Supremes fifth consecutive number one hit in America, *Back In My Arms Again* was something of a re-write of *This Old Heart Of Mine*, containing much the same hook. However, Holland-Dozier-Holland had the idea of writing the individual Supremes into the lyrics, with Diana name-checking both Mary Wilson and Florence Ballard during the course of the song. At this point in their career, it was still The Supremes, with Diana Ross' elevation to group leader still some two years off.

Back In My Arms Again knocked The Beach Boys' *Help Me Rhonda* off the top of the Billboard Hot 100 and spent a week at the summit. It also dethroned label-mate Marvin Gaye's *I'll Be Doggone* from the top of the R&B chart, where it also spent a solitary week. The single's performance in the UK, however, was somewhat disappointing, peaking at #40 and way off the heights attained by any of their earlier chart hits.

TOM BAIRD

Born in Vancouver, Canada on 27 April 1943, Tom Baird made his name for his production work and writing for Rare Earth, both the label and the band, but was active on many other sessions around Hitsville. He was a member of Canadian group The Classics, formed in Vancouver in 1961 as CFUN Classics, a group that did public promotion for radio station CFUN before incorporating their own material into their repertoire. They recorded a couple of singles in the mid 1960s for Valiant (as The Canadian Classics) and GNP Crescendo before Tom crossed the border to begin working for Motown.

He first came to prominence co-writing Bobby Taylor & The Vancouvers' *Does Your Mama Know About Me* and would later write and produce The Commodores, Gladys Knight, Diana Ross and Stevie Wonder, among countless others. He was at his most active for the Rare Earth label, again writing and producing many of the artists on the label but also linking with Nick Zesses and Dino Fekaris in a trio called Matrix. Tom produced Rare Earth between 1970 and 1972 and in 1974 formed a new band called HUB with Peter Hoorelbecke (better known by his stage name Pete Rivera, a member of Rare Earth) and Mike Urso, the group taking their name from their initials and recording two albums for Capitol.

This group was brought to an untimely end when Tom was killed in a boating accident in November 1975; Tom was due to go sailing with Pete Rivera off the coast of Los Angeles when he learned Pete would be a late as he had to return home for a short while. Rather than wait Tom decided to undertake some solo practice and went off into open waters, was probably hit on the head by a sail, tipped into the sea unconscious and subsequently drowned. A search organized by the Coast Guard failed to find his body, as did an air search conducted by Pete Rivera. The body was eventually found some time later by local fishermen, with his date of death being recorded as 25 February 1976.

CHET BAKER

Equally well known as a trumpeter and singer, jazz musician Chet Baker should have become a bigger success, but a well publicized drug problem, which invariably led him to pawning his musical instruments, proved virtually insurmountable.

Born Chesney Henry Baker in Yale, Oklahoma on 23 December 1929, Chet made his reputation with stints with Charlie Parker and Stan Getz before linking up in 1952 with Gerry Mulligan in a piano-less quartet that was widely admired. Unfortunately Gerry Mulligan's own drug problems brought the quartet to a halt after a little over a year, with Chet subsequently recording a vocal album for Pacific Jazz in the mid fifties, **Chet Baker Sings**, which whilst successful alienated his core jazz fan base. Chet's battles with drug addiction would see him expelled from West Germany and Britain, endure several spells in prison and also become the victim of a severe beating that resulted in the loss of several teeth and with it the ability to actually play the trumpet for a spell.

Once he had been fitted for a set of dentures he resumed his career, recording one solo album for CTI (**She Was Too Good To Me** in 1974, which would hit #31 on the jazz chart) and reuniting with Gerry Mulligan for a highly regarded series of concerts at Carnegie Hall that were issued as two CTI albums (the first volume would hit #22 on the jazz chart). Chet effectively moved to Europe in 1978, where he recorded and toured extensively, although he invariably returned home to America at least once a year right up until his death on 13 May 1988. He was found lying in the street outside his hotel bedroom window in Amsterdam, with the autopsy revealing heroin and cocaine in his body.

ALBUMS: SHE WAS TOO GOOD TO ME (1974), CARNEGIE HALL CONCERT (1975), CARNEGIE HALL CONCERT VOLUME TWO (1975)

THE BAKER'S WIFE (THEATRICAL SHOW)

Motown partnered legendary Broadway producer David Merrick to fund a short run for the Stephen Schwartz penned musical 'The Baker's Wife' in 1976. Despite featuring Topol as the lead, the show underwent numerous changes during its six month run across the United States, with plans for a Broadway run and cast recording coming to an ignoble end in November 1976.

HARRY BALK

By the mid 1960s, the three main music men of Detroit were Berry Gordy, Ed Wingate and Harry Balk, with all three effectively ending up inside the same camp; Berry Gordy's at Motown. Harry's career in music had predated his rivals, having been responsible for producing Johnny & The Hurricanes and Del Shannon, run his own record labels Twirl, Bigtop and later Impact and Inferno and written a number of hits with Irving Micahnik. Born in Michigan on 15 October 1925, Harry was also a movie theatre owner in Detroit but would ultimately play a greater part in musical history during his involvement with Motown.

By 1968 his fledgling labels Impact and Inferno were, like Ed Wingate's various imprints, proving to be something of a thorn in Motown's side, so much so that Berry bought out his rivals one by one and folded their operations into his own. Whilst this would mean several Inferno and Impact artists eventually turned up on Motown, most notably The Detroit Wheels, Michael Denton and The Volumes, Harry was soon installed in a more creative position, including being put in charge of the launch of the Rare Earth label. He was also responsible for pushing for the release of Marvin Gaye's *What's Going On* single, even though he was aware that Gordy disliked it. In the event, Harry and Barney Ales' hunch paid off, resulting on one of the biggest album successes Motown ever enjoyed. Harry would later form another record label, Avatar Records based in Malibu and continue his entrepreneurial skills.

BALL OF CONFUSION – THE TEMPTATIONS [SINGLE]

Norman Whitfield had originally intended for *War* to be declared the follow-up single to *Psychedelic Shack* by The Temptations but found stiff opposition within Motown to this idea. With The Temptations having broken through into the pop charts on a regular basis, it was felt by many that the anti-war message in *War* would alienate too many of their new found pop fans. Whilst Norman Whitfield accepted the argument (at least as far as The Temptations were concerned, for he would rework the song with Edwin Starr and score a worldwide hit) he still felt it vital that The Temptations should use their new found position to pass comment on what was happening domestically and internationally, writing *Ball Of Confusion* as a compromise.

Despite this, *Ball Of Confusion* is a masterful single in its own right. If the lyrics are somewhat watered-down, at least as far as *War* is concerned, then the music is anything but. As funky as anything The Temptations recorded, *Ball Of Confusion* throws in comment on all manner of problems facing America at this particular point in time. Indeed, there is so much comment the group initially had reservations about whether they could pull off the quick-fire vocal delivery satisfactorily, with Dennis Edwards, Eddie Kendricks, Paul Williams and Melvin Franklin all taking lead at some point. It should be noted, however, that Norman and lyricist Barrett Strong would be proven wrong on one aspect of the single; despite the observation 'The Beatles' new record's a gas', The Beatles wouldn't release another single!

Released in May 1970, the end result was a smash, hitting #3 pop and #2 R&B in the US and #7 in the UK. As the song was effectively specially recorded in the wake of *War* being rejected as a single, *Ball Of Confusion* did not appear on any of The Temptations contemporary albums, although it is to be regularly found on compilations. Norman Whitfield would revisit the song with both The Undisputed Truth and Edwin Starr, whilst Tina Turner also recorded a cover version in conjunction with Martyn Ware and Ian Craig Marsh of Heaven 17 – the success of the track led indirectly to Capitol Records signing Tina as a solo artist.

FLORENCE BALLARD

Considered by many to be the supreme Supreme, both as a singer and for her looks, her life ended tragically young with her career virtually in tatters. Born Florence Glenda Ballard in Detroit, Michigan on 30 June 1943, the eighth of thirteen children and known as either Flo or Blondie (due to her auburn hair and light complexion), she quickly developed a reputation around her neighbourhood as a talented singer.

One day in 1958, Flo was sitting outside her home with her elder sister Maxine when a bright red Cadillac pulled up alongside them. The driver Milton Jenkins got out and initially approached Maxine, asking her whether she would be interested in joining a female singing group he was putting together. Whilst Maxine was taken by the dapper man on her doorstep (Maxine and Milton would subsequently marry in 1961, after the divorce from her husband, a Marine stationed overseas, came through) she seemingly had little or no interest in singing, although Flo did, eventually signing a contract pretty much there and then which was endorsed by her mother Lurlee. Since Flo also seemed to know the names of several other would-be singers, Milton instructed her to bring along another likely singer later that week.

At school a day or so later, Flo told Mary Wilson of this potential opening and arranged for the pair of them to journey over to Milton's place for an audition. Also there on the same day was Betty McGlown (the girlfriend of Paul Williams of The Primes) and Diane Ross, another local girl who had established something of a reputation of her own for her singing abilities. Thus The Primettes were born, although Milton Jenkins' abilities extended no further than being able to get them a succession of live dates but no recording contract. That they would eventually land through the efforts of Robert Bateman and Richard Morris, with The Primettes recording their first single for LuPine Records, *Tears Of Sorrow* (written by Flo, Diana and Richard Morris and with Diana singing lead) backed with *Pretty Baby* (written by Flo, Diana, Mary and Morris and with Mary on lead) appearing in August 1960.

Irrespective of who sang lead, Flo was seen as the outgoing member of the group; mischievous and fun-loving. However, her personality underwent a severe change during 1960 when, having become separated from her brother Billy at a dance at Detroit's Graystone Ballroom, she accepted a lift from local high school basketball player Reginald Harding. Instead of taking her home as promised, he drove to a secluded parking lot and raped her at knifepoint. Flo kept the attack secret from everyone for weeks, reluctant to reveal the trauma she had undergone even to her group-mates until, many weeks later, Flo told them the whole story. After that, the subject was never discussed again, resulting, as far as Mary Wilson was concerned, in Flo retreating into a shell, cynical and mistrustful of others (although Harding was never charged with rape, his basketball career stuttered owing to spells in prison, drug addiction and at least two instances when he threatened to shoot his manager and a teammate; he was to be shot dead in 1972).

Meanwhile Betty McGlown had left The Primettes to be replaced by Barbara Martin and the group was badgering Motown Records for a contract, finally being signed in January 1961. Although Berry thought the girls had potential, he did not like their name and so had Janie Bradford write up a list of alternatives, from which Flo picked the replacement; although Diana Ross and Mary Wilson later stated they were not over-enthused with the new name, thinking it too masculine. The name Flo chose was The Supremes, perhaps her last truly meaningful contribution to the group.

As well as her work with the newly christened group, Flo kept busy around Hitsville, appearing on numerous sessions doing backing vocals and handclaps, as did the other group members. Flo also briefly toured with The Marvelettes, filling in for Wanda Young whilst she was on maternity leave. According to Marvelettes lead singer Gladys Horton, Flo supplied vocal advice before she went into the studio to record *Please Mr. Postman*, even though The Supremes had yet to register a hit record.

Whilst The Supremes shared lead vocals on their early recordings and live dates, all that was to change with Berry Gordy's insistence that Diana be made lead singer on all singles from 1963 onwards, leaving *Buttered Popcorn* the only Supremes 45 ever released that featured Flo as the showcased singer. Whilst Mary was content to provide backing vocals on the material provided, Flo was not (Barbara Martin left the group in 1962 and The Supremes continued as a trio), putting her on a collision course with Berry Gordy.

Flo did get several leads on album tracks and live dates, with one highlight of The Supremes live show being *People* from the Broadway musical *Funny Girl*, which remained a staple part of The Supremes live show for several years. In 1966, prior to an appearance at the Copacabana in New York, Flo complained of a sore throat and was unable to take her moment in the spotlight; Diana Ross sang the song on the night and later, at the insistence of Berry Gordy, was assigned the song on a permanent basis. An already fractured relationship between employer (Berry Gordy) and employee (Florence Ballard) was heading towards an abrupt end.

According to later reports, Berry and Flo bickered and argued almost constantly, with Berry finding fault in almost everything Flo did. The criticism stung, resulting in Flo drinking more than she should, turning up late on a regular basis and putting on weight. Just prior to a date at the Flamingo Hotel in Las Vegas in July 1967, Flo and Berry argued backstage, with Berry again criticising Flo's weight. When The Supremes took to the stage, Flo made a point of deliberately sticking her stomach out, inflaming Berry Gordy to such an extent he effectively sacked her on the spot, refusing to allow her to go back on stage for the second performance. As the troubles between Berry and Flo had headed towards their peak, Motown had already been grooming a replacement Supreme, with Cindy Birdsong taking over on a permanent basis. It should be noted, however, that whilst Flo's weight problem is often cited as a major reason for her exit from The Supremes, Cindy Birdsong wore many of her outfits once she had become a permanent member of the group!

With the official reason for her departure being given as exhaustion, Flo returned to Detroit to ponder her next move. At the same time Flo negotiated her release from Motown, she also arranged her wedding to former Motown chauffeur Tommy Chapman. The release from Motown came in February 1968, with the label paying $139,804 in royalties and earnings as full and final settlement (during their time as members of The Supremes, Flo and Mary had been paid a weekly wage of $225; the assumption is that Diana Ross may have started on this wage too but been later paid more as befitted her rank as group leader), and a week later Flo and Tommy were married. Tommy had ambitions of becoming a manager and negotiated a deal with ABC Records, which Flo signed in March 1968. Unfortunately, the terms of her departure from Motown had stipulated that she could not make any mention of her time as a Supreme or that she had even recorded for Motown in any promotional material, making ABC's job of marketing her extremely difficult.

Two singles appeared and disappeared with speed, *It Doesn't Matter How I Say It (It's What I Say That Matters)* and *Love Ain't Love*, resulting in a planned album being shelved and her contract cancelled. Disappearing equally quickly was the settlement money from Motown, lost in Chapman's management company Talent Management Inc., which had been set up by Tommy and lawyer Leonard Baun. When Flo took a closer look at Baun's track record, she discovered a lawyer facing several charges of embezzlement from previous clients. Flo fired him and began a lengthy legal battle that was not resolved until 1975.

With the termination of her ABC contract, Flo did a number of live dates before the birth of twins, Michelle and Nicole in October 1968. Flo returned to the stage in January 1969, performing at Richard Nixon's inaugural ball in Washington D.C. before going into semi-retirement to look after her babies, although even with her solo career effectively in tatters, Flo remained loyal to the Motown cause, especially over the manner of her removal from The Supremes.

"I've told people over and over again that we didn't have any 'fight'. We had arguments and things just like sisters have because we grew up just like sisters and we were together all those years. Now as far as the so-called 'jealousy' is concerned, Mary Wilson and I always knew that Diana had the most commercial type voice, so she took most of the leads. We knew that all along...so I just wish people wouldn't read more into my leaving than there is actually there. All I have to say is that I wish the group all the success in the world. They're doing their thing, and Flo Ballard is going to do hers."

That 'thing' turned out to be an attempt to extract additional royalties from Motown, which floundered in 1971, the same year that her third child Lisa was born. Unfortunately, her marriage collapsed soon after, with Tommy leaving the family home which, as money problems mounted, was subsequently foreclosed. Briefly lured out of retirement in 1974 by Mary Wilson, who with a new line-up of The Supremes (Mary, Cindy and Scherrie Payne) invited Flo to a concert in Valencia, California and encouraged her onstage to sing; Flo did go on stage but was more than happy to stand at the side and play the tambourine.

With no interest in reviving her professional career at the time, Flo returned to Detroit and applied for welfare, bringing a flurry of media activity focussing on the decline of one of The Supremes. In 1975 Flo received an insurance payout and started to turn her life around, purchasing a house on Shaftesbury Avenue, reconciling with her husband and deciding to return to singing. A performance at the Ford Auditorium in Detroit in June 1975, backed with The Deadly Nightshade was extremely well received, leading to numerous requests for interviews from both press and television.

Before Flo could begin shopping around for a new record deal, however, she was taken ill on the morning of 21 February 1976 and admitted to hospital complaining of numbness in her extremities. The following morning, at 10.05 am, she died, with the official cause of death being given as coronary artery thrombosis, a blood clot. Several people, including one of her sisters, continue to question the official cause, pointing to the presence of an unidentified substance in her body and have pushed (unsuccessfully) for Flo's body to be exhumed and re-examined.

Flo's funeral drew a crowd of 5,000 lining the streets and some two thousand to the church, including both Mary Wilson and Diana Ross. While Mary sat and sobbed among the congregation, Diana Ross sat in the front row with one of Flo's daughters, Lisa, on her lap; that was the image that appeared in the national papers the very next day. Even at the end of the service, fate had a final twist in store for Flo; the organist played *Someday We'll Be Together* as the congregation filed up the aisles. Unfortunately, whilst the lyrical sentiments might have been well intentioned, it did not go unmissed that the song, the last released by Diana Ross & The Supremes, was recorded entirely by Diana *without* The Supremes, and certainly not Florence 'Flo' Ballard, who had left the group two years beforehand.

In a sense, Flo had foreseen that her time as a Supreme was never going to be for the long haul, stating, "We were bound someday to go our separate ways. But the best part was back at the beginning. All of it was a lot of work before we made it. We lived like sisters."

FURTHER READING: LOST SUPREME: THE LIFE OF DREAMGIRL FLORENCE BALLARD (2008)

HANK BALLARD & THE MIDNIGHTERS

Henry Bernard Ballard was born in Detroit, Michigan on 18 November 1927 and after a spell working in the automotive industry in Detroit joined The Royals in 1953, a group that also included Henry Booth, Charles Sutton, Sonny Woods and Alonzo Tucker. Signed to Federal Records, the group would enjoy a big R&B hit with *Get It* before changing their name to The Midnighters in order to avoid confusion with The 5 Royales.

Meanwhile, the newly christened Hank Ballard was proving himself to be an excellent writer as well as singer, coming up with *Work With Me Annie* in 1954 that would go on to become an R&B chart topper and a #22 pop hit as well as inspiring a slew of answer records and cover versions. Hank Ballard & The Midnighters would go on to enjoy a further sixteen R&B hits over the next eight years, including the R&B chart toppers *Annie Had A Baby* and *Let's Go Let's Go Let's Go* and the crossover hit and Grammy nominated *Finger Poppin' Time* (#7 pop and #2 R&B). This latter track was featured on the soundtrack to 'The Flamingo Kid' and released on Motown in December 1984. The Midnighters disbanded in 1965, after which Hank launched a solo career, although with little success and reformed The Midnighters in the mid 1980s, touring with them until 2002. A cousin of The Supremes' Florence Ballard, Hank died from throat cancer on 2 March 2003.

BALLERINA GIRL – LIONEL RICHIE [SINGLE]

Lionel Richie's third solo album **Dancing On The Ceiling** had already given rise to three Top Ten pop smashes when *Ballerina Girl* was scheduled for release in November 1986. The lead track, as delicate a ballad as any he had produced previously, was certainly guaranteed interest as a single in its own right, but the decision to couple it with *Deep River Woman*, a country flavoured track that featured backing vocals by Alabama, a long standing and successful country rock group, proved something of a master stroke.

Lionel was no stranger to the country market, having successfully written and produced Kenny Rogers on *Lady* some six years previously, and the presence of Alabama ensured continuing interest from this sector. *Ballerina Girl* would become the fourth consecutive Top Ten single from the album, hitting #7 pop and #5 R&B (and making the Top 20 in the UK, where it peaked at #17), but *Deep River Woman* charted at #71 in its own right on the pop chart and made an impressive #10 on the Hot Country Singles chart.

BANCO

Italian progressive rock group Banco was formed in Rome in 1969 by brothers Vittorio (born in Marino on 23 January 1951) and Gianni Nocenzi (born in Marino on 27 December 1952) as Banco del Mutuo Soccorso (the name means 'the bank of self-help', or piggy bank). Inspired by British rock group Emerson, Lake & Palmer, Banco recorded their debut album in 1972 and were later signed by ELP to their Manticore label.

In 1975, by which time the group consisted of Francesco DiGiacomo (born in Siniscola on 22 August 1947, vocals), Vittorio Nocenzi (keyboards), Gianni Nocenzi (keyboards), Rodolfo Maltese (born in Orvieto on 26 February 1947, guitar), Renato D'Angelo (bass) and Pierluigi Calderoni (born in Rome on 14 December 1949, drums), Banco released their self titled fourth album, which received a US release through Motown, who were then the licensees of the Manticore label. The group continues to perform live, although haven't recorded any new material since 1997. DiGiacomo was killed in a traffic collision on 21 February 2014.

ALBUM: BANCO (1975)

THE BAND

A Canadian rock group formed in Toronto by Robbie Robertson (born in Toronto on 5 July 1944, guitar and vocals), Richard Manuel (born in Stratford on 3 April 1945, piano and vocals), Garth Hudson (born in London, Ontario on 2 August 1937, organ), Rick Danko (born in Simcoe on 9 December 1943, bass and vocals) and Levon Helm (born in Marvell, Arizona on 26 May 1942, drums and vocals), they were originally members of Ronnie Hawkin's backing group The Hawks. They left Hawkins in 1964 and toured and recorded with Bob Dylan, eventually recording under their own steam as The Band in 1968.

Their debut album featured the hit single *The Weight* (US #63, UK #21), which was later featured on the Motown soundtrack album **More Songs From The Big Chill**, released in April 1984. Manuel committed suicide by hanging himself after a concert on 6 March 1986. Danko died in his sleep on 10 December 1999. Helm died from throat cancer on 19 April 2012.

ROSE BANKS

Rose first came to prominence as a member of Sly & The Family Stone, a group that also included her brothers Sly and Freddie Stone. Keyboardist and vocalist Rose, who was born Rose Mary Stewart in Vallejo, California on 21 March 1945, joined the group in 1968 and enjoyed several major hits before the group imploded in 1975. Her husband, Hamp 'Bubba' Banks, a former manager and co-producer of Sly & The Family Stone wasted little time in arranging a solo career for his wife, recording several tracks that were played to Motown executives.

Whilst they expressed interest in signing her, the company also insisted she record a number of songs from the Jobete catalogue, resulting in a somewhat diluted debut album in **Rose**, issued in May 1976 (it appeared two months later in the UK). Despite the appearance of former Family Stone members Freddie Stone and Cynthia Robinson, production from Motown stalwart Jeffrey Bowen and a well received slot supporting Marvin Gaye on tour, the album disappeared without trace and only one single, *Whole New Thing* made any kind of impact, hitting #50 on the R&B chart. Shortly after Rose left Motown and concentrated on providing backing vocals for artists as diverse as Michael Jackson, Ringo Starr and Robbie Williams.
ALBUM: ROSE (1976)

IMAMU AMIRI BARAKA

Writer and poet Amiri Baraka was born Everett LeRoi Jones in Newark, New Jersey on 7 October 1934 and studied religion at Rutgers, Columbia and Howard universities. He left in 1954 without having obtained a degree and joined the US Air Force, where he attained the rank of sergeant. He was later given a dishonorable discharge (Soviet writings were found among his belongings after an anonymous tip-off) for violation of his oath of duty and moved to New York where he wrote poetry (his first book was published in 1961) and founded the Black Arts Repertory Theater School.

After winning an Obie award for his play 'Dutchman' in 1963 he began to take an active interest in and became leader of the Black Nationalist movement, subsequently changing his name to Imamu Amiri Baraka. He dropped the 'Imamu' name (which means 'spiritual leader') in 1970, but his full Muslim name was present on both of his albums released by the Black Forum label in April 1972, **Black Spirits** and **It's Nation Time – African Visionary Music**. The albums featured Baraka reading selections from his volumes 'Tales', 'Spirit Reach', In Our Terribleness' and 'Nation Time' blended with African Visionary Music performed by Lonnie Liston Smith, Idris Muhammad, Gary Bartz and other jazz notables. He died on 9 January 2014.
ALBUMS: BLACK SPIRITS (1972), IT'S NATION TIME - AFRICAN VISIONARY MUSIC (1972)

J.J. BARNES

James Jay Barnes spent a year signed to Motown, working in the studio almost every day (according his later recollections) with a succession of producers but released nothing during his time with the label, at least in the US. Like Edwin Starr, J.J. (born in Detroit, Michigan on 30 November 1943) was inherited by Motown following the acquisition of Ric-Tic and Golden World, with Berry Gordy purchasing the labels in order to eliminate the opposition, at least locally. By the time he joined Motown J.J. had already scored a Top Twenty R&B hit with *Real Humdinger* (#18) under his own name and a Top Ten hit as a member of The Holidays with Edwin Starr and Steve Mancha with *I'll Love You Forever* (#7), but apart from a couple of composing credits (*Show Me The Way* by Martha & The Vandellas and *Don't Make Hurting Me A Habit* by The Marvelettes) his time at Motown was wasted.

"They had me in the studio almost every day with one producer or another. I cut things with Richard Morris,

Sylvia Moy, James Dean, William Weatherspoon, Clarence Paul and Norman Whitfield. And some of the material was good. I never really knew what they were doing. When they took us over, I was doing okay, but they seemed to ignore Edwin and me. It was as if they weren't interested so I got the hell out as soon as I could."

Released from his Motown contract he later recorded for Groovesville, Perception, Buddah, Volt and several other labels, with little success, but a later tour of England with Edwin Starr and a recording contract with Contempo Records reinforced his position as one of Northern Soul's favourite artists. It was in the UK that his only (Tamla) Motown single got released, *Real Humdinger* being issued in September 1973.

ROBERT BATEMAN

A founder member of The Satintones, the first vocal group to be signed to Motown, Robert Bateman was with the group for their six singles and undertook backing vocal and engineering work before switching to writing and production, working initially in conjunction with Brian Holland under the moniker Brianbert. The pair, along with Georgia Dobbins and William Garrett wrote Motown's first number one hit, *Please Mr. Postman* for The Marvelettes, and Robert had a hand in writing the follow-ups *Twistin' Postman* and *Playboy* as well as conducting the audition that saw Mary Wells signed to the label.

After this success in Detroit, Robert headed to New York in search of further acclaim, co-writing Solomon Burke's R&B hit *If You Need Me* with Wilson Pickett and Sonny Sanders. Robert would later produce one of Florence Ballard's two ABC singles, *Love Ain't Love*, although he had greater success as a writer, with *If You Need Me* being covered by The Rolling Stones, Tom Jones and Wilson Pickett.

THE BEACH BOYS

Originally formed in Hawthorne, California in 1961 by brothers Brian (born in Hawthorne on 20 June 1942, keyboards and bass), Carl (born in Hawthorne on 21 December 1946, guitar) and Dennis Wilson (born in Hawthorne on 4 December 1944, drums), cousin Mike Love (born in Los Angeles, California on 15 March 1941, saxophone and vocals) and Al Jardine (born in Lima, Ohio on 3 September 1942, guitar) as Carl & The Passions, they underwent a name change to The Pendletones before settling on The Beach Boys to reflect the inspiration for their early singles, all about surfing and beach life in California. They quickly became one of the biggest American bands of their age, scoring worldwide hits, with *Wouldn't It Be Nice* one of their most recognisable, a US #8 hit in 1966. The track appeared on the album **More Songs From The Big Chill** soundtrack released in April 1984.

Dennis Wilson drowned on 28 December 1983 at the age of 39 (his family's request that he should be buried at sea was only granted after the personal intervention of President Ronald Reagan). Carl Wilson, who was listed as a 'conscientious objector' during the Vietnam War (and was briefly jailed for refusing to undertake bedpan changing duties at the Los Angeles' Veterans Hospital in lieu of military service) died from cancer on 6 February 1998.

CARL BEAN

Formerly a singer with gospel outfit the Alex Bradford Gospel Troupe, Carl Bean (born in Baltimore, Maryland on 26 May 1944) had recorded as Carl Bean & Universal Love for ABC Records before turning to Broadway and appearing in several shows.

When Motown expressed an interest in reviving *I Was Born This Way*, originally released by Valentino in 1975, songwriter Bunny Jones suggested Carl Bean be the man to do it. With production by Philadelphia stalwarts Norman Harris, Ron Kersey and Talmadge 'TG' Conway, the track proved popular in the clubs and reached #15 on Billboard's National Disco Action Top 40 in 1977.

Bean later recorded for Airwave Records before being ordained a bishop and founding the Unity Fellowship Church in Los Angeles, a church that actively welcomes lesbian, gay and bisexual African Americans.

FURTHER READING: I WAS BORN THIS WAY (2010)

THE BEATLES

Although The Beatles never recorded for Motown, they never made any secret of their admiration for the label and its artists, championing the likes of Mary Wells in particular at almost every opportunity. That admiration led to their second American album containing cover versions of three Motown songs; *Please Mr. Postman*, originally by The Marvelettes, *Money* by Barrett Strong and *You Really Got A Hold Of Me* by Smokey Robinson & The Miracles (a fourth track, *Devil In Her Heart* was originally by fellow Detroit group The Donays). John Lennon does the lead vocal on all three tracks; *Please Mr. Postman* was recorded in nine takes, *You Really Got A Hold On Me* was edited from takes 10 and 11, and *Money* took seven takes.

Ever the businessman, Beatles' manager Brian Epstein telephoned Berry Gordy to negotiate a reduced royalty rate for the three tracks. Whilst the standard rate was two cents per track, Epstein was prepared to pay one and a half cents, believing that Motown would agree because they would see it as an honour to have three of their songs recorded by The Beatles. Berry Gordy refused the initial approach and also rejected a second request the following morning, although he was told by Epstein that he had until 12:00 that day in which to wire an answer. Berry Gordy called all of Motown's executives into his office to discuss the matter, with the assembled throng giving differing views. Finally, Berry Gordy sent word to Brian Epstein, two minutes before the deadline, that he would agree to the reduced rate. Two hours later, Motown learned that the songs were already recorded and Capitol had stock of **The Beatles Second Album** on its way to radio stations and stores! Fortunately, the album sold over two million copies in the United States, giving Motown and Berry Gordy some compensation for backing down at the last moment!

Over the ensuing years, Berry would repay the compliment, with several Motown artists recording songs written and made famous by The Beatles, including The Four Tops (*Eleanor Rigby* and *The Fool On The Hill*), Stevie Wonder (*We Can Work It Out*), Marvin Gaye (*Yesterday*) and Edwin Starr (*My Sweet Lord*), and releasing the album **Tribute: Motown Meets The Beatles**, although it was not reported whether Berry tried to get Brian Epstein or The Beatles' publishers to accept a reduced royalty rate!

BEAUTY IS ONLY SKIN DEEP – THE TEMPTATIONS [SINGLE]

Beauty Is Only Skin Deep features David Ruffin on lead vocals, but by all accounts it could have been the other Ruffin, his elder brother Jimmy, who took it into the charts. Norman Whitfield wrote the melody in 1964 and recorded the instrumental backing track in April of that year, but it was to take a further two years before it was presented to Eddie Holland to write the lyrics. The finished song was offered to Jimmy Ruffin, who turned it down (he had just completed recording *What Becomes Of The Broken Hearted* at the time) and then The Miracles, who recorded a version that eventually appeared on their **Away We A Go-Go** album towards the end of 1966.

By then Norman had achieved a major hit with *Ain't Too Proud To Beg,* which guaranteed him a shot at the next Temptations single and got them to record *Beauty Is Only Skin Deep* as a potential follow-up. That it was chosen as a single by Billie Jean Brown of the Quality Control Department caused the group to complain bitterly directly to Berry Gordy that they thought the song was the wrong choice; Berry backed Billie Jean Brown, who saw *Beauty Is Only Skin Deep* sail to the top of the R&B chart and hit #3 on the pop chart, their second pop Top Ten hit. For good measure, it made the Top 20 in the UK, peaking at #18.

JOE BECK

Guitarist Joe Beck was born in Philadelphia, Pennsylvania on 29 July 1945 and made his name as a session guitarist and producer, working with artists as diverse as Gil Evans, James Brown, Frank Sinatra, Paul Simon and Miles Davis during the course of his career. By the 1970s he was an in-house guitarist at CTI/Kudu and shared arrangement chores with David Matthews, as well as recording the album **Beck** for the Kudu label (#140 pop and #14 on the jazz chart) and helming Esther Phillips' albums **What A Diff'rence A Day Makes** and **With Beck**. Joe later recorded for Warner Brothers and a series of highly regarded albums for DMP before he died from lung cancer on 22 July 2008.

ALBUM: BECK (1975)

BEHIND A PAINTED SMILE – THE ISLEY BROTHERS [SINGLE]

What would become The Isley Brothers' second UK Top Ten hit was originally recorded in 1967 and appeared on the **Soul On The Rocks** album. *Behind A Painted Smile* also briefly surfaced in America as the B-side to the non-charting single *All Because I Love You*, but following the UK success of a revived *This Old Heart Of Mine* (#3 in November 1968) and then *I Guess I'll Always Love You* (#11 in February 1969), Tamla Motown promoted the song to the A-side for release in April 1969. Written by Ivy Jo Hunter and Beatrice Verdi and produced by Hunter, *Behind A Painted Smile* returned The Isley Brothers to the upper reaches of the UK chart, spending five weeks in the Top Ten and peaking at #5. It was something of a last hurrah for The Isley Brothers at Motown, for by the time the single reached its peak, the group had already exited Motown in order to revive their own T-Neck label.

BEHIND THE GROOVE – TEENA MARIE [SINGLE]

Following the success of Teena's debut album **Wild And Peaceful** and the hit single *I'm A Sucker For Your Love* (#8 R&B and #43 in the UK), both of which heavily featured Rick James as writer, co-singer and producer, attention turned to the follow-up album. With Rick James unavailable, it was Teena's own suggestion that Motown approach famed producer (and husband of the late Minnie Riperton) Richard Rudolph to secure his input, Teena believing she was not quite ready to fully helm her own album. Teena would write or co-write ten of the albums eleven tracks, including the album's opener *Behind The Groove* with Rudolph.

A sure-fire smash thanks to heavy club play, *Behind The Groove* converted that popularity to strong sales and would become the biggest single of Teena's career, at least as far as the UK was concerned, hitting #6 in June 1980. In the US it had to settle for a rather more modest position of #21 R&B, missing out on the pop charts altogether.

BEING WITH YOU – SMOKEY ROBINSON [SINGLE]

In the summer of 1980 Kim Carnes enjoyed a US pop Top Ten hit with *More Love*, a revival of a 1967 Smokey Robinson song. Shortly after the song peaked, Smokey contacted Kim's producer George Tobin to offer both his thanks and a new song he had written entitled *Being With You*. Unbeknown to Smokey, George and Kim had had a falling out over the recording of her follow-up single *Bette Davis Eyes*, with the result the pair were no longer working together.

Still, George arranged to meet with Smokey and listen to the song, which Smokey performed live in his office in Los Angeles. At the end of the song, George offered to record it on Smokey at his expense, reasoning that Smokey would have a proper demo of the song at the very least. Whilst Smokey had never worked with an outside producer before he accepted the offer and the song was recorded a day later. Whilst Motown didn't hold out much hope on the single being a hit, Berry's attitude changed once the single got a foothold on the charts and he instructed Motown to put all their marketing muscle behind it. It would eventually top the R&B Chart and stall at #2 on the pop charts, held off the summit by Kim Carnes' *Bette Davis Eyes*, but its success increased the pressure on the UK arm to similarly deliver a major hit.

Released in April 1981, initial sales proved somewhat sluggish, but the eventual appearance of a promotional video, filmed at Berry Gordy's beach house helped push the single along and, after making its first chart appearance on 9 May, it propelled itself to the top of the chart four weeks later, knocking Adam & The Ants' *Stand And Deliver* off the top. It would remain there for two weeks before being replaced by Michael Jackson's reissue of *One Day In Your Life*, the only occasion in which one Motown record replaced another at the top of the British charts. Sales of *Being With You* enabled Smokey to collect gold discs from both the UK and US trade bodies, made all the sweeter by the fact it was Smokey's silver anniversary year in the record industry.

BEING WITH YOU – SMOKEY ROBINSON [ALBUM]

Smokey had enjoyed the impromptu session with George Tobin that resulted in the single *Being With You*, enough to entrust him with the recording of a whole album. It was still Smokey providing much of the material (four of the eight tracks), but the end result was one of his most commercial albums and easily his most successful. Indeed, just as the single had done, the success of **Being With You** caught many at Motown by surprise, with the album eventually going on to earn a gold disc for sales in excess of half a million copies. It also performed well on the respective charts, becoming Smokey's only Top Ten success on the pop chart and an R&B chart topper, again the only time he achieved that feat up to that point. In the UK it became his only charting solo album, reaching a peak of #17.

BEN – MICHAEL JACKSON [SINGLE]

One of the surprise movie hits of 1971 was 'Willard', a horror film directed by Daniel Mann concerning a social misfit (Willard, played by Bruce Davison) whose only friends are a couple of rats he raised at home,

Ben and Socrates. Its success prompted a sequel from Phil Karlson, with 'Ben' picking up the story where 'Willard' had ended, with Willard being replaced by an equally lonely young boy in Danny (played by Lee Armstrong). In the film Armstrong sings the Don Black and Walter Scharf composed song *Ben*, but in order to attract greater interest to the film, the producers (Bing Crosby Productions) searched for a name singer to re-record the song as the film's theme.

According to legend, Donny Osmond was originally to perform the theme but was on tour with his siblings when the track was to be recorded, resulting in Berry Gordy successfully lobbying for Michael Jackson to take over the task. Given that Michael was known to collect exotic pets, including at one point a number of rats, the song and the singer made perfect partners. Appearing over the end credits in the film (Michael was said to have seen the film on many occasions, excited to see his name appear on screen), it eventually appeared on vinyl in July 1972 (held back until November in the UK owing to the success of the UK-only single *Ain't No Sunshine*) and proved a greater success on the pop charts than the R&B ones, topping the former and peaking at #5 on the latter. In topping the pop charts, it enabled Michael to become the third youngest solo chart topper, behind Stevie Wonder and Donny Osmond! In the UK, its belated release did little to hamper its progress up the charts, coming to rest at #7 and becoming his fourth consecutive Top Ten hit.

Ben would go on to win a Golden Globe for Best Song and was also nominated for an Academy Award (Oscar) for Best Original Song; although Michael performed the song at the ceremony, it lost out to *The Morning After* from 'The Poseidon Adventure'. The song was revived in 1985 by Marti Webb and taken back into the Top Ten, peaking at #5, whilst two years later Toni Warne reached #50 with her version.

BEN – MICHAEL JACKSON [ALBUM]

Michael Jackson's second solo album for Motown, **Ben** was entirely built around the success of the title track, itself the theme to the film of the same name. There were to be no further singles lifted from it, although one, *Everybody's Somebody's Fool* was apparently scheduled and then withdrawn. As with the Jackson 5 albums, the material was drawn from the same Jobete pool, alongside cover versions of other notable songs, including *People Make The World Go 'Round* by The Stylistics. Unlike Jackson 5 albums, however, The Corporation was conspicuous by their absence, with no fewer than six different productions teams taking Michael through the ten tracks on display.

Whilst this might imply a disjointed album, the end result was actually very well received, both critically and commercially. A #5 pop hit (his first solo Top Ten album) and #4 R&B, it would go on to break the Top 20 in the UK, peaking at #17. With worldwide sales of over five million copies, it remains one of his most successful Motown solo albums.

LaBRENDA BEN

A female singer reportedly brought to Motown by George Fowler, LaBrenda recorded two singles for the Gordy label, although her debut single was originally to have been released on Motown itself. The song in question was *Camel Walk*, originally released by Saundra Mallett & The Vandellas in July 1962 on Tamla, albeit unsuccessfully. Five months later, LaBrenda's version was released, with the initial pressings appearing on the Motown label and credited to LaBrenda Ben & The Vandellas, but this was withdrawn and the single appeared instead on Gordy credited to LaBrenda Ben & The Beljeans!

It may well be that The Vandellas were beginning to make a name for themselves and Motown wished to distance them from any involvement in the LaBrenda single; if so it worked for LaBrenda's version went the same way as Saundra Mallet's. LaBrenda released one further single, *Just Be Yourself*, which has attracted interest from Northern Soul enthusiasts, and recorded a number of other un-released tracks.

LEO BENDIX

An extremely obscure British singer who had one single scheduled on the MoWest label in the UK, *Holdin' On You* backed with *Don't Take Your Love From A Clown* due for release in July 1974 but subsequently dropped. This appears to have been the closest Leo Bendix got to a recording career, for nothing else on any label appears to have been released. The scheduled top side *Holdin' On You* was supposedly recorded by The Rockits, also signed to MoWest in the UK but similarly unreleased.

BENNY BENJAMIN

It is an ongoing matter of debate as to which musician contributed more to the dynamic Motown sound of the 1960s – drummer Benny Benjamin or bass player James Jamerson. Even those within Motown are undecided, for more than a few producers refused to even commence sessions until both men were in their respective places in the 'Snakepit'.

Born William Benjamin in Mobile, Alabama on 15 July 1925, Benny was Motown's first drummer, working with Berry Gordy from 1958 having learnt his craft with various big bands. Despite, or perhaps even because of his jazz background Benny brought something special to every recording session, as Berry Gordy would later confirm.

"He was so good on the drums and had a feel no one could match. He had a distinctive knack for executing various rhythms all at the same time. He had a pulse, a steadiness, that kept the tempo better than a metronome. Benny was my man."

Benny might have been Berry's man, but he could still drive his boss and the other producers to the very edge of frustration, especially with his errant timekeeping with regards to arriving at the studio. Indeed, his excuses for turning up late grew evermore fabricated and humorous, and whilst few believed the stories, Benny's status as one of the most beloved of the Funk Brothers ensured they were tolerated, perhaps even enjoyed. Like most of the Funk Brothers, Benny supplemented his Motown income with moonlighting sessions for other labels, adding to his lateness for reporting for duty at Hitsville and increasing his tiredness when he got there; on one occasion he fell asleep at his drum kit and awoke with a start to begin drumming whilst calling out 'Papa-zita, papa-zita, papa-zita', earning himself the nickname Papa Zita from there on in.

As the decade wore on heroin and alcohol addiction began to affect Benny's work to such an extent that Uriel Jones and Richard 'Pistol' Allen began doing more of the sessions. Benny suffered a stroke and died on 20 April 1969 at the young age of 43, but is still fondly remembered as the greatest drummer ever to work at Hitsville. He was inducted into the Rock & Rock Hall of Fame in 2003.

GEORGE BENSON

George Benson's credentials as a guitarist were never in question, but the almost effortless way he switched from being a jazz guitarist to singer surprised many. Born in Pittsburgh, Pennsylvania on 22 March 1943, he began his career as an R&B singer and recorded a number of tracks for RCA when aged only eleven as Little Georgie. It was as a guitarist, however, that he made his name, first as a member of Brother Jack McDuff's band and then as a solo artist, recording a couple of highly acclaimed albums for Columbia in the 1960s. He then recorded for Verve before being taken by producer Creed Taylor to A&M in 1968, where he was seen as the heir apparent to Wes Montgomery.

When Creed Taylor subsequently set up CTI as an independent label in 1970, George followed him, still considered a jazz guitarist, although a lone vocal single, *Supership*, charted on both the pop and R&B charts (at #105 and #98 respectively; the single also reached the Top 30 in the UK thanks to support from the Northern Soul crowd, although CTI was distributed by Polydor in this territory). The CTI albums distributed by Motown also performed relatively well, with **Bad Benson** hitting #78 pop and topping the jazz chart, aided by a stirring version of Dave Brubeck's *Take Five*. In December 1976 CTI released **In Concert Carnegie Hall**, George's last album for the label, which featured across all three charts at #122 pop, #43 R&B and #6 jazz. Thereafter George switched to Warner Brothers, where under the direction of producer Tommy LiPuma he broke out of the jazz market and enjoyed major crossover success.

ALBUMS: BAD BENSON (1974), IN CONCERT CARNEGIE HALL (1976)

SHELLY BERGER

A fair percentage of the credit for getting artists such as The Supremes and The Temptations on national television shows, for helping The Jackson 5 break into superstardom in short order and many of the Motown artists maintaining their popularity even after the hit records had slowed down goes to manager Shelly Berger. Even so, his Motown career almost ended no sooner than it had begun; employed by the Los Angeles office in 1966, he did not make a good impression with Berry Gordy the very first time they met, with the result Berry contemplated getting rid of him soon after. Fortunately, the misunderstanding was soon cleared up and Shelly would go on to play an integral part in the careers of many of his artists, going on to manage The Temptations for some 42 years.

Born Sheldon Berger in The Bronx, New York on 15 July 1925 and a graduate from Boston University, Shelly initially intended pursuing a career as an actor but eventually opted to work off stage. He joined

Motown in 1966 with a brief to help their acts get television and film tie-ins before going on to effectively run the West Coast office. He was subsequently appointed manager of The Temptations and The Supremes and was instrumental in getting an Ed Sullivan appearance for The Supremes and then the legendary 'T.C.B.' networked show for both.

"The 'Ed Sullivan Show' was the launching pad in the entertainment business, but Sullivan's show was only interested in the artists' singing their hit records," Shelly would later relate. "This was a snag for Motown, because with The Supremes, who constantly made hits, we held our breath while Berry Gordy dealt with Sullivan's people, requesting that they do one of their hits and also include other lesser-known material. When we did the Sullivan show, which was broadcast live, we were concerned with the quality of the artists' presentations. To prevent worry about the balance of the sound Berry Gordy requested pre-recorded orchestration and background vocals for their artists' performance on live television. They were amazed at the terrific sound. From that time on, shows were sending artists into the studio to pre-record their material."

When Berry signed The Jackson 5, he immediately appointed Shelly their manager, with the result Shelly decided he would not send the young group out on the road for anything less than $25,000 a show, an unheard of figure then, even more so for an act without a hit record to their name. By the time The Jackson 5 had racked up four number ones with their first four releases, they got their $25,000 a night.

Whilst Otis Williams and Melvin Franklin were largely responsible for hiring the numerous Temptations that passed through the group during their lengthy career, it invariably fell to Shelly to deliver the fateful news to those who were being fired. Shelly left Motown in the early 1980s to form his own talent management company, Star Direction, an apt name given the continued support he was able to give The Temptations and even Berry Gordy and Suzanne De Passe during the course of a career in the entertainment industry that spanned more than 55 years.

BERNADETTE – THE FOUR TOPS [SINGLE]

Whilst its status as one of the definitive Motown tracks of all time has seldom been queried, a veritable debate has sprung up around *Bernadette* (alongside several other key tracks), namely who exactly plays the backing music?

Whilst logic and several recollections point to the track being recorded in Detroit at Hitsville with James Jamerson, noted bassist Carol Kaye has laid claim to playing the part in Los Angeles in sessions supervised by Gene Page. Whilst Motown had opened studios in Los Angeles as early as 1966 (*Love Is Here And Now You're Gone* by The Supremes was over-dubbed in Los Angeles by Page under supervision by Holland-Dozier-Holland), it is extremely doubtful that HDH allowed anyone other than James Jamerson to perform bass on their tracks. Indeed, Brian Holland signed a sworn affidavit in 1989 attesting to James Jamerson performing on the track in an attempt to halt the mounting speculation. It is possible that Carol Kaye performed a demo of the track or recorded a version used as a backing track for a television appearance, but if Holland-Dozier-Holland state that James Jamerson appeared on the version that was released as a single, the case becomes a pretty solid one.

Indeed, the bass is an integral part of a song about a male's excessive desire for and jealousy over his girlfriend, with Bernadette being a composite of women HDH had personally encountered and which Brian Holland was responsible for coming up with the idea of giving her a specific name. Irrespective of the inspiration or aggravation, *Bernadette* was another smash hit for The Four Tops, hitting #3 R&B, #4 pop and #8 in the UK. Of all HDH hits, and there were many, it was the one that most impressed label boss Berry Gordy, as he revealed in his autobiography 'To Be Loved'.

"I loved them all but for me, *Bernadette* would epitomize the Holland-Dozier-Holland genius for capturing a listener's ear and not letting it go. It also helped fuel my belief that Levi Stubbs of The Four Tops could interpret and deliver the meaning of a song better than anybody. He made Bernadette live. I wanted to meet her myself."

ERIC BERRY

British singer and actor Eric Berry was born in London on 9 January 1913 and made his Hollywood debut in 'The Edge Of The World' in 1937. Although never an A list star, he kept busy in both Hollywood and on Broadway, making his debut in 'The Boy Friend' in 1954. In 1972 he landed the role of Charles in the Broadway production of 'Pippin', a show that would go on to become his most successful, running for some four and a half years. He appeared on the cast recording soundtrack, alongside the likes of Ben Vereen and Irene Ryan, and 'Pippin' was his last appearance on Broadway, although he made a number of minor acting appearances thereafter. Eric died in Laguna Beach in California on 2 September 1993.

THE BIG CHILL (FILM SOUNDTRACK)

A 1983 film starring Kevin Kline, Glenn Close, Jeff Goldblum, Tom Berenger and William Hurt, 'The Big Chill' concerned seven old friends from college gathering together at a winter house in South Carolina after the death of another friend. The film was also to have starred Kevin Costner, who was cast in the role of the dead friend (who committed suicide), but his 'appearances' were limited to a number of still shots of various body parts. Something of a surprise hit, the film would collect three Oscar nominations, although it won none.

Motown released the soundtrack album in September 1983, a various artist compilation that in addition to featuring Motown artists Marvin Gaye, The Temptations and The Miracles also contained hit tracks by The Young Rascals, Three Dog Night, Aretha Franklin, Procol Harum and The Exciters. The album was also a success, hitting #17 pop and #40 R&B, selling a million copies after six months and two million within a year. The album has since gone on to sell more than six million copies in the US alone.

The success of the soundtrack prompted the release of a second album, **The Big Chill: More Songs From The Original Soundtrack**, issued in April 1984, which also fared well on the chart, peaking at #85. This collection featured Motown artists The Four Tops, Martha Reeves & The Vandellas, Marvin Gaye and The Marvelettes alongside Creedence Clearwater Revival, The Beach Boys, Percy Sledge, The Rascals, The Steve Miller Band, The Spencer Davis Group and The Band. One integral song in the film, The Rolling Stones' *You Can't Always Get What You Want* lived up to its title and was conspicuous by its absence; presumably licensing issues prevented its inclusion.

ALBUMS: THE BIG CHILL SOUNDTRACK (1983), THE BIG CHILL: MORE SONGS FROM THE ORIGINAL SOUNDTRACK (1984)

BIG TIME (1977 FILM)

Smokey Robinson not only wrote the score to 'Big Time', he also invested a sizeable chunk of his own money into the project, confident that he would earn it all back.

"The movie is my project so that's why I did the soundtrack. I think that soundtracks are being done by more contemporary artists in this day and age than they were in the past. I also financed the entire film and have been involved since the writing of the script, right down to promoting the film. Christopher Joy, Leon Isaacs and myself adapted a short story and then directed the movie between us, [although Andrew Georgias got the credit]. That meant I actually became involved in the daily shooting, down to the cutting and post production as editor. I've got close to half a million dollars invested in it, although I feel confident that I'll make that back because it's a quality movie."

The story, about a small time con-artist who gets between the FBI and a suitcase filled with money also featured Smokey doing what he does best, writing music. The album's better cuts were the theme and reprise, with the single hitting #38 on the R&B charts and the album one place lower at #39, with neither crossing over onto the pop chart. And therein lay the problem; as a late entry to the blaxploitation genre, the market for 'Big Time' was somewhat limited, resulting in Smokey Robinson losing most of his money.

ALBUM: BIG TIME (1977)

THE BIG WHEELS OF MOTOWN – VARIOUS ARTISTS [ALBUM]

The **Motown Chartbusters** series might have outlived its usefulness on the British chart, but there was always room for a Motown compilation that gathered together the label's biggest hits from over the years, as **The Big Wheels Of Motown** would prove. Released in September 1978, the twenty track compilation featured major hits from Marvin Gaye, Stevie Wonder, Smokey Robinson & The Miracles, The Jackson 5, Mary Wells and The Temptations. Accompanied by television advertising it became a major hit, peaking at #2 and only held off the top spot by the **Grease** soundtrack. It would go on to spend eighteen weeks on the chart, selling over 100,000 copies and earning a gold disc in the process.

ACKER BILK

British male singer and clarinettist Bernard Stanley Bilk was born in Pensford, Somerset on 28 January 1929 and took up the clarinet whilst in the guardhouse in Egypt in 1947. He formed his own band in 1958 and went on to become one of the most popular bands during the traditional jazz boom of the era. *Stranger On The Shore* was written by Acker (his nickname is Somerset slang for 'friend') for his daughter Jenny and was subsequently used as the theme to a BBC TV drama series called 'Stranger On The Shore'. Released as a single in October 1961, it hit #2 in the UK, spending more than a year on the chart, and topped the US chart for one week in May 1962 (one of the few instrumentals to top the Billboard chart). It was subsequently featured in the soundtrack to 'The Flamingo Kid', released by Motown in December 1984. Acker was made an M.B.E. in the 2001 New Year's Honours list.

THE BINGO LONG TRAVELING ALL-STARS & MOTOR KINGS (1976 FILM)

Based on the book by William Brasher and inspired in part by the professional baseball team the Indianapolis Clowns, who took to touring with comic acts to present a baseball version of the Harlem Globetrotters, 'Bingo Long' was produced by Motown Productions for Universal Pictures. Aside its three major stars in Richard Pryor, Billy Dee Williams and James Earl Jones, 'Bingo Long' attracted the attention of Steven Spielberg during its planning stages, with him being considered as both a director and producer. The success of 'Jaws' meant he could have the choice of any film that met his fancy, ultimately deciding upon 'Close Encounters Of The Third Kind.'

Instead the role of director went to English-born John Badham, who had worked in television for many years and for whom 'Bingo Long' was his directorial debut. He didn't make a bad job of it too, turning in a film that has at times been described as one of the best films of its genre. There again, he would go on to direct 'Saturday Night Fever' a year later, most definitely the best of *its* genre. Despite being a Motown Productions film, the accompanying soundtrack, which featured two vocal tracks from Thelma Houston, appeared on the MCA label.

CINDY BIRDSONG

Whilst Marlene Barrow of The Andantes substituted for Flo Ballard for a number of live dates, she was never intended to be a permanent replacement. Instead, Berry Gordy and Diana Ross had been grooming Cindy Birdsong for the task, one she took on officially in July 1967.

Born Cynthia Ann Birdsong in Mount Holly Township, New Jersey on 15 December 1939, Cindy had aspirations of becoming a nurse until she was asked to join The Ordettes by a friend, Patsy Holt in 1960. A year later the group got their first recording contract with Newtown Records, where label owner Harold Robinson suggested a name change, with The Ordettes becoming The Blue Belles, after another label owned by Robinson, Blue Belle Records, and Patsy Holt becoming Patti LaBelle.

In 1962 the group scored their first hit with *I Sold My Heart To The Junkman,* although it is doubtful they actually appeared on it, for another Newtown group, The Starlets, recorded *I Sold* which Harold Robinson released as by The Blue Belles and had them promote it into the chart, peaking at #13 R&B and #15 Pop. It is not clear whether the version that sold features Patti LaBelle and her Blue Belles or The Starlets, but whilst Patti and her group emerged from the resulting scandal unscathed, the same could not be said for The Starlets, who apart from a $5,000 per singer award against Robinson saw their career come to an abrupt end.

In 1963 Patti LaBelle & Her Blue Belles, as they were now christened embarked on their own recording career and would score a further five hits for Newtown, Parkway and Atlantic Records over a period of four years, although none were major hits. Despite the lack of significant recording success, Patti LaBelle & Her Blue Belles were impressive live performers, appearing at venues across the country. Indeed, they were said to have developed a friendship during this time with Diana Ross, Flo Ballard and Mary Wilson of The Supremes, who were performing at many of the same venues at much the same time (The Supremes opened for the Blue Belles during 1963, before they'd scored a hit), although it was also said that there was friction between the two groups because The Supremes were often to be found shopping for outfits at the same boutiques as Patti LaBelle and the Blue Belles. Whilst Patti LaBelle would later claim to have been angry to have seen The Supremes wearing outfits that her group had intended wearing, it was reportedly during this time that Diana Ross in particular grew friendly with Cindy, advising her one what make-up to wear and the like.

When in 1967 Flo Ballard's behaviour got more erratic, it was Diana's suggestion that Cindy be considered a possible replacement. There was a physical resemblance between Flo and Cindy, resulting in the audience during those shows being unaware whether it was Flo or Cindy onstage (Cindy had spent many weeks rehearsing all of Flo's moves and lines). Despite being given several chances to mend her ways, Flo didn't and was dropped from The Supremes for good in July 1967. According to Patti LaBelle, the first she knew of Cindy Birdsong's move from The Blue Belles to The Supremes was when she read about it, prompting a rift between Cindy and her old group members that wasn't repaired until the early 1980s, although Cindy was quick to play down the dispute.

"All I was told was they wanted me there. I was met at the airport by Motown executives and driven to Berry Gordy's house where the group was having a meeting with him. I was still a member of Patti's group and didn't even tell her I was going to Detroit because I planned to return. So, the door of the room swung open and Florence came out in tears. Her mother came out with her. Oh, she was so upset, so shaken, she didn't even see me. It was then I realised I was to replace her. I felt so bad, but later on Florence understood why I did it."

The arrival of Cindy also heralded a new name for Motown's female group, who now became Diana Ross & The Supremes. Whilst this may have meant Cindy got to perform on The Supremes hits, this was only for live dates, for Diana Ross and assorted session singers did the actual singles and many of the album cuts!

However, the new found fame did have drawbacks, with Cindy the target of a potential kidnap in December 1969, being snatched at knifepoint from her Hollywood apartment and bundled into a car that roared off into the night towards the Long Beach Freeway. California was already in a heightened state, given that this event was barely three months since the notorious Sharon Tate and LaBianca murders by the Charles Manson Family. Cindy fought with her kidnapper during the thirty minutes or so they raced along the freeway, leaping out of the moving car in a panic when her attacker threatened her with all manner of outcomes once he met up with his two accomplices. Cut and bruised but otherwise unharmed, Cindy was taken to hospital where she made a rapid recovery. Some four days later, her would-be kidnapper Charles Collier, a maintenance man at the apartment where she lived, turned himself in to the police.

The departure of Diana Ross for a solo career in 1970 saw Jean Terrell join the The Supremes as the new lead singer, with Cindy and Mary getting the chance to feature more prominently, especially on three albums recorded with fellow Motown act The Four Tops. After marrying Charles Hewlett, Cindy fell pregnant with her first child and took her leave of The Supremes in April 1972. She returned in late 1973, replacing her replacement Lynda Laurence, who was also pregnant! After contributing to two further hit albums, **The Supremes** and **High Energy** Cindy left The Supremes a second time in February 1976.

Then Cindy finally got to achieve one of her life's ambitions, working as a nurse at UCLA Medical School for a number of years. In 1983 she was coaxed out of retirement to join with Diana and Mary for the 'Motown 25' television special. Having originally agreed to join FLOS – Former Ladies of The Supremes – in 1985, Cindy dropped out to pursue a solo career and recorded for Hi-Hat Records, without success. In 1999 she reunited with The Blue Belles for an R&B Foundation Award for Lifetime Achievement and, five years later linked with Mary Wilson and Kelly Rowland of Destiny's Child to perform a medley of The Supremes' hits on the television special 'Motown 45'.

ZELL BLACK

Singer and songwriter Zell Black first came to prominence writing with her husband Gary Black, penning *Pickin' Daisies* for Dotti Holmberg in the early 1970s. Zell then picked up a contract with Motown, which saw the single *I Been Had By The Devil* released by the label in February 1974 after an earlier single, *I'd Hate Myself In The Morning* had been scrapped. Two further singles for Curb and Warner Brothers followed before she joined up with Andy Mulikoff, Mike Millwood and David Morby in the Kenny Nolan produced Persia project that released one album on Casablanca.

BLACK FIGHTING MEN

To give the album its full name, **Guess Who's Coming Home: Black Fighting Men Recorded Live In Vietnam** was recorded, edited and narrated by Wallace Houston Terry (born in New York City on 21 April 1938, died on 29 May 2003), the renowned journalist, author and historian. Terry had been sent to Vietnam in 1967 as 'Time' deputy bureau chief and would become the first black war correspondent on full time duty. During the course of his two years in the country he interviewed scores of G.I.'s, which would form the basis for the 1967 'Time' cover story 'The Negro In Vietnam' and eventually the album released on the Black Forum label in 1972. The album would also form the basis for Terry's Pulitzer Prize nominated book

'Bloods: The Oral History of the Vietnam War by Black Veterans.'
ALBUM: GUESS WHO'S COMING HOME (1972)

BLACK FORUM RECORDS

Active between 1970 and 1973, Black Forum Records was a spoken word label, issuing albums featuring progressive political and pro-civil rights speeches and poetry. The label itself was run by Motown executives Ewart Abner, Junius Griffin (a journalist and former speech writer for Martin Luther King) and George Schiffer, the latter the company's contract lawyer who also worked as a civil rights attorney for the Congress of Racial Equality in New York.

The label's mission statement was carried on the back of the sleeves; 'Black Forum is a medium for the presentation of ideas and voices of the worldwide struggle of Black people to create a new era. Black Forum also serves to provide authentic materials for use in schools and colleges and for the home study of Black history and culture. Black Forum is a permanent record of the sound of the struggle and the sound of a new era.'

It was launched in October 1970 with albums from Dr Martin Luther King (who had released three albums on the Gordy label earlier; two in 1963 and one posthumously in 1968 and whose 1970 album was **Why I Oppose The War In Vietnam**), Stokely Carmichael and Langston Hughes and Margaret Danner. Two years later four albums were released, including something of a compilation album in **Black Men Fighting In Vietnam** before the label came to a halt in 1973 following the release of Elaine Brown's eponymous album and the label's only single, *No Time*, also by Elaine. Whilst none of the eight albums were big sellers, their cultural impact was significant, with **Why I Oppose The War In Vietnam** winning the 1970 Grammy Award for Best Spoken Word Recording.

BLACK RUSSIAN

Dissident Jews Serge Kasputin (guitar and percussion) and his wife Natasha (piano and vocals) were members of the Sovremennik, the Soviet Union state run pop orchestra, whilst Natasha's brother Vladimir Schnieder (piano) was a member of The Singing Hearts. Both groups found what they could play severely controlled by the state, as Vladimir would later explain.

"We'd sing 37 songs on how good the Communist Party is, and at the end – if we were lucky – we were allowed to play a mellow song like *Killing Me Softly* or *Ain't No Sunshine*. But never rock. If it wasn't ideologically sound, it was out."

In 1976 all three applied to immigrate to Israel, falsifying documents to show they had relatives there. But Israel was not their intended destination; they had set their sights on America, arriving in New York with no instruments (they had been confiscated by the authorities when they left Moscow) and little or no money.

The original line-up also included lead singer Tommy Hill and drummer Richard Smith, but Hill would leave after discovering his vocal style was being stolen and Smith died from cancer. After working menial jobs and scraping enough money together for a demo, the remaining Russian members headed out to Los Angeles and got their tape to Motown, who signed the group to a five year deal in 1980. In the end the group issued just one eponymous album, with two singles also being issued in the UK (*Mystified* and *Leave Me Now*) before they were dropped. Natasha died from cancer on 2 July 2008.

ALBUM: BLACK RUSSIAN (1980)

BILL BLACK'S COMBO

Best known as a member of Elvis Presley's original trio, eventually leaving over a dispute over poor wages, Bill Black holds an important place in music history. Born William Patton Black Junior in Memphis, Tennessee on 17 September 1926 and the oldest of nine children, Bill first recorded for Sun Records in 1954 as a member of the country group Doug Pointdexter & The Starlite Wranglers. Also a member of the group, who recorded just one single for Sun, was guitarist Scotty Moore, with Sam Phillips linking Scotty and the bass playing Bill with Elvis Presley later the same year. Billed as Elvis Presley, Scotty & Bill, the trio recorded a number of singles for Sun and undertook a number of tours over the next couple of years, with Bill said to possess a much better stage presence than the youthful but inexperienced Elvis.

Both Bill and Scotty continued to work with Elvis until 1958 but a growing dispute over wages and royalties (both had been granted a 25% share of royalties at the outset of Elvis' career, but when Elvis moved to RCA and started selling millions of records and earning millions of dollars, both found their wages frozen at $200 a week) saw both exit the trio.

Bill would join a local Memphis group that evolved into Bill Black's Combo and secured a recording deal with Hi Records, scoring a number of hits at the start of the 1960s as well as undertaking a tour with The Beatles when the Fab Four first toured the United States (such was the esteem with which Paul McCartney held Bill, Linda McCartney later bought his stand-up bass as a birthday present for her husband). Bill developed a brain tumour and died on 21 October 1965 following three operations at the age of just 39. A compilation of hits from Bill Black's Combo was released by Motown in 1983 as part of the brief deal with Hi Records. Bill was inducted into the Rock & Roll Hall of Fame as a sideman in 2009.

COMPILATION: GREATEST HITS VOLUME 2 (1983)

BLACKBERRIES

Venetta Lee Fields (born in Buffalo, New York in 1941), Clydie King (born Clyde Mae Crittendon in Dallas, Texas on 21 August 1943) and Sherlie Matthews (born in Los Angeles, California on 10 November 1934) were among the most in-demand backing singers from the mid-60s through the 70s, working with the likes of Diana Ross, Quincy Jones, Aretha Franklin, Barbra Streisand, The Supremes, Stevie Wonder, Pink Floyd, Neil Diamond, Leonard Cohen and Steely Dan, among countless others. Eventually the three decided to form their own vocal group under the name Blackberries and recorded for Motown, largely because Sherlie was signed to Motown as a songwriter/producer. In addition, they already had a 'foot in the door' as the 'house' background singers for the label.

Sherlie also chose the name, Blackberries "to note our ethnicity and in deference to Berry Gordy." They continued to perform background work plus appearing on stage and TV, while recording their own material, most of which was written by Sherlie and Deke Richards with Marva Holiday. Even though the album contained several potential hits only one track has surfaced, *Kidnapped* appearing on the fourth volume of the **Cellarful Of Motown** series. Another track, *Somebody Up There* backed with *But I Love Him* was scheduled for release on MoWest in June or July 1972 but got pulled from the schedule (although it duly appeared on **The Complete Motown Singles Volume 12A** and was chosen as the reproduced vinyl single for the entire package).

The Blackberries believed that the resulting album was buried for reasons unknown, except for the fact that a Motown executive stated that the label was not equipped to handle "our unique approach to pop music and secondly we were the first girl group to record using all three of us, alternatively, as lead and back-up singers. Motown didn't have enough faith in our new concept to take a chance; today it's the common denominator."

BLAKE & HINES

A duo formed in Detroit, Michigan by multi-instrumentalist Cory Blake and singer Andra 'Detroit Dray' Hines (born Andra Philander Hines in Detroit on 11 January 1964), they recorded one eponymous album for Motown in 1987 produced by Paul Ring and Tim Eaton which gave rise to two hit R&B singles in *Sherry* (#50) and *Road Dog* (#59). Their Motown contract was not renewed after this album, with the pair subsequently signing with Larry Blackmon's Atlanta Artists label before going their separate ways in the 1990s.

ALBUM: BLAKE & HINES (1987)

CORNELL BLAKELY

'Bouncing' Cornell Blakely didn't actually record *for* Motown, but virtually everything connected with his career between 1961 and 1963 had the Motown stamp on it – songs written by Motown staffers, recorded at Hitsville and published by Jobete. The reason he wasn't signed to the label was because he already had a manager in James Hendrix when he was first introduced to Berry Gordy, and Hendrix wasn't prepared to give up ownership of Cornell or his recordings.

Instead, Berry and James entered into an agreement whereby Cornell would record at Motown and the finished masters would be leased to another company on a 50/50 profit split, with the initial release being *You Ain't Gonna Find* (written by Berry). The label that released them was Rich Records in Nashville, which would eventually pick up national distribution through Ace Records and then Mercury Records before it went bankrupt. With several sides already recorded, Berry and James revived the Rich label name for themselves, issuing *I've Got That Feeling* backed with the appropriately named *I Want My Share* B-side.

ARTHUR BLANCH

Australian country singer Arthur Ernest Blanch was born in Wollum near Tamworth in New South Wales on 1 November 1928 and grew up on the family's sheep farm where he learned to play guitar as a child. Married in 1954 to Berice, he toured Australia as both a solo performer and as a duo with his wife, with their daughter Jewel being born in 1958. They first recorded for W&G in 1963 as The Blanch Family and a year later the family had their first crack at the American market, recording for Dot Records in 1965 as Little Jewel & The Blanch Family.

They returned to the US in 1968 and spent ten years there, with Arthur's one and only Motown connected single being *The Little Man's Got The Biggest Smile In Town*, released on MC Records in July 1978. Arthur returned to Australia in 1980 and settled near Brisbane.

BLAZE RECORDS

A label formed by Barney Ales, it was included in the same deal that took Prodigal into Motown in 1975. It released just one single, Jack Ashford & The Sound Of New Detroit's *Do The Choo Choo Parts 1 & 2* issued in September 1975.

BLINKY

Born in Oakland, California on 21 May 1944, Sondra Lee Williams established her name as a gospel singer with The Cogic Singers (the name standing for Children of God in Circulation), alongside Andrea Crouch, Sandra Crouch, Billy Preston, Frankie Karl (who would later record for Motown as Franki Karh'rl), Edna Wright and Gloria Jones. Still using her birth name (Blinky was a nickname applied because of her habit of blinking intensely), Sondra recorded for Vee-Jay and then Atlantic Records (the album **Hark! The Voice** appeared under the name Sondra 'Blinky' Williams) before signing with Motown in 1968.

Her initial single, *I Wouldn't Change The Man He Is* received rave reviews but few sales, prompting Motown to pair her with Edwin Starr in an attempt to re-create the success Marvin Gaye had enjoyed with a succession of female singing partners, especially as Edwin Starr was just coming off a sizeable hit in *25 Miles*.

"Neither Edwin nor myself had much confidence in the product because we had so little say, or little input. Motown had so much confidence in this project. Many of the songs were thrown at us at once. Every writer and producer seemingly were offering us material."

The resulting album **Just We Two**, produced by Frank Wilson, was pleasant enough but the lack of a sure-fire hit single and promotional support from Motown meant it sank without trace. This lack of success resulted in three scheduled albums (**Sunny And Warm** and **Softly** on Motown and **Blinky** on MoWest) being shelved, although a handful of singles appeared on the Soul and MoWest subsidiaries over the next three years (and Blinky also appeared in the soundtrack to 'Lady Sings The Blues' performing *T'Ain't Nobody's Bizness If I Do*). These also failed to sell and by 1974 Blinky had moved on to Reprise Records, later becoming a backing singer.

ALBUM: JUST WE TWO (1969)

BLOODSTONE

Bloodstone had been something of a regular feature on the charts for some six years prior to pitching up at Motown in 1978, with their 1973 debut *Natural High* becoming a Top Ten hit on both the pop and R&B chart. Formed in Kansas City, Missouri in 1962 by Charles Love (born in Salina, Kansas on 18 April 1945, guitar), Willis Draffen (born in Kansas City on 18 March 1945, guitar), Charles McCormick (bass) and Harry Williams (drums), the group's breakthrough came after they moved to England and linked up with producer Mike Vernon, the founder of the Blue Horizon label and whose other production credits included Fleetwood Mac.

Vernon would produce five albums for Bloodstone, of which their 1973 R&B #2 debut **Natural High** was their biggest seller, although by the mid-1970s their better days were seemingly behind them, an appearance in the 1975 blaxploitation film 'Train Ride To Hollywood' notwithstanding.

They signed with Motown in 1978 and released **Don't Stop!** in January the following year, an album produced by Winston Monseque and Al Johnson but which failed to stop their slide in sales.

Whilst Motown may have struggled to know how to promote them, their next home, the Isley Brothers' T-Neck label had infinitely more success, charting an album and five singles over two years, including the R&B top ten hit *We Go A Long Way Back*. With hindsight it can be seen that whilst Bloodstone may have been the right group for Motown, it just wasn't

the right time when they came through the doors. Willis Draffen died on 8 February 2002. Charles Love died from pneumonia on 7 March 2014.
ALBUM: DON'T STOP (1979)

BLOWIN' IN THE WIND – STEVIE WONDER [SINGLE]

What would become something of an anthem for the civil rights movement was a song written by Bob Dylan in just ten minutes, according to his later recollections. The original two verse song, based on a Negro spiritual *No More Auction Block* was first performed by Dylan at Gerde's Folk City in April 1962 and then with the addition of a middle third verse, recorded for release on his 1963 album **The Freewheelin' Bob Dylan**. *Blowin' In The Wind* had an immediate impact, with Mavis Staples (of The Staple Singers) later stating her astonishment that a young white singer could write a song that so effectively and powerfully captured the frustration and aspirations of the black community. She was not alone, for Sam Cooke would record a version in 1964 and use the song as inspiration for his own *A Change Is Gonna Come*.

The first act to record the song was The Chad Mitchell Trio, but hesitancy on the part of their record company (Mercury) over the song's lyrics prevented its release, allowing Peter, Paul & Mary (managed by Bob Dylan's manager Albert Grossman) to get their version out on to the market first, selling 300,000 copies in its first week and more than a million during its chart run, where it peaked at #2 and was kept off the summit by Little Stevie Wonder and *Fingertips*! Stevie was also attracted to *Blowin' In The Wind* and began featuring it into his live show for a couple of years, with the positive audience reaction prompting Stevie and his producer Clarence Paul to eventually record it in January 1966.

"We did it as a kind of duet. For one, because we sang a lot together when his voice was changing and also, because Stevie used to forget the words of the song. So I said like 'How many years' and Stevie starts singing 'How many years can a mountain exist…' The song went down really well in the gigs we did."

Also helping out on the session vocally was Levi Stubbs of The Four Tops, but despite the song's pedigree Berry Gordy was not entirely convinced of its potential and, according to the producer, berated Clarence for having used the song as an opportunity to advance his own singing career! Berry eventually relented and released it as a single in June 1966, and despite it being only three years since Peter, Paul & Mary's seemingly definitive version, the continuing battle for civil rights was such that Stevie's version would top the R&B chart and make #9 on the pop chart. In the UK it would become only his second charted single and peak at #36.

BLUE SCEPTER

Originally formed as SRC, which stood for The Scott Richard Case, they played in many of the rock ballrooms in and around Detroit in the 1960s and auditioned for Motown during the decade but were turned down. They recorded three albums for Capitol Records, with limited success, prompting something of a final stab at stardom and a name change, linking up with Rare Earth Records as Blue Scepter in 1972. By this time the line-up consisted of John Scott Richardson (vocals), Gary Quackenbush (guitar), Byron Coons (bass), Al Wilmot (bass) and E.G. Clawson (drums), with their only single for Rare Earth being a cover of The Pretty Things' *Out In The Night*.

When this failed to sell, the group disbanded. Gary Quackenbush later linked with another former Rare Earth signed group The Sunday Funnies, joining them in 1973 and remaining with them until they folded in January 1975. Clawson died on 23 July 2003 (at the age of 56) whilst Al Wilmot died during 2005.

BOB & EARL

Bobby Byrd (born Robert James Jennings in Tenalia, Texas on 2 July 1929) and Earl Lee Nelson (born in Salt Lake, Louisiana on 8 September 1928) formed the first incarnation of Bob & Earl in 1960, the pair having met whilst they were members of The Hollywood Argyles. Byrd also had a solo career, recording under the moniker Bobby Day (he wrote and recorded *Little Bitty Pretty One* and scored the first hit with *Rockin' Robin*, later successfully revived by Michael Jackson) and after Bob & Earl proved unable to land a major hit, Byrd/Day left the duo. In his place, Earl recruited Bobby Relf (born Robert Nelson Relf in Los Angeles, California on 10 January 1937), with the pair recording for a number of labels over the next few years, again without much success.

In 1963 Bob & Earl were with Marc Records and went into the studio to record *Harlem Shuffle*, a song they had written themselves, with Barry White handling arrangements (as well as playing piano) and Fred Smith the production. Released in December 1963, the single would go on to hit #3 R&B and #44 pop, although Bob & Earl struggled to follow this success (apart from a minor hit single three years later) and went their separate ways, with Earl enjoying some chart action as Jackie Lee. In 1969 *Harlem Shuffle* was revived in the UK and became a Top Ten pop hit, peaking at #7, prompting a brief reunion by Relf and Nelson for a lucrative European tour before disbanding for good in 1970.

Harlem Shuffle was featured on the 1986 compilation **Hits From The Legendary Vee-Jay Records** released on CD by Motown. Bobby Byrd died from cancer on 15 July 1990. Bobby Relf died on 20 November 2007. Earl Nelson died on 12 July 2008.

BOB & MARCIA

Jamaican duo Bob Andy (born Keith Anderson in Kingston in 1944) and Marcia Llyneth Griffiths (born in Kingston on 23 November 1949) first teamed up in 1970 to record a reggae flavoured cover version of Nina Simone's *Young Gifted And Black*, with the single becoming a #5 UK hit on Harry J's label in March.

This UK success prompted Motown to pick up the single and the option of an album the same year, with the single being subsequently released in July 1970. When this failed to chart, the album remained unreleased, although Bob & Marcia did manage to score again in the UK, with *Pied Piper* on the Trojan label making #11 in 1971.

Their pairing came to an end in 1974, after which Marcia became a member of The I-Threes (Bob Marley's backing singers) whilst Bob, a former member of The Paragons, resumed his solo career. He would later become A&R and Promotions Director for Tuff Gong, the label founded by Bob Marley. Receiving the Jamaica Prime Minister's Award for Excellence in 2003, he was given the Order of Distinction in the rank of Commander in 2006 for his services to reggae music.

BOB & PENNY

Signed to Mike Curb's MC Records, Bob and Penny's sole Motown album **Presenting Bob & Penny** was supposedly released in the US in October 1977 as MC6-507S1 and allocated a release number in the UK, but no copies (promotional or commercial) have thus far emerged on either side of the Atlantic to confirm its existence.

MICHAEL BODDICKER

Film composer and session musician Michael Boddicker was born in Cedar Rapids, Iowa on 19 January 1953 and made his name as a keyboard player on sessions for the likes of Michael Jackson, Earth Wind & Fire, Cheap Trick, Randy Newman, The Dazz Band, Lionel Richie, Kenny Loggins, The Pointer Sisters, Quincy Jones and Barbra Streisand, among countless others. Having written the scores to numerous television and film projects, he became involved in the film 'Get Crazy' in 1983, performing the track *Starscape* on the soundtrack.

GEORGE BOHANON

Jazz musician George Roland Bohanon was born in Detroit, Michigan on 7 August 1937 and learned to play the trombone at the age of eight, going on to study at the Wayne State University and the Detroit Institute of Musical Arts. In 1961 he was hired by Motown and would go on to accompany such artists as Marvin Gaye, Smokey Robinson, Diana Ross and Smokey Robinson during his seven years with the company.

He also got to record two albums under his own name, with **Boss Bossa Nova** (featuring sidemen Kirk Lightsey, Joe Messina and Cecil McBee) and **Bold Bohanon** being released on the Workshop Jazz label (although the latter album may have existed as promotional pressings only), but whilst Motown may have recorded jazz material during the early 1960s, their promotional support behind it was seldom more than fleeting, which also applied to the only single issued, *Bobbie* backed with *El Rig* in May 1962.

George remained at Motown until 1968 when he moved out to Los Angeles, later becoming a member of Karma who recorded for A&M and recording with the likes of Norman Connors, Etta James and Freddie Hubbard, among countless others. He also briefly crossed paths with Motown again, arranging a couple of tracks on Celebration's eponymous album on MoWest in 1973.

ALBUMS: BOSS BOSSA NOVA (1963), BOLD BOHANON (1964)

GARY U.S. BONDS

In the space of a little over two years, Gary U.S. Bonds registered five Top Ten hits out of just seven releases, including a number one. Whilst other artists may have had a comparable track record, the fact that Gary achieved his hits in the rock and roll genre made it all the more impressive.

Born Gary Levohn Anderson in Jacksonville, Florida on 6 June 1939, he signed with Frank Guida's Legrand Records label in 1960, with Frank suggesting a name change to U.S. Bonds in the hope that his records would get confused with a public service announcement for government bonds and therefore get more airplay. The ruse worked, to an extent, with *New Orleans* making #6 and *Quarter To Three* going all the way to the top, but the public were confused into thinking U.S. Bonds was the name of a group, so subsequent releases were credited to Gary U.S. Bonds. There were a further three Top Ten hits to come, *School Is Out, Dear Lady Twist* and *Twist, Twist Senors*, but by the end of 1962 the hits had tailed off.

There was still enough allure in his name for him to headline a European tour in 1963 ahead of The Beatles, although as the decade progressed he would slip down the roster.

In 1975 he linked up with Prodigal for a one-off single in an attempt to return to chart glory, *Grandma's Washboard Band* getting some radio play but few sales. Gary U.S. Bonds would make a comeback six years later, his return orchestrated by Bruce Springsteen.

BOOGIE DOWN – EDDIE KENDRICKS [SINGLE]

The success of *Keep On Truckin'*, Eddie Kendricks' first major success as a solo singer, piled the pressure on producer Frank Wilson and his co-writing team of Leonard Caston and Anita Poree. Taking a leaf out of the Holland-Dozier-Holland school of song-writing, they set about crafting a follow-up with much the same feel.

"We were basically interested in making sure we did not lose what we had gained with *Keep On Truckin'*. We knew that they were both club records. They were groove tracks with a gospel, churchy kind of background feel. We did an awful lot in terms of just letting the background ride over the vamp, so most of those songs were half-background grooves and the other half, of course, were leads."

Recorded at Motown's studios and Crystal Sound Recording in Los Angeles, the final version ran to just over seven minutes, but anyone wishing to enjoy the full length version would have to buy the album, for the single was heavily edited for release in December 1973. Although similar to *Keep On Truckin'*, *Boogie Down* kept Eddie's name in lights, again topping the R&B charts and hitting the Top Ten pop (at #9), and like its predecessor, earned Eddie a second Grammy nomination for Best R&B Vocal Performance, missing out once again to Stevie Wonder and *Boogie On Reggae Woman*. In the UK it peaked at a rather lower #36 and would be his last charting single until 1985 when he combined with Hall & Oates and David Ruffin for *A Nite At The Apollo Live!*

BOOGIE ON REGGAE WOMAN – STEVIE WONDER [SINGLE]

Whilst it may have seemed with hindsight that Stevie Wonder spent much of the 1970s working on one album project after another, the reality was completely different; according to the recording logs kept by associate producers Malcolm Cecil and Robert Margouleff, Stevie was recording song after song, getting down on to tape every idea that entered his head as quickly as possible lest the idea disappear before it was recorded for prosperity. Then, when Motown's demand for an album had to be met, the three would convene at the office of Stevie's lawyer Johanan Vigoda and pick the songs that would make up the album. It was during this selection process that the feel of an album was created, mixing and matching the tempo of the songs to create one seamless entity.

Boogie On Reggae Woman was recorded in 1973, right in the middle of the sessions that would eventually turn up on **Innervisions**, but for some reason Stevie didn't feel the song was right for that particular album. A year later, Robert Margouleff argued convincingly enough for it to be included on **Fulfillingness' First Finale**, and, as Stevie was also in control of what was issued as singles from his albums, for it to be released on 45 in December 1973 as the follow-up to *You Haven't Done Nothin'*. Two years later than anticipated, therefore, *Boogie On Reggae* entered the battle for chart honours and won almost convincingly, hitting #1 R&B, #3 pop and a respectable #12 in the UK.

The following March at the Uris Theatre in New York, Stevie beat his label mates Eddie Kendricks (*Boogie Down*) and Marvin Gaye (**Marvin Gaye**), former label-mate Johnny Bristol (*Hang On In There Baby*) and George McCrae (*Rock Your Baby*) to win the Grammy for Best R&B Vocal Performance, one of four awards he collected that evening.

THE BOONE FAMILY/PAT BOONE

Singer turned actor Pat Boone (born in Jacksonville, Florida on 1 June 1934) made his name in the 1950s by recording a series of R&B songs and making them palatable to the white market, so it was somewhat ordained that he should do much the same for Motown some twenty years later. By then he was recording and touring with his wife Shirley Lee Foley (born on 24 April 1934) and their four daughters, Cheryl 'Cherry' Lynn (born in Denton, Texas on 7 July 1954), Lindy Lee, Deborah 'Debby' Ann (born in Hackensack, New Jersey on 22 September 1956) and Laury Gene.

They initially performed and recorded gospel music, including the albums **The Pat Boone Family** and **The Family Who Prays** for Boone's own Lion & Lamb label. In 1974 they came up with the idea of doing an updated version of The Marvelettes' *Please Mr. Postman* and interested Berry Gordy enough for him to release the single on Motown (it was released on MoWest in the UK). Unfortunately, The Carpenters had much the same idea at much the same time, with the result the two versions went head to head for sales. The Carpenters made it to #1 in the US and #2 in the UK; The Boone Family made only brief appearances on the Cashbox and Record World charts. Two further singles also raided the Jobete and Motown catalogue, *When The Lovelight Starts Shining Thru' His Eyes* and *My Guy*, both released under the moniker The Boones, but even with a subtle credit change they failed to sell.

Whilst pop success might have eluded the family, they did at least make a showing on the country charts, with Pat and Shirley taking *I'd Do It With You* to #84 and Pat alone scoring a #34 hit with *Texas Woman*. Pat recorded four solo albums for Motown; **Texas Woman** appeared on Hitsville in September 1976 and **The Country Side Of Pat Boone** on MC the following August, with **Country Days And Country Nights** on the same label getting as far as promotional copies in October 1977 although finished stock was presumably pulled, as was a further album in **Indiana Girl** on Melodyland. Daughter Debby launched her own solo career in 1977, scoring a major hit with *You Light Up My Life*.

ALBUMS: TEXAS WOMAN (1976), THE COUNTRY SIDE OF PAT BOONE (1977)

BOTTOM & CO

A studio project assembled by James Brown's former musical director Richard Griffith, Bottom & Company featured Jesse Boyce (bass and vocals), Freeman Brown (drums and vocals), John Helms (guitar and vocals), Sanchez Harley (saxophone and vocals), George Woods (trumpet and vocals) and Fred Birdwell (keyboards and vocals). They recorded one album for the Gordy label, **Rock Bottom** in 1976, with their two hit singles *You're My Life* (#96 R&B) and *Here For the Party* (#93 R&B) having previously appeared on Motown.

ALBUMS: ROCK BOTTOM (1976)

JEFFREY BOWEN

Jeffrey Bowen made his name during two spells with Motown, usually working with mentors Holland-Dozier-Holland. He was introduced to Motown by Mickey Stevenson, however, and earned writing and production credits with Marvin Gaye before leaving Motown in order to link with Holland-Dozier-Holland at their Invictus and Hot Wax labels. There he met, managed and later married British female singer Ruth Copeland (there are claims he married Bonnie Pointer in 1978, but these are unsubstantiated) as well as working with a wide variety of artists for both his employers (Chairmen Of The Board) and outside projects (Three Dog Night). He returned to Motown midway through the 1970s, producing and writing with the likes of The Commodores (*I Feel Sanctified*), The Temptations (the albums **In A Mellow Mood**, **A Song For You** and **Wings Of Love**) and Bonnie Pointer.

THOMAS 'BEANS' BOWLES

One of the many understated legends of Motown, Thomas Bowles was born in South Bend, Indiana on 7 May 1926 and earned the nickname String Bean, later shortened to 'Beans' as a young man on account of standing six foot five inches tall. As a saxophonist he was one of the first musicians to walk through the doors of Hitsville, performing on the second Motown album, **Twistin' Around The World** by The Twistin' Kings, effectively a studio band assembled to capitalise on the twist craze sweeping America in 1961. Tracks such as *Twist Ala B.G.* (Berry Gordy) and *Twisting Ales Style* (Barney Ales) sat alongside the singles *White*

House Twist and *Congo Twist* but sold little on either single or album, bringing a halt to The Twistin' Kings. Similarly, a planned album release on the Workshop Jazz label was cancelled, although at least twelve tracks were recorded between October 1962 and July 1964 (six of these finally appeared as downloadable tracks on the album **Unreleased 1962: Jazz Volume 2** in December 2012). Beans did get to appear on many hits however, most notably *What's Going On* (Marvin Gaye), *Baby Love* (The Supremes) and *Heat Wave* (Martha & The Vandellas). It was his suggestion to Berry Gordy that led to the Motortown Revue's heading out on the road, where in addition to performing with the band Beans was responsible for the bed checks, ensuring the younger singers and musicians were safely tucked up in bed (and in particular their own beds) at night! Indeed, his duties led to Esther Gordy Edwards saying, "I called him a mother hen for the girls and a father figure for the boys."

Beans was also signed to Motown as an artist and, upon being sacked by the company after entering local politics, had to negotiate with Motown in order to get back the rights to his own name! Despite his sacking, he was later employed by Smokey Robinson as musical director for his road band. He died after a lengthy battle with cancer on 29 January 2000.

JANIE BRADFORD

Janie Bradford spent some twenty years at Motown, initially as receptionist, then writer and later as Director of Writer's Relations. Born Jannil Bradford in Ohio Township, Missouri on 2 June 1936, it was her writing that earned her a place in Motown history, for she co-wrote *Money (That's What I Want)* with Berry Gordy, which was recorded by Barrett Strong and became the label's first hit, albeit leased to Anna Records. Other songwriting credits for Janie include *Too Busy Thinking About My Baby* (Marvin Gaye), *Contract On Love* (Stevie Wonder) and *Hip City* (Junior Walker) over the course of her time at Motown. With *Money* alone having been recorded by more than 200 artists (including The Beatles), it adds weight to Janie's statement, "I believe if you have an idea, a dream, you can't just think about it, you have to go out and do it. And don't let anything get in your way. If the elevator stops, take the stairs!"

DELANEY BRAMLETT

Delaney Alvin Bramlett spent five decades in the music business but enjoyed the peak of his success over the just three years, between 1969 and 1972. Born in Pontotoc County, Mississippi on 1 July 1939, he moved to Los Angeles in the early 1960s after a stint with the US Navy. There he set himself up as a singer and songwriter and also became a member of the house band on the television show 'Shindig'.

In 1967 he married Bonnie Lynn O'Farrell and together they picked up assorted friends over the next few years and toured extensively. These friends included, at various times, Eric Clapton, Rita Coolidge, Dave Mason, Duane Allman and Leon Russell, with the first Delaney & Bonnie & Friends album **Accept No Substitute** appearing and charting in 1969 on Elektra, although an album recorded for Stax in 1967 remained in the can until their sudden arrival on the charts. A further five albums charted before 1972 was out, but then both the group and the Bramlett's marriage disintegrated, with both going on to record solo.

Delaney recorded for Atco, Atlantic, CBS and MGM before signing with Prodigal in 1977 for **Delaney And Friends – Class Reunion**. The 'friends' this time around were Patti Quatro (sister of singers Suzi and Michael Quatro) and Spider Taylor (guitar), Stu Perry and Jim Keltner (drums) and vocalist (and former MC Records artist) Susie Allanson. The material drew upon Jobete's own catalogue, with *I Wish It Would Rain* one of the standout cuts. According to several sources, Delaney recorded a second album for Prodigal, **Delaney Bramlett With Steve Cropper**, but no catalogue number exists nor have copies ever surfaced. Delaney died from complications of gall bladder surgery on 27 December 2008.

ALBUM: DELANEY AND FRIENDS – CLASS REUNION (1977)

BRASS MONKEY

Although included in part of the deal that saw British rock acts assigned to the Rare Earth label for release in the US, Brass Monkey may well have been put together specifically in order to make up the numbers. That being the case, the group was assembled by songwriters and producers Guy Fletcher and Doug Flett, a pair that were particularly hot at the time having penned hits for The Hollies, Elvis Presley, Cliff Richard and Cilla Black, among others.

Brass Monkey was fronted by vocalist Ben Case, who was born Peter Lee Stirling but would later find fame as Daniel Boone, scoring two UK hits with *Daddy Don't You Walk So Fast* and *Beautiful Sunday*. Also in the group as guitarist was Ken Summer, who had first come to prominence as a member of Emile Ford's Checkmates, where he went under the name Ken Street. Brass Monkey was rounded out with Mike Morgan (guitar), Les Hurdle (bass) and Dougie Wright (drums), with their eponymous album featuring material largely written by Fletcher and Flett (six of the eight tracks). **Brass Monkey** was released in the US in April 1971, having been preceded by the single *Sweet Water* which was released in January.

Both album and single would receive European release on the Philips label, although neither made much of an impact. Guy Fletcher was honoured in the 2005 Her Majesty The Queen's Birthday honours list with an O.B.E. (Order of the British Empire) for services to British music.

ALBUM: BRASS MONKEY (1971)

BOBBY BREEN

Canadian born singer and actor Bobby Breen (born in Montreal, Quebec on 4 November 1927) was playing vaudeville in Toronto from the age of four and went to Hollywood to pursue his dreams in 1935. He appeared on Eddie Cantor's radio show in 1936 which led to a contract with RKO the same year, going on to make nine films over the next six years. Unfortunately, his film career effectively ended as he entered his teens, prompting a switch to singing and performing in nightclubs around the country.

He also hosted his own television show in New York but spent much of the next two decades trying to reclaim former glories, even appearing on a television show entitled 'The Comeback Story' in which he detailed his struggles. That was in 1953; in 1963 he was signed by Berry Gordy, who was still trying to find a credible white singer to present to MOR audiences.

His first single was a revival of Marv Johnson's *How Can We Tell Him* backed with the Smokey song *Better Late Than Never*. When this failed, Berry and his brother Robert wrote *You're Just Like You* (with the writing credit given to Martin and Kay and the publishing company listed as Stein & Van Stock rather than Jobete, but by issuing the single on Motown any subterfuge was surely lost), written and recorded to sound like a MOR standard. This also failed and a proposed album **Better Late Than Never** was subsequently cancelled. Bobby did achieve a certain degree of notoriety in 1967; he appeared on the cover of The Beatles' **Sgt Pepper** album, in between George Harrison and Marlene Dietrich.

BRICK HOUSE – THE COMMODORES [SINGLE]

Lionel Richie's emergence as a songwriter of exquisite ballads, highlighted by the success of *Easy*, *Just To Be Close To You* and *Sweet Love* may have propelled The Commodores in to the upper echelons of the charts, but the band hadn't forgotten their origins and still knew how to lay down a funky groove that could get an audience up on their feet. *Brick House* was one such number, with William King of the band coming up with the basic idea for the song lyrics one night (apparently he mumbled them in his sleep, with his wife thoughtfully writing them out on a pad which she left on the bed in the morning!).

During a temporary lull in a recording session, William explained his idea to the rest of the band, who instantaneously came up with a groove to match the lyrics. Ostensibly about a woman with a great body, the lyrics were slightly amended for the recording session, with Walter 'Clyde' Orange the lead vocalist. Released as the follow-up single to *Easy*, the change of pace did little to dent the group's sales, resulting in a #5 pop and #4 R&B hit single.

In the UK, Motown coupled the single with *Sweet Love*, which had not been a hit when originally released and were rewarded when the double A-side hit #37. Both *Brick House* and *Easy* earned nominations for Best R&B Song at the 1978 Grammy Awards but lost out on the night to Leo Sayer and Vini Poncia's *You Make Me Feel Like Dancing*.

The success of *Brick House*, however, did eventually give The Commodores one of their most bizarre honours; in 1991 the group was inducted into the National Association of Brick Distributors' Brick Hall of Fame in recognition of the publicity generated by the single!

JOHNNY BRISTOL

Although his career began and ended as a performer, Johnny Bristol made his name at Motown as both a songwriter and producer, turning out a succession of hits on a variety of artists.

Born Johnny William Bristol in Morganton, North Carolina on 3 February 1939, Johnny met fellow would-be singer Jackey Beavers whilst serving in the US Air Force and as Johnny & Jackey the pair made a number of recordings for Anna Records (*Lonely & Blue* in 1959) and Tri-Phi (*Someday We'll Be Together, Carry Your Own Load* and *Baby Don'tcha Worry* between 1961 and 1962).

Johnny followed Tri-Phi owner Harvey Fuqua into the Motown stable when Berry Gordy bought the label, linking with Fuqua for both songwriting and production duties. He also married Berry's niece Iris, thus further becoming part of the Motown family.

Both with and without Harvey Fuqua, Johnny helmed a large number of hits for Motown, including Junior Walker's *How Sweet It Is, Take Me Girl I'm Ready, Way Back Home, Walk In The Night* and *What Does It Take,* The Four Tops *What Is A Man,* The Velvelettes' *These Things Will Keep Me Loving You,* Marvin Gaye & Tammi Terrell's *If I Could Build My World Around You,* Gladys Knight & The Pips' *I Don't Want To Do Wrong* and *Daddy Could Swear I Declare,* Edwin Starr's *25 Miles* and, most notably, *Someday We'll Be Together* for Diana Ross and the Supremes. This latter track was a revived version of Johnny & Jackey's release from 1961, with Johnny supplying the male vocal on the single that was originally to have been a debut solo single for Diana Ross but was subsequently released as the final Diana Ross & The Supremes single.

Motown's switch from Detroit to Los Angeles, coupled with a contract dispute resulted in Johnny severing his ties to the label.

"When you worked for them, you weren't able to work for any other record company. I stayed there about ten years and I guess I produced just about everyone on the label. It's all about money. I really had no other choice because of the offers they made me. I was one of their top five producers and when they came to me – I never talked to Berry Gordy – about my contract they made me a very insulting offer and I felt I couldn't take it."

Instead Johnny opted to remain in Michigan before joining CBS Records as a producer. There he worked with Randy Crawford, Marlena Shaw, Boz Scaggs and Johnny Mathis before announcing his desire to resume his own recording career. When CBS showed no interest he signed for MGM, scoring an international hit with *Hang On In There Baby* (#3 in the UK and #2 R&B and #8 pop in the US) and several other R&B hits, earning him a nomination for Best New Artist at the 1975 Grammy Awards! He also got a nominated for Best R&B Vocal Performance for the single although lost out on the night to Stevie Wonder and *Boogie On Reggae Woman*.

The **Hang On In There Baby** album also included *Love Me For A Reason,* later a smash hit for The Osmonds (and later Boyzone), proof Johnny's songwriting was still top of the tree. After a further album for MGM Johnny moved to Atlantic for two albums as well as continuing with outside production work, most notably Tom Jones and Tavares. Johnny would later work extensively in Europe, linking with Amii Stewart on a medley of *My Guy-My Girl*, which became his last UK chart entry, and Ian Levine's Motorcity label, for whom he recorded a number of tracks. Johnny returned to the US and recorded with his daughter Shanna before he died in Brighton Township, Michigan of natural causes on 21 March 2004.

BRITISH MOTOWN CHARTBUSTERS – VARIOUS ARTISTS [ALBUM]

EMI announced the launch of the Tamla Motown label in March 1965 with the release of six albums, with the compilation **A Collection Of 16 Big Tamla Motown Hits** (despite the title not every track on the album had been a hit) getting the imprint off to a perfect start by hitting #16 on the album chart. This particular range would run to eight albums (**Hitsville USA** was the second and **Motown Magic** the third before the series adopted a more traditional numbering system), with Volumes 4, 5 and 6 all making something of a showing on the chart.

By the time the eighth and final volume was released, Tamla Motown had launched another compilation series, one which was to become infinitely more successful, **Motown Chartbusters**. The very first volume was released in October 1967, with liner notes by Mike Raven (an acknowledged authority on both soul and blues music, one of the first DJ's on Radio 1 and host of Mike Raven's Blues Show on the newly launched national radio station), and became an instant success, hitting the Top Ten in its second week and eventually hitting #2, kept off the top of the chart by the soundtrack to 'The Sound Of Music'. It would, however, go on to spend more than a year on the chart and its success ensured there would be further volumes of Motown Chartbusters.

BRITISH MOTOWN CHARTBUSTERS VOLUME 2 – VARIOUS ARTISTS [ALBUM]

Record buyers who had only recently discovered the delights of Tamla Motown were well served with a succession of compilation albums throughout 1967 and 1968. In addition to **British Motown Chartbusters** released in October 1967, there was the ongoing **A Collection Of 16 Big Hits**, which would continue up to

Volume 8 and the four volume series **Motown Memories**.

Whilst these were relatively successful, nothing matched the sales achieved by the first edition of chartbusters, and another collection of sixteen hits were gathered for release in November 1968 as **British Motown Chartbusters Volume 2**.

This time around Tony Blackburn, DJ on Radio 1's flagship breakfast show provided the liner notes, thus establishing a link between Tony and Tamla that would prove extremely beneficial in the years to come. The second volume also made it into the Top Ten of the British album chart, peaking at #8 in February 1969.

The album was still at #10 on the chart when it disappeared from the listing altogether; on 15 February 1969 British Market Research Bureau took over compilation of the charts that would be published in Record Retailer magazine (later better known as Music Week) and cut back the listing from a Top 40 that had been regularly published in New Musical Express to a Top 15 for Record Retailer.

MORRIS BROADNAX

Born in Detroit, Michigan on 9 February 1931, Morris Ervin Broadnax auditioned for Mickey Stevenson in 1961 as a singer. Whilst Mickey didn't think much of him as a vocalist, he did like the songs he'd performed, all of which were Morris' own compositions, so Mickey offered him a job as a staff writer for Jobete. Morris mainly worked with Clarence Paul and Stevie Wonder, helping compose such hits as *Until You Come Back To (That's What I'm Gonna Do)*, later a massive hit for Aretha Franklin, *Just A Little Misunderstanding* (a hit for The Contours) and *All I Do,* which Stevie eventually included on his **Hotter Than July** album. Morris remained at Motown until 1969 and tried to organise the first Motown Alummi Association in 1989 but gave up owing to lack of interest at the time. He died from congestive heart failure on 17 February 2009.

ROY BROOKS

Although Roy Brooks excelled as a sportsman as a youngster, earning a scholarship to Detroit Institute of Technology on the strength of his ability at basketball, his greater love of music won over. Born in Detroit, Michigan on 9 March 1938, he learned to play the drums as a youngster and dropped out of school after three semesters in order to tour with Yusef Lateef. A five year stint with Horace Silver followed, after which he recorded the album **Beat** for the Workshop Jazz label. Utilising Hugh Lawson on piano, Eugene Taylor (bass), Junior Cook (tenor saxophone), George Bohanon (trombone) and Richard 'Blue' Mitchell (trumpet) alongside Roy on drums, the album was recorded in a single day in October 1963 and released the following August.

Thereafter he moved to New York and freelanced for a wide variety of artists on the hard bop jazz scene, including James Moody, Wes Montgomery and Milt Jackson. Despite his prowess as a drummer, his career was littered with bizarre behaviour, with much of the 1970s and 80s being spent undertaking treatment for a mental disorder. These reached a peak the following decade, culminating in spells incarcerated or institutionalised, and after leaving prison in 2004 he was put into a nursing home where he died on 15 November 2005.

ALBUM: BEAT (1964)

ARTHUR BROWN

British rock and roll singer Arthur Wilton was born in Whitby, North Yorkshire on 24 June 1944, but would ultimately become better known as Arthur Brown, or more appropriately, The Crazy World Of Arthur Brown. After fronting numerous R&B bands he formed The Crazy World Of Arthur Brown in 1967 with Vincent Crane (keyboards), Nick Greenwood (bass) and Drachen Theaker (drums), although Theaker was subsequently replaced by Carl Palmer (later of Emerson, Lake & Palmer). Despite releasing numerous albums and singles, only one ever set the charts alight; *Fire* issued in 1968 topped the UK charts and peaked at #2 in the US. Arthur also had a spell as a solo artist, recording **Dance With Arthur Brown** for the Gull label in 1974 that was issued in the US the following year as part of the deal between Motown and Gull.

ALBUM: DANCE WITH ARTHUR BROWN (1975)

BILLIE JEAN BROWN

A former student at Cass Technical High School, Billie Jean Brown (born on 12 May 1941) joined Motown in 1960 as an assistant to Loucye Gordy, writing sleeve notes and sending out letters chasing payment for records sold. She would eventually become head of

Quality Control, a position that would make her one of the most important executives at Motown, especially during the company's early days.

It was Billie Jean's job to have all the week's recordings ready for appraisal at the meeting, and she would often select records based on what she thought might sell, irrespective of the opinions of the artists and producers themselves; *Beauty Is Only Skin Deep* by The Temptations was her choice as a single, even though the group wanted to issue something else. The group appealed the decision directly to Berry Gordy, who called Billie Jean into his office, together with copies of *Beauty Is Only Skin Deep* and the group's preferred choice. After listening to the two songs, he agreed to issue Billie Jean's choice, which eventually topped the R&B chart.

As Berry Gordy said of her, "Billie Jean was feared by almost every producer in the room because they knew she 'had my ear.' She had as keen a sense of what was a hit as anyone I knew. And she knew it. That's why she sat there like a diva in the last act waiting for her solo. She was expressionless, nothing moving except her squinting eyes, which darted back and forth from one hopeful producer to another as if to say 'Yes, I hold your fate in my hands.'"

Billie Jean held the fate of the producers in her hands for nineteen years, during which time she also sat in judgement on several of the songs *she* wrote, including *Here Comes The Judge* by Shorty Long and *I Promise To Wait My Love* by Martha Reeves & The Vandellas, before leaving Motown in order to take up a law degree.

EDDIE 'BONGO' BROWN

Originally introduced to Motown as Marvin Gaye's valet, Eddie 'Bongo' Brown found greater fame as a member of The Funk Brothers. Born in Clarksdale, Mississippi on 13 September 1932, he made his first recordings in 1962, eventually going on to become the leading percussionist at Motown, appearing on virtually all of the label's key releases for the next ten years. As well as his recording contributions, Eddie was also known as the joker within the Motown pack, often bringing recording sessions to a halt with a joke that had the other players unable to continue because they were laughing too much.

Despite his undoubted ability Eddie was unable to read music, so when the writers and producers handed him sheet music of the song they were about to record, he would invariably replace it with an adult magazine and stare at that whilst playing the bongos, congas, gourd or claves! One of the few musicians to make the move to Los Angeles when Motown moved in 1972, Eddie continued to appear on key releases, including Marvin Gaye's **Let's Get It On** and Stevie Wonder's **Songs In The Key Of Life**. Eddie died from heart disease on 28 December 1984.

ELAINE BROWN

Political activist, writer and singer Elaine Brown was born in Philadelphia, Pennsylvania on 2 March 1943 and moved to Los Angeles in the 1960s looking to pursue a career as a songwriter. After working as a cocktail waitress, she became interested in the Black Panther Party following the assassination of Martin Luther King, joining as a rank and file member and then getting involved in the party's activities, including helping set up the Free Breakfast for Children programme.

Encouraged by the party to record her songs, she linked with producer Horace Tapscott for the album **Seize The Time**, released by Vault in 1969 and including *The Meeting*, the Black Panther Party national anthem. Her next album came in 1973 when her eponymous album was released by Motown on the Black Forum imprint, arranged by Horace but produced by Fonce Mizell and Freddie Perren, with the single *No Time* backed with *Until We're Free* becoming the only single to be issued on the Black Forum imprint. This was to prove her last album, for the following year she assumed leadership of the Black Panther Party in place of the fleeing Huey Newton, wanted on murder charges.

Elaine was Chairwoman for three years and later left the party in order to raise her daughter, later writing her memoirs and returning to political activism as a member of the Green Party.

ALBUM: ELAINE BROWN (1973)

SEVERIN BROWNE

The younger brother of fellow singer Jackson Browne, Edward Severin Browne was born in Heidelberg, Germany on 19 December 1949 (his father was a US serviceman stationed there at the time) and learned to play piano and guitar at a young age. He followed Jackson into the record industry, although when he auditioned for Berry Gordy in 1972, he intended becoming a songwriter only – it was Berry who convinced him to record his songs himself.

He would record two albums for Motown but the company put little or no promotion into either effort, **Severin Browne** and **The New Improved**, despite positive reviews for the latter. In the UK **The New Improved** was re-packaged as **Love Songs** and issued on MoWest, as were the singles *Love Song* and *Romance*. Severin left Motown after the two albums and promised never to record an album again – he kept the promise for more than twenty years!

ALBUMS: SEVERIN BROWN (1973), THE NEW IMPROVED (1974)

BROWNMARK

A former bass player in Prince's band Mark Louis Brown (born in Minneapolis, Minnesota on 16 May 1962) left The Revolution in 1986 and signed with Motown as a solo performer under the name Brownmark (the name having been bestowed upon him by Prince). He recorded two albums for Motown in the 1980s, **Just Like That** and **Good Feeling** (which appeared in 1989), with the former featuring his only hit single, *Next Time* (#48 R&B). He later founded and produced the group Mazarati before taking a sabbatical from the music business, subsequently re-appearing with a new project called Cryptic.

ALBUMS: JUST LIKE THAT (1987)

ELBRIDGE 'AL' BRYANT

A founder member of The Temptations, tenor singer Elbridge Bryant was born in Thomasville, Georgia on 28 September 1939 and moved to Detroit as a youngster, where he became friends with Otis Williams. When Williams suggested forming a group, Al as he was known was one of the first to join, also linking with James 'Pee-Wee' Crawford, Vernard Plain and Arthur Walton in Otis Williams & The Siberians.

After an unsuccessful single the group changed name to El Domingos, with Melvin Franklin and Richard Street replacing Arthur Walton and Vernard Plain. A further name change to Otis Williams & The Distants saw two moderately successful local singles for Northern Records before, in 1960, Otis, Melvin and Al linked with two former members of The Primes, Eddie Kendricks and Paul Williams, to form The Elgins. After earning little or no money from their Northern recordings, The Elgins turned up at Motown in 1960 looking for a deal, although they were told to find themselves a new name, eventually settling on The Temptations and landing a deal.

The group was to see some six singles released over the next three years, with only *Dream Come True* appearing on the chart (at #22 R&B), although the group was kept busy touring, performing and doing backing work around Hitsville. It was the lack of success that pushed Al into conflict with the rest of the group, for whilst Otis, Melvin, Paul and Eddie spent every available moment rehearsing and polishing up their act, Al had a wife, a child and day job as a milkman and was absent from his duties to the group. Even when he was in attendance, he would invariably complain to whoever would listen all the way back to Detroit that he didn't need the hassle of trying to become successful, especially if he had to get up early the next morning for his job at the dairy.

Matters reached a head in 1963 when, after a particularly well received live date and the group deciding on whether to go back for an encore, an altercation backstage saw Al smash a beer bottle into Paul William's face that required hospital treatment. Despite this, Paul convinced the rest of the group to give Al another chance, but a similar disagreement at the Motortown Revue Christmas show was the final straw for all concerned, with Al sacked and David Ruffin eventually brought in as his replacement.

Whilst Al sang with a number of local Detroit groups after his sacking from The Temptations, success eluded him and he was to die of cirrhosis of the liver in Orange County, Florida on 26 October 1975.

SONNY BURKE

Keyboard player Reginald 'Sonny' Burke (born in Illinois on 25 October 1945) played with Odell Brown & The Organizers and Mahalia Jackson before becoming a member of soul jazz combo Clarence Wheeler & The Enforcers in 1970. Thereafter Sonny played with Stanley Turrentine, Dizzy Gillespie, Margie Joseph, Aretha Franklin and John Handy but found greater fame as a songwriter (he co-composed *Serpentine Fire*, a massive hit for Earth, Wind & Fire) and arranger (Narada Michael Walden's **Awakening** and Smokey Robinson's **Warm Thoughts** albums). In between, he was scheduled to release an album for Motown in 1975, **Free Delivery**, but for some reason this was pulled from the schedule and presumably remains in the can.

THE BURNADETTES

A female gospel group led by musical director Joseph Norris and signed by Motown's gospel imprint Divinity, The Burnadettes recorded an album's worth of material in 1962 that never saw the light of day. A year later their only single *First, You Got To Recognize God,* produced by writer George Fowler and backed with the Clarence Paul produced *I'm Going Home* was issued to little fanfare.

DORSEY BURNETTE

Rockabilly singer Dorsey Burnette was born in Memphis, Tennessee on 28 December 1932 and formed The Rock And Roll Trio with his younger brother Johnny and friend Paul Burlison. They disbanded in 1957 and Dorsey recorded solo for a variety of labels, including briefly pitching up at Motown and recording for Mel-O-dy, including *Jimmy Brown* in 1964 (it would get a British release in October 1965 on Tamla Motown), although Dorsey's heart wasn't really in it owing to the death by drowning of his brother in August 1964.

Dorsey returned to Motown and its country label Melodyland in 1975, scoring minor hits on the country chart with *Molly (I Ain't Gettin' Any Younger)* (#28), *Lyin' In Her Arms Again* (#97) and *Ain't No Heartbreak* (#74) and an album for the MC imprint in 1977, **This Is Dorsey Burnette**, again without success. He died from a massive coronary on 19 August 1979.

ALBUM: THIS IS DORSEY BURNETTE (1977)

JERRY BUTLER

Born in Sunflower, Mississippi on 8 December 1939, Jerry grew up in Chicago and performed in the same church choir as Curtis Mayfield. The pair then joined R&B group The Roosters in 1957, securing a recording contract with Vee-Jay and a new name, The Impressions in 1958. Their single, *For Your Precious Love*, billed as Jerry Butler & The Impressions, much to the disgust of the other group members, eventually became a hit after being released on Vee-Jay, Falcon and then Abner Records, hitting #3 on the R&B chart and #11 pop.

A follow-up release, *Come Back My Love* made the Top 30 of the pop charts, prompting Jerry to leave The Impressions and take Curtis Mayfield with him as a song-writer. Jerry would enjoy several sizeable hits throughout the 1960s, including R&B chart toppers with *He Will Break Your Heart, Let It Be Me, Hey Western Union Man* and *Only The Strong Survive* for Vee-Jay and Mercury. It was during this hit run, in 1965, that Jerry invited Tammi Terrell (then still known as Tammy Montgomery) to perform at a series of nightclub dates, one of which in Detroit was attended by Berry Gordy who signed the young female singer as a solo artist to Motown.

Jerry meanwhile, who had signed with Mercury in 1966 following the collapse of Vee-Jay, would remain with Mercury until 1976 when he himself joined Motown at the prompting of Ewart Abner. Jerry would record three solo albums in **Love's On The Menu** (a #49 R&B hit), **Suite For The Single Girl** (#22 R&B and #146 pop) and **It All Comes Out In My Song**) and two albums with Thelma Houston in **Thelma & Jerry** (#20 R&B and #53 pop) and **Two To One**. The closest Jerry came to major success was with the singles lifted from **Suite**, with *I Wanna Do It To You* becoming a #7 R&B hit (as well as #51 pop) and *Chalk It Up* hitting #28 R&B.

When his contract expired Jerry opted to team up with Kenneth Gamble and Leon Huff at Philadelphia International, later recording for Fountain and dueting with Patti Austin on CTI. In November 1986 four Jerry Butler associated tracks, *For Your Precious Love, Moon River, He Will Break Your Heart* and *Let It Be Me* with Betty Everett appeared on the compilation CD **Hits From The Legendary Vee-Jay Records.** In recent years Jerry has turned his attentions to politics, being elected Commissioner for Cook County in Illinois in 1985, a position he still holds.

ALBUMS: LOVE'S ON THE MENU (1975), SUITE FOR THE SINGLE GIRL (1977), THELMA & JERRY (1977), IT ALL COMES OUT IN MY SONG (1977), TWO TO ONE (1978)

GARY BYRD

Perhaps better known as a radio deejay than performer, Gary Byrd was born Gary De Wit in Brooklyn, New York on 14 March 1949 and first linked with Stevie Wonder in the 1970s, writing the lyrics for *Black Man* and *Village Ghetto Land* for the **Songs In The Key Of Life** album. Seven years later Wonder and Byrd collaborated again on *The Crown*, the first (and so far only) release on Stevie Wonder's Wondirection label. The success of the single, at least as far as the UK was concerned, increased Byrd's profile, resulting in him being given his own gospel show for BBC Radio entitled 'Sweet Inspiration.' Gary later returned to the

C

G.C. CAMERON

George Curtis Cameron was just 23 years of age (he was born in McCalls Creek, Mississippi on 21 September 1945) when he was chosen to replace Chico Edwards as lead vocalist with The Spinners, by which time the group had already been with Motown for some seven years and registered just three R&B hits. Fortunately, G.C.'s friendship with Stevie Wonder led to an offer by Stevie to produce a number of tracks on The Spinners, one of which, *It's A Shame*, not only returned them to the R&B charts (it peaked at #4) but also the pop charts in the US (#14) and the UK (#20).

Although The Spinners were to enjoy one further hit single from their recordings with Stevie Wonder, they had already made up their mind to jump ship from Motown when their contract expired in 1971. G.C. Cameron was not in a position to follow them to Atlantic.

"My contract with the Spinners was a separate contract and there was much more time left on it. I could not leave, when the Spinners left. Motown made sure I stayed. A lot of people thought that I just left the group. Motown owned all the names. Motown registered everything, but they let the Spinners go with that name. It was part of the deal that Gwen Gordy (later his wife) and the Motown machine made."

Never a major priority for the label, he nevertheless scored a number of R&B hits, including *It's So Hard To Say Goodbye To Yesterday*, featured in the film 'Cooley High' and later to provide Boyz II Men with a major R&B and pop hit. He also recorded three albums, **Love Songs And Other Tragedies, G.C. Cameron** and **You're What's Missing From My Life**, had a fourth album cancelled and recorded with Syreeta on **Rich Love Poor Love**.

After leaving Motown towards the end of the 1970s he signed with Malaco before touring as an independent artist. He rejoined The Spinners in 2000 for two years and then replaced Barrington 'Bo' Henderson in The Temptations, singing lead on their Grammy nominated *How Sweet It Is (To Be Loved By You)*. After four years with The Temptations, G.C. left in order to concentrate on his own 'G.C. Cameron Review.'

ALBUMS: LOVE SONGS AND OTHER TRAGEDIES (1974), G.C. CAMERON (1976), YOU'RE WHAT'S MISSING FROM MY LIFE (1977) RICH LOVE POOR LOVE (1977)

CHOKER CAMPBELL

Born Walter Luzar Campbell in Shelby, Mississippi on 21 March 1916, Choker dreamed of being a star in his own right, just like the vocalists he backed at the Hitsville studio. After several years as a saxophonist and flautist for the in-house band at Motown, Choker pressured Berry Gordy into letting him issue a record under his own name, having recorded a live album at the Graystone Ballroom. After receiving a blunt refusal, Choker left the studio and restricted himself to performing with the touring band, a unit completely separate from the in-house studio band The Funk Brothers.

In March 1965 Berry relented enough to allow the release of the album **Hits Of The Sixties** (credited to Choker Campbell & Orchestra), which comprised twelve of the more famous Motown songs that had actually been recorded more than a year previously. From this *Come See About Me* (credited to Choker Campbell's 16 Piece Band) was issued as a single stateside, whilst in the UK *Mickey's Monkey* appeared on Tamla Motown (credited to Choker Campbell's Big Band!).

After a few more years touring with the likes of The Temptations, The Four Tops, The Supremes, Stevie Wonder, Marvin Gaye and other top draw names, Choker left Motown and settled in Canada where he formed both a band and a record label, Campbell Artist Productions. He later returned to Detroit where he died on 20 July 1993.

ALBUM: HITS OF THE SIXTIES (1965)

MICHAEL EDWARD CAMPBELL

Born in Anderson, Indiana songwriter and vocalist Michael Edward was proficient enough in the former to have songs recorded by The Jackson 5 (*Joyful Jukebox Music*, co-written with Tom Bee of Xit) and Stoney & Meatloaf and talented enough at the latter to record one album for Motown. Prior to this he was a member of the bands Abstract Reality and Scorpion and released a single on MoWest (under the truncated name Mike Campbell), *Angel Got A Book Today*, issued in January 1973.

A year later came his only album, largely written and produced by Tom Baird and featuring such stellar names as Joe Sample on keyboards, Bob Babbitt on bass, Ernie Watts on saxophone and Gloria Jones and Veneta Fields on backing vocals. However, neither the eponymous album nor the only single lifted *Roxanne (You Sure Got A Fine Design)* did much by the way of sales. Only the single was issued in the UK, put out on the Rare Earth label, which is perhaps where it should also have been in the US. He later became an actor under the name Michael Champion, appearing in 'Total Recall', 'Toy Soldiers' and 'Beverly Hills Cop', among other films.

ALBUM: MICHAEL EDWARD CAMPBELL (1974)

CAN'T SLOW DOWN - LIONEL RICHIE [ALBUM]

After the international success of his eponymous debut album, Lionel Richie was faced with the all-important second album syndrome. The fact that he had consistently come up with the goods whilst a member of The Commodores, together with the sales enjoyed by both the album and singles from **Lionel Richie** would count for little or nothing if **Can't Slow Down** failed to live up to expectations.

"I always like to lighten things up now and again" he would later reveal. "I don't really like to fall into the trap of giving people what they expect, or come to expect, from me. I too like the lushy strings and the tearful ballads, but I wanted to do something special. I was also afraid of falling into the middle-of-the-road market with slow songs because that's not what I want to do right now. I was looking for more up-tempo songs this time that wouldn't sound like everyone else's. Michael Jackson seems to have that market sewn up for the next few years or so, and I wanted to create my own unique sound. I prefer to write new songs for new projects, although I'm sure I must have some good songs in store by now that I've forgotten about."

Such was the rich vein of form Lionel had hit in his songwriting, the original line-up for the album omitted *Running With The Night*, *Hello* and *All Night Long*, but fortunately common sense prevailed and these were put back into the final mix. The advance release of the single *All Night Long (All Night)* indicated that Lionel was prepared to move his musical horizons from the prevalent sound of his debut album, with the result that **Can't Slow Down** featured virtually something for everyone – the up-tempo dance groove of *All Night Long*, the rock influenced *Running With The Night*, even country with *Stuck On You*.

The area of the market that he had effectively made his own, R&B ballads, was well serviced thanks to *Penny Lover* and *Hello*, and upon the album's release on 11 October 1983, it was obvious that this wasn't just a good album, it had the prospect of becoming a great one. A total of five tracks (from only eight on the album) were issued as singles, with all five hitting the Top Ten of both the R&B and pop charts in the US. The album itself sold spectacularly, topping the R&B charts (for twenty three weeks), the US pop charts (for three weeks) and the UK charts (also for three weeks) and even made #55 on the US country charts! Having hit #1 on Billboard's pop chart in December 1983, it would go on to spend 59 consecutive weeks inside the Top Ten and over three *years* on the chart in total!

Not surprisingly, after becoming the best selling album of 1984, **Can't Slow Down** was named Album of the Year at the Grammy Awards, with Lionel and James Anthony Carmichael also being named joint Producer of the Year. Total worldwide sales of the album exceed twenty million copies, and with over ten million of those sales coming domestically, **Can't Slow Down** became the first Motown album to be awarded a Diamond Award from the RIAA, having surpassed the ten million copies threshold on 19 December 1985.

ACE CANNON

One of the leading session musicians in Nashville from the late 1950s, alto saxophonist Ace Cannon began his professional career as a member of Bill Black's Combo. Born John Cannon in Grenada, Mississippi on 5 May 1934, Ace spent two years with the Combo before being offered a solo deal with Hi Records, scoring a country hit with *Tuff*, which also featured the Combo as backing musicians. In 1983 Motown released the **Memphis Golden Hits** album as part of the brief deal licensing deal with Hi/Cream Records.

ALBUM: MEMPHIS GOLDEN HITS (1983)

VIN CARDINAL

A soul singer and percussionist born in San Fernando, Trinidad, Vin found fame in Sweden first, where he moved in the 1960s. Together with his band The Queens, he toured across continental Europe as well recording a number of albums that became regional hits. He moved to the US in the early 1970s, where he signed with Motown in 1973. He released one single, *There'll Be No City On The Hill* backed with (in Vin's case the misnamed) *Never Been To Spain*. He was unable to replicate his European success but continues to tour around the world.

JAMES ANTHONY CARMICHAEL

Indelibly linked with The Commodores and Lionel Richie, James Anthony Carmichael was already an industry veteran when he first linked up with the Motown group. Born in Harrodsburg, Kentucky on 12 October 1920, James first made his name as an arranger, working for Mirwood Records (The Olympics, Jackie Lee and The Furys) and Warner Brothers (Bill Cosby) among others during the 1960s before pitching up at Motown as the decade came to a close.

There he worked with the Jacksons, both collectively and individually, Marvin Gaye, Diana Ross, Eddie Kendricks and Gladys Knight before linking up with The Commodores for their second album, **Caught Up**. The success of that and following albums transformed The Commodores from a band with potential into a worldwide phenomenon and one of the few Motown acts of the time able to sell both singles and albums in quantity.

When Lionel Richie exited the band for a solo career in 1982, he made sure he secured the services of James Anthony Carmichael as co-producer (to such an extent The Commodores opted to produce themselves thereafter) and was rewarded when **Lionel Richie** shifted four million copies in the US and its successor **Can't Slow Down** more than ten million. This latter album earned both Lionel and James the 1984 Grammy Award for Producer of the Year, the ultimate accolade. Lionel then opted to bring in other producers for subsequent albums, although James did work with him again in 1998 on the disappointing **Time** album, the pair unable to recapture former glories.

STOKELY CARMICHAEL

Born in Port of Spain, Trinidad & Tobago on 29 June 1941, Stokely moved to New York at the age of eleven where he was reunited with his parents, who had emigrated nine years previously, Stokely having been raised by his grandmother. It was at school that he first became interested in activism, joining the Nonviolent Action Group (NAG) and eventually becoming active within the Civil Rights Movement.

He also participated in the Freedom Rides of the Congress of Racial Equality (CORE), for which he was frequently arrested and jailed (he would later claim to have been arrested more than 30 times for such activism). Stokely marched alongside Martin Luther King and others on James Meredith's 'March Against Fear', during which he made what is recognised as the first Black Power speech.

He is also credited with coining the phrase 'institutionalised racism' and in 1968 made a speech with H Rap Brown at a Free Huey (Newton) rally. This would eventually be released in October 1970 as one of the first albums on the Black Forum label, but by then Stokely himself had distanced himself from the Black Panther Movement, moving to Guinea-Conakry where he adopted the name Kwame Ture. He died from prostate cancer on 15 November 1998 despite two years of treatment in New York.

ALBUM: FREE HUEY (1970)

JEAN CARN

Chiefly known for the stir created by her four albums for Philadelphia International during the 1970s, Jean Carn (born Sarah Jean Perkins in Columbus, Georgia on 15 March 1947; she took her stage name from her former husband Doug Carn) had already made something of a name for herself thanks to earlier work with Earth Wind & Fire and Norman Connors. Her Philadelphia International albums produced several charting singles, with the result she was already an established artist by the time she joined Motown in 1982.

Her only album for the label, **Trust Me**, saw one hit single in the shape of *If You Don't Know Me By Now*, a Philadelphia International number originally made famous by Harold Melvin & The Blue Notes, which featured The Temptations and made #49 on the R&B chart.

Jean also paired with Bobby M for an update of Al Green's *Let's Stay Together*, which made #74 R&B and became her only UK charting single when it peaked at #53 in 1983. Although there was supposedly a second album recorded, Jean Carn's departure from the label ensured it remained in the vaults.

ALBUM: TRUST ME (1982)

JOHN CARPENTER

Film director and composer John Howard Carpenter was born in Carthage, New York on 16 January 1948 and made his name, at least in Europe, with his 1976 directorial debut 'Assault On Precinct 13'. He would go on to helm such films as 'Halloween', 'Escape From New York', 'Starman', 'Escape From L.A.' and 'Village Of The Damned'. He also composed the music for several of these and would undertake both duties on 'Christine', his 1983 adaptation of the Stephen King novel. He linked with Alan Howarth on the track *Christine Attacks* that was featured on the soundtrack album released by Motown.

DIAHANN CARROLL

Born Carol Diahann Johnson in New York on 17 July 1934, Diahann made her name as an actress, achieving her breakthrough on the television contest 'Chance of a Lifetime.' After winning the show for three consecutive weeks, she secured several singing engagements in New York before landing her first major acting role in 'Carmen Jones'. Diahann then appeared on Broadway and picked up another major film role, for 'Porgy And Bess', although her voice in this was dubbed by opera singer Loulie Jean Norman. That there was really no need to have her voice dubbed was shown in 1962 when she won a Tony award, the first by a black woman, for her role in 'No Strings' and also picked up a Grammy Award nomination for Best Female Pop Vocal Performance for the title song.

Her singing career was launched in 1957 with the album **Diahann Carroll Sings Harold Arlen Songs**, with her career thereafter consisting of successful acting roles in film (she would collect an Academy Award nomination for Best Actress for 'Claudine') and television (her first Emmy Award nomination for 'Naked City' in 1963 and a Golden Globe win for 'Julia' in 1968), with at one point Diahann seriously considered for the role of Billie Holiday in 'Lady Sings The Blues', which of course went to Diana Ross.

In 1974 Diahann signed with Motown and released one eponymous album in April. A scheduled single, *I've Been There Before* was pulled after the album failed to ignite any interest, enabling Diahann to return to her acting career, most notably as a three year member of the cast of 'Dynasty' from 1984. Diahann, who has been married four times and survived breast cancer, continues her acting career today.

ALBUM: DIAHANN CARROLL (1974)

LYNDA CARTER

Lynda Jean Carter was born in Phoenix, Arizona on 24 July 1951 and became better known as an actress, most notably in the television series Wonder Woman, her first leading role, which aired on ABC between 1975 and 1977 (as 'The New Original Wonder Woman') and then moved to CBS (as 'The New Adventures Of Wonder Woman').

After two successful seasons CBS dropped the show but retained Lynda, giving her a showcase special. Her brief involvement with Motown came when Motown Productions, in conjunction with CBS, assembled the television movie 'The Last Song', with Lynda performing the Ron Miller and Kenny Hirsch penned title song.

Released in September 1980 in the UK, where Lynda was undertaking something of a tour and promotional work, the single bombed and resulted in the planned release in the US being pulled and the option on a further recording contract not being taken up.

RON CARTER

Born in Ferndale, Michigan on 4 May 1937, Ron began his career playing the cello but switched to bass at the Cass Technical High School in Detroit when it became apparent that African Americans weren't considered apt for classical music! That, however, did not stop Ron from performing with the Philharmonic Orchestra of the Eastman School of Music or prevent him from gaining a bachelor's degree at Eastman or going on to earn a master's degree in double bass performance from the Manhattan School of Music.

It was jazz that gave Ron his first job after graduation, most notably with Chico Hamilton, before linking up with Miles Davis in the frontman's second great quintet in 1963, alongside Herbie Hancock, Wayne Shorter and Tony Williams. A member of the Miles Davis touring group for the next five years and the recording group for a further two, Ron became a house musician at CTI from its early days in 1967 when the label was distributed by A&M, recording several albums under his own name and appearing on virtually everything else the label issued as well as being a one time member of the New York Jazz Quartet.

The two albums released during CTI's time distributed by Motown both made a showing on the charts, with **Spanish Blue** making #37 R&B and #10 jazz and **Anything Goes** peaking at #21 on the jazz chart. Ron would later record extensively for Milestone and Blue Note, his reputation as jazz music's greatest bass player of his generation untouched. In all, Ron is believed to have appeared on some 2,500 albums, making him one of the most recorded bass players of all time.
ALBUMS: SPANISH BLUE (1975), ANYTHING GOES (1975)

CARTOONS

The meteoric rise of The Jackson 5 saw all manner of commercial opportunities arise for both Motown and the act themselves, with a television special entitled 'Goin' Back To Indiana' being taped in July 1971 for airing in September on ABC.
The same network also announced a cartoon series, Jackson 5ive, to launch the same month. Produced by Rankin/Bass and Motown Productions, the series was a fictionalised account of the group's career, with the boys undertaking a wide variety of tasks to drum up publicity.
The 'tasks' were set by the group's manager Berry Gordy and each week two of The Jackson 5's songs would be featured. A specially recorded medley of *I Want You Back*, *ABC*, *The Love You Save* and *Mama's Pearl* served as the theme. Although the series was supposedly all about The Jackson 5, they didn't actually appear in it, apart from posing for promotional photographs which then morphed into cartoon images.
Michael's voice was provided by Donald Fullilove, Marlon by Edmund Sylvers (who as a member of the family group The Sylvers would enjoy considerable recording success that mirrored The Jackson 5's career), Jermaine by Joel Cooper, Tito by Mike Martinez and Jackie by Craig Grandy. Berry Gordy's voice was provided by Paul Frees; only Diana Ross provided her own voice to the series.
The first series ran from 11 September 1971 to 15 January 1972 (a total of 17 episodes) and a second series aired from 9 September to 14 October 1972 (six episodes). The two series were re-run during 1984 and 1985 when Michael Jackson mania was at its height.
A DVD/Blu-Ray collection of four discs featuring all 23 episodes was released by Classic Media in January 2013 (Region 1, the US only).

SERIES ONE EPISODES [AND SONGS FEATURED]
It All Started With... [*ABC* and *Goin' Back To Indiana*]
Pinestock U.S.A. [*I'll Be There* and *Young Folks*]
Drafted [*I Want You Back* and *2-4-6-8*]
Mistaken Identity [*I'll Bet You* and *16 Candles*]
Bongo, Baby, Bongo [*My Little Baby* and *It's Great To Be Here*]
The Winners' Circle [*The Love You Save* and *How Funky Is Your Chicken*]
Cinder Jackson [*Reach In* and *Can I See You In The Morning*]
The Wizard Of Soul [*The Love I Saw In You Was Just A Mirage* and *Oh How Happy*]
The Tiny Five [*The Wall* and *I Will Find A Way*]
The Groovatron [*Maybe Tomorrow* and *Nobody*]
Ray & Charles: Superstars [*(Come Round Here) I'm The One You Need* and *(We've Got) Blue Skies*]
Farmer Jacksons [*My Cherie Amour* and *Honey Chile*]
Jackson Island [*Ready Or Not (Here I Come)* and *La La Means I Love You*]
The Michael Look [*Darling Dear* and *I Don't Know Why I Love You*]
Jackson Street U.S.A. [*Petals* and *She's Good*]
Rasho-Jackson [*One More Chance* and *I Found That Girl*]
A Rare Pearl [*Never Can Say Goodbye* and *Mama's Pearl*]

SECOND SERIES
Who's Hoozis? [*Rockin' Robin* and *Wings Of My Love*]
Michael White [*Sugar Daddy* and *I Wanna Be Where You Are*]
Groove To The Chief [*I'm So Happy* and *In Our Small Way*]
Michael In Wonderland [*Got To Be There* and *Maria (You Were The Only One)*]
Jackson And The Beanstalk [*Love Is Here (And Now You're Gone)* and *Girl Don't Take Your Love From Me*]
The Opening Act [*Little Bitty Pretty One* and *If I Have To Move A Mountain*]

CASTON & MAJORS

Husband and wife team Leonard Caston (born in Chicago, Illinois on 13 November 1943) and Carolyn Majors (born in Greenville, South Carolina) recorded one eponymous album for Motown, released in November 1974 (March 1975 in the UK). Despite the presence of such luminaries as Syreeta and Leonard's own writing abilities, which had taken the likes of Eddie Kendricks to the top of the charts the album did little, resulting in a planned follow-up album being scrapped and Leonard and Carolyn returning to their original day jobs.

In Leonard's case this meant as a writer and producer, for Carolyn that of a backing singer for the likes of Eddie Kendricks, Minnie Riperton, Philip Bailey and The 5th Dimension. Tamla Motown in the UK made a concerted effort to try and get a hit out of the project, releasing no fewer than three singles (*Child Of Love*, *Sing* and *I'll Keep A Light In My Window*) over the course of six months, all to no avail. The album was reissued on CD in Britain in 2013 on the BBR label, with the abandoned second album included as bonus material.

ALBUM: CASTON & MAJORS (1974)

LEONARD CASTON

Although he undertook several attempts at a recording career, as a member of The Valiants and in partnership with Carolyn Majors, it is as a song writer that Leonard Caston made his name at Motown.

Born in Chicago, Illinois on 13 November 1943, Leonard served in the US Army before returning to Chicago and joining The Radiants who were to enjoy a hit with *Voice Your Choice* on Chess Records in 1965. Leonard left the group soon after in order to become a staff writer, producer and musician for Chess, producing *Hold On* for his former group and *I Had A Talk With My Man* by Mitty Collier.

Following the death of Leonard Chess and the sale of the label to GRT, Leonard relocated to Detroit in order to try his luck at Motown, going on to record an album for Rare Earth entitled **Jesus Christ Greatest Hits** credited to The God Squad Featuring Leonard Caston and produced by Henry 'Hank' Cosby. After hanging around the offices trying to get someone, anyone, to listen to the songs he had written he found a mentor in Frank Wilson, who after using *Nathan Jones* (co-written by Leonard with Kathy Wakefield) on The Supremes suggested that he join the team working on Eddie Kendricks solo material.

Along with Frank and Anita Poree, Leonard came up with *Keep On Truckin'* (a #1 R&B and pop hit in the US and #18 UK), *Boogie Down* (#1 R&B, #2 pop and #39 UK), *Son Of Sagittarius* (#5 R&B and #28 pop) and the track that is often heralded as Motown's first full-blown attempt at catering for the burgeoning disco scene, the majestic *Girl You Need A Change Of Mind* (#13 R&B and #87 pop).

"We were very compatible as a creative team. Before I became a production partner, I was a writing partner. And then I just kind of grew into that kind of position because Frank began to respect my creative ability to the degree he thought we would be a better dynamic if we became production partners."

Leonard also wrote with Kathy Wakefield, penning *I Can't Quit Your Love* which was recorded by both The Four Tops and The Jackson 5. In 1974 Leonard got the chance to record himself, pairing up with Carolyn Majors for **Caston & Majors** and later pairing up with her as man and wife. Whilst the album did little (the album was released in the UK, where three singles were also lifted), Leonard continued writing and producing for a slew of acts, including Minnie Riperton.

A growing drug problem halted his musical career and both he and his wife later relocated to Harrisburg, Pennsylvania where he became Minister of Music of the Dayspring Ministries church.

ALBUMS: JESUS CHRIST GREATEST HITS (1972), CASTON & MAJORS (1974)

THE CATS

A Dutch rock group formed in Volendam in 1962 as The Mystic Four by Piet Veerman (born on 1 March 1943, guitar and vocals), Cees Veerman (born on 6 October 1943, guitar and vocals), Jaap Schilder (born on 9 January 1943, guitar and piano) and Arnold Muhren (born on 28 January 1944, bass) they name-changed a year later to The Blue Cats.

The name was subsequently shortened to The Cats in 1966 and drummer Theo Klouwer (born on 30 June 1947) added to the line-up. By then they were extremely popular across continental Europe, especially their homeland and Germany, and in the UK had a deal with EMI that would ultimately see them part of the launch for the Rare Earth label.

Their 1970 Rare Earth release, entitled **45 Lives**, appears to be a compilation of sorts, with several of the tracks having been previously issued in Europe by Imperial/Bovema, including the track issued as a single, *Marian*. Their European popularity didn't carry across the Atlantic, with their album doing little business, although they continued recording throughout the decade and both Veerman brothers releasing solo albums. Cees Veerman died on 15 March 2014.

ALBUM: 45 LIVES (1970)

CELEBRATION

Celebration was a vocal sextet assembled by songwriters and producers Deke Richards with Sherlie Matthews, supposedly in an attempt to replicate the success of Fifth Dimension. Deke in particular had high hopes for the group, one of the most enjoyable he had worked with during his time at Motown.

"Celebration were such nice people, talented and a pleasure to work with. The group was quite versatile. I think that was part of the problem; there was no true identity as the style of songs on the [album] is all over the place, almost like a rainbow."

The group attracted favourable live reviews and dropped their debut eponymous album, featuring lead vocals by Charles Dennis 'Chuck' Bedford with Rosalind, Wendy, Kitty, Richard and Bill in July 1972 on MoWest with a subsequent single *Since I Met You There's No Magic* the following January being pulled off the schedule and released on Motown instead in June 1973.

Chuck Bedford later became a member of Shanghai and sang on their debut album before being replaced by Cliff Bennett. He also released a couple of solo singles on Bell and Rockfield in Britain.

ALBUM: CELEBRATION (1972)

A CELLARFUL OF MOTOWN

No record company has milked its back catalogue quite like Motown, with the seemingly never ending release of greatest hits, best of's and themed compilations. As good as many of these are, there are only so many times you want the same tracks turning up in your collection, for most seem to be perpetually based around the same selection of hits by stellar names.

Fortunately, no record company has mined its back catalogue quite like Motown, and the four volume (at the time of writing) **A Cellarful Of Motown** is quite possibly the best Motown series to have hit the shops for the last twenty or so years. The series, which was inspired by the British phenomenon of Northern Soul and the unquenchable thirst for 60's Motown stompers, was launched in 2002 with the first volume gathering together 40 tracks that had lain in the vaults for near on forty years. The initial response based on the tracks on display was why were these titles not made available previously? Virtually everyone could and should have made it as a single release, leading to the inescapable conclusion that it must have been virtually impossible to get anything approved by the famed Quality Control meetings.

Further volumes appeared in 2005, 2007 and 2010, giving a total of 179 tracks that were finally made available for public consumption, and, more importantly, the quality continued in the same rich vein that had been prevalent on the first edition.

Not every track conformed to Northern Soul, with The Dalton Boys' *Take My Hand* being almost a carbon copy of the kind of thing The Beatles were doing at the time (1965), but over the course of four volumes there are scores of tracks to savour, including gems from Yvonne Fair (with and without Chuck Jackson), Stevie Wonder, The Temptations, The Originals and countless others, including many artists for whom this series represented their first appearance on a Motown release. Several reviewers have passed judgement that the reason these tracks were not issued at the time of recording was that whilst they might have been perfect for the Northern Soul market, they were not necessarily perfect for what Motown was or wanted to be. Assuming we will never really know why they weren't released, we can only rejoice that they have finally come out – better late than never.

ALBUMS: VOLUME 1 (2002), VOLUME 2 (2005), VOLUME 3 (2007), VOLUME 4 (2010)

GENE CHANDLER

Born Eugene Dixon in Chicago, Illinois on 6 July 1927, he was a member of The Dukays and quickly became established as the main singer, fronting *The Girl Is A Devil* for Nat Records in 1961. Producers Carl Davis and Bill Sheppard recorded four more sides on The Dukays, with Nat picking up on *Night Owl*, leaving Carl and Bill to shop around for a further deal on the remaining tracks. One of these, *Duke Of Earl*, was snapped up by Vee-Jay, although to avoid confusion the single was released as a solo effort by Gene Chandler (Johnny Chandler, a popular actor of the era, was Gene's favourite) and were rewarded with a double chart topper, with *Duke Of Earl* spending five weeks on top of the R&B chart and three atop the pop listing.

Duke Of Earl prompted a slew of answer records, including *I Out-Duked The Duke* by Little Otis that was picked up by Motown. The follow-up *Rainbow* also scored, hitting #11 pop and #47 pop, with the flip side *You Threw A Lucky Punch* (an answer record to Mary Wells' *You Beat Me To The Punch*) also registering at #25 R&B and #49 pop. In 1986 both *Duke Of Earl* and *Rainbow* appeared on the compilation album **Hits**

From The Legendary Vee-Jay Records, issued on CD by Motown.

BRUCE CHANNEL

Born Bruce McMeans in Jacksonville, Texas on 28 November 1940 he adopted the stage name Bruce Channel when he performed on the Louisiana Hayride radio show. He linked up with harmonica player Delbert McClinton and the pair performed country music across the United States and recorded unsuccessfully for Teenager and King Records. Then in 1962 Bruce was invited to record a single he and Margaret Cobb had written in 1959 for Bill Smith and his label Le Cam based in Fort Worth, the single being *Hey! Baby*, which Bruce had made an integral part of his show.

When copies began selling locally, Smith sold the master to Smash Records, who shifted more than a million copies in getting the single to the top of the US pop chart. The single took off internationally too, hitting #2 in the UK and Bruce getting an invitation to tour the country. The support act was the then unknown Beatles, who according to legend were impressed enough by the harmonica break in *Hey! Baby* to incorporate a similar refrain into their single *Love Me Do*.

Two minor hits on Smash followed (at least in the US), together with another release on Le Cam before Bruce's career appeared effectively over. He then turned up at Motown, the lure of his success two years previously enough to get a deal with Mel-O-dy. Although he wrote material at Mel-o-day under his real name Bruce McMeans, his only releases were the Joe Hayes and Jack Rhodes penned *Satisfied Mind* and *You Make Me Happy*, written by Jimmy Curtis in a style reminiscent of *Hey! Baby*.

Unfortunately for Bruce, Mel-O-dy's profile as a country label meant his single sank without trace and his deal came to an abrupt end, even though he later claimed to have recorded some six tracks, several of which featured the involvement of HDH.

CHARLENE

Originally signed by Motown in 1973, Charlene Duncan had been dropped by the label when her only major hit single took off, prompting a frantic worldwide search trying to locate her in order to re-sign her to the company!

Born Charlene Marilyn D'Angelo in Hollywood, California on 1 June 1950, Charlene was married at the age of 16 and signed to Motown under her married name of Charlene Duncan. Her first single, *All That Love Went To Waste* was issued on Motown in January 1974 but flopped, resulting in her being dropped by the label. Charlene subsequently returned to Motown via Prodigal, where she scored her debut hit, *It Ain't Easy Comin' Down*, which made #97 in March 1977.

By then her first album **Charlene** was also in the shops, although six months after the albums original release in November 1976, it was repackaged with one track replaced and issued as **Songs Of Love**, with *I've Never Been To Me* edited to remove the spoken bridge. From the album *Freddie* became a minor hit single, hitting #96 and prompting the release of *I've Never Been To Me*, which stalled at #97. After one further single for Motown, *Hungry/I Won't Remember Ever Loving You* in June 1980 that went nowhere, Charlene was dropped by the company a second time.

In February 1982, Florida DJ Scott Shannon of WRBQ-FM began playing *I've Never Been To Me* at the suggestion of a girlfriend. The audience response was such that the record began getting plays across the country, prompting a re-issue on Motown, complete with the spoken bridge and a search for Charlene – they found her in England, where she had re-married (she was now Charlene Oliver) and worked in a sweet shop in Ilford!

The single would eventually hit #3 on the pop charts (it missed the R&B charts altogether) and, more impressively, top the UK charts and herald a quick burst of activity for Charlene, releasing both a follow-up single in *It Ain't Easy Comin' Down* and a Spanish version of *I've Never Been To Me* (the first release on Motown's Latino label) in June 1982. Despite releasing a further three albums for Motown, the only other hit record was *Used To Be*, a duet with Stevie Wonder that made #46 on the singles chart in 1983. Despite a cameo appearance in 'The Last Dragon', Charlene was unable to add to her hit tally and left Motown in 1985. She would however continue her singing career and return to the US to live in California.

ALBUMS: CHARLENE (1976), SONGS OF LOVE (1977), I'VE NEVER BEEN TO ME (1982), USED TO BE (1982), THE SKY IS THE LIMIT (1982), HIT AND RUN LOVER (1984)

THE CHARTERS

Another little known group that pitched up at Motown (in this case on the Mel-O-dy label) for just one release, only to disappear without trace thereafter. According to Motown this was a self-contained group from Toledo, Ohio whose only single *Trouble Lover* was written by Ray Reynolds, Ron Moore and John Williams and produced by Reynolds and Moore, with the group or producers then approaching Motown with a finished master for sale. Whilst promotional copies have surfaced since the supposed September 1962 release, no finished stock has emerged, implying that poor radio reaction may have meant the official release was subsequently scrapped. It is believed the group later recorded for Tarx, Merry Go Round and Alva Records, assuming that it is the same group on all three labels.

CHESS RECORDS

As crucial to Chicago as Motown would become to Detroit, Chess Records was founded in 1950 by émigré brothers Leonard and Phil Chess. The label soon became pre-eminent in the Windy City and something of a magnet for talent across the United States, covering numerous musical genres. Chess Records also handled national distribution for a number of label start ups, including Gwen Gordy and Harvey Fuqua's Anna Records, which would lead to Motown's first major hit in *Money* by Barrett Strong.

Berry Gordy was also able to secure a brief deal direct with the brothers for six masters on The Miracles, *Bad Girl* backed with *I Love You Baby*, *It* backed with *Don't Say Bye Bye* (credited to Ron [Ronnie White] and Bill [Smokey Robinson] and issued on Chess' Argo imprint) and *I Need A Change* backed with *All I Want Is You* (which unlike the other two singles was never released on Motown or Tamla). *Bad Girl* became a minor hit, peaking at #93, but slowly Berry managed to acquire enough funding to be able to handle his own national distribution, bringing an end to his brief deal with Chess Records.

THE CHIFFONS

Three classmates from the James Monroe High School in the Bronx, New York got together to form a vocal group in 1960, with Judy Craig (born in The Bronx on 6 August 1946), Barbara Lee (born in The Bronx on 16 May 1947) and Patricia Bennett (born in The Bronx on 7 April 1947) the original members. Two years later songwriter Ronnie Mack suggested they should add Sylvia Peterson (born in The Bronx on 30 September 1946) to the line-up, with their initial recordings appearing under the moniker of The Four Pennies.

They became The Chiffons in 1963, just as *He's So Fine* was about to be released, with the single going on to top the US charts and hit #16 in the UK. Their major follow-up was *One Fine Day* (#5 US and #29 UK), with both tracks subsequently appearing on the soundtrack to 'The Flamingo Kid', released by Motown in December 1984. Judy Craig left the group in 1969 but returned following the death by heart attack of Barbara Lee on 15 May 1992.

CHISA RECORDS

South African trumpeter Hugh Masekela moved to America in 1960 following the Sharpesville massacre and in protest at the government's Apartheid policy. After recordings for a variety of labels, including Uni where he received a Grammy nomination for *Grazin' In The Grass*, he formed his own Chisa label in 1966 and initially secured distribution through Uni, subsequently being distributed by Revue, Vault and Buddah as well as a brief spell as an independent. He inked a deal with Motown in 1970, by which time his roster included the likes of The Crusaders, Monk Montgomery and Letta Mbulu.

The deal with Motown lasted just two years, with The Crusaders (who were no strangers to Motown, as both Joe Sample and Wilton Felder had appeared on many of Motown's West Coast studio sessions) also releasing albums on Motown and MoWest. For some reason, when the deal with Chisa was brought to an abrupt end in June 1971, Motown retained the rights to the seven albums that had been released, together with one that had not, **Mosadi** by Letta Mbulu.

Chisa would subsequently link with Blue Thumb and release ten albums (including five by The Crusaders) before closing down, with The Crusaders switching to parent label ABC Records when Blue Thumb was phased out (and moved on again to MCA when ABC was phased out). The Chisa label was never given a release in Britain; those albums that were issued were released on the Rare Earth label.

KEN CHRISTIE AND THE SUNDAY PEOPLE

A little known gospel rock group that were assigned to the Rare Earth label, releasing two singles during 1971. Kenneth Beavers and Roger Griffin wrote all four tracks the group recorded, *Don't Pay Me No Mind* backed with *Listen To Your Soul* being released in February and *The Reverend John B. Daniels* backed with *Jesus Is The Key* following in June. All four tracks, which appear to be the only records made by the group, were produced by Mike Valvano. The group did perform live, however, appearing at the Detroit Discovery 1971, something of two day showcase for Rare Earth acts at the Rackham Building.

LOU CHRISTIE

Best known for his 1965 US #1 *Lightnin' Strikes*, Lou Christie pursued a number of different musical styles during the course of his career, with varying results. Born Lugee Alfredo Giovanni Sacco (his first name is sometimes listed as Luigi) in Glenwillard, Pennsylvania on 19 February 1943 he recorded for a number of New York and Pittsburgh labels, most notably *The Jury* which appeared on the Robbee label as Lugee & The Lions.

His first hit, however, came with *The Gypsy Cried*, which was eventually picked up for national distribution by Roulette and credited to Lou Christie without his knowledge (he would later claim "I was pissed off about it for 20 years. I wanted to keep my name and be a one-named performer, just 'Lugee'"), which featured what would later become Lou's trademark vocal style of verses sung in his normal register and then a dramatic shift to falsetto for the choruses. *The Gypsy Cried* peaked at #24 and was followed by an even bigger hit in *Two Faces Have I* (#6 pop in the US) and a modest Top 50 placing for *How Many Teardrops* before Lou was drafted into the US Army and his career brought to a temporary halt.

After his discharge he signed with MGM, for whom he recorded his smash hit *Lightnin' Strikes* in 1965, registering several other hits for the label before signing with Columbia in 1969. It was a subsequent move to Buddah that first linked him with writer and producer Tony Romeo and scoring a major international hit with *I'm Gonna Make You Mine*, which peaked at #2 in the UK. After a spell living in England at the start of the 1970s Lou teamed up with Tony Romeo again in 1974 and recorded an eponymous album (although it has since become better known as **Beyond The Blue Horizon** after the minor hit single that was extracted) that was issued on Three Brothers Records, probably the least known part of the CTI set-up. Although the single peaked at #80 on the pop chart, it missed the country chart altogether, prompting something of a retirement from the music industry for a lengthy spell.

Lou subsequently found work as a ranch hand, offshore oil driller and carnival barker before returning to the music scene and appearing on the oldies circuit.
ALBUM: LOU CHRISTIE (1974)

CHRISTINE (FILM SOUNDTRACK)

Based on the book of the same name written by Stephen King, 'Christine' was an American horror film about a car with a feeling that ran amok killing any enemies of its owner. Directed by John Carpenter and starring Keith Gordon, John Stockwell, Alexandra Paul and Harry Dean Stanton, 'Christine' was successful, grossing over $20 million. John Carpenter and Alan Howarth wrote and performed much of the incidental music in the film, with Varese Sarabande releasing a film score album.

Motown meanwhile picked up the soundtrack rights which were released in November 1983. Featuring well known tracks by George Thorogood & The Destroyers, Buddy Holly & The Crickets, Johnny Ace, Robert & Johnny, Little Richard, Dion & The Belmonts, The Viscounts, Thurston Harris, Danny & The Juniors and Larry Williams, alongside an incidental piece by John Carpenter and Alan Howarth, the album reached #177 on the pop chart. It is somewhat unique among Motown soundtracks in so much as none of the artists on display had any connection to Motown (although Little Richard would have a compilation album released by the company two years later) either before or after release.
ALBUM: CHRISTINE SOUNDTRACK (1983)

KEITH CHRISTMAS

British singer and songwriter Keith Peter Christmas was born in Wivenhoe, near Colchester on 13 October 1946 and first recorded for RCA in 1969. After a spell with B&C Records he signed with Emerson, Lake & Palmer's Manticore imprint, for whom he recorded the album **Brighter Day** in 1974. Released in the US in May the following year it contained his version of *My Girl*, which had been issued as a single a month earlier.
ALBUM: BRIGHTER DAY (1974)

CHUCK-A-LUCKS

Students from North Texas State College in Denton, Adrian McClish (also known as Adrian Keith), Reuben Noel and Jim Bob Nance initially worked under the moniker as The Dipsy Doodlers immediately after the Second World War. By 1950 Nance had been replaced by Charlie Dickerson and the trio performed semi-professionally for several years before Noel and Dickerson were drafted to serve in Korea. When the group reconvened in 1953, the name Dipsy Doodlers had been appropriated by several other groups and so they decided on Chuck-A-Lucks.

Their mixture of vocals and comedy made them a popular draw around Texas, resulting in recordings for Lin and Jubilee, without success, but they still had their touring to fall back on. It is likely they were persuaded to record for Motown by Al Klein, the company's sales representative for the Texas area who was given responsibility for running the Mel-O-dy label by Berry Gordy early in 1963. Deciding to focus on comedy and country, two areas Chuck-A-Lucks excelled in, Klein produced their only Mel-O-dy single *Sugar Cane Curtain*, which was released in February 1963. It flopped and the group moved on, later recording for Shannon Records.

CITIZENS ON PATROL (FILM SOUNDTRACK)

The fourth in the 'Police Academy' series of comedy films, 'Citizens On Patrol' starred regulars Steve Guttenburg, Bubba Smith, David Graf, George Gaynes, Michael Winslow, Bobcat Goldthwait and Tim Kazurinsky. Although the film received poor reviews when it opened in April 1987, the strength of the franchise was sufficient to enable it to debut as the top grossing film that week and go on to earn nearly $30 million.

The film was also the only release in the franchise to have an accompanying soundtrack, which was issued by Motown in April 1987, with in-house artists Stacy Lattisaw and Chico DeBarge being joined by The S.O.S. Band, Brian Wilson (of The Beach Boys), Michael Winslow, Family Dream, Darryl Duncan (later to become a Motown artist), Garry Glenn (also subsequently signed as a solo artist by Motown) and Southern Pacific.

Despite the relative success of the film, the album did little, with none of the three subsequent 'Police Academy' films bothering with an accompanying soundtrack. The franchise, however, would gross nearly $240 million across the seven films (an eighth instalment is planned for release in 2014).
ALBUM: CITIZENS ON PATROL SOUNDTRACK (1987)

THE CLAMS

Devised as a 'Spike Jones tribute band', The Clams formed in 1974 with bass player Tony Levin, his brother and keyboardist Pete Levin and drummer Steve Gadd, with Michael Holmes (piano) and Vinnie Pasternack (guitar and washboard). According to Pete Levin, the group lasted for two days, recording one single in The Carpenters' parody *Close To You* backed with *The First Time Ever I Saw Your Face*, which was picked up by CTI and assigned to the Three Brothers label, which was intended for popular material.

Only 100 copies were pressed for promotional purposes, one of which found its way to Bruce Morrow at WNBC in New York, who reportedly 'played it to show his listeners the kind of crap he got in the mail every day from record companies'. Bruce might not have liked it but his listeners did, resulting in the phones lighting up and the record getting added to the playlist. Word of the record's growing popularity saw it added to the other radio stations fortunate enough to get a copy of the record and, bizarrely, it actually made the Top 40 of the charts based on airplay alone (although not, as is often claimed, the Billboard chart). Pete Levin later reported that the CTI staffer who'd picked up The Clams record was fired by Creed Taylor!

THE CLAN

Whilst several writing and production teams scored hits for Motown during the 1960s, no one did it as well or as consistently as Holland-Dozier-Holland, scoring twelve of the sixteen number one pop hits the label had accumulated up to the end of 1967. Indeed, that figure looks even better when you consider that their tally was twelve out of the fourteen the label managed between 1964 and 1967, with Smokey Robinson with *My Guy* and *My Girl* on Mary Wells and The Temptations respectively being the only shoe-ins. When HDH went on strike during 1967, eventually to leave and set up their own Invictus and Hot Wax labels, it was more than a challenge to Gordy and his autocratic way of running a business, it threatened the very continuance of his labels. Since he believed the publicity HDH received had possibly turned their heads, or at least made them vulnerable to outside offers, he decided to hide the composition of future teams, reasoning that if rivals weren't aware of who was doing what at Motown, they wouldn't be approached with lucrative offers.

His first such attempt at putting together a team saw Pam Sawyer, R. Dean Taylor, Frank Wilson, Hank Cosby and Deke Richards virtually locked into a suite at Detroit's Pontchartrain Hotel in September 1968, with the team instructed to come up with something worthy of Diana Ross & The Supremes. Although the five had never collaborated together previously and spent much of the first few hours doing little more than passing time drinking and getting to know each other, by the second day their labours began to bear fruit, eventually coming up with *Love Child*. Whilst the writing credits mentioned them all by name, the production credit was given to The Clan.

The subject matter of the track *Love Child* ensured Motown had to field criticism over the message that was being conveyed, but Berry Gordy must have been astonished when he then found several reports questioning whether The Clan was some kind of reference to the Ku Klux Klan! Not surprisingly, The Clan was quietly dropped soon after, with the next conglomeration going under the moniker The Corporation.

CHRIS CLARK

Although Chris Clark's recording career promised much and delivered little, her abilities in other areas made her an important part of the Motown family for more than two decades. Born in Santa Cruz, California on 1 February 1946, Chris auditioned for Hal Davis at the age of 18 in Motown's West Coast office and, suitably impressed arranged for her to journey to Detroit to audition for Berry Gordy. Upon hearing the tape, Berry stated that he was not too much taken with the songs but liked her voice, so asked her to perform *a capella*. The song she chose was Etta James' *All I Could Do Was Cry*, a song co-written by Berry, who subsequently signed the six foot tall, platinum blonde blue eyed soul singer!

Whilst her chart career consists of just one hit single, *Love's Gone Bad*, which made #41 on the R&B chart on the V.I.P. label in 1966, the recordings she made did earn her the sobriquet 'White Negress' in England (it was intended and received as a compliment, although Chris herself raised many an eyebrow when she relayed the story in several radio interviews), where she was seen as America's answer to Dusty Springfield. These included her debut album on Motown, **Soul Sounds**, released on Motown in August 1967 and **CC Rides Again** on Weed in 1969, the only album release on that label. By 1969 Chris, who enjoyed a romance with Berry Gordy, switched to the office side of Motown, becoming vice president of the new film division, where, in 1972, she would help write the script to 'Lady Sings The Blues' and earn an Oscar nomination. In 1981 she was put in charge of creative affairs, a position Chris held until 1989 when she left the company.

A keen photographer (Chris had utilised these skills on several Motown artists over the years), Chris has exhibited with dealers and art galleries across the United States. Like many of her former Motown colleagues, Chris was involved in Ian Levine's Nightmare/Motorcity Records re-recordings of the late 1980s. A 2005 double CD release in the UK gathered her two albums together with 25 previously unissued tracks, leading to a revival of interest and even some live dates from Chris.

ALBUMS: SOUL SOUNDS (1967), CC RIDES AGAIN (1969)

DEE CLARK

Delecta Clark (his forename is sometimes shown as Delectus) was born in Blytheville, Arkansas on 7 November 1938 and raised in Chicago, going on to become a member of Thr Hambone Kids and making his first recordings in 1952. He then joined The Goldentones in 1953, a group that evolved into The Kool Gents and was snapped up by Vee-Jay in 1956. Assigned to the Falcon and then Abner label, the group also recorded a novelty record as The Delegates.

It is as a solo performer, however, that Dee Clark made his name, scoring a Top Ten R&B hit with *Nobody But You* in 1958. His biggest hits for the label were *Hey Little Girl* (#2 R&B in 1959) and *Raindrops* (#3 R&B in 1961), both of which were featured on the 1986 compilation CD issued by Motown, **Hits From The Legendary Vee-Jay Records**. He suffered his first heart attack in 1987 but recovered sufficiently to resume performing, although was advised not to by his doctor. He died from a second and fatal heart attack on 7 December 1990.

TOM CLAY

Controversial DJ Tom Clay (born Thomas Clague in New York on 20 August 1929) began his radio career in the 1950s and made his name with radio stations in Detroit, Cincinnati, Ontario and Los Angeles, with his first brush with Berry Gordy coming in 1958 when Berry penned *Marry Me* which was released on Chant Records. He openly admitted to having been involved in payola, which cost him at least one job, and was later embroiled in a fraud case involving The Beatles and a Clay-inspired 'Beatle Booster Club' which promised personal Beatles' items for each listener who sent in $1 – over 85,000 CKLW listeners sent in a dollar but received little or nothing in return, nor was the money returned.

By the early 1970s Tom was working temporarily for KGBS and came up with the idea of creating a message song that would "get across the idea of what we needed was love even though we were up to our armpits in hate, war and killing." The tape created featured clips of speeches by the late John F Kennedy, his brother Bobby and Martin Luther King, together with schoolgirl definitions of hatred and with the accompaniment of The Blackberries and the Burt Bacharach Orchestra. The resulting tape, entitled *What The World Needs Now Is Love/Abraham Martin And John* was heard by Berry Gordy, an admirer of Clay's radio work from his days in Detroit (according to legend, Berry felt he had to release the record as Tom Clay had been largely instrumental in breaking Marv Johnson many years before). Assigned to the MoWest label, the single proved a surprise smash, peaking at #8 on the pop chart and #32 R&B, prompting a resulting album **What The World Needs Now Is Love** that also charted, making #92 pop.

Unfortunately, the success of the single did not land Tom a permanent job with KGBS nor herald a recording career, with much of the next two decades spent doing voice-overs in Los Angeles. He died from lung and stomach cancer on 11 November 1995.

ALBUM: WHAT THE WORLD NEEDS NOW IS LOVE (1971)

JILL CLAYBURGH

Oscar nominated actress Jill Clayburgh was born in New York City on 30 April 1944 and began her career in theatre in Boston, subsequently making her Broadway debut in 1968 in 'The Sudden & Accidental Re-Education Of Horse Johnson'. In 1972 Jill landed the role of Catherine in 'Pippin', holding the role for the next four and a half years and appearing on the cast recording album that was released by Motown in December 1972.

Jill also appeared in the 1980 film 'It's My Turn', for which Motown issued the soundtrack, although she was not required to perform on the album. After picking up Oscar nominations for her performances in 'An Unmarried Woman' and 'Starting Over' Jill died from leukaemia on 5 November 2010, with the posthumously released 'Bridesmaids' her final screen appearance.

REVEREND JAMES CLEVELAND AND THE PUSH EXPO CHOIR

Gospel singer, arranger and composer The Reverend Doctor James Cleveland was born in Chicago, Illinois on 5 December 1931 and began singing as a boy soprano at the Pilgrim Baptist Church. He continued singing into his teenage years but strained his vocal chords in the process, resulting in his distinctive gravelly voice that would later make his reputation. With the change of voice came a change in focus, with James concentrating on polishing up his skills as a pianist and arranger, attributes that would result in his subsequent elevation into one of the most important gospel stars of his generation.

His only Motown involvement came with the soundtrack to 'Save The Children', with James contributing *Praise Him With A Stringed Instrument* alongside the PUSH (People United To Save Humanity) Expo Choir. James Cleveland died, reportedly from AIDS, on 9 February 1991.

JOEY CLICK

Joey Click graduated from Oklahoma State University with a degree in Business Administration but switched to country music soon after. He released one single on the MC imprint, *California Girl* backed with *I Married You To Be With You* appearing in July 1978, although the single made little or no impact. Thereafter Joey became a session bass guitarist, recording with Radney Foster, Trace Adkins, Holly Sunn, Irene Kelley and Josh Turner among others and subsequently touring as a member of Turner's backing band.

CLOUD NINE – THE TEMPTATIONS [SINGLE]

He may never have recorded for the company but Sly Stone's influence on Motown in general and Norman Whitfield in particular is undeniable. The Temptations had been hot throughout 1968, but their succession of love and romance based singles differed little from what a lot of other R&B vocal groups were doing at the time. Then along came Sly & The Family Stone and *Dance To The Music*, a song Otis Williams brought to the attention of Norman Whitfield at one of their regular meetings. Whilst equally impressed, Norman expressed the opinion that he thought the overall sound was little more than a passing fancy.

He obviously had second thoughts a short while later, for he attended a producer's workshop at Golden World studios and was immediately taken by the wah wah guitar effect of new Funk Brothers recruit Dennis Coffey and decided to use it as an integral part of *Cloud Nine*. There were lengthy rehearsals with each musician before a note was committed to tape, Norman coaxing them all as the overall sound he envisaged, with Uriel Jones (drums), Eddie Brown (percussion), James Jamerson (bass) and of course Dennis Coffey vital to the finished instrumental recording. On 1 October 1968 he brought The Temptations into the studio, including new recruit Dennis Edwards, for them to lay down their vocals, although according to Dennis, the producer had no distinct instructions for them to follow.

"Norman never said, 'Sing it this way.' He said, 'Sing what you feel.' So I really produced myself. And that's basically how it was for every song we'd do. It was more or less organised chaos, for a long time. We'd start at like midnight, 'cause that's when Norman liked to work, and stumble out of there at like six or seven A.M. But I think we gave him what he wanted – more than he wanted."

Norman also borrowed another trick from Sly & Family Stone, with all five Temptations trading vocals on the song, which lyrically focused on the ability of the singer to suspend reality by journeying to cloud nine. There were many, Berry Gordy among them, who thought the cloud nine reference to be an allusion to drugs, thus putting him on yet another collision course with Norman Whitfield (the two were already involved in a battle over the non-release of *I Heard It Through The Grapevine* by Marvin Gaye). When Norman and Barrett Strong, who wrote the lyrics, refused to alter them in any way, shape or form, Gordy and Quality Control eventually conceded and readied the record for release in October 1968.

Different enough to anything not only The Temptations but Motown as a whole had ever released before, *Cloud Nine* heralded Norman's own embracement of the psychedelic soul scene, one he was to return to time and time again over the next four years. *Cloud Nine* also had the desired effect on the record buying public, with the single becoming a #6 pop and #2 R&B smash. In the UK the single was held back until August 1969 as Tamla Motown pushed out a succession of re-releases that had missed out on chart honours the first time around; it eventually made #15 towards the end of October that year. By then the single had already entered Motown folklore; on 12 March 1969, after six unsuccessful nominations, Motown won its first Grammy Award, *Cloud Nine* picking up the award for Best Rhythm & Blues Performance by a Group. Not bad for a passing fancy, as Norman would surely have admitted.

CLOUD NINE – THE TEMPTATIONS [ALBUM]

Built around the success of the *Cloud Nine* single, the resulting album is referred to as the start of The Temptations excursion into psychedelic soul, with the album cover continuing the link. Yet apart from the title track and the second single, *Runaway Child Running Wild*, much of the rest of the album is effectively the same kind of material The Temptations had been recording for the previous four or five years. The one exception is The Temptations' take on *I Heard It Through The Grapevine*, a song that had already been recorded by Smokey Robinson & The Miracles, Gladys Knight & The Pips and Marvin Gaye, and given Norman Whitfield's track record one suspects that had neither Gladys or Marvin's versions been hits or still not been released, The Temptations would have had a single release on it too! The two singles and *Grapevine* make up the whole of the first side, itself something of a pointer for future Temptations albums, with *Runaway Child Running Wild* being stretched out beyond nine minutes.

The flip side, containing seven tracks, sees most of the group being given an opportunity at handling lead vocals, with Dennis Edwards leading on *Gonna Keep On Tryin' Till I Win Your Love*; the song would be re-recorded for 1971's **Sky's The Limit** with Eddie Kendricks handling lead. The new look and new sound found favour among Temptations fans, with the album hitting #4 pop and #1 R&B in the US and #32 in the UK.

DENNIS COFFEY

Dennis learnt to play the guitar at the age of 13 and was earning a living as a professional musician before he was out of his teens. Born in Detroit on 1 November 1940, Dennis linked up with The Royaltones, performing sessions for the likes of Del Shannon before signing a recording contract with Nat Tarnopol, manager of Jackie Wilson, Although nothing came of the contract, Dennis was kept busy with session work, working for the likes of Motown and Ric-Tic.

He would eventually come to be more closely associated with Motown, especially after Gordy bought Ric-Tic, but his playing helped define such Ric-Tic originals as Edwin Starr's *SOS* and The San Remo Strings' *Hungry For Love*. By the mid 1960s he was effectively a Motown regular, performing on such hits as The Temptations *I Wish It Would Rain*, *Cloud Nine* and *Ball Of Confusion*, all three of which fully utilised the wah wah effect he introduced, as well as several outside engagements such as Freda Payne's *Band Of Gold*.

In the early 1970s he pursued his own career as an artist, film scorer and producer and achieved considerable success with the film score to 'Black Belt Jones' and the single *Scorpio*. Indeed, *Scorpio* was a million selling Top Ten success, also enabling Dennis to become the first white artist to appear on 'Soul Train' and leading to three successful albums on Sussex and one on Westbound. Dennis appeared in the 2002 film 'Standing In The Shadows Of Motown', further proof of the important part he had played as a musician some 35 years previously.

STEPHEN COHN

Born and raised in Los Angeles, California Stephen Cohn earned a degree in music from the California State University at Northridge. He then joined The Pleasure Fair as a guitarist as well as assisting on vocal arrangements as the group released their eponymous debut album in 1967. In the early 70s Stephen was working on his own project for small production company Watermark, who went under before the album was completed.

"So I shopped for a label to complete and release it. I walked into Motown one day and met Karl Bornstein, who was the manager of a Motown group. Karl was enthusiastic about my music and became my manager. With his help and with the help of my father, Morris Cohn who was an attorney, I got a contract with Motown. It took a year to negotiate the agreement, making it a very stressful period for me, full of political intrigue with many delays and frustrations."

The eponymous album, featuring assistance from such musical notables as Ben Benay (guitar), Lincoln Mayorga (piano), Jim Gordon (drums) and Larry Carlton (guitar), finally appeared in September 1973, accompanied with something of a marketing campaign.

"It was an expensive but misguided promotional campaign which included a performance tour, trade ads and a billboard on the Sunset Strip. Motown saw me as an opportunity to break into the white, pop market. However, their marketing skills in this area of the business were naïve. They didn't understand my music and really didn't know how to sell it."

Despite this, Stephen began work on a second album, although all his efforts in the studio would eventually get caught in the round of executive shuffles taking place at Motown.

"It was never finished as there was a change of leadership in the A&R Department and the new chief didn't like what I was doing. *Power Is* (released as a single in January 1974) was part of this second round and was released as a single. Karl and I ended up doing our own promotion on the single."

With the second album scrapped, Stephen went on to other pastures and would eventually make a name for himself as a composer and performer of classical, new age and film scores, winning an Emmy Award for his chamber orchestra score for the documentary 'Dying With Dignity.' Whilst his Motown career didn't pan out as he hoped, Stephen still remembers his time with the iconic label.

"All in all, I left Motown without regret but with a good education in music production."

ALBUM: STEPHEN COHN (1973)

ANGELA COLE

Angela Cole (her full name is Angela Coleman) began singing at the age of three and by the time she was six was signing gospel music professionally around the Los Angeles area. Her voice, coupled with her tender years soon had her marked as an artist to watch and by the time she was ten she had already performed with Barry White, Stevie Wonder and Sarah Vaughan.

Producer Hal Davis signed her to Motown in 1987, when she was still only fourteen, and produced her album **Turn Up The Beat**, from which one single was released (*L-O-V-E Love*) backed with the title track. It

represented something of a change in musical style for Angela, for what became her only album saw her forsake gospel in favour of R&B, including updated versions of *Get Ready* and *Let's Get Serious*.
ALBUM: TURN UP THE BEAT (1987)

THELMA COLEMAN

Former nurse Thelma Louise Coleman was Berry Gordy's first wife, the pair marrying in 1953 after Berry returned from the US Army in Korea. Their union resulted in three children, Hazel Joy, Berry Gordy IV and Terry James, with the three children's names being contracted into the name of his publishing company Jobete. Berry and Thelma divorced in 1959 but obviously remained on amicable terms, for in the early 1960s, when Thelma launched her own record company imprint Thelma Records (although the funding came from her parents Robert and Hazel Coleman and the company was run by Don Davis), Berry helped write several of their releases.

Thelma would also write several songs released by Motown, most notably with future Temptation Richard Street, who also recorded earlier in his career for Thelma Records. Thelma Records is also the label that gave several future Motown alumni their start in the business, most notably Norman Whitfield. Operative between 1962 and 1966, Thelma Records was eventually purchased by Berry Gordy, although few of the artists appear to have followed the label into the Motown fold.

COLUMBIA RECORDS

One of the major record labels in the US, Columbia Records licensed one single from Tamla Records, Herman Griffin's *True Love* being snapped up and reissued in April 1961, six months after its original release. Columbia would also provide manufacturing facilities during Motown's early days, although Berry later excluded the company wherever possible in retaliation for Columbia remixing an old Four Tops single to try and make it sound like the type of hits the group was enjoying during the middle of the decade.

COME SEE ABOUT ME – THE SUPREMES [SINGLE]

The Supremes' third consecutive pop chart topper in the US (although it only managed to hit #2 on the R&B chart), *Come See About Me* is rightfully regarded as one of the classic Supremes tracks in America. Recorded in July 1964 (before *Baby Love*) and included on the **Where Did Our Love Go** album, the song was another that The Supremes themselves felt had a simplistic, even childish feel, but given the success HDH were enjoying as writers and producers, no one was going to deviate too far from a winning formula. Indeed, when *Come See About Me* hit the top of the chart, which it did in December 1964 (replacing Bobby Vinton's *Mr Lonely*), it enabled The Supremes to become the first act in Billboard's history to have three number one singles lifted from one album. After a week at the top, *Come See About Me* dropped a place, only to return to the summit three weeks later and topple The Beatles' *I Feel Fine* in the process.

The Supremes' single had also to compete against a rival version by Nella Dodds, with her single on the Wand label making it as far as #74 on the US charts and was supposedly being readied for release in the UK in order to steal a march on the original. When Berry Gordy found out, he instructed Stateside (Motown's UK distributor at the time) to rush release The Supremes version, just as Motown had done in the US to head off the competition.

Whether Stateside had intended releasing the single is not known (they had not released the **Where Did Our Love Go** album, preferring to alter the track listing to **Meet The Supremes**, the group's debut album originally released in 1962 with little fanfare either side of the Atlantic but which in its revamped UK form, including *Where Did Our Love* but not *Baby Love* or *Come See About Me*, hit #13), but a rather lacklustre final chart placing of #27, especially after the previous single had topped the UK charts, was a disappointing blow to say the least. If there was any consolation, then it was that Nella Dodds' version similarly fell by the wayside.

The song would be revisited again by several artists, with Junior Walker & The All Stars enjoying a #8 R&B and #24 pop US hit in 1967, whilst twenty years later Welsh rock and roll revivalist Shakin' Stevens hit #24 in the UK with his take on it.

COME TO ME - MARV JOHNSON [SINGLE]

Although not a Top Ten hit, *Come To Me* by Marv Johnson is worthy of special mention purely for the fact that it was the very first single issued on any of Berry Gordy's labels, being assigned the catalogue number T101 on the Tamla label when released in January 1959. The label for this release shows the company's address being 1719 Gladstone Street, Detroit 6, which was also the address for Jobete.

Written by Berry with Marv and produced by Berry, the song began making significant waves around Detroit, prompting Berry to look for some assistance in getting national distribution. It was Andre Williams who provided a name and number for a contact at United Artists in New York, with Berry able to secure a deal after several other labels rejected it. Part of the deal, however, was that United Artists would also pick up Marv Johnson's contract, although Berry would produce the first two albums Marv recorded for his new home.

In the US the single would go on to become a #6 R&B and #30 pop hit, the single also being the first chart presence for The Rayber Voices and master musicians James Jamerson and Benny Benjamin. Berry would also finalise a deal with the London American label in the UK, and whilst the single failed to chart, it does hold the distinction of being the only Motown connected single released in the UK on the old 78RPM format.

THE COMMODORES

The various members of the group first met at the Tuskegee Institute in Alabama, where Lionel Richie (born in Tuskegee on 20 June 1949) was keyboardist and saxophonist, Thomas McClary (born in Eustis, Florida on 6 October 1949) played guitar and William King (born in Alabama on 30 January 1949) the trumpet in a band called The Mystics. At the same time, there was another Tuskegee outfit called The Jays, which comprised Andre Callahan (drums), Michael Gilbert (bass) and Milan Williams (born in Okolona, Mississippi on 28 March 1948) on keyboards. The Jays underwent something of a change, jettisoning Callahan and Gilbert and bringing in Walter 'Clyde' Orange (born in Florida on 10 December 1946) and Ronald LaPread (born in Tuskegee on 4 September 1946) respectively.

In 1968 an internal disagreement ended The Jays, with Clyde, Milan and Ronald accepting an offer to join forces with The Mystics and form a new group. The new six-piece agonised for hours on a group name, with Clyde eventually handing William a dictionary and telling him to throw it in the air.

"We decided that where it came down, we'd blind pick a word on that page. The word was 'commodore'. It's an old navy ranking from the old days which isn't used anymore. I guess we were lucky because we could have ended up being The Commodes!"

The Commodores quickly established a healthy reputation locally and during the summer vacation of 1969 journeyed to New York in order to try and get a date at Smalls Paradise. Their first approach was a disaster, not helped by the group having their equipment and outfits stolen from outside the club, but they managed to make contact with an old acquaintance, Benny Ashburn, who put them up at his home and arranged with Pete Smalls to give them another chance at his Monday night auditions. Smalls was unaware that at that time New York was filled with students from Tuskegee who had followed their local group to the Big Apple, and the reaction to The Commodores audition ensured they got a three week residency at Smalls Paradise followed by another at the Cheetah Club. When summer finished they headed back to Tuskegee and their respective studies.

A year later they were back in New York to record with producer Jerry 'Swamp Dog' Williams for Atlantic Records, who released a single *Rise Up/Keep On Dancin'* but scrapped a planned album when the single failed to sell (the album had since turned up frequently on various budget labels). After their Atlantic contract was cancelled, the group again turned to Benny Ashburn for assistance, who arranged a showcase gig for them at Lloyd Price's Turntable Club and invited key record executives and media personnel to the date.

Among them was Suzanne De Passe of Motown, who was looking specifically for a group to accompany The Jackson 5 on their forthcoming tour. Impressed with The Commodores, she signed them initially for a forty two date tour from New York to Hawaii; The Commodores would eventually tour with The Jackson 5 for some three years. By this time they had been signed by Motown's west coast outlet MoWest and initially been assigned to writers and producers Pam Sawyer and Gloria Jones, recording the single *The Zoo (The Human Zoo)* which was released in March 1972. Tom Baird was then handed the group, producing the Clyde Orange co-written *Don't You Be Worried*, whilst Willie Hutch produced the B-side on the single issued in January 1973.

With MoWest coming to an end two months later, The Commodores were switched to the main Motown label as work continued on their debut album. Whilst several of the songs were those provided by Motown and in-house writers, The Commodores were coming up with their own material for consideration, much of which was as good if not better.

The key track was an instrumental written by Milan Williams, which the group produced themselves with James Anthony Carmichael. It was originally given the title *The Ram*, but when an acetate was played to Berry Gordy, he thought it sound like a machine gun and the name stuck. It proved so good a name for the single the resulting album was also christened **Machine Gun**. The single proved their breakthrough, making #7 R&B, #22 pop and even managed to crack open the British charts, peaking at #20. There was a follow-up too, with *I Feel Sanctified* scoring #17 R&B and #75 pop in their homeland, although in the UK Tamla Motown went with a revival of *The Zoo*, which made #44. The album made a rather more modest #178 pop and #22 R&B, but it encouraged Benny Ashburn to become their full time manager and for the group to insist on even greater control over subsequent albums.

Their second album, **Caught In The Act** was therefore produced by the group with James Carmichael and, even at this early stage, two distinct styles were emerging within the group and their writing. The success of the funk themed *Machine Gun* and *I Feel Sanctified* was continued with the title track, which became their first R&B chart topper and top twenty pop hit (peaking at #19) and *Wide Open,* whilst Lionel Richie penned the ballad *This Is Your Life*, which hit #13 R&B. The album sold exceptionally well, hitting #7 on the R&B chart and #26 pop and heralded the arrival of Motown's latest group of stars.

Whilst the third album, **Movin' On** was not laden with hits, there were many interesting tracks on display; the haunting instrumental *Cebu*, the up-tempo *Hold On* and, the crowning moment, Lionel Richie's *Sweet Love*. The only single released from the album, *Sweet Love* cracked the Top Ten of both the R&B and pop charts, although it missed out on chart honours in the UK at the time (which did not stop it being a firm favourite of the group's live shows whenever they played the UK). The lack of singles did not hinder the album's sales, making #29 pop and #7 R&B.

By now The Commodores were well into their stride; 1976's **Hot On The Tracks** contained *Just To Be Close To you*, a #1 R&B and #7 pop hit, with the album spending six weeks on top of the R&B chart and reaching #12 on the pop album listing, enough to turn The Commodores from a support group (they had just completed touring with The O'Jays and effectively stolen the show) to headliners in their own right. The key to this change was the material they were churning out; whilst R&B radio quickly jumped on tracks such as *Fancy Dancer* and *Let's Get Started*, it was Lionel Richie's lush ballads that were winning over pop stations.

That diversity was heightened by their 1977 album **Commodores** (re-christened **Zoom** in the UK), their first R&B chart topper and a top five pop success (it hit #3), largely fuelled by the singles *Brick House* (#4 R&B, #5 pop) and *Easy* (#1 R&B, #4 pop), leading to their first world tour, sadly cut short when Ronald LaPread's wife Kathy died of cancer. The group did issue a live double album following this success, which also included one new studio track in *Too Hot Ta Trot*, recorded especially for the film 'Thank God It's Friday', a joint Casablanca Filmworks and Motown production. With Casablanca singer Donna Summer in one of the lead roles, The Commodores were given a cameo role (having previously appeared in the Motown production of 'Scott Joplin' in 1977 as The Minstrel Singers) performing in the nightclub around which the film is based (in reality a club called Osko's based on South La Clenega Boulevard). Apparently the group was told shortly before filming that a new song was required and hastily wrote *Too Hot Ta Trot* to order (it would go on to top the R&B chart but only make #24 pop and #38 in the UK).

Despite the success of *Brick House* and *Too Hot Ta Trot*, The Commodores main success was being achieved with their soft-soul ballads, and the epitome of that style was to be found on their next album **Natural High**. Right from release, Lionel Richie's *Three Times A Lady* was the stand-out cut, going on top the R&B and pop charts on both sides of the Atlantic. However, in the UK, in an attempt to help shift extra copies of the album, *Flying High* was issued as the first single and would make #37; in the US it was the second single and peaked at #38 pop and #24 R&B. Whilst these were to be the only singles lifted, the album matched the performance of its two predecessors in hitting #3 pop and #1 R&B on its way to becoming the group's first platinum seller and, perhaps as a result of the delayed release of *Three Times A Lady*, became their first UK Top Ten entry.

Following this success Motown issued a greatest hits collection in time for the Christmas market, resulting in a #23 US and #19 UK hit. By now all eyes were on the group to see whether they could match their previous glories, with competition within the group itself at its keenest. Since most albums at the time consisted of eight tracks, the five members of the group would write up to ten songs each that would be played to the rest of the group for consideration for final selection. Lionel Richie had pretty much cornered the ballad market, and two of his compositions would find their way on to next album **Midnight Magic**, *Sail On* and *Still*. Whilst not too dissimilar from *Three*

Times A Lady in their overall feel, it was *Sail On* in particular that would garner Lionel interest from outside The Commodores, with a host of artists expressing an desire in working with him. Whilst he was still committed to The Commodores, Lionel turned down such requests, including one from Kenny Rogers, who had been impressed with *Three Times A Lady* and felt Lionel could write material that would provide his career with a lift. As he had done with everyone else, Lionel conveyed his gratitude but would reluctantly be unable to assist as The Commodores were in the middle of another headlining coast to coast tour.

Fate was waiting to lend a hand, for a week after turning Kenny down Lionel found himself with three weeks with which to kicks his heels after Clyde had an accident falling off his motorcycle and the group was forced to cancel the rest of the dates. Lionel contacted Kenny and later the same day was in a studio working on *Lady*, a single that returned Kenny Rogers to the top of both the pop and country charts and sold more than six million copies.

It also marked the beginning of the end of Lionel as a member of The Commodores, for after three years of unrivalled success, 1980's **Heroes** album was a relative failure. Whilst it still managed to attain platinum status, sales lagged well behind the previous four albums, with both singles *Old-Fashioned Love* and *Heroes* under-performing on the charts. Then Lionel had further success as a songwriter, agreeing to supply a song to Franco Zeffirelli's film 'Endless Love' starring Brooke Shields. He also agreed to Zeffirelli's suggestion that the song be recorded as a duet, with the then former Motown recording star Diana Ross the star of choice. The resulting single, a pop and R&B chart topper, convinced Lionel that it was time to strike out on his own.

He was to leave after one last album with The Commodores, 1981's **In The Pocket**, a vastly under-rated album from their catalogue. Whilst there was another Lionel ballad to savour in *Oh No*, the first single lifted was *Lady (You Bring Me Up)*, not the Lionel penned song that had given Kenny Rogers' career a fillip, but a song written by William King, his wife Shirley and Harold Hudson, a member of The Commodores' own backing group The Mean Machine. The success of this *Lady* suggested that the future might not be all doom and gloom for those who remained behind, but events in 1982 conspired against them. Whilst Lionel had begun recording his solo debut whilst still officially a member of The Commodores, it soon became obvious that he wasn't returning, nor was producer James Anthony Carmichael, who had opted to work with Lionel rather than the group.

After auditioning a couple of potential lead singers, neither of whom were in the same league as Lionel Richie (there again, who was?), it was decided to spread the vocals around those who remained. Then in August 1982 manager Benny Ashburn, who had been considered a seventh Commodore during the group's career, collapsed and died from a heart attack. As William King said, "He was the glue. Losing Benny was more of a blow to The Commodores than if Richie had quit 20 times."

Motown issued two further compilations within six months of each other, **All The Great Hits** peaking at #37 in December 1982 and **Anthology** at #141 in June 1983 whilst the remaining members worked on their next album, with **Commodores 13** being released in September 1983. Lacking Lionel's abilities as a writer and front man, **13** limped into the chart at a very lowly #103, with the only single *Only You* peaking at a distant #54 pop and #20 R&B.

In 1982 Thomas McClary left the group, destined for a very brief solo career, which resulted in The Commodores *having* to find new members to come on board. They finally settled on Sheldon Reynolds (born in Cincinnati, Ohio on 13 September 1989) as guitarist and James Dean 'J.D.' Nicholas (born in Watford, England on 12 April 1952), a former singer with Heatwave that the group met whilst performing on 'Soul Train'. With Nicholas and Clyde sharing lead vocal duties, the next incarnation of The Commodores was ready to assume their place at the top of the Motown tree.

It came with a song inspired by the death of Marvin Gaye, with the tribute song *Nightshift* also giving a name check to Jackie Wilson and becoming a trans-Atlantic smash, topping the R&B chart and peaking at #3 pop in both the US and UK. The resulting album, also entitled **Nightshift** also returned the group to the upper echelons of the chart, hitting #12 pop, #1 R&B and #13 in the UK. Subsequent singles might have lacked the obvious appeal of *Nightshift*, but both *Animal Instinct* and *Janet* helped shift copies of the album in the kind of quantities they had previously enjoyed with Lionel Richie on board.

A dispute with Motown over the scheduling of their next album would eventually prompt The Commodores to walk out of the door and head for Polydor, although Ronald LaPread decided it was time for him to quit the group and he eventually settled in New Zealand with his new wife.

The Commodores' sojourn at Polydor started brightly, with *Goin' To The Bank* hitting #2 on the R&B chart. However, the inability of this and the resulting album

United to fare even adequately on the main pop charts left the group feeling that they weren't seen as a major priority for their new label or its promotion departments, resulting in them leaving after **Rock Solid** failed to live up to its name, barely making #101 on the pop charts. By then the group had seen Sheldon Reynolds depart to join Earth, Wind & Fire, and Milan Williams became the next of the original group members to leave, allegedly over a disagreement with the rest of the group over performing in South Africa. The man who effectively kick-started The Commodores' hit career with *Machine Gun*, Milan was to die of cancer on 9 July 2006. Today The Commodores, Walter 'Clyde' Orange, J.D. Nicholas and William King, continue to record for their own label and tour worldwide almost annually.

ALBUMS: MACHINE GUN (1974), CAUGHT IN THE ACT (1975), MOVIN' ON (1975), HOT ON THE TRACKS (1976), THE COMMODORES (1977), LIVE! (1977), NATURAL HIGH (1978), MIDNIGHT MAGIC (1979), HEROES (1980), IN THE POCKET (1981), 13 (1983), NIGHTSHIFT (1985)

COMPILATIONS: GREATEST HITS (1978), ALL THE GREAT HITS (1982), ANTHOLOGY (1983), 14 GREATEST HITS (1984), ALL THE GREAT LOVE SONGS (1984), GREAT LOVE SONGS WITH THE COMMODORES (1985)

COMMODORES – THE COMMODORES [ALBUM]

Perhaps the album that elevated The Commodores in to the superstar bracket, thanks to the sheer diversity of material present. Lionel Richie's growing penchant for ballads was more than adequately displayed on *Easy*, the biggest single taken from the album (#4 pop, #1 R&B and a #9 hit in the UK), whilst William King came up with the original concept behind *Brick House*, a #5 pop and #4 R&B hit. Whilst that may have been it as far as hit singles was concerned (at least in the US, for in the UK *Zoom*, by which name the album was titled, was coupled with *Too Hot Ta Trot* and made #38 in 1978), there was still much to enjoy, with several of the album's tracks quickly becoming an integral part of the group's live repertoire. Chief among them was *Zoom*, written by Ronald LaPread and Lionel Richie. Lionel also linked with Thomas McClary for three tracks, proof of his rapidly growing worth. Whilst **Commodores** repeated their earlier success on the R&B charts, becoming their second consecutive chart topper, it also became the major pop breakthrough, eventually peaking at #3 and spending more than a year on the album listings.

COMMODORES LIVE! – THE COMMODORES [ALBUM]

After almost ten years out on the road, The Commodores had developed a live show that was second to none. They also had a wealth of material upon which to draw, meaning the only problem for the band was what to perform and what to leave out. Recorded during their coast to coast US tour of 1976 and largely featuring material performed at the dates in Atlanta and Washington D.C., **Commodores Live** showed them at their very best. From their early days of performing at small clubs, they could now fill large auditoriums yet lose none of the intimacy, as is evidenced by the in-between songs patter from Lionel Richie. Indeed, **Commodores Live** is an abject lesson in how to present a live album, one that Parliament and their **P Funk Earth Tour** from the same year could have done with taking on board, since the Parliament album seems to feature more of the audience than it does the band! No such problems with The Commodores album, which ran to two records and had a new studio cut, *Too Hot Ta Trot* as something of a bonus. The album was another success, peaking at #3 pop and #2 R&B and proved their UK breakthrough, hitting #60.

THE COMPLETE MOTOWN SINGLES

The most complex and adventurous reissue programme ever undertaken by Motown (and quite possibly by any record company), and yet ultimately the most rewarding. As the name might imply, it is a series of issues covering *every* single issued by Motown and its assorted labels between 1959, when the first was released, all the way through to the end of 1972. Each package contains five or six CDs containing every single released or even scheduled for release in the year in question, together with a vinyl reissue of a key single of the relevant era. Volume one covers the years 1959 through to 1961; thereafter each year is afforded a single volume all the way through to 1971 and 1972, where there were so many singles issued it was necessary to put two packages together. Each release features both the A side and B side, and where relevant remixes and radio edits, which are packaged with a hefty booklet giving full recording details and information on the artist, together with essays by those who were there at the time (the only exceptions are those singles that were licensed in from EMI, to which Universal did not hold the rights). The end result is breath taking, the whole series little short of a musical treasure trove.

ALBUMS: VOLUME 1 (2004), VOLUME 2 (2005), VOLUME 3 (2005), VOLUME 4 (2006), VOLUME 5 (2006), VOLUME 6 (2006), VOLUME 7 (2007), VOLUME 8 (2007), VOLUME 9 (2007), VOLUME 10 (2008), VOLUME 11A (2009), VOLUME 11B (2009), VOLUME 12A (2013), VOLUME 12B (2013)

CONCEITED RECORDS

Conceited Records was formed by Ron Perry and Louis Williams and secured a joint label deal with Motown in 1985, with their artist roster comprising Lushus Daim & The Pretty Vain, Troy Johnson and Mello-Mackin-D & Mr Stretch. All three artists were produced by Leon Sylvers III, formerly a member of family group The Sylvers and an extremely successful writer and producer for Solar Records (The Whispers, Shalamar and Lakeside, among others) before undertaking freelance assignments. Both Lushus Daim and Troy Johnson had albums released on Motown/Conceited, Mello-Mackin-D & Mr Stretch just one single.

BARDELL CONNER

Singer and dancer Bardell first came to prominence in the 1975 touring production of 'Don't Bother Me, I Can't Cope' before landing the role of Calvin in the Broadway revival of 'Guys And Dolls' in 1976 and appearing on the cast recording album. He later returned to Broadway for the musical comedy 'My One And Only'.

THE CONTOURS

Berry Gordy had spent a couple of fruitless hours searching for The Temptations in June 1962, with no sign of the group around the Hitsville studio. After a while he called off the search and stood on the stairway listening to The Contours rehearsing a song in the studio and, liking the sound they were coming up with, decided the song that had been earmarked for The Temptations, *Do You Love Me*, would be given over to The Contours instead. By then The Contours had spent some three, fruitless years at Motown and were in as desperate a need for a hit as The Temptations.

The Contours had first formed as The Blenders in 1959, with lead vocalist Billy Gordon, Billy Hoggs, Joe Billingslea (born in Hamtrack, Michigan on 14 November 1937) and Billy Rollins honing their craft on the street corners, especially around 12th Street, with the group writing a song called *12th Street* which they performed at their first Motown audition. By then they had replaced Rollins with Leroy Fair, added Hubert Johnson (born on 14 January 1941) and changed their name to The Contours, taking the moniker from the name of another company they auditioned for, Contour Recording.

Berry passed on the group the first time around, telling them to come back in a year or so, but Hubert's cousin happened to be Jackie Wilson, the same Jackie Wilson that had helped launch Berry on his career as a writer. Jackie took a listen to the enthusiastic group and placed a call to Berry, convincing him that the group was worth taking a chance on there and then.

Whether it was reluctantly or not, Berry signed The Contours and soon had them in the studio, where a Gordon and Hoggs song was polished off by none other than Smokey Robinson, produced by Berry and released as *Whole Lotta Woman* in February 1961. Leroy left the group soon after this single, to be eventually replaced by Sylvester Potts (born on 22 December 1938), and he had an immediate impact, linking with Billy Gordon to work with Mickey Stevenson on their follow-up, *Funny*, a doo-wop ballad that was released in August 1961.

Although it failed to chart, it does hold a place in musical history for being the first Motown single entirely released with the now famous map of Detroit on the label. Whilst chart success might have eluded them, the group was in hot demand as a live draw, with their energetic routine, complete with gymnastics, flips and splits all across the stage the direct opposite to the routines other acts on Motown were performing. About the only group member who didn't throw himself about the stage was Huey Davis (born on 17 August 1939), a new recruit who stood almost to one side playing the guitar.

Then came the day that The Contours got their hands and voices on *Do You Love Me*, with Billy Gordon performing vocal acrobatics to pull off a version that sounded exactly as Berry Gordy had envisaged it. Released as single in June 1962, it powered its way up to the top of the R&B chart and peaked at #3 on the pop chart, the record's rise up both charts being helped by the fact the group was out on tour with their label-mates as part of the Motortown Revue. Indeed, Berry marked the cards of all the others on the tour, especially the females, telling them to give The Contours a wide berth, for their offstage antics were just as boisterous as their onstage ones and proof that they were, in his words, 'a bunch of hoodlums.'

In October that year The Contours debut album, entitled **Do You Love Me (Now That I Can Dance)** in order to capitalise on the success of the single, became the first release on the newly instigated Gordy label. Kicking off with the hit single, naturally, the two previous misses were joined with what would become the group's second hit single, *Shake Sherry*, another frantic rocker penned and produced by Berry but perhaps too similar to their massive hit; it had to be content with a rather more modest placing of #43 on the pop chart and #21 R&B. After that success, Berry seemingly got tired of the group, assigning them to other producers and writers for subsequent releases.

First in the studio with the group was Berry's then wife Raynoma, who wrote *You Get Ugly* with her brother Mike Ossman, but the song was not entirely to the group's liking and stiffed. Next came Berry's ex-wife Thelma, who combined with The Monitors' Richard Street to write *Can You Do It*, a song also similar in style to *Do You Love Me* but which was ideal to the then popular dance craze the jerk. *Can You Do It* did at least return them to the charts, hitting #41 pop and #16 R&B in the spring of 1964, and inspired another dance orientated track, this time *Can You Jerk Like Me*, written by Mickey Stevenson and Ivy Hunter and which hit #47 pop and #15 R&B at the turn of the year. The flip side of *Jerk, That Day When She Needed Me* also attracted considerable chart action, hitting #37 on the R&B charts in its own right.

Whilst the group had scored one massive and three minor hits over the course of three years or so, priorities at Motown had changed and The Contours had slipped down the pecking order, a situation that the group resolved to confront Berry with collectively. Unfortunately, the group didn't present a united front, with internal conflicts effectively bringing about a hiatus as Billy Gordon was seen to have sided with the company in their dispute, prompting a mass walk out by The Contours.

A newly constructed group, based around Billy Gordon and featuring Council Gay, Jerry Green and Alvin English then returned the group's name to the charts, the Smokey Robinson and Bobby Rogers penned *First I Look At The Purse* hitting #57 pop and #12 R&B in August 1965. That was to prove a final bow for Billy Gordon, for a growing drug problem had made him unreliable. In his place came Joe Stubbs, the younger brother of The Four Tops' Levi, and Sylvester Potts also returned in place of Alvin English. Joe Stubbs reign as lead singer was short lived but did produce another minor hit, *Just A Little Misunderstanding*, written by Stevie Wonder, Morris Broadnax and Clarence Paul barely scraping into the pop chart at #85 but powering much higher on the R&B listing, hitting #18. Something of a storming dance number, *Misunderstanding* would much later prove to be the group's only UK chart entry, hitting #31 in 1970 as Northern Soul made a habit of reviving seemingly long forgotten Motown classics.

Joe Stubbs exited the group soon after to eventually link up with 100 Proof Aged In Soul, with The Contours taking a look at Clarence Paul's recommendation Dennis Edwards as a potential replacement. As it turned out, Dennis' first lead vocal would turn out to the last Contours single on Gordy, *It's So Hard Being A Loser,* originally intended for Jimmy Ruffin, disproving its title in making #79 pop and #35 R&B in 1967.

The following year their Motown contract expired and the group disbanded, Dennis going on to join The Temptations and the rest seemingly scattered to the four corners of the country. Joe Billingslea revived the group with both new and old members in the mid-1970s for a number of live dates as the nostalgia craze began to kick in, but it could hardly be called a fully fledged reunion as most of the group held full time day jobs in between touring. Former member Hubert Johnson committed suicide on 11 July 1981, but in 1988 the group was suddenly back in the limelight after *Do You Love Me* was included in the hit film 'Dirty Dancing'. Reissued as a single, it would hit #11 pop the second time around, prompting a quick revival of the group that subsequently joined the 'Dirty Dancing Concert Tour' and performed before audiences totalling two million over the next eight months. Buoyed by that success and level of acceptance, The Contours continued touring and even returned to recording, signing with Ian Levine's Motorcity label in 1990. By the new century, there were *two* versions of The Contours out on the road – The Contours with Joe Billingslea and The Contours featuring Sylvester Potts!

ALBUM: DO YOU LOVE ME (1962)

COOK COUNTY

A studio concept assembled by producer Vic Caesar (born in Chicago, Illinois on 27 May 1931), Cook County consisted of Everett D Bryson (percussion), Steve Turner (drums), Bill Von Ravensberg (bass), George Gaffney (keyboards), Dennis Kilman (guitar), Bruce Wyndham (guitar), Vic Caesar (vibes) and a horn section of Ralf Rickert, Bob Ojeda and Gene Goe (trumpets) and Peter Christlieb, Jim Coile and Pat

Rizzo (saxophones). Their only album for Motown was **Pinball Playboy (Playboy Theme)**, two themes apparently close to Caesar's heart; he lived at the Playboy Mansion for some ten years, where he held the Donkey Kong top score of 785,000!
ALBUM: PINBALL PLAYBOY (PLAYBOY THEME) (1979)

COOLEY HIGH (FILM SOUNDTRACK)

Set in Chicago in 1964, 'Cooley High' is still highly regarded among the proliferation of high school films, being considered one of the best of the genre. Starring Glynn Turman and Lawrence Hilton-Jacobs with a supporting cast comprising Garrett Morris, Cynthia Davis, Corin Rogers and Maurice Leon Havis, the plot focuses on the exploits of school friends Leroy 'Peach' Jackson (Turman) and Richard 'Cochise' Morris (Hilton-Jacobs) and was written by Eric Monte, who had grown up in Chicago around the era the film was set. Given the time frame, Motown was the ideal choice for the soundtrack, with G.C. Cameron also providing a new song in *It's So Hard To Say Goodbye To Yesterday*, which would hit #38 on the R&B chart (and later attract a much more successful cover version from Boyz II Men) to go alongside classic tracks from The Supremes, Stevie Wonder, The Marvelettes, The Miracles, The Four Tops and Mary Wells. Incidental music for the film, some of which also appeared on the double album soundtrack, was written and performed by Freddie Perren. Whilst not a blockbuster in terms of box office receipts, 'Cooley High' attracted enough attention to warrant ABC consider turning it into a television series, but after the pilot was poorly received, it was subsequently adapted into 'What's Happening!!' which ran for some three years.
ALBUM: COOLEY HIGH SOUNDTRACK (1976)

MARTY COOPER

Martin James Cooper was born in Denver, Colorado and moved to Los Angeles whilst still a teenager, attending the University of Southern California and UCLA before dropping out in order to pursue a career in the music industry. He recorded his first single (as Marty Cooper) for the Crest label in 1958 and would later record as El Clod, but he forged a more successful career as a composer (his biggest hit was *Peanut Butter*, written with H.B. Barnum, whilst Stevie Wonder covered his *Hey Harmonica Man*) and producer, most notably in conjunction with Jack Nitzsche.

Marty also had a spell as an A&R executive for RCA, where he also recorded extensively and launched his own imprint Holiday Records. After sporadic attempts at becoming an artist in his own right Marty recorded an album for Barnaby Records in 1972 and later one single on MC, with *Like A Gypsy* released in October 1977. Marty later signed for Barry White's label Unlimited Gold, **Sing You A Story, Spin You A Rhyme** being released in 1980.

PHIL CORDELL

A multi-talented instrumentalist and writer, Phil Cordell was born in London on 17 June 1947 and on leaving school in 1963 joined local Enfield band The Challengers. They would subsequently change their name to The Prophets and record several sides with Joe Meek, although nothing was released. After this mishap Phil formed Tuesdays Children but left in 1967 for a solo career and received considerable attention for his single *Red Lady*. His next major hit was *I Will Return*, a Top Ten UK success released under the pseudonym Springwater on which he played all of the instruments.

Another pseudonym, Dan The Banjo Man saw him recording for Rare Earth, with the singles *Dan The Banjo Man*, *Black Magic* and *Red River Valley* appearing between 1973 and 1975, whilst he was also responsible for Riverhead and the cover of *I Can't Let Maggie Go* on MoWest. It would appear that Phil was responsible for not only his own recordings but also writing and producing a number of other artists assigned to the label. Two years later, in 1977, he recorded the album **Born Again** for Prodigal, which was released in the UK in October 1977 and scheduled but never released in the US (although it was released on CD in Japan in 2006). He recorded for a variety of labels after his Motown days came to an end and died on 31 March 2007.
ALBUM: BORN AGAIN (1977)

CORLISS

Corliss Nelson is an Albuquerque based guitarist and violinist whose folk rock/country rock styled album was released on the Natural Resources label in May 1972 (and was issued on Rare Earth in the UK). Produced by John Wagner and written by Corliss (all but one track), the album was a brave venture into hitherto uncharted territory for Motown, but presumably sales were not sufficient to warrant any further solo excursions for Corliss. He would maintain his connection with John Wagner, however, appearing on the John Wagner Coalition album **Shades Of Brown** in 1976 as well as several other albums and projects that Wagner helmed.

ALBUM: CORLISS (1972)

THE CORPORATION

Bobby Taylor may have been responsible for finally getting The Jackson 5 to Motown and would produce their early recording sessions, but Berry Gordy was simply not going to allow what could be a real potential money spinner to remain in inexperienced hands. Whilst Taylor did his sessions, unsure whether anything he did would see the light of day, Berry was putting together another team, one that would include himself in perhaps his greatest hands-on approach since the very early days of the Motown story.

It began with Deke Richards, a former member of The Clan, who was actually working with fellow writers Alphonzo 'Fonce' Mizell and Freddie Perren on a track called *I Wanna Be Free*, which they intended recording on the other group that had gone out of their way to get The Jackson 5 to Motown, Gladys Knight & The Pips. When he heard the initial backing track and guide vocal, Berry reasoned that with a few changes, including one he called 'giving it the Frankie Lymon treatment', it would be an ideal track with which to announce The Jackson 5's arrival on an unsuspecting public. *I Wanna Be Free* thus became *I Want You Back*, a single that blasted Motown back up to the top of the charts, both pop and R&B. And, just as he had done earlier with The Clan, Berry chose to cloak the new writing and production team in anonymity, dubbing them The Corporation.

Over the next couple of years, The Corporation kept the hits coming, penning *ABC*, *The Love You Save*, *Mama's Pearl*, *Maybe Tomorrow* and *Goin' Back To Indiana*. The Corporation would briefly be expanded to include a fifth member in Christine Yarian (Freddie Perren's wife) before disbanding in 1972. The names of the members eventually got out into the public domain, but by the time they did, The Jackson 5 had registered so many hits it barely mattered.

BILL COSBY

One of the leading stand-up comics, Bill Cosby (born William Henry Cosby in Philadelphia, Pennsylvania on 12 July 1937) has enjoyed considerable success on television and with his stand-up routines. In the latter category he scored his first hit album in 1964 with **Bill Cosby Is A Very Funny Fellow, Right!** and would go on to win the Grammy Award for Best Comedy album on three occasions; **Wonderfulness**, **Revenge** and **To Russell, My Brother, Whom I Slept With**.

The star of his own long-running television series 'The Bill Cosby Show', he also appeared in several other television shows and films. He had two brushes with Motown, releasing **The Congressional Black Caucus** with Ossie Davis on the Black Forum label in April 1972 and **Bill Cosby 'Himself'** in November 1982. This latter album, a much more obvious comedy album made #64 pop and #33 on the R&B chart although a planned single, *Just The Slew Of Us* (a parody of Grover Washington Jr.'s *Just The Two Of Us*) was unreleased.

ALBUMS: THE CONGRESSIONAL BLACK CAUCUS (1972), BILL COSBY 'HIMSELF' (1982)

HANK COSBY

Born Henry Cosby in Detroit, Michigan on 12 May 1928, Hank was raised in the city and learned to play the tenor saxophone whilst serving with the US Armed Forces in Korea in the 1950s. Upon his discharge he joined the Joe Hunter band, where he came across many of the players who would propel the Motown sound to celebrity, Joe Hunter, James Jamerson and Benny Benjamin in particular. They were regularly backing Jackie Wilson out on the road when they all came across Berry Gordy for the first time and eventually all would gravitate to the Hitsville studio where there was regular work and a steady income (although until they were on the regular payroll, this crew of musicians were still in demand with other artists, with John Lee Hooker's *Boom Boom* benefitting from their involvement).

Hank was soon put to work trying to come up with a song that might work for the then christened Little Stevie Wonder, a precocious talent in and around the Motown plot in search of the right material to showcase his undoubted talent. Together with Clarence Paul, he came up with *Fingertips*, a song Stevie quickly introduced to his live set and which was subsequently recorded live in Chicago. The success of the single, which topped both the R&B and pop chart, saw Hank working closely with Stevie in the ensuing years, penning much of the material during Stevie's 'Little' days and then guiding and collaborating with him as Stevie took greater control of his own material. Key among these tracks, of course, was the song that effectively announced his triumphant return, *Uptight*, for which Stevie came up with the melody, Sylvia Moy wrote the lyrics and Hank took care of creating the arrangement, with all three sharing the composer credits. This little team would craft some mighty big hits over the next four years, including *I Was Made To Love Her, I'm Wondering, Shoo Be Doo Be Doo Da Day, Never Had A Dream Come True* and, perhaps the standout track, *For Once In My Life.*

As Stevie began working towards total autonomy, Hank found other outlets for his own creativity, becoming part of The Clan that wrote and produced *Love Child* and *Living In Shame* for Diana Ross & The Supremes and also penning songs for Martha Reeves & The Vandellas, Marvin Gaye and countless others. However, all of this success counted for little when Motown moved out of Detroit to Los Angeles, with Hank eventually leaving the label and spending time first in New York for CBS Records and then Los Angeles for Fantasy Records (where he produced Martha Reeves again and former Motown act Softouch) as well as outside production work for the likes of Blood, Sweat & Tears.

He retired from the music industry in 1980 and headed home to Detroit.

"Once upon a time, man, I thought Detroit was the greatest place in the world," he would later tell writer Bill Dahl. "Couldn't nobody tell me no different. I went in the Army and I couldn't get back there fast enough. And then they had the '67 riot. It's been a different place ever since."

Sadly his retirement was hindered by ill-health and at his funeral following his death on 22 January 2002, Stevie Wonder performed *My Cherie Amour,* a fitting finale for one of Motown's true greats.

THE COURTSHIPS

The Courtships was a Trenton, New Jersey vocal trio formed by Billy Procter with Donald Robbins and Bruce Rembert whose *It's The Same Old Love* was written and produced by Gary Knight and Gene Allan (part of Jerry Ross' production group) and arranged by Thom Bell. Released on single on Tamla in April 1972 (with the group name incorrectly truncated to The Courtship) it did little, with the November follow-up *Love Ain't Love (Till You Give It To Somebody)* getting pulled, although it did later appear on the Glades label and was released in Britain by Jonathan King's UK label (although the release was flipped, with *Oops It Just Slipped Out* promoted as the A side and *Love Ain't Love* as the B side). Interestingly enough, whilst the record might have appeared on Tamla, the backing musicians were MFSB, effectively the pride of Philadelphia!

THE COYOTE SISTERS

Pop-rock trio The Coyote Sisters weren't actually sisters at all, comprising Leah Kunkel (who was the sister of Cass Elliot), Marty Gwinn Townsend and Renee Armand. They signed with the Morocco imprint in 1984 and scored a minor hit single with *Straight From The Heart (Into Your Life)*, which made #66, although the follow-up *I've Got A Radio* and their eponymous album missed the chart and the group was subsequently dropped.

ALBUM: THE COYOTE SISTERS (1984)

CAROLYN CRAWFORD

First prize in the 1963 Tip Top Bread talent contest, sponsored by radio station WCHB, was a Motown recording session. Although entry to the contest required the competitors to submit a certain number of wrappers from Tip Top bread, the competition drew a healthy response with both the quantity and quality of competitors surprising the organisers.

"You had to enter with a tune that you liked. If you were picked for the finals, you had to go out and collect bread wrappers. I went around restaurants, cafes and hotels for these wrappers – boy, you had to work hard as well as sing!"

The eventual winner was local Detroit girl Carolyn Crawford, who was thirteen, fourteen or fifteen at the time of the competition (it has been suggested that she was only 13 but claimed to be 15 in order to gain entry), who secured top spot after spotting Berry Gordy on the judges panel and electing to perform Mary Wells' *Laughing Boy,* complete with an ad-libbed verse of her own writing.

Whilst the competition stated that the prize was a session, not the guarantee of a single (or anything subsequent) Carolyn performed well enough on the two tracks that were initially cut, *Forget About Me* and *Devil In His Heart* (the A side written by Carolyn, the B side by Berry Gordy) for the single to be issued on Motown in October 1963. Whilst the single didn't become a hit, it fared well enough to earn Carolyn further sessions and two more singles. The first, *My Smile Is Just A Frown (Turned Upside Down)*, written by Smokey Robinson, Janie Bradford and Mickey Stevenson, was released in August 1964 and would become a minor hit, reaching #39 on the R&B chart. December's follow-up, the Berry Gordy composed *When Someone's Good To You*, missed out on the charts but would become her first single released in the UK, appearing on the Stateside label in February 1965. Whilst not a chart hit, it became a monster track on the Northern Soul circuit, with copies changing hands for several hundred pounds.

"I had a contract from '63 to '67 but I came in the middle of the company changing over their business operation. I got lost in the shuffle so to speak. I don't think anyone knew what to do with me so I was pushed aside and by '65 I was through. For two years I sat around and did nothing. I couldn't go to work because I was still signed to Motown. So I sat out my contract, which I regret. I felt Motown could have given me a release."

Carolyn eventually left Motown after three singles in four years and later recorded for Roulette and became a member of Hodges James Smith & Crawford. In the 1970s she returned to do backing vocals, subsequently signing with Philadelphia International and becoming a member of Chapter 8, a Detroit soul group. She also made a brief return to the charts, scoring with *Coming On Strong* on Mercury as Caroline Crawford.

HANK CRAWFORD

Born in Memphis, Tennessee on 21 December 1934 as one of seven children, Bennie Ross Crawford would go on to become one of the leading jazz saxophonists of all time. Hank began his career as a musical director for Ray Charles, elevated to the position having first joined with Ray as a baritone saxophonist. By the time Hank took his leave of Ray in 1964, he had already begun recording solo for Atlantic Records, going on to record some ten albums for the label by the end of the decade. He then switched to Kudu, where Creed Taylor had established something of a blueprint for wider acceptance; recording a number of well known pop and soul songs but giving them a distinct jazz feel. Hank felt the concept suited his music to perfection, wanting to aim his music towards "the average listener, rather than the jazz diehard. I found out as a young musician growing up in Memphis that if you weren't reaching people, and having them tap their foot, then there was nothing happening."

Hank would record eight albums for Kudu, four of which were distributed by Motown, with **Don't You Worry 'Bout A Thing** (#29 on the jazz chart), **I Hear A Symphony** (#159 pop, #17 R&B and #11 jazz), **Hank Crawford's Back** (#167 pop, #42 R&B and #16 jazz) and **Tico Rico** (#28 jazz) getting punters tapping their feet and making a splash on the charts. When CTI later hit problems Hank moved on to Milestone, remaining with the label for nearly twenty years. Hank also formed a successful partnership with organist Jimmy McGriff in the 1980s which lasted the rest of the partners' careers. Hank died on 29 January 2009 at age of 74 from complications from a stroke.

ALBUMS: DON'T YOU WORRY 'BOUT A THING (1975), I HEAR A SYMPHONY (1975), HANK CRAWFORD'S BACK (1976), TICO RICO (1977)

THE CREATIONS

A little known group from Detroit, Michigan who released the first single on Mel-O-dy, *This Is Our Night* coupled with *You're My Inspiration* which was released in July 1962. Producer Andre Williams had a hand in writing both sides with Robert Williams, Juan Wingard and Charles Holman, with the last three gentlemen believed to be the members of the group for what was their only single release.

CREEDENCE CLEARWATER REVIVAL

American rock group Creedence Clearwater Revival was formed at high school at El Cerrito, California by John Fogerty (born in Berkeley, California on 28 May 1945, guitar and vocals), Tom Fogerty (born in Berkeley on 9 November 1941, guitar), Stuart Cook (born in Oakland, California on 25 April 1945, keyboards and bass) and Doug 'Cosmo' Clifford (born in Palo Alto, California on 24 April 1945, drums). Their first dates were under the name Tommy Fogerty and the Blue Velvets, their first recordings as the Golliwogs for Fantasy in 1964. They adopted the name Creedence Clearwater Revival in 1967: 'Creedence' was the name of a friend, 'Clearwater' came from a beer commercial and 'Revival' was intended to reflect their music.

Bad Moon Rising was an international smash in 1969, hitting #2 on the US chart (and selling more than a million copies) and topping the British chart for three weeks. The track was featured on the soundtrack album **More Songs From The Big Chill** released by

Motown in April 1984. Tom Fogerty, who left the group in 1971 (the group disbanded a year later) died on 6 September 1990 from tuberculosis.

MARSHALL CRENSHAW

Born in Detroit, Michigan on 11 November 1953, Marshall Howard Crenshaw was raised in Berkley and learned to play the guitar at the age of ten. After forming his own band he landed the role of John Lennon in the off-Broadway show 'Beatlemania' and made his debut recording for Alan Betrock's Shake Records. He was subsequently signed by Warner Brothers and scored his first hit in 1981, with his debut album arriving the following year. Equally at home as a writer, performer and actor, he appeared on the soundtrack to the 1983 film 'Get Crazy' performing *It's Only A Movie*.

HOWARD CROCKETT

A shoulder injury sustained as a youth caused Howard Crockett to change career paths, switching from an intended pursuit as a professional baseball pitcher to a country musician. Born Howard Elton Hausey in Yellow Pine, Louisiana on 25 December 1925, his ability at baseball had scouts from the Brooklyn Dodgers taking a look, but a severe shoulder injury brought an end to his career.

After a stint in the US Navy, he began writing songs, taking three of them to the 1955 Louisiana Hayride, where he auditioned for Johnny Horton. One of these, *Honky Tonk Man* was considered good enough for Horton to record (with Horton and his manager also taking two thirds of the composing credit and therefore royalties), becoming his first major hit.

On the strength of this success, Howard moved to Texas, still writing songs but also looking to launch his own singing career, picking up a contract with Dot Records, for whom he would record two singles before linking with Smash, although all of his material was considered too similar in style to Johnny Horton for Howard to have enjoyed a successful career. Still, the success of *Sugar Coated Baby*, another Howard composition that provided Johnny Horton with a posthumous hit was probably enough to get him a contract with Mel-O-dy in 1963.

Howard would record and release five singles (as well as writing nine of the label's 20 releases) between October 1963 and April 1965, when Mel-O-dy shut its doors, but none of these made much of an impact.

Howard would record for a number of small labels for the rest of the decade, including Soft, Blackfoot, Charay and Stop, bouncing back with a hit record in 1973 on Dot, *Last Will And Testament*. He died from cancer on 27 December 1994, two days after his 69th birthday.

SCATMAN CROTHERS

Better known as an actor, most significantly as Louie the Garbage Man on 'Chico And The Man', Benjamin Sherman Crothers (born in Terre Haute, Indiana on 23 May 1910) became Scatman when he auditioned for a radio show and the programme director didn't think his own name was catchy enough; Scat Man was the result, later truncated to Scatman by Arthur Godfrey. His early career saw him singing and dancing before making his film debut in 1950 and his first credited role in 1953. He also worked extensively in television, appearing in 'Starsky And Hutch', 'Dragnet', 'Sanford And Son', 'The Gong Show' and countless others. In 1973 he made a one-off album for Motown, **Big Ben Sings**, something of a blues album. Diagnosed with lung cancer in late 1985, he died from pneumonia on 22 November 1986.

ALBUM: BIG BEN SINGS (1973)

THE CROWN – GARY BYRD [SINGLE]

Gary Byrd and Stevie Wonder first worked together on the latter's **Songs In The Key Of Life**, with Gary supplying the lyrics to *Village Ghetto Land* and *Black Man*. It was this latter track that was to prove something of an inspiration for their 1983 outing; where *Black Man* had highlighted the contributions to civilisation made by black men (and women), *The Crown* took its start with the Ancient Egyptians and gave a historical narrative of human progress with special emphasis on contributions made by those of African heritage. Whilst Gary rapped his way through the six minutes plus of the song, Stevie Wonder and Crystal Blake were on hand to sing the chorus and one verse on what was the only release on Stevie's Wondirection label.

"When I did the vocal, Stevie first had me running for the voice. He warmed me up in the studio. After that, he pressured me to do segments of the song, to top the song. It was some time after the record had been pressed that I actually heard the completed record."

Only available as a 12" single, presumably because those involved didn't want to edit it down for a 7" release, the single did little in the US, peaking at #69 on the R&B chart. In the UK, however, the combination of enterprising lyrics, a dance beat and the involvement of Stevie Wonder was enough to turn it into a major pop hit, reaching the Top Ten and spending three weeks stalled at #6.

"What happened in the UK was exciting, almost a phenomenon. We felt the UK was a very good market for the record but we were really surprised at the level of success."

By comparison, the record's subsequent failure in the US was a disappointment.

"The single got caught up with Motown's new distribution deal with MCA but there were other things, like they really didn't know what I was about. I have operated in radio and promotion and the record thing before so I know how these things work, and the single wasn't moving in the way I wanted it to in the US. And also if a project doesn't work with Stevie Wonder's involvement, well, you know something is wrong."

CRUISIN' – SMOKEY ROBINSON [SINGLE]

By 1979 Smokey Robinson had enjoyed six years as a solo artist, racking up eleven pop hits without ever cracking the Top Ten. Indeed, not one of the eleven had even made the Top 20, a disappointing return for an artist who was seemingly a permanent resident on the R&B chart, where during the same time scale he had registered one #1 hit (*Baby That's Backatcha*) and no fewer than six more Top Ten hits. Then in May 1979 Motown released the album **Where There's Smoke** on the Tamla label, a seven track album divided into 'Smoke' and 'Fire' sides. Perhaps it was because *Cruisin'* was the final track on the second (Fire) side, but for reasons unexplained Tamla chose a disco update of The Temptations hit *Get Ready* as the lead single from the album, which flopped at #82 on the R&B chart.

In August Tamla tried again, this time selecting Smokey Robinson and Marv Tarplin's sensuous composition *Cruisin'*. The result was an instant return to the R&B Top Ten, peaking at #4, and emulating that position on the pop chart, becoming Smokey's biggest hit single since *The Tears Of A Clown* in 1970 (which, of course, had originally been recorded in 1967!). This single success carried over to the album too, with **Where There's Smoke** finally awakening from its low chart slumber to reach #17 pop and #8 R&B. At the year's end *Cruisin'* would pick up a Grammy nomination for Best R&B Vocal Performance, Male, which was ultimately won by Michael Jackson and *Don't Stop 'Til You Get Enough*. The single missed out on British chart honours, although a later cover version by D'Angelo would hit #31 in 1996 after it had reached #53 in the US.

THE CRUSADERS

The Crusaders would see four albums released by Motown (two as The Jazz Crusaders and a further two under their truncated name) in three years but would remain an integral part of Motown's west coast operation for several years either side of their being signed by the label.

Originally formed in Houston, Texas as The Swingsters in the early 1950s by Joe Sample (born in Houston on 1 February 1939, keyboards), Wilton Felder (born in Houston on 31 August 1940, saxophone), Wayne Henderson (born in Houston on 24 September 1938, trombone), Hubert Laws (born in Houston on 10 November 1939, flute) and Nesbert 'Stix' Hooper (born in Houston on 15 August 1938, drums), they established their credentials as a tight R&B group before heading out to California in early 1960.

By then they had changed their name to The Jazz Crusaders and secured a contract with Pacific Jazz (although minus Hubert, who headed off to New York), for whom they would record a dozen albums between their 1961 debut and 1969. In between recording their own material, the individual group members found themselves much in demand as session musicians, with Joe Sample and Wilton Felder in particular being utilised extensively by Motown's west coast operation, although Wilton was invariably used as a bass player rather than a saxophonist.

In 1970 they switched labels to Chisa, recording two hit albums in **Old Socks New Shoes, New Socks Old Shoes**, which became a #90 pop, #12 R&B and #6 jazz success, (in Britain the album was released on the Rare Earth label) and **Pass The Plate**, which made #168 pop and #12 jazz in 1970. Soon after they accepted advice to drop 'Jazz' from their name, thus expanding their potential market, with *Pass The Plate* being their first single release under their new name.

In 1972 they released **Hollywood** on MoWest (an album that hinted at future success, peaking at #45 on the R&B chart) before the group left Motown the same year for ABC/Blue Thumb and more autonomy.

That did not stop them returning on several occasions as musicians, or their former label putting out a compilation album **At Their Best** on the main Motown label in September 1973, by which time the group was even appearing on the national pop charts with the singles *Put It Where You Want It* and *Don't Let It Get You Down*. Wayne Henderson died from heart failure on 4 April 2014.
ALBUMS: OLD SOCKS NEW SHOES, NEW SOCKS OLD SHOES (1970), PASS THE PLATE (1971), HOLLYWOOD (1972)
COMPILATION: AT THEIR BEST (1973)

CRYSTAL MANSION

Formed in 1962 as a covers band called The Secrets, this progressive rock band name changed to Crystal Mansion in 1968. Featuring Johnny Caswell (piano and vocals), Sal Rota (keyboards and vocals), Ronny Gentile (guitar), Mario Sanchez (guitar, piano and vocals), Bill Crawford (bass) and Rickey Morley (drums), Crystal Mansion attracted the attention of Capitol Records and released their debut album in 1968. They were dropped after that one album and then turned up at Jerry Ross' Colossus label for a single before Ross took them to Motown in 1972, being assigned to the Rare Earth label and releasing another eponymous album (although not with the same tracks as their earlier Capitol album). This was to be their only release for Rare Earth, the band being dropped when the album failed to sell, although they later resurfaced at 20th Century and recorded yet another eponymous album in 1979 before disbanding.
ALBUM: CRYSTAL MANSION (1972)

CTI RECORDS

Originally formed in 1967 by legendary jazz producer Creed Taylor, CTI (which stood for Creed Taylor Incorporated) began life as a subsidiary of A&M Records but went independent in 1970. In 1971 Taylor launched another label, Kudu (he would later add Salvation, Greenestreet and Three Brothers imprints over the next few years) and scored major hits with Deodato, whose jazz version of *Also Sprach Zarathustra* became an international hit single, followed by the likes of George Benson (*Supership*) and Esther Phillips (*What A Diff'rence A Day Makes*), as well as crossing over from the jazz to the pop charts with artists such as Grover Washington Jr. and Bob James.

As Harvey Fuqua had discovered more than a decade earlier, such success stretched Creed Taylor's line of credit to such an extent that he looked for outside distribution, finally signing with Motown in 1974, with releases by the likes of Joe Farrell, Milt Jackson, Chet Baker, Ron Carter, Bob James, Hubert Laws and George Benson appearing on CTI and Grover Washington Jr., Hank Crawford and Esther Phillips released on Kudu. By 1976 it became apparent to Creed Taylor that the deal with Motown wasn't working, isolated success for Grover Washington Jr. notwithstanding.

When Taylor began negotiating a way out of the company, he was forced to relinquish not only Grover Washington's back catalogue but Grover himself, who would go on to record two good albums of his own for Motown before also departing for even greater success at Elektra. Creed Taylor meanwhile struggled on with CTI for a further four years before filing for bankruptcy. He would revive the label briefly in the 1980s and again in the 1990s and remains active in overseeing reissues of his earlier work.

D

DADDY'S HOME - JERMAINE JACKSON [SINGLE]

Just as Michael Jackson's debut solo album had revived an old song in *Rockin' Robin*, so Motown employed much the same tactic for Jermaine's solo outing. In his case, the revived song was *Daddy's Home*, originally written by James Sheppard and William Miller and a hit for Shep & The Limelites. Sheppard had previously been a member of The Heartbeats, a doo-wop group that enjoyed a 1957 hit in *A Thousand Miles Away*, another composition by Sheppard and Miller. *Daddy's Home* would become a major hit following its release in 1960, peaking at #2 pop, although its success was somewhat tarnished by a later court case whereby the publishers of *A Thousand Miles Away*, Kahl Music, sued the publishers of *Daddy's Home*, Keel Music, and won their case for copyright violation, which brought to an end both the Limelites and their record company.

Daddy's Home was subsequently revived in 1970 by PJ Proby, although it was not a hit, with the result

Jermaine's version, produced by The Corporation and issued in November 1972 was being presented to a whole new generation. Jermaine was able to secure a Top Ten hit, peaking at #9 pop and #3 R&B, a marked improvement from the performance of the debut single *That's How Love Goes*. *Daddy's Home* did little in the UK, with the song remaining virtually unknown to British record buyers until 1981 when Cliff Richard scored a #2 hit.

THE DALTON BOYS

Claimed to be the first white group signed by Motown, with their relatively few singles appearing on the V.I.P. label, the Dalton Boys began as a folk group formed by brothers Dan, Jack and Wally Dalton. After appearing in folk clubs on both the east and west coast, the three brothers returned to Detroit where Jack and Wally teamed with Gary Montgomery and adopted a more rock sound for their debut V.I.P. 1965 release *I've Been Cheated* (written by Hank Cosby, Mickey Stevenson and Bob Montgomery). Although the record became something of local hit in and around Detroit, it failed to crossover onto any chart. The B-side was originally to have been *Take My Hand*, something of a Beatles' like workout written by Bob and Jack which might have got some airplay, but despite appearing on promotional copies of the single at the last moment this was changed to the instrumental track *Something's Bothering You*. Jack and Gary later moved to California where they formed another group called Colours that recorded two albums for Dot Records, which were both influenced by The Beatles.

DANCING IN THE STREET – MARTHA REEVES & THE VANDELLAS [SINGLE]

One of several tracks that defined the Motown sound, *Dancing In The Street* retains both its popularity and importance right up to today. According to Mickey Stevenson, he was inspired after seeing a group of black and white children playing in the street under the spray of a burst water hydrant (although writer Don Mancha would later claim to have sold a ballad tune called *Old Southern Beat* to Mickey, which was subsequently reworked as *Dancing In The Street*). When Mickey took the song into the studio to record, Marvin Gaye, who played piano on it, passed the comment that it sounded like 'dancing in the street', thus attaching the title and earning himself a co-composer credit.

The original recording, which in addition to Marvin featured Joe Messina on Telecaster, James Jamerson on bass, Fred Waites on drums and Ivy Hunter on percussion, had a demo vocal done by Marvin Gaye, yet Motown decided that the song would work better with a female singer. It was apparently initially offered to Mickey's wife Kim Weston but she turned it down (in later interviews she would state she was unaware she ever had first refusal on it), with Martha Reeves being brought in instead. After a temporary mishap, with her original vocal being unrecorded as the engineer had forgotten to turn on the tape, Martha turned in a majestic vocal performance.

"I was very upset. I was angry enough not to want to sing it again but somehow I kind of put my feelings behind me. But there's a bit of urgency that you will hear in the version that they finally kept. I only did it the twice. There were no dub-ins, that's why it has the live-sounding feeling. I think there's some anger in there too."

As a pop record, it worked to perfection, hitting #2 shortly after its release in the summer of 1964 (kept off the top of the chart by Manfred Mann's *Do Wah Diddy Diddy*), #8 R&B and #28 in the UK on the Stateside label. The record's chart placing, however, is only a small part of the story surrounding *Dancing In The Street*, for with the name checks to several cities where the civil rights struggle was strongest there were those who saw the song as some kind of a call to arms, claims that apparently gained some credence as there had been race riots in New York and Philadelphia shortly before the record was released. Whilst Martha and others connected with the record have played down any such connection, when Detroit itself exploded with rioting in July 1967 that left some 43 people dead, the record was pulled from a great many radio stations.

In 1969 the single was reissued in the UK, where it was coupled with The Vandellas earlier hit *Quicksand* and sailed up to #4 on the chart. By coincidence, when the record was reissued anti-racist demonstrations had developed into widespread rioting in London as protesters fought running battles with the police. That the song could have a positive impact was evidenced in 1985 when a version by David Bowie and Mick Jagger topped the UK charts and made #7 in the US as part of the worldwide Live Aid project.

DANCING MACHINE – THE JACKSON 5 [SINGLE]

It has often been claimed that Motown somewhat missed the boat where disco was concerned, overtaken and left in the slipstream of several other companies who got on that particular bandwagon the minute it rolled into town. The reality is somewhat different, of course, for there are several key cuts released that could conceivably fall into the disco category. After all, this is the label that gave us *Keep On Truckin'* and *Boogie Down* by Eddie Kendricks, *Machine Gun* by The Commodores and *Skywriter* by The Jackson 5, all of which owed part of their popularity to the burgeoning club scene.

And then there was *Dancing Machine*, released in February 1974 and another early entrant from The Jackson 5, which was not only a huge club favourite but carried that appeal onto the chart. The song was written by Hal Davis, Don Fletcher and Weldon Dean Parks, with Hal providing the initial inspiration. Among the musicians who effectively drove the single along were James Gadson on drums, William Salter on bass and Joe Sample on keyboards, but what *really* sent the single into orbit was an appearance on the television show 'Soul Train', upon which Michael Jackson debuted the dance the Robot. Much as he would do nearly ten years later on the 'Motown 25' special, Michael's dancing turned what was merely a single into an event, enough to send *Dancing Machine* up to #2 pop and #1 R&B, subsequently earning a Grammy nomination for Best R&B Song (won by Stevie Wonder for *Living For The City*).

That it missed out charting altogether in the UK has long been attached to the cancellation of a proposed British tour at around the time the single was released; Joseph Jackson leaked the group's arrival details to certain sections of the press, who duly published them, causing some consternation among the group's security staff, who mindful of the then recent stampede at fellow teen sensation David Cassidy's concert in London that had seen several hundred injured and one dead, advised against the group setting foot in the UK altogether. With little positive publicity with which to promote it, *Dancing Machine* slipped by unnoticed.

DANCING ON THE CEILING – LIONEL RICHIE [SINGLE]

Written by Lionel with Carlos Rios and Michael Frenchick, *Dancing On The Ceiling* (which would become the title of his third solo album), was a joyous, dance orientated track, similar in style to Lionel's earlier massive hit *All Night Long*. To help promote the single no expense was spared on the accompanying video, which would eventually cost some $400,000. Shot over a total of four days (three days in the studio and one day on location), the video was reminiscent of Fred Astaire's dance routine in the 1951 film 'Royal Wedding'. This was no coincidence, for directing the video was Stanley Donen (Lionel met Stanley at the Oscars ceremony), who had directed the original film some 35 years previously. Donen would later claim that Lionel adapted to dance routines in the rotating room easier and quicker than Fred Astaire, praise indeed! With such a memorable video and a radio friendly manner, the single proved another major success, peaking at #2 on the US pop chart, #6 R&B and #7 in the UK.

DANCING ON THE CEILING - LIONEL RICHIE [ALBUM]

The runaway success of Lionel Richie's two previous solo albums had raised the bar to extraordinary levels, as producer James Anthony Carmichael duly noted.

"Whether or not you'll sell more records than your last should be the concern of your label. The artist's job is to simply be true to himself and make music that represents who he is."

It helped, of course, that *Say You Say Me* had been such a major hit and would go on to win Lionel an Oscar. Originally, the album was to have been called **Say You Say Me**, but almost a year had passed since the single had been in the charts, too long as far as those involved in the album project were concerned, hence the change to **Dancing On The Ceiling**.

Recording had taken Lionel all around North America; to Seattle for Eric Clapton's guitar solo on *Tonight Will Be Alright* and Nashville for *Deep River Woman*. Since the latter track had a distinct country flavour, Lionel pinpointed country superstars Alabama as the act he wanted to accompany him on the song. He flew into Nashville to meet the group over dinner and asked what time they should get together the next day to record their vocals. He was told eight o'clock and assumed they meant in the evening, so was rather surprised to get an early wake-up call at six o'clock in the morning! According to Lionel, he was physically in the studio by 8.30am but his mind didn't turn up until 2.00pm!

Released on 15 July 1986, the album would prove to be packed with hit singles just as its predecessors had been, with four Top Ten hits being culled. The single activity translated itself to album sales, with the album hitting #1 on the pop chart and #4 R&B as well as reaching #2 in the UK. At home, total sales exceeded four million, less than half its predecessor **Can't Slow Down**, but still well ahead of what Lionel's contemporaries were managing at the time.

DANNY & THE JUNIORS

American vocal group Danny & The Juniors was formed in Philadelphia, Pennsylvania in 1955 by Danny Rapp (born in Philadelphia on 10 May 1941), David White (born in Philadelphia on 1 September 1940), Frank Maffei (born in November 1940) and Joe Terranova (born in Philadelphia on 30 January 1941) as the Juvenairs. Their debut hit was *At The Hop* originally written as *Do The Bop* and changed at the suggestion of Dick Clark, going on to top the US chart for seven weeks. The follow-up, *Rock And Roll Is Here To Stay* was a Top Twenty hit, peaking at #19, and subsequently appeared on the soundtrack to 'Christine', released by Motown in November 1983. Danny Rapp committed suicide on 5 April 1983.

BOBBY DARIN

Born Walden Robert Cassotto in The Bronx on 14 May 1936 Bobby was something of a sickly child, suffering rheumatic fever from the age of eight, a condition that severely weakened his heart. Indeed, he was to overhear a doctor telling his mother that he would be lucky to live beyond the age of 16, a revelation that he used to motivate himself to make the most of whatever time he had. Fortunately, his talent as a musician, able to play the guitar, piano and drums, as well as an exceptional singing voice *and* the ability to write material offered him an escape from the poverty he suffered at home.

His first break came in 1955 when he linked with Don Kirshner in a writing partnership (having adopted the name Bobby Darin, the surname apparently derived from a Chinese restaurant called Mandarin Duck), leading to a contract with Decca Records the following year. Bobby also got a number of writing assignments, including a couple of tracks for Connie Francis, with the young singer and young writer being attracted enough to consider eloping. Unfortunately Connie's father hated Bobby Darin so much he waved a gun in his face and told him to stay away from his daughter for good.

Whilst his personal life may have suffered a setback, the same could not be said for his musical career, for a switch to Atco in 1958 saw the first of 25 pop hits over the course of the next five years, including the smash *Mack The Knife,* which helped him win the Grammy Award for Best New Artist in 1959 and was one of four million sellers he would release. Record success was just the start of his achievements, for he was noted as an exceptional performer (Sammy Davis Jr. once said the one act he never wanted to follow was Bobby Darin), which in turn led to film offers, with Bobby picking up an Oscar nomination for Best Supporting Actor in 'Captain Newman, MD' in 1963.

He switched labels to Capitol in 1963, at the same time modifying his musical style and recording several folk songs, including his 1966 Top Ten hit *If I Were A Carpenter*. Whilst his music could never be said to have been political, he was interested enough to help Senator Bobby Kennedy with his Presidential campaign in 1968 and was present at the Ambassador Hotel in Los Angeles on the night Kennedy was murdered. In the immediate aftermath Bobby Darin sold his house and most of his possessions and went to live in a trailer near Big Sur. Further fuelling his gloom was the revelation the same year that he had been raised by his grandparents and the girl he thought was his sister was actually his mother!

When he left the trailer and his self-imposed exile, he formed his own record label, Direction Records, who released a steady stream of folk and protest music. In 1970 he signed with Motown (there is considerable speculation that he was behind The Ding Dongs album released on Motown, even if the material was most definitely *not* folk or protest), with the single *Melodie* being released in April 1971, although his first album **Live At the Desert Inn Finally**, which was to be released in the summer of 1971 was shelved (it would eventually appear in 1987 on CD).

That same year Bobby underwent heart surgery to try and repair earlier damage, with much of the rest of the year spent recuperating. His debut album finally appeared in July 1972, an eponymous album that should have benefitted from the fact that Bobby had his own variety show on NBC that ran for more than a year. As it was the only appearance Bobby made on the chart whilst at Motown was with *Happy*, a version of the love theme from the film 'Lady Sings The Blues', which would make #67 in January 1973.

In June of that year he married Andrea Yeager (his second marriage, his first one in 1960 to actress Sandra Dee, which had occurred soon after the break-up of his relationship to Connie Francis, ended in divorce in 1967), but less than six months later his health took a dramatic turn for the worse. He missed taking medication for his heart problems prior to a dental visit and developed systematic infection and

was rushed to hospital to undergo surgery to repair the two artificial heart valves that had been inserted in 1971, but on 20 December 1973, shortly after a six hour operation he died in the recovery room. The following February Motown issued a memorial album, **Bobby Darin 1936-1973**, which mixed his Motown recordings with live versions of his earlier Atco hits.
ALBUMS: BOBBY DARIN (1972)
COMPILATION: 1936-1973 (1974)

THE DARNELLS

Technically, there never was a Motown group called The Darnells; this is in fact Gladys Horton (of The Marvelettes) singing with Louvain Demps, Marlene Barrow and Jackie Hicks (better known within Motown as The Andantes). The only single released under The Darnells moniker was *Too Hurt To Cry, Too Much In Love To Say Goodbye* backed with *Come On Home*, issued on Gordy in October 1963. According to later reports, the song, written and produced by Holland-Dozier-Holland was done specifically to sound like Phil Spector, with Berry Gordy having instructed HDH to show the musical world that Motown could beat Spector at his own game if they so wished. Whether Motown put any promotional muscle behind it is open to debate, but it managed to limp into the chart at #117 pop. In the UK it had to be content with being one of four tracks featured on the Stateside issued EP *R&B Chartmakers No 3* in June 1964.

IRENE DATCHER

Female singer and dancer Irene Datcher first came to prominence in the role of Agatha in the 1976 Broadway revival of 'Guys And Dolls', appearing on the cast recording album released by Motown in December of that year. This would be Irene's only appearance on Broadway, although she has recorded sporadically over the years, most notably providing backing vocals for the likes of James Blood Ulmer, Jean-Paul Bourelly and Tarika Blue.

DWIGHT DAVID

Dwight David Turner (born in Beckley, West Virginia on 4 February 1947) began his career as a serious singer, winning a talent contest at the Apollo Theater and later singing back-up for several doo-wop and soul groups. In 1966 he was invited by producer Clay McMurray to record a cover version of *Stand By Me*, in which Dwight (under the name Spyder Turner) did vocal impressions of Jackie Wilson, David Ruffin, Billy Stewart, Smokey Robinson and Chuck Jackson. Picked up by MGM, it would go on to hit #3 R&B and #12 pop, with a follow-up *I Can't Make It Anymore* also hitting the pop chart. However, dissatisfied with the way he was being promoted by MGM he left the label and would spend much of the next ten years or so touring and recording only sporadically.

Towards the end of the 1970s he began working with Norman Whitfield, releasing two albums in **Music Web** and **Only Love** and co-writing Rose Royce' *Do Your Dance*, a top forty hit on both sides of the Atlantic. He recorded the theme to the Berry Gordy film 'The Last Dragon' in 1985, which duly became his only single for the label when backed with an instrumental version.

BILLY DAVIS

Whilst Billy Davis never recorded for Motown, he is still something of a key figure in its early development. Born Roquel Davis in Detroit on 11 July 1932, his earliest experience in the industry was as a writer and manager, with Billy penning a number of songs for his cousin Lawrence Payton's group The Four Aims (later to become The Four Tops). Recording a demo, Billy sent it to Chess Records in Chicago hoping to get the group a contract; they did, for one single, but Chess were impressed with Billy's songs and gave them to several artists to record.

Back in Detroit Billy began dating Gwen Gordy and through her was introduced to her brother Berry. Equally impressed with Billy's writing abilities, the pair began penning a number of songs that would eventually be submitted to another of Billy's cousins, Jackie Wilson. With Billy using the pseudonym Tyran Carlo, the pair would write a number of hits, including *Reet Petite, To Be Loved* and *Lonely Teardrops*, among others. Despite this success, very little of the money generated was finding its way back to the writers, eventually leading to Berry and Billy turning their writing attentions to other artists, most notably Marv Johnson and Barrett Strong.

In 1958 Billy helped Gwen set up the Anna label with national distribution through Chess whilst still writing with Berry, including *Got A Job* (The Miracles), *Money* (Barrett Strong) and *You Got What It Takes* (Marv Johnson). When Etta James covered another

Gordy/Davis song, *All I Could Do Was Cry* in 1960, Chess Records invited Billy to head up their A&R department. There he would be responsible for a succession of hits, most notably producing *Rescue Me* by Fontella Bass in 1965. Three years later he was lured to New York to join advertising agency McCann-Erickson, where his major claim to fame would be helping create the Coca Cola jingle that would eventually become *I'd Like To Teach The World To Sing (In Perfect Harmony)*. A life-long friend of the Gordy family, Billy died on 2 September 2004.

HAL DAVIS

Hal Davis' involvement with Motown was of such significance he was considered 'Mr Motown' by those in the business in Los Angeles, and they continued to call him by that affectionate nickname even when Berry Gordy was in earshot!

Born Harold Edward Davis in Cincinnati, Ohio on 8 February 1933, Hal had entered the music business as a singer at the age of 13, with future TK president Henry Stone his manager. He then switched to writing and production, formed his own label and had a degree of success with Giselle Hawkins and *Amazon*. Looking to be closer to the real centres of the music business, Hal moved to Los Angeles in 1960, taking his operation with him but finding the going hard, although he did record a number of titles under his own name, including *Read The Book Of Love* on Del-Fi, *I'll Tell It* on M.J.C. and *My Only Flower* for Federal. Then came the introduction to the first Mr Motown.

"I first met Berry in 1962. He was out here (Los Angeles) at a convention at the Ambassador Hotel, and he was looking for someone to run a west coast office for Motown. At the time, to survive, I was cooking for the county. When I went to meet Berry, I came right from the county with dough on my fingers. I met Berry and he was impressed; I had everybody out here signed up. My record company was set up in the front room of my house and my publishing company was set up in the bathroom. Berry related to that. That and my hustle got me into the job. The next week I got the letter from Motown telling me I had gotten the job."

It was not just Hal's hustle, of course, that so convinced Berry that Hal and Marc Gordon would be the ideal personnel to front up Motown's west coast operation; it was their uncanny knack of unearthing talent, all of which they sent on to Detroit. That and their ability to accurately reproduce the famed Motown sound in the studios in Los Angeles are testament to their abilities. Among the artists they auditioned in Los Angeles and sent on to Detroit with a glowing reference were sisters Brenda and Patrice Holloway and Blinky Williams, and among those who came out west to record was Stevie Wonder.

"We started at 6290 Sunset by setting up all the facilities for producers. At that point we had a number one artist in Stevie Wonder. Stevie came out to the coast, so one day we went out to the beach. Stevie had never been to the beach. He just sat there taking in all the sounds and out of that came *Castles In The Sand*. Next came *Harmonica Man*, which was a smash. Then we got involved in the American International soundtracks. That was Motown's and Stevie's first picture, and it opened the door for the Motown office. We got out of the trial basis; we had really proved ourselves."

Over the ensuring years Hal would continue to prove himself, most notably with his production on The Jackson 5, with the five youngsters quickly putting aside their fears of the Hal's imposing figure.

"I liked them, but they were afraid of me in the beginning, because I always wore a beret and mirrored glasses. Sometimes recording with those boys was just so much fun. We'd do the serious part, the recording of the music and vocals and then sit around listening back to what we'd achieved. And woe betide me if I fell asleep during the sessions; I'd often wake up to find the boys had written on my face or were trying to set my shoelaces on fire. Boy, we had some fun back then!"

With the fun came the hits, with Hal being involved with the group throughout their time at Motown, guiding them from the bubblegum soul of their early singles through to the transition to disco.

"I got a tune called *Dancing Machine*, with a lot of electronic sounds. This was the beginning of disco – it sold about four million copies."

Almost without consciously trying, Hal helped define disco during the 1970s – *Love Hangover* by Diana Ross and *Don't Leave Me This Way* by Thelma Houston just two smash hits he helmed, with Thelma's record earning two Grammy nominations, for Best Rhythm & Blues Song and Best R&B Female Vocal Performance, winning the latter. The former nomination, which saw the song's writers Kenny Gamble and Leon Huff gain a nomination, may have missed out on the award but they sent a letter of gratitude to Hal for the amazing job he had done on their song – it held pride of place in his office at Motown. Hal showed little sign of losing his enthusiasm for recording as the decade wore on, teaching a succession of artists the studio ropes.

"I shape my groove by the act. It doesn't just take me – it takes the act, too. I have to relate to them and they have to relate to me. It's worked for me. My records have always set precedents. And I want my records to set precedents in the future."

Hal would be a fixture of Motown for nearly thirty years, setting precedents along the way. He died on 18 November 1998, with one Mr Motown, Berry Gordy reading the eulogy for the other Mr Motown, at his funeral.

OSSIE DAVIS

Perhaps better known as an actor, Raiford Chatman Davis was born in Cogdell, Georgia on 18 December 1917. A county clerk filling in his birth certificate misheard his mother's pronunciation of his initials R.C. and entered Ossie as his name instead, the name under which he made his reputation. He dropped out of Howard University in order to pursue an acting career, joining the Rose McClendon Players in Harlem in 1939. He made his film debut in 1950 in 'No Way Out' and would become a regular for the next 55 years, appearing in such films as 'The Hill', 'Gladiator' and 'Jungle Fever'. He also directed five films, including 'Cotton Comes To Harlem' and 'Gordon's War' as well as making countless television appearances.

In 1972 he linked with Bill Cosby for the Black Forum album **The Congressional Black Caucus**, indicative of his role as a social activist. He was found dead in a Miami hotel room on 4 February 2005, with his death believed to have been caused by a heart problem.

ALBUM: THE CONGRESSIONAL BLACK CAUCUS (1972)

SAMMY DAVIS JR.

A singer who scored several major worldwide hits, including *Love Me Or Leave Me, That Old Black Magic* and *Something's Gotta Give,* a member of The Rat Pack and one of the first artists lured to Frank Sinatra's Reprise label, Sammy Davis (born in Harlem, New York on 8 December 1925) was effectively one of music's establishment. Despite this, his first appearance on a Motown record was uttering 'hear ye, hear ye' on Shorty Long's parody *Here Comes The Judge*, a song based on Sammy's routine on the 'Rowan & Martin Laugh-In'.

That record introduced him to Motown and thereafter he and Berry Gordy negotiated a recording contract, with **Something For Everyone** being released in May 1970. Although not a success, it did prompt further discussions between Sammy and Berry that resulted in a boutique label, Ecology Records. There was to be just one single, *In My Own Lifetime* released in March 1971, after which the pair disagreed over the future musical direction the label and artist should pursue. Sammy would return in 1984, releasing *Jello Detroit* on the main Motown label. He died from throat cancer on 16 May 1990.

ALBUM: SOMETHING FOR EVERYONE (1970)

THE SPENCER DAVIS GROUP

British group The Spencer Davis Group was formed in Birmingham, West Midlands in 1963 by Spencer Davis (born in Swansea, West Glamorgan on 14 July 1941, guitar), Steve Winwood (born in Birmingham on 12 May 1948, guitar, keyboards and vocals), his brother Mervin (known universally as 'Muff', after the character in British children's television programme 'Muffin The Mule', born in Birmingham on 15 June 1943, on bass) and Pete York (born in Redcar, Cleveland on 15 August 1942, drums). Initially named the Muff-Woody Jazz Band, then Rhythm & Blues Quartet, they were spotted by Island Records boss Chris Blackwell who promptly signed them up (although Blackwell's label was still in its embryonic stage and licensed their product to Fontana) and changed name to The Spencer Davis Group (the name was suggested by Muff Winwood since Spencer was the only member of the group who actually enjoyed doing interviews). They scored minor hits (usually covers of American hits) until their major chart breakthrough with *Keep On Running*, written by another Blackwell protégé, Jamaican Jackie Edwards in 1965. *Gimme Some Lovin'* in 1966 was their first international smash, hitting #2 in the UK and #7 in the US, and was featured on the album **More Songs From The Big Chill** released on Motown in April 1984.

DANNY DAY

Armed with a portfolio of songs he had written, Jim Webb went from one publishing office to another looking for a job. He arrived at Motown's offices in Los Angeles and was ushered in by Frank Wilson, with the producer giving Jim a contract. His first song, *This Time Last Summer* impressed Hal Davis and Marc Gordon enough for them to record it soon after, with the track, coupled with *Please Don't Turn The Lights Out* being credited to Danny Day (in fact it was Hal Davis himself) and released on the V.I.P. label in June 1965. Whilst the single did little, it was proof enough of Webb's abilities as a songwriter. Unfortunately, Motown didn't appear to know what to do with him or his songs; *By The Time I Get To Phoenix* was offered to Paul Petersen, who turned it down and it would later become a smash for Glen Campbell, by which time Jim was a former Motown employee.

THE DAZZ BAND

Bell Telefunk and Mother Braintree, two bands from Cleveland, Ohio combined in 1976 to form a new entity, Kinsman Dazz, named after a lounge where they worked as the house band. Leading the ensemble was Bobby Harris (guitar), with Michael Wiley (bass), Mike Calhoun (guitar and percussion), Kenny Pettus (percussion), Wayne Preston (saxophone) and Isaac 'Ike' Wiley (Michael's brother, drums).

They were signed to 20th Century by Joe Lewis, with their debut album being produced by Philip Bailey (Marvin Gaye had apparently been originally lined up to produce but fell ill, with the band subsequently requesting and getting Bailey from Earth, Wind & Fire). Their eponymous debut gave rise to a minor hit in *I Might As Well Forget About Loving You*, which made #46 R&B and #104 pop, prompting a quick return to the studio for a second album.

By then the band had expanded, adding Les Thaler (trumpet) and Ed Myers (trombone), with **Dazz** containing another R&B hit in *Catchin' Up On Love*, which made #33 in 1979. The following year 20th Century shut the doors on its record operation, although the band's pedigree and track record was such that they weren't left out in the cold for too long, being signed by Motown in 1980.

They took the decision to truncate their name to Dazz Band and underwent further changes in their line-up, which now consisted of Bobby Harris, Pierre DeMudd (trumpet, flugelhorn and vocals), Sennie Skip Martin (trumpet and vocals), Eric Fearman (guitar), Kevin Frederick (keyboards), Kenny Pettus and the Wiley brothers.

Still following a musical style reminiscent of Earth Wind & Fire, the band dropped their debut album in 1980, **Invitation To Love**, which would see two R&B hit singles in the title track (#51) and the earlier released *Shake It Up* (#51). **Let The Music Play** in 1981 saw the band modify its sound and reap the benefits on the chart, with the album hitting #154 pop and a very encouraging #36 R&B. One single made the chart, *Knock! Knock!* peaking at #44 on the R&B chart.

The following year saw Dazz Band hit pay-dirt, with *Let It Whip* topping the R&B singles chart for five weeks and reach #5 on the pop chart, whilst the parent album **Keep It Live** would also top the R&B chart and reach #14 on the pop chart. Better was to follow, for *Let It Whip* would go on to pick up a Grammy nomination for Best Rhythm & Blues Song and win the award for Best R&B Performance by a Group with Vocal. The album benefitted from the attention, eventually shifting sufficient copies to earn a gold disc, helped also by a further R&B top 20 hit in *Keep It Live (On The K.I.L.)*.

Whilst this would represent as good as it got for the Dazz Band, there were still moments to savour over the next few years, racking up a further three R&B Top Ten singles hits in *On The One For Fun*, *Joystick* and *Let It All Blow* (the latter track also became their only single to crack the UK charts, hitting #12 in 1984) and putting a further four albums on the chart, with three (**On The One**, **Joystick** and **Jukebox** also going as far as the Top Twenty. As the band progressed so their sound changed, becoming a bit more rock orientated by the time their final Motown album **Hot Spot** hit the stores, and group members were also beginning to move on, with Marlon McClain and Keith Harrison replacing Eric Fearman and Kevin Frederick in 1985.

With their albums receiving ever decreasing sales and impact, the band left Motown in 1986 bound for Geffen, later joining RCA and still looking to rekindle their glory days.

ALBUMS: INVITATION TO LOVE (1980), LET THE MUSIC PLAY (1981), KEEP IT LIVE (1982), ON THE ONE (1983), JOYSTICK (1983), JUKEBOX (1984), HOT SPOT (1985)

SUZANNE DE PASSE

In 1967 The Supremes were due to appear on the 'Ed Sullivan Show' in New York, with Berry Gordy flying in and being introduced to a friend of Cindy Birdsong's, a nineteen year old by the name of Suzanne Celeste De Passe (born in New York on 19 July 1947). A couple of months later the pair crossed paths again, this time in Miami, where Suzanne took the opportunity of bringing to Berry's attention problems she had been having in getting Motown staff to return her calls when trying to book acts.

According to Berry's autobiography, 'To Be Loved', the conversation effectively ended with Berry asking her if she could run Motown any better, to which she replied that she'd love the opportunity. Two weeks later, Berry had Suzanne flown to Detroit and put on the payroll, although at the time he had no definite plans as to how to utilise her talents and abilities.

"I think what happened was that, up to that point, Berry thought I was bright but didn't know what I was going to do."

Eventually he found a role, that of Creative Assistant, something of a catch-all title that saw her liaising with television companies to try and get Motown acts on the bill, assembling a wardrobe for the soon to be launched Jackson 5 (indeed she also played a significant part in getting the group to Motown in the first place), chaperoning them on their early tours and turning her hand to pretty much any activity her boss requested.

The area in which she undoubtedly excelled was television and film, going on to help knock the script to 'Lady Sings The Blues' into shape (for which she received an Academy Award nomination) and edit and co-ordinate the soundtrack, abilities that eventually saw her promoted to head of Creative.

"The evolution of the job was shaped by the fact that Berry was more confident about my abilities than I was. I can tell you when I took over that job, I had absolutely no idea how a deal was struck, no idea how the pie was split up for royalties, no idea what happened to a record after the tape leaves the studio and heads towards the marketplace."

In 1978 Suzanne was moved sideways to head up the movie production company MPI, overseeing an ever-expanding list of film and television projects. The crowning glory of the 1980s was 'Motown 25', a television special that saw the greats still at Motown such as Stevie Wonder, The Temptations and The Four Tops, among others, being joined by many returning superstars, such as Diana Ross, Marvin Gaye and Michael Jackson, with the latter stealing the show and ensuring its place in television history thanks to his moonwalk dance to accompany his then current single *Billie Jean* (out on single for Epic). The show won an Emmy, with Suzanne collecting another of the highest television accolades for 'Motown Returns To The Apollo' in 1985.

Berry Gordy sold the record division to MCA in 1988 and merged Motown Productions into a new entity Gordy/De Passe Productions, selling the entire company to Suzanne a year later. Renamed De Passe Entertainment, the company has continued to produce successful television programming, most notably with two excursions back into Motown territory; 'The Jacksons: An American Dream' (1992) and 'The Temptations' (1998).

DEBBIE DEAN

Debbie had several stabs at success during the late 1950s, recording as Penny Smith, Debra Dion and Debbie Stevens for ABC and Roulette before pitching up at Motown in 1960. Debbie, who was born Reba Jeanette Smith in Corbin, Kentucky on 1 February 1928, thus became the first white solo artist to be signed to Motown and quite possibly its first artist aimed fair and square at the pop market. Her debut single as Debbie Dean was *Itty Bitty Pity Love*, released in August 1961, but it was pulled almost immediately in favour of *Don't Let Him Shop Around*, an answer record to The Miracles' *Shop Around*, a month later. This too failed despite the presence of The Miracles as background singers, and after one final single *Everybody's Talking About Me* in March 1962, Debbie was dropped from the label.

She relocated to California where she would release two singles for Sue and Treva Records, reverting back to the name Debra Dion, neither of which sold. A couple of years later, still working the California nightclub scene, she came to the attention of Deke Richards, who became the leader of her backing band and wrote a song that the pair spent whatever money they could raise recording a demo, although the funds ran out before Debbie's vocal could be added. Undeterred, Debbie called up Berry Gordy when he happened to be visiting Los Angeles and managed to secure an appointment, at which Debbie sang to the backing tape created by Deke; it was enough to get the pair a writing contract with Motown and Jobete.

There she would help compose *I Can't Dance To That Music You're Playing* (recorded by Martha & The Vandellas) and *Honey Bee* (The Supremes), among others, as well as recording several songs herself with Deke Richards (under the his real name Dennis Lussier) as producer. Only one of these was released, *Stay My Love* on V.I.P., but when that went the same way as her earlier singles, a second single *You Asked Me* was scrapped. Debbie died on 17 February 2001.

JAMES DEAN

Best known for his compositions with William Weatherspoon, James enjoyed a brief but hugely successful spell at Motown, penning such hits as *What Becomes Of The Brokenhearted*, a major hit for Jimmy Ruffin. Born James Anthony Dean in Detroit, Michigan on 7 February 1943, he graduated from Hamtramck High School and served in the US Army before pitching up at Motown in 1964, where his cousins Brian and

Eddie Holland were already well ensconced. Teamed up with William Weatherspoon, James wrote numerous hits, including *Brokenhearted, Farewell Is A Lonely Sound* and *I've Passed This Way Before*, all for Jimmy Ruffin, but the pair were unable to gain access to the upper rank of artists at Hitsville.

James Dean and William Weatherspoon parted company in 1968 when Holland-Dozier-Holland left Motown, but whilst William linked with HDH at their Invictus and Hot Wax labels, James opted to throw his lot in with Don Davis, writing material with John Glover for the likes of The Dells, The Dramatics, Johnnie Taylor and The Soul Children. He would later co-write *You Don't Have To Be A Star*, a pop and R&B chart topper for Marilyn McCoo and Billy Davis Junior. Based in Detroit for his entire career, James died from cancer of the spine on 9 April 2006 at the age of 63.

DeBARGE

Whilst Tommy and Bobby DeBarge were enjoying a degree of success as members of Switch, their younger siblings back home in Grand Rapids, Michigan could only watch with envy. Within two years, however, they were old enough to pursue their own musical dreams, with Bunny (born Etterlene DeBarge in Grand Rapids on 15 March 1955, vocals), El (born Eldra DeBarge on 4 June 1961, keyboards and vocals), Mark (born on 19 June 1959, trumpet, saxophone and vocals) and Randy (born William Randall DeBarge on 6 August 1958, bass and vocals) becoming the next members of the DeBarge family to walk through the doors of Motown.

Like their elder brothers, DeBarge were signed to the Gordy label and mentored by Jermaine Jackson, which would immediately bring comparisons to The Jackson 5. This would not be a bad thing, since at least it gave Motown a something of a start in their marketing campaign. The initial album, released as **The DeBarges** in April 1981 was a somewhat hesitant start, failing to chart and found the group still in search of both a direction and an identity.

That was to change with the release of **All This Love**, the first album to also feature brother James (born on 22 August 1963) and the group's name slightly shortened to DeBarge. The new album did the business, making #24 on the pop chart and #3 R&B, earning the group a gold disc into the bargain. It helped that the album could boast three hit singles, with *I Like It* and *All This Love* cracking the Top Ten of the R&B chart, at #2 and #5 respectively.

Building on this success, **In A Special Way** would become another gold album and give the group the first of their two R&B chart toppers in *Time Will Reveal*, a self-penned number that showed creative juices flowed all the way through the family. The group would then take something of a two year break from recording, but even without any new releases to report, the media were still had plenty to write about when it came to DeBarge – in 1984 James DeBarge eloped with Janet Jackson, seemingly against the wishes of both sets of parents. After initially living on the Jackson family compound, the pair would split up and the marriage was annulled in 1985; nearly twenty years later, rumours abounded that the pair had a daughter Renee born during this brief marriage that was subsequently raised by another member of the Jackson family, but whilst the rumours emanated from the DeBarge family, no confirmation was forthcoming from the Jacksons.

After a two year gap the group returned in 1985 with **Rhythm Of The Night**, an album that would at last enable them to crossover to the more lucrative pop market. The difference was in the material; whereas their previous albums have been almost entirely written by the group and concentrated on ballad material, this time around the compositions were largely derived from not only outside the group but outside Motown as well, with Motown feeling that a more up-tempo song might break them out of R&B. Key among the tracks was the title track, a song written by Diane Warren that was said to kick start her career as a serious writer. It certainly helped that the song was also included on the soundtrack to the Motown film 'The Last Dragon', with the accompanying free publicity helping propel the single to the top of the R&B chart and to #3 pop and also become the group's breakthrough in the UK, peaking at #4. The success of the single drove the album up the charts, hitting #19 pop and #3 R&B and earning the group their first platinum disc.

Three further singles were pulled from the album, *Who's Holding Donna Now* (#2 R&B, #6 pop), *You Wear It Well* (#7 R&B and #46 pop) and another Diane Warren composition, *The Heart Is Not So Smart* (#29 R&B and #75 pop). The final two hits were released under the moniker El DeBarge With DeBarge, a move that appeared to indicate Motown was preparing El for a future solo career. Indeed, both El and Bunny would sign solo deals with Motown, a move that angered some within the DeBarge family, most notably Etterlene 'Mama' DeBarge, the mother of the seven DeBarge children who had recorded for Motown thus far. Whilst acknowledging that Motown

had told El they would make him a star, she felt the way it was handled split not just a group but a family.
Soon after Bunny and El signed their solo contracts, the remaining members of the group left Motown and would eventually sign with the Striped Horse label. James, Mark and Randy were joined by Bobby in the new line-up but this was to be a short-lived affair as personal problems mounted for virtually all of the DeBarge brothers – Chico and Bobby were arrested and imprisoned for drug trafficking in 1989 and Randy, Tommy, Mark and James all underwent treatment for drug abuse. The group disbanded soon after sentence had been imposed on the two brothers. At Bobby's intake process it was revealed that heroin use had resulted in him contracting AIDS, from which he died on 16 August 1995.
ALBUMS: THE DeBARGES (1981), ALL THIS LOVE (1982), IN A SPECIAL WAY (1983), RHYTHM OF THE NIGHT (1985)
COMPILATION: GREATEST HITS (1986)

BUNNY DeBARGE

Born Etterlene DeBarge (named after her mother) in Grand Rapids, Michigan on 15 March 1955, Bunny had been the female lead singer in the family group DeBarge from their inception in 1979 through to 1986. During the course of those seven years, Bunny proved she was more than just a singer, helping pen songs for both the group and artists outside, with *Hold On To My Love* being recorded by fellow Gordy act High Inergy and *Love Over And Over Again*, a Top Ten R&B hit for Switch. According to her own later comments, the recording and touring schedule DeBarge had to undertake resulted in virtually all of the group suffering a drug problem, with Bunny succumbing to hard drugs and then prescription drugs over the course of their career.
In 1986 both Bunny and El DeBarge were offered solo deals with Motown, with Bunny releasing **In Love** in January 1987. The album would barely make #172 pop and #52 R&B on the charts, with one single, *Save The Best For Me (Best Of Your Lovin')* the lone single success, peaking at #18 on the R&B chart. Despite this modest success, Bunny was dropped by the Gordy label soon after and rather than look for a deal elsewhere retired in order to try and battle her ongoing drug problem. It would take until the middle of the next decade, by which time Bunny had become a born-again Christian and her return to a studio would see her record gospel music.
ALBUM: IN LOVE (1987)

CHICO DeBARGE

Although a member of the DeBarge clan, Chico (born Jonathan Debarge in Grand Rapids, Michigan on 23 June 1966) was never a member of the family group. Instead he arrived at Motown as a solo performer in 1986, blessed with many of the talents that his siblings had already displayed, including as a writer and producer. The eponymous album by the tenor singer (the only male member of the DeBarge family to sing tenor – the rest of his brothers sang falsetto) gave rise to the hit single *Talk To Me*, which hit #7 R&B and would be his only pop crossover hit when it peaked at #21. The single success did help shift copies of the parent album, which whilst never reaching the kind of heights the family group had attained still managed a respectable #90 pop and #25 R&B.
His follow-up album, **Kiss Serious** was largely produced by former Prince sideman Brownmark and would produce two minor hits in *Rainy Night* and *Kiss Serious* (#18 and #53 respectively on the R&B chart), with the album making #63 R&B. His career was brought to an abrupt halt in 1988 when he was arrested, along with his brother Bobby and charged with drug trafficking (at the time, Chico was to have been appearing in an anti-drug telethon for the Sheriff's Department in Los Angeles!). The pair was sentenced to five years in prison, with Chico resuming his career upon his release.
ALBUMS: CHICO DeBARGE (1986), KISS SERIOUS (1987)

EL DeBARGE

The lead singer of the family group DeBarge, El was born Eldra DeBarge in Grand Rapids, Michigan on 4 June 1961 and was inspired by the success of his brothers Bobby and Tommy and their group Switch to pursue a musical career of his own. Having mastered the piano at an early age, El would drop out of school in 1977 in order to perform with his elder brothers, with Bobby and Tommy helping El and their other siblings get a deal with Motown.
Happy to do as Motown dictated on their first album, its relative failure convinced El that the group should take more responsibility for production and song writing on future efforts. Whilst Bunny DeBarge therefore became the lead female voice, El quickly became the male lead as well as writing much of the material and handling production. When DeBarge scored a major hit with *Rhythm Of The Night*, included on the soundtrack to 'The Last Dragon', Berry Gordy

convinced El it was time to pursue a solo career, an offer El readily accepted.

It was another film soundtrack that provided the biggest hit from his eponymous album, *Who's Johnny* being featured in the hit film 'Short Circuit', with the single topping the R&B chart and making #3 pop. Further hits were lifted from the album, including *Love Always* and *Someone*, the success of which enabled the album to make #172 pop and #8 R&B and earn a gold disc.

It would take three years before a follow-up album hit the streets, **Gemini** being released in 1989, by which time Motown had changed hands and El DeBarge was not the priority he had been previously. Despite providing another Top Ten R&B hit in *Real Love* (#8), the album struggled to reach #35 on the chart and El DeBarge left the label, eventually signing with Warner Brothers. Like his siblings, El would have his own drug problems over the years, being arrested on several occasions and eventually sent to prison in 2008 after violating the terms of an earlier probation.

ALBUM: EL DeBARGE (1986)

KIKI DEE

Motown would sign several British artists as a result of a joint deal with EMI Records, picking up a number of rock acts for its Rare Earth label, but the honour of being the first British artist directly signed went to Kiki Dee.

Born Pauline Matthews in Bradford, Yorkshire on 6 March 1947, she began her professional career as a backing singer, both on the road and in the studio before being spotted in 1963 by a Philips representative at a show, who taped her performance and sent it to Jack Baverstock at Fontana Records. Pauline was invited to London to work with Mitch Murray, at which point a name change was suggested – Pauline's original choice was Kinky Dee, but eventually settled on the less risqué Kiki Dee.

Despite hitting the charts in several European countries, most notably Italy, Kiki was unable to get a chart breakthrough in the UK. In the summer of 1969 she was signed by Motown and flew into Detroit in September in order to begin work on her debut for her new label. Unfortunately, **Great Expectations** was unable to live up to its title, despite getting released in most of the major markets around the world. The album and first single appeared in the summer of 1970 on Tamla (*The Day Will Come Between Sunday And Monday*), with a further single released on Rare Earth in March 1971, *Love Makes The World Go Round*.

Following the expiration of her Motown contract Kiki signed with Elton John's Rocket label and finally got her name on the charts, some ten years after her recording career began. In 1976, she accompanied Elton on top of the charts on both sides of the Atlantic with *Don't Go Breaking My Heart*.

ALBUM: GREAT EXPECTATIONS (1970)

JACK DEJOHNETTE

Born in Chicago, Illinois on 9 August 1942, Jack made his name as a drummer, pianist and composer within the jazz world, working with the likes of Freddie Hubbard, Keith Jarrett, Sonny Rollins, Miles Davis and Joe Henderson, among others. Jack did not record for Motown, nor was he actually signed to CTI, but he was equally billed alongside Freddie Hubbard and Stanley Turrentine on their **In Concert Volume 2** album issued on CTI in 1974, along with Ron Carter, Herbie Hancock and Eric Gale.

ALBUM: IN CONCERT VOLUME TWO (1975)

THE DELLS

Several friends at the Thornton Township High School in Harvey, Illinois formed themselves into The El-Rays in 1952, with Johnny Funches (born in Chicago, Illinois on 13 July 1935), Marvin Junior (born in Harrell, Arkansas on 31 January 1936), Laverne Allison (born in Chicago on 22 June 1936), Mickey McGill (born in Chicago in 17 February 1937), Lucius McGill (born in Chicago in 1935) and Chuck Barksdale (born in Chicago on 11 January 1935) the initial members. Lucius McGill left the group soon after, with the remaining members picking up a recording deal from Checker Records, although when this was unsuccessful they changed name to The Dells in 1955.

Signing with Vee-Jay they scored a major hit with *Oh What A Nite,* which hit #4 R&B in 1956 and sold over a million copies. A follow-up hit proved somewhat elusive, matters not helped when the group was forced into a temporary lull following a serious car accident in 1958. They regrouped in 1961, with Johnny Carter (born in Chicago on 2 June 1934), formerly of The Flamingos replacing Johnny Funches. This new line-up would eventually return to the charts in 1965 when *Stay In My Corner* hit #23 R&B and bubbled under the pop chart at #122. The Dells left Vee-Jay for

Cadet in 1967 and scored nearly thirty R&B hits over the next ten years. Both *Oh What A Nite* and *Stay In My Corner* were included on the compilation album **Hits From The Legendary Vee-Jay Records** issued by Motown on CD in November 1986. Funches died from emphysema on 23 January 1998. Johnny Carter died from lung cancer on 21 August 2009. Marvin Junior died from kidney failure on 29 May 2013.

MICHAEL DENTON

Alongside Berry Gordy, one of the major movers on the Detroit music scene was Harry Balk, who during the sixties ran the Inferno and Impact record labels and would have Mitch Ryder & The Detroit Wheels under contract, with The Wheels having a couple of singles released under the Motown umbrella. Earlier in the decade Harry had first come into contact with Mickey Denton, a young singer brought to his attention by manager John Brooks.

Born Gasper Badalamenti in Detroit, Michigan on 6 August 1942 Mickey signed a management contract with Brooks at the age of 17, with Brooks also coming up with the rather more manageable stage name. Whilst Harry Balk was particularly looking for singers who wrote their own songs when he auditioned Mickey in 1961, he was taken enough with the voice to take a chance. Mickey thus joined a stable of artists that included Del Shannon and Johnny & The Hurricanes at Bigtop Records and recorded several singles, none of which charted.

The rest of the decade was spent hopping from label to label in search of that elusive hit, including Amy, World Artists and Impact. The closest he came to a hit was with *One (Is The Loneliest Number)*, which Mickey recorded but couldn't get released as Impact was in the process of being sold to Motown; by the time the deal was done, Three Dog Night had also done the song and taken it to number one.

Mickey also tried to get his manager and label head to agree to him recording *Easy To Be Hard* and *Eli's Coming*, both of which were eventually recorded by Three Dog Night and became big hits!

"After that, I don't think I had another song played in Detroit except for one, and that was only because of who the songwriter was, and that was on the Rare Earth label from Motown. They released one single on me [as Michael Denton] because Ron Miller wrote the song, *Just Another Morning*, but it got played only on the black stations, and not on the white stations. And the flipside was called *Arma' Geden* and produced by Tom Baird. There were some things done at Motown that were shelved. I think *I'm Sticking With You* and *Little Egypt* we did while at Impact, those never got out. But at Motown, we recorded *Didn't We* the Jimmy Webb song, with a huge 32-piece orchestra. It was the flipside of *MacArthur Park* which went to something like #4 in July of 1968. Lots of people ended up recording *Didn't We* but we were playing the Richard Harris version."

Having had no success as a solo performer, Mickey moved to New York to put together a band called New York Express that would record an album for Atlantic's Cherie imprint. New York Express would also remain hitless, but that didn't greatly worry Mickey.

"I was very successful. I was a performer for 35 years and made money without a hit record. Now how many people can say that?"

PAUL DESMOND

Best known for his work with Dave Brubeck, Paul was an accomplished saxophonist, songwriter and arranger as well as possessor of a unique brand of humour. Born Paul Emil Breitenfeld in San Francisco, California on 25 November 1924, he played the violin as a child (even though his father expressly forbade him) before switching to the clarinet whilst at high school. He finally concentrated on the saxophone at San Francisco State College, and joined the Army band when he was drafted. It was whilst still serving during the Second World War (although his unit was never involved in combat) that he first met Dave Brubeck, linking up again in 1951 in the Dave Brubeck Quartet. The quartet would remain a popular staple on the jazz circuit for some sixteen years, scoring a major hit with *Take Five* (which Paul wrote) and numerous successful albums.

When Brubeck disbanded the quartet in 1967 in order to concentrate on composing, Paul signed a solo deal with Creed Taylor at A&M, following the A&R man when he left to form CTI. Paul would record five albums for CTI under his own name, including **Pure Desmond** in 1975, the only album issued via Motown (which would peak at #15 on the jazz chart). Paul would also appear on numerous other CTI albums by Jim Hall, Chet Baker and Don Sebesky and later recorded for Horizon Records. A known heavy drinker, when it was revealed he had contracted lung cancer (because of his equally heavy smoking) he declared himself happy that his liver had emerged unscathed, announcing, "Pristine, perfect. One of the great livers of our time. Awash with Dewar's and full of health." He died on 30 May 1977 at the age of 52.

ALBUM: PURE DESMOND (1975)

DETROIT 9000 (SOUNDTRACK)

Lamont Dozier co-wrote the theme to the film 'Detroit 9000' with Luchi De Jesus, with Laura Lee, who was signed to Holland-Dozier-Holland's Hot Wax label appearing in the opening scenes as a singer. Motown scheduled the soundtrack for April or May 1973 but subsequently pulled the release off the schedule. The film, meanwhile, has gone on to attain cult status, thanks largely to Quentin Tarantino's efforts.

THE DETROIT WHEELS

The Detroit Wheels had begun their career in the early 1960s when Jim McCarty (guitar), Earl Elliott (bass) and Johnny 'Bee' Badanjek (drums) began backing white singer William Levise, who regularly performed local black clubs such as The Village. Levise joined the band, adopting the name Billy Lee and the group became The Rivieras. After discovering another group with the same name, they elected upon another change, with Billy Lee becoming Mitch Ryder (courtesy of a phone book) and the band The Detroit Wheels. By then the group had got a recording contract thanks to producer Bob Crewe, who took them to New York to record their debut hit *Jenny Take A Ride*, a Top Ten hit in 1965.

A further six hits followed before Crewe engineered Ryder out of the group and into a solo career, with Badanjek fronting the Detroit Wheels and eventually signing with Harry Balk at Inferno Records. Their time with Motown would see two singles issued, *Linda Sue Dixon* (a song glorifying LSD) in April 1968 and *Think (About The Good Things)* in September the same year. Inferno was closed soon after this release, with what was left of The Detroit Wheels linking up with Mitch Ryder in 1969 in a new outfit called Detroit.

THE DEVASTATING AFFAIR

The only album The Devastating Affair recorded for Motown, **Devastating Affair Mountain** for the MoWest label was scheduled for release in September 1973 but shelved. Formed by vocalists Andrew Porter, Greg Wright, Harold Johnson, Karin Patterson and Olivia Foster, the group did see three singles hit the streets, *I Want To Be Humble* in January 1972 on MoWest (the first single released on the imprint) and two on Motown, *That's How It Was (Right From The Start)* in July 1973 and *You Don't Know (How Hard It Is To Make It)* in September 1974 (the latter track also appeared on the Magic Disco Machine album **Disc-O-Tech**). Whilst their own recording career proved difficult to get off the ground, the group was much in demand as backing singers, most notably on Diana Ross' **Everything Is Everything** album and a number of her duets with Marvin Gaye. Harold Johnson later became a member of another Motown act, Finished Touch.

HANK & CAROL DIAMOND

Husband and wife pair Hank and Carol Diamond released one single on the Workshop Jazz label, *Exodus* (the theme to the film of the same name) backed with *I Remember You*, issued in May 1962. They apparently recorded an album's worth of material that never saw the light of day. Hank later recorded for World Pacific (his *Soul Sauce* from 1966 was extremely popular on the Northern Soul scene) and the pair also performed jazz clubs for several years. Following Hank's death Carol continued her singing career, eventually forming a duo with her daughter Angel.

JOEL DIAMOND

A long term music industry veteran, Joel was born in Passaic, New Jersey on 20 February 1943 and headed music publishers MRC Music, working on songs such as *This Girl Is A Woman Now, Na Na Hey Hey* and *I'm Gonna Make You Love Me* (the latter a hit for The Supremes and The Temptations). Joel would later work for CBS Music Publishing, where he further improved his list of contacts among artists, manager, producers and record company heads, culminating in an eventual offer from Polygram to establish his own label, Silver Blue Records, also setting up his own publishing and production company at the same time. After several hits with other artists Joel produced his own albums, first through Columbia and then Casablanca before linking with Motown for a one-off single in 1981, *Theme From Raging Bull* which would make #82 on the pop charts in February.

DIAMOND AWARDS

Motown was one of the few major record companies not a member of the RIAA (the Recording Industry Association of America) throughout the 1960s and much of the 70s. Much of the reason for this was Motown's refusal to allow any outside organisation to undertake audits of its accounts, so any sales awards given to its artists during this period were figures that Motown claimed to have sold; there was no way of confirming these figures. Motown did hold their own ceremonies for publicity purposes, with the Jackson 5's first three singles all being granted platinum status (sales of over one million copies). On another occasion, they held a ceremony for Marvin Gaye and presented him with a gold single award – whereas the RIAA award used a proper metallic disc, Motown's was merely an ordinary single spray painted gold, so when Marvin Gaye got home and played the awarded disc, he discovered it to be a Supremes record!

Motown became a member of the RIAA in 1976; in 1999 RIAA introduced the Diamond Award to signify albums that sold a minimum of ten million copies in the United States. To date, two Motown albums have qualified for a Diamond Award; Lionel Richie's **Can't Slow Down**, and Stevie Wonder's **Songs In The Key Of Life**. It should be noted, however, that RIAA's certification policy allows for each disc or record in a multi-disc set or from the vinyl era to be counted, so although **Songs In The Key Of Life** is granted Diamond status, as a double album its actual sales are only five million. In later years Boyz II Men's **II** would join the ranks of Motown Diamond albums with sales of twelve million copies.

DIANA – DIANA ROSS [ALBUM]

There was no hotter songwriting or production team in 1979 than Bernard Edwards and Nile Rodgers, collectively known as Chic. Unknown barely two years previously, a succession of hits under their own name (*Le Freak* and *Good Times* had topped both the pop and R&B charts) and outside productions on Sister Sledge (*He's The Greatest Dancer* and *We Are Family* had been R&B chart toppers) and Norma Jean Wright (*Saturday*) had elevated them into the men with the Midas touch.

More importantly, they had shown that whilst they could come up with the goods on singles, their expertise carried over to the album market, where their productions were shifting millions of copies. It was noted, however, that their expertise extended to having a degree of control over virtually every aspect of a recording, even down to ideas for the cover, the order in which singles would be released and so on. Sister Sledge, who had not even cracked the Top 30 of the R&B singles chart prior to linking up with Bernard and Nile, were happy to hand over responsibility and reaped the rewards, with their **We Are Family** album selling a million and hitting #3 on the pop chart. Norma Jean, or perhaps her record label Bearsville were not quite so pliant; **Norma Jean** stalled at #134.

By comparison, Diana Ross' career was in the doldrums; her last Top Ten album had been in 1976 and even a reunion with Ashford and Simpson on **The Boss** had not been as successful as might have been hoped. According to legend, it was one of Diana's children who turned her on to Chic, playing either Chic or Sister Sledge virtually non-stop and alerting their mother of the possibilities of working with the two producers. It was not to be a match made in heaven, although the initial discussions were cordial and Bernard and Nile fully understood that what Diana was looking for was something of a new sound, one that would be unlike any of her previous Motown recordings.

"Diana Ross was the first star I ever worked with," Nile later related, "the first star I ever was able to do what I was suggesting they [Atlantic Records] might do with the Rolling Stones or Bette Midler, which was basically, 'Diana, we've got you covered. We are going to write every song, we're going to do everything and we are going to create the story.'"

To this end Bernard and Nile set about writing material with Diana specifically in mind, covering ballads and up-tempo material in equal measure.

"The album **diana**, which is her biggest-selling album ever, is basically the biography of Diana Ross. We interviewed her for a couple of days and then wrote songs about Diana Ross, about the things she wanted to do, about the things in her life, the unresolved things, the things that she was making us feel. If we were filmmakers it would have been a film. If we were magazine writers and newspaper writers it would have been an article. Because we are composers it wound up being a record."

The recordings sessions themselves were not without difficulties, with the producers learning too late in the day that Diana Ross was not someone you told directly they were singing flat; her response had been to walk out of the studio and fly to the south of France, disrupting the recording for several months! After ironing out their differences, the team re-assembled to complete the sessions, with Bernard and Nile then moving on to the mixing stage. Eventually, the work done to their satisfaction, they sent the tapes over to

Motown. Unfortunately, the finished album was *not* to Diana Ross' satisfaction!

"When I first listened to the tapes they sounded pretty much like Chic or Sister Sledge. In fact, they were a bit too disco and that's not what's happening today. You have to remember that both Nile and Bernard have only been in the industry for two or three years and in re-mixing the album I felt that I may be able to put a little of Diana Ross into the product. In many cases all I've done is change some of the musical interludes."

Whatever Diana and her team had done did not meet with the approval of Chic, resulting in something of a war of words between the two camps. Bernard Edwards set out their opposition to the end result.

"We're definitely not happy with the album. When we finished it and turned it in, Diana wasn't happy with her vocals. So, she almost went for a re-mix, and still felt her voice was too thin. So we gave her the tapes to do what she felt she wanted and despite the fact that it shouldn't have been done contractually, another re-mix was done. The album was on the streets before we had even heard it. We started to take some kind of legal action to have the album stopped but we decided against it. Apparently, Diana loves it so we thought we would just sit back and see what happens. If we made a mistake, it was in giving the tapes away so that changes could be made, but you live and learn, and we've definitely learned."

Time proved to be something of a great healer. Nile Rodgers had been as aghast as his partner Bernard when he first heard the remix, even intending taking up the matter directly with Diana.

"I was shocked when they finally sent the songs to me again. I was furious and got on the phone right away and called Motown. I was asked to listen to the album and then talk to Diana. I calmed down and listened to it about ten times. Then, I had to say, hey, I know where they're coming from. I understand what they're doing. But, initially, I was not prepared for that kind of shock."

The remix was done by Diana and Motown engineer/producer Russ Terrana and the finished album is certainly a lot sparser than previous Edwards-Rodgers productions. It was said that the producers were so furious with the eventual mix they asked for their names to be removed from the album, but copies had already gone out and it was too late. Despite the verbal battle and the issues either side may have had, the one thing that cannot be ignored is that the album ended up being the most successful solo album of Diana Ross' career!

The publicity may have been temporarily bad, but it did not hinder the album's rise up the charts – an R&B chart topper, a #2 hit on the pop chart (it proved unable to dislodge Barbra Streisand's **Guilty** off the summit) and a UK placing of #12 made this a welcome return to chart form. In addition, of the three tracks lifted as singles, *Upside Down* topped both pop and R&B charts domestically and reached #2 in the UK, *I'm Coming Out* made the Top Ten pop and R&B (#13 in the UK) and *My Old Piano* was another UK top ten success.

All told, **diana** would go on to sell a reported ten million copies worldwide, including more than a million copies in both the US and the UK. In 2003, the public was given the chance to hear what all the fuss was about – Universal released a deluxe double CD edition that contained the album as it was originally released coupled with Bernard Edwards and Nile Rodgers original mixes - we all definitely learned something.

DIANA AND MARVIN - DIANA & MARVIN [ALBUM]

Although this appears to be an album of duets performed by Diana Ross and Marvin Gaye, overseen by Ashford & Simpson (one track), Berry Gordy (one track), Mark Davis and Margaret Gordy (one track), Bob Gaudio (one track) and Hal Davis (the remaining six tracks), apart from an early, aborted session, the two singers recorded their vocal parts separately.

Problems sprung up at that first session when Marvin arrived, supposedly stoned, and proceeded to light up the first of several joints, quickly turning the recording booth into a veritable fog of marijuana. This alarmed Diana, who was heavily pregnant with her second child, and when Marvin refused to extinguish it, she ran off to complain directly to Berry Gordy. Despite an appeal by Berry, Marvin refused to alter *his* way of getting through a session. Indeed, it has been suggested that Marvin's refusal to temper his behavior was done deliberately to annoy Berry Gordy, rather than Diana Ross, since Marvin felt Berry had been devoting so much time and attention to making Diana a star he had ignored other artists on the label. If that is the case, then Berry would get his own back at the end of the collaboration; after much negotiation, Berry apparently conceded that Marvin would get top billing on the album, only to switch the credit later on! Since Marvin expected to chain smoke copious amounts of marijuana at every session, it was eventually agreed to record the two stars separately and then paste them together to make it appear like an album of duets. They would also have to reconvene in order to pose for the pictures on the cover, but by then Diana had given birth and smoke clouds in the background would have been a bit of a giveaway!

Diana & Marvin proved infinitely more popular in Europe that it did in America, barely making the Top 30 in the US (it would peak at #26 on the pop chart, although it did find favour on the R&B listings, making #7), but becoming a Top Ten hit in the UK, peaking at #6. Three singles were released in the US, of which *You're A Special Part Of Me* became the biggest hit in peaking at #12 pop and #4 R&B. It says much about the musical differences between the two sides of the Atlantic that although this track was released in the UK, Tamla Motown had doubts about its ability to make a decent dent in the charts and hastily arranged for a solo Diana single, *All Of My Life* to be released in time for Diana's forthcoming UK tour. Once Diana had been and gone, Tamla Motown returned to the duets album and pulled off *You Are Everything*, originally recorded by The Stylistics on Avco. Since The Stylistics version had not been a hit in the UK, Diana and Marvin's version had the field to themselves, resulting in a #5 hit, with the follow-up another Thom Bell and Linda Creed composition on The Stylistics, *Stop, Look, Listen (To Your Heart)*, which would make #25.

An attempt to produce another UK hit out of *My Mistake (Was To Love You)* turned out to be a mistake, but since the album had already attained gold status, pretty much every possible sale had been wrung from the project.

DIANA ROSS – DIANA ROSS [ALBUM]

A lot of thought and attention may have gone into the decision to spin Diana Ross out of The Supremes and into a solo career, but by the time 1975 came around, it hadn't quite panned out as expected. There were occasional bursts of chart glory, plus the positive publicity gained from her performance in 'Lady Sings The Blues', but sustained success had proved elusive. There was another number one hit to enjoy when the theme to the film 'Mahogany', *Do You Know Where You're Going To* was released in October 1975, around about the time Diana was recording what would become her second self titled album.

The key to the eventual success of the album, of course, would be the worldwide smash *Love Hangover*, but even then the momentum could have been lost, for Motown originally went with *I Thought It Took A Little Time (But Today I Fell In Love)* as the first single and only issued *Love Hangover* some two weeks later when they learned a note for note cover version was being readied for immediate release on The 5th Dimension. Thus Motown's hand was forced, but as Diana's version easily outstripped the cover, the situation was somewhat rectified.

Many purchasers of the album bought it purely for the full length seven minute plus *Love Hangover*, whilst the two number one hits (the 'Mahogany' theme was added as something of a bonus) were joined by *I Thought* and *One Love In My Lifetime*, also issued as a single and becoming a #25 pop and #10 R&B hit. All of this helped shift the album, which would go on to become Diana's most successful since 1973, hitting #5 pop and #4 R&B and hitting #4 in the UK, where it would eventually attain gold status.

DIANA ROSS AND THE SUPREMES GREATEST HITS - DIANA ROSS & THE SUPREMES [ALBUM]

The version of this album released in the US in August 1967 is a double album containing twenty tracks, packaged with an inner paneled fold out poster of Diana, Mary and Flo (although by the time the album was released Flo had ceased to be a member of The Supremes, having been fired and replaced by Cindy Birdson a month previously), which was designed to pull apart and then for each individual poster be framed. The album also contains sleeve notes by actress Carol Channing that were supposedly originally written for another album that was subsequently cancelled!

The version of the album released in the UK in January 1968, which has the same front cover, was a single disc containing sixteen tracks. Irrespective of the territory or the packaging, the result was a smash, topping the chart in the US for five weeks and the UK for three. It would also head the R&B chart for twelve weeks in a row. It would thus become only the second greatest hits compilation to top the US chart (after Johnny Mathis) and the second double album set to have achieved the feat (after Judy Garland).

DIANA ROSS & THE SUPREMES JOIN THE TEMPTATIONS - DIANA ROSS & THE SUPREMES & THE TEMPTATIONS [ALBUM]

By 1968, a collaborative album between Motown's two flagship acts, The Supremes and The Temptations made sense, not least because it would divert attention away from the fact that The Supremes were no longer recording with HDH.

Instead, over the course of four months, The Supremes and The Temptations gathered at studios in Detroit (both Hitsville and the newly acquired Golden World studio) and Los Angeles under the guidance of Frank Wilson and Nickolas Ashford to record eleven tracks, most of which were drawn from the Jobete catalogue.

Among the exceptions was *I'm Gonna Make You Love Me*, written by Kenny Gamble, Jerry Williams and Jerry Ross, with Kenny Gamble later to set up Philadelphia International with Leon Huff, a label that would rival Motown during the 1970s, whilst Jerry Ross would spend some time at Motown recording a number of projects.

The album marked the first recorded appearance of Dennis Edwards as a Temptation following his replacing David Ruffin (somewhat late in the day as far as the recording sessions were concerned, resulting in David's original vocals being erased and replaced by Dennis'), but he, like the rest of his group, got little chance to shine as the album featured Diana singing lead on every track accompanied by one or two of The Temptations.

Radio play on *I'm Gonna Make You Love Me* from advance promo copies eventually dictated that be the first single lifted, with the album being released in November 1968 and rising to the top of the R&B chart and #2 pop. It did even better in the UK, knocking The Seekers of the summit and spending four weeks at #1, the first and only time The Temptations would top the British charts and a second chart topper for Diana Ross & The Supremes.

DIANA ROSS AND THE SUPREMES 20 GOLDEN GREATS - DIANA ROSS & THE SUPREMES [ALBUM]

Compiled in the UK and sold throughout Europe, **20 Golden Greats** was actually eighteen hit singles and two tracks that had not been UK hits in *My World Is Empty Without You* and *Love Is Like An Itching In My Heart*, the tracks culled from the years 1964 to 1969. With the aid of a distinctive cover (basically three lips in front of three microphones!) and an extensive television advertising campaign, the album became a major seller, topping the UK chart for seven straight weeks.

This came at a time when the British charts were awash with nostalgia, with various greatest hits packages by The Shadows, Johnny Mathis, Connie Francis, Elvis Presley (whose **40 Greatest Hits** was dethroned by Diana Ross & The Supremes) and then Cliff Richard & The Shadows taking their turn at the top of the chart, all aided by equally extensive and expensive television campaigns. According to the many rock orientated magazines of the time, the most successful (doubtful) and groundbreaking (debatable) album of 1977 was by The Sex Pistols, which would knock Cliff Richard off the top of the chart (now that was at least ironic!), but come the end of December, Diana Ross & The Supremes' **20 Golden Greats** was only just behind Abba's **Arrival** as the best selling album of the year.

DIANA ROSS PRESENTS THE JACKSON 5 – THE JACKSON 5 [ALBUM]

There are two versions of how The Jackson 5 came to sign for Motown – the official version was that Diana Ross had seen them perform at a benefit concert in Gary, Indiana for Mayor Richard Hatcher and went and told Berry Gordy that this was an act he *had* to sign.

The true version, which eventually emerged years later, is that it was Gladys Knight and Bobby Taylor (lead singer of The Vancouvers) who were most vociferous in singing the young group's praises around Hitsville, with Bobby even putting them up on the floor of his apartment the night before their audition. Having got them in through the door of Motown, Bobby was at least given an opportunity to work with them on material that would eventually form the bulk of their debut album. Given little or no new material with which to work, Bobby plucked several tracks from the Jobete catalogue, including *Standing In The Shadows Of Love, My Cherie Amour, Who's Lovin' You* (Michael's version of this is widely reckoned to be the definitive version of the song, and the loudest voice in praise belongs to Smokey Robinson, who wrote and originally recorded it), *Chained, (I Know) I'm Losing You* and *Born To Love*. Outside of Jobete, Bobby took The Delfonics' *Can You Remember*, Sly Stone's *Stand,* a track from the group's Steeltown days in *You've Changed* and the oddball *Zip-A-Dee-Doo-Dah*.

It was late summer when Berry took his first listen at what had been recorded and realised that there wasn't a standout track that could be released as a single, and so just as he had done previously with Diana Ross and The Supremes, Berry decided it was time for a hands-on approach. He assembled a group of songwriters, which would be christened The Corporation, appropriated a song they had been working on for Gladys Knight & The Pips, which would become *I Want You Back*, and added it alongside another Corporation composition in *Nobody* on the eventual album.

With Diana Ross' endorsement on the front and notes on the back **Diana Ross Presents The Jackson 5** already stood a good chance of being successful, but with *I Want You Back* topping the pop charts, it became a near-on certainty. The album would eventually top the R&B chart and peak at #5 pop, whilst in the UK it still managed a respectable #16. The fact that the rest of the album sounded little like the *I Want You Back* single did not appear to matter, only sales, and in that respect the album worked.

DICKEY & THE POSEIDONS

A studio creation of producers and song writers Mel Larson and Jerry Marcellino with arranger James Carmichael, the single *Where Were You When The Ship Went Down* backed with *Tidal Wave* was released in 1974 in a few territories without success. In Italy the single was released in a picture sleeve of a girl in a bikini; they had obviously taken the titles quite literally!

DIFFERENT SHADES OF BROWN

Formed in Springfield, Ohio in 1969, Different Shades Of Brown was originally a quintet, joined Motown as a quartet and left as a trio. The original group consisted of Nate Newsome (born on 1 November 1944), Ronald Logan (born on 12 May 1947), Steven Warfield (born on 28 June 1950), James Griffiths and Trent Smith. Smith left the group before they'd even acquired a name, with Marvin Sutton (born on 13 January 1950) his eventual replacement.

After much practice they had formulated a stage routine, enough to get them a support slot with The Dells in 1971, and word of mouth soon had their praises being sung at Motown, most notably by producer Clay McMurray. They signed in 1972 (by which time Griffiths had left) and released their debut single *Label Me Love* on the Tamla label in May 1972, although soon after the recording was finished, Ronald Logan left and was replaced by Nate Alexander (born on 13 November 1945).

By then Motown had also left Detroit, requiring the group to travel to Los Angeles for recording sessions, although their second single *When The Hurt Is Put Back On You*, released on the Motown label in July 1973 was a left over from their Hitsville recordings. Sutton left the group just before they requested a termination of their contract and Different Shades Of Brown disbanded soon after. Nate Newsome and Marvin later linked up with Ellsworth Senior and Mike Harris in an outfit called The Lovemakers who recorded a couple of sides for Island, with the producer none other than Clay McMurray.

VINCENT DiMIRCO

A Puerto Rican singer and songwriter based in New York, Vincent's main claim to fame is writing *Up The Ladder To The Roof*, which would become The Supremes' first hit after the departure of Diana Ross for a solo career. Vincent submitted the song to Motown with a view to recording it himself, but producer Frank Wilson felt it would sit better with a female group. Vincent did get to play guitar on The Supremes version, however.

He wrote a small number of other songs whilst at Motown, including *Once I Have You I Will Never Let You Go* and *There's A Place We'd Like To Know* (recorded by The Originals), *I Almost Had Her (But She Got Away)* (The Four Tops), *Take Me Clear From Here* (David Ruffin and later Edwin Starr) and *Thank Him For Today* (The Supremes), although *Up The Ladder To The Roof* was the only one released as a single. In 1971 Vincent finally got his own recording session with Norman Whitfield, with *I Can Make It Alone* backed with *Come Clean* eventually being released on Rare Earth in April 1972, although the artist credit carried the slightly modified name of Vincent DiMarco.

THE DING DONGS

Gimme Dat Ding, written by Albert Hammond and Mike Hazelwood, proved to be a transatlantic success for The Pipkins (a vocal duo formed by Tony Burrows, the leading British session singer of the day, and songwriter Roger Greenaway), hitting the Top Ten. It also prompted a cover version by The Ding Dongs that was scheduled for release in April 1970 (a month after The Pipkins had reached the Top Ten in the UK, but before its release in the US) but was subsequently shelved.

The Ding Dongs did, however, release an album in July 1970 entitled **Gimme Dat Ding**, something of a ragtime outing produced by Tom King (formerly of The Outsiders) and arranged by David Van De Pitte. Whilst the suppliers of the furniture were credited on the album sleeve, The Ding Dongs were not, but it is most likely to have been Bobby Darin, who had recorded as

The Ding Dongs in 1958 (he released a single under that moniker for Brunswick at a time he was under contract to Atlantic) and had recently joined Motown as an artist.
ALBUM: GIMME DAT DING AND OTHER DINGS (1970)

DION & THE BELMONTS

American male singer Dion Francis DiMucci was born in The Bronx, New York on 18 July 1939 and made his first recordings in 1957. The following year he formed The Belmonts (named after Belmont Avenue in the Bronx), enlisting Angelo D'Aleo (born in The Bronx on 3 February 1940), Fred Milano (born in The Bronx on 22 August 1939) and Carlo Mastrangelo (born in The Bronx on 5 October 1938). The group enjoyed some nine major hits, most notably with *A Teenager In Love* and *Where Or When* before Dion went solo in 1960, topping the chart with *Runaround Sue* in 1961 (it peaked at #11 in the UK) and coming close with *The Wanderer* (it hit #2 US and #10 in the UK). *I Wonder Why,* their first hit in 1958 appeared on the 'Christine' soundtrack in November 1983, *Runaround Sue* appeared on 'The Flamingo Kid' soundtrack in December 1984. Fred Milano died from lung cancer on 1 January 2012.

DISCO STAN

Stanton Scott Sheppard linked with fellow writer and producer Ron Rancifer as Disco Stan for the Prodigal single *Funky Cocktail*, released in April 1976. After the single flopped, Sheppard would become a member of Motown group Flavor, later linking with Tony Lane to form Sheppard Lane Music and manage DJ Quik. Ron Rancifer meanwhile became part of Smokey Robinson's backing group and a noted songwriter around Motown, penning *Only You* for Quiet Storm.

DIVINITY RECORDS

Both Tamla and Motown had seen gospel material released in their early days, prompting Berry Gordy to set up a dedicated gospel label in July 1962 and appointing George Fowler to run it. Given the name Divinity, it would release four singles (two by The Wright Specials and one apiece by The Gospel Stars and The Burnadettes) before being shuttered in May 1963. One further single by Liz Lands was shelved, although the artist would release two singles on Gordy.

THE DIXIE CUPS

The Dixie Cups was formed in New Orleans, Louisiana in 1963 by Barbara Ann Hawkins (born in New Orleans on 23 October 1943), Rosa Lee Hawkins (born in New Orleans on 24 September 1944) and their cousin Joan Marie Johnson (born in New Orleans on 15 January 1945), as The Meltones and were discovered by Joe Jones performing at a high school talent show. Jones took them to Jerry Leiber and Mike Stoller's Red Bird label where they recorded their debut hit *The Chapel Of Love*, despite the fact that both the Ronettes and the Crystals had failed to have hits with the song. The Dixie Cups' version hit #1 in America (although the girls claim they never saw any money other than a couple of hundred dollars as a result of the hit) and had a number of other, minor hits, including *You Should Have Seen The Way He Looked At Me* (#39 in 1964). Both *The Chapel Of Love* and *You Should Have Seen* featured on the soundtrack to the documentary film 'Girl Groups: The Story Of A Sound' released in November 1983.

DO I DO – STEVIE WONDER [SINGLE]

One of four new compositions Stevie put on his career retrospective **Original Musiquarium I** in 1982, *Do I Do* was the second single lifted from the album, after *That Girl*. On the album, *Do I Do* is a ten minute plus musical romp mixing jazz with R&B, with bebop jazz trumpeter Dizzy Gillespie the featured musician on the track. Unfortunately, Dizzy's solo was removed from the single edit (as was Stevie rapping towards the end), although the full length version can be heard on the 12" single (released in Europe only).

Released on either side of the Atlantic in May 1982, it would hit #2 pop and #2 R&B in the US and peak at #10 in the UK. This chart success was reflected at the end of year Grammy Award nominations, with *Do I Do* picking up nominations in the Best R&B Song (along with Stevie's *That Girl*) and Best R&B Vocal Performance, Male categories, although for once Stevie came home empty handed, losing out to *Turn Turn Your Love Around* as Best R&B Song and former labelmate Marvin Gaye and *Sexual Healing* for Best Vocal Performance.

DO YOU LOVE ME – THE CONTOURS [SINGLE]

The competition between Berry Gordy and Smokey Robinson to come up with the songs that would keep Motown at the forefront showed no sign of abating during 1962; if anything it became more intense. The succession of hits pouring from Smokey's pen showed he had learned well from his teacher, but Berry could often be relied upon to use his greater experience to good effect when it mattered. In June 1962, Berry bounced right back with *Do You Love Me*.

"Getting the concept for this song was easy. I just thought back to the days when I could never get girls I really liked because I couldn't dance. It took me about two hours to write it. But recording it was a little more complicated."

The complication was down to one man, James Jamerson, who used the recording session to show just how good a jazz musician he was, much to the chagrin of Berry Gordy, who didn't want jazz licks in what was essentially a dance record. Eventually, after several retakes, the threat of sacking and several outbursts, Berry got the instrumental track down to his liking.

After the musicians left the studio, Berry added his own voice to make a demo. The initial version was good enough to release as it was but Berry had other ideas, selecting it as one for The Temptations, still then looking for a major hit. Unfortunately, on the day of the scheduled session The Temptations were nowhere to be found (in a later interview, Melvin Franklin of The Temptations stated that they were at a local church, where they'd gone to watch The Dixie Hummingbirds, The Harmonizing Four and The Swan Silvertones), so Berry packed The Contours into the studio, mainly because lead singer Billy Gordon had a vocal style reminiscent of Berry's.

By being in the right place at the right time, The Contours got their big break, with *Do You Love Me* going on to become a #1 R&B and #3 pop hit at much the same time the group was heading out onto the road with the first Motortown Revue. In fact, their performances on the Revue proved one thing; The Contours *could* dance, and dance very well, with their energetic routines one of the highlights of the show.

Do You Love Me was also released in the UK, being assigned the catalogue number CBA 1763 on the Oriole American label and issued in September 1962. It was perhaps too raucous for British tastes and failed to chart, although the song itself became popular among the numerous British beat groups that sprung up towards the end of the year.

One of these was Faron's Flamingos, who also recorded for Oriole and released a version of *Do You Love Me* in May 1963, again without success, although this may have been because the publishing company of the B-side, Leeds Music, pushed their track *See If She Cares*. Whilst touring the UK with several other beat groups, one expressed an interest in *Do You Love Me* and asked Faron's Flamingo's leader, William 'Faron' Ruffley, for a copy of the lyrics. Faron wrote them out by hand and gave them to Brian Poole, who learned the song and then recorded a version with The Tremeloes. Released as a follow-up to their Top Ten hit *Twist And Shout*, it would hit the top of the charts on 10 October 1963, despite the presence of versions by The Dave Clark Five (who hit #30), Frank Bacon & The Baconeers, The Moonrakers and Ray Pilgrim out on the market at the same time.

The song would provide British group Deep Feeling with a #34 hit in 1970, Duke Baysee reached #46 in 1995 and Mademoiselle #56 in 2001. The Contours, meanwhile, were to enjoy a hit with *Do You Love Me* all over again in 1988 after the track had been featured in the hit film 'Dirty Dancing', hitting #11 on the Billboard Hot 100 in June 1988 with exactly the same version that had been a hit in 1962.

ROBERT DOBYNE

Born in Brent and raised in Bessemer, Alabama, Robert Dobyne was the former lead singer with The Artistics and lead vocalist on The Hit Pack's only Motown outing. Robert also recorded a number of sides as a solo artist, but for some reason these were not released at the time, eventually appearing some forty five years later as part of the **Cellarful Of Motown** series (*All I Need Is A Chance*, an apt title, appeared on Volume 4). Robert wrote or co-wrote a number of songs that were covered by others at Motown, most notably *Say You* (The Monitors and The Temptations) and *Never Leave Your Baby's Side* (Martha & The Vandellas), but he had to leave Motown in order to pursue his own recording career, eventually turning up at Kama Sutra.

DOCTOR MY EYES – JACKSON 5 [SINGLE]

Just as they had done with Michael Jackson and *Ain't No Sunshine*, the staff at the Tamla Motown office in London kept a keen eye on what was happening on the charts around the world and most particularly in America. It was therefore noted that whilst composer Jackson Browne had enjoyed a major Top Ten US hit with *Doctor My Eyes*, the single had made no impact in the UK whatsoever. When a new version by The Jackson 5 turned up on the **Looking Through The Windows** album, a mental note to issue it at some point in the future was duly logged.

Whilst the title track became a success on both sides of the Atlantic, the UK office was unsure whether the American follow-up *Corner Of The Sky* was right for their market. Instead they held fire, releasing the seasonal single *Santa Claus Is Comin' To Town* (which would peak at #43) and readying *Doctor My Eyes* for release in February 1973. The ploy worked, with *Doctor My Eyes* returning the group to the Top Ten of the chart, peaking at #9 and becoming the sixth Top Ten hit of their career in Britain.

DR STRUT

Motown made something of a conscientious effort at getting into the jazz fusion market towards the end of the 1970s, signing the likes of Dr Strut and Ahmad Jamal in rapid succession. Dr Strut had been formed in 1977 as The Legendary Dynamic Groovadelics by Kevin Bassinson (keyboards), Tim Weston (guitar), Peter Freiberger (bass), David Woodford (flute and saxophone), Everett Bryson (percussion) and Claude Pepper (drums). They signed with Motown in 1979, with Berry Gordy, who apparently suggested their new name, calling them 'the flagship of the new jazz division'.

Their two albums for the label, an eponymous debut in May 1979 being followed by **Struttin** in February 1980 sold relatively well, with the first hitting #48 on the jazz chart and the second going a little further in peaking at #33. A third album was recorded, entitled **Soul Surgery**, but before it could be released Berry and Motown lost interest in jazz and Dr Strut left the label. The third album did appear in 1982, released on the Agharta/Canyon label.

ALBUMS: DR STRUT (1979), STRUTTIN' (1980)

DON'T LEAVE ME THIS WAY – THELMA HOUSTON [SINGLE]

It is somewhat ironic that it should be Hal Davis who helmed two of Motown's biggest disco hits of the mid-1970s, as he spent so much time in the studio, he could hardly have been fully aware of what was happening in the clubs! Yet the one thing that Hal had, better than almost anyone else at Motown at the time, was a real sense of how to make a song groove and bring out vocal performances that suited the songs in question. In May 1976, Diana Ross had taken *Love Hangover* to the top of the pop and R&B chart, and some nine months later, Thelma Houston would emulate that with *Don't Leave Me This Way*.

The song had first appeared on Harold Melvin & The Bluenotes' 1975 **Wake Up Everybody** album, but Philadelphia International had chosen to go with the title track and *Tell The World How I Feel About 'Cha Baby* as singles, with the former topping the R&B chart and making #12 pop. Most of the club's, however, had jumped on *Don't Leave Me This Way*, a seven and a half minute gem powered by Teddy Pendergrass' lead vocal.

Hal thought the song might be a good vehicle for Thelma Houston, an artist who was struggling to establish an identity within Motown. Gathering much the same core of musicians who had played on *Love Hangover*, Hal went for an even more obvious disco groove, running for 5.40 minutes. He had in mind doing an extended mix, but apparently ran into problems with the union representative present at the recording session!

"We were doing the session and it was three minutes before six. The union man came in and told us we only had three minutes. We didn't have a rehearsal or anything, we just did it. It was so hot that I called Berry and woke him up. He wasn't feeling too well and was mad that I woke him up, but I took it over to his house to play it for him. He told me 'It better be good, or you're fired.' But as I played it for him I saw his face light up."

Released in the US in December 1976, by February it was similarly lighting up the top of the pop and R&B chart, spending a week at the summit of both charts. The record's release in the UK was delayed until January 1977, giving CBS (Philadelphia International's UK licensee) time to ready the release of Harold Melvin & The Bluenotes original. Faced with a choice, the British public sided slightly with the original, pushing it to #5 on the chart whilst Thelma had to settle for a final placing of #13 – one wonders how well the song would have done if there had been only one version out at the time, especially as nearly ten years later, The Communards took it all the way to the top with a hi-energy treatment.

Thelma might have lost the race for UK chart honours but was more than adequately compensated when the Grammy Awards were announced, with *Don't Leave Me This Way* winning Thelma the trophy for Best R&B Vocal Performance, Female. The song's writers, Kenny Gamble and Leon Huff also picked up a nomination for Best Rhythm & Blues Song; whilst they didn't win, they sent a heartfelt letter of thanks to Hal Davis that took pride of place in his office at Motown. And this was a man whose office was virtually decorated with awards and nominations, the fruits of a lengthy career in music. Whilst Thelma never hit the same heights again, *Don't Leave Me This Way* is as good a legacy as any, with a re-recording making the Top 40 of the UK charts in 1995 (it peaked at #35).

DON'T MESS WITH BILL – THE MARVELETTES [SINGLE]

Without a Top Ten pop hit to their name since 1962, in 1966 The Marvelettes were temporarily switched from their usual writing and production team to none other than Smokey Robinson. Written especially with Wanda Young in mind, which would require switching the usual lead singer within the group, Smokey would later deny the title was aimed at his erstwhile writing and production rivals; it was just a name that fitted with the stanza of the song. Irrespective of how the title came about, *Don't Mess With Bill* returned The Marvelettes to the upper reaches of the chart, hitting #7 pop and #3 R&B, their best performance since topping the chart first time out in 1961.

NORMA DONALDSON

Born in New York on 8 July 1928, Norma made her name as an actress, appearing in a number of small roles on television and in film before landing the role with which she is best known, that of Dr Pauline Ravelle in the long running television drama 'General Hospital'. Prior to this, Norma made sporadic appearances on Broadway, commencing in 1959 with a role in 'Jamaica' and culminating with the role of Miss Adelaide in the 1976 revival of 'Guys And Dolls'. Norma died on 22 November 1994 in Los Angeles at the age of 66.

DONOVAN BUILDING

Whilst Motown's building on West Grand Boulevard is an iconic image of the label, in 1968 Berry Gordy moved the business operation to the Donovan Building on Woodward. Designed by Albert Kahn, the building opened in 1923 with shops on the ground floor and various offices renting the upper ten floors. Several reasons have been floated for the move, ranging from a panic reaction to the Detroit riots of 1967, simply having outgrown the base at West Grand Boulevard despite having bought up several of the houses through to wishing to present a much more professional image.

One of Hitsville's attractions (and probably the reason why it has become something of a Mecca for tourists ever since) is its old-world charm – you can imagine the artists gathering in the kitchens for a meal before and after recording sessions, and you can also imagine scores of would-be singers hanging around outside praying and hoping that they might get the opportunity to make a pitch to a writer or producer on their way in.

The Donovan Building by comparison was the complete opposite, with CCTV covering the entrance, visitors having to be screened before admittance and other security measures – no one could just walk up to the door and come in without an invite. Even the recording artists had to have an identity card to get in and out! Yet even Berry Gordy did most of his business at a suite at the Pontchartrain Hotel in the city. The Donovan Building, dubbed the Motown Center whilst the record label was in residence, became derelict when Motown moved operations to the West Coast and despite several plans to revamp the building or build a new centre in its place, with each passing year the building became more and more of an eyesore. So much so that when Detroit was awarded the right to host the 2006 Super Bowl, the then Mayor Kwayme Kilpatrick approved plans for its immediate demolition in order to provide sufficient car parking space.

Whilst no recordings ever took place at the Donovan Building, it was still a relatively important hub within the Motown machine, as evidenced by the recording sheets and other items of considerable interest that flew into the streets once the giant demolition balls started rolling.

DOROTHY, OMA & ZELPHA

Female vocal trio Dorothy, Oma & Zelpha released one single on Hugh Masekela's Chisa label in 1969, *Gonna Put It On Your Mind* backed with *Henry Blake*. Formed by Dorothy Berry (the former wife of songwriter Richard Berry), Oma Heard and Zelpha Crawford (previously a member of The Wooden Nickels), they had established a reputation as backing singers in Los Angeles prior to their only single outing. Oma had previously been signed to the V.I.P. label and released a solo single in 1964 (subsequently withdrawn) as well as recording a number of unreleased duets with Marvin Gaye.

RONNIE DOVE

Born in Herndon, Virginia on 7 September 1935 Ronnie began his musical career singing in clubs in Baltimore. There he formed a backing group, The Belltones, and spent some four years touring the area and working the clubs before finally paying for their own debut recording, *Lover Boy* on Dove Records. Ronnie would eventually drop The Belltones and it was as a solo performer that he signed with Diamond Records in 1964, going on to register twenty pop hits over the next five years, with *One Kiss For Old Times' Sake* and *Right Or Wrong*, making #14 pop (*Right Or Wrong* also crossed over to the top five of Cashbox' R&B chart).

By 1971 his hit career on the pop charts was at an end and Ronnie was recording more country repertoire, firstly for Decca and then for a succession of small and smaller labels as the years progressed.

He joined Melodyland at the tail end of 1974, with his debut single *Please Come To Nashville* being released the following February. Ronnie would record four singles for the label before switching to the Hitsville label for a further two singles. He was then part of the block of artist absorbed into the MC label, with Ronnie recording two albums during the course of 1977, **New Old-Fashioned Love** and **Livin' In The Country** (both exist as promotional copies but are unlikely to have been commercially released). His only MC single outing, *Angel In Your Eyes (Brings Out The Devil In Me)* backed with *Songs We Sang As Children* was issued in August 1978 to little or no fanfare and Ronnie continued his musical travels, later opening his own club in Baltimore where he was a regular performer.

ALBUMS: NEW OLD-FASHIONED LOVE (1977), LIVIN' IN THE COUNTRY (1977)

THE DOWNBEATS

Michigan group The Downbeats consisted of Johnny Dawson, Robert Fleming and Cleo 'Duke' Miller, with Dawson and Fleming having previously been members of local groups The Sensations and The Five Emeralds. They signed with the Tamla label in late 1961, releasing one single the following February, *Your Baby's Back* coupled with *Request Of A Fool*. The Downbeats appear to have spent the next two or three years in limbo, with only a couple of recording sessions and no releases, with even a scheduled album in **Introducing The Downbeats** remaining unissued. However, two of the sessions, *You Say You Love Me*, in November 1963, and *Do You Know What I'm Talkin' About* in June 1964, were to have been coupled as a single for the V.I.P. label in early 1965, although the number allocated, V.I.P. 25007, had already been used for The Velvelettes' *Needle In A Haystack* in April 1964! All three of The Downbeats would eventually resurface in The Elgins with Saundra Mallett and not only record but register a number of hits on the V.I.P. label.

LAMONT DOZIER

All three of the most successful writing and production team within Motown attempted solo careers; one can but wonder how musical history would have panned out had any of them had even a modicum of sustained success.

Lamont Herbert Dozier was born in Detroit, Michigan on 16 June 1941 and grew up listening to his father's jazz records and classical music his aunt played on the piano and sang in the local Baptist gospel choir - this early schooling in different aspects of music was to serve Lamont well in his later professional career.

It was at McKenzie High School in 1955 that Lamont joined his first group, linking with Ty Hunter, Leon Ware, Gene Dyer and Kenny Johnson as The Counts, who later changed their name to The Romeos. After two years of local performances, The Romeos got their first recording contract with Fox Records in 1957 and issued two singles, *Gone, Gone Get Away* and *Moments To Remember You By*. Whilst the first made little impact outside of Detroit, the second did enough business to attract the attention of Atco Records, although by the time that interest had converted itself into a deal for national distribution The Romeos had disbanded.

Lamont and Ty Hunter would later resurface in The Voice Masters, a group who got a deal with Gwen Gordy's Anna label, with Lamont appearing on several singles before getting a chance at a solo outing. The first to be scheduled was *Popeye (The Sailor Man)* backed with *Let's Talk It Over*, but owing to potential legal problems with King Features (the owners of the Popeye character), the single was re-recorded with the same music but new lyrics as *Benny The Skinny Man* (although it retained the same catalogue number, Anna 1125). It failed, as did a second single on the Check-Mate label, *Just To Be Loved* backed with

I Didn't Know (What A Good Thing I Had), after which Lamont followed the various artists and personnel from Anna into Hitsville.

He was still thought of as a singer and signed with Mel-O-dy as Lamont Anthony, with his first single coming in June 1962 with *Dearest One*. Co-written by Lamont with Brian and Eddie Holland, this was a landmark single, the first to be written and released by the trio. *Dearest One* didn't exactly set the cash registers ringing, but its historical relevance as the first HDH composition has ensured continued interest.

The trio would reconvene a year later for *What Goes Up, Must Come Down*, again written by the three but featuring Lamont accompanied by The Four Tops and The Andantes on vocals and Brian on piano. It too failed, with the three then letting their own recording careers drift in order to concentrate on writing and production. That phase of their career at Motown is dealt with elsewhere, suffice to say for the next five years Holland-Dozier-Holland would rack up a portfolio of hits unrivalled in popular music history.

When the trio exited Motown in dispute over the remuneration their efforts warranted it was to form their own Invictus and Hot Wax labels, although the welter of lawsuits that bounced backwards and forwards between HDH and Motown prevented them from being credited on their own label's releases. It is thought that employees of the company were therefore named as writers and producers in an effort to cover any HDH involvement, although the style of material released by Freda Payne, Chairmen Of The Board and others was such the belief that HDH (along with many members of The Funk Brothers) moonlighted holds considerable credence.

An out of court settlement of part of the dispute in 1972 at least enabled HDH to appear on the label copy and Lamont and Brian briefly resumed their own recording careers, scoring internationally with *Why Can't We Be Lovers* and domestically with *Don't Leave Me Starvin' For Your Love, Slipping Away* and *New Breed Kinda Woman*.

Lamont left the Holland brothers in 1973 in order to pursue his own solo career with ABC, with his **Black Bach** album gaining him a Best New Artist accolade from Billboard magazine. He would later record for Warner Brothers (his *Going Back To My Roots* was a huge club hit and would provide Odyssey with a pop hit) and Columbia before relocating to Britain.

There he resumed his writing and production career and worked with the likes of Simply Red, Alison Moyet, Boy George and Eric Clapton, although his best known work was with Phil Collins on the film soundtrack to 'Buster'. Indeed, Phil and Lamont's composition *Loco In Acapulco* by The Four Tops became a huge international hit, Phil's cover of *You Can't Hurry Love* topped the UK charts and made the Top Ten in the US and *Two Hearts* won a Grammy Award for Best Song Written Specifically for a Motion Picture and a Golden Globe for Best Original Song as well as picking up an Oscar nomination. Following this success Lamont would resume his own recording career, most notably with Atlantic.

DREAMGIRLS

Playwright Tom Eyen and composer Henry Krieger developed what would eventually become the Broadway smash musical 'Dreamgirls' over the course of some three years, from 1978 to 1981. In the musical Effie White, Deena Jones and Lorrell Robinson are members of The Dreamettes, a hopeful vocal trio from Chicago trying to make it into the big time, with their career being masterminded by local car dealer turned manager Curtis Taylor Jr. The Dreams, as they are later named, suffer internal conflicts and managerial pressure during the course of their career, with the vocal emphasis of the group being switched from Effie to Deena, Effie eventually being squeezed out of the group, which is now named Deena Jones & The Dreams, and Deena's own exit in order to pursue a film career.

Both Eyen and Krieger went to great lengths to deny the story was a basic retelling of The Supremes story, but Mary Wilson loved the show enough to title her first autobiography 'Dreamgirl: My Life As A Supreme' and Diana Ross liked the music enough to perform *Family* at a free concert in Central Park. A huge success on Broadway, 'Dreamgirls' would be nominated for thirteen Tony Awards and win six, whilst the soundtrack album would collect two Grammy Awards.

One of the shows backers on Broadway was record company mogul David Geffen, who also ensured he had first option on the film rights, which eventually hit the screens in 2006, with Jennifer Hudson as Effie, Beyonce Knowles as Deena and Anika Noni Rose as Lorrell. Jamie Foxx took the role of Curtis Taylor Jr. and Eddie Murphy starred as R&B star Jimmy 'Thunder' Early.

If 'Dreamgirls' the musical had merely hinted at The Supremes as inspiration, 'Dreamgirls' the film was blatant in its interpretation. The setting was switched from Chicago to Detroit and several of The Supremes album covers of the era were adapted into album covers for The Dreams. Mary Wilson still remained a fan, attending the Los Angeles premiere and being moved to tears, later stating it was, "'closer to the truth than they even know." Others were not so happy, with Diana Ross and Smokey Robinson among the most critical. Smokey even went as far as saying that the producers owed an apology for the way the character largely based on Berry Gordy was portrayed; an apology was issued and Berry duly accepted it.

Irrespective of the accuracy of the musical or film, there can be no denying that the main beneficiaries of the success both enjoyed have been, probably in this order, Mary Wilson, The Supremes and the current owners of the Motown catalogue. In 2011 Berry Gordy announced he was working on his own Broadway musical about the Motown label, one which would give his side of the story on Motown's formation. 'Motown The Musical' eventually opened in April 2013.

DUKE JUPITER

Duke Jupiter was established in 1973 by Marshall Styler (keyboards and vocals), Greg Walker (guitar and vocals), George Barajas (bass and vocals) and Earl Jetty (drums). In 1974 guitarist Don Maracle joined the band, facilitating their signature dual-harmony lead guitar arrangements. With manager Pete Morticelli at the helm, they made a name for themselves in Upstate New York, which led to a three-record deal with Mercury Records, **Sweet Cheeks** (1978), **Taste The Night** (1979) and **Band In Blue** (1980). When Earl Jetty passed away Dave Hanlon joined the band as drummer for their second and third albums. In 1980 Maracle and Hanlon left the group and Dave Corcoran joined as drummer and vocalist.

Duke signed with CBS subsidiary Coast To Coast Records and recorded two albums in **Duke Jupiter 1** (released in 1982, with the extracted single *I'll Drink To You* being extensively played on AOR radio and the video receiving heavy rotation on MTV, activities that were enough to propel the single to #53 on the Billboard chart) and **You Make It Look Easy** (1983). George Barajas passed away from cancer in 1982 and Ricky Ellis came onboard as bassist.

At the height of their popularity in June 1982, Duke Jupiter played a live show at Ontario Beach Park (Rochester, New York) that attracted an unprecedented crowd of 50,000. Local police and fire officials called it a public hazard and banned rock concerts at the beach, as well as banning Duke Jupiter from city-sponsored performances in Rochester.

In 1984 Duke Jupiter signed a two-record deal with Morocco Records, which was an attempt by Motown to enter the rock and roll market. **White Knuckle Ride** would become Duke's only charting album with Morocco, peaking at #122. Their *Little Lady* video was regularly seen on MTV and also aired on the Solid Gold TV show. Motown then decided their foray into rock was not working, shut down Morocco and switched Duke Jupiter to the Motown label for their last album. This was despite a failed attempt at terminating the two album contract, with Motown eventually releasing an unfinished version (rough mixes only) of **Line Of Your Fire**. Lack of commitment and no promotion resulted in poor sales for this 1985 release. Worn down from years of touring, and discouraged by disappointing record label support, Duke Jupiter disbanded after a farewell concert in 1986. Due to popular demand, the group has had several reunions in their hometown of Rochester, with their 2010 reunion attended by 10,000 fans.

ALBUMS: WHITE KNUCKLE RIDE (1984), LINE OF YOUR FIRE (1985)

DARRYL DUNCAN

Born in Chicago, Illinois in 1963, Darryl Duncan learned to play the piano at an early age and was still in high school when he joined his first band. Upon leaving school he became a songwriter for A&M, relocating to Los Angeles and penning songs for the likes of Chaka Khan and Maurice White. He also undertook production duties for Sarah Dash and Billy Always before landing a contract with Motown as a solo singer in 1987, with a track on the soundtrack to 'Citizens On Patrol' his initial release. His January 1988 album **Heaven** would yield a minor hit single in *James Brown Part 1*, which made #71 on the R&B chart, but by then Motown was in the process of being sold and Darryl's product got lost in the upheaval this caused.

His songwriting, however, continued to garner acclaim, with Darryl writing and producing seven tracks on R. Kelly's debut and having the likes of Michael Jackson, Barry White, Jerry Butler and Jeffrey Osborne record his material. Darryl would later carve out a career writing music for video games for Electronic Arts before returning to Illinois to set up his own company, GameBeat, to service this industry.

ALBUM: HEAVEN (1988)

DUNN & RUBINI

Don Dunn began his career in California in 1960s, writing songs for an assortment of artists. He linked with Michel Rubini (born in Los Angeles, California on 3 December 1942), a multi-talented writer, keyboard player, producer and arranger in 1976 for an album and two singles on Prodigal. **Diggin' It** would see the title track and *Imaginary Girl* issued as singles to little avail, with the pair drafting in singer and guitarist Chuck Smith to form Friendly Enemies for a further album on Prodigal.

ALBUM: DIGGIN' IT (1976)

DON DUNN

Songwriter and guitarist Donald Lewis Dunn (his name was shortened to Don Dunn so as to avoid confusion with the Stax musician Donald 'Duck' Dunn) had his songs recorded by artists as diverse as Joe Cocker, Jose Feliciano, Rare Earth, Kenny Rogers and Diana Ross before linking with Michel Rubini in Dunn & Rubini. In between the pair becoming the trio Friendly Enemies with the addition of Chuck Smith, Don recorded a one-off single for Prodigal in March 1977, *Ruby*, although this was not commercially released. After leaving Prodigal, Don would journey to Nashville to continue his writing career, later teaching songwriting in San Diego.

ADA DYER

Chicago, Illinois born Adaritha Dyer played with a number of local bands in nightclubs and colleges before being spotted by manager Paul Wilson. Wilson paid for a number of demos to be cut, one of which eventually found its way to jazz drummer and producer Norman Connors, who invited her to do an updated version of one of her songs, *Invitation* in 1979, subsequently using it as the title track to his album. Ada also appeared on his **Take It To The Limit** the following year, the recognition enough to see her abandon her studies in computers and relocate to New York. There she joined electro-funk group Warp 9 and scored a couple of R&B hits before quitting the group in 1984 and undertaking considerable session work (although she would be almost reunited with Warp 9 a couple of years when they signed with Motown!).

It was at one such session that she worked with James Anthony Carmichael of The Commodores and Lionel Richie fame, ultimately beginning work on what would be her debut album in 1987. Released the following year on Motown, **Meant To Be** gave rise to the R&B hit *I Bet Ya, I'll Let Ya* which hit #33 on the R&B charts. A second single, *I Don't Feel Like Crying*, penned by L.A. Reid and Babyface got lost in the management reshuffles at Motown after the company's sale and flopped. A second eponymous album was planned for 1990 but suffered an even worse fate, effectively being pulled after promotional copies had been despatched.

ALBUM: MEANT TO BE (1988)

THE DYNAMIC SUPERIORS

Formed in high school in Washington D.C. in 1963 by George Spann, George Wesley Peterbank Jr., Michael McCalpin and brothers Tony and Michael Washington as The Superiors, they got their first live dates in local clubs by lying about their ages. Their act was mainly based around flamboyant lead singer Tony, whose was open about his homosexuality and often performed in drag.

The group would spend some ten years trying for a break, releasing one obscure single on Sue Records in 1969, although such was their determination to succeed they operated a strict no-marriage clause within the group lest it detract from their quest. They were finally spotted performing at a DJ convention in Atlanta, signed with Motown in 1974 and handed over to Nickolas Ashford and Valerie Simpson for their debut recordings.

A stunning first outing with *Shoe Shoe Shine* took them into the charts, hitting #68 pop and #16 R&B, followed by *Leave It Alone*, a bigger R&B hit in peaking at #13 but which bubbled under the Hot 100 at #102. The success of the two singles helped their eponymous album register a #36 R&B listing, but unfortunately the group had effectively peaked at that point.

A second album helmed by Ashford and Simpson, **Pure Pleasure** gave rise to two minor hits in *Nobody's Gonna Change Me* (#51 R&B) and *Deception* (#53 R&B), with the parent album also making #36 R&B and would be their last appearance on the pop chart at #130. A change of producers to Hal Davis, Pam Sawyer and Marilyn McLeod saw a change of emphasis towards a more disco sound, but both the album **You Name It** and lifted single *I Can't Stay Away (From Someone I Love)* missed out on the chart. The group's final Motown outing, **Give And Take** was produced by

Brian Holland and saw a minor hit single in an update of *Nowhere To Run*, which made #53 in 1977.

Dropped by the label soon after, The Dynamic Superiors tried in vain to secure a new contract elsewhere without much success (although an album for Venture, entitled **Magic Wand** found them working with Tony Camillo in 1980) and disbanded soon after although the surviving members reformed in 2005. Tony has reportedly died from AIDS, whilst Michael McCalpin is also deceased.

ALBUMS: THE DYNAMIC SUPERIORS (1975), PURE PLEASURE (1975), YOU NAME IT (1976), GIVE AND TAKE (1977)

CLIFTON DYSON

Spiritual soul singer and writer Clifton Dyson had several stabs at stardom, fronting his own group Dyson's Faces that released a couple of highly regarded albums in the mid 1970s on Dy-Rich. He then went solo and continued recording for a number of small labels. It was the All-American label, another small label operating out of Hollywood that first released *Body In Motion (Want Your Body In Motion With Mine)*, with the buzz enough for Motown to pick it up for national distribution in February 1980. The single was also released in Germany, but Motown obviously passed on the album that was supposedly available.

E

BRENDA LEE EAGER

Born in Mobile, Alabama on 8 August 1947, Brenda Lee Eager began singing in her local church at the age of three and was performing professionally from the age of seventeen. After relocating to Chicago Brenda joined Jerry Butler's group as a backing singer and also performed on several duets with Jerry, with *Ain't Understanding Mellow* becoming their biggest hit when it peaked at #3 R&B and #21 pop in 1972. The pair would also perform *(They Long To Be) Close To You* for the 'Save The Children' soundtrack released by Motown in 1974.

EARTHQUIRE

Formed by Tata Vega (born Carmen Rose Vega in Queens, New York on 7 October 1951), Brie Brandt, Laurie Anne Ball and Mike Gorfaine (all on vocals), with musical accompaniment from Greg Mathieson (keyboards), Bob Crosby (saxophone), Charlie Stephens (bass) and Jim Varley (drums), Earthquire released one album on Natural Resources, an eponymous album issued in January 1973. Produced by Tom Wilson, the album would also see one single lifted, with *Sunshine Man* trying to capitalise on the summer by being released in June 1973. Both the album and single flopped, although three members of the group went on to make some impact in music; Brie Brandt would later become a member of female rock group Fanny, Mike Gorfaine would launch his own talent agency and Tata Vega enjoyed a solo recording career, most notably with Motown.

ALBUM: EARTHQUIRE (1973)

LORI EASTSIDE

Originally a singer with although never a full time member of The Coconuts, Lori appeared on two of Kid Creole's albums and would subsequently record with Coati Mundi. In 1983 she briefly became an actress/singer, appearing in the film 'Get Crazy' as lead singer of the girl band Nada, featuring on the tracks *You Can't Make Me* and *I'm Not Gonna Make It* that appeared on the accompanying soundtrack. Lori would later become better known on the other side of the film industry; as a casting director she has discovered a number of talented individuals, including Michael Pitt.

EASY – THE COMMODORES [SINGLE]

Despite the success of *Just To Be Close To You*, The Commodores received flak from some quarters, with Milan Williams claiming that several radio stations thought the group's repertoire was 'too black'. There could be no such complaints about the lead single from their next album **The Commodores** (released in the UK as **Zoom**), *Easy* being released in May 1977 in all major territories. Written by Lionel Richie, *Easy* would prove to be a single that was almost impossible to categorise, ending up making a major dent on the pop, R&B and even country charts. In the US, it would top the R&B chart and peak at #4 pop, whilst in the UK in became The Commodores' first Top Ten hit, reaching #9.

Easy was also one of three Motown associated songs nominated for the Grammy Award for Best R&B Song in 1978, alongside the group's own *Brick House* and *Don't Leave Me This Way*, written by Kenny Gamble and Leon Huff but brought back to popularity by Thelma Houston. With the field also featuring Maurice White and Al McKay's *Best Of My Love*, the award went to Leo Sayer and Vini Poncia for *You Make Me Feel Like Dancing*!

In 1988 *Easy* was revived in the UK following the song's use in an advertisement for the Halifax Building Society and would reach #15 second time around. Fifteen years later, in 2003 *Easy* was heavily sampled in Cam'ron's *Hey Ma*, a #7 R&B, #3 pop and #8 UK hit. Even today *Easy* retains its appeal, featuring on the opening credits to Sky TV's 'Goals On Sunday' programme.

THE EASYBEATS

Like many of their contemporaries, The Easybeats were inspired by the worldwide success of The Beatles. Indeed, for a two year spell, Easyfever swept across Australia at much the same pace as Beatlemania. Formed in Sydney in 1964, the group comprised Stevie Wright (born in Leeds, England on 20 December 1948, vocals), George Young (born in Glasgow, Scotland on 6 November 1947, rhythm guitar), Harry Vanda (born Harold Wandon in The Hague, Holland on 22 March 1947, guitar), Dick Diamonde (born in Hilversum, Holland on 28 December 1947, bass) and Gordon 'Snowy' Fleet (born in Bootle, England on 16 August 1946, drums) and took their name from television programme 'Easybeat'.

Domestic success throughout 1965 and 1966 prompted the group to head for England in 1966 where they initially worked with freelance producer Shel Talmy, with *Friday On My Mind* becoming an international hit, leading to tours around the world with The Rolling Stones. Fleet began to resent the amount of time he was away from his family and left the group in 1967, being replaced by Tony Cahill. Despite the addition of Cahill, The Easybeats were already on the decline, with their brief flirtation with Motown coming in 1969 when *St Louis* was licensed and issued on the Rare Earth label, peaking at #100 on the pop chart. A proposed album, **Easy Ridin'** was scheduled for release in September the same year but was subsequently cancelled when the group disbanded.

BILLY ECKSTINE

Born in Pittsburgh, Pennsylvania on 8 July 1914, William Clarence Eckstine was intent on a professional football career but a broken collar bone brought those dreams to an end and he concentrated on music thereafter. His musical career began in 1939 when he joined Earl Hines band, spending four years as vocalist and occasional trumpeter and fronting their R&B chart topper *Stormy Monday Blues* in 1942.

Billy left in 1943 and the following year formed his own big band, which over the next few years would play host to such talents as Dizzy Gillespie, Miles Davis, Dexter Gordon, Charlie Parker and Art Blakely, with Sarah Vaughan the vocalist. Billy racked up an impressive number of R&B hits, most notably with *Last Night, A Cottage For Sale, Prisoner Of Love* and *You Call It Madness But I Call It Love* and two pop hits in *The Bitter With The Sweet* and *Passing Strangers*, the latter a duet with Sarah Vaughan.

By the time Billy joined Motown in 1965, he had been without a hit for eight years, but his signing still represented something of a coup for Berry Gordy, eager as he was to get established names on his labels. His first outing, *Down To Earth* backed with *Had You Been Around* (the titles were reversed in the UK) was released in May 1965 and was followed by the album **The Prime Of My Life** six months later. There would be a further five singles and two albums, **My Way** and **For The Love Of Ivy** released over the course of the next three years, with a further album **Live At Lake Tahoe** subsequently cancelled and the **Gentle On My Mind** album released in the UK only in July 1969. Prestigious as his signing was, interest in jazz at Motown had already diminished by the time Billy landed at the label, making promoting him a somewhat difficult task.

Billy would later move to the other major R&B label, Stax, where he recorded for their Enterprise imprint in 1969, with Isaac Hayes producing the first of his four albums for the label. Known throughout the business as Mr B, he died on 8 March 1993.

ALBUMS: THE PRIME OF MY LIFE (1965), MY WAY (1966), FOR THE LOVE OF IVY (1968), GENTLE ON MY MIND (1969)

ECOLOGY RECORDS

A very short-lived label established by Berry Gordy and veteran singer Sammy Davis Jr., the label was destined to have just one artist, who released just one single. After recording an album for Motown in 1970, Sammy and Berry had agreed the formation of a boutique label, Ecology, for future Sammy Davis Jr. releases, although after *In My Own Lifetime* the pair disagreed on the future direction the label should take but agreed to end their association.

DUANE EDDY

Born in Corning, New York on 26 April 1938, Duane Eddy learned to play the guitar at the age of five and after a brief spell recording as one half of the duo Jimmy & Duane (with Jimmy Delbridge), launched a solo career masterminded by producer and writer Lee Hazlewood. The distinctive 'twangy' guitar effect was created by recording in a 2,000 gallon water storage tank as the studio they invariably used in Phoenix did not have an echo chamber.

Duane's hit career commenced in 1958 on Jamie Records with the album **Have Twangy Guitar Will Travel** and over the next five years he would be a regular on both the Top 100 and album charts, scoring Top 20 hits with *Rebel Rouser, Cannonball, Forty Miles Of Bad Road, Because They're Young* (the theme to the film of the same name, which also starred Duane), *Pepe* and *Dance With The Guitar Man* as well as the albums **Have Twangy Guitar Will Travel**, **The Twangs The Thang** and **$1,000,000.00 Worth Of Twang**.

Motown picked up the rights to the Jamie catalogue in 1986, releasing a compilation album as well as re-issuing **Have Twangy Guitar Will Travel** and scheduled two reissues for the European market that were subsequently shelved.

ALBUMS: HAVE TWANGY GUITAR WILL TRAVEL (1986), COMPACT COMMAND PERFORMANCES (1988)

DENNIS EDWARDS

Born in Birmingham, Alabama on 3 February 1943, the son of a minister, Dennis and his family moved to Detroit in 1950. Whilst at high school Dennis had sung with the Mighty Clouds Of Joy gospel group, but it was with his eye on soul that he formed Dennis Edwards & The Firebirds in 1961. He recorded an obscure single for International Soulsville in 1965, *I Didn't Have To (But I Did)* (so obscure that it invariably sells for £1,500 on the Northern Soul circuit) before being recommended to The Contours as lead singer in 1967. His tenure would last for only one single, *It's So Hard Being A Loser,* with the group's contract expiring the following year.

Then came the call to join The Temptations, a call that Dennis was initially reluctant to accept. He was known to be a fan of David Ruffin and was even having a relationship with David's estranged wife Sandra (with, it has to be said, David's full blessing), and only accepted on the advice of David!

"He'd drop by sometimes, and that's what he did that night. I opened the door and he said he was leaving the group — that's how he put it, he didn't go into details or nothin' — and that I was gonna be hired to replace him. I'm standing there half asleep and here's the guy I idolised laying this on me, and I'm like, what the hell?"

His first official engagement came on 9 July 1968 at Valley Forge, a show that became notorious for being the first time no fewer than *six* Temptations were on stage at the same time — David Ruffin sneaked up to the stage and took the microphone during *Ain't Too Proud To Beg;* Dennis sang the opening line of 'I know you wanna leave me' and David completed the refrain 'But I refuse to let you go'! The stunt would be repeated a further three times over the next month before David finally accepted he was an ex-Temptation.

Dennis' first recording session with The Temptations came with *Cloud Nine*, and whilst the original intention following the departure of David had been to spread the lead vocals around the group in order to make them less reliant on the likes of David Ruffin, the reality was that Dennis' vocal was so powerful it suited the kind of material Norman Whitfield and Barrett Strong were coming up with. Aside from *Cloud Nine*, therefore, Dennis would be largely responsible for powering such songs as *Papa Was A Rollin' Stone*, *Runaway Child Running Wild* and *Don't Let The Joneses Get You Down,* among others.

As well as taking over David Ruffin's vocal responsibilities within the group, Dennis adopted some of his negative traits, including a growing drug problem and eventually the same kind of unreliability that had marked the end of David's spell with the group. Matters were not helped during the recording of The Temptations album **Wings Of Love**, with producer Jeffrey Bowen utilising Dennis and backing singers to the exclusion of The Temptations. He also spent time filling Dennis' head with the idea of embarking on a solo career, words Dennis took to heart. Eventually The Temptations tired of his attitude and showed him the door in 1977, by which time Dennis was already recording a solo album.

Unfortunately, Motown showed little or no interest in taking the album, leaving Dennis out in the cold for the next three years or so, helping his uncle with laying concrete driveways. Dennis would return in 1980 at much the same time The Temptations returned to Motown, but the consistent hitmaking days were behind them. Two years later Dennis would sing with David Ruffin for real, Eddie Kendricks also rejoining the group as part of the reunion tour and album. Yet Dennis had still not beaten his drug demons and was fired from the group a second time in 1984.

This time he found Motown more receptive to the idea of a solo career, linking him with producer Dennis Lambert for **Don't Look Any Further**. Lead single *Don't Look Any Further* featured Siedah Garrett and proved irresistible, making #72 pop but a massive #2 R&B hit, also hitting #45 in the UK. Helped by a further hit single in *(You're My) Aphrodisiac* (#15 R&B), the album would make #48 on the pop chart and #2 R&B. The follow-up album, 1985's **Coolin' Out** did not fare so well, peaking at #36 on the R&B chart and featuring two minor R&B hit singles in *Amanda* (#77) and *Coolin' Out* (#23).

In 1987 Dennis was enticed back into The Temptations for a third and final time (at much the same time a re-release on *Don't Look Any Further* was hitting #55 on the UK chart), replacing his replacement Ollie Woodson, only for the tables to be turned two years later when Woodson came back in and Dennis went out. He then linked with David Ruffin and Eddie Kendricks for a series of tours but no records, although Dennis and Eddie did record *Get It While It's Hot* for the A&B label in 1990.

With David's death in 1991 and Eddie's the following year, Dennis assembled a new group of singers and began touring as Dennis Edwards & The Temptations, prompting a legal battle with Otis Williams and the original Temptations. A compromise was eventually worked out, with Dennis touring under the moniker The Temptations Review Featuring Dennis Edwards, a unit that features Paul Williams Jr. (original Temptation Paul Williams' son), David Sea, Mike Patillo and Chris Arnold and continues to tour today.

ALBUMS: DON'T LOOK ANY FURTHER (1984), COOLIN' OUT (1985)

LEFTY EDWARDS

Born in 1927, Charles 'Lefty' Edwards was a mainstay of many Detroit jazz bands, recording with the likes of Dave Bartholomew, Todd Rhodes, Carl Davis, Wyonie Harris and Eddie 'Lockjaw' Davis during the 1940s and 50s. Like several other Detroit jazz musicians, he was enticed to Hitsville by the promise of being able to record an album of his own, which he duly did between February and May 1963.

The album **The Right Side Of Lefty Edwards** was subsequently released on the Workshop Jazz label in June 1964 and featured Edwards (alto and tenor saxophone), Joe Messina (guitar), Johnny Griffith (piano), Vance Matlock (bass) and Ben Appling (drums). Whilst not a big seller domestically and ignored completely in the UK, Lefty Edwards' album was one of five issued in Belgium by Motown's licensor Disques Artone Fonoplatten in December! He died on 11 July 1994 aged 67.

ALBUM: THE RIGHT SIDE OF LEFTY EDWARDS (1964)

THE EL DORADOS

Formed in Chicago, Illinois in 1952 as Pirkle Lee & The Five Stars, the group comprised Pirkle Lee Moses, Arthur Bassett, Louis Bradley, Jewel Jones and James Maddox. They changed name to The El Dorados in 1954, shortly before picking up a recording contract with Vee-Jay Records, although their initial recordings were all unsuccessful. Their luck changed with *At My Front Door*, released in August 1955 which would go on to top the R&B chart and make the pop Top Twenty, but sustained success proved elusive (they registered just one more appearance on the R&B chart) and they were dropped by Vee-Jay in 1958. Their major hit, which was also known as *Crazy Little Mama* was featured on the CD compilation **Hits From The Legendary Vee-Jay Records**, issued by Motown in 1986. Moses died from a brain tumour on 16 December 2000.

THE ELGINS

Technically, there were two groups called The Elgins connected with Motown. The first had come through the door in 1960 but Motown hadn't liked the name, which reminded them of the watch company. Asked to choose a new moniker, they eventually settled on The Temptations. Two years later, former Sensations and The Five Emeralds' singers Robert Fleming, Johnny Dawson and Cleo 'Duke' Miller signed to the Tamla label as The Downbeats and released one single in *Your Baby's Back*.

When their career stalled, Motown suggested they add a female lead vocal to the line-up, with former solo singer Saundra Edwards (nee Mallet) given the role. Handed over to the HDH team, the group recorded *Darling Baby* for release in December 1965. Early pressings that went out were credited to The Downbeats (copies of this are worth a reported $200), but late in the day Berry Gordy got the group name changed to The Elgins.

Irrespective of what they were called, the group was to enjoy a major hit first time out, with *Darling Baby* making #4 R&B and #72 R&B. This was followed by *Heaven Must Have Sent You*, another R&B Top Ten hit (#9) and improving their pop placing by peaking at #50. August 1966 would see the release of the group's only album, **Darling Baby**, which even included Saundra's 1962 single with The Vandellas in order to pad the album out. The group featured on the chart once more in 1967, with *It's Been A Long Long Time* backed with *I Understand My Man* stopping at #35 R&B and a lowly #92 pop.

The group disbanded later the same year, but in 1971 a huge upsurge in all things Motown in the UK resulted in *Heaven Must Have Sent You* hurtling all the way to #3 on the pop chart. With Saundra unwilling to rejoin the group, Fleming, Dawson and Miller recruited Yvonne Vernee Allen (previously a member of The Donays) in her place and undertook a UK tour at much the same time *Put Yourself In My Place*, originally the flip side to *Darling Baby* was slowly rising up the chart, eventually coming to settle at #28.

There was speculation that Motown might be interested in resigning the group, but with a US reissue of *Heaven Must Have Sent You* attracting little interest the idea was quietly put to bed. Towards the end of the 1980s, another line-up of The Elgins (with Allen, Dawson, Jimmy Charles and Norbert McLean) recorded for Ian Levine's Motorcity project, with Saundra Edwards also recording a number of tracks.

ALBUM: DARLING BABY (1966)

THE EMOTIONS

Formed in Chicago, Illinois as The Heavenly Sunbeams by sisters Jeanette (born in Chicago in February 1951), Wanda (born in Chicago on 17 December 1951) and Sheila Hutchinson (born in Chicago on 17 January 1953), they name changed to The Emotions in 1968 upon signing with Stax' Volt imprint. They scored a Top Ten R&B and Top 40 pop hit with *So I Can Love You* and were to enjoy thirteen hits over the next five years. Following the collapse of Stax they linked with Earth Wind & Fire frontman Maurice White at Columbia, scoring a number one pop and R&B hit with *Best Of My Love* in 1977 and aiding Earth Wind & Fire's international hit *Boogie Wonderland* in 1979, winning Grammy Awards for both.

After leaving Columbia's ARC label in 1981 they eventually resurfaced at Red Label in 1984 and scored three minor R&B hits, but their day in the sun had effectively ended by the time they joined Motown in 1985. By this time the group consisted of Sheila, Wanda and Adrianna Harris, who recorded a solitary album, **If I Only Knew.** This would see two singles lifted, *Miss Your Love* and *If I Only Knew Then (What I Know Now)* but whilst well received critically, sales proved disappointing and the group was dropped from the roster.

ALBUM: IF I ONLY KNEW (1985)

END RECORDS

Renowned record producer George Goldner (born on 9 February 1918) formed his first record label, Tico Records, towards the end of the 1940s. The following decade he was at the forefront of Rock & Roll, either discovering or recording the likes of Bill Haley & His Comets, Frankie Lymon & The Teenagers, Little Anthony & The Imperials and a slew of other acts. He also created many labels, among them End, Gone, Gold Disc and Mark-X, but a heavy gambling addiction invariably meant he sold the labels to his one-time business partner Morris Levy, including the infamous Roulette Records imprint.

In 1958, however, there was something of mutual admiration between owner George Goldner and would-be writer Berry Gordy, who met at United Sound Studios in Detroit when George was in town for a session. Although nothing formal was agreed at the time, George gave Berry $100 as a down payment in case they did any business together in the future. That came around sooner than they all could have imagined, for a short while later Berry approached George with the master for The Miracles' *Got A Job*, which was duly issued on 19 February 1958, Smokey's birthday. The single attracted some attention, enough for Goldner to commit to a follow-up release in *Money* backed with *I Cry*, released later the same year and would re-issue it in 1961 after the group had made their major chart breakthrough with *Shop Around*. End also released a number of Berry Gordy compositions and productions that were not Motown associated including The Five Stars' *Blabber Mouth.*

End Records continued until 1964, when Goldner was again forced to sell his assets to Morris Levy. George would try again with Red Bird Records, a label formed with Jerry Leiber and Mike Stoller, but by 1966 his partners were so desperate to get out of the deal they sold back their shares for $1, shortly before the Mafia-run label also ended up in the hands of Morris Levy. George died from a heart attack on 15 April 1970.

ENDLESS LOVE – DIANA ROSS & LIONEL RICHIE [SINGLE]

Lionel Richie was still a member of The Commodores when he was invited to a meeting with film director Franco Zeffirelli and producer Jon Peters in 1981.

"They called me and asked did I have a song for their new movie. I didn't have so I went to see the movie, although I didn't really want anything else to do at that time. Then Polygram said all they wanted was an instrumental and I could do that on a weekend, that would have been easy – no problem. Next thing I know, I get told they want lyrics, and wanted me to sing them. So I agreed; still a weekend thing – no problem. Then I hear them say, 'We've got Diana Ross to sing it with you' – now I have a problem. This was turning into a bigger project by the minute but it turned out to be a wonderful weekend. One major aspect though had to be sorted out, namely, where the two of us would record the track. You see, Diana was in Atlantic City doing some concerts, and I was in New York, and neither of us had the time to visit each other. So, we decided to meet in Nevada. She finished her concert at one in the morning and drove down, and I flew in. We started around three, three-thirty, and finished around six, six-thirty. Diana, once she showed, was a real professional. Diana Ross knows how to be Diana Ross. She kills a song."

Endless Love would duly feature in the film starring Brooke Shields and would top both the R&B and pop charts, for seven and nine weeks respectively, shifting more than a million copies domestically and pick up nominations for Best Original Song at the Academy Awards and Record of the Year and Song of the Year at the Grammy Awards (it lost out to *Arthur's Theme* at the Academy Awards and *Bette Davis Eyes* at the Grammy's). *Endless Love* would also travel better than the film, hitting #7 in the UK and the Top Ten of most charts around the world. In 1994 Luther Vandross and Mariah Carey recorded a cover version that hit #2 in the US and #3 in the UK.

EP'S

A total of 26 Motown-connected EPs were released in Britain between October 1961, when *Shop Around* by The Miracles made its bow on the London American label and March 1967, with Marvin Gaye's *Originals From Marvin Gaye* the final such release. *Shop Around* was the only EP release by London American, with the next EP not appearing until January 1964 when Stateside released the first of their five issues. The Tamla Motown label issued nineteen EPs, of which six featured on the Record Retailer chart, including *Four Tops Hits*, which spent a total of twenty weeks at the chart summit, swapping places with *The Beach Boys Hits* for much of the year although on 28 October 1967, *The Four Tops Hits* was at number one on the chart whilst the earlier release *The Four Tops* was at number two. A separate EP chart was discontinued after 16 December 1967, and Motown's only other EP release since then has been the *Something Special* additional four tracks that were included in the Stevie Wonder album **Songs In The Key Of Life.**

THE EQUADORS

Fortunately, there are relatively few Motown artists for whom there is next to no biographical information, but unfortunately The Equadors are one of those few. Several propositions have been put forward, ranging from a mysterious Rex Robertson (who had a hand in writing both sides of their release) accompanied by four other vocalists, who could have been name checked during their single, which would make them John, Marvin, Sam and Charlie, another group featuring Harvey Fuqua, Billy Roquel Davis and Etta James, or finally a Philadelphia vocal group. In short, no one knows, and since *Someone To Call My Own* backed with *You're My Desire*, issued on Miracle in September 1961 did nothing, no one bothered to ask.

ERIC & THE VIKINGS

Formed in high school in Detroit, Michigan in 1970, The Vikings consisted of Eryke McClinton, Phil Taylor and Cliff Moore. After graduating from McKenzie High the trio continued singing, making their debut live performance as opening act for Isaac Hayes. They got their first recording contract soon after for former Motown staffer Richard 'Popcorn' Wylie's Soulhawk label, with Richard penning their big local hit *Vibrations (Made Us Fall In Love)* with Anthony Hester. The group appeared on Motown in 1972, where they would have two singles released. *It's Too Much For Man To Take Too Long* was scheduled for Tamla but appeared on Gordy in April 1972, whilst *I'm Truly Yours* was scheduled for Motown but subsequently released on Gordy in September 1973.

BETTY EVERETT

Born in Greenwood, Mississippi on 23 November 1939, Betty moved to Chicago in 1957 and recorded for a number of small labels in the city before landing at Vee-Jay in 1963. After a false start with her initial single, Betty registered a major hit with an update of *You're No Good,* a #5 R&B and #51 pop hit in November 1963. Three months later she scored the biggest hit of her career, with *The Shoop Shoop Song (It's In His Kiss)* topping the R&B chart for three weeks and making #6 pop. Betty returned to the top of the R&B chart later the same year, her duet with Jerry Butler *Let It Be Me* also spending three weeks at the summit. All three hits were featured on the CD compilation album **The Hits From The Legendary Vee-Jay Records**, issued by Motown in November 1986. Betty died on 19 August 2001.

THE EXCITERS

Originally formed as an all female quartet in Queens, New York by Brenda Reid (born in New York in 1945), Carol Johnson, Lillian Walker and Sylvia Wilbur under the name The Masterettes, the group performed numerous local shows, usually in conjunction with an all male group known as The Masters, who included in their line-up Herb Rooney (born in New York City in 1941 and later to become Brenda's husband). Sylvia left soon after the group recorded their debut single for Le Sage, being briefly replaced by Penny Carter.

The girls were duly snapped up by Jerry Leiber and Mike Stoller, who also gave them the name The Exciters, and at an early recording session Herb got drafted in to round out the sound (he was present to help out on the arrangements), with the group reverting back to a quartet with the departure of Penny. They scored their first major hit with *Tell Him* in 1962, written by Leiber and Stoller and a #4 pop and #5 R&B hit as well as making #46 in the UK (its progress was somewhat hampered by the presence of a cover version by British singer Billie Davis that hit the Top Ten). The song has gone on to feature in numerous film soundtracks, including 'The Big Chill', released by Motown in September 1983. Herb reportedly died sometime during the 1990s. Carol Johnson died on 7 May 2007 at the age of 62.

F

YVONNE FAIR

Best known for her hit single *It Should Have Been Me* (at least as far as the UK is concerned), Yvonne Fair spent a frustrating eight years or so at Motown, releasing just one album during her time with the company.

Born Flora Yvonne Coleman in Richmond, Virginia on 21 October 1942, she dropped out of school after the eleventh grade and married Leroy Fair, giving birth to their son Leroy Junior shortly after. Although the marriage was shortlived, Yvonne (she had never been fond of her given first name and had always been known as Yvonne) retained her married name for professional purposes.

That began in 1961 when she joined the all-female vocal group The Chantels, who had enjoyed four R&B hits in the 1950s; by the time Yvonne joined, supplementing the group following the departure of founder Arlene Smith, the group had one more big hit in them, *Look In My Eyes*, which hit #6 R&B and #14 pop on Carlton Records. Yvonne then joined James Brown's revue, where she made her first solo recordings, *I Found You* (James Brown would later rework this into *I Got You (I Feel Good)* and score a major hit) and *It Hurts To Be In Love* for King and *Say Yeah Yeah* (written by Dessie Rozier, which was a pseudonym for James Brown) for Dade Records over the next couple of years. Yvonne also had a relationship with her boss, giving birth to their daughter Venisha (Brown was still married but legally separated from his wife at the time) before leaving the revue and linking with Chuck Jackson.

It was Jackson who took her to Motown in 1967 where she was signed to the Soul label, although her initial

recordings were duets with Chuck that never saw the light of day. Working with producers Harvey Fuqua and Johnny Bristol, Yvonne released her debut solo single in 1969, *Stay A Little Longer* without success and nothing further was issued for the next five years. Yvonne appeared in the 1972 film 'Lady Sings The Blues' and then began working with producer Norman Whitfield, scoring a modest #32 R&B hit with *Funky Music Sho Nuff Turns Me On* (which features Marvin Gaye on vocals) on Motown in 1974. Further minor success followed with *Walk Out The Door If You Wanna* (#60) and *Love Ain't No Toy* (#90) and a subsequent album **The Bitch Is Black!**, released in May 1975. Only *Funky Music* had been released in the UK, without success, although in November 1975 Tamla Motown released *It Should Have Been Me*, almost as a last ditch attempt to try and generate some interest in both the artist and her album. That *It Should Have Been Me* should become such a major hit was a surprise, so much so that the follow-up *It's Bad For Me To See You* failed to make a dent, leaving Yvonne a one-hit wonder in the UK. The UK success did prompt Motown to issue *It Should Have Been Me* as a single in the US, where it belatedly made #85 pop in May 1976. With Norman Whitfield having left Motown to form his own label, Yvonne's Motown career came to an end at this point. Having married former Little Anthony & The Imperials and future O'Jays singer Sammy Strain, Yvonne retired from recording, although she did work as personal manager for Dionne Warwick. Yvonne died from prostate cancer on 6 March 1994, her undoubted talent never fully realised.
ALBUM: THE BITCH IS BLACK! (1975)

FAMILY DREAM

The LA Dream Team was a hip hop group formed in 1984 by Rudy Pardee (born in Cleveland, Ohio on 29 June 1957), Chris Wilson and Lisa 'Miss Rockberry' Love, recording a number of albums for MCA. In 1987 Pardee contributed to the soundtrack to the film 'Police Academy 4 – Citizens On Patrol', with the track *Rescue Me* being credited to the Family Dream. Written by Pardee with Michael Perison and Victor Brooks, it would hit #75 on the R&B chart when released as a single. The L.A. Dream Team also provided backing to Michael Winslow on the title theme. Motown planned on releasing a Family Dream album in 1987 although this was subsequently cancelled. Pardee died in a scuba diving accident on 30 August 1998.

FANTACY HILL

A self-contained rock group formed in Detroit, Michigan in 1974 by Danny Mullins (guitar and vocals), George Durbin (guitar and vocals), Jose Conrado (bass and vocals), Gerson Migliaco (percussion and vocals) and Doug Golema (drums), Fantacy Hill released two albums on the Prodigal label. The first, **Fantacy Hill** appeared in August 1976, having been preceded by the single *Minnie Ha Ha*. Their follow-up **First Step** was released in January 1978, with *Sanity Baby* being issued in June the same year.
ALBUMS: FANTACY HILL (1976), FIRST STEP (1978)

THE FANTASTIC FOUR

The success The Fantastic Four and Edwin Starr in particular enjoyed on Ed Wingate's Ric-Tic label eventually prompted Berry Gordy to swoop, buy up the label, its artists and contracts and remove one of the last vestiges of local competition. Once they got into Motown, the former Ric-Tic artists had varying degrees of success, with several being unceremoniously knocked off their perch, none more so than The Fantastic Four.

Formed in Detroit, Michigan in 1965 by brothers Ralph and Joseph Pruitt, 'Sweet' James Epps and William Hunter (subsequently being replaced by Wallace 'Toby' Childs), they linked with Ric-Tic in 1966 and saw their first single released in December of that year, with *Girl Have Pity* issued as Ric-Tic 119. A second single in *Can't Stop Looking For My Baby* in February 1967 also failed to register on the chart, but it was to be their third single, *The Whole World Is A Stage* that provided their breakthrough, crashing into the Top Ten of the R&B chart (#6) and making a minor dent pop (#55). The follow-up did nearly as well, with *You Gave Me Something (And Everything's Alright)* hitting #12 R&B and #68 pop, and subsequent chart hits in *To Share Your Love* with *As Long As I Live (I Live For You)*, *Goddess Of Love* and *I've Got To Have You* kept their profile high.

Unfortunately, it was too high, for with backing supplied by moonlighting Funk Brothers and Ric-Tic also enjoying hits by Edwin Starr and J.J. Barnes, such success was too close to home for Berry Gordy to tolerate. The Fantastic Four, undoubtedly Ric-Tic's best-selling act at the time, were on their way to another major hit with *I Love You Madly*, originally issued as Ric-Tic 144 but subsequently switched over to Soul 35052 once the sale deal had gone through. Aided by Motown's marketing machine, it would come to rest at #12 R&B and #56 pop, although it missed out in the UK despite getting a release two months after its US debut. Access to Motown's marketing and promotional expertise was one thing, but The Fantastic Four were virtually left kicking their heels during their time at Hitsville. They saw only three singles released, none of which bothered the charts, and even their only album actually issued, February 1969's **The Best Of The Fantastic Four** drew upon their Ric-Tic recordings.

James Epps later explained their disappointment with Motown.

"We were just like one big happy family [at Ric-Tic] and I think that's why those records were so different from anything else. Everyone was involved in the music and that was what really mattered. I think we were all upset when the company closed, it was like closing a page of your life. We were the last that Ed Wingate kept but when he arranged that we join Motown, he felt we would stand the best chance of succeeding."

Wingate's optimism, sadly, proved wrong.

"We never felt the company was interested in us and we were never able to concentrate on what we should have been doing."

Thoroughly disillusioned by their time at Motown, the group went into semi-retirement in 1970, being coaxed back in 1973 with a line-up of Joseph Pruitt, James Epps, Cleveland Horne and Robert Newsome. Signed by Eastbound, they hit the charts with *I'm Falling In Love (I Feel Good All Over)* and then moved over to the Westbound imprint and scored further hits, most notably with *B.Y.O.F. (Bring Your Own Funk)*, produced by Dennis Coffey and which became their only UK hit, making #62 in 1979. The group continued working for the next few decades, although Cleveland Horne died from a heart attack on 13 April 2000. The Fantastic Four effectively came to an end later that year when lead vocalist 'Sweet' James Epps also died from a heart attack, on 11 September 2000. Joseph Pruitt died on 18 November 2008. Wallace Toby Childs predeceased them in September 1979. The last original member Ralph Pruitt died on 3 June 2014.

COMPILATION: THE BEST OF THE FANTASTIC FOUR (1969)

FAREWELL IS A LONELY SOUND – JIMMY RUFFIN [SINGLE]

Originally recorded in March 1967, the James Dean, William Weatherspoon and Jack Goga penned *Farewell Is A Lonely Sound* first appeared on Jimmy Ruffin's February 1969 album **Ruff 'N' Ready**. By then, the Soul label had already released three of the tracks as singles without any success whatsoever and in October the same year made one final throw of the dice to find a track that hit, opting for *Farewell Is A Lonely Sound*. Agonisingly close to making the chart, it bubbled under for two weeks, unable to lift itself beyond #104. In the UK, however, Jimmy's star was still very firmly in the ascendency, aided by the success of *I've Passed This Way Before*, which hit #33 in August 1969. The single had indeed passed this way before, having made #29 in February 1967.

The upshot was that British audiences were receptive to Jimmy, turning *Farwell Is A Lonely Sound* into a major hit, and one that *didn't* require the Northern Soul crowd to propel it up the chart. Jimmy's second Top Ten hit in what would eventually become his adoptive home, *Farewell Is A Lonely Sound* would make it to #8, the first of four consecutive Top Ten hits in Britain. The single was reissued again in 1974 after *What Becomes Of The Broken Hearted* became a Top Ten hit for the second time and again made a healthy chart showing, peaking at #30 towards the end of the year.

FAREWELL MY SUMMER LOVE – MICHAEL JACKSON [SINGLE]

As 1983 gave way to 1984, there was no bigger artist in the music world than Michael Jackson. Sales of the **Thriller** album were still way above the industry norm, with the title track and its accompanying video the latest in a long stream of singles success. Just as they had done earlier Motown watched the sales action with interest and once more delved in to their extensive back catalogue for a track that had never previously seen the light of day. Then it had been *One Day In Your Life*, now it was *Farewell My Summer Love*.

Originally recorded in 1973 as part of the sessions for the **G.I.T.** album and written by Keni St Lewis, the track was given an up to date remix and sent out to radio. Whilst a moderate success domestically, where it would peak at #37 R&B and #38 pop, *Farewell My Summer Love* resonated with British record buyers, enough for it to lift itself as far as #7 on the pop chart in June 1984. What made the final chart placing all the more remarkable was that it was achieved *without* an accompanying video, an art-form in which Michael Jackson was proving to be the new master. Eight years later British male vocal group Chaos took their take on the song to #55 on the chart.

FAREWELL MY SUMMER LOVE - MICHAEL JACKSON [ALBUM]

At much the same time the *Farewell My Summer Love* single was hitting the streets, Motown released a whole album's worth of 'new' material. Originally recorded between January and September 1973, the tracks were shelved and supposedly lost, only to be re-found in 1984 when Motown were looking to put previously unreleased Michael Jackson material out onto the market. Since the original material would have had a very dated sound (Michael was barely fifteen years of age when the original recording sessions took place), Motown commissioned a series of over-dubs and remixes, utilising the likes of Tony Peluso, Michael Lovesmith, Steve Barri and Tom Baird to bring the sound as up-to-date as was possible.

It has been said that Michael's appeal alone was responsible for getting it as far as #46 on the US pop charts, but once again it impressed the British market, hitting #9 and selling over 100,000 copies to earn a gold disc. Total worldwide sales are estimated at three million copies (a considerable number of these may well have been shifted in the aftermath of Michael's death in 2009), enough to have fully justified the search of the vaults for this previously lost album.

JOE FARRELL

Born Joseph Carl Firrantello in Chicago, Illinois on 16 December 1937, saxophonist and flautist Joe Farrell was one of the CTI All-Stars and would also become a founding member of Chick Corea's Return To Forever. Having spent the 1960s playing with the likes of Maynard Ferguson, Thad Jones and Charles Mingus, Joe linked with Creed Taylor and CTI in 1970, releasing his debut album that same year. He would record seven albums for the label, with **Upon This Rock** (a #24 jazz hit in 1974) and **Canned Funk** (#30 jazz in 1975) being released via Motown.

When CTI shut its doors Joe recorded crossover albums at Warner Brothers and straight ahead albums for Xanadu as well as with the CTI super group Fuse One, The Mingus Dynasty and Louis Hayes' group. He died from bone cancer on 10 January 1986 at the age of 48, reportedly having fallen on lean times owing to a drug habit.

ALBUMS: UPON THIS ROCK (1974), CANNED FUNK (1975)

THE FAYETTES

The Fayettes got their only credit on later pressings on the Hattie Littles' September 1962 single on Gordy *Your Love Is Wonderful*, providing backing vocals to the flip side *Here You Come*. They would subsequently become better known as The Vandellas, signing their own recording contract with Motown on 21 September 1962.

FEAR

Punk rock group Fear was formed in Los Angeles, California in 1977 by Lee Ving (born Lee James Jude Capallero in Philadelphia, Pennsylvania on 10 April 1950, guitar and vocals) and Derf Scratch (born Frederick Charles Milner III in Monmouth, New Jersey on 30 October 1951, bass), the pair recruiting Burt Good (guitar) and Johnny Backbeat (drums) in the first incarnation. Good and Backbeat left the group after recording one single and were replaced by Philo Cramer and Split Stix (born Tim Leitch) respectively.

After achieving notoriety for their performance on 'Saturday Night Live' in 1982, the group was invited to appear in 'Get Crazy', also contributing to the soundtrack released on Motown's Morocco imprint. Today Lee Ving is the only original member of Fear still with the group. Scratch died on 28 July 2010.

FEELS SO GOOD – GROVER WASHINGTON JR. [ALBUM]

As the follow-up album to the hugely successful **Mister Magic**, **Feels So Good** was assured of attention, with many punters waiting expectantly to see whether Grover could repeat the magic. **Feels So Good** employed much the same style, studio, crew of musicians (with one or two additions, including Louis Johnson of The Brothers Johnson on bass, Randy Brecker on trumpet and Steve Gadd on drums) and source of material, yet there were those who were not impressed, accusing Grover of 'bastardizing' jazz. His response was quite straight forward.

"My music is for the everyday person – people music. There's no pretense. It's honest. It transmits feelings and moods. That's about all you can hope to achieve. Music was never meant to stand still. That is one of the main reasons why I try to deal with a lot of different music. I don't want to be known as just a one-dimensional cat."

So it proved, with **Feels So Good** matching its predecessor to the letter, topping the jazz and R&B chart and hitting #10 on the pop listings, also giving vent to Grover's abilities as a songwriter (he composed three of the album's five tracks).

DINO FEKARIS

Born in Pittsburgh, Pennsylvania on 21 January 1945, Dino is best known for the Grammy award winning song *I Will Survive*, written with Freddie Perren and which Gloria Gaynor took to the top of both the US and UK charts in 1979. He joined Motown at the tail end of the 1960s as a producer and writer, initially linking with Nick Zesses and working with the likes of The Naturals. Their first major success came with Rare Earth, for whom they penned *I Just Want To Celebrate* and *Hey Big Brother,* with Nick and Dino also linking up with fellow writer and producer Tom Baird in the band Matrix. The trio also wrote together, penning *Love Me* for Diana Ross, a #38 UK hit in 1974.

Dino exited Motown during the middle of the 1970s and eventually linked with another former Motown staff writer, Freddie Perren, penning hits for Peaches & Herb, for whom *Reunited* was a US chart topper in 1979, the same year Dino and Freddie were hot with Gloria Gaynor, winning the Grammy Award for Best Disco Recording for *I Will Survive*. Whilst much of Dino's Motown work has been largely overlooked in the years that have passed, *I Will Survive* has become an anthem for both the feminist and gay movements.

JOSE FELICIANO

Largely known the world over for his 1968 interpretation of The Doors' track *Light My Fire*, taken to #3 pop in the US (and #29 R&B) and #6 in the UK, a year after Jim Morrison *et al* had taken it to the top of the US charts, Jose Feliciano was hardly expected to rack up a lengthy series of hit singles during his time at Motown. Rather, his signing would enable Motown to make significant strides in shifting albums in the hitherto untapped Latino market.

Born on 10 September 1945 in Lares, Puerto Rico and blind since birth, Jose Montserrate Feliciano Garcia moved to Spanish Harlem in New York City with his family when he was five. He first learned to play the accordion and then the guitar, spending fourteen hours a day absorbing influences such as rock and roll, jazz and classical. After being spotted whilst performing in Greenwich Village at the age of eighteen, he signed with RCA in 1964 and released his first album the same year. His breakthrough came four years and three albums later, with **Feliciano!** containing the aforementioned smash *Light My Fire* and sending the album almost to the chart summit.

Over the next decade and a half, Jose would receive an estimated thirty two gold album awards, two Grammy Awards and become the leading Latino artist of the time. He joined Motown in 1981 and released his first eponymous album in October 1981, hitting #61 on the R&B chart and enjoying a rare R&B hit single as *I Wanna Be Where You Are* made #63. Further success came with his Spanish language release **Escenas De Amor (Love Scenes)**, which would make #3 on the US Latin Album chart. Jose would release one further album for the company, **Romance In The Night** in March 1983.

ALBUMS: JOSE FELICIANO (1981), ESCENAS DE AMOR (LOVE SCENES) (1982), ROMANCE IN THE NIGHT (1983)

THE FESTIVALS

Originally formed in Dallas, Texas by brothers Vaughan and Woody Price, Earl Moss and Leon Thomas, The Festivals first came to prominence in 1966 with a series of singles for Smash Records, although with little or no success. After a brief stop with Blue Rock they resurfaced at Jerry Ross' Colossus Records in Philadelphia and released a further three singles, two of which, *You're Gonna Make It* and *Baby Show It* hit the Top 30 of the R&B chart.

They followed Jerry to Motown in 1972 and got one outing, *Green Grow The Lilacs*, a song Motown had already tried out on Soupy Sales, The Originals and Joe Harnell. The Festivals' Gordy single went nowhere, with the group recording one further known single for Lo Lo before seemingly disbanding.

F.G.O.

Mike Harris (lead vocals), Scott Weatherspoon (keyboards), Mike Banks (bass and keyboards) and Raphael Merriweathers (percussion and drums) met at school whilst members of various other groups but would eventually come together as F.G.O. (For Girls Only) and sign for Motown in 1986. Their time at the label can only be described as frustrating, with two singles (*Nice Girls* and *I'll Be Around*) and one album (**Give Her What She Wants**) scheduled for 1987 release, all being cancelled before they went to the press, although it is believed that the 12" version of *Nice Girls* was released in March 1987. The group then disbanded, although they would later reconvene in Detroit collective Members Of The House.

ERNIE FIELDS JR.

The son of legendary band leader Ernie Fields, saxophonist Ernie Junior played with his father during the 1950s and by the middle of the next decade was well established as a bandleader, producer and musician in his own right. He is credited with revitalising the career of Bobby 'Blue' Bland in the early 1970s and was utilised as a session musician on countless recordings, including the likes of Rick James, Marvin Gaye, Teena Marie, Stevie Wonder and B.B. King. His one Motown single, released as a 12" single only, was *Ride A Wild Horse* issued in 1978. Ernie wrote the music for the blaxploitation film 'Disco Godfather' and would later tour with Fred Wesley.

THE FIFTH DIMENSION

Motown could have signed The 5th Dimension right from day one but passed, only to come to rue the decision several times over in the following years. Originally formed as The Versatiles in Los Angeles, California in 1965, the line-up comprised Marilyn McCoo (born in Jersey City on 30 September 1943), Florence LaRue (born in Philadelphia, Pennsylvania on 4 February 1944), Billy Davis (born in St Louis, Missouri on 26 June 1938), Lamont McLemore (born in St Louis on 17 September 1939) and Ron Townson (born in St Louis on 20 January 1933).

They submitted an audition tape to Marc Gordon, then running Motown's Los Angeles office, who was impressed enough to forward it to Detroit for further consideration, although the tape and the band were eventually turned down. The group would record one single for Bronco before moving on to singer Johnny Rivers' Soul City label, where they once again came across Marc Gordon, who would become their manager. Both Rivers and Gordon recommended the group ditch their name and come up with a catchier moniker, eventually settling on The Fifth Dimension.

After a hesitant start the group hit their stride with *Go Where You Wanna Go*, a #16 pop hit in 1967 that missed the R&B chart. Indeed, The Fifth Dimension found greater acceptance in pop circles than in R&B ones, racking up two number one hits with *Aquarius/Let The Sunshine In* and *Wedding Bell Blues* whilst never getting beyond #2 on the R&B chart. As well as five million selling singles for Soul City and later label Bell (to whom Rivers sold Soul City) in 1970, The Fifth Dimension charted 13 albums for these two labels and won a total of six Grammy Awards.

They switched to ABC in 1976 and came up on Motown's radar once again, with their hastily recorded version of *Love Hangover* considered a viable threat to Diana Ross' own original version. The result was Diana's original was rush released and became major hit, whilst The Fifth Dimension had to settle for a #39 R&B and #80 pop hit.

The group joined Motown in 1978, by which time husband and wife Marilyn McCoo and Billy Davis had departed for a career as a duo. The line-up that signed with Motown therefore featured Florence LaRue (who had married the group's manager Marc Gordon), Lamonte McLemore, Mic Bell, Terri Bryant and Lou Courtney. The group would record two albums for Motown, **Star Dancing** being released in January 1978 and **High On Sunshine** a year later, with *You Are The Reason (I Feel Like Dancing)* their lone hit single, making #66 on the R&B chart in March 1978. Townson died from kidney failure on 2 August 2001 whilst former manager Marc Gordon died after a lengthy illness on 16 June 2010.

ALBUMS: STAR DANCING (1978), HIGH ON SUNSHINE (1979)

A FINE MESS (FILM SOUNDTRACK)

Written and directed by Blake Edwards, 'A Fine Mess' was originally envisaged as a remake of the Laurel & Hardy 1932 Oscar winning short 'The Music Box'. However, after poor initial reviews and reported studio interference the film was re-edited and became something of a standard chase comedy. Starring Ted Danson and Howie Mandel with music by Henry Mancini, the film was so poorly received upon release in April 1986 that Blake Edwards went on American television talk shows and advised the public to avoid the film at all costs! With the film going on to receive even poorer reviews, the soundtrack should have similarly disappeared without trace, but somehow it

managed to limp into the chart at #183. Motown artists The Temptations, Smokey Robinson, Chico DeBarge, Mary Jane Girls, Nick Jameson and Keith Burston and Darryl Littlejohn were joined by Christine McVie (formerly of Fleetwood Mac), Los Lobos, Billy Vera & The Beaters and Henry Mancini on the ten track soundtrack, the only worthwhile thing to come out of a film that lived up to its name.
ALBUM: A FINE MESS SOUNDTRACK (1986)

FINGERTIPS PART 2 – STEVIE WONDER [SINGLE]

Berry Gordy may have been mightily impressed with Stevie's abilities on almost any musical instrument he cared to pick up, but the truth of the matter was that aside from marketing him as a much younger version of Ray Charles, which they would do later, Berry had little or no idea how they were going to get across to the public just how talented this youngster was. His first three singles, released in 1962, lacked a real sense of direction and, whilst they were all competently recorded, there was nothing in the grooves that leapt out and forced the listener to pay real attention. However, Berry had noticed Little Stevie was a captivating live performer, where audiences could see just how much fun the performer was having; if there was a way of capturing that excitement on record, Berry might have a hit record on his hands.

As it happened, a live date at the Regal Theater in Chicago provided all of them with the ammunition they needed. Partway through Stevie's slot, he launched into *Fingertips*, a song written by Hank Cosby and Clarence Paul. Whilst there was a song in there somewhere, what made the recording was Stevie's exuberant harmonica playing, during which he ad-libbed into a quick rendition of *Merrily We Roll Along*. On the recording, as the song drew to a close and the MC called for one more round of applause for Little Stevie Wonder, the youngster bounded back on stage and carried on playing where he had left off, leaving Larry Moses, one of the musicians about to take his place as a member of the backing band for the next act to perform, to shout 'what key, what key' as he tried to pick up on the song that was being played.

When Berry Gordy heard the recording, he reasoned that this was the perfect vehicle to release as a Little Stevie Wonder single. It did not matter that the actual recording was too long to be released as a single; a simple edit produced *Part 1* and *Part 2*, with the ad-lib featured *Part 2* promoted as the main side. The hunch paid off, for in quick time *Fingertips* was sitting on top of the pop (for three weeks) and the R&B (for six weeks) charts, becoming Motown's second US chart topper, with a hastily assembled live album also hitting the market to capitalise on this sudden success and also topping both charts.

FINISHED TOUCH

All five members of Finished Touch were staff writers for Jobete, given an opportunity to record some of their own material under a collective group name. Mike and Brenda Sutton, Michael McGloiry, Harold Johnson and Kenny Stover therefore recorded an album **Need To Know You Better**, released in July 1978, from which the single *Sticks And Stones (But The Funk Won't Ever Hurt You)* hit #88 on the R&B chart. Two further singles were lifted but didn't get much in the way of promotion, resulting in a second album **Finished Touch** being cancelled. Husband and wife duo Mike and Brenda would later go and record with some success for SAM and Rocshire in the 1980s.
ALBUM: NEED TO KNOW YOU BETTER (1978)

ALBERT FINNEY

Infinitely better known as an actor than as a singer, Albert was born in Salford, Lancashire on 9 May 1936, graduated from the Royal Academy of Dramatic Art (RADA) and made his first stage appearance in 1958 in 'The Party'. His first film success came with 'Saturday Night And Sunday Morning', with his best known roles being in 'Tom Jones' and as Hercule Poirot in 'Murder On The Orient Express'.

A regular on stage too, it was his performances in the musicals 'The Lily White Boys' and 'Scrooge' that prompted a call to record an album, with Albert also electing to write his own material. The album was released on Motown in July 1977 as **Albert Finney's Album**, with two singles also being lifted in *Those Other Men* and *A State Of Grace*. He returned to acting after this brief interlude, continuing to earn plaudits and awards along the way. However, whilst he picked up nominations for Oscars, Emmy's and Golden Globes during his career, he is equally well known for two awards he refused to collect, turning down a C.B.E. (Commander of the Order of the British Empire) in 1980 and a knighthood in 2000, claiming the British awards system perpetuated snobbery!
ALBUM: ALBERT FINNEY'S ALBUM (1977)

THE FIVE SMOOTH STONES

A gospel group that was the brainchild of writer, producer and arranger Frank Kavelin (the son of Al Kavelin, the owner of Lute Records which had The Hollywood Argyles), The Five Smooth Stones featured Frank, John Colar, Tim Hawkins, his later wife Edie Hayes and Jackie Fishell. They released one single on the Chisa label in 1969, *I Will Never Love Another*, although recorded several tracks which presumably remain in the vault. Frank meanwhile worked with several other Chisa artists, including arranging duties for Monk Montgomery and his Motown released album **It's Never Too Late**. John Colar later became a member of LA Rhythm Kings.

FIZZY QWICK

Female singer Debravon Lewis (born in Solano County, California on 9 February 1953) had been a member of New Wave group Tiggi Clay, adopting the moniker Fizzy Qwick for this project. Two years after Tiggi Clay recorded their only album, Fizzy Qwick issued an eponymous solo album, from which two singles were lifted, *Hangin' Out* and *You Want It Your Way, Always*, with the material written and produced by her previous partners in Tiggi Clay.
ALBUM: FIZZY QWICK (1986)

ROBERTA FLACK & QUINCY JONES

Female singer Roberta Flack was born in Black Mountain, North Carolina on 10 February 1939 (although some sources state the year of birth to be 1937) and learned to play piano at an early age. After gaining a full scholarship to Howard University at the age of 15, Roberta began graduate studies in music but was forced to give this up following the sudden death of her father. Instead she became a teacher during the day and performed in clubs in the evening and at weekends, subsequently being spotted by Les McCann who helped get her a contract with Atlantic in 1968. She scored her first hit with a cover of *You've Got A Friend* and would go on to top the charts with *The First Time Ever I Saw Your Face* in 1972 and return to the summit in 1973 with *Killing Me Softly With His Song* and 1974 with *Feel Like Making Love*.

Quincy Delight Jones meanwhile, was born in Chicago, Illinois on 14 March 1933 and raised in Seattle, Washington. He began his career as a jazz trumpeter with Lionel Hampton but would go on to forge a hugely successful career as a musical director, producer, arranger, writer and artist, enjoying a career that has stretched across some six decades. Robert and Quincy linked up for the track *On A Clear Day (You Can See Forever) – Killer Joe* for the 'Save The Children' soundtrack released by Motown in April 1974.

THE FLAMINGO KID (FILM SOUNDTRACK)

A 1984 comedy film starring Matt Dillon, Hector Elizondo, Jessica Walter, Janet Jones, Martha Gehman and Richard Crenna, 'The Flamingo Kid' was directed by Garry Marshall and opened in December 1984. The film was relatively successful, grossing over $23 million, with Walt Disney announcing plans for a remake some 25 years later. Motown ensured the soundtrack album was released at the same time as the film, resulting in a #130 pop chart placing. Among the Motown artists featured on the soundtrack were Martha & The Vandellas, Barrett Strong and Maureen Steele, with Jesse Frederick, The Chiffons, Acker Bilk, Dion, Little Richard, The Impressions, Hank Ballard & The Midnighters and The Silhouettes completing the twelve track line-up.
ALBUM: THE FLAMINGO KID SOUNDTRACK (1984)

FLAVOR

Vocal trio Flavor was formed by Stanton Scott Sheppard, Chauncey Matthews and Fred Brown Jr., with their debut single in 1976 *Don't Freeze Up* on Bunky Records (run by Sheppard's father Bill as a division of Scepter Records) getting enough interest for the group to sign a deal with Ju-Par, then distributed by Motown. The single was duly reissued on Ju-Par in February 1977, with the album **In Good Taste** following in May (released on the Motown label in Britain in August), although neither made any impact on the charts. The group remained with Ju-Par after its distribution deal with Motown came to an end, later changing their name to Livin' Proof. Stan Sheppard had previously recorded as Disco Stan for Prodigal and would later become a member of Triple S and Skool Boyz.
ALBUM: IN GOOD TASTE (1977)

FLIGHT

A progressive jazz rock group formed in Florida in the early 1970s, Flight recorded two albums for Capitol before linking with Motown in 1980. By the time their only album for the label, **Excursion Beyond** was released, the group consisted of Jim Michael Yaeger (keyboards), John DeNicola (bass), Ted Karczewski (guitar and bass), Pat Vidas (trumpet and vocals) and Steve Shebar (drums) and their sound had become lighter and fusion based.

John DeNicola would later make a name for himself as a songwriter, helping pen *(I've Had) The Time Of My Life* for the film 'Dirty Dancing', for which he would win an Academy Award and Golden Globe Award and receive a Grammy nomination.

ALBUM: EXCURSION BEYOND (1980)

FLOY JOY – THE SUPREMES [SINGLE]

Smokey Robinson had been just one of many writers who tried to provide The Supremes Mark I with a hit during their early days at Motown, although with slightly more success than the likes of Berry Gordy. Where Gordy's attempts had missed the charts, Smokey could claim to have been responsible for two of the group's earliest hits in *Your Heart Belongs To Me* (#95 pop) and *A Breath Taking Guy* which made it as far as #75. Then Holland-Dozier-Holland took over and for the next four or five years turned popular and R&B music on its head with a succession of hits. The departure of HDH from the Motown stable came at a heavy price for all concerned, not least The Supremes who struggled to match the quality of earlier releases. In 1969 they were paired with Smokey once again for *The Composer*, which hit #27 pop and #21 R&B. By 1971 The Supremes were now without Diana Ross who had left for a solo career, and sessions for an album to be called **Promises Kept** with Frank Wilson were eventually abandoned.

The Supremes Mark II turned to Smokey once again and were pleasantly surprised at the quality of songs he had written with them in mind, most of which seemed to bear more than a little trace of HDH influence – time would tell if they contained the same kind of magic. The first fruits of their joint labours was *Floy Joy* (originally titled *Floyd Joy*), a song that harked back to their earlier glories. With Jean Terrell and Mary Wilson sharing lead vocals, *Floy Joy* did at least return the group to the upper reaches of the chart – in the US it make #16 pop (it was to be the group's final appearance in the Top 20) and #5 R&B. However, it was to be in Britain that the song found its true home, hitting #9 in April 1972.

KING FLOYD

King Floyd didn't actually record *for* Motown, although the company would release an album and single under his name whilst his popularity was at its peak. Born in New Orleans, Louisiana on 13 February 1943 he was singing from the age of twelve and got his first professional engagement at sixteen (with fake I.D.), although his initial plans at a musical career were put on hold whilst he served in the military. Upon his return he made his way to New York where he would briefly sign with James Brown's Try Me label, although nothing was recorded. King then headed west and signed with Original Sound, who released his first single in 1965. He would also record for Uptown and in 1968 did a whole album for Mercury's Pulsar label, but when that failed to sell, King Floyd decided to head for home and took a job with the post office.

Soon after arriving back in New Orleans he bumped into producer Wardell Quezergue of Malaco Records, who convinced him to give it another shot. Those initial sessions resulted in *Groove Me*, which was turned down by several labels (including Stax) before being issued on the Atlantic affiliate Chimneyville. The single was originally released with *What Our Love Needs* as the top side until a New Orleans disc jockey flipped it, and by the beginning of 1971 the single was on top of the R&B chart and on its way to the Top Ten of the pop chart.

When it became known that there was an earlier album by King Floyd (the 1968 Pulsar recordings) available for purchase, Motown led the chase and issued **Heart Of The Matter** in April 1971 to capitalise on his new found fame. They also lifted a single in *Heartaches*, but King Floyd's only subsequent appearances on the charts were to be with new material on Chimneyville. He died on 6 March 2006 following complications brought about by a stroke and diabetes.

ALBUM: HEART OF THE MATTER (1971)

ROBERT FOLK

Film and television music composer Robert Folk was born in New York on 5 March 1949 and graduated from the Juilliard School in the city. He would go on to compose the music to more than 65 films, including

'American Pie: Band Camp', 'Ace Ventura: When Nature Calls' and 'The Slayer' as well as all of the films in the 'Police Academy' franchise. He therefore contributed the track *The High Flyers* to the soundtrack of 'Police Academy 4: Citizens On Patrol' that was released by Motown in 1987.

FONTANA RECORDS

London American had been Motown's temporary home in Britain between May 1959, when Marv Johnson's *Come To Me* had been released, through to The Miracles *Ain't It Baby* in June 1961. Despite four direct Motown releases (they would also release subsequent Marv Johnson singles, as well as one by Paul Guyten), London American and Decca were too large to fully do justice to the fledgling Motown label. Thus in the late summer of 1961, Berry Gordy switched distributors in the UK to the Fontana label. Part of the Philips group of companies, Fontana had also had success in taking American repertoire and turning it into British chart material, most notably with Johnny Mathis, Marty Robbins and Buddy Greco.

There were high hopes that their smaller operation might make them hungrier for success, but despite having Motown's first US chart topper, *Please Mr. Postman* by The Marvelettes with which to kick off the union, Fontana were no more able to get a hit than their predecessor. The deal with Fontana would be extremely short-lived, covering two singles by The Marvelettes and one apiece from The Miracles and Eddie Holland, but by March 1962, barely four months after entering into an agreement, Fontana were quietly dropped.

FOR ONCE IN MY LIFE – STEVIE WONDER [SINGLE]

There are Motown records that have sold more copies and there are Motown records that have received more airplay, but for sheer popularity, no Motown song can come close to *For Once In My Life*. Written by staff writer Ron Miller with Orlando Murden and reportedly inspired by the birth of Miller's daughter, *For Once In My Life* was supposedly written with Barbara McNair in mind. However, the earliest recording was a demo version done by Jean DuShon, supervised by Miller, which was considered good enough to subsequently get released by Chess Records' Cadet imprint.

According to legend, Berry Gordy was not happy to hear that one of his writers had given a song to an outside singer and so had Miller make the song available to several Motown artists. It is also claimed that the first male vocalist to record the song was Japanese-American actor Jack Soo, who reportedly cut two albums for Motown in the 1960s that were never released. Other versions, of course, were recorded and released, including The Temptations (it would be become something of a show stopper for Paul Williams), The Four Tops, The Supremes and Stevie Wonder.

"I wrote *For Once In My Life* like a Tony Bennett ballad," Ron would explain. "It was beautiful. And then – along comes Stevie. He put a harmonica solo in it and he put the tempo up and made a whole different song out of it."

Indeed, just about every other version until Stevie's stuck true to the ballad nature of the song, including a version by Tony Bennett that hit the lower reaches of the chart in 1967.

"*For Once In My Life* was a great tune, but it lacked excitement" was Stevie's retort. "The other interpretations were beautiful – but too old fashioned. I wanted to do the song the way I felt it. You know the bit where I go 'wow'! That is after the music starts you become aware of the mood of the song – and then you just have to go 'wow'. Even though it was a ballad and I loved it as that I felt the tune could be done in the form of rejoicing in meeting someone who needed me. I was excited and recorded it that way."

Stevie's version sat in the can for more than a year until Billie Jean Brown brought it into a Quality Control meeting and pushed for it to be released as a single. Motown eventually relented and were rewarded when it hit #2 pop and #2 R&B (behind Marvin Gaye's *I Heard It Through The Grapevine*, another single Motown had been reluctant to release!), also matching that success in the UK where it became Stevie's biggest hit to date in peaking at #3. The single proved successful enough to earn Stevie his second Grammy nomination for Best R&B Vocal Performance, Male, missing out on the night to Otis Redding and *Sittin' On The Dock Of The Bay*. However, in 2006 Stevie joined Tony Bennett on his album **Duets: An American Classic** and performed a ballad version that would go on to win the Grammy Award for Best Pop Collaboration with Vocals!

Stevie's solo version however has come to be considered the definitive version of *For Once In My Life*, although that has not stopped artists as diverse as Dorothy Squires, John Farnham, Ella Fitzgerald, Cilla Black, Andy Williams, Dean Martin, Frank Sinatra, Gladys Knight & The Pips, The Osmonds, Desmond

Dekker, Michael Ball, Michael Bolton, Michael McDonald, Michael Buble and scores of others offering their own interpretations. In short, it has become one of the most valuable songs in the entire Jobete catalogue.

DARLA FOSTER

Discovered by legendary producer and writer Stan Kesler, Darla Foster recorded one single for the Melodyland imprint, although there is some doubt as to whether *Say Love (Or Don't Say Anything At All)* backed with *He Makes The Wrong Seem Right* was actually released, for whilst promotional copies surfaced in September 1975, finished stock has not. Whilst Stan Kesler has continued to add to his legend, Darla seemingly never recorded again.

JERRY FOSTER

Ultimately better known as a songwriter, Jerry Foster had several attempts at pursuing a recording career under his own name, with varying degrees of success. Born in Tallapoosa, Missouri on 19 November 1935, Jerry was still a serving sergeant in the US Marines when he launched a musical career, becoming both host and resident singer on WSAV-TV in Savannah, Georgia in 1956. The following year he signed his first recording contract, inking with Backbeat Records in December but not actually releasing anything until January 1959. A further two years passed with little or no action on his career, prompting him to take up songwriting.
He teamed up with Bill Rice and after the pair moved to Nashville in 1967 found there were plenty of artists eager to record their material, with Jeannie C Riley earning a Grammy nomination for her version of *Back Side Of Dallas* in 1969. Further recognition came in 1972 when the pair received a record 10 citations from the ASCAP Awards, a record they themselves beat in 1974 with eleven. That same year Jerry formed a production company with Bill Hall, but by 1976 the hankering for a return to his own recording career saw Jerry sign with Hitsville. He would record two singles for the label, *I Knew You When* and *Family Man* before resuming his writing career, including another Grammy nomination for *Here Comes The Hurt Again* by Mickey Gilley in 1981. Whilst his impact as a singer might have been minimal, his writing has had a long lasting effect.

"I received a phone call, while being interviewed by a Florida radio station, from a young lady who told me that at one time she became pregnant out of wedlock causing her father and mother to disown her. She said that she had checked into a motel intending suicide. The radio in the room played a Foster/Rice song, *Rosie Cries A Lot* by Ferlin Husky, causing her to change her mind about dying. She told me that, thanks to our song, mother and baby were doing fine and the little one is adored by her (the mother's) parents. I never understood why the song affected her in the way it did, but thank God it did! We writers never know, most of the time, the impact some of our work can have."

THE FOUR TOPS

If The Supremes were the female jewel in Motown's crown, then The Four Tops would have a very strong case for being their male equivalent. Aside from their body of work, which contains many of Motown's biggest hits, the sheer longevity of the group has ensured their place in the pantheon of popular music; with a unity akin to marriage, it is fitting that they remained together 'til death us do part.'
Growing up in Detroit, Michigan, Levi Stubbles (born in Detroit on 6 June 1936), Renaldo 'Obie' Benson (born in Detroit on 14 June 1936), Lawrence Payton (born in Detroit on 2 March 1938) and Abdul 'Duke' Fakir (born in Detroit on 26 December 1935) were all high school students when they first got together at a local birthday party. Resolving to stick together, they adopted the name The Four Aims and with the assistance of Lawrence' cousin Billy Roquel Davis got a one-off single deal with Chess Records.
Changing their name to The Four Tops so as to avoid any confusion with the popular singing group The Ames Brothers, the group headed to Chicago to record *Could It Be You*, released in 1956 to little or no fanfare. Meanwhile the group earned a veritable reputation for the quality of their live work, performing in numerous clubs and even getting picked to support Billy Eckstine on one of his tours.
There were sporadic recording opportunities over the next few years, with Red Top, Columbia and Riverside issuing singles with much the same results as their Chess outing. Their reputation continued to grow and Berry Gordy made several attempts at signing them to Motown during its early days. He did get them into Hitsville on one occasion and put a contract in front of them, but their insistence on taking it away and letting

a lawyer have a look at the fine print resulted in the deal remaining unsigned.

Instead, The Four Tops continued their nomadic existence for a couple more years until eventually they decided to take Berry up on his offer, although whether they received legal advice prior to signing on the dotted line is not known. What is known that the group was keen to pursue their own interest in jazz and worked with Mickey Stevenson on a number of standards ranging from *Nice 'N' Easy, Stranger On The Shore, I Left My Heart In San Francisco, Young And Foolish* and *On The Street Where You Live*. Although the resulting tracks were intended for release as the album **Breaking Through** on Workshop Jazz in 1964, the release was pulled. Instead, at the eleventh hour, Berry Gordy convinced the group to work with Holland-Dozier-Holland, the production and songwriting trio who were also highly active with The Supremes.

It was a decision that was to prove crucial to the career of The Four Tops and the future prosperity of Motown. Their first session produced *Baby I Need Your Lovin'*, a track that highlighted Levi Stubbs' gruff but distinctive lead vocal, superbly accompanied by the remaining three Tops harmonies and, rounding out the sound, the female backing supplied by The Andantes. *Baby I Need Your Lovin'* exploded across the airwaves and would go on to peak at #11 pop and #4 R&B. Whilst those chart positions would be bettered by many of The Four Tops' own singles, the importance of the track can be judged by the fact that it has received more radio play than any other Motown track, indicative of its importance in establishing the famed Motown sound.

After a couple of smaller hits in *Without The One You Love (Life's Not Worth While)* and *Ask The Lonely*, The Four Tops and HDH started to raise the pace, with *I Can't Help Myself* surging to the top of the pop and R&B charts in 1965 and becoming their UK chart breakthrough in making #23. Three months later, the group hit again with *It's The Same Old Song*, a prophetic title given that the song was crafted out of bits and pieces left off of *I Can't Help Myself*. Irrespective of how the song came together, it proved to be another major smash, hitting #5 pop and #2 R&B and cracked the UK Top 40 at #34.

The sudden success The Four Tops were enjoying at Motown prompted Columbia to brush the dust off one of their 1960 recordings, with *Ain't That Love* coming to a halt at #93. This Columbia anomaly aside, The Four Tops were making a dual attack on the charts during the middle 1960s, with their albums also doing healthy business, even if the sometimes patched up nature of the long players issued by Motown meant that many buyers tended to stick to the singles. Still, an R&B chart topper with their debut album was followed by the #3 success of **Four Tops Second Album** which also peaked at #20 on the pop chart, proof the group could crossover.

It helped that they never disappointed whenever they were given the opportunity of appearing on television, and whilst their performances didn't have the same kind of crafted choreography that was taking The Temptations to the limit, The Four Tops were no slouches when it came to putting on a show. Meanwhile, HDH and The Four Tops kept the hits rolling, with *Reach Out I'll Be There* in 1966 the undoubted pinnacle of their career. An across the board chart topper, spending two weeks apiece at the top of the R&B and pop chart and three weeks at the summit in the UK, *Reach Out I'll Be There* just exploded around the world, even if its eventual success caught the group by surprise. It also set something of a template that *Standing In The Shadows Of Love* and *Bernadette* were quick to follow, both also becoming Top Ten hits on both sides of the Atlantic.

By this time, The Four Tops' stock was so high they could afford to stretch out a bit on their albums, with **Four Tops On Top** mixing the blueprint HDH sound with both pop and jazz standards. That was swiftly followed by a live album and four months later **Four Tops On Broadway**, with both albums being packed with MOR repertoire. Despite this they still performed well on the charts, with **Four Tops Live** topping the R&B chart and hitting the Top 20 pop whilst **On Broadway** making #15 R&B.

The Four Tops growing fan base needn't have become unduly worried, however, for they were back in the studio putting the finishing touch to **Reach Out**, built around the success of the single along with *Bernadette, 7 Rooms Of Gloom* and *I'll Turn To Stone*, all of which would be released as singles. When Motown delved back in the album at a later date to issue *If I Were A Carpenter* and *Walk Away Renee* it became apparent that something was amiss.

That something was Holland-Dozier-Holland, who went missing from the studio having effectively gone on strike as their dispute with Berry Gordy escalated. No group suffered more from the loss of HDH than The Four Tops, as the group themselves readily admitted. The hits enjoyed on the singles chart during 1967 and 1968 were effectively material that had been recorded prior to the dispute, so as the summer of 1968 loomed, the group was in need of new writers and new producers.

Initially assigned the task was Ivy Jo Hunter, who worked with Vernon Bullock, Jack Goga and new

Jobete writer Pam Sawyer on *Yesterday's Dreams*, a minor pop (#49) and R&B (#31) hit, although it performed slightly better in the UK where their fanbase remained loyal. Over the next two years Britain helped keep The Four Tops near the top, turning *I'm In A Different World*, *What Is A Man* and *Do What You Gotta Do* into Top 30 hits at a time when the group was struggling to make any kind of impact at home.

Also keeping their name hot was a compilation of their biggest hits, **The Four Tops Greatest Hits** which topped the UK charts (and also became a #4 hit in their homeland), but **Yesterday's Dreams** featured just one HDH track and perhaps suffered as a result, peaking at #91 and #37 in the US and UK respectively, even if it did hit #7 R&B. **The Four Tops Now!** was similarly devoid of a major hit or real direction, reflected in its rather tame #74 pop and #18 R&B showing, missing out in the UK altogether.

It was obvious that The Four Tops needed new inspiration, which finally arrived when Frank Wilson was assigned their producer. The new collaboration cut their teeth with **Soul Spin**, effectively an album that went down the same path as its predecessors in gathering material both inside and outside of Hitsville, including the by now obligatory Beatles cover (for this album read *Got To Get You Into My Life*), but which was something of a trial run for future glories. Certainly, both parties learned something from the experience of recording the album together, with Frank in particular identifying the kind of material The Four Tops excelled with. Frank delved far back into musical history for the group's next single, *It's All In The Game*, which whilst a minor pop hit proved its worth on the R&B chart (#6) and in the UK (#5). Just as HDH had done a few years previously, the success prompted Frank to step up a gear or two, coming up with the melody to *Still Water (Love)* to which Smokey Robinson added the lyrics. Whilst this was not a new writing combination in the sense of others established at Motown, it was still potent enough to have *Still Water* sail into the Top Ten of the chart in the UK (it would have to settle for a rather more modest #11 in the US, although it did hit #4 on the R&B chart). Frank would also helm the last major Four Tops album success, with **Still Waters Run Deep** featuring the usual potpourri of material, ranging from *L.A. (My Kind Of Town)* and *Everybody's Talkin'*, with the album settling just outside the Top 20 at #21 and just inside the Top 30 in the UK at #29 (it managed much better on the R&B chart where it hit #3).

Six months later came the next Four Tops album **Changing Times**, which struggled to make a significant headway on the chart, not even cracking the Top 100.

Water would again provide the inspiration for another major hit, with a remake of Ike & Tina Turner's *River Deep Mountain High*, done in collaboration with The Supremes would make #14 pop, #7 R&B and a #11 hit in the UK. The resulting album, **The Magnificent 7** found greater favour in the UK, where it peaked at #6, but the concept worked well enough to see three albums released by the two Motown supergroups, with **The Return Of The Magnificent Seven** and **Dynamite** making brief chart appearances in the US. Remarkably, neither album charted in the UK, a strange outcome given the success the very first album had enjoyed. No doubt the fact that there wasn't a single with the same kind of strength as *River Deep* to be found on any of the albums played a part in the stagnating album sales.

Meanwhile, The Four Tops continued their by now diminishing assault on the singles chart, with *Just Seven Numbers (Can Straighten Out My Heart)* and *(It's The Way) Nature Planned It* the only two to make the Top Ten of the R&B chart; *MacArthur Park* at #38 being the only single to actually break into the Top 40 by this stage. With Motown planning to move lock, stock and barrel to Los Angeles in 1972, The Four Tops opted to head out of a different door and began shopping around for a new label before the year was out.

They would eventually sign with Dunhill/ABC and be made a major priority for the label, exactly the reason why they had decided to leave Motown in the first place, resulting in major hits such as *Keeper Of The Castle*, *Ain't No Woman (Like The One I've Got)* and *Are You Man Enough* all making the Top Ten on the R&B chart (and the first two also made the Top Ten on the pop chart too). The Four Tops would later record for Casablanca, with *When She Was My Girl* a major hit in 1981, and RSO before taking part in the 'Motown 25' television special. On a night of many highlights, the battle between The Four Tops and The Temptations would prove hard to top, resulting in the two groups going out on the road together for a series of highly acclaimed live dates. The group also briefly returned to Motown and scored another couple of hits in *I Just Can't Walk Away* and *Sexy Ways* before moving on to Arista and further success towards the end of the 1980s.

The one constant during all of this time was the group itself, with no changes to the line-up all through their heyday and beyond. That run was finally brought to an end with the death of Lawrence Payton on 20 June 1997, with former Temptation member Theo Peoples brought in as his replacement. The new line-up was in place for eight years before The Four Tops suffered their next loss, Obie Benson succumbing to cancer on

2 July 2005. Three years later Levi Stubbs, who had already left the group after suffering a stroke, died peacefully in his sleep on 17 October 2008. The group had actually had a much earlier brush with disaster; in 1988 they were delayed during a recording session in Europe and had to change their flight back home to America. Had they got on the scheduled plane, they would have been among the 259 crew and passengers and 11 people killed on the ground as Pan Am flight 103 exploded over Lockerbie. The sole surviving original member of the group, Abdul Fakir, continues to lead a Four Tops group on tour around the world, with Roquel Payton (Lawrence's son), former Motown solo artist Ronnie McNeir and Harold 'Spike' Bonhart for company. The group was inducted into the Rock & Roll Hall of Fame in 1990.

ALBUMS: THE FOUR TOPS (1965), FOUR TOPS SECOND ALBUM (1965), ON TOP (1966), LIVE (1966), REACH OUT (1967), YESTERDAY'S DREAMS (1968), NOW (1969), SOUL SPIN (1969), MAGNIFICENT SEVEN (1970), STILL WATERS RUN DEEP (1970), CHANGING TIMES (1970), RETURN OF THE MAGNIFICENT SEVEN (1971), DYNAMITE (1971), NATURE PLANNED IT (1972), BACK WHERE I BELONG (1983), MAGIC (1985), HOT NIGHTS (1986)

COMPILATIONS: GREATEST HITS (1967), GREATEST HITS VOLUME 2 (1971), THE BEST OF THE FOUR TOPS (1973), THE FOUR TOPS STORY (1973), ANTHOLOGY (1973), SUPER HITS (1976), 19 GREATEST HITS (1984)

THE FOUR TOPS – THE FOUR TOPS [EP]

A four track compilation featuring *I Can't Help Myself*, *Ask The Lonely*, *Something About You* and *It's The Same Old Song*, **The Four Tops** EP was released in the UK in February 1966. For some unfathomable reason, it took seven months to register on the chart, finally making an entrance on 29 October at #9. Three weeks later it reached its peak of #2, going on to spend a total of 60 weeks on the EP chart until the listing was discontinued on 16 December 1967. Midway through **The Four Tops**' chart run it was joined on the listings by **Four Tops Hits**, with the two holding the top positions on the chart on the 28 October 1967.

FOUR TOPS GREATEST HITS – THE FOUR TOPS [ALBUM]

The Supremes may have been the first Motown associated act to top the British charts with their single *Baby Love* in 1964, but The Four Tops were the first act to top the album and single chart on the Tamla Motown label. *Reach Out I'll Be There* had topped the singles chart in 1966 and a succession of Top Ten singles followed, including *Standing In The Shadows Of Love*, *Bernadette*, *Walk Away Renee* and *If I Were A Carpenter*, making them Motown's most successful artist in Britain. A greatest hits package, therefore, could not fail, and the fact that it would go on to dethrone The Beatles' **Sgt Pepper** album only added to its achievement. Although it was to spend a solitary week at the chart summit (and reach as high as #4 in the US, it should be noted), it lost the top spot to label-mates Diana Ross & The Supremes and their greatest hits package. Whilst the middle 1960s are often held as Motown's glory days, by 1968 the label had still not lost its shine, as the success of The Four Tops and then The Supremes would confirm.

FOUR TOPS HITS – THE FOUR TOPS [EP]

Released in March 1967, almost a year to the day after the first Four Tops EP, **The Four Tops Hits** was something of a mini hits compilation, featuring *Reach Out I'll Be There*, *Loving You Is Sweeter Than Ever*, *Standing In The Shadows Of* Love and *Baby I Need Your Loving*. This particular EP proved even more popular than its predecessor, spending a total of 41 weeks on the listing (in effect for as long as the EP chart continued to be compiled as a separate feature) and never once dropped below #5. A total of 22 of those 41 weeks were spent at #1, including a ten week stretch from 18 March to 20 May, and as noted earlier, on 28 October 1967 it held the pole position whilst **The Four Tops** was at #2.

FOUR TOPS LIVE – THE FOUR TOPS [ALBUM]

Recorded at the Upper Deck of the Roostertail in Detroit, **Four Tops Live** managed to capture on vinyl the extra special magic that made The Four Tops a very top live draw. They had performed their show on countless occasions, knew the routines backwards and forwards, yet still spent much of the afternoon of a Monday during autumn preparing for what had become known as the legendary 'Motown Mondays'. The fact that it was The Four Tops and in Detroit was always going to draw a capacity crowd, but the crowd would also include several other Motown luminaries, including all three Supremes who joined The Four

Tops on stage during the course of the evening, Marvin Gaye and The Everly Brothers. The end result is an album that has been described as one of the best live albums ever recorded, on par with James Brown's **Live At The Apollo**. The quality of the album can be gauged by the fact that it performed exceptionally well on the charts, topping the R&B chart and making #4 on the UK pop register.

FOUR TOPS ON TOP – THE FOUR TOPS [ALBUM]

By 1966 The Four Tops had been making steady progress on the US album charts but had yet to make their chart breakthrough in the UK. All that was to change with **Four Tops On Top**, which would hit #32 in the US (and #3 R&B) but became a Top Ten hit in the UK, reaching as high as #9. That it should be this album that enabled them to break through was something of a surprise, for **On Top** was hardly crammed with hits. Indeed, the only singles on display were *Loving Is You Is Sweeter Than Ever* (#45 US, #21 UK) and *Shake Me Wake Me (When It's Over* (#19 in the US and missed the chart altogether in the UK). Whilst HDH supplied four of the tracks on display, the whole of the second side of the album comprised cover versions, including *Michelle* (Lennon and McCartney), *In The Still Of The Night* (Cole Porter) and *Bluesette* (Toots Thielemans and Norman Gimbel).

FOX FIRE

Fox Fire was an obscure country rock group who had one single released on Prodigal in 1975, *Bump In Your Jeans* backed with *Such A Long Time* with both sides produced by Nick Cenci. As the single did little they don't appear to have made the move when Prodigal was subsequently bought by Motown, although Nick Cenci joined the company and worked in the publicity and promotions department.

ARETHA FRANKLIN

Aretha Louise Franklin was born in Memphis, Tennessee on 25 March 1942 and began her career recording religious material for the Wand label in 1956. A switch to secular music was suggested by Sam Cooke in 1960 and she signed to Columbia on the strength of her demos, although sustained success eluded her until she moved to Atlantic Records in 1966.

There Aretha soon earned her nickname First Lady of Soul with a series of hit singles and albums. The winner of eighteen Grammy Awards, her 1967 smash hit (#8 pop and #2 R&B) *Natural Woman* appeared on the soundtrack to 'The Big Chill' in September 1983, and the following month Aretha featured on The Four Tops album **Back Where I Belong**, guesting on the track *What Have We Got To Lose*.

JOE FRAZIER

Infinitely better known as a boxer, he first came to prominence winning an Olympic gold medal in Tokyo in 1964 in the heavyweight division. 'Smokin' Joe', who was born Joseph William Frazier in Laurel Bay, South Carolina on 12 January 1944, turned professional in 1965, going on to become Heavyweight Champion of the World in 1970. It is the fights he had with Muhammad Ali in 1971, 1974 and 1975 (the 'Thrilla in Manila') that ensured his reputation as a fighter, even if he lost the last two fights against Ali. He retired after another defeat to George Foreman in June 1976, training local boxers in Philadelphia and making a cameo appearance in the film 'Rocky'.

His recording career took in two singles for Motown, *First Round Knock-Out* being issued on Motown in November 1975 and the following April *Little Dog Heaven* being released on Prodigal. He made a brief return to the ring in 1981 for one fight but seemingly not to the recording studio. He died from liver cancer on 7 November 2011.

JESSE FREDERICK

Born Jesse Frederick James Conaway in Salisbury, Maryland in 1948, he would later drop his last two names in an attempt to distance himself from his father, a leading figure in the poultry processing industry! Instead, Jesse opted to pursue a career in music, recording his debut album for Bearsville in 1971, although his spell with the label would end frustratingly with numerous tracks unreleased.

By the end of the decade Jesse had switched to writing the music for television and film, including the 1984 release 'The Flamingo Kid'. As well as writing much of the score Jesse appeared on the soundtrack with the opening number *Breakaway*.

THE FREEMAN BROTHERS

Johnny and Jerry weren't actually brothers, with the duo being formed by Johnny Mitchell, a former lead singer of the doo wop group The Majestics, and Gerald Williams, who was really an orchestra leader. The pair first linked in 1963, recording *You Got Me On A String* for the International Allied label, subsequently recording for Mala (*Every Day It's You* backed with *I'm Counting On You*) and Jovial (*Come And Get These Memories*) before signing with Motown's Soul imprint in 1965.

They issued just one single, with Johnny's composition *My Baby* being produced by Berry Gordy and Mickey Stevenson and released in March 1965. When the single did little The Freeman Brothers moved on, subsequently recorded for Format and Sprout. Gerald Williams was reportedly shot to death in Harlem in or around 1971.

FRESH

Formed in 1975 by Bill Pratt (vocals), Paul Marshall (guitar), Elaine Mayo (rhythm guitar), Milo Marton (bass), David Kaffinetti (keyboards) and Fred Allen (drums), Fresh signed with MCA in 1976 and released their debut album the following year. Despite gaining a slot as a support act to Rufus & Chaka Khan the album failed to sell and they were dropped from the label.

They then moved on to Prodigal, by which time George Englund had joined on saxophone and Kaffinetti replaced by Frank Savino. Prodigal issued two albums by Fresh, **Feelin' Fresh** in January 1978 and **Omniverse** in October the same year, but after they failed to sell, a third eponymous album was scrapped. The group disbanded soon after.
ALBUMS: FEELIN' FRESH (1978), OMNIVERSE (1978)

FRIENDLY ENEMIES

Michel Rubini and Don Dunn had recorded an album for Motown in 1976 under the moniker Dunn & Rubini and two years later added Chuck Smith to the line-up and adopted the name Friendly Fires for an album on Prodigal. With Michel playing keyboards and handling all arrangements and production, Don on vocals and Chuck on guitar and vocals, Friendly Fires issued **Round One** in April 1978.
ALBUM: ROUND ONE (1978)

FRIENDLY PERSUASION

A studio creation of writers Miki Antony and Phil Chapman with co-producer Peter Anders, Friendly Persuasion had one single released on Rare Earth in the UK, *Remember (Sha La La)* backed with *I'll Always Do The Best I Can* appearing in November 1974. The group name had been used four years previously, in 1970 by Paul Raven on a track written by Ed Seago and Mike Leander, *Make A Wish Amanda*. By 1974 Paul Raven was better known as Gary Glitter, although there is no indication that *Remember* has any connection to Glitter or the Glitter Band.

FULFILLINGNESS' FIRST FINALE - STEVIE WONDER [ALBUM]

The four year, four album relationship between Stevie Wonder and Malcolm Cecil and Robert Margouleff may have come to an end by the time **Fullingness'** was released, but it was certainly a fitting finale. The social commentary that had dominated its predecessor **Innervisions** was largely abandoned, although not entirely, with *You Haven't Done Nothin'* an attack on politicians who had promised but failed to deliver, with President Nixon the main target. Whilst there had been something of a theme running through **Innervisions**, **Fullingness'** was later described as a collection of songs. The main reason for this was because the tracks had been recorded at various stages during the Wonder/Cecil/Margouleff relationship, with *They Won't Go When I Go* dating as far back as 1971 and *Boogie On Reggae Woman* finished in time for consideration on **Innervisions** but left off the album as it didn't fit with the rest of the material. On **Fullingness'** it stands out as one of the most joyous tracks on what is otherwise a more sombre offering.

The album was released on 22 July 1974 and seven weeks later topped the US pop charts, where it would spend two weeks, as well as going on to collect Grammy Awards for Best Male Pop Vocal Performance and Album of the Year. Stevie thus became only the second artist (after Frank Sinatra) to have won back to back Album of the Year accolades. In the UK the album had to settle for a rather more modest chart peak of #5, but this was still a new chart high for Stevie in this territory.

THE FUNK BROTHERS

Entries for the individual members of what became known as the Funk Brothers can be found elsewhere in this book, but it is worth commenting on their collective achievements; without the Funk Brothers, there would have been no Motown and certainly no Motown Sound.

Initially they had no name since this ad hoc group of musicians were used purely on studio recordings at Hitsville, with the occasional opportunity to record on their own seeing them being billed as whatever fitted the purpose; The Twisting Kings on **Twist The World Around**, The Swinging Tigers on *Snake Walk* and The Soul Brothers for an album and several singles with Earl Van Dyke.

Benny Benjamin is credited with giving the 'group' the now accepted moniker, pausing as he was leaving the studio after a particularly productive session and telling the assembled musicians, "You all are the Funk Brothers." Still largely uncredited until Marvin Gaye insisted on naming the individual musicians on his 1971 **What's Going On** album, the thirteen accepted members of the Funk Brothers were Joe Hunter, Earl Van Dyke and Johnny Griffith (keyboards), Robert White, Eddie Willis and Joe Messina (guitar), James Jamerson and Bob Babbitt (bass), Benny Benjamin, Richard 'Pistol' Allen and Uriel Jones (drums), Jack Ashford and Eddie 'Bongo' Brown (percussion).

Even with Marvin Gaye's patronage, the Funk Brothers remained largely unknown outside of the music world, but their worth inside it was never taken for granted, as their frequent moonlighting sessions for rival companies and singers would confirm.

All that changed with the release of the book and subsequent film 'Standing In The Shadows Of Motown', a project that began as something of an homage to James Jamerson but which ended as a fitting tribute to the entire ensemble. And whilst pundits continue to argue over what contributed most to the success of Motown, drummer Uriel Jones is in no doubt, as he discussed in the film.

"People always say it was everything but the musicians. They'd say it was the artists, the producers, the way the building was constructed, the wood on the floor, or maybe even the food. But I'd like to see them take some barbecue ribs or hamburgers and throw them down in the studio and shut the door and count off 'One-two-three-four' and get a hit out of it. The formula was the musicians."

HARVEY FUQUA

The many plaudits directed in the direction of Harvey Fuqua usually focus on his abilities as a singer, songwriter or producer, but it may well be that his main attribute was as a spotter of talent; probably only Berry Gordy himself was as canny at unearthing rough talent and fashioning it into polished diamonds. Born in Louisville, Kentucky on 27 July 1929, he was a cousin of Charlie Fuqua of The Ink Spots. That family connection may well have inspired Harvey to form his own group in 1951, linking with Bobby Lester, Alexander Graves and Prentiss Barnes as The Crazy Sounds. The group would later move to Cleveland in Ohio where local DJ Alan Freed took them under his wing, rechristening them The Moonglows and signing them to his Champagne label in 1953. Later the same year the group moved to Art Sheridan's Chance label and enjoyed some local success before Chance was shut down.

At the suggestion of Ewart Abner, Harvey duly presented the group to Leonard Chess at Chess Records and was rewarded with a recording deal that would result in hits such as *Sincerely, See Saw, Please Send Me Someone To Love* and *Ten Commandments Of Love*. By the time of this last smash, a new Moonglows was in place, Harvey having sacked the original group and installed the members of Washington D.C. group The Marquees, Reese Palmer, James Knowland, Chester Simmons and Chuck Barksdale (on loan from The Dells) together with Marvin Gaye as the new group.

The new line-up was a short lived affair, Harvey dismantling the group by giving all but Marvin Gaye the fare money back to Washington D.C. Harvey took Leonard Chess' advice and went to Detroit to hook up with Gwen Gordy, owner of Anna Records (named after another of the Gordy sisters), taking Marvin with him. Initially working for Anna Records, Harvey produced a number of tracks on Lamont Anthony (later to become much better known as Lamont Dozier) and Johnny Bristol among others as well as enjoying a burgeoning relationship with Gwen. The pair married in 1961, shut down Anna Records and launched two new labels, Harvey and Tri-Phi with a roster that would include Junior Walker & The All Stars, The Spinners, Johnny & Jackey and Shorty Long. Despite the impressive array of talent, Harvey was bedevilled by success since having a hit would mean pressing more and more records and income flowing out with little guarantee of royalties and revenue coming back in.

Eventually, when Berry Gordy offered an opportunity of coming into the Motown fold, Harvey took it with both hands, bringing much of his roster (including the now Anna Gordy smitten Marvin Gaye) with him. It was the way all of the acts associated with Harvey possessed such a professional stage presence, cultivated by endless rehearsals instigated by Harvey himself that indirectly led to the creation of the Artist Development Department, with Harvey installed as its head.

However, whilst he undoubtedly made a significant contribution to Motown through this route, of equal value was the abilities he brought as both a writer and producer for the label and its various imprints. Often paired with Johnny Bristol, he would handle the very first of Marvin Gaye and Tammi Terrell's duets, sessions on Gladys Knight & The Pips, Junior Walker and David Ruffin, scoring a huge catalogue of hits.

He left Motown in 1971 and landed a production deal with RCA Records, taking New Birth from obscurity to stardom and later discovering Sylvester and doing much the same again. In 1982 he was drafted in to assist Marvin Gaye in turning what had been a disjointed series of recordings into a return to former glories and Grammy award winning **Midnight Love**. Having briefly resurrected The Moonglows in 1972, Harvey would do so again towards the end of the century and record **Harvey & The Moonglows 2000** for his own Resurging Artist label. He died from a heart attack whilst in hospital in Detroit on 6 July 2010.

G

GAIEE RECORDS

An extremely short-lived label that released only one single, Gaiee was formed by songwriter Bunny Jones, who co-wrote *I Was Born This Way* with Chris Spierer and recorded the track in 1975 with vocalist Charles Harris, giving him the stage name Valentino. As the song title and label name might imply, the record was intentionally aimed at the gay market, and after Jones had sold 15,000 copies out of the back of her car, Motown picked up the track for nationwide distribution. The single failed to break, with Gaiee and Valentino being quietly dropped thereafter, although the song was revived by Carl Bean in 1977 and released on Motown.

ERIC GALE

Born in Brooklyn, New York on 20 September 1938, Eric was the leading jazz guitarist of his generation, both as a session musician and as a band leader. He linked with CTI and Kudu Records in 1973 and recording his debut album **Forecast** the same year as well as being the featured guitarist on numerous recordings, although his own solo career didn't take off until he switched to Columbia. Eric did not record for Motown but he was equally billed alongside Freddie Hubbard and Stanley Turrentine on **In Concert Volume 2** issued on CTI in 1974, along with Ron Carter, Herbie Hancock and Jack DeJohnette. Eric died from lung cancer on 25 May 1994.

ALBUM: IN CONCERT VOLUME TWO (1975)

PATRICK GAMMON

Born in Seattle, Washington on 15 January 1956, Patrick Gammon started his professional career with local group Family Affair in 1973 before auditioning and winning a place with Ike & Tina Turner's Revue. He was to spend two years with the Revue before taking a leave of absence, spent in Germany doing television, session work and writing with Gerhard Augustin. The two set up Patrick's first record, *Party Hardy* appearing on the Galaxy label in 1976, followed by a deal with Chrysalis that resulted in nothing being released owing to a difference of opinion as to which direction he should pursue.

"Chrysalis wanted me to be a black Elton John – but all I got was a lot of talk and a lot of studio time, but no record releases."

A brief deal with Metronome raised enough money for Patrick and Gerhard to finance their own demo, which they got to Motown and resulted in an album deal in 1979. His only album, **Don't Touch Me** was released in May, with *Cop An Attitude* being released as a single a month later. After being dropped by Motown he returned to Europe to continue his career.

ALBUM: DON'T TOUCH ME (1979)

STU GARDNER

Keyboard player Stu Gardner released only two singles on Chisa, *Home On The Range (Everybody Needs A Home)* appearing in September 1969 and *Expressin' My Love* in February 1970, but he had worked with Hugh Masekela and Stewart Levine on several occasions previously. Indeed, Stewart and Hugh produced Stu's 1967 album **To Soul With Love** which appeared on Revue, with the musicians including several others who were an integral part of the later Chisa label, including Wayne Henderson of The Jazz Crusaders.

This album was released at a time interest in Stu was at its height, helped by an appearance in the film 'Point Blank' starring Lee Marvin. After his brief time with Chisa, Stu would work with Bill Cosby on his television show (Columbia would release two albums of music from the show during the 1980s) and record for Stax as Stu Gardner & The Sanctified Sound.

SIEDAH GARRETT

Whilst her solo career has not achieved the level of success many predicted, Siedah has still made a significant mark on Motown. Born in Los Angeles, California on 24 June 1960 she was a member of Plush who recorded an eponymous album for RCA in 1982. Two years later she was credited on Dennis Edwards' big club hit *Don't Look Any Further*, a track which should have enabled both Siedah and Dennis to become major solo performers. It didn't work out for either artist, with Dennis eventually rejoining The Temptations.

Meanwhile, Siedah appeared on Michael Jackson's **Bad** album in 1987, dueting on *I Just Can't Stop Loving You*, albeit uncredited, which topped the charts on both sides of the Atlantic. After appearing on several Quincy Jones albums and touring with Michael Jackson on his 'Dangerous' world tour, Siedah became a member of Brand New Heavies. As a songwriter Siedah has collected a Grammy Award (for Best Song Written for a Motion Picture in 2007 for *Love You I Do*) and two nominations for an Academy Award for Best Original Song (for *Love You I Do* and *Real In Rio*).

MARVIN GAYE

Trouble man or just a stubborn kind of fellow; no artist has polarized opinion at Motown quite like Marvin Gaye. Born in Washington D.C. on 2 April 1939, Marvin Pentz Gay was the second child of four born to Marvin Gay Sr. and his wife Alberta, respectively a Pentecostal minister and schoolteacher. Gay Sr. imposed an iron will on his children and punished any shortcoming severely, resulting in a fractured relationship throughout Marvin's childhood that would continue into adulthood.

Although his father had hoped that all four children would follow him into the church, Marvin developed a love of doo-wop and R&B at an early age and would often run away from home in order to attend local concerts, often against his father's wishes or orders. Having been inspired by watching others perform, Marvin was soon forming his own groups, including The Dippers with Johnny Stewart (the brother of R&B singer Billy Stewart) and then The D.C. Tones with Reese Palmer and Sondra Lattisaw (the mother of future Motown singer Stacy Lattisaw).

In 1956 Marvin took the decision to fly from the family nest, enlisting in the US Air Force with the aim of becoming a pilot. This would turn out to be a major mistake, for Marvin showed no aptitude whatsoever to military life and was soon involved in a battle of wills with his superiors even tougher than that he had engaged with his father. Disobeying orders and even faking mental illness, Marvin was discharged eight months later with a ringing mark against his name. 'Airman Gaye is uncooperative, lacks even a minor degree of initiative, shows very little interest in his assigned duties, and does nothing to improve his job knowledge' read his discharge papers. 'He has been a constant problem to his supervisor and to the First Sergeant ever since he has been assigned to this Squadron.'

Back home in Washington D.C. Marvin took a job as a dishwasher to make ends meet but still harboured hopes of making it in the entertainment business, eventually hooking up again with Reese Palmer with James Nolan and Chester Simmons in a group called The Marquees. They were eventually discovered by Bo Diddley, who helped them get a deal with Okeh Records for whom they recorded the single *Wyatt Earp* backed with *Hey Little Schoolgirl*. Whilst a minor local success it was not to the level of success the group had hoped for, with Okeh also losing interest in the group once the single had failed.

It was through Chester Simmons, who was also working as Bo Diddley's driver and valet that they got their introduction to Harvey Fuqua. Harvey informed them that he was on the verge of disbanding the original Moonglows and that he considered them good enough to become the new line-up, a move that took effect in January 1959. He also got them a new recording contract with Chess Records who recorded six sides on them, looking to reproduce the kind of success the old Moonglows had enjoyed with *Ten Commandments Of Love* and *Please Send Me Someone To Love*. None of the singles made a serious dent in the chart, with Nolan and Palmer eventually leaving the group in 1960.

By then Harvey and Marvin had also moved on, heading to Detroit where Leonard Chess had suggested Harvey link up with Gwen Gordy, who was running her own Anna Records label. Harvey would also set up his own Harvey and Tri-Phi labels with Marvin signing to the former and working as a drummer on many of the sessions, including The Spinners hit *That's What Girls Are Made Of*. There was more than just music being made at the new company, for Harvey soon became romantically involved with Gwen Gordy and Marvin was attracted to her sister Anna. Both relationships would eventually lead to marriage (and divorce!), Gwen and Harvey tying the knot in 1961, with Marvin and Anna overcoming a seventeen year age gap and eventually marrying in 1964 (Motown claimed for many years the pair had married in 1961, but their marriage certificate shows the date as being 8 January 1964).

Not long after Harvey and Gwen married they closed their respective labels and merged their various artist rosters into Berry Gordy's burgeoning Motown label. According to Marvin, his 'audition' consisted of him gatecrashing the Motown Christmas party in 1960 and singing and playing *Mr Sandman* at the piano. Suitably impressed, Berry Gordy signed Marvin along with many of the other artists associated with Harvey Fuqua (it was later revealed that not only did Berry Gordy sign Marvin as a performer, he acquired a 50% interest in the artist too, a deal Marvin only became aware of several years later).

Although Marvin was now signed to Motown and assigned to the Tamla label, both artist and label owner were on a clash course; Motown and its imprints might have been making headway in the R&B field, but Marvin had visions of becoming the new Nat King Cole and wished to record standards and jazz material. Eventually Berry reasoned that the way to get the best out of Marvin would be to allow him his head on his initial release and then reel him in to tow the company line when it failed to sell. Thus *Let Your Conscience Be Your Guide* would become the first Marvin Gaye single in May 1961 (he added the 'e' to his surname because it sounded more professional, to follow in the footsteps of Sam Cooke and to further distance himself from his father), followed a month later by the album **The Soulful Moods Of Marvin Gaye**. Whilst the single and *Never Let You Go* were in the traditional Motown style, the rest of the album carried an abundance of standards from the pens of Cole Porter, Irving Berlin and Richard Rodgers and Lorenz Hart, including a second single in a cover of The Chordettes' *Mr Sandman*.

As Berry Gordy predicted it failed to sell (and even Marvin was beginning to doubt whether he would find fame through this route, stating "None of these records were in a commercial bag. I needed something more orientated to the teenagers. Harvey kept telling me that. Berry kept telling me that, and I knew that."), although how much promotional support was put behind the album is open to debate; the album certainly stands more than adequate comparison with anything Nat King Cole and Ray Charles were releasing at the time.

With his own recording career still at the departure gate, Marvin busied himself by working as a session drummer and even janitor at Hitsville, although the one area he did not make much effort was with the Artist Development Department. This refusal to attend grooming sessions did not make him popular within Motown, with several rival artists believing Marvin was using his newly acquired family connections to avoid having to attend. Marvin would later state he regretted not attending as much as he should and felt his live performances could have benefitted from the work the department did.

Yet his worth to the company could be measured by his appearance on recordings by The Contours, Mary Wells, The Marvelettes and numerous others as well as developing his own writing skills, helping pen The Marvelettes hit *Beechwood 4-5789*, a Top 20 pop and Top Ten R&B hit in 1962. The same team responsible for this hit (Marvin along with Mickey Stevenson and George Gordy) would also come up with Marvin's first hit. Using a comment by Anna Gordy aimed at Marvin, the team came up with *Stubborn Kind Of Fellow*, released in July 1962 and which would go on to become a #8 hit on the R&B chart and crossover to #46 on the pop listings; the Gordy's had won the first round of the perpetual arguments they were to have with Marvin.

Further hit singles in *Hitch Hike* (#12 R&B but Marvin's debut inside the Top 40 of the pop chart, hitting #30) and *Pride And Joy* (#2 R&B and #10 pop) strengthened Berry's argument, although they were not sufficient to propel the parent **Stubborn Kind Of Fellow** into the chart, an album that in addition to these three singles also included the original version of *Wherever I Lay My Hat*, later a UK number one for Paul Young. Indeed, it should be noted that whilst Marvin may have seen himself as something of a crooner, he was actually one of the early vanguards of the Motown sound, with many of his early singles being covered by British artists such as The Rolling Stones, The Who and Dusty Springfield, among others.

That catalogue of hits continued to grow as 1963 gave way to 1964; *Can I Get A Witness* (#3 R&B, #22 pop) and *You're A Wonderful One* (#3 R&B and #15 pop). As well as making his first major television appearance ('American Bandstand'), 1964 also saw the first of what would eventually become something of a trademark, an album of duets with the then First Lady of Motown Mary Wells. **Together** would become an album chart debut for both acts when hitting #42 and give rise to two major hits in *What's The Matter With You* and *Once Upon A Time* (both sides of the same single charted separately), although Mary was on her way out of Motown and heading for pastures new before the album had run out of steam.

With or without Mary Wells, Marvin Gaye was still a bankable name, as hits such as *Try It Baby* and *Baby Don't You Do It* would prove. Motown tried to recreate the earlier duet magic by pairing Marvin with Kim Weston, initially for the single *What Good Am I Without You* and later for the album **Take Two**, although the chemistry between the two didn't quite reach the heights Marvin's work with Mary Wells had attained.

Solo success, however, proved to be more than adequate compensation, with *How Sweet It Is To Be Loved By You* (#3 R&B and #6 pop and his UK chart debut at #49) being followed by his first chart topper *I'll Be Doggone*, which hit number one on the R&B chart and made #8 pop. Before the year was out Marvin would come to rest at the top of the chart again, with *Ain't That Peculiar* also making #8 pop. Despite this success the ongoing battle between what Motown wanted him to record continued; **How Sweet It Is To Be Loved By You** was a #4 R&B hit but limped to #128 on the pop chart, but these positions easily surpassed **A Tribute To The Great Nat King Cole**, the latter album a long held desire of Marvin's but which failed to register with the record buying public. New hits would eventually come with old recordings; *It Takes Two* had originally been recorded by Marvin and Kim Weston in November 1965 but was allowed to sit on the shelf gathering dust for more than a year. Then Berry Gordy got wind that both Kim and her husband Mickey Stevenson were about to jump ship for MGM and decided to release *It Takes Two* and the album **Take Two** as something of a parting shot, seeing the single make #4 R&B, #14 pop and a #16 UK success, although the album did little. Whilst this success ultimately did little for Kim it certainly aided Marvin, for by now his reputation was almost reliant on being paired with a quality female singer.

He found the perfect foil with Tammi Terrell, with the original intention being to allow Tammi to establish a reputation on the back of Marvin's name before pushing her as a serious solo artist in her own right. That the second part of the equation never quite happened was down to her health issues, but in the meantime she and Marvin produced a tidy catalogue of titles that remain as fresh and exciting now as they were when originally released.

When Nick Ashford and Valerie Simpson had written *Ain't No Mountain High Enough,* their intention was to record the song on Dusty Springfield, but then the call came to join Motown and the song was requisitioned, despite Dusty's protests. It was handed to Harvey Fuqua and Johnny Bristol, who had in mind doing the song on Tammi on her own, but when Berry Gordy suggested linking her with Marvin, his vocals were added to the recording to create a seamless duet. It struck a similar chord with the public too, hitting #3 R&B and #19 pop and picking up a Grammy nomination for Best R&B Performance by a Duo but somehow missing out in the UK.

Nickolas Ashford and Valerie Simpson would later request permission to produce their own compositions on Marvin and Tammi (Berry would take the precaution of having Johnny Bristol and Harvey Fuqua produce versions of the same songs as a back-up), with much the same result; Marvin and Tammi were almost meant to record together.

Whilst they were never romantically linked, despite Motown's publicity campaign hinting at an out of studio relationship, it was the empathy between the two that came across on record. Thus *You're Unchanging World, Your Precious Love, If I Could Build My Whole World Around You, Ain't Nothing Like The Real Thing* and *You're All I Need To Get By* vaulted into the Top Ten of the R&B chart (the latter two actually topping the chart), with all but *You're Unchanging Love* also making the Top Ten of the pop listings. There was also success to be garnered on the album chart, with the pair's **United** making #7 R&B and #69 pop. Having proved their worth on record, Marvin and Tammi were sent out on the road for a series of live dates, with Tammi's presence doing much to alleviate Marvin's usual shyness when it came to performing live. Unfortunately, Tammi had begun to complain of migraines and dizziness, although she claimed she was well enough to perform. All was well until 14 October 1967 at the Hampden-Sydney College when Tammi collapsed onstage midway through a show. After being rushed to hospital, where she was diagnosed as having a malignant brain tumour, Tammi spent a considerable time recuperating and whilst she would at times be well enough to record, her performing days were at an end. So too for a considerable time were Marvin's, devastated by the extent of Tammi's illness.

Motown may have had considerable duet recordings still in the can and would get to complete several more before Tammi's untimely death, but Marvin had to resurrect his solo career. His studio visits became infrequent, but the times he was at Hitsville produced a solid body of work, including *You* (a #7 R&B and #34 pop hit) and *Chained* (#8 R&B and #32 pop on a song Marvin would later claim was almost autobiographical since he felt chained to the Motown system) which returned him to the upper reaches of the chart. He was to sail all the way to the top with his next solo outing, Norman Whitfield's persistence at getting *I Heard It Through The Grapevine* released paying off when it spent seven weeks at the top of the pop and R&B chart and three weeks in the UK for good measure.

Little time was wasted in capitalising on this new found success, Motown issuing *Too Busy Thinking About My Baby* (#1 R&B and #4 pop) and *That's The Way Love Is* (#2 R&B, #7 pop), interspersed with further duets with Tammi in *Good Lovin' Ain't Easy To Come By* and *What You Gave Me*, the latter another Top Ten R&B hit at #6. Yet this success only papered over what was an increasingly difficult time for Marvin, battling the breakdown of his marriage to Anna and Tammi Terrell's rapidly declining health. Whilst Marvin may have been aware of just how fragile Tammi had become and therefore prepared for the worse, her eventual death on 16 March 1970 left him devastated and sent him into personal and professional seclusion.

Marvin would spend the best part of a year mourning the loss of Tammi and all Motown could do was sit and wait for him to work his sorrow out and return to recording. For a time it appeared he had no wish to return to music whatsoever, contemplating a switch in career to become a professional football player with the Detroit Lions (he also had plans on becoming an actor, but apart from bit roles in 'The Ballad Of Andy Crocker' with Lee Majors in 1969 and 'Chrome And Hot Leather' in 1971 nothing further evolved), going as far as working out in order to get himself physically fit enough for a trial. That proved unsuccessful, although he did become friendly enough with two players, Mel Farr and Lem Barney, to include them on what would eventually become his *piece de resistance*.

The spark that coaxed him back in to the studio was provided by musician Al Cleveland and Four Tops member Renaldo 'Obie' Benson, who played him the basics of a song they had entitled *What's Going On*. Marvin helped complete the composition and initially planned on recording it on The Originals, a group he had already assisted in getting to the upper echelons of both the pop and R&B charts with *Baby I'm For Real* and *The Bells*, titles he had written and produced. However, both Al and Obie argued persuasively enough that *What's Going On* would be better suited to Marvin himself, a suggestion Marvin eventually took on board and entered the Hitsville studio in June 1970 to record the track, together with *God Is Love*, another song that hinted at a radical change in musical direction.

When the completed single was delivered Berry Gordy refused to release it, feeling the political overtones of the song would struggle to find favour among the radio programmers and thus unlikely to be commercially successful. Rather than go back and record something more radio friendly, Marvin stuck to his guns, appealing to Berry and other executives within the company in a non-stop attempt to get *What's Going On* out into the market. He would eventually find two key allies in Harry Balk and Barney Ales, who no doubt played their part in convincing Berry that the single was worth taking a chance with. Berry eventually relented, despite his continued belief that it was radically different from not only what Motown was doing but popular music itself; it would become the fastest selling Motown single and power its way to the top of the R&B chart for five weeks and hit #2 pop.

Proved wrong on the single, Berry Gordy was quick to admit his error and demanded an album along similar lines. The end result some four months later was what has been described as the first soul concept album **What's Going On**, a *tour de force* that topped the R&B charts for nine weeks, peaked at #6 pop and sold more than two million copies during the year or so it was a fixture on the chart. Despite being a concept album that dealt with social issues, **What's Going On** had enough commercial appeal to give rise to two further smash singles in *Mercy Mercy Me (The Ecology)* and *Inner City Blues (Make Me Wanna Holler)*, both of which topped the R&B charts and made #4 and #9 respectively on the pop chart. Marvin returned to the theme for the single *You're The Man*, a #7 R&B hit that was probably too barbed in its attack on President Nixon, stalling at a much more distant #50 pop, with the result Marvin abandoned plans for an album of the same name. Instead he took yet another change in musical direction, scoring the film 'Trouble Man', from which the title track returned him to the Top Ten of both the R&B and pop listings.

By now having returned tentatively to live work, Marvin made other changes in his life during the course of 1972. Like virtually the rest of Motown he exited Detroit for California, settling in the Topanga Canyon Boulevard region and beginning work on his next album. Having dealt with issues of the mind on **What's Going On**, Marvin turned to the body for **Let's Get It On**, an album that would surpass its predecessor, shifting more copies and topping the R&B and pop charts in Cashbox and Record World (it would have to settle for #2 in Billboard), aided by the singles *Let's Get It On*, *Come Get To This* and *You Sure Love To Ball*. *Let's Get It On* would become Marvin's second pop chart topper, with *Come Get To This* also becoming a Top Ten R&B hit; *You Sure Love To Ball* was possibly too sexual a title for mainstream success. That would come with a series of duets with Diana Ross; having announced that he would never record with another female artist in the wake of Tammi Terrell's death, Marvin relented and recorded **Diana & Marvin** in 1973. Problems during the early sessions resulted in the two artists recording their respective parts separately, a move that lead to some claiming the album lacked the spontaneity of his work with Tammi, Kim and Mary, but whilst the album struggled for acceptance in the US, it did brisk business in the UK, where it helped both artists further establish their reputations.

Further personal problems, including the total collapse of his marriage to Anna in 1975 kept Marvin out of the studio for a considerable time, Motown filling the void between official albums with 1974's **Marvin Gaye Live** album, another R&B chart topper that made a respectable #8 on the pop chart and garnered a Grammy nomination for Best R&B Vocal Performance, Male. When eventually coaxed back into the studio, it was to record an album that had been written by Leon Ware and Diana's brother T-Boy Ross. Effectively a continuation of the themes on **Let's Get It On**, **I Want You** performed well, with the album and its title track topping the R&B chart (as well as collecting a Grammy Award nomination for Best R&B Vocal Performance, Male) and the album hitting #4 pop as well as becoming his highest charting solo album in the UK when it made #22.

With Leon Ware having eschewed the opportunity of doing a follow-up album (he would retain the songs written and eventually release them as **Musical Massage** under his own name), the lack of new studio material was kept at bay by another live recording, this time **Live! At The London Palladium** appearing in March 1977, going on to sell more than two million copies, largely helped by the smash hit single *Got To Give It Up*, a single that gave more than a nod to the then popular disco scene.

Whilst the single and album's success maintained Marvin's professional reputation, his personal life was continuing on a downward spiral. Mounting financial problems, a messy divorce from Anna, a growing dependency on drugs, the eventual collapse of his second marriage to Janis Hunter (the pair had their first child, a daughter Nona Marvisa in September 1974 and a son Frankie in November 1975, before finally tying the knot in October 1976) and legal battles with former band members had prompted the European tour that culminated in the **Live!** album and raised sufficient funds to enable him to avoid imprisonment for non-payment of alimony and child support to Anna.

According to Berry Gordy, it was he who came up with the idea of getting Marvin to record an album with the royalties being paid to Anna as settlement in their divorce, although Berry's original idea had been for Marvin to record a series of songs supplied by Motown's in-house writers and producers. Instead, Marvin decided to do the album himself, initially intending to do an album that was little more than an obligation album but eventually, with his professional pride suitably aroused, coming up with **Here, My Dear**. A double album of varied musical styles, **Here, My Dear** laid out the entire Marvin Gaye and Anna Gordy relationship on vinyl, with recording taking some eighteen months to finish. When released in December 1978, it was panned by critics and avoided by punters (over the years its status has improved considerably), although one interested listener was Anna Gordy, who was distressed enough at seeing her relationship with her former husband enter the public domain and considered issuing a $5 million invasion of privacy suit.

Whilst nothing came of the threat, others were still pursuing Marvin relentlessly, including the I.R.S. for several million owed in taxes. He took himself off to Hawaii, initially to do a couple of live dates but then deciding to remain on the island rather than face whatever might be coming his way should he return to the American mainland. By the end of the decade, Marvin was at his lowest ebb, a planned album of ballads having been discarded (originally intended as **The Ballads**, the album would eventually be released in 1997 as **Vulnerable**), a further album to be entitled **Love Man** scrapped after the lead single *Ego Tripping Out* failed to set the charts alight and his second marriage now at an end.

He accepted an invitation to tour Europe, a territory where he enjoyed superstar status to the point he could be forgiven for most of his foibles. Unfortunately, there were some marks even Marvin could not overstep and his apparent snubbing of Princess Margaret at a charity show proved to be a step too far. The event at the Lakeside Country Club had been organised some time previously, the type of gathering Berry Gordy had always hankered after, but on the night Marvin wasn't interested, despite the pleas of a Motown employee. In desperation he telephoned Peter Prince, head of Motown's European office, who also tried to convince Marvin to make the date.

"Marvin was adamant he was not going to go to the Lakeside Country Club, although he could not come up with a valid reason for not showing up. He had lost his temper, was throwing plates at the hotel walls and showed no sign whatsoever of listening to reason. I was trying to point out what an honour it was for him to be asked to perform like this, but he wasn't listening. So I rang Berry and explained the situation to him and to ask his help in getting Marvin moving. Berry rang Marvin and I gather Marvin complained to him that Jeffrey Kruger [the tour's British promoter] and I had threatened him with a shotgun! He also claimed Michael Roshkind and I were threatening all kinds of things to try and get him there, but it was just crazy."

Marvin did eventually make his way to the Lakeside Country Club, but by the time he got there, all of the dignitaries had long since departed.

Roundly criticised in the media and castigated by Berry Gordy, who had always been supremely proud whenever any of his artists were invited to entertain or meet royalty, it appeared to be the lowest point in his Motown career.

There was, however, one further, final twist of the knife to come; having been working on a new album, **In Our Lifetime?**, Marvin sent rough mixes of the album to Motown to gauge response ahead of release, although the more logical conclusion was that in such financial straits at the time, Marvin had asked Motown's European offices for an advance against his next album and had been instructed to send over some kind of confirmation that he was actually working on an album before any money would be handed over. Instead, with Motown having not had a studio album for some two years, they edited and remixed the album and dropped the question mark from the title and issued **In Our Lifetime** in January 1981. That it would make #31 pop and #6 R&B (and hit #48 in the UK) cut no ice with Marvin; he would never record for the label again. Even the little promotion Marvin did in support of the album was farcical; a television interview had been arranged in Manchester, which required Marvin and the plugger flying up from London's Heathrow Airport. Whilst the pair sat in the departure lounge waiting for the flight, Marvin excused himself in order to visit the toilet, climbed out of a window and grabbed a taxi back into the city centre, leaving the bemused plugger to wonder where on earth his errant star had gone!

Marvin eventually headed to Belgium, where he reduced the amount of drugs he was doing and managed to get both mind and body back into some kind of shape. Eventually, attention turned to a resumption of his recording career, with several labels said to be interested in signing him, assuming he could prove to be clear of his Motown contract.

Of all the suitors it was Columbia Records (CBS in the UK) who came up with the best proposition, sorting out a deal with Motown and the I.R.S. and handing full creative control to Marvin for his next album. When progress proved slow, he brought in his former mentor Harvey Fuqua as something of a production assistant and sounding board for the numerous musical ideas swirling around in his head. Built around the sublime *Sexual Healing* single, **Midnight Love** would be a glorious return to former glories, with the single becoming a major hit in all territories (it topped the R&B chart for ten weeks and would make #3 pop in the US and #4 in the UK). The attendant album was also a success, topping the R&B chart and hitting the Top Ten on both sides of the Atlantic.

When he eventually returned to the US, he did so in triumph, singing the *Star Spangled Banner* anthem at the NBA All-Star Game, collecting two Grammy Awards for *Sexual Healing*, the first of his career after six unsuccessful nominations (he was escorted to the awards evening by former wife Anna Gordy) and even settling his long standing feud with Berry Gordy, appearing on the 'Motown 25' television special.

Unfortunately, being back in America brought Marvin back in close proximity to the demons that had driven him to Europe in the first place; a haphazard tour in 1983 saw him once again over indulging in drugs, paranoid about his safety and once again having financial problems.

The tour came to an end in August 1983 and Marvin headed home to Crenshaw in Los Angeles, where he had bought a mansion for his parents. There a still volatile relationship with his father would simmer for several months before exploding in one final, tragic event on the day before his forty fifth birthday. On 31 March 1984, Marvin lay ill in bed from drug misuse until woken up by the noise of his parents arguing over a misplaced insurance document. Marvin admonished his father, although there was no physical contact between either. However, the next day the argument between his father and Alberta exploded again, with Marvin telling his father not to talk to Alberta like that and reportedly hitting his father. At some point Marvin Gay Sr. pulled a handgun from under a pillow and fired two shots, hitting his son once near the heart and once in the shoulder. It was later reported that Marvin was still alive for a short period after being shot, but the first paramedics on the scene refused to enter the building until the location of the gun was revealed; several members of the family believe the delay prevented potential life saving treatment being applied. Rushed to the California Hospital Medical Center, Marvin was pronounced dead on arrival at 1.01pm. His funeral four days later attracted a crowd of some 10,000 mourners, including many of his former Motown stable mates, both his ex-wives and his three children. A few days later, Anna took the three children on a boat trip to dispose of his ashes in the Pacific Ocean.

Whilst much of his recorded work enjoyed a resurgence of interest in the aftermath of his death, attention turned almost immediately to the status of new material he had been working on prior to his death. Motown and Columbia collaborated on two further releases, **Dream Of A Lifetime** and **Romantically Yours**, albums of varying quality given the unfinished nature of the original material. If the new material has yet to find lasting favour, the same cannot be said for the rest of his work; *I Heard It Through The Grapevine* made a return to the UK Top Ten in 1986 (#8), whilst various compilations have resulted in six appearances on the UK album chart, the most recent in 2006. Marvin was inducted into the Rock & Roll Hall of Fame in 1987.

ALBUMS: THE SOULFUL MOODS OF MARVIN GAYE (1961), THAT STUBBON KIND OF FELLOW (1963), RECORDED! LIVE ON STAGE (1963), WHEN I'M ALONE I CRY (1964), TOGETHER (1964), HELLO BROADWAY (1964), HOW SWEET IT IS TO BE LOVED BY YOU (1965), A TRIBUTE TO THE GREAT NAT KING COLE (1965), MOODS OF MARVIN GAYE (1966), TAKE TWO (1966), UNITED (1967), IN THE GROOVE (I HEARD IT THROUGH THE GRAPEVINE (1968), YOU'RE ALL I NEED (1968), MPG (1969), EASY (1969), THAT'S THE WAY LOVE IS (1970), WHAT'S GOING ON (1971), TROUBLE MAN (1972), LET'S GET IT ON (1973), DIANA & MARVIN (1973), LIVE! (1974), I WANT YOU (1976), LIVE! AT THE LONDON PALLADIUM (1977), HERE, MY DEAR (1978), IN OUR LIFETIME (1981)

COMPILATIONS: GREATEST HITS (1964), GREATEST HITS VOLUME 2 (1967), MARVIN AND HIS GRILS (1969), SUPER HITS (1970), GREATEST HITS (1970), ANTHOLOGY (1974), GREATEST HITS (1976), EARLY YEARS: 1961-1964 (1980), EVERY GREAT MOTOWN HIT OF MARVIN GAYE (1983), 15 GREATEST HITS (1984), 21 CLASSIC DUETS (1986), 20 GREATEST HITS (1986), A MUSICAL TESTAMENT 1964-1968 (1988)

FURTHER READING: DIVIDED SOUL: THE LIFE OF MARVIN GAYE (1985)

GAYLORD & HOLIDAY

Originally formed in 1949 as The Gaylords, the group comprised Ronald Fredianelli (born in Detroit, Michigan on 12 June 1930), Bonaldo Bonaldi and Don Rea and originally recorded *Tell Me You're Mine* (based on an Italian song *Per Un Bacio D'amour*) in 1952 with the intention of selling copies in Bonaldi's father's store. The recording was considered good enough for a copy to be sent to Mercury Records, who subsequently signed the trio up. *Tell Me You're Mine* would hit #2 on the chart (in the pre-rock and roll days) and lead to several other hits, most notably *The Little Shoemaker*, recorded with Hugo Perelli. By this time Ronald had been drafted in to the military, although he continued his singing career, even scoring a hit under the name Ronnie Gaylord, with *Cuddle Me* making #13.

He rejoined The Gaylords upon his discharge, with Bonaldo also changing his name to Burt Holiday and the group enjoying three more minor hits. Gaylord & Holiday continued as a duo when Don Rea left and in 1975 signed with Barney Ales' Prodigal label for the novelty hit *Eh Cumpari*, which hit #72. They also released the album **Second Generation** and moved to Motown when Prodigal was bought by Berry Gordy. With the company uncertain where to position them, they were placed on the Natural Resources label for the album **Wine, Women And Song**, from which *Angelina (The Waitress At The Pizzeria)* was issued as a single, the only 45 released by the label. Ronnie died on 25 January 2004 with Burt continuing to tour with Ronnie's eldest son, Ron Gaylord Jr.

ALBUMS: SECOND GENERATION (1975), WINE, WOMEN & SONG (1976)

GENERAL KANE

Originally formed by Mitch McDowell as General Caine, in honour of an officer who had encouraged his musical aspirations whilst in military school, the group arrived at Motown in 1986 already seasoned professionals. Mitch was born in San Bernardino, California in 1954 and formed his first group, Booty People, soon after leaving military school. They would record one album for ABC before Mitch put together General Caine and signed with Groove Time Records for two albums, **Let Me In** (released in 1978) and **Get Down Attack** (1980).

The group then switched to Tabu where they had a further two albums issued, **Girls** (1982) and **Dangerous** (1983), with the albums providing two minor R&B hits. After a subtle name change to General Kane the group was signed by Motown in 1986, by which time the line-up consisted of Mitch (guitar, bass, keyboards and vocals), Brenda Jackson (keyboards and vocals), Kevin Goins (formerly of Quazar, guitar and vocals), Tony Patler (guitar), Danny Macon (vocals), Craig Owen (vocals), Darryl 'Daddy-O' Haywood (vocals), Nelson Hardwick (vocals) and Tony Patler (vocals).

Their first Gordy offering was the hard hitting single *Crack Killed Applejack*, an anti-drug message song that struck a chord and made #12 on the R&B chart, prompting the resulting album **In Full Chill** to also make the listings at #46. The group slimmed down and switched to the main Motown label for their next release but also expanded their musical horizons, being rewarded when *Girl Pulled The Dog* hit #33 and the attendant album **Wide Open** hit #57. The group left Motown soon after, with Mitch leaving the music business and opening a bail bondman business in his home town of San Bernadino in 1990. There he was shot to death with his nephew on 22 January 1992 during a robbery.

ALBUMS: IN FULL CHILL (1986), WIDE OPEN (1987)

GEORGIO

Although born in San Francisco, California in 1966, Georgio Allentini was raised in Minneapolis, Minnesota and learned to play a variety of instruments whilst still a youngster. An early demo he made was eventually handed to Prince at Paisley Park, but although he and Brownmark made moves to sign Georgio to the label, he turned them down because, it was said, they just wanted him as a singer. Instead he paid for his own more professional demo of *Sexappeal* which aired on Los Angeles radio station KJLH as part of an amateur music day and was pressed up by local label Picture Perfect Records via Macola. After 9,000 copies sold in four days, Georgio signed with Motown on a reported seven year multi album deal.

There was to be only two albums on Motown, **Sexappeal** in 1987 and **Georgio** a year later, although he would score five R&B hits, including *Sexappeal* (#16 and crossed over to hit #96 pop), *Tina Cherry* (#5 R&B and #59 pop), *Lover's Lane* (#26 R&B and his only UK chart hit at #54), and *Bedrock* and *I Don't Want To Be Alone*, both of which peaked at #37. Whether it was for publicity purposes or ego is not known but his limited Motown career was blighted by attempts to fuel rivalries with Michael Jackson and Prince.

ALBUM: SEX APPEAL (1987)

GET CRAZY (FILM SOUNDTRACK)

A musical comedy starring Malcolm McDowell (as Reggie Wanker, a character based on Mick Jagger), Allen Garfield, Daniel Stern, Gail Edwards, Howard Kaylan (best known as a member of The Turtles), Lori Eastside (formerly a singer with Kid Creole & The Coconuts) and Lou Reed, 'Get Crazy' was something of a troublesome film even before it was released, with friction between the director (Allan Arkush) and producer (Herbert F Solow) the root of the problems. Arkush had worked at the Fillmore East and wanted to make a film that drew upon his experiences.

"Everything in that movie is based on real stuff, and I wish I could remake it as a realistic movie. But the only way I could get it made at the time was to do the 'Airplane!' version of it. There was this small company called Sherwood Productions that had some capital. We had meetings, and they liked my idea of a comedy set in a theatre like the Fillmore. 'Airplane!' was really big then, and what they wanted was that kind of whacky comedy. We started working on the script… and I realized during that process that the executive, Herb Solow, was pretty much of a jerk. Whatever I'd suggest, he'd counter with another suggestion. It was just the way he was: everything he heard, he said no to… but he would take the germ of what you said, and put his own spin on it."

Arkush and Solow also clashed repeatedly over the cast, with virtually every character being the subject of a tug of war between director and producer.

"The part of the little sister was supposed to be played by Mariska Hargitay, who was so beautiful, you wanted to fall on the floor. Herb wanted Stacey Nelkin. We wanted Jerry Orbach to play the owner; he was much more like Bill Graham. Herb went with Allan Garfield. Every role, there was an argument. He actually talked me into Daniel Stern in the lead instead of Tom Hanks… who was hilarious, and I think he'd only done 'Bosom Buddies' at that point. So it was one stupid decision after another."

Once the cast had been finally agreed, all of the actors were required to sing in the film (Malcolm McDowell, who was not a singer by any stretch of the imagination, was so adamant that he sing he insisted on a clause in his contract to that effect, rather than have his vocals dubbed), with the soundtrack subsequently appearing on Motown's rock imprint Morocco in August 1983.

The tracks by Malcolm McDowell and Sparks were subsequently combined for release as a single, with the soundtrack also featuring Marshall Crenshaw, The Ramones, Fear, Michael Boddicker and Bill Henderson alongside Lori Eastside and Howard Kaylan. Despite the strength of the names on the album, the soundtrack flopped, as did the film, although Allan Arkush wasn't entirely surprised.

"The scam they came up with to release it was to sell the shares in it to some Wall Street tax shelter group, and then put it out so it would lose money, just like 'The Producers'! So nobody saw it – on purpose! It was so horrible to work so hard on something, and then see it just thrown away. The audiences that saw it didn't get it. They didn't understand how there could be a rock concert with all these different kinds of acts. My take on it? It's a movie with three thousand punch lines, but only a thousand jokes. There's too much zaniness, and not enough human comedy. It's just too bizarre."

If the film *was* designed to lose money then it succeeded spectacularly, grossing barely $1.5 million at the box office. Despite this, the film has gone on to become something of a cult classic, at least among those who favour rock and roll films, who have had to fulfil their appetite with VHS copies that were released later on in the decade; the film is not available on DVD and is unlikely to be released owing to copyright issues with the soundtrack.

ALBUM: GET CRAZY SOUNDTRACK (1983)

GET READY – THE TEMPTATIONS [SINGLE]

Ordinarily, any record that tops the R&B chart would be described as a success, but the fact that *Get Ready* failed to carry that success over to the pop charts effectively spelt the end of Smokey Robinson's almost exclusive hold on The Temptations. This stall in The Temptations' run of success had not been anticipated, for Smokey had written what he thought to be his most direct song and had Eddie Kendricks restored to lead vocalist on a number that has proved to be a much longer lasting favourite than the song it beat out, *Ain't Too Proud To Beg*.

Indeed, at Motown's Quality Control meeting, after reviewing the two tracks, the assembled throng agreed that *Get Ready* appeared to be the more obvious hit. *Get Ready* spent a week at the top of the R&B charts but hit a wall at #29 on the pop chart and would spend only seven weeks on the listings. In the UK the single missed the chart altogether the first time out, but was reissued in 1969 in the wake of The Temptations then current success with Diana Ross & The Supremes, *I'm Gonna Make You Love Me*. In a smooth marketing move, *Get Ready* was coupled with *My Girl*, which had been a minor hit in 1963 when originally issued, and the new pairing bounced all the way to #10. In 1987 Australian female singer Carol Hitchcock revived the song and was rewarded with a #56 British hit.

GET READY – RARE EARTH [SINGLE]

The Temptations' 1966 hit *Get Ready* had been part of The Sunliners live repertoire for a good few years, with the group continuing to feature the song when they subsequently evolved into Rare Earth. Their first recording of *Get Ready* appeared on their 1968 Verve album **Dreams/Answers**, but once they signed with Motown, Barney Ales was keen to have the group do an update, largely because he had seen the response when performed live. An initial version recorded for possible release was scrapped, with the need for an album then becoming a priority.

To this end it was suggested that the group try to capture their live show as closely as possible, with Rare Earth allocated a slot at two o'clock in the morning. The group set up their own equipment and proceeded to knock out the album over the course of the very early morning, with *Get Ready* being stretched out to twenty one and a half minutes; it would eventually take up the whole of one side of the resulting album. Audience applause was dubbed in at the end, giving the album its required live feel.

For the single release, a much more manageable 2:46 edit was issued on the Rare Earth label (it was released on Tamla Motown in the UK, the only Rare Earth single to appear on the iconic label) and achieved all that was expected; although a minor R&B hit that peaked at #20, it sailed all the way to #4 on the pop chart, selling a reported million copies in the process.

GIRL GROUPS: THE STORY OF A SOUND (FILM SOUNDTRACK)

Originally a tribute book to classic 1960s girl groups written by Alan Betrock in 1982, the concept was taken by director and producer Steve Alpert, who produced a documentary that was released the following year. According to Steve, what would ultimately be a 65 minute film took considerably longer to produce.

"This film took almost a year of my life, a very stressful year at that since it is always difficult to juggle the creative storytelling aspect of making a film with the realities of budget and music/clip clearance. We went to ABC for footage from the show, 'Hullabaloo' that they did not even know they had. We dug up stuff in Detroit. I flew there during a blizzard that winter and found footage from a local afternoon programme, 'Teen Town', that was Detroit's local 'American Bandstand'. That stuff was sitting in a damp basement at a TV station in Windsor, Canada on two-inch video, long extinct even then in 1982."

Among the other problems facing the creators was clip clearance, with Steve negotiating directly with Motown for what would be the company's first outside licensing venture. As part of the deal agreeing to provide material for the film, Motown insisted that the producers buy a minimum of ten clips. They also insisted on having the rights to release an accompanying album, which duly appeared in November 1983 (January 1984 in the UK). Alongside Motown luminaries Diana Ross & The Supremes, Mary Wells, The Velvelettes, Martha Reeves & The Vandellas and The Marvelettes were classic 1960s groups The Shangri-Las, The Dixie Cups, The Shirelles and The Angels, with Alan Betrock also supplying sleeve notes for the album.

Whilst not a major seller, its importance in showcasing the major artists of the era can be gauged by the fact it was reissued on CD in 1987. The documentary meanwhile was released on VHS soon after airing, although has yet to appear on DVD.

ALBUM: SELECTIONS FROM THE SOUNDTRACK OF 'GIRL GROUPS: THE STORY OF A SOUND' (1983)

GARRY GLENN

Born in Detroit, Michigan on 12 May 1955, Garry achieved considerable fame as a songwriter, penning *Caught Up In The Rapture* (Anita Baker), *Intimate Friends* (Eddie Kendricks), *Share Your Love* (Earth, Wind & Fire), *Winning Streak* (Pieces Of A Dream) and *Gonna Make You Mine* (Natalie Cole) among other hits.

In 1980 he launched his own singing career, recording one album for PPL Records. He also made one album for Motown (having previously contributed to the soundtrack to 'Citizens On Patrol'), with **Feels Good To Feel Good** being released in August 1987 and making #70 on the R&B chart, whilst two of the lifted singles, *Do You Have To Go* and *Feels Good To Feel Good* (which features The Emotions' Sheila Hutchinson) also made #37 on the R&B chart. Garry died from kidney failure on 18 September 1991.

ALBUM: FEELS GOOD TO FEEL GOOD (1987)

GO HOME – STEVIE WONDER [SINGLE]

With **In Square Circle** having already given rise to the number one smash *Part Time Lover*, Motown was keen to maintain the momentum with another hit single. To this end *Go Home* was chosen as the follow-up, a song in which Stevie tries to tell a young woman to go home when the woman in question wants to stay. A simplistic song idea, *Go Home* may have lacked its predecessors immediate appeal but still performed well on the charts, making #2 on the R&B chart and #10 pop following its release in November 1985, although it fared considerably worse in the UK where it barely made #67.

GOLDEN HARMONEERS

One of Motown's earliest attempts at gospel music, the Golden Harmoneers was an obscure Detroit, Michigan based group that are believed to have shared members with another local group, The Sons of Zion. The one known member, George Anderson (born in Beach, Mississippi in 1927) also sang with The Heavenly Chandlers during his career. The Golden Harmoneers released one single on Motown, *I Am Bound* backed with *Precious Memories* in August 1961. George died from leukemia on 20 April 2003.

GOLDEN WORLD/RIC-TIC/WINGATE/J&W RECORDS

Golden World Records was formed late in 1961 after Ed Wingate had rejected overtures from Berry Gordy to become a partner in Motown; instead Ed and his business partner JoAnne Bratton (the then wife of champion boxer Johnny Bratton) wanted to launch their own musical venture. Golden World initially comprised two entities, a record label and publishing company, although unlike Motown, Golden World at that time had neither studio nor writers to call their own. And whilst much of the talent in Detroit naturally gravitated to Hitsville, Golden World undertook the unusual step of advertising for singers and songwriters, locating producer, arranger, conductor and pianist George 'Teacho' Wiltshire and singer Sue Perrin in this manner, with Sue's *I Wonder* backed with *Put A Ring On My Finger* the very first release in January 1962.

By September 1963 the fledgling company had established its own offices based at 11801 12th Street (Rosa Parks), although for several releases the address was given as 4039 Buena Vista, JoAnne's home address. Over the next few years, Golden World became a viable alternative to Motown, with several artists making the journey from one side of Detroit to the other in order to work with or for Golden World. Their roster included the likes of The Sunliners (later to become Rare Earth), Gino Parks (a former Motown recording artist), The Reflections (who would score one of Golden World's biggest hits with *Just Like Romeo And Juliet*, a #6 pop hit in 1964), The Debonairs, The Parliaments (the George Clinton led group), Carl Carlton, Juanita Williams, Barbara Mercer and The Adorables, whilst in the production booth could be found Freddie Gorman, Bob Hamilton, Sonny Sanders and Richard 'Popcorn' Wylie.

Aside from Golden World, Ed and JoAnne also launched a number of other labels, including Wingate, J&W (possibly named from the initials Jackson, JoAnne's maiden name, and Wingate) and Ric-Tic. This latter label was named in honour of JoAnne's son Derek, affectionately known as Ric-Tic, who was killed in an accident in January 1962, the label making its bow a month later with Joyce Webb's *You've Got A Whole Lot Of Living To Do*.

At much the same time, Ed and JoAnne made the decision to set up their own recording facilities, having recorded virtually all of their earlier singles in New York. It was JoAnne who located a former electrical store at 3246 West Davison Avenue, bringing in Bob D'Orleans and Kem Hamman who between them would build a brand new studio from scratch. Whilst the various labels enjoyed sporadic success, it was to be the arrival of J.J. Barnes, Edwin Starr and The Fantastic Four that propelled them into the big league. With musical backing invariably provided by moonlighting Funk Brothers (if caught they were each fined $1,000 by Berry Gordy, but Ed Wingate usually reimbursed them the cash out of his own pocket, so pleased was he with the end results), Edwin would hit the charts with *Agent Double-O-Soul* and *Stop Her On Sight (S.O.S.)*, hits which may well have proved to be the catalyst for Berry Gordy moving to quell this Detroit rival.

In 1966, Berry paid a reported $1 million for virtually all of Golden World and two years later acquired Ric-Tic, including the roster of artists (Edwin Starr was on tour in the UK when the sale went through, returning to the US to find he had been acquired by Motown) and studio. The studio facilities at 3246 West Davison were considered at the very least the equal of those at Hitsville, with the result the former Golden World studios became known as Motown Studio B and continued recording whilst the company was still based in Detroit.

WILLIAM GOLDSTEIN

A graduate from Columbia University, William Goldstein was brought to Motown in 1975 under contract as an artist, composer and producer. He would release two singles under his own name for the Motown label, *Spirit Of 76 (A.M. America)*, a celebration song for the American bicentennial released in November 1975 (having originally been the theme to the ABC morning show AM America), and *Midnight Rhapsody*, credited to William Goldstein & The Magic Disco and released in July 1976.

It was the latter project that saw William at his most active at Motown, producing a significant number of tracks on the Magic Disco Machine series of albums. William was also utilised on the soundtrack to 'Bingo Long' and later 'Norman Is That You' during his time with the company. After leaving Motown William made a name for himself as a composer for television and movies, scoring 'Fame', 'Twilight Zone' and 'Oceanquest'.

TOMMY GOOD

Born and raised in Detroit, Michigan in 1937, singer Tommy Good fronted The Tabs and recorded for Nasco and Dot at the tail end of the 1950s. He was signed by Motown in 1964 and would see only one single released (supposedly by public demand, but Motown staged a fake protest march on Hitsville by hired schoolchildren to demand the release of his single), although *Baby I Miss You* became a favourite on the Northern Soul scene.

Although Tommy also recorded for Harry Balk's Impact label as a member of Inner Circle and later became a member of The Good-Rainwater Company, his main career was a designer for Chrysler. Joining the company in 1961, he remained in their employ until he retired in 1999. The continuing popularity of his one single on Gordy, however, eventually prompted a return to music, with Tommy being one of several former Motown artists who appeared at the Soul Weekender in Northampton in 2006, with Universal issuing an anthology CD to coincide with the event.

CUBA GOODING

Although Cuba Gooding came to Motown as an untried solo singer, he had already made a more than considerable mark on pop and R&B music as the lead singer of The Main Ingredient.

Born in New York on 27 April 1944, Cuba grew up with Tony Silvester, Luther Simmons Jr. and Donald McPherson in Harlem. Silvester, Simmons and McPherson first linked up as The Poets in the mid 1960s, recording a number of singles for Jerry Leiber and Mike Stoller's Red Bird label. They then name changed to The Insiders and moved to the RCA label, although in 1966 they switched monikers to The Main Ingredient, still searching for their first hit. That eventually came in 1970 with *You've Been My Inspiration*, but for lead singer Donald McPherson the success would prove to be short lived, for not long after the group made their breakthrough, he was struck down with leukaemia. Whilst the group waited for him to recover, they drafted in backing singer Cuba Gooding as a temporary replacement, subsequently making the change permanent following McPherson's death on 4 July 1971.

With Cuba now the focal point of the group, The Main Ingredient would score a significant number of hits, including *Everybody Plays The Fool, Just Don't Want To Be Lonely* and *Rolling Down A Mountainside*, the latter a cover of the Leon Ware penned song that had been first recorded on Motown by Third Creation (The Main Ingredient would also have a minor hit with another of Leon's songs, *Instant Love*). Despite the hits, Tony Silvester left the group in 1976 and was replaced by Carl Tomkins, but The Main Ingredient disbanded a year later, with Cuba moving to Motown as a solo artist.

Assigned to the production team of Dennis Lambert and Brian Potter his debut album **The 1st Album** was much anticipated and received favourable reviews, but apart from a minor hit single in *Mind Pleaser* which crept onto the R&B chart at #91 in 1978, the album did not take off as expected. A second album found Cuba working with Michael Lovesmith on **Love Dancer**, released in April 1979, but this fared no better than its predecessor.

Following the lack of success in his solo career, Cuba reformed The Main Ingredient with Tony Silvester and Luther Simmons Jr. and signed with RCA, although Cuba would score another solo hit for Streetwise in 1983 with *Happiness Is Just Around The Bend*, a remake of a Main Ingredient hit from 1974.

ALBUMS: THE 1ST CUBA GOODING ALBUM (1978), LOVE DANCER (1979)

MARC GORDON

Ultimately best known for guiding the careers of The Fifth Dimension, Tony Orlando & Dawn, Thelma Houston and Willie Hutch, among others, Marc Gordon ensured his place in Motown folklore by setting up the Los Angeles office with Hal Davis in the early 1960s. As head of the West Coast office, Marc had responsibility for producing and co-producing many of the Motown artists who found themselves in California, including Stevie Wonder's various beach projects, The Supremes and Marvin Gaye.

He left Motown in 1966, not long after Motown turned down an audition tape by The Versatiles that he had forwarded to Detroit. It proved to be a costly mistake for Motown, for Marc made contact with the group soon after, convinced them to come up with a better name and guided them through a succession of Grammy Awards and platinum record successes as The Fifth Dimension. Marc, who married Florence LaRue of the group would later form his own Rocky Road label and enjoy success with Al Wilson and Climax. Ill for a number of years, he died on 16 June 2010 at the age of 74.

ROSCOE GORDON

Born in Memphis, Tennessee on 10 April 1928, Roscoe Gordon made his early recordings for Sam Phillips' Sun Records in 1952. Those early masters would be sold by Phillips to both RPM and Chess Records, with both labels releasing exactly the same single, although RPM enjoyed the bigger hit. In 1960 Roscoe briefly signed with Vee-Jay, scoring a Top Ten R&B hit with *Just A Little Bit*, which peaked at #2 and became his only appearance on the pop chart at #54. The later hit was featured on the CD compilation **Hits From The Legendary Vee-Jay Records** issued by Motown in November 1986. Roscoe, who retired from the music industry in 1962 and bought an interest in a laundry died from a heart attack on 11 July 2002.

GORDY FAMILY

Motown Records might have been the brainchild of Berry Gordy, but in time virtually every member of his immediate family made their way to Hitsville and helped turn a dream into reality. Anna, Gwen and Robert (all of whom have separate entries within this book) were active in various aspects of recording, either as writers, producers or, in the case of Robert, as actual artists.

Berry's other siblings and even his parents undertook various duties within the organisation. Eldest brother Fuller (born on 9 September 1918) was one of the last of the Gordy's to join the organisation, having begun his working career within the printing industry, even handling print for Motown before deciding to shut up shop and join Berry at Hitsville. Initially procurement manager, Fuller would eventually rise to overseeing facilities, purchasing and personnel whilst the company was located in Detroit, eventually moving out to California in 1973 where he became Vice President of administration. Not only was he employed by Motown, his daughter later married Johnny Bristol. He died on 9 November 1991.

Esther Gordy was born in Oconee, Georgia on 25 April 1920 and was therefore the eldest of the Gordy sisters. She was Berry's secretary (unpaid, according to her later recollections) when he first began in the business as a writer for Jackie Wilson. When Tamla first opened its doors in 1959, Esther was co-ordinator of the management company (later going on to head ITM for some ten years), secretary and general office staff, with her husband George Edwards (a local politician) serving as Motown's comptroller. According to Berry, it was Esther who first realised the importance of what was being created at Hitsville, carefully preserving all manner of pictures, contracts and other items of memorabilia. One of the few family members who did not move to California, Esther founded the Motown Historical Museum at the site of the former Hitsville Studios and continued to be involved in the day to day running of this venture right up until her death on 24 August 2011.

Brother George (born on 7 January 1926) was the fourth Gordy child and Berry's first business partner, helping set up the ill-fated 3D Record Mart. Although this business collapsed, George obviously had faith in Berry and his business acumen, joining Motown in 1960 and co-writing several hits, including *Stubborn Kind Of Fellow* and *What Christmas Means To Me* as well as serving as a producer. Sadly, he died some three weeks before Esther in 2011.

The other Gordy sister, Loucye was married to saxophonist Ron Wakefield, who also joined Motown as a full time staff member in 1963. Loucye ran the publishing company Jobete until her sudden death from a cerebral haemorrhage on 24 July 1965.

Even mother and father Bertha and Berry (affectionately known as Pops around Hitsville) did their bit, with Bertha signing all of the expense cheques and Pops undertaking general maintenance work and acting as a mentor to many of the artists signed to the label. When Pops died in 1978, Motown released a tribute album in his memory. Bertha died three years later, in 1981.

GORDY RECORDS

Miracle Records wasn't only a confusing imprint for a company that had the recording group The Miracles on its roster, it was also something of an outpost at Hitsville, with only The Valadiers *Greetings (This Is Uncle Sam)* making an appearance on the chart. Then in early 1962, Berry Gordy got wind that his former wife Thelma Coleman was starting up her own record label, which she intended calling Gordy Records, utilising her former married name.

Pressed into action, Berry pre-empted her by registering the name himself, switching much of the Miracle roster to Gordy and intending the label to become a home for R&B as opposed to the eclectic mixture that had appeared on Miracle. Employing the slogan 'It's what's in the grooves that count', over the course of the next twenty years Gordy Records was home to the likes of The Temptations, Martha & The Vandellas, Edwin Starr, The Contours, Undisputed Truth, Luther Allison, Leon Ware, High Inergy, Rick James, Teena Marie, Switch, DeBarge, Mary Jane Girls and Dennis Edwards, among others. Somewhat fittingly, The Temptations had the honour of releasing both the first single on the imprint, *(You're My) Dream Come True* in April 1962 and the last, *Someone* in February 1987.

ANNA GORDY

The third of Berry Gordy Sr. and Bertha's eventual eight children, Anna Ruby Gordy was born in Oconee, Georgia on 28 January 1922. Together with her equally vivacious younger sister Gwen, Anna was quickly established as one of the faces on the Detroit social scene, with the pair sharing the photo and cigarette concession at Detroit's Flame Show Lounge during the 1950s. Whilst their compatriots, including their other sisters Esther and Loucye invariably settled down into married life, Anna and Gordy had developed a taste for show business having rubbed shoulders with the likes of Billie Holiday, Sam Cooke and Jackie Wilson and wanted more of it.

Both Anna and Gwen would be drawn into the musical world, initially with their own nationally distributed label Anna Records. Although the label was named after Anna, she was little more than a part-founder, with the musical input coming from Gwen and her then boyfriend Billy Roquel Davis. Anna Records would eventually hit the same kind of financial problems that beset many start up labels, despite a major hit with Barrett Strong's *Money*, ironically a single they leased from brother Berry Gordy's new Tamla set up.

By 1961, Anna Records was no more, but Gwen Gordy had not remained idle, linking up with new boyfriend and later husband Harvey Fuqua to form the Harvey and Tri-Phi labels. Harvey had arrived in Detroit with a protégé in tow; one Marvin Gaye, who quickly established a relationship with Anna Gordy. Although there was a seventeen year age gap between the two, Marvin was smitten, and Anna equally so. Although the Motown publicity machine would claim that the pair married in 1961, around about the time Harvey and Gwen tied the knot, in reality the actual marriage did not take place until 8 January 1964.

Irrespective of when they married, Anna and Marvin were often more than just a romantic item, with the pair co-writing several of Marvin's early recordings for Tamla. On other occasions Marvin would take experiences and phrases that occurred during his relationship and use it to his advantage; it was Anna asking him why he was so stubborn during one argument that subsequently became the major hit *Stubborn Kind Of Fellow*.

By all accounts, the marriage between Anna and Marvin was fraught almost from the start, with several artists convinced Marvin was using his family connections to gain leverage over Berry Gordy. However, as revealed many years later, a major problem within the relationship was Marvin's apparent desire to have children and Anna's inability to give birth. Then, on 17 November 1965 the pair presented to the world their son, christened Marvin Pentz Gaye III, a child they said was their biological son. A short while before his death, Marvin admitted the boy was actually adopted by him and Anna, although he held off from revealing who the biological parents might have been. The answer came several years later and was as shocking a story as could be possibly imagined; Marvin fathered the child with Anna's niece Denise, the daughter of George Gordy. To make matters worse, Denise was 15 years old at the time she gave birth and the whole story was apparently concocted to preserve Marvin's image as the leading Motown male star!

Despite the addition of a child, the relationship between Anna and Marvin became more and more volatile, with Anna accusing Marvin of conducting affairs with Mary Wells, Kim Weston and Tammi Terrell (effectively every female Motown star he sang with). There were also rumours floating in the other direction too, with stories of Anna's own infidelity causing the arguments between the two to become even more vociferous, even in public.

In between the arguments, however, Anna and Marvin found time to continue their occasional songwriting partnership, penning such hits as *Baby I'm For Real* and *The Bells* for The Originals and *God Is Love* and *Flying High (In The Friendly Sky)* on Marvin's seminal **What's Going On**. Despite this recording success, the romantic relationship became more and more strained, with break-ups and make-ups in abundance, especially after they moved to California in 1971.

By 1973 the pair was no more, Marvin having taken up with a woman 17 years his junior in Janis Hunter, a relationship that would result in two children. Upon the birth of the second child in 1975, Anna and Marvin reached agreement for a divorce, although such were the financial demands made by Anna, the case became a prolonged legal battle between the pair. It was eventually agreed that a significant part of the financial settlement should come from Marvin's advance for a new album and the rest to be made up by royalties from that album. The result was **Here, My Dear**, in which Marvin laid out on record virtually every aspect of their relationship. Anna did contemplate initiating a $5 million invasion of privacy suit against her former husband when she first heard the album but decided against it in the long run.

Ironically, the pair reconciled their differences after their divorce, even more so when Marvin's second marriage collapsed, with the lawyer who had handled their bitter divorce expressing considerable and understandable surprise at seeing the former protagonists kissing and cuddling whenever they met!

Anna eventually became something of a recluse, although she would appear at family parties and reunions and kept in touch with Marvin during his flights to Hawaii and later Belgium. When he returned in triumph to the United States in 1982 following the success of *Sexual Healing* and **Midnight Love**, it was Anna who accompanied him to collect his well deserved Grammy awards. Indeed, the pair became so close this second time around several friends expected the pair to remarry, but in the end both Anna and Marvin were happy to remain friends.

Devastated by Marvin's death in April 1984, Anna took his three children and several family friends on a boat to scatter Marvin's ashes in the Pacific Ocean. Her public appearances thereafter became sporadic; appearing in 1987 with Marvin III to accept Marvin Gaye's induction into the Rock & Roll Hall of Fame and three years later attending with all of Marvin's children as his star was unveiled on the Hollywood

Walk of Fame. Anna died after several years of declining health on 31 January 2014.

BERRY GORDY

Berry Gordy's place in music history is assured; as a writer and producer he would be guaranteed a seat at the top table of legends, but his influence, motivation and vision in founding the Motown organisation puts him in a class of his own.

Born in Detroit, Michigan on 28 November 1929, the seventh of eight children born to Berry Gordy Sr. and Bertha Fuller Gordy, it was hoped (at least by his father) that Berry would go into the family business, which at the time was plastering. Ever rebellious, however, Berry Jr. dropped out of high school whilst in the eleventh grade in order to become a professional boxer in the featherweight division.

His first fight saw him beat Frankie Branchetti on 1 December 1947 at the Maple Leaf Gardens in Toronto, but even then he was engaged in another battle, struggling to overcome a growing interest in music. Boxing won out for the next three years, during which time Berry had fought seventeen bouts, winning twelve, drawing two and losing the other three. By November 1950 however, his passion for music had taken over and, according to Berry's autobiography, the opportunity of seeing a battle of the bands between Duke Ellington and Stan Kenton proved more alluring than seeing a battle between two boxers – he hung up his gloves for good after winning a points decision against Joe Nelson on 11 January 1950.

For the next six months he filled his spare time writing songs about all manner of subjects, even sending off one he felt was ideal for Doris Day and submitting another in reply to a magazine advertisement to have it properly written up as sheet music.

After six months however, the only meaningful post he received was his call-up papers, informing him he had been drafted into the US Army and was to report to Fort Custer. A reluctant soldier, Berry served in Korea during the war, where he first met up with Billy Davis who had been drafted on the same day. From their numerous conversations it seemed the pair shared a common interest in music and they resolved to use their army severance pay to set up in the music business once they were demobbed.

That came in 1953, with Berry heading back to Detroit and waiting for Davis to show up with his half of the money needed for their venture, a record store. Davis seemingly spent his money on clothes before signing any agreement with Berry, with the result that Berry Gordy Sr. borrowed money from the church credit union and loaned it to his son. Brother George also became a partner, although the two argued over the prospective name for the new shop, Berry favouring the 3D Record Mart with the subtitle The House That Jams Built and George wanting House of Jazz as the subtitle. After Berry Sr. intervened, it was George's suggestion that won out, an apt name given that Berry was particularly into jazz music and initially filled the store with nothing else. Unfortunately, potential customers who ventured into the store were looking for the latest Muddy Waters or John Lee Hooker releases rather than jazz and soon exited with their money still in their pockets. By the time Berry Jr. realised that the store should be catering to what the customers wanted rather than what Berry wanted them to buy, it was almost too late; the flurry of sales that resulted from the changing of stock was not enough to rescue the store from bankruptcy.

After a brief spell as a door to door salesman selling cookware Berry's need for a full time job took on greater importance, for he married his first wife Thelma Coleman, a nurse in 1953, with their first child Hazel Joy being born the following August. The following October, a son named Berry IV was born, followed the next August by a second son, Terry James. The names of his children would prove inspirational in his later music venture, but in the meantime with a growing family to feed, Berry was forced into looking for full time employment. With the help of Thelma's parents he got a job at the Ford foundry, although he walked out after a day. Three weeks later Thelma's mother got him another job, this time at the Lincoln-Mercury plant where he worked the assembly line fastening upholstery and chrome strips.

Berry endured the job for some two years before handing in his notice, determined to make a real go at the music business, initially as a songwriter.

"My sister sent me to a publishing company where the owners managed Jackie Wilson. They liked my songs and my ideas so I got involved with that. We wrote the first six or seven Jackie Wilson hits; *Reet Petite, To Be Loved, Lonely Teardrops, That's Why I Love You So* and two or three others. A guy named Dick Jacobs over at Decca Records would always call me when they would record a song for Jackie; for *Lonely Teardrops* they actually flew me into the company to be in on the session. I enjoyed working with Dick Jacobs quite a lot. Or at least I enjoyed talking to him – he always gave me a lot of credit, which built my ego up quite a lot. But I didn't actually make money from those songs that I was writing, because by the time I got my royalties I owed everybody in town, especially my family."

By the time of the later hits, however, Jackie's manager Al Green had died and been replaced by Nat Tarnopol. A disagreement over getting a Gordy tune used on the B side to the next single prompted Berry to terminate his relationship with Jackie Wilson. His co-writers, Billy Roquel Davis and Gwen Gordy decided to set up their own label, named Anna after another Gordy sister, and asked Berry to go into business with them. Reluctant to tie himself to anyone else, Berry turned them down, although Anna Records would prove to be a useful outlet for several records that Berry had a hand and more in over the next year or so. There were other labels to which Berry leased tracks, including End Records, who took The Miracles' *Got A Job* and Carlton Records, who leased Bob Kayli (in reality Berry's younger brother Robert) and *Everyone Was There*, a #96 hit in 1958. Despite these hits and earlier successes with Jackie Wilson, Berry still had difficulty making a living out of music, with one publisher holding out on handing over income Berry felt was rightfully his. In the end he decided to set up his own publishing company, founding Jobete (the name was taken from his three children –JOy, BErry and TErry; Gordy had always been keen on name contractions, calling the backing group he and future wife Raynoma assembled The Rayber Voices) to protect his songwriting interests.

Then came the producer's royalty for *Got A Job*, with Berry receiving a cheque for $3.19. Present when he opened the envelope had been Smokey Robinson, lead singer and chief songwriter of The Miracles (who Berry was also managing at the time); when he saw the sum involved, he told Berry he might as well start his own record label since they couldn't do any worse than that.

"The reason I wrote songs was because I loved writing. The reason I produced songs was because I didn't like the way they were being produced, other than the ones with Wilson and Dick Jacobs. And because I was not making a profit, I felt I would have to sell them, too. Hence I got into selling the records, and Motown was formed. The point is, I would just as soon have been a songwriter, and stayed there. But through my experiences as a writer, I found that the songwriters were not getting what I consider a fair shake. They were not making money. So my idea was that if songwriters could make money, how wonderful, and how big a company could grow."

Berry approached the family loan fund and was able to get an $800 loan to fund the very first recording, *Come To Me* by Marv Johnson. Initially released on the Tamla label, *Come To Me* started to attract interest beyond Detroit, with the result that Berry had soon run out of money trying to ensure there was sufficient stock to meet demand. Fortunately, the local stir created by *Come To Me* caused ripples of interest in New York, with United Artists eventually buying not only the master but Marv's contract too, although with Berry being retained to handle production for his first two albums for his new label.

United Artists would also pick up on Eddie Holland and *Merry-Go-Round*, whilst Chess Records took The Miracles' *Bad Girl* and some five other masters that Berry had at the time. Any money Berry received was quickly reinvested in further recordings, with the aptly titled *Money (That's What I Want)* by Barrett Strong the next hit to roll off the production line. That single was picked up by sister Gwen's label Anna Records, which had national distribution through Chess Records. A #2 R&B and #23 pop hit, *Money* would bring in vital revenue for the embryonic company, which in September 1959 expanded still further with the launch of the Motown label and the release of The Miracles' *I Love Your Baby*. This single too was picked up by Chess as soon as sales started looking as though they would take off, although Chess was unable to deliver a hit this time around.

Gradually the need for assistance in getting national distribution began to tail off, although Barrett Strong's follow-up to his smash, *Yes, No, Maybe So* was handed over to Anna for continuity purposes. Finally, in September 1960 Motown was able to deliver its own national hit, with Mary Wells' *Bye Bye Baby* (a song written by Mary and intended for Jackie Wilson) putting the label on the map when hitting #8 R&B and #45 pop.

There would still be singles that were leased out of the company, with Herman Griffin's *True Love* appearing on the Columbia label in April 1961 (six months after its original Tamla release), but it did not take long for the news to filter throughout Detroit that the Tamla and Motown labels were making a mark on the music scene. The hits would come mainly with R&B, with The Miracles' *Shop Around* becoming the label's first chart topper when it hit #1 on the R&B chart and sailed almost as close on the pop chart, stalling at #2. It sold over a million copies, providing the company with further funds for growth.

Whilst the hits may have been R&B, Berry was open minded musically, with the result artists from virtually every musical genre beat a path to the doors of Hitsville (now firmly established at 2648 West Grand Boulevard) looking for a deal. Some, such as Nick & The Jaguars, arrived with a finished single and sold the master rights to Berry, others came looking for a more conventional contract. It did not matter if the music did not fit easily into the Tamla and Motown label ethos; Miracle Records was launched with *Don't Feel Sorry For Me* by Jimmy Ruffin and would follow this up with releases by Little Iva (in actual fact Raynoma Liles) and Gino Parks. In 1962 Mel-O-dy was launched, with much of its repertoire country music brought to the company by Al Klein, whilst Gordy Records was established in 1962, largely to prevent Berry's former wife Thelma Coleman from registering the name.

Berry did much more than create labels for the artists, he also established something of a blueprint that would eventually enable Motown to enjoy unprecedented success for the next two decades or so. Remembering his days at Lincoln-Mercury, Berry set Motown up as a musical assembly line; staff were required to clock in and out, the musicians would provide the musical accompaniment to every track the company recorded, a studio vocal group (The Andantes) would be on permanent call to provide backing vocals as required and a pool of writers and producers would create the material on which the company would build its future.

It would take some two years before the company fully found its feet, but Berry was able to use that two years as something of a learning curve. There were vital lessons learnt, not least of which was the need to follow a hit with a record as similar as it was possible to be, thus virtually ensuring further sales and success. Ultimately, the goal was to release more hits than misses. Whilst the balance was tilted more towards the misses in the first couple of years, by mid 1961 the company was beginning to turn it around.

Much of the credit for this must go to another of Berry's master strokes, the creation of the Quality Control Department, with the weekly meeting involving creative and sales staff voting on prospective releases; once they got into their stride, nearly everything the company released would go on to become a hit. Berry also installed into the company a competitive edge (singer Chris Clark would famously state that at Motown, even chess was a blood sport), combined with a sense of family. Members of the company would gather each year for a picnic, a day that usually also featured a football game between sides selected by Berry and Barney Ales.

"We just had certain things that we believed in. We believed in making quality records, or making the records that were commercial but were also good. We had no real models, other than all the other record companies who had hits; if a company had a hit, that was a company that I looked at. Of course, it's hard to pick even one company, but I remember there was Nat King Cole and the Capitol people over there that I liked – I thought they had a lot of feeling and soul. There was a label that at one point came up with hit after hit, I think it was Liberty Records; Bobby Vee was on there. And there were a lot of blues labels. There was a guy named Don Robey from the south, a black record company, who I had sent some songs to several years before; I always enjoyed writing blues, and since they had quite a few blues artists there, when I would write a blues I'd send it to them."

Equally important was the ability in getting the right people in to do the job; the predominantly white salesforce run by Barney Ales raised eyebrows around the company, but their sales together with Barney's ability to ensure the money came in enabled the company to prosper.

If Motown in its formative years was reliant on its founder for pretty much everything, with Berry writing and producing much of the early repertoire, by 1963 there were others who had stepped up to the plate. Yet unlike almost every other record company at the time, Berry was not merely a figurehead, an executive who would be relied upon to provide a quote or two when times got good. Whilst his name may have been missing from the records that were being released, his influence could be felt on each and every one of them. He maintained his interest in several of the acts, most notably The Supremes, not least as he became involved with the singer he would ultimately describe as his most important creation, Diana Ross. The relationship between the two, which would result in the birth of a daughter, Rhonda Ross Kendrick in 1971 (Berry also fathered a son Kerry by his second wife Raynoma in 1959, a daughter by girlfriend Jeana Jackson and another son, Kennedy by his mistress Margaret Norton in 1964), led to some resentment within the company, with several artists believing that their careers were overlooked because of the personal relationship between the label boss and the lead singer of one of its artists.

There would be other problems for Berry to contend and deal with, with Mary Wells opting to walk out of the company as soon as she reached the age of twenty one and launching a lawsuit claiming that her original contract was void as she had been a minor when she had first put pen to paper. There would be other singers who came and went, although the Mary Wells walkout was a bitter pill for Berry to swallow. Even so, that was nothing compared to the furore when his ace writing and production team Holland-Dozier-Holland went on strike in an attempt to secure greater financial reward for their efforts. Whether Berry considered the initial strike as little more than a bluff to try and get him to the negotiating table is not known, but a flurry of lawsuits that bounced between the two camps set in motion a long and drawn out fight.

The end result was that Motown lost its chief hit making team, a loss from which took some considerable time to recover. Berry had missed the initial strike because he had relocated himself to California, where it was not only the warmer climate that he looked to soak up. In the entertainment capital of the world, Berry began formulating new plans; hit records were to be just the start for what would become a multi-faceted company, looking to expand its horizons and make films and television shows. With hindsight it can be seen that Berry's move into films caused him to lose sight of what had made the company successful in the first place, although 'Lady Sings The Blues' was successful enough to prove that Berry might have been right all along. The same year he pushed Diana Ross into superstardom with a starring role in 'Lady Sings The Blues', Berry moved his entire operation to Los Angeles, eventually shutting down all facilities in Detroit.

It was not a move that was well received in Detroit (indeed, even to this day it causes considerable bitterness among those who were left behind), with even some of the fabled Funk Brothers not part of the new regime that sprung up at the new home on Sunset Boulevard. Irrespective of the ire Berry caused in his hometown, the focus for the next few years was films, with Berry even directing Diana Ross in 'Mahogany'.

Meanwhile, the exodus that had begun with Mary Wells and HDH continued, with the likes of Gladys Knight & The Pips, Edwin Starr and even The Four Tops heading for pastures new. Berry had a brief return to concentrating on recording with Motown's new discovery The Jackson 5, with Berry one of The Corporation that crafted a succession of number one hits for the group. Eventually, however, The Jackson 5 would walk out the door, Berry's refusal to allow them to record their own material a bridge too far for their father and manager Joseph Jackson. Even paramour Diana Ross and brother-in-law Marvin Gaye left, for RCA and Columbia respectively.

By the start of the 1980s, Motown's best days were beginning to be an ever fading memory, although there would still be moments that harked back to the glory days, with Lionel Richie's emergence as a major star one of the positives from the era. So too was Stevie Wonder's continued success, even if the hits of the 1980s weren't quite as big or vital as those he had enjoyed in the 1970s.

For many years Motown was the most important and most successful black owned corporation in the United States, but maintaining that position became a harder task as the decade wore on. Berry came close to selling Jobete at the start of the 1980s but backed out of the deal when he could not get Stevie Wonder's approval. Then in 1986 he came even closer to selling Motown to MCA, only to back out of the deal at virtually the eleventh hour. Two years later, when MCA came back for another attempt to prise the company from Berry's grip, they found him more responsive. Thanks in part to the fact there were other suitors interested, most notably Virgin, Berry was able to get MCA to up their original offer from 1986 by some 50 percent, paying $61 million for the name and record catalogue, the masters and the remaining artists' recording contracts. The deal went through on 29 June 1988, with Berry setting up the Gordy Company to handle his remaining interests in publishing (Jobete), film and television production (Motown Productions would change name to Gordy-De Passe Productions) and several other projects.

Eventually Berry would sell or hand over all the other assets; Jobete would be sold piece by piece to EMI Music for a total of $321.3 million and Gordy-de Passe Productions would be handed over to Suzanne De Passe. His personal life was equally rewarding, with a further son Stefan (his eighth child) being born to Nancy Leiviska (Stefan is today better known as Redfoo, one half of LMFAO with Skyler Gordy, Berry's grandson). In 1990 he married his girlfriend of eight years Grace Eaton, his third marriage, although this too ended in divorce in 1993. He published his autobiography 'To Be Loved' in 1994 and retired to Palm Desert in California although by 2011 he was working on a stage musical that will tell the story of Motown; something of an answer musical to 'Dreamgirls'. This duly opened on Broadway in April 2013 as 'Motown The Musical'.

FURTHER READING: TO BE LOVED (1994)

GWEN GORDY

Whilst virtually all of Berry's brothers and sisters would be drawn to the Motown Corporation, it was Gwen who would enjoy the greatest success within the industry, her own abilities as a songwriter and talent spotter only marginally behind those of her brother.

Born Gwendolyn Gordy in Detroit, Michigan on 26 November 1927, Gwen had joined with sister Anna selling cigarettes and photographs at Detroit's Flame Show Lounge during the 1950s before linking up with her brother and her then boyfriend Billy Roquel Davis and co-writing several hits for Jackie Wilson. Whilst

Berry was putting together his business plan for Tamla and Motown, Gwen had already got a head start, forming Anna Records in 1959 with Davis and enjoying a hit with a single that had originally appeared on Tamla, Money by Barrett Strong.

Billy Roquel Davis would eventually move to Chicago in order to work more directly with Chess Records (who handled national distribution for Anna), with Gwen then linking up with Harvey Fuqa and launching the Harvey and Tri-Phi labels in conjunction with the man who would become her husband in 1961 (even after the pair divorced in the late 1960s, Gwen went by the name Gwen Gordy Fuqua).

Eventually Gwen and Harvey folded their various recording interests into Berry's Motown Corporation, with Harvey becoming a staff producer and writer and Gwen initially taking control of the Artist Development department as well as becoming a fashion model. Subsequently returning to writing (she has more than 75 copyrights to her credit), Gwen took a more active role in many aspects of the company, including discovering High Inergy, following the labels move to California in the 1970s.

Gwen would maintain her own publishing interests (her Old Brompton Road Publishing company controls numerous copyrights, including Anita Baker's *Sweet Love*) even after effectively retiring from the business, settling on a ranch and breeding horses. Gwen died from cancer on 8 November 1999 at her home in San Diego and was buried in Detroit.

LESLEY GORE

Discovered by Quincy Jones whilst singing at a hotel in Manhattan, Lesley Gore became an overnight teen sensation with her debut single. Born Lesley Sue Goldstein in New York on 2 May 1946, Lesley was raised in New Jersey and was attending Dwight School for Girls when she was signed by Mercury, with *It's My Party* becoming a chart topper in 1963 (it would also make #9 in the UK). Whilst that was her only chart topper, Lesley returned to the Top Ten with each of her next three singles, thus becoming a major star.

Rather than pursue every lucrative offer that came her way, she opted to stick with her school studies with the result her musical career was basically confined to weekend engagements. Whilst this initially had little impact on her recording career, eventually the opportunity to move into films and television would pass her by. Within four years the hits had dried up too, although Lesley remained on the label for a further two years whilst she tried to resolve a number of legal issues.

Eventually given a release in 1969, Lesley would return in 1972 with **Someplace Else Now**, her only album for the MoWest label. Regardless of whether it was too long since her last hit or just changing musical tastes isn't clear, but her album did little and Lesley would remain musically quiet for a further four years before resurfacing on A&M. She has recorded sporadically since, with her last album appearing in 2005.

ALBUM: SOMEPLACE ELSE NOW (1972)

FREDDIE GORMAN

Although Freddie Gorman would make a veritable name for himself as a member of The Originals, he had already been something of a regular around Hitsville for a good few years and played an integral part in the first number one hit the company achieved.

Born Frederick Cortez Gorman in Detroit, Michigan on 11 April 1939, Freddie was still in high school when he made his recording debut as a member of The Qualitones, recording *Tears Of Love* for Josie Records in 1955. By 1957 he had joined with Brian Holland in The Fideletones, recording for Aladdin Records in 1959, although the group splintered soon after and Freddie went back to his then day job as a postman. After completing his round, Freddie would invariably pop into the Hitsville complex, where Brian Holland was by now a staff writer and producer, and was therefore present the day Georgia Dobbins came in with the suggestion of a song entitled *Please Mr. Postman*. Utilising his on the job knowledge, Freddie contributed to the lyrics of what would go one to become The Marvelettes number one smash.

However satisfying co-penning a number one hit may have been, Freddie was after a recording contract and duly got one a short while later, with *The Day Will Come* backed with *Just For You* being issued in October 1961 on the Miracle label. Although Brian and Freddie continued their songwriting partnership a little while longer, Brian eventually began writing more and more with his brother Eddie and Lamont Dozier, with Freddie discovering most of the songs he had been working on were completed by the time he finished his post round and got back to Hitsville.

Freddie eventually left the company and with a new writing partner, Bob Hamilton, eventually resurfaced at Motown's rival Golden World, releasing two singles on the Ric-Tic imprint. When Berry bought out his local rival Freddie found himself back at Motown, this time being put into the newly assembled vocal group

The Originals. Freddie would eventually make a solo album, **It's All About My Love** being released on Rene Records in 1997. He died from lung cancer on 13 June 2006.

THE GOSPEL STARS

Based in Detroit, Michigan The Gospel Stars had recorded since the late 1940s for Davis Claiborne Records of Washington. In 1960 they signed with Tamla, by which time the all female vocal group comprised Elizabeth Davis, Etta Gooch, Sandra Gooch, Mae Gooch, Lois Russell and Lillian Woods.

The group would have one album and two singles released by the label, with **The Great Gospel Stars** being the very first album released by any of Berry Gordy's labels. As such it has become an album of much interest, with copies (when they can be found) shifting for more than $500 a time. The lead track *He Lifted Me* was lifted as a single in March 1961, whilst two years later *Give God A Chance* (recorded in 1961 but held off the original album release) was issued on the Divinity label.

ALBUM: GREAT GOSPEL STARS (1961)

GOT TO BE THERE – MICHAEL JACKSON [SINGLE]

As strange as it may seem, Michael Jackson owed the launch of his solo career to Donny Osmond! When The Jackson 5 first exploded on the musical scene, they had the market pretty much to themselves, racking up four consecutive number one hits. By 1971, however, they had a rival family group with which to contend, The Osmonds, who hit number one with their first outing *One Bad Apple*. As the two groups traded hits, Donny Osmond was projected for a solo career at the start of 1971, topping the charts with his second single *Go Away Little Girl*.

Whilst Motown had not seriously considered pushing Michael as a solo singer, the feeling within Hitsville was that Michael was a much better singer than Donny and could outperform his rival as well as remaining an integral part of The Jackson 5. Despite his initial reluctance, Berry Gordy gave the go ahead, with Hal Davis selected to produce the first single, *Got To Be There*.

Written by Elliot Willensky, a former research scientist for the National Institute of Health who had given up the job in 1969 in order to become a songwriter, *Got To Be There* was recorded in June 1971, although Berry did not like the initial mix nor the fact that it was another ballad; three of The Jackson 5's previous four singles had been ballads, with their last release *Maybe Tomorrow* becoming their first single to fail to hit the Top Ten. A remix was ordered and despite initial reservations was released as a single in October the same year. A #4 hit on both the pop and R&B chart, *Got To Be There* also made #5 in the UK, the success in both territories sufficient to ensure that Michael Jackson was not only lead singer with The Jackson 5, he was a bona fide solo star too.

GOT TO GIVE IT UP – MARVIN GAYE [SINGLE]

Hal Davis had originally toyed with the idea of having Marvin Gaye record *Love Hangover* until Berry Gordy suggested Diana Ross as a more suitable candidate. Since Marvin had criticised disco music as lacking substance, it is doubtful whether he would have bettered the version that Diana did, but the success she enjoyed was certainly noted.

When Marvin did eventually return to the studio at the tail end of 1976, he had in mind doing something of an answer record to Johnny Taylor's *Disco Lady*, a club smash that had gone on to top the pop charts. Tentatively titled *Dancing Lady*, the first of what would be three recording sessions for the single took place at Marvin's Room (his own studio complex in Los Angeles) on 13 December 1976, with Johnny McGhee (guitarist with L.T.D.), Frankie Beverly (lead singer and percussionist with Maze), Fernando Harkness (saxophone), Bugsy Wilcox (drums) and Jack Ashford (percussion) helping out on the session.

Just as he had done with *What's Going On*, Marvin wanted to create a party atmosphere for the record and invited friends and family along for the next series of sessions, including his brother Frankie, little sister Zeola, girlfriend Janis Hunter and 'Soul Train' host and friend Don Cornelius. The recording sessions were wrapped up by 17 December and mixing of the single, which was now titled *Got To Give It Up* completed by mid January.

The full length version was stretched out to 11:48 and would take up the entire fourth side of the **Live At The London Palladium** album, released in the US on 15 March 1977. A 4:12 edit, entitled *Got To Give It Up Part 1* was released as a single the same month and was soon vaulting its way up the chart, going on to top the R&B and pop chart in the US, the first time he achieved the double since *Let's Get It On* in 1973. In the UK *Got To Give It Up* would peak at #7, his first solo Top Ten hit since 1969.

The single also earned Marvin a Grammy nomination for Best R&B Vocal Performance, Male, although he lost out to Lou Rawls and **Unmistakably Lou**. The success of the single helped the parent album shift more than two million copies worldwide, proof that disco did have substance after all. The song has also proved durable, with female singer Aaliyah taking a 1996 update to #37 on the UK charts.

Got To Give It Up would also provide the inspiration for *Blurred Lines*, a massive 2013 hit for Robin Thicke with T.I. and Pharrell Williams, selling some 15 million copies, although the inspiration and/or similarities between the two would become the subject of a legal battle between Robin Thicke and Marvin Gaye's children.

GOTHAM

Formed by Schuylar 'Sky' Ford (vocals and guitar), Alfred 'Pee Wee' Ellis (born in Bradenton, Florida on 21 April 1941, saxophone), Frank Vicari (born in New York City on 11 April 1931, saxophone), John Gatchell (born in New York City on 27 November 1945, trumpet), John Eckert (trumpet and flugelhorn), Lionel 'Linc' Chamberland (born in Norwalk, Connetticut on 13 September 1940, guitar), Chris Qualles (bass) and Jimmy Strassburg (drums), jazz rock group The New York Street Band was signed by Motown in 1972 and assigned to the Natural Resources imprint.

Pass The Butter was produced by Tom Wilson and issued in July 1972, with the group's name changed to Gotham for their only release. Whilst the album wasn't a success, several of the tracks have been sampled in more recent years. There was reportedly another album's worth of material recorded, but this remains unreleased. Linc Chamberland died from leukemia on 24 June 1987. John Gatchell died on 9 June 2004. Frank Vicari died on 20 October 2006.
ALBUM: PASS THE BUTTER (1972)

THE GRAFFITI ORCHESTRA

A studio band arranged by Ernie Freeman, with their only single released on Prodigal. The Graffiti Orchestra was just one of many artists recording cover versions of John Williams' theme to *Star* Wars that was released in 1977, with Meco enjoying by far the biggest hit. The Graffiti Orchestra version was released in several territories, without success.

RITA GRAHAM

The daughter of a barber, Rita was born in Charleston, West Virginia on 16 October 1949 and moved to California whilst in her late teens initially intending to become a schoolteacher. She eventually opted for music and after fronting Rita & The Tiaras Northern Soul favourite *Gone With The Wind Is My Love* for Dore records in 1967 would eventually link up with Ray Charles, who produced her debut album **Vibrations** in 1968 and then made her one of The Raelettes. Rita spent a year with Ray Charles before linking with Mike Post in Rye & Rita Jean, recording eight singles for Bell before touring with Oscar Peterson and Redd Foxx.

After landing a part in the musical 'Selma', Rita signed a one off deal with CBS and then recorded the single *Rich Man Poor Man* (the arranger was her former husband Charles Blaker) that got picked up and released by Prodigal in June 1976. Despite healthy airplay, Prodigal and Motown were unable to turn it into a hit, resulting in this being her only outing for the label. Rita would later tour with the Harry James Orchestra, Mercer Ellington and the Duke Ellington Orchestra before forming a duo with guitarist Kenny Burrell.

GRAMMY AWARDS

The Grammy Awards were launched in 1959 by the National Academy of Recording Arts and Sciences (NARAS) to recognise outstanding achievement in the recording industry. The very first awards ceremony, held on 4 May 1959, presented a total of 22 trophies to fourteen recipients. Over the years the ceremony would grow in both size and scope, with Motown collecting the first of its 94 nominations in 1964, when *Heat Wave* by Martha & The Vandellas was nominated for Best Rhythm & Blues Recording, a category that was virtually the exclusive preserve of Ray Charles, who won the trophy for four consecutive years. The label's first award came in 1968 when *Cloud Nine* by The Temptations was named Best Rhythm & Blues Performance by a Group, and by the time the label was sold in 1988, Motown singles, albums and compositions had picked up 26 awards.

Stevie Wonder is the label's most decorated performer, having gone on to collect no fewer than twenty two trophies (up to and including 2011), a figure that places him fifth on the list of all time winners and the second most successful male artist. Stevie is also the fourth youngest artist to have won the Album of the Year award, a feat achieved in 1973 for **Innervisions**, and was only the second artist (after Frank Sinatra) to have won the Album of the Year award on three occasions, achieved in 1977. Diana Ross was nominated on no fewer than seven occasions during her time at Motown (six for her solo recordings and once with Lionel Richie) without ever winning, whilst Marvin Gaye also garnered six nominations without a trophy. Both artists eventually won, although Diana's Grammy was a Lifetime Achievement Award presented in 2012. Details of the individual awards and nominations received can be found within the entries for the artist, single or album.

GRAMMY HALL OF FAME
Introduced in 1973, The Grammy Hall of Fame Award honours recordings that are at least twenty five years old and have 'a qualitative or historical significance.' Open to both albums and singles, Motown has received several of these prestigious awards, with the recipients and the year of the award as follows:

Ain't No Mountain High Enough - Marvin Gaye & Tammi Terrell (1999)
Dancing In The Street – Martha & The Vandellas (1999)
For Once In My Life – Stevie Wonder (2009)
I Heard It Through The Grapevine – Marvin Gaye (1998)
I Want You Back – The Jackson 5 (1999)
Innervisions – Stevie Wonder (1999)
Mercy Mercy Me (The Ecology) – Marvin Gaye (2002)
My Girl – The Temptations (1998)
My Guy – Mary Wells (1999)
Papa Was A Rollin' Stone – The Temptations (1999)
Reach Out I'll Be There – The Four Tops (1998)
Shotgun – Junior Walker & The All Stars (2002)
Shop Around – The Miracles (2006)
Songs In The Key Of Life – Stevie Wonder (2002)
Stop! In The Name Of Love – The Supremes (2001)
Superstition – Stevie Wonder (1998)
Talking Book – Stevie Wonder (1999)
The Tears Of A Clown – Smokey Robinson & The Miracles (2002)
The Tracks Of My Tears – The Miracles (2007)
War – Edwin Starr (1999)
What's Going On – Marvin Gaye (1998)
Where Did Our Love Go – The Supremes (1999)
You Are The Sunshine Of My Life – Stevie Wonder (2002)
You Keep Me Hangin' On – The Supremes (1999)
You Really Got A Hold On Me – The Miracles (1998)

GRAMMY AWARDS – OTHER CATEGORIES

The numerous special awards are handed out at the Grammy Awards and are awarded without nomination for achievements over many years rather than a specific year. These are the various Motown recipients.

LIVING LEGEND AWARD
Introduced in 1990, the Grammy Living Legend Award is intended to recognise 'ongoing contributions and influence in the recording field.' It is not only open to recording artists, reflected in a change in the award's recognition; it is now labelled 'in the music industry' rather than recording field. The following Motown artists have been honoured:
Smokey Robinson (1990)
Michael Jackson (1993)

LIFETIME ACHIEVEMENT AWARD:
Marvin Gaye (1996)
Stevie Wonder (1996)
Smokey Robinson (1999)
The Funk Brothers (2004)
The Four Tops (2009)
Michael Jackson (2010)
Diana Ross (2012)
The Temptations (2013)
The Isley Brothers (2014)

TRUSTEES AWARDS:
Berry Gordy (1991)
Holland-Dozier-Holland (1998)

MUSICARES PERSON OF THE YEAR
Stevie Wonder (1999)

CORNELIUS GRANT

Unofficially known as the sixth Temptation, Cornelius Grant's professional life was intertwined with Motown's premier vocal group between 1964 and 1982. Born in Fairfield, Texas on 27 April 1943, Cornelius acquired his first guitar from a Sears & Roebuck catalogue and taught himself how to play by the age of nine. Three years later Cornelius moved with his family to Detroit and was enrolled into Mumford High, although much of his spare time was spent playing with local bands. Initially working with Mary Wells and then Marvin Gaye, Cornelius linked up with The Temptations in 1964 and would remain with the group for nearly twenty years as guitarist, arranger and musical director.

He was also a more than competent songwriter, co-writing The Temptations' hits *I Know I'm Losing You,* and *You're My Everything* and *Take Me In Your Arms And Love Me,* a hit for Gladys Knight & The Pips. Whilst he was utilised as a musician on numerous recording sessions (most notably *I Heard It Through The Grapevine* by Gladys and The Pips), Cornelius found recording sessions restrictive and preferred being out on the road, subsequently touring much of the world with The Temptations. A partner in D.O.C. Productions, a company formed with Melvin Franklin and Otis Williams of The Temptations, Cornelius would produce two groups, Swiss Movement and Quiet Elegance. He remained in The Temptations' employ until 1982 when he left to become a reporter for 'The Hollywood Reporter'. He would later launch a magazine of his own as well as a line of cigars and set up a non-profit organisation Starz of Tomorrow.

GREATEST HITS 2 - DIANA ROSS [ALBUM]

Diana Ross' first American compilation of greatest hits, which charted at #13 on the album charts in August 1976, featured a slightly amended track listing for British consumption. As Diana had hit the British charts in 1972 with her first collection of greatest hits, the 1976 version was titled **Greatest Hits 2**, although it did feature exactly the same cover picture as its American counterpart. It took six weeks to reach its peak of #2, agonisingly held off the top of the British charts by The Beach Boys and their **20 Golden Greats**, which would remain at the chart summit for each of the three weeks that Diana's album was at #2. Diana's album would go on to attain gold status (with the sales levels that were in place at the time, this meant the manufacturers, EMI, had received more than £500,000 in revenue) during the course of the 29 weeks it spent on the listings.

GREATEST HITS VOLUME 2 – SMOKEY ROBINSON & THE MIRACLES [ALBUM]

The Miracles first volume of hits had appeared in March 1965 as a double album package containing twenty two tracks. Over the next three years the group would register a significant number of hits, ranging from the sublime *I Second That Emotion* to the dance orientated *Going To A Go-Go*. In January 1968 Tamla gathered together another twelve tracks, delving back into the group's hit catalogue to resurrect *Come On Do The Jerk* (making its first appearance on a Miracles album) and bringing the story up to date with the afore-mentioned *I Second That Emotion*. The end result was **Greatest Hits Volume 2**, an album that would become one of the group's best sellers and their most successful as far as the charts were concerned, hitting #7 pop and #2 R&B.

PAULA GREER

Born in Chicago, Illinois in 1932, Paula initially found a degree of fame as both a model and ballad singer, but it was when she concentrated on the latter that her professional career took off. Originally the house singer for Chicago's Crown Propeller, Paula became a regular on the city's nightclub circuit during the 1950s and, after being spotted by Mickey Stevenson, was eventually signed by Motown's Workshop Jazz label. Although two albums were scheduled, only one was actually released, **Introducing Paula Greer** appearing in January 1963. A second album with the Johnny Griffith Trio, **Detroit Jazz** was scheduled for the following month but never released, and since there appears to be no sign of the original master tapes it is not known if the album was actually recorded.
There were acetates made for a further two albums, however, although these also remained unreleased. Paula had no further luck with her planned single releases, for *I Want To Talk About You* got no further than the promotional single stage and did not feature on the one album that was released, although her second single *I Did* appeared on both 7" and on her album. The Workshop Jazz material was seemingly the only recordings of her entire career, although she remained a regular performer back in Chicago for a considerable number of years after her Motown flirtation. Paula died on 7 September 2007 following a lengthy illness aged 75 years.
ALBUM: INTRODUCING PAULA GREER (1963)

AL GREEN

One of the most successful soul singers of the early 1970s, Al Green was undoubtedly an artist Motown would have loved to have had on their roster, although they would have to settle for releasing a compilation album midway through the following decade. Born Albert Greene in Forrest City, Arkansas on 13 April 1946, Al scored his first hit in 1967 fronting Al Greene & The Soul Mates, but it was after signing with Hi Records of Memphis in 1969 as Al Green that he would enjoy his greatest success. Teaming up with producer Willie Mitchell, Al scored a major hit album (although no hit singles) with **Green Is Blues**, establishing something of a format with this album that was to serve him well for the next decade; a number of originals, mixed with well known cover versions, including one or two from the Jobete catalogue. In the case of **Green Is Blues** it was *My Girl*, but it was his revival of *I Can't Get Next To You* that scored big, becoming a #11 R&B hit in 1970.

Thereafter Al became a permanent fixture in the charts, most notably with original hits such as *Tired Of Being Alone, Let's Stay Together* (a pop and R&B chart topper), *I'm Still In Love With You, You Ought To Be With Me, Livin' For You, L-O-V-E (Love)* and *Full Of Fire*, all of which were co-written by Al and topped the R&B charts. When Al's spiritual crisis resulted in him switching to gospel music, Hi Records hit problems, resulting in a brief distribution deal with Motown during the 1980s. One of the few new releases (although virtually his entire Hi catalogue was reissued at mid-price) was **14 Greatest Hits**, a compilation of his best known hits released as part of the same series that saw Little Richard, Jimmy Reed and others appearing on the Motown label. That was as close as Motown got to Al Green, and vice versa.
ALBUM: 14 GREATEST HITS (1984)

KATHE GREEN

Born in California on 22 September 1944 and the daughter of actor Johnny Green, Kathe Jennifer Green appeared in a number of television series at the start of the 1960s but made her first serious involvement in show business in 1968 when she dubbed the singing voice of Mark Lester in the film 'Oliver!', for which her father was musical director. The same year Kathe appeared in the Peter Sellers film 'The Party' and made her first album the following year for Deram Records, working with producer Wayne Bickerton on **Run The Length Of Your Wildness**, writing ten of the album's thirteen tracks.

In 1975 Kathe signed with Motown, with producer Frank Wilson assembling a stellar cast to work on her debut album. Kathe herself wrote or co-wrote with David Shire all but one of the tracks, with David Shire alone providing the other, whilst the likes of Leonard Caston (keyboards), James Jamerson (bass), Eddie 'Bongo' Brown (percussion), Jeff Porcaro (drums) and Ray Parker Jr. (guitar) were among the musicians on board.

Seemingly, however, not long after the 6' 1" blonde model turned singer and keyboard player signed with the company Motown lost interest, with a single *Love City* scheduled for release in March 1975 and then getting pulled. A single finally appeared in November, *Beautiful Changes*, but little was done to promote it. Her album was subsequently scheduled for April, coinciding with the eventual release of the *Love City* single, but whilst the single made the streets, the album appeared two months later, banished to the Prodigal label.
ALBUM: KATHE GREEN (1976)

SUSAYE GREENE

Born in Houston, Texas on 13 September 1949, Susaye's main claim to fame is that of being the last official member of The Supremes, replacing Cindy Birdsong in 1976. Susaye began her professional career at an early age, appearing on Harry Belafonte's 1963 album **Streets I Have Walked**. After relocating to New York as a teenager, Susaye appeared in a number of commercials and eventually graduated from the NYC High School of Performing Arts.

After recording a one-off single (*Please Send Him Back*) for an obscure New York label, Susaye became a member of the Raelettes, Ray Charles' backing group. Susaye then briefly fronted New Birth (the single *Until It's Time For You To Go* was produced by Harvey Fuqua) before joining Stevie Wonder's backing group Wonderlove. There she partnered Deniece Williams, both as a singer on stage and as a writer off it, with *Free*, which was originally intended as a track for Earth Wind & Fire being produced by Maurice White and taken to number one by Deniece.

By then Susaye had accepted an offer to join The Supremes as replacement singer for Cindy Birdsong, although Susaye later revealed that she had also been asked to supply material for the group to record. As it happened, although Susaye recorded two albums as a member of The Supremes, **High Energy** and **Mary, Scherrie & Susaye**, not one of the tracks was written by Susaye, although she did get to sing lead on several.

With The Supremes disbanding after a farewell concert in June 1977, Susaye and Scherrie linked for an album entitled **Partners** in 1979, on which the girls shared both songwriting and executive production credit. Although not intended as a one-off album, both went their separate ways after its release, with Susaye linking up with Stevie Wonder once again (she co-wrote *I Can't Help It* with Stevie, which was recorded by Michael Jackson).

Whilst touring England in 1984 Susaye met her future husband, eventually settling in Britain and recording with the likes of Courtney Pine and for Ian Levine's Motorcity label. Susaye and her husband returned to the US in 2000, where Susaye eventually resumed her solo career.

ALBUM: PARTNERS (1979)

HERMAN GRIFFIN

Given his role in hastening Mary Wells' departure from the company, Motown history has not been particularly kind to Herman Griffin. Irrespective of his role in that chain of events, Herman still left other lasting impressions.

Born Herman Lewis Griffin in Selma, Alabama on 25 November 1936, he was known as an acrobatic and energetic performer and after being spotted by Berry Gordy in 1958 recorded one of the first Jobete published songs, *I Need You* which was released on the HOB label. Herman would later switch to the Anna label for *Hurry Up And Marry Me* (something of a prophetic title given later developments) before joining the Tamla label in 1960 for *True Love (That's Love)*.

That same year he married Mary Wells, although the marriage was in trouble right from the start owing to the relative youth of the pair and Herman's desire to have greater control over her career. His own career at Hitsville would see one further single issued in *Sleep (Little One)*, released on the Motown label in June 1962 before he was out of the company and began engineering his wife's eventual walkout. Whilst Mary would eventually sign with 20th Century, her career never hit the heights she had enjoyed at Motown and her marriage quickly disintegrated.

Herman meanwhile recorded for a number of small labels, including Double L, Mercury, Magic Touch and Spring and also did some recordings for Ian Levine's Motorcity label towards the end of the 1980s. He died on 11 November 1989.

JOHNNY GRIFFITH TRIO

Classically trained pianist Johnny Griffith was born in Detroit, Michigan on 10 July 1936 and graduated from the University of Detroit with a degree in music. Despite his background, jazz was his favoured music and he began his professional career backing the likes of Sarah Vaughan, Dinah Washington and Aretha Franklin.

He was drawn to Motown in 1961 in the hope of getting a recording deal, eventually recording at least two albums for the Workshop Jazz label; **Jazz**, credited to the Johnny Griffith Trio (with Vance Matlock on bass and Ben Appling on drums) and **Detroit Jazz**, on which his trio backed Paula Greer, although it is doubtful whether this latter album was actually released.

However, it was as one of The Funk Brothers that he made his mark at Hitsville, with his best performances claimed to be *Stop In The Name Of Love* and *I Heard It Through The Grapevine* (Marvin Gaye's version). Unlike the rest of the Funk Brothers, Johnny was not under exclusive contract to Motown so appeared on numerous outside recordings, including *Higher And Higher* (Jackie Wilson), *Have You Seen Her* (The Chi-Lites) and *Cool Jerk* (The Capitols).

He died from a heart attack on 10 November 2002, with his funeral service taking place at the James H. Cole Funeral Home, next door to the Motown Museum and where Johnny and several other Funk Brothers would clandestinely sneak off for a drink during their recording heyday!

ALBUM: JAZZ (1963)

LINDA GRINER

After singing gospel from the age of eight, Washington D.C. born Linda Griner went to the Howard University and was then sent to the Ophelia Modeling School, her place being sponsored by a nightclub manager called Angelo Benedetti. Thereafter Linda put together a nightclub act (although she was still a teenager) and ended up supporting The Miracles in 1962 at the Howard Theater, with Smokey Robinson watching her act from the side of the stage and after her performance offered her an immediate contract with Motown. However, when she arrived in Detroit it was discovered that at 15 years of age, Linda was too young to sign, with Motown putting her back into school at the Woodrow Wilson High School in Detroit.

Her only single for Motown, *Good Bye Cruel Love* backed with *Envious* was written and produced by Smokey Robinson and recorded in June 1962, although its release was held back until January 1963, by which time Motown may have cooled on Linda, resulting in little or no promotion on the single, although it would later become something of a hit on the Northern Soul circuit. Smokey is supposed to have recorded an album's worth of material on Linda, none of which has ever surfaced, but Linda would go on to enjoy a successful recording career with a more sophisticated jazz style for Columbia, Dot, Mercury, Brunswick and others as Lyn Roman.

LARRY GROCE

Larry Groce recorded in a variety of styles, commencing his career with an album of hymns and arriving at MC Records soon after scoring his only major hit with a novelty record in 1976. Born in Dallas, Texas on 22 April 1948, Larry moved to New York after graduating from college and became a regular performer at the organic food restaurant 'Focus'.

His first recording contract came with Daybreak Records (an imprint of RCA) in 1970, with the album **The Wheat Lies Low** appearing the same year. His only hit came in 1976 with the satiric novelty song *Junk Food Junkie,* recorded live at McCabe's nightclub in Santa Monica and a #9 hit on Warner Brothers/Curb records.

When Curb left Warner Brothers to set up MC Records as a joint venture with Berry Gordy in 1977, Larry Groce followed, releasing the album **Please Take Me Back** in November 1977. He would later record extensively for Walt Disney Records and become a radio host, a position he still maintains.
ALBUM: PLEASE TAKE ME BACK (1977)

ROBERT GUILLAUME

A legendary actor and performer he was born Robert Peter Williams on St Louis, Missouri on 30 November 1927 and later studied at St Louis University and Washington University. After serving in the US Army Robert opted to pursue a career as an actor, joining the Karamu Players in Cleveland and going on to make his Broadway debut in 1961 in 'Kwamina'. In 1976 he joined the cast of 'Guys And Dolls', with his role of Nathan Detroit earning him a Tony Award nomination, also appearing on the Motown released cast recording.

His best known stage role, however was that of The Phantom in 'The Phantom Of The Opera', replacing the original lead Michael Crawford. On television he is best known for portraying Benson in both 'Soap' and its spin-off series 'Benson', a role that would win him the Emmy Awards for Outstanding Lead Actor (1985 for 'Benson') and Outstanding Support Actor ('Soap' in 1979). He has also won a Grammy Award for Best Spoken World Album for Children for **The Lion King** in 1995.

GUINN GAMILY

A family group formed in Philadelphia, Pennsylvania in 1970 by Margie (vocals), Bonnie (vocals), Michael (vocals), Skip (vocals) Earl (guitar) and Randy Guinn (bass) they first recorded as New Experience for the Philly World label. They were joined by Lori Fulton (vocals) in 1985 before signing with Motown later the same year. Their only album for the label, **Guinn** featured *People Will Be People, Open Your Door* and *Dreamin'*, the latter song being later covered by Vanessa Williams and taken into the Top Ten.
ALBUM: GUINN (1986)

GULL RECORDS

British record label Gull Records was formed in 1974 by Derek Everett, Monty Babson and David Howells and had an eclectic roster, ranging from heavy metal merchants Judas Priest (whose better days lay ahead of them) all the way through to multi-racial pop group Blue Mink (whose better days were in the past). The following year, in 1975, Motown picked up the label for American distribution, also giving Gull Records its own label imprint.

The deal was to see four albums (by Steve Ashley, Arthur Brown and Isotope) and one single (by Typically Tropical) released during the twelve months or so that the deal lasted. Two further albums were scheduled, Judas Priest's **Rocka Rolla** (this was eventually issued by Janus on import) and **Tea Break Over, Back On Your 'Eads** by If but subsequently cancelled. In the UK Gull remained in business until 1984, racking up hits by Carol Douglas and Cleveland Eaton in addition to Typically Tropical and The Diversions in the faux reggae category.

GUNG-HO

A British group formed by former Boomtown Rats members Simon Crowe (born on 14 April 1955, vocals, drums, programming and sequencing) and Johnnie Fingers (born John Moylett on 10 September 1955, keyboards, programming and sequencing) with female singer Yoko Kurokawa, Gung-Ho had several singles on the Magnet label in the UK, one of which was initially picked up for Motown, *Play To Win*. Intended for release in June 1987 it was subsequently pulled from the schedule.

GUYS AND DOLLS (BROADWAY SHOW)

Frank Loesser's 'Guys And Dolls' (based on two short stories by Damon Runyon, 'The Idyll Of Miss Sarah Jones' and 'Pick The Winner') was one of the major Broadway successes of the 1950s, running for some 1,200 performances following its opening in November 1950. The show also successfully transferred to London's West End, where it opened in May 1953 and ran for 555 performances. In 1976 an all-black cast production previewed at the Broadway Theatre, with the performers including Robert Guillaume, Norma Donaldson, James Randolph, Ernestine Jackson and Ken Page.

What made the show significantly different was the musical production, which was arranged by Danny Holgate and Horace Ott with a distinct Motown style, although whilst the modern take on the material worked on the gospel inspired numbers, those that were transformed into disco outings horrified many! Despite this, the show was a success, the twelve previews (from 11 July 1976) giving way to a run of 239 performances before the show closed down on 13 February 1977. The show's producers meanwhile struggled to find a record company prepared to take a chance on a cast recording album, with Motown eventually entering the fray and assigning William Goldstein to handle production chores. The cast recording was released in December 1976 and whilst not a major seller has continued to attract interest, subsequently being re-released on CD in 1991.

ALBUM: GUYS AND DOLLS SOUNDTRACK (1976)

H

CONNIE HAINES

Connie Haines was another of the music industry veterans signed by Berry Gordy in an attempt to target the MOR market. Born Yvonne Marie Antoinette JaMais in Savannah, Georgia on 20 January 1921, she moved at the age of five with her family to Jacksonville and quickly became interested in music. In 1930 she made her first performance on radio and earned the moniker Baby Yvonne Marie – The Princess of the Air, overcoming rheumatic fever and singing seated on a piano bench.

In 1935 she won a talent contest on Fred Allen's syndicated show on NBC and used this as a springboard to a professional career, joining Harry James orchestra as a singer alongside Frank Sinatra. It was Harry James who suggested a name change as her own was too long to fit on billboards, with 'Haines' selected as it rhymed with 'James'. After financial problems forced Harry James to let several of his band go, Connie and Frank hitched up with Tommy Dorsey, where she would enjoy considerable success on record and eventually film.

By 1965 when she signed with Motown, however, Connie's hit recording days were but a distant memory. She recorded several songs for the company, including the first version of *For Once In My Life* (which remains unreleased), with her only issue being the Smokey Robinson penned *What's Easy For Two Is So Hard For One*, originally a hit for Mary Wells. Connie died from myasthenia gravis on 22 September 2008.

JIM HALL

With a career that lasted for well over fifty years, Jim Hall was rightfully regarded as one of the greatest jazz guitarists of all time. Born James Stanley Hall in Buffalo, New York on 4 December 1930, Jim grew up in a musical environment and learned to play the guitar at the age of ten thanks to his mother giving him one as a Christmas present. His professional career began in 1955 when he joined Chico Hamilton's quintet, later performing with the Jimmy Giuffre Three. He would later work with Ella Fitzgerald, Lee Konitz, Sonny Rollins, Art Farmer and Paul Desmond; in short the cognoscenti of the jazz world.

After extensive studio work throughout the 1960s, Jim began his own solo recording career in the 1970s, following which he recorded extensively for MPS, World Pacific, Pacific Jazz, Milestone, Horizon, Telarc, Concord and CTI, with his 1975 album **Concierto** being widely considered his greatest recording and among the very best albums in the entire CTI catalogue; it would reach #17 on the jazz chart. His most recent solo album, **Conversations** appeared in 2010 on

ArtistShare. He died peacefully in his sleep on 10 December 2013 at the age of 83 years.
ALBUM: CONCIERTO (1975)

DAVE HAMILTON

Dave Hamilton was already an experienced guitarist when he hooked up with Motown as a studio musician, having toured with the Helen Pennilton Quartet at the age of 18 and formed his own band, The Noc-Tunes who recorded for Sensation.
Born in Savannah, Georgia on 15 January 1920, he was one of the first musicians used by Berry Gordy (he played on Jackie Wilson's *Lonely Teardrops*), with his session work leading to the opportunity of recording his own album for Workshop Jazz. **Blue Vibrations** was released in January 1963, from which *Late Freight* was issued as a single the following month. Dave also moonlighted outside of Motown and appeared on John Lee Hooker's *Boom Boom*.
He left Motown in 1965 to set up his own labels Tempo and Topper and the Da Da studio with singer and songwriter Rony Darrell based in Detroit. Later on in the decade Dave set up another couple of labels, TCB and Democratic before he died in 1995.
ALBUM: BLUE VIBRATIONS (1963)

JACK HAMMER

Born Earl Solomon Burroughs in New Orleans, Louisiana on 16 September 1925 Jack began writing at the age of fourteen, with *Fujiyama Mama* being recorded by Annisteen Allen but would later be covered by Wanda Jackson. After briefly recording for Roulette and Kapp, Jack submitted a song he had written, *Great Balls Of Fire,* to the team putting together the soundtrack for the film 'Jamboree'. Whilst they didn't think much of the song itself, the title appealed and so with Jack's permission they asked noted writer Otis Blackwell to write a song based on the title, with the credit split equally.
In 1961 Jack moved to Europe, subsequently recording several twist singles and an album for Ronnex in Belgium, where he became known as The Twistin' King, as well as singles for Polydor, Oriole and United Artists. *Colour Combination* backed with *Swim* was originally recorded for Young Blood in Europe and was picked up for American release on the Soul label, being issued in October 1971.

Jack eventually returned to the US and pursued a number of occupations, including becoming a painter, playwright (he wrote a musical on the life of Jimi Hendrix, a former friend) and actor (he appeared in 'Bubbling Brown Sugar') as well as continuing to compose music.

JOHNNY HAMMOND

Born John Robert Smith in Louisville, Kentucky on 16 December 1933, he became known as Johnny 'Hammond' Smith thanks to the musical instrument with which he made his reputation and later adopted the shortened moniker Johnny Hammond, thus avoiding confusion with jazz guitarist Johnny Smith. After spells with Paul Williams and Chris Columbo and as an accompanist for Nancy Wilson, Johnny formed his own group and began recording for Arrow Records in 1959.
After a ten year sojourn at Prestige, he joined Kudu in 1971 and recorded a series of highly acclaimed jazz funk albums, most of which utilised the CTI in-house core of musicians, including Grover Washington Jr., Eric Gale, Airto Moreira and Bob James, among others. The only album distributed by Motown, 1974's **Gambler's Life**, was produced by Larry and Fonce Mizell, who after their writing spell with Motown established a healthy reputation on the jazz funk market thanks to their work with Donald Byrd. As such Johnny's album was released on the Salvation label rather than Kudu.
Johnny later switched to Milestone, where Larry and Fonce also helmed his highly regarded **Gears** album, with *Los Conquistadores Chocolates* and *Shifting Gears* enjoying considerable success in the UK. Johnny died from cancer on 4 June 1997.
ALBUM: GAMBLER'S LIFE (1974)

HERBIE HANCOCK

An exceptionally gifted pianist, keyboardist, composer and arranger, Herbert Jeffrey Hancock was born in Chicago, Illinois on 12 April 1940 and made his name during his spell with Miles Davis' second great quintet. He launched his own solo career in 1962 with Blue Note, but it is his body of work for Columbia, most notably **Headhunters**, **Thrust** and the soundtrack to 'Death Wish' that took him to the forefront of the jazz funk movement.

Herbie did not record for Motown (although he did appear as a guest musician on several albums, most notably Stevie Wonder's **Songs In The Key Of Life**), nor was he actually signed to CTI, but he was equally billed alongside Freddie Hubbard and Stanley Turrentine on their **In Concert Volume 2** album issued on CTI in 1974, along with Ron Carter, Jack DeJohnette and Eric Gale.

ALBUM: IN CONCERT VOLUME TWO (1975)

CHIP HAND

The son of an aide to future President Lyndon B Johnson, Lloyd 'Chip' Hand was born on 5 April 1954 and began his musical career singing demos at the age of fifteen. The following year he won a talent contest and with it a contract with RCA Records, who released several singles during the early 1970s. In 1973 he provided the lead voice for the Hanna & Barbera cartoon 'Butch Cassidy & The Sundance Kids', with Butch (based on David Cassidy's character in The Partridge Family) being a teenage undercover agent posing as a member of a rock group!

Two years later came his only outing on Motown, with *Wait Until September* backed with *Dreamtime Lover* being issued in September 1975. Whilst it wasn't successful Chip carved out a full career doing voice-overs, singing on commercials and also writing. He died on 8 June 2009.

BERT 'JACK' HANEY & BRICE 'NIKITER' ARMSTRONG

Comic duo Bert Haney (born in 1927) and Brice Armstrong (born in Dallas, Texas on 3 January 1936) came up with the concept of doing a 'cut-in' disc, whereby a story could be created by utilising snippets of other hits. In this case, the storyline (written by Bert, who would assume the 'Jack' character) concerns a meeting between US President John (Jack) Kennedy and Soviet Premier Nikita Khrushchev at the Kremlin, made all the more topical as when this was released on Mel-O-dy in March 1963, the Cuban missile crisis was still very fresh in the memory. *The Interview (Summit Chanted Meeting)* would be their only Motown outing together, although Brice would record several more tracks and release another single under the name Ray Oddis. Bert meanwhile went on to become a news anchor at WPIX in New York.

THE HAPPENING – THE SUPREMES [SINGLE]

The 1967 release 'The Happening' is today a largely forgotten film, most notable for marking an early appearance of Faye Dunaway. In the film she was joined by Anthony Quinn, Michael Parks and George Maharis, with the plot line being four hippies kidnap a retired Mafia boss in order to hold him for ransom. The soundtrack for the film was written by noted composer Frank De Vol, with HDH asked to contribute a couple of songs based on De Vol's score. After watching a print of the film, HDH wrote two songs, *The Happening* and *All I Know About You* which were originally recorded in Los Angeles but subsequently rejected by the Motown producers.

They re-recorded the tracks in Detroit and the finished tracks were coupled for release as a single in March 1967. The last single to be issued with the artist credit as simply The Supremes, *The Happening* would go on to become the group's tenth US chart topper, spending a solitary week at the top of the Billboard chart. A rather more modest #12 R&B hit, the single did peak at #6 in the UK, although the film itself fared poorly in all markets.

HAPPY BIRTHDAY – STEVIE WONDER [SINGLE]

It is one of the quirks of the recording industry that Stevie Wonder's homage to Martin Luther King Jr., in which he uses the power of song to call for a national holiday in honour of the civil rights leader, should fail to chart at all in the United States but became the biggest hit of his British career at the time of release!

One of the standout tracks from his **Hotter Than July** album, itself a return to former glories after the disappointing reception to his film soundtrack **Secret Life Of Plants**, *Happy Birthday* was not initially considered for release as a single.

"The one thing I do not want is for the meaning of the record to be overshadowed by any commercial consideration. We might think about putting the record out as a collectors item maybe, but I would have to be sure that the intention was right! This particular song means a lot to me."

After *Master Blaster*, *I Ain't Gonna Stand For It* and *Lately* had all attained Top Ten status in the UK, Motown's licensee EMI requested permission to release *Happy Birthday* as the fourth release. Permission was granted, reportedly because EMI had all but guaranteed that the single would become Stevie's first UK chart topper.

The eventual release carried an undoubted American bias, with the picture sleeve containing an original notation by Stevie from the album that read, "It is believed that for a man to lay down his life for the love of others is the supreme sacrifice. Jesus Christ by his own example showed us that there is no greater love. For nearly two thousand years now we have been striving to have the strength to follow that example. Martin Luther King was a man who had that strength. He showed us, non-violently, a better way of life, a way of mutual respect, helping us to avoid much bitter confrontation and inevitable bloodshed. We still have a long road to travel until we reach the world that was his dream. We in the United States must not forget either his supreme sacrifice or that dream. I and a growing number of people believe that it is time for our country to adopt legislation that will make January 15, Martin Luther King's birthday, a national holiday, both in recognition of what he achieved and as a reminder of the distance which still has to be travelled."

Happy Birthday failed to top the UK chart, but only by one place, held off the top by Shakin' Stevens and *Green Door*, although the single has enjoyed regular plays at clubs around the world ever since, usually in honour of a birthday celebration. Whilst *Happy Birthday* may have missed out on topping the UK charts, it did achieve something far more important to Stevie Wonder; on 2 November 1983 President Ronald Reagan signed into law the creation of a national holiday for Martin Luther King Jr.

"Somewhere Dr King is smiling, not because his birthday is a holiday, but because he too is convinced that we are moving in the right direction. I know that Dr King appreciates that this day is a day for all Americans to celebrate love, peace and unity. It is not a cure-all, but it is a healing aid."

The very first national public holiday was held on 20 January 1986 and on the third Monday of January every subsequent year.

JOE HARNELL

Born in The Bronx, New York on 2 August 1924 Joe Harnell learned to play piano at the age of six and joined his father's jazz ensemble at fourteen. After attending the University of Miami he played with Glenn Miller's Air Force Band until his discharge in 1946, upon which he studied under Aaron Copland and Leonard Bernstein. Initially a member of Lester Lanin's band, Joe would go on to work with Judy Garland, Maurice Chevalier and Marlene Dietrich before linking with Peggy Lee as a pianist and arranger.

His own recording career began in 1962 whilst he was recuperating from a car accident; Kapp Records asked him to put together an album to capitalise on the then hot bossa nova craze. The resulting album would enable Joe to win the 1962 Grammy Award for Best Performance by an Orchestra for Dancing for *Fly Me To The Moon*. Subsequent albums established him at the forefront of the easy listening market, including his 1969 album **Moving On** released on Motown in November 1969, from which two singles were lifted, *Midnight Cowboy* and *My Cherie Amour*. Joe would later move to Los Angeles and establish his reputation all over again as a composer and arranger for film and television, including his Emmy award winning score for 'V'. He died from heart failure on 14 July 2005.

ALBUM: MOVING ON (1969)

CHARLES HARRIS TRIO

Charles Harris was born and raised in Baltimore, Maryland in 1916 and learned to play the double bass whilst still a youngster. He began playing professionally whilst at college and joined Lionel Hampton in 1941 soon after graduating. Charles remained with Lionel for eight years, touring extensively before returning to Baltimore in 1949, working in a band called Three Strikes & A Miss before accepting an offer to join Nat King Cole's trio. After a lengthy spell with Nat, Charles eventually returned home to Baltimore, playing locally whilst working as a furniture salesman.

The closest he got to Motown was a proposed album for the Workshop Jazz label, with recording sessions for the album taking place at Hitsville in April and May 1963 under the direction of Mickey Stevenson and Hank Cosby. A total of six tracks were recorded, ranging from standards such as *Our Day Will Come* and *The Days Of Wine And Roses* to original material *Jackie* and *She's Gone* but the album was subsequently cancelled. Charles died from cancer on 9 September 2003 in Baltimore, Maryland.

EDDIE HARRIS

Jazz musician Eddie Harris was born in Chicago, Illinois on 20 October 1934 and studied music at Roosevelt University. Having excelled on the piano, vibraphone and saxophone, he chose to concentrate on the tenor saxophone, working in New York City before returning home to Chicago and landing a contract with Vee-Jay Records. His debut album **Exodus To Jazz** featured a jazz arrangement of Ernest Gold's theme to 'Exodus' and quickly became a radio hit, with its eventual release as a single seeing it reach #16 on the R&B chart and #36 pop. It is also claimed to be the first jazz single to be certified gold, indicating sales in excess of 500,000 copies.

Eddie would later record for Columbia and Atlantic, also switching instruments to the electric piano along the way. *Exodus* was a featured track on the CD compilation **Hits From The Legendary Vee-Jay Records** issued by Motown in November 1986. Eddie died from cancer on 5 November 1996.

SAM HARRIS

He may have come to national prominence by winning the inaugural season of 'Star Search' in 1984, but Sam Harris had already been pursuing a musical career for eight years. Born Samuel Kent Harris in Cushing, Oklahoma on 4 June 1961, Sam left home at the age of fifteen and worked in regional and repertory theatre before arriving in Los Angles and attending UCLA. He would then spend two years playing small clubs around the city before getting his break with 'Star Search', which resulted in a Motown contract.

This would see two albums released, with **Sam Harris** peaking at #35 and earning a gold disc and **Sam-I-Am** hitting #69 in 1986. Sam also enjoyed three hit singles with *Sugar Don't Bite* (#36) and *I'd Do It All Again* (#52) becoming his biggest hits. Surprisingly, the song with which he is most closely associated, *Over The Rainbow* missed out on the chart altogether. Once his Motown contract came to an end Sam went on to other entertainment avenues, appearing on stage and in film and helping create the television series 'Down To Earth'.

ALBUMS: SAM HARRIS (1984), SAM-I-AM (1985)

THURSTON HARRIS

Born in Indianapolis, Indiana on 11 July 1931, Thurston Theodore Harris made his first recordings as a member of the Lamplighters in 1953, but whilst the group would ultimately go on to become The Tenderfoots, The Sharps and The Rivingtons, they did so without Thurston, who launched a solo career in 1957. He scored what would prove to be his biggest hit with his take on Bobby Day's *Little Bitty Pretty One*, which would become a #2 R&B and #6 pop hit (and features his erstwhile group The Sharps on backing vocals). Whilst subsequent success proved elusive (his only other hit was *Do What You Did*, a #14 R&B and #57 pop hit the following year), *Little Bitty Pretty One* remains a popular track and has featured in numerous films, including 'Christine', for which Motown released the soundtrack in November 1983. Thurston died from heart failure brought about by acute alcoholism on 14 April 1990.

PETE HARTFIELD

Very little is known about singer and songwriter Pete Hartfield, who arrived at Motown to record one single for the Miracle label, with *Love Me* backed with *Darling Tonight* being released in September 1961. Since the Miracle label was not considered a major priority, it is doubtful whether any promotional effort was put behind Pete's single. His recording career apparently dates back to 1953 and he later recorded for Baby Records as well as funding his own PH label for a release by Pete Hartfield & Flint Connexion.

HARVEY RECORDS

One of two labels formed by Harvey Fuqua in Detroit, Harvey Records was introduced in November 1961 with Eddie Burns' *Orange Driver*. Unlike sister label Tri-Phi, Harvey Records registered no hits on its twelve releases, although given the financial problems having a hit record caused Tri-Phi, perhaps it is just as well! In addition to Eddie Burns, the roster included Loe & Joe (Lorri Rudolph and Joe Charles), The Five Quails, Keith Moss, Harvey & Ann (Harvey Fuqua and Ann Bogan, with Ann later a member of The Marvelettes) and, most notably, Junior Walker & The All Stars. Harvey released its final single in May 1963 (Keith Moss' *Satisfaction Guaranteed*), after which Harvey Fuqua folded his labels and took his key acts to Motown.

THE HEADLINERS

Originally formed as The Tornadoes in Fort Lauderdale, Florida, the group recorded a couple of singles for small labels without endangering the chart at the start of the 1960s. By 1963, Bobby Lewis (guitar and vocals), Ray Clayton (piano and saxophone), Lonnie Londin (bass) and Larrie Londin (born Ralph Gallant, drums) had taken on a new name The Headliners, and were spotted performing by Berry Gordy and Diana Ross.

Signed to the V.I.P. label in 1964, the group released their first single for the label in October, *Tonight's The Night*, and a follow-up in November the following year, *We Call It Fun*. Although the group did perform a Motortown Revue concert, Motown called it a day on their recording career soon after.

OMA HEARD

As well as his duets with Mary Wells and later Kim Weston, Marvin Gaye recorded a number of tracks with another female singer at Motown, Oma Heard. Sometimes credited under her married name of Oma Drake (her husband was guitarist Phil Drake), she was already an experienced singer by the time she arrived at Hitsville in 1964. Whilst Oma was kept busy in the recording studio during her first few months at Motown, only one single, *Lifetime Man* backed with *Mr. Lonely Heart* was released, appearing on the V.I.P. label in September 1964. However, not long after release the record was recalled, supposedly due to contractual disagreements between Oma and Motown (these apparently related to her diet, which ultimately saw her dropped by the company!).

Her duets with Marvin were similarly unreleased, with four tracks finally appearing on a Marvin collection in 1990 and a further track on **A Cellarful Of Motown Volume 4** in 2010. The previous edition of **Cellarful** also included one of Oma's solo tracks. There is also some considerable confusion surrounding Oma at Motown, not least because of the presence of another female singer called Oma Page recording at Hitsville at much the same time. The master tapes for the Marvin Gaye and Oma Heard recordings were mislabelled Marvin Gaye & Oma Page, but an extensive search of the Motown vaults has so far uncovered only one track, *When Someone's Good To You* by Oma Page (who, just to further confuse matters, was the sister of songwriter Billy Page, who wrote a number of the tracks that were recorded by Marvin and Oma Heard!).

Oma Heard meanwhile carved out an extensive career as a backing singer under her married name of Oma Drake and even returned to Motown as one third of the group Dorothy, Oma & Zelpha that released a single on the Chisa label in 1969.

HEART

Not to be confused with the later group of the same name led by the Wilson sisters, this Heart was formed in Albuquerque, New Mexico by Carl Silva (drums, harmonica and vocals), Bob Barron (bass), Danny Burnett (guitar) and Arnold Bodmer (piano). They recorded their debut eponymous album for the Look label, with production guru John Wagner at the helm. After releasing **Have A Heart** on King in 1970, the group slimmed down to just Carl and Bob and recorded another eponymous album for the Natural Resources label that was released in May 1972, also produced by John Wagner with Leon Danielle.

This album featured Carl on lead vocals, drums, keyboards, guitar and mouth harp, whilst Bob was responsible for bass guitar, lead guitar, slide guitar and backing vocals. When the album did little Carl and Bob went their separate ways; Carl reportedly manages a shoe shop whilst Bob performs in a band called Combo Special.

ALBUM: HEART (1972)

HEARTS OF STONE

Despite hailing from Philadelphia, Pennsylvania, Hearts Of Stone eventually gravitated towards Detroit and Motown, recording their only album in 1970. Originally known as The Four Pennies, Carl Cutler, John Myers, Floyd Lawson and Lindsay Griffin got their first contract with Brunswick in the mid-1960s, recording two singles that sold locally but couldn't break out nationally. The group then headed across the border to Canada in pursuit of work and eventually produced a set of demos that were hawked around various labels in the search of a deal.

They received the most positive response from Motown, who invited them to Detroit, signed them to a contract with V.I.P. and assigned Hank Cosby their producer. Although the group had a portfolio of songs they had written themselves, like virtually every other artist signed to the company their album would have to contain a number of songs from the Jobete catalogue. Motown also insisted on a change of name for the group, with Hearts Of Stone being selected as it represented the tough times the group had endured out on the road for the last five or so years. The resulting album **Stop The World – We Wanna Get On** saw two singles lifted that were penned by the group, *It's A Lonesome Road* (co-written by Hank Cosby) and *If I Could Give You The World*, with the album well received, enough for the group to be invited back to

record another. Unfortunately, internal conflicts within the group over relocating to Detroit got back to Motown who cooled on the group, with the second album remaining unreleased.
ALBUM: STOP THE WORLD - WE WANT TO GET ON (1970)

HEAT WAVE – MARTHA & THE VANDELLAS [SINGLE]

Whilst the song's lyrics deal with the singer being in love with a guy who has her heart 'burning with desire', *Heat Wave* owed some of its popularity because it was released at a time when a heat wave was affecting various parts of America, with the record providing a musical background to several weather reports on television. Of course, this was not the only reason for its success, for *Heat Wave* is also taken as the record that announced the arrival of the Motown sound. Written and produced by HDH, *Heat Wave* was the follow-up single to *Come And Get These Memories*, which had been a chart breakthrough for Martha & The Vandellas.

Heat Wave proved a resounding success, topping the R&B charts (albeit the Cashbox chart since Billboard would not print another R&B chart until January 1965) and hitting #4 on the pop chart. It also became the first Motown record to be afforded the honour of being nominated for a Grammy Award, being selected in the Best R&B Vocal Performance by a Group category in 1964, although it lost out on the night to Ray Charles and *Busted* (his fourth straight win in the category). *Heat Wave* also holds the honour of being the first single released in the UK under Motown's new arrangement with EMI's Stateside label.

HEAVEN HELP US ALL – STEVIE WONDER [SINGLE]

Reminiscent in style to Bob Dylan's *Blowin' In The Wind* which Stevie successfully covered in 1966, *Heaven Help Us All* was another song with a message. Written by Ron Miller, who had obviously forgiven Stevie for the way he had recorded *For Once In My Life*, it would mark the last time Stevie would release a Ron Miller composition as a single. It proved a fitting way to bow out, for with production by Ron and Tom Baird, *Heaven Help Us All* brought out a gospel singing style seldom heard from Stevie. The single would go on to become a #9 pop and #2 R&B hit, also making #29 in the UK.

HEAVEN MUST HAVE SENT YOU – THE ELGINS [SINGLE]

Originally intended for The Supremes, *Heaven Must Have Sent You* was recorded by The Elgins as the follow-up to the double sided hit *Put Yourself In My Place* and *Darling Baby*. As instantly catchy as anything HDH were turning out on The Supremes, *Heaven Must Have Sent You* did fair business when originally released in September 1966, making #9 R&B and a healthy #50 on the pop chart, even though it did little in the UK.

Five years later, when seemingly the whole of Britain was undertaking a Motown revival, *Heaven Must Have Sent You* sailed all the way to #3 on the chart, prompting a search for The Elgins, who had disbanded in 1967. With original lead female vocalist Saundra Mallett not interested in reprising her role in the group, The Elgins recruited Yvonne Allen for a hastily arranged UK tour, resulting in a reissued *Put Yourself In My Place* also featuring on the charts.

The success Tamla Motown in the UK enjoyed with *Heaven Must Have Sent You* saw V.I.P. re-releasing the single in the US, albeit without the success their counterparts over the Atlantic enjoyed. *Heaven Must Have Sent You* meanwhile would enjoy its own revival, Bonnie Pointer taking it to #11 in 1979. The Supremes' version finally appeared on CD in 1990, and the song's relevance to HDH was revealed when they chose 'Heaven Must Have Sent You' as the title of their Grammy nominated career retrospective.

HELLO – LIONEL RICHIE [SINGLE]

The third single to be lifted from Lionel Richie's **Can't Slow Down** album, *Hello* proved to be the biggest hit from the album. A hit around the world, *Hello* would top the pop, R&B and adult contemporary charts in the US and the UK pop charts, spending six weeks at the top of the UK chart on its way to earning a gold disc. Much of the reason for this was the accompanying video, in which Lionel sings about unrequited love for a blind art student (played by Laura Carrington), only to discover that she has feelings for him, as evidenced by the clay likeness of his head she has been sculpturing. Not surprisingly, this image has been parodied many times since the original appeared in 1984!

Hello was nominated for Song of the Year at the 1985 Grammy Awards, one of three nominations Lionel received, although it was the only category he lost, with *What's Love Got To Do With It* by Graham Lyle and Terry Britten winning the award. Later cover versions of *Hello* include Jhay Palmer Featuring MC Image (who hit #69 in the UK in 2002) and Glee Cast, who took their version to #35 on both the American and British charts in 2010.

BILL HENDERSON

Actor and singer William Randall Henderson was born in Chicago, Illinois on 19 March 1926 and began his professional career with Ramsey Lewis, later performing and recording with the Oscar Peterson Trio and Nancy Wilson. He landed his own recording contract with Vee Jay and subsequently became an actor, appearing in the films 'Trouble Man', 'Silver Streak', 'Mother Jugs And Speed' and, in 1983, 'Get Crazy'. This latter role enabled him to both act and sing, contributing *The Blues Had A Baby And They Named It Rock And Roll* for the accompanying soundtrack released on Morocco.

FINIS HENDERSON

Born in Chicago, Illinois the son of a noted manager and the vice president of Sammy Davis Enterprises, Finis Henderson's career started conventionally, joining the Chicago Community Music Foundation, The Dynamic 4 and then becoming a member of Weapons Of Peace. Formed in 1970 by Finis with Lonell Dantzler, Bill Leathers, Randy Hardy and David Johnson, Weapons Of Peace secured a recording contract with Hugh Heffner's Playboy label and scored three R&B hits, with *Just Can't Be That Way (Ruth's Song)* also becoming a club hit in 1976. Finis moved to Los Angeles in 1980 and switched to comedy, appearing at the Comedy Store where he was discovered by Richard Pryor and invited to become his opening act!

Whilst for the next two years his job was to make people laugh, he still possessed considerable talent as a songwriter and singer, resulting in a guest appearance on Bill Wolfer's acclaimed **Wolf** album on the track *Call Me*. After teaming up with former Earth Wind & Fire guitarist Al McKay, Finis briefly resumed his own musical career, signing with Motown in 1983 and releasing **Finis** in April of that year. A #42 success on the R&B chart, the album would produce the minor hit single *Skip To My Lou* which made #48 in June 1983. A second single *Lovers* missed the chart and Finis left the label soon after. These days his act mixes music and comedy, with his impersonations of Sammy Davis, Willie Nelson, Julio Iglesias and Michael Jackson highly recommended!
ALBUM: FINIS (1983)

WES HENDERSON

Originally a bass playing member of Little Daddy & The Bachelors, Wes Henderson was born in Edmonton, Alberta in Canada on 11 May 1942. Voted Best Band at the 1964 Pacific National Exhibition, The Bachelors recorded one single with RCA, *Too Much Monkey Business*. Fronted by Tommy Melton, the group would go through a number of name changes, including Four Niggers And A Chink, The Calgary Shades, Four Coloured Fellows And An Oriental Lad and finally The Four N's And A C. Whilst the names were intended to reflect their multi-racial line-up, promoters found them offensive, with the result the group struggled to get bookings.

In 1965 they reformed under Bobby Taylor with a much more acceptable name, The Vancouvers and eventually landed a deal with Motown, by which time Wes had switched to guitar. Whilst much of the focus on Bobby Taylor & The Vancouvers has revolved around Bobby Taylor and to a lesser extent Tommy Chong, Wes Henderson was an integral part of the group and a strong song-writer. Along with Tommy Chong, Wes was sacked from the group in 1968 by Johnny Bristol after the pair went absent without leave (they were required to attend an interview for their Green Cards), with Wes subsequently turning up on the Rare Earth label the following year with a solo single, *In Bed*. Written by Wes with Lynn Henderson and Tom Baird, the song would also be covered by Rare Earth and Matrix for the Rare Earth label and subsequently be recorded by Three Dog Night. Despite favourable reviews and reception to Wes' single, it failed to chart and remained his only solo release for the label.

VIRGIL HENRY

Virgil Henry had a circuitous journey to getting a record out on the Tamla label, one that saw him record under three different names for a variety of labels. His first release was under his birth name Gil Blanding, with *Rules* appearing on the tiny Long Island based Ready label in 1966 (it would later go on to become a monster Northern Soul tune) before amending it a couple of months later to Virgil Blanding for *Girl Wasn't Born* issued on Verve. Two years later, still as Virgil Blanding he surfaced at Moon Shot for *Birth Of A Man*. By 1970 he had linked with producer and songwriter Jerry Ross at his Colossus label, where he released *I'll Be True* and *I Can't Believe You're Really Leaving* as Virgil Henry.

When Jerry had some significant success as a writer, with Diana Ross & The Supremes & The Temptations covering *I'm Gonna Make You Love Me* (which Jerry had written with Kenny Gamble and Leon Huff), Berry contacted him about working directly with Motown. This brief partnership saw The Courtship, Crystal Mansion, The Festivals and the Jerry Ross Symposium release singles, as well as a reissue for the former parking lot attendant Virgil Henry, with *I Can't Believe You're Really Leaving* backed with *You Ain't Sayin' Nothin' New* being issued on the Tamla label in November 1971.

According to Jerry, Motown put little or no promotional effort behind this or any of his other singles, with the result it sank without trace. Virgil also disappeared at much the same time, although in 2009 he resurfaced on a Northern Soul forum and, after explaining that he was trying to find copies of his original singles, found that the members of the forum clubbed together to buy him a set.

This prompted the response from Virgil, "I wanted to thank you for your kind gift and heartfelt generosity. It is nice to know that there are angels like you and you cannot believe how touched I have been just knowing that my music has been appreciated. That you have enjoyed my work and felt as I did when I created these songs from my heart as God directed me."

GENE HENSLEE

A native of Boswell, Oklahoma, Gene had formed the Rancho Valley Boys in the 1940s in Artesia, New Mexico. His solo career had begun with Imperial in 1953, where he became acknowledged as something of a rockabilly legend, even if nothing ever crossed over to make the charts. The same fate would await his only outing with Motown, with *Shambles* backed with *Beautiful Women* appearing on the Mel-O-dy label in January 1964. Gene later recorded for United Artists, Brownfield, Starday, Jubilee and Billie Fran but still found chart success eluded him.

DANNY HERNANDEZ & THE ONES

The Ones had already passed through Motown in 1968 when the company picked up their local Lansing hit *You Haven't Seen My Love* from the Fenton label. Then the group comprised Danny Hernandez, Kerry and Kevin Nicholoff and Mark Boomershine, and after the failure of the single and its follow-up, the group returned home to Lansing to lick their wounds. When the Nicholoff brothers departed, Danny put together a new line-up with a rotating list of members. Danny had first performed with Pepe & The Problems and attracted attention even then, but his subsequent arrival in The Ones made them the group to catch in Lansing.

"We were doing James Brown stuff because Danny could do it," Kerry Nicholoff remembered. "He was a great showman and guitar player. He'd drop down to his knees and all that. That's what he did."

Even rival bands were impressed, as Loren Molinaire of The Dogs, another group out of Lansing recalled.

"Danny was kind of like the Hispanic James Brown with a guitar – he was quite the showman. People take that stuff for granted now. Back then, rock and roll was still fresh and new. Live music was a big deal, so when a band came to town it was a big deal."

The showman in Danny resulted in the new Ones getting a second crack at Motown with *As Long As I've Got You* being released on the Rare Earth label in September 1970, but despite the single being released on a more natural label home, it didn't crack the charts. Whilst The Ones departed the label a second time, Danny and The Ones kept touring until 1975. Danny died in Florida in 2000 at the age of 53.

HEROES – THE COMMODORES [ALBUM]

Although not as immediate as their previous album **Midnight Magic**, **Heroes** represented something of a shift in musical style for The Commodores. There were no ballads as delightful as *Still* or *Sail On*, no up-tempo numbers to drive fans to the dance floor like *Brick House*, yet **Heroes** was still an important album in the growing Commodores catalogue. Much influenced by gospel and with several tracks carrying something of a spiritual message, such as *Jesus Is Love*, *Wake Up Children* and *Mighty Spirit*, The Commodores' reputation for turning out strong albums was sufficient to propel **Heroes** to #7 on the pop chart and #3 R&B, although it peaked at a much more modest #50 in the UK. With the impending departure of front man Lionel Richie for a solo career, **Heroes** would mark The Commodores' final appearance in the Top Ten of the album charts.

HE'S MISSTRA KNOW IT ALL – STEVIE WONDER [SINGLE]

Whilst *Higher Ground* and *Living For The City* had been major US hits, their respective performances in the UK had been less than expected. When time came to select a third single therefore, Tamla Motown decided upon a different track for UK audiences; *Don't You Worry 'Bout A Thing* was issued by Tamla in the US (and would become a #16 pop and #2 R&B hit), with Tamla Motown selecting *He's Misstra Know It All*.

It proved to be a wise choice, for *He's Misstra Know It All* is still considered one of Stevie's most popular tracks in the UK, the contrast between hard-hitting lyrics and a swinging rhythm track proving to be instantly radio friendly and receiving similar acceptance at retail. The end result was a Top Ten hit, with the single reaching #10 in May 1974, thus becoming the best performing chart single in the UK from the **Innervisions** album.

Surprisingly, given its UK success, *He's Misstra Know It All* was not selected for release in the US, finally appearing as the flip side to *Sir Duke* in 1977. Tamla Motown did issue *Don't You Worry 'Bout A Thing* as the fourth single from the album, but it proved to be a single too far, missing out on the chart altogether. In 1992 the track attracted a jazz funk cover version from Incognito and would become a Top 20 hit, peaking at #19.

HERE COMES THE JUDGE – SHORTY LONG [SINGLE]

Television's 'Rowan & Martin's Laugh-In' provided the inspiration for what would become Shorty Long's biggest hit. Former vaudeville star Dewey 'Pigmeat' Markham can lay claim to having originated the title and later developed the phrase into something of a regular feature on the show, often in conjunction with Sammy Davis Jr. Recognising the appeal of at least the phrase, Quality Control head Billie Jean Brown mentioned to Berry Gordy that Motown should get a song out on to the market that capitalised on 'Here comes the judge.'

It was eventually agreed to have Shorty Long record the song that was penned by Billie Jean, Shorty and Suzanne De Passe. Several heavyweights gave their support, with Pervis Jackson of The Spinners providing the bass voice and Sammy Davis Jr. the spoken introduction (Sammy's involvement led, indirectly, to a brief recording deal with Motown). By the time the record was released, however, several other artists had had much the same idea, including Pigmeat Markham, who had his own *Here Comes The Judge* written by Pigmeat, Bob Astor, Dick Allen and Sarah Harvey out on Chess. Ultimately it was Motown (through the Soul subsidiary) who won the day, with Shorty's *Here Comes The Judge* becoming a #4 R&B and #8 pop hit, also making #30 in the UK for good measure.

Pigmeat's recording also made #4 R&B but stalled at #19 on the pop chart, the same position it reached in the UK, although circumstances dictated *Here Comes The Judge* would be the only hit for Pigmeat and the final hit for Shorty.

HETHERINGTON

British singer, songwriter and guitarist John Hetherington released one single on the British MoWest label, *Teenage Love Song* backed with *That Girl's Alright* appearing in July 1973. He had begun his recording career with RCA in 1970 when aged 20 and would later record for the Neighborhood label, also having a very brief spell signed with the Uni label in the US.

HI RECORDS

Hi Records was formed in Memphis, Tennessee in 1957 by singer Ray Harris, record store owner Joe Cuoghi, Bill Cantrell and Quinton Claunch along with three silent partners. After enjoying initial success with Bill Black's Combo, Hi Records hit its creative peak during the early 1970s, most notably thanks to Al Green. Al was invariably joined on both the soul and pop charts by the likes of Ann Peebles, Willie Mitchell and O.V. Wright, but following Al's switch to gospel Hi Records lost its way. In 1977 the label was sold to Al Bennett of Cream Records, necessitating a switch of emphasis from Memphis to Los Angeles, but Willie Mitchell left the label and Hi Records became little more than a credible back catalogue.

The catalogue was licensed to Motown for a brief spell at the start of the 1980s, but with the entire catalogue to delve into, Motown concentrated on just a handful of artists, reissuing virtually all of Al Green's repertoire alongside single releases by Ann Peebles, Ace Cannon,

Bill Black's Combo and Willie Mitchell. When CDs were launched, Motown doubled up various Al Green albums but did little else with Hi until a later lawsuit instigated by Al Bennett's daughter Adalah Bennett Shaw returned the entire catalogue back to Cream.

HIGH INERGY

Scoring such a huge hit with their debut single set High Inergy a bar they would struggle to reach for the rest of their career. Formed in Pasadena, California by Linda Howard, Michelle Martin and sisters Barbara and Vernessa Mitchell, they initially worked under the name High Energy until they were spotted by Gwen Gordy whilst performing at Pasadena's Bicentennial Performing Arts Programme, who quickly signed them to the Gordy label (Berry Gordy's label, that is) and insisted on a subtle name change to High Inergy.
The group exploded out of the traps with *You Can't Turn Me Off (In The Middle Of Turning Me On)*, a delightful ballad written by Marilyn McLeod and Pam Sawyer and produced by Kent Washburn which hit #12 pop and #2 R&B in April 1977. The immediate success of the single enabled the accompanying album, **Turnin' On** to score on the chart too, hitting #28 pop and #6 R&B, although alarm bells may have rung when the second single *Love Is All You Need* could only make #89 pop and #20 R&B.
A second album released in June 1978, **Steppin' Out** would produce two minor R&B hits in *We Are The Future* (#77) and *Lovin' Fever* (#51), with the album suffering accordingly by only making #42 pop and #46 R&B. The group was dealt a blow when co-lead singer Vernessa left soon after the release of **Steppin' Out** in order to pursue a career in gospel music, leaving High Inergy a trio.
Subsequent albums continued the downward spiral, **Shoulda Gone Dancin'** peaking outside the Top 100 on the pop charts (#147), and a lowly #72 on the R&B chart. The title track, lifted as a single did little to alleviate the gloom, bubbling under the pop chart and only making #50 on the R&B listings. High Inergy were to release five further albums, but only two of these made any kind of dent on the chart, with **Hold On** making #70 R&B in 1980 and **Groove Patrol** #60 three years later, the latter aided by the presence of Smokey Robinson on two tracks. By 1984 however High Inergy decided to call it a day. Linda died from unknown causes on 17 December 2012.
ALBUMS: TURNIN' ON (1977), STEPPIN' OUT (1978), SHOULDA GONE DANCIN' (1979), FRENZY (1979), HOLD ON (1980), HIGH INERGY (1981), SO RIGHT (1982), GROOVE PATROL (1983)

HIGHER GROUND – STEVIE WONDER [SINGLE]

Stevie Wonder's ground breaking album **Innervisions** was released on 3 August 1976 and was quickly shaping up to be the most successful of his career, even after three days of sales. Then disaster struck as a car in which Stevie was a passenger, being taken to a concert in Durham in South Carolina, was involved in a collision with a logging truck, with Stevie being stuck in the head and suffering a broken skull and contusion of the brain. He was rushed to hospital, still in a coma and everyone began to fear the worse. He was to remain in an unconscious state for four days, with aide Ira Tucker singing loudly into his ear the lead single from that album, *Higher Ground*.
Stevie would eventually recover, although he lost his sense of smell and would later claim that he had almost anticipated his close brush with death.
"I wrote *Higher Ground* before the accident, but something must have been telling me that something was going to happen to make me aware of a lot of things and to get myself together. This is like my second chance for life, to do something, or to do more, and to value the fact that I'm alive. And, if I felt that not living would be better, to conclude it."
That it should be *Higher Ground* that brought him around proved somewhat prophetic, for the song dealt with the singer being given a second chance. Written in May 1973 when Stevie was enjoying a burst of creativity, *Higher Ground* was a funk driven song reminiscent of the earlier *Superstition*, with Stevie playing all of the instruments.
The single's relevance to the life and near death of Stevie Wonder was obvious, but its almost universal acceptance was not based on sympathy; it fully deserved its final placing of #4 pop and #1 R&B and should have done better than its #29 peak in the UK. In 1990 American group Red Hot Chili Peppers took a rock version to #54 on the British chart.

TOMMY HILL

A graduate from New York's John Jay College of Criminology, Tommy Hill was briefly a singer with Black Russian but quit the group after discovering they had been utilising his vocal phrasing. Whilst Black Russian would go on to record an album for Motown,

Tommy remained in New York and eventually linked up with writer and producer Rick Tarbox.

One of the songs the pair produced, *Flame* was picked up by Motown in July 1981, with the company requesting an instrumental version for the B side, which was eventually called *Superstar Of Love*. With no 12" version and little promotion, the single did little business, as Rick later recalled.

"This was very disappointing as we had worked hard on the two songs. We later found out that the whole project was a tax right off for Motown so they did not want the project to become successful; rather they were trying to lose money to make up for not having to pay taxes. Yet bizarrely, having been the producer of the record I was on Motown's payroll, and every two weeks a car would deliver a check for $125, in the hope that new songs would be written and given to Motown."

In the event every song that was submitted was rejected, with *Flame* evidently Tommy's only single release. He would leave the industry and move to Washington D.C., where he became part of the government law enforcement. According to Rick, Tommy quit his job in 2010 and moved to Los Angeles to try and get back into the music business but committed suicide when this was unsuccessful.

THE HILLSIDERS

Described as 'another of Al Klein's obscure discoveries', The Hillsiders recorded one single for the Mel-O-dy label, *You Only Pass This Way One Time*, something of an apt title for a group whose single came and went in March 1965. Written by Roland Pike and produced by Al Klein and Barney Ales, the folk group went the way of virtually all of Mel-O-dy's artists; back to obscurity.

JOE HINTON

Often confused with a gospel singer with the same name, this Joe Hinton was a singer, songwriter and producer who worked with the likes of Johnny Bristol, Pam Sawyer and Hank Cosby during the course of his Motown career. He first recorded as Little Joe Hinton on Arvee and would later record as Jay Lewis, both solo (for Capitol) and with his wife Zilla Mays (on ABC). Whilst he only recorded one single at Motown, with *Let's All Save The Children* on Soul in January 1971 (one further track *What A Friend We Have In Jesus* with Impact Of Brass appeared on Motown's **The Key To The Kingdom**) he wrote many songs whilst at Hitsville, including *Gotta Hold On To This Feeling* for Junior Walker & The All Stars in 1970. Joe later recorded for Hotlanta during the mid 1970s.

THE HIT PACK

Another of the virtually anonymous groups that breezed into Hitsville, recorded a track or two and then breezed out again, with few any the wiser to who they were or what they did. In the case of The Hit Pack, recent research suggests that they were a four piece vocal group featuring Robert Walker, Robert Staunton (these two wrote and produced both sides of The Hit Pack single), Charles Jones and Robert Dobyne (and these two briefly recorded as Dobyne & Jones for Motown), with Dobyne the lead vocalist. The group name had previously been used on a single for Colpix (which was also written by Staunton and Walker with Artie Kornfield), their only single for Soul, *Never Say No To Your Baby* backed with *Let's Dance* was released on both sides of the Atlantic in 1965 with little or no sales in either territory.

The group recorded one other track for Motown, *Didn't I* which remains in the vault. Meanwhile, all three Robert's (Staunton, Walker and Dobyne) remained at Motown for a few years writing and or producing a variety of artists, including The Monitors debut hit *Say You*.

HITSVILLE RECORDS

When Motown ran into legal problems with the Melodyland label, the decision was taken to rename the country outlet Hitsville, a name that Berry had registered some years previously. The roster, including T.G. Sheppard, Rick Tucker, Pat Boone and Wendel Adkins were switched over to the new label, which made its bow in May 1976 with T.G. Sheppard's *Solitary Man*. Run by Mike Curb and Ray Huff, the label would remain active until March 1977, when the MC label was launched, with the artists moving once again to their new label home.

HITSVILLE U.S.A.

Although Hitsville has come to be most associated with the recording studio, it should be noted that the Hitsville U.S.A. moniker applied to the whole complex, one that grew over the course of some ten years to encompass some nine buildings on West Grand Boulevard. It is a matter of some debate as to which is the world's most famous recording studio; Abbey Road in London or Hitsville in Detroit.

Certainly both had a varied history up to the point they became recording facilities, 3 Abbey Road being a Georgian townhouse built in 1830 that one hundred years later was acquired by the Gramophone Company and converted into studios. It earned its place in folklore when The Beatles began recording there in 1962, turning out a succession of hit singles and albums up to 1970, including the famous **Abbey Road** album in 1969 (the pedestrian crossing on which The Beatles were photographed was granted Grade II listed status, meaning it has been afforded the status of being particularly important with more than special interest; every day Beatles fans from around the world walk across the same crossing to have their photograph taken, much to the chagrin of motorists using Abbey Road!). A glance at the Abbey Road facilities reveals that this is indeed a grand studio complex.

By comparison, Hitsville U.S.A. looked like a cottage industry! Based at 2648 West Grand Boulevard, the house was a photographers' studio when Berry Gordy purchased it on 2 August 1959, subsequently turning it into both a recording studio and administrative offices for his growing Motown empire. The recording studio was located at the back of the house and was open 22 hours a day (it was shut between 8.00am and 10.00am for maintenance) with Berry and Raynoma's living quarters upstairs, directly above the sign informing the world that this was Hitsville U.S.A.

"I actually found Hitsville while I was married to Berry," said Raynoma Lilles. "That house was unbelievable, because it already had a studio built on the back. It was there that the 'Motown sound' took shape. It was a completely natural sound. All we did was put up some theatre curtains and maybe a rug. There was nothing contrived about it. All of the rhythm players – like James Jamerson, Eddie Willis, Ivy Jo Hunter – had this natural talent that Berry and I could really relate to. That was the original, the funky Motown sound."

In April 1961 Berry purchased 2644/46, which became the offices of the Jobete Publishing Company. In January he purchased two more houses, at 2650 and 2652/4, with the former becoming the executive offices of Berry, Esther Edwards and Ralph Setzer and the latter Motown Administration. The Finance Department was housed in 2656 when this was purchased in March 1965, whilst January 1966 saw the purchase of 2657, the only property directly opposite Hitsville which became the home of Artist Development. There were to be three further acquisitions in 1966, with 2662/4 and 2666/8 becoming the Motown Sales & Marketing locations following their purchase in July 1966. A week previously 2670/2 was acquired and International Talent Management became the new occupiers.

Berry moved into more opulent surroundings in 1967 with the purchase of a stately mansion at 918 West Boston Boulevard in the affluent Boston-Edison neighbourhood, with the home quickly becoming known as The Motown Mansion (Berry gave his former home to his sister Gwen and her husband Marvin Gaye).

A year later, in 1968 Berry moved all administrative staff into the Donovan building on the corner of Woodward Avenue and Interstate 75, with Hitsville's studio becoming Studio A and the recently acquired Golden World complex Studio B. The various buildings have had a somewhat chequered history since their Motown connection; the Donovan building was demolished in 2006 to make way for car parking for the Super Bowl when it was hosted in Detroit, 2644/46 now serves as the entrance to the Motown Museum and 2650 burned to the ground in 1971.

The whole complex, however, remains steeped in a rich history, as Raynoma fondly remembers.

"People did whatever it was necessary to do. Everybody did something, from maintaining the exterior of the building, painting and so forth, to what we called 'snack time', when someone had to cook and serve lunch. My specialty was chilli, so I usually did the cooking. Smokey Robinson usually was the one who had to mop up! The salaries back then were very interesting. Smokey was making three dollars a week. But you know, this is how interested everyone was in just being a part of it and watching it grow. It was fun, something that was in our blood, not just a job. It was a bunch of people who really believed, working together for a specific goal. It was a happening."

BRIAN HOLLAND

One third of the legendary writing and production team with his brother Eddie and Lamont Dozier, Brian was the only one of the three not to release a single or otherwise on the Motown label. However, like the other two he did start his professional career as a singer before finding his true vocation lay behind the other side of the studio glass.

Born in Detroit, Michigan on 15 February 1941, Brian made his recording debut in 1958 for the small Kudo label in Detroit, with his single *(Where's The Joy?) In Nature Boy* being credited to Briant Holland And The Band. It was the flip side, however, that was more revealing, *Shock* being written by Berry Gordy and his brother Robert, bringing Brian into the Gordy fold for the very first time.

Never the most confident of solo singers, Brian opted to join The Satintones, becoming lead vocalist, although his greater strength was as a pianist and he would perform this function on Barrett Strong's hit *Money*. Eventually his singing duties at Motown became less and less and his time behind the console grew, with Brian working with a variety of writing partners, including Mickey Stevenson (with whom he wrote a number of songs for his brother Eddie).

Brian's first regular writing partner was another member of The Satintones, Robert Bateman, with the pair writing and producing under the Brianbert moniker. Their first major hit came in 1962 with *Please Mr. Postman* for The Marvelettes, the first number one the company achieved. Bateman left the company soon after and Brian linked with Lamont Dozier and Freddie Gorman, although within a year Gorman had been replaced by Eddie Holland and by 1963 the triumvirate was in place.

Whilst it is the body of work that they produced over the next four years that has ensured their place in musical folklore, it should also be remembered that both Brian and Eddie fulfilled other functions at Hitsville. When Billie Jean Brown took an eighteen month furlough to go to Spain with her husband, Berry Gordy appointed Brian the new head of Quality Control (brother Eddie was similarly appointed A&R Director when Mickey Stevenson left the company), putting the Holland brothers in control of probably the two most important areas of the company's activities.

By the tail end of 1967 the brothers and Lamont Dozier felt that their efforts as writers, producers and executives were worthy of greater remuneration, resulting in an initial strike and then walkout by the team. Legal challenges prevented them from writing or producing anyone else, at least publically, although all three were undoubtedly active, even if they were forced to release their work under pseudonyms.

When the legal battles were over and the Invictus (with distribution by Capitol) and Hot Wax (distributed by Buddah) labels were up and running, Brian would make a brief return to the studio floor, being credited by name on *Don't Leave Me Starvin' For Your Love* and *Slipping Away*, which were #13 and #46 R&B hits respectively. Brian also contributed to *Why Can't We Be Lovers* and *New Breed Kinda Woman*, although both carried a more prominent credit for Lamont Dozier.

Lamont would head off for a solo career in 1973, with Brian and Eddie eventually bringing the curtain down on their label set-up midway through the 1970s. Brian would make a number of returns to Motown, producing The Jackson 5 on several tracks on **Moving Violation** and *Keep Holding On* among others for The Temptations. Non-Motown productions included Donny and Marie Osmond's 1978 album **Winning Combination**, but in truth little or none of his material could match the sheer magic that he, Lamont or Eddie had produced a decade previously.

CHRIS HOLLAND & T-BONE

Hailing from New Jersey, Chris Holland originally recorded under his real name of Arnie Corrado for Date as a 17 year old in 1966, with *My World* his debut single. Also recording for Columbia, Capitol and Mercury, Arnie would issue singles under his own name, as Bobby Corrado and, for two singles, including his one outing on Rare Earth in 1972, Chris Holland & T-Bone. His single *Get Me Some Help* backed with *If Time Could Stand Still* was released in May 1972 but received no help in making the charts. Nine years later the song at least made a minor dent in the British charts, with Martinique vocal duo Ottawan (perhaps best known for *D.I.S.C.O.* and *Hands Up*) taking it to #49.

EDDIE HOLLAND

The vocal similarities between Eddie Holland and Jackie Wilson were such that Berry Gordy used Eddie to do demo versions of songs that would be submitted to Jackie for consideration. When Berry had a fall out with Wilson and his team, he kept Eddie on and helped shape his early career, one which would result in four R&B and pop hits during Motown's early days. Indeed, these hits made Eddie the most successful of the pre-teamed Holland-Dozier-Holland trio and, seemingly destined for a long and fruitful career of his own. That he didn't, preferring to stay in the background as a writer and producer, was down to one thing; a dislike of performing live.

Born in Detroit, Michigan on 30 October 1939, Eddie dropped out of college soon after meeting Berry Gordy, no doubt convinced by his argument that a successful recording career lay in wait. After severing his working relationship with Jackie Wilson, Berry Gordy was convinced he had a readymade replacement in Eddie Holland and got him a deal with Mercury Records, who issued *Little Miss Ruby* backed with *You* in 1958.

The following year Berry founded Tamla Records and brought Eddie into the fold, writing and producing both sides of *Merry-Go-Round* and *It Moves Me*, initially released in February 1959. When Berry inked a nationwide deal with United Artists for Marv Johnson's *Come To Me*, he also added Eddie Holland's single for release on the major too, being re-released in May 1959. The United Artists deal would see a further three singles released, *Because I Love Her*, *Magic Mirror* and *The Last Laugh*, all of which failed to make much of a dent.

By the time the deal had run its course, Berry Gordy had the last laugh and Motown was better able to promote and sell in house. Eddie's first single back at Motown, therefore, would go on to become the biggest hit of his career, with *Jamie* hitting #6 R&B and #30 pop in October 1961 (it would be released in the UK on Fontana but failed to chart). It had been written by Barrett Strong and Mickey Stevenson and was intended as a single for Barrett until he left the company, with Eddie overdubbing his vocals on the tracks that already existed.

Getting a follow-up hit, however, proved rather more difficult, with *You Deserve What You Got* backed with *Last Night I Had A Vision* (both sides written by Eddie and his brother Brian with Mickey Stevenson) being released in April 1962 and vanishing almost immediately. This may have been because Motown had decided to release something a little stronger the following month, with *(If) Cleopatra Took A Chance* backed with *What About Me* hitting the streets at much the same time Eddie's debut album was released.

In August Motown would try again with two tracks lifted from the album, with *If It's Love (It's Alright)* and *It's Not Too Late* being coupled for single release, again without success. Eddie's December 1962 single *Darling, I Hum Our Song* kept the hitless streak going, but far more revealing was the identity of the song's writers; Brian Holland, Lamont Dozier and Eddie Holland, one of the earliest songs the three had crafted.

By the following year the three were spending more and more time in the control booth, although Eddie would still make the occasional recording, with *Baby Shake* being issued in April 1963 and *I'm On The Outside Looking In* in October the same year, with the latter track originally intended for Sammy Turner but released with Eddie's vocals overdubbed. Neither of these were hits but Eddie was not far away, eventually returning to the chart with *Leaving Here*, which would become a #27 R&B and #76 pop hit in January 1964. That surprise success put on hold Eddie's plans to effectively retire from recording and performing, since Motown demanded a follow-up.

It came with *Just Ain't Enough Love*, which would peak at #31 R&B and #54 pop in June 1964 and be bettered by *Candy To Me*, which hit #29 R&B and #58 pop. After that success Eddie called time on recording, making good his threat to concentrate on writing and production. For the next four years Eddie would provide the lyrics to a slew of hits on a variety of artists before walking out of Motown in 1968.

Whilst Brian and Lamont would revive their own recording careers with varying degrees of success during the 1970s, Eddie resisted the temptation, although he was the subject of an excellent compilation of all his recorded work released by Ace Records in the UK in 2011.

ALBUM: EDDIE HOLLAND (1962)

HOLLAND-DOZIER-HOLLAND

Individually they had recording careers that resulted in varying degrees of success, but collectively they are quite possibly the most successful writing and production team in popular music. As will have been noted in their respective solo entries, Brian Holland, Lamont Dozier and Eddie Holland arrived at Motown as performers but graduated to songwriting and production, sometimes out of choice and sometimes out of necessity.

The original writing trio had been Brian Holland, Lamont Dozier and Freddie Gorman, but once Eddie called time on his recording career and became available, it was Holland-Dozier-Holland from there on in. It was 1962 that the trio was launched on an unsuspecting record buying public, with *Dearest One* recorded by Lamont Dozier being generally acknowledged as their first joint composition. It was to be the following year that HDH became an established unit, producing *Locking Up My Heart* by The Marvelettes following a direct request from Berry Gordy to help elevate the group back into the upper reaches of the chart.

Whilst *Locking Up My Heart* was a hit, albeit a minor one, it would be their work with another female group at Motown that earned them their legendary status. That group *could* have been Martha & The Vandellas, who took *Come And Get These Memories* into the Top Ten R&B and Top Thirty pop charts and *Heat Wave* even higher and seemingly had first option on whatever HDH were coming up with during 1963. There were exceptions, with The Miracles (*Mickey's Monkey*), Marvin Gaye (*Can I Get A Witness*) and Mary Wells (*You Lost The Sweetest Boy*) all registering hits, something that eluded The Darnells (*Too Hurt To Cry Too Much In Love To Say Goodbye*).

It was their ability to knock out hits, however, that prompted Berry to place The Supremes in their care, finally getting them into the Top Thirty with *When The Lovelight Starts Shining Through His Eyes*. Then, after a minor hit on The Miracles (*I Gotta Dance To Keep From Crying*) it was back to the top division artist, Martha & The Vandellas for *Quicksand* and *Livewire*. Whilst HDH achieved considerable back to back hits on most of their artists, the exception in their formative years were The Supremes, who saw *Run Run Run* (actually recorded before but released after *When The Lovelight*) barely scrape into the Hot 100 at much the same time Marvin Gaye and The Vandellas were enjoying much higher chart placings with *You're A Wonderful One* and *In My Lonely Room* respectively.

Then came the decision that changed everything at Motown; *Where Did Our Love Go* was offered to The Marvelettes, who turned it down as being too simple and childish a song to amount to much. Berry Gordy suggested recording it on The Supremes, who were equally less than enamoured but were in such need of a hit they had to tow the company line; it went all the way to number one and for the next four years or so The Supremes and HDH became a combination that would dominate the charts.

If HDH's success at Motown had only been the result of their work with The Supremes it would be impressive, but to replicate that success with The Four Tops whilst also hitting with an abundance of artists they were assigned speaks volumes. After vaulting to the top of the charts with *Where Did Our Love Go*, HDH developed the Midas touch, with virtually everything registering high up the charts – there were five straight #1 hits on The Supremes, back to back Top Ten hits on The Four Tops and a return to the Top Ten for Marvin Gaye; all of this achieved by the opening months of 1965! Indeed, it was a level of chart domination to rival that of The Beatles.

Equally impressive was their production talents; songs such as *Where Did Our Love Go* and *Baby Love* might have appeared twee and little more than the epitome of sweet soul, but thanks to HDH's efforts in the studio, coaxing majestic performances out of Diana Ross, assisted by fellow Supremes Florence Ballard and Mary Wilson, they helped define soul music during the middle 1960s. Their work with The Four Tops, meanwhile, pushed the boundaries even further. Aided by exceptional playing by the Funk Brothers and the male vocals mixed in deftly with the female backing (The Andantes, whose contributions to these recordings cannot be understated) proved simply irresistible.

For the next two years, the upper reaches of the charts around the world were awash with HDH compositions and productions, with The Isley Brothers, The Elgins, The Miracles and Kim Weston as well as The Four Tops and The Supremes all reaping the benefit. Unfortunately the more successful the trio became, the more they began to question whether or not they were receiving their full dues.

In 1967, at the very peak of their creative powers, their relationship with Berry Gordy went into meltdown. According to HDH, the dispute was over the amount of control of their work they had and receiving greater reward for the fruits of their labours. Initially they undertook a work slowdown, which affected not only their own songwriting but also other aspects of the workings at Hitsville, since both Eddie and Brian held key positions within quality control and production. By the time Berry Gordy became fully aware of the problem (having relocated to California), HDH were no longer working at or for Motown.

A flurry of lawsuits officially kept HDH out of the studio for the next couple of years, although there were rumours that the trio were still working in any one of Detroit's other studios, undertaking outside production work and laying the foundations for their own labels. Motown must have heard the rumours and invariably sent spies, lawyers and agents out and about with a brief of catching any or all the trio undertaking work when legally prohibited from so doing but never managed to actually catch them in the act.

When the legalities cleared a little a couple of years later, HDH were free to set up their own Invictus and Hot Wax labels (later adding the Music Merchant label), going on to enjoy varying degrees of success with artists such as Freda Payne, Chairmen Of The Board, 100 Proof Aged In Soul, The Glass House, The Honey Cone and Laura Lee. The legal battle with Berry Gordy still hung the air, resulting in the composer and production credits on several of the Invictus and Hot Wax releases bearing names of others within those organisations. Those with an ear, however, could detect not only HDH over each and every one of them but moonlighting Funk Brothers on the musical backing for good measure.

The legal dispute was settled in 1972, but the settlement came at a time when the first cracks in their partnership were beginning to show. Lamont Dozier left in 1973 in order to resume his solo career, with Brian and Eddie continuing with Invictus and Hot Wax for a further couple of years before dissolving the labels. Fortunately, their relationship with Motown was repaired, so much so that Brian undertook a number of production assignments for the label, including The Jackson 5 and The Temptations.

Unfortunately, by the time he returned his better days as both a writer and producer were effectively behind him. Indeed, whilst history has consistently viewed the five years or so that HDH ruled the charts as responsible for not only the best Motown music of all time, much of it is considered the best popular music of all time. The financial rewards that HDH so desired came their way; in 1982, when they had little or nothing out on the market by way of new releases, their collective income from royalties from earlier recordings actually exceeded what they had received in 1966! Popular music, therefore, continues to ponder the question as to what HDH may have achieved had they remained at Hitsville whilst at the height of their creative powers.

BRENDA HOLLOWAY

With a little more patience Brenda Holloway could have been a major star at Motown; she had the looks, the voice and the songwriting ability to take her above many of her rivals, but in her own mind being stuck out in Los Angeles whilst Detroit was the hub of activity counted against her.

Born Brenda Jereal Holloway in Atascadero, California on 21 June 1946 she grew up in Los Angeles and studied the violin at both elementary and high school as well as singing in church with her younger sister Patrice. Brenda also got to sing with future Whispers members Walter and Wallace Scott whilst still in school and also recorded for the first time whilst still a teenager. Record shop owner Kent Harris brought Brenda to the attention of Bob Keane, the head of Del-Fi Records, who was impressed enough with the precocious youngster's talent to have her record *Echo* for the Donna label in 1962.

The same label later released *I'll Find Myself A Guy* by The Wattesians, an all-girl group put together by Hal Davis with Brenda, Priscilla Kennedy, Pat Hunt and a fourth member called Barbara. The group provided backing vocals to the likes of Johnny Rivers and Ike & Tina Turner when they performed in the Los Angeles area. The following year (1963) found Brenda virtually ever-present in the studio, recording variously as a member of The Four J's (with Patrice, Priscilla and Pat) on 4-J with *Will You Be My Love,* with Hal Davis as Hal and Brenda for *It's You* (released by Minasa and Snap), with Jess Harris for *I Never Knew You Looked So Good Until I Quit You* on Brevit, with Gloria Jones' brother Robert Jackson as Bonnie & Clyde for *I Get A Feeling*, with the same song also being released on Era and credited to The Soul-Mates and solo for *I Ain't Gonna Take You Back* on Catch and *Every Little Bit Hurts*, which was written and produced by Ed Cobb for potential release on Del-Fi but subsequently held back.

Most of these recordings were produced by Hal Davis (the exception being *Every Little Bit Hurts*) and it was he who eventually helped get Brenda something of an audition for Berry Gordy, at which she sang a version of Mary Wells' *My Guy*. Suitably impressed with her vocal abilities (and, it is said, equally taken by the tight fitting gold outfit she wore), Berry offered a recording contract on the proviso Brenda graduate from high school first.

Her first Motown session saw her re-record *Every Little Bit Hurts*, this time done in more of the style of the guide vocal that had been provided by Barbara Wilson (the wife of producer Frank Wilson), although the actual session was not without its problems as Brenda didn't believe she could better Barbara's version and only relented after firm instructions from Hal Davis. The flip side was to be *Land Of A Thousand Boys,* a song written by Brenda herself, with both tracks being recorded at Armin Steiner's studio. Released on the Tamla label in late March 1964, the single would go on to become the biggest West Coast produced single for the Motown stable at the time, finally reaching #3 R&B and #13 pop. Its progress up the chart was helped by Brenda appearing on the Motortown Revue and Dick Clark's 'American Bandstand', subsequently going out on the road as part of Clark's 'Caravan Of Stars' tour that summer (unbeknown to Brenda, her presence on the tour helped get The Supremes the kick-start their career needed, for so keen had Dick Clark been to get Brenda on board, he accepted Esther Gordy-Edwards imposing The Supremes on the tour as part of the deal). As the tour progressed, so The Supremes' record *Where Did Our Love Go* moved up the charts and the group moved up the roster, displacing Brenda in the process.

However, the success of *Every Little Bit Hurts* had given Brenda a toe-hold on chart material herself, resulting in her similarly Ed Cobb penned follow-up *I'll Always Love You* also making something of a dent, albeit a rather more lowly #60 on the pop chart. Motown also rush released an album, **Every Little Bit Hurts** in the wake of this success, with all but one of the twelve tracks being recorded in Los Angeles, the exception being the Clarence Paul production *A Favor For A Girl (With A Lovesick Heart)* that was recorded on Brenda's first trip to Detroit. Overall the album followed the then standard Motown formula; a hit or two, a few originals, a few covers from the Jobete catalogue and a couple of standards. Formulaic it might have been but Brenda's voice stood out, particularly on the ballads.

Her star was seemingly on the rise, helped by the sudden departure of Mary Wells for a contract with 20th Century; Berry Gordy quickly announced plans to make Brenda Holloway the new female star at Motown. That gave her access to the same pool of writers and producers who had helped Mary Wells to the top, including Smokey Robinson, who would write and produce *When I'm Gone,* a song originally intended for Mary (Brenda was played Mary's version in order to get a feel for how Smokey envisioned the recording) which returned Brenda to the upper reaches of the chart, hitting #25 pop and #12 R&B.

Smokey also provided *Operator*, a song Mary had originally recorded in 1962 as the flip side to *Two Lovers*. Brenda's version made it to #78 on both the pop and R&B charts and no further, despite supposedly benefitting by Brenda being out on the road again, this time supporting The Beatles on their debut US tour. The failure of the Berry Gordy penned *You Can Cry On My Shoulder* to make a proper impact (it bubbled under at #116), followed by *Together 'Til The End Of Time* also missing out on the Hot 100 (it bubbled under at #125) convinced Brenda that her career was not becoming a priority as promised, a feeling that was surely reinforced when her scheduled second album **Hurtin' & Cryin'** was pulled off the schedule. *Hurt A Little Everyday,* released in August 1966 became her only single to not feature on any chart, with the result that an eponymous album scheduled for release at the end of the year was also removed, along with the single *'Til Johnny Comes*.

In March 1967 Brenda at last returned to the chart, taking the Frank Wilson composition *Just Look What You've Done* to #69 on both charts, but already work was underway on what would go on to become one of the most valuable assets in Jobete's catalogue. Brenda and Patrice began working on the song, with Brenda using her sadness at the end of a relationship to inspire an anthem about being happy. Frank Wilson added considerably and the rough song was played to Berry Gordy, who suggested a couple of changes and produced Brenda's version in Motown's West Coast studio. Brenda and Berry had different opinions as to how *You've Made Me So Very Happy* should sound, with Berry's interpretation holding sway on the final cut. It was still a successful single, returning Brenda to the Top 40 (it would peak at #39 on both pop and R&B charts), but as far as Brenda was concerned it merely reinforced her opinion that she was no longer a priority for the label.

Brenda wrote Berry a letter expressing her disappointment at the way she was being treated, feeling the label was trying to groom her for Las Vegas when all she wanted was to make hits. Brenda left Motown and, following her marriage to Reverend Alfred Davis at the age of 22 effectively retired from the music business, her name briefly returning to the limelight when Tamla Motown in the UK issued something of a compilation album in **The Artistry Of Brenda Holloway** in October 1968. The following year saw Blood Sweat & Tears record a cover version of *You've Made Me So Very Happy*, turning the song into something of a jazz rock hybrid and being rewarded with a gold selling single that hit #2 pop (Brenda would later successfully sue Motown for her cut of the royalties this version generated).

Brenda would return to the recording studios in 1972 for Holland-Dozier-Holland's Music Merchant label, but in the main she was happier out of the limelight, singing backing vocals for the likes of Joe Cocker. A gospel album was issued in 1980 and later in the decade Brenda was one of several former Motown artists to record for Ian Levine and his Motorcity label. Brenda even returned to live performing in the 1990s, including one date with Blood Sweat & Tears and a triumphant performance at the Northern Soul festival in Skegness in 2013. Her most recent recordings saw her perform with Cliff Richard on his **Soulicious** concept album.

ALBUM: EVERY LITTLE BIT HURTS (1964)
COMPILATION: THE ARTISTRY OF BRENDA HOLLOWAY (1968)

PATRICE HOLLOWAY

The youngest of the three Holloway children, Patrice was born in Los Angeles, California on 23 March 1951 and grew up showing the same kind of musical dexterity as her older sister Brenda. The pair proved more than capable singers and writers, with Patrice also adept on drums, guitar, cello, autoharp and violin. Patrice and Brenda began writing songs together whilst Patrice was still a young teenager, with Brenda going on to record several of their joint compositions during her time with Motown, including *You've Made Me So Very Happy*, which would attract a million selling cover version by Blood, Sweat & Tears. Having made one single (*Do The Del-Viking*) for the Taste label in 1963 produced by Hal Davis, Patrice followed her elder sister into Motown's arms later the same year.

Her only Motown release (although it is believed she recorded several tracks), however, was with the Frank Wilson penned *Stevie*, a tribute to Little Stevie Wonder. It was claimed they were boyfriend/girlfriend and may have spent some time together when Stevie was in California filming and recording. *Stevie*, the single meanwhile was the first release on the V.I.P. label in December 1963, but an unexplained contractual problem arose soon after the single appeared in record stores in Detroit, with the result Motown pulled the single and thus called time on Patrice' Motown career.

Patrice would later record for Capitol, but it was as Valerie Brown, a member of Josie & The Pussycats that she made her mark, a Hanna-Barbera television production that linked her with Kathleen Dougherty and Cheryl Stoppelmoor (later to become better known as Cheryl Ladd). When her time with The Pussycats came to an end, Patrice briefly resumed a solo career but eventually became content to provide backing vocals for a variety of artists, including Billy Preston, Bill Withers, Thelma Houston and Neil Young, among others. Reportedly suffering ill health throughout her entire professional life, Patrice died from a heart attack on 1 October 2006.

HOLLYWOOD WALK OF FAME

The Hollywood Walk of Fame, which stretches for 1.3 miles east to west on Hollywood Boulevard from North Gower Street to North La Brea (plus a short segment of Marshfield Way between Hollywood and La Brea) and 0.4 miles north to south on Vine Street, was suggested in 1953 by the then president of the Hollywood Chamber of Commerce. To date, more than 2,500 stars have been sited at 6 feet intervals, of which more than 390 have been awarded for contribution to recorded music.

Whilst there are several artists who have been awarded stars who have at some point recorded for Motown, such as Sammy Davis Jr. and Bobby Darin, this list is those who have received their stars wholly or largely for their Motown work, together with the specific address at which to find the star. Interestingly, the cover to The Miracles 1976 album **City Of Angels** depicts a girl stepping over The Miracles star; at the time, The Miracles did not have a star on the Hollywood Walk of Fame – this was finally rectified on 20 March 2009.

The Four Tops – 7060 Hollywood Boulevard
The Funk Brothers – 7065 Hollywood Boulevard
Marvin Gaye – 1500 Vine Street
Berry Gordy – 7000 Hollywood Boulevard
Michael Jackson – 6927 Hollywood Boulevard
The Jacksons – 1500 Vine Street
Gladys Knight – 7083 Hollywood Boulevard
The Miracles – 7060 Hollywood Boulevard
Lionel Richie – 7018 Hollywood Boulevard
Smokey Robinson – 1500 North Vine Street
Diana Ross – 6712 Hollywood Boulevard
The Spinners – 6723 Hollywood Boulevard
The Supremes – 7060 Hollywood Boulevard
The Temptations – 7060 Hollywood Boulevard
Stevie Wonder – 7050 Hollywood Boulevard

It was announced on 20 June 2013 that Holland-Dozier-Holland had been awarded a joint star on the Hollywood Walk of Fame. Neither a date nor a location has yet been specified, but the recipients have five years to schedule ceremonies from the date of selection or they expire.

BUDDY HOLLY & THE CRICKETS

Charles Hardin Holley was born in Lubbock, Texas on 7 September 1936 and began his career recording country music until the success of Elvis Presley dictated a musical change. He formed a duo with Bob Montgomery and recorded a number of demos as Buddy and Bob (with Larry Welborn on bass), with Decca expressing interest in signing Holly as a solo artist. Holly formed a new band with Sonny Curtis (born in Meadow, Texas on 9 May 1937) and Don Guess, touring as Buddy Holly & The Two-Tunes; recordings of this time later appeared as Buddy Holly & The Three-Tunes as drummer Jerry Allison (born in Hillsboro, Texas on 31 August 1939) had been added to the line-up. In February 1957 Buddy gathered The Crickets of Jerry Allison, Niki Sullivan (born in South Gate, California on 23 June 1937) and Joe Benson Maudlin (born on 8 July 1940) to re-record *That'll Be The Day*, the success of which landed Holly a solo deal with Coral, a subsidiary of the Brunswick label that The Crickets recorded for.

Although *Not Fade Away* was recorded by The Crickets in 1957 it never became a hit for the group, although it did chart thanks to a cover version by The Rolling

Stones. The Crickets' original, however, appeared on the soundtrack to 'Christine' released in November 1983.

On 3 February 1959 Buddy, Ritchie Valens and the Big Bopper were killed when their plane crashed near Mason City, Iowa. It was later reported that the crash was due to pilot error: after a successful take off, pilot Roger Peterson experienced vertigo and flew straight into the ground. Niki Sullivan died from a heart attack on 6 April 2004.

THE HONEST MEN

A Dutch rock group formed in Enschede in 1966 by Henk Bruinewoud (guitar and vocals), Aloys Van Der Zwaan (guitar and vocals), Simon Duivelaar (guitar and vocals), Johan Aldenkamp (bass and vocals) and Henry Lubben (drums) they added Martin Hofman (flute and vocals) in 1968. After making minor ripples in Europe with a number of singles, most notably on the Havoc label, they found one of these, *Cherie* backed with *Baby* being picked up for release by Motown on the V.I.P. label in April 1968. They bowed out in 1971 with a cover of the Beatles' *Help*, with Bruinewoud later becoming a member of Buffoon.

JOHN LEE HOOKER

Born in Clarksdale, Mississippi on 22 August 1917, John Lee Hooker was taught to play the guitar by his grandfather and made his recording debut in 1948. Domestic success came in the 1940s and 1950s; international success was not attained until the 1990s, when he became one of the oldest artists to hit the top three of the album chart and go on to collect four Grammy awards.

His 1962 recording *Boom Boom*, which is said to feature several moonlighting members of the Funk Brothers on musical accompaniment, was the biggest hit of his Vee-Jay sojourn, hitting #16 R&B and #60 pop in June 1962 (it would become a British Top Twenty hit more than thirty years later!) was featured on the CD compilation **Hits From The Legendary Vee-Jay Records** released by Motown in November 1986. John Lee Hooker was still touring and recording into his eighties and died on 21 June 2001, shortly before he was due to tour Europe.

BOB HORN

Singer and songwriter Bob Horn had one outing on Motown, *You've Gotta Try A Little Love* backed with *Static Free* appearing on the main Motown label in March 1975. As well as writing his single, Bob also co-produced with arranger Mark Davis, although this would appear to have been his only attempt at pursuing a recording career, for nothing else has appeared on any other label since this release.

LAWRENCE THOMAS HORN

The chief recording engineer at Hitsville between 1964 and 1967, Lawrence Horn was given a producer's credit on several singles, including Junior Walker's #1 R&B hit *Shotgun*. He also mixed just about every single the company released during that period, making him as key a member of the staff as the producers and writers.

Unfortunately, he was to achieve greater notoriety several years after leaving Motown; in May 1996 he was found guilty for plotting the murder of his wife, his 8-year old severely retarded son and an overnight nurse. Horn, who had been laid off by Motown in 1990 and fallen deeply into debt, stood to gain from a $1.7 million trust fund from a malpractice settlement following the hospital incident that left his son Trevor a quadriplegic. He hired James Edward Perry for $6,000, who used a manual entitled 'Hit Man: A Technical Manual for Independent Contractors' and following it almost to the letter shot Horn's former wife Mildred and nurse Janice Saunders and suffocated Trevor by cutting off his air supply on 3 March 1993.

Perry was sentenced to death but this was overturned on appeal and a second trial sentenced him to three life terms – he died in prison in December 2009. Horn was found guilty on three counts of first degree murder and one of murder conspiracy and sentenced to life without parole. The families of the victims later sued Paladin Press of Colorado, the publishers of 'Hit Man' and received significant compensation and the withdrawal of the book.

LENA HORNE

Berry Gordy made several marquee signings during the 1960s, artists that he hoped would appeal to a more mainstream audience and help establish his group of labels as a major force in American music. The likes of Billy Eckstine and Sammy Davis Jr. were instantly recognisable names, yet as far as their respective recording careers were concerned, their better days were behind them. The same can also be said for Lena Horne, who signed with Motown in 1976 and suffered the ignominy of having her only recording for the company scheduled but remain unreleased.

Born Lena Mary Calhoun Horne in Brooklyn, New York on 30 June 1917, Lena joined the chorus of the Cotton Club as a sixteen year old and worked her way up as a performer at the club before heading to Hollywood in pursuit of a film career. Lena landed a number of small roles, but her political leanings together with her colour meant major opportunities were few and far between; she was considered for the role of Julie LaVerne in 'Show Boat' but lost out to Ava Gardner as the Production Code in force at the time had a ban on interracial relationships. To further fuel her indignation at not landing the part, Lena learned that Ava initially lip-synched to Lena's recordings, which was offensive to both actresses.

Although denied a worthwhile opening in Hollywood, Lena found plenty of opportunities on Broadway (receiving a Tony Award nomination for Best Actress in a Musical for 'Jamaica'), television, nightclubs and recordings, with her 1957 live album becoming one of the best selling of the year. Having made her first recording in 1941, Lena would go on to enjoy a career that stretched over six decades, picking up her first Grammy nomination in 1961 for Best Female Solo Vocal Performance for **Lena At The Sands**. The first of her four awards came in 1981 for Best Pop Vocal Performance, Female for **Lena Horne: The Lady And Her Music** (the album also collected the award for Best Cast Show Album the same year).

Her brief Motown stint came with 'The Wiz', with Lena appearing in the film as Glinda The Good Witch and contributing *Believe In Yourself* to the soundtrack. Scheduled for release as a single in May 1976, promotional copies were pressed and distributed but a full release was pulled. Lena continued her recording career for many more years, collecting her final Grammy Award in 1995 for Best Jazz Vocal Performance for **An Evening With Lena Horne**. Her final studio album appeared in 1998, after which she officially retired, although she was coaxed back into a studio in 2000 to contribute to the **Classic Ellington** project. Lena died from heart failure on 9 May 2010 at the age of 92.

THE HORNETS

There is little doubt that everything to do with The Hornets was inspired by The Beatles, from the group's name to the overall sound of their only single, *Give Me A Kiss*. Whilst Johnny Powers (born John Pavlik in Detroit, Michigan in 1938), the former Sun Records rockabilly singer who was working at Hitsville as a would-be songwriter but sang on this has tried to play down any Beatles intention, the A-side to The Hornets single is considered by many to be close enough to *I Want To Hold Your Hand* to have run the risk of incurring a plagiarism suit if it had taken off!

Written by Mike Valvano, Andre Williams and Jerome Sims and performed by Johnny and Mike with musical backing by the house band, *Give Me A Kiss* failed to sell, thus thankfully remaining under the legal radar. It might also be the only recording released that features Johnny Powers, who had signed a five year contract with Motown in 1960 yet never released anything under his own name, quietly walking out of the back door when the contract expired in 1965.

WILLIE HORTON

Born in Arno, Virginia on 18 October 1942, Willie Wattison Horton is better known as a baseball player, a former left fielder and designated hitter turning out for six American League teams, most notably the Detroit Tigers between 1963 and 1977. In 1967 he tried to halt the escalating riots that engulfed Detroit, standing on his car dressed in his Detroit Tiger kit and appealing for calm, albeit unsuccessfully. He subsequently recorded the single *Detroit Is Happening*, written by Holland-Dozier-Holland and Frank De Vol with special lyrics by Ron Miller (and which was therefore a rewrite of The Supremes hit *The Happening*) and featuring backing vocals from Mary Wilson and Flo Ballard. The single carried a Motown catalogue number but was effectively credited to the City Of Detroit label.

HOTTER THAN JULY - STEVIE WONDER [ALBUM]

Secret Life Of Plants might have made the upper reaches of the chart for Stevie Wonder but it was widely regarded as a commercial and critical failure when compared with any of its three or four predecessors. Only one major hit single had been lifted, *Send One Your Love*, leading to suggestions that

Stevie might have reached the peak of his creativity. By the start of the 1980s however, Stevie was keen to show that he had lost none of his musical sharpness, penning *Let's Get Serious* for Jermaine Jackson, *You Are My Heaven* for Roberta Flack and Donny Hathaway and *Betcha Wouldn't Hurt Me* for Quincy Jones.

A meeting with Bob Marley at the Black Music Association in Philadelphia in the summer of 1979 proved inspirational, with Stevie penning *Master Blaster (Jammin')* and recording the track in his newly acquired Wonderland Studios in Los Angeles. Further sessions found Stevie incorporating other musical influences into his music; the country flavoured *I Ain't Gonna Stand For It*, ballad material in *Rocket Love* and *Lately*, the harder hitting social commentary of *Cash In Your Face* and, lifted from his own back catalogue *All I Do* originally recorded by Tammi Terrell in 1966 but never released. The crowning glory, however, was *Happy Birthday,* the song that Stevie was to use in the long and hard fought campaign to get Martin Luther King's birthday recognized as a national holiday in America.

The album, entitled **Hotter Than July** was initially intended for release in September 1980 but then delayed, as had most of Stevie's albums in the past. This time, however, the delay was merely a matter of days rather than months, for that same month EMI Records in London hosted a listening party for assorted journalists at Abbey Road studios, attended by Stevie himself, who was in London for a series of hugely successful live dates. The album was released in October 1980 and was an instant success, peaking at #2 in the UK and #3 in the US, attaining platinum status in both territories (it was his first officially sanctioned platinum disc in the US, following Motown joining the RIAA). Its commercial success could be gauged by the reception the various singles received; in the UK, all four (*Master Blaster, Lately, I Ain't Gonna Stand For It* and *Happy Birthday*) made the Top Ten, proof that Stevie was not only back but back to his best.

THELMA HOUSTON

Despite a Motown career that would stretch across six solo albums, two albums of duets with Jerry Butler and critical acclaim for much of her output, it is Thelma Houston's lot to be remembered for just one single.

Born Thelma Louise Jackson in Leland, Mississippi on 7 May 1946, Thelma and her three sisters were raised by a cotton picking mother before the family moved to Long Beach in California. There Thelma graduated from school, got married, had two children and divorced in quick fashion before getting a job in the health care field.

"My first job was in a hospital as a nurse's aide, emptying bedpans, changing beds, all that kind of thing. Then I went to another hospital. I think I was eighteen and worked on the 11-7 shift at night. Actually, I never worked in a job long enough to get a vacation. I just got kinda restless and lost interest. I've worked with geriatric patients, worked as a telephone operator, then at a school for physically handicapped children, in physical and occupational therapy."

Fortunately, her over-riding love of music saw her become a member of the Art Reynolds Singers, performing the lead vocal on their recording of *Glory Glory Hallelujah* on Capitol. "I was singing around Long Beach, California, must have been in '67. I was booking myself in and was totally ignorant of the music industry. Mind you, I had a regular job singing at the weekends. Then I met Marc Gordon, sometime in '69. He became my manager and recommended I sign with ABC, which I did."

Former Motown employee Marc Gordon not only got Thelma a deal with Dunhill Records (an imprint of ABC), he also brought in Jimmy Webb to produce **Sunshower**, a critically acclaimed outing that reflected well on both the producer and artist.

"ABC said it was going to be a hit. When it wasn't I was really disappointed."

Several other Dunhill singles followed, with the Laura Nyro penned *Save The Country* becoming a #74 pop hit in 1970, but the end of her time with ABC was approaching and Thelma was on the lookout for a new deal.

"ABC and I split on friendly terms and I told Marc that I wanted to go to Motown. But he didn't like the idea. It's not often that I make major decisions; when I do I've thought about the situation very carefully and weighed up the fors and against. I always wanted to go to Motown, even my instincts told me it was the place to go. So I did, and I never regretted it."

In 1970 therefore Thelma was signed by Motown and assigned to the MoWest label, although the promise suggested by her Dunhill debut was left unfulfilled during her time on MoWest. An eponymous album was issued as her label debut in July 1972 but lacked both a strong single or proper promotion from Motown, with several singles coming and falling by the wayside. In July 1973 Thelma was switched to the Motown label, with her second single for the label, *You've Been Doing Wrong For So Long* at least featuring on the R&B chart, peaking at #64 and no higher in the summer of 1974, although it did pick up a Grammy nomination for Best R&B Vocal Performance, Female.

A brief, almost cameo appearance in the Motown film 'Bingo Long', a brief spell as part of the cast for 'The Marty Feldman Comedy Machine' and performing backing vocals for Jermaine Jackson at least kept her working as her Motown career threatened to fizzle out. Indeed, her best chance of scoring a major hit was lined up as *Do You Know Where You're Going To* until the song was withdrawn and handed to Diana Ross for the theme to the film 'Mahogany'.

"We did it with just the basic background. It was never finished off properly and I guess was hidden away. Certainly it was never issued in the States. Then 'Mahogany' was in the works and Michael Masser was asked to write the score. He resurrected the song for the title track, and as Diana was the star of the movie, it was only natural she would sing it. I didn't feel denied. Let's put it this way; if I was the star of a movie, I wouldn't expect someone else to sing the credit. I'd want to do it myself."

Finally, having been knocking on the door of success for so long, the big break came in 1976 thanks to Hal Davis. Having heard Harold Melvin & The Bluenotes' *Don't Leave Me This Way*, Hal reasoned that a disco version, similar in style to the one he had fashioned with Diana Ross and *Love Hangover*, might prove to be the breakthrough single for Thelma. Once again, Hal's chart radar was on the button, with *Don't Leave Me This Way* topping both the R&B and pop charts for a week (in the UK it failed to reach the Top Ten, although its progress was hindered by CBS rush-releasing the Harold Melvin & The Bluenotes original that made #5) and going on to win Thelma the Grammy for Best R&B Vocal Performance, Female.

Whilst that would prove to be as good as her Motown career got, as least far as the charts were concerned, there were several other moments of vocal inspiration. *Don't Leave Me This Way*'s parent album **Anyway You Like It** would go on to become a #11 pop and #5 R&B hit, helped by a further minor hit in *If It's The Last Thing I Do*, a Tommy Dorsey revival that made #12 R&B and #47 pop, even though it had originally been recorded in 1973 and held back. Whilst her star was still rising, Thelma recorded the first of two albums of duets with Jerry Butler, with **Thelma & Jerry** hitting #53 pop and #20 R&B and the extracted *It's A Lifetime Thing* making #84 R&B (the second album, **Two To One** was issued in June 1978 and did little of note). *I'm Here Again*, the lead single from her **The Devil In Me** album from 1978 was a virtual note for note copy of *Don't Leave Me This Way* but lacked its predecessor's appeal, only registering on the R&B chart at #21.

There was to be a two year hiatus until Thelma returned to the charts, with *Saturday Night Sunday Morning* initially appearing on the **Ready To Roll** album (released in October 1978) and being added to **Ride To The Rainbow** the following May, soon after the single had reached its peak of #19 R&B and #34 pop, her last appearance on the chart for any of the Motown labels (her later repertoire appearing on the Tamla label, making Thelma one of the few artists to have had releases on as many as three label imprints). Thelma left Motown for RCA where she was briefly reunited with Jimmy Webb for **Breakwater Cat** in 1980. Subsequent releases on RCA, MCA and Reprise saw her working with luminaries such as Lenny Kravitz, Jimmy Jam & Terry Lewis, Glen Ballard and Dennis Lambert, among others, but her career never again visited the heights attained with *Don't Leave Me This Way*. Her rendition of *Don't Leave Me This Way* frequently appears in the upper echelons of any list of the greatest dance tracks of all time (and would make a return appearance in the UK Top 40 in 1995), although Thelma herself would later state that the disco backlash left her without an adequate fan base.

"I've been in this business for a while, and I do have other things in my catalogue. I can, and have, released other things and haven't followed a particular trend. So, no, it wasn't my intention to become involved in discos. I feel that in America particularly, you're only as good as your last hit record. Unless your name is kept in the public eye, people tend to forget."

ALBUMS: THELMA HOUSTON (1972), ANY WAY YOU LIKE (1976), THE DEVIL IN ME (1977); THELMA & JERRY (1977), TWO TO ONE (1978), READY TO ROLL (1978), RIDE TO THE RAINBOW (1979), SUNSHOWER (1981), REACHIN' ALL AROUND (1982)

HOW SWEET IT IS TO BE LOVED BY YOU – MARVIN GAYE [SINGLE]

American comedian Jackie Gleason's weekly television show unwittingly inspired Eddie Holland to come up with the basic idea for *How Sweet It Is*, with the title coming from a regularly repeated phrase on the show. According to Eddie, whilst the hook came quickly, the rest of the song took some considerable time, so much so that by the time Marvin Gaye was brought into the studio on 24 July 1964, he had not had time to fully memorise the song and had to sing whilst reading from lyric sheets during the course of the session.

If the recording session itself was somewhat hurried, the finished song is anything but and rightfully returned Marvin to the Top Ten, peaking at #6 pop and #4 R&B. Whilst the song is one of many most usually associated with Marvin Gaye, it has been recorded by a slew of artists over the years, including fellow Motown artist Junior Walker and James Taylor, both of whom enjoyed sizeable hits with their versions. Other artists to have covered the song include Cissy Houston, whose version appeared on a Grammy Award winning gospel album, The Isley Brothers and The Elgins.

ALAN HOWARTH

Sound designer and composer Alan Howarth was born in South River, New Jersey on 6 August 1948 and became best known for his frequent collaborations with film director John Carpenter. The pair worked together on the film 'Christine' in 1983, with both being credited on the track *Christine Attacks* that was featured on the soundtrack album released by Motown.

REUBEN HOWELL

Often wrongly credited as being the first white solo American artist to record for Motown, Reuben (born on 9 August 1945) did at least get to enjoy a lengthier Motown career than many of his predecessors. Reuben joined Motown in 1973 and would record two albums, from which a total of four singles were eventually lifted. Both **Reuben Howell** and **Rings** showed him to be one of the leading exponents of what had become known as blue eyed soul, although such was Motown's desire to hide his ethnicity, his debut album was released without his picture on the cover. Even those singles that were issued in picture sleeves clouded his image to the extent it would be almost impossible to guess he was a white singer.
Several of his recordings made an impact on the Northern Soul circuit, including *You Can't Stop A Man In Love,* although nothing made much of a dent on the charts. After his Motown career came to an end Reuben moved to Florida where he recorded an extensive number of tracks at the Playground Studios in Valparaiso. Reuben died from a massive heart attack on 5 January 2004 at the age of 59 years.
ALBUMS: REUBEN HOWELL (1973), RINGS (1974)

HOWL THE GOOD

Evolving out of Detroit group Distant Passage, Allan Odom (vocals), Ira 'Wiley' Pack (guitar and vocals), Neil Fayne (also known by his birth name Neil Faigenbaum, guitar, bass and vocals), Tom Schneider (keyboards and vocals) and Dennis Harrison (drums) found something of a benefactor in local builder Harry Weitzer. Inspired by Frijid Pink, another Detroit group that had enjoyed some success after recording in England, Distant Passage convinced Harry that British recording sessions were the way to success, and the group duly travelled to Olympic Studios in London, where they were teamed with producer Gary Wright. Gary had become something of a fixture on the British music scene (despite being born in America), recording with George Harrison, among others, and his abilities were a good fit for the folk-rock influenced Detroit group. Wright would play keyboards on their album and also came up with a new group name, with Howl The Good being something of a rough translation of Hywel Dda, a tenth century Welsh king. Howl The Good's eponymous album was released in April 1972, with the single *Long Way From Home* backed with *Why Do You Cry* issued at the same time. Despite positive reviews, neither sold sufficiently and the group appear to have disbanded shortly after.
ALBUM: HOWL THE GOOD (1972)

FREDDIE HUBBARD

One of jazz music's greatest horn players, Freddie Hubbard was already an acclaimed name by the time he signed with CTI. Born Frederick Dewayne Hubbard in Indianapolis, Indiana on 7 April 1938, Freddie made his name working with the Montgomery brothers, Wes, Buddy and Monk whilst still a teenager. After moving to New York in 1958 he played with many of the great names in jazz before making his debut album a couple of years later and then joining Art Blakey's Jazz Messengers. Freddie spent five years in the group before leaving to set up his own band as well as performing on countless sessions for the likes of Herbie Hancock, Ornette Coleman, John Coltrane, Oliver Nelson, Eric Dolphy and Wayne Shorter.
He signed with Blue Note during the decade, releasing some eight albums for the iconic label as a front man and appearing on nearly thirty as a sideman. He switched to CTI at the start of the 1970s, recording a series of highly acclaimed and well received albums that kept his name at the forefront of jazz, although several critics would claim his later CTI albums were

something of a sell out. Despite this he continued to enjoy commercial success, with the compilations **The Baddest Hubbard** (#127 pop, #16 R&B and #9 jazz) and **Polar AC** (#167 pop, #32 R&B and #11 jazz) crossing over on several charts. His collaborations with Stanley Turrentine also enjoyed chart action, albeit on the jazz charts (**In Concert** hit #12, the second volume reached #28), confirming Freddie's status as a bona fide jazz star. After recording extensively for Columbia he began hopping from label to label from 1980 onwards, releasing his final album on Time Square Records shortly before his death on 29 December 2008 after suffering a heart attack.

ALBUMS: FREDDIE HUBBARD & STANLEY TURRENTINE IN CONCERT VOLUME ONE (1974), THE BADDEST HUBBARD (1974), POLAR AC (1975), IN CONCERT VOLUME TWO (1975)

FRED HUGHES

Although born in Arkansas Fred Hughes moved to Compton, California where he attended Compton High School during the day and sang with The Cymbals at night. It was as a member of the group he made his first recordings, later working with The Creators, but he made a bigger impact as a solo performer. Signed by Vee-Jay Records he scored a major hit with *Oo Wee Baby, I Love You* in 1965, hitting #3 R&B and #23 pop and registering a further hit, but the label's subsequent demise brought his career to a temporary halt. *Oo Wee Baby* was featured on the CD compilation **Hits From The Legendary Vee-Jay Records** released by Motown in November 1986.

LANGSTON HUGHES & MARGARET DANNER

Writer James Mercer Langston Hughes was born in Joplin, Missouri on 1 February 1902 and became known as one of the earliest proponents of jazz poetry. Raised by his maternal grandmother, Langston wrote his signature poem 'The Negro Speaks Of Rivers' in 1920 and had his first poetry collection book, 'The Weary Blues' published in 1925. He would later write novels and short stories, but it is for his poetry, always espousing racial consciousness, that he is best remembered.

Margaret Esse Danner was born in Pryosburg, Kentucky on 12 January 1915 and began writing poetry whilst still in junior high school. After attending Loyola University, Northwestern University and Roosevelt College, Margaret became assistant editor of the 'Poetry: A Magazine Of Verse, assuming this role in 1951. By then Margaret had begun a correspondence with Langston Hughes, a relationship that would endure for the rest of his life.

In 1963 the pair were recorded discussing and reading their poetry, although the recordings were initially shelved. Seven years later they were dusted off and released as **Writers Of The Revolution**, the first release on Motown's Black Forum label. Langston Hughes died on 22 May 1967 whilst Margaret Danner died in Chicago on 1 January 1984.

ALBUM: WRITERS OF THE REVOLUTION (1970)

IVY JO HUNTER

Ivy Jo Hunter is one of several unsung heroes of Motown, a noted songwriter who warranted just three brief mentions in Berry Gordy's autobiography, all of which misspelt his name! A very private man, both during his Motown heyday and after, Ivy Jo was born George Ivy Hunter on 28 August 1940 and raised in Detroit, Michigan, showing a musical aptitude at an early age and going on to play with the Detroit Symphony and Detroit City Orchestra.

Although he was equally adept on the trumpet, euphonium and keyboards, he studied economics at Cass Technical High School, even though his musical abilities were such he wrote his first song at the age of 15, his composition helping local group The Velveteers win a talent contest. After graduating from high school he joined the army, returning to Detroit after his discharge looking for work. He first turned to singing, performing at the 20 Grand and then Phelp's Lounge, where he was spotted by Hank Cosby, who suggested Ivy Jo make his way to Hitsville and audition for Mickey Stevenson.

Impressed as he was with Ivy Jo's singing, Mickey thought he had more potential as a songwriter and producer and got him a deal with Motown in 1962. Mickey and Ivy Jo would co-write many songs together, most notably *Dancing In The Street* for Martha & The Vandellas, but the emergence of Holland-Dozier-Holland as the chief songwriters at Hitsville meant that much of Mickey and Ivy Jo's work was overlooked.

Matters weren't helped when Mickey Stevenson left Motwn in 1966, with Ivy Jo falling further in the pecking order. He did manage to record several tracks during the course of his eight years or so with the company, although only two singles were ever released, *I Remember You (Dedicated To Beverly)* backed with *Sorry Is A Sorry Word* on V.I.P. in March 1970 and *I'd Still Love You* backed with *I Can Feel The Pain* the following May. These were released at a time when Ivy Jo was in dispute with Motown, his request for a bonus having been turned down and resulting in him being considered a disruptive element by the company.

A planned album, **Ivy Jo Is In This Bag** was never released and, for a time, neither was Ivy Jo himself, as Raynoma revealed in her autobiography. "Having never recovered from being pegged as a troublemaker, Ivy was cut off from projects as punishment. He asked to be released from his contract, but the company refused, giving him nothing to do but walk the halls of the Donovan Building. Double indemnity. When the release (his second single) was finally issued, Ivy left in bitterness."

He found work elsewhere for many a year, playing keyboards on Funkadelic's *Mommy, What's A Funkadelic* and producing former Dramatics' lead singer Wee Gee's album. By the end of the 1980s he was working with Ian Levine and his Motorcity project, co-writing Frances Nero's hit *Footsteps Keep Following Me*.

JOE HUNTER

Motown's first pianist, Joseph Edward Hunter was born in Jackson, Tennessee on 19 November 1927 and moved with his family to Detroit shortly before his twelfth birthday. It was thanks to his mother that he learned to play the piano, watching her giving lessons in the family home and naturally taking to the instrument. Joe played in a number of bands whilst serving in the army, including bands that featured drummer Elvin Jones and another future Motown pianist in Earl Van Dyke.

After his discharge, Joe returned to Detroit and became a mainstay in the local music scene, performing in clubs during the week and in church on Sunday. In 1956 he began playing with Hank Ballard & The Midnighters, but it was after being spotted playing at Little Sam's club in 1958 that he came to the attention of Berry Gordy. Berry asked him to join his set-up as pianist, with Joe going on to perform on early Motown hits by Marv Johnson (*Come To Me*) and Barrett Strong (*Money*).

At this time, however, Motown was not able to offer him full time work, so Joe accepted an invitation to go out on the road with Jackie Wilson, appearing on later Motown singles whenever he happened to be in Detroit long enough to make it down to Hitsville. These sessions included The Contours' *Do You Love Me* and Martha & The Vandellas' *Heat Wave*, his involvement sufficient to garner him a place in the Funk Brothers roll of honour.

Joe left Motown to become a freelance pianist in late 1963, going on to work with Jimmy Ruffin, Junior Parker, Edwin Starr and several other artists on Golden World and Fortune Records. Joe was still working as a full time musician in and around Detroit at the time of his death on 2 February 2007 at the age of 79.

WILLIE HUTCH

Born Willie McKinley Hutchinson in Los Angeles, California on 6 December 1944 Willie was raised in Dallas, Texas and began singing whilst in his teens as a member of The Ambassadors. He also began writing at an early age, penning his debut single in 1964, *Love Has Put Me Down* which was issued on the Soul City label. Thus it was this talent that earned him his first break in the industry, going on to write and co-produce several tracks on Fifth Dimension's 1967 album **Up Up And Away**.

Three years later he took a late night call from Hal Davis, who was busy in the recording studio working on a song for The Jackson 5. Hal had a title which Berry Gordy liked and a few musical ideas but no lyrics, something Willie excelled in. After working all night on the song, Hal and Willie presented the finished music to Berry Gordy at 8.00am the next morning. Suitably impressed, Berry had The Jackson 5 record the song that same day, with *I'll Be There* going on to become both the group and Motown's biggest selling single of the time.

Berry was also to sign Willie Hutch to a more permanent deal, giving the writer and producer the opportunity to work with the likes of Smokey Robinson, Marvin Gaye, Diana Ross, Junior Walker and The Four Tops as well as further recordings with Michael Jackson and The Jackson 5. Having released his debut album in 1969 (**Soul Portrait** was issued by RCA, followed by **Seasons For Love** the following year) Willie was also keen to pursue his own recording career, something Motown were more than happy to accommodate.

His first Motown outing came with the soundtrack to the blaxploitation film 'The Mack' in 1973, with the album making #114 pop and #17 on the R&B charts. Two singles also charted, *Brothers Gonna Work It Out* (#67 pop, #18 R&B) and *Slick* (#65 pop and again a #18 placing R&B). The success of **The Mack** would see

Willie asked to score another film in 'Foxy Brown', which although more successful at the box office didn't do quite as well on the charts. Whilst none of Willie's albums exactly set the stores alight, he was a steady seller, with all eight of his albums making at least the R&B album chart, with **Concert In Blues** in 1976 reaching #22 R&B and #163 pop. On the singles chart, Willie was to register a Top Ten R&B hit with *Love Power* in 1975 (#8 and also making #41 on the pop chart) from an impressive tally of twelve hits between 1973 and 1978.

After **Havin' A House Party** was issued in May 1977 (#26 on the R&B chart), Willie left Motown for a brief sojourn at Norman Whitfield's label. He returned to Motown in 1982 having released two further albums, **In Tune** and **Midnight Dancer** during his time on Whitfield Records. Whilst his return to Motown was not as successful as his earlier career, he was still an important member of the recording roster, including penning a number of tracks for the soundtrack to 'The Last Dragon'. He also continued with outside writing and production work, most notably for Aretha Franklin and G.C. Cameron and got to feature on the UK singles chart, with *In And Out* making #51 in 1982 and *Keep On Jammin'* #73 in 1985.

Willie left Motown for good at the end of the decade, eventually relocating back to Dallas, and whilst his own recordings were somewhat sporadic, his name would frequently appear on the charts as his music was invariably sampled by modern rappers and dance acts and old tracks were reused in modern films. He died on 19 September 2005, survived by his six children.

ALBUMS: THE MACK (1973), FULLY EXPOSED (1973), FOXY BROWN (1974), MARK OF THE BEAST (1974), ODE TO MY LADY (1975), CONCERT IN BLUES (1976), COLOR HER SUNSHINE (1976), HAVIN' A HOUSE PARTY (1977), IN AND OUT (1983), MAKING A GAME OUT OF LOVE (1985)

SHEILA HUTCHINSON

Born in Chicago, Illinois on 17 January 1953, Sheila was a member of The Emotions with her sisters Wanda and Jeanette, enjoying considerable success on Stax and then Columbia during the 1970s. They signed with Motown in 1985, with Sheila also guesting on *Feels Good To Feel Good* by Garry Glenn, a #37 R&B hit in 1987. Sheila is still a member of The Emotions, performing today with sisters Wanda and Pamela.

I

I AIN'T GONNA STAND FOR IT - STEVIE WONDER [SINGLE]

One of the few excursions into almost country territory for Stevie Wonder, *I Ain't Gonna Stand For It* first appeared on the **Hotter Than July** album. Whilst not the most obvious choice as a single, it made perfect sense after the reggae influenced *Master Blaster*, offering proof of the sheer diversity of Stevie's material. Featuring Ben Bridges on pedal steel guitar and Charlie and Ronnie Wilson from The Gap Band on backing vocals, the single was released in December 1980, going on to reach #10 in the UK and only just lower in the US, where it would peak at #11 pop and #4 R&B. In 2001 the song attracted a cover version by none other than Eric Clapton for his album **Reptile**. This version was also released as a single but failed to chart, although the parent album made the Top Ten on both sides of the Atlantic.

I CAN'T GET NEXT TO YOU – THE TEMPTATIONS [SINGLE]

Psychedelic soul had served The Temptations well and made them consistent chartmakers, but fortunately Norman Whitfield knew when to change the musical style, abandoning the social commentary that had dominated their material for the previous eighteen months in favour of a love song for *I Can't Get Next To You*. Still, typical of Norman is was not your usual type of love song, but rather one of the funkiest declarations of undying love ever committed to vinyl. The lyrics were written by Barrett Strong, but it was the arrangement and in particular the vocals that made the song so irrepressible, with each of the five Temptations (Dennis Edwards, Melvin Franklin, Eddie Kendricks, Paul Williams and Otis Williams) being given the opportunity to shine.

A sure-fire smash, *I Can't Get Next To You* topped both the R&B and pop charts, The Temptations first time at the pop summit since *My Girl* some four years previously. The single would also reach #13 in the UK, whilst the song would be revisited by Al Green (who took it to #11 R&B chart in 1971), Annie Lennox and even Westlife over the ensuing years.

I CAN'T HELP MYSELF – THE FOUR TOPS [SINGLE]

Holland-Dozier-Holland had given The Four Tops their breakthrough hit in *Baby I Need Your Loving* in 1964 but had then been side-tracked into turning the previously 'no hit Supremes' into a hit act in their own right. Meanwhile, others assigned to The Four Tops hadn't managed to step up to the same plate, with the result The Four Tops were back looking for a hit too. Just as HDH had done with The Supremes, they looked at material they had written previously for inspiration, with Lamont Dozier taking the harmonics and chord structure to *Where Did Our Love Go* to create *I Can't Help Myself*. As they would with most of their songs, the backing music was created, recorded and polished before the lyrics were completed. Lamont however did have one phrase he wanted to work into the song, 'Sugar Pie Honey Bunch', which apparently was the standard greeting his grandfather gave visitors to his wife's beauty parlour.

With the phrase, *I Can't Help Myself* becomes more than just a perfectly compelling piece of music, rising as a standard bearer for much of HDH's work for the next three years. The Four Tops, whose contribution to the song should not be overlooked, were about to take their place at Motown's top table, hitting as they did the top of both the pop and R&B charts in 1965, for two weeks and nine weeks respectively. In the UK the single became their chart debut, hitting #23, but bettered this by a long way five years later when it was reissued and hit #10. That the song is another of HDH's classics can be gauged by the fact that Donnie Elbert, who had a brief chart career mainly covering HDH material, took the song to #11 in the UK in 1972.

I HEAR A SYMPHONY – THE SUPREMES [SINGLE]

After five consecutive number one hits, The Supremes had suffered something of a blip when *Nothing But Heartaches* had failed to get any higher than #11 on the pop charts. According to legend, Berry Gordy had responded to this disappointment with an internal memo to all staff at Hitsville, 'We will release nothing less than Top Ten product on any artist, and because The Supremes' worldwide acceptance is greater than the other artists, on them we will only release number one records.'

The challenge, therefore, was for HDH to return The Supremes to what was seen as their rightful place on the chart; at the very top. The earlier success had been achieved with catchy pop songs, with the writing and production team vowing to amend the sound for *I Hear A Symphony*. The result, which Mary Wilson would claim was one of the group's own favourites among their superlative portfolio, was a grand and complex number that still contained almost instant appeal.

The use of something of a classical theme was not new, indeed at much the same time as *I Hear A Symphony* was released, The Toys' had issued *A Lover's Concerto*, a single that bore a more than passing resemblance to The Supremes' single. The final result was that The Supremes won the race to the top of the chart, hitting #1 for two weeks and making #2 on the R&B chart (Berry's memo was entirely concerned with success on the pop chart, with R&B acceptance considered something of a bonus). In the UK the single had to settle for a much more modest #39 chart placing. The song has attracted several cover versions, including Stevie Wonder in 1966, The Jackson 5 in 1970 and even a jazz-funk version by Hank Crawford, the title cut to his 1975 Kudu album.

I HEAR A SYMPHONY – THE SUPREMES [ALBUM]

The Supremes enjoyed a truly remarkable year in 1964, with three number one hit singles and continued that success into the following year, stretching their unbroken run of chart toppers to five. Motown was quick to capitalise on this success, getting the girls recording all manner of material, designed to appeal to different sectors of the recording buying public. There were tribute albums to The Beatles and Gerry & The Pacemakers (**A Bit Of Liverpool**, released in Britain as **From Us To You**), country and western music (**The Supremes Sing Country And Western And Pop**) and Sam Cooke (**We Remember Sam Cooke**), with some of the repertoire duly finding its way into the group's live repertoire.

Also to be found on those live shows were assorted standards and cover versions, prompting Motown to consider having The Supremes record an entire album of standards, which was to be called **There's A Place For Us**. The album was recorded but subsequently shelved, the company opting instead to utilise some of the recordings (which included *Stranger In Paradise, With A Song In My Heart, Wonderful Wonderful* and *Without A Song*) and mix them cover versions of then current hits in *Yesterday* (The Beatles, with The

Supremes version being produced by Norman Whitfield), *A Lover's Concerto* (The Toys) and *Unchained Melody* (The Righteous Brothers). Rounding out the album were four Holland-Dozier-Holland compositions, including the eventual hits *I Hear A Symphony* and *My World Is Empty Without You*. The album was released in February 1966 and became a major hit in the US, peaking at #8 on the pop chart and topping the R&B listings.

I HEARD IT THROUGH THE GRAPEVINE – GLADYS KNIGHT & THE PIPS [SINGLE]

If the only version of *I Heard It Through Grapevine* that had made the charts had been by either Gladys Knight & The Pips or Marvin Gaye, it would still be regarded as one of the greatest songs in the Motown catalogue. The fact that both artists scored million selling hits with it, barely a year apart, and both earned Grammy nominations is further proof of its stature. The background story to Marvin Gaye's version can be found elsewhere, but it was to be Gladys Knight & The Pips who scored a major hit with it first time around.

The basic idea for the lyrics came to Barrett Strong whilst he was walking down a street in Chicago; he had heard people use the grapevine phrase on numerous occasions, but no one had written a song about it. So he got with Norman Whitfield and together they wrote *I Heard It Through The Grapevine*, supposedly the first song the pair ever collaborated on.

According to folklore, the song was offered to The Isley Brothers, who turned it down, and it was subsequently recorded by Smokey Robinson and The Miracles. This version was seemingly played at one of the weekly Quality Control Meetings and rejected, with Berry Gordy supposedly remarking that it was one of the worst songs he had ever heard (a version by Smokey and The Miracles appears on their 1968 album **Special Occasion**, although it is believed that this version is in fact a re-recording).

Undeterred, Norman worked out another arrangement that was intended for The Temptations, although at the last moment Marvin Gaye was brought into the studio to do the vocal (The Temptations did get to record the song, their version, which was closer in style to The Pips version appearing on **Cloud Nine** released in March 1969). Marvin's version was also presented to the Quality Control Meeting and Berry Gordy's opinion of the song had not changed one iota; the recording went back onto the shelf.

If there was one quality that Norman Whitfield possessed, however, it was persistency, and so he would have a further go at getting the song out to the market. This time he targeted Gladys Knight and The Pips, playing them the basic backing tracks, handing them the lyrics and giving them a rough idea of how he envisaged the third version of the song would sound, which was something along the lines of Aretha Franklin's *R.E.S.P.E.C.T*. Whilst Gladys would later state that she and her fellow group members initially felt somewhat slighted by being given a hand me down track, they were impressed enough with the basic qualities to get together regularly over the next couple of weeks working out an arrangement that worked for both the song and the group, as Edward Patten would later explain.

"We took it home, worked hard to give it a new treatment and Norman hardly had to do anything. That one wasn't nothing until we took it."

They returned to Detroit in June 1967 and sang their new arrangement to Norman, who was that excited he opted to record it there and then. Ejecting a bemused Smokey Robinson from the Hitsville studio, Norman and The Pips recorded much of the track that very day, with Norman returning a couple of days later for some additional overdubs. When presented to the Quality Control Meeting, there were no dissenting voices, with *I Heard It Through The Grapevine* being released on the Soul label in September 1967.

Despite criticism from Gladys that Motown put little promotional support behind the single, it would still soar up the chart, topping the R&B chart for six weeks and peak at #2 on the pop chart, held off the top by The Monkees and *Daydream Believer*. Since the single went on to become the best selling released by Motown up to that point, it is doubtful that the company held back on its promotion.

Berry Gordy must have relented quite considerably as far as the song itself was concerned, for it would also be recorded by Bobby Taylor & The Vancouvers (it appears on their eponymous album released in September 1968), Rustix (it's on their **Bedlam** album released August 1969), Sounds Nice (this of course was an album bought in from EMI in the UK and appears on the **Love At First Sight** album released September 1970), The Undisputed Truth (it's on their eponymous album released July 1971), Rare Earth (it's on **Grand Slam** released September 1978) and Bettye Lavette (it's on her **Tell A Lie** album released in 1982).

I Heard It Through The Grapevine had a significant effect on Gladys Knight and The Pips too, elevating them briefly into the top rank of Motown artists and earning the group a Grammy nomination for Best R&B Vocal Performance, Female (ironically losing out to

Aretha Franklin's *R.E.S.P.E.C.T.*). Had matters regarding the song come to rest there and then, it is likely that the group's Motown career would have turned out somewhat differently, with them being offered first call on material rather than relying on songs that other artists turned down. As it was, Norman Whitfield's persistence, most particularly concerning the version by Marvin Gaye that still sat in the can at Hitsville, ensured Gladys and The Pips had barely a year to enjoy their new found prestige at Motown.

I HEARD IT THROUGH THE GRAPEVINE – MARVIN GAYE [SINGLE]

Gladys Knight & The Pips' version of *I Heard It Through The Grapevine* had proved to Berry Gordy and the rest of Motown that the song could be a major hit, but co-writer and producer Norman Whitfield was still convinced that a better, if not definitive version of the song sat in the Motown vaults gathering dust; he was determined to get it out on the market.

As noted earlier, Marvin Gaye's version, which was deliberately styled to give it a Ray Charles-inspired feel, was recorded after Smokey Robinson & The Miracles' version. The original musical backing tracks were intended for The Temptations but subsequently used on Marvin's version, with the vocals being recorded in February 1967 and strings and horns added two months later. The final version was duly played at a Quality Control meeting and rejected as a single the first time around in preference to *Your Unchanging Love*.

According to many, the difference in sound that Norman had achieved on Marvin Gaye's version counted against releasing it as a single; Motown's policy at these Quality Control meetings was to play the top five records on the Billboard chart, with *I Heard It Through The Grapevine* being considered such a stylistic departure from what was selling at the time no one (apart from Norman) could see it making much of an impression. When Gladys Knight & The Pips scored the then biggest hit of their career with it in 1967, the song itself was at least vindicated.

In the summer of 1968 Motown was busy assembling the latest Marvin Gaye album for release on Tamla and found themselves a track or two short of the required twelve to complete the listing for **In The Groove**. Norman convinced Billie Jean Brown to use *I Heard It Through The Grapevine*, with the track appearing as the fourth track on side one of an album released to the market in August 1968.

Soon after promotional copies (along with the single *Chained*) had been sent to DJs around the country, Motown marketing executive Phil Jones received an urgent telephone call from E Rodney Jones (no relation) of Chicago's WVON, who had played *Grapevine* at a live date and then on air and noticed an extraordinary public reaction to the track. Phil Jones duly sought out Billie Jean Brown to pass on the information, and whilst Billie Jean still felt that the company had effectively scraped the bottom of the vaults to get the track on the album, agreed to present it once again to Quality Control for consideration as a single.

This time around, the song had a successful track record thanks to Gladys Knight & The Pips and Marvin's version was already creating something of a stir; it was agreed to release it as a single in November 1968, although even Marvin shared some of the hesitancy about the track.

"I never thought a great deal about the song after recording it. In fact, I wasn't too optimistic about it at all. I had no idea it would be released and sell nearly four million copies."

Despite being nearly two years old and in the minds of record buyers a cover version of Gladys Knight & The Pips recent hit, Marvin Gaye's version of *I Heard It Through The Grapevine* proved irresistible, hitting the top of the pop and R&B chart in December 1968 (it knocked The Supremes' *Love Child* off the summit of the pop chart) and remained there for seven straight weeks. Not only was it the biggest hit of Marvin's career up to that point, it was the best selling Motown single of the time, racking up more than four million sales.

The single also repeated its success in the UK, being released in February 1969 and topping the chart for three weeks. Flush with this success, **In The Groove** was duly repackaged as **I Heard It Through The Grapevine** and would become a #2 R&B hit. Just as Gladys Knight & The Pips version had done a year earlier, Marvin's rendition garnered a Grammy Award nomination for Best R&B Vocal Performance, Male (along with label mate Stevie Wonder and *For Once In My Life*, Marvin lost out to Otis Redding and *Sittin' On The Dock Of The Bay*). Long considered one of the best Motown singles of all time, Marvin's version of *I Heard It Through The Grapevine* was reissued in the UK in 1986 following use in the Levi Jeans commercial and returned to the Top Ten, peaking at #8 (it had previously provided post-punk female group The Slits with a minor hit, peaking at #60 in 1979).

In the US, where the song has been covered by artists as diverse as Creedence Clearwater Revival, Roger Troutman (who topped the R&B charts in 1981, making *I Heard It Through The Grapevine* the only song to have topped the chart by three different artists) and Trini Lopez, the most bizarre cover version and hit was registered by The California Raisins, a clay-animated singing group with lead vocals by Buddy Miles whose rendition first appeared on a television commercial on behalf of the California Raisin Advisory Board and made #84 in 1988.

I JUST CALLED TO SAY I LOVE YOU – STEVIE WONDER [SINGLE]

Perhaps fearful that Stevie Wonder's latest film venture might develop into another sales disaster, Motown's Jay Lasker initially refused to release the soundtrack to 'The Woman In Red'. He eventually relented when Stevie played him another song he intended adding to the album, *I Just Called To Say I Love You*, probably the most commercial track he had ever written.

The melody itself was written several years before the lyrics, with the song being completed for the 1984 film and soundtrack release. Issued as a single, it became the biggest hit of Stevie's career, selling over four million copies worldwide, including 1.75 million in the UK, where it would become Stevie's only solo number one hit, eighteen years after making his chart debut. The record sold a little more than half that figure in the US but still managed to top both the pop and R&B charts, his first number one on the former since *Sir Duke* in 1977 and the latter since *That Girl* in 1982.

The chart success resulted in both the singer and the song collecting a slew of nominations, including Grammy's for Song of the Year, Best Pop Vocal Performance and Best Pop Instrumental Performance (none of which were won), and the Golden Globe and Academy Awards for Best Original Song (both of which were). There was some controversy at the Academy Awards presentation, with Stevie dedicating the award to the then imprisoned Nelson Mandela, with the result Stevie's music was banned from the air in South Africa!

A year after release, Lee Garrett and Lloyd Chiate launched a lawsuit claiming Stevie's song infringed upon one they had written in 1978 called *I Just Called To Say*. Lee Garrett was well known to Stevie, having co-authored several hits for both Stevie and other artists, including *Signed Sealed Delivered*, *Let's Get Serious* and *It's A Shame*. In May 1986 Lee withdrew from the $10 million lawsuit, acknowledging at the time that there had been no infringement and that the only thing the two songs shared was much the same title (Stevie and Lee would manage to repair their personal relationship in the wake of the withdrawal). Chiate continued with the lawsuit and ultimately lost the claim, which was subsequently upheld by a San Francisco appeals court in 1992.

Stevie's assertion that he himself had written the melody several years prior to 1984 caused him some problems with the Motion Picture Academy, whose rules and regulations for songs nominated for consideration stated that the song be written specially for the film. Although the Academy considered at one point withdrawing the Oscar because of the claim, Stevie's eventual success in winning the lawsuit ensured he got to keep both the Oscar and Golden Globe.

I JUST WANT TO CELEBRATE – RARE EARTH [SINGLE]

By the time Rare Earth came to record their third album for Motown, the group had settled on a new line-up, one that would look to maintain the momentum established by **Get Ready** and **Ecology** and the singles *Get Ready* and *(I Know) I'm Losing You*. Whilst major singles success had come with rock interpretations of classic Motown songs, **Ecology** had given notice of a new potential stream of success; Tom Baird's songwriting and production on *Born To Wander* had seen the group score a third major hit, even though its final chart placing of #17 pop and #48 R&B had been less than either of its predecessors.

The new line-up were keen to feature more of their own compositions on **One World** and were also working with Tony Clarke, best known for his work with The Moody Blues and having also helmed The Four Tops' hit *It's All In The Game*. Unfortunately, the sessions with Tony Clarke didn't work out quite as everyone had hoped, resulting in Tom Baird being brought in take over production duties. By the time the sessions were all but wrapped up, Tom realised that there wasn't a standout track for potential single release. Having worked closely with Motown staff writers Dino Fekaris and Nick Zesses, Tom felt a song the pair had recently written entitled *I Just Want To Celebrate* might prove the ideal vehicle for Rare Earth. They were less than enamoured with either the suggestion or the track but eventually relented, recording it in less than a week in May 1971.

Duly released as a single, *I Just Want To Celebrate* would become something of an anthem for Rare Earth, hitting #7 pop (it was to be their final Top Ten pop hit) and #30 R&B. In the UK the single was flipped, with the Pete Rivera composition *The Seed* promoted as the top side and *Celebrate* as the B side; neither track made an impression. Helped by the success of the single, **One World** would make #28 on Billboard Top 200, the last Top 30 album the group was to enjoy.

(I KNOW) I'M LOSING YOU – THE TEMPTATIONS [SINGLE]

The Temptations' musical director and guitarist Cornelius Grant was fooling around in the studio with touring bass player Bill Upchurch when producer Norman Whitfield stopped by. Intrigued by what he had heard, Norman had the pair play the short riff over and over, encouraging Cornelius to add some chords as he went along. Norman soon heard what he wanted to hear and quickly raced off to the studio, utilising Cornelius on guitar, James Jamerson on bass, Earl Van Dyke on piano and percussionists Eddie 'Bongo' Brown and Jack Ashford. Once the music was completed, Norman brought Eddie Holland in to write the lyrics, which were duly written in short order.

Originally titled *You Got My Soul* and then *I Don't Wanna Lose You*, the song was recorded by The Temptations on 16 September 1966, with David Ruffin on lead vocals and eventually given the title *(I Know) I'm Losing You*. From its distinctive guitar opening, *(I Know) I'm Losing You* sounded like a sure-fire hit, yet when Norman presented it to the Quality Control meeting, Berry Gordy turned down its release. This was neither the first nor the last time Berry Gordy failed to share Norman Whitfield's vision, although this was undoubtedly one of the most serious rifts between the pair; Norman went so far as to state that if Motown did not release *(I Know) I'm Losing You*, he would not record another note for the company. Faced with losing one of his most creative producers or losing face, Gordy opted for the latter and the single was duly released in November 1966. An R&B chart topper for four weeks (it was the group's fourth straight R&B #1, all within the year, an unprecedented feat), the single would also make #8 on the pop chart and return the group to the Top 20 in the UK, peaking at #19 in January 1967.

(I KNOW) I'M LOSING YOU – RARE EARTH [SINGLE]

Rare Earth had scored something of a surprise hit with their version of *Get Ready*, stretching the track out to over twenty minutes for the album version and scoring on the pop charts with a heavily edited single version. Their debut album had been self-produced and relatively successful, but Motown felt that an older, more experienced hand in the studio might be the difference between a minor hit and a major hit. When work began on their second album **Ecology**, therefore, Tom Baird was put in charge of the project. As the album neared completion, Motown began to have second thoughts, especially over whether anything might be worthy of release as a single.

Thus Norman Whitfield was brought in to oversee the recording of *(I Know) I'm Losing You*, previously a major hit on The Temptations and a song that Rare Earth already performed on their live list. When Norman heard the initial Rare Earth version, he felt it was too close to The Temptations version to warrant inclusion (the similarity between the two versions was quite deliberate), so in the studio he encouraged the group to try different things. He was the master at taking one song and producing a completely different feel for it time and again, something he had already proved with *I Heard It Through The Grapevine*.

A lengthy session ensued, with Norman bringing one instrument after another to the fore, finishing with some 45 minutes of music on tape. An initial edit brought the finished album version down to nearly eleven minutes, whilst a single edit of 3.36 that captured all of the key elements of the recording was readied for release in July 1970. Once again, Norman Whitfield proved his worth; the Rare Earth version actually performed better on the pop charts than the original, hitting #7, one place higher than The Temptations version four years previously. The single also repeated Rare Earth's success on the R&B chart, similarly peaking at #20. Following the success of the single the **Ecology** album performed well, making #15 pop and #4 R&B.

I SECOND THAT EMOTION – SMOKEY ROBINSON & THE MIRACLES [SINGLE]

In December 1966 Smokey Robinson and Al Cleveland went early Christmas shopping at Hudson's department store in Detroit, with Smokey looking to buy something special for his wife Claudette, who had recently suffered the death of prematurely born twins. The pair stopped at the jewellery counter, with Smokey picking out some pearls that he and the saleslady admired. When Smokey expressed his hope that Claudette might like them too, Al went to say 'I second that motion' but got the last word wrong, thus giving Smokey the title inspiration.

After making their way out of the store, Smokey and Al hurried over to Hitsville to complete the song, which was finished later the same day. Despite coming up with the idea and the song inside a day, the track wasn't recorded until the following September, being recorded at Hitsville over the course of two days. The finished version was slightly longer than that which was released, Berry Gordy insisting in the removal of a whole verse to make the song much sharper (much to Smokey's disappointment!). Rightly considered one of Smokey's finest compositions, *I Second That Emotion* was released in October 1967 and would return The Miracles to the Top Ten of the charts for the first time since 1963, eventually hitting #4 on the pop chart and topping the R&B chart (it knocked Gladys Knight & The Pips' *I Heard It Through The Grapevine* off the summit).

In the UK it could only make #27; the true worth of the song was revealed in 1969 when Diana Ross, The Supremes and The Temptations hit #18 and 1982 when British synth group Japan took a cover version to #9. Seven years later Alyson Williams and Chuck Stanley revived it once again and reached #44 on the UK chart.

I WANT YOU – MARVIN GAYE [ALBUM]

After the worldwide success of **Let's Get It On**, Marvin Gaye again hit a creative wall, unable to come up with material or even a concept that would continue his musical renaissance. Meanwhile singer, writer and producer Leon Ware was working on his second album (although his first for Motown, since his eponymous album had been released on United Artists in 1972), writing material with Arthur 'T-Boy' Ross, the brother of Diana Ross. The pair had already scored a major hit in 1972 with *I Wanna Be Where You Are*, which Michael Jackson had taken into the Top 20 of the pop chart and #2 R&B, thus establishing their credentials as writers. Somewhere along the way, Leon and T-Boy played the demos of the material they had written to Berry Gordy, who was mightily impressed.

So impressed, in fact, he suggested that they offer the songs to Marvin Gaye for him to record! Whilst this would mean Leon would have to start his album from scratch, the opportunity of not only writing for Marvin but also producing him was too good to turn down. Marvin was equally impressed with the demos that were played and, creative juices flowing once again, would co-write four tracks with Leon. One of these, *Soon I'll Be Loving You Again* was also co-written by T-Boy Ross, but during the recording session for the song, T-Boy gave too many instructions as to how *he* envisaged the song that he was effectively fired from the project, leaving Marvin and Leon to craft **I Want You** between them.

Recorded and mixed at Marvin's own studio on Sunset Boulevard throughout 1975, **I Want You** represented something of a stylistic departure for Marvin, incorporating a light disco style whilst still exploring the sexual themes that were evident on **Let's Get It On**. The album artwork was equally striking, featuring an adaptation of Ernie Barnes' painting 'The Sugar Shack'. When Marvin first approached Barnes with a view to utilising the painting on the album cover, Ernie offered to make it more personalised, adding several individual song titles to banners that hung from the rafters.

The album was released in March 1976, followed two weeks later by the title track being issued as a single. Whilst the single topped the R&B charts, it halted at #15 on the pop chart, although it would later garner a Grammy Award nomination for Best R&B Vocal Performance, Male (Marvin again lost out to Lou Rawls). The album however proved rather more resilient, topping the R&B chart and peaking at #4 on the pop chart as well as making #22 in the UK. The album sold in excess of a million copies in the US, a rather modest tally compared with his two previous albums, and received a mixed reception from the media, but in the years since release, **I Want You** has become regarded as both influential and crucial.

I WANT YOU BACK – JACKSON 5 [SINGLE]

When Deke Richards, Fonce Mizell and Freddie Perren first began writing together, their intention was to get their songs to Glady Knight & The Pips, an act they believed to be out in the cold at Motown and thus requiring a major hit. Those early sessions resulted in a song that went by the name of *I Wanna Be Free*, but when Berry Gordy first heard the backing track, he reasoned that it might prove to be a better vehicle for a new group he had signed to the label, The Jackson 5. Turning *I Wanna Be Free* into *I Want You Back* wasn't just a case of changing the gender from female to male; the song underwent a major overhaul, with Berry also insisting that the finished sound should invoke memories of Frankie Lymon & The Teenagers. The main story thread to the song changed too, with the end result being a song where the narrator (Michael Jackson) decides he has been too hasty in ditching his partner and deciding 'I want you back'. The fact that the lead singer wasn't even a teenager (even if Michael was two years older than Motown claimed him to be) didn't appear to matter.

Largely recorded in Los Angeles (the original music was certainly recorded at Dave Hassinger's Sound Factory, although there is still some ongoing debate over whether James Jamerson appeared on the final version or not and whether he recorded his part in Detroit or out west), the final version was played to Berry Gordy for approval. He was more than happy with the record, the group had been rehearsed to perfection and the back story, whereby Diana Ross was given a large part of the credit for bringing the young group to Motown's attention, was firmly in place; little or nothing could now stop *I Want You Back* marching up the charts.

With songwriting and production credit given to The Corporation, *I Want You Back* by The Jackson 5 was released on the Motown label on 7 October 1969. On 10 January 1970, it hit the top of the R&B charts, replacing Diana Ross & The Supremes' final single *Someday We'll Be Together*, a fitting swap since it marked the end of one era and the beginning of another. *I Want You Back* would remain at the summit of the R&B charts for four weeks, but on 31 January came greater glory; the single ended B.J. Thomas' *Raindrops Keep Fallin' On My Head* run at the top of the pop chart.

The Jackson 5 single performed almost as well internationally, peaking at #2 in the UK where it was unable to dislodge Lee Marvin's *Wand'rin' Star* from the number one spot. Largely envisaged by Berry Gordy as being in a style reminiscent of the bubblegum pop that was hitting the charts at the time of its original release, *I Want You Back* would prove to have a much better pedigree than many of its rivals; the single would become a smash all over again in 1988 when remixed and taken to #8 on the UK chart. In 1998 it again reached the British Top Ten, this time via a cover version by female vocal group Cleopatra which hit #4.

I WAS MADE TO LOVE HER – STEVIE WONDER [SINGLE]

After getting his Motown career back on track with *Uptight*, Stevie Wonder had become a virtual resident in the Top Ten of the R&B charts, helped by the success of *Nothing's Too Good For My Baby, With A Child's Heart, Blowin' In The Wind, A Place In The Sun* and *Hey Love*. Stevie was also taking on a much bigger role in co-writing his own material, usually aided by Hank Cosby and Sylvia Moy. His girlfriend of around this time (1966), Angie Satterwhite, would inspire several songs, most notably *My Cherie Amour, Angie Baby* and *I Was Made To Love Her*, with Stevie seemingly unafraid to put into song the emotions and feelings he was experiencing.

According to Hank Cosby, the first time Stevie presented the rudiments of *I Was Made To Love Her* there was little more than four bars of music and rough but not yet ready lyrics. Hank, Sylvia and Stevie's mother Lula Mae Hardaway helped flesh out the lyrics, with Hank deciding that the four bars of music would bear repeating to fill out the song. The recording sessions were undertaken in March 1967, although once again there is some considerable dispute as to where the track was actually recorded. According to the Motown logs, the track was entirely recorded in Detroit, with the session tapes revealing some playful vocal banter between Stevie and drummer Benny 'Papa Zita' Benjamin during the course of the session. Also known is that this was one of the first tracks on which Stevie played the clavinet, then a relatively new electronic keyboard still in its infancy. However, *I Was Made To Love Her* is another track that bass player Carol Kaye claims to have appeared on and that it was recorded in Los Angeles.

Irrespective of where it was recorded, *what* was recorded was another piece of Stevie Wonder magic. Released as a single on 18 May 1967, *I Was Made To Love Her* would become Stevie's fourth R&B chart topper, peak at #2 on the pop chart and become his international breakthrough hit, making #5 in the UK. Whilst *I Was Made To Love Her* is undoubtedly a personal number, written about his relationship with Angie, the song itself has been recorded over the years by artists as diverse as The Beach Boys, Jimi Hendrix (Stevie played drums on the BBC sessions that produced Hendrix' version), Boyz II Men, Michael Jackson, Tom Jones, Michael McDonald and Whitney Houston, among others.

I WISH – STEVIE WONDER [SINGLE]

The burst of success enjoyed by **Talking Book**, **Innervisions** and **Fulfillingness' First Finale** had made Stevie Wonder the most successful and important artist on the Motown roster. When the time came to renew his contract in 1975, Berry Gordy reasoned that almost any price was worth paying if it ensured Stevie remained within the Motown family. The eventual deal that was inked on 9 April 1975 was said to total some $13 million, then an almost unheard of financial guarantee against future earnings. The deal was confirmed without Motown requiring sight and sound of the new material Stevie was working on; his reputation and the musical progress he had made over the previous decade was more than enough for Berry Gordy to commit to such a sum.

So Stevie remained in the Motown family and it was at one such gathering, the annual Motown picnic in the summer of 1976, that inspired one of the last songs to be written for the **Songs In The Key Of Life** project but which would become the lead single. According to Stevie he had thoroughly enjoyed the picnic, even though he personally was troubled by a toothache during the course of the day. The pain had been a distraction, but the laughing and joking that had been prevalent put Stevie in a good mood, one he wished to continue as he made his way over to Crystal Industries recording studio in Hollywood later that day. The music came quickly, with the joyful, bouncy feel coming across on the song. The lyrics, however, took a little more time, for Stevie initially toyed with the idea of making the song something much more spiritual before realising that the lyrics would have to match the joyful nature of the music. Fortunately, he was inspired to look back beyond his career and back to a time when he had been a young boy, enjoying picnics and other pursuits for the very first time.

To help out on the track, Stevie enlisted Raymond Pound (drums), Nathan Watts (bass), Raymond Maldonado (trumpet), Trevor Lawrence (tenor saxophone), Steve Madaio (trumpet) and Renee Hardaway (Stevie's sister on background vocals). The hype that surrounded **Songs In The Key Of Life** (when released it was his first album release in some two years) ensured a phenomenal amount of interest in the album when it finally appeared in September 1976, followed two months later by the single *I Wish*. Irrespective of the fact it had been more than two years since his previous single release, *I Wish* would have been a hit at any point in Stevie's career; that it would smash its way to the top of both the R&B and pop charts is indicative of its instant appeal, further confirmed when the Grammy Award for Best R&B Vocal Performance, Male was bestowed on the single.

In the UK the single had to be content with making #5, the slight delay in getting the single to the market (it was not released until December 1976) perhaps hindering its progress. However, in 1999 *I Wish* was musically revisited by Will Smith on his single *Wild Wild West* (and used as the theme to the film of the same name) and topped the US charts whilst peaking at #2 in the UK. The accompanying video also featured a guest appearance from Stevie Wonder.

I WISH IT WOULD RAIN – THE TEMPTATIONS [SINGLE]

Both The Temptations and Gladys Knight & The Pips would enjoy hits with *I Wish It Would Rain*, with David Ruffin's performance on The Temptations version widely considered one of his finest recordings, but the song itself owed much to the personal angst being suffered by songwriter Roger Penzabene.

Norman Whitfield and Barrett Strong started off the song, which originally had a different set of lyrics and was titled *At The End Of A Hard Working Day* and then *I Saw The Light Life And Breath*. The music was recorded in April 1967, at which point Norman had Jimmy Ruffin in mind as the singer (he had previously been offered another song that would become a major hit for The Temptations, *Beauty Is Only Skin Deep*), although by the time brother David came to record the song in August, Roger had written new lyrics that put in song the problems he was having with his wife Helga, who had recently left him in order to be with her lover.

Roger was present at the recording session when David laid down his lead vocal and, according to all those who were present, spent much of the time crying in the control room as life was brought to the song. Released in December 1967, *I Wish It Would Rain* had hit written all over it, as it proved when it topped the R&B chart and made #4 pop. It also became a minor hit in the UK, creeping into the lower reaches of the Top 50 at #45.

By the time the single was a hit, however, Roger Penzabene could stand his internal pain no more, taking his own life on New Year's Eve, a week after the single had been released in the US. Roger therefore missed not only the song becoming a smash but also a nomination for a Grammy Award, with *I Wish It Would Rain* being nominated for Best Rhythm & Blues Song, where it lost out to Otis Redding and Steve Cropper's *(Sittin' On) The Dock Of The Bay*. Five years after The Temptations had enjoyed their success, British rock group The Faces enjoyed a #8 UK hit with their interpretation, featured alongside *Pool Hall Richard* as a double sided single.

IF

British jazz rock group If was formed in 1969 by Dick Morrissey (born in Horley, Surrey on 9 May 1940) and over the next six years became established as one of the leading bands of the genre. They did extensive tours around the world and recorded some eight albums during that spell, although mainstream success somehow eluded them. By the time **Tea Break Over, Back On Your 'Eads** was released in 1975, the rest of the group comprised Gabriel Magno (keyboards), Geoff Whitehorn (guitar), Walt Monaghan (bass and vocals), Carlos Martinez (percussion) and Cliff Davies (drums and vocals).

The album was released in the UK on Gull Records and was scheduled as part of the label's deal with Motown in the US, although the release was subsequently cancelled. If disbanded soon after, with Morrissey going on to perform with the Average White Band and Herbie Mann before enjoying considerable success with Jim Mullen in Morrissey Mullen. Dick died from cancer on 8 November 2000.

IF I COULD BUILD MY WHOLE WORLD AROUND YOU – MARVIN GAYE & TAMMI TERRELL [SINGLE]

By November 1967, Tammi Terrell was in hospital following her collapse on stage the previous month, but Motown were keen to maintain the momentum she and musical partner Marvin Gaye had enjoyed with two major single hits and a well received album earlier that year. As the end of the year loomed, the decision was taken to extract another single from their **United** album. Initially the intention was to issue *Two Can Have A Party* as the top side, a song written and produced by Harvey Fuqua and Johnny Bristol (with Thomas Kemp also having contributed to the song writing process), only for the track to be held back for later release. Instead, *If I Could Build My Whole World Around You* was chosen, another Fuqua-Bristol composition, this time in conjunction with Vernon Bullock.

Since *If I Could* was written specifically as a duet (*Two Can Have A Party* was written for Tammi as a solo artist), with the vocal interchange between Tammi and Marvin much more pronounced, the switch in lead titles made commercial sense. On the flip side was *If This World Was Mine*, written by Marvin Gaye and recorded with both Marvin and Tammi singing into the same microphone. Both the A and B sides of the single release, issued on Tamla in November 1967, would make the charts; *If I Could Build My Whole World Around You* would hit #10 pop and #2 R&B (and reached #41 in the UK), whilst *If This World Was Mine* would peak at #68 pop and #27 R&B. *Two Can Have A Party* would eventually get a release, appearing in July 1968 as the B side to *You're All I Need To Get By*.

IF I WERE A CARPENTER – THE FOUR TOPS [SINGLE]

The Four Tops' **Reach Out** was to prove something of a mini greatest hits compilation, at least as far as the UK was concerned, where no fewer than five tracks made the Top Ten, including the number one transatlantic smash *Reach Out I'll Be There*. Whilst The Four Tops are often held to be the perfect vehicle for HDH's material, Levi Stubbs' abilities as a vocalist were such that he could breathe new life into almost any song. **Reach Out** had been seemingly padded out with a couple of non-HDH compositions, including covers of The Monkees hits *Last Train To Clarksville* and *I'm A Believer*, and also to be found were cover versions of *Walk Away Renee* and *If I Were A Carpenter*.

The latter song had been written by Tim Hardin and provided Bobby Darin with a major hit in 1966, hitting #8 in the US and #9 in the UK. Following the success Tamla Motown enjoyed in the UK with the extracted *Walk Away Renee*, the company opted to try their luck with *If I Were A Carpenter* for the follow-up. Although it was some seventeen months old by the time it was issued as a single, it still found favour, surpassing the well-known Bobby Darin version when it reached #7 in the UK in April 1968 (a later recording by Robert Palmer would also become a British hit, peaking at #63 in 1993).

The UK success prompted Motown to issue it in the US, where it managed a respectable #20 pop and #17 R&B. It was the UK success, however, that kept The Four Tops name in the headlines whilst they waited for the ongoing legal battles between Berry Gordy and HDH to resolve themselves enough for the group to get back into the studio to record new material.

IF I WERE YOUR WOMAN – GLADYS KNIGHT & THE PIPS [SINGLE]

Gloria Jones and Pam Sawyer met for a barbecue lunch and a bottle of champagne and during the course of the meal discussed a song idea they had. Whilst the rest of the world was pushing for female liberation, Pam and Gloria had more romantic visions, especially how most of the women they knew tended to give their all in relationships. The basics of the song were written in some thirty minutes, according to Gloria, although the more polished version that came to be recorded came about after they showed what they had written to Clay McMurray.

A former assistant to Norman Whitfield, Clay recreated the bass line and made a number of changes to the lyrics and began trawling through the

Motown artist roster looking for the ideal outlet for the song. His initial thought was for Blinky, but she was apparently unavailable at the time. His second choice was for The Supremes, but Frank Wilson's recent success with the group had ensured that he would continue to get first option on recording that particular group. It was when Clay played the backing track to Norman Whitfield that the ideal group became obvious.

"If you record that on Gladys Knight & The Pips', Norman said, 'you'll have a number one record."

Clay was convinced, but Gladys wasn't, at least at first. Since the song was written almost entirely from a woman's point of view, there appeared little or nothing for The Pips to contribute, but a subtle change in lyric to 'If you were my woman' ensured Bubba, Ed and William could play a major part in the eventual success of the song. Arranged by Paul Riser, *If I Were Your Woman* was recorded by a less than enthusiastic Gladys Knight in August 1970, although her professionalism was such that she still threw everything she had into the recording, confident that the track would merely be used as an album track. Convinced he had a major hit on his hands, Clay McMurray put it forward for consideration as a single, only to hear that Quality Control had turned it down. Clay decided to approach Berry Gordy direct, informing him that the track was similar in style to an earlier Gladys Knight & The Pips' hit in *Letter Full Of Tears*, a slow, ballad song with which the group had enjoyed phenomenal success.

Berry was finally convinced and readied the track for release in October 1970, only to receive a call from a bemused Gladys, who was still dead set against releasing it as anything other than an album cut. Berry won her round, apparently by placing a bet with her that the single would become a number one hit. Gladys would later state that whilst she lost that particular bet, she received more than adequate compensation when it became the group's second R&B chart topper on the Soul label when it hit the top spot for a week in January 1971 (it would have to settle for peaking at #9 on the pop chart).

The single's writing credits list the composers as LaVerne Ware, Pam Sawyer and Clay McMurray; since Gloria Jones had previously had a recording career under her real name, she wished to distance her songwriting and chose LaVern Ware for her initial writing career. *If I Were Your Woman* would go on to earn two Grammy nominations, for Best Rhythm & Blues Song (it lost out to Bill Withers' *Ain't No Sunshine*) and Best Rhythm & Blues Performance by a Duo or Group (won by Ike & Tina Turner's *Proud Mary*) and become the title of the group's next album.

Despite Gladys' initial reluctance to record or release *If I Were Your Woman*, the track has become one of the defining moments in the group's career, so much so that in 2001 Gladys recorded something of a sequel in *If I Were Your Woman 2* for her album **At Last**. All of this success makes that fact the single completely missed the UK chart totally mystifying, to say the very least.

IF YOU REALLY LOVE ME – STEVIE WONDER [SINGLE]

Having spent much of his childhood and teenage years recording what Motown had wanted him to, Stevie Wonder approached adulthood looking to exert greater control of his material and future career. His final album before he officially 'came of age' was **Where I'm Coming From**, written by Stevie and his soon to be wife Syreeta, with Stevie virtually abandoning accepted Motown practice in song composition and selection. Whilst the album was not resplendent with hit singles, one or two tracks stood head and shoulders above the rest. In the US, the most obvious single was *If You Really Love Me*, a stop start number that featured extensive horn work reminiscent of Chicago.

A radical departure from his earlier work, *If You Really Love Me* had enough about it to hit #8 pop and #4 R&B in the US following its July 1971 release. In the UK the single had a rather more chequered route to the chart. Initially it was relegated to the flip side of *Never Dreamed You'd Leave In Summer*, a strange single choice released in July 1971 that struggled to gain acceptance at radio and thus failed to make any kind of impact on the chart. The following January Tamla Motown tried again, this time promoting *If You Really Love Me* to the top side and coupling it with another album cut, *Think Of Me As Your Soldier*. Rescued from obscurity, *If You Really Love Me* made the most of its second chance, hitting #20 in February and returning Stevie to the chart after a seven month absence.

SUZANNE IKEDA

Whilst she would become better known for her activities behind the scenes at Motown, especially as a 'creative confidant' to Michael Jackson, Suzee Ikeda started her career at the company as a singer. Born Susan Wendy Ikeda in Chicago, Illinois on 25 August 1947 to Japanese parents (it is claimed she was the first Asian-American artist signed by the company, but

Jack Soo pre-dated her, even if none of his material has yet been released), Suzee was signed by MoWest in 1971 and released her first single, a cover of the Disney tune *Zip-A-Dee-Doo-Dah* in October of that year. The following June came the follow-up *I Can't Give Back The Love I Feel For You* which also missed the chart, and in April 1973 her final single, *A Time For Me To Go* was released on the main Motown label.

With her recording career at an end, Motown utilised her ability to interact with the artists by naming her production assistant on Diana Ross and Marvin Gaye's album, and Suzee would later work with the likes of The Temptations, Commodores, Jose Feliciano and others in a similar capacity.

I'LL BE DOGGONE – MARVIN GAYE [SINGLE]

Marvin Gaye had enjoyed a major success with *How Sweet It Is To Be Loved By You*, written and produced by Holland-Dozier-Holland. Unfortunately, with HDH also writing for The Supremes and The Four Tops almost on a full-time basis, they did not have the time (nor possibly the right material) to come up with a follow-up for Marvin. Instead, he was put in care of the other permanently hot writing and production team around Hitsville, Smokey Robinson and various members of The Miracles.

I'll Be Doggone was written by Smokey, Pete Moore and the band's guitarist Marv Tarplin, with Smokey and Pete working on the lyrics, to which Marv put the music. Whilst it was Smokey and The Miracles song, the performance was undoubtedly Marvin Gaye's.

"He'd interpret my material like he'd written it himself," said Smokey, "improvising and improving the original concept."

This combination was enough to turn *I'll Be Doggone* into the required hit, topping the R&B chart for one week and hitting #8 on the pop chart following release in February 1965.

I'LL BE THERE – JACKSON 5 [SINGLE]

When Berry Gordy first signed The Jackson 5, he all but promised the group would kick off their career with three consecutive number one hits. It was more bravado than a guarantee, but when their first three singles did top the charts (*I Want You Back*, *ABC* and *The Love You Save*) the pressure was on to keep the phenomenal run going as long as possible. The Corporation, the team behind those first three number ones, had little or no material stashed away for consideration for the fourth single, so attention turned to the West Coast office of Hal Davis, where his collection of writers and producers had their own creative pool to dip into.

It was bass player, arranger and writer Bob West who came up with the original idea for *I'll Be There,* a song that sat around the office for a time gathering dust until Hal Davis picked it up and gave it a listen. Impressed with what he heard, he brought the song to the attention of Berry, who liked the tune and the title but not much else. Still, there was enough left over for Hal, Bob and Willie Hutch to knock into shape, with Willie responsible for much of the new lyrical content. Initially unsure as to which thread to pursue, Willie had written two variations of the song.

"One was more or less a brotherhood kind of lyric, and the other was more guy-girl" he later related. "But I kept the brotherhood aspect in both songs at the beginning: *You and I must make a pact/We must bring salvation back.* I thought that's good, either way it goes."

When the initial rewrite was presented to Berry, he insisted the guy-girl aspect be played upon more, so Hal, Willie and Berry worked at the song until all were satisfied with the end result. Arranged by original author Bob West, the musical backing tracks were recorded at the Sound Factory Studio with Hal's usual cream of West Coast session musicians, including Art Wright, David T Walker and Louis Shelton on guitar, Bob West on bass, Joe Sample on keyboards, Gene Pello on drums and Jackie Johnson on tambourine. The group vocals were recorded at the Record Plant, and whilst the song might have suited Jermaine Jackson on lead (he had to settle for a lead role on the bridge), the backing track was recorded high, thus forcing Michael to the very limits of his vocal register. On the spot coaching from Berry Gordy, Willie Hutch and Suzanne Ikeda enabled Michael to produce a stunning performance.

There was also a little levity brought to the session; the song's title recalled an earlier Four Tops hit in *Reach Out I'll Be There*, so Berry had Michael throw in a line from that song into The Jackson 5's one; 'Just look over your shoulder, honey', although Michael sang 'shoulders', with Berry deciding to keep the mistake in the finished recording. The end result was a radical departure from the three up-tempo numbers that had blasted The Jackson 5's career off the launch pad, but *I'll Be There* was to become the group's biggest hit, proof that their popularity was growing at such a rate their fanbase would accept a switch in tempo.

I'll Be There was released in August 1970 and would become the group's fourth consecutive chart topper (on both the pop and R&B charts), selling more than three million copies whilst it reigned for six weeks on the R&B chart and five on the pop. It did almost as well in the UK, hitting the Top Ten in its fifth week of chart action and spending five weeks stalled at #5. It moved up a place a week later but never got beyond the #4 position. That was partially remedied two decades later when Mariah Carey performed the song on MTV Unplugged with Trey Lorenz; her version hit #2 in the UK in July 1992 but did even better in the US where it topped the chart for two weeks.

I'LL PICK A ROSE FOR MY ROSE – MARV JOHNSON [SINGLE]

The singer who recorded and released the very first Motown associated single, Marv Johnson enjoyed a brief spell of success when United Artists picked up his contract in 1959 but found the momentum difficult to maintain when taken away from the hit factory that was being created in Detroit. He returned to the fold in 1965, but by then other artists at Motown had surpassed his potential and he quickly found himself relegated to undertaking backroom duties. There was still the occasional chance at recording, one of which resulted in a most surprising upturn in his career fortunes.

I'll Pick A Rose was written by James Dean, William Weatherspoon and Marv himself, and there is some indication the initial recording sessions were undertaken in 1966. Two years later the track was dusted down, polished up and released on the Gordy label in October 1968 (the recording logs for the song show that the actual recording sessions, for both music and vocals, were undertaken in January and February 1968) to little or no interest in the US.

In December 1968 the single was released by Tamla Motown in the UK and found almost instant favour, hitting the chart in mid January and peaking at #10 in February 1969. The success of the single prompted the rush release of an album of the same name (which remains unissued in the US) and a tour of the territory that had taken Marv so close to its heart. The revival of Marv's career was enough to produce a further hit, the revived US R&B hit from 1966 *I Miss You Baby (How I Miss You)* becoming a Top 30 hit in the wake of his live performances.

I'LL SAY FOREVER MY LOVE – JIMMY RUFFIN [SINGLE]

No artist benefitted more from the disparity between American record buyers and their British counterparts than Jimmy Ruffin. His US chart career peaked almost as soon as it started in 1966, with *What Becomes Of The Broken Hearted* destined to be his only Top Ten hit in his homeland. In Britain, however, the same song not only made the Top Ten on two separate occasions, it kick-started a career that would result in no fewer than five Top Ten hits out of nine chart entries; no wonder Jimmy Ruffin eventually took up permanent residence in the UK.

I'll Say Forever My Love was written by James Dean, William Weatherspoon and Stephen Bowden, with James and William producing the October 1967 session that was eventually released in February 1968 in the US on Soul and the following month on Tamla Motown in the UK. The initial release saw *I'll Say Forever My Love* make #77 on the US pop chart but miss out altogether on both the R&B chart and in the UK.

By May 1970, however, Jimmy had enjoyed something of a revival of fortunes in the UK, with a reissue of *I've Passed This Way Before* from February 1967 making #33 the second time around, enabling the follow-up *Farewell Is A Lonely Sound* to make the Top Ten. Flush with this success, Tamla Motown opted to try again with *I'll Say Forever My Love*, their decision vindicated when it sailed into the Top Ten, coming to rest at #7.

I'M COMING OUT – DIANA ROSS [SINGLE]

Songwriter and producer Nile Rodgers got the idea for *I'm Coming Out* shortly after agreeing to helm an album with musical partner Bernard Edwards for Diana Ross; out one evening at the Gilded Grape, a notable nightclub in New York, Nile spotted a number of Diana Ross impersonators and quickly realised that Diana had become an icon within the gay community.

"What would it be like if Diana celebrated her status among gay men in song? I shared the anecdote with Bernard, who agreed that it would be a cool idea to have Diana talk with her gay fans in slightly coded language."

Nile had also agreed to produce an album on Meco Monardo, a former session musician who had scored a major pop hit with *Star Wars Theme-Cantina Band*, a disco version of the theme from the smash hit film 'Stars Wars'. As part of the deal, Nile asked Meco to organise the horn section for Diana's album, with Meco finishing the task inside three hours. When the rest of the horn section left the studio, Nile asked Meco to stay behind and record a trombone solo for *I'm Coming Out*, with Meco eventually recording four different solos which Nile intended mixing into one. Diana's unhappiness with the original mix saw Russ Terrana being given the master tapes to produce a version of the album to Diana's satisfaction, with the result that the trombone solo that appeared on the album was the first version only.

I'm Coming Out was released as the second single from the **diana** album and was nearly as successful as its predecessor *Upside Down*; it made #5 pop and #6 R&B and would go on to hit #13 in the UK (it was released as the third single from the album in that territory, following *Upside Down* and *My Old Piano*). Perhaps just as importantly, *I'm Coming Out* was almost instantly installed as the opening number in Diana's live show, a position it still holds.

I'M GONNA MAKE YOU LOVE ME – DIANA ROSS & THE SUPREMES & THE TEMPTATIONS [SINGLE]

I'm Gonna Make You Love Me was written by Kenny Gamble, Jerry Williams and Jerry Ross and first provided Dee Dee Warwick with a minor hit single in 1966, making #13 R&B and #88 pop. Jerry Ross had produced that version, with Nickolas Ashford and Valerie Simpson providing backing vocals, with Jerry later producing versions by Jerry Butler and Jay & The Techniques, both of which also featured Ashford & Simpson on backing vocals. In 1967 the song was offered to British singer Dusty Springfield, who turned it down but handed it over to labelmate Madeline Bell, with her version being produced by John Franz. Initially little more than an album track on **Bell's A Poppin'**, the track was eventually released as a single in early 1968 and would go on to make both the pop (#26) and R&B charts (#32), where its presence would have been noted by Motown executives busy with preparations for a forthcoming television special featuring Diana Ross & The Supremes and The Temptations.

It was Suzanne De Passe who suggested the song to producer Frank Wilson, who was working in conjunction with Nickolas Ashford on the album that would eventually accompany the special. By all accounts Diana's vocal was recorded in Los Angeles and supervised by Frank Wilson, before Nickolas Ashford overdubbed Eddie Kendricks' lead role in Detroit. The track initially scheduled for release was *The Impossible Dream*, taken from the Broadway show 'Don Quixote, Man Of La Mancha' but this was switched at the last minute after numerous radio stations began playing *I'm Gonna Make You Love Me* from the advance copies of the album they had received. It proved the right decision, with the single making #2 on both the pop and R&B charts and hitting #3 in the UK. The success of the single in the US also led, indirectly, to Jerry Ross doing a number of productions on behalf of Motown, having firmly established his songwriting talent.

I'M LIVIN' IN SHAME – DIANA ROSS & THE SUPREMES [SINGLE]

Written by the same team responsible for *Love Child* and intended as something of a sequel to that hit, *I'm Livin' In Shame* was inspired by the plot to the film 'Imitation Of Life'. Once again it was Pam Sawyer who came up with the initial idea, which would carry the working titles *The Eyes Of Love* and *I Live In Shame* until the eventual title was bestowed upon it. Recorded in December 1968 and released in January 1969, the single would become a sizeable hit, peaking at #8 R&B and #10 pop, even hitting #14 in the UK.

The title alone carried with it some stigma, and Diana Ross would later claim that whilst she liked the melody she could not relate to the lyrics. Despite becoming a Top Ten hit, *I'm Livin' In Shame* was never featured as part of The Supremes stage show. As it turned out, it was to be the last single The Clan were directly responsible for, with the various members moving on to other projects, some collectively, some individually.

I'M READY FOR LOVE – MARTHA & THE VANDELLAS [SINGLE]

Although Holland-Dozier-Holland's main priority by 1966 was ensuring both The Supremes and The Four Tops were permanent residents on the chart, their creativity was such that The Elgins, The Miracles, Marvin Gaye and The Isley Brothers also got a chance at chart action with HDH compositions and productions.

Also queuing at the Hitsville door were Martha Reeves & The Vandellas, who enjoyed a major Top Ten hit with *Nowhere To Run* with HDH in 1965 but then saw their next three singles struggle for acceptance. Glad though they were to be reunited with HDH for *I'm Ready For Love*, which was recorded as part of the sessions for their forthcoming album **Watchout!**, The

Vandellas were seldom given the opportunity of recording brand new material; *I'm Ready For Love* was effectively a discarded backing track dating back to 1964! Still, The Vandellas breathed considerable life into the track, enough for the single to hit #9 pop and #2 R&B, as well as making #22 in the UK, with the parent album eventually making #116 on the pop chart and #14 R&B.

I'M STILL WAITING – DIANA ROSS [SINGLE]

Deke Richards had come up with the basic idea for *I'm Still Waiting* whilst recovering in hospital from a slipped disc, eventually recording the song on Diana Ross for her second solo album **Everything Is Everything** (although its inclusion was somewhat in the balance, for Deke would later state that Berry didn't like it when it was first played to him). Despite the success of her debut album and its attendant singles, **Everything Is Everything** didn't exactly set the till registers ringing, even if it did make the Top Ten of the R&B chart (it would peak at #5 R&B and #42 pop) in the US.

In the UK, however, Diana could do little wrong, having scored Top Ten pop hits with *Ain't No Mountain High Enough* and *Remember Me* and with certain sections of the media eagerly looking forward to the release of **Everything Is Everything**. One DJ in particular, Tony Blackburn of Radio 1's Breakfast Show (at its peak, he had a listenership of 20 million), leapt upon the track *I'm Still Waiting*, making it his record of the week whilst it was still an album track and effectively telling Tamla Motown that he would continue to play it if the label were to release it as a single. He was as good as his word too, continuing to plug the song so much that it could not help but become a major hit. Released on 23 July 1971 it hit the top of the charts three weeks later and would remain there for four weeks, becoming the biggest solo hit of Diana's career in the UK.

Such is the record's resonance with British audiences, it became a hit all over again for Diana in 1976 (it peaked at #41) and via a remix in 1990 (peaking at #21). The song has also been frequently revived and taken back into the charts, with Courtney Pine Featuring Carroll Thompson (#66 in 1990) and Angelheart Featuring Aletia Bourne (#74 in 1997) both enjoying minor hits. Yet for some reason, American audiences remained unmoved; a belated US issue on Diana in October 1971 after it hit #1 in the UK saw it barely make #63 pop and #40 R&B.

I'M STILL WAITING - DIANA ROSS [ALBUM]

Following the success of the single *I'm Still Waiting,* a UK chart topper, Tamla Motown requested permission to issue the **Surrender** album as **I'm Still Waiting,** although retaining the same cover photograph that had appeared on the American release. The album also had the smash hit single as the lead track by way of a bonus, thus expanding the original eleven track American album into a twelve track package for British consumption.

Inadvertently, the album became a contrast of styles; one track written and produced by Deke Richards (the bonus track *I'm Still Waiting*) alongside eleven tracks produced by Ashford and Simpson, of which they wrote all but one! The marketing ploy worked, for whilst **Everything Is Everything** had peaked at #31, despite the presence of the number one single, **I'm Still Waiting** became a Top Ten chart success and ultimately earned a silver disc sales award.

IMPACT OF BRASS

Formed in 1968 in South Florida by trumpet player Wally McMurray with former students at the University of Miami, The Impact Of Brass played locally at Crossways Airport Inn Lounge and made their first album for United Artists in 1968. Their deal with Rare Earth was effectively a licensing deal for a finished album, with the group by then rounded out to include McMurray, Ed Bevil (trombone), Val Houston (trombone), Mark Hurwitz (woodwind), Doug Smith (trumpet), George Dukas (trumpet), John Clausi (guitar), Ken Conklin (bass), Steve Wittmack (bass and keyboards) and Rick Docen (drums). Their album **Down At The Brassworks** was released in September 1971, having been preceded by the single *Never Can Say Goodbye.* The group linked with Joe Hinton for *What A Friend We Have In Jesus* on Motown's **The Key To The Kingdom** and later recorded an album for Polydor.

ALBUM: DOWN AT THE BRASSWORKS (1971)

THE IMPRESSIONS

An American R&B group formed in Chattanooga, Tennessee in 1957 by Arthur Brooks, Richard Brooks, Sam Gooden (born in Chattanooga on 2 September 1939), Fred Cash (born in Chattanooga on 8 October 1940) and Emanuel Thomas as the Roosters. Gooden and the Brook brothers relocated to Chicago, Illinois in 1958 and linked up with Jerry Butler (born in Sunflower, Mississippi on 8 December 1939) and Curtis Mayfield (born in Chicago on 3 June 1942), renaming the group The Impressions in the process. The success of their first hit *(For Your Precious Love)* prompted Butler to leave for a solo career in 1958, with Fred Cash his replacement.

Mayfield then reformed the group with Cash and Gooden in Chicago, with the Brooks brothers remaining in New York. Curtis Mayfield penned most of the group's material, including their 1963 R&B chart topper *It's All Right*, which also crossed over to become a major pop hit, peaking at #4. The track was featured on the soundtrack to 'The Flamingo Kid' released in December 1984. Two years later, *For Your Precious Love* appeared on the compilation CD **Hits From The Legendary Vee-Jay Records.** Curtis was paralysed from the neck down when a lighting gantry fell on him in 1990 and died on 26 December 1999.

IN AND OUT OF LOVE – DIANA ROSS & THE SUPREMES [SINGLE]

The original backing tracks for what became *In And Out Of Love* were recorded in Detroit in March 1967, at much the same time HDH were recording future hits *The Happening* and *Reflections*. Yet six weeks later, in Los Angeles, HDH redid the music, at the time christened *Summer Good Summer Bad*. Owing to a hectic touring schedule, one that took the group to virtually all four corners of the country, The Supremes lead and background vocals remained unrecorded until 12 June (this would be one of Florence Ballard's last recording sessions as a member of The Supremes), with The Andantes coming into Hitsville a day later to lay down their backing vocals. Nearly four weeks later the strings were added, with the by now titled *In And Out Of Love* finally ready for release on 25 October 1967. Something of a departure in style for the group, with a distinct country flavour, the single was not as immediate a success as its predecessors and had to settle for a final chart position of #16 R&B and #9 pop, as well as only making #13 in the UK.

IN MY HOUSE – MARY JANE GIRLS [SINGLE]

The biggest hit the Mary Jane Girls enjoyed, *In My House* was also their most controversial release. Written and produced by mentor Rick James, it was chosen as the lead single from the second album **Only Four You** in February 1985 and quickly vaulted the charts, peaking at #7 pop, #3 R&B and hit #1 on the Hot Dance Club Play chart, ultimately helping the parent album attain gold status.

However, whilst record buyers might have wholeheartedly approved of the single, the Parents Music Resource Center did not. Established in 1984 to draw attention to music they felt contained inappropriate lyrical content for children, the PMRC objected to the song's supposed sexual content (the Mary Jane Girls refuted the allegation, claiming the song was about love, not sex) and placed it at #13 on their Filthy Fifteen songs recommended for banning by radio stations across the country. Only one other Motown track made the listing, with Vanity's *Strap On Robbie Baby* being placed at #4!

IN SQUARE CIRCLE - STEVIE WONDER [ALBUM]

Originally intended for release in 1984, **In Square Circle** kept slipping back in the release schedule, with its delay, according to Stevie, down to a number of factors.

"I'd been working a lot on making Martin Luther King's birthday a national holiday and was also working on **The Woman In Red** soundtrack, and it just took me a long time to get the songs I wanted together. I usually come up with the music first and then come up with an idea about the song. I sing a lyric out loud and change it right away if it sounds like too many words. I practice piano every day and sing other people's songs when I do."

That delay had seen an album entitled **People Move, Human Plays** rumoured, scheduled and then withdrawn, with record buyers none the wiser as to what the album would have featured. Finally, five years after his last 'proper' release in **Hotter Than July** in 1980, Stevie was ready, previewing the album in March 1985 at the annual record retailers convention in Florida. The reaction to **In Square Circle**, which finally hit the streets in September 1985, was immediate; aided by a smash hit single in *Part-Time Lover*, **In Square Circle** returned Stevie to the top of the R&B charts, also going on to make #5 on the pop charts in both the UK and the US.

Further single success came from *Go Home* and *Overjoyed*, the latter an instrumental track that had originally been intended for **The Secret Life Of Plants**, only to be held back and revisited, with vocals, for **In Square Circle**. The album would on to sell more than two million copies in the US and attain gold status in the UK, as well as collecting the Grammy Award for Best R&B Vocal Performance, Male.

INDIANA WANTS ME – R. DEAN TAYLOR [SINGLE]

"I was living in a fleabag hotel and one night I heard these sirens and somebody was breaking in to a store below. I looked out and police had surrounded this store and I turned my tape-recorder on. I saw 'Bonnie And Clyde' a couple of times and with those two things that's how I came to write *Indiana Wants Me*."

The tale of a man on the run after murdering someone who had insulted his wife, *Indiana* was written by R. Dean Taylor, who had greater success at Motown as a writer than a performer, but his own recording, which he also produced, would become his only US Top Ten hit. The song was also unique in that the original single release featured a police siren on the opening that was subsequently removed after complaints from radio listeners who heard the song whilst driving and thought they were being pulled over by the police for real!

Released on Rare Earth in April 1970, it would go on to become a #5 pop hit on the Billboard chart, actually topping the Cashbox listing as well as in his Canadian homeland, although it failed to make the R&B chart. In the UK the release was held over until February the following year, but when issued on the Tamla Motown label it sailed all the way to #2, held off the chart summit by Dawn's *Knock Three Times*.

INFERNO RECORDS

Formed by Harry Balk in Detroit in 1967, Inferno Records released four records before Berry Gordy bought the label out in 1968, with a further three singles being issued whilst it was briefly an imprint within Motown, including one release from Volumes and two by The Detroit Wheels. The label disappeared after the last release in September 1968, with Balk going on to become an executive within Motown and helping set up the Rare Earth label.

INNER CITY BLUES (MAKE ME WANNA HOLLER) – MARVIN GAYE [SINGLE]

Marvin Gaye had first collaborated with part-time lyricist and full time lift operator James Nyx on *We Can Make It Baby* in 1970, which Marvin had subsequently produced on The Originals. When Marvin eventually began work on what would become the **What's Going On** album, he kept the relationship with James going. The pair collaborated on three numbers that wound up on the album, the most notable being a song that was initially known as *The Tail End*. Based on a musical variation of a Drifters number, the lyrics initially consisted of social and political issues as observed by Marvin and James, with James spotting a newspaper headline that gave the song its more obvious name, *Inner City Blues* (the end rejoinder of *Make Me Wanna Holler* came from Marvin).

Work on the track began at Hitsville in March 1971, along with something of a guide vocal. The lead vocals would eventually be re-recorded in Los Angeles in May, by which time the whole of the **What's Going On** project was effectively pulled together. *Inner City Blues (Make Me Wanna Holler)* was to be the third single lifted from the album and the third straight R&B chart topper, also making #9 on the pop chart. The whole album was little short of a masterpiece and deserved every award, honour and accolade going, yet only *Inner City Blues* ended up with a nomination for a Grammy, being selected in the Best R&B Vocal Performance, Male category. It lost out on the night to Lou Rawls and *Natural Man*, a decision that rattled Marvin to such an extent he contemplated taking physical revenge on Lou, although common sense prevailed on the night. Even more bizarre was the lack of response from British record buyers, with only *Save The Children* making any chart impact, albeit a lowly #41; *Inner City Blues* joined previous releases *What's Going On* and *Mercy Mercy Me (The Ecology)* in missing out altogether.

INNERVISIONS - STEVIE WONDER [ALBUM]

The commercial and critical success enjoyed by **Talking Book** raised expectations for Stevie's next album. As would become the norm with new Stevie Wonder material, the album went through a number of reported titles and release dates before finally hitting the streets. At one point the album was to be called **The Last Days Of Easter**, with Stevie having an idea for the cover image.

"It should have been an old man, a very old man, who's been through it all and can now sit and look on at the confusion. He would have wisdom and contentment." Then Stevie scrapped the idea and changed the title. "People would only relate it to Easter and not the other things I'll be saying."

And Stevie had much to say, with the nine track album being a much more spiritual affair than its predecessor. There was hardly a subject left untouched; the anti-drug message of *Too High*, poverty and racism in *Living For The City*, reincarnation in *Higher Ground* as well as more standard, ballad fare in *All In Love Is Fair* and *Golden Lady*. Recorded at Media Sound in New York and Record Plant in Los Angeles, **Innervisions** was virtually the work of one man, with Stevie playing all instruments on seven of the nine tracks. The cover, painted by Efram Wolff and depicting Stevie as a visionary despite his blindness gave a further instinct as to the material contained within, making the whole package a veritable tour de force.

As the album neared completion, Stevie undertook a number of interviews to explain the concept for the forthcoming album. He already had something of a premonition that something major was about to happen to him, even stating in an interview with 'Rolling Stone' that he foresaw his own death. The publicity campaign was topped off with a media playback in New York, with assorted media personnel being met in Times Square, blindfolded and then driven around the city in a coach.

"The idea of the blindfolds was to try to give people an idea of what's happening in my mind. When you look at something, your hearing is distracted by your eyes."

When the album was officially released on 3 August 1973, Stevie was asleep in a car being driven by his cousin John Harris. They were behind a logging truck, which made an abrupt stop and caused a log to smash through the windscreen and hit Stevie in the head, resulting in a fractured skull and contusion of the brain. In a coma for a week, there were fears that Stevie's premonition was going to come true, but thanks to round the clock hospital care and friends and relatives whispering into his ear to try to rouse him from his coma, Stevie eventually regained consciousness. Whilst the accident robbed him of his sense of smell, his musical talent was left intact.

Meanwhile, **Innervisions** was shaping up to be Stevie's most successful album to date, taking just six weeks to reach its pop peak of #4 and also going on to top the R&B charts, his second consecutive chart topper and selling more than a million copies in the process. In the UK **Innervisions** would become his first album to crack the Top Ten, peaking at #8 and spending more than a year on the listings. That the album was a commercial success was never in question, but it also became a huge critical success too, being awarded the Grammy award for Album of the Year, one of four awards Stevie won that evening (the other three all related to his earlier **Talking Book** album). There was also an award for Malcolm Cecil and Robert Margouleff, who picked up the trophy for Best Engineered Recording, Non-Classical.

INTERNATIONAL TALENT MANAGEMENT

Berry Gordy didn't only start a record company to release records on the artists he signed, he also created a management company to look after their careers. Despite being something of a conflict of interest, for almost ten years or so every recording artist signed by Motown and its group of labels was managed by International Talent Management Inc. However, Berry would admit there was a conflict, for a deliberate reason.

"People used to attack me and say it was a conflict of interest; I was the manager, I was the record company, I was the publisher, and I would say, yes, of course, conflict of interest, but it's in their favour!"

The company was run for some ten years by Berry's sister Esther.

"I recall that Mary Wells' was Motown's first hit artist, while The Temptations were the first all-male group on the label. But when The Marvelettes released *Please Mr. Postman* the girls had never been on a bus, let alone a stage, so that was definitely interesting."

ITM, as it became known, not only managed the artists but also took care of getting bookings, handled their accounts and gave financial advice and career guidance. From July 1966 it was housed at 2670/2 West Grand Boulevard, but by the end of the decade many of the artists had begun to make their own management arrangements, rendering ITM virtually obsolete.

THE ISLEY BROTHERS

The Isley Brothers were already ten year music industry veterans and had experience of running their own label when they joined Motown, although sustained success had proved somewhat elusive. Originally formed in Cincinnati, Ohio by O'Kelly Jr. (born on 25 December 1937), Rudolph Bernard (born on 1 April 1939), Ronald (born on 21 May 1941) and Vernon Isley (born in 1942), the four came together in 1954 after encouragement by their father, O'Kelly Sr.

The Isley Brothers accompanied their mother and father on the gospel circuit, although tragedy soon overtook them when Vernon was hit and killed by a motorist whilst out cycling in 1954, with the remaining siblings going into temporary retirement. The three brothers were eventually coaxed back and spent two years performing in Baptist churches before deciding to switch musical genres and head for New York in 1956, all with the blessing of their parents.

Soon after arriving in New York the brothers got their first recording deal, signing with Teenage Records for their debut *Angels Cried*. The next couple of years saw them record for a succession of small labels and perform as the opening act for various bigger R&B acts on package tours. On one of these they were spotted by a talent scout from RCA Victor, performing a cover version of Jackie Wilson's *Lonely Teardrops*. Their performance was good enough to earn them their first major label contract, with their second single being a self-composed number entitled *Shout* which became their chart debut, peaking at #47 towards the end of 1959.

Unable to replicate that success at RCA, The Isley Brothers continued their nomadic existence, eventually turning up at Scepter Records' Wand imprint. They initially intended recording a cover version of *Make It Easy On Yourself*, only to find another act had beaten them to it, so instead accepted the advice of producer Bert Berns to record a cover version of The Top Notes' Atlantic Records miss *Twist And Shout*. As raucous a performance as *Shout* had been three years previously, *Twist And Shout* restored the group to the charts, making #19 pop and #2 R&B in 1962, although the song itself would later become more commonly associated with The Beatles.

The Isley Brothers scored another minor hit with another twist orientated record, *Twistin' With Linda*, which made #54 pop later the same year. The Isley Brothers were soon on the move again, switching to United Artists (where they would record the first version of *Who's That Lady*), their own T-Neck imprint and later Atlantic, at which point their backing musicians included Jimi Hendrix.

By 1965 the group was struggling to make any kind of impact and after receiving an invitation to join Motown put T-Neck into storage and signed with the Tamla imprint. Handed over to HDH, the group could have been forgiven for thinking they had become a major priority for the label, but HDH had no intention of giving The Isley Brothers brand new material to record. Instead, *This Old Heart Of Mine (Is Weak For You)* was dusted down, a song that had originally been intended for Kim Weston or The Four Tops (Kim Weston had been assigned the track and the only thing that prevented The Four Tops from recording it was they were on tour at the time).

Regardless of how they came by the song, The Isley Brothers turned in a commanding performance, enabling the single to hit #6 R&B and #12 pop in the US and #47 in the UK in 1966. The first time out at Tamla proved to be as good as it got, at least as far as the US was concerned, for subsequent hits *Take Some Time Out For Love* (#66 pop), *I Guess I'll Always Love You* (#31 R&B and #61 pop and #45 in the UK), *Got To Have You Back* (#47 R&B and #97 pop), *That's The Way Love Is* (#125 pop) and *Take Me In Your Arms (Rock Me A Little While)* (#22 R&B and #121 pop) represented their full singles chart career whilst with Tamla.

One of their two albums also charted, although there was some considerable controversy surrounding the cover to their debut **This Old Heart Of Mine**, with a white boy and girl on a beach rather than a picture of the group. The group may not have made the cover but they did at least make the chart, with the album struggling to #140 on the pop chart but performing much better at R&B where it made #15.

By the time **Soul On The Rocks** was released in 1967, the cracks between Motown and The Isley Brothers were already beginning to widen, and whilst there were several potential hit singles to be found on the album, the fact that nothing made any impact in the US would indicate that Motown had lost interest in the group. The feeling was somewhat mutual, for when Motown offered a contract renewal in 1968 The Isley Brothers turned it down, preferring to return home to New Jersey in order to reactivate T-Neck.

There were to be other hits on Motown, but these occurred on the other side of the Atlantic, where Tamla Motown took the decision to reissue *This Old Heart Of Mine* in 1968 and saw it make #3 the second time around. Flush with this success, *I Guess I'll Always Love You* was given another airing, this time going to the very brink of the Top Ten when it stopped at #11. A track from the **Soul On The Rocks** album, *Behind A Painted Smile* returned them to the Top Ten, peaking at #5 in May 1969.

As *Behind A Painted Smile* began its descent down the chart, The Isley Brothers first outing on T-Neck (released on the Major Minor label in the UK), *It's Your Thing* was going in the opposite direction. The single would hit the top of the R&B chart and #2 pop in the US and #30 in the UK, but its success prompted a lawsuit from Motown, who claimed the track had actually been recorded whilst the group was still contracted to the label. A lengthy lawsuit was finally settled nearly eight years later when a federal judge upheld an earlier jury decision that the song had been recorded *after* the group left Motown, even if the song itself had been written whilst the group was under contract.

At the time of the settlement, The Isley Brothers had been expanded by the addition of two further brothers (Ernie and Marvin) and a cousin (Chris Jasper) and were ruling both the pop and R&B charts with their own brand of R&B and funk. It would result in smash albums such as **3+3**, **The Heat Is On**, **Harvest For The World** and **Showdown**, along with major hit singles in *That Lady, Summer Breeze, Live It Up, Fight The Power, Harvest For the World* and *The Pride*. Motown tried to capitalise on The Isley Brothers' new found fame with a hastily packaged **Doin' Their Thing – Best Of The Isley Brothers**, whilst in the UK the run of hit singles was maintained by *Put Yourself In My Place*, but the musical difference between their Motown recordings and their own work on T-Neck was vast.

Indeed, Ernie Isley recalls asking Ronald, who wrote most of *It's Your Thing* why the group didn't record the song whilst they were with Motown. He told him, 'Because it would have been done differently, with a different arrangement. And he said that there was a certain way they wanted the song to go, and a certain direction they wanted their career to go in.' The final assessment would be that The Isley Brothers made the correct career decision; they enjoyed greater success away from Motown than they had within and with a musical style that was all their own. The six piece line-up would remain together until 1984 when the three younger members (Ernie, Marvin and Chris) splintered off into Isley Jasper Isley, with the three older brothers retaining The Isley Brothers moniker. The group was inducted into the Rock & Roll Hall of Fame in 1992. O'Kelly died from a heart attack on 31 March 1986, Marvin died from diabetes on 6 June 2010.

ALBUMS: THIS OLD HEART OF MINE (1966), SOUL ON THE ROCKS (1967), BEHIND A PAINTED SMILE (1969)
COMPILATIONS: DOIN' THEIR THING (1969), GREATEST HITS (1970), SUPER HITS (1976)

ISOTOPE

British jazz rock group Isotope was formed in 1972 by guitarist Gary Boyle (born in Bihar, India on 24 November 1941), recruiting Brian Miller (keyboards), Jeff Ovid Clyne (born on 29 January 1937, bass) and Nigel Morris (drums), who toured extensively before landing a recording contract with Gull Records in 1974 and recording an eponymous debut album the same year. Soon after release Clyne and Miller left and were replaced by Hugh Hopper (born in Cantebury on 29 April 1945) and Laurence Scott (born on 7 February 1946) respectively.

This new line-up recorded the follow-up album **Illusion**, which was released in the UK in 1974 and issued in the US by Motown a year later. This was the only album issued via Motown, although Isotope would record one further album, **Deep End** for Gull in 1976 before disbanding. Hugh Hopper died from leukaemia on 7 June 2009. Jeff Clyne died from a heart attack on 16 November 2009.
ALBUM: ILLUSION (1975)

IT SHOULD HAVE BEEN ME – YVONNE FAIR [SINGLE]

Ask American Motown fans who scored the hit with *It Should Have Been Me* and they will probably answer Gladys Knight & The Pips. Ask their British counterparts the same question and they will reply without hesitation Yvonne Fair. The song, written by Norman Whitfield (it is widely believed to have been his very first Motown composition) and Mickey Stevenson, had originally been recorded by Kim Weston, appearing on the flip side to her 1963 single *Love Me All The Way* (although initially *It Should Have Been Me* had been the A side until DJ reaction to *Love Me All The Way* prompted a switch). Five years later Norman revived it on Gladys and her Pips, slowing down the tempo to match the mood of the song and was rewarded with a #9 R&B and #40 pop hit. Kim Weston's original had not been released in the UK and Gladys version missed the charts altogether, meaning the song at least was relatively untested in the market.

In 1975 Norman revisited it once again, this time on Yvonne Fair, retaining the slow tempo but increasing the bitterness in the lyrics courtesy of a majestic vocal performance from Yvonne. Whilst undoubtedly a risky single release, especially after the first release from **The Bitch Is Black**, *Funky Music Sho' Nuff Turns Me On*, had failed to gain much interest, *It Should Have Been Me* proved to be a surprise hit. And not just a hit, but a veritable monster, finally coming to rest at #5 on the UK chart. The success in the UK prompted Motown to try in the US, but it stalled at #85. Yvonne Fair was unable to fully capitalise on the hit in either the UK or the US, and *It Should Have Been Me* would turn out to be the last hit Norman Whitfield enjoyed on the Tamla Motown label, for he was shortly to depart Motown in order to set up his own, eponymous label.

IT'S ALL IN THE GAME – THE FOUR TOPS [SINGLE]

In 1911 Charles Dawes was a Chicago bank president by day and amateur pianist and flautist in his spare time. One day he came up with a melody that he played to a friend, the violinist Francis MacMillen, who in turn took it to a local publisher. The tune, known as *Dawes Melody In A Major* was duly published, accompanied by pictures of Charles Dawes wherever it was sold. This prompted Dawes to remark that he would be pilloried by his friends, stating "They will say that if all my notes in my bank are as bad as my musical ones, they are not worth the paper they were written on."

The tune became immensely popular, despite the apprehension and much to the chagrin of Charles Dawes, who would serve as Vice President under Calvin Coolidge and help set up the Dawes Plan to collect war reparations from Germany after the First World War (for which he shared the 1925 Nobel Peace Prize). His tune, meanwhile, continued to attract interest, being recorded and performed by the likes of Tommy Dorsey. Soon after Dawes death in 1951, lyricist Carl Sigman added a set of sentimental lyrics to create the song *It's All In The Game*, which was recorded by Dinah Shore, Sammy Kaye and Tommy Edwards, who had the biggest hit at the time.

The song became something of a standard over the next six or seven years, being recorded by Louis Armstrong and Nat King Cole and in 1958 was revived by Tommy Edwards as part of his make or break final session for MGM. It turned out to be make, for it sailed to the top of the charts, thus making Charles Dawes the only Vice President and Nobel Prize Winner to have composed a number one hit! It also topped the charts in the UK and five years later nearly made it all the way again when Cliff Richard had a version that peaked at #2.

Tommy Edwards' version had long been a favourite of Frank Wilson, who suggested it to The Four Tops and produced a compelling revival that did much to restore the group's stock around the world. Whilst a relatively minor #24 US pop hit, it made #6 on the R&B chart and reached as far as #5 in the UK in July 1970, the third time the song had got into the upper echelons of the chart.

IT'S MY TURN (FILM SOUNDTRACK)

Written by Eleanor Bergstein and directed by Claudia Weill, 'It's My Turn' was envisaged by the producers Martin Elfand and Jay Presson Allen as a romantic comedy. To this end they instructed that an erotic dance scene between the two stars, Michael Douglas and Jill Clayburgh, be deleted from the final cut of the film. Whilst the scene did not make 'It's My Turn', screenwriter Eleanor Bergstein used it as the basis of the 1987 film 'Dirty Dancing'.

'It's My Turn' meanwhile received mixed reviews upon release, and with the film struggling for acceptance the accompanying soundtrack was similarly hampered. The one saving grace was the title song, written by Carole Bayer Sager and Michael Masser and performed by Diana Ross which became a major hit, although it wasn't enough to rescue the soundtrack, which aside from Diana Ross featured fellow Motown act Ozone, Tony Travalini and orchestrated music by Patrick Williams. The album was released in October 1980, just as the film opened, but both soon sank without trace.

ALBUM: IT'S MY TURN SOUNDTRACK (1980)

IT'S MY TURN – DIANA ROSS [SINGLE]

Just as 'The Happening' became better known for The Supremes' title song, so 'It's My Turn' was to suffer much the same fate, rescued in part by the title song. The producers of 'It's My Turn' assigned the soundtrack to Motown, with much of the music written by Patrick Williams. Also hired were Carole Bayer Sager and Michael Masser, who wrote the theme song that was duly recorded and released as a single in the wake of Diana's recent hits with Chic' producers Nile Rodgers and Bernard Edwards. Released in September 1980, *It's My Turn* did brisk business, ending up hitting #9 pop (and made #9 on the Adult Contemproary Tracks chart) and #14 R&B in the US as well as #16 in the UK. The song would be recorded by Aretha Franklin the following year.

IT'S THE SAME OLD SONG – THE FOUR TOPS [SINGLE]

The Four Tops became so hot with *I Can't Help Myself* that not only Motown stood to benefit; in July 1965 Berry Gordy got wind that Columbia Records intended reissuing an old Four Tops record, *Ain't That Love* and had had the single remixed so as to sound as close to the famed Motown sound as they could with the material at their disposal. The presence of a rival Four Tops record was something that was to be avoided at all costs, not least because it would threaten the group's future releases on Motown. Berry instructed

Holland-Dozier-Holland to come up with an official follow-up as quickly as possible; legend has it the entire record was recorded, mixed and promotional copies pressed inside a day! The backing track had been recorded in May, complete with strings, but there were no lyrics and therefore no title. Indeed, the lyrics were still being written when The Four Tops arrived at Hitsville in order to record their parts!

It has been said that the eventual title was a somewhat tongue in cheek reference to HDH's policy of re-using bits of previous songs, either by isolating key sections or playing the same chords in reverse order. Either way, this policy had served them well in the past and would continue to do so in the future. Thus *It's The Same Old Song* is often said to be a re-write of *I Can't Help Myself*, but if that was all it was, it would not have performed as well as it did on the charts. Rather, *It's The Same Old Song* is a logical and natural progression from *I Can't Help Myself* and earned its chart placing on merit. It would peak at #5 on the pop chart and #14 R&B; in the UK progress was slower, with the single having to contend with a final placing of #34. Six years later, British studio group The Weathermen (effectively Jonathan King) took their version to #19 in the UK.

IT'S THE TEMPTATIONS – THE TEMPTATIONS [EP]

One of four EP's released in Britain by Tamla Motown in February 1966, **It's The Temptations** was a four track collection featuring *My Baby, Since I Lost My Baby, It's Growing* and *The Way You Do The Things You Do*. All four tracks had previously been released as singles, with only *It's Growing* making any kind of dent in the chart, peaking at #45 and spending just two weeks on the listings. The EP would also take its time making an impact, finally hitting the EP chart in February 1967 and peaking at #8.

IT'S WONDERFUL (TO BE LOVED BY YOU) – JIMMY RUFFIN [SINGLE]

By the end of the 1960s, Jimmy Ruffin's Motown career had reached a stalemate, with a succession of surprising releases, little or no promotion on those that were issued and a seeming reluctance to hand him over to the bigger name writers and producers. Whilst Jimmy could therefore be forgiven for thinking he was virtually unwanted at Hitsville, internationally it was a completely different story. There was something about his voice that motivated record buyers, so much so that they were snapping up his records as soon as they hit the shops. And not just new material either; a reissue of *I've Passed This Way Before* had become a Top 40 hit in the autumn of 1969 and kick started a Jimmy Ruffin revival that was to see his next three singles all land inside the Top Ten.

It's Wonderful was written and produced by James Dean and William Weatherspoon, the same team responsible for *Farewell Is A Lonely Sound* and *I'll Say Forever My Love* and was lifted from his **Ruff 'N' Ready** album released a year previously. Coming on the back of two Top Ten hits, *It's Wonderful* already had one foot in the door, but it would go on to become the biggest hit of his career up to that point in peaking at #6. Despite this British success, Motown in Detroit was unmoved; the single remained unreleased and, perhaps sensing that his time at the label was coming to an end, Jimmy took the decision to move to Britain permanently. That he continued to enjoy a hit recording career was Motown's loss, not Jimmy's.

I'VE NEVER BEEN TO ME - CHARLENE [SINGLE]

Written by Ron Miller and Kenneth Hirsch, *I've Never Been To Me* had originally been recorded by Charlene in 1976 for her eponymous album, with the version that appeared on the album being the full length version complete with a spoken bridge. It was subsequently edited to remove the bridge for release as a single on Prodigal in July 1977 and became a very minor hit, peaking at #97. A British release a month later went nowhere, and in 1980 Charlene was dropped by Prodigal, subsequently returning moving to Britain.

In February 1982, Florida DJ Scott Shannon played the record on WRBQ-FM at the suggestion of a girlfriend. The audience response was immediate, with the phones lighting up as listeners requested repeat plays. Eventually word got back to Motown that there was a buzz happening on the single in Florida and it might be worth reissuing. Released on the Motown label, the single would become a major hit the second time around, peaking at #3. It was also reissued in the UK on Motown and performed even better; entering the chart at #73 on 15 May 1982, it took seven weeks to sail to the top of the chart, knocking Adam Ant and *Goody Two Shoes* off the summit. A week later it was itself replaced by Captain Sensible and *Happy Talk*, but the single would go on to attain silver status (sales in excess of 250,000 copies) and spend five of its twelve weeks on the chart inside the Top Ten.

Although it had taken time for Charlene's version to catch fire, the song itself had proven popular almost from day one, attracting cover versions from Randy Crawford, Nancy Wilson (who scored the first hit, a minor #47 R&B placing in 1977), Mary McGregor, Walter Jackson, The Temptations, Howard Keel and even Ned's Atomic Dustbin!

J

JAKE JACAS

London-born trombonist and singer Jake Jacas studied classical music at the Knellar Hall School of Music. He began his musical career as Colin Jacas, working as a backing singer for Marc Bolan before he became a full time member of British soul group Gonzalez in 1979, appearing on their album **Move It To The Music**. Jake then had a one-off single deal with Motown in Europe, the self-composed *Hold Me* backed with an instrumental version being his only release in June 1985, although he later recorded **The Very Best of Jake Jacas** and with Bettye Lavette for Ian Levine's Motorcity label. He is better known for being a member of Sade's backing group between 1985 and 1989, appearing on the albums **Promise** and **Stronger Than Pride** and undertaking two world tours.

CHUCK JACKSON

The slew of hits Chuck Jackson recorded during the first six years of his career brought envious glances from many within the industry, most notably Smokey Robinson, who long coveted Chuck for the Motown roster.

Born in Winston-Salem, North Carolina on 22 July 1937, Chuck was raised in Latta in South Carolina where he began his career as a gospel singer with The Raspberry Singers. At the age of thirteen he moved to Pittsburgh where eventually he would be drawn to pursue a professional career in music, taking a song he had written (*Willette*, named after a girl Chuck knew) to the manager of The Dell-Vikings. The group had recently scored a number of hits but suffered from having an ever-changing line-up and hopping from one label to another. Chuck's arrival proved fortuitous, with *Willette* being recorded by the group for Joe Averbach's Fee Bee label and Chuck installed as lead singer.

In 1960 The Dell-Vikings were on the same bill as Jackie Wilson at the Howard Theater in Washington, with Jackie subsequently inviting Chuck to open for him at the Apollo Theatre a month or so later. On his opening night, representatives of Scepter Records were in the audience and were impressed enough to offer him a solo recording contract on the spot.

Assigned to the Wand label, Chuck scored a major hit first time out with *I Don't Want To Cry*, which would make the Top 40 pop and Top Five R&B, kicking off a run of some twenty six hits over the next six years. It was not only as a solo artist that Chuck made his name either, for a number of duets with Maxine Brown and Doris Troy also charted. It was, however, his work with noted songwriter Burt Bacharach that established his reputation, with *I Wake Up Crying* and *Any Day Now* his biggest hits. It was not only record buyers who took to Chuck Jackson, for Smokey Robinson noted his rise and constantly told him he should try his luck at Motown. By 1967 and with the hits at Wand beginning to dry up, Chuck took Smokey's advice and began negotiations with Motown.

Not only did Motown finally get their hands on Chuck Jackson, they also got Yvonne Fair as part of the package. Chuck and Yvonne had worked together for a number of years, with Yvonne initially used to sing live the female parts that had been recorded by Maxine Brown, but Yvonne's force of personality was such that she eventually got a healthy slot of her own on Chuck's revue. Chuck and Yvonne thus signed with Motown in September 1967, with the pair recording a number of duets during their initial days at Hitsville, even though the recordings were left on the shelf for many years.

As a solo performer, Chuck was handed over to Smokey Robinson and Al Cleveland, who produced Chuck's debut outing *(You Can't Let The Boy Overpower) The Man In You*, a revival of The Miracles' 1964 hit, which was released in February 1968 and peaked at #94 on the pop chart (it would be flipped for release in the UK, with *Girls Girls Girls* being promoted as the top side, without success). Later the same month came **Chuck Jackson Arrives**, an album containing songs drawn from the Jobete catalogue but without any real focus or concept. With his Motown career already stalling, it would be more than a year until any new material arrived, with April 1969's *Are You Lonely For Me Baby* at least returning him to the Top 30 of the R&B chart, peaking at #27, although it was unable to shift beyond the #107 and bubbling under slot on the pop chart.

Chuck's second Motown album retained much the same formula as his debut, meaning **Goin' Back To Chuck Jackson** featured an array of Jobete material as well as a couple of covers from outside. *Honey Come Back* at least became a minor hit, reaching #46 pop and #43 R&B (but missed out in the UK), but it was a significant drop from the heady days he had enjoyed at Wand. By November 1969 Chuck had been moved off the Motown label and placed with V.I.P., but *The Day My World Stood Still* showed that his career had stood still. Chuck was to release three further singles for V.I.P.; *Two Feet From Happiness* in May 1970, *Pet Names* in January 1971 and *Who You Gonna Run To* in July 1971. Sandwiched in between these releases was his final album, **Teardrops Keep Falling On My Head** which was issued in September 1970. After the failure of his final single in July 1971, Chuck left the company and headed over to ABC.

"It was a bad move to go to Motown. Motown was not a Chuck Jackson record company. They didn't know the New York sound. I'm not talking about the studios now, I'm talking about the singer. They didn't know how to cut me. I'm sure that was a lot of it."

Chuck found a degree of success with ABC and later All Platinum and EMI American, although none were able to restore him to the kind of successes he had enjoyed in the 1960s with Wand. Despite this, he retains his popularity in the UK, where he is still a regular performer.

ALBUMS: ARRIVES (1968), GOING BACK TO CHUCK JACKSON (1969), TEARDROPS KEEP FALLING ON MY HEAD (1970)

ERNESTINE JACKSON

Born in Corpus Christi, Texas on 18 September 1942, Ernestine made her name as an actress and singer, making her Broadway debut in 1967 in the role of Irene Molloy in 'Hello Dolly'. In 1976 she landed the role of Sarah Brown in the revival of 'Guys And Dolls', a role that would earn her a Tony Award nomination for Best Actress (Music), her second nomination (she had earlier been nominated for Best Supporting Actress for her role in 'Raisin'). Ernestine appeared on the soundtrack album released by Motown and has since gone on to add to her acting credits, appearing in 'The Bonfire Of The Vanities', 'Girls Town' and 'Steam' as well as the television series 'Law And Order', 'Swift Justice' and 'Roots: The Next Generation'.

JACKIE JACKSON

The second child born to Joseph and Katherine Jackson, Sigmund Esco Jackson was born in Gary, Indiana on 4 May 1951 and given the nickname Jackie by family relatives. Growing up Jackie had aspirations of becoming a professional baseball player, but when his younger brothers formed themselves into a group, The Jackson Brothers, Jackie took his place alongside his siblings. Whilst much of the focus on The Jackson 5 was on Michael and Jermaine, Jackie's high tenor was used to stunning effect on a succession of hit singles.

When plans were announced to have Michael and Jermaine undertake parallel solo careers, Jackie got one as well, although without anywhere near as much promotional support as either of his brothers. This was despite having The Corporation and Berry Gordy on hand supplying material and production on the album; with nothing released as a single and Motown's full marketing force behind Michael and Jermaine, **Jackie Jackson** disappeared from sight almost as soon as it was released in October 1973 (it was released in the UK in January 1974).

Jackie married Enid Spann the following year (1974), with whom he would have two children, Siggy (born on 29 June 1977) and Brandi Jackson (born on 6 February 1982). Along with all the original Jackson 5 members bar Jermaine, Jackie left Motown in 1975 bound for CBS and more creative control. Jackie would play an important role in the group's later successes, most notably on the **Victory** album and the singles *Wait* and *Torture*, although he was unable to take part of the tour – officially he was out of action owing to a knee injury incurred during rehearsals, but it was later claimed the injury was being due to Enid running him over in a parking lot after catching him with another woman! Jackie and Enid divorced in 1987, with Jackie subsequently marrying Victoria Triggs in 2001. He revived his solo career in 1989 when he recorded **Be The One** for Polydor Records. Today Jackie runs his own record labels, Jesco Records and Futurist Entertainment, with his son Siggy (recording as DEALZ) one of the artists.

ALBUM: JACKIE JACKSON (1973)

JERMAINE JACKSON

The fourth child born to Joseph and Katherine Jackson, Jermaine LaJuane Jackson was born in Gary, Indiana on 11 December 1954. Along with Tito and Jackie, Jermaine would pull his father's treasured guitar out of the closet and play whilst their father was at work, with all three becoming more than capable on the instrument before the strain of three young, inquisitive hands managed to break one of the strings. After surviving the inevitable backlash from Joe, the three were given the chance to show off what they had learned for themselves; when they passed that test, Joseph encouraged them to form a group.

The group, which began as The Jackson Brothers with Jermaine on lead guitar and lead vocals, would eventually evolve into The Jackson Five, with Jermaine having to switch to bass guitar and devolve lead vocal duties to Michael. It was this later incarnation that got a deal with Motown in 1968, and although the initial focus was on Michael, Jermaine proved an ideal counterpoint, providing the lead vocals on numerous album tracks and a significant joint lead vocal on I'll Be There.

The success of Michael's parallel solo career caused Motown to consider other members of the group for similar treatment, with Jermaine the next in line, due in part to the fact he had already proven a more than capable lead singer and because the fan mail for Jermaine was almost as great as that for Michael. Jermaine was handed over to a variety of writing and production teams for his July 1972 debut, including Hal Davis, The Corporation (both of whom he had already worked with during the course of his Jackson 5 career), Johnny Bristol, Gloria Jones and Pam Sawyer and Jerry Marcellino and Mel Larson.

After a minor hit with the first single That's How Love Goes (#23 R&B and #46 pop), Jermaine scored a million selling hit with Daddy's Home, a revival of Shep & The Limelites 1961 hit. The success of the two singles helped propel sales of the **Jermaine** album, which would eventually come to rest at #6 R&B and #27 pop, being only just below the chart positions achieved by Michael's solo debut. As work began on his second album, **Come Into My Life**, Jermaine could have been forgiven for thinking he would supplant Michael as the major priority at Motown, not least because of his burgeoning relationship with Berry Gordy's eldest child, daughter Hazel Joy. The pair were to marry in December 1973 in a star-studded, celebrity packed ceremony (one notable absentee was Marvin Gaye, who had previously been married to Berry's sister Gwen and felt that Jermaine was replacing him as the Prince of Motown), not long after Jermaine had graduated from high school!

It took some time for Jermaine to become the heir apparent at Motown, with the May 1973 release **Come Into My Life** barely registering on the chart (#30 R&B and #152 pop) and a subsequent September single release in You're In Good Hands also stalling (#35 R&B and #79 pop). It was not only Jermaine as a solo artist who was suffering; even The Jackson 5's recordings were running out of steam, due in part because of Motown's refusal to allow the group to mature musically.

By 1975 Joseph was shopping for a new deal outside of Motown, a decision that was always going to cause Jermaine anguish, for whichever side he took, he would incur the wrath of his father or father-in-law. In the end, Jermaine opted to remain at Motown when the brothers left for Epic, an option that prompted Joseph to lividly exclaim "My blood runs through Jermaine's veins, not Berry Gordy's." It wasn't only his new-found family ties that bound Jermaine to Motown; Jermaine still believed the label was the right home for him and the rest of his brothers, as he would later state.

"Motown was gonna make us like The Beatles. We were The Jackson 5 and that's all I wanted."

Berry certainly pulled out all of the steps for Jermaine's next album, the August 1975 release **My Name Is Jermaine** assembling a veritable who's who of producers and songwriters in an effort to prove to The Jackson 5 that they had made the wrong decision in leaving Motown. Unfortunately the abundance of writers and producers resulted in a disjointed album that struggled to hit #29 R&B and only #164 pop, with the only single lifted Let's Be Young Tonight barely faring any better (#19 R&B and #55 pop).

As the 1970s progressed Jermaine's career did not, a situation not helped by the eventual elevation of The Jacksons (they lost the rights to the name The Jackson 5 following their departure from Motown) to superstar status, both as a group and for Michael as a solo performer. Whilst the group registered gold with **The Jacksons** and platinum with **Destiny**, Jermaine still found himself languishing well down the charts, 1977's **Feel The Fire** getting no higher than #36 R&B and #174 pop.

In 1979 Michael Jackson released **Off The Wall** and threw down a challenge to Jermaine and Motown. Enlisting the help of Stevie Wonder, Jermaine not only rose to the challenge, he met it head on. Stevie was responsible for writing and producing three tracks on the album, including one that was revived from 1975 in You're Supposed To Keep Your Love For Me. However, the standout track was to be the album's title track, Let's Get Serious, on which Stevie also contributed his distinctive vocal; the end result was a sure-fire smash that powered its way to the top of the R&B chart and #9 pop, also becoming Jermaine's chart debut in the UK when it hit #8. Fuelled by the success of the single, the album would also become a major success, hitting #1 R&B and #6 on the pop chart (it would have to settle for a rather more modest resting place of #22 in the UK). Further single success came from *You're Supposed To Keep Your Love For Me*, which hit #32 R&B and #34 pop, with *Burnin' Hot* being extracted for release in the UK and making #32. Jermaine's eponymous follow-up album, released in December 1980 also topped the R&B chart, although its performance on the pop chart was below expectations at #44 and it also failed to make any impact in the UK. There was some compensation on the singles chart, with *Little Girl Don't You Worry* making #17 R&B and the follow-up *You Like Me Don't You* hitting #13 R&B, #50 pop and #41 in the UK.

In addition to his own solo career, Jermaine also found himself mentoring other acts within Motown, most notably DeBarges, another family group that had evolved out of the earlier group Switch. However, his days at Motown were heading towards the end, with two further albums in **I Like Your Style** (a #31 R&B and #86 pop hit) and **Let Me Tickle Your Fancy** (#9 R&B and #46 pop, with the title track hitting #5 R&B and #18 pop on the singles charts) unlikely to challenge brother Michael's then near domination of the charts.

"I just felt I wanted to be on my own, to be out. We talked it over for a long time, then went to Berry and told him of my decision. We looked at it from all sides and he understood. He said he wanted me to be happy and if this move would make me happy I should do it."

Jermaine subsequently resurfaced at Arista in 1984 where he resumed his solo career and recorded with and produced Whitney Houston (who he was later reported to have been involved in a romantic liaison), worked with Pia Zadora on the theme to the film 'Voyage Of The Rock Aliens' and also linking up with his siblings for a series of albums and tours following their successful reunion for the television broadcast 'Motown 25' in 1983. He also moved into television production, including the award winning 'The Jacksons: An American Dream' in 1992. His marriage to Hazel, with whom he had three children, ended in divorce in 1988, by which time he was involved with Margaret Maldonado (and had a further child by another, un-named woman), who would become his common-law wife. This relationship resulted in two children before Jermaine married Alejandra Genevieve Oaziaza (a former girlfriend of Randy Jackson, with whom she had two children) resulting in a further two children. Jermaine married for a third time to Halima Rashid in 2004. He converted to Islam in 1989, taking on the name Mohammad Abdul Aziz, although his continued television work is invariably produced under his original name of Jermaine Jackson.

ALBUMS: JERMAINE (1972), COME INTO MY LIFE (1973), MY NAME IS JERMAINE (1975), FEEL THE FIRE (1977), FRONTIERS (1978), LET'S GET SERIOUS (1980), JERMAINE (1980), I LIKE YOUR STYLE (1981), LET ME TICKLE YOUR FANCY (1982)

REVEREND JESSE JACKSON

The civil rights activist and Baptist minister was born Jesse Louis Burns in Greenville, South Carolina on 8 October 1941, changing his name to Jesse Jackson when his mother married a year later (his father was a married neighbour of Jesse's mother Helen Burns). An exceptional sportsman as a teenager, Jesse had the chance of pursuing minor league professional baseball but rejected this in order to attend university of a football scholarship. He graduated in sociology and was working towards a master's degree when he dropped out of college in order to focus on the civil rights movement full time, working closely with Dr Martin Luther King and James Bevel.

On 25 December 1971 Jesse helped establish Operation PUSH (People United to Save Humanity, although Jesse later changed the name to People United to Serve Humanity), something of an effort to improve economic opportunities for the poor of all races. The following year, Operation PUSH staged a Black Exposition in Chicago's Amphitheater, with more than thirty of the top African American artists of the day performing in concert. The highlights of the show were subsequently released as a double album 'Save The Children', with Jesse Jackson featured on the album twice. Since then The Reverend Jesse Jackson (he was ordained a Baptist minister in 1968) has continued to be an often outspoken critic of American domestic policy as it relates to the plight of the poor in general and African Americans in particular. He also twice stood as the Democratic candidate for presidential nomination (in 1984 and 1988) and served as a shadow Senator for the District of Columbia between 1991 and 1997.

MICHAEL JACKSON

The eighth of the ten children born to Joseph and Katherine Jackson, Michael Joseph Jackson was born in Gary, Indiana on 29 August 1958 and displayed his musical talents at a very early age. When Joseph had the three oldest brothers form themselves into a group in 1962, four year old Michael itched to be a part of the set up, creating his own percussion instruments out of discarded boxes until such time Joseph bought proper instruments.

However, it was as a vocalist along with his dynamic dance moves that his true talent shone, with Michael looking to all intents and purposes a pre-teen version of James Brown. Eventually the family group, initially known as Ripple & The Waves but ultimately to become The Jackson Five, was built around Michael, with previous lead singer Jermaine relegated to secondary lead in order to accommodate Michael's new found centre stage position.

Joseph rehearsed all of the brothers relentlessly but reserved the most punishing routines for Michael, resulting in the most vicious punishment should he get a single word or dance step wrong. Whilst this robbed Michael of his entire childhood and left him variously physically and emotionally abused, it also instilled in Michael the desire to strive for perfection, ultimately paving the way for his later success.

After a brief recording spell with Steeltown, the group landed a much bigger contract with Motown, although their arrival at the label took the personal intervention of Gladys Knight and then Bobby Taylor. The newly christened Jackson 5 were launched on to the market in August 1969 and proved an instant sensation, the quality of the material that was specially created for them being matched by their obvious stage presence. Of the five, it was Michael out front that caught the eye, displaying a maturity well beyond his age (even more so given that Motown knocked two years off his real age in an attempt to make him appear even cuter), enough to convince Berry Gordy that not only could Michael front the group, he could maintain a parallel solo career.

In announcing the decision to the family, Berry was quick to stress that this *wasn't* the first step in launching an entirely new career for Michael. The group wasn't going to become Michael Jackson & The Jackson 4 (as had happened with Smokey Robinson and Diana, who had been elevated to the front of The Miracles and The Supremes respectively), neither was it going to be to the detriment of the group as whole. There was material that Berry felt would be a perfect fit for Michael as a solo artist that did not work within a group environment.

The first fruits of this new career came in October 1971 with the Elliot Willensky penned *Got To Be There*, which would hit #4 on both the R&B and pop chart and reach #5 in the UK. The similarly titled album was released the following January in the US and, with The Jackson 5 still very much flavour of the time, it would go on to make #2 on both the R&B and pop charts. For the second single, Motown went with a revival of *Rockin' Robin* which had provided Bobby Day with a #2 hit in 1958. It would peak at a similar position in the US, kept off the top of the pop chart by Roberta Flack and *First Time Ever I Saw Your Face*, as well as making #3 in the UK. **Got To Be There** made a belated appearance in the UK in April 1972, just as *Rockin' Robin* was reaching its chart peak, but despite having already played host to two Top Ten hits, the album could do no better than #37 on the chart. The Top Ten single count increased by one in the UK, Tamla Motown opting to extract *Ain't No Sunshine*, the Bill Withers penned number that had provided its author with a massive US hit but which had failed to register in the UK. Tamla Motown's bravery was vindicated when Michael's single hit #8, and whilst Bill's version remains popular, in the UK it is Michael's version that is considered definitive. In the US it was the Leon Ware and T-Boy Ross penned *I Wanna Be Where You Are* that was lifted as a single, and whilst it peaked at #2 on the R&B chart, it stalled at #16 pop.

Michael's next hit came with his ode to a rat; the title track to the film 'Ben' was originally intended for fellow teen sensation Donny Osmond to record, but with he and his siblings on tour at the time of the planned recording session, Michael stepped in to record it and made it his own. *Ben* would go on to become his first solo chart topper, spending a week at the summit of the pop chart in October 1972 and reaching #5 R&B. Released in November in the UK, it would become his fourth consecutive Top Ten hit when peaking at #7. Such was the success of the single it garnered writers Don Black and Walter Scharf nominations for a Golden Globe for Best Song (which it won) and an Academy Award for Best Original Song (which it lost to *The Morning After* from 'The Poseidon Adventure', despite Michael performing at the awards ceremony). Fortunately for Motown, the popularity of *Ben* and Michael was sufficient to help the parent album making #5 pop and #4 R&B, for the rest of the album was an uneven collection of covers and new material that lacked real focus; the album would have to settle for peaking at #17 in the UK, with little else that was released as a single bothering the Top 40.

By the end of 1972, a rift had grown between Motown (for which read Berry Gordy) and The Jackson 5 (for which read Joseph Jackson). At the heart of the battles was Berry's refusal to even consider allowing Michael or any of his siblings the opportunity of recording self-composed material, either as solo singles (by then both Jermaine and Jackie had also undertaken parallel solo careers) or album tracks, collectively or singularly. The Jackson 5, Michael, Jermaine and Jackie could record only what Motown instructed them to, irrespective of their wishes or desires to grow as artists.

Thus the ragbag collection of material that had been utilised to compile **Ben** was repeated on **Music And Me**, which featured a depressed looking Michael on the cover, which was made even more poignant with the picture of Michael holding an acoustic guitar, even though he wasn't allowed to perform anything other than vocals on the album itself. Michael appeared disinterested on the cover and record buyers expressed their disinterest too, with the album limping in at #92 pop and #24 R&B in the US and failing to chart at all in the UK. Motown initially intended hurrying another album on to the market in the wake of **Music And Me**, but the surprising success of The Jackson 5 single *Dancing Machine* prompted Motown to halt all recording on the solo project and concentrate on marketing the group album instead.

When **Forever Michael** appeared in January 1975, most of the material and recordings were already nearly a year old. With the rift between the Motown and Jackson camps by now a chasm, little or no promotion or marketing was put behind the release, resulting in a derisory #101 position on the pop chart, even if it did confound everyone by reaching #10 on the R&B chart. Meanwhile, negotiations between Joseph and Berry had reached an impasse; Joseph was adamant that the group wanted greater creative control, as had already been given to Marvin Gaye and Stevie Wonder, whilst Berry was equally firm in his position that Motown knew best.

Joseph eventually got the group a contract with Epic Records (although initially *without* the autonomy that had proven a deal-breaker in the negotiations with Motown), with the result Michael, Tito, Jackie and Marlon jumped ship. Only Jermaine remained at Motown, as he had married into the family, with Randy replacing him in the revamped Jacksons. The deal was announced at a press conference in June 1975, although The Jacksons would not be able to officially sign for Epic until the following March.

Whilst Motown were resigned to losing Michael and his brothers (although not without a legal challenge) there was still enough material left in the can to keep a succession of albums hitting the streets. First off was a compilation album **The Best Of Michael Jackson**, an album released in August 1975 that chart-wise reflected the difference in buying habits in the US and UK; in the US, where such a compilation was usually seen as an admission that an artist had run its course, the album peaked at #44 R&B and a distant #156 on the pop chart, whilst in the UK, where such releases were (and still are) commonplace, it would eventually perform admirably in reaching #11 (albeit six years later when everything Michael touched turned to gold or platinum).

The Jacksons duly bade their farewells to Motown and took up residence at Epic and the next chapter of their careers. The desire to retain greater control over what they recorded and released might have been the motivating factor in their departure from Motown, but The Jacksons didn't find it much different at Epic. Instead, they were handed over to writers and producers from Motown's chief rivals in the R&B field at the time, Philadelphia International and Kenny Gamble and Leon Huff. The Jacksons were to record two albums with the Philadelphia kingpins at the helm, **The Jacksons** and **Goin' Places**, with the first album earning the group their first, official gold album for sales in excess of half a million copies, even if the overall reception to both had been somewhat lukewarm. Indeed, neither had caused enough of a stir to prompt Motown to delve in to their extensive back catalogue and put out a competing album.

Yet, unbeknown to all parties, Motown was to loom large in the Michael Jackson story again. In 1977 Motown had picked up the film rights to 'The Wiz', a theatrical show featuring music and lyrics written by Charlie Smalls that had been a major hit on Broadway, running to over 1,600 performances and making a star out of the lead performer Stephanie Mills. Sidney Lumet had been brought in to direct and with him came a reluctant Quincy Jones to oversee the soundtrack (according to later reports, Quincy only took the assignment as a favour to Lumet), who in turn would enlist Nickolas Ashford and Valerie Simpson and Luther Vandross to help flesh out Charlie Smalls' original score.

Manoeuvres behind the scenes had seen Diana Ross land the role of Dorothy, even though her presence required a considerable re-write of the script, since 33-year old Diana could not expect to convincingly portray sixteen year old Dorothy in the film; even adapting the script to make Dorothy a 24 year old schoolteacher required a stretch of the imagination. Whilst the lead role was given to completely the wrong person, the casting of Richard Pryor as The Wiz and Michael Jackson as the Scarecrow was inspired, none more so than Michael landing his first major role.

Michael accepted the role almost as soon as it was offered, despite the opposition of his father Joseph, who could not see what Michael stood to gain by once again doing something completely divorced from his brothers. Michael refused to listen to his father's arguments and opted to take the role, confident that it would be the first step in a successful multi-level entertainment career. As such Michael gave his all, spending hour upon hour studying tapes of gazelles, cheetahs and panthers in order to learn how to move gracefully.

More importantly, at least as far as his future musical career was concerned, he struck up an instant rapport with producer Quincy Jones, resulting in one of the few musical high spots in *Ease On Down The Road*. The film would garner some notoriety and a slew of nominations (four Academy Awards, including Best Original Music Score, although it failed to win in any category for which it was nominated), but proved to be a commercial disaster. Only Quincy, Michael and Richard emerged from the debacle with their reputations unblemished, with Quincy and Michael enjoying the experience enough to seriously contemplate working together in the future.

In fact, the decision to have Quincy Jones helm the **Off The Wall** album wasn't a clear-cut decision, with Michael telephoning Quincy to ask his advice as to which producer he should consider engaging. Quincy gave him just one name, his own, and Michael readily agreed. Released in August 1979, **Off The Wall** exceeded all expectations, selling over seven million copies in the US alone and giving rise to no fewer than four Top Ten pop hits, also matching that tally in the UK.

This time Motown did attempt to capitalise on his new found popularity, releasing *One Day In Your Life* as a single and utilising the title for an accompanying album that featured four tracks from The Jackson 5 alongside six Michael solo efforts. In the US, the single peaked at #42 R&B and #55 pop, with the album making #41 R&B and #144 pop. Once again, it was in the UK that both found a better market, with the single becoming Michael's first single chart topper (in what was a unique event for Motown in the UK, *One Day In Your Life* replaced Smokey Robinson's *Being With You* at the chart summit) and the album reached #29. There was enough momentum to propel a second single, *We're Almost There* into the Top 50 at #46, even if the overall sound on the **One Day In Your Life** album and assorted singles was in complete contrast to the slick feel of **Off The Wall**.

It was not only as a solo performer that Michael was making his presence felt on the charts, for he had taken a much greater role in The Jacksons, enabling their **Destiny** and **Triumph** albums reach heights that had proven beyond The Jackson 5 even at their peak. Both albums went platinum, aided by a succession of hit singles and a tour, with the latter Michael undertaking in order to placate his father and brothers rather than any real desire to go out on the road. Indeed, by 1981 everything Michael did or planned was centred on what was best for Michael Jackson as a solo performer, not what was best for The Jacksons.

This had put him on a collision course with his father and manager Joseph, but Michael had avoided that issue by appointing his own lawyer in John Branca and allowing him virtually all of the rights usually associated with a manager. That left Michael free to do what he felt he did best, which was create music.

Michael and Quincy reconvened in August 1982 to begin work on the follow-up album **Thriller**, utilising much the same pool of writers and musicians to craft the album. Michael was initially unhappy with the mix and threatened to pull the album off the release schedule (it was intended to be out in time for the crucial Christmas market in 1982), much to the horror of Columbia head Walter Yetnikoff. Fortunately, a mix that Michael was happy with was completed in time for the album to hit the streets on 30 November 1982. The performance of the first single, a duet with Paul McCartney on *The Girl Is Mine* that had preceded the album with a release in October had hardly been a ringing endorsement for the forthcoming album, but the album was critically well received and, more importantly, been an immediate commercial success in selling a million copies within the first week. Maintaining that level of album sales was reliant on the singles performing well, with *Billie Jean* quickly installed as the second single and scheduled for release in January 1983.

Michael agreed to film a video, with Steve Barron brought in to direct the clip. Taken to MTV, it was initially refused airtime on the grounds that the station's viewers were not into R&B, that it was more rock orientated. Enraged, Walter Yetnikoff called the head of MTV and told him that in light of MTV's refusal to air *Billie Jean*, he was going to pull every Columbia and Epic artist and video from the station and inform the media why he had done so, basically accusing MTV of racism. MTV backed down and aired the video and were pleasantly surprised that the clip received a positive reaction, enough for it to be given medium and then heavy rotation on the station. The repeated airings were sufficient to significantly add to the sales of **Thriller**.

However, it was Motown that would provide the vehicle that elevated **Thriller** (and *Billie Jean*) beyond being an exceptional album into an industry phenomenon. Motown had previously celebrated its tenth and twentieth anniversaries with low-key promotions, but with the twenty fifth anniversary looming, it was decided to produce a real song and dance occasion. Several of the artists that the producers wished to feature on the show had long left Motown, requiring lengthy negotiations between Motown and management in order to get them back, even for only one night. Gradually, they all signed up for the event, although one of the last holdouts was Michael Jackson, necessitating a personal visit from Berry Gordy to convince him of the worth of the evening. Berry and the producers were keen to have Michael join with his brothers for a Jackson 5 segment, something Michael was happy to agree to. However, it appeared that the sticking point was Michael's request for a solo slot, with Berry believing that Michael would use the section to highlight some of his solo successes at Motown, such as *Got To Be There* or *Ben*.

Michael had no intention of being stuck in the past; he wanted to showcase his new material, using the section as something of a plug for his latest album and perhaps show Motown just how much he had developed as an artist. Whilst Berry was reported to be unhappy with this decision (especially as the other artists who were coming back to Motown for the evening would be performing *their* Motown material), he reluctantly agreed, reasoning that Michael back with his brothers in The Jackson 5 and then performing solo was better than not having them at all. Once Berry agreed to his terms and conditions, Michael began his preparations for the evening's event.

No one, not even his brothers, was aware of quite what Michael had in mind for the show. He rehearsed long and hard with the rest of his siblings in ensuring the time they got on stage performing a medley of their biggest hits would work to perfection on the evening, but when not rehearsing with them he effectively shut himself away working on a routine that would stun the watching world. A dance routine on 'Soul Train' known as backsliding had captivated Michael when he had viewed it three years earlier, and although the routine had been retired he tracked down the dancer responsible and hired him to teach him the moves.

On 25 March 1983, Michael joined his brothers, including Jermaine for the first time since they had left Motown eight years previously, at the Pasadena Civic Auditorium for the taping of the 'Motown 25: Yesterday, Today, Forever' special. After performing a medley of Jackson 5 hits, Michael headed towards the centre of the stage as his brothers made their exit to the wings.

Introducing the next part of his performance, Michael said, "Those were magic moments with all my brothers – including Jermaine. But, you know, those were the good songs. I like those songs a lot. But especially I like...the new songs." A recording of *Billie Jean* blared out over the auditorium speakers, with Michael lip-syncing the lyrics as he danced around the stage. Then came the moment that transformed Michael's career forever; at the instrumental bridge, he performed a spin, hitched up his trousers and moonwalked gracefully across the stage. Just in case anyone missed it first time around, he repeated the move towards the end of the song. When the song ended, the auditorium erupted in pandemonium as the crowd clapped and cheered, resulting in the filming having to be halted in order to restore some resemblance of order.

The effect on sales of **Thriller** and the assorted singles lifted was simply phenomenal, with the album selling over 27 million in the US alone (total worldwide sales are reported to be somewhere between 65 and 110 million copies) as well as elevating Michael into the unrivalled 'King of Pop'. Motown would make sporadic attempts to get a piece of Michael Jackson business, releasing assorted singles and albums from their vast library collection and with varying degrees of success.

Happy (Love Theme From 'Lady Sings The Blues') was issued in the UK and reached #52 following its July 1983 release, whilst nearly a year later *Farewell My Summer Love* made #38 pop and #37 R&B in the US and a surprising #7 in the UK. They might have been hits, as was the hastily assembled **Farewell My Summer Love** album (#46 pop in the US and #9 in the UK), but they were mainly appealing to record buyers who were busy acquiring everything Michael released, since none of the Motown issues sounded anything like the material on **Thriller** or follow-up albums **Bad**, **Dangerous** or **HIStory**.

That extensive Motown catalogue continued to sell over the years, with a remixed version of *I Want You Back* credited to Michael Jackson & The Jackson 5 hitting #8 in the UK in May 1988, and undergoing a huge sales spike following Michael's tragic and untimely death on 25 June 2009 as he prepared for what was planned to be his final, farewell tour. His memorial service at Staples Center on 7 July 2009 was attended by many of his musical peers, with a fair number of his former Motown label-mates performing musical tributes and Berry Gordy and Smokey Robinson speaking fondly of their memories of the former child star. Inducted into the Rock & Roll Hall of Fame in 1997 as a member of The Jackson 5, Michael was inducted as a soloist in 2001.

ALBUMS: GOT TO BE THERE (1972), BEN (1972), MUSIC AND ME (1973), FOREVER, MICHAEL (1975), ONE DAY IN YOUR LIFE (1981), FARWELL MY SUMMER LOVE (1984)

COMPILATIONS: THE BEST OF MICHAEL JACKSON (1975), THE BEST OF MICHAEL JACKSON (1980), 18 GREATEST HITS (1984), 14 GREATEST HITS (1984), 16 GREATEST HITS (1984), ANTHOLOGY (1986), ORIGINAL SOUL (1987)

FURTHER READING: MOONWALK (1988)

MILT JACKSON

Milt Jackson enjoyed a career that stretched more than fifty years, during which he was virtually unchallenged as the greatest jazz vibes player of his generation.

Born Milton Jackson in Detroit, Michigan on 1 January 1923, he learned to play the guitar at seven and switched to the piano at eleven before finally settling on his instrument of choice, the vibraphone a few years later. Discovered by Dizzy Gillespie playing in local clubs (where he also acquired the nickname 'Bags' on account of the bags under his eyes as a result of the many late nights he performed), he was invited to join Dizzy's quintet and subsequently his big band, establishing an unrivalled reputation on the vibes and being invited to record with the likes of Charlie Parker, Thelonius Monk, Woody Herman, Coleman Hawkins and countless others.

He formed his own quartet in 1950, a group that would eventually evolve in the Modern Jazz Quartet and go on to tour and record for some twenty years before disbanding owing to financial pressures in 1974 (it would subsequently reconvene during the following decade). Milt also recorded solo extensively for many of the great jazz labels, including Blue Note, Atlantic Prestige, Impulse, Riverside, Savoy, Verve, Pablo and CTI, for whom his 1974 album **Olinga** was distributed by Motown (and would reach #32 on the jazz chart). He died from liver cancer on 9 October 1999 at the age of 76.

ALBUM: OLINGA (1974)

THE JACKSON 5

One of the last great groups to roll off the Motown conveyor belt, The Jackson 5 quickly became a phenomenon in the industry, but Berry Gordy's reluctance to grant permission for the group to record their own material ultimately cost him as they headed for the exit in search of autonomy.

Assembled in their hometown of Gary, Indiana in 1964 by Joseph Jackson, a blues guitarist and former member of The Falcons, the initial line-up was known as The Jackson Brothers and consisted of Jackie (born Sigmund Esco in Gary on 4 May 1951), Tito (born Toriano Adaryll in Gary on 15 October 1953) and Jermaine (born in Gary on 11 December 1954) with friends Reynaud Jones and Milford Hite on guitar and drums respectively. A year later another Jackson brother, Marlon (born in Gary on 12 March 1957 – his twin brother Brandon died at birth) joined on tambourine and congas, with Michael (born in Gary on 29 August 1958) joining the group in 1966.

Joseph drilled and rehearsed the youngsters relentlessly, working on song and dance routines hour after hour, all in the hope that they might accomplish in the music business what he personally had been unable to. After appearing in and winning several talent contests the group underwent a number of changes, with Jones and Hite being replaced by Johnny Jackson (no relation) on drums and Ronnie Rancifer on keyboards, with Tito becoming lead guitarist and Jermaine switched to bass guitar.

After a spell as Ripple & The Waves, they name-changed to The Jackson Five and began performing at local clubs, even venturing as far afield as Chicago and New York. It was in New York at the Apollo Theatre in Harlem that the group was first spotted performing at Amateur Night, with the interested observers being Gladys Knight and Sam Dees and Dave Prater. Gladys Knight sent word of The Jackson Five's abilities to Motown, although no one at the company acted on the tip-off, and Sam & Dave, who recorded for Motown's chief rival Stax Records, felt the label might not be the ideal home for the group.

The Jackson Five did get a recording contract, however, signing with Gordon Keith and his local Steeltown label in October 1967. The group recorded a total of eleven tracks, with *Big Boy* being issued as a single in January 1968, also planning on a second single in *We Don't Have To Be Over 21 (To Fall In Love)* and an album should the initial single take off. *Bad Boy* went on to sell over 10,000 copies locally, although the second single did not do anywhere near as well, with the result the planned album was scrapped at the time.

However, whilst out on the road promoting *Bad Boy* and performing at the High Chaparral Club in Chicago the boys were spotted by another artist with Motown connections, Bobby Taylor, who ensured they at least got an audition. Berry wasn't present at the group's audition, but fortunately the event was taped and played to him later. After viewing the tape, Berry had little hesitation in snapping the group up, giving manager Joseph Motown's then standard contract to sign; a 6% royalty against 90% of the wholesale price, plus $12.50 for each song recorded, but only if released.

Berry handed the group over to Bobby Taylor for their initial recording sessions and got Motown's legal department to get the group out of their existing contract with Steeltown. Whilst Bobby Taylor recorded a number of tracks on the group (mainly standards and cover versions from the Jobete catalogue), Gordy had in mind a much grander launch for the group, putting together The Corporation (Freddie Perren, Deke Richards and Fonce Mizell with Gordy himself) to create new material and, with the aid of Motown's publicity department, created a new back-story.

According to the press release that went out with their initial single, *I Want You Back*, they had been discovered performing a benefit concert in Gary by Diana Ross, who had personally intervened on their behalf to get them an audition at Motown. The ruse was designed to work on two fronts; give greater prominence to Diana Ross, who was about to launch her own solo career and give credibility to a new, unknown group.

Gordy made a number of other subtle amendments, with the group's name now changed to Jackson 5 and two years being chopped off Michael's age. The group made their new debut in August 1969, opening for Diana Ross at the Los Angeles Forum, followed two months later by the release of their debut single. The initial response at radio was difficult, but all that changed when Motown managed to get the group on a number of prime television shows, most notably 'The Ed Sullivan Show'. After that, the record vaulted up the charts, hitting #1 on both the pop and R&B charts.

Just before their ascendency on the singles chart their debut album hit the streets, with the single helping the album **Diana Ross Presents The Jackson 5** to similar lofty heights, peaking at #5 pop and topping the R&B chart, as well as making #16 in the UK. That album became the blueprint for later Jackson 5 albums, and barely six months later the sophomore album **ABC** was released. This time the major hit single count was two, with both *ABC* and *The Love You Save* topping both the R&B and pop charts (and making a perfectly respectable #8 and #7 in the UK), with the rest of the album drawing extensively from the Jobete catalogue. The album also sold well, topping the R&B chart for twelve weeks and making #4 pop, although it fared less well in the UK, despite the single's success, only getting as far as #22.

By the time the third album, unimaginatively titled **Third Album** was released, America was in the grip of Jackson 5 mania. According to Motown, all three of the group's singles had sold in excess of a million copies, and sales of their two albums had also easily topped that sales plateau. Plans were afoot for a cartoon series (broadcast, where else, on ABC Television, in 1971) and branded products that covered the full gamut of fan paraphernalia; lunch boxes, stickers, sew on patches, colouring books and a host of other items were licensed and branded with the Jackson 5 logo. Of course, the merchandising opportunities would only last as long as the hits did, and still The Jackson 5 hadn't finished churning out the number one hits. *I'll Be There* became the group's fourth consecutive chart topper (and also made #4 in the UK), and *Mama's Pearl* only stopped one place short, peaking at #2 on both the R&B and pop charts (it had to settle for a #25 position in the UK). Aided by the singles, **Third Album** did brisk business, ultimately going on to sell a reported six million copies worldwide, making it the most successful of the group's Motown albums.

A whirlwind twelve months or so was brought to a close with the release of another album, the obligatory **Christmas Album**, with the cover of *Santa Claus Is Comin' To Town* the stand out track (it would become a minor UK hit in 1972, peaking at #43) on an album that topped the Christmas charts. Whilst the group would continue to feature heavily at the upper reaches of the chart, their most commercially successful era was already behind them.

Whilst **Maybe Tomorrow** would give rise to the smash hit *Never Can Say Goodbye*, another ballad that found instant favour and topped the R&B chart (it had to settle for a #2 peak on the pop chart and stalled at #25 in the UK), the title track barely scraped to #20, resulting in the album also faltering to #11 on the pop chart (although it became their fourth R&B #1). The **Goin' Back To Indiana** project was a live television special soundtrack that saw the group 'return' to Gary along with special guests Diana Ross, Bobby Darin, Bill Cosby and several American football and basketball stars, although only The Jackson 5 appeared on the resulting album, a #16 pop hit that became the group's first album *not* to top the R&B chart, peaking at #5.

At the year's end, Motown gathered together their impressive singles portfolio for the release of **Greatest Hits**, along with a new track in *Sugar Daddy*. The single would become another Top Ten hit (and made #3 R&B), helping the album scale the top of the R&B charts and reach #12 pop (and #23 in the UK) on its way to racking up over five million sales worldwide. The group seldom got to enjoy the fruits of their labours, for their routine had become an almost constant round of recording followed by touring.

Work on what would be their fifth studio album **Lookin' Through The Windows** was hastily arranged so as to avoid problems with Michael's voice breaking, something Motown were known to privately fear might leave him vocally deficient. Yet a bigger problem was looming over the choice of material they were recording; whilst The Jackson 5 had been happy to record anything and everything Motown put in front of them in the early days of their career, by 1972 they were no longer comfortable with the bubblegum pop they were being presented. **Lookin' Through The Windows** was little different from any of its predecessors, containing the usual cover versions of Jobete material, a couple of newer covers and one or two new songs from The Corporation. The album would perform adequately on the charts, peaking at #7 pop and #3 R&B (and would go one to reach #16 in the UK), but their singles were no longer guaranteed a presence in the Top Ten. *Little Bitty Pretty One* stalled at #13 pop and #5 R&B (although it was redeemed in the UK where it hit #9), whilst the title track slipped further down the listings at #16 pop and #5 R&B.

The resentment that had begun to surface during the recording sessions for **Lookin'** developed even further come **Skywriter**, with both Michael and Jermaine expressing their reluctance to perform the song *Touch* and its lyrics concerning satisfying a woman in bed. **Skywriter** performed badly, barely scraping to #44 pop and #15 R&B, with only one single (*Hallelujah Day*) making the Top 40 and another being cancelled altogether. The group looked miserable on the cover, perhaps sensing that Motown would still not budge on the issue of allowing the group to record their own material, by now a major factor in the growing rift between label and artist.

If **Skywriter** had been disappointing, then **G.I.T. Get It Together** just flopped, at least as far as the pop audience was concerned, barely reaching #100 (the disparity between what was selling in the pop market as opposed to the R&B market can be seen by the chart placing on the R&B chart – it reach #4!), although a belated release for the single *Dancing Machine* proved an irresistible choice, topping the R&B chart and finishing only one place lower pop. The success of the single prompted a revamp of the group's next album, with the single being added to the selection and providing the album with its name. It was enough to send the album to #16 pop, even if R&B buyers remained unconvinced by the subterfuge. However, this sudden burst of success in the disco field was one that Motown would explore further on what would become The Jackson 5's final Motown album, **Moving Violation**. Recorded between October 1974 and March 1975, the album saw the brothers working with not only Hal Davis but also a returning Brian Holland, Mel Larson and Jerry Marcellino. Better than many other disco albums that were being churned out at the time, **Moving Violation** performed no more than adequately, making #36 pop and #6 R&B.

By the time it was released in May 1975, Joseph Jackson was busy shopping around for a new deal, with both he and his sons deciding that Motown's refusal to allow them greater creative control was holding them back. In June 1975 a press conference announced that The Jackson 5 would be leaving Motown following the expiry of their contract and would be signing with Epic Records, the new deal to take effect on 10 March 1976.

Berry Gordy slapped an immediate writ alleging breach of contract and demanded $5 million in damages. The group subsequently counter-sued, thus enabling the general public to learn some of the hitherto secret facts and figures about Motown and its business; The Jackson 5 had recorded some 469 tracks for Motown during their time with the company, of which only 174 had at that point been officially released. Whilst the group had been promised payment of $12.50 for each released track, they were also responsible for the costs incurred on those *not* released, with the group said to owe Motown some $500,000. The writs also revealed that the group's royalty rate had been pegged at 2.7%, despite the group having shifted millions of records worldwide and generated many millions in income.

Yet even the royalty rate paled into insignificance alongside the most revealing fact of all; despite arriving at Motown as The Jackson Five, it was Berry Gordy who had registered the name, meaning the family no longer owned the rights. The lawsuit was eventually settled in Berry Gordy's favour, with Motown receiving $600,000 and the group having to change their name to The Jacksons when they eventually signed for Epic Records. And it wasn't all of the Jackson brothers who made the switch either, with Jermaine, who had married Berry's daughter Hazel in December 1973, opting to stick with Motown and pursue a solo career rather than move to Epic as part of the group (his place would be taken by Randy, born Steven Randall Jackson in Gary on 29 October 1961).

Despite having made retention of creative control something of a cornerstone in their contract negotiations with Epic, The Jacksons didn't get things all their own way right from the start. Instead they were shipped out to Philadelphia to work with Kenny Gamble and Leon, the erstwhile founders of Philadelphia International Records, who in the 1970s had become Motown's chief rivals in the R&B field. Whilst Kenny and Leon and their team of writers oversaw the first two albums, **The Jacksons** and **Goin' Places**, they did at least involve the brothers in much of the production process, even if it was their names that got top billing. Autonomy finally came with their third album for the company, **Destiny**, which was followed four months later by the release of Michael Jackson's **Off The Wall** album, elevating him into the top group of artists.

The rest of the Jackson clan would remain in Michael's shadow for the next couple of decades, although there was the odd occasion when his particular brand of stardust sprinkled itself on their shoulders, none more so than when Michael and his brothers returned to celebrate Motown's twenty-fifth anniversary and partake in the television special. Michael's moonwalk to *Billie Jean* was as much a surprise to them as it was to the rest of the audience; the subsequent screening sent him even further into orbit.

It is of course indicative of just how big a star Michael had become that virtually every repackaging of The Jackson 5 hits should invariably carry the artist credit Michael Jackson & The Jackson 5; despite Berry Gordy's original assurance that the group would not be billed as such it occurred because attaching Michel's name to an album was worth several thousand additional sales, especially in the UK, as was proven by the success of **18 Greatest Hits** (a chart topper on the Telstar label in 1983), **The Best Of Michael Jackson & The Jackson 5** (#5 and a gold selling album on Polygram in 1997), **The Motown Years** (#4 in 2008) and **The Very Best Of** (another gold selling album in 2009 following Michael's death).

After the release of **Thriller**, Michael concentrated almost exclusively on his solo career, linking with his siblings for the occasional album and tour (the latter usually at the behest of his father, who still saw Michael as the main way for the family to generate vast income). The success of the **Destiny** and **Triumph** albums proved The Jacksons, both collectively and individually had great songwriting and production abilities, talents that could have served Motown well had they been encouraged.

However, it is doubtful that Michael Jackson would have become quite as big a star had he remained; Epic and Walter Yetnikoff's clout, especially when it came to forcing MTV to change their programming policy, was way above anything Berry Gordy could have contemplated. There again, Walter Yetnikoff never contributed to a song as instantly compelling or appealing as *I Want You Back* or *ABC*. The group was inducted into the Rock & Roll Hall of fame in 1997.

ALBUMS: DIANA ROSS PRESENTS THE JACKSON 5 (1969), ABC (1970), THIRD ALBUM (1970), CHRISTMAS ALBUM (1970), MAYBE TOMORROW (1971), GOIN' BACK TO INDIANA (1971), LOOKIN' THROUGH THE WINDOWS (1972), SKYWRITER (1973), GET IT TOGETHER (1973), DANCING MACHINE (1974), MOVING VIOLATION (1975)
COMPILATIONS: GREATEST HITS (1971), ANTHOLOGY (1976), JOYFUL JUKEBOX MUSIC (1976), BOOGIE (1979)

JAKATA

West coast rockers Jakata formed in Long Beach, California and signed with Motown's rock imprint Morroco in 1983. Comprising Steve Kragen (vocals and horns), Jimmy Felber (keyboards and vocals), Chuck Coffey (bass and vocals) and Chris Myers (drums), noted guitarist Robbie Nevil also guested on their album.

They released one album in **Light The Night**, from which two singles were lifted, *Hell Is On The Run* and *Golden Girl*. Only the singles were released in Britain, although both were afforded release on 12" vinyl. A second album **Designs Of The Heart** was scheduled for release in 1986 but subsequently got shelved as the group was dropped from the label.

ALBUM: LIGHT THE NIGHT (1983)

AHMAD JAMAL

Legendary jazz pianist Ahmad Jamal was born Frederick Russell Jones in Pittsburgh, Pennsylvania on 2 July 1930 and began playing the piano at the age of three before taking formal lessons from Mary Caldwell Dawson from the age of seven. He moved to Chicago in 1950 and the following year made his first recordings, for the Okeh label, assembling his own trio and retaining the basic piano, guitar and bass line-up for much of his career. Converting to Islam in 1952 and adopting the name Ahmad Jamal, he set about making a different name for himself over the next five decades or so, with his position within the jazz genre said to be second only to Charlie Parker.

He had recorded scores of albums prior to joining Motown, including more than twenty for the Cadet label, but in 1980 he swung by Motown for **Night Song**, released on both sides of the Atlantic in October (the United States) and December (the UK). Whilst not a spectacular seller, it did at least enable him to enhance his reputation, especially in the UK, where the light fusion sound gained him many new admirers.

ALBUM: NIGHT SONG (1980)

JAMES JAMERSON

For years James Jamerson was one of the music industry's best kept secrets, widely acknowledged by his peers as one of the greatest bass players of all time yet almost entirely unknown by the general public.

Born James Lee Jamerson in Charleston, South Carolina on 29 January 1936 (the original year of birth that James gave was 1938, but in the late 1970s he finally got sight of his birth certificate and discovered he was two years older than he believed), his parents divorced in the early 1950s, with his mother Elizabeth moving to Detroit in 1953 in order to look for work, subsequently sending for her son a year later.

James was already proficient on piano by the time he arrived in Detroit, but it was at the Northwestern High School that he first picked up an upright bass he found lying on the floor of the music room. James spent hours practising on his new instrument, encouraged by his teacher William Helstein, and as well as playing in the school jazz band quickly found he was in demand with visiting jazz acts, including Yusef Lateef, Kenny Burrell and Hank Jones. Indeed he became so popular, both as a local hero and with visiting musicians that the Detroit police department gave him special dispensation to perform at clubs that served alcohol, despite his being under the legal age.

Shortly before graduating, James married Annie Wells and turned down a music scholarship from Wayne State University, reasoning that he could better support his wife by continuing with his already considerable music enterprises. Immediately after graduating, James linked up with Washboard Willie & The Super Suds of Rhythm, a blues group that expanded his musical knowledge but also introduced him to alcohol for the first time, something James had hitherto avoided. It was whilst performing with the Super Suds that James got spotted by others within the industry, with Johnnie Mae Matthews inviting James down to a number of recording sessions at Northern Records.

As word of his abilities carried around the city, James found himself invited to perform on sessions for other labels, including Fortune, Harvey Fuqua's Anna and Tri-Phi, often travelling from one session to another with his upright bass sticking through the sun roof of his car. This brought him into direct contact with many of the musicians who would gravitate towards Hitsville, including Hank Cosby, Joe Hunter and Benny Benjamin. For a time James divided his time between touring with Jackie Wilson and doing sessions, recording in Chicago for Vee-Jay (he appears on John Lee Hooker's *Boom Boom*) and in Detroit for Motown.

Eventually, Berry Gordy came to realise the importance of the studio musicians, in particular James Jamerson and Benny Benjamin, and sought to have them under exclusive contract. That proved rather more difficult than Berry imagined, for both were in demand and frequently moonlighted on other recording sessions, including those for rival Detroit labels Golden World and Ric-Tic. Although invariably caught out and fined, Benny and James' importance to the Golden World recordings was such that Ed Wingate would pay the fines on their behalf! Of course, their importance to Motown's output was such sessions would be cancelled if either Benny or James were unavailable, with many of the producers at Hitsville of the opinion that only Benny and James could deliver what was wanted or required.

In 1968 James asked for and received a salary of $52,000 a year, topping this up with frequent club dates, bonuses and other recording sessions, proof of his worth in creating the famous Motown sound. The following year, however, things began to unravel, with the death of Benny from a stroke brought about by heroin and alcohol addiction and James' own alcohol consumption also being a cause for some concern. Despite occasionally failing to show up for sessions and his increasing dependence on alcohol, James' abilities as a bass player (he had switched to the electric bass in 1961) were such that even Berry Gordy shied away from giving him his cards. On his day, no one could play the bass better, as James would prove on later recordings such as Marvin Gaye's **What's Going On** album.

Yet when Motown made the move to California, James was not invited along, having to find out the hard way that Hitsville had been shut down and almost all of the facilities had headed out West. James would eventually follow in 1973, turning up at Motown's new complex on Sunset Boulevard and initially being barred entry, although such was his reputation it wasn't long before he found himself a key part of the musical scene in California. And not just for Motown, for there were still plenty of artist and labels keen to utilise the undoubted talents of James Jamerson; Joan Baez, Marvin Gaye, Maria Muldaur, Hues Corporation, The Sylvers, Rhythm Heritage, Marilyn McCoo & Billy Davis, Dionne Warwick and Robert Palmer featured James either in the studio or out on the road, and all reaped the benefits.

By the end of the 1970s however, James was suffering from chronic alcoholism and was no longer as in demand as ten years previously, resulting in him putting his name down on the union list of available musicians. The man who had provided the bass line to such stellar recordings as *I Heard It Through The Grapevine* (both versions), *Baby I Need Your Loving, Reach Out I'll Be There, I Can't Help Myself, Bernadette, Papa Was A Rollin' Stone, I Was Made To Love Her, Where Did Our Love Go, Baby Love, Jimmy Mack* and countless others dismissed them all by merely stating he had done 'all the Motown shit'.

Largely forgotten by the 1980s, James was not invited to the 'Motown 25' television celebration, even though he had played a part as crucial as any of the artists on display that evening (although contrary to popular myth that he had to buy a ticket from a tout outside, James went backstage and was immediately admitted and spent some time chatting to various former Motown personnel but left when his friend was not admitted to the auditorium). That lack of recognition was perhaps the final blow from a label that he had helped create; he was to die from cirrhosis of the liver, heart failure and pneumonia some four months later, on 2 August 1983.

Belated recognition came in 1989 when James was the subject of the book 'Standing In The Shadows Of Motown', later turned into an acclaimed film, followed in 1997 when The Funk Brothers received a long overdue segment in the 'Motown 40: The Music Is Forever' television special. James was inducted in to the Rock & Roll Hall of Fame in 2000 as a sideman, received the Grammy Lifetime Achievement Award in 2004 as a member of The Funk Brothers and in 2009 was inducted into the Fender Hall of Fame. His true legacy, however, is to be found on the hundreds of recordings he featured on, the vast majority of them hits, which would serve to inspire a slew of bass players around the world, and not all of them from the R&B field.

FURTHER READING: STANDING IN THE SHADOWS OF MOTOWN (1989)

BOB JAMES

One of the true stalwarts of the CTI label, Bob made his name as a keyboard player and arranger as well as enjoying a hugely successful career as a recording artist in his own right. Born Robert McElhinney James in Marshall, Montana on 25 December 1939, pianist and keyboard player Bob was discovered by Quincy Jones performing at the Notre Dame Jazz Festival in 1963, subsequently recording **Bold Conceptions** with Ron Brooks (bass) and Robert Pozar (drums) for Mercury later the same year and following it up with **Explosions** in 1964. He then toured extensively as musical director for Sarah Vaughan for a number of years before becoming a studio musician, working with the likes of Quincy Jones and Grover Washington Jr.

In 1972 he became an in-house member of the team at CTI, writing and arranging the likes of Hubert Laws, Stanley Turrentine, Johnny Hammond, Hank Crawford and Grover Washington Jr. among others. Two years later he got the chance to record under his own name (the album was not initially intended for commercial release but was conceived as a way of Bob showcasing his arranging abilities) with **One** featuring *Nautilus*, a track which would be later heavily sampled on the hip hop circuit, and *Feel Like Making Love* (Bob performed on Roberta Flack's original version), a #88 pop hit and with the album peaking at #2 on the jazz chart as well as #48 R&B and #85 pop. The following year **Two** provided *Take Me To The Mardi Gras*, another staple of the hip hop genre, with the album again peaking at #2 jazz but bettering its R&B and pop performance at #28 and #75 respectively.

Bob would continue to record extensively for CTI before launching the Tappan Zee label via Columbia, with his best known composition *Angela* in 1978, the theme to the television comedy series 'Taxi' being the label's biggest hit. Bob continues to record today, both solo and as a member of Fourplay.

ALBUMS: ONE (1974), TWO (1975)

KEEF JAMES

Born Keith Felstead in Kent in December 1946 he played guitar in several school bands and wrote his own songs. Upon leaving school he trained to become an accountant but kept playing music part-time, eventually getting an audition that led to a one-off album deal with Rare Earth Records.

Produced by Andrew Loog-Oldham and Adrian Miller, **One Tree Or Another** featured ten Keef James compositions given full orchestral treatment, but with the label unsure where to position him, the album disappeared upon its release in May 1972 (it finally appeared in Britain the following February). Keef would later become part of country covers band Tequila Nights until he lost his battle with cancer in December 2005.

ALBUM: ONE TREE OR ANOTHER (1972)

RICK JAMES

Rick James had two spells as a Motown artist, the second infinitely more successful than the first as he provided the label with its first real serious entry into the funk market.

Born James Ambrose Johnson Jr. in Buffalo, New York on 1 February 1948, he was the third child out of eight, although the father would eventually abandon the family home and leave the raising of the children to the mother, who allegedly ran errands for the Mafia in order to make ends meet. Rick also spent his youth flirting with trouble with the authorities, being charged with petty crime and other misdemeanours, although music was beginning to take a hold in his life following a talent contest win whilst in high school.

He dropped out of school at the age of 15 and, in order to avoid the draft, signed up for the Naval Reserve, which required that he spent two weekends every month in training. However, the local success his vocal group The Duprees was enjoying soon meant he was unable to even commit to this and in 1964, upon being ordered to report for active duty on the USS Enterprise, he fled to Toronto to avoid arrest.

There he met almost immediately with Garth Hudson and Levon Holm (later to become members of The Band) and formed The Sailorboys, with Rick adopting the alias Ricky James Matthews as he tried to hide in the Toronto underground. Rick would eventually form The Mynah Birds and record a one off single for Columbia in late 1964, *The Mynah Bird Hop* backed with *Mynah Bird Song* which was released early the following year without success.

By the end of the year, however, the group had come to the attention of Motown, signing a seven year contract with the label in January 1966. Returning to the US with Rick were John Taylor (rhythm guitar), Neil Young (guitar), Bruce Palmer (bass) and Rickman Mason (drums), with the five being put into the Hitsville studio to work with in-house writers and producers Mike Valvano and R. Dean Taylor to record the single *It's My Time*, which was scheduled for release in March 1966. Before it saw the light of day, however, a series of insurmountable problems surfaced. Mynah Bird manager Maury Selman had been paid an advance to cover the recording costs for an entire album but had seemingly disappeared with the money; when the group informed him he was sacked, he told Motown that Ricky Matthews was in fact James Ambrose Johnson, for whom there was an outstanding arrest warrant relating to his having absconded from the US Navy.

Motown pulled the single and proposed album and told Ricky he should turn himself in to the authorities. When he did, he was sentenced to serve a year at the Brooklyn Brig, with the Mynah Birds disbanding whilst he was serving his time. Upon release, he returned to Canada where he was arrested on stolen property charges and sentenced to further time in prison before being deported back to America.

He would eventually gravitate back to Motown, initially with a new Mynah Birds line-up that he had assembled with Neil Merryweather, recording an updated version of *It's My Time* before disbanding soon after. Then Rick spent a while at Motown as a songwriter and producer, working with Smokey Robinson & The Miracles, Bobby Taylor & The Vancouvers and The Spinners, albeit under an assumed name.

It was as a performer that Rick saw his future, so in 1968 he and Greg Reeves moved to Los Angeles and formed the rock group Salt & Pepper, drafting in Steve Rumph and Michael Rummans. After a spell in London, where Rick would form the blues influenced group Main Line, Rick returned to the US, working as a session musician on a number of projects. One of these, Bruce Palmer's solo album **The Cycle Is Complete** would eventually lead to working more extensively with Ed Roth, initially in Heaven And Earth and then Great White Cane. Great White Cane recorded an album for Lion Records in March 1972 with the line-up being rounded out with horn players Bob Doughty and Ian Kojima, drummer Norman Wellbanks, guitarist Paul C Saenz, and keyboard player John Cleveland Hughes, although the group disbanded in the summer of the same year after the album failed to sell.

Rick James eventually emerged as a solo performer in 1974, recording *My Mama* for A&M, although without success. Two years later Rick produced a number of demos with Aidan Mason and Peter Cardinali, including *Get Up And Dance* and an early version of *Mary Jane*. The demos were of good enough quality to get Rick a contract with Motown, but the Rick James who eventually emerged had undergone both a visual and aural makeover. Attending a couple of concerts gave Rick the inspiration to braid his hair and adopt a more flamboyant live show, whilst the success the likes of Parliament and The Ohio Players were enjoying convinced Rick to inject his music with his own brand of funk, which he christened punk funk.

His debut album **Come And Get It**, issued in April 1978, was almost entirely written, arranged and performed by Rick, who also co-produced with Art Stewart and was helped by the success of the singles *You And I* ("I wrote *You And I* about my ex-old lady. She was the main woman in my life for many years and it's crazy because as we broke up the song became a hit") and *Mary Jane*, with the former topping the R&B chart and #13 pop (and also becoming Rick's UK chart debut in hitting #46) and the latter making #3 R&B and #41 pop. Yet the release of *Mary Jane* in particular stoked the flames of controversy.

"*Mary Jane* is one of several titles for marijuana which is the greatest thing since ice cream and I'm not afraid to admit it. I wanted to treat it like a girl because I like to look at it like it's a girl. Kids are no longer kids. They are able to decipher and decide what they want. You can't sit down and tell a thirteen year old anything about anything because they pretty well know what's going on. Their brothers and sisters were junkies and/or prostitutes, they've been through the marijuana trip, and they may even smoke it. I don't propagate anything. I don't say 'everyone smoke grass'. I say 'I love Mary Jane'. It makes me feel good, it hasn't lowered my IQ, nor has it been detrimental in any way. There is nothing wrong with marijuana, scientifically or any other way. Another thing I'd like to know is, why don't people ever put down Bob Marley for his use of marijuana? He used it as his whole religion."

Controversial or not, **Come And Get It** would hit #13 pop and #3 R&B and become a double platinum seller, with Rick capitalising on his new found fame by putting together a backing group, The Stone City Band and heading out on the road. In between time he recorded his follow-up album, **Bustin' Out Of L Seven**, released in January 1979 and which offered more of the same, hitting #16 pop and #2 R&B, but the lack of a massive hit single meant the album had to contend with only selling half the quantity of its predecessor.

By the time of Rick's third album, **Fire It Up**, released in October 1979, Rick had serious competition on the funk front. On paper the decision to invite Prince along as a support act for a large part of the **Fire It Up** tour made sense, but what was billed as the Battle of Funk soon became a virtual walkover for the pretender. Matters were not helped by Rick's claim that Prince was lifting many aspects of his show and incorporating them into his own set (Prince would also procure other elements from Rick, such as building a roster of artists that would serve as an outlet for an array of tracks), thus setting in motion a rivalry that would last for years.

With his own solo career off and running, Rick turned his attentions to his backing band, The Stone City Band, writing, producing and arranging their debut album **In N' Out**. In time, Rick would also turn his attentions to Teena Marie, The Mary Jane Girls, Bobby Militello and Val Young, composing and producing hits on all. In amongst all of the outside production work, Rick still had his own solo career to attend to, although his fourth album **Garden Of Love** was considered something of a dip in fortunes compared with any of its predecessors. Much of the failure of **Garden Of Love** was down to the switch in musical style; having sprung to fame with his own brand of funk music, the pop and R&B orientated album only served to alienate his fan base.

Less than a year later, Rick James returned with **Street Songs**, an album that went back to the basics and proved a winner both critically and commercially. As well as reaching #3 on the pop chart and topping the R&B listings, the album would garner a Grammy Award nomination for Best Rhythm & Blues Vocal Performance, Male and an American Music Award for Favourite Soul/R&B Album. It also proved to be the biggest selling album of his career, earning a platinum disc as sales topped the three million mark. The singles also hit the mark too, with *Give It To Me Baby* topping the R&B chart (and reaching #40 pop) and *Super Freak* peaking at #3 R&B and #16 pop – both tracks would later become heavily sampled during the hip hop and rap era.

Even at the height of his career, problems were beginning to mount, both personally and professionally. Whilst he kept churning out hit albums, with **Throwin' Down** and **Cold Blooded** going gold, neither came anywhere near matching the success of **Street Songs**. More importantly, by 1985 he was at loggerheads with Motown over his ever-growing roster of artists. His undoubted talents as a writer and producer had been positively welcomed at Motown at the start of his career; he had collaborated with Smokey Robinson and The Temptations and returned them to the upper reaches of the chart. These, alongside his successes with Teena Marie (several of the songs she recorded on her debut album were originally to be recorded by Diana Ross, but when Motown informed Rick they only wanted him to produce four tracks on Diana, not a whole album, he pulled out of the project) and The Stone City Band as well as non-Motown projects such as Eddie Murphy had made him a veritable one man hit making machine at the start of the eighties.

As the decade wore on his increasing use of drugs, coupled with the complex status of his roster, drove a wedge between himself and Motown. After one final album for Motown, **The Flag** in 1986, Rick left to sign a lucrative deal with Warner Brothers, and without Rick to champion their cause at Motown, both Mary Jane Girls and The Stone City Band dissolved in 1987. Rick's music career never returned to its former status, yet he was seldom out of the news as the years progressed; an arrest for assault in 1991 and a further assault charge in 1993 (he was still on bail for the original charge) meant a two year prison sentence and a $2 million civil suit action brought by one of his victims. Released from prison in 1996 (reportedly drug-free) he resumed his recording career but suffered a stroke in 1998, which required the fitting of a pacemaker to aid his breathing.

On the morning of 6 August 2004, he was found dead in his home in Los Angeles with the cause later being given as pulmonary failure and cardiac failure; the traces of alprazolam, diazepam, bupropion, citalpram, hydrocodone, digoxin, chlorpheniramine, methamphetamine and cocaine found in his body were not apparently life-threatening.

ALBUMS: COME AND GET IT (1978), BUSTIN' OUT OF L SEVEN (1979), FIRE IT UP (1979), GARDEN OF LOVE (1980), STREET SONGS (1981), THROWIN' DOWN (1982), COLD BLOODED (1983), GLOW (1985), THE FLAG (1986)
COMPILATION: REFLECTIONS (1984)
FURTHER READING: CONFESSIONS OF RICK JAMES: MEMOIRS OF A SUPER FREAK (2007)

NICK JAMESON

In recent years Nick Jameson (born in Columbia, Missouri on 10 July 1950) has enjoyed a high profile thanks to his acting ability, most notably in the television dramas 'The Critic', '24' and 'Lost'. He had previously made a name for himself as a musician and producer, firstly as a member of The American Dream and then as a temporary member of British band Foghat, who he also produced.

After launching a solo career with Warner Brothers in the late 1970s, Nick recorded two albums for Motown during the 1980s, with **A Crowd Of One** being issued in July 1986 (from which the single *Weatherman* was released the same month) and also contributed to the soundtrack to 'A Fine Mess'. He also undertakes voice over work, appearing in 'Star Wars: Clone Wars' as Palpatine.
ALBUM: A CROWD OF ONE (1986)

PHILLIP JARRELL

Phillip Jarrell has pursued a wide variety of careers and not all of them in the music business. He first found fame as a songwriter, co-penning Mary MacGregor's number one hit *Torn Between Two Lovers* in 1976. That in turn led to a brief recording career with Prodigal, who released his **I Sing My Songs For You** in September 1977. The album featured his own take on *Torn Between Two Lovers*, as well as *I'm Dyin'*, which was released as a single in November.

Phillip later recorded for 20th Century but eventually moved to Shanghai where he opened a fashion photography studio. Four years later he broke a foot falling down some steps and whilst recuperating decided to switch to designing guitars, a function he continues to this day.
ALBUM: I SING MY SONGS FOR YOU (1977)

JAY & THE TECHNIQUES

A brief flurry of chart activity for Smash Records in 1967 and 1968 saw Jay & The Techniques briefly touch the upper echelons of the chart. Formed in Allentown, Pennsylvania by Jay Proctor (vocals), George 'Lucky' Lloyd (vocals), Dante Dancho (guitar), Chuck Crowl (bass), Ronnie Goosley (saxophone), Jon Walsh (trumpet) and Karl Landis (drums), with Paul Coles Jr. and Danny Altieri subsequently replacing Landis and Walsh respectively at much the same time Jack Truett was added on organ, the multi-racial group linked with producer Jerry Ross and turned out a a major hit first time of asking with *Apples, Peaches, Pumpkin Pie*, which hit #6 pop and #8 R&B in July 1967. Thereafter their singles were more pop than soul, with *Keep The Ball Rollin'*, *Strawberry Shortcake* and *Baby Make Your Own Sweet Music* keeping their name in the charts, even if the returns were diminishing. Fortunately they had touring to fall back on and spent the next few years travelling both domestically and internationally.

In 1972 Jerry Ross contacted them again as he had an in at Motown, with *Robot Man* being written and produced by Jerry Akines, Johnny Bellman, Vic Drayton and Reggie Turner (formerly members of The Formations and something of a hit songwriting team in and around Philadelphia for the likes of Black Ivory and The Spinners) and released on Gordy in December 1972. According to Jay Proctor, it is not him that does the lead vocal and he was not too sure that many if any of The Techniques actually appeared on the record either! It was to be their only single for the company before they resumed their touring.

MILTON JENKINS

At one point Milton Jenkins had the likes of Eddie Kendricks, Paul Williams, Diana Ross, Florence Ballard and Mary Wilson all under contract. Then the various personnel were members of The Primes and their sister group The Primettes, who would go on to become world renowned under their new monikers of The Temptations and The Supremes respectively. Yet Milton Jenkins disappeared into the history books almost as quickly and as quietly as he arrived, his role in the creation of two of the powerhouses of American popular music almost entirely overlooked.

Very little is known about the personal life of Milton Jenkins, largely by his design. Born in Birmingham, Alabama, he moved to Cleveland when he was in his early thirties and hooked up with a young singing group going by the name of The Cavaliers, a four piece group comprising Eddie Kendricks, Paul Williams, Kell Osbourne and Wiley Waller. When Milton realised that Cleveland was not the centre of the musical universe, he upped and headed for Detroit in 1957, persuading The Cavaliers to join him. The Cavaliers would subsequently relocate and change their name to The Primes, although Wiley eventually dropped out and they continued as a trio.

When Milton reasoned that The Primes needed a sister group, possibly at Paul Williams' urging, he didn't have far to look, subsequently drafting in Flo Ballard (the sister of Milton's girlfriend and later wife Maxine Ballard), Flo's friend Mary Wilson, Paul Williams' girlfriend Betty McGlown and a local girl who came highly recommended in Diane Ross. Milton had great plans for his two groups and, seemingly, an almost unlimited supply of money to help him achieve those goals, although the source of the money was something of a mystery, as Mary would later recall.

"We never knew exactly where Milton's investment capital came from – he never had a nine-to-five job, and he never volunteered any information. Of course, to the streetwise, the answer was probably obvious. Because we were so young, we didn't really think too much about it. Milton was one of the most interesting people any of us had ever met."

If the source was mysterious, the trappings of 'success' were obvious; Milton drove around in a bright red Cadillac, which would invariably be parked directly outside the Flame Show bar. Always immaculately dressed, apart from carrying his arm in a sling (the result of a broken arm sustained in a car accident – as Milton hated doctor's, he refused to go and have the injury properly set), he had apparently set up home in a former hotel, just across the street from where the musical action was happening in Detroit.

Whilst Milton had the contacts to get The Primes and Primettes significant live action, he could get neither a recording contract. Then in 1959, Milton disappeared off the scene, his withering arm finally requiring hospital treatment, if he survived since gangrene had set in due to the original bad set. After an emergency operation, he required months of recuperation and told no one, other than Maxine Ballard, of his whereabouts, leaving The Primes and Primettes to get on with their careers without him.

By the time he had reappeared it was too late, with both groups forging their own paths into Motown. Instead, he swapped his sharp suits for the more demure overalls required for his job of cutting the grass on behalf of the Detroit Parks Department. At night he was still a regular on the music scene, at least for a while, organising talent shows at the Twenty Grand. He and Maxine eventually married in 1961 (Maxine was already married to a Marine who was stationed overseas at the time she first met Milton) and have two children together, although Milton's attempts to fashion a recording and singing career for Maxine were ultimately doomed to failure.

For some reason he never made any attempt to capitalise on his involvement in the early days of The Temptations or The Supremes (or the fact that his contracts with the various members were still enforceable), never tried to use his family connection to Flo Ballard nor made any attempt to offer his managerial talents to Berry Gordy or Motown. The closest Milton got to a Motown connection was cutting the grass at Flo's house twice a week, an arrangement that seemingly lasted until his death from cancer during 1973.

JENNIFER

French female singer and actress Chantal Benoist was born in Paris on 18 June 1954 and began her career as a fashion model in 1972. Four years later her then boyfriend Michel Deloir, a successful record producer, persuaded her to record a number of disco songs, with *Do It For Me* becoming a hit across Europe under the pseudonym Jennifer or Disco Jennifer on Big Box Records.

Motown picked the single up for release in the UK and US and issued it in April 1977 (promotional copies of the US 12" combined Jennifer's single with Syreeta's *One To One*), although it failed to hit in either territory. As a result Motown passed on the resulting album, **Walking In Space**, even though this had been mastered at Motown's studios.

JIMMY MACK – MARTHA & THE VANDELLAS [SINGLE]

According to Lamont Dozier, the inspiration for *Jimmy Mack* came during a BMI Songwriting Awards dinner in 1963 in New York. One of the winning song's had been *He's So Fine*, recorded by The Chiffons and written by Ronnie Mack, which had gone on to become a #1 hit. Unfortunately, Ronnie Mack had died soon after The Chiffons had recorded the song, with his mother attending the BMI dinner to collect the award on his behalf. Her speech touched Lamont, who began tinkering on the piano when he got back home and came up with the refrain 'Jimmy, oh Jimmy Mack, where are you coming back'.

The song was recorded by Martha & The Vandellas in June 1964 and reportedly rejected by the head of Quality Control Billie Jean Brown, resulting in it sitting in the can for the next couple of years. According to most sources, the track might have remained canned but for a chain of events instigated by Martha Reeves herself.

Frustrated by what she felt was Motown prioritising The Supremes, whereby they got access to the best songs by the best writers and producers and the full weight of Motown's marketing capabilities behind them once released, she approached Berry Gordy directly in order to push for The Vandellas to get some chart action. Berry ordered all of The Vandellas recorded material to be brought to a meeting in order to try and find something worthy of release and settled on *Jimmy Mack*, supposedly astonished that the track had been allowed to gather dust for so long.

However, the track had been included on The Vandellas' 1966 album **Watchout!** and had already begun to garner radio plays (Motown later took out an advertisement in Billboard' thanking stations in Boston and Cleveland 'for bringing this record to our attention'), sufficient for HDH to take The Vandellas and The Andantes back into the studio in January 1967 for some additional overdubs in order to bring the sound up to date.

Released in February 1967, *Jimmy Mack* would prove a return to form for Martha and The Vandellas, topping the R&B chart (only their second R&B chart topper after *Heat Wave* in 1963) and making #10 on the pop chart. The record also proved popular in the UK, with the initial release in March 1967 hitting #21 and being revived three years later when it came to rest at exactly the same chart position. The flip side on The Vandellas single, *Third Finger Left Hand* might also have scored a hit for the group; it was revived in 1972 by British duo The Pearls (Sue Glover and Sunny Leslie) and taken to #31 pop in the UK.

JOANNE & THE TRIANGLES

A family group formed in Los Angeles, California by Rickie Page (born June Kuykendall and after her marriage became June Motola) and her daughters Joanna, Sheilah (also known as Susie) and Becky, Joanna & The Triangles had one release on V.I.P. in February 1964, *After The Showers Come Flowers*, written by Guy Hemric and Jerry Styner and produced by Hal Davis and Marc Gordon. Rickie had previously spent eight years writing and recording variously solo or with her daughters and sister. After this one outing on V.I.P., Rickie would move to Nashville with her husband George Motola and record for Epic, later becoming a member of The Nashville Edition. The three daughters meanwhile would record under a slew of different names; The Bermudas, The Georgettes, The Majorettes, Becky & The Lollipops and Beverly & The Motorscooters, all without success.

JOBETE MUSIC

If there was one lesson Berry Gordy learned during his time writing for Jackie Wilson, it was that copyrights were all important. Indeed, it was the fact that Nat Tarnapol refused to allow Berry to write both sides of a single that effectively brought Berry's writing relationship with Jackie to an end; royalty income on a single was split 50/50 between the top and flip sides, irrespective of how many more radio plays one received over the other. And whilst a single might sell well initially, that revenue stream had a limited life. Publishing, however, would continue to earn, from the initial radio play and sales, and then whenever the song was covered by another artist or used in a commercial or film.

Thus the first company that Berry set up was not a record label but a publishing company, Jobete Music, deriving the name from his three children, Joy, Berry and Terry. When he later set up the Tamla and Motown labels, the writers that were signed to the company were also signed to Jobete, so any income their compositions earned would benefit the company. Berry would also form a number of sub-divisions of Jobete; when he signed Ron Miller, he felt his songwriting resembled old classics and rather place them on Jobete, which had established a reputation for R&B, launched a new company to handle Miller's songs. The company was culled from a Detroit telephone book and called Stein & Van Stock, which Gordy reasoned 'sounded old line, classy and Jewish'. The ruse worked too, for when *For Once In My Life* was published and later covered by Andy Williams and Frank Sinatra, Billboard magazine reviewed the song as an old classic from Stein & Van Stock Publishing!

Over the years Jobete (and Stein & Van Stock) would create and acquire more than 15,000 copyrights, including several of the most successful in popular music history; all of the Holland-Dozier-Holland hits, the early hits of Stevie Wonder (Stevie would later take a leaf out of Berry's book and form his own publishing company Black Bull), the works of Norman Whitfield, Ashford & Simpson, The Corporation, Marvin Gaye, Smokey Robinson and scores of others.

The value of those copyrights can be gauged by the fact that Brian Holland, Lamont Dozier and Eddie Holland earned more in royalty income in 1982, when they had little or no new recorded material released than in *any* year during their glory days of the middle 1960s! Jobete thus became one of the most lucrative and coveted publishing empires in the business. Berry Gordy sold Motown Records to MCA and Boston Ventures for $61 million in June 1988 but retained ownership of Jobete.

He sold part of Jobete to EMI Music Publishing, a long term suitor, in July 1997, receiving $132 million for a fifty percent stake. At the time, it was reported that Jobete's annual income was $25 million. In April 2003 Berry sold a further 30% of the company for $109.3 million, giving EMI ownership of 80% of the catalogue. The remaining 20% was sold the following year, with the sale costing EMI a further $80 million. Thus the total cost of acquiring Jobete over the three sales amounted to $321.3 million, more than five times the value of the record company.

MABLE JOHN

The first female singer signed to Motown, Mable John initially made herself useful around Hitsville as a backing singer, waiting for her chance to record. Born in Bastrop, Louisiana on 3 November 1930, Mable came to Detroit via Arkansas with her parents and their growing family (which included her brother, famed blues singer Little Willy John), settling in a new housing estate in the city.

After graduating from Pershing High School, Mable took a job as a representative at the Friendship Mutual Insurance Agency, where Berry Gordy's mother Bertha was her immediate superior. Mable would later spend two years at the Lewis Business College before again running into Bertha Gordy, who told her that her son was now writing songs and needed singers to record them. Mable made contact with Berry, who would go on to play piano for her at a number of nightclub dates before getting her a contract with United Artists that came to nothing.

When Berry started his own label, he made sure Mable was on board, with Mable signing background vocals on a number of tracks before getting her own release in August 1960, with *Who Wouldn't Love A Man Like That* being issued on the Tamla label. Unfortunately, Mable's blues style was already on its way out, at least at Motown, and her single did little. A follow-up appeared the following year, *No Love* being released in June 1961, although two weeks later a second version, with a shorter introduction and the addition of strings, was released in an attempt to garner radio play. Both versions failed, as did her next single *Action Speaks Louder Than Words*, released in November 1961, and it appeared to Mable that the company's growing reliance on R&B and pop meant they were never going to be able to break a blues singer into the mainstream.

Nothing further appeared until 1963 when *Who Wouldn't Love A Man Like That* was revisited, with the production credit being given to Holland and Dozier, although Mable would later claim that it was Stevie Wonder who handled the production! Several other producers had a go at getting the best out of Mable, but eventually she realised she was not going to make it at Motown and asked Berry for a release from her contract. Although sorry to see her go, Berry duly agreed. Mable would subsequently record for Stax, a label more in tune with her desired sound and registered a number of hits before leaving in 1968 and joining The Raelettes. Mable left secular music in 1973 and began a new career as a manager of gospel acts.

ROBERT JOHN

Robert John Pedrick was born in Brooklyn, New York on 3 January 1946 and recorded his first single and hit at the age of twelve, with *White Bucks And Saddle Shoes* by Bobby Pedrick Jr. on Big Top making #74. He would then front Bobby & The Consoles on Diamond Records, enjoying a number of local hits but nothing that broke nationally. In 1968 he changed name to Robert John and had several hits, most notably with *The Lion Sleeps Tonight* (#3) in 1972, *Sad Eyes,* a US chart topper in 1979 and *Hey There Lonely Girl* (#31) in 1980. In 1983 he recorded a one-off single for Motown, with *Bread And Butter* (a cover of The Newbeats 1964 hit) becoming his last hit single when it peaked at #68.

MARV JOHNSON

Although never one of the major Motown names, Marv Johnson's place in history is assured as the first artist to release a record on the fledgling Tamla label. Born Marvin Earl Johnson in Detroit, Michigan on 15 October 1938 he was a member of The Serenaders when discovered by Berry Gordy and persuaded to pursue a solo career, although Marv needed little persuasion, having already released his first solo record on Kudo in 1958, *My Baby-O*.

Berry and Marv went into United Sound Studios in Detroit in late 1958 to work on a number of tracks, with *Come To Me* being released as Tamla 101 in January 1959. It made an almost immediate impact, alerting the United Artists label that this might be a single worth picking up on a national deal and was subsequently reissued as United Artists 160 and became a #6 R&B and #30 pop hit. United Artists not only picked up the single; they optioned Marv as well, although the arrangement with United Artists allowed Berry to continue writing and recording with his first protégé.

The next few years saw Marv score a number of major hits on both the pop and R&B charts, most notably with *You Got What It Takes* and *I Love The Way You Love*, with both also breaking into the UK charts when licensed to London, with *You Got What It Takes* making #7. Berry kept Marv supplied with material up until 1961, at which point he decided to concentrate all of his efforts on his burgeoning Motown empire, leaving Marv to the mercy of whatever writers and producers United Artists could muster. The quality diminished as time passed, with other artists becoming bigger priorities and Marv slipping down the pecking order.

He left United Artists in 1965 and joined Motown, being assigned to the Gordy label, but unfortunately others within Hitsville had not only matched Marv's earlier exploits but surpassed them. Thus whilst he recorded a number of tracks, the closest he came to chart glory was with *I Miss You Baby (How I Miss You)*, a #39 R&B hit in 1966. With his recording career seemingly going nowhere, Marv convinced Berry that he could do a job for Motown in other areas, working on sales and promotion.

Then in 1968, a couple of his earlier Motown recordings were dusted down and readied for release, his first single release in some two and a half years. Whilst *I'll Pick A Rose For My Rose* did nothing in the US, its subsequent release on Tamla Motown in the UK became a Top Ten hit, nine years after he had last appeared in the upper reaches of the chart.

A hastily arranged tour of the UK saw him receive the kind of adulation that had accompanied his heyday in America, whilst an equally hastily assembled album, comprising several tracks that have still not been issued in the US, also did brisk business, aided by a revived *I Miss You Baby* cracking the Top Thirty. After his brief, second brush with fame, Marv returned to his backroom job at Motown, working for the company throughout the 1970s and also writing for a number of artists. By the end of the following decade, Marv was itching to get back to singing, eventually performing on a number of Motown Revue shows and also recording an album for Ian Levine's Motorcity label. He was still performing when he died from a stroke at a concert in Columbia in South Carolina on 16 May 1993.

ALBUM: I'LL PICK A ROSE FOR MY ROSE (1969)

STACIE JOHNSON

Songwriters and producers Deke Richards and Sherlie Matthews discovered Stacie Johnson, a thirteen year old singer at the time she was brought into the Motown fold. Born on 28 November 1960, Stacie was initially assigned to the MoWest label, with her debut single *Woman In My Eyes* scheduled for release in February 1973. This was subsequently transferred across to the Motown label and issued in April the same year with a cover version of *Every Little Bit Hurts* on the flip side, with an album also being planned for May release. According to Deke, Motown felt that Stacie sounded too similar to Michael Jackson, resulting in them putting little or no promotional effort behind the single and pulling the album. After her brief time at Motown Stacie would continue singing, working as a backing singer as well as fronting a Los Angeles group called Hot Cakes and Hawaiian group Lemuria.

TERRY JOHNSON

By the time Terry 'Buzzy' Johnson got to record his first singles for Motown, he was already a five year veteran at Hitsville, having been recruited in 1964 as a writer and producer. Born Isaiah Johnson in Baltimore, Maryland on 12 November 1938, he formed The Whispers (not the same group who later recorded for Solar) in 1954 with four high school friends and wrote and sang lead on both their singles for Gotham Records out of Philadelphia.

Two years later he joined The Flamingos, replacing the recently drafted Johnny Carter, and proved his worth not only as a singer but also as a writer, arranger and producer for the next five years or so. Soon after Tommy Hunt's departure from the group, The Flamingos split into two separate entities, with Terry leading one with Nate Nelson that went under the monikers The Modern Flamingos, The Fabulous Flamingos and Terry Johnson's Flamingos for a couple of years. They also recorded as The Starglows for Atco in 1963, but a year later Terry accepted an invitation from Smokey Robinson to join Motown as a writer and producer.

There he wrote and produced for Bobby Taylor & The Vancouvers, The Four Tops, Martha & The Vandellas, The Supremes, The Temptations and The Miracles, including the latter's major 1969 hit *Baby, Baby Don't Cry*. That same year Terry recorded two singles under his own name for the Gordy label, *My Springtime* and *Whatcha Gonna Do*, later releasing *Stone Soul Booster* under the name Buzzie. He remained in Detroit when Motown headed west, briefly serving Harold Melvin & The Blue Notes as musical director and later reviving Terry Johnson's Flamingos. He was inducted into the Rock & Roll Hall of Fame as a Flamingo in 2001.

TROY JOHNSON

California born and raised vocalist Troy Kent Johnson had mastered the piano, saxophone and bass guitar by the time he was thirteen, attributes that were enough to get him a post with various local bands over the next few years. He first recorded in 1984, performing *I Must Be Doing Something Right*, the theme song to Michael Caine's film 'Blame It On Rio'. His singing career then stalled until he met Leon Sylvers, a producer and writer who had been responsible for hits by The Whispers, Shalamar and Gladys Knight. Both Leon and Troy worked on Lushus Daim's Motown debut (Troy as a writer, backing singer, arranger, keyboard player and co-producer) before Sylvers produced Troy's debut **Getting A Grip On Love** which appeared on Motown in March 1986.

The album would give rise to a minor hit single in *It's You*, which hit #65 on the R&B chart. Thereafter Troy moved on to RCA as a solo performer as well as writing for the likes of Lakeside before undergoing a religious conversion and putting his career on hold. He returned recording gospel material in 1993 for the Word label and later established his own imprint Sought After Entertainment.

ALBUM: GETTING A GRIP ON LOVE (1986)

GLORIA JONES

Born Gloria Richetta Jones in Cincinnati, Ohio on 19 October 1945, she moved to Los Angeles at the age of seven and in 1959 helped form The Cogic Singers (the name standing for Children of God in Circulation) with Andrea Crouch, Sandra Crouch, Billy Preston, Frankie Karh'rl and Edna Wright. It was whilst singing in church that Gloria was discovered by Hal Davis and invited along to Motown's West Coast operations to do background work on numerous sessions along with Brenda and Patrice Holloway.

Through Hal Gloria also got an introduction to noted songwriter and producer Ed Cobb, who in 1965 recorded Gloria on *Tainted Love*, a single that was issued on the Champion label (although *Tainted Love* was the flip side to *My Bad Boy's Comin' Home*). The following year Gloria recorded her debut album, with **Come Go With Me** being released on the Uptown label, part of EMI/Capitol. Gloria would also record a couple of singles for Minit, but even as she pushed her own solo career, she continued doing work at Motown.

That led to introductions to other backroom staff at the label, most notably Pam Sawyer, with Gloria eventually forming something of a songwriting partnership with Pam and landing a writing and production deal with Motown, although since she was still considered a singer, her early writing credits were issued under the pseudonym LaVerne Ware. Pam and Gloria would write and produce the likes of Gladys Knight & The Pips (earning a Grammy nomination for Best R&B Song for *If I Were Your Woman*), The Four Tops (*Just Seven Numbers*) The Commodores (*The Zoo*) and Marvin Gaye and Diana Ross (*My Mistake*), although Gloria still hankered after her own recording career.

In 1973 Gloria recorded **Share My Love** on Motown, with *Why Can't You Be Mine* coupled with *Baby, Don't Cha Know* being issued as a single. However, neither album nor single received much in the way of promotion, largely down to Gloria's decision to leave the label in order to join Marc Bolan (they had first met in 1969 whilst Gloria was touring with the musical 'Hair') in his backing band. As well as singing backing vocals Gloria also wrote numerous tracks with Marc, with the blossoming romance also leading to the birth of the couple's son Rolan. Marc helped Gloria get another recording contract, with **Vixen** being produced by Marc (also featured is an update of *Tainted Love*, which by 1976 had become a huge track on the Northern Soul circuit) as well as containing a number of tracks co-written by Gloria and Marc.

Gloria also undertook a number of outside writing and production assignments, including penning *Haven't Stopped Dancing Yet*, a hit from British R&B group Gonzalez. However, in September 1977 Gloria and Mark had enjoyed a meal at a Mayfair restaurant, after which Gloria was driving the couple home to Richmond when her Mini car smashed into a tree in Barnes. Neither was wearing a seat belt with the result that Marc was killed instantly and Gloria was found lying unconscious on the bonnet with a broken jaw. Gloria did not learn of Marc's death until the day of his funeral and when she was eventually well enough to leave hospital found Marc's fans had looted whatever of his possessions they could from the home in Richmond. With Marc's divorce from his wife June still not finalised at the time of his death, there was no provision in his will for Gloria, so she returned home to Los Angeles with her son Rolan, eventually returning to the music industry. Gloria would release the album **Windstorm** in 1978 and **Reunited** in 1981 (the latter album being produced by Ed Cobb) as well as linking up with former Cogic Singers members for a 1984 reunion album.

ALBUM: SHARE MY LOVE (1973)

JONAH JONES

By the time Jonah Jones signed with Motown in 1968, he was a Grammy Award winning trumpeter that had made his name with a succession of jazz styled standards. Born Robert Elliott Jones in Lousville, Kentucky on 31 December 1909, he began his professional career performing on 'Island Queen', a riverboat that worked the Kentucky to Ohio route on the Mississippi River. He would then go on to play with Horace Henderson, Jimmie Lunceford, Stuff Smith, Benny Carter and Fletcher Henderson before becoming the featured soloist with Cab Calloway. He formed his own quartet in the 1950s and won a Best Jazz Performance – Group Grammy for **I Dig Chicks** on Capitol in 1960.

He would record two albums for Motown, **Along Came Jonah** in 1969 and **A Little Dis, A Little Dat** the following year, but Motown did little by way of promotion on either album or the one single culled, *For Better Or Worse*. Jonah continued playing until he was in his 80s before he died at the age of 90 on 30 April 2000.

ALBUMS: ALONG CAME JONAH (1969), A LITTLE DIS, A LITTLE DAT (1970)

RED JONES

Along with Joe Frazier on Prodigal, Red Jones was one of the few sports connected personalities to record for Motown. Born Nicholas Ittner Jones in Charlotte, North Carolina on 16 April 1905, Red Jones was a baseball umpire, beginning his career in the South Atlantic League in 1936. After graduating through the Piedmont League and Southern Association League, he became an American League umpire in 1944 and umpired 889 games over the next five years. This spell gave Red a host of anecdotes about the game, which Motown had recorded in conversation with Detroit sports broadcaster Al Ackerman and released as **Red Jones Steeerikes Back** in August 1969. Red Jones died in Miami on 19 March 1987.

ALBUM: RED JONES STEEERIKES BACK (1969)

URIEL JONES

Benny Benjamin's value to Motown and The Funk Brothers may have been such that it would effectively take two men to replace him, but neither Richard 'Pistol' Allen nor Uriel Jones need stand in his shadow. Uriel was born in Detroit on 13 June 1934 and toured with Marvin Gaye at the start of the 1960s before being invited into Hitsville to provide cover for the increasingly unreliable Benny Benjamin. As such Uriel took it upon himself to copy Benny's style as best as he possibly could, but over time would prove to have his own distinctive drum sound.

Indeed, Paul Riser said of him, "Uriel's drum sound was the most open and laid back and he was the funkiest of the three guys we had. He had a mixed feel and did a lot of different things well."

Among those different things was the introduction to *Cloud Nine*, the Norman Whitfield production on The Temptations that heralded in a whole new sound for Motown, psychedelic soul. He could also turn it down, excelling on Ashford & Simpson's productions on Marvin Gaye and Tammi Terrell. Like the rest of the Funk Brothers, Uriel moonlighted for other labels and performed at jazz clubs around Detroit, usually in tow with Richard 'Pistol' Allen. Indeed, the two would often greet each other with the retort 'Morning Piss, Morning Urine', supposedly a variation on their nicknames, although Uriel was known as Possum down in the snakepit.

Uriel, who was working on Marvin Gaye's **What's Going On** album when Motown exited Detroit, decided to remain in the city and played the club circuit for many years. Like his former musicians, he received due recognition for what they had all achieved in the studio with the release of the book and subsequent film 'Standing In The Shadows Of Motown', which in turn led to a number of live dates. He died in Dearborn, Michigan on 24 March 2009 from complications after a heart attack.

WADE JONES

Wade Jones never recorded for Motown and seemingly didn't record for anyone else after doing two tracks with Berry Gordy in 1959. The relevance to Motown, however, is that Wade Jones' tracks have come to be considered as something of a trial run for the launch of the Tamla label. Berry Gordy and Raynoma Liles had set up Rayber, company that offered a service as a company that would record any would-be singer, providing arrangements, backing vocals (from The Rayber Voices) and production and providing them with a finished copy disc that could be sent to record labels and publishing companies. Wade Jones' *I Can't Concentrate* (written by Wade) backed with *Insane* (written by Berry and Smokey Robinson) was the only disc that was actually pressed up, appearing on the Rayber label sometime between January and April 1959.

This being the case, Marv Johnson's *Come To Me* was actually released ahead of Wade's single, although Wade's was undoubtedly recorded before Marv's. Wade Jones reportedly sounded similar in style to Sam Cooke but would appear to have had little luck in placing his single with a major company, and for some reason was not offered a further deal with Tamla when Berry launched his own label. Thus *I Can't Concentrate* appears to have been the only single Wade ever recorded and released.

PORTER JORDAN

Although Porter Jordan recorded one album of country music for the MC imprint, he had an extensive musical background, having first recorded for Hanna & Barbera's label in the mid 1960s. He then made his name working as a composer and musical supervisor on numerous films, including 'The Thing With Two Heads' in 1972 and 'Dixie Dynamite' in 1976.

His **Porter Sings Porter** album on MC was scheduled for release in October 1977, but whilst promotional copies were produced, it is unknown whether the album was made available commercially. A single *What We Do Two By Two*, however was issued in February 1978.

ALBUM: PORTER SINGS PORTER (1977)

JOURNEY THROUGH THE SECRET LIFE OF PLANTS - STEVIE WONDER [ALBUM]

In 1973 authors Peter Tomkins and Christopher Bird wrote a pseudoscientific book entitled 'The Secret Life Of Plants', a study of plants supposedly being sentient which was later described as 'A fascinating account of the physical, emotional and spiritual relations between plants and man.' A few years later director Walon Green announced plans to turn 'The Secret Life Of Plants' into a documentary film, mainly utilizing time-lapse photography, with producer Michael Braun approaching Stevie Wonder with a view to having him provide the film soundtrack.

"It was such a great challenge for me and I enjoy challenges," was Stevie's response. "I hadn't ever given much thought to writing a score before Michael approached me, but I'd always figured if I ever did one it would be for a film that would raise society's consciousness about black people. But this film interested me, being about plants, and it seemed a good place to start."

Michael had to explain each scene in exact detail, conveying what was happening on screen, how long each scene lasted and the type of tempo that would be required to musically compliment the action. Thus the soundtrack was three years in the making, **Secret Life Of Plants** expanding into a double album with the addition of three extra, unrelated tracks, with recording further delayed after Stevie decided to add 'sounds of nature' and then sent aides out into the wildlife in order to capture those sounds.

The album was originally intended to be released at the same time as the film had its premier, but alarmed executives at Paramount suddenly announced that the film was temporarily shelved, meaning the album would be released as a soundtrack to a film that no one could view, further hindering its chances. Stevie however remained upbeat about the albums' prospects.

"It's about the emotional, physical and mental relationship between plants and between men and plants. It's a musical way to help people understand and appreciate the film, even though I cannot see it. I achieved what I wanted to do. I appreciate it may throw some people because it's not what they expect from me. When people are basically hearing the kind of music they expect, they can tolerate a few songs that are out of the ordinary. But the songs on this album are in an unusual context for me and I think my fans will accept it, but I'm not totally sure."

Neither was Berry Gordy, who ordered the initial two million copy run to be halved (and would later state that the remaining million was still 'around nine hundred thousand too many'), even though the elaborate packaging, which was perfumed and contained a Braille message from Stevie was retained. Stevie himself went to town promoting the album, hosting release parties in Malibu and at the Bronx Botanical Garden as well performing selections from the album at the Lincoln Center's Metropolitan Opera House with the National Afro-American Philharmonic Orchestra.

Released on 30 October 1979, the fact that it was following the ground-breaking **Songs In The Key Of Life** and accompanied a film no one had seen resulted in the album being savaged in many reviews, even though the songs themselves featured some of the finest melodies of Stevie's career. The fact that it was his first album of new material for three years was enough to earn the album instant sales, resulting in a final chart placing of #4 pop and R&B in the US and #8 in the UK, but Stevie's reputation took such a battering he brought forward plans for his next album, **Hotter Than July** in order to placate fans and critics alike.

JU-PAR RECORDS

A Detroit label launched in 1976 by John 'Juney' Garrett and Richard Parker and based at 13801 West 8 Mile Road, Ju-Par had a brief twelve month distribution deal with Motown in 1977, releasing albums by the Ju-Par Universal Orchestra, Flavor and Sly, Slick & Wicked and two singles, by Flavor and the Ju-Par Orchestra.

Ju-Par went back to being an independent label when the Motown deal ended, with Flavor subsequently changing name to Livin' Proof. About the only Ju-Par act who did not have a record distributed by Motown was The Esquires, one of the best known names on the label!

JU-PAR UNIVERSAL ORCHESTRA

A studio group assembled by former David Carroll & His Orchestra pianist Dick Boyell (who also plays keyboards on this project) and producer Bruce Swedien with Phil Upchurch (guitar), Lou Satterfield (bass), Ralph Craig (trombone), Ken Soderdlom (saxophones), Rich Rudoll (flute), Art Hayle (trumpet), Murray Watson (trumpet) Quinton Joseph (drums) and Derf Walker (percussion) with a string section comprising Elliot Golub, Ev Zlatoff Mirsky, Carl Fruh, Len Chausow, Sam Thaviu and Sal Bobrov and vocalists Kitty Haywood, Bonnie Herman and Vivian Haywood. Their only album **Moods & Grooves** was issued on Ju-Par and gave rise to the single *Funky Music*, which tantalisingly stalled at #101 on the pop chart.

ALBUM: MOODS & GROOVES (1977)

JUDAS PRIEST

Taking their name from a Bob Dylan album track, *The Ballad Of Frankie Lee And Judas Priest*, this heavy metal band was formed in Birmingham, West Midlands in 1969 by Ken 'KK' Downing (born in Birmingham on 25 August 1951, guitar) and Ian Hill (born in Birmingham on 20 January 1952, bass). By 1971 the line-up consisted of Downing, Hill, Rob Halford (born in Birmingham on 25 August 1951, vocals) and John Hinch (born in Lichfield on 19 July 1947, drums), adding second guitarist Glenn Tipton (born in Birmingham on 25 October 1948) in 1974, the same year they signed with Gull Records.

The recording sessions for their debut album **Rocka Rolla** were not without their problems, with the album suffering from poor sound quality and being released to little or no fanfare in September 1974. The album was scheduled for release in the US via Motown but was subsequently cancelled, although copies eventually appeared on import through Janus.

JUST MY IMAGINATION (RUNNING AWAY WITH ME) – THE TEMPTATIONS [SINGLE]

By 1970 The Temptations were top of the musical tree, but it came at a price, with growing friction between Eddie Kendricks and the rest of the group. Eddie had moved into management (Posse would have a release on V.I.P. in 1972), production and had a boutique label in EJK Records and was in earnest discussions with Frank Wilson about launching a solo career. Even though the rest of the group was aware of Eddie's plans, such was the rift that no one felt any compulsion about trying to convince him that his future lay with The Temptations, as Otis Williams would later admit.

"At the time Eddie and I weren't getting on. That's how it is in a group. You have personality clashes. He wanted to go solo, take control of his own destiny. We didn't know that this would be his last recording with us. We'd start at seven at night and go right through to the wee small hours. It was a tedious process, Norman was quite a taskmaster and he'd fry your nerves. Eddie didn't leave the studio until morning, having delivered a wonderful sweet, tender, sincere performance."

Under the circumstances, *Just My Imagination* would prove to be a swansong not just for Eddie but also for Paul Williams, but what a track with which to mark the end of an era. According to the later recollections of co-writer Barrett Strong, *Just My Imagination* had been conceived towards the end of the 1960s but, when he showed it to fellow writer Norman Whitfield, The Temptations were in the middle of a run of psychedelic hits and Norman had no inclination to slow the tempo. After the relative failure of *Ungena Za Ulimwengu (Unite The World)*, Norman decided to revisit *Just My Imagination*, although Barrett had no idea how Norman envisaged the song, not least because he didn't tell him!

The backing tracks were laid down with Eddie Willis on guitar, Bob Babbitt on bass (although there is speculation that the bass player was James Jamerson), Jack Ashford on marimba, Jack Brokensha on tympani and Andrew Smith on drums. Five days later the group added their vocals, with Paul Williams also being given a significant lead role, effectively his last for The Temptations, as Otis conceded.

"Paul has the line, 'Every night on my knees I pray.' This leads into Eddie singing 'Dear Lord, hear my plea. Don't ever let another take away from me, or I will surely die.' It was getting to the point where we were going to have to let Paul go, health-wise. It's a bad memory. It was difficult. He was a wonderful person, kind of like the soul of the group, but illness was taking him out of the game."

Eddie completed his distinctive lead vocals long after the rest of The Temptations had left the studio for the night, and a couple of days later, a few members of the Detroit Symphony Orchestra recorded the strings and harp to complete the track.

Otis Williams' would later state, "We loved the song with just the basic tracks, but we were totally knocked out when we heard the finished record, with all the strings. Arranger Jerry Long, who studied in Paris and scored movies, did a wonderful job capturing the song's magical, dreamy sadness. It was, I think, Eddie's finest moment. We were up half the night recording the song, and when I left at six in the morning, Eddie was still putting down his vocals. Things between us were very bad [the pair had recently had a major altercation during a show at the Copacabana], but I called him the next day to let him know I was concerned about how hard he worked and appreciated his efforts."

Otis wasn't the only one; *Just My Imagination* was released as a single on 14 January 1971, with the group performing the track on the 'Ed Sullivan Show' at the end of the month. The rift between Eddie and the rest of the group was evident on the show, with Eddie sitting well away from the rest of The Temptations, but irrespective of the internal wrangling, there was no escaping just how magical a song *Just My Imagination* was, or indeed still is.

It entered the Billboard chart a week after that performance and hit the very top of both the R&B and pop chart in March (for three weeks) and April (for two weeks) respectively, also going on to become a Top Ten success in the UK, hitting #8. By the time it topped those charts, Eddie had officially announced his departure from the group (temporarily replaced by Ricky Owens and then permanently by Damon Harris) and Paul Williams had also been advised to retire by his doctor. Thus *Just My Imagination* marked not just a chart topper but a full stop to the second great Temptations line-up; there can have been no better way for the five-some to bow out.

The song has attracted a considerable number of cover versions, ranging from The Rolling Stones, Donald Byrd, Rose Royce, Dianne Reeves, Larry Carlton, Bette Midler, Modern Romance and, in 1998, family trio The McGanns scored a minor British hit with an update that peaked at #59.

JUST TO BE CLOSE TO YOU – THE COMMODORES [SINGLE]

Sweet Love had been Lionel Richie's major contribution to The Commodores' third album, **Movin' On**, with the track becoming a Top Ten hit on both the pop and R&B charts. When the group gathered to compare material that was intended for the fourth album **Hot On The Tracks**, it was another Lionel ballad that stood out, *Just To Be Close To You*. Conceived as a more mellow follow-up to *Sweet Love*, *Just To Be Close To You* had to overcome the odds in order to become a success, not least because the group faced reluctance from the pop stations to add the track to their playlists, claiming it to be 'too black'. Milan Williams was aghast at the statement.

"Certain stations considered our music too black for listeners. *Just To Be Close To You* was one. But if that tune was too black to be played on a pop station, then how the hell did it get to number seven in the national charts!"

Thomas McClary agreed. "Statements about music being too black are hindering the people that are listening to the music and they are also hindering the artist. Whatever we create should be accepted and rejected by people as a whole. Why should we have to sell 800,000 copies at #1 in the R&B chart before we get accepted as pop?"

Just Be Good To Me may well have been the track that broke down that resistance, for it did hit #7 on the pop chart and top the R&B chart, with the group having little trouble in attaining Top Ten status on either chart over the next five years. For some reason, the track did little in the UK, having to contend with peaking at #62 (although even that lowly position was an improvement on *Sweet Love*, which failed to chart altogether when originally released).

JUST TO SEE HER – SMOKEY ROBINSON [SINGLE]

Having been responsible for writing and producing almost all of his material for some twenty years, Smokey Robinson began the 1980s relinquishing several of the reins, scoring a major hit with *Being With You* with George Tobin in the producers chair. The rest of the decade would see Smokey work with an assortment of other writers and producers, frequently re-creating some of the magic that had made *Being With You* such as success.

Nowhere was this bettered than on his 1987 album **One Heartbeat**, which was helmed by Peter Bunetta and Rick Chudacoff, with the stand out track being the Jimmy George and Louis Pardin composition *Just To See Her*. Freed from the responsibility of overseeing all of the material, Smokey was able to do one of the things he truly excelled in; delivering a vocal performance of sheer perfection. The public obviously thought so, turning *Just To See Her* into a Top Ten hit on both the pop and R&B listings (at #8 and #2 respectively, although it could only manage #52 in the UK), and the following February his peers showed their appreciation, presenting Smokey the Grammy Award for Best R&B Vocal Performance, Male, the very first Grammy Award of his long and illustrious career.

KAGNY & THE DIRTY RATS

Berry Gordy's son Cliff Liles (by his second wife Raynoma Liles Gordy) had a second stab at recording fame following an earlier spell with Apollo. This time around the bass playing singer linked with Steven St James (vocals), Marq Torien (guitar and vocals) and Jerry Blaze (drums) to form Kagny & The Dirty Rats and released an eponymous album in March 1983.

The first single lifted, *At 15* bubbled under the Billboard charts at #110 and saw considerable import action in the UK (neither album nor single was released in that market), but despite cameo appearances from Junior Walker, The Temptations and Rick James, the album flopped. By the time Kagny released a solo single *Sundown At Sunset*, family interest at Motown had switched to Rockwell and a projected Kagny album **Mind Control** was cancelled.

ALBUM: KAGNY & THE DIRTY RATS (1983)

FRANKI KAH'RL

Frankie Karl Springs was born in Los Angeles, California on 25 June 1945 and was a member of The Cogic Singers during the 1960s, alongside other future Motown singers Blinky, Billy Preston and Gloria Jones. After serving in the US Air Force Frankie returned to Los Angeles and formed The Tripps, a group that would subsequently be renamed The Dreams when they recorded *Don't Be Afraid (Do As I Say)* in 1968, a song written and produced by Gene Dozier and released on his own DC label.

Don't Be Afraid became a minor hit, reaching #23 R&B and #93 pop, but the cost of getting the record even that far had wiped out whatever funds Dozier had and he would accept an offer to link up with Kenny Gamble and Leon Huff at their Chess backed Neptune Records label.

Frankie meanwhile found the success enabled him to tour extensively as a support artist for the likes of Gladys Knight & The Pips, Aretha Franklin, The Jackson 5, The Commodores and Tavares, among countless others. He was briefly a member of The Music Makers, along with Bobby Warren, Skip Starkey and Bobby

Evans, who got a brief deal with Motown but were forced to change their name to Marbaya for their only release.

Eventually Frankie returned to Motown as a solo artist, recording and releasing *I'm In Love* for the Gordy label in January 1977 as Franki Kah'rl. This was to be his only release for the label and he died on 30 July 2008.

FRED KARLIN

Born Frederick James Karlin in Chicago, Illinois on 16 June 1936, Fred initially studied jazz but would go on to establish a name for himself as one of the most prolific film music composers, with the likes of 'Westworld' and 'Futureworld' among the more than 100 films he scored. He also composed much of the accompanying music to the 1980 film 'Loving Couples' which was released on Motown in November 1980. He died from cancer on 26 March 2004.

HOWARD KAYLAN

Born Howard Kaplan in New York City on 22 June 1947 he was raised in Los Angeles and helped form the successful rock and roll group The Turtles, who enjoyed a number of hits during the 1960s. When he left the group somewhat acrimoniously in 1969 alongside Mark Volman he joined Frank Zappa's Mothers Of Invention, although legal issues prevented him from using his own professional name Howard Kaylan or mentioning his previous involvement with The Turtles. The pair thus recorded as Flo & Eddie, with Howard also undertaking a number of acting roles. One of these was as Captain Cloud in the 1983 film 'Get Crazy', with Howard also contributing to the soundtrack album.

BOB KAYLI

Bob Kayli scored a minor novelty hit in 1958, peaking at #96 with *Everyone Was There* on the Carlton label. In fact Bob Kayli was just a stage name – his real name is Robert Gordy (born in Detroit, Michigan on 15 July 1931), the younger brother of Berry Gordy. A year after his Carlton outing he recorded a single for sister Gwen's Anna label, with *Never More* being released in August 1959. Robert joined brother Berry's organisation in 1961 and would record a further two singles as Bob Kayli, *Small Sad Sam* (a cover of Phil McLean's parody of *Big Bad John*) on Tamla and *Hold On Pearl*, which was scheduled for Tamla but eventually released on Gordy (a further track, *There's Always Room For Love In A Movie* later surfaced on Volume 3 of the **Cellarful Of Motown** series).

After this brief recording flurry, Robert had a spell working as a postman before eventually returning to Motown where his first job was as an engineer.

"I didn't know anything about it, but I got a job under Mike McLean – they paid me 65 cents an hour, which shows you how much I knew. But we felt Mike was a genius, and he certainly taught me a great deal. At that time he was building the first eight-track machine in the east; I put together the electronics, learned how to read the schematics, helped with the writing and so on."

Robert learned well enough to become a recording engineer and also undertook some production work on the likes of The Supremes, The Temptations, The Isley Brothers and Soupy Sales. Following the death of sister Loucye in 1965, Robert lobbied to take over her role as head of the publishing company Jobete.

"It was a trial by fire. I really had to learn publishing on the job. When Loucye died, in fact, Berry first rejected my offer to go into Jobete. 'What do you know?' was his reaction; but I said, 'Believe me, I'll learn'. We were the number one chart publisher for the next fourteen years."

He learnt well enough to be named executive vice president in 1970, a position he held until he left the company in 1985. Robert also made a cameo appearance in the film 'Lady Sings The Blues' playing a drug dealer called The Hawk.

KEEP ON TRUCKIN' - EDDIE KENDRICKS [SINGLE]

Eddie Kendricks had in mind pursuing a solo career even as he toured the world with The Temptations, with divisions between the other members and Eddie being such that when he announced his intention to go it alone, they didn't try to stop him. His parting gift to them would be *Just My Imagination*, a song that ranks right up there with his greatest performance. It was officially announced that he had left the group in March 1971, but Eddie had already been shopping around for a producer to work with, eventually settling on Frank Wilson after all parties had received the necessary clearances for Motown.

Whilst *Just My Imagination* had kept The Temptations name up in lights, it did not guarantee Eddie an instant hit when his solo material hit the streets. Indeed, by August 1973, his two albums had performed reasonably well on the R&B chart but had proved incapable of making the all important crossover onto the pop market. Equally worrying was the fact that all six of his singles to date had failed to make the R&B Top Ten or the pop Top 40 – Eddie's solo career was in need of a boost. By the third album, the team assembled by Frank (Leonard Caston and Anita Poree) had got used to working with each other, making their songwriting sessions much more productive.

"When Leonard and I would get together, we would look at just different pieces of grooves. Things would start musically, and if we really liked it, we'd work at coming up with the melody and the structure. Then we'd get with Anita Poree. She'd come up with the basic lyric idea, and we'd work together to completion."

Keep On Truckin' takes the groove explored on *Girl You Need A Change Of Mind* to its next level.

"We'd cut the tracks first and then get with Eddie and rehearse," continued Frank. "Both Leonard and I could sing falsetto, so we could actually select a key and everything without him."

If anything, this sounds almost exactly the way Norman Whitfield was putting together The Temptations' albums and singles, but the system obviously worked, for *Keep On Truckin'* sounded like a sure-fire smash right from day one. Not only did the single power its way all the way to the top of the R&B chart, it would do the same on the pop chart, spending two weeks at the top of both piles. It would also become his chart breakthrough in the UK, making a respectable #18 on the pop chart.

In New York, where the club scene was beginning to blossom, many were playing the full length eight minute version that was to be found on the accompanying album – one wonders how many extra copies of the single might have been sold if the 12" single, almost compulsory for club hits by the middle of the decade, had been around a few years earlier. At the year's end, the record became one of three Motown singles nominated for a Grammy in the Best R&B Vocal Performance category, along with Stevie Wonder's *Superstition* and Marvin Gaye's *Let's Get It On*, with Stevie emerging triumphant at the awards evening.

KEITH & DARRELL

Nephews of Motown legend Smokey Robinson, Keith Larnell Burston and Darrell Littlejohn could have been forgiven for thinking that their family ties would result in a hit career with Motown. Unfortunately even with Smokey's close involvement as a producer, nothing happened for the pair in the charts, despite several attempts.

They first recorded *Feel The Fever* in 1979 and this was scheduled for release in October 1979, but whilst promotional copies did the rounds, a full release was pulled. Three months later they tried again, with *Kickin' It Around* but much the same fate befell this single. Their third release, written by Smokey, *You're My Gardener* did appear in July 1981 but lack of promotion led to little or no sales.

The pair returned in December 1983 with *Work That Body*, but time had not created a market for the pair and once again the single failed to sell. One final effort, released under the moniker Burston & Littlejohn appeared in June 1986, but whilst the title may have been *Rich And Famous*, Keith and Darrell achieved neither.

KAREN KELLY

Born in San Diego, California, Karen toured with Charley Pride in 1966 and would also record for Capitol, ABC and Sound 7 Stage Records. Her one outing for Melodyland came in April 1975 when her composition *The Dessert* (which had originally been recorded in Nashville in 1970 for consideration by Capitol but unissued) backed with *Annie* was produced by then husband Tommy Allsup. Karen later recorded for Southland Records where she wrote and released *You Don't Have To Be From Texas (But It Helps)*. Despite the title, Karen later moved to Hendersonville in Tennessee where she still lives.

EDDIE KENDRICKS

If the sum total of Eddie Kendricks' contribution to Motown history had been his time spent as one of the lead vocalists with The Temptations, it would be impressive, but to have then added a hugely successful solo career over the next six years ensures Eddie a position as one of the key personnel involved with the company during its history.

Born Edward James Kendrick in Union Springs, Alabama on 17 December 1939, he moved with his family (Eddie had a sister and three brothers) to Birmingham where he met Paul Williams, who would become a life-long friend. The pair began by singing in the church choir before linking with Kell Osborne, Jerome Averette and Wiley Waller in 1955 to form The Cavaliers, a doo-wop group that earned a reputation in and around Birmingham. Soon, however, The Cavaliers felt restricted in Birmingham and looked to go elsewhere in the hope that they could get a foothold in the music business.

Whatever money they had got them (minus Averette) as far as Cleveland, where they came to the attention of would-be manager and impresario Milton Jenkins, who heard them singing at a party and invited them to Detroit (although Waller did not make the journey). Upon arriving in the Motor City Milton Jenkins re-christened the group The Primes, also starting a female version of the group called The Primettes, who would eventually become The Supremes.

Despite gaining a good reputation for the quality of their live performances (the choreography being arranged by Paul, with Eddie responsible for the wardrobe), The Primes made little or no headway in getting a recording deal, with Kell deciding to opt for a solo career and heading out to California and Eddie becoming disillusioned and returning home to Birmingham. Eventually Paul decided they should give it another go in Detroit and persuaded Eddie to make the journey back to Michigan with him.

As luck would have it, another of the local groups had also undergone something of an upheaval, with Eddie and Paul linking with Otis Williams, Melvin Franklin and Al Bryant to form The Elgins in 1960. A successful audition for Berry Gordy led to the offer of a contract with Motown, although with the proviso they change their name since there was already another group called The Elgins. After discussing several options, the group finally settled on The Temptations.

Whilst the group scored a minor R&B hit with their third single release, the Eddie led *Dream Come True* (#22 in May 1962), mainstream success proved more elusive, with The Temptations being handed over to a succession of different writers and producers in search of a distinguishable sound. That included working with Berry Gordy, Mickey Stevenson, Norman Whitfield, Clarence Paul (the recordings they did with Clarence were released with the artist credit of The Pirates) and Brian Holland and Eddie Holland, although with little or no success.

The Temptations' fortunes changed with two unrelated events; the sacking of the disruptive and at times disinterested Al Bryant, who was replaced by David Ruffin, and the decision to give Smokey Robinson a shot at getting the group a hit. His first outing was *The Way You Do The Things You Do,* with Eddie again chosen as the lead singer. It proved to be the breakthrough The Temptations needed, topping the R&B chart and landing at a very respectable #11 on the pop chart. Eddie would also head up the next three hits, *I'll Be In Trouble, The Girl's Alright With Me* and *Girl (Why You Wanna Make Me Blue)* before David Ruffin took over on *My Girl*. Eddie's next lead should have been a major hit, but when *Get Ready* did not perform as had been expected (at least as far as the US was concerned, for in the UK it made the Top Ten), Norman Whitfield took over writing and production duties on The Temptations from there on in.

Norman utilised David as lead singer on virtually all the group's recordings for the next three years or so, fuelling David's already inflated ego to such an extent that he pushed for the group to become known as David Ruffin & The Temptations, driving a wedge between himself and the rest of the group. Eddie had his own issues too, most notably with Otis Williams, but whilst the group was having hits and enjoying their success, these issues remained in the background. Matters would come to a head in 1968 when David Ruffin pushed his luck once too often and was unceremoniously ejected from the group, with Dennis Edwards coming in as his replacement.

Dennis Edwards' arrival coincided with a radical change in material the group was about to record, with Norman exploring psychedelic soul with a vengeance over the next couple of years. Whilst initially this propelled The Temptations to the very top of the musical tree, in time Eddie in particular began to bemoan the fact that they were getting as far away from their musical roots as one could imagine. In particular, the dreamy love songs of their earlier recording career were but a distant memory, and Eddie's own lead vocals were restricted to trading vocals with Diana Ross on a number of singles.

Eddie had rekindled his relationship with David Ruffin, who spoke at length to convince Eddie he needed to pursue his own solo career. By his own later admission, Eddie had contemplated leaving The Temptations as far back as 1965 but had put his plans back as he was unsure as to what support he might get from the Motown machine. With the rift between him and Otis and Melvin growing ever wider, Eddie began making plans for his eventual departure, forming a management company that handled Posse, who were signed to the V.I.P. label, a production company and his own EJK label.

He also sounded out producer Frank Wilson as to whether he would be interested in producing him once he was free from his Temptations commitments and received a positive response. Thus his parting shot for The Temptations proved to be *Just My Imagination*, ironically a song that harked back to the group's glory days. A solid chart topper on both the R&B and pop charts, it hit the chart summit soon after Eddie had officially announced his departure from The Temptations, as fitting an end to his tenure as could be imagined.

Eddie took time to hit his stride with his solo career, with the lack of a sure-fire single on **All By Myself** resulting in the album struggled to #80 on the pop chart (although Eddie's loyal R&B fans didn't desert him, helping the album attain a lofty #6 position), with *It's So Hard For Me To Say Goodbye* (a #37 R&B and #88 pop hit) and *Can I* (which also peaked at #37 on the R&B chart) the sum total of Eddie's chart action.

Despite the lowly chart positions, Frank Wilson had already begun assembling the team that would turn Eddie into a bona fide star, most notably songwriter and pianist Leonard Caston, who in turn worked with fellow writers Kathy Wakefield and Anita Poree. It was Leonard and Anita that came up with the strongest cut on Eddie's second album **People...Hold On**, the near on eight minute epic *Girl You Need A Change Of Mind*. Whilst ostensibly a song aimed at the burgeoning women's rights movement, it found its true home in the nightclubs, with the percussion break becoming very much a template for dance records in the future, including several of Eddie's own. Backed by his band The Young Senators, Eddie might have expected to have scored a major hit with *Girl*, yet Tamla released the album's opener *If You Let Me* as the lead single, which peaked at #66 pop and #17 R&B. The correct single was issued next, in January 1973, but the edited version lacked much of the appeal of the full length version, resulting in a peak of #87 pop and #13 R&B, and with the album also slipping down the listings, barely making #131 pop and #13 R&B.

Despite the lowly chart positions, Frank, Leonard and Anita believed they had found something of a niche for Eddie and looked to recapture the same kind of groove that had propelled *Girl* to club acceptance. That came with *Keep On Truckin'*, one of Motown's finest dance tracks of the era and a sure-fire smash if ever there was one. It was certainly the standout track from Eddie's third album, imaginatively entitled **Eddie Kendricks**, but once again the Motown marketing machine made fans wait; the album was released in May 1973, with *Keep On Truckin'* quickly getting extensive plays in clubs and on radio, but Eddie's next single turned out to be *Darling Come Back Home*, released in June. After barely troubling the charts (it would peak at #67 pop and #26 R&B), matters were finally rectified with the release of *Keep On Truckin'* in August 1973. In order to accommodate the original eight minute album version, the single featured Part 1 and Part 2, with the single literally flying up the chart to top both the pop and R&B chart, selling over three million copies in the process and helping the parent album hit the Top 20 of the pop chart (#18) and #5 R&B. It garnered a Grammy nomination for Best R&B Performance by a Male, losing out to Stevie Wonder, but became his first chart hit in the UK, where it peaked at #18.

Frank and his team wasted little time in capitalising on the success of *Keep On Truckin'*, quickly crafting a fourth album that was both named after and built around *Boogie Down*, which was effectively *Keep On Truckin'* Part 3. *Boogie Down* proved almost as irresistible as its predecessor, topping the R&B chart once again and coming to rest at #2 on the pop listings, held off the summit by Terry Jacks and *Seasons In The Sun*, as well as becoming a Top 40 hit in Britain. It also picked up a Grammy award nomination for Eddie, who once again lost out to Stevie Wonder! Further hit singles in *Son Of Sagittarius* and *Tell Her Love Has Felt The Need* ensured the **Boogie Down** album was also a solid seller, topping the R&B chart even if its pop performance wasn't quite as good as previously, peaking at #30. It would not have been apparent at the time but this point marked the peak of Eddie's solo career, for nothing he recorded or released after *Boogie Down* managed to make even the Top Ten of the pop charts, even though he retained his R&B audience for the duration of his career.

That audience turned his fifth album **For You** into a Top Ten hit (#8), but it failed to even break into the Top 100 of the pop listings, stalling at #108. Matters were probably not helped by the relative failure of the two singles released, *One Tear* (#71 pop and #8 R&B) and *Shoeshine Boy* (#18 pop and an R&B chart topper), when compared to previous releases. Frank Wilson and his team produced one further album on Eddie, **The Hit Man** being released in June 1975 and making #63 pop and #9 R&B, whilst the singles *Get The Cream Off The Top* (written by Brian and Eddie Holland) and *Happy* both made the Top 10 of the R&B charts but failed to even crack the Top 50 pop.

With Frank Wilson having ended his relationship with Motown soon after **The Hit Man** was released, Eddie cast his eye outside of the company in his search for a new production and creative team. By the mid 1970s, just about the hottest musical place to be was Philadelphia, where Kenny Gamble and Leon Huff had created a serious rival to Motown with their Philadelphia International label. Just like Motown, there was a team of writers and producers, featuring the likes of Norman Harris, Allan Felder, Bunny Sigler and Ron Kersey, an in-house group of musicians collectively known as MFSB and a favoured studio in

Sigma Sound Studio, located right in the heart of the city at 212 N. 12th Street. Philadelphia International had also developed something of their own sound, much the same way that Motown had a decade earlier, and Eddie hoped to tap into that sound for his next album **He's A Friend**.

It was Eddie's idea to record in Philadelphia, a decision Motown weren't entirely happy with, agreeing reluctantly but with the proviso that the publishing on the album would be split equally with Stone Diamond, Motown's own publishing house. Whilst the music still kept in touch with what was happening in clubs and discos around the world, **He's A Friend** had a spiritual message in its lyrics, most notably the title track (released as a single it would become Eddie's last Top 40 pop hit, peaking at #36 whilst reaching #2 on the R&B chart), whilst Eddie's fans who hankered after his glory days with *Just My Imagination* would have been more than happy with *The Sweeter You Treat Her*. **He's A Friend** was also a return to form on the album charts, reaching #38 pop and #3 R&B, chart positions which must have been particularly galling for Motown since it showed that Eddie Kendricks had gone outside the company to record and had done so successfully.

The success of **He's A Friend** prompted a return visit to Philadelphia a year later for further sessions, resulting in the album **Goin' Up In Smoke**. Norman Harris again took care of production, crafting an album that was every bit as strong as its predecessor, with the title track along with *Music Man, Born Again* and *Thanks For the Memories* becoming key club tracks and even made #11 on Billboard's Hot Dance chart. Yet despite club acceptance for the tracks on display, Motown's promotional efforts were sadly lacking, resulting in the album barely making #144 on the pop chart and #22 on the R&B listings. The culled singles also fared less than was to be expected, with none making the pop chart and *Goin' Up In Smoke* struggling to a #30 peak on the R&B chart.

Frustrated that he had slipped down the rankings at Motown, Eddie let it be known that he intended leaving the label when his contract was up, which would occur after he had delivered a further album. Motown seemingly couldn't wait, going through their extensive library and dusting off several of the tracks he had previously worked on with Leonard Caston to put together **Slick**, released in August 1977. Despite the haphazard manner in which **Slick** had been assembled, there were several high spots, most notably with the extracted single *Intimate Friends*, which made #24 on the R&B chart as the parent album peaked at #47.

After the release of the album Eddie got his release from the label, even though it meant relinquishing all rights to any material he had written whilst at Motown. Although this would impact on Eddie's future earnings, he wanted out that badly he accepted the terms. Whilst his later albums might have suffered from lack of promotion, his name and reputation was sufficient to have a number of labels interested on signing him. He eventually opted for a two album deal with Arista (a longer deal was reportedly on offer, but having already been signed to one label for the best part of sixteen to seventeen years, he was not about to commit to more than two albums) and created enough of a stir with his debut album **Vintage '78** for Motown to hastily put together a greatest hits package **At His Best** to pick up any leftover sales.

His second Arista album, **Something More** did not do as well, largely because of the label pushing the wrong material, so with his Arista contract done, Eddie switched to Atlantic (who had also taken The Temptations from Motown a couple of years previously), but this turned out to be a wrong move as **Love Keys** did little. By 1981 Eddie was without a label, and his former group mates The Temptations were also out of sorts, having returned to Motown after their Atlantic stint but unable to recapture former glories.

The invitation to reunite with the group, along with David Ruffin, was one to be taken seriously, resulting in the album **Reunuion**, for which The Temptations became a seven member band (featuring David Ruffin, Otis Williams, Melvin Franklin, Eddie Kendricks, Dennis Edwards, Richard Street and Glenn Leonard), a hit single in *Standing On The Top* (which would make the R&B Top Ten) and a financially lucrative tour. The tour was not without its problems, with David Ruffin's old demons resurfacing on a regular basis, resulting in him missing several shows, to the financial detriment of the other six group members, whilst Eddie's voice was beginning to show signs of wear and tear, exasperated by his lifelong smoking habit.

Eddie eventually exited The Temptations a second time (as did David Ruffin), and with no firm record offers on the table decided to launch his own label, Ms Dixie to release **I've Got My Eyes On You**. The album proved something of a drain on Eddie's finances and suffered promotion and distribution problems, halting its progress soon after release. For the next couple of years Eddie was out of the spotlight, spending much of his time pursuing lawsuits for unpaid royalties against his former record labels, with his only recording being *Surprise Attack*, which made #87 on the R&B chart on the CornerStone label.

In 1985 he accepted an invitation to record and tour with Hall & Oates, long time admirers of The Temptations, also linking up again with David Ruffin.

The success of the venture kick-started both Eddie and David's career once again, leading to a record deal with RCA, where they recorded **Ruffin & Kendrick** (Eddie had taken to dropping the 's' from his name when he discovered Motown owned the rights to his professional name!). Whilst the album was not as successful as might have been hoped, it did enough business and produced a couple of minor hit singles in *I Couldn't Believe It* (#14 R&B) and *One More For The Lonely Hearts Club* (#43 R&B) to keep the pair in demand for live performances.

Eddie and David would later link up with Dennis Edwards and tour as 'The Former Leads of The Temptations' on the nostalgia circuit for a couple of years, with Eddie and Dennis also recording *Get It While It's Hot*, a Jermaine Jackson production for A&B Records. Eddie, David and Dennis were still out on the road, although David was still prone to being a no-show from time to time, still a slave to a cocktail of drugs. Matters reached a tragic conclusion in June 1991, soon after the three had completed a successful European tour, when David was found dead in mysterious circumstances. Eddie and Dennis struggled on for a while, even drafting in another former Temptation in Damon Harris, but Eddie's health was beginning to fail.

He then learned he was suffering from lung cancer, undoubtedly a result of his lifelong smoking habit (he quit the moment he found out he had cancer), resulting in the removal of one of his lungs in an attempt to forestall the inevitable. Although he continued performing, the cancer returned and Eddie underwent chemotherapy before dying on 5 October 1992.

ALBUMS: ALL BY MYSELF (1971), PEOPLE...HOLD ON (1972), EDDIE KENDRICKS (1973), BOOGIE DOWN! (1974), FOR YOU (1974), THE HIT MAN (1975), HE'S A FRIEND (1975), GOIN' UP IN SMOKE (1976), SLICK (1977)
COMPILATION: AT HIS BEST (1978)

AL KENT

Born Albert Prentis Hamilton in Detroit, Michigan in 1937, Al originally recorded for a number of small labels in New York before landing at Golden World as a songwriter. He resurrected his own recording career with Wingate and Ric-Tic and reportedly worked at Hitsville for several years following the acquisition of Ed Wingate's various labels by Motown. Whilst nothing was ever released stateside by Motown, Al's original Ric-Tic recordings were hugely popular on the Northern Soul circuit in Britain, resulting in *You Gotta Pay The Price* and *Ooh Pretty Lady* appearing on the compilation album **Ric-Tic Relics** in 1973. The latter track also appeared on another British compilation album the same year, **Motown Disco Classics Volume Four**. Al left Motown and joined Armen Boladien at Westbound where he was reunited with The Fantastic Four, writing and producing much of the material on the albums **Alvin Jones** and **Spanky Wilson**.

KIDD GLOVE

In 1984 Paul Sabu was persuaded to enter a rock contest in Los Angeles, even though he had done little research and wasn't sure what the prize was. As it turned out, the competition had been organised by Motown's Morocco imprint and was intended to turn up the perfect rock artist. Paul, born on 2 January 1960 to Indian-born actor Sabu and Marilyn Cooper, won the competition and discovered the prize was a Motown recording contract.

Put with songwriters Michael Price and Daniel Walsh and producers Steve Barri and Tony Peluso, Paul adopted the moniker Kidd Glove and released his eponymous debut album in February 1984, with two singles being lifted in *Good Clean Fun* and *Killer Instinct*. This was to be his only album for the label, with a planned album under his own name being scrapped, although he would later record for Heavy Metal America and Capitol, among others.
ALBUM: KIDD GLOVE (1984)

BOBBY KING

Born in Detroit, Michigan on 4 November 1943 Bobby was the son of a preacher and one of thirteen children. In 1968 he moved to Los Angeles with one of his brothers, Billy, and performed as The Relations for five years. After performing as a preacher in a gospel musical, Bobby was offered a recording contract with Warner Brothers in 1973 which led to two single releases. Thereafter he worked as a backing singer for the likes of Billy Preston, Boz Scaggs, George Harrison and Ry Cooder before returning to Warner Brothers in 1981 for another contract. Producer Steve Barri worked with him on his eponymous album, but it got lost in the company's other releases.

When Barri joined Motown, he invited Bobby to the label, producing his **Love In The Fire** with Brian Potter, from which the club hit *Lovequake* was released in

April 1984. The album also contained *Close To Me*, a duet with Alfie Silas that made #73 on the R&B charts later the same year.
ALBUM: LOVE IN THE FIRE (1984)

MARTIN LUTHER KING

Born Michael Luther King Junior in Atlanta, Georgia on 15 January 1929, he changed his name at the age of 15 in honour of his father. His grandfather James King had been pastor of the Ebenezer Baptist Church in Atlanta between 1914 and 1931, his father then taking the position from 1931 and Martin Luther King Junior serving as co-pastor from 1960.

However, it was as a civil rights activist that he made his name, helping form and becoming president of the Southern Christian Leadership Conference (SCLC) in 1957 which would be at the forefront of King's non-violent protests to combat racial discrimination and secure greater rights for African Americans. Always eloquent in his public speaking, plans were afoot to record and release King's speeches at the very start of the 1960s, with Atlantic Records undertaking a number of discussions with a view to issuing an album, although nothing ever came of it.

In June 1962, however, Dootsie Williams, the owner of the Los Angeles based label Dootone Records set up a recorder at the Zion Hill Baptist Church in Los Angeles and, when questioned by Martin Luther King's representatives as the reason for the recording told them it was for the church. Three months later **Martin Luther King At Zion Hill** appeared on the Dooto label, despite no permission for a release having been granted. The SCLC spent five months trying to get Dooto to withdraw the record, finally obtaining a court injunction to halt further sales and an account of income. According to the statements provided by Dooto, the record had generated income of some $4,750, but out of that came costs for recording, manufacturing and marketing which had resulted in a loss of $98.30!

Irrespective of the validity of the accounts, the figures revealed that recordings could generate income that would be of benefit to the SCLC (all of the Dooto income ended up in the pockets of Dootsie Williams). Thus when Berry Gordy approached the SCLC with a view to releasing something of an 'official' record, the response was positive, with Motown signing an exclusive agreement to record Martin Luther King's speech at the Cobo Hall in Detroit on 23 June 1963.

Berry would later reveal that what had particularly impressed him during the course of negotiations was King's insistence that every cent of the royalties would go directly to the SCLC, refusing to take anything for himself. Similarly, when King won the Nobel Peace Prize in 1964 and with it a cheque for $54,123, it was handed over the to the SCLC in its entirety.

The recording would not appear until August 1963, by which time King had generated considerable media attention for his March on Washington For Jobs and Freedom, which Motown (it was issued on Gordy) would capitalise upon by naming the album **The Great March To Freedom** and releasing it on the very day of the march! The key 'track' amongst the eleven on the album was the closer, which Motown had titled *I Have A Dream* and which is now regarded as one of the greatest public speeches in American history. Despite this, Martin Luther King was reportedly unhappy with Motown exploiting the value of the speech to promote the album.

Motown also recorded the speech King and others made at Washington with a view to issuing these on record too, but the SCLC obtained another injunction preventing Motown and another two labels, Mr Maestro and 20th Century Fox, from utilising anything from the recordings. Less than a month after obtaining the injunction, King dropped the suit against Motown, clearing the way for **The Great March On Washington** to be released, which also featured the *I Have A Dream* speech in its entirety, which had been delivered from the steps of the Lincoln Memorial to a crowd in excess of quarter of a million marchers.

I Have A Dream would make a third appearance on a Gordy album, being part of the tribute album **Free At Last** released two months after Martin Luther King had been assassinated in Memphis on 4 April 1968 (the track was also issued as a single on 8 April 1968). There would also be one final King album released via Motown, with **Why I Oppose The War In Vietnam** being issued on Black Forum in October 1970. A recording of a speech he gave at the Ebenezer Baptist Church in Atlanta on 16 April 1967, it would go on to win the Grammy Award for Best Spoken Word Album.

ALBUMS: THE GREAT MARCH TO FREEDOM (1963), THE GREAT MARCH ON WASHINGTON (1963), FREE AT LAST (1968), WHY I OPPOSE THE WAR IN VIETNAM (1970)
COMPILATION: COMPACT COMMAND PERFORMANCES (1987)

GEORGE KIRBY

Comic George Kirby was born in Chicago, Illinois on 8 June 1923 and began his career as a blues singer, recording for Aristocrat Records in 1947. He switched to comedy in the 1950s and by the following decade was a regular on mainstream television. In 1969 he was a special guest on 'The Temptations Show', both as a singer and comedian and subsequently appeared on the accompanying soundtrack album. He later hosted his own special, which in turn led to a series, but by 1977 he had fallen on hard times and was imprisoned after selling drugs to an undercover policeman. He died from Parkinson's Disease on 30 September 1995.

GLADYS KNIGHT & THE PIPS

A successful group either side of their stint with Motown, Gladys Knight & The Pips' sojourn at Hitsville promised much but achieved only a percentage of the success their undoubted talents deserved.

Gladys Maria Knight was born in Atlanta, Georgia on 28 May 1944 and was singing almost as soon as she could talk. She joined the choir of her local church where her natural talent convinced her mother to put her name forward for the Ted Mack Amateur Hour television at the age of seven in 1952. Gladys won three heats, finally walking off the stage at the Madison Square Garden final with a cheque for $2,000 after her rendition of *Too Young* won her first prize. In addition to the cash Gladys also won the opportunity of joining Ted Mack's touring show, spending a year on the road before returning home to Atlanta.

It was during a birthday celebration for elder brother Merald 'Bubba' (born in Atlanta on 4 September 1942) that Gladys, along with sister Brenda and cousins Elenor and William Guest (born in Atlanta on 2 June 1941) first held an impromptu singing session, with the end result considered good enough for the five youngsters to spend several weeks rehearsing. The five then began singing on a more formal basis at the local church, subsequently involving a further cousin in James Wood as manager. It was Wood who came up with the name for the group, utilising his own nickname for his suggestion The Pips.

This early incarnation of The Pips first recorded for Brunswick Records in 1958, although *Whistle My Love* failed to sell and both Brenda and Elenor left the group, being replaced by yet another cousin in Edward Patten (born in Atlanta on 2 August 1939) and family friend Langston George.

By 1961 the group had secured something of a residency at the Builder's Club in Atlanta, where owner Clifford Hunter would install some primitive recording equipment. One night, after a show, he asked The Pips to try out the equipment, with one of the songs performed, a version of Johnny Otis' *Every Beat Of My Heart* sounding good enough to release as a single. Hunter and his partner Tommy Brown set up the Huntom label and pressed up a few hundred copies which garnered a good local reaction. Word of the single travelled beyond Atlanta, with Bobby Robinson of the New York based labels Fire and Fury hearing a copy and sending word down to Atlanta that if they were prepared to come to New York he would record them.

The Pips sold whatever personal items they could to raise the fare and upon arriving in New York were sent straight into the studio to re-record *Every Beat Of My Heart*, with *Room In My Heart* as the flip side. As Fury readied their version for release, word reached The Pips that the Huntom Records original version had been sold to Vee-Jay Records, an established R&B label, with the result the two versions competed against each other for radio play and sales.

Vee-Jay's better marketing and distribution channels proved crucial, enabling their version to top the R&B chart and reach #6 on the pop chart (in November 1986 this version was featured on the compilation **Hits From The Legendary Vee-Jay Records**), although Fury's version credited to Gladys Knight & The Pips also performed well, peaking at #15 R&B and #45 pop. More importantly, Fury had The Pips signed to a contract, resulting in the follow up *Letter Full Of Tears* hitting #3 R&B and #19 pop, although subsequent Fury singles did little before the company folded.

By the time Fury closed its doors (at least temporarily), both Langston George and Gladys had left the group, Langston permanently and Gladys in order to start a family. The remaining Pips continued to tour and work for a while, waiting for Gladys to return to the fold. That came about in 1963, with Gladys Knight & The Pips signing a new recording deal with Maxx Records towards the end of the year.

Owner Larry Maxwell teamed them with writer and producer Van McCoy, who scored a hit first time out with *Giving Up* (#6 R&B and #38 pop), which in turn prompted both Vee-Jay and Bobby Robinson's new Enjoy label to delve into their respective catalogues for further material by the group. Despite scoring a number of regional hits, most notably with *Lovers Always Forgive*, Maxx Records filed for bankruptcy barely a year after The Pips had signed on, leaving the group out in the cold once again.

Fortunately, their reputation as a live group preceded them, having worked with choreographer Cholly Atkins long before Motown got their hands on him, resulting in a constantly full touring diary and regular work. Eventually word of their predicament reached

Berry Gordy, who offered the group a recording contract with his Soul imprint. The decision to sign with Motown was not a universal one, with Gladys the lone dissenting voice, citing her belief that The Pips would not be treated as a front line artist.

"When I was singing alone with a band Smokey asked me to join Motown, but I didn't feel I was ready then because they had so many female acts. I was still hesitant about signing with The Pips in 1965, but we have this thing where majority rules and I was out-voted. Outside of Motown I think we were the only group doing anything. I felt we'd just be into a whole lot of company politics and wouldn't get a fair shake while waiting in line to get over. In some ways I was proven wrong. Being with an establishment and not knowing what things are like, you have to learn. The main thing the four of us agreed on was that we wanted to sell records and if we could accomplish that we would worry about the rest of it later."

Bubba later expanded on their view of joining Motown. "But we decided that we didn't have that much to lose. Because if we hit it big at Motown, that meant we would hit it *big*. But if we didn't at least we could get over there and get the experience, work with the best writers and producers, and all of that. We could learn ourselves how to become better writers and producers. So here was a win-win situation for us, by going over there, even if we did not get a hit record."

Hindsight will show that both viewpoints proved correct, for whilst The Pips certainly benefitted from the experience, they got the best writers and best producers too infrequently to maintain their challenge at the upper reaches of the chart, as Gladys would later complain.

"At the time we didn't have any say in what we recorded, or who we recorded with. We're the type of people who like to be co-operative and whatever was set up, we'd do our best and make it work. Since it was Motown's procedure to assign a producer to an artist, we left it up to them. We must have worked with every producer they had, except Holland-Dozier-Holland, who were reserved for the suppies [superstars]. But we started working with Ivy Hunter who did *Dancing In The Street*. Ivy had the gutsiest things but they didn't get any further than the shelf."

Their tenure began promisingly enough, being handed over to Norman Whitfield for their label debut *Just Walk In My Shoes*, which was written by the Lewis sisters and bubbled under the Hot 100, unable to improve on its #129 peak following its June 1966 release. The group then spent the next eight months or so working on their debut album, with their next single not appearing until March 1967. *Take Me In Your Arms And Love Me* proved to be a major success, but not in the US, where it struggled to #98 on the pop chart. Instead, the single would become the group's chart breakthrough across the Atlantic in Britain, where it sailed all the way to #13.

Back home in America, the title track to their forthcoming album was released as the third single. *Everybody Needs Love* had been recorded by several artists at Motown, including The Temptations, The Velvelettes, The Miracles, Mary Wells and Jimmy Ruffin, with only The Temptations version attracting any kind of interest when it was an album cut on their **The Temptin' Temptations** release. In the hands of Gladys Knight & The Pips, however, it became a significant hit, returning the group to the Top 40 of the pop chart (it would reach #39) and becoming a major R&B hit in peaking at #3. The success of the single helped the resulting album, with **Everybody Needs Love** also making a sizeable showing on the chart in reaching #60 pop and #12 R&B.

It was to be another hand-me down song that really broke big, with Gladys Knight & The Pips having worked out a vocal arrangement to *I Heard It Through The Grapevine* for themselves. The mixture of Norman's studio capabilities and Gladys and The Pips vocal dexterity turned *Grapevine* into a smash, topping the R&B chart and peaking at #2 pop, unable to shift The Monkees and *Daydream Believer* from the top of the chart. However, it did sell some 2.5 million copies, making it the biggest selling single of Motown's entire history, up to that point (its performance in the UK was somewhat stilted, halting at #47, a very disappointing position given the earlier success of *Take Me In Your Arms And Love Me*) and collected a Grammy nomination for Best R&B Vocal Performance, Female.

Unfortunately for Gladys Knight & The Pips, Norman Whitfield was still convinced he had an even better version of *Grapevine* by Marvin Gaye still sitting in the can, which he would eventually get released a year later and see it become an even bigger hit. The net result was that eventually Gladys and the Pips would have to drop *Grapevine* from their live routine, since many audiences felt they were just doing a cover of 'Marvin's song'!

Battling for top division recognition where material was concerned, Gladys and the Pips had other growing issues with Motown, not least of which was the fact that their championing of a young group they had encountered out on the road was being ignored. Motown would eventually see and sign The Jackson 5, but Gladys, Ed, Bubba and William's role in getting Motown alerted to their talents would be erased from history, at least the history that Motown wrote.

In the meantime, Gladys and the Pips concentrated on their own career, which saw them score another Top 40 hit with *The End Of Our Road*, a new song that would become a #15 pop and #5 R&B hit (true to form, Norman would later produce a version on Marvin Gaye). The lead track to what would become their second Soul album, **Feelin' Bluesy**, it already indicated that their earlier momentum had been lost, with the album repeating its #12 R&B placing but tumbling well down the rank on the pop chart, unable to get beyond #158. That may well have been a result of the fact that much of the album featured tracks that had been recorded by others at Motown, most notably *That's The Way Love Is* (Marvin Gaye) and *It Should Have Been Me* (Kim Weston), although the latter was extracted as a single and hit #40 pop and #9 R&B.

Rather than alter the format, Norman Whitfield kept revisiting material for the third album **Silk 'N' Soul**, which would feature covers of The Temptations' *I Wish It Would Rain* (although it did well enough as a single, hitting #41 pop and #15 R&B) and *You're My Everything*, *The Look Of Love*, *You've Lost That Lovin' Feelin'*, *The Tracks Of My Tears* and *Yesterday*.

By the time the group recorded **The Nitty Gritty** in 1969, their displeasure at constantly having to revisit some of Motown's earlier glories was an open secret. Yet Norman would not let up, having them cover *Cloud Nine* and *(I Know) I'm Losing You*. When given new material, such as Ashford & Simpson's *Didn't You Know (You'd Have To Cry Sometime)* they showed they could still deliver the goods, with *Didn't You Know* hitting #63 pop and #11 R&B. The album's other big hit, *The Nitty Gritty* was not a new track, having originally been written by Lincoln Chase and first recorded by Shirley Ellis in 1963, but in the hands of Gladys Knight & The Pips it became a major hit, peaking at #19 pop and #2 R&B. The album, meanwhile, at least restored the group to chart glories, a #81 placing on the pop listings and #11 R&B. The success of *The Nitty Gritty* did at least offer a temporary respite, for having seen Gladys Knight & The Pips enjoy a hit with a psychedelic update of an obscure song, Norman crafted something along similar lines in *The Friendship Train*, a #17 pop and #2 R&B smash.

"It was a good song to put into our act, because it brought a lot of action," said William. "We would let the audience participate and stuff. They would shake hands and make a friend in the audience. That was a good tune for us."

How good it was could be heard on **All In A Knight's Work**, a live album issued in September 1970, with a greatest hits package having been released six months earlier in order to keep the group's name in lights as the decade came to a close. Gladys and the Pips were still competing with The Temptations for direct access to Norman's better songs, with *You Need Love Like I Do (Don't You)* being recorded by both groups at much the same time. It was Gladys' version that was released as a single, hitting #25 pop and #3 R&B.

Eventually Norman opted to concentrate his main efforts on The Temptations, handing control of Gladys Knight & The Pips over to his protégé Clay McMurray, whose first offering to the group was *If I Were Your Woman*, a song he'd written with Pam Sawyer and Gloria Jones. Gladys was less than enamoured with the song and even felt the final version was little more than an album track, even going so far as to try and convince Berry Gordy *not* to release it as a single. Yet the single surpassed everyone's expectations, including Gladys' when it soared to #9 pop and topped the R&B charts as well as picking up two Grammy nominations, for Best Rhythm & Blues Song and Best R&B Performance by a Group.

Just to prove that the group had learned well from their time at Motown, Gladys, Bubba and William linked with producer Johnny Bristol and former Marvelette Katherine Anderson Schaffner to write the group's next hit, *I Don't Want To Do Wrong*, which hit #17 pop and #2 R&B following its June 1971 release. Clay returned in September, writing and producing the sublime *Make Me The Woman That You Go Home To*, which was released as a single two months later and deserved much better than its final chart placing of #27 pop and #3, although the resulting album **Standing Ovation** would give rise to another medium sized hit in *Help Me Make It Through The Night* (#33 pop and #13 R&B) in March 1972. *Help Me* would also become a belated hit in the UK, where virtually all of Gladys Knight & The Pips singles had inexplicably missed the charts. Then, in June the group's Northern Soul stomper from 1966, *Just Walk In My Shoes* was reissued and hit #35. Flush with that success, Tamla Motown issued *Help Me* in October the same year and saw it hit #11 on the chart, the group having finally registered back to back hits.

International success should have provided a welcome respite, for back at home relations between The Pips and Motown were beginning to unravel, due in part to the company's decision to relocate their headquarters to Los Angeles, a move the group was known to be unhappy with. The **Neither One Of Us** album was to prove to be their final hurrah at Motown, although the group undoubtedly bowed out on a high. It was the title track that stood out from the crowd, with the song and the writer (Jim Weatherly) having been brought to Gladys and the Pips attention by producer

Joe Porter. Although Porter is officially listed as the producer, much of the credit should have gone to the group, who worked out the vocal harmonies and arrangement among themselves prior to the actual recording session.

Neither One Of Us was a sure-fire smash, topping the R&B chart and sailing to #2 pop (although having to settle for a rather more modest #31 in the UK, the group's fourth consecutive chart hit). And, after three previous misses, it enabled the group to collect a Grammy Award, beating the competition in the Best Vocal Performance, Group category. Spurred on by the single's success, the album also vaulted the charts, also becoming an R&B chart topper and hitting #9 pop. This success, late in the day as far as their Motown career was concerned, caused several of the group to question whether it might be worth remaining with Soul for the foreseeable future. But, as Bubba would later state, negotiations with Motown were not easy.

"Once we finished **Neither One Of Us,** our contract ran out with Motown. Our seven years was up. And we tried to negotiate with them to re-sign with the company, but they didn't want to negotiate with good faith, as far as paying us what we felt like what we deserved. They wouldn't give us the kind of perks that we wanted in the contract. So we decided that that was not a good deal for us. After that point, we said okay, we started talking to Buddah Records. That's when the real success started coming."

In fact, it was to be not only Gladys Knight & The Pips that Motown ended up losing, for when the group signed with Buddah, they took Jim Weatherly with them, scoring with the chart topping, Grammy award winning *Midnight Train To Georgia*, along with a succession of other tracks from Jim and Curtis Mayfield.

Motown meanwhile continued to mine the back catalogue, hitting #19 pop and #2 R&B with *Daddy Could Swear I Declare,* another song the group had co-written. In 1975, in an attempt to halt the almost constant reissues and releases from Motown, Gladys Knight & The Pips launched a legal suit against Motown Records, Multi-Media Management and Jobete for $1 million in damages, ownership of the compositions that had been recorded whilst the group was signed to Soul together with full accounting and payment of royalties due from the four albums Motown had released since their recording contract had expired.

Gladys Knight & The Pips went on to enjoy a hit-laden career with Buddah, with Gladys also breaking into films (appearing in 'Pipe Dreams') before legal problems towards the end of the decade meant Gladys and the Pips could not record together, with the male members recording two albums for Casablanca whilst Gladys negotiated her way out of Buddah.

The four were reunited at Columbia, also linking up again with Ashford & Simpson on such hits as *Bourgie Bourgie* and topping the R&B singles chart on a further two occasions. The group remained together until 1987, when Gladys kick-started a solo career that fully justified her moniker of The Empress Of Soul. The group was inducted into the Rock & Roll Hall of Fame in 1996. Ed Patten died following a stroke on 25 February 2005.

ALBUMS: EVERYBODY NEEDS LOVE (1967), FEELIN' BLUESY (1968), SILK 'N' SOUL (1969), NITTY GRITTY (1969), ALL IN A KNIGHT'S WORK (1970), IF I WERE YOUR WOMAN (1971), STANDING OVATION (1971), NEITHER ONE OF US (1973)

COMPILATIONS: GREATEST HITS (1970), ALL I NEED IS TIME (1973), KNIGHT TIME (1974), A LITTLE KNIGHT MUSIC (1975), 20 GOLDEN GREATS (1979), 17 GREATEST HITS (1984), ANTHOLOGY (1986)

FURTHER READING: BETWEEN EACH LINE OF PAIN AND GLORY: MY LIFE STORY (1997)

KOKO-POP

Former Rick James saxophonist Chris Powell formed KoKo-Pop in Columbus, Ohio towards the tail end of 1983 with himself on lead vocals, Recco Philmore (bass and vocals), Eric O'Neal (keyboards) and Keith Alexander (guitar). Whilst the individual group members were in demand as session musicians, appearing on recordings by Teena Marie, Willie Hutch, Stargard, Rose Royce and The Temptations among others, it was a demo tape submitted to Motown that got them a two album deal the same year, with their eponymous debut being released in May 1984. The album would produce two minor R&B hits in *Baby Sister* (#51) and *I'm In Love With You* (#62), whilst the follow-up album **Secrets Of Lonely Boys**, released in September 1985 would play host to the single *Brand New Beat* (#84 R&B).

ALBUMS: KOKO-POP (1984), SECRETS OF LONELY BOYS (1985)

KUBIE

Singer and songwriter David Kubinec played with Pieces Of Mind in Germany before helping form The

World Of Oz in 1967 and Mainhorse Airline in 1969. According to legend, when he decided he wanted to pursue a solo career, he turned up unannounced at the home of producer and manager Adrian Millar and performed some new material he had written. With the help of Andrew Loog Oldham, they seemingly got him a contract with MoWest, with the album **Kubie** and single *Glad That You're Not Me* scheduled for release at the tail end of 1972.

Whether the label or Millar and Oldham had second thoughts about Kubie as a solo artist is not known, but both releases were cancelled. Instead a group was created with Kubie, Graeme Quinton-Jones, Chris Bailey and Peter Kirke with the moniker The Rats, who duly recorded exactly the same material. This was released as the album **Rats First** on the Goodear label, although there is no evidence to suggest this was ever offered to Motown. The album sank without trace, its progress not helped by a dissolving of the first Rats line-up, which meant that the group trying to promote the record (Roddy MacKenzie and Jeff Allen had replaced Graeme Quinton-Jones and Chris Bailey) hadn't actually been responsible for recording it. David Kubinec did get to release one album, **Some Things Never Change**, produced by John Cale and given both European and American distribution by A&M Records in 1978.

KUDU RECORDS

A sister label to Creed Taylor's CTI Records, Kudu was launched in 1971 and was intended as 'a black awareness label, more commercial oriented than CTI and indigenous to the black popular music of the United States.' Whilst Taylor held back on some of the packaging expense that marked CTI releases, Kudu proved every bit as popular as its bigger sibling, although it became a hit label by accident; Hank Crawford was scheduled to record for the label in September 1971 but was unable to make the session (he was arrested the night before in Memphis on a two year old driving charge), with Grover Washington Jr. being given the slot instead and the resulting album **Inner City Blues** becoming a success on the soul and jazz charts.

There were to be some sixteen albums issued on Kudu whilst distributed by Motown between 1974 and 1976, including four more from Grover Washington Jr. Alongside Grover came Esther Phillips, Hank Crawford, Joe Beck, Ron Carter, Johnny Hammond, Idris Muhammad and Phil Upchurch and Tennyson Stephens, with Esther's **What A Diff'rence A Day Makes** another steady seller. It was, however, the success of Grover Washington Jr. that enabled Creed Taylor to terminate his distribution deal with Motown early, even if the cost, which included losing Grover and his back catalogue, was somewhat exorbitant.

L

LADY SINGS THE BLUES (1972 FILM)

Billie Holiday had been one of the greatest jazz singer's of all time, although her troubled private life had been responsible for bringing about her early demise at the age of 44 in 1959. Four years earlier, Billie had written her autobiography (alongside ghostwriter William Duffy), the film rights to which had eventually ended up with producer Jay Weston. His initial discussions on bringing the Billie Holiday story to the big screen had seen him sign up director Sidney Furie and obtain financial backing from Cinema Center Films, with a number of actresses linked to the starring role, most notably Diahann Carroll.

Then Weston happened to see the television special 'Diana', in which Diana Ross not only sang but also did a few passable impersonations of classic comedians! Thinking that Diana Ross might also be an ideal candidate for the role, he eventually spoke at length about the matter with Berry Gordy. Whilst Gordy was desperate to get Motown in to the film industry, he tried to sound only vaguely interested, reasoning that if the producers *really* wanted Diana Ross, they would come back and make a concrete offer. Gordy's ruse worked, for Weston did come back with an offer that was acceptable, although there would be a few twists and turns along the way.

The first of these was the fact that Cinema Center Films did not see Diana Ross in the role of Billie Holiday, to the extent they pulled their financial backing. Jay Weston eventually found alternative funding from Paramount Films, with the budget set at $2 million.

The first problem that confronted the film was the script, which had initially been written by Sidney Furie and Terence McCloy, but which lacked any real vigour. Despite Furie's protestations, Berry Gordy brought in Motown executive Suzanne De Passe and his former girlfriend Chris Clark to beef up the script, allowing them artistic licence in creating dialogue and even characters within the film; one of the key musicians who had worked with Billie had been saxophonist Lester Young (who actually gave her the name 'Lady Day'), who would be replaced by Richard Pryor playing 'The Piano Man', whilst her surviving husband Louis McKay was nothing like that depicted in the film, with the character an amalgamation of her previous relationships. Berry Gordy initially had in mind casting Levi Stubbs of The Four Tops in the role of McKay, but as the group would be on tour across Europe when filming commenced was forced to look elsewhere. A series of readings were held, including Billy Dee Williams, who was being championed by Suzanne De Passe. Williams not only delivered the worst reading, his screen test was no better, but Gordy noticed the chemistry between Diana Ross and Billy Dee Williams that ultimately got him the part.

Several other Motown artists got in on the act, including Yvonne Fair, the Lewis sisters Kay and Helen, Scatman Crothers and Robert Gordy. Principal photography on the film commenced in December 1971 and quickly ran into problems, largely because of conflicts between director Sidney Furie and associate producer Berry Gordy (the title was largely an honorary one, since at this point in time it was not Gordy's money that was funding the film but Paramount's), with Gordy feeling his special knowledge of Diana Ross gave him an insight on how she should be handled on the set, how she should be photographed, what stage direction to give; in short everything that would ordinarily be Sidney Furie's domain!

The disagreements eventually resulted in Furie walking off the set in fury, only returning after he and Gordy had agreed an uneasy truce. The additional stage direction, change of wardrobe and other conflicts soon had the film running towards the upper limit of the budget, with no more than half the planned movie having been filmed. Needing to get the budget increased, Berry Gordy arranged an early morning meeting with Paramount Studios head Frank Yablans, known throughout Hollywood as a tough negotiator.

After listening to Gordy's account of how the film was progressing Yablans turned down the request for a budget increase and told Gordy, "If you're out of money, I suggest you end the film right where it's at." Berry Gordy virtually exploded at the suggestion, since ending the film at that point would be impossible. That cut no ice with Yablans. "Easy. Just fade to black and put letters on the screen that say T-H-E E-N-D." The blunt assessment forced Gordy to change tack; what would Berry Gordy have to do to save the film. The options were equally cursorily delivered. "Pay everything over $2 million and you'll get your money back after deferments, distribution fees, prints and ads, and everything else. Or, just bring me a cheque for the $2 million and the film is yours to do whatever you want."

The meeting came to an abrupt end at that point, with Gordy returning the following morning bearing a cheque for $2 million, although he did not get the full release from Yablans, who backtracked and insisted the film would still have to be contractually distributed by Paramount. Now however Berry Gordy was in control of virtually every aspect of the film and gave the director carte blanche to film scene after scene in pursuit of the ultimate film on Billie Holiday.

There were still one or two problems to contend with, not least of which was a further meeting between Gordy and Yablans soon after filming had been completed. Yablans and his executives were keen to see what progress had been made and instructed Gordy to bring a rough print to a screening at the company's New York office. Although Berry had only just started editing the film and was reluctant to show an unpolished version, he did as requested, inserting 'scene to come' and 'music to come' boards where necessary to show the film as he envisaged it. The screening lasted for four hours, after which Yablans took Gordy into his office and told him the film was in serious trouble, most notably because it was twice as long as it needed to be. Rejecting Yablans offer of a film doctor or two who could pull the shot scenes into a passable film, Berry returned to Los Angeles and set about learning the fine art of film editing himself, aided by director Sidney Furie, principal editor Argyle Nelson and photographer Lawrence Schiller (whose main role during the editing process was to take shots from scenes and turn them into montages that maintained the story line without adding too much to the running time).

The initial version the team came up with ran to two hours fifteen minutes, still some fifteen minutes longer than Frank Yablans had instructed, with the result the next major scene to go was one that featured Robert Gordy as the dope peddler The Hawk. Realising that Robert and the rest of the Gordy family would be seeing the film at preview, Berry re-inserted the scene and, after a positive audience reaction, decided to keep the film at that length, irrespective of Yablans instructions.

The official world premier for the film was held at Loews State Theatre in Times Square in October 1972, with many of the film's cast and crew in attendance. The notable absentee was Diana Ross, heavily pregnant and forbidden by her doctor to fly across the country in order to attend. Despite Diana's absence the premiere went well, with the film going on to break the theatre's attendance record and secure a closing slot at the Cannes Film Festival. It would also go on to become a critical and commercial success as it earned just short of $20 million at the box office in the US, picking up a number of awards and honours and with the soundtrack topping the pop charts.

Diana was nominated for two Golden Globes (Best Actress and Most Promising Newcomer, winning the latter category), a BAFTA Film Award (Best Actress), New York Film Critics (Best Actress) and, most pleasingly, an Academy Award for Best Actress. 'Lady Sings The Blues' also picked up Academy nominations for best art direction, best costume design, best score and adaptation and best screenplay. Whilst the other four nominations honoured several of the other crew members who had contributed to the success of the film, it was the Best Actress nomination for Diana Ross that, in the mind of Berry Gordy, vindicated his decision to take greater control of the film.

Unfortunately, Berry thought he could be equally persuasive with the voters on the Academy panel, undertaking an enormous publicity campaign in the trade papers that ultimately served only to alienate those he sought to influence. Instead of a coronation at the Dorothy Chandler Pavilion in Los Angeles on 27 March 1973, there was a wake, with Liza Minnelli beating Diana in the Best Actress category and 'Lady Sings The Blues' being overlooked in the other four nominated categories. The film has retained its popularity in the ensuing years, being released on video in 1996 and on DVD in 2005.

LADY SINGS THE BLUES (OST) - DIANA ROSS [ALBUM]

Although credited to Diana Ross, **Lady Sings The Blues** was the soundtrack to the film featuring Diana Ross and as such also features extensive contributions from the likes of Michel Legrand and Gil Askey. It was Gil who was responsible for pulling the album together, handing a stock of Billie Holiday records to Diana Ross so that she could learn Billie's phrasing and vocal style as well as selecting the key tracks from Billie's career, such as *Strange Fruit* and *Fine And Mellow*.

Other Motown artists appearing on the album included Blinky and Michelle Aller, whilst Michel Legrand provided the main theme, which he composed, arrange and conducted. A double album, **Lady Sings The Blues** was released in December 1972 shortly after the film had its premier, and whilst several within Motown felt the album to be Berry Gordy's folly since much of the material was old show tunes (according to sales manager Phil Jones, "As far as Berry was concerned, this might as well have been the only album we had to sell"), the film's success helped push the album to the top of the charts, displacing **Dueling Banjos** by Eric Weissberg and Steve Mandell and enjoying a two week residency at the summit.

LADY (YOU BRING ME UP) – THE COMMODORES [SINGLE]

Featured on The Commodores album **In The Pocket**, the group's last with Lionel Richie as a member, *Lady (You Bring Me Up)* would become one of two Top Ten hits extracted from the album. *Lady* was written by group member William King, his wife Shirley and Harold Hudson, the latter a keyboard player and trumpeter who was a member of Mean Machine, The Commodores' own backing group. Harold had joined The Mean Machine in the 1970s and had been contributing compositions since the **Midnight Magic** album. This, however, was the first of his co-written songs to be released as a single, and the lead single from the album at that.

It proved to be another Top Ten hit for the group following its release in June 1981, peaking at #8 pop and #5 R&B, although it struggled in the UK, where it only made it as far as #56. *Lady* did go on to garner a nomination for the Grammy Award for Best Rhythm & Blues Song, although it lost out to *Just The Two Of Us*. In 1998 American female vocal group Simply Smooth scored a minor British hit with a cover version, peaking at #70.

PHILLIP LAMBRO

Film music composer and conductor Phillip Lambro was born in Wellesley Hills, Massachusetts on 2 August 1935 and educated at the Music Academy of the West in California. After undertaking military service he turned to film composing, with 'Murph The Surf' and 'Crypt Of The Living Dead' among his best known works. However, he is equally known for the one film he did *not* score; originally hired to compose the music for the 1974 film 'Chinatown' his submission was rejected by the producer at the last minute (although sections of his music can be heard on the original trailer for the film). Motown released the soundtrack to 'Murph The Surf' in June 1975, Perseverance Records released his score for

'Chinatown' (as 'Los Angeles, 1937') in 2007, a year after reissuing 'Murph The Surf' on CD.

MAJOR LANCE

One of the most successful and popular soul singers of the 1960s, Major Lance was another of the artists whose better days were well behind them when they showed up at Motown. Born in Winterville, Mississippi on 4 April 1939 (Major Lance was his birth name, not a nickname or stage name), Major moved to Chicago at a young age and attended the same school as Jerry Butler and Curtis Mayfield, Wells High School. After initially considering a career as a boxer, Major switched to music and formed The Floats with Otis Leavill, although it was as a solo performer that he made his recording debut, with *I Got A Girl* (written and produced by Curtis Mayfield) appearing on Mercury in 1959.

After a number of odd jobs over the next three years, Major resurfaced at OKeh Records in 1962, again linking with Curtis Mayfield. After a false start with *Delilah*, Major scored a smash hit with *The Monkey Time*, hitting #2 R&B and #8 pop in 1963. Over the next five years he would make frequent visits to the upper reaches of both the R&B and pop charts, topping the former with *Um Um Um Um Um Um* in 1964 as well as registering his only UK hit at #40.

Major left OKeh in 1968 and recorded for Dakar and scored a minor R&B hit with *Follow The Leader*, although his domestic popularity was beginning to wane. Major reunited with Curtis in 1970, recording two singles for the Curtom label, both of which charted on the R&B charts, before moving on to Volt for a further three singles.

Major then moved to England, where his earlier recordings for OKeh had made him something of an absent star on the Northern Soul Scene, culminating in his critically acclaimed **Live At The Torch** issued by Contempo in 1973.

The following year Major returned to America and settled in Atlanta, subsequently signing with Playboy Records. He then set up the Osiris label with Booker T & The MG's drummer Al Jackson, but this was shuttered by Major after Al was murdered by two burglars at his home. Thereafter his career hit a downward spiral, only briefly revived with his signing with the Soul imprint in 1978.

The brief union would see a single (*I Never Thought I'd Be Losing You*) and album (**Now Arriving**) being released in April and July of that year, with the bulk of the album that was produced by Kent Washburn utilising backing tracks that had originally been recorded for a planned album on Jamal Trice. Unfortunately, Major's subsequent four year imprisonment for selling cocaine brought an abrupt end to his Motown career (resulting in the scrapping of a planned second album **Major, Just Messin' Around**), although following his release he found his earlier recordings were once again popular, this time on the beach music scene. A heart attack suffered in 1987 prevented him from touring extensively, although he was able to undertake a few minor tours and dates. He gave his last public performance at the Chicago Blues Festival, dying from heart failure on 3 September 1994 at the age of 55.
ALBUM: NOW ARRIVING (1978)

LIZ LANDS

Born Elizabeth Lands in the Georgia Sea Islands on 11 February 1939 and raised in New York, Liz married blues singer Tommy Brown and became actively involved in Dr Martin Luther King's Southern Christian Leadership Conference. It was whilst performing with Harry Belafonte at a benefit show for the SCLC that Liz was spotted by Berry Gordy, who was impressed with her five octave voice.

Signed initially to the gospel imprint Divinity, her first single was to have been *We Shall Overcome* backed with *Trouble In This Land* in 1963 (credited to Liz Lands & The Voices Of Salvation) but was subsequently cancelled. Instead Liz was switched to the Gordy label for *May What He Lived For Live*, a tribute to the then recently assassinated President John F Kennedy which was rush-released in December 1963.

The following March Liz linked with The Temptations for what would be her second and final Gordy single, *Midnight Johnny*. Liz resurfaced some three years later on the One-Derful label for one single and then formed her own label with her husband, T&L Records. Liz would also record for Ian Levine's Motorcity label in the 1990s. Her death was reported on 11 January 2013, although there was no further information or confirmation.

THE LaSALLES

The LaSalles were originally formed in Buffalo, New York by Carl Cisco, Kathy Lynn Leppen, Nickolas Ameno and Tony DiMaria. They first recorded for Philadelphia's Swan label in 1964, releasing three singles as Kathy Lynn & The Playboys and one as The Rockin' Rebels before signing a one-off single deal with V.I.P. that saw *La La La La La* (originally recorded by Little Stevie Wonder in 1962) released in June 1966 and credited to The LaSalles. The single had barely hit the streets when the group signed with Swan again, as The Buena Vistas, although another Rockin' Rebels single appeared in 1966 on the Itzy Records label.

JAY LASKER

Jay Lasker began his record industry career with Decca Records in 1945, joining the company after coming out of the army at the end of the Second World War. A branch manager by 1951, Jay was elevated to Vice President of Sales in 1956 and spent five years in the role before moving on to Reprise in 1961. After a short spell at Vee-Jay, Jay moved on to become a partner and president of Dunhill Records, subsequently becoming president of the company when ABC bought Dunhill in 1966 and formed ABC Dunhill. From ABC Dunhill Jay moved on briefly to Ariola America Records before joining Motown in 1980 where he became president and was heavily involved in the reissues programme the company introduced later in the decade. He retired owing to illness in 1987 and died from cancer on 13 June 1989 at the age of 65 years.

THE LAST DANCE – VARIOUS ARTISTS [ALBUM]

After countless compilations that focussed purely on hits, **The Last Dance** represented something of a change. The theme running through the album was that all of the tracks were slow tempo or ballads, traditionally the kind of songs played as the last dance of an evening across Britain's clubs and discos. Over the years, Motown songs had featured heavily in this segment, so a compilation of some of the better songs would surely be successful.

And so it proved, with **The Last Dance** topping the chart barely three weeks after its release in January 1980, thanks once again to an extensive television advertising campaign. It would remain there for two weeks before being dislodged by The Shadows' **String Of Hits**. Featuring obvious hits from The Commodores (*Three Times A Lady* and *Still*), Diana Ross (*I'm Still Waiting* and *Do You Know Where You're Going To*), Michael Jackson (*Ben* and *Got To Be There*) and Stevie Wonder (*My Cherie Amour* and *He's Misstra Know-It-All*), the twenty track album sold over 100,000 copies, earning a gold disc.

THE LAST DRAGON (1985 FILM)

Produced by Berry Gordy and directed by Michael Schultz, the martial arts and musical film 'The Last Dragon' was released in 1985 after the martial arts craze had peaked, resulting in somewhat negative reviews. Despite the criticism, 'The Last Dragon' would go on to become a financial success at the box office, in turn helping the soundtrack album, available on the Motown label, do considerable business. Written by Louis Venosta and starring Taimak Guarriello, Motown artist Vanity, Christopher Murney and Julius Carry, 'The Last Dragon' began filming in New York in April 1984, with a projected budget of $10 million. It was released eleven months later and would gross over $25 million at the box office, subsequently becoming considered something of a cult classic.

The soundtrack album featured tracks from Dwight David, Vanity, Alfie Silas, Charlene, Willie Hutch (solo and with The Temptations), DeBarge, Stevie Wonder, Smokey Robinson and Syreeta and Rockwell, with DeBarge' *Rhythm Of The Night* becoming a smash hit single, topping the R&B chart and making the Top Ten in both the US and UK. The album itself would peak at #29 R&B and #59 pop for what was Motown Productions last ever feature film venture.

ALBUM: THE LAST DRAGON SOUNDTRACK (1985)

LATELY – STEVIE WONDER [SINGLE]

The **Hotter Than July** album had already given rise to two Top Ten hits in *Masterblaster* and *I Ain't Gonna Stand For It* when Motown in the UK opted for a ballad as the third release. Lyrically the story of a woman cheating on her husband, it ranked alongside previous Wonder ballads in being simplistic in its musical arrangement, with only a bass and piano accompanying Stevie on vocals.

Yet its simplicity worked, at least as far as the UK was concerned, for it would peak at #3 and earn him a silver disc sales award, despite the presence of a reggae cover version by Rudy Grant that peaked at #58. Stevie's version didn't carry quite the same weight in the US, where it had to settle for a chart position of #64 pop and #29 R&B, but the value of the song was revealed in 1993 when Jodeci recorded a cover version and hit #4 pop and topped the R&B listings.

LATINO RECORDS

An extremely brief label imprint of Motown, Latino opened and shut its doors in 1982, during which time just three singles and two albums were released. As the name implies, it was intended to target the growing Latino market in the United States, yet the first single released on the label was by Charlene Duncan, a Spanish language version of her hit *I've Never Been To Me* entitled *Nunca He Ido A Mi*. Isela Sotelo's single *Angelito* was subsequently transferred to the Motown label, whilst the final single release was by Jose Feliciano, *Samba Pa Ti* being released in October 1982. Jose was also responsible for one of the two albums released on the label, **Escenas De Amor (Love Scenes)** being issued in July 1982, a month before Pedro Montero's **Amor Secreto**.

STACY LATTISAW

Stacy Lattisaw was not even a teenager when she began recording, having begun her professional career at the age of eleven. Born in Washington D.C. on 25 November 1966, Stacy was snapped up by Cotillion Records at the age of twelve and handed over to legendary producer Van McCoy. Her debut album **Young And In Love** in 1979 yielded only a minor hit in the title track (which peaked at #91 R&B) and following McCoy's death from a heart attack the same year Stacy was assigned Narada Michael Walden as her next producer. Adopting a more dance orientated stance paid dividends, with *Dynamite!* and *Jump To The Beat* topping the dance charts, with the former becoming a #8 R&B hit and the latter peaking at #3 on the UK pop charts.

Over the next five years Stacy was a regular on the charts, scoring four Top Ten hits on the R&B charts and recording a number of duets with former school friend Johnny Gill. In 1985 Stacy and her management began shopping around for a new deal, with Motown their preferred option after Stacy had been out on the road supporting The Jacksons, even though The Jacksons no longer recorded for the company.

"I watched The Jacksons' show from the wings every night and every night I learned something new. I tried to copy the way he [Michael] related to an audience. He got so involved in every performance he did and the way he communicated with the public was something I wanted to do. We negotiated with different companies before deciding on Motown, and they didn't have a female singer like myself."

The signing of Stacy was seen as an attempt to fill a vacancy created by the departure of Teena Marie, another female artist who appealed to a younger audience. Motown assembled several production and writing teams for her label debut **Take Me All The Way** in 1986, including Kashif, Leon Sylvers, Michael Narada Walden, Jellybean and Steve Barri.

"It was Motown's choice to work with different producers. We wanted to produce an album of variety to show what I could do. There was a mixture of up-tempo and ballads in there."

Fuelled by the success of the singles *Nail It To The Wall* (#4 R&B and #48 pop) and *Jump Into My Life* (#13 R&B), the album would register at #36 R&B and #131 pop, which whilst not quite near the chart performances Teena Marie had achieved was still a promising start to Stacy's career at Motown. Her follow-up album **Personal Attention** also featured an assortment of producers, including Brownmark, Ron 'Have Mercy' Kersey, Lou Pace, Vincent Brantley and Aaron Zigman and Jerry Knight.

"I'm aware of my musical growth and I think this is probably the best album I've ever done," Stacy explained at the time. "It is a very exciting time for me right now. I feel this album is more me because I enjoyed singing these songs. It was as if they were written with me in mind. I'm now at the stage where I have to believe in a song before I can sing it."

Whilst the album performed better on the R&B chart (peaking at #24) it failed to connect with pop buyers, reaching a lowly #151. This was despite three hit singles, including *Every Drop Of Your Love* (#8 R&B) and *Let Me Take You Down* (#11 R&B). The subsequent sale of Motown resulted in Stacy slipping down the priority list, although her third and final Motown album **What You Need** made a good showing on the R&B charts in hitting #16 and produced an R&B chart topping single in *Where Do We Go From Here*, which Stacy recorded with Johnny Gill. Thereafter Stacy retired from the industry in order to raise a family, although she subsequently recorded gospel music.

ALBUMS: TAKE ME ALL THE WAY (1986), PERSONAL ATTENTION (1988), WHAT YOU NEED (1989)

LYNDA LAURENCE

Born Lynda Tucker born in Philadelphia, Pennsylvania on 20 February 1949, Lynda began her career with The Pendelles, a group that also featured her sister Sundray (who sang under the moniker Cindy Scott). In time, both Lynda and Cindy would join Stevie Wonder's vocal backing group, then known as The Third Generation and later Wonderlove.

After three years with Stevie Wonder, Lynda was recommended to Mary Wilson by Lamont Dozier as a potential replacement for the pregnant Cindy Birdsong in The Supremes. She appeared on the cover to album **Floy Joy**, although Cindy had performed on all the tracks, making Lynda's first vocal appearance was with the Jimmy Webb produced album that subsequently followed.

Lynda used her close relationship with Stevie to the group's advantage in 1973, getting him to write and produce *Bad Weather*. In October that year Lynda announced she was leaving The Supremes in order to raise a family, with her replacement being a returning Cindy Birdsong. Lynda returned to backing vocal work, most notably for Stevie Wonder on his **Songs In the Key Of Life** album and also linked with her then husband Trevor Lawrence for the Wilton Place Street Band project, which saw the release of *Disco Lucy*, a disco version of the theme to 'I Love Lucy'.

Lynda would record solo during the 1980s under the name Norma Lewis and then in 1985 linked up with former Supremes Jean Terrell and Scherrie Payne in The Former Ladies of The Supremes (known as The FLOS), touring worldwide to this day. Lynda also made several solo recordings at the start of the 1990s for Ian Levine's Motorcity Records.

LAURIE RECORDS

Formed in New York City in 1958, Laurie Records was started by brothers Robert and Gene Schwartz and Allan Sussel. Sussel had previously bank-rolled Jamie Records, a label named after his eldest daughter, and when that failed had launched Laurie, named after his other daughter. Laurie Records would become successful thanks to a roster that included Dion & The Belmonts, The Mystics, The Jarmels, The Royal Guardsmen, Gary U.S. Bonds (via its Legrand imprint), Bobby Goldsboro, The Chiffons and several licensed tracks from Gerry & The Pacemakers, when the British invasion was at its height.

Laurie Records also licensed Lee & The Leopards *Come Into My Palace*, which had originally been released on Gordy in April 1962, without success. Laurie Records reissue in October 1963 was similarly overlooked.

BETTYE LaVETTE

Although a doyen of the Detroit music scene for a good many years, Bettye LaVette spent only a brief part of her recording career with Motown and that didn't come until 1982, after the label had vacated the city. Born Betty Jo Haskin in Muskegon, Michigan on 29 January 1946, she was raised in Detroit and showed an early aptitude for singing. After being discovered by Johnnie Mae Matthews, she first recorded for LuPine at the age of 16, with a test pressing of *My Man-He's A Loving Man* being snapped up by Atlantic Records in 1962 and becoming a #7 R&B and #101 pop hit (credited to Betty LaVett).

After a further single release on Atlantic Betty returned to LuPine and recorded *Witchcraft In The Air*. Betty moved to New York for a while, becoming the featured vocalist with the Don Gardner and Dee Dee Ford Revue and recording a one-off track for consideration by Scepter Records. She eventually resurfaced at Calla Records, scoring a minor hit with *Let Me Down Easy* in 1965, but subsequent singles didn't fare as well and Betty became something of a recording nomad, appearing at Silver Fox, SSS International and her own TCA imprint.

In 1972 she returned to Atlantic, signing with the Atco label but success still proved elusive, with the result Betty moved into musicals and recorded sporadically. After small hit on Epic (1975's *Thank You For Loving Me* which hit #94 R&B) and an attempt at disco on West End (*Doin' The Best I Can* in 1978) Betty disappeared off the music radar, finally re-appearing in 1982 when she signed with Motown.

A slight change of name to Bettye LaVette and a musical switch saw her in Nashville, working with producer Steve Buckingham on her album **Tell Me A Lie**. The album would give rise to a hit single in *Right In The Middle (Of Falling In Love)*, which hit #35 R&B and #103 pop, but executive changes at Motown resulted in her album not being properly promoted and Bettye was dropped from the label. She would record with Ian Levine's Motorcity label in 1989, whilst many of her earlier recordings remain popular on the Northern Soul scene.

ALBUM: TELL ME A LIE (1982)
FURTHER READING: A WOMAN LIKE ME (2012)

HUBERT LAWS

The second of eight children, Hubert Laws was born in Houston, Texas on 10 November 1939, with several of his brothers and sisters later following him into the professional musical arena, including saxophonist Ronnie and singers Eloise and Debra. Having learnt to play piano, mellophone and alto saxophone, Hubert switched to the flute in high school almost as an afterthought, filling in a flute solo performance with the school orchestra.

However he came by it, Hubert had found his instrument of choice and would play the flute both at high school and with a local band known variously as The Swingsters and Night Hawks before settling on the name The Jazz Crusaders. Hubert moved with the other Crusaders to Los Angeles before winning a scholarship to the Juilliard School of Music in New York, driving all the way in a ten year old Plymouth Sedan with his life savings in his pocket.

"It was the fall of 1960. I was down to my last fifty bucks and wondering what to do when the phone rang and it was a call offering me my first job at Sugar Ray's Lounge in Harlem. Times were tough then, but I haven't looked back since."

Equally at home with classical music (having performed with the New York Metropolitan Opera Orchestra and the New York Philharmonic Orchestra) and jazz and R&B, Hubert launched his solo career with Atlantic Records in 1964 with **The Laws Of Jazz**. However, it is the body of work he recorded at CTI that firmly established his name, mixing jazz and classical on **The Rite Of Spring** and electrifying the jazz funk crowd with his 1975 album **The Chicago Theme**. The title track, written and arranged by label mate Bob James, became a #53 hit on the R&B singles chart, with Hubert's composition *Inflation Chaser* also attracting heavy club play in the United Kingdom. **The Chicago Theme** would become one of the biggest albums of Hubert's career, hitting #2 Jazz, #18 R&B and #42 pop. After CTI Hubert recorded extensively for Columbia and later Music Masters in 1990s, where he revisited and reconsidered his past CTI recordings.
ALBUM: THE CHICAGO THEME (1975)

LAURA LEE

Born Laura Lee Newton in Chicago, Illinois on 9 March 1945, Laura moved with her mother to Detroit as a child and was eventually adopted by the Reverend E Allan Rundless. Laura's adopted father had previously been a member of The Soul Stirrers and assembled a new gospel group with his wife Ernestine, The Meditation Singers, a group that also featured Della Reese. Laura joined the group as a teenager and spent several years touring the country before launching a secular solo career in 1965, mainly working in R&B clubs in and around Detroit.

In 1966 she recorded a one-off single for Ric-Tic, with *To Win Your Heart* backed with *So Will I* being released in March, although the following year Laura signed with Chess Records. After several fruitless recording sessions in Chicago, Laura was sent to Muscle Shoals to work with Rick Hall, resulting in several R&B and pop hits, most notably with *Dirty Man* and *Up Tight Good Man*. Laura then had a brief spell with Cotillion before returning to Detroit and signing for Holland-Dozier-Holland's Hot Wax label.

The three albums Laura recorded for Hot Wax resulted in several big hits, including *Women's Love Rights* (#11 R&B and #36 pop) and *Rip Off* (#3 R&B and #68 pop). It was the impending British release of *Rip Off* (written by another former Motown writer in William Weatherspoon) that prompted Tamla Motown in the UK to dust off *To Win Your Heart* in September 1972 (the track also featured on a UK only compilation album, **Ric-Tic Relics**, released in 1973), although neither single made any chart headway. Laura then switched to the Invictus label in 1974 before moving on to sign for Ariola, but shortly after signing she fell seriously ill and retired from the industry. She returned in 1983 with a gospel album for Myrrh Records and, having been ordained as a minister in 1990, has continued to record gospel music.

LEE & THE LEOPARDS

Fronted by Detroit singer Lee Henry Moore with Prentiss Anderson and George Ross, Lee & The Leopards had one release on Gordy, with Mickey Stevenson, Brian Holland and Lee Moore composing *Come Into My Palace*. The doo-wop single was issued in April 1962 and was only the second release on the Gordy label but failed to make the charts.

The single was leased to Laurie Records in October 1963 and still did little business, with Lee & The Leopards moving on to Fortune Records where they adopted their sound to give it a blues feel. Lee Moore, under which name he would later record, retained that sound for his solo work on Diamond Jim and Tri City.

LEGEND

A vocal group led by songwriter, singer and producer Eddie Coleman Jr., Legend had one release on the Tamla label, *Shake It Lady* backed with *Lay Your Body Down* (with both sides written by Eddie with Randall Fowler and Gwen Gordy Fuqua) being issued in September 1980.
Eddie also wrote and produced a number of tracks on High Inergy, The Stone City Band and G.C. Cameron and later formed Steel 4 Reel. Legend meanwhile released one further single on the Spider Web Records label, *Let Your Body Move*.

MICHEL LEGRAND

One of the best known writers of film and television scores, Michel has over 200 credits to his name which have won him three Oscars and five Grammy Awards. Born in Paris, France on 24 February 1932 he came to prominence after the release of 'The Umbrellas Of Cherbourg' in 1964, with countless studios approaching him with requests to score a variety of films, with his best known being 'The Thomas Crown Affair', 'Ice Station Zebra', 'Wuthering Heights' and 'The Summer Of '42'.
In 1972 he was brought in to the 'Lady Sings The Blues' project, writing and arranging both the *Love Theme* and *Closing Theme* for the soundtrack album. *Love Theme From 'Lady Sings The Blues'* was coupled with Gil Askey's *Any Happy Home* and originally scheduled for release on MoWest in March 1973, although it subsequently appeared on the main Motown label the same month.

LET IT WHIP – THE DAZZ BAND [SINGLE]

Reggie Andrews and Ndugu Chancler had briefly been writing partners towards the end of the 1970s before going their separate ways, with Ndugu recording for Epic and Reggie taking a staff job at Motown. The pair linked up again in 1980, writing a number of songs for Switch and Reggie hiring Ndugu for a number of recording sessions at Motown. After The Dazz Band had enjoyed some success with their first two albums for the label, Motown took the decision to appoint Reggie as producer for their third effort, **Keep It Live**, with Reggie and Ndugu offering the group a song they had written entitled *Let It Whip*.

The lead track on the album, *Let It Whip* was not Motown's original choice as the lead single release, preferring to go with a ballad, but almost as soon as the album hit the streets, calls came in demanding that *Let It Whip* be released as a single. It proved to be the correct choice, with the single topping the R&B charts for five weeks (non-consecutively) and peak at #5 pop. The song would earn Reggie Andrews and Ndugu Chancler a Grammy nomination for Best R&B Song (they lost out to *Turn Your Love Around,* which had been a hit for George Benson), although more than adequate compensation was achieved when the group won the award for Best R&B Performance by a Group with Vocals.

LET'S GET IT ON – MARVIN GAYE [SINGLE]

According to co-writer Ed Townsend, *Let's Get It On* is a song about dealing with life, inspired by Ed's own battles with alcohol addiction. When Marvin first heard the song, he was still contemplating doing an album that continued the social issues he had first explored on **What's Going On**, and to that end had Kenneth Stover write a new set of lyrics with a political flavour. Ed wasn't enamoured with the new version, contending that the song would work better if it retained the romantic flavour of the original. Marvin and Ed then collaborated on a third set of lyrics but retained the original musical backing and went to the other extreme, producing a song that was overtly sexual in its message.
It may have helped that Marvin's latest girlfriend Janis Hunter was present in the studio when the song was recorded, her presence inspiring Marvin to deliver a majestic performance. Whilst the single's subsequent release in June 1973 did receive some criticism for the suggestive lyrics, it proved altogether irresistible, going on the top both the R&B (for six weeks) and pop charts (for two weeks) and selling more than two million copies in the first six weeks of release. In Britain it received a rather more conservative reception, peaking at #31 on the pop chart, even if the song would become a staple of his later live dates. The single also earned Marvin a Grammy Award nomination for Best R&B Vocal Performance, Male but lost out to Stevie Wonder and *Superstition*.

LET'S GET IT ON – MARVIN GAYE [ALBUM]

The phenomenal success of **What's Going On** gave Marvin greater creative and artistic control of his musical career and earned him a much more lucrative contract from his employers, but with it came greater expectations. Struggling to decide upon a direction for his follow-up album, Marvin initially worked on a few tracks that continued the social and political themes of his blockbuster, but creatively the juices weren't flowing.

Then he met with writer and producer Ed Townsend, who played him the basics of a song he had written entitled *Let's Get It On*. When Marvin expressed his interest in working with him on the song and a possible album, Ed was quick to ensure that he had a proper deal in place, one which would guarantee him fifty percent of the royalties. After a couple of false starts, with Marvin taking Ed's song and getting Kenneth Stover to write a new set of lyrics that didn't meet with Ed's approval, prompting a virtual re-write from Marvin and Ed, the pair set down to craft an album.

Of the eight tracks on display, four were co-written by Marvin and Ed, comprising the entire first side of the album. These, highlighted by the eventual smash hit single and album title track *Let's Get It On*, were much more sensually and sexually charged than anything Marvin (or for that matter any other R&B singer) had ever recorded and released previously.

Let's Get It On proved to be an inspiration to Marvin too, for he delved into his own back catalogue and revisited songs that had been written three or so years previously and worked them up to fit the groove and tempo of *Let's Get It On*, including *Distant Lover* (co-written with his wife Gwen and Sandra Greene around 1970), *Come Get To This* (which dated back to the early recording sessions for **What's Going On**) and *You Sure Love To Ball*.

Let's Get It On was recorded at Golden World Studios in Detroit and Hitsville West in Los Angeles and featured a veritable who's who of the recording scene, including James Jamerson and Wilton Felder on bass, Paul Humphrey and Uriel Jones on drums, David T Walker, Eddie Willis, Melvin 'Wah Wah Watson' Ragin and Robert White on guitar, Eddie 'Bongo' Brown on percussion, Joe Sample on keyboards and Marvin on piano. Also present in the studio for the sessions was Janis Hunter, who would ultimately become Marvin's second wife. As such, **Let's Get It On** was as much a musical love letter as a ground-breaking album, and whilst several of the songs may have contained personal messages to Janis, they found a wider audience and acceptance.

Let's Get It On surpassed even **What's Going On** on the charts and sales, topping the R&B chart for ten weeks and peaking at #2 on the pop chart. It also bettered its predecessor in the UK, making a one week appearance at #37 when **What's Going On** had failed to chart at all. Helped by the hit singles *Let's Get It On* (an R&B and pop chart topper), *Come Get To This* and *You Sure Love To Ball*, the album would sell over three million copies upon its release, offering further proof that Motown were no longer just a successful singles company.

LET'S GET SERIOUS – JERMAINE JACKSON [SINGLE]

By 1980 Jermaine Jackson's solo career had stalled. Whilst his brothers were enjoying collective success as The Jacksons and Michael, of course, solo success with Epic Records, Jermaine hadn't been anywhere near the pop Top Ten for eight years. Indeed, he was equally absent from the R&B charts, with only one Top Twenty entry in that same eight year period. Enter Stevie Wonder to revive his career at a time he most needed it.

According to several stories put out at the time of release, Stevie had written and recorded *Let's Get Serious* for himself but was persuaded by Berry Gordy to give the song to Jermaine so that his career would be given something of a kick-start. However, according to Lee Garrett, who had written on and off with Stevie for a considerable period of time, Stevie had contacted Lee to inform him that he'd been asked to work with Jermaine but was struggling to complete the one song that he thought might be ideal. As Lee remembered it, Stevie had a basic track but no lyrics or title, which Lee eventually provided. Once Lee attached a title to the track, the lyrics and melody came easy to Stevie, who not only produced the track but also sang along with Jermaine on various sections of the track.

Even without Stevie's presence the song would have been a hit, but combined Jermaine and Stevie were unstoppable, resulting in *Let's Get Serious* powering its way to the top of the R&B chart for six weeks (the first and only R&B solo chart topper of his Motown career) and hitting #9 pop. It also proved a monster hit in the UK, where it became his first hit single and came to rest at #8. At the year's end *Let's Get Serious* was nominated for two Grammy Awards, Best Rhythm & Blues Song and Best R&B Vocal Performance, Male but lost out to *Never Knew Love Like This Before* (written by Reggie Lucas and James Mtume for Stephanie Mills) and *Give Me The Night* by George Benson respectively.

LET'S GET SERIOUS – JERMAINE JACKSON [ALBUM]

Stevie Wonder provided much of the ammunition that enabled Jermaine Jackson to get his solo career back on track in 1980, writing and producing the monster hit *Let's Get Serious*. Stevie also wrote and produced two further tracks on the accompanying album, *Where Are You Now* and the follow-up single *You're Supposed To Keep Your Love For Me*, which had originally been recorded in 1975 for a proposed Stevie album.

The original version featured Stevie with Michael and Jackie Jackson on background vocals but had subsequently been scrapped. When Stevie was invited to produce for Jermaine, he picked the track out and remixed it, removing Michael and Jackie's vocals in the process. As a Jermaine solo single it maintained the momentum established by *Let's Get Serious*, going on to hit #32 on the R&B chart and #34 pop. The rest of the seven track album was produced by Jermaine himself, with *Burnin' Hot* going on to become a UK hit and peaking at #32. The album proved to be the biggest success of Jermaine's career, topping the R&B chart and reaching the hitherto unattainable Top Ten of the pop listings, peaking at #6. **Let's Get Serious** also did brisk business internationally, becoming his UK chart debut and reaching #22.

LETTA

British audiences first encountered Letta Mbulu in 1961 when she was part of the cast in the musical 'King Kong', a South African production that became a major West End success. When the production ended, Letta returned to her South African homeland, where she had been born in Soweto on 23 August 1942. Angered by the continuing apartheid policies of the South African government, Letta headed to America in 1965 and quickly linked up with several ex-patriots, including Hugh Masekela, Miriam Makeba and Jonas Gwangwa, all of whom had also appeared in 'King Kong'.

After recording for Columbia and Capitol during the decade, Letta became one of the first artists signed to Hugh Masekela's Chisa label, releasing the album **Letta** in October 1970 and single *I Won't Weep No More* the following March. Her second album was scheduled for May 1971 as **Mosadi** in the US but was never released. It did appear, however, in South Africa two years later as **I'll Never Be The Same** (there may also have been a compilation album **Letta Mbulu – Gold** released on Tamla Motown in Europe in 1977). Letta moved on and would record for Fantasy and A&M during the 1970s, appearing on Quincy Jones' **Roots** album and later the soundtrack to 'The Color Purple'. The 1980s saw her performing with Michael Jackson on *Liberian Girl* before Letta and her husband ended their South African exile after 26 years, returning home in 1991.
ALBUM: LETTA (1970)

CHICO LEVERETT

A member of The Satintones, Charles 'Chico' Leverett recorded and released one single for the Tamla label before The Satintones had even got around to recording. Chico wrote both sides of *Solid Sender* backed with *I'll Never Love Again* with several of The Satintones helping out on backing vocals, along with Robert Bateman and Sonny Sanders, with the single released on Tamla in April 1959. Chico would also co-write The Satintones' debut for the label, *Going To The Hop* backed with *Motor City*, with the flip side playing a part in the naming of Berry Gordy's second label; according to Chico, Berry announced a competition to provide a name for the label, with Chico suggesting Motor City in deference to Detroit's position as the car capital of America, which Berry subsequently amended to Motown.

Meanwhile frustration that his solo single didn't sell and the lack of recordings on The Satintones prompted Chico to leave the group in 1961 and move to Reading, Pennsylvania, subsequently reviving his solo career with a number of recordings for Bethlehem in 1963. Chico would also be one of the former Motown artists who recorded for Ian Levine's Motorcity Records label in the 1990s.

THE LEWIS SISTERS

Pianist Helen Lewis graduated from UCLA with a degree in music and was joined in California by her sister Kay in 1955, herself a music graduate from Michigan State University. They found an early champion in jazz pianist Les McCann, who helped get them a contract with Liberty Records and played on their 1959 debut album **Way Out...Far**, on which the sisters performed a dozen well known standards. A year later they linked up with producer Russ Garcia for **Voices, Strings & Percussions** on Verve, an album of Tchaikovsky songs on which their voices were used like violins.

They then switched to pop music, recording a one-off single for Aura before going to Motown in Los Angeles to audition for Hal Davis and Marc Gordon, subsequently being signed as artists early in 1965. The first single, *He's An Oddball* was recorded in California and released on V.I.P. in May 1965. Whilst it did little sales-wise, the sisters were already proving themselves an asset to Motown, performing backing vocals on sessions by Chris Clark and submitting several songs to Jobete for consideration by other artists. These included *Just Walk In My Shoes* (Gladys Knight & The Pips), *Happiness Is Guaranteed* (Martha & The Vandellas) and, released much later but considered their masterpiece, *This Love-Starved Heart Of Mine* (Marvin Gaye). This latter song they wrote with Al Wilson in mind and he did record it but Hal and Marc were unable to get him a deal with Motown.

The Lewis sisters were meanwhile sent to Detroit to record their second single for Motown, with Berry Gordy writing and producing *You Need Me*. Despite the boss' involvement and billing them as The Singing School Teachers, *You Need Me* didn't sell and marked the end of their Motown recording career. They continued to write for Jobete for at least another year and would make a cameo appearance in the film 'Lady Sings The Blues', whilst Kay's daughter Lisa also had a brief Motown recording career as Little Lisa. Helen, who married Arthur Mastor and became Helen Lewis-Mastor, was also awarded an M.A. in Education and a Phd in Psychology, whilst Kay initially married John Miller and became Kay Lewis Miller. Kay later built her own recording studio with her second husband Bob Smith.

RAMSEY LEWIS TRIO

Ramsey Emmanuel Lewis Jr. was born in Chicago, Illinois on 27 May 1935 and began taking piano lessons at the age of four. He formed his first trio with Eldee Young (bass) and Isaac 'Redd' Holt (drums) in 1956. By 1973 the line-up comprised Ramsey, Cleveland Eaton (born in Fairfield, Alabama on 31 August 1939, bass) and Morris Jennings (drums), with the trio appearing in the film and on the soundtrack to 'Save The Children', performing a version of the Thom Bell and Linda Creed composition *People Make The World Go Round*.

LIBRA

An Italian progressive rock group from Rome, Libra was formed in 1973 by Federico D'Andrea (guitar and vocals), Nicola Di Staso (guitar and vocals), Alessandro 'Sandro' Centofanti (born in Sulmona on 23 June 1952, keyboards), Dino Cappa (born in Candela on 25 June 1948, bass and vocals) and David Walter (drums). They recorded an album with producer Danny Besquet in the autumn of 1974, **Musica E Parole**, also recording an English version of the album at the same time. Besquet initially got them a deal with Ricordi, who issued the Italian language version in February 1975, but continued shopping for a bigger deal.

He got one with Motown, who gave him a ten album contract which he began to fulfil by leasing the English language version of their album. This was released as **Libra** in August 1975, by which time the group (with a new drummer, Walter Martino having replaced David Walter) were in the United States rehearsing for an American tour with Frank Zappa, Chicago and Steppenwolf.

Libra also recorded a follow-up album whilst in the country, a much more commercial offering that was released in May 1976 as **Winter Day's Nightmare**. By then the group had already returned home to Italy and temporarily disbanded, although a new line-up assembled in 1977 for a further album on Ricordi. D'Andrea died after being knocked down by a car on 28 November 1978.

ALBUMS: LIBRA (1975), WINTER'S DAY NIGHTMARE (1976)

RAYNOMA LILES

Whilst much of Motown's early history has tended to focus almost exclusively on Berry Gordy, his then girlfriend and later second wife Raynoma also played an important part in establishing the label.

Born Raynoma Mayberry in Detroit, Michigan on 8 March 1937, she married her first husband Charles Liles, a would-be musician, with the marriage resulting in the birth of a son, Cliff Liles in December 1955. However, the marriage didn't last and Raynoma resorted to singing in order to provide for herself and her young child, winning a local talent contest.

"The emcee recommended that I go and see Berry, who had some acts. I went to his place and auditioned with my sister. He watched and everything, and then said, 'What else can you do?' That's how impressed he was. I had about a hundred songs that I'd written – most of them were lousy, but they were songs. I'd been writing since I was about twelve. I guess Berry thought the songs could have been better...but I went in to work with him and his company."

Raynoma could also write and arrange music, which were attributes Berry did need, so she set to work helping form vocal backing group the Rayber Voices with Brian Holland, Robert Bateman and Sonny Sanders.

Raynoma and Berry also formed the Rayber Music Writing Company, an outfit that would record a song for a fixed fee of $100. Berry and Raynoma would later form the publishing company Jobete (the ownership of the company has been mired in confusion ever since; according to Raynoma, she was a joint owner of the company, even though it was named after Berry's three children by his first wife Thelma, and her name was removed from the director's list on Berry's instructions) and then the Tamla record label.

Raynoma also had a son by Berry, Kerry being born in June 1959, the birth of whom eventually prompted Berry to divorce Thelma and marry Raynoma in 1960. At first Raynoma was a key member of the team at Hitsville, appearing on many sessions as a backing singer, releasing her own single under the moniker Little Iva & Her Band (*When I Need You* appearing on the short-lived Miracle label in February 1961) and co-writing several tracks.

Despite her worth to the company, her personal relationship with Berry was unravelling, fuelled in part by his affair with another Motown employee, Margaret Norton. By 1963 the marriage between Raynoma and Berry was at an end (largely because Raynoma had threatened Margaret with a gun!), although Raynoma expressed her wish to continue working for the company. It was therefore agreed that Raynoma should open up an office for Jobete in New York, where the likes of George Clinton, George Kerr, Sidney Barnes and J.J. Jackson were signed up as songwriters.

Unfortunately, the cost of maintaining an office in New York soon proved exorbitant, leaving Raynoma severely short of cash. It is not known whether Berry refused to help or whether Raynoma's spending exceeded whatever money was allocated to the office, but in desperation Raynoma ignored the pleas of Eddie Singleton (then her partner, later her third husband) and came up with a plan to have 5,000 copies of Motown's biggest hit, *My Guy* by Mary Wells, pressed up and sold off the books. Once again, it is not clear who informed the F.B.I. (some say it was Berry Gordy himself), but Raynoma was arrested and had to explain to Berry exactly what she had done. Berry was furious and had the New York office shut down, although he did not press charges against his former wife.

Indeed, their relationship after the event appears to have been quite amicable, with Berry even lending Raynoma and Eddie the money to launch their own label in Washington D.C., Shrine Records. The label did not last long, with Raynoma eventually drawn back towards Motown, undertaking a wide variety of tasks for the company, most notably acting as personal assistant to Diana Ross. That was probably the most bizarre appointment of all the jobs and positions Raynoma held within the organisation, since it pitted Berry's second wife and the mother of his fourth child against his long time girlfriend and the mother of his seventh child!

Raynoma remained with Motown for a total of eighteen years in her various capacities before being let go as the company was paring back on costs. Raynoma then set about writing her autobiography (at the time she wrote it, she had reportedly fallen on hard times and was living with her former husband Eddie Singleton and his wife Barbara!) which was published in 1990.

FURTHER READING: BERRY, ME AND MOTOWN: THE UNTOLD STORY (1990)

LIONEL RICHIE - LIONEL RICHIE [ALBUM]

Lionel Richie had enjoyed considerable success as a writer within The Commodores, penning most of the group's major hits such as *Just To Be Close To You*, *Easy* and *Three Times A Lady*, but with the group being run on democratic lines, Lionel's songs had to compete with whatever material the rest of the group had written when it came to recording an album. Yet when outside artists and producers came looking for material, it was invariably Lionel that they called, with his success with *It's My Turn* (recorded by Lionel and Diana Ross for the film of the same name) and *Lady* (recorded by Kenny Rogers) further fuelling his confidence.

Although still officially a member of The Commodores, Lionel began work on his eponymous debut in 1981, bringing in long time Commodores' producer James Anthony Carmichael to co-produce the album. Once again it was the ballads that proved the strongest material, with *Truly*, *You Are* and *My Love* all hitting the Top Ten of the pop and R&B charts. **Lionel Richie** quickly became one of the biggest albums of 1982, selling more than four million copies in the US and topping the R&B chart whilst hitting #3 pop and #9 in the UK. The success of **Lionel Richie** also ensured there was no going back to The Commodores; his solo career was well and truly underway.

LITTLE LISA

Eight year old Lisa Lewis often accompanied her mother Kay to the studios for recording sessions, sitting quietly in the background whilst Kay and her sister Helen worked on a number or two. One of these, which the sisters had written, proved problematic and, as the studio costs racked up, those involved were desperate to get a good demo committed to tape. Lisa was equally desperate to get home, so announced that she could sing it! Hal Davis duly switched on the tape, Lisa stood on a box to reach the microphone and began singing. Her vocal was good enough to have Berry Gordy commit to a single, with *Hang On Bill* (a re-working of Bob Kayli's *Hold On Pearl*) backed with *Puppet On A String* being issued in August 1965 on V.I.P. (although another track, *Because I Love Him* was supposedly scheduled for release on Motown in June '65).

Lisa performed the B side on a Christmas episode of 'Hullabaloo' and told the viewers that aside from a new doll and dress, what she wanted most for Christmas was for her record to be a hit. Lisa didn't get her wish that year but would later record as Lise Miller and hit with *Love Is* on Canterbury in 1967 and, as Lisa Miller feature on Sergio Mendes' *Never Gonna Let You Go,* a #4 hit in 1983.

LITTLE MISS SOUL

Patrice Jefferson recorded several tracks for Motown during 1970, most notably with producers Duke Browner and Clay McMurray. Given the moniker Little Miss Soul, it appeared as though Motown had high hopes for the singer but for some reason nothing was released at the time; the only track that has thus far emerged is her version of *You've Made Me So Very Happy* which duly appeared on the 2007 compilation **A Cellarful Of Motown Volume 3**.

LITTLE OTIS

Veteran record producer George Leaner would set up his own One-derful record label in Chicago in the spring of 1962, later adding the M-Pac and Mar-V-Lus imprints to his portfolio. Earlier that year, however, he had produced something of an answer record to Gene Chandler's *Duke Of Earl* single on Little Otis and needed national distribution. He approached Berry Gordy who picked up the single, one of the first finished master deals the company had done. Little Otis was in fact Otis Hayes, who was born in Greensboro, North Carolina on 13 June 1936 and started his musical career in New York before moving to Chicago some three or four years later. Whilst *I Out-Duked The Duke* did little, largely because Chandler's hit inspired so many other tracks trying to jump on the bandwagon, Otis Hayes would become one of the staff writers for Leaner's growing stable of artists.

LITTLE RICHARD

Born Richard Wayne Penniman in Macon, Georgia on 5 December 1932, Little Richard made his first recordings in 1951 but made his breakthrough in 1955 with the release of *Tutti Frutti* on the Specialty label. Over the next four or five years, Little Richard was a regular on the charts, establishing himself as the self-proclaimed 'Architect of Rock & Roll'. However, in late 1957 he had converted to Christianity and announced his retirement from secular music and his intention to record gospel music (his presence on the chart was maintained by recordings left in the can). Although he returned to secular music in 1962 the momentum was lost and not one of his latest releases cracked the Top Ten of the R&B chart.

In 1986 he was one of several artists given a CD release by Motown as part of the **Compact Command Performances** series, featuring fifteen re-recorded versions of his greatest hits. An original recording, *I Don't Know What You've Got (But It's Got Me)* from 1965 (which is reputed to feature Jimi Hendrix on guitar) appeared on the compilation album **Hits From The Legendary Vee-Jay Records** issued on CD in November 1986.

ALBUM: COMPACT COMMAND PERFORMANCES (1986)

HATTIE LITTLES

Hattie Littles spent four years signed with Motown, recording some ten singles yet only one was ever released. Born in Shelby, Mississippi in 1937, Hattie was discovered by Clarence Paul performing in Detroit in 1962, having won a talent contest at Lee's Sensation Lounge and assigned to the Gordy label. Her first single was to have been *Back In My Arms* in 1962, but this was pulled and replaced in September with *Your Love Is Wonderful*. When nothing happened sales-wise, Hattie slipped down the priority list to such an extent that her only other appearance on the release schedule was in January 1965, when *Conscience I'm Guilty* was listed on the forthcoming V.I.P. singles list, but this remained unreleased. Despite this, Hatti was almost constantly out on the road.

"I was the opening act and toured on and off with them for quite some time. I think I did different gigs with The Spinners, then Jimmy Ruffin. We worked Cleveland together. I also toured with my cousin Choker Campbell, so I was busy most of the time."

Hatti also went out on the road with Marvin Gaye, a personal favourite of many around Hitsville.

"Marvin Gaye spells g-o-s-p-e-l. He was the type of person you could talk to, who would listen. He'd never cram advice down your throat, but if you needed advice, he would try his very best to help you out. He was never critical, never used fancy words, never called you stupid or things like that. He always had time, and he was like that with everyone, not just me."

Despite the fact her recordings struggled to see the light of day, Hatti stuck around Hitsville.

"I was happy. Motown was a family. I don't know whether everyone actually liked each other or not, but I do know it was like coming home. Motown had a nice, homely feeling and I stayed because I had these feelings. I sang better with those feelings. Everything felt right, if I hadn't felt anything how could I expect anyone listening to me to feel anything!"

Eventually, however, Hatti did leave Motown and its family, and whilst the departure might have been amicable, what happened after saw her life began to unravel, suffering alcoholism and drug abuse during the 1960s and, so it is said, spending time in prison after killing her abusive husband. In the 1980s she was discovered again singing gospel in Detroit and subsequently signed by Ian Levine's Motorcity label, recording *and* releasing three albums and several singles. She died from a heart attack in June 2000.

LIVE AT LONDON'S TALK OF THE TOWN - DIANA ROSS & THE SUPREMES [ALBUM]

Situated on the corner of Charing Cross Road and Leicester Square in the heart of London, the Talk of the Town had been built in 1900 and opened as the London Hippodrome for circus and variety performances. It later became a theatre but in 1958 the interior was removed and replaced by a nightclub, with the venue changing name to The Talk of the Town at the same time. It soon began to attract the biggest names in show business, including Frank Sinatra, Shirley Bassey, Tom Jones, Sammy Davis Jr., Cliff Richard and, in February 1968, Diana Ross & The Supremes.

The first opportunity for British audiences to see Florence Ballard's replacement Cindy Birdsong, The Supremes' show proved a massive success, with assorted stars and celebrities in attendance, including Mick Jagger and Paul McCartney. The group presented a mixed show that contained standards (*With A Song In My Heart*, *Stranger In Paradise* and *You're Nobody Till Somebody Loves You*), several medleys, including a tribute to The Beatles and many of their own biggest hits in both medley and long form, with the orchestra being conducted by Jimmy Garrett.

The whole show was recorded and, no doubt inspired by the success of a live album from the same venue by Tom Jones (which hit #6 in the UK in 1967) was released in the UK in March 1968 as a twelve track album (only four songs from the group's stage show were omitted). The album proved a major European success, peaking at #6 in the UK, although it was more modestly received in the US following its release in August, having to settle for a #57 placing on the pop chart, even if it did repeat its #6 berth on the R&B listings. The success of the album, as least as far as the UK was concerned, prompted subsequent albums from The Temptations and Stevie Wonder also recorded at the Talk of the Town. In 1982 the venue reverted back to being called The Hippodrome.

LIVING FOR THE CITY – STEVIE WONDER [SINGLE]

Following the release of **Innervisions**, the track *Higher Ground* became ironic because of Stevie's subsequent car accident, but there was little doubt as to what the centrepiece of the album was, *Living For the City*. In its album form it was a seven and a half minute musical journey from Mississippi to New York, encountering poverty and racism, and whilst the central character arrives in New York full of hope at the prospect of a new beginning, finds himself tricked into transporting drugs and is sentenced to ten years in prison.

To get the strength of the message across, Stevie employed the vocal services of his brother Calvin Hardaway, close aide Ira Tucker Jr. and lawyer Johann Vigoda on the spoken interlude, but it is the power in

Stevie's voice that ensured the message hit home. The power was deliberately sought, as producer Malcolm Cecil later revealed.

"We had to find a way to get the vocal rougher and harder, sound like someone who'd been through some real shit, so we decided the only thing to do was try and get Steve real angry and get his voice hoarse, so when we were recording that vocal for the last verse again we kept on doing stuff that would get him angry and one of the things he hates is stopping the tape, you know if he doesn't say stop the tape in the middle of a vocal then... well, we broke that rule! We kept on stopping the tape, 'Come on Steve, you can do better than that, this is shit' and I was really shirty with him, and we got him hoarse, we wouldn't give him tea, he likes his tea with no milk in it, with the lemon to clear the throat, We didn't give him the tea. He was getting real upset; I think he's still upset with me about that, but we got a great track!"

Not only a great track but following its October 1973 release as a 3:41 edit (much of the spoken interlude is omitted) a massive hit too, with the single hitting the top of the R&B chart and #8 pop in the US and #15 in the UK. At the year's end, the song won the Grammy Award for Best Rhythm & Blues Song, giving Stevie back to back awards in the category following *Superstition*'s triumph twelve months previously. Eight years later British group Gillan recorded a rock version and scored a #50 hit in the UK.

LODI

In 1962 brothers Robert and John Carlos Cecchino adopted new names, Beau Charles and John Charles respectively and formed a group in their New Jersey homeland. Named after Knickerbocker Road, which ran through their hometown in Bergenfield, the Knickerbockers had a several personnel changes until settling down with a line-up that consisted of Beau (guitar and vocals), John (bass and vocals), William Crandall (a vocalist and saxophonist who adopted the name Buddy Randell) and Jimmy Walker (drums). They were spotted playing in New York by producer Jerry Fuller who got them a contract with Challenge Records based in Los Angeles. Although they were to enjoy three hits, the biggest of which was *Lies* (which was also the title of their only charting album) in 1965, Challenge had distribution problems and their records were not the sellers they had anticipated.

Walker left in late 1967 to replace Bill Medley in The Righteous Brothers and Randell would leave soon after, although he did briefly rejoin in 1970. The Charles brothers meanwhile kept a variation of the group going into the 1970s and in 1971 were signed by MoWest, by which time the rest of the group featured Ritchie Costanza (vocals) and Eric Swanson (drums). Here they released a single *Happiness* (August 1971) and a similarly titled album (October 1972) under the moniker Lodi but when neither sold the group disbanded. The Knickerbockers have reformed twice since then, the most recent occasion being in 1990.
ALBUM: LODI (1972)

THE LOLLIPOPS

Whilst history has thus far not revealed the names of all the members of The Lollipops, undoubtedly their key member was Arenita Walker, who not only sang with the group but was also responsible for writing much of the material that did get released. They first surfaced on Harry Balk's Impact label in 1967 with *Loving Good Feeling* being produced by Barney 'Duke' Browner. When Harry sold his labels to Berry Gordy, The Lollipops were one of several acts that became part of the sale, with *Cheating Is Telling On You*, written by Duke and Arenita, being scheduled for released on the Gordy label in July 1969. It was subsequently pulled and eventually issued in October on the V.I.P. label, and after the group recorded several unissued tracks, they appear to have disbanded.

Arenita would continue to make a name for herself as a writer and wrote under the moniker Tony Walker and then T-Baby before linking up with Bootsy Collins in Godmama in 1981. The Lollipops previously unissued tracks have since turned up on **Tamla Motown Connoissuers Volume 2** and **A Cellarful Of Motown Volume 3** and **4**.

LONDON AMERICAN RECORDS

The story of how Berry Gordy took his first independent production, *Come To Me* by Marv Johnson and did a deal with United Artists for national distribution has entered folklore, but it should also be observed that not long after he concluded a deal with United Artists for the United States, he also managed to secure a deal that saw Motown product released internationally. His first such deal was with Decca's London label, which by 1959 had significant expertise in turning American recordings into British hits, having taken Andy Williams, The Everly Brothers, The

Chordettes and Pat Boone among others into the charts.

Motown's releases were to be assigned the London American label, supposedly to further identify their origin, but not one of the four singles released (Marv Johnson, Barrett Strong and two by The Miracles) made a dent in the chart, although Marv Johnson would make an impact with his later United Artists recordings that were also licensed to London American. London American also released *The Hunch* by Paul Gayten in November 1959, a single that is often shown to have a Motown lineage, but Paul was an Anna Records artist and was never signed to any Motown label. There was also an EP by The Miracles released in October 1961, but London American's main claim to fame is that Marv Johnson's *Come To Me* is the only Motown connected single released in Britain as a 78 RPM disc.

SHORTY LONG

One of the most under-rated artists to have recorded for Motown, Shorty Long had just made his major breakthrough when tragedy struck at the age of 29 years of age. Born Frederick Earl Long in Birmingham, Alabama on 20 May 1940 he inevitably acquired the nickname Shorty as a young man owing to his size, standing five foot and one inch tall. Yet beneath the small stature there lurked a musical powerhouse, able to play piano, organ, drums, guitar, trumpet and harmonica with equal ability.

After working as a DJ in Birmingham, Shorty went out on the road touring with The Ink Spots, subsequently moving to Detroit in 1959. There he eventually signed with Harvey Fuqua's Tri-Phi label, releasing three singles in *I'll Be There* and *Too Smart* (in 1962) and *Going Away* the following year.

When Harvey folded his operation into the Motown set-up, Shorty followed and was assigned to the Soul label, where he linked with producer and writer Mickey Stevenson for his label debut *Devil With The Blue Dress* in March 1964. It should have been a major smash but could only hit #125 pop and #26 R&B, although a truer reflection of the song came in 1966 when Mitch Ryder & The Detroit Wheels recorded a cover version and hit #4.

Shorty's follow-up *It's A Crying Shame* lived up to its title and missed the charts altogether in August 1964 and even a British only release *Out To Get You* in April 1965 failed to make an impact. Soul held high hopes for the next single released more than a year later in August 1965, with *Function At The Junction* being written by Shorty and Eddie Holland. Yet even this failed to hit the mark, stalling at a lowly #97 on the pop chart and #42 R&B and missing out in the UK. A remake of *Chantilly Lace* didn't fare any better in February 1967, even if it garnered some considerable radio play. Though not considered among his better songs, *Night Fo' Last* did at least return Shorty to the charts, hitting #75 pop and #42 R&B at the start of 1968.

A suggestion by Billie Jean Brown to write a song based on a television catchphrase at last provided Shorty a major hit, with *Here Comes The Judge* hitting #8 pop and #4 R&B following its May 1968 release, also becoming Shorty's only UK hit when it peaked at #30. Motown wasted little in capitalising on the success of the single, pushing out a similarly titled album that contained the hits and those that should have been, although there were one or two omissions. Although subsequent singles *Don't Mess With My Weekend*, *I Had A Dream* and *A Whiter Shade Of Pale* would ultimately all miss the charts, Motown still sanctioned Shorty producing himself on his planned second album **The Prime Of Shorty Long**. Unfortunately the album was released posthumously, for on 29 June 1969 he and his friend Oscar Williams drowned in Detroit River when his small boat capsized off Sandwich Island, Ontario after a large freighter passed by creating major waves.

ALBUMS: HERE COMES THE JUDGE (1968), THE PRIME OF SHORTY LONG (1969)

LOOKIN' THROUGH THE WINDOWS – THE JACKSON 5 [SINGLE]

Songwriter Clifton Davis had already proved his worth to The Jackson 5, penning their international smash *Never Can Say Goodbye* in 1971. Later that year he came up with another sure-fire hit in *Lookin' Through The Windows*, which would also become the title track to the group's fifth studio album. Arranged by James Anthony Carmichael and John Bahler, it showed producer Hal Davis at his best, extracting a solid performance out of a group that were beginning to show signs of rebelling against the accepted Motown way of doing things. Whilst the song did not exactly strike a chord at home in the US, where it stalled at #16 pop and #5 R&B, in the UK it would make the Top Ten. Undoubtedly helped by the group's participation in the Royal Variety Performance in October 1972, the subsequent release of the single saw *Lookin' Through The Windows* become the group's first UK chart hit in almost eighteen months, finally peaking at #9.

LOOKIN' THROUGH THE WINDOWS – THE JACKSON 5 [ALBUM]

The fifth studio album recorded by The Jackson 5, **Lookin' Through The Windows** represented something of a watershed for the group. There was growing resentment within the group about the quality of material they were being asked, for whilst they were still appearing at or near the top of the charts, it was still the same bubblegum pop they had commenced their career with. An additional problem to contend with was Michael's voice, with several within Motown unsure how he would emerge once his voice had broken, meaning the sessions for the album had to be completed as quickly as possible, lest the album could not be finished to everyone's satisfaction. That problem was duly avoided, with Michael barely stretched on the usual assortment of Jobete covers, a couple of new songs and other material to round the album out to eleven tracks (one of which, *Don't Let Your Baby Catch You* actually dated back to sessions from February 1970). In the US the album would give rise to two hit singles in *Little Bitty Pretty One* (#13 pop and #8 R&B) and the title track (#16 pop and #5 R&B), whilst in the UK the two hits would be the title track and *Doctor My Eyes*, both which hit the Top Ten. The album itself also did good business, shifting some 3.5 million copies worldwide as it became the final Jackson 5 album to break into the pop Top Ten, peaking at #7 and #3 R&B as well as reaching #16 in the UK, where it also became the first Motown disc to be achieve a BPI sales award, hitting silver status on 1 January 1974.

LOS LOBOS

Spanish-American group Los Lobos was formed in Los Angeles, California in 1974 by David Hidalgo (born in Los Angeles on 6 October 1954, guitar, accordion and vocals), Cesar Rosas (born in Hermosillo, Mexico on 26 September 1954, guitar and vocals), Conrad Lozano (born in Los Angeles on 21 March 1951, bass) and Luis Perez (born in Los Angeles on 29 January 1953, drums), adding Steve Berlin (born in Philadelphia, Pennsylvania on 14 September 1955, saxophone) in 1983. Best known for the 1987 film 'La Lamba', for which they contributed eight tracks, they had previously featured on the soundtrack to 'A Fine Mess' a year earlier, with *I'm Gonna Be A Wheel Someday* written especially for the film.

LOST NATION

Progressive rock band Lost Nation was formed in Detroit, Michigan by Ron Stults (vocals), Craig Webb (guitar), Larry Zelanka (keyboards), Art Wolff (bass) and Ron Fuller (drums). They were to release one album on Rare Earth in September 1970, with **Paradise Lost** being entirely written by the group and produced by Ollie McLauglin. The only album the group ever recorded it lived up to its name, getting lost soon after release, although both Larry Zelanka and Craig Webb later joined another Detroit rock group, Frijid Pink. Zelenka was used as a guest keyboard player on their studio recordings whilst Webb became a group member in 1972.
ALBUM: PARADISE LOST (1970)

LOVE CHILD – DIANA ROSS & THE SUPREMES [SINGLE]

When Holland-Dozier-Holland downed their tools and went on strike, one of the biggest acts to suffer from the withdrawal of their labours was Diana Ross & The Supremes. The group enjoyed four consecutive #1 hits in 1966 and 1967, but by the summer of 1968 they were struggling, with *Forever Came Today* and *Some Things You Never Get Used To* barely scraping the Top Thirty.

According to Berry Gordy, Diana and The Supremes were Motown's flagship act and, come what may, they had to have a major hit, not only to restore them to the upper reaches of the chart but also to show HDH and any other writer or producer considering leaving the company that Motown could and would survive without them.

Since there was no one individual that Berry felt capable of achieving that, he created a team, drafting in Frank Wilson, R. Dean Taylor, Pam Sawyer, Hank Cosby and Deke Richards, shutting them into a suite at the Ponchetrain Hotel in Detroit on Friday 13 September and instructing them not to emerge until they had something tangible that could be recorded. After twenty four hours or so, the team had little more than two separate pieces of music which were duly played to Berry when he checked by the hotel to see what progress had been made. As the musicians in the group played their respective parts to Berry, Pam told him of her idea about a child born out of wedlock, with the title *Love Child* eventually being suggested as the two pieces of music were crafted together.

With a title, subject matter and basic melody and chorus in place, the lyrics came easily, so by the time

Berry came back to the hotel, the actual song was very near completion. The recording sessions began barely four days after the writing team had first assembled, with Diana Ross entering the studio to lay down the lead vocal on 19 September (neither Mary Wilson or Cindy Birdsong appeared on the recording, apparently the second successive Supremes single *not* to feature The Supremes), with The Andantes providing the backing vocals. Whilst the individual writers were all credited by name (with the exception of Hank, whose name does not appear), the production credit was given to The Clan, a name Berry had conceived in order to hide their identities lest the culture of producers as celebrities arise again.

The subject matter alone ensured the record was going to attract interest, some of it negative, but the strength of the melody and the hard-hitting lyrics over-rode any criticism. Less than three weeks after The Clan had gathered at the Ponchetrain Hotel, the first fruits of their labours was being delivered to record stores, with Diana Ross & The Supremes showcasing the song during their appearance on 'The Ed Sullivan Show'. Thereafter the record stormed the charts, topping the pop chart (it knocked The Beatles' *Hey Jude* off the summit of the Billboard chart) and #2 R&B, also making #15 in the UK. After two weeks at the summit, *Love Child* gave way to Marvin Gaye and *I Heard It Through The Grapevine*, something of a unique way of keeping it in the family.

LOVE HANGOVER – DIANA ROSS [SINGLE]

Hal Davis was sitting in a colleague's office when he first heard a demo of *Love Hangover*, a song penned by in-house writers Marilyn McLeod and Pam Sawyer. The original version was effectively a slow-paced ballad, but Hal had in mind turning it into something different and gathered together the cream of Los Angeles' studio musicians, including Henry Davis on bass, James Gadson on drums and Joe Sample on keyboards, later adding Art Wright on guitar. The original three minute ballad became virtually two songs welded together, with the first half giving way to a distinctive disco groove. Now all he needed was someone to do the vocals.

It was Berry Gordy's idea that the song be tried out on Diana Ross, although she was initially reluctant, not wishing to go down the disco route. So when Diana arrived at the studio, Hal was careful to set the right atmosphere for the evening's session. First off there would be the obligatory cocktail of his own making with which he started virtually every session; orange juice, vodka and rum. This, he said, was to break the ice, but according to some reports Diana was a little bit drunk when the session finally kicked off.

The first part of the song Diana could record in her sleep, but as the song began to pick up tempo, Diana expressed her doubts about being able to carry it off. So Hal had the lighting changed, bringing in a strobe light to create a mini disco within the studio. A couple more sips of the cocktail and the tape was switched on again, and this time Diana sailed through the song. Indeed, she started to actually enjoy herself, giggling here and there, ad-libbing and turning in a spontaneous performance. Hal kept it all in for the final version, rightly reasoning that the fun they had recording it would come across on the actual record, as Diana would later confirm.

"It was a spontaneous thing that we captured on record and if I had to go back in and do it again, I couldn't have. The music was me and I was the music. Things came out of my mouth that I didn't even expect."

The track was featured on Diana's self titled album released in February 1976, with *I Thought It Took A Little Time (But Today I Fell In Love)* scheduled for release as a single the following month. However, almost from the release of the album clubs around the world began picking up on *Love Hangover*, so much so that The 5th Dimension quickly recorded a virtual note for note cover and scheduled it for release towards the end of the month.

When Motown learned of this potential rival, an emergency executive meeting was called and the decision to rush release Diana's original was taken, lest any sales be lost to the 5th Dimension. It turned out to be the correct decision, with Diana's version entering the chart at exactly the same time as the rival version, but whilst Diana's would go all the way to the top of the pop and R&B chart (and, for good measure, Record World's Disco File Top 20), The 5th Dimension stalled at #80.

Diana's version of *Love Hangover* also collected two Grammy nominations, for Best R&B Song and Best R&B Vocal Performance, Female, although it lost out to *Lowdown* by Boz Scaggs and David Paich in the former category and *Sophisticated Lady* by Natalie Cole in the latter. Of course, the fact that Motown were effectively pushing two Diana Ross singles at the same time proved detrimental to *I Thought*, which would limp to #47 pop and #61 R&B. In the UK the confusion was enough to halt *Love Hangover* at #10 whilst *I Thought* made #32, but *Love Hangover* has gone on to earn its place in Motown folklore, bringing about successful covers by The Associates and Pauline Henry. Diana's version was also remixed in 1988 and became a minor chart but massive club hit all over again, including hitting #3 on Billboard's club chart.

LOVE IS HERE AND NOW YOU'RE GONE – THE SUPREMES [SINGLE]

In August 1966, The Supremes and their regular writing and production team of Brian Holland, Lamont Dozier and Eddie Holland had supplanted themselves to Los Angeles, ostensibly to record a couple of tracks for a forthcoming film, 'The Happening'. Motown had hired Columbia Studios on Sunset Boulevard (not far from where Motown would eventually set up office), chiefly because the studio had often been used for the production of film scores.

Since the cost of hiring the studio, along with some sixty assorted musicians, was somewhat extortionate, HDH decided to make as much use of the studio time as was possible, eventually recording some four completed songs. Whilst they were unhappy with the sound achieved on *The Happening* and would re-record the track in Detroit and Hitsville, they were more than happy with *Love Is Here And Now You're Gone*, which was orchestrated by another long term associate, Gene Page. Despite having worked with Diana Ross for some three years, there were still the occasional disagreements between artist and producers, which Motown musician Earl Van Dyke described as, "You can call it 'edge', but she never liked to do a lot of takes. She had that prima donna shit going then. You know how that is." Lamont Dozier was a little more diplomatic.

"Diana was always a thorough professional. If she heard something wrong, you wouldn't have to stop her, she'd stop herself and say, 'I'll do that again.' Once she was into it, she liked to go from beginning to end without stopping. She may have felt it wasn't necessary to do it over. She would do it if you pressed the issue, but we found out that it was – like Earl said – best to get it over with, rather than cause yourself a lot of headaches."

Regardless of how many takes it took, *Love Is Here* captured The Supremes to perfection, with the single eventually going on to top both the pop and R&B chart as well as hitting #17 in the UK.

LOVE IS LIKE AN ITCHING IN MY HEART – THE SUPREMES [SINGLE]

Between *Where Did Our Love Go* in 1964 and *In And Out Of Love* in 1967, The Supremes released fifteen official singles (plus two Christmas titles), topping the chart on ten occasions. Such was their domination of the singles chart that anything that made only the Top Ten was considered a failure and anything that missed the Top Ten was a disaster.

Fortunately, the latter category contains only one single (*Nothing But Heartaches*), but the former category contains four singles that any artist would have been proud to record. *Love Is Like An Itching In My Heart* was something of a stylistic departure for The Supremes, being a more dance-orientated number than their earlier efforts. Recorded in June 1965 and released in April the following year, the single got the perfect promotion push, with The Supremes performing the song on 'The Ed Sullivan Show' soon after release. It is certainly one of the group's stellar performances and deserved a better fate, having to settle for a final placing of #9 pop and #7 R&B.

LOVE MACHINE (PART 1) – THE MIRACLES [SINGLE]

The success of *Do It Baby* opened up a whole new audience for The Miracles, who had struggled to establish an identity following the departure of former lead singer Smokey Robinson and the arrival of Billy Griffin. Although the group did not actively court the dance crowd, *Do It Baby* owed part of its success to that sector of the market, a fact that would have been duly noted when it came to recording follow-up material.

City Of Angels was a concept album, based on the arrival of a man following his estranged girlfriend to Hollywood, where she is set on becoming a star. The key track of the album was *Love Machine*, written by Billy with Warren 'Pete' Moore, aided by Bobby Rogers' growling vocal and some stunning synthesizer work by producer Freddie Perren. The track ran for 6:52 on the album, with a simple edit producing Part 1 and Part 2 for single release.

Whilst the single did become a firm favourite of the disco crowd (most of whom preferred the full length album version), the 2:55 single edit was also radio friendly, enabling the single to become the biggest single of The Miracles' post Smokey Robinson career. It topped the pop charts and hit #5 on the R&B listings on its way to selling 4.5 million copies domestically.

It also translated that success internationally, peaking at #3 in the UK, where it became the group's only chart entry without their former lead singer. *Love Machine* may have been a key track in a concept album for The Miracles but that has not stopped several other artists from recording cover versions, most notably Thelma Houston and British pop duo Wham!

LOVE SCULPTURE

Welsh rock group Love Sculpture emerged out of another Cardiff based band, The Human Beans. Formed in 1966, the group was centred on guitarist and singer Dave Edmunds (born in Cardiff on 15 April 1944), with John Williams (born in Cardiff on 19 January 1946) on bass and drummer Terry Riley, although he was later replaced by Rob 'Congo' Jones (born in Barry on 13 August 1946).

Inspired by Keith Emerson's classical arrangements for E.L.P., Love Sculpture recorded an updated version of *Sabre Dance* by Aram Khachaturian, which became a surprise UK pop hit in 1968, peaking at #5 following radio support from John Peel. As the single was carving its way up the chart, it was reported that the group had signed a US deal with London Records that would guarantee them £250,000 per album.

Despite this deal, their debut album **Blues Helping** was issued in the UK by Parlophone in December 1968 and by Rare Earth in the US six months later. It would fail to chart in both territories, as did their second album, after which the group disbanded following an American tour. Edmunds would go on to enjoy considerable success as a musician, hitting number one in the UK (and #4 in the US) with a revival of Dave Bartholomew and Pearl King's *I Hear You Knocking* and producing the likes of The Stray Cats, Paul McCartney and Status Quo, among others.

ALBUM: BLUES HELPING (1969)

THE LOVE-TONES

Just as The Andantes were Motown's female backing singers of note, so The Love-Tones were briefly their male equivalents. Although their contributions were usually credited, they were seldom if ever allowed to release anything under their own name, with the result their contribution to Motown would be easy to overlook. However, Carl Jones, Mickey Stevenson, Joe Miles and Stan Bracely had recorded under their own name, their 1956 debut being *Talk To An Angel* on Plus Records and issued a 1962 single, *When I Asked My Love* on their own Love-Tone label. Whilst at Motown they appeared on recordings by Marvin Gaye (*Soldier Boy*), Henry Lumpkin (*Mo Jo Hanna*), Marv Johnson (*Let Yourself Go*) and Gino Parks (*For This I Thank You*). They exited Motown in 1962 and seemingly broke up thereafter, although they reformed for a series of recordings for Ian Levine's Motorcity label in the 1990s.

LOVE WILL CONQUER ALL – LIONEL RICHIE [SINGLE]

The third single lifted from Lionel Richie's **Dancing In The Ceiling** album, *Love Will Conquer All* was written by Lionel with Greg Phillinganes and Cynthia Weil. Greg had been involved with Lionel ever since he launched his solo career, whilst Cynthia, who had long been a writer of considerable note, usually with her husband Barry Mann, had joined the Richie pool of writers for his second album. *Love Will Conquer All* was not immediately obvious as a hit as either of its predecessors (*Say You Say Me* and the title track) but still performed exceptionally well, hitting #9 pop, #2 R&B and topping the Adult Contemporary chart for two weeks. It would also scrape into the UK charts, peaking at #45 following its September 1986 release.

THE LOVE YOU SAVE – JACKSON 5 [SINGLE]

The success of *I Want You Back* had begat *ABC*, with elements of the former appearing the latter and both going on to top the R&B and pop charts. For the third Jackson 5 single released in May 1970, The Corporation followed much the same creation process, utilising elements from *ABC* and *The Love You Save* and the same 'walking chord progression'. Freddie Perren explained the thinking behind the creation of a Jackson 5 single.

"There was a little play between Jermaine and Michael, we always tried to get that in there. We found out Tito had a commercial bass voice and we would put little trick things in with him. We had a little list of things, a checklist, that we followed."

Deke Richards took it a little further. "The only difference was we just had to come up with a new punch and groove for the beginning, and a new, different structure for the verse."

If the public had felt they were being short-changed, they would not have bought the single. Instead, The

Jackson 5 managed to repeat the feat of replacing The Beatles at the top of the pop chart, knocking *The Long And Winding Road* off the summit and spending two weeks at the top. Their reign at the top of the R&B chart was even longer, a total of six weeks, whilst the single hit a very respectable #7 in the UK.

MICHAEL LOVESMITH

A native of St. Louis, Missouri, Michael Larry Smith first came to prominence as a writer and musician, working with The Isley Brothers and Isaac Hayes during the 1960s. In the early 1970s he moved with his brothers Danny and Louis to Los Angeles where they signed to Holland-Dozier-Holland's Music Merchant label as The Smith Connection, scoring a Top Thirty R&B hit with *(I've Been A Winner, I've Been A Loser) I've Been In Love*. Michael also worked for the label set-up as a producer, most notably for Honey Cone. When Brian and Eddie resumed their working relationship with Motown, Michael went with them, which in turn led to working with Jermaine Jackson and then G.C. Cameron and Syreeta.

Michael's own recording career was resurrected in August 1981 with the formation of Lovesmith alongside his brothers Aaron, Danny and Louis (effectively an expansion of The Smith Connection), although their eponymous album **Lovesmith** was little more than a vehicle for Michael. Both singles, *Shame On You* and *I Fooled Ya* attracted quiet storm play, but the album failed to sell well.

Two years later Michael tried again, this time as a solo artist with the release of **I Can Make It Happen**, with *Baby I Will* from the album becoming his chart breakthrough, albeit at a lowly #80 on the R&B chart. Whilst solo success proved to be somewhat elusive, Michael was still in demand as a writer and producer, both inside and outside of Motown, with artists of the calibre of Aretha Franklin, Gladys Knight and Bobby Brown.

His own recording career at Motown would see two further album releases in **Diamond In The Raw** (1984) and **Rhymes Of Passion** (1985), with the latter album containing the minor hit *Break The Ice* which hit #82 R&B in August 1985 as well as his only British hit, *Ain't Nothin' Like It* which peaked at #75 in October the same year. He left the label in 1988 and continued writing for a slew of artists, including Barry White and later Smokey Robinson.

ALBUMS: LOVESMITH (1981), I CAN MAKE IT HAPPEN (1983), DIAMOND IN THE RAW (1984), RHYMES OF PASSION (1985)

LOVING COUPLES (FILM SOUNDTRACK)

Written by Martin Donovan and directed by Jack Smight, 'Loving Couples' featured several top class stars among the cast, including Shirley MacLaine, James Coburn, Stephen Collins and Susan Sarandon. The plot centred on an adulterous relationship between Greg (played by Stephen Collins) and Evelyn (Shirley MacLaine), with their respective injured parties Walter (James Coburn) and Stephanie (Susan Sarandon) comforting each other with their own clandestine relationship. Despite the A list cast, the film was something of a flop, barely making $2.8 million at the box office following its October 1980 release. The accompanying soundtrack was largely written by Fred Karlin and also featured The Temptations, Syreeta, Billy Preston and Jermaine Jackson. With the film struggling for acceptance, the soundtrack quickly disappeared without trace too.
ALBUM: LOVING COUPLES SOUNDTRACK (1980)

HENRY LUMPKIN

The general consensus seems to be that Henry Lumpkin was too heavy to have become a star, even if his voice marked him as distinctive. He would record three singles for the Motown label, *I've Got A Notion* backed with *We Really Love Each Other* was the first, issued in January 1961. Although it wasn't a hit, Berry Gordy believed in the top side enough to produce a version on Marv Johnson for United Artists later the same year.

Henry's second single appeared twelve months later, with *What Is A Man (Without A Woman)* coupled with *Don't Leave Me* (this flip side had originally been recorded by Marv Johnson!). Henry had one more go at scoring a hit with Motown, with *Mo Jo Hanna* backed with *Break Down And Sing* being released in July 1962. Although another recording session was booked for later in the year, Henry had already left the company and would resurface the following year at Pageant (*Make A Change* and *I'm A Walkin' (For J.F.K.)*) and later Buddah (where he linked up with Robert Bateman again) with two singles, *Soul Is Taking Over* backed with *If I Could Make Magic* (1967) and *Honey Hush* backed with *Your Sweet Lovin'* (1968). Both sides of his first single appeared on the 1968 Buddah showcase compilation album **Classmates**.

KENNY LUPPER

Kenneth Michael Lupper began his professional career playing keyboards for the likes of Aretha Franklin and Billy Preston as well as many of the artists active on the gospel circuit. He made his first album **Testify** for the gospel label Creed Records in 1975 before joining Motown as a songwriter the following year. Kenny would write for Diana Ross and Jermaine Jackson whilst at the company and also got to record a single under his own name, *Passion Flower* being released on the Tamla label in March 1978. Background vocals on this single were provided by High Inergy, a group Kenny would also work with as a writer, performer and producer during his time on the label. By 1981 Kenny was with AVI Records, for whom he recorded an album that featured much the same material that had appeared on his Creed Records outing.

LUSHUS DAIM & THE PRETTY VAIN

Inspired in part by the success Prince had enjoyed with Vanity 6 and Rick James had with Mary Jane Girls, the signing of Lushus Daim sent the Motown publicity machine into overdrive in 1985. She was, so they said, the seventh child of the seventh son and born in the seventh month, and Lushus Daim was her given birth name. Research would tend to indicate that she was born in Los Angeles on New Year's Eve in 1969, although she did spend several years growing up in Germany with her three brothers and three sisters as her father was stationed overseas with the military.

Having caught the eyes and ears of two music executives, she moved to Los Angeles and began work on her debut album with famed producer Leon Sylvers. **More Than You Can Handle** would eventually be released as a joint project by Conceited Records and Motown, with two minor hit singles in *More Than You Can Handle* and *The One You Love* making #53 and #33 respectively on the R&B charts. Whilst Lushus Daim could frequently be seen driving around Los Angeles with a distinctive personalised number plate, there is considerable speculation that she did *not* appear on the cover of her own album, a model being used instead! Lushus eventually retired from the music business in order to concentrate on raising her three children.

ALBUM: MORE THAN YOU CAN HANDLE (1985)

M

MAGIC

Originally formed in Lansing, Michigan in 1968 as Next Exit by Duane King (guitar), his brother Nick (bass), Mike Motz (guitar), Clyde Hamilton (organ) and Gary Harger (drums), they changed their name to Magic the following year and financed their own debut single. Hamilton and Motz then left the group, with Joey Murcia joining on guitar at the same time. A native of Miami, Murcia convinced the group he could get them a deal with TK Records, with the group upping sticks and moving to Florida as a result. They would record one album in Florida, with **Enclosed** being issued on the Armadillo label (this was Magic's own label but with TK handling marketing and distribution).

In 1970 the group returned to Detroit to look for another deal and eventually producer Scott Regan got them a contract with Rare Earth. **Magic** featured Stevie Wonder on keyboards on several tracks and upon release in September 1971 received favourable reviews, leading to hopes that the group was on the verge of breaking big. Unfortunately, Motown's flight from Detroit to Los Angeles resulted in the group being left without a label and whilst they recorded several demos with a view to finding a new home, the group eventually disbanded.

ALBUM: MAGIC (1971)

THE MAGIC DISCO MACHINE

The first Magic Disco Machine album **Disc-O-Tech** in 1975 was a studio project that featured producers Clayton Ivey and Terry Woodford, Gloria Jones and Paul Riser, Freddie Perren, Frank Wilson, Hal Davis and Jerry Marcellino and Mel Larson with the vocals being provided by The Devastating Affair and The Sisters Love. The second album the following year was largely the work of producer William Goldstein, with contributions from Clayton Ivey and Terry Woodford, George Gordy and Larry Brown, Hal Davis and Raynard Miner. The project did result in one minor hit single, with *Control Tower* from the first album making #106 on the pop chart.

ALBUMS: DISC-O-TECH (1975), MOTOWN MAGIC DISC MACHINE VOLUME 2 (1976)

MAGIC LADY

Former Enchantment, Bob Seger and The Soul Searchers backing singer Linda Stokes (guitar and vocals) formed Magic Lady in Detroit, Michigan with Jackie Steele (bass) and Kimberly Ball (keyboards). With Linda's husband Michael Stokes handling production, the group originally recorded for Arista, releasing their debut album in 1980. Two years later they resurfaced at A&M for **Hot 'N' Sassy**, with *Red Hot Stuff* becoming a minor hit on the R&B chart as #52.

By the time they joined Motown in 1988, Kimberly Ball had left and the group was a duo, recording an eponymous album split into two distinct styles, with side A being 'Magic Mood' and side B 'Lady Groove'. The album gave rise to another R&B hit in *Betcha Can't Lose (With My Love)* which made #45 as well as becoming a minor British pop hit, peaking at #58. Nothing further has been heard from the group since that release.

ALBUM: MAGIC LADY (1988)

THE MAGNIFICENT 7 – THE SUPREMES & THE FOUR TOPS [ALBUM]

Both The Supremes and The Four Tops were in a commercial lull when producer Frank Wilson suggested the idea of recording together in 1970. The Four Tops' fall from grace had been greater, with their last appearance in the Top Ten of the album chart having been three years previously. The Supremes meanwhile had at least enjoyed sporadic success with the albums they recorded with The Temptations, which would be used as a template for **The Magnificent Seven**, the title referring to the number of singers present on the album.

Whilst it was Frank's idea to record the album and he would serve the project as Executive Producer, the actual material itself was produced by three teams in Ashford & Simpson, Duke Browner and Clay McMurray. The key track turned out to be *River Deep Mountain High*, originally recorded by Ike & Tina Turner and a Phil Spector production that had done little or nothing in the US when originally released in 1966 but had become a UK Top Ten hit. As far as the US was concerned, the track had yet to prove its worth, something The Supremes & Four Tops were able to do in taking it to #14 pop and #7 R&B, adding a healthy #11 position in the UK for good measure.

It was in the UK that the album made its mark too, for whilst the project floundered in the US to a #113 pop and #18 R&B peak, it would sail all the way to #6 in Britain, restoring both The Supremes and The Four Tops to the Top Ten. Whilst the album was only a moderate success in the US, it did prompt a later reunion between the two acts, released as **The Return Of The Magnificent Seven** in November 1971.

MAHOGANY (1975 FILM)

Flush with the critical and commercial success of 'Lady Sings The Blues', Berry Gordy began scouting around for further film vehicles for Diana Ross. Her nomination for an Academy Award meant there was no shortage of offers, with scripts and treatments arriving almost daily, but one thing Berry was keen to explore was a film that didn't rely on Diana's abilities as a singer.

The search for the right film would take a couple of years, with all being rejected until Rob Cohen, a film producer who was head of Motown Productions, brought 'Mahogany' to a working lunch with Berry, manager Shelly Berger and writer Bob Merrill. The concept itself was simplicity, with Diana to play a young woman who dreams of being a big fashion designer and eventually achieves her goal, only to realise whilst in Europe that what she had always aspired to was happiness and that was to be found back home in her own neighbourhood. Add to the mix a love interest, which Berry wanted to offer to Billy Dee Williams following the chemistry he and Diana had created whilst filming 'Lady Sings The Blues', and a crazed photographer, to be played by Anthony Perkins, and 'Mahogany' sounded as though it was a perfect fit for Diana Ross.

Based on a short story by Toni Amber, the screenplay was written by Bob Merrill and then rewritten by John Byrum. To direct Berry initially hired British director Tony Richardson, whose previous credits included 'Tom Jones' and 'Ned Kelly'. Shooting began in December 1974 in Chicago but hit problems inside two weeks, not least because Tony Richardson wanted to shoot the film *his* way, whilst Berry, who was putting up all of the money, wanted at least some degree of control as to how it was being spent.

The daily rushes did little to inspire confidence, but the final disagreement between the two focused on which bit-part actor would play the protagonist in a rape scene. Tony wanted a big guy, but the one he chose couldn't act, whilst Berry preferred a little guy who could act but didn't, in the eyes of Tony Richardson, look much like a rapist! The dispute finally boiled over on set, with Berry giving Tony his marching orders and taking over direction of the film himself.

Despite having no experience of helming a film, Berry did know how to direct and control artists, and in his eyes actors and actresses were merely artists by another name. By February 1975 he had effectively completed the film, although there was to be another on set explosion, this time involving Diana who refused to reshoot a final scene, walked off set and packed her bags ready to return home.

By October 1975 the film was complete, with the editing being conducted during the same time frame as Berry was having to contend with the departure of most of The Jackson 5 from Motown to Epic Records, and was the subject of several advance screenings. It quickly became apparent that the film was not going to be the success all concerned hoped or expected it to be, as Berry Gordy would later admit.

"In the past I seldom took what critics said personally, but the advance reviews on 'Mahogany' were so bad they made the negative ones on 'Lady Sings The Blues' sound like love letters."

There was a degree of hope, for Michael Masser's soundtrack album became a Top Twenty pop and R&B success whilst the theme song, *Do You Know Where You're Going To* (which was buffed into shape by lyricist Gerry Goffin) would top the pop chart and make #5 in the UK.

Ultimately, however, 'Mahogany' did not fare anywhere near as well as its predecessor. 'Lady Sings The Blues' worked because the audience knew Diana as a singer first and foremost and could therefore relate to her playing the role of a singer, even one with as tragic a life story as Billie Holiday. Having praised her performance in 'Lady Sings The Blues', those same critics turned on her when 'Mahogany' opened, so much so that whilst the film did well at the box office (it would gross some $7 million and play to sell-outs theatres across the country), the negative reviews tended to be louder than the positive ones.

ALBUM: MAHOGANY SOUNDTRACK (1975)

THE MAIN INGREDIENT

Originally formed in New York in 1964 as The Poets by Donald McPherson (born in Indianapolis on 9 July 1941), Tony Silvester (born in Colon, Panama on 7 October 1941) and Luther Simmons Jr. (born in New York on 9 September 1942), they made their initial recordings for Jerry Leiber and Mike Stoller's Red Bird label. They then moved on to RCA, where they also changed their name a first time to The Insiders before settling on The Main Ingredient in 1966. After numerous singles and albums fell by the wayside, the group's prospects began to improve when Bert DeCoteaux took over as producer, scoring their first hit with *You've Been My Inspiration* in 1970.

Soon after achieving their breakthrough, Donald McPherson was struck down by leukaemia, passing away on 4 July 1971. A distraught Silvester and Simmons eventually drafted in Cuba Gooding (born in New York on 27 April 1944) as his replacement. The new trio got off to the perfect start, with *Everybody Plays The Fool* hitting #2 R&B and #3 pop on its way to selling more than a million copies, with the group later performing the song in the film and on the soundtrack to 'Save The Children'. Tony Silvester left for a solo career in 1976, with Cuba doing likewise a year later and signing with Motown. Gooding, Silvester and Simmons would reconvene as The Main Ingredient in 1979 and again in 1986. Tony Silvester died from multiple myeloma on 26 November 2006.

THE MAJESTICS

Richard Street (born in Detroit, Michigan on 5 October 1942) links not only The Majestics to The Monitors but later to The Temptations for good measure. Richard had grown up in Detroit and sang with Melvin Franklin in a local group (one which would also include future Supreme Barbara Martin) before moving on to join Otis Williams & The Distants. Whilst half of this group would eventually become The Temptations, they did so without Richard, who joined The Majestics towards the end of the 1950s.

The Majestics already had a recording pedigree, having cut *Hard Times* backed with *Teenage Gossip* for Robert West's Contour label and some four singles for Chex Records (they also recorded some demos at Thelma Records, the label run by Berrry Gordy's ex-wife). It was here that they began to get closer to Motown, for also at Chex were Johnny Mitchell and The Volumes, both outfits also recording for Motown later in their careers.

By the time The Majestics signed up in 1963 their line-up consisted of Richard Street, John 'Maurice' Fagin and his wife Sandra and Warren Harris. The group initially worked on a song they had originally demoed whilst at Thelma Records, *Hello Love* backed with *The Further You Look, The Less You See*, which was scheduled for release on V.I.P. in the summer of 1964. Shortly before release Motown had a change of heart and pulled the single, sending the group back into the studio to work on some new material.

More than a year later, The Majestics' *Say You* backed with *All For Someone* got as far as having promotional copies pressed up and despatched, only for Motown to learn that there was another group using the name The Majestics, with this version recording for the Linda label in Los Angeles. Rather than face a legal battle over the rights to the name, Motown opted to re-name their group The Monitors, who did finally get material released on the V.I.P. and Soul imprints. Richard Street died on 26 February 2013 after a lengthy illness.

FURTHER READING: BALL OF CONFUSION: MY LIFE AS A TEMPTIN' TEMPTATION (2014)

SAUNDRA MALLETT

Although Saundra Mallett was signed by Motown as a solo singer, every one of her singles features her fronting one group or another. Her first recording was *Camel Walk* backed with *It's Gonna Be Hard Times*, with both sides being written and produced by Berry Gordy. The top side was intended to launch a new dance craze, something it failed to do, but of greater relevance is the credit under which it was released. Originally the single was going to be credited to Saundra Mallett & The Dominettes, but at the last minute Motown instructed the female group to come up with a better name; they opted for The Vandellas. Released in July 1962 the single did little, with Saundra's Motown career effectively placed on hold whilst she married and settled down. Three years later, as Sandra Edwards she returned to Motown and was placed with The Downbeats on the V.I.P. label, but again Motown instructed the group to change their name at the last minute; they became The Elgins.

HENRY MANCINI

One of the leading film composers and conductors of all time, Enrico Nicola Mancini was born in Cleveland, Ohio on 16 April 1924 and raised in Pennsylvania. He attended the Julliard School in New York and became in-house composer for Universal Pictures in 1952. The winner of twenty Grammy Awards (out of 72 nominations, more than any other artist) and four Oscars, he is perhaps best known for his body of work with long time collaborator Blake Edwards, most notably 'The Pink Panther' series. It was another Edwards vehicle responsible for his brief involvement with Motown, contributing the track *Stan And Ollie* to the film and soundtrack of 'A Fine Mess'. Henry died from cancer on 14 June 1994.

MANDRE

Born in Nebraska on 7 December 1948, Michael Andre Lewis formed his first band at the age of fifteen with Lester Abrams before forming Andre Lewis & The New Breed and then touring with Buddy Miles. In 1972 he and his then wife Paulette Parker formed the group Maxayn, with Paulette adopting the name Maxayn Lewis for the purposes of the group. With Andre on keyboards and Maxayn on keyboards and vocals, they were joined by Hank Redd (guitar) and Emilio Thomas (percussion) and recorded three albums for Capricorn. The key to the Maxayn project was Andre's use of synthesizer's, and when he wanted to evolve the project still further, it became Mandre, a space-age and intergalactic project that was said by Motown to be 'funkier than Parliament.' As the music sounded out of this world, Andre adopted the persona of 'The Masked Marauder, a mystery man sent from space to create peace on Earth through the sound frequencies.' He also wore a mask, custom-made by famed costume designer Bill Whitten, which although designed so as to make it easier to breathe during performances was seldom used since Mandre remained very much a studio based creation.

However, the project did result in three well received albums in **Mandre** (released in 1977 and a #64 pop hit), **Mandre II** (released in 1978) and **M3000** (released in 1979 and a #74 R&B hit), with the single *Solar Flight (Opus 1)* becoming a minor hit but dance floor favourite. Andre recorded one further album under the Mandre moniker, **4** appearing on his own Future Groove label. Six years later he moved to Germany but subsequently made his name and reputation as a session musician, working with the likes of Buddy Miles, Johnny 'Guitar' Watson and Labelle. He returned to the United States where he died in Shreveport, Louisiana on 31 January 2012.

ALBUMS: MANDRE (1977), MANDRE II (1978), M3000 (1979)

REVEREND COLUMBUS MANN

The son of Reverend Bromley Mann Senior of Nashville, Tennessee, Columbus had been a member in church since his infancy and was touring with his father from the age of six. A member of All Nations Church of God in Christ, he was also State Musical Director of Northerwestern Michigan. By 1961, the Reverend Columbus Mann preached every Sunday at the True Love Church in Detroit.

One Sunday sitting in the pew was George Fowler, then working at Motown. Fowler was that impressed with the sermon he persuaded Berry Gordy to come along the very next week, with the result the Reverend Mann was signed to the Tamla label. His only single, *They Shall Be Mine* (written by the Reverend and Mattie Clark) backed with *Jesus Loves* (also written by Reverend Mann) was produced by Berry Gordy and released in September 1961, but after the single did little sales wise the Reverend left the label.

He would then record for several local labels, including Tru-Sound, who issued an album with Mann and the Pentecostal Choir in May 1962. Whether Berry Gordy had Reverend Columbus Mann back in the studio or had enough recordings in the can is a matter of debate, but in December 1962 Tamla issued **They Shall Be Mine**, today one of the most sought after Tamla albums. This was to be his final Tamla release, although he would issue a live album **He Satisfies Me** with The Pentecostal Choir on Wingate in May 1966 and later issued **Got To Be Ready** on the Creed label.

ALBUM: THEY SHALL BE MINE (1962)

MAMA'S PEARL – THE JACKSON 5 [SINGLE]

It would not have been apparent at the time, but after knocking out four consecutive #1's with their first four single releases, The Jackson 5's run of chart domination had come to an end. The single that brought the run to an end was *Mama's Pearl*, a good record but, in the words of co-writer Deke Richards, not a great record, "and great is what we had to have if we were going to remain on top and for the J5 to continue to be king of the hill."

According to later sources, *Mama's Pearl* began life as a song entitled *Guess Who's Makin' Whoopie (With Your Girlfriend)* but changed title and lyrics in order to maintain Michael's youthful and innocent persona. Unfortunately, *Mama's Pearl* went head to head with another group who portrayed a youthful and innocent image, The Osmonds, whose *One Bad Apple* proved impossible to shift from the top of the charts. *Mama's Pearl* did make it to #2 on the Billboard pop chart (and even topped the chart in Record World) and a similar position on the R&B chart, unable to prevent Johnnie Taylor's *Jody's Got Your Girl And Gone*, The Temptations *Just My Imagination* or Marvin Gaye's *What's Going On* from leapfrogging to the summit (although it did top the Cashbox R&B chart). In the UK the single reached a rather more modest #25, the first Jackson 5 record to fail to reach the Top Ten.

MANTICORE RECORDS

One of the earliest boutique record labels, Manticore was launched by British rock group Emerson, Lake & Palmer in 1973, initially in partnership with Island Records. When a two year distribution deal in the United States with Atlantic Records came to an end in 1975, Motown picked up the label in January 1975 (possibly as a replacement rock label instead of the slowly declining Rare Earth imprint) and would release a total of six singles and seven albums in the two years before the label was shut down in 1977.

MARBAYA

Originally known as The Music Makers, the group was formed by Frankie Karl, Bobby Warren, Skip Starkey and Bobby Evans. Shortly before the release of their single *Follow Me – Mother Nature* backed with *And I Thought You Loved Me* in January 1973, it was discovered that there was another group known as The Music Makers, prompting this group to change their name. The single was eventually released on Motown in September 1973. Former Cogic Singers and The Chevrons singer Frankie (born in Los Angeles on 25 June 1945), who also fronted Frankie Karl & The Dreams and recorded solo for Motown as Frankie Kah'rl, died on 30 July 2008.

TEENA MARIE

Born Mary Christine Brockert in Santa Monica, California on 5 March 1956, she was known as Tina as she grew up in an area known as Venice Harlem in Los Angeles. Whilst she showed an early appreciation of music, and in particular Motown, her early steps in show business were as an actress, appearing in the television series 'The Beverly Hillbillies' at the age of eight, billed as Tina Marie Brockert.

After a couple of years performing in a semi-professional band with her brother, she attended the Santa Monica College and studied English Literature whilst also sending out audition tapes to several record companies. In 1976 she was a member of a group that auditioned for Motown for a proposed film project, but although the film was subsequently scrapped several at the label, most notably Berry Gordy, were impressed enough with her abilities to offer her a solo contract.

Teena would spend the next couple of years recording with a variety of producers, although nothing was released and her career appeared to be going nowhere. Then came a fortuitous meeting with Rick James, who was scheduled to produce a forthcoming album on Diana Ross but opted to work with Teena after hearing her sing.

The resulting album, **Wild & Peaceful** was largely written and entirely produced by Rick and was originally going to be credited to Teena Tryson but changed to Teena Marie, the name by which she would be known for the rest of her career. The album was extremely well received and hit #98 on the pop chart and #18 R&B, with the absence of an artist picture on the front cover misleading many purchasers into believing that Teena must have been an African American singer. That subterfuge was continued with the release of the single *I'm A Sucker For Your Love*, which was effectively a duet with Rick James, with both Rick and Teena performing the song on 'Soul Train' and thus revealing Teena's ethnicity. It made little difference to the single, which bubbled under the Hot 100 at #102 but proved a major R&B success, hitting #8, and also became Teena's UK chart breakthrough when it hit #43. A revival of Smokey Robinson and Ronald White's 1965 composition *Don't Look Back* gave Teena her second single success, hitting #91 R&B.

With Rick unavailable to helm her sophomore album, Teena specifically asked for Richard Rudolph, the husband of the late Minnie Riperton, even though Teena was given the opportunity of producing the album herself. Rudolph proved an inspired choice, for the pair would collaborate on the album's major hit single *Behind The Groove*, which hit #21 R&B and powered its way to #6 pop in the UK. **Lady T** (a nickname she acquired around Motown) did at least feature Teena's picture on the cover and would become a major seller, repeating the #18 R&B placing of its predecessor but rising to #48 on the pop chart.

Motown were quick to capitalise on this new found popularity, issuing her third album **Irons In The Fire** later the same year, with the lead single *I Need Your Lovin'* becoming the major hit, returning Teena to the Top Ten of the R&B chart (it peaked at #9) and into the Top Forty pop (#37) as well as a welcome return to the UK chart at #28. **Irons In The Fire** also marked the first album entirely produced and largely self-written by Teena, proof that her abilities knew no bounds. Teena also found time to guest on Rick James' hit album **Street Songs**, performing a duet on *Fire And Desire*, even though she was reportedly ill with a fever at the time the track was recorded.

What would prove to be her final Motown album, **It Must Be Magic** lived up to its title. With the album hitting #2 R&B and #23 pop, sales of over 500,000 copies earned her a gold disc, her first such album award. The album was undoubtedly helped by the success of the singles *Square Biz* (#3 R&B and #50 pop), *Young Love* (#41 R&B) and *Portuguese Love* (#54 R&B), but legal problems lay just around the corner.

When Teena submitted the tape for her follow-up album, it was rejected. Stunned, Teena asked for a release from the label, which was also turned down. Teena would then launch a legal battle that resulted in a decision known as The Brockert Initiative, which effectively made it illegal for a record company to keep an artist under contract without releasing new material on that artist. The case also revealed the restrictive contract that Motown had locked Teena into, in so much as she was paid a weekly wage rather than advances and royalties, so that whilst her albums had generated income in excess of $2 million, Teena had received a paltry $100 a week for six and half years!

It was an unhappy end to her time with Motown, but Teena would later state, "It wasn't something I set out to do. I just wanted to get away from Motown and have a good life. But it helped a lot of people, like Luther Vandross [who challenged the length of time an artist could be signed to one label] and the Mary Jane Girls [also signed to Motown], and a lot of different artists, to be able to get out of their contracts."

Teena would resume her recording career with Epic and also set up her own publishing company Midnight Magnet. Over the course of the next seven or so years Teena enjoyed varying success, although Epic's strengths in the pop market ensured she performed somewhat better on the pop listings than she had during her time with Motown. Teena also managed to top the R&B chart, *Ooo La La La* in 1988 becoming her only R&B chart topper.

Diminishing sales by the end of the decade saw her dropped from the Epic roster, resulting in a hiatus from the recording industry as she brought up her daughter. Teena would sporadically return, funding **Passion Play** in 1994 on her own Sarai Records and then appearing on the Cash Money Classics label in 2004 with **La Dona**, a Top Ten success and another gold selling album. After one further album for the label Teena joined the revived Stax imprint for **Congo Square** in 2009, a Top Twenty pop and Top Ten R&B hit.

Teena was found dead at her home on 26 December 2010, the death believed to have been connected to an incident six years previously when a large picture frame had fallen on her head whilst she was asleep in a hotel room. The blow caused serious concussion and would lead to seizures for the rest of her life, with it later being reported that she had suffered a grand mal epileptic seizure less than a month before her death at the age of 54.

ALBUMS: WILD & PEACEFUL (1979), LADY T (1980), IRONS IN THE FIRE (1980), IT MUST BE MAGIC (1981)
COMPILATION: 14 GREATEST HITS (1986)

MARK III TRIO

An obscure instrumental group from Detroit, Michigan, The Mark III Trio comprised John Lewis, Edwin Ray Kelly and Richard Lewis, with all of their material being produced by Ricardo Lewis. They recorded for Wingate and In (a label that was probably owned by Ricardo Lewis), with their recordings for In being subsequently leased to Atco, part of Atlantic. Their one recording for Wingate, *G'wan (Go On)* backed with *Good Grease* became a favourite on the Northern Soul scene, prompting the inclusion of *G'wan* on the British compilation album **Ric-Tic Relics** in 1973. Mark III Trio meanwhile may well have recorded with noted jazz musician Jack Taylor; further clouding the known history of the group is the presence of another trio with exactly the same name, at much the same time and recording similar repertoire! The other Mark III Trio featured Grover Washington Jr., later to achieve considerable solo success, including a spell with Motown.

JOEY MARTIN

Little known country singer Joey Martin released one single on the Melodyland label, with *Anything To Keep From Going Home* backed with *Ruby Is A Groupie* being released in October 1975 to little or no fanfare. The top side, written by Dennis Linde and Alan Rush would become better known thanks to a version by Tommy Overstreet whilst the flipside would later be recorded by its writer Bobby Braddock. Joey Martin meanwhile doesn't appear to have released any further singles.

TONY MARTIN

One of Berry Gordy's several attempts at breaking into the lucrative MOR market, veteran singer Tony Martin joined Motown in 1964. He was born Alvin Morris in Oakland, California on 25 December 1913 and was a saxophonist with Tom Gerun's band before leaving the band and heading for Hollywood in 1936, adopting the name Tony Martin and marrying singer and actress Alice Faye the following year (this marriage would end in divorce in 1941).

After appearing in several films (he made his first, 'The Farmer In The Dell' in 1936) he resumed his musical career, fronting several hits for Ray Noble and then going solo with Decca. Following the Japanese attack at Pearl Harbour in December 1941, Tony enlisted in the armed forces, first with the US Navy (he left owing to unsubstantiated rumours he had obtained his commission by bribery) and then the US Armed Air Forces, being assigned to Glenn Miller's band.

At the end of the hostilities, for which he was awarded a Bronze Star, Tony resumed his acting and singing career, signing with Mercury and then RCA and scoring a significant number of hits in the late 1940s through to the mid 1950s. By 1957 his career seemed spent, with his last hit single being *Do I Love You (Because You're Beautiful)* peaking at #82 and 'Let's Be Happy' his last film starring role.

He signed with Motown in 1964, with *Talkin' To Your Picture* being released in December of that year and peaking at a distant #133 on the chart. In August the following year they tried again, with *The Bigger Your Heart Is (The Harder You'll Fall)* missing the chart altogether, as did his final outing for the label, *Ask Any Man* in January 1966, resulting in the album **Live At The Americana** being scrapped.

Tony, who married actress Cyd Charisse in 1948 and would enjoy a union of sixty years until her death in 2008, left the label soon after and made one brief comeback single for Dunhill in 1967 with *Theme From The Sandpebbles (And We Were Lovers)*. Whilst he may not have made much of a dent at Motown, Tony's career has seen him honoured with no fewer than four stars on the Hollywood Walk of Fame; for motion pictures (6436 Hollywood Boulevard), radio (1760 Vine Street), television (1725 Vine Street) and recording

(6331 Hollywood Boulevard). He died at the age of 98 from natural causes on 27 July 2012. His son, Tony Martin Jr., was also a Motown recording artist as one half of the duo Martin & Finley.

MARTIN & FINLEY

Soft rock duo Martin & Finley were formed by Tony Martin Junior and Guy Finley. Tony was born in Los Angeles, California on 28 August 1950, the son of legendary performer Tony Martin and actress Cyd Charisse, with Tony mastering guitar and keyboards whilst growing up. Guy Finley was born in Los Angeles on 22 Febuary 1949, the son of talkshow pioneer Larry Finley.

The duo was signed by the MoWest label in 1972, releasing a couple of singles before being switched to the main Motown label, even though Rare Earth might have been a better home for them. As a result, their only album, **Dazzle 'Em With Footwork** was originally scheduled for release on MoWest and subsequently got switched to Motown, appearing in June 1974. Produced by Bob Gaudio the album saw them working with an abundance of stalwart musicians, but Motown were unsure how to promote or market the album and it disappeared from view soon after release.

Whilst the pair went their respective ways soon after, Guy remained at Motown for a while and wrote a number of songs for other artists before abandoning music altogether in 1979 and journeying to India in order to study self-awareness. Tony, who had apparently been ill for a number of years and had returned home to live with his ageing father, died on 10 April 2011.
ALBUM: DAZZLE 'EM WITH FOOTWORK (1974)

THE MARVELETTES

Whilst they were never able to match the success of their first single, the fact that The Marvelettes scored the very first #1 pop smash of the more than fifty the company would accumulate ensures them a lasting place in Motown history.

Gladys Catherine Horton (born in Gainesville, Florida on 30 May 1945) moved to Detroit, Michigan with her parents and assembled a vocal group among her school friends at Inkster High School in 1960, with Georgeanna Marie Tillman (born in Detroit on 6 February 1943), Katherine Anderson (born in Ann Arbor, Michigan on 16 January 1944), Juanita Cowart and Georgia Dobbins, with the group adopting the name The Casinyets (a play on the phrase 'can't sing yet').

The following year the group entered a local talent contest and came fourth. Although only the first three finishers had been promised an audition for Motown, two teachers believed in the girls' abilities enough to persuade a Motown connected acquaintance to give them an audition too. The girls duly passed the audition in April 1961, although they were told that they were to return when they had an original song to record. Fortunately, the group had something that could be worked into a full blown song, partially written by group member Georgia Dobbins and another Inkster resident William Garrett.

The group, minus Georgia who left because of family commitments and replaced by Wanda Young (born on 9 August 1943) returned to Motown and showed the in-house team what they had, with Brian Holland, Robert Bateman and Freddie Gorman knocking the song into shape. With Gladys on lead vocal, *Please Mr. Postman* was recorded in August and released on Tamla before the month was out. Following an internal meeting at Motown, it was also decided to change the name of the group and eventually settled on The Marvelettes, reasoning that the name would be easier to market than the jokey Casinyets.

Released on 21 August 1961, the single literally tore up the charts, finally coming to rest at the very top of the pop and R&B listings, the very first time any Motown connected record had achieved the feat. With success came demands, both to record follow-up material and go out on the road. Motown wasted little time in getting the girls back in to the studio, recording an eleven track album that was effectively one smash hit and ten filler tracks, with compositions from the likes of Berry Gordy, Smokey Robinson, Marv Johnson, Brian Holland, Janie Bradford and Robert Bateman. Although **Please Mr. Postman** was not a major seller, it did at least keep the girls' name in vogue following its release in December 1961. Touring proved more problematic, since most of the girls were still attending high school when the single started breaking. At one point Motown considered gathering any five girls together and getting them out to fulfil dates, a proposal that was met with astonishment by the real group members.

According to Katherine, "Hell was going to freeze over before that happened! At that point, we made a decision that we would go ahead and leave school. But it was also under the auspices that we were going to have tutors. We had our schoolwork from Inkster High, and our teachers, and all like that. But we did not have tutors."

Instead, Berry appointed his sister Esther as their legal guardian, accompanying the group on their numerous tours and live dates as they helped promote *Please Mr. Postman* and its follow-up hit *Twistin' Postman* (#34 pop and #13 R&B), released in January 1962.

Fortunately the postman phase was ushered out in 1962, with the group being given the opportunity to record some fresher material. The first of these was *Playboy*, the basics of which Gladys Horton took into Hitsville, where Brian Holland, Robert Bateman and William 'Mickey' Stevenson worked it into another piece of audio magic. It restored the group to the Top Ten of both the pop and R&B charts, hitting #7 pop and #4 R&B, whilst both sides of the follow-up *Beechwood 4-5789* and *Someday Someway* would make an impression on the R&B chart, hitting #7 and #8 respectively. The top side made #17 on the pop chart for good measure.

Whilst The Marvelettes proved themselves to be something of a force to be reckoned with on the singles chart, the album listings proved a little more difficult to crack, although Motown undoubtedly gave it their best shot. Two albums were released inside four months during the year, **Smash Hits Of '62** appearing in April (when it was later reissued as **The Marvelettes Sing,** the group's name was misspelled as The Marveletts on the front cover!) and **Playboy** in July. The year was to close with mixed fortunes, with another hit in the shape of *Strange I Know* (#49 pop and #10 R&B) being countered by a crucial mistake made on air by Juanita during 'American Bandstand', a mistake that obviously played on her mind in the ensuing months and would eventually lead her to leave the group, citing a 'nervous breakdown.'

The group would continue as a quartet for their next album **The Marvelous Marvelettes** which would give rise to the hit single *Forever* (#78 pop and #24 R&B), with the flip side *Locking Up My Heart* also making an impression (#44 pop and #25 R&B), but The Marvelettes status as the leading female group within Motown was about to be usurped by The Supremes. Whilst the group was finding it difficult to reclaim their place on the singles chart, their stature as a live act continued to grow, as the **Recorded Live! On Stage** album issued in June 1963 would confirm. And whilst The Supremes were waiting in the wings to take over their mantle, their stock at Motown was still considerably high, enough to prompt Smokey Robinson to attempt to get them back on to the charts. He accomplished this with *As Long As I Know He's Mine,* a #47 pop but big R&B hit, where it peaked at #3. Smokey would repeat the magic with *He's A Good Guy (Yes He Is)* (#55 pop and #18 R&B) and *You're My Remedy* (#48 pop and #16 R&B) during 1964, at much the same time The Supremes began hitting the very top of both charts.

One third of the team responsible for getting The Supremes to the top, Eddie Holland, linked with Norman Whitfield to craft The Marvelettes next hit, *Too Many Fish In The Sea*, a return to former glories and a #25 pop and #5 R&B hit. Yet as big a hit as it was, it was later revealed that Gladys Horton, on behalf of the group, had rejected an even bigger hit that had been offered to them. Holland-Dozier-Holland had written *Where Did Our Love Go* with The Marvelettes in mind, only for Gladys to turn it down on the grounds it was too childish. Of course, it was the song's simplicity that was ultimately its strength, as The Supremes would prove in taking it to the top of both the pop and R&B charts.

Whilst turning down the song might have been a bad commercial move in the long run, it was the group's growing maturity that had been behind the decision. The nervous school friends who had been launched in 1961 with *Please Mr. Postman* had developed into sophisticated young women, requiring a change in stage costumes and material to record. There were changes afoot within the group too, with Wanda marrying Bobby Rogers of The Miracles, Katherine marrying The Supremes' handler Joe Schaffner and Georgeanna marrying Billy Gordon of The Contours. Georgeanna would also retire, suffering from leukaemia and lupus, conditions that would ultimate lead to her untimely death on 6 January 1980.

The remaining three Marvelettes meanwhile continued their Motown career, which for the next four years or so comprised entirely of singles (aside from a compilation **Greatest Hits** issued in 1966 that made #84 pop and #4 R&B), with mixed results. Mickey Stevenson and Ivy Jo Hunter wrote and produced *I'll Keep Holding On*, the #34 pop and #11 R&B follow-up to *Too Many Fish*, whilst Clarence Paul joined Mickey and Ivy to compose *Danger Heartbreak Dead Ahead*, a #61 pop and #11 R&B hit, but still a long way off the group's previous hits. Fortunately Smokey Robinson returned to the group's aid in June 1965, producing them on a song entitled *Don't Mess With Bill*. Whilst the obvious assumption to make would be that the song was about Smokey himself, he quickly denied it, claiming the name was just one that fitted the song to perfection. And so it did, with Wanda Young turning in a solid performance, ably backed by Gladys and Katherine and helping guide the single to #7 pop and #3 R&B, the group's first appearance in the pop Top Ten since *Please Mr. Postman*.

Despite the success of the single Motown still refrained from issuing an album, a stance that would have been unthinkable some four or five years earlier when virtually every hit single was quickly followed by an album in order to wring out every last possible sale. By contrast, in 1966 The Marvelettes released just two singles, *You're The One* in April (it would hit #48 pop and #20 R&B) and *The Hunter Gets Captured By The Game*, a single that Smokey had to fight to get released in December. His efforts were rewarded when the single made it to #13 pop and #2 R&B. *The Hunter* would be the key track on **The Marvelettes**, issued in March 1967, although there would also be another major hit in a cover of Ruby & The Romantics' *When You're Young And In Love*, written by Van McCoy. This would go on to be a #23 pop and #9 R&B hit, as well as becoming the group's only UK chart entry when it hit #13, and helped the album attain a #13 berth on the R&B charts.

That proved to be something of a last hurrah for the group, for it was later revealed that only lead singer Wanda was actually being used on recording sessions, the female backing invariably being provided by The Andantes. Whilst Katherine and Gladys were at first philosophical about the decision, citing Motown's need to have a steady stream of material ready for release, which often meant recording whilst the group was supposed to be out on the road, in time the realisation that The Marvelettes recordings only featured one Marvelette became a bone of contention.

Former lead singer Gladys Horton was the next to leave following her marriage, with Harvey Fuqua suggesting her replacement, Cleveland, Ohio born Anne Bogan (Anne had been previously signed to Harvey's Tri-Phi label, where she recorded with Challengers 3). With Anne on board the group once again sported at least two lead vocalists, with both being used on the group's next album, **Sophisticated Soul**. As strong an album as the group had previously recorded, it would play host to no fewer than five hit singles, of which *My Baby Must Be A Magician, Here I Am Baby* and *What's Easy For Two Is Hard For One* were the biggest hits, all making the Top Twenty of the R&B chart. Such activity helped the album too, peaking at #41 on the R&B listings.

The group's next album, **In Full Bloom** did not fare anywhere near as well, despite featuring a varied assortment of tracks. By the time **In Full Bloom** hit the streets, The Marvelettes were beginning to reach the end.

"It wasn't a decision that we necessarily made" Katherine later observed. "The decision was pretty much made for us. We did have some internal problems, but we were not receiving the assistance of Motown in trying to correct some of those internal problems. Because the only original two that were still there was Wanda and myself. And we had internal problems within the group with Wanda. And they were making no effort whatsoever to help to try to resolve some of those problems. Motown, of course, was really beginning to catch on fire then."

Whilst Wanda, Anne and Katherine initially went their own ways, Motown did try to revive the group in 1970 for the album **Return Of The Marvelettes**, but once again only one Marvelette was actually present during the recording sessions, The Andantes rounding out the sound. According to Katherine, Motown did contact her with a view to her making herself available for photo sessions, but her response was, "Since I'm not good enough to sing on it, or to be a part of it, then I'm not good enough to be on the album."

Motown were therefore forced to use stand-ins on the cover too, although the album did little (it did hit #50 on the R&B chart) and officially The Marvelettes came to a halt at that point. Anne Bogan would leave Motown and link up again with Harvey Fuqua in New Birth whilst Gladys would tour extensively on the nostalgia circuit. However, since The Marvelettes name was owned by Motown and none of the former members were able to use the name in its entirety, Gladys usually performed as Gladys Horton of The Marvelettes. After recording for Ian Levine's Motorcity label in the 1990s she resumed her touring schedule. She died in a nursing home in Sharman Oaks in California on 26 January 2011 following a series of strokes.

ALBUMS: PLEASE MR. POSTMAN (1961), THE MARVELETTES SING (1962), PLAYBOY (1962), THE MARVELOUS MARVELETTES (1963), RECORDED LIVE! ON STAGE (1963), THE MARVELETTES (1967), SOPHISTICATED SOUL (1968), IN FULL BLOOM (1969), RETURN OF THE MARVELETTES (1970)

COMPILATIONS: GREATEST HITS (1966), ANTHOLOGY (1975), 23 GREATEST HITS (1986)

FURTHER READING: THE ORIGINAL MARVELETTES – MOTOWN'S MYSTERY GIRL GROUP (2004)

MARVIN GAYE LIVE – MARVIN GAYE [ALBUM]

Never the most comfortable of live performers, Marvin Gaye had deliberately avoided performing live following the collapse and subsequent death of Tammi Terrell. Besides, at the start of the 1970s he had transformed himself into a serious artist, one whose better work was to be found on his albums rather than singles. Two factors in particular were to get him out on the road again, the first being the enormous success **What's Going On** and **Let's Get It On** had enjoyed, which had increased demands from punters to see him back on stage, and his own spending, always extravagant but which was spiralling out of control thanks to his drug habit.

He was therefore almost compelled to go out on the road since that was one sure way he could generate vast sums of money. On 4 January 1974 he was scheduled to appear at the Oakland Coliseum, a 14,000 capacity venue that was packed to the rafters for Marvin's appearance, with the audience quickly settling Marvin's nerves and anxieties. Whilst an audience that vast made it somewhat difficult to present an intimate show, Marvin delivered everything the expectant crowd had come to see, including a new song *Jan*, dedicated to Janis Hunter, later to become his second wife.

His 1960s hits were rolled into one long medley (although conspicuous by its absence was *I Heard It Through The Grapevine*), with much of the rest of the show focussing on the two blockbuster albums. The show was taped and subsequently issued as **Marvin Gaye Live!** in June of that year and, as if to prove Marvin's fears about touring totally wrong, would become almost as big a success as the two albums that had first inspired the tour. The album would top the R&B chart and reach #8 on the pop listings, selling well over a million copies in the process. The album would also be aided by the release of the live single *Distant Lover*, itself a #28 pop and #12 R&B hit. At the end of the year the album earned a Grammy Award nomination for Best R&B Vocal Performance, Male, although for the second year in succession Marvin lost out to Stevie Wonder, this time to *Boogie On Reggae Woman*.

MARVIN GAYE LIVE AT THE LONDON PALLADIUM – MARVIN GAYE [ALBUM]

Despite his continuing popularity as a recording artist, by October 1976 the life of Marvin Gaye was troubled. He had recently divorced his first wife Anna Gordy and married his second, Janis Hunter, but he had developed something of a drug habit to combat stage fright and had seemingly taken on board other demons. Yet whilst the troubles may have been mounting at home, in Europe he was still highly revered, as the sell out notices for his series of dates at The London Palladium would confirm.

Although it had been only three years since he had released a live album (see above), a decision was taken to record the dates at The London Palladium, not least because it would mark the first time his later **I Want You** recordings would be featured. It proved an inspiring decision, for away from the trials and tribulations of home, Marvin gave a series of masterful performances, interacting well with his audience and seemingly enjoying himself on stage like never before.

The resulting show would cover three sides of the **Live At The London Palladium** album, with many of his greatest hits presented in a series of medleys. To complete the album Marvin had been working on his entry into the disco market, *Got To Give It Up*, which would run for nearly twelve minutes and take up the whole of the fourth side of the album. The album would become a major success, selling over two million copies and topping the R&B chart for two weeks and peaking at #2 pop, although surprisingly it did not make an impression in the UK, where the album was recorded. The album was also helped by the phenomenal success of *Got To Give It Up*, itself a double chart topper.

THE MARY JANE GIRLS

A short-lived but highly successful girl group, The Mary Jane Girls were assembled as part of a ruse by their protégé Rick James. Rick had been working with female singer Joanne McDuffie, with her singing lead vocals and the Waters Sisters providing backing vocals on a number of tracks that Rick hoped to get Motown interested in. Motown was interested in the project but were led to believe that Rick was working with a female group, not a solo singer, so rather than lose the deal altogether, Rick also recruited Kimberly Wuletich, Candice Ghant and Ann Bailey, who were chosen more for their looks than their actual singing abilities (although Candice had previously been a member of Softouch, who released one single on Prodigal and an album on Fantasy).

The group's name was also something of an in-joke, given Rick's affinity with marijuana. However, to maintain the ruse Rick created alternative personalities for the four, renaming them Jojo (Joanne), Maxi (Kimberly), Candi (Candice) and Cheri (Ann). Only Jojo actually performed on the group's debut album **Mary Jane Girls**, released in April 1983. A month earlier the girls had released their debut single, *Candy Man*, which would bubble under the Hot 100 at #101 but hit #23 on the R&B chart, also making an appearance on the chart in the UK where it hit #60. The follow-up *All Night Long* was even bigger, for whilst it again failed to break into the Hot 100 (it again stalled at#101), it hit #11 R&B and #13 in the UK. There was to be a third major hit single lifted from the album, *Boys*, which peaked at #102 pop, #29 R&B and #74 in the UK. Motown also extracted a fourth single in *Jealousy* but this proved to be a single too far as it barely made #84 on the R&B listings. However, aided by the singles the album would make #56 pop, #5 R&B and #51 in the UK.

By the time Rick began work on the second album, again only utilising the vocal talents of Jojo, Cherri had departed the group and been replaced by Yvette Marine, who was given the moniker Corvette for the group. Rick would also devise persona to go with the name, with Jojo becoming as female version of Rick James, Maxi a dominatrix, Candi the vamp and Corvette taking over the Valley Girl role previously played by Cherri.

The second album, **Only Four You** would become an even bigger success than their debut, hitting #18 pop and #5 R&B and earning a gold disc for sales of over 500,000, although it missed out the UK chart altogether. The singles proved to be even bigger successes than anything that appeared on the predecessor, with *In My House* becoming an across the board smash, hitting #7 pop, #3 R&B and #1 on the Hot Dance Club Play chart. This was despite being mired in controversy, with the Parents Music Resource Center placing it on their notorious Filthy Fifteen list of singles they wanted banned from the radio airwaves. *Wild And Crazy Love* would become another Top Ten R&B hit, whilst *Break It Up* also made a showing on the charts.

Mary Jane Girls would make one further appearance on the chart, a cover of Frankie Valli & The Four Seasons' *Walk Like A Man* being produced for inclusion on the soundtrack to the film 'A Fine Mess'. The title proved apt, for by the middle of the 1980s Rick James was embroiled in a dispute with Motown over the status of his various bands, resulting in him departing the label and The Mary Jane Girls single *Shadow Lover* getting little or no promotion.

With Rick no longer available to mentor the group, a planned third album **Conversation** was shelved and the four girls disbanded in 1987. Although there were frequent rumours and stories that they planned to reunite, most notably with Jimmy Jam and Terry Lewis to handle production, nothing ever came of it.

ALBUMS: MARY JANE GIRLS (1983), ONLY FOUR YOU (1985)

HUGH MASEKELA

Born Hugh Ramopolo Masekela in the Kwa-Guqa Township of Witbank, South Africa on 4 April 1939, he began his musical career singing and playing piano as a child. He switched to the trumpet at the age of 14, inspired by the film 'Young Man With A Horn'. A one-time member of The Huddleston Jazz Band, fronted by Trevor Huddleston, Hugh joined The Merry Makers and would also play in the orchestra for the musical 'King Kong', which played in London's West End for two years (and also featured Miriam Makeba).

Hugh returned to South Africa after this success and formed the Jazz Epistles with Abdullah Ibrahim, recording the first contemporary South African jazz album but was compelled to leave the country after the Sharpeville Massacre. He initially settled in London, where he studied at the Guildhall School of Music. He later moved to America in order to study classical trumpet at the Manhattan School of Music and would subsequently record for Mercury, Verve and Uni before setting up the Chisa label, initially with distribution through Uni Records.

Chisa would subsequently be distributed by Revue, Vault and Buddah before linking with Motown in 1970. Hugh's own output during the eighteen months or so that Motown handled the label included the albums **Reconstruction** and **Hugh Masekela & The Union Of South Africa**, with the latter album (which Hugh himself considers his masterpiece) featuring Jonas 'Mosa' Gwangwa (from the Orlando Township in Johannesburg, vocals and trombone) and Caiphus 'Caution' Semenya (from the Alexandra Township in Johannesburg, vocals and alto saxophone).

When the deal with Motown was brought to an abrupt end, Hugh lost the rights to all seven albums that had been released, plus one that had not. Hugh and several of his artists moved on from Motown to the Chisa label distributed by Blue Thumb, with Hugh issuing three albums as part of this deal. He would later record for Casablanca, A&M, Jive, Warner Brothers, RCA and Columbia, releasing his most recent album in 2011, **We Are One** on Vega Records.

ALBUMS: RECONSTRUCTION (1970), HUGH MASEKELA & THE UNION OF SOUTH AFRICA (1971)

MASTER BLASTER (JAMMIN') – STEVIE WONDER [SINGLE]

Stevie Wonder was a long time admirer of reggae superstar Bob Marley, with the pair performing together at a concert at the National Stadium in

Kingston in 1975. The pair renewed their acquaintance in the summer of 1979 when they shared the stage at a Black Music Association conference in Philadelphia. At the time Stevie was putting the finishing touches to the soundtrack album **Journey Through The Secret Life Of Plants**, but the performance with Bob Marley inspired Stevie to quickly write down the lyrics to what would become *Master Blaster (Jammin')*.

The music and melody also came easily, for at the time Stevie had immersed himself in a lot of reggae music, although neither the song nor the style was a ready fit for the soundtrack. Instead Stevie held the song over for nearly a year, eventually recording it at his newly acquired Wonderland Studio with many of his usual musicians, including Nathan Watts on bass, Benjamin Bridges and Rick Zunigar (guitars), Isaiah Sanders (organ), Dennis Davis (drums), Earl DeRouen (percussion), Hank Redd (saxophone) and Larry Gittens (trumpet) with backing vocals from Marva Holcolm, Angela Winbush, Shirley Brewer and Alexandra Brown Evans.

Released in September 1980 as the lead single from the **Hotter Than July** album, the single proved a worldwide smash, topping the R&B chart and hitting #5 pop in the US and peaking at #2 in the UK, unable to overtake another group who had adopted reggae rhythms in their music, The Police with *Don't Stand So Close To Me*.

At the end of the year the single would gain a nomination for a Grammy Award for Best R&B Male Vocal Performance although it lost out to George Benson and *Give Me The Night*. Shortly after the single's release, Bob Marley's health began to quickly deteriorate; having initially been diagnosed with cancer in a toe in 1977, by October 1980 the cancer had spread throughout his body. Bob died in a hospital in Miami on 11 May 1981, with that year's Reggae Sunsplash, held at the Jarrett Park Cricket Ground in Montego Bay in August being dedicated as a memorial to Bob Marley. Stevie appeared on the final night, performing with Third World (who he would later produce) on *Master Blaster (Jammin')* and *Redemption Song*.

MASTERPIECE – THE TEMPTATIONS [SINGLE]

Musically, at least, *Masterpiece* lives up to its title, a grand slice of cinematic soul and a natural progression from *Papa Was A Rollin' Stone*. And there, as far as The Temptations was concerned, lay the problem with the material they were being asked to record by Norman Whitfield in 1973. There was nothing wrong with it as a piece of music, it was just that *Masterpiece* is more about the musicians and the producer than it was The Temptations.

In its original form it ran to almost fourteen minutes, with the group contributing little more than three minutes of vocals. Even in its single edited form, it took a minute before The Temptations entered the fray, although the wait was certainly worth it. Called *Masterpiece* because Norman Whitfield thought it the perfect blend of all the musical elements, it performed as well on the charts as *Papa*, topping the R&B chart (which *Papa* failed to do) and peaked at #7 on the pop chart, although it was perhaps too similar to its predecessor to make an impact in the UK. However, the success of the single only served The Temptations in further alienating them from their writer and producer Norman Whitfield. The recording of the **Masterpiece** album was not a necessarily pleasant one for the group.

MASTERPIECE – THE TEMPTATIONS [ALBUM]

Dennis Edwards was the voice that breathed life into *Papa Was A Rollin' Stone*, The Temptations massive hit and Grammy Award winning epic from 1972, but even he was beginning to query how little the group was being asked to contribute to what was, after all, their own album.

"I just wish we had the opportunity to do more vocally on the album. I just don't think we did enough."

Yet in a sense The Temptations were the victims of their own success. With each successive single (and album), the demands to go out on the road and perform, where the *real* money was to be made, grew even greater. Whilst they travelled the globe on a succession of tours, Norman Whitfield remained ensconced in Detroit writing material for their albums. Even the musicians and arrangers were sometimes aghast at the sheer length of the material they had to perform, as arranger Paul Riser recalled.

"I'm sitting up writing, flipping pages, flipping pages, and the musicians are at the studio, waiting, because I didn't realise the song was that long."

Masterpiece would eventually stretch out to nearly fourteen minutes, requiring significant pages of sheet music, yet The Temptations' vocal parts filled only three minutes of Norman Whitfield's epic.

Barrett Strong had left the Whitfield-Strong partnership in order to resume his own recording career, meaning Norman was now responsible for everything in studio, lyrics and music. Once again, when short of material, he delved into his own catalogue for material that could be revamped, although in the case of *Law Of The Land*, he came up with a version that actually bettered The Undisputed Truth's original (so much so it was released in the UK as a follow-up single to *Masterpiece* and hit #41 on the pop listings).

Soon after release Temptations fans took it upon themselves to actually write to the group to complain about how little they appeared on the album, with critics also weighing in by disparagingly referring to them as 'The Norman Whitfield Singers.' Yet **Masterpiece** was every bit a success as its predecessor **All Directions,** again topping the R&B chart and peaking at #7 on the pop chart and making #28 in the UK. It was helped by the success of the singles, with the title track being joined by *Plastic Man* and *Hey Girl (I Like Your Style)* in becoming hits, albeit with varying degrees of success, with the latter two hitting #40 and #35 pop and #8 and #2 R&B respectively. Norman Whitfield was happy with the album and what it achieved.

"I wanted to try some songs that had the scope and feeling of a movie. The group had some scepticism about taking on the material. But their technique is so all-encompassing that once we had reached an understanding about what they were singing, The Temps were able to summon up the necessary extra energy the songs demanded. Look, trends were changing and I was only interested in keeping them on top and in keeping them current. A transition was needed, but I admit I never really confided in them as to what I was doing."

No doubt the fact that Norman's image on the back cover is bigger than any of The Temptations image on the front only added to the group's angst, but they would be back for one further album, **1990** recorded later the same year.

MATRIX

All three members of Matrix had full time day jobs at Motown as writers and producers for other artists but took the opportunity to record an album of their own for Rare Earth in 1972. Nick Zesses, Dino Fekaris (born in Pittsburgh on 24 January 1945) and Tom Baird (born in Vancouver on 27 April 1943) were responsible for writing and producing many of the acts that appeared on the Rare Earth label, although not exclusively, since their compositions and productions appeared on virtually all of Motown's imprints.

Matrix' eponymous album appeared in October 1972, with many of the songs having been previously listed as being recorded for an album by a group called Other People, although there is no confirmation that the album was ever released. Two years later, in June 1974 Matrix released another single, *Streakin' Down The Avenue* on the main Motown label. All three continued their writing and production chores at Motown, with Tom Baird becoming a de facto member of Rare Earth and linking with Pete Hoorelbeke and Mike Urso from the group in a new outfit called Hub. They recorded two albums for Capitol before Tom was killed in a freak boating accident in November 1975. Dino Fekaris later linked with Freddie Perren and won a Grammy for Gloria Gaynor's *I Will Survive*.
ALBUM: MATRIX (1972)

JOHNNIE MAE MATTHEWS

The Johnnie Mae Matthews depicted in the 1998 television mini-series 'The Temptations' is a manipulative, forceful and single-minded woman who uses Otis Williams & The Distants as a means of promoting her own interests and funding her own lifestyle. Later, when Otis and his new group are on television performing as The Temptations, Johnnie Mae Matthews is shown almost aghast at the success of the group, as though wondering 'what if.' Whilst Otis Williams has frequently said that the producers allowed for a certain degree of artistic licence in telling The Temptations story, no one comes out of the series with their reputation as tarnished as Johnnie Mae Matthews. Much of the portrayal may be spot on, especially having the group's name emblazoned on a car and bristling when the group had the temerity to ask for royalties, prompting them to leave her label and move on to Motown, but Johnnie Mae Matthews had been a force in the Detroit music scene prior to picking up on Otis Williams and his group and would remain so for many years after their departure.

Born in Bessemer, Alabama on 31 December 1922, Johnnie Mae had arrived in Detroit in 1947, got married and started her own family. Once the children were no longer babies, she began pursuing her own musical career, joining local group The Five Dapps and performing lead vocals on *You're So Unfaithful*, the B-side to their first outing *Do Wop A Do*. Johnnie Mae did more for the next single, borrowing $85 out of her husband's paycheque to form her own record company, Northern Recording Company, which she based at 2608 Blaine.

With sessions usually held at the nearby Special Studio or at the radio station WCHB, Northern Recording

Company started out as little more than a vehicle for Johnnie Mae's own recording efforts, with *Dreamer* and then *Mr Fine* appearing in 1959. As big a city as Detroit was in 1959, the musical pool was still a relatively small one, and many of the musicians Johnnie Mae used on her recordings would eventually become integral parts of the Funk Brothers across the city at Motown, including Joe Hunter, Eddie Willis, Uriel Jones, James Jamerson and Norman Whitfield. Add to this Otis Williams & The Distants brief recording stint, together with both Jimmy and David Ruffin and Mary Wells also being guided at some point and a different Johnnie Mae Matthews is revealed; one who obviously had a feel for the music that was being made in Detroit, and who could make it the best. And her instincts not only extended to recording, for she was also savvy enough to know the machinations of the industry, with Berry Gordy later acknowledging the help she gave him in getting national distribution for The Miracles' *Shop Around*.

According to many, Berry tried on several occasions during the 1960s to get Johnnie Mae Matthews to join Motown, although whether this was as a singer or in an administrative role has never been revealed. Instead, Northern Recording Company struggled on throughout the decade, with one or two singles making a local ripple without ever becoming a national smash before closing their doors temporarily. The following decade she turned her attentions to a local funk group Black Nasty, which featured two of her children, Artwell and Aubrey, in the line-up. Johnnie Mae produced their only album, **Talking To The People**, which was issued on Stax in 1973. This group later changed their name to ADC and in 1978, with Northern revived, released *Long Stoke* to acclaim. The track and the band were subsequently picked up by Cotillion and enjoyed a Top Ten hit with *Long Stoke*, a national charting album and five further R&B hits over the next four years. Johnnie Mae died after a long battle with cancer on 6 January 2002.

CURTIS MAYFIELD

Curtis Lee Mayfield was born in Chicago, Illinois on 3 June 1942 and joined The Impressions in 1957, as both lead singer and songwriter, also penning a number of hits for Jerry Butler and numerous other artists. He formed the Curtom label in 1968 with Eddie Thomas (The Impressions' manager), utilising the catchphrase 'We're A Winner' from his former group's 1967 hit and launched his own solo career in 1970. With the release of the soundtrack album **Superfly** in 1972, he was at the peak of his career and seen as a serious rival to Marvin Gaye and Stevie Wonder as a standard bearer for soul music.

In 1973 Curtis performed *Give Me Your Love,* one of the key cuts from 'Superfly' on the soundtrack to 'Save The Children', subsequently released by Motown in 1974. His later career didn't quite match the earlier promise, although he made sporadic appearances on the R&B chart and also continued to write and record for a host of outside artists. On 13 August 1990 he was performing an outdoor concert in Brooklyn, New York when a gust of wind blew a lighting rig on top of him, leaving him paralysed from the neck down. The accident also led him to develop diabetes, a condition that led to his right leg having to be amputated in 1998. He died on 26 December 1999 as a result of the injuries sustained in 1990.

MC RECORDS

Notable record company executive Mike Curb, who had made his name at MGM during the 1960s, approached Berry Gordy with the idea of a joint label in 1977, to be called MC Records and specialising in country music. With Motown's own country music labels Melodyland and then Hitsville having had limited success, the proposal made some commercial sense. MC Records would schedule sixteen albums before the joint venture was terminated in November 1977, although how many of these albums actually saw the light of day is still open to debate (probably no more than three), for several appear on the listings as having been released but no known commercial copies have ever surfaced, even though several promotional editions exist. Mike took several of the artists and started a new joint venture with Warner Brothers, where their better ability at marketing and promoting country music would pay dividends.

THOMAS McCLARY

Guitarist Thomas McClary was born in Eustin, Florida on 6 October 1949 and helped form his first band The Matadors whilst still in high school. In 1968 Thomas was in the line waiting to enrol at Tuskegee Institute in Alabama when he heard the person behind him whistling an Eddie Harris tune. Recognising a fellow music fan, Thomas turned round to ask him if he was a musician, only to be told that he wasn't but he knew a few guys on campus who were. A meeting was duly arranged, with Thomas McClary being taken along to meet potential musicians by none other than Lionel Richie! Of course, both Thomas and Lionel would go on to be core members of The Commodores, a group who set out with the goal of becoming 'The Black Beatles'. To an extent they accomplished that goal, breaking their attendance record in The Philippines and racking up a succession of smash hit albums and singles.

Whilst the group's success was largely due to Lionel's abilities as a writer of sublime ballads, Thomas was no slouch when it came to supplying material too, writing or co-writing such hits as *Slippery When Wet, Cebu, Fancy Dancer* and *Brick House,* among others. Lionel left The Commodores in 1982, followed shortly after by Thomas McClary. Both men were destined for solo careers with Motown, but obviously with vastly different results. Whilst Lionel linked with former Commodores producer James Anthony Carmichael and enjoyed even greater success than he had achieved within the group, Thomas produced his own eponymous album, released in November 1984. The album would give rise to one minor hit single, *Thin Walls* reaching #57 on the R&B chart, although the album did little and was not even released in the UK. Thomas would subsequently return to Florida where he moved into gospel music, serving as Director of Music at his local church between 2002 and 2007 and later recorded the gospel album **Revolution Not A Revival** in conjunction with his son Ryan.

ALBUM: THOMAS McCLARY (1984)

MIKE McLEAN

In January 1961 twenty one year-old Mike McLean responded to an advertisement in the *Detroit News* for an Electronic Technician, with knowledge of Ampex equipment a necessity. Mike answered each and every technical question asked of him by Berry Gordy and a couple of days later was invited back for a second interview, at which he received the job offer for $50 a week as a maintenance technician. Over the course of the next eleven years, Mike proved knowledgeable not just on Ampex equipment but on virtually all matters electronic, building Motown's first three track and then eight track recorders, usually at a quarter of the price buying a brand new one would cost, with the additional benefit to Mike of being promoted to Engineering Department Head in 1964. Mike remained with Motown until 1972, when the company left Detroit, and later headed west to California where he worked in the film industry, again on the technical side.

MICKEY McCULLERS

Detroit, Michigan native Mickey McCullers owed his chance at Hitsville to his good friend Smokey Robinson, who took him into the studio in December 1961 to record *I'll Cry A Million Tears*. Six months later they went back and recorded another track, *Same Old Story,* which was subsequently released the following month as the A side on Tamla. According to Claudette Rogers in the notes to **The Complete Motown Singles Volume 2**, Mickey had a great voice in person but it changed when he got in front of a microphone. Two years later Motown tried again, this time releasing *Who You Gonna Run To* backed with *Same Old Story* on the V.I.P. label but it was the same old story; the single didn't sound right and Mickey's recording career came to an end.

CARRIE McDOWELL

Something of a childhood singing sensation, Carrie McDowell first came to prominence on Bill Riley's television talent show 'Talent Sprouts' at the age of eight. Born in Des Moines, Iowa on 11 May 1963, Carrie then appeared on several other television shows and released a one off single with MGB (*Over The Rainbow*) before her mother took her back to Iowa to attend school. After leaving school Carrie spent time in New York before heading west to Los Angeles and signing with Motown. Her first single was released as *Casual Sex* in February 1987 but subsequently re-promoted three months later as *Uh Uh, No No Casual Sex (Part 1)* to further enhance the safe sex message and became a minor hit, peaking at #65 R&B and making #68 in the UK. A further single, *When A Woman Loves A Man* was lifted off her eponymous album, after which Carrie left Motown. She later married guitarist Michael Hodge and recorded gospel and country music with her husband under the name Two Hearts.

ALBUM: CARRIE McDOWELL (1987)

MALCOLM McDOWELL

The 1983 film 'Get Crazy' was responsible for English actor Malcolm McDowell making a brief appearance on Motown's Morocco imprint, with *Hot Shot* being released as the flip side to Sparks' *Get Crazy* title track. Michael John Taylor was born in Hosforth, Yorkshire on 13 June 1943 and is best known for his portrayal of Alex DeLarge in 'A Clockwork Orange', a role that seemed to set the benchmark for his later film career, since he usually plays villains of one description or another. Receiving the script of 'Get Crazy', Malcolm was intrigued by the character he was asked to portray, a parody of Mick Jagger called Reggie Wanker, 'twenty years of rock and roll and still on top'. He also noticed that his character was expected to sing in the film and insisted on a clause in the contract stipulating that he perform his own vocals rather than have his voice dubbed. Unfortunately he failed to read the entire script before shooting commenced, so was somewhat surprised when he arrived on set and was asked by another actor how he planned to play the conversation with his penis! Not surprisingly, the film and soundtrack did little or no business.

DON McKENZIE

Don McKenzie was apparently a DJ to whom Berry Gordy owed a favour, perhaps in return for playing some other Motown releases on air. To this end, Don was given the opportunity of recording a single on the Miracle label, with *Whose Heart (Are You Gonna Break)* backed with *I'll Call You* being released in November 1961. He had previously released at least one single on the Ridge imprint, a label that Berry Gordy may well have had an interest in, and also recorded near on an album's worth of material during his brief spell at Hitsville. Whilst the rest of the material was supposedly standards, nothing other than this single ever appeared.

MARILYN McLEOD

Born in Detroit, Michigan in 1942, Marilyn McLeod came from a musical family, with both her parents achieving some notorierty as singers (her mother was also a pianist), her older brother Ernie Farrow was a bass player and sister Alice married fame jazz musician John Coltrane. Marilyn showed an early aptitude as a song writer, eventually signing with Motown's publishing arm Jobete in 1970, subsequently following the company out to California in 1972. Her best known compositions came in conjunction with Pam Sawyer, with the pair penning *Love Hangover* for Diana Ross and *You Can't Turn Me Off (In The Middle Of Turning Me On)* on High Inergy, among others. Marilyn also hankered after a recording career, having a brief spell as a member of Nu Page and also fronting a promotional single by Pure Magic, albeit without success. Marilyn left Motown in 1985 and in 2010 fulfilled her singing ambitions, relasing the album **I Believe In Me** on Twinn Records, a label she had formed with fellow former Motown writer Janie Bradford.

BARBARA McNAIR

Barbara Jean McNair was born in Chicago, Illinois on 4 March 1934 and raised in Racine in Wisconsin. After studying music at the American Conservatory of Music in Chicago, Barbara appeared on the Arthur Godfrey Talent Scout Show and the Ed Sullivan Show, subsequently landing a recording deal with Coral Records. She would later record for Signature, Roulette and KC, but found greater success as an actress, both in films (including 'Spencer Mountain', her 1963 debut), television (guest roles in 'Dr Kildare', 'I Spy' and 'Hogan's Heroes') and on stage (appearing on Broadway in 'The Body Beautiful' and 'The Pajama Game').

After a brief deal with Warner Brothers, Barbara signed with Motown in 1966, working with Berry Gordy on a couple of single releases and then producer Frank Wilson on her label debut album **Here I Am**. The album contained her version of *For Once In My Life*, subsequently a major hit for Stevie Wonder but which was reportedly written by Ron Miller with Barbara very much in mind. Only *Here I Am Baby* made any kind of chart impact, bubbling under at #125 on the Hot 100.

Whilst her recording career then stalled, her acting career continued to prosper, as did her general popularity to such an extent she undertook a nude photo session for 'Playboy' magazine in the October 1968 issue. The resulting publicity may not have helped her singles but Motown did capitalise with the release of the album **The Real Barbara McNair** in April 1969, using one of the 'Playboy' shots as the album's front cover. Barbara left Motown thereafter but landed her own television series which would run for three seasons. In December 1976 her husband Rick

Manzie was murdered in what was later reported to be a Mafia related hit, with the resulting publicity doing little to help her career. Barbara died from throat cancer on 4 February 2007.
ALBUMS: HERE I AM (1966), THE REAL BARBARA McNAIR (1969)

RONNIE McNEIR

Lewis Ronald McNeir was born in Camden, Alabama on 14 December 1951 and moved to Detroit at an early age. Self taught on the piano, he won a talent contest whilst still a teenager and got to release the single *Sitting In My Class* for the Deto label. In 1972 he moved to California, performing in local churches where he was spotted by former Motown personnel Kim Weston and Mickey Stevenson. Ronnie would record his debut album **Ronnie McNeir** at Kim's private studio, the album being issued by RCA, although Ronnie would subsequently return home to Detroit to become a studio musician.

Several of these sessions were at the United Sound Studio, where he came to the attention of former Motown vice president Barney Ales, then running his own Prodigal label. He signed Ronnie to a solo deal, with the singles *Wendy Is Gone,* released in March 1975 and *Saggitarian Affair* in November the same year scoring on the R&B charts at #51 and #63 respectively. Whilst the parent album, also entitled **Ronnie McNeir** did not chart, it made sufficient progress for Ronnie to be switched to the main Motown label when Prodigal was absorbed into Berry Gordy's empire.

Ronnie would record one album, **Love's Coming Down**, from which the single *Selling My Heart To The Junkman* was released in June 1976, as well as working with Smokey Robinson on the soundtrack to 'Big Time'. He began work on a new Motown album but this was neither completed nor released, with Ronnie subsequently working with The Four Tops on a number of tracks before becoming their musical director. Ronnie would become a member of The Four Tops in 1999 when Levi Stubbs became too ill to tour owing to cancer.
ALBUMS: RONNIE McNEIR (1975), LOVE'S COMING DOWN (1976)

STERLING McQUEEN

Sterling McQueen landed his only meaningful Broadway role in the 1976 revival of 'Guy And Dolls', performing as Rusty Charlie in both the run at the theatre and on the cast recording soundtrack issued by Motown in December 1976.

CHRISTINE McVIE

Anne Christine Perfect was born in Bouth, near Ulveston in England on 12 July 1943 and began her career with Shades Of Blues before joining Chicken Shack in 1967. After marrying John McVie of Fleetwood Mac she left Chicken Shack and briefly formed the Christine Perfect Band (apparently in response to a poll in 'Melody Maker' that had voted her 'Female Singer of the Year' in 1969), although the following year she joined the expanding Fleetwood Mac in place of Peter Green. Her marriage to John McVie came to an end, although Christine remained in the band and subsequently launched a solo career in 1984. In 1986 Christine appeared on the soundtrack to the Blake Edwards film 'A Fine Mess', contributing *Can't Help Falling In Love*.

MELLO-MACKIN-D & MR STRETCH

Rapper Mello-Mackin-D (born Darrick Scott) and vocalist Mr. Stretch (born Lawrence Bowens) were discovered in Pomona in California by Leon Sylvers. A former member of the family singing group The Sylvers, Leon had made a bigger name for himself as a writer and producer, most notably for the Solar Records stable of artists. He co-wrote (with Darrick Scott) Mello-Mackin-D's only Motown single, *Back To School* being released in September 1985 and also featuring a second rapper in OGD.

MEL-O-DY RECORDS

The Mel-O-dy label was introduced by Motown in June 1962 with a single by The Creations, *This Is Our Night* and was shuttered a little over three years later after the release of *All The Good Times Are Gone* by Howard Crockett. For much of its life it was run as a country music label under the guidance of Al Klein, who was at the time Motown's sales representative for Texas and the south, and Al also wrote and produced several of the tracks that were released. However, the non-country singles contain some real surprises, including singles by The Vells (effectively The Vandellas), The Pirates (a one-off outing for the group otherwise known as The Temptations) and Lamont Dozier. Other material that was not out and out soul (such as novelty) was also released on Mel-O-dy before it was shut down.

MELODYLAND RECORDS

Berry Gordy had briefly recorded and released country music during Motown's formative years, all of which were issued on the Mel-O-dy label before it was shut down. In 1974 Berry decided to have another go at the genre, creating the Melodyland label and establishing a separate office in Nashville. The label caused quite a stir when its first artist acquisition turned out to be Pat Boone and it would also acquire several other big names, including T.G. Sheppard.

According to legend, Sheppard was shopping his potential hit *Devil In The Bottle* to Atlantic Records, whilst next door executives of Melodyland were so impressed with the sound coming through the walls they collared the singer on his way out of the building! It proved to be a master stroke, for the single launched both the label and the artist with a #1 country hit.

In all Melodyland would sign some fifteen artists and release thirty singles and two albums. It was the success of another single, *The Biggest Parakeets In Town* by Jud Strunk that brought about Melodyland's demise, for as the song gained in popularity, the Melodyland Christian Center Church, which had also been releasing records under the same label name, took umbrage at both the song and Motown's use of the name. The complaint led to a Motown spokesman commenting, "You don't mean to tell me that churchgoers don't drink or participate in a little nooky from time to time!"

Although the church had not registered the name Melodyland neither had Motown and so a potential legal battle loomed. Motown could have prevailed and won the use of the name but decided the resulting publicity such a move would bring was not worth the trouble. Instead, Berry changed the name of the country label in 1976 to Hitsville, which Motown *had* registered.

MERCED BLUE NOTES

Originally formed in 1956 as a backing group for Roddy Jackson, The Merced Blue Notes (named after the town in which they were formed) found a sponsor in the local fire chief, George Coolures, who would accompany them on stage at the local Civitan Club after Jackson had left for greener pastures. After releasing several obscure records for several obscure labels, The Merced Blue Notes turned up at Harvey Fuqua's Tri-Phi label in Detroit in 1961.

By this time the line-up of the group comprised Ken Craig (guitar and vocals), Gilbert Fraire (bass), Bobby Hunt (keyboards), Bill 'Tiger' Roberton (saxophone) and Carl Mays Jr. (drums). They would record two singles for the label, *Midnite Session (Part 1)*, backed with *Part 2*, which appeared in 1962, and *Whole Lotta Nothing* the following year. They joined the Soul label itself when Fuqua sold his Harvey and Tri-Phi labels into the Motown fold, but despite recording at least one single (*Do The Pig* backed with *Thumpin'* briefly appeared on the release schedule for late 1964 but never saw the light of day; it was reportedly approved by the Quality Control Department but remained unreleased, with the masters being handed over to the group for them to find a deal independently) they left the label early in 1965 and, after releases on Mammoth and Galaxy the same year split up shortly after.

MERCY MERCY ME (THE ECOLOGY) – MARVIN GAYE [SINGLE]

Against Berry Gordy's expectations, *What's Going On* became the hit that Harry Balk, Barney Ales and Marvin Gaye promised him it would, which only heightened the expectancy for the forthcoming album. Yet Marvin was in no rush, slotting in the sessions for what became **What's Going On** with try-outs for his other fancy, playing professional football for the Detroit Lions. Arranger David Van DePitte would later reveal that he spent many an hour sitting around Marvin's home, waiting for the arrival of the singer so that they may continue with the recording, only for Marvin to be a no-show and put the sessions off until a later day. Somehow however the album did take shape, although the initial mix done in Detroit was not entirely to Marvin's satisfaction, so he took the tapes out to California and remixed them with Lawrence Miles.

He finally delivered the completed album to Motown ready for a May 1971 release, also selecting the album's second track *Mercy Mercy Me (The Ecology)* as the next single to be lifted the following month. Written solely by Marvin, the song concerned itself with the environment but did so by musically paying homage to jazz, yet another radical departure from what Marvin's counterparts in soul and R&B were doing. The single proved irresistible, topping the R&B charts for two weeks and peaking at #4 on the pop listings. Its jazz credentials can be gauged by the fact it quickly attracted a cover version by Grover Washington Jr., who would also record a version of another of the key tracks from **What's Going On**, *Inner City Blues*, which provided Grover with his album title to his 1972 album. In 1991 British singer Robert Palmer recorded something of a medley of *Mercy Mercy Me* with another Marvin Gaye associated song, *I Want You* and scored a #9 hit in the UK and #16 in the US.

BILLY MERRITT

Billy Merritt recorded one single for Mel-O-dy, *Why Go Out Of Your Way* backed with *I'll Go Anywhere*, which was scheduled for release in April 1963 but remained unissued. There is considerable speculation that Billy Merritt was in fact a pseudonym for Michigan steel guitarist Freeman Cowgar (born on 12 January 1933), who wrote both sides of the abandoned Merritt single. Freeman not only played the steel guitar he manufactured them as well, under the brand name The Cougar, for some thirty years up until his death from cancer on 7 August 2002.

THE MESSENGERS

Originally formed in high school in Winona, Minnesota in 1962 by Greg Bambenek (guitar), Roy Berger (guitar), Greg Jeresek (bass), Chip Andrews (keyboards) and Jim Murray (drums), The Messengers continued playing when they went to university in Milwaukee. After recording for Soma Records the group got a brief contract with USA Records, for whom they recorded a cover of *In The Midnight Hour*. This started getting some local reaction, leading to the group being given a support slot on the Dave Clark Five tour and being spotted by Motown producer Jeffrey Bowen in Chicago. Bowen offered them a contract, which Jeresek, Jeff Taylor (vocals), Peter Barana (bass) and Augie Jurishica (drums) eagerly accepted, although Mark Kapov (guitar) and Jesse Roe (keyboards) turned it down.

Whilst the remaining four began work on what would become their debut release on Soul, a Chicago DJ assembled another group to go out as Michael & The Messengers to promote *In The Midnight Hour*, which was becoming a regional hit but which would get no further than #116 on the chart. Fortunately, the imposter group wasn't able to push the single or a follow-up done in a similar style (*Romeo & Juliet*, which stalled at #129) into a major hit, meaning The Messengers could release *Window Shopping* backed with *California Soul* without having to clear up any confusion in the minds of record buyers.

The group's first spell with Motown was not entirely problem free, with the decision to place them on the Soul label when their music was rock orientated only the first they had to contend with. Also assigned to R. Dean Taylor for writing and production, the group felt Taylor's own desire to become a recording artist thwarted The Messengers since he would invariably hold back his better songs for his own recording sessions. *Window Shopping* came and went without much notice, peaking at #132 and the group left the label soon after. They returned in 1969 to record an eponymous album for the Rare Earth label, which was released in August 1969, and again in 1971, with *That's The Way A Woman Is* becoming their only chart hit, peaking at #62 in September of that year.

ALBUM: THE MESSENGERS (1969)

JOE MESSINA

Guitarist with the Funk Brothers, Joe Messina was afforded the moniker 'the white brother with soul' in deference to his abilities. Born in Detroit, Michigan on 13 December 1928 Joe picked up the guitar at an early age and by his mid twenties had become a member of the ABC Television studio band, backing artists such as Sonny Stitt, Lee Konitz, Donald Byrd, Charlie Parker and Stan Getz as they appeared on various shows produced by the company. Joe's own inclinations lay towards jazz and he would also perform in jazz clubs in and around Detroit, which ultimately led to him being picked by Berry Gordy to become one of the Funk Brothers in 1959. For the next thirteen years or so he was an integral part of the musical crew that drove countless Motown recordings up to the top of the charts, his role often made all the more challenging by having to double James Jamerson's bass lines on numerous recordings. When Motown headed west for Los Angeles in 1972, "Joe put down his guitar for almost thirty years, but he quickly got his chops back in late 2000 to play on 'Standing In The Shadows of Motown'', according to the Funk Brothers website.

MICKEY'S MONKEY – THE MIRACLES [SINGLE]

A chance encounter in the rehearsal room at Hitsville between Smokey Robinson and Lamont Dozier resulted in the return to the Top Ten of both the pop and R&B charts for The Miracles. Smokey walked in to hear Lamont playing a basic riff that sounded as though it was influenced by Bo Diddley, although at the time he had no more than the song's chorus of 'Lum dee lum dee la' lyrically worked out. Encouraged to both complete the song *Mickey's Monkey* and record it on The Miracles, Lamont did just that, with the backing track recorded on 9 July 1963 and The Miracles entering the studio a day later to lay down their vocals. In order to create something of a party atmosphere The Miracles also brought in a number of friends, including various members of The Supremes, The Temptations, Martha & The Vandellas, The Marvelettes and local DJ and personality Jay Gibson. Just over two weeks later the single was released, with Bobby Rogers of the group having also worked out a dance routine to accompany the song. The single soon scaled the chart, hitting #3 R&B and #8 pop, with the song going onto become such a guaranteed crowd pleaser that with The Miracles invariably used it as their closing number when out on the road for the Motortown Revues.

MIDNIGHT BLUE

A self-contained R&B group formed in Columbus, South Carolina, they first came to prominence with a cover version of Jerry Leiber and Mike Stoller's *I Who Have Nothing*, a single that had been produced locally and issued on the Samarah label. Produced by Myron Alford and Daniel Hodge with lead vocals by Debra Bailey (Debra was later replaced by Sharon Harmon), the single attracted sufficient interest for Motown to licence it for national release in February 1981. Whilst the single did little, the group did at least get to support The Temptations on tour.

MIDNIGHT MAGIC – THE COMMODORES [ALBUM]

The worldwide success of **Natural High** and in particular the classic single *Three Times A Lady*, gave The Commodores a seemingly impossible target for their next album **Midnight Magic**. Yet even before the sessions commenced for what would be their seventh studio album, manager Benny Ashburn was telling anyone who would listen that The Commodores had material that potentially could be even bigger smashes. His confidence was based on two songs in particular that Lionel Richie had written after *Three Times A Lady*, which Lionel would subsequently submit to the group meeting that decided what material would go on to the album. Both songs, *Still* and *Sail On*, made the final cut, although the other group members would also contribute worthwhile material, with Milan Williams' *Wonderland* becoming the third hit single lifted from the album. Released in July 1979, **Midnight Magic** would replicate its predecessors chart positions, hitting #3 pop and topping the album chart, although it was slightly down in the UK where it had to settle for peaking at #15.

MIKE & THE MODIFIERS

Formed in Detroit, Michigan towards the end of the 1950s, Mike & The Modifiers consisted of Mike Valvano (born in Detroit in 1943, vocals), Mike Ondercin (guitar), Ronnie Greb (rhythm guitar) and Rick Greb (drums). They made enough of a noise locally to get a seven year contract with Motown in 1960, although much of their time with the label appears to have been spent doing anything *but* recording, most notably chauffeuring the likes of Stevie Wonder between gigs. They were to get only one single released, *I Found Myself A Brand New Baby* being written by Mike Valvano with Clarence Paul and issued on Gordy in July 1962. It was also afforded a British release on Oriole the same October, but was probably a year or two ahead of its time – the British invasion hadn't even started in Britain at the time the single was released, let alone crossed the Atlantic.
Whilst the rest of the Modifiers negotiated their way out of both their contracts and Motown, Mike Valvano stayed as a producer, writer, backing musician (his chief claim to fame is providing the foot stomps on The Supremes' hits *Baby Love* and *Where Did Our Love Go*) and had another very brief attempt at a recording career as a member of The Hornets. He also recorded a one off single *Watch Your Step* as Mike Varo in 1964, written by Johnny Powers that was left in the vault,

subsequently being released in 2007 on the compilation album **A Cellarful Of Motown Volume 3**. Mike evidently left Motown sometime during the mid 1960s, although he continued to write and penned a number of songs for Frijid Pink. Problems securing royalties from Frijid Pink's management caused Mike severe financial hardship, eventually accepting an offer to return to Hitsville and write and produce for a number of the artists signed to Motown's rock imprint Rare Earth, including XIT and Stoney & Meatloaf. He died following a stroke on 10 April 2002.

AMOS MILBURN

Something of an elder statesman by the time he arrived at Motown, Amos Milburn had been a major star throughout much of the 1940s and 50s, having scored highly with a succession of blues songs based on drink. Born in Houston, Texas on 1 April 1927 as one of thirteen children, he learned to play the piano at the age of five and was soon putting together his own songs. He joined the US Navy in 1942 and at the war's end returned to Houston to form a sixteen piece band, earning a veritable reputation locally for his abilities as both a performer and organiser.

Eventually in 1946 he was invited to record for Aladdin Records in Los Angeles and over the next eight years recorded some 75 tracks. It was not until 1948 that any of them attracted attention, but once the first cracked the R&B chart, *Chicken Shack Boogie*, which hit number one, the rest followed in a torrent. Over the next six years a further eighteen crashed into the Top Ten, including further chart toppers in *Bewildered* (1948), *Roomin' House Boogie* (1949) and *Bad Bad Whiskey* (1950). Somewhat fittingly, his last charted record would be *Good Good Whiskey* in 1954, after which Aladdin hit problems and were unable to sell his records much beyond his Houston base.

Amos left the label in 1957, subsequently recording a couple of tracks for Ace and King without success. When the opportunity came to link up with Motown in 1962, it was a deal that made sense to both parties; Amos would be able to get back into the recording studio and Motown got an artist with bona fide credentials, then very important to a label that was still finding its way. Assigned to producer Clarence Paul, Amos recorded an album **The Return Of The Blues Boss** that would eventually see light of day in July 1963. Preceding this were two singles, *My Baby Gave Me Another Chance* and *My Daily Prayer*, released in February and July 1963 respectively. Among the musicians backing Amos was Little Stevie Wonder, whilst the album was a mix of traditional Amos Milburn material with obligatory Jobete copyrights.

By the time the album was released, Motown had begun to establish a foothold on the charts with a more urgent R&B musical style than Amos' blue-based recordings. It was to be his only album for the label although he continued working and occasionally recording, most notably with Johnny Otis, for several more years. He died following a stroke on 3 January 1980.

ALBUM: THE RETURN OF THE BLUES BOSS (1963)

BOBBY MILITELLO

Jazz musician Robert Philip Militello was born in Buffalo, New York on 25 March 1950 and made his name performing with Maynard Ferguson between 1975 and 1979, on saxophone and flute. In 1982 he formed his own fusion group RPM, performing locally in Buffalo where Rick James would become a regular attendee. James got Bobby a contract with Motown's Gordy label, although fellow fusion artist Lenny White produced his debut album for the label, **Bobby M Blow**, which resulted in two singles being lifted, *How Do You Feel Tonight* and *Let's Stay Together*. The latter track was originally recorded as an instrumental, but Bobby had other ideas.

"Once the track was recorded we felt in order to give it the full potential it shouldn't stay an instrumental but should have a vocal. Not a male vocal because that would have been too much like Al Green's version. So we decided to give the song a whole different spectrum. I wanted Jean Carn and as she was signed to Motown everything came together quickly."

Not only quickly but successfully too, making #74 on the US R&B chart and #53 pop in the UK. By the time the album came out, Bobby had accepted an invitation to join Dave Brubeck's band and took his leave of Motown.

ALBUM: BOBBY M BLOW (1982)

RON MILLER

Born Ronald Norman Gould in Chicago, Illinois on 5 October 1932 (his father died while Ron was still a child and his mother remarried, hence his adopted name Ron Miller) he showed an early aptitude as a songwriter, writing a tribute to the Chicago Cubs baseball team whilst still a teenager. After graduating from high school Ron served in the US Marines for a while but returned to Chicago and undertook menial jobs to survive while still determined to make a go of it in the music business as a writer. One of these involved becoming a pizza delivery man and one such delivery found him in the hotel room of Motown producer Mickey Stevenson. When Ron found out he badgered Mickey into listening to his songs. Suitably impressed, Mickey persuaded Ron to move to Detroit where he was signed on as a songwriter.

He scored his first hit in 1966 with Stevie Wonder and *A Place In The Sun*, co-written with Bryan Wells. Ron would write several hits for Stevie in the coming years, most notably *For Once In My Life*, which was written about the birth of Ron's daughter and originally intended for Barbara McNair, *Yester-Me Yester-You Yesterday* and *Heaven Help Us All*. Ron's ability to write material that sounded as though they were old show tunes and standards initially caused Berry Gordy some problems since he believed several artists would be turned off recording material from the Jobete catalogue, subsequently setting up Stein & Van Stock Publishing to handle the bulk of Ron's songs. This plan obviously worked, with *For Once In My Life* being described by trade magazine Billboard as an old classic and receive some 270 different recorded cover versions.

Ron would later write for Diana Ross (co-writing *Touch Me In The Morning*) and Charlene (*I've Never Been To Me*) and others outside of Motown, including Celine Dion, Barbra Streisand and Michael Bolton. He also wrote a couple of Broadway musicals, 'Daddy Goodness' and 'Cherry'. After combating emphysema and cancer, Ron died from a cardiac arrest on 23 July 2007.

THE STEVE MILLER BAND

American rock group The Steve Miller Band was formed in San Francisco, California in 1966 by Steve Miller (born in Milwaukee, Wisconsin on 5 October 1943, guitar and vocals), James 'Curley' Cooke (guitar and vocals), Lonnie Turner (bass and vocals) and Tim Davis (drums and vocals). Signed to Capitol in 1967, they recorded their debut album in 1968 and would go on to register a slew of hits, most notably *The Joker*, *Rock 'N Me* and *Abracadabra*, all of which topped the US charts. *Quicksilver Girl* was a track written for their second album, released in 1968, and was subsequently featured in the film 'The Big Chill', appearing on the album **More Songs From the Big Chill**. Cooke died from cancer on 16 May 2011.

STEPHANIE MILLS

Stephanie Dorthea Mills was born the fifth of six children in Brooklyn, New York on 22 March 1957 and first showed her vocal abilities as a child, singing gospel music at the Cornerstone Baptist Church in her hometown. By the age of nine, her talent was such that she was appearing on Broadway in the play 'Maggie Flynn', the same year she would win the Amateur Hour Talent Contest at the Apollo Theatre for six straight weeks. That victory, coupled with her growing reputation on Broadway, brought her an opening slot on a tour with The Isley Brothers.

Michael Barbiero secured Stephanie her first recording contract, signing her to ABC/Paramount for one album, for whom she would record **Movin' In The Right Direction** in 1975. However, it was landing the role of Dorothy in the Broadway production of 'The Wiz' later the same year that raised her profile, with Jermaine Jackson and his wife Hazel suitably taken with both the show and Stephanie's performance to raise the matter with Berry Gordy. Gordy would subsequently sign Stephanie as a solo artist and secure the film rights to 'The Wiz', with the expectation that the film version would enable Motown to launch Stephanie as a bona fide star.

Whilst Stephanie was despatched to work with writers and producers Hal David and Burt Bacharach for her debut album **For The First Time**, released in November 1975, intense lobbying behind the scenes would see Diana Ross land the role of Dorothy, even though her selection required a major rewrite to the plot of the film. Without the attendant publicity the film might have brought, Stephanie's album received little promotion and even less attention, despite Bacharach and David's involvement. Stephanie recorded a number of other tracks but Motown showed little interest in releasing them or promoting her career, with the result she left in 1978, bound for 20th Century.

Her three albums for the label all attained gold status to signify sales in excess of 500,000 copies of each, prompting Motown to delve into its catalogue for the release of **Love Has Lifted Me**, issued in November 1982. Perhaps too dated and dissimilar to her 20th Century successes, this album also did little. Stephanie would continue her recording career with Casablanca and MCA, scoring platinum and gold successes with the latter label.

ALBUMS: FOR THE FIRST TIME (1975), LOVE HAS LIFTED ME (1982)

MIRACLE RECORDS

The third label created by Berry Gordy, Miracle Records lasted eleven months before the label was shuttered and the artists Berry wished to retain switched over to other imprints. During its brief life, Miracle would see a total of twelve singles released, with The Valadiers' *Greetings (This Is Uncle Sam)* the only hit. Whilst several of the singles released might have done better, the label suffered from confusion caused by The Miracles as a group, together with a rather bizarre slogan in 'If it's a hit, it's a Miracle!'

THE MIRACLES

The importance of The Miracles to Motown can be gauged by the fact that Berry Gordy once stated, "Without The Miracles, Motown would not be the Motown it is today." The first of the supergroups to roll off the Motown conveyor belt, the group not only racked up a veritable number of hits for themselves, they also helped a considerable number of the other artists who came through the doors of Hitsville.

William 'Smokey' Robinson (born in Detroit, Michigan on 19 February 1940), Ronald White (born in Detroit on 5 April 1939) and Warren 'Pete' Moore (born in Detroit on 19 November 1939) were all school friends at Northern High School when they decided to form a vocal group in 1955, giving themselves the name The Five Chimes and drafting in Clarence 'Humble' Dawson, Donald Wicker and James 'Rat' Grice to round the group out. Within six months Wicker, Dawson and Grice had departed, being replaced by cousins Emerson 'Sonny' Rogers and Bobby Rogers (born in Detroit on 19 February 1940; it was later discovered that both Bobby and Smokey were born on the same day in the same hospital, although they did not meet until they were 15 years of age). Emerson was drafted in 1956 and was replaced in the group by his sister Claudette Rogers (born in New Orleans, Louisiana on 1 September 1942), by which time the group had also adopted the name The Matadors. In 1958 the group acquired another member, guitarist Marv Tarplin (born in Atlanta, Georgia on 13 June 1941), poached from The Primettes (later to become The Supremes), with Marv becoming known over the ensuing years as 'The Miracles' Secret Weapon'.

Like many local Detroit acts, The Matadors sought an audition with anyone they thought might be in a position to help further their career, which in late 1957 meant Nat Tarnopol, the manager of Jackie Wilson. Tarnopol thought The Matadors sounded and looked too similar to The Platters and turned them down, but as they were leaving the office, they were approached by one of Jackie Wilson's writers in Berry Gordy, who expressed an interest in working with the group. After listening to every song in Smokey's portfolio, Berry made a number of suggestions on song composition and structure, thus starting a friendship that continues to the present day.

Smokey proved to be a quick learner when it came to song writing, turning up a couple of months into the relationship with the basics of a song called *Got A Job*, something of an answer record to The Silhouettes recent hit *Get A Job*. The song itself was fleshed out by Berry and Billy Davis (the song writing credits on the single show Berry Gordy and Tyran Carlo, the other name under which Billy Davis wrote) and recorded at the United Sound Studios in January 1958, with Berry subsequently striking a deal with George Goldner to release it on his End label. Berry also decided the group needed a name change since The Matadors implied an all-male group, with Smokey picking out their new moniker The Miracles. The single, backed with *My Mama Done Told Me* was eventually released on 19 February, both Smokey and Bobby's eighteenth birthday, and would earn the princely sum of $3.19 in royalties.

Another single appeared before the year was out, *I Need Some Money* backed with *I Cry* being issued by End (further complicating the issue was the appearance of *Your Love (Is All I Need)* backed with *I Love You So* on End's parent label Fury, but this group of Miracles was a backing group assembled by Carl Hogan that featured John Brisbane, Jerry Moore, Ronnie Bright and Irving Lee Gail). Berry's sister Gwen used her influence to get the group's next single *I Need A Change* backed with *All I Want Is You* released by Chess, a link that would shortly prove useful in getting the group their first hit. In the meantime, Berry decided on a change of focus, releasing the single *It*, something of a novelty item about an alien and credited to Bill & Ron and licensed to Argo after it had briefly appeared on the Tamla label.

Then Berry and Smokey collaborated on *Bad Girl*, a doo wop item that was released on the Motown label (the only Miracles record released on the Motown label, the switch occurring because Berry had initially decided that the Tamla label would house all of the solo artists and Motown the groups, although he subsequently rescinded the decision) and started attracting some strong local interest. Still unable to fully service any record on a national basis, Berry licensed the single to Chess and saw it hit #93 on the pop chart.

It was after this success that Motown became a fully fledged independent record company, responsible for all sales and marketing, although it very nearly looked as though Berry would have to launch his own operation without The Miracles; one of the labels to which Berry had leased a Miracles record tried to take over the group's contract (Berry was managing the group at this time) and, although he quickly realised he was in a poor position, Berry called a meeting of local but prominent deejays and informed them of the situation. When word got around that the deejays intended boycotting any and all releases from that company until they handed back The Miracles' contract, the label backed down and delivered The Miracles back to Berry Gordy.

It is therefore fitting that the first chart topper Motown enjoyed came with The Miracles. *Way Over There* might have been the track to do it, but after it started creating a stir locally, selling a reported 60,000 copies, Berry decided it would sound better if it had strings, similar to the sound The Drifters were scoring big with. Unfortunately, by the time the re-recorded version was available the momentum had been lost. Berry Gordy nearly made the same mistake a second time with the next single, *Shop Around*. This time copies had got around to the local radio stations but every time Berry heard it played, he felt that something was missing, that extra ingredient that would turn the good song into a great one. At three o'clock one morning Berry could stand it no more, calling the group up on the telephone and dragging them into the recording studio to re-cut the song. Fortunately, the company had sufficient time to recall the initial copies and get a much more pop sounding version out on the streets, which subsequently exploded at both radio and retail, topping the R&B charts and hitting #2 pop (it actually hit #1 on the Cashbox chart), selling more than a million copies in the process, the company's first million selling release. The success of the single had side benefits too, with The Miracles becoming the first Motown act to appear on the television show 'American Bandstand', performing on Dick Clark's show on 27 December 1960. Motown would also issue an answer record, with Debbie Dean hitting #92 on the pop chart with *Don't Let Him Shop Around* in 1961. Although Berry's name was listed as a co-composer, his contribution on The Miracles' songs was becoming less and less as Smokey Robinson took more control.

In time Smokey was writing not just hit material for The Miracles but also many of the other artists signed to the various Motown labels, including The Temptations, Mary Wells and countless others, effectively becoming a one-man hit factory within Hitsville. It has been suggested that Smokey's work on other acts detracted from The Miracles own output during that time, but the evidence would suggest otherwise, since everything the group recorded over the ten years or so charted.

That run continued through with *Ain't It Baby* (#45 pop and #15 R&B), *Mighty Good Lovin'* (#51 pop and #21, with the flip side *Broken Hearted* also making a brief chart appearance at #91 pop), *Everybody's Gotta Pay Some Dues* (#52 pop and #11 R&B) and *What's So Good About Goodbye* (#35 pop and #16 R&B, with the flip *I've Been Good To You* also getting some action and bubbling under the pop chart at #103). *What's So Good About Goodbye* proved more than anything Smokey's ability to take an innocuous comment and turn it into as hit song.

"I was looking at TV one night, and this woman and this man were talking. They were saying goodbye. They were lovers, you know, and she was asking him, 'What's good about that?' That's was where it came from."

Whilst Smokey could work his magic on a single, the album's **Hi We're The Miracles** and **Cookin' With The Miracles** were too disjointed for wider consumption. Indeed, The Miracles fared less well than almost all their label-mates on the album chart until 1965 when Smokey's name was elevated to centre stage. Meanwhile, on the singles chart the group could do little wrong, taking *I'll Try Something New* into the Top Forty (#39 pop and #11 R&B) and then scoring their second million seller with *You've Really Got A Hold On Me* (#8 pop and #1 R&B). This latter hit happened almost by accident, for Tamla originally released the single with *Happy Landing* as the plug side, only to see radio switch sides and play *You Really Got A Hold On Me* as the top side. It proved a masterstroke, for the song would become a major hit and attract a number of cover versions, most notably by The Beatles on their second album. Yet The Miracles still struggled to shift meaningful copies of their own albums, with **I'll Try Something New** being a sadly under-rated album that saw the group delve into the American songbook for several tracks on the second side, all of which were masterfully performed and executed. The group returned to the charts with *A Love She Can Count On*, a #31 pop and #21 R&B hit at much the same time the group achieved their first album success, **The Fabulous Miracles – You Really Got a Hold On Me** peaking at #118.

Whilst the initial flurry of chart activity on The Miracles had come with material penned largely by Smokey Robinson, the group's next major hit came with a song that had been instigated by Lamont Dozier. Smokey happened to be passing the rehearsal room where Lamont was playing the brief snippets of music, a Bo Diddley influenced riff that Lamont and Eddie Holland eventually fleshed out in to *Mickey's Monkey*, which Smokey ensured The Miracles got the first crack at. With Bobby Rogers devising an intricate dance routine to go with the song, *Mickey's Monkey* became both a major hit (#8 pop and #3 R&B) and a firm favourite of the group's live repertoire, becoming something of a showstopper for many years after.

The same writing team provided The Miracles with the follow-up *I Gotta Dance To Keep From Crying*, which whilst not as big a hit as its predecessor did at least keep the group active, peaking at #35 pop and #17 R&B. In the meantime the group had returned to the chart with **Recorded Live! On Stage**, the first of the group's successful live albums (although somewhat unique in so much as it omitted *Mickey's Monkey*, although the group managed to work *Way Over There*, the album's closer, into an excellent call and response battle with the audience) that made #139 on the pop listings.

Christmas was also a cause for celebration, with The Miracles releasing **Christmas With The Miracles**, one of Motown's first forays into the seasonal market in October 1963 and another success, hitting #15 on the Billboard Christmas chart. The following year, 1964, would see the group restored to its original full complement with the return from military service of Pete Moore but suffer the loss of Claudette, who decided to retire from the stresses and strains of touring. Smokey and Claudette had wanted to start a family almost as soon as they had been married in 1959, but Claudette was to suffer seven miscarriages along the way.

"Becoming a mother was very, very important in my life. I had gotten to the point after so many miscarriages that I didn't think I would ever have children of my own. Smokey and Berry Gordy were the ones who really felt first and foremost that my health was suffering and that I should come off the road."

Claudette would continue to appear on various recordings and would make her presence known as the inspiration for several songs Smokey wrote (most notably *My Girl*), but on stage the group continued with the four male singers and Marv Tarplin. Meanwhile the group was back on the album chart, Lamont Dozier and Eddie Holland crafting an entire album of dance inspired material on **Doin' Mickey's Monkey**, which hit #113 following its release in November 1963. After working with HDH The Miracles were back in the care of Smokey for the delightfully titled *(You Can't Let The Boy Overpower) The Man In You*, which deserved a better fate than #59 pop and #12 R&B (Chuck Jackson would later revive the song as his first Motown outing), which could also be said for both *I Like It Like That* and *That's What Love Is Made Of*, both of which reached the R&B Top Ten but peaked outside the Top Twenty pop.

The group's final hit single of 1964, *Come On Do The Jerk*, had originally been intended as the follow-up to *Mickey's Monkey* but held back as *Mickey's Monkey* proved to have a longer lifespan than originally envisaged. Instead, *Come On Do The Jerk* was held back until November 1964, appearing at much the same time as The Contours released the similarly inspired *Can You Jerk Like Me*. This was a chart battle that was ultimately won by The Contours, who hit #15 R&B and #47 as opposed to The Miracles' #22 R&B and #50 pop. *Come On Do The Jerk* (and its flipside *Baby Don't You Go*) was to become something of a forgotten item in The Miracles catalogue, left off any album until it finally appeared on a second greatest hits package in 1968.

Perhaps the oversight was down to the realisation that The Miracles wasn't a group that followed dance trends but set their own agenda with their sublime material and wondrous harmonies, two traits that really rose to the top during 1965. The year kicked off with *Ooo Baby Baby*, a song that had begun life as little more than a phrase the group incorporated on stage, as Smokey would later recall.

"We used to sing a medley of love songs. It was some of the songs we had done, some songs that other artists had done. There was a song called *Please Say You Want Me Too*, which was by a group called The Schoolboys. That was like the last song in the medley. We had that there, and right after we sang *Please Say You Want Me Too*, we were on stage, and spontaneously we started to sing 'Ooo, baby baby.' So we left that in, and everywhere we went, when we would sing that thing, when we got to 'Ooo, baby baby,' even though people had never heard that, they loved it. So we said, 'Hey, we're going to write a song like that!'"

Although they were on tour in Europe when *Ooo Baby Baby* was released (the group would perform *Ooo Baby Baby* on the 'Ready Steady Go! Motown special to rapturous acclaim), the song quickly became something of a signature tune for The Miracles, powering its way to #4 R&B and #16 pop, even if it missed out in the UK, despite added exposure of 'Ready Steady Go!' Whilst *Ooo Baby Baby* was great, the follow-up was even better. *The Tracks Of My Tears* would become Berry Gordy's favourite song by the group and, judging by its final chart placing of #2 R&B and #16 pop, found favour with a wide and varied audience too. It still missed out in the UK, although four years after its original release it was coupled with the long time Northern Soul favourite *Come On Do The Jerk* and would make the Top Ten on reissue. By then The Miracles had already achieved their British breakthrough, which came with another of the group's excursions into dance territory.

"We did a lot of go-gos," explained Bobby Rogers. "You had a go-go in Chicago, and there was the Whiskey A Go Go in California. We used to work these two spots. That's how we wrote that song."

That song turned out to be *Going To A Go-Go*, partially inspired musically by none other than The Rolling Stones. It was something of a back-handed compliment, since The Rolling Stones was just one of several British groups who were utilising the Motown style (or their interpretations of it), but as *Going To A Go-Go* proved, the originators did it better. A #2 R&B and #11 pop hit (even the flip side, *Choosey Beggar* had enough about it to reach #35 R&B), *Going To A Go-Go* got the group onto the British chart for the first time, reaching #44 in March 1966 after it had been played extensively across Northern Soul venues.

Back home in the US, The Miracles had hit a rich vein of form, one which converted into healthy sales across both the singles and album chart, with the compilation album **Greatest Hits From The Beginning** (a double album package that despite the title omitted some of the group's hits, including *Come On Do The Jerk*) hitting #21 pop and #2 R&B being followed by **Going To A Go-Go** doing even better, a #8 pop and R&B chart topping album. **Going To A Go-Go** benefited from hosting no fewer than four R&B Top Ten hits (*Ooo Baby Baby, The Tracks Of My Tears, Going To A Go-Go* and *My Girl Has Gone*), virtually all of which having also found favour on the pop listings and made the Top Twenty.

Despite having been the architects of their own success with many of their singles up to 1966, the group found themselves working with others around the Hitsville lot during the year, including Frank Wilson on *Whole Lot Of Shakin' In My Heart (Since I Met You)* and Holland-Dozier-Holland on *(Come 'Round Here) I'm The One You Need*, with the latter number by far the most successful, hitting #17 pop and #4 R&B as well as a minor UK hit at #37. The only album to appear was **Away We A Go-Go**, something of an attempt to continue to cash in on the success of the *Going To A Go-Go* single, even though the track did not appear on the long player.

What did appear, however, was a slight change of artist credit to Smokey Robinson & The Miracles and, on the back cover, Claudette made her first photographed appearance since **The Fabulous Miracles** in 1963. The first single to carry the new moniker was *The Love I Saw In You Was Just A Mirage*, where Smokey was back in charge of production duties (with Pete Moore), a #10 R&B and #20 pop hit following its release in January 1967. Claudette, meanwhile, would inspire the follow-up single *More Love*, as Smokey would later relate.

"We had many miscarriages. Every time I went to the hospital after a miscarriage, Claudette was in there and she was apologising to me: 'Oh, I'm so sorry, baby. I let you down.' And all that stuff like that. And I'd always tell her, 'You didn't let me down, because even though I wanted those babies, and it would have been a great thing, I know you. I didn't know those babies, but I know you. You're the person who's been in my life since I was 14 years old. I love you. You're okay, I'm fine! We'll try again on another baby.' After one of those times, I went home and I said, 'I'm going to write a song to her.' And I wrote *More Love* because I wanted her to know that was how I felt. Like I said, it would have been great to have the babies, but we didn't. But we had each other, so that was what was important to me."

Written from the heart (and in Smokey's words designed "Hoping the words would heal her heart"), *More Love* touched a nerve following its release as a single, hitting #5 pop and #23 pop. Despite the intensely personal message and declaration, *More Love* would be covered by Barbara McNair and later Kim Carnes (whose version would be responsible for bringing together producer George Tobin and Smokey in 1980), with varying degrees of success. *More Love* was featured on the album **Make It Happen** released in August 1967 and another big selling album, hitting #28 pop and #3 R&B the following month. Unbeknown to all at Motown, however, was that the album carried what was to become Smokey Robinson & The Miracles' biggest selling hit, a worldwide smash in *Tears Of A Clown*; when the album was released, the track languished as the closer on side two, until revived some three years later.

In the meantime, Smokey and in-house writer and producer Al Cleveland had crafted another gem in *I Second That Emotion*, a song born out of a malapropism by Al when the pair went out shopping for Christmas presents. Taking the amusing but incorrect phrase as their inspiration, the pair created a masterful song that returned the group to the Top Ten of the pop chart for the first time since 1963 (at #4) and their first R&B chart topper since 1962 (as well as hitting #27 in the UK). The momentum was maintained with *If You Can Want*, which peaked at #11 pop and #3 R&B and kept the group on the British listings, albeit at a relatively lowly #50. The domestic success meanwhile continued unabated, with *Yester Love, Special Occasion, Baby Baby Don't Cry* and

Doggone Right all hitting the R&B Top Ten, even if their pop fortunes fluctuated wildly (only *Baby Baby Don't Cry* made the Top Ten).

With success came demands, with the group regulars on television and on tour, with Ed Sullivan making the same kind of malapropism as Al Cleveland when the group appeared on his show in 1968, introducing the group as Smokey & The Little Smokeys! Big Smokey (Robinson) wasn't that inspired to write a song around *this* faux pas, although the group's performance of The Beatles' *Yesterday* more than made up for it. That track would be featured on the album **Special Occasion**, the only new album the group released during 1968, although the material contained within featured some old cuts, including the group's own take on *I Heard It Through The Grapevine*, which was actually the first recorded version of this iconic song.

By the end of 1968 Smokey had pretty much made up his mind to leave the group and launch a solo career, although he knew that the timing for such a move would be crucial. In an ideal world, he would leave when the group was on top, meaning it would be easier for them to continue touring and earning, whilst his profile would also be high. Perhaps the other group members had already guessed his intentions, for there was a somewhat fraught atmosphere for a time, both in and out of the studio.

And The Miracles were busy in the studio during 1969, eventually releasing three albums, including a second live album. The live platter, recorded at Detroit's Roostertail Restaurant during 1968 was something of a departure from their normal live show, since the performance and material were aimed more at the supper club market, featuring their interpretations of such standard pop songs as *Walk On By, Up Up And Away, Yesterday* and *Theme From Valley Of The Dolls* as well as their hits. The album carried enough of the latter to ensure the album was something of a success, hitting #71 pop and #6 R&B.

The group's two other long players released during the year were also a mixed bag collection of material, with **Time Out** making #25 pop (although it failed to reach the R&B chart) and **Four In Blue** #78 pop and #3 R&B. The former album benefitted from hosting no fewer than four Top 40 hits (*Doggone Right, Abraham Martin & John, Here I Go Again* and *Baby Baby Don't Cry*); the latter suffered from having no singles lifted whatsoever. Smokey might have felt that now was probably as good a time as any to exit the group (especially as he had finally become a father), but events transpiring nearly four thousand miles away would put those plans on indefinite hold.

Tamla Motown was enjoying something of a revival of interest in Britain, with all manner of artists benefitting from a reissue programme that had seen hitherto ignored and overlooked singles being given a second lease of life. Following the Top Ten success of *Behind A Painted Smile* by The Isley Brothers, Tamla Motown decided the next single to be revisited was The Miracles' *Tracks Of My Tears*, one of Smokey's finest lyrical moments that had missed the chart altogether when originally released. Coupled with the Northern Soul favourite *Come On Do The Jerk*, it made #9 the second time around and subsequently prompted the British arm of the company to search for a logical successor. It was found on the album **Make It Happen**, with *Tears Of A Clown* being extracted as a single and powering its way to the top of the British chart. Flush with this success, Tamla in the US tried the same tactic and were equally rewarded when *Tears Of A Clown* spent two weeks at the top of the Billboard pop chart.

The success of old material came at a time the newer material wasn't hitting quite the same heights, although there was still much to enjoy on **What Love Has Joined Together** (one of the shortest Miracles' albums, featuring just six tracks and a running time of under half an hour) and **A Pocket Full Of Miracles**, both of which made the Top Ten of the R&B chart although enjoyed widely varying degrees of acceptance on the pop listings, peaking at #97 and #56 respectively.

The chart topping *Tears Of A Clown* forced Smokey to abandon his plans for a solo career for at least eighteen months, with extra demands to go out on the road having to be managed alongside the need for new material, both for the group and others who relied on Smokey for their shot at stardom. Add to this two young children at home (a son, Berry was born in 1968, being joined by a daughter Tamla the following year) and it was apparent that Smokey would be unable to put off the inevitable for much longer. The Miracles released one album in 1971, **One Dozen Roses**, containing *I Don't Blame You At All* (something of a return to form, hitting #18 pop and #7 R&B and a #11 hit in the UK), *Crazy About The La La La* (#56 pop and #20 R&B) and *Satisfaction* (#49 pop and #20 R&B), with the album becoming a #92 pop and #17 R&B hit.

By the start of 1972, the end was in sight, even if the group's biggest hit of the year, *We've Come Too Far To End It Now* might have suggested otherwise. Almost entirely produced by Johnny Bristol (and featuring next to nothing that was written by Smokey or any of the other Miracles), **Flying High Together** was to become the final studio album recorded by The Miracles with Smokey Robinson. After that, it was time to prepare for a parting of the ways.

"The Miracles were part of my satisfaction on the road," said Smokey. "I was with the guys I loved so much and got along with perfectly well. The only part I found I hated about the whole thing was the travelling, the hotels, food in restaurants, and so on. It was driving me up the wall. Also I had two very young children and I wanted to be able to be their father rather than a celebrity they saw every now and again. These are the factors that made me decide I had to stop."

Whilst Smokey was planning his exit from the group, so the rest of the Miracles began preparing for live after his departure, as Pete Moore explained.

"As Smokey told us he was leaving a year before he actually left we had plenty of time to work things out. Even so, his leaving was quite psychological and a lot of people just didn't want to recognise the group without him. We weren't so much disappointed as a little hurt when he left because we'd been associated with him for so many years that it was sad."

The saddest point came with Smokey's final live appearance with his erstwhile group mates, a series of three performances at the Carter Barron Amphitheatre in Washington D.C. on the 14th, 15th and 16th of July 1972, with the performances being recorded and subsequently released as the album **1957-1972 Live**, featuring material drawn from their entire career, with the album hitting #75 pop and #14 R&B in the aftermath. The final curtain on Smokey and The Miracles was to be the poignant single *I Can't Stand To See You Cry*, released in November 1972 and a #45 pop and #21 R&B hit.

The rest of The Miracles, meanwhile, were working with Smokey's replacement, Billy Griffin. Actually, replacement isn't exactly the right term, since Smokey was irreplaceable, but in time Billy Griffin would prove more than adequate compensation. Born in Baltimore, Maryland on 15 August 1950, Billy had sung with a group called Last Dynasty and won a television talent programme with NBC, for which the first prize was a recording deal with RCA. Last Dynasty never took up the deal, due in large part because Billy had been tipped off by Damon Harris that there was a possibility of an opening with The Miracles and had journeyed down to Detroit to audition, as Pete Moore later explained.

"When we got back to Detroit, we made an announcement that we were looking for a replacement for Smokey. Then we got a lot of calls, we did a lot of interviews and auditions. Billy was living in Baltimore at the time. He came to Detroit from Baltimore, and he was about the fifth or sixth person that we listened to and auditioned. When we heard him and saw him, we knew he was the person. He was a nice-looking kid, he was a good songwriter, he was very enthusiastic, and he knew a lot about the group because as a kid, he studied what we did."

Billy was introduced by none other than Smokey as the newest Miracle during that final performance at the Carter Barron Amphitheatre, as the group undertook their final encore of *Going To A Go Go*. "I'd like to have you meet a young man who is a really beautiful cat. He's going to join The Miracles, and sing with them. How about it, for William Griffin!"

Billy Griffin and the rest of The Miracles were handed over to an assortment of in-house writers and producers, with Leon Ware and Arthur T-Boy Ross coming up with *What Is A Heart Good For*, a song that received a good reception and seemed likely to be the group's first post-Smokey single, only for the decision to be later rescinded, Motown supposedly feeling it was too close to the material the group had recorded with Smokey. Instead, *Don't Let It End ('Til You Let I Begin)* would be the first single lifted off the **Renaissance** album, something of a minor success when it peaked at #56 pop and #26 R&B following its release in July 1973 (the album appeared three months earlier). Despite the failure of the single and album, The Miracles were more than happy with the end results, as Ronnie White would later confirm.

"We feel that this album is a lot more varied than our previous work, when Smokey did most of the writing and producing. We used a lot of the best Motown producers for different cuts."

Perhaps there lay the problem; with so many involved, the album lacked a distinct direction or unique sound, something that would have to be addressed on their next album if they were to emerge from the shadow of their former leader. What came wasn't so much a unique sound, although the first single *Give Me Just Another Day* did allow the group to add a further string to their bow, for whilst much of their major success with Smokey had been with sublime ballads, this latest single showed they could mix it up. A minor hit when released in November 1973, the single would bubble under the pop charts at #111 and scrape into the Top 50 of the R&B chart (#47). That single had been written by husband and wife songwriting team Freddie Perren and Christine Yarian, and the same pairing was responsible for the follow-up (and eventual title track to the album) *Do It Baby*. Seen by some as a blatant attempt to cash in on the disco craze, *Do It Baby* had enough about it to smash into the charts, hitting #13 pop and #4 R&B, assisting the album to the lofty heights of #41 pop and #4 R&B, the highest charting album the group had enjoyed in some five years.

The follow-up **Don't Cha Love It** was perhaps too similar to enjoy widespread appeal, although the title track made #78 pop and #4 R&B, with the album also hitting #96 pop and #7 R&B, aided by the limited success of another single extract, *Gemini* (#101 pop and #43 R&B). Even as *Gemini* was sliding down the chart, The Miracles were planning their next offering, one which would see them take greater control of their material, as Billy Griffin noted.

"The seed for the idea came one day when I was looking out of the window at a Holiday Inn in Hollywood, thinking about all the people who must come here with aspirations of making it. I commented to Pete about it, and the millions who must come here and never do make it – the dreams that are broken. **City Of Angels** was the result. It was a soul opera...the first of its kind. It was different from a concept album like Marvin's **What's Going On** because it told a story. We wrote the opera around two songs. *Love Machine* was going to be the hit record for the central character, and the other was *My Name Is Michael*. That was actually written for Michael Jackson, but he'd finished his own album before he got to hear it, so Pete and I included it as part of ours. It was almost what Michael Jackson could have said in looking back on his life."

It was *Love Machine*, however, that was central to the album, a driving track that found favour across every chart imaginable, including pop (#1), R&B (#5) and Britain (#3, becoming the group's only post Smokey success). Produced by Freddie Perren, **City Of Angels** deserved a better fate than peaking at #33 pop and #29 R&B (Billy would later claim "Motown didn't grasp the whole album"), although the album's importance has long since surpassed the lowly chart positions. There is no doubt the album was ahead of its time, as was reflected on the cover, which features a pair of female legs stepping over The Miracles star on the Hollywood Walk of Fame; the group didn't get one until 2009.

What would turn out to be the group's final album for Motown appeared in September 1976, with **The Power Of Music** lacking a hit single and slipping down to #178 pop and #35 R&B, although the album was later revealed to be little more than a contractual obligation album, since the group was already shopping for a new deal and recording not only **Power Of Music** but the subsequent album too.

"To put it simply, it's like a marriage," Billy would state after the group had left Motown. "After eighteen years of being 'married' to Motown, we woke up one day to realise we needed a new 'love' – one with more enthusiasm, more willingness to work with us and, to a degree, more money to put behind the Miracles."

They found that money at Columbia/CBS, where they would release two albums, only one of which made any impact on the charts. After that the group splintered, with Billy undertaking a solo career, with some international success before turning to writing and production, most notably for Take That at the launch of their career. The rest of The Miracles, meanwhile, effectively retired.

"I think everybody was tired. I knew I was," said Ronnie White. "After so much travelling, it just really wears you down."

The group has enjoyed sporadic reunions, most notably for the ceremony celebrating the star on the Hollywood Walk of Fame in 2009 and their long overdue induction into the Rock & Roll Hall of Fame in 2012, two accolades among many the group has collected over the years. Pete Moore looked back across the years to assess The Miracles' success and impact.

"We never thought it would be what it ultimately became. How could five kids back in Detroit at that time envision what would happen to us? It was just a joyride. We started rehearsing in Claudette's basement, and we went from Claudette's basement to sitting in Ed Sullivan's dressing room, talking to Bob Hope and Charlton Heston. It was a dream come true."

Ronnie White died from leukaemia on 26 August 1995. Marv Tarplin died on 30 September 2011. Bobby Rogers died after a lengthy illness on 3 March 2013.

ALBUMS: HI WE'RE THE MIRACLES (1961), COOKIN' WITH THE MIRACLES (1961), I'LL TRY SOMETHING NEW (1962), THE FABULOUS MIRACLES – YOU REALLY GOT A HOLD ON ME (1963), RECORDED LIVE! ON STAGE (1963), CHRISTMAS WITH THE MIRACLES (1963), DOIN' MICKEY'S MONKEY (1963), GOING TO A GO-GO (1965), AWAY WE A GO-GO (1966), MAKE IT HAPPEN (1967), SPECIAL OCCASION (1968), LIVE! (1969), TIME OUT (1969), FOUR IN BLUE (1969), WHAT LOVE HAS JOINED TOGETHER (1970), POCKETFUL OF MIRACLES (1970), THE SEASON FOR MIRACLES (1970), ONE DOZEN ROSES (1971), FLYING HIGH TOGETHER (1972), 1957-1972 LIVE (1972), RENAISSANCE (1973), DO IT BABY (1974), DON'T CHA LOVE IT (1975), CITY OF ANGELS (1975), THE POWER OF MUSIC (1976)

COMPILATIONS: GREATEST HITS – FROM THE BEGINNING (1965), GREATEST HITS VOLUME 2 (1968), ANTHOLOGY (1974), GREATEST HITS (1977), 18 GREATEST HITS (1984), ANTHOLOGY (1986), 22 GREATEST HITS (1986)

MISTER MAGIC – GROVER WASHINGTON JR. [ALBUM]

After the success of the his first three albums for Kudu, high hopes were held for Grover Washington Jr.'s fourth release **Mister Magic**, and it didn't disappoint. Recorded at the Van Gelder Studios in Englewood Cliffs, it featured the usual crew of CTI house musicians alongside some of the biggest names in the jazz movement at the time, including Bob James (who in addition to playing keyboards also arranged and conducted the entire album), Eric Gale (gutar), Gary King and Phil Upchurch (bass), Harvey Mason (drums), Ralph MacDonald (percussion), Jon Faddis and Marvin Stamm (trumpets), Wayne Andre and Tony Studd (trombones), Phil Bodner and Jerry Dodgion (saxophones), a string section that comprised Al Brown, Max Ellen, Paul Gershman, Harry Glickman, Harold Kohon, Harry Lookofsky, Charles McCracken, Joe Malin, David Nadien, Matthew Raimondi, Alan Shulman and Manny Vardi and Grover on alto, soprano and tenor saxophone.

Featuring only four extended tracks, **Mister Magic** was a tour de force, with the title track being extracted as a single, peaking at #16 R&B and #54 pop. Released on 5 February 1975, the album sailed all the way to the top of the jazz and R&B charts as well as hitting #10 on the pop listings, becoming the best selling jazz album up to that point. If there was one album that vindicated Motown's decision to pick up the CTI stable for distribution, **Mister Magic** was that album, and things would only get better for Grover Washington Jr.

BARBARA MITCHELL

Better known as a member of High Inergy, who recorded a number of hits for the Gordy label, Barbara didn't actually record any solo material for Motown. Instead, she was the featured female performer on Smokey Robinson's 1983 single *Blame It On Love*, a #35 R&B and #48 pop hit, and one other track that was featured on High Inergy's album **Groove Patrol**, *Just A Touch Away*. Barbara left Motown when High Inergy disbanded in 1984 and would later record gospel music for a number of labels, most notably Atlanta Artists.

MARTY MITCHELL

Bass guitarist and singer Marty Mitchell hailed from Birmingham, Alabama and first recorded for Atlantic Records in 1974, releasing two singles that same year. In 1976 he signed with Motown's Hitsville imprint, recording and releasing a cover of Frankie Valli's *My Eyes Adored You* backed with *Devil Woman*, which hit #87 on the country chart. Work on his only album continued throughout the rest of the year, with **You Are The Sunshine Of My Life** being released on the MC label in November 1977. The title track was extracted as a single and did well on the country chart, peaking at #34, but with Motown eventually severing ties with the MC label, Marty was one of several artists that got lost in the cull.

WILLIE MITCHELL

Although better known as a producer, most notably for the likes of Al Green and Ann Peebles, Willie was also a successful artist in his own right. Born in Ashland, Mississippi on 1 March 1928 he learned to play the trumpet whilst attending the Rust College. He moved to Memphis after army service in 1954, leading the orchestra at the Manhattan Club and the house band for a local label. In 1961 he was signed by Hi Records, an independent label that had enjoyed initial success with rockabilly and would later score several country hits. As an artist Willie would enjoy eight R&B hits between 1964 and 1969, including the Top Ten smash *Soul Serenade*, but as the decade wore on Willie began to play a greater role in shaping the label. From 1969 onwards he shifted the musical focus away from country and more towards R&B, signing and producing Al Green, Ann Peebles, Syl Johnson and O.V. Wright. It was Al Green who was the ultimate star at Hi, with a succession of hit singles and albums that crossed over to the pop charts. Green's eventual switch to gospel music, coupled with Hi Records' sale to Cream saw Willie work with a variety of artists from all musical genres, including Wet Wet Wet, Tina Turner, Rod Stewart and Keith Richards. A compilation of Willie's greatest hits was released on Motown in 1982 as part of the brief licensing deal with Hi/Cream Records. Willie died from a cardiac arrest in Memphis on 5 January 2010.

ALBUM: THE BEST OF WILLIE MITCHELL (1982)

FONCE MIZELL

Alphonso 'Fonce'Mizell was born in New York on 15 January 1943 and, along with younger brother Larry (born in New York on 17 February 1944) was given a trumpet as a youngster and subsequently joined the school band. They formed their first group The Nikons with another classmate Freddie Perren and cut a few demos before they graduated from high school. All three then attended Howard University, where Fonce studied under Donald Byrd, Larry earning a degree in engineering and Fonce a degree in music. Whilst Larry took an position with Grumman Aerospace and would eventually work on the Apollo Space Programme, Fonce and Freddie relocated to Los Angeles and initially worked with independent label Larco.

An introduction to Deke Richards brought both Fonce and Freddie into the Motown stable as staff songwriters, with Fonce becoming one of The Corporation who penned the majority of The Jackson 5's early hits. Larry meanwhile earned a masters degree from New York University and left Grumman in order to join his brother in Los Angeles, becoming a session musician on several Motown recordings.

Whilst Fonce continued to write and produce for Motown, it was not an exclusive arrangement, enabling him to link up with Donald Byrd in 1972 and work on the **Street Lady** album (produced by Larry, with Larry, Fonce and Freddie responsible for the vocal arrangements) and **Blackbyrd**. The contrasts couldn't have been greater; producing bubblegum soul on The Jackson 5 and classic jazz funk on Donald Byrd. Eventually Larry and Fonce formed their own production company Sky High Productions, with Freddie Perren also a part of the team, and would produce the likes of Bobbi Humphrey, L.T.D., Johnny Hammond, Gary Bartz, A Taste Of Honey and Mary Wells outside of Motown and Michael Jackson, Edwin Starr and The Miracles within. Freddie Perren set up his own production company in 1978, with the Mizell brothers eventually scaling down their work, with A Taste Of Honey's 1979 album **Another Taste** the last album the pair produced. Fonce died from heart failure on 5 July 2011.

DOUG MOMARY

Best known as the co-creator and writer of the children's television programme 'New Zoo Revue', written with his wife Emily Peden and which ran from 1972 to 1977, Doug recorded an album for the MC label. The eponymous album was scheduled for release in November 1977 but subsequently got pulled as the deal with Mike Curb's label came to an abrupt end.

THE MONITORS

When Chex Records shut its doors, The Majestics joined the rush of artists heading towards Hitsville, signing with Berry Gordy's V.I.P. label after a spell with his ex-wife's Thelma label in 1963. By then the group had been recording locally since 1959 and comprised Richard Street (born Richard Allen Street in Detroit, Michigan on 5 October 1942), John 'Maurice' Fagin and his wife Sandra and Warren Harris.

At Hitsville The Majestics set to work on a song they had previously recorded as a demo at Thelma, *My Love*, which was written by Thelma Coleman Gordy, Richard Street and Warren Harris and readied for release in October 1964. However, shortly before release Motown had a change of heart and pulled the single, sending the group back into the studio to work on new material with a variety of producers. It would take another year before The Majestics were ready to release another single, with the Richard Dobyne, Robert Walker and Robert Staunton composition and production *Say You* backed with *All For Someone* scheduled for release in December 1965.

Then another problem arose soon after promotional copies had been despatched, with Motown discovering that The Majestics name was being used by another group. The Detroit variation of The Majestics could have maintained their claim to the name, since they undoubtedly held seniority, with the other variation being one based in Los Angeles that had seemingly begun their recording career in 1963 on Linda Records. Instead, a decision was taken to re-christen the Detroit group The Monitors, the name that appeared on commercial copies of the single.

Fortunately, despite the hiccups surrounding their start with Motown, *Say You* became their debut hit, reaching #36 on the R&B chart, with the song generating enough interest to attract a cover version by The Temptations. The Monitors next single release was also a cover version, with Mickey Stevenson and Hank Cosby resurrecting The Valadiers' minor 1961 hit *Greetings (This Is Uncle Sam)*. The sentiments of the song were even more poignant in 1966, especially when sung by The Monitors, and whilst the single barely made #100 on the pop chart, it would peak at #21 on the R&B listings, ultimately their biggest hit, as Richard Street would later acknowledge.

"It was our biggest record, because the Vietnam War jumped off. The soldiers and the guys who got drafted loved that song because they did not want to go over there and fight. When we'd sing that in a nightclub, they would just stand up and applaud forever. We went all over the world with that one song."

The group was able to make it three hits out of three releases when *Since I Lost You Girl* hit a lowly #117 on the pop chart, but the lack of a major hit necessitated the four group members undertaking other work in order to earn a living.

In the case of Richard Street, this meant a spell in Motown's Quality Control Department as well as touring with The Temptations to provide off stage vocal back-up for the increasingly unreliable Paul Williams.

The Monitors resumed their own recording career in 1968, with *Step By Step (Hand In Hand)* scheduled for release on the V.I.P. label in July 1968, only to eventually appear on the Soul label. The group also got to issue an album, with **Greetings! We're The Monitors** recalling their hit single from two years previously! However, since it gathered their singles from the previous three years (but not all of the flip sides) it lacked the consistency to do any real business. When Richard Street was eventually co-opted into The Temptations as a permanent replacement for Paul Williams in 1971, The Monitors had run their course and disbanded. The group partially reunited in the late 1980s (Richard Street was still a member of The Temptations at the time) and recorded an album for Ian Levine's Motorcity label. Richard Street, who married The Velvelettes' Cal Gillis in 1969 (they divorced in 1983) died after a lengthy illness on 26 February 2013.

ALBUM: GREETINGS! WE'RE THE MONITORS

PEDRO MONTERO

Mexican actor and singer Pedro Montero was born on 6 February 1942 and made his name locally before moving to the United States. There he appeared in the television movies 'Moonlight' and 'Falcon's Gold' as well as pursuing a singing career, being one of the first artists signed to Motown's Latin imprint. His only album, **Amor Secreto** produced by Manuel Acune in 1982 was described in Billboard magazine as 'The lush Motown treatment to this collection of Mexican songs on the side of the romantic ballad, but a pride and scorn number like *La Perfumada* proves that this suave ranchero can also hang tough.' Pedro died in Los Angeles on 28 March 1987, with his album being reissued in 1993 on CD and cassette.

ALBUM: AMOR SECRETO (1982)

MONK MONTGOMERY

The eldest of the three musical Montgomery brothers who would make a reputation in the field of jazz, William Howard Montgomery was born in Indianapolis, Indiana on 10 October 1921. Although Monk is widely regarded as the first musician to introduce the electric bass to jazz, his own professional career did not start until he was already 30 years of age. Indeed, it would appear that he was encouraged to pursue a career in music by his guitarist brother Wes, who came to fame touring with Lionel Hampton and worked an introduction to Hampton, with Monk subsequently becoming a member of the band in 1951. Wes and Monk would later link with another vibraphonist, their brother Buddy and record several albums as The Mastersounds and The Montgomery Brothers as well as forming the Montgomery Johnson Quintet with Alphonso Johnson. By 1969 Monk had signed with Chisa Records and his **It's Never Too Late** album would be the first album issued under the deal with Motown, recorded with The Jazz Crusaders and hitting the streets in January 1970. Monk recorded a follow up album, **Bass Odyssey** in May 1971 that variously featured Monk with Joe Sample (keyboards), Andy Simpkins (bass), Kent Brinkley (bass), Mike Carven (drums), Stix Hooper (drums) and Wayne Henderson (trombone), but by this time the Chisa and Motown deal was coming to an end, with Motown retaining the rights to all of the albums and singles issued during their tie-up. After freelancing with Cal Tjader, Monk returned to the recording studio in 1974 for an album on Philadelphia International before settling in Las Vegas, where he died from cancer on 20 May 1982.

ALBUMS: IT'S NEVER TOO LATE (1970), BASS ODYSSEY (1971)

MARION MOORE

Singer and performer Marion made her Broadway debut in 'Treemonisha' in 1975, a musical that ran for 64 performances at the Palace Theatre. Marion then landed the role of Martha in the following year's revival of 'Guys And Dolls', which would go on to become her only leading role on Broadway.

MORE HITS BY THE SUPREMES – THE SUPREMES [ALBUM]

The title might imply that this was something of a greatest hits package, but such was hit-making capabilities of The Supremes by 1965, the album was actually a standard LP release, the group's sixth. Yet it managed to live up to the title, producing three massive singles hits in *Stop! In The Name Of Love*, *Back In My Arms Again* (both of which topped the pop chart) and *Nothing But Heartaches*, a #11 pop and #6 R&B hit. Entirely written and produced by Holland-Dozier-Holland, **More Hits By The Supremes** became The Supremes' most successful album since **Where Did Our Love Go** in 1964. Shifting more than a million copies upon its release in July 1965, **More Hits** would hit #6 pop and #2 R&B, offering further proof that by 1965, The Supremes could do no wrong in the eyes of record buyers. In Britain the album was released in December 1965 but for some reason failed to chart at all, a surprise given the success the group enjoyed on the singles listings during the course of the year.

MOROCCO RECORDS

A short lived rock imprint that was active between 1983 and 1984, Morocco derived its name as a truncated version of Motown Rock Company. Among the artists who secured album releases were Duke Jupiter, Tiggi Clay, The Coyote Sisters, Wolf & Wolf and Kidd Glove as well as the soundtrack to 'Get Crazy'. When Morocco was closed down, both Duke Jupiter and Tiggi Clay were transferred over to the main Motown label.

MORROCCO MUZIK MAKERS

Formed by students at two Dayton, Ohio schools, Dunbar and Roosevelt, The Morrocco Muzik Makers originally got together in 1956. Although featuring an ever-changing line-up, the core members were Edward 'Little Woo Woo' Early (vocals), Jack Hart (organ), Earl McDaniel, Tyrone Harris and Ronald Green (saxophones), Melvin Owens (guitar), Don McWaters (percussion) and Ralph Hopper and Sonny Patterson (drums). Having made a name backing a number of visiting musicians, the group was offered a Motown deal, although not all the group agreed to the deal. Thus the group who journeyed to Detroit to record their one and only single in February 1963 were Early, McDaniel, Harris, Curtis Alexander and William Buckins (trumpets), Booker Dotson (organ) and Harold Williams (guitar). The group also took along future Ohio Players bass player Marshall Jones for the session, which would feature Marvin Gaye on drums and Martha & The Vandellas on background vocals. The Morrocco Muzik Makers single *Back To School Again* backed with *Pig Knuckles* was issued in August 1963, by which time the group was back in Dayton and performing behind other acts visiting the city.

THE MOTOR CITY CREW

Kerry Ashby Gordy and Benny Medina became friends at high school, with Benny eventually moving into the Gordy household, a move that would eventually provide the inspiration for the television series 'Fresh Prince of Bel-Air'. Both Benny (born on 24 January 1958, the son of legendary jazz drummer Ahmad Medina) and Kerry (born in Detroit on 25 June 1959, the son of Berry Gordy) became members of Apollo who recorded one album for Motown. Both then worked at Motown in the A&R department as writers and producers before coming up with the Motor City Crew project that saw the single *Let's Break* released in September 1983. Benny and Kerry both eventually left Motown for other positions in the industry, with Benny currently CEO of The Medina Company in artist management and Kerry forming Kerry Gordy Enterprises handling intellectual property and branding.

MOTOWN CHARTBUSTERS VOLUME 3 – VARIOUS ARTISTS [ALBUM]

By 1969 the Motown Chartbusters series had settled into something of a winning routine, with a release planned for around October each year, just in time for the traditional gift season of Christmas. This regular release pattern would be copied in years to come, most notably by the 'Now That's What I Call Music' series, proof that Tamla Motown was ahead of the game when it came to marketing and capitalising on buying habits.

The third volume of chartbusters, which dropped the 'British' tag but which was still heavily biased towards singles that had proven their worth in the UK, was presented in an eye-catching silver foil sleeve, whilst another radio DJ in Alan Freeman provided the liner notes. Easily the strongest line-up of tracks since the series began, the sixteen tracks included ten that had or would reach the Top Ten of the singles chart, including the chart-topper *I Heard It Through The Grapevine* by Marvin Gaye. The remaining six tracks also enjoyed a healthy chart presence, making **Motown Chartbusters Volume 3** an album that really lived up to its name. Released in October 1969, it entered the chart at #4 on 25 October and moved up to #2 the following week, nestling behind The Beatles' **Abbey Road. Volume 3** spent six consecutive weeks at #2 before briefly running out of steam, dropping down to #4 and then moving back up to #2, again behind The Beatles, on 17 January 1970. After slipping to #3 for two weeks, the album returned to #2, this time behind Led Zeppelin and their second album before finally being elevated to pole position on 14 February 1970.

That **Motown Chartbusters Volume 3** was a hugely popular album is not in any doubt since it sold sufficient copies to earn a gold disc and spent nearly two years on the listings (including 29 consecutive weeks in the Top Ten), but far more telling was the fact that in reaching number one, it became the first compilation album to top the British chart since the chart had been launched in 1956. It also ensured future volumes would be eagerly awaited by the record buying public.

MOTOWN CHARTBUSTERS VOLUME 4 – VARIOUS ARTISTS [ALBUM]

Motown Chartbusters Volume 4 might not have housed any singles chart toppers, and the number of Top Ten hits was down to a mere nine, but the album itself was still a solid and successful seller. Tony Blackburn returned to pen the accompanying liner notes, coining the phrase TTT (Tremendous Tamla Talent) to describe the delights that awaited the listener on the album. With the three earlier volumes having blazed a trail up the charts, the pressure was on for **Volume 4** to emulate previous editions; it entered the chart at #4 on 24 October 1970 and dethroned Led Zeppelin and their third album a week later to become only the second compilation to top the British album chart. The success of the series in general prompted a slew of copycat compilations, with Trojan's **Reggae Chartbusters** series perhaps the best known. **Motown Chartbusters Volume 4** meanwhile would spend some forty weeks on the chart, proof that Motown continued to weave its magic in the UK.

MOTOWN CHARTBUSTERS VOLUME 5 – VARIOUS ARTISTS [ALBUM]

Motown Chartbusters Volume 5 was the only album in the series that was not released to coincide with the traditional Christmas market, appearing in March 1971, some five months after its predecessor **Volume 4**. It was also the first album in the series to carry images of some of the artists on the front cover, offering proof that by March 1971 many of the artists who recorded for Tamla Motown were household names. Everything else about the album remained the same; sixteen tracks of which twelve were Top Ten hits, including the revived number one smash *Tears Of A Clown* by Smokey Robinson & The Miracles. The album was eagerly anticipated upon release, going on to debut on the chart in pole position, the only Motown connected album to achieve that feat, and would go on to register three weeks at the chart summit during the course of its 36 weeks on the chart.

MOTOWN CHARTBUSTERS VOLUME 6 – VARIOUS ARTISTS [ALBUM]

By the time **Motown Chartbusters Volume 6** hit the shops in October 1971, the British album chart had changed its rules, with numerous budget albums included in the listings. Many of these were soundalike cover versions by anonymous studio musicians, including one album, **Smash Hits Supreme Style** that carried the posing question 'Can you tell the difference between these and the original sounds?' That this album made #36 whilst **Hot Hits 6** and **Top Of The Pops Volume 18** topped the chart would suggest that many thousands of record buyers couldn't tell the difference, but the increased competition made the battle for chart honours even harder. Having briefly flirted with utilising images of the artists on **Volume 5**, **Volume 6** featured a futuristic image by legendary artist Roger Dean (perhaps best known for his album sleeves for Yes, Osibisa and Uriah Heep), with the reverse bearing the legend 'Motortown Review 2008'. The album entered the chart at its peak position of #2, immediately behind Rod Stewart and **Every Picture Tells A Story**, but despite spending a further eleven weeks in the Top Ten proved unable to go that one step further.

MOTOWN CHARTBUSTERS VOLUME 7 – VARIOUS ARTISTS [ALBUM]

As quickly as they arrived budget albums were once again excluded from the chart, but in their place came renewed competition, this time from the likes of K-Tel, Ronco and Arcade, whose heavily television promoted packages of dynamic, fantastic and star tracks took over the upper echelons of the chart. To combat this threat, EMI went to town with their packaging for **Motown Chartbusters Volume 7**, producing a gimmick slot machine cover that spun round to reveal three images of each artist in the window. However, with K-Tel in particular having an extremely strong presence on the chart (including all three top positions at one point), **Motown Chartbusters Volume 7** did well to even reach the Top Ten, peaking at #9 in its third week of chart action. It would go on to register sixteen weeks on the chart.

MOTOWN CHARTBUSTERS VOLUME 8 – VARIOUS ARTISTS [ALBUM]

Featuring a somewhat prophetic cover of an eclipse, **Motown Chartbusters Volume 8,** released in October 1973 was the last of the long running series to make the Top Ten of the British album chart, peaking at #9 and spending fifteen weeks on the listing, although sales were still sufficient to earn another gold disc. The series didn't come to an end with **Volume 8**, for **Volume 9** made #14 a year later, although subsequent volumes (10 in 1979, 11 in 1980 and 12 in 1982) failed to register. Fortunately, EMI and Tamla Motown came up with an alternative series, **Motown Gold** that ensured a continued chart presence. Over the years the Motown Chartbusters series proved to be extremely popular and huge sellers, a 'Now That's What I Call Music' for Motown music in the 1960s and 1970s. The continued popularity of the series can be gauged by the fact that all twelve albums were subsequently reissued on CD on the Spectrum label (part of Universal), and the original vinyl releases continue to sell well on sites such as ebay. The Telstar album Motown Chartbusters released in 1986 is not part of this collection.

A MOTOWN CHRISTMAS - VARIOUS ARTISTS [ALBUM]

Motown and its numerous artists had recorded Christmas material almost from the start of the label, with The Twistin' Kings (effectively The Funk Brothers recording under an assumed name) having included *Christmas Twist* for their debut album in December 1961. As the decade progressed, other artists recorded rather more standard Christmas material, such as *I Saw Mommy Kissing Santa Claus* (The Jackson 5), *Little Drummer Boy* (The Temptations), *Jingle Bells* (Smokey Robinson) and *White Christmas* (The Supremes). In 1968 Motown released **Merry Christmas From Motown**, an album that would hit #24 on the special Christmas chart Billboard published that year. Five years later, the album was expanded into a twenty four track double album package and, as **A Motown Christmas** would hit #1 on the same chart.

MOTOWN DANCE PARTY – VARIOUS ARTISTS [ALBUM]

One of the last Motown compilations released prior to the company's sale to MCA and Boston Ventures, **Motown Dance Party** was a double album featuring forty tracks. Compiled specifically for the European market, the album featured a wide cross section of hits, covering artists such as The Elgins, Mary Wells, The Four Tops, The Isley Brothers, Stevie Wonder, The Jackson 5 and The Temptations, among others. It would also become a major success, peaking at #3 on the UK album chart in May 1988, shortly before the change in chart rules that saw compilation albums being given their own chart. Sales of over 100,000 earned another gold disc.

MOTOWN GOLD – VARIOUS ARTISTS [ALBUM]

Released in October 1975, **Motown Gold** was a hugely successful compilation album, benefitting in particular from a rather adventurous sleeve design that attracted some considerable attention at the time. Containing eighteen tracks, all of them having previously been hits in the UK, the album would go on to reach #8 on the British album chart and attain gold status. The success of **Motown Gold** prompted the release of a second volume two years later, with **Motown Gold Volume 2** peaking at #28 and reaching silver status for sales in excess of 60,000 copies.

MOTOWN HISTORICAL MUSEUM

Long before Berry Gordy began formulating plans to move Motown out of its historic home in Detroit, another of the Gordy clan was busy filing and saving various artefacts connected with the label and its activities. Esther Gordy Edwards had been an executive at Motown, serving as a senior vice president and company secretary during the company's early, formative years. When Motown moved lock, stock and barrel to Los Angeles in 1972, Esther chose to remain in Detroit, where she continued to turn up for work each and every day, even as the rest of the organisation migrated or moved away around her.

Her days were invariably punctuated by knocks on the door at 2648 West Grand Boulevard, with virtually each and every caller wishing to have a glimpse of the legendary Studio A, the original recording venue where countless hours of memorable music had been created. Esther lost count of the number of visitors to the tiny complex but by 1985 the numbers turning up had not diminished but increased, with visitors coming from all four corners of the globe wishing to drink in the Motown magic for a while. It was then Esther contacted Berry and told him "Berry, I think we made history and didn't know it."

At this point the Hitsville USA building was converted in to a museum and was declared a Historic Site by the State of Michigan two years later, in 1987. Many of the early exhibits were those same artefacts Esther had saved from the rubbish tips many years previously, with the museum undergoing a complete overhaul in 1995 when a gallery was added, along with the early offices and the upper rooms, where Berry lived with his growing family, were similarly opened up to visitors.

The current mission of the museum is 'To preserve the history and legacy of Motown Records Corporation through the conservation of Motown's original site on West Grand Boulevard in Detroit, Michigan, U.S.A. To educate and motivate people, especially youth, through exhibitions and programs that promote the values of vision, creativity and entrepreneurship. To build awareness of the global impact of Motown and its artistic contributions to entertainment.' Esther Gordy Edwards continued to promote those values right up to her death on 24 August 2011, with the Motown Museum having received more than a million visitors since its opening.

MOTOWN PRODUCTIONS

Formed in 1968, Motown Productions initial focus was on television programming, in particular specials featuring the likes of Diana Ross & The Supremes and The Temptations in 'TCB' and 'G.I.T. On Broadway' in 1968 and 1969 respectively. Flush with the success of these two ventures, Motown Productions would be responsible for specials featuring The Temptations, Smokey Robinson, Diana Ross and The Jackson 5. The Jackson 5 would also be the subject of a successful cartoon series, aired on ABC between 1971 and 1973.

It was films, however, that interested Berry Gordy the most and, after looking through a considerable number of suitable film vehicles, finally settled on 'Lady Sings The Blues', a bio-pic on Billie Holiday starring Diana Ross that became a critical and commercial success. Diana Ross' second film venture, 'Mahogany' did not fare anywhere near as well, whilst her selection in the lead role in 'The Wiz' was roundly criticised, not least because she was felt to be too old for the role she played. Other Motown Productions met a mixed reception, ranging from the joint production with Casablanca FilmWorks 'Thank God It's Friday', 'Scott Joplin' (another bio-pic) and 'Big Time', which failed at the box office. There were some critical successes, however, with 'Bingo Long', 'Almost Summer' and 'The Last Dragon' well received. The failure of 'The Wiz' however forced Motown Productions to rethink its strategy, reverting back to the one area it knew well, television.

Here it racked up a considerable number of successes, including 'Motown 25' and 'Motown Returns To The Apollo', but it was not the same dominant force it had been during its formative years. Berry Gordy sold Motown Records to MCA in 1988 and a year later Motown Productions to Suzanne De Passe.

MOTOWN RECORDS

Tamla might have been the first label Berry Gordy founded as part of his empire, but it is the Motown brand that has proved the more iconic name.

"Because of its thriving car industry, Detroit had long been known as the 'Motor City'. In tribute to what I had always felt was the down-home quality of warm, soulful country-hearted people I grew up around, I used 'town' in place of 'city'. A contraction of 'Motor Town' gave me the perfect name, Motown."

Motortown would also be used in later years, although this was reserved for the tours and revues the early Motown pioneers undertook rather than a label name. The actual Motown label itself was launched in September 1959, by which time nine records had already appeared on the Tamla imprint, with varying degrees of success, with Marv Johnson and Eddie Holland's releases subsequently picked up by United Artists and Barrett Strong's *Money* had been leased to Anna Records. Motown's first single and the only time The Miracles appeared on the label ("My original plan was to put out all the solo artists on the Tamla label and the groups on the new Motown label" said Berry) was *Bad Girl*, which would get snapped up by Chess Records before the month was out, resulting in the first commercial release being The Satintones *My Beloved*, issued in October 1959.

Nearly a year later Motown would release its first major self promoted hit in Mary Wells' *Bye Bye Baby*, whilst the following year the same artist's release *I Don't Want To Take A Chance* became the first single to utilise the now famous Detroit map design (on later pressings) and have a picture sleeve. By then the whole company was known as Motown Record Corporation, which Berry incorporated on 14 April 1960, adopting the slogan 'The Sound of Young America'. Yet Motown came to be more than a name for a corporation or a label, it came to stand for an ideal and a sound, and not just in America; Motown would resonate around the world.

MOTOWN REVUE

It was Thomas 'Beans' Bowles who came up with the idea of sending Motown's acts out on the road as a revue, which he discussed with Berry and Esther at length during early 1962. Henry Wynne of Supersonic Attractions was responsible for booking the dates, which covered much of the USA but in a haphazard fashion. With all of the acts also managed by Motown's own in-house management company ITM, it would also mean vital cash for the company. The running order would depend on who had a hit record at any one time, whilst whoever performed better would be placed further down the roster.

On 22 October 1962, members of The Miracles, The Marvelettes, The Contours, The Supremes and The Vandellas and Marv Johnson, Marvin Gaye and Singing Sammy Ward, together with musicians led by Choker Campbell and tour manager/chaperone Beans Bowles set off from Detroit in a bus out into the unknown (Mary Wells also appeared on the tour, but as befitted her status as Motown's premier star, she was driven from venue to venue in her own car after she had attained some consistent chart success). On the bus, early demarcation zones were set; the musicians sat at the back, which they dubbed 'Harlem', while the artists and management personnel were seated at the front, dubbed 'Broadway.' Whilst the idea of sending virtually the entire Motown roster out on the road might have been appealing, both as a way of generating publicity and income, the overall experience was not what had been expected, as Beans Bowles explained.

"Berry packed far too many people on the bus. We were always overcrowded. And he booked way too many dates. The strain was bad. We had a bad accident in November '62, my driver was killed and we were lucky not to have others."

Beans Bowles was travelling ahead of the musicians from one gig in Greenville, South Carolina to another in Tampa, Florida and carrying the tour's earnings of some $15,000 in cash (contemporary reports stated a total of $3,387 was recovered in cash in two suitcases from the wreckage), when the car in which he was a passenger smashed into a station wagon, killing the driver Eddie McFarland instantly and trapping Beans inside the vehicle. Beans was later told in hospital that the first state patrolman to turn up to the site of the accident was the only honest one for some fifty miles – all of the money, vital to Motown, was still intact. Meanwhile, the artists were facing a different set of problems, both on the road and at their stop-off points.

"Every few days we would stop at a cheap motel to bathe and wash some clothes," said Mary Wilson. "We seldom got to sleep one in a bed, but compared to sleeping sitting up on a hard bus seat, being able to lie on any mattress was heaven. Living in cramped quarters, eating irregularly, going days without the most basic comforts – this was a baptism by fire, but none of us complained. With every bump in the road, bad meal, or sleepless night, we knew we were one step closer to being real professional performers, and we cherished every moment."

Perhaps not every moment, for when visiting the southern states, the party (musicians and artists alike) found that they could not buy food or book rooms because of their colour, a state of affairs that particularly angered Martha Reeves.

"It's an awful insult when you walk around and you got money and you can't eat."

On at least one occasion, southern hospitality extended to taking pot-shots at the bus (several of the party thought rocks had been thrown, only to discover the truth when they stopped a safe distance away and investigated further), but overall, despite the hardships and hassles, the tour was a success.

The dates on that historic tour were:

26 October – Howard Theater, Washington D.C.
2 November – Franklin Theater, Boston
3 November - New Haven Arena, New Haven Connecticut
4 November – Memorial Auditorium, Buffalo, New York
5 November – Raleigh City Auditorium, Raleigh, North Carolina
6 November – County Hall, Charleston, South Carolina
7 November – Country Club, Augusta, Georgia
8 November – Bamboo Ranch Club, Savannah, Georgia
9 November – National Guard Armoury, Birmingham, Alabama
10 November – City Auditorium, Columbus, Georgia
11 November – Magnolia Ballroom, Atlanta, Georgia
12 November – Fort Whiting Auditorium, Mobile, Alabama
13 November – State Fair Grounds, New Orleans, Louisiana
14 November – College Park Auditorium, Jackson, Mississippi
15 November – Memorial Auditorium, Spartanburg, South Carolina
16 November – City Armoury, Durham, North Carolina
17 November – Township Auditorium, Columbia, South Carolina
18 November – Capitol Arena, Washington Arena
19 November – Day off
20 November – Civic Auditorium, Greenville, South Carolina
21 November – Palladium, Tampa, Florida/The Palms, Bradenton, Florida
22 November – The Armoury, Jacksonville, Florida
23 November – Auditorium, Macon, Georgia
24 November – National Guard Armoury, Daytona Beach, Florida
25 November – Harlem Square, Miami, Florida
26 November – Skating Rink, Orlando, Florida
27 November – Field House, Tallahassee, Florida
28 November – Cheraw, South Carolina
29 November – Long High School, Charlotte, North Carolina
30 November – New Park Center, Louisville, Kentucky
1 December – Memorial Auditorium, Memphis, Tennessee
2 December – City Auditorium, Nashville, Tennessee
3 December – Fairground Coliseum, Pensacola, Florida
4 December – Day off
5 December – Mosque Auditorium, Richmond, Virginia
6 December – Day off
7 December – Apollo Theater, New York
8 December – Apollo Theater, New York
9 December – Apollo Theater, New York
10 December – Apollo Theater, New York
11 December – Apollo Theater, New York
12 December – Apollo Theater, New York
13 December – Apollo Theater, New York
14 December – Apollo Theater, New York
15 December – Apollo Theater, New York
16 December – Apollo Theater, New York
17 December – Syria Mosque, Pittsburgh, Pennsylvania

Despite the problems the Motortown Revue faced, it went out on the road again in 1963, and then, in 1965, spread its range even further. The Supremes had visited Britain for the first time in October 1964, shortly after the success of *Where Did Our Love Go* and just ahead of *Baby Love* topping the charts. They returned to Detroit and enthused to Berry Gordy about the reception they had received, prompting Berry to consider sending a revue over at some point the next year.

Working with British promoters Harold Davison and Arthur Howes, an ambitious tour of 21 dates across three weeks, to coincide with the launch of the Tamla Motown label, was arranged for March 1965. Headlined by The Supremes, the tour also featured Martha & The Vandellas, Stevie Wonder, Smokey Robinson & The Miracles, The Earl Van Dyke Six (who would back all of the other acts on the tour) and, to provide local interest, British group and special guests Georgie Fame & The Blueflames with compere Tony Marsh. Whilst the shows were well received critically, the attendances were somewhat sparse, as Mary Wilson later recalled.

"It was a flop. What's the use in denying it. The audiences were good but they were kinda thin. We didn't get too many people along. So, it's like being wise when it's too late, but in my opinion the show was too specialised for British audiences. We should have had a few more British groups with us. Another thing is that the British people wait until the end of a number before they show their appreciation. We found that a bit strange at first, but then we got used to it. Other times it's disappointing. You might be feeling good and you want everyone to be happy and sing."

The Supremes weren't the only ones disappointed, with one promoter later stating, "By the time people got to know how good the show was, the Revue had moved to another venue. I didn't make any money at all but I have to admit those Motown people know how to put on a very good show."

There were two shows at each of the venues, with the tour running as follows:

20 March – Astoria, Finsbury Park (6.40 & 9.10)

21 March – Odeon, Hammersmith (6.00 & 8.00)
22 March – Day off
23 March – Colston Hall, Bristol (6.30 & 8.45)
24 March – Capital, Cardiff (6.00 & 8.30)
25 March – Odeon, Birmingham (6.45 & 9.00)
26 March – ABC, Kingston (6.45 & 9.00)
27 March – Winter Gardens, Bournemouth (6.00 & 8.30)
28 March – Odeon, Leicester (5.40 & 8.00)
29 March – Day off
30 March – Odeon, Manchester (6.15 & 8.45)
31 March – Odeon, Leeds (6.20 & 8.40)
1 April – Odeon, Glasgow (6.40 & 9.00)
2 April – ABC, Stockton (6.15 & 8.30)
3 April – City Hall, Newcastle (6.30 & 8.45)
4 April – Empire, Liverpool (5.40 & 8.00)
5 April – Day off
6 April – ABC, Luton (6.30 & 8.45)
7 April – ABC, Chester (6.15 & 8.30)
8 April – City Hall, Sheffield (6.20 & 8.50)
9 April – ABC, Wigan (6.20 & 8.35)
10 April – Gaumont, Wolverhampton (6.30 & 8.40)
11 April – Gaumont, Ipswich (5.30 & 8.00)
12 April – Guildhall, Portsmouth (6.30 & 8.30)

MOTOWN SOUNDS

A studio project assembled by writer and producer Michael Lovesmith (as Michael L. Smith), featuring Michael, Sammy Burke and John Barnes (keyboards), Greg Peree, Jay Graydon, David T. Walker, Lee Ritenour and Roland Bautista (guitars), Jermaine Jackson, Henry Davis and Scott Edwards (bass), Dave Garibaldi, Ollie E. Brown and James Gadson (drums), Julius Wechter and Oliver Brown (percussion) and Gary Coleman and Michael Smith (synthesizers). The project would result in the album **Space Dance** in January 1979, with the title track being released as a single two months later.
ALBUM: SPACE DANCE (1979)

MOTOWN 25: YESTERDAY, TODAY, FOREVER (TV SPECIAL)

In early 1983, Motown Vice-President Suzanne De Passe concocted a plan to honour Motown's approaching twenty-fifth anniversary with a gala performance, featuring as many of the great and good artists as could be persuaded to reunite. The show was to be staged at the Pasadena Civic Auditorium in Los Angeles on 25 March 1983 (although this employed a little artistic licence, since the actual 25th anniversary should have been staged in 1984, not 1983), with the proceeds to be donated to the National Association of Sickle Cell Disease.

The first major problem for Suzanne and her team was that several of the major names they wished to feature had already departed Motown, including Marvin Gaye, Diana Ross, The Four Tops and, most notably, Michael Jackson and his siblings, whilst several others had effectively disbanded, including The Miracles and The Supremes. Whilst Suzanne's own, persuasive approaches were sufficient to get many of the former artists to reunite for the evening, several others would only do so if Berry Gordy asked them personally, most notably Marvin Gaye and Michael Jackson. And even then there were provisos, with Michael Jackson only agreeing to perform with his brothers if he was given a slot for his own post-Motown solo material. Faced with the prospect of having a Motown special without Michael Jackson, Berry acceded to the request.

Scripted by Buz Kohan, Suzanne De Passe and Ruth Robinson and hosted by Richard Pryor, the actual show ran for some five hours, which was edited for a one hour TV special for later broadcast. The special lived up to its name, with the highlights including Michael Jackson's performance of *Billie Jean* (he lip-synched the song, but it was his moonwalk dance routine that stole the plaudits, resulting in his then current album **Thriller** exploding sales wise) and The Four Tops and The Temptations trading vocal blows. By comparison, Adam Ant's version of *Where Did Our Love Go* was both surprising and embarrassing, although it was not helped by Diana Ross almost hijacking his performance by suddenly appearing on stage and dancing along.

"Being on the show was like Hollywood with people like Jack Nicholson in the front row. I thought I was doing all right when suddenly everybody cheered. I thought, great, I've cracked it. I turned around and ten yards away was Diana Ross dancing. I didn't know she was coming on. I go over to her, dance a bit and as I turn round, she's gone. What can you do to follow that?"

Diana had something to follow it, which although omitted from the television airing became the most talked about occurrence on the night. According to Mary Wilson, she and Cindy Birdsong had been told they would be introduced by Diana, at which point they were to enter the stage and join in on the song *Someday We'll Be Together*. Any doubts the audience may have had of lingering hostility between Diana and her former bandmates were dispelled by Diana's introduction; 'This is Cindy Birdsong, and *that's* Mary Wilson.'

"We started singing *Someday We'll Be Together*. Then something went wrong," Mary would later write in her autobiography. "Diana seemed genuinely confused. Attempting to distance herself from us, she took two steps closer to the audience. As agreed, Cindy and I stepped two paces forward too. Diana again moved forward; we followed. The third time it happened, Diana turned and forcefully shoved me aside. The audience gasped, appalled. Diana's eyes widened in shock at the realisation that I wasn't about to back down, and that all these people had just witnessed her little tantrum. She got so flustered she lost her place in the song, so I sang a line, thinking Diana would compose herself and assume the lead again in a few seconds. I kept singing lead. The only thing that she could think of doing was to begin to talk while I sang. She proceeded to speak to Berry, out in the audience. 'Berry, come on down,' I called whilst the music continued. With that comment, Diana grabbed my microphone and pushed it away from my face. 'It's been taken care of!' she snapped at me with fire in her eyes."

Out in the audience, a worried Suzanne De Passe quickly sent Smokey Robinson on to the stage to try and defuse the situation, although by the time he arrived on stage, Berry and a host of other artists had also convened for what would be the show's finale, *Reach Out And Touch (Somebody's Hand)*. Diana herself played down the contretemps after the show, preferring to focus on other aspects of the evening.

"It was amazing. There were some people there I hadn't seen in thirteen years. Berry Gordy is like a daddy to everybody who was there, and it was just real warm thoughts there. Like Michael and Stevie, they were all backstage with me, and seeing Billy Dee Williams after I hadn't seen him for a long time...and even Suzanne De Passe was crying backstage. It was just wonderful. I know that the people in the audience saw a glorious special but they didn't really see everything."

There was some criticism about the omissions, with Gladys Knight & The Pips, The Marvelettes, Edwin Starr and Jimmy Ruffin among the many artists excluded. The musicians who had made it all possible, The Funk Brothers, were also missing from the roll of honour (it was rumoured James Jamerson had to buy a ticket from a tout, but this was not the case, for he appeared backstage and talked with many of the artists he'd helped in his and their heyday), as were the numerous writers and producers. However, since it had proved impossible to pay tribute to all of those who had played their part in Motown's success story in the five hour recording, the hour long special only served to further highlight their omission.

The show was a major success when aired on NBC on 16 May 1983 and attracted an audience of 47 million, going on to win an Emmy Award for Outstanding Variety Program for its writers and director Don Mischer and producer Suzanne Coston. The show was released on video in 1991 (minus, of course, evidence of the Diana Ross and Mary Wilson bust-up, footage of which is said to reside in a safe to which only Berry Gordy and Suzanne De Passe have access) but has yet to appear on DVD, music and performance clearance issues said to be behind its non-appearance. Suzanne De Passe would later go on to organise Motown tributes to coincide with other anniversaries, although none had the magical moments like Michael Jackson's moonwalk, nor, thankfully, the confrontation between Diana and Mary.

Smokey Robinson & The Miracles Medley - *Shop Around-You Really Got A Hold On Me-Tears Of A Clown-Going To A Go-Go*
Speech Made By Dick Clark
Stevie Wonder Medley - *Uptight (Everything's Alright)-Signed, Sealed, Delivered I'm Yours-My Cherie Amour-Sir Duke-You Are The Sunshine Of My Life*
Songwriters Scene
Band Teaser
The Four Tops With And Versus The Temptations - *Reach Out (I'll Be There)- Get Ready-It's The Same Old Song-Ain't Too Proud To Beg-Baby I Need Your Loving-My Girl-I Can't Get Next To You-I Can't Help Myself (Sugar Pie, Honey Bunch)- (I Know) I'm Losing You*
Video Of Little Michael Jackson Singing Frank Sinatra
Marvin Gaye - *Yesterday, Today, Forever-What's Going On*
Martha & The Vandellas - *(Love Is Like A) Heat Wave*
DJ's Interlude
Mary Wells - *My Guy*
Junior Walker - *Shotgun*
T.G. Sheppard - *Devil In The Bottle*
Jose Feliciano - *Lonely Teardrops*
The Commodores - *Brick House*
Adam Ant - *Where Did Our Love Go*
Lionel Richie - *You Mean More To Me* [Taped Performance]
The Jacksons - *I Want You Back-The Love You Save-Never Can Say Goodbye-I'll Be There*
Michael Jackson - *Billie Jean*
Ballet Interlude
Motown Sound
Debarge - *The Way Of Love*
High Energy - *Pretender*
Smokey Robinson & Linda Ronstadt - *Ooh Baby Baby -*

The Tracks Of My Tears
Motown Singing
Smokey Robinson - *Being With You-Cruisin' Together*
Richard Pryor Speech
Diana Ross - *Ain't No Mountain High Enough*
Diana Ross & The Supremes - *Someday We'll Be Together*
Diana Ross & The Supremes - *Reach Out And Touch (Somebody's Hand)* [With Full Cast]

MOTOWNOPOLY

Produced by Late For The Sky in 2003, Motownopoly is based on the world's best selling board game Monopoly but with famous Motown tracks substituting for the traditional properties. The tokens are also changed to give a musical connection, featuring the likes of a guitar, saxophone, gold disc and jukebox. There is also a six track Motown CD to listen to whilst playing the game, but since the average Monopoly game lasts for 90 minutes, this will need to be played on repeat a fair number of times!

MOWEST RECORDS

Motown had a presence of sorts in Los Angeles from 1963, with Marc Gordon and Hal Davis establishing an office from which they arranged West Coast sessions for visiting Motown artists as well as scouring around for talent they could send east to Detroit. By the end of the 1960s however, Berry Gordy had in mind moving the entire Motown operation to California in order to be nearer to both the film and music industries, with the former very much headquartered in Los Angeles.

MoWest was set up in 1971 as something of an advance guard, with Berry hiring industry veteran Dave Pell to head up the new label. A noted jazz saxophonist, producer and a former president of the Grammy's, Dave Pell was an ideal frontman for the new label, attracting an eclectic mixture of artists to the label, including the blue eyed soul of Frankie Valli & The Four Seasons, hippy rock from Odyssey, garage rock from Lodi, jazz from The Crusaders along with more traditional R&B from the likes of The Commodores, Syreeta, Thelma Houston and G.C. Cameron.

The label would release a total of ten albums and 40 singles during its two year life, with a separate MoWest label also being formed in the UK, where in addition to the issuing material direct from their American counterparts, the label revamped the artist roster to include country artist T.G. Sheppard and made local signings such as The Rockits, Hetherington, Phil Cordell and Leo Bendix (whose single was not released). The biggest success the label scored was with the Tom Clay single *What The World Needs Now Is Love/Abraham Martin And John*, with many associated with MoWest feeling that as soon as any of their artists gained a modicum of success, they were quickly switched over to the mainstream Motown or Tamla labels, a fate that awaited The Commodores, Syreeta, Thelma Houston and G.C. Cameron. That is if they could get the initial promotional push, another major bone of contention between MoWest in California and Motown in Detroit.

MoWest was shut down in 1973, by which time Motown had transplanted itself in California. The imprint was retained in the UK until 1976, although the label had been effectively wound up a year previously. This extended lifespan did at least result in MoWest getting one single onto the British charts, with Frankie Valli & The Four Seasons' *The Night*, originally released in 1972 and reissued three years later becoming a Top Ten hit. In June 2011 Light In The Attic Records released a sixteen track compilation album, **Our Lives Are Shaped By What We Love: Motown's MoWest Story 1971-1973.**

SYLVIA MOY

One of nine children born to Floyd and Beulh Moy, Sylvia Rose Moy was born and raised in Detroit in 1939 and studied and performed jazz and classical music whilst at school, only to find greater fame writing songs when she got to Motown. Her best known work was for Stevie Wonder, co-writing such hits as *My Cherie Amour, I Was Made To Love Her, Uptight* and *Shoo-Be-Doo-Be-Doo-Da-Day*, with Sylvia also responsible for Stevie being retained by the label when he reached puberty; uncertain as to how his career might pan out, Berry Gordy was considering letting Stevie go but agreed to Sylvia's request that they try one more single on him and see how it went. That single turned out to be *Uptight*, resulting in a contract extension for Stevie. Sylvia was also the first female staff producer at Motown and would write hits for a number of other artists on the label. She did not pursue a recording career of her own until 1989 when she was briefly linked to Ian Levine's Nightmare label. Inducted into the Songwriters Hall of Fame in 2006, she continues to write and produce at her studio in Detroit.

IDRIS MUHAMMAD

Born Leo Morris in New Orleans, Louisiana on 13 November 1939, he learned to play the drums as a boy and became a professional musician at the age of sixteen. After playing with The Neville Brothers he became a well known drummer, appearing on sessions and dates with everyone from Fats Domino, Sam Cooke, Jerry Butler and Curtis Mayfield. In the 1960s he adopted a new moniker, Idris Muhammad, taking the name when he and his then wife Dolores 'LaLa' Brooks (a former member of The Crystals) converted to Islam. It was under this name that he made his reputation, particularly within jazz circles, although eager to expand his musical horizons Idris paid for lessons with Paul Barbarin, a former drummer with Louis Armstrong.

"All of the seasoned guys used to say if you want to learn how to play drums, you got to take lessons with Paul Barbarin. So I asked Mr. Barbarin to come to my house so I could take a lesson. He came by. He said 'OK, sit down at the drums and play the intro to *Bourbon Street Parade*.' He said play a waltz, and I played a waltz. He said play a mambo, and I played a mambo. He said play a cha-cha, and I played a cha-cha. He said, 'Listen, son. I'm a very busy man. One day you're gonna be a great drummer, but when they say to you that you're great, let it go in one ear and out the other ear. Now gimme my two dollars.'"

Eventually everyone came to realise how great Idris Muhammad was, working with artists in every musical genre and performing with the stage production of 'Hair'. His own recording career began with Prestige in 1970, and after two albums on that label joined Kudu, where he would record a total of four albums, of which two were distributed by Motown. **House Of The Rising Sun,** released in 1976 is widely regarded as his definitive album and proved extremely popular on both the jazz (a #24 hit) and R&B listings (it reached #51). The following year, **Turn This Mutha Out**, which contained a nod towards the growing disco scene, did even better, appearing on all three available listings in pop (#127), R&B (#16) and jazz (#17). Idris later recorded for Fantasy, Evidence and more recently Cannonball Records. He died on 29 July 2014.

ALBUMS: HOUSE OF THE RISING SUN (1976), TURN THIS MUTHA OUT (1977)
FURTHER READING: INSIDE THE MUSIC: THE LIFE OF IDRIS MUHAMMAD (2012)

GERRY MULLIGAN

Widely regarded as one of the greatest baritone saxophone players jazz ever produced, Gerry Mulligan's career spanned some five decades and took in collaborations with most of the greats. Born Gerald Joseph Mulligan in New York City on 6 April 1927, he began his career as an arranger for Tommy Tucker, Gene Krupa and, most notably Miles Davis. It was with Miles Davis that Gerry made his first recordings, appearing in the Birth Of The Cool nine piece band. In 1952 he formed a quartet whose other star member was Chet Baker, but Gerry's growing drug problem resulted in him being sent to prison and the original quartet disbanded, although following his release in 1954 he formed a new partnership with Bob Brookmeyer.

Over the following years Gerry would tour with his own quartet, sextet and Concert Jazz Band, recording extensively for a variety of labels as well as writing and arranging. In 1968 he joined Dave Brubeck's quartet, with whom he toured for the next four years or so. In 1974 he reunited with Chet Baker for a concert at New York's Carnegie Hall on 24 November, with Bob James (keyboards), John Scofield (guitar), Ron Carter (bass), Harvey Mason (drums) and Dave Samuels (vibraphone) the accompanying musicians for a concert that was recorded and released by as two separate albums by CTI in 1975 (the first would hit #22 on the jazz chart).

Gerry continued recording and touring for the next two decades, most notably a Rebirth of the Cool project following Miles Davis death, whilst his final recording was a quartet album issued in 1995, stretching his professional career beyond fifty years.

"I think I managed not to be an adult in just about every imaginable area. A band is most fun when you're in rehearsals. When you're working you have no time to enjoy it."

Gerry enjoyed his career and life right to the end, dying from complications following knee surgery on 19 January 1996.

ALBUMS: CARNEGIE HALL CONCERT (1975), CARNEGIE HALL CONCERT VOLUME TWO (1975)

DEE MULLINS

Born Dwight Mullinaux in Grafford, Texas on 7 April 1937, country singer Dee Mullins had his first stab at success with his wife, Patsy Simmons, recording a series of duets for Mercury, Dixie and D Records towards the end of the 1950s. By 1960 the pair had divorced, with Patsy leaving the music business and Dee was working solo. In 1964 he signed with Mel-O-dy, with Howard Hausey, who had previously written several hits for Johnny Horton, writing both sides of his only single for the company, *Love Makes The World Go Round* and *Come On Back (And Be My Love Again)*, which was released in January 1965. After this lack of success, Dee moved on, later recording several highly rated sides for Shelby Singleton's Plantation and SSS labels.

MURPH THE SURF (FILM SOUNDTRACK)

Jack Roland Murphy first found notoriety in October 1964 when he and his accomplices Alan Kuhn and Roger Clark robbed the American Museum of Natural History in New York of several artefacts, including the Star of India, Eagle Diamond and de Long Ruby. The gang was captured two days later and all of the items, with the exception of the Star of India, recovered. The heist earned Murphy a three year sentence and inspired the 1975 film 'Murph The Surf', with the soundtrack by Phillip Lambro appearing on Motown in June 1975.

Jack Murphy meanwhile had been unable to see the film made in his honour when it originally opened; in 1968 he was convicted of murder and attempted robbery and sentenced to life in prison. After he had participated in a prison chaplaincy programme, Bible studies and mentored other prisoners, the authorities reconsidered his status and, despite originally being given no chance of parole until 2225, Murphy was released on licence in 1986. The 'Murph The Surf' soundtrack was also released once again; Perseverance Records including it in their reissue programme of Phillip Lambro material in 2007.
ALBUM: MURPH THE SURF SOUNDTRACK (1975)

THE MUSIC MAKERS

The Music Makers were scheduled to release *Follow Me-Mother Nature* on MoWest in January 1973, although shortly before the record was issued, it was discovered there was another group with the same name. The Motown group changed their name to Marbaya to avoid any potential confusion.

MY CHERIE AMOUR – STEVIE WONDER [SINGLE]

One of Stevie Wonder's most endearing songs from his 1960s catalogue, *My Cherie Amour* endured a somewhat long and arduous journey before it finally found acceptance with the public. The song itself had been written in 1966, inspired by a then dancer girlfriend (as well as The Beatles' *Michelle*), and had been completed inside an hour. As was his style at the time, giving each and every one of his songs a female name, it was known as 'Oh My Marcia' and was given an early airing to Berry Gordy, who felt it had potential but would need the benefit of additional work from Stevie's in-house production and writing team of Hank Cosby and Sylvia Moy. It was Sylvia who would come up with the most significant change, amending the title from a song about Marcia to the more internationally favourable *My Cherie Amour.*

Yet even with all of the key elements in place, the recording and eventual release dragged on over a considerable time. Backing tracks were recorded at Hitsville in November 1967, with the strings and horns being added some ten days later. Stevie's vocals were recorded in January 1968, but the song didn't make an appearance until a year later, when it was coupled with *I Don't Know Why* and released as a single. For some reason, Motown opted to promote *I Don't Know Why* as the top side, with the single hitting #16 R&B and #39 pop. Tamla Motown in the UK made much the same move, with *I Don't Know Why* making #14 on the 'Record Retailer' chart when it was released in March 1969. Quite who was responsible for flipping the single remains lost in time, but soon after it began picking up radio plays, *My Cherie Amour* started its march back up the charts, hitting #4 on both the R&B and pop charts in the US.

By the summer of 1969, Stevie was touring the UK (his supporting act was female vocal group The Flirtations, with Stevie involved in a relationship with one of the members) and was surprised at the positive reaction *My Cherie Amour* received from the audiences. Tamla Motown wasted little time in re-promoting the single to radio, this time with *My Cherie Amour* as the plug side and were rewarded when it matched its chart performance in hitting #4 in August, becoming only his third Top Ten hit in the territory. Over the course of the ensuing years, *My Cherie Amour* has become one of the most popular songs in the Jobete catalogue, attracting cover versions from The Rolling Stones, The Jackson 5, Andy Williams, Engelbert Humperdinck, Quincy Jones and Smokey Robinson & The Miracles.

MY FRIENDS

Brought into Motown by Ralph Terrana, My Friends was formed around a nucleus of Ken Rich (guitar and vocals), Greg Kobe (keyboards and vocals) and Dave Kiswiney (bass and vocals) with a variety of personnel behind the drum kit. Whilst they recorded a number of tracks with the intention of recording an album, only one single was ever released on the Rare Earth label, the Ken Rich penned *I'm An Easy Rider* backed with *Concrete And Clay* being issued in August 1971. The group disbanded soon afterwards, with Kiswiney going on to play with Ted Nugent.

MY GIRL – THE TEMPTATIONS [SINGLE]

The Temptations might have registered five R&B hits by the time 1965 came around, but only one of these, *The Way You Do The Things You Do* had been a significant hit, topping the R&B chart and crossing over to #11 pop. What they needed now to really kick start their career was a major hit, one that would have the ability to top both charts, and it was a task that their then writer and producer Smokey Robinson had made a major priority. According to Smokey, he and fellow Miracle Ron White came up with the song while the group (The Miracles) was on the road and performing at the Apollo Theater.
"I was going in different directions with The Temptations at that time because Paul Williams and Eddie Kendricks had done all the lead vocalising at that point, and I knew David was a dynamic singer. We wanted to try some songs with David and *My Girl* was the very first one."
In 'The Temptations' television series, Smokey is shown going through the song line by line and the group pretty much falling for its obvious appeal immediately. However, it does seem somewhat strange that The Miracles did not keep the song for themselves, for their last single had been a major chart disappointment.
Whatever the reason, the track as produced by Smokey and Ron worked to perfection, setting a standard for future Temptations releases that would last for more than a decade. And, just as he had set out to do, Smokey had crafted a song that could and did top both the R&B and pop chart, spending six weeks on top of the former and one week the latter (it would also pick up a Grammy nomination for Best Rhythm & Blues Recording). In the UK, where it became The Temptations first hit, it had to settle for a rather more modest #43 first time around.

The song, of course, would go on to become something of a standard in music circles, having been taken back into the charts by the likes of Eddie Floyd, Otis Redding, Hall & Oates, The Whispers, Suave and, with the other half of the male/female divide written by Smokey and Ron, *My Guy,* by Amii Stewart and Johnny Bristol (Amii would revisit the medley in 1986 with Don Estus). Finally, in 1991, having been featured in the Macauley Culkin film 'My Girl', The Temptations version finally achieved its rightful place on the UK chart, hitting #2 in February 1992 for two weeks, kept off the top by *Stay* by Shakespear's Sister.

MY GUY – MARY WELLS [SINGLE]

Mary Wells' career had hit something of a drought during the latter stages of 1963, one that continued into the early months of the following year. The search for an elusive hit had seen her handed over to writers and producers other than Smokey Robinson, but nothing that was recorded sounded much like a major hit, resulting in Berry Gordy deciding that come March 1964, the company would release an album of all the previously unreleased material in order to try and recoup some of the recording costs. When the album was cobbled together, it was discovered that it was a track or two light, so Smokey was asked to come up with some material that would pad it out. The song Smokey came up with was *My Guy*.
"I can look at a lot of things from a woman's point of view. I grew up with women after all, my mom, my two sisters, my nieces, and I'm a life observer. For *My Guy*, I pictured Mary, a woman who was a star already, with a boyfriend who was a miner or a factory worker. Naturally, she had lots of guys trying to lure her away, but she was devoted."
On 2 March 1964, Smokey gathered the cream of Hitsville musicians, including Eddie Willis (guitar), James Jamerson (bass), Johnny Griffith (piano), Benny Benjamin (drums), Dave Hamilton (vibes), Herb Williams, Russ Conway and John Wilson (trumpets) and George Bohanon and Paul Riser (trombones) to lay down the musical accompaniment. A day later, Mary Wells and The Andantes came in to lay down the vocals, with Mary virtually hoarse by the end of the session as she delivered what is regarded as one of her finest ever performances. It was obvious as soon as *My Guy* was completed that this was no ordinary, throw away album track but a majestic return to form for Mary, Smokey and Motown.
Released just ten days later, on 10 March 1964, *My Guy* exploded onto the charts, becoming Mary's first

#1 hit (it would top both the R&B and pop chart, for seven and two weeks respectively) and, for added good measure, become Motown's first UK hit when it was issued on the Stateside label, hitting #5. Its UK performance was aided by Mary's presence in the country on tour with The Beatles, but *My Guy* was such an instant hit it would probably have become a hit even if she had been absent. Such was the single's success, Berry Gordy handed out bonuses to all those involved, with The Andantes collecting $500 for their contribution, their very first recording bonus. Those involved weren't to know it, of course, but *My Guy* would become Mary's last solo single for Motown; not long after its success, her manager and husband succeeded in luring her away from the label.

The song meanwhile has attracted a considerable number of successful cover versions, ranging from Petula Clark (a #70 hit in 1971), Sister Sledge (#23 in 1982) and, as noted above, as part of a medley with *My Girl* for Amii Stewart & Johnny Bristol (#63 in 1980).

MY LOVE – LIONEL RICHIE [SINGLE]

The third single lifted off Lionel Richie's debut solo album, after *Truly* and *You Are, My Love* continued his rich vein of chart form, at least as far as the US was concerned. Featuring country singer Kenny Rogers on backing vocals, *My Love* was another of Lionel's attempts to cross over to other areas of music, away from his R&B roots. It succeeded too, hitting #5 on the pop chart and topping the Adult Contemporary Chart as well as making a respectable #6 on the R&B chart following its release in April 1983. In the UK it was a rather more modest hit, peaking at #70.

MY OLD PIANO – DIANA ROSS [SINGLE]

"Bernard and I talked endlessly with Diana, went to her apartment to see who this woman was. Once we met her and became friends, she started to reveal things about herself that no one knew. No one understood that she was driven, complex and intellectual."

Nile Rodgers and Bernard Edwards were already hot on the charts with their own recordings and outside production work for Sister Sledge and Norma Jean when they were drafted in to work similar magic on Diana Ross, taking their inspiration from what she said and what they observed.

"When I went to her apartment and saw the grand piano, I didn't know if she played it or not, and I didn't care. Feeling it in the space makes you know something else about a person. So I was writing based on compiling Diana Ross information."

That information would surface as *My Old Piano*, the second track on the second side of the album **diana**. After *Upside Down* had become a major hit both sides of the Atlantic, attention turned to the follow-up. Whilst the US went from *I'm Coming Out*, which had already gained notoriety among her large gay following, in the UK *My Old Piano* was selected, being coupled with *Where Did We Go Wrong* (an old album track from 1978) and was released on both 7" and 12" in September 1980.

Again finding favour in the clubs, *My Old Piano* would return Diana to the Top Ten in the UK, peaking at #5. The difference between the two markets can be gauged by the fact that when eventually released in the US in January 1982 it bubbled under at #109, although by then Diana was no longer a Motown artist, which may have affected whatever promotional muscle the company put behind the single.

MY WHOLE WORLD ENDED (THE MOMENT YOU LEFT ME) – DAVID RUFFIN [SINGLE]

According to the Motown logs, *My Whole World Ended* had originally been intended for The Temptations, where David Ruffin would have sung lead (those same logs also show the musical backing tracks to have been recorded in July 1968 and assigned to The Temptations). It is debatable as to whether the track would have been released as a single by The Temptations however, as Norman Whitfield had a vice like grip on the group at the time and was churning out hit after hit.

In the event, David Ruffin did get to lead on the song; it became his solo debut following his departure from The Temptations in June 1968. After being dismissed from the group, David's intention had been to leave Motown altogether, but when he broached the subject with the hierarchy found they expected him to honour his management contract with International Talent Management which had been signed in October 1966 and was valid all the way through to October 1970. Thus David found himself still bound to the company (although in an attempt to keep him onside, Berry Gordy switched him from the Gordy label to Motown), being handed over to Johnny Bristol and Harvey Fuqua for his debut recordings, with the pair penning his debut along with Pam Sawyer and Jimmy Roach.

Joining David in the studio for the session in November 1968 were The Originals, who provide the backing vocals for *My Whole World Ended*, with the single being coupled with *I've Got To Find Myself A Brand New Baby* and being released in January 1969. David's distinctive vocal, still recognisable to music fans as the recently departed Temptations singer, helped turn the song into a major hit, hitting #2 R&B and #9 pop, an impressive performance first time out. Unfortunately, it would be another six years before he reached such heights again.

MY WORLD IS EMPTY WITHOUT YOU – THE SUPREMES [SINGLE]

Whilst much of Holland-Dozier-Holland's early success with The Supremes (and to an extent The Four Tops) came by re-using bits and pieces of music from one song to the next, this is more likely an example of the lyrics of one song inspiring a whole new song. The phrase 'This world is empty without you' was utilised in the song *Darling Baby*, which was originally intended for The Supremes but subsequently recorded by The Elgins in October 1965 (it would appear as the flip side to *Put Yourself In My Place*). Eddie Holland affected a slight change of emphasis to 'My world is empty without you', with the backing tracks recorded eight days after *Darling Baby* and the vocals some six weeks later.

Irrespective of when the vocals were recorded, one missing element was Flo Ballard. It is not known whether she was not informed of the session or was staging her own, silent protest at what she perceived was a snub by removing her torch song *People* from The Supremes' live show (although the song would be reinstated but with Diana performing lead), but for whatever reason, Flo failed to show up for the recording at Hitsville. Rather than wait for her arrival, HDH drafted in The Andantes' member Marlene Barrow to perform Flo's part.

Of course, The Andantes were already performing on pretty much every Supremes record anyway, with Diana's voice the only one that was said to be irreplaceable. The end result was such that no one could tell the difference on record, perhaps the first step in Flo's eventual departure from the group. Whilst not as immediate as some of The Supremes' earlier hits, *My World Is Empty Without You* still performed well, hitting #10 R&B and #5 pop, although for some reason it missed the chart altogether in the UK, an unwanted feat that only *Nothing But Heartaches* had previously achieved.

THE MYNAH BIRDS

When Toronto band The Sailorboys folded in 1964, its members wasted little or no time in putting together a new band, with Jimmy Livingstone (born in Nova Scotia on 28 February 1938, vocals) being joined by Ian Goble (guitar), Goldy McJohn (born John Raymond Goadsby in Toronto on 2 May 1945, keyboards), Nick St Nicholas (born Klaus Karl Kassbaum in Plon, Germany on 28 September 1943, bass) and Rick Cameron (drums), with James Ambrose Johnson (born in Buffalo, New York on 1 February 1948), who went by the name Ricky James Matthews, joining soon after.

They adopted the name The Mynah Birds at the suggestion of early manager Colin Kerr and recorded their first single, *The Mynah Bird Hop* for Columbia in Canada in late 1964. Whilst recording success proved elusive, the band got encouraging reviews for their live work, eventually leading to a seven year contract with Motown in January 1966. By this time the group consisted of Ricky, John Taylor (born John Yachemac in Welland, Ontario on 12 June 1946, rhythm guitar), Neil Young (born in Toronto on 12 November 1945, guitar), Bruce Palmer (born in Toronto on 9 September 1946, bass) and Rickman Mason (born in Brantford, Ontario on 2 December 1945, drums), with the group being quickly put into the studio to record *It's My Time*, a song written by Ricky with in-house writers Mike Valvano and R. Dean Taylor.

The single, to be coupled with *Go On And Cry* was scheduled for release in March 1966 but was subsequently cancelled when problems began mounting. The group's manager, Maury Selman, had been paid an advance that was supposed to cover the recording of a whole album, but he had pocketed it. When the group sacked him, he retaliated by informing Motown that Ricky was in fact AWOL from the US Navy and there was an outstanding warrant for his arrest. Motown told him to give himself up, which he did and would spend a year in naval prison.

With the head of the band out of action, Young and Palmer saw no point in hanging around, selling their equipment and heading for California where they would eventually form Buffalo Springfield, with that group evolving into Crosby Stills Nash & Young. Ricky would eventually return to Motown in 1968 where he became an in-house writer and later, as Rick James, one of its star recording artists. Jimmy Livingstone died on 1 June 2002. John Taylor died on 27 September 2002. Ricky Matthews/Rick James/James Johnson died on 6 August 2004. Bruce Palmer died on 1 October 2004.

N

NATHAN JONES – THE SUPREMES [SINGLE]

Penned by staff writers Kathy Wakefield and Leonard Caston, *Nathan Jones* might well have remained little more than an album track but for an experiment in the studio. Frank Wilson had recorded the song for inclusion on The Supremes' forthcoming album **Touch** and was at Hitsville one night when engineer Russ Terrana offered to show him a phasing technique he had developed. Taking a tape at random from the pile that made up the forthcoming album but intending to use the technique on another, perhaps unrecorded track, both men agreed the effect was good enough to be retained on the final mix of *Nathan Jones*. The actual recording featured Jean Terrell on lead vocals, supported by Mary Wilson, Cindy Birdsong and, uncredited, Clydie King of The Blackberries, with the end result something of a favourite of Mary Wilson's.

"*Nathan Jones* was the most unusual hit of our career, with its unorthodox blues-based structure and unison lead singing. Jean's vocals are pulled out of the mix ever so slightly, then our three voices break into harmony. As with almost everything Frank did for us, we loved this the minute we heard it. The psychedelic electric guitar and electronically treated vocals made *Nathan Jones* a great, unique record."

Whilst the single was something of a minor success in the US (where it would peak at #8 R&B and #16 pop following its release in April 1971), it found its true home in the UK, where the mix of a sixties feel with seventies sound effects was enough to propel it to #5 on the chart, thus becoming the 25th British chart hit of The Supremes career.

In 1988 the song was covered by Bananarama and taken to #15 on the UK chart. The only serious chart rival to The Supremes in terms of hits scored, Bananarama had previously enjoyed a major hit in 1982 with another old Motown number, The Velvelettes' *He Was Really Saying Something*.

NATURAL HIGH - COMMODORES [ALBUM]

The success of **The Commodores** album (released as **Zoom** in the UK) gave the group two mountains to climb with their next release; would there be anything as uplifting as *Brick House* or as sublime as *Easy* on their follow-up album?

In the event, The Commodores probably bettered the ballad but couldn't find anything quite as good on their up-tempo material. Right from the release of the album **Natural High**, one track stood head and shoulders above all others, with Lionel Richie surpassing himself on *Three Times A Lady*. The album was released in May 1978, *Three Times A Lady* being issued the same month in the US, with the single helping the album and vice versa; the album would eventually hit #3 pop and top the R&B chart (their third such chart topper).

In the UK the album was also released in May, but in an attempt to aid album sales, Motown opted to issue *Flying High* as the lead single, even though *Three Times A Lady* was already on heavy rotation across the radio stations. Whilst the ruse may not have helped the single too much (it stalled at #37), the delay in releasing the single certainly aided the album, which would go on to become the group's first Top Ten success in the UK, peaking at #8 and earning a gold disc for sales in excess of 100,000 copies.

NATURAL RESOURCE RECORDS

Launched in 1972 with the slogan 'Natural Sounds For Natural People', the Natural Resource label was originally used for the company's rock artists, although geared more towards the soft rock market. The label was initially operative for eight months, during which time it released a total of seven albums, by Two Friends, Heart, Corliss, Gotham, Road, Earthquire and Northern Lights. The label was then inactive for three years before being revived for an album by Gaylord & Holiday, only to be shut once again. It was revived a second and final time in 1978 when it became something of a reissue label before being shuttered for good in August 1979.

THE NATURALS

The sudden rise in popularity of The Stylistics effectively ended any chance V.I.P. signed act The Stylists had for achieving notoriety, with their only single *What Is Love* disappearing without trace soon after release in June 1971. The group, fronted by John Barnett (who worked during the day as a manager of a fast food restaurant) settled into a routine of doing backing vocals around Motown until they got a second shot at stardom, with Dino Fekaris and Nick Zesses writing and producing both sides of their September 1972 Motown single *The Good Things (Where Was I When Love Came By)* backed with *Me And My Brother*. In an attempt to distance themselves from the earlier release, the group was rechristened The Naturals, but this too proved problematic; an Atlanta, Georgia group formed by Johnny Simon, Robert Fitzpatrick Jr., Michael Williams and William Thomas beat them onto the chart with their Calla Records hit *I Can't Share You*. Rather than share the name, the Motown group disbanded, with guitarist and singer Edward Arrington Jr. heading off for a solo career in New York.

JERRY NAYLOR

Jerry Naylor's main claim to fame is that he became lead singer with The Crickets following Buddy Holly's death in 1959, linking up with Jerry Allison, Sonny Curtis and Glen Hardin in the reformed Crickets in 1960. Jerry (born Jerry Naylor Jackson in Chalk Mountain, Texas on 6 March 1939) would go on to front several international hits over the next five years before launching a successful solo career in 1965.

This would eventually bring him to Motown in 1974 and the Melodyland and Hitsville labels, where he released seven singles and an album, with **Love Away Her Memory** being aimed at the country market. *Is That All There Is To Honky Tonk,* released as a single on Melodyland in November 1974 made most headway, hitting #27 on the country chart, although *If You Don't Want To Love Her* on MC in January 1978 made #37 on the same listing.

In more recent times, Jerry has revealed that he used his international fame as a singer as something of a cover for work as a secret agent for the CIA, undertaking some hundred or so missions after he had been recruited in 1968.

ALBUM: LOVE AWAY HER MEMORY (1977)

NEITHER ONE OF US (WANTS TO BE THE FIRST TO SAY GOODBYE) – GLADYS KNIGHT & THE PIPS [SINGLE]

Jim Weatherly attended the University of Mississippi on a football scholarship, where he would become All Southeastern Conference Quarterback. Despite his abilities as a footballer, Jim had dreams of becoming a successful musician, moving to Los Angeles in 1966 with his rock band The Gordian Knot. Widely feted, with the likes of Nancy Sinatra singing their praises, they were tipped for stardom but their only album for Verve sank without trace.

Jim then turned to songwriting, with one of his compositions being picked up by producer Joe Porter, slated to helm an album on Gladys Knight & The Pips. That song was *Neither One Of Us*, which had a distinct country flavour (although Gordian Knot had been soft rock), which he subsequently presented to Gladys and the Pips for consideration. The group worked out the vocal harmonies, with Porter organising the backing tracks, which featured the cream of Los Angeles' session musicians. The Pips had half finished the track and were due to fly back to Detroit when they did an about-turn and returned to the studio in order to complete the song that night, so convinced were they that they had a potential hit on their hands.

Released in December 1972, the single appeared just as the Pips' contract with Motown was about to expire, so if the single became a major hit, it would only serve to strengthen their bargaining power. *Neither One Of Us* duly became a smash, topping the R&B chart for four weeks (their third such chart topper after *I Heard It Through The Grapevine* and *If I Were Your Woman*) and hitting #2 on the pop chart (although it only peaked at #31 in the UK). Yet Motown showed little or no interest in bettering the contract offer that was already on the table, and with Gladys Knight & The Pips unprepared to accept the terms, either financially or creatively, opted to leave and sign with Buddah.

Wisely, they took Jim Weatherly with them; he would pen subsequent hits *Midnight Train To Georgia* and *Where Peaceful Waters Flow* and earn a recording contract with Buddah as well. *Neither One Of Us* would go on to earn Gladys and the Pips a Grammy Award for Best Pop Vocal Performance, Group, their first success after three previous nominations. The country sensibilities of *Neither One Of Us* were satisfied in 1973 when Bob Luman scored a #7 country hit, whilst in 1982 David Sanborn gave the song a jazz treatment.

NEITHER ONE OF US – GLADYS KNIGHT & THE PIPS [ALBUM]

Despite *Neither One Of Us* shaping up to become one of the biggest hits of Gladys Knight & The Pips'

Motown career, the company showed little or no interest in negotiating a better deal. The Pips were discontent with playing second fiddle at Motown, where they were seldom given access to the top writers or producers (Jim Weatherly, who penned *Neither One Us*, was discovered by producer Joe Porter), quite apart from the financial rewards they were receiving, which were well below what the group thought they were worth. Thus the album, titled after the hit single, was a contract fulfilling album as far as the group was concerned, comprising material produced by five producers or teams and material largely drawn from the Jobete catalogue.

The exceptions were *Neither One Of Us*, of course, and *Who Is She (What Is She To You)*, a gender change from the Bill Withers original. Despite the lack of any real continuity, the album did well in the aftermath of the single, hitting the top of the R&B chart and even crossing over to hit #9 on the pop chart, making it the best selling and best performing album of their entire seven year Motown career. By the time the album sales really began to kick in, Gladys and the Pips had moved on to Buddah Records, although they would become embroiled in a legal battle with Motown over unpaid royalties for this and previous recordings.

FRANCES NERO

The same talent contest that had brought Carolyn Crawford into the Motown fold was also responsible for getting Frances Nero a brief contract. Born in Asheville, North Carolina on 13 March 1943, Frances was married with two young children at the time she entered the WHCB sponsored contest, which by now was decided purely on performance and talent (no bread wrappers to submit!), with Frances beating future Motown artist Ronnie McNeir in the final reckoning. Her prize ended up as a single release on the Soul label (hers was the first Soul single to use the 'swirl' design), *Keep On Lovin' Me* backed with *Fight Fire With Fire*, with both tracks having originally earmarked for The Marvelettes. This single did little upon its release and Frances spent three frustrating years at Motown trying to get another single out. Eventually she asked to be released from her contract and after a brief deal with the Crazy Horse label settled back into life as a housewife.

Whilst that is effectively the end of Frances' story with regards to Motown, fate still had a trick in store; *Keep On Lovin' Me* would become a firm favourite on the Northern Soul scene (although unissued as a single in Britain, it would appear on the 1973 compilation *Motown Disco Classics Volume Four*) and when Ian Levine launched Nightmare Records recording former Motown artists, Frances was one of those coaxed out of retirement. One of her recordings, *Footsteps Following Me,* an original written by Ian with Steven Wagner and Ivy Jo Hunter was recorded for Nightmare in 1990 but remixed and reissued on Debut the following year, hitting #17 on the UK charts.

NEVER CAN SAY GOODBYE – THE JACKSON 5 [SINGLE]

Long before he found fame as an actor, Clifton Davis wanted to be a songwriter and had put together a small portfolio of songs that he hawked around a number of publishers. One of these happened to be Jobete, for whom he auditioned a number of potential songs, including one entitled *Never Can Say Goodbye*. Fortunately for Clifton, the thin walls at the company's base on Sunset Boulevard meant that the piano playing carried into the next room, in which legendary producer Hal Davis (no relation) was trying to conduct a meeting with Jerry Marcellino.

Intrigued by the melody and convinced it was a hit, Hal called an abrupt end to his meeting and popped next door to ensure he got first option on the song. Introduced to Clifton, he promised to record the song immediately on The Jackson 5, heading into the studio at the Sound Factory that very night with arranger Gene Page to lay down the backing tracks. Two days later he brought The Jackson 5 in record their vocals, extracting a dynamic performance from the group.

Excited with what he had got on record, Hal played the potential single to the various departmental heads at Motown, only to find that whilst they loved the song and thought it a hit, they didn't think it right for The Jackson 5. The song, so they said, was 'too adult', a radical departure from the kind of teenage love songs that had proved so successful in the past. A month slipped by with Hal getting no nearer to securing a release before he opted to try the same kind of technique that had been responsible for him obtaining the song in the first place. After another rejection, Hal returned to his office, had a couple of drinks for Dutch courage and put the acetate on the record player, turning the volume right up in the process. In the very next office was Berry Gordy, who heard the single and rushed into Hal to tell him it was a smash.

Countermanding the order to hold the single, Berry arranged for it to be released in March 1971, with it going on to top the R&B chart and #2 pop as well as hitting #33 in the UK. The song itself would pick up a nomination for Best Rhythm & Blues Song (one of three Motown nominations in the category that year, alongside *If I Were Your Woman* and *Smiling Faces Sometimes*) although was beaten on the night by Bill Withers' *Ain't No Sunshine*. Almost from release, *Never Can Say Goodbye* attracted cover versions, with Isaac Hayes, Andy Williams and Smokey Robinson & The Miracles all releasing versions. The most notable covers have been by Gloria Gaynor in 1974, who turned the song into a disco smash, and a Hi-NRG version in 1987 by British group The Communards.

NEVER HAD A DREAM COME TRUE – STEVIE WONDER [SINGLE]

Written by Stevie with long term collaborators Hank Cosby and Sylvia Moy, *Never Had A Dream Come True* had been penned in early 1967, with the initial backing tracks being laid down at Hitsville in February of that year. Strings were added a year later, but for some reason the track sat in the can for more than two years before being resurrected in late summer 1969, at which point Stevie recorded his lead vocal. It was originally intended for release as Tamla 54188 in September 1969 until the company opted to revive another old recording in *Yester-Me Yester-You Yesterday* (which was an even older track, having been recorded in January 1967), which became a major international smash and restored Stevie to the upper reaches of the chart.

Never Had A Dream Come True was eventually released (as Tamla 54191) in January 1970 as the follow-up, and whilst it struggled to replicate the American success of its predecessor, having to settle for a #11 R&B and #32 pop position, it maintained Stevie's profile in the UK. No doubt aided by the Northern Soul flavoured flip side *Somebody Knows Somebody Cares*, the single would crack the Top Ten, peaking at #6 following its UK release in March 1970.

NEW YORK JAZZ QUARTET

Pianist Roland Hanna (born in Detroit, Michigan on 10 February 1932) first formed the New York Jazz Quartet in the early 1970s, despite the fact the name had been used towards the end of the 1950s by another group fronted by flautist Herbie Mann. Roland's group also utilised a flute player in Hubert Laws (born in Houston, Texas on 10 November 1939), along with noted bass player Ron Carter (born in Ferndale, Michigan on 4 May 1937) and drummer Billy Cobham (born in Panama on 16 May 1944).

Despite the pedigree of the individual players, this incarnation of the New York Jazz Quartet did little, resulting in Roland disbanding this line-up in 1974 and re-assembling the group with tenor saxophone and flautist Frank Wess (born in Kansas City, Missouri on 4 January 1922), initially retaining Ron Carter but subsequently replacing him with George Mraz (born in Czechoslovakia on 9 September 1944) and drummer Ben Riley (born in Savannah, Georgia on 17 July 1933), with Richard Pratt and Grady Tate filling in for Riley whenever he was indisposed.

This version of The New York Jazz Quartet signed with Creed Taylor's Salvation label, for who they would record one album marketed and distributed by Motown, **Concert In Japan.** Recorded in the Kaikan Hall in Tokyo on 2 April 1975, the album was released later the same year but did little. Roland would also record three other albums for Salvation fronting a trio, although these were only released in Japan. Given an honorary knighthood by President William Tubman of Liberia and known as Sir Roland Hanna for much of his career, he died on 13 November 2002.

ALBUM: CONCERT IN JAPAN (1975)

ALLAN NICHOLLS

Ultimately to find greater recognition within the film world, Allan Nichols had a successful musical career too. Born in Montreal, Canada on 8 April 1945, he helped form J.B. & The Playboys who signed with RCA in 1964 and scored several hit singles in Canada. The group name changed in May 1966 to The Jaybees (to avoid confusion with Gary Lewis & The Playboys), initially still with an RCA recording contract but switching to Columbia the following year. Allan then formed The Carnival Connection in August 1967, recording briefly for Capitol before moving to New York where he landed the part of Claude in the musical 'Hair'. The notoriety of the musical was sufficient to get him a number of recording deals, including a chart hit on Avco Embassy and a release on Rare Earth, *Coming Apart* (which holds the distinction of being the first Motown related single released in stereo) being issued in November 1970. Thereafter Allan concentrated on his film career, appearing in 'Popeye', 'A Perfect Couple' and 'Cradle Will Rock' and directing 'Dead Ringer' and 'I Am A Hotel'.

NICK & THE JAGUARS

Hailing from Pontiac, Michigan, Nick & The Jaguars are likely to have already crossed Berry Gordy's path before getting a chance to record under their own name, for the group had recorded as The Biscaynes for the Ridge label (a label that many believe was owned or at least part-owned by Berry Gordy) and had provided the musical accompaniment to The Ferros' 1958 Fortune Records outing *Come Home My Love* and *Tough Cat*. Nick & The Jaguars were a three piece group comprising Nick Ferro on drums with his brother Johnny and Marv Weyer on guitar (Johnny writing both sides of the Fortune release and the Tamla single), with Nick's father Gus credited with getting them an introduction to Berry Gordy. In August 1959, when their single *Ich-i-bon #1* backed with *Cool And Crazy* was released, Motown had still to establish a unique sound, so the release of The Jaguars' single, which predated the sound of Dick Dale (later known as The King of the Surf Guitar) was an ambitious move on the part of the company. Nick & The Jaguars single did little, although the group has entered the record books for being the first white act to appear on any Motown label. Whilst history lost track of the Ferro's soon after their Tamla release, Marv Weyer would go on to become a well known rockabilly and country guitarist.

THE NIGHT – FRANKIE VALLI & THE FOUR SEASONS [SINGLE]

Frankie Valli & The Four Seasons' time with Motown subsidiary MoWest was disappointing for both the group and the label. Of the three planned albums (two by the group and a solo effort from Frankie), only one was ever released, with **Chameleon** being issued in May 1972 to a lukewarm reception. Indeed, it was the failure of the album that resulted in the single *The Night*, written by Bob Gaudio and Al Ruzicka, being taken off the American release schedule, even though promotional copies had been pressed and distributed. The single was issued on MoWest in the UK in October 1972 but made little or no impact upon its initial release.

Three years later, just as MoWest was being effectively closed down in the UK (it had already been shuttered in the US), the Tamla Motown office in the UK noticed the increasing demand for *The Night*, which since its release had become something of a growing favourite on the Northern Soul scene. The single was duly reissued to cater for that demand and, crossing over onto the pop chart would eventually hit the Top Ten, peaking at #7 in May 1975. Not only was this Frankie Valli & The Four Seasons' only hit for Motown, it was the only charted record for MoWest in the UK. Later cover versions include Intastella (#60 in 1995) and Soft Cell (#39 in 2003).

NIGHTSHIFT – THE COMMODORES [SINGLE]

Getting to the top had been a long and arduous challenge for The Commodores, but no sooner had they arrived than it all seemed to disintegrate around them. There was the death of their manager Benny Ashburn in 1982, followed a year later by the departure of their lead singer and chief songwriter Lionel Richie, who took producer James Anthony Carmichael with him. A year later guitarist and founding member Thomas McClary also opted to pursue a solo career, leaving the three original members to regroup collectively and creatively. They drafted in JD Nicholas and Sheldon Reynolds as singer and guitarist respectively, along with producer Dennis Lambert.

Dennis wasn't a straight replacement for James Anthony Carmichael since he brought much more to the studio than just his production qualities. He had also made his name as a songwriter, having enjoyed hits on the country (*Don't Pull Your Love* by Glen Campbell), rock (*We Built This City* by Starship) and R&B charts (*Keeper Of The Castle* by The Four Tops) during the course of a lengthy career, and by 1982 he was working with Franne Golde, herself no stranger to chart success. Just as they had done previously, the various members of The Commodores presented their completed songs and work in progress, with Dennis and Franne the interested listeners.

"Each member wanted to write, so they each submitted ideas. One of them, by Walter Orange, was this little groove he had going, which was the bass line to *Nightshift*. Dennis played me a few things, and then he played me that. The only thing in the song was, 'Marvin, he was a friend of mine.' When Dennis said, 'We need to make this like *Rock And Roll Heaven*,' I said, 'Great, let's do it.'"

Rock And Roll Heaven harked back to 1974, a Righteous Brothers song co-produced by Dennis that paid homage to the likes of Otis Redding, Janis Joplin and Jim Morrison. The soul credentials of The Commodores dictated that the update should focus more on the fallen Marvin Gaye and Jackie Wilson, with Dennis reportedly checking through chart reference books in order to get the titles of hit singles by the pair in order to incorporate them into the lyrics. Recorded inside two days, with Walter Orange leading on the first verse and new arrival JD Nicholas the second, *Nightshift* was released in December 1984 in the US and the following month in the UK.

The result was a return to the Top Ten of the charts for the first time in four years in the US and six in the UK, hitting #3 on the pop charts on both sides of the Atlantic and topping the R&B chart for good measure. The single would go on to garner two Grammy Award nominations, being beaten for the Best R&B Song by *Freeway To Love* by Jeffrey Cohen and Narada Michael Walden but winning The Commodores the award for Best R&B Performance by a Group.

NOLEN & CROSSLEY

Guitarist and singer Curtis Anthony Nolen first linked with keyboard player and singer Raymond Crossley in Passage, a gospel group formed by former Brothers Johnson member Louis Johnson. Soon after completing recording of a one-off album, the pair was signed by Motown, being assigned to the Gordy label for their debut album **Nolen & Crossley**, which was released in January 1981. Their follow-up appeared a year later, with **Ambience** being released in February 1982. Although neither of their albums or attendant singles charted, they were highly regarded around Motown, penning material for DeBarge collectively whilst Curtis also served as an A&R Director and was responsible for signing Rockwell to the label.

ALBUMS: NOLEN & CROSSLEY (1981), AMBIENCE (1982)

NORMAN, IS THAT YOU (FILM SOUNDTRACK)

A 1970 play written by Ron Clark and Sam Bobrick, 'Norman, Is That You' was originally about a Jewish couple coming to terms with their son's homosexuality. The film rights were picked up by 'Rowan & Martin's Laugh-In' later the same year, and by the time the film was made in 1976 it had undergone something of a change, with the Jewish couple becoming African American. Starring Redd Foxx and Pearl Bailey, the film became only a moderate success, which may account for the scrapping of a proposed soundtrack release which featured music composed and conducted by William Goldstein with lyrics by Ron Miller, although singles by Smokey Robinson (*An Old Fashioned Man*) and Thelma Houston (*One Out Of Every Six*) were released in October 1976.

NORTHERN LIGHTS

A psychedelic pop group formed by Christian St James (guitar and vocals), Yvonne Solomonides (flute, recorder and vocals), Carol Hutchinson (keyboards and vocals) and Mike Blundel (bass, percussion and vocals) they signed with Motown's subsidiary label Natural Resources in 1972 and released their only album, **Vancouver Dreaming** in January 1973.

Much of the material was written by Jeffrey Comanor, something of a veteran staff writer who had released his own solo album in 1969 on A&M and would later become best known for his film score to the film 'Midnight Cowboy'. According to the brief sleeve-notes, the inspiration for the album came from comedians Zero Mostel, Stan Freburg, Murray Roman and Jonathan Winters, the relevance of which is unknown.

ALBUM: VANCOUVER DREAMING (1973)

NOTHING BUT A MAN (FILM SOUNDTRACK)

One of Motown's earliest ventures into the film soundtrack market, 'Nothing But A Man' was the story of a railroad worker and his school teacher wife facing discrimination in 1960s America. Sidney Poitier had been offered the lead role of Duff Anderson but turned it down, with Ivan Dixon eventually taking the role, and Abbey Lincoln played his wife Josie. Co-written and directed by Michael Roemer (with Robert Young the other co-writer), 'Nothing But A Man' was well received critically but did little at the box office, although its subsequent release on DVD forty years after release has increased the film's profile. The soundtrack was an eleven track compilation of well known Motown numbers, featuring Martha & The Vandellas, Little Stevie Wonder, The Miracles, Holland & Dozier, The Marvelettes and Mary Wells.

ALBUM: NOTHING BUT A MAN SOUNDTRACK (1965)

NOWHERE TO RUN – MARTHA & THE VANDELLAS [SINGLE]

Following the worldwide success of *Dancing In The Street*, Martha & The Vandellas found themselves even more in demand for live dates, fulfilling concerts the length and breadth of the country. At Hitsville, meanwhile, Holland-Dozier-Holland were learning that whilst success might breed success, it also brought the added pressure of trying to keep coming up with quality material for an ever-growing list of Motown clients, including The Four Tops, The Supremes and The Vandellas. *Nowhere To Run* was originally written as an instrumental and went by the working title of *Nowhere To Run Nowhere To Hide*, with the backing tracks being cut towards the end of September 1964. Somewhere along the way HDH decided the tune was ideal for Martha & The Vandellas, utilising the same car chain percussion that had worked so well on *Dancing In The Street*, this time to even greater effect. A little over three weeks later, Martha, Rosalind Ashford and Betty Kelly came in to lay down their vocals.

"I loved the lyrics the minute I heard them," Martha would later state. "One of the reasons that I so strongly identified with the song was because of the pace, urgency, and pressure under which it was recorded. We had worked so hard on the road, and were not given a moment to rest. I was very ill that day. I could barely walk, so it seemed like it was I who had nowhere to run and nowhere to hide."

Towards the end of the year The Vandellas also found enough time to record a promotional film for the single, miming the lyrics whilst being filmed at a local Ford motor plant. The video was shot at the behest of presenter Murray The K, who subsequently gave the clip an airing on one of his television specials (for an added attraction, when *Nowhere To Run* was eventually released, it carried the flip side *Motoring*!), thus enabling Martha & The Vandellas to claim to have shot the very first pop video. Although not as big a hit as *Dancing In The Street*, *Nowhere To Run* was still a major success, hitting #5 R&B and #8 pop. In the UK the single was one of six debut releases on the newly inaugurated Tamla Motown label, being given the catalogue number TMG 502 (The Supremes' *Stop In The Name Of Love* was TMG 501) and became the group's second major hit, peaking at #26.

Both the song and Martha & The Vandellas version have been heavily used in films and as samples in the years since its original release, most notably in the films 'Warriors' in 1979 (where it was covered by Arnold McCuller) and 'Good Morning Vietnam' in 1988. Following its use in the latter film, the track was coupled with James Brown's *I Got You (I Feel Good)* as a double A-side and released on the A&M label, where it made #52 in the UK.

NU PAGE

Although the only known picture of Nu Page shows a line-up of one female and four male group members, the actual group was little more than a studio creation by producer Robert Gordy with writers Marilyn McLeod, Melton Bolton and Horace Jones. Their only outing appeared on MoWest in February 1973, *When The Brothers Come Marching Home* backed with *A Heart Is A House*, on which Marilyn, Melton and Horace were augmented by session musicians.

BOBBY NUNN

Born in Buffalo, New York in 1952, Bobby Nunn began his recording career with schoolfriend Eugene Coplin, with the pair recording a number of tracks in Bobby's father's homebuilt studio, of which *You Gave Me Love* (credited to Bob & Gene) was released on Mo Do Records and attracted some local attention. Bobby moved to Los Angeles in the 1970s and formed Splendor with his brother Billy, Sascha Meeks and Richard Shaw, who got a contract with Columbia and released one album in 1979. When Splendor disbanded, Bobby switched to session work as a keyboard player and singer, most notably for Rick James, subsequently getting a solo contract with Gordy in 1982.

He scored first time out with *She's Just A Groupie*, a #15 R&B hit (it stalled at #104 on the pop chart), propelling his album **Second To Nunn** to #14 on the R&B chart and #148 pop. The album would also give up another minor hit, with *Got To Give Up On It* making #36 R&B as Bobby returned to the studio to work on his next long player. **Private Party** appeared in September 1983 (released in the UK the following January) and yielded two hits in the title track (#66 R&B) and *Hangin' Out At The Mall* (#50 R&B), although a third track, *Don't Knock It (Until You Try It)* would become his UK chart breakthrough, making #65 in February 1984. Although Bobby started work on a third album, **Fresh** never saw the light of day. After being dropped by Motown, Bobby became a freelance songwriter and producer, with the Grammy Award nominated *Rocket 2 U* by The Jets his best known success.

ALBUMS: SECOND TO NUNN (1982), PRIVATE PARTY (1983)

JAMES NYX

Although not a prolific songwriter (according to most figures, he had no more than 35 songs actually published), James Nyx left a lasting legacy during his brief time involved with Motown, having co-written three songs on Marvin Gaye's groundbreaking **What's Going On** album.

Born in Indianapolis, Indiana on 3 May 1914, James moved to Detroit at an early age where he married his first wife, by whom he would have six children. He would later remarry and have a further two children, providing for his rapidly expanding family with a succession of menial jobs. Employed by Harvey Fuqua at Harvey's Tri-Phi/Harvey Records office as a janitor and general handyman, James used his easy access to Harvey for his own use, showing him song lyrics he had written. He got his first break when Harvey collaborated with him on *What Can You Do Now*, which Harvey himself recorded with Ann Bogan and released on Harvey Records in 1963.

When Harvey and his wife Gwen Gordy sold their recording operation to Motown, James followed his previous employers into Hitsville, initially as janitor but later as the lift operator at the Donovan Building. James kept on writing lyrics too, eventually working with another of Harvey's former protégés, Marvin Gaye, on *We Can Make It Baby*, which was recorded by The Originals in 1970. James' work with Marvin on The Originals proved fortuitous, for when Marvin then began assembling material for **What's Going On**, James was on hand to assist, co-writing *Inner City Blues (Make Me Wanna Holler), What's Happening Brother* and *God Is Love*.

When Motown left Detroit for the West Coast, James opted to remain in his adopted city, subsequently getting a publishing deal with KellGriff Music, although little or nothing was actually recorded or released. However, with *Inner City Blues* in particular having become a staple diet on both the R&B and rap circuit for both cover versions and samples, the royalty income from that track alone undoubtedly made James Nyx one of the best paid lift operators around! He died on 16 July 1998, his passing seemingly unnoticed by the music world.

RAY ODDIS

Brice Armstrong (born in Dallas, Texas on 3 January 1936) recorded under the assumed name of Ray Oddis for his only single on the V.I.P. label, an attempt at something of a seasonal novelty offering with *Randy The Newspaper Boy* released in November 1964. Bert Haney, who had partnered Brice on his earlier Motown outing, wrote the flip side *Happy Ghoul Tide*, with both sides being produced by Al Klein, who had previously run the Mel-O-dy label. *Happy Ghoul Tide* had previously been released in 1962 on the Duchess label and credited to Brice Armstrong & The All American Ghouls.

ODYSSEY

Not to be confused with the late 1970s group that scored a number of club orientated hits that crossed over onto the pop charts, this Odyssey was formed by Royce Jones (born in Los Angeles, California on 15 December 1954, vocals), Billy Pierce (vocals), Kathleen Warren (keyboards and vocals), Warner 'Doc' Schwebke (born on 6 June 1948, bass), Don Peake (guitar), Donnie Dacus (born in Galena Park, Texas on 12 October 1951, guitar) and Gene Pello (drums). Largely made up of session musicians rather than a working band, Odyssey's eponymous album was produced by Karl Bornstein and Michael Goldberg and released on MoWest in May 1972 (February 1973 in the UK), with the C.L. Robert James penned single *Our Lives Are Shaped By What We Love* appearing stateside in August 1972. The group apparently disbanded after Donnie Dacus expressed his desire to leave the group, with Royce Jones later singing lead and backing vocals for Steely Dan and Ambrosia. Doc Schwebke died on 15 November 2008.
ALBUM: ODYSSEY (1972)

OH NO – THE COMMODORES [SINGLE]

The second single lifted from The Commodores' **In The Pocket** album, *Oh No* was another of Lionel Richie's trademark ballads and the last he would record with the group. As a parting shot it kept the group hot on the charts, reaching #4 pop and #5 R&B and making #44 in the UK, although it would be The Commodores' last appearance in the Top Ten of either the pop or R&B charts for four years.

THE O'JAYS

Formed in Canton, Ohio in 1958, The O'Jays would ultimately become as vital and successful for Philadelphia International Records as The Temptations and The Four Tops were for Motown. The group originally formed as a five piece under the name The Triumphs, with Eddie Levert (born in Canton on 16 June 1942), Walter Williams (born in Canton on 25 August 1942), William Powell (born in Canton on 20 January 1942), Bill Isles and Bobby Massey as members. They later recorded as the Mascots and name-changed to The O'Jays (after Cleveland DJ Eddie O'Jay) in 1963. Isles left in 1965, Massey in 1972 and the group continued as a trio. Having previously worked with Kenny Gamble and Leon Huff at Neptune, The O'Jays signed with their Philadelphia International label in 1972 and made their major chart breakthrough with *Back Stabbers* at the turn of 1973, going to register numerous Top Ten pop hits over the next few years. The O'Jays appeared on the soundtrack to 'Save The Children' performing *Sunshine*, a track from their **Back Stabbers** album. William Powell, who was replaced in the group in 1975 by Sammy Strain, died from cancer on 26 May 1977.

KIM O'LEARY

A singer and songwriter born in Melbourne, Australia, Kim O'Leary studied drama with the Melbourne Theatre Company and then spent four years with various rock and blues groups touring Australia. In 1977 she linked with Geoff Bridgford to formed One Foundation, relocating to America and working a number of clubs before going solo in 1981, aided by Nick Jaimeson. Kim would eventually link up with Motown in 1987 on the recommendation of Stevie Wonder's management company. Her only single for the company, *Put the Pieces Back* was heavily featured on the Adult Contemporary chart and led to a publishing contract with Jobete, although a planned eponymous album was pulled off the schedule. Kim, who was later a member of Freezone and Kalizzmo eventually returned home to Australia.

ONE DAY IN YOUR LIFE – MICHAEL JACKSON [SINGLE]

Written by Sam Brown III and Renee Armand, *One Day In Your Life* was recorded by Michael in December 1974 and originally featured on his album released the following year, **Forever Michael**. Whilst it remained as nothing more than an album track in the US, it was chosen for release as a single in the UK, appearing on the Tamla Motown label in April 1975. It did little at the time, being somewhat out of sorts with the rest of the material Michael and his siblings were recording. However, six years later and with Michael dominating the charts the world over with his **Off The Wall** album, it was decided to release the single for the first time in the US and give it a second chance in the UK. Perhaps still too dated for mass consumption in the US, where it had to settle for a #55 pop and #42 R&B peak, it found its mark in the UK where it would go on to top the singles chart. On hitting the top spot, it knocked Smokey Robinson's *Being With You* off the summit, the first and only time one Motown record replaced another in the UK. It would go on to spend two weeks at the top, selling more than 500,000 copies and earning a gold disc award.

ONE HEARTBEAT – SMOKEY ROBINSON [SINGLE]

The title track to Smokey's million selling album, *One Heartbeat* was the second single released from the album after *Just To See Her*, itself a Top Ten pop and R&B hit. Written by singer/songwriter Brian Ray and keyboard player Steve LeGassick, a former member of Tommy Tutone, *One Heartbeat* was produced by Peter Bunetta and Rick Chudacoff. Continuing Smokey's renewed success, *One Heartbeat* was another Top Ten hit across the board, hitting #3 on the R&B listings and #10 pop. It also made a healthy showing on the Adult Contemporary chart, where it peaked at #2 following the single's release in October 1987.

THE ONE WHO REALLY LOVES YOU – MARY WELLS [SINGLE]

Berry Gordy had taken care of Mary Wells' first recordings for Motown, often getting her to sing at the very limits of her range in order to capture the dynamism of her voice. In December 1961 she was handed over to Smokey Robinson, who decided upon a completely different vocal style, but ultimately with even greater success. The first fruits of their professional relationship came with the single *The One Who Really Loves You*, a song Smokey had written specifically with Mary in mind.

Smokey had noted the success Harry Belafonte was having on the chart and incorporated a similar Calypso beat, maintained to perfection by drummer Benny Benjamin, with the rest of the Funk Brothers adding their own variation of a Caribbean beat. Rounding out the sound was the vocal accompaniment of The Love-Tones, who vocal contribution was duly noted on the second pressing of the single. The end result was the biggest hit of Mary's career up to that point, hitting #2 on the R&B chart and #8 on the pop listings. In the UK that single was never released, possibly owing to the switch in licensees from London American to Fontana.

THE ONES

You Haven't Seen My Love was a single that started to get a bit of action in the Lansing area, enough for Motown to join a slew of labels keen to pick it up for national distribution. It had been recorded by The Ones, a group formed by Danny Hernandez (guitar and vocals), Kerry Nicholoff (keyboards), his brother Kevin, who also went by the name Carey (bass) and Mark Boomershine (drums), with Carey and Danny having written the song and Bob Baldori produced the session.

Originally released on the Fenton label, it has also appeared on Baldori's Spirit label before Motown came calling. Faced with a choice of homes for the single, the group picked Motown, mainly for the creditability of being in the same company as Smokey Robinson and The Temptations. The Motown reissued single couldn't build on the early success in Lansing, only hitting #117, and a follow-up single issued in August 1968, *Don't Let Me Lose This Dream* also missed the chart. In 1970 a new version of The Ones, featuring only Danny Hernandez from the original line-up, returned to Motown and signed with the Rare Earth label, releasing *As Long As I've Got You* in September.

THE ONION SONG – MARVIN GAYE & TAMMI TERRELL [SINGLE]

Of the numerous tracks released and credited to Marvin Gaye & Tammi Terrell, none have had their recording origins so closely investigated as *The Onion Song*. Whilst co-writer Valerie Simpson was present in the studio at the time the song was recorded (as well she might as she is also listed as co-producer) and has admitted helping Tammi out on the vocals, there is considerable speculation that the single is almost entirely the work of Marvin and Valerie, with Tammi little more than an innocent bystander. Tammi, of course, had been struck down by a brain tumour, requiring some eight operations before she finally succumbed to the illness in March 1970.

The sessions for *The Onion Song*, originally intended for The Supremes but re-assigned to Marvin and Tammi, began in January 1969 with the recording of the backing tracks. Marvin eventually recorded his vocal on 15 March 1969, with further vocal recording sessions taking place two days later at the Golden World studio. Whilst Tammi was in attendance at these sessions, it is reported that she was in a wheelchair at the time. Valerie has stated that all she recorded was a guide vocal, but Marvin would later claim that the female voice heard on the finished version is undoubtedly that of Valerie, not Tammi. He would further strengthen his argument by claiming that Motown both knew and acknowledged that Tammi did not appear on the song, with her failing health and the financial implications this would have on her and her family justifying the switch.

Whoever is the female voice, they contributed their half of what has become one of Motown's finest moments, at least as far as British fans are concerned. Released on 17 March 1969, the single would sail into the Top Ten in the UK, peaking at #9, and continue Marvin Gaye's hot streak as far as British audiences were concerned. It was also Tammi's sixth and final appearance on the Record Retailer chart, as well as her biggest hit in Britain. The British success was duly noted and *The Onion Song* was subsequently released in America on 20 March 1970, the very day that the funeral of Tammi Terrell was taking place in Philadelphia, some four days after her death. Despite the additional publicity such an event would have generated, *The Onion Song* was unable to replicate its British success, stalling at #18 R&B and a lowly #50 pop.

ORANGE SUNSHINE

Little is known about Orange Sunshine, other than they originated from St. Louis, Missouri and were discovered by Don Boddie, who wrote and produced their only Motown connected single *Who's Cheating On Who* which was released on Prodigal in December 1975. The single was certainly recorded in St. Louis, with Boddie producing the single under his Show Me Town Enterprises moniker.

ORIGINAL MUSIQUARIUM 1 - STEVIE WONDER [ALBUM]

In 1977, some twelve months after **Songs In The Key Life** had become a major smash, Motown readied career retrospective **Looking Back**, a three disc collection of Stevie Wonder's recordings from 1962 through to 1971. Featuring hits and misses, the album was intended to satisfy the demand for Stevie Wonder product until he was once again ready to release new material. Whilst Stevie controlled all repertoire from 1971 onwards, he had enough clout within the company to control pretty much everything that was being released under his name, and **Looking Back** was not an album he much cared for, even if it sat nicely with the various other anthologies and retrospectives that Motown were releasing on other artists. Although some 200,000 copies were pressed, Stevie would not allow the album to be officially released, with the finished stock filtering onto the deletions market and some stock finding its way over the Atlantic. Stevie eventually relented and the remaining stock was issued as something of a limited edition, although Motown executives had learned their lesson and didn't try to pressure Stevie into releasing a greatest hits or similar package for a further five years.

Then, in 1982, Motown president Jay Lasker learned that Stevie might be financially stretched, perhaps enough to welcome the injection of cash that a retrospective album would undoubtedly bring. Lasker and Motown's original budget for the album was said to have been $2 million, with Stevie getting it increased to $3 million, the extra being justified by Stevie's plan to make the album a double disc package and add four brand new tracks to go alongside the obvious hits. With the contract signed, Stevie announced his forthcoming project to the assorted media.

"There are many songs that I write, many songs that could have gone on, say, **Innervisions** or **Talking Book** which are in the can, and I had to make a decision about those songs. I've never done an album consisting of all the songs I've done over the last two years, a kind of review, so I decided it was best to do that now."

Such words were music to the ears of Jay Lasker and Berry Gordy, who duly sat back to wait for delivery of the tapes, something only Stevie and his camp could provide since they retained the master recordings. The first package that arrived in December 1981 was the tape for one of the brand new recordings, *That Girl,* which was duly issued on Tamla in January 1982 and became the major hit all and sundry expected. Unfortunately, the single was just about all the correspondence and communication Motown got from Stevie; the tapes for the album did not appear until April, by which time sales of *That Girl* had peaked and some of the sales momentum lost.

The double album itself was finally rush released onto the market the following month, containing eleven of Stevie's singles that had been Top 40 hits, an album track not previously released as a single in *Isn't She Lovely* (something of a signature song for Stevie's daughter Aisha) and four new tracks. Despite the lateness of its arrival, **Original Musiquarium 1** still managed to do brisk business, hitting #4 pop and topping the R&B chart, on its way to attaining gold status. In the UK the album would peak at #8 and earn a gold disc for sales in excess of 100,000 copies.

THE ORIGINALS

Freddie Gorman had already been through Hitsville once, joining the company at the start of the 1960s with aspirations of becoming a successful singer and/or producer. At the time Motown had utilised his experience as a postman to help craft the company's first number one hit in *Please Mr Postman*, with Freddie also assisting Brian Holland on a number of other compositions. Aside from a brief solo career (just one single being released on the Miracle label), Freddie struggled to realise his main goals of singing and production, so eventually left Motown and wound up at Golden World.

There he was able to do both functions, but the success he was to enjoy helped raise the profile of the company to such an extent Berry Gordy moved swiftly to halt the competition, buying up the label and its various assets, including Freddie Gorman.

So in 1965 Freddie found himself back at Motown, where Lamont Dozier suggested putting together a vocal group to Walter Gaines (born in Detroit, Michigan on 15 August 1936), with C.P. Spencer (born

Cratham Plato Spencer in Detroit on 13 January 1938), Ty Hunter (born in Detroit on 30 November 1943) and Freddie (born Frederick Cortez Gorman in Detroit on 11 April 1939) accepting the invitation. Unfortunately, Ty was unable to obtain a release from his contract with Chess Records, so to round out the group they approached Hank Dixon (born in Detroit on 17 December 1939), who had sung with the others during the 1950s. The Originals approach came just at the right time, for he had recently returned to Detroit after getting out of the army after eight years.

"They had a girl in the group at the time and I guess the guys didn't like the idea of having a girl in there, so when I got out of the army they took me in right away."

The newly created foursome found almost instant work at Motown as backing singers, effectively becoming the male version of The Andantes and appearing on a slew of hits by Jimmy Ruffin, Marvin Gaye, David Ruffin and Shorty Long, among others. Finally, The Originals got their own shot at stardom, working with Clarence Paul on an updated version of Huddie Ledbetter's *Goodnight Irene*. Also rounding out the vocal was Levi Stubbs' younger brother Joe (born in Detroit in 1942), on something of a temporary placement from The Contours, as Hank explained.

"They [Motown] were trying to find a place for him, so they put him with us, but it didn't work out."

The fact that *Goodnight Irene* was originally intended for The Four Tops might have had something to do with Joe's secondment to The Originals, but the single did little following its release on Soul in December 1966 and the original Originals went back to vocally assisting others around Hitsville. Their cause wasn't helped by the subsequent departure of Holland-Dozier-Holland, a setback Freddie duly noted.

"We went to Motown with Holland-Dozier-Holland to produce us. Then they left. So there we were at Motown without a producer. It was kind of an awkward position."

When Motown finally released a second single in January 1969, *We've Got A Way Out Of Love,* it was with a track HDH had been working on prior to their departure, recorded in August 1967 but never quite finished.

"That was one we had done just before they left," said Freddie. "It was supposed to have some strings and horns and things of that sort on it. It was just the rhythm tracks and the vocals."

There is speculation that the single's release was done to spite HDH, but in the event it was The Originals who suffered, with the disc doing nothing. A subsequent release, *Green Grow The Lilacs* saw them working with Ron Miller and Tom Baird, who were at least on hand to complete the single, but it too failed to find a market. By the middle of 1969, therefore, The Originals were feeling somewhat out of sorts at Motown, struggling to find any kind of momentum, seldom getting their own sessions and with no one to champion their cause.

Enter Marvin Gaye, who went back a while with several of the group, most notably Walter Gaines and C.P. Spencer, all of whom had recorded for the Anna label some ten years previously. Marvin did his homework, listening to the group and their sound and eventually approached the group with a song he thought might be ideal.

"So he put us together and said he had a song for us" remembered Freddie. "We went over to his house and it was *Baby I'm For Real*. We started working on it. Everybody just knew right off. He had the idea of switching parts. You had four different leads on *Baby I'm For Real*."

In fact, the song wasn't especially written for The Originals, with the initial sessions being conducted with Bobby Taylor in mind (equally bizarre was the fact The Originals masqueraded in the studio as The Vancouvers on those sessions!) before it was transformed into something of a signature song for The Originals. Yet its release wasn't quite so straightforward, with the track languishing on the group's album **Green Grow The Lilacs**, which had been released in July 1969. The group themselves took copies of the album around numerous radio stations, picking out the tracks they thought would be worthy of interest. At WCHB the song selected was *Baby I'm For Real*, which got three plays inside an hour and virtually demanded release by Motown thereafter. Fortunately, Motown had already got calls from retailers about the track, so the single was released in September and would go on to become the group's debut hit, topping the R&B chart and making a more than healthy #14 on the pop listing.

In light of the success of the single, Motown repackaged the album as **Baby I'm For Real**, a ploy that worked enough for the album to hit #18 on the R&B chart (it was a rather more modest #174 on the pop chart). Richard Morris had got the producer's credit for *Baby I'm For Real* as Marvin wasn't registered at Motown as a producer, but following the single's success, that situation was quickly remedied, enabling Marvin to work openly with the group on their follow-up. That was *The Bells*, written with the group in mind and with Marvin knowing exactly what he was trying to achieve.

"You'd do it over and over until he heard it," said Freddie. "You were thinking it was okay, but there was something he was listening for, and that's what he wanted to hear. But we didn't mind working with him, because we were all group people, and we loved the harmonies. He was a harmony man and a group man, and we all understood each other."

The Bells would become the group's second straight hit, selling more than a million copies as it peaked at #4 R&B and #12 pop, also taking pride of place as the opening track to The Originals second album **Portrait Of The Originals** (#47 R&B and #198 pop). The single hit tally continued with Marvin's *We Can Make It*, paired with *I Like Your Style*, with the top side making #74 pop and #20 R&B and the flipside also getting an honorary mention on the R&B chart. *I Like Your Style* had been written by the group along with Pam Sawyer, proof that The Originals could not only carry a good song, they could write one too. Their dalliance with Marvin came to an end at that point, although there could have been one final hit wrung out of their collaboration. The group recorded *Just To Keep You Satisfied*, which was submitted to the weekly Quality Control departmental meeting but rejected on the grounds those present found the phrase 'I want your body' in the background somewhat objectionable. The single might have been rejected, but many of the same elements would subsequently re-appear on Marvin's **Let's Get It On** album, where such phrases were commonplace!

The Originals meanwhile moved on from Marvin and into the hands of Clay McMurray for their third album **Naturally Together**, released in September 1970 (barely four months after **Portrait** had hit the streets) and a #44 R&B success thanks to continued single success with *God Bless Whoever Sent You* (#53 pop and #14 R&B). A change of producer to Johnny Bristol for *I'm Someone Who Cares* brought down the curtain on the group's first spell of success, a single that bubbled under the pop charts at #113 without ever troubling the R&B listing.

Spencer left for a solo career in 1972 and was replaced, ironically, by Ty Hunter, who since ditching his solo career with Chess had fronted the Glass House on Invictus Records. Ty arrived just as the group had completed their **Definitions** album, but without a hit single the album fared little chance of crossing over. Matters weren't helped by the departure of Motown from Detroit, with the sales and marketing departments joining the same westward drift to California. Two years later The Originals upped and followed them, linking with Stevie Wonder for *Game Called Love*, a single with something of a country flavour that also disappeared without trace.

In 1975 The Originals finally got their chance to work with HDH, or at least one third of that creative team, with Lamont Dozier helming the sublime **California Sunset**, an album that marked the group's arrival not only in California but also back on the charts, peaking at #51 R&B. The group was to make one final appearance on the chart, *Down To Love Town* being extracted from the album **Communique** and finding a new market for The Originals, topping the dance chart and hitting #47 pop and #93 R&B. The same single would provide the title track to the group's final Motown album in 1977, where much of the rest of material tried to appeal to the same kind of market, with *Call Me Your Six Million Dollar Man*, *Hurry Up & Wait* and *Been Decided* all getting extensive club plays as album tracks and hitting #6 on the specialist club chart (plans to release *Six Million Dollar Man* as a single hit legal problems with ABC, the makers of the television series of the same name).

With their Motown contract at an end The Originals moved over to Fantasy where they recorded two albums and welcomed back a returning C.P. Spencer, thus making the group a quintet for a short while. Sadly, Ty Hunter died on 24 February 1981, with the group effectively coming to a halt as a recording entity after one final album for the Phase II label (although they continued to tour for some considerable time thereafter). Joe Stubbs died on 6 February 1998. C.P. Spencer died from a heart attack on 20 October 2004. Freddie Gorman died from lung cancer on 13 June 2006. Walter Gaines died on 17 January 2012.

ALBUMS: GREEN GROWS THE LILACS (1969), PORTRAIT OF THE ORIGINALS (1970), NATURALLY TOGETHER (1970), DEFINITIONS (1972), GAME CALLED LOVE (1974), CALIFORNIA SUNSET (1975), COMMUNIQUE (1976), DOWN TO LOVE TOWN (1977)

ORIGINALS FROM MARVIN GAYE – MARVIN GAYE [EP]

One of the last EPs issued by Tamla Motown in the UK (along with **Four Tops Hits**), **Originals From Marvin Gaye** was released in March 1967. A six track compilation featuring *Can I Get A Witness?*, *Stubborn Kind Of Fellow*, *Baby Don't You Do It*, *You're A Wonderful One*, *Hitch Hike* and *Pride And Joy*, the EP entered the chart at #9 on 15 April and moved up to #3, its peak position, a week later. The EP was to enjoy eight weeks on the listing, enabling Tamla Motown to garner three of the Top Ten positions during that run.

ORIOLE RECORDS

Ivor Novello-award winning composer John Schroeder (who co-wrote Helen Shapiro's *Walkin' Back To Happiness*) had worked as an A&R assistant to Norrie Paramor at Columbia Records before joining Oriole as head of A&R in 1962. One of his first moves was to establish an Oriole American imprint and secure the British licensing rights to Motown, with Berry Gordy and Barney Ales travelling over to London to sign the deal. The first singles were released in September 1962 and over the next year a total of nineteen would be issued in the UK on the Oriole American label.

Despite seeing the first British releases by such artists as Marvin Gaye, Stevie Wonder, Mary Wells and The Contours, not one of the nineteen made an impact on the charts, even though they were well received. Indeed, John Schroeder later related that The Beatles had become such fans of Motown he had to send Ringo Starr a copy of every release! The Oriole deal came to an end in September 1963, with Motown moving on to the Stateside label for UK distribution.

OSCARS

The American Academy of Motion Picture Arts and Sciences Award, more commonly known as The Oscars, are the most prestigious awards of the film industry and were inaugurated in 1929. It was for the Billie Holiday bio-pic 'Lady Sings The Blues' that Motown earned its first nominations for an Oscar, collecting five in the categories of Best Actress (Diana Ross), Best Art Direction (Carl Anderson and Reg Allen), Best Costume Design, Best Music, Original Song Score and Adaptation (Gil Askey) and Best Writing, Story and Screenplay (Terence McCloy, Chris Clark and Suzanne De Passe). Of all the nominations, the one award Berry Gordy coveted above all others was for Best Actress, especially as it was Diana Ross' first film. Unfortunately, Gordy's desire to win the award led to a highly criticised advertising campaign that hindered rather than helped Diana's chances of landing the statuette. Indeed, rather than entice the members entitled to vote for the award, Gordy's campaign drove them away, resulting in Liza Minnelli winning for 'Cabaret'. And 'Lady Sings The Blues' failed in all four other categories too.

Diana Ross' next film vehicle also picked up an Oscar nomination, with *Do You Know Where You're Going To*, the Michael Masser and Gerry Goffin written theme to 'Mahogany' being beaten by *I'm Easy* from 'Nashville'.

Fortunately, Motown has been able to collect two Oscars, both in the field of music. Stevie Wonder won the Best Film Song award in 1984 for *I Just Called To Say I Love You* from the film 'Woman In Red', whilst twelve months later Lionel Richie collected the same award for *Say You, Say Me* from 'White Nights'. Lionel Richie had been nominated in 1981 for *Endless Love* from the film of the same name – he sang the song with Diana Ross!

OTHER PEOPLE

A short lived duo formed by Nick Zesses and Dino Fekaris, Other People was to have released an album on Rare Earth entitled **Head To Head**, but the bulk of the songs intended for their release were subsequently recorded by Matrix, a trio of Nick, Dino and Tom Baird.

OZONE

Benny Wallace (guitar), Jimmy Stewart (keyboards) and Charles Glenn (bass) had been members of Nashville, Tennessee funk group The Endeavors who called it a day in 1977. Undaunted, the trio regrouped, recruiting Thomas Bumpass (trumpet), William White (flute), Greg Hargrove (guitar) and Paul Hines (drums) and formed a new group called Ozone. Their musical abilities alone soon got them regular work, most notably backing Billy Preston and Syreeta, both of whom were signed to Motown at the time.

Using this as an introduction, Ozone was able to land a contract with the label in 1979, releasing their debut album **Walk On** in April 1980, their profile helped by appearing on Teena Marie's album **Irons In The Fire** (the group featured on the single *Chains* as well as handling horn arrangements for the album). Featuring all self-composed material and production from Lee Young, the album would give rise to one minor hit single, the title track landing at #94 on the R&B chart.

Encouraged by this, the group began work on a follow-up, with **Jump On It** being released in January 1981. Neither the album nor the two single releases (*Ozonic Bee Bop* and *Mighty-Mighty*) made any headway on the chart, but Ozone was rewarded with an extension on their contract. Their third album provided them with something of a breakthrough, **Send It** hitting #61 on the R&B chart whilst the single release *Gigolette* made #73, assisted by a guesting Teena Marie who appeared on half of the tracks.

Eighteen months later the group released their fourth album **Lil' Suzy**, which saw action on both the pop (#152) and R&B chart (#45), with the title track also becoming a small hit, bubbling under the pop chart at #109 and reaching #59 R&B. Their final releases came in 1983, with the album **Glasses** (a #50 R&B hit) containing the hit single Strutt My Thang, which peaked at #55 R&B. Unfortunately, whilst Ozone were undoubtedly an integral part of the Motown music machine during the early 1980s, also appearing on albums by DeBarge and Teena Marie as well as recording with the likes of Luther Vandross and Sammy Davis Jr. outside the company, their own recordings were never afforded priority status. The group disbanded soon after the release of their final Motown album.
ALBUMS: WALK ON (1980), JUMP ON IT (1981), SEND IT (1981), LIL' SUZY (1982), GLASSES (1983)

BRUNI PAGAN

Puerto Rican female singer Bruni was raised in New York City and worked in a hospital whilst studying at college at night, eventually majoring in English and business administration. After singing backing vocals for Herbie Mann she landed a solo contract with Elektra, releasing the Patrick Adams and Pete Warner produced debut **Just Bruni** (with a guest appearance by Herbie Mann) in 1979. Whilst the album would give rise to a minor R&B hit in Fantasy, it did make an impact on the club charts. After recording one-off single for Emergency Records, Bruni had one release on Motown in 1984, the 12" single You Turn Me On written, produced and arranged by Rick James and which similarly garnered some club activity, although not enough to warrant any further releases.

KEN PAGE

Singer and actor Ken Page was born in St Louis, Missouri on 20 January 1954 and began his career at the local Muny outdoor theatre. He made his Broadway debut in 'The Wiz' as The Lion in 1975 and subsequently appeared in the revival of 'Guys And Dolls' as Nicely-Nicely Johnson. He has since gone on to appear regularly on Broadway, including 'Cats', Ain't Misbehavin'' and 'It Ain't Nothin' But The Blues' and several television series appearances.

LAWANDA PAGE

Born Alberta Peal in Cleveland, Ohio on 19 October 1920 but raised in St Louis, Missouri, this female comedienne would make her name as LaWanda Page, most notably in the television comedy 'Sanford & Son' in the role of Aunt Esther. Prior to this LaWanda had earned a veritable reputation as a fire-eater (she was dubbed The Bronze Goddess of Fire) and stand-up comedienne, with Laff Records issuing several best-selling albums of hers during the 1970s. These included **Watch It Sucker**, originally released in 1972 and which reputedly earned a gold disc. It was scheduled for reissue by Motown in July 1982 but subsequently cancelled. LaWanda died from complications of diabetes on 4 June 2006.

PAL

Despite forming in Los Angeles and signing with Motown worldwide, PAL never got a record issued in America, their success in Europe counting for little or nothing in their homeland. Sisters Rhett and Sinden Cellier (their real names were Laretta and Lanetta Collier) linked up with Rebekha Sweet and circulated a demo tape to several record companies, including Motown in the hope of getting a deal. After several rejections (including, it is said, six times by Motown!) the group found something of a champion in Steve Buckley at Capitol, although he was leaving the company for Motown and took PAL with him!
An adventurous European marketing campaign aimed at getting the group exposure was formulated, with Motown releasing the single Talk We Don't and the album **Truth For The Moment**. The single, helped by a video that was aired considerably across Europe did well in several markets, but this was not enough to get a record released in the US (although promotional copies of a different single, Panic, may have been pressed up). Instead, they got the ultimate release in 1988 and disbanded soon after.
ALBUM: TRUTH FOR THE MOMENT (1986)

LELAND PALMER

Born in Port Washington, New York on 16 June 1945, Leland made her Broadway debut in 1964 in 'Hello Dolly' and would go on to earn Tony Award nominations for her performance of Miss Jimmie in 'A Joyful Noise' and Fastrada in 'Pippin'. It was this latter musical that saw Leland briefly recording for Motown, appearing on the cast recording album issued in December 1972.

PAPA WAS A ROLLIN' STONE – THE TEMPTATIONS [SINGLE]

Like many of Norman Whitfield's compositions and productions *Papa Was A Rollin' Stone* required something of a prototype before he finally achieved aural perfection with a second version. In this case, the original was recorded by The Undisputed Truth, whose version (which seemingly borrowed the bassline from Donny Hathaway's *The Ghetto*) was released in June 1972 and became a #24 R&B and #63 pop hit in the US, even if it missed out on chart success in the UK.

At much the same time The Undisputed Truth's version was working its way up the chart, Norman was back in the studio working on a new Temptations album, eventually to be released under the title **All Directions**. With his co-writer Barrett Strong having departed, Norman was responsible for selecting and/or writing all of the material that would make up the album. Once again he delved into his own expanding song catalogue for material, revisiting *Funky Music Sho' Nuff Turns Me On* and *Papa Was A Rollin' Stone*. If The Undisputed Truth's original had been a tight, funk influenced song, then The Temptations' version of *Papa Was A Rollin' Stone* was to be a musical extravaganza.

The group was again out on the road when Norman began the recording sessions for the track, drafting in his chosen musicians, most notably Melvin 'Wah Wah' Ragin, whose guitar dominates the song. When The Temptations went into the studio to record their vocals, there was already a fractious atmosphere, due mainly to the group realising just how little they were expected to sing on what was, ultimately, their own album.

However, a couple of myths and legends have sprung up surrounding that recording session, both concerning Dennis Edwards, who was to feature as the lead vocalist. The first, detailed in Otis Williams' autobiography and repeated in 'The Temptations' television movie, is that he requested Norman change the very first line of the song as that was the day his own father had died and the emotions were still too raw for him to deliver the line. Notwithstanding that the song had already been recorded by The Undisputed Truth with the supposed offending date, Dennis himself discounted that particular myth.

"My daddy died on the third of October. I did mention this to Norman but only as a fact, like to say, you know, it was October, that would be the day that my daddy died. That was all there was to it."

Dennis did, however, agree that Norman had pushed him to the very edge of his patience, getting him to record the first line over and over again before he was finally satisfied.

"It upset me. I kept asking 'when do I come in, when do I come in?' I got so mad that I sang 'It was the third of September, That day I'll always remember' very tightly, not my usual style. But Norman was good at psyching us up, and I realised, it was the attitude he wanted."

Whilst the rest of The Temptations were equally against the track, they all played their part in turning *Papa Was A Rollin' Stone* into a veritable classic. With the recording sessions complete, The Temptations went back out on the road, with the **All Directions** album being released in July 1972. Much to the group's dismay, radio stations began playing the full length version of *Papa Was A Rollin' Stone* as soon as the album landed on their desks, with audiences the length and breadth of the country requesting the group feature it in their playlist. Sensing they had a potential hit on their hands, Motown requested an edit for single release, which in itself was not going to be an easy task if it was to retain as much of the magic as was possible.

On the full length version, the introduction alone accounted for some four minutes of music, which Norman managed to cut down to some two minutes for the single. Whilst virtually the complete musical middle section was removed altogether and an early fade out brought into effect, the single version ran to near on seven minutes, unprecedented in popular music. Even the bits that were removed were utilised, with Norman creating an instrumental version of the track for the flip side of the single.

What was left was still almost perfection, as the single would go on to prove. Released on the 3rd of September 1972, *Papa Was A Rollin' Stone* exploded across the board, becoming the group's fourth pop chart topper and hitting #5 on the R&B chart. The single received a British release in January 1973, the delay being down to Tamla Motown still extracting singles from an earlier Temptations album towards the tail end of 1972 (*Smiling Faces Sometimes* from **Sky's The Limit** was issued in October 1972, with **All Directions** finally being afforded a British release in November 1972), but even then it managed to hit #14 on the Record Retailer chart. The Temptations' own catalogue of hits contains some of Motown's finest moments, but it is doubtful if any have ever bettered *Papa Was A Rollin' Stone,* even if the group themselves were not entirely convinced, as Otis later conceded.

"We fought tooth and nail not to record *Run Charlie Run* and *Papa Was A Rollin' Stone*, a fantastic song – for somebody else. We were God dammed sick of that kind of crazy song. We wanted to sing romantic ballads again. We felt we had begun to lose our audience with the crazy shit Norman was doing. The good thing was that we thought *Papa* would be a failure. We almost were rooting for that, so we could go back to singing love ballads."

Instead, *Papa Was A Rollin' Stone* would go on to win three Grammy Awards, indicative of its almost universal appeal. The song The Temptations fought against recording would lift the award for Best R&B Vocal Performance by a Group. The bits cut out of the top side of the single to create an instrumental flip won Best R&B Instrumental Performance (collected by Norman and arranger Paul Riser), and the combined eleven minutes won Best Rhythm & Blues Song for Norman and Barrett Strong. The original version was remixed in 1987 and became a hit all over again, at least in the UK, where it peaked at #31.

The song was equally popular, with the best performing cover versions on the British chart coming from Was (Not Was) in 1990, which hit #12, and a chart topping version by George Michael in 1993, part of a *Five Live EP* with Queen, Lisa Stansfield and Seal, offering further proof of the song's pedigree. As Dennis Edwards so succinctly put it, "I was wrong about that record. I'm glad I was wrong."

EDDIE PARKER

Born in Saginaw, Michigan Eddie Parker recorded a succession of singles for small labels that have since gone on to find favour on the Northern Soul scene. His first such outing came in 1966 with *I'm Gone*, recorded in Detroit with producers Jack Ashford and Lorraine Chandler and issued on the Awake label. Two years later he linked with the pair again, this time recording *Love You Baby* for the Ashford label, which again struggled for sales on release but has since gone on to become a firm Northern favourite. When Jack Ashford and Lorraine Chandler had a go at launching their third label, Triple B, it was again Eddie Parker who inaugurated the imprint, this time with *I Need A True Love* in 1970.

After other releases went nowhere, Eddie kept out of the studio for four years until coaxed back in 1975, with Ashford and Chandler producing *Body Chains*, released on Prodigal. Another single eventually appeared on the Los Angeles label Miko, but after a brief spell spent running his own label, Eddie eventually turned his back on recording in order to concentrate on the church. He is occasionally persuaded to perform his old material, most recently at the Prestatyn Soul Weekender in 2005.

GINO PARKS

Hailing from the same district as Eddie Kendricks and Paul Williams of The Temptations, Gino Parks also found his way to Hitsville from Birmingham, Alabama. Born Gene Purifoy on 26 June 1933 he sang with various gospel groups locally before moving to Detroit in 1954, deciding to stay in the city after visiting his mother there one Christmas. After singing in a number of clubs from 1956, Geno (as he preferred his named spelt) got the chance to record for Fortune Records, as a member of The Don Juans and later solo. When little or nothing happened with any of his material, he accepted an offer in 1960 to join Berry Gordy's set up.

It had originally been intended to link him with Henry Lumpkin and Robert Bateman in the trio Hank, Gino & Bob, inspired by The Coasters. Gino (as he would be billed on his singles) recorded *Blibberin' Blabberin' Blues* for the Miracle label as a solo singer, with the single slated for release in April 1961. Whether copies were actually released remains debatable, but the single was certainly close enough to The Coasters sound to have perhaps warned Motown off, fearful of another injunction in the wake of The Satintones' *Tomorrow And Always*.

Gino barely had time to get despondent, for soon after he was in the studio when Mary Wells was a no show and used the studio time to record *That's No Lie* and *Same Thing (Will Happen To You)* that *was* released on Tamla in June 1961. There would be one further single, with *Fire* backed with *For This I Thank You* being issued in July 1962. Aside from a couple of singles on Golden World and Crazy Horse a few years later, Gino retired from the music business and went to work for Chrysler and later the Atlanta Life Insurance Company until his retirement.

PART-TIME LOVER – STEVIE WONDER [SINGLE]

The news that Stevie Wonder's planned 1984 album release would be delayed was hardly a surprise, but fortunately the reason for the delay wasn't Stevie's seemingly endless pursuit of musical excellence but rather him switching musical projects midway through in order to undertake a film soundtrack. That would result in **The Woman In Red** and *I Just Called To Say I Love You*, two massive sellers that re-affirmed Stevie as a major player.

By the time Stevie was ready to release the album, which had switched titles from **People Move Human Plays** to **In Square Circle**, expectations were once again raised. Fortunately, the wait proved worth it, with the album finally appearing on the release schedules for September 1985. A month before the album hit the streets came the first single, *Part-Time Lover*, a track on which Stevie played all instruments and brought in singer Luther Vandross to do some of the lead vocal work and backing vocals by the likes of Syreeta and Philip Bailey. The presence of such luminaries aided the single to such an extent it became Stevie's first R&B and pop chart topper since *Sir Duke* in 1977 as well as hitting #3 in the UK. The single would go on to earn a Grammy Award nomination for Best Male Pop Vocal Performance, losing out to Phil Collins and *Against All Odds*, the second consecutive year Stevie had lost out to Phil Collins in the category after *I Just Called To Say I Love You* lost in 1985 to the **No Jacket Required** album.

BUNNY PAUL

When Bunny Paul was persuaded to sign a brief contract with the Gordy label in 1963, she was already something of a seasoned professional, having enjoyed a professional career since the 1940s. Born in Detroit, Michigan on 21 May 1924, Bunny would record more than fifty singles for various labels, both big and small, in a wide variety of styles, most notably rockabilly. Unfortunately, despite her stunning good looks and strong voice, Bunny invariably got lost in record industry politics, seldom collecting any royalties from the singles that sold and struggling to be considered a priority as she moved from one label to the next.

Her move to Capitol in 1955 promised much, with Cashbox gushing about her debut. 'Bunny Paul, a tremendous performer both on wax and in person, and an artist with loads of potential, debuts on the Capitol label with a tremendous new piece of material that could establish her as a top female vocalist. It´s a driving rhythm and blues item titled *Please Have Mercy*. A powerhouse of an arrangement with Bunny singing right from the toes. One of the best things she´s done to date.'

Despite Cashbox' endorsement the single flopped, as did a further four outings and her contract was not renewed. Bunny returned to Detroit and would record for Dash, Point and Roulette over the next few years as well as performing live. Her career then suffered massive jolts, with her twins being still born and then in 1960 she developed a brain tumour, which initially left her unable to talk or walk properly.

Three years later, despite still not feeling well, Bunny was persuaded to cut a couple of sides for Motown, being coaxed through the recording sessions for *I'm Hooked* and *We're Only Young Once* by producer Clarence Paul (no relation). With assistance from a young Martha Reeves on backing vocals, Bunny managed to give a good performance on the A-side, reminiscent of her earlier rockabilly tracks. Although *I'm Hooked,* released in May 1963 on Tamla, picked up significant radio play, the record would get overtaken and overlooked by the sudden British invasion and Bunny decided to call a permanent halt to her career.

CLARENCE PAUL

Although best known as a writer and producer for Stevie Wonder, most notably during his 'Little' days at Motown, Clarence Paul began his career as a singer, recording both gospel and secular music. Born Clarence Otto Pauling in Winston-Salem, North Carolina on 19 March 1928, Clarence grew up in a musical family and helped form gospel group The Royal Sons Quintet with his brother Lowman. By the time the group changed name to The 5 Royales and began their recording career, Clarence was serving in the US Army in the Korean War.

When he returned home he recorded secular music for a number of labels, including Federal, Roulette, Hannover and Pride, shortening his name to Clarence Paul in order to avoid confusion with his brother. He moved to Detroit in the early 1960s where he was introduced to Motown by Mickey Stevenson, becoming an in-house writer and producer. After early work on artists as diverse as The Valadiers, Hattie Littles, Gino Parks, Mike & The Modifiers and Henry Lumpkin, Clarence scored his first number one hit with *Fingertips Part 2* on Little Stevie Wonder in 1963. And Clarence was not only responsible for Stevie's output in the studio, for many at Motown said Clarence was something of a father figure to the precocious youngster, teaching him vocal techniques, accompanying him on tour and ensuring he kept out of trouble.

Clarence was responsible for writing or producing many of Little Stevie's early hits, including *Hey Love, Until You Come Back To Me* (later a major hit for Aretha Franklin), *I'm Wondering* and *Work Out Stevie Work Out* as well a number of songs for other artists, most notably *Hitch Hike* by Marvin Gaye and *Just A Little Misunderstanding* by The Contours.

His best known production was probably on *Blowin' In The Wind*, the Bob Dylan song recorded by Stevie with Clarence prompting him so that it sounded like a duet. Berry and several other Motown executives accused Clarence of using the song to promote his own singing career, an accusation that could not have been further from the truth!

He remained with Motown until the 1970s when he left in order to link up with Mickey Stevenson at Venture Records where he was appointed head of A&R. Clarence died from complications of heart disease and diabetes whilst lying in hospital at the Cedars-Sinai Medical Center in Los Angeles on 6 May 1995, with Stevie Wonder at his side. His body was later returned to Winston-Salem and buried alongside his brother Lowman (who died in 1973) at the Piedmont Memorial Gardens.

ERNIE PAYNE

Born in Acadia Parish, Louisiana on 13 April 1945, Ernie Payne made his first stab at success as one half of Dinsmore Payne with Rick Dinsmore, releasing an album on United Artists in 1973. The album was entirely composed by Ernie, proof of his songwriting abilities, and when Dinsmore Payne disbanded Mike Curb was quick to sign Ernie to Motown's country label, Melodyland. Only one single was released, *Take Me (The Way That I Am)* backed with *Talk To Jeanette* appearing in December 1975. Three years later Ernie came by Motown again, being signed to Mike Curb's MC label for *Neon Riders And Sawdust Gliders* backed with *The Very Last Love Letter* which was issued in April 1978.

Motown's involvement with the MC label came to an abrupt end and Mike Curb took the label and much of its roster to Warner Brothers, with *Neon Riders* subsequently appearing on the Warner Brothers label in January 1979. Despite this it would not be until 2004 that Ernie released his debut album, touring Europe for the first time in support of that album. He died in Los Angeles on 17 September 2007.

SCHERRIE PAYNE

The younger sister of fellow singer Freda, Scherrie Payne was born in Detroit, Michigan on 14 November 1944 and is best known for her spell as lead singer of the Supremes. After graduating from Michigan State University with a Bachelor of Science degree, Scherrie had a spell teaching at the Grayling Observatory in Detroit as well as recording a number of unreleased tracks for the Revilot label. It was Eddie Holland's pursuit of Freda that got Scherrie her start in the business, as Scherrie would later recall.

"Freda was on the telephone with Eddie. She was just getting ready to sign with the company [Invictus]. She was on the phone in the kitchen and I was in the living room playing the piano. I knew she was talking to him so I was deliberately playing very loudly, singing a song I had made up. I knew he was gonna call me to the phone. Sure enough, Freda said, 'Oh, Eddie wants to talk to you.' So he asked what was that I was playing, I said, 'It was just a song I made up,' he said 'You write songs? I said, 'Yeah,' I guess he knew I sang a little bit. He said, 'Would you be interested in auditioning for our company?' I said, 'Sure, I don't care.' So he says, 'We'll send a car around for you and I'll take you over to Lamont Dozier's house.'"

Although Scherrie successfully auditioned for Eddie and Lamont, they did not have in mind a solo career, especially since they were about to sign Freda in that capacity. Instead, Scherrie was drafted into a new group, Glass House, alongside Ty Hunter, Pearl Jones and Larry Mitchell. Whilst Freda's career got off to a blistering start with *Band Of Gold*, Glass House also hit the ground running, with *Crumbs Off The Table* making #7 R&B and #59 pop. Over the next three years the group would register a total of six R&B hits and record two albums, **Inside The Glass House** (1971) and **Thanks I Needed That** (1972) and undergo a number of line-up changes, although nothing released managed to match the appeal of their debut single. Invictus also tried releasing solo efforts by Scherrie and Ty Hunter, all to no avail.

The group finally went their separate ways following the release of their second album, with Scherrie touring with Charo as a backing singer but giving serious consideration to leaving the industry altogether. In 1973 a phone conversation between Mary Wilson and Lamont Doxier gave Scherrie her next big break; with Jean Terrell having exited The Supremes, Mary called Lamont to ask for suggestions for a possible replacement. Lamont gave her Scherrie's telephone number and after a brief conversation Scherrie was invited along for an audition.

Despite standing only five feet two, Scherrie had become known throughout the industry as 'The little lady with the big voice' and it was that voice that convinced Mary that she had found the new lead singer for The Supremes. Her first two years with the group was spent touring and perfecting her live performances, with Motown showing little interest in getting the group into the studio for recording purposes. Mary finally managed to convince Motown to give them some studio time in 1975, resulting in the album **The Supremes** being released in June 1975. Although not a major seller (it would hit #152 pop and #25 R&B), *He's My Man* attracted considerable attention from the dance crowd to get released as a single, where it would peak at #69 R&B.

That success, such as it was, would provide a blueprint for the group's subsequent album **High Energy** (which reunited The Supremes with Brian and Eddie Holland), with Scherrie sharing lead vocal duties with Susaye Greene, who replaced Cindy Birdsong in the group in February 1976. All three singers (Mary, Scherrie and Susaye) would handle lead vocals on what was to become the final Supremes studio album, **Mary, Scherrie & Susaye**, released in October 1976, with the Holland brothers again at the helm.

Whilst Mary would eventually secure a solo recording contract with Motown and release one album (Scherrie was also offered a solo deal, which resulted in one single, *Fly*, which was withdrawn in the US but released in the UK in January 1978), Scherrie and Susaye linked up for the album **Partners**, produced by Eugene McDaniels and an album on which both Scherrie and Susaye sang lead and wrote material. With little or no promotion behind it the album failed to find a market, with both singers opting for solo careers in the aftermath.

Motown showed little interest in signing either, with the result they left the company, Scherrie becoming a backing singer for the likes of James Ingram, Jose Feliciano, Thelma Houston, The Brothers Johnson and Luther Vandross as well as touring with her sister Freda. In 1982 Scherrie launched something of a solo career with Altair and later Megatone Records, and four years later was instrumental in getting several former members of The Supremes back together for the FLOS project (Former Ladies of The Supremes), which continues to tour around the world.
ALBUM: PARTNERS (1979)

ANN PEEBLES

Best known for the hits *Part Time Love* and *I Can't Stand The Rain*, Ann Peebles was a vastly under-rated talent. Born in St Louis, Missouri on 27 April 1947, Ann began singing in the choir at the church where her father was minister and sang with the family group The Peebles Choir. Her introduction to secular music came through Oliver Sain, who added her to his revue and took her on tour around the country.

It was in Memphis in 1968 that Ann got her big break, being introduced to Gene 'Bowlegs' Miller who in turn took her to Hi Records where head producer Willie Mitchell was in the process of switching the company's musical emphasis from country to R&B. Ann was signed to a contract and put together with in-house writer Don Bryant (who she would marry in 1974) to work on material. Both *Part Time Love* and *I Can't Stand The Rain* made the Top Ten of the R&B chart, with Ann's other hits including *I'm Gonna Tear Your Playhouse Down* (later covered by Paul Young), *Breaking Up Somebody's Home* and *I Pity The Fool*. By the end of the 1970s however, Hi Records had been sold and Ann had taken a hiatus in order to concentrate on raising her family. Following a licensing deal between Motown and Cream Records, a compilation of her greatest hits was issued on Motown in 1982.
ALBUM: I CAN'T STAND THE RAIN (1982)

PENNY LOVER – LIONEL RICHIE [SINGLE]

Lionel Richie's **Can't Slow Down** album produced no fewer than five Top Ten hits, a tally that maintained his status as one of the superstars of popular music of the 1980s. The fifth and final single, released in September 1984 was *Penny Lover*, another ballad written by Lionel and his then wife Brenda Harvey Richie. Aided by a promotional video directed by Bob Giraldi, the director for previous hits *Running With The Night* and *Hello*, *Penny Lover* would peak at #8 on both the pop and R&B chart and make #18 in the UK. The single also performed exceptionally well on the Adult Contemporary chart, spending four weeks at #1.

ROGER PENZABENE

After graduating from Mumford High School in Detroit in 1963, Roger (his forename is also sometimes spelt 'Rodger', although virtually all Motown material shows it as 'Roger') accepted an offer from school friend and guitarist Cornelius Grant to join him at Hitsville, with the latter thinking that the former's way with words might make him a useful acquisition to the team of writers at Motown. And so it proved, for Roger was to show that his ability to craft lyrics that actually meant something could be the difference between a miss, a small hit and a monster hit.

Unfortunately, Roger also used his songwriting as a way of getting out into the open matters that were troubling him at home, with his wife Helga's affair with another man the subject matter for more than a few of his poignant lyrics. Whilst he is chiefly remembered for a trio of songs performed by The Temptations (*You're My Everything*, *I Could Never Love Another* and *I Wish It Would Rain*), all of which highlight the internal struggle he was going through, he co-wrote many other fine songs, including *Take Me In Your Arms And Rock Me*, *The End Of The Road* and *Save My Love For A Rainy Day*.

In all Roger would help write 15 songs that are a part of the Motown canon, but it is with *I Wish It Would Rain* that his legacy reached its peak. Roger was at the recording session and as David Ruffin (who described Roger as "A nice, white Jewish songwriter with long hair who wrote great songs at Motown. For a long time, people thought he was black because he kept a tan – truthfully") sang the emotionally charged song (Helga had recently left to be with her lover), Roger was actually sobbing in the control booth. Roger committed suicide on 31 December 1967, a week after the track was released, with The Temptations learning of the tragic blow whilst on their way to a New Year's Eve date in New Jersey. Apparently, it was raining particularly hard on the day they were told the news.

FREDDIE PERREN

The body of work he produced whilst at Motown would ensure Freddie Perren a place in music history, but his accomplishments after leaving the company's employ place him among the most successful writers and producers of all time.

Born in Englewood, New Jersey on 15 May 1943, Freddie graduated from the Dwight Morrow High School in 1961 and subsequently attended the Howard University in Washington D.C. where he first met Fonce Mizell and Larkin Arnold. Both Freddie and Fonce moved to California in 1968 where they met up with guitarist Deke Richards, a former member of the in-house writing team at Motown known as The Clan. The three began working on material for Gladys Knight, including a song *I Wanna Be Free*, but were eventually diverted into rebuilding the song into *I Want You Back*, the debut single for The Jackson 5 which was credited to The Corporation (Freddie, Fonce, Deke and Motown head Berry Gordy). The Corporation would pen subsequent hits *ABC*, *The Love You Save*, *Mama's Pearl* and *Maybe Tomorrow* as well as numerous album tracks for The Jackson 5, with Freddie's wife Christine Yarian (they met in 1967 and married three years later) also briefly becoming a member before the team was disbanded in 1972.

Freddie and Fonce retained their partnership however, going on to score the blaxploitation film 'Hell Up In Harlem' with Edwin Starr the featured vocalist and 'Cooley High', which showcased *It's So Hard To Say Goodbye To Yesterday* by G.C. Cameron and later a major hit for Boyz II Men. Freddie was also responsible for The Miracles (with new member Billy Griffin) adopting a much funkier sound, penning and producing *Do It Baby* which in turn would inspire Billy and Warren Moore to come up with the concept album **City Of Angels** and the smash hit *Love Machine*, with Freddie responsible for production.

Freddie left Motown shortly after with no set plan or idea as to which direction to go until old college friend Larkin Arnold, by then a vice president at Capitol Records, suggested he work with The Sylvers, a family group similar in style to The Jackson 5 (Edmund Sylvers had actually provided the voice of Marlon Jackson on the television cartoon series!). Freddie was soon back in the charts, linking with writer Kenny St Lewis on *Boogie Fever* (a pop and R&B chart topper) and *Hot Line* and the successful albums **Showcase** and **Something Special**.

When The Sylvers opted to produce themselves, Freddie switched to Tavares, another family group, producing three albums in **Sky High** (the production company formed by Larry and Fonce Mizell would be named Sky High Productions), **Love Storm** and **Future Bound** and the hit singles *Don't Take Away The Music* and *Heaven Must Be Missing An Angel*. However, it was the inclusion of a remake of The Bee Gees' *More Than A Woman* on the soundtrack to 'Saturday Night Fever' and Freddie's production on *If I Can't Have You* by Yvonne Elliman (the Bee Gees, who wrote the song, preferred Freddie's version to their own!) that would enable Freddie to take a share in the Grammy Award for Album of the Year.

In 1978 he formed his own production company MVP Productions based at his own Mom & Pop's Company Store studio, signing Peaches & Herb and getting them a deal with Polydor. Along with another former Motown writer in Dino Fekaris, Freddie turned the fortunes of Peaches & Herb's round, giving them the up-tempo smash *Shake Your Groove Thing* and the ballad smash *Reunited*, a pop and R&B chart topper. Incorporating both up-tempo and down tempo elements enabled Freddie and Dino to craft a song they would forever be remembered for, with *I Will Survive* by Gloria Gaynor topping the pop charts on both sides of the Atlantic, sell over four million copies in the US and more than half a million in the UK as well as winning the Grammy Award for Best Disco Recording (the only time the award was presented).

Freddie would later work with another young group New Edition, but by the end of the 1980s he was largely inactive as both a writer and producer. After suffering a stroke in 1993 he spent the next eleven years battling to recover his health but died on 16 December 2004.

PAUL PETERSEN

Ultimately better known as an actor than a singer, Paul Petersen (born William Paul Petersen in Glendale, California on 23 September 1945) was seemingly yet another attempt by Berry Gordy to generate record sales out of a personality from another field, again with little or no success. Paul had first come to prominence as a Mouseketeer on the 'Mickey Mouse Club', which led to a film role in 'Houseboat' with Sophia Loren and Cary Grant before landing his best known role on 'The Donna Reed Show', playing her son Jeff Stone. Paul would remain with the show for eight years, during which he also made his first stab at recording success, signing with Colpix and enjoying six hits over a period of eighteen months, including a Top Ten hit with *My Dad* in 1962. He signed with Motown in 1967, after he had left 'The Donna Reed Show', so with hindsight the lack of a weekly promotional outlet may well have helped stall his time at Hitsville, with *Chained* (May 1967) and *A Little Bit For Sandy* (August 1968) failing to replicate his earlier success.

P.F.M.

Italian progressive rock group P.F.M. (the name stood for Premiata Forneria Marconi, which translates to 'award-winning Marconi bakery') formed in 1970 and achieved considerable domestic success during their early career. They were spotted by Greg Lake of Emerson, Lake & Palmer in 1973 whilst ELP were on tour in Italy and were signed to Manticore Records, ELP's boutique label for the US and UK. By this time the group consisted of Bernardo Lanzetti (vocals), Franco Mussida (guitar and vocals), Flavio Premoli (keyboards and vocals), Mauro Pagani (flute, violin and vocals), Patrick Djivas (bass and vocals) and Franz Di Cioccio (drums and vocals). The first album, **P.F.M. Cook** was a live recording that had previously been released in Italy as **Live In The USA**, whilst the follow-up **Chocolate Kings** was released in 1976, the last album issued under the Manticore agreement.

ALBUMS: P.F.M. COOK (1974), CHOCOLATE KINGS (1976)

ESTHER PHILLIPS

Born Esther Mae Jones in Galveston, Texas on 23 December 1935, she was spotted at an amateur talent contest in 1949 by Johnny Otis, who was so impressed with her talent he recorded a number of tracks for Modern Records. These were billed as 'Little Esther Phillips' (the name apparently came from a petrol station), although her first hit wouldn't come until 1950 and *Double Crossing Blues* issued on Savoy.

Esther left Johnny Otis at the end of 1950 and signed directly with Federal Records, but without his guidance and a growing addiction to drugs Esther wasted much of her talent for the rest of the decade. She made her comeback in 1962 recording for a number of labels, including Atlantic and Roulette, as well as coming to the attention of The Beatles, who flew her over to Europe after hearing her version of *And I Love Him*.

In 1971 she signed with Kudu and would go on to record seven albums for the label, scoring a major hit first time out with her version of Gil Scott-Heron's *Home Is Where The Hatred Is*, something that was almost an autobiographical song for Esther. Her 1974 album **Performance** was the first under the agreement between CTI and Motown and hit both the jazz (#27) and R&B charts (#46), but it was the following year's **What A Diff'rence A Day Makes** (also known as **Esther Phillips With Beck**) that enabled her to crossover, with the disco influenced title track becoming a Top 20 US and Top Ten UK hit (although it should be noted that her records were distributed in the UK by Polydor, who held the CTI and Kudu distribution rights), exposing her to a whole new generation of record buyers. The album was a major seller too, hitting #3 jazz, #13 R&B and cracking the Top 40 of the pop chart, peaking at #32. However, her continued drug use still punctuated her career and led indirectly to the liver and kidney failure that was to lead to her early death on 7 August 1984.

ALBUMS: PERFORMANCE (1974), WHAT A DIFF'RENCE A DAY MAKES (1975)

WILSON PICKETT

Born in Prattville, Alabama on 18 March 1941, the fourth of eleven children, Wilson endured a troubled childhood, eventually running away from home in order to live with his father in Detroit. He eventually found salvation in singing, joining the gospel group The Violinaires before switching to the secular market with The Falcons. He helped write the group's 1962 hit *I Found A Love* and would subsequently record solo for Correct-tone and Double L (a label owned by Harold Logan and Lloyd Price) before Atlantic signed him in 1964.

There he created a catalogue of major hits, including *In The Midnight Hour, Mustang Sally, Land Of 1,000 Dances* and *Funky Broadway,* recorded in Memphis at Stax' studio and Fame Studios in Muscle Shoals. Wilson remained with Atlantic until 1972 when he switched to RCA, but his subsequent recordings never quite reached the heights set by his earlier work and after three years he was dropped from the label.

He recorded sporadically thereafter and signed with Motown in 1987 where he worked with producer Robert Margouleff on **American Soul Man**, which would give rise to the US R&B hit *Don't Turn Away* (#74) and the UK pop hit *In The Midnight Hour* (#62), a remake of his best known number. His extensive back catalogue ensured he was in demand for concert appearances in the ensuing years and he continued to tour until ill health brought a halt in 2004. He died from a heart attack on 19 January 2006.
ALBUM: AMERICAN SOUL MAN (1987)

CHRISTOPHE PIERRE

Christophe Pierre made his only Broadway appearance in the 1976 revival of 'Guys And Dolls' in the role of Benny Southstreet, appearing on the soundtrack album and was one of several original members of the cast who reprised their roles in a touring version in 1977.

PIPPIN (BROADWAY SHOW)

Written by Stephen Schwartz, the musical 'Pippin' opened at the Imperial Theater on Broadway on 23 October 1972 and ran for 1,944 performances prior to closing on 12 June 1977. The show also opened in London's West End in 1979 and was revived on Broadway in 2013. The original Broadway production featured Eric Berry as Charles, Jill Clayburgh (Catherine), Leland Palmer (Fastrada), Irene Ryan (Berthe), Ben Vereen (Leading Player) and John Rubinstein (Pippin), with Dorothy Stickney replacing Irena Ryan after Irene's death in April 1973. Motown signed a deal to back the Broadway production and release the cast recording album, which was duly issued in December 1972 (it was also released on CD in 1986), with the album going on to hit #129 on the album chart. The show itself earned back several millions during the course of its six year run, a substantial return on Motown's initial investment of $140,000. Motown subsequently released two singles by Irene Ryan from the album, both appearing shortly before her death.
ALBUM: PIPPIN CAST RECORDING (1972)

THE PIRATES

In September 1962 Berry Gordy got word that a record that was strong on local radio, *Mind Over Matter (I'm Gonna Make You Mine)* by Nolan Strong & The Diablos on Fortune Records had hit something of a sales road block. Whilst Fortune had managed to press up sufficient stock to meet the anticipated demand, the records were languishing in a warehouse rather than being sent out to record stores.

Spotting an opportunity to seize the initiative, Berry sent a five man vocal group into the studio with Clarence Paul to record a cover version of *Mind Over Matter*, with Clarence instructed to come up with a version that could cross the sales divide between black and white, with the finished master, coupled with *I'll Love You Till I Die* scheduled for release the following month.

When it appeared, it was a profound shock to all concerned, for the five men who had sung on the record were Eddie Kendricks, Paul Williams, Otis Williams, Melvin Franklin and Al Bryant, better known as The Temptations, even if they were still awaiting their first major hit.

According to Otis Williams, Berry said, "We're gonna try you guys as The Pirates. If it's a hit, you guys'll be The Pirates from now on, no more The Temptations."

It would appear that even Berry was unsure whether the move would pay off, shuttling the disc off to the Mel-O-dy graveyard rather than one of his first rank labels. Unfortunately for Berry, Fortune Records managed to resolve their distribution problem and got their stock out of warehouses and into stores, where it became something of a regional if not national success. Fortunately for the group, the Mel-O-dy single died a death (although the company tried promoting both sides in an attempt to generate some sales activity) and The Pirates were pressganged back into The Temptations.

Otis concludes, "I mean, sure, we wanted a hit, but it was like, the *Pirates?* They got to be kidding. We wanted no part of that. No way we wanted to come out with eye patches and swords."

P.J.

Al Green (not the R&B singer of the same name) was the owner of the Flame Show Bar in Detroit and also helped give a considerable number of acts their break in show business, including Jackie Wilson, Johnnie Ray, LaVern Baker and Della Reese, going on to manage most of them. He also discovered a female singer by the name of Patti Jerome, getting her a recording deal with Derby Records in 1954.

Born Patricia Morris in New York on 5 August 1925, Patti recorded her debut single *Travelin' Light* which was released on Derby's R&B subsidiary Central Records, although there was little promotion done on the record and Patti moved on to Jubilee Records for *Yoo Young To Die* in July 1954. Patti later recorded for Josie, Mercury/Wing and Rama before coming to the attention of Harry Balk. The pair married in 1958, with Patti then following Harry across the various labels he was associated with, recording for Big Top, Twirl and American Arts before joining him at his latest venture, Impact in 1965.

As well as recording several solo sides, Patti also recorded a duet with Mickey Denton, although by 1968 Harry Balk had sold his recording interests to Berry Gordy and had joined Motown where he would help set up the Rare Earth label. Patti went with him to Motown too, releasing *(I've Given You) The Best Years Of My Life* backed with *It Takes A Man To Teach A Woman How To Love* on the V.I.P. label in April 1971, billed as P.J. Eight months later she would release another single in *T.L.C. (Tender Loving Care)* with the same B side for the Tamla label, but would go on to achieve better results as a writer for Jobete.

When Motown shut down its Detroit base and moved to California, the Balk's went with them, although Patti went into the film industry rather than back to music, appearing in a number of films including 'Sgt Pepper', 'Alligator' and 'Buddy Buddy'. Having battled several illnesses during the late 1990s, Patti died in Los Angeles on 24 September 2000.

A PLACE IN THE SUN – STEVIE WONDER [SINGLE]

Motown and Stevie Wonder wasted little time on capitalising on his new found success with **Uptight** and the *Blowing' In The Wind* single, heading back into the studio to record **Down To Earth** with much the same mixture of songs as its predecessor. This time around the Bob Dylan cover was *Mr. Tambourine Man*, but instead of a cover, the first single release was a Ron Miller and Bryan Wells original entitled *A Place In the Sun*.

Released in the US in October 1966 (and in the UK two months later), it would go on to become a major hit, equalling the #9 pop peak of *Blowin'* and hitting #3 on the R&B charts. It also proved to be more appealing to UK audiences, where it reached #20, some sixteen places higher than its predecessor. Stevie would also record an Italian version entitled *Il Sole E Di Tutti*, which translates to *The Sun Is For Everyone*, with the I Cantori Moderni di Alessandroni choir. Although the Italian version attracted a cover version by Dino (the stage name of Eugene Zambelli) that was released ahead of Stevie's, it was Stevie's version that became the biggest hit, topping the Italian chart in November 1968.

THE PLANETS

Following the demise of Liverpool group Deaf School in 1978, bass guitarist Steve 'Average' Lindsey released a couple of singles as Steve Tempo and then began putting together a new band to be called The Secrets. This never quite materialised, instead evolving into New Wave synth pop group The Planets who got a contract with the small Rialto label. With Steve handling writing, production, bass, guitar and drums, the rest of the group comprised Danny Kustow (guitar), John Turnbull (guitar), Tony Wimhurst (guitar), Mickey Gallagher (keyboards) and Charlie Charles (drums).

The group enjoyed two minor hit singles in *Lies* and *Don't Look Down* and might have had success with

their debut album **Goon Hilly Down** but for Rialto hitting financial problems. The album was picked up for release in the US in February 1980 by Motown, although repackaged and entitled **The Planets**, with *Break It To Me Gently* being released as a single two months later.
ALBUM: THE PLANETS (1980)

PLATINUM HOOK

A self-contained R&B group formed by Tina Renee Stanford (vocals), Stephen Daniels (drums and vocals), Robert Douglas (keyboards), Elisha 'Skip' Ingrams (bass), Victor Jones (guitar), Robin David Carley (saxophone and flute) and Glenn Wallace (trombone), Platinum Hook signed with Motown in 1978.
Producer Greg Wright provided two of the cuts on their debut eponymous album, but it was the George Clinton cover *Standing On The Verge (Of Getting It On)* that provided them with their only hit, spending a solitary week at #72 in the UK in September 1978. Their second album **It's Time** saw them undergo a subtle change of style to disco, but this too missed the mark and the group left Motown soon after, with a third album **Ecstasy Paradise** remaining unreleased. Platinum Hook subsequently resurfaced at RCA four years later for a mini album.
ALBUMS: PLATINUM HOOK (1978), IT'S TIME (1979)

PLAYBOY – THE MARVELETTES [SINGLE]

Georgia Dobbins had been responsible for bringing The Marvelettes first major hit *Please Mr. Postman* into Hitsville and it was another Marvelette, Gladys Horton who originated their second Top Ten hit *Playboy*. As before, the song was knocked into shape by Brian Holland, Robert Bateman and Mickey Stevenson, with Brian and Robert producing the session in November 1961, with Gladys on lead vocals. With The Marvelettes enjoying some success with *Twistin' Mr. Postman* (a #34 pop and #13 R&B hit), the release of *Playboy* was held over until April 1962.
When finally released it hit #7 pop and #4 R&B, but success came with a price to pay; during the course of promoting the single, the group appeared on the Dick Clark show 'American Bandstand', with Marvelette member Juanita Cowart making a nervous slip during the course of an interview. Taking the slip to heart, Juanita stopped performing live and would subsequently leave the group. *Playboy* also marked the final Motown contribution for Robert Bateman, who headed off to New York to set up his own label operation.

PLEASE MR. POSTMAN – THE MARVELETTES [SINGLE]

Five young schoolgirls auditioned for Motown in April 1961, having been given a roundabout introduction to the company via Berry Gordy's driver and bodyguard. Then billed as The Casinyets passed the audition, they were told to come back to the label when they had an original song that could be recorded. They had little more than a basic idea, based on some lyrics and a title concocted by Georgia Dobbins and a tune that was originally a blues style piece by William Garrett, who lived in the same Inkster area as the girls.
It was enough to get them back into Motown however, where Brian Holland, Robert Bateman and Freddie Gorman would flesh out the basic idea into a fully blown song. Freddie Gorman's contribution proved especially beneficial, for he was actually a postman during the day and, keen to move into the music business, spent much of his spare time hanging around the Hitsville complex. Song writer Georgia Dobbins left the group before the recording session owing to a family conflict (her mother was taken ill and it was said her father was against her singing in a group) but did at least help the remaining four girls find a replacement in Wanda Young. In early August 1961, all was ready for recording, with Gladys Horton selected as the lead vocalist on the song, *Please Mr. Postman* and a musical backing provided by Marvin Gaye and Benny Benjamin on drums, James Jamerson on bass, Popcorn Wylie on piano and Eddie 'Bongo' Brown on percussion.
The single was readied for release before the month was out, although no one at Motown was particularly happy with the jokey name the group had given themselves, finally electing to call them The Marvelettes. Released on 21 August on the Tamla label, *Please Mr. Postman* was certainly the most commercial release the fledgling label had released up to that point and proved to be a major success, sailing to the top of both the pop and R&B chart, knocking Jimmy Dean's *Big Bad John* off the summit. It may have remained at the top for only a week (although it would spend seven weeks at the summit of the R&B chart) and for The Marvelettes proved impossible to equal, let alone better, but its status as the very first #1 hit on any of Motown's labels makes it a historic record.

It was also an immensely popular song, with The Beatles incorporating it into their stage act in 1962 and recording it for their second album **With The Beatles**. In 1974 it was revived once again by brother and sister act The Carpenters, who took it to the top of the pop chart for a second time and hit #2 in the UK.

BONNIE POINTER

Born Patricia Eva Pointer in Oakland, California on 11 July 1950 and linked with her younger sister June (born in Oakland on 30 November 1953) in 1969 in an act that worked as Pointer, A Pair. When Anita (born in Oakland on 23 January 1948) joined the act, the name changed to The Pointer Sisters, with the trio getting a brief contract with Atlantic Records. By the end of 1972 the act had expanded still further with the addition of Ruth (born in Oakland on 19 March 1946) and adopted 1940s attire and vocal style. They scored their breakthrough hit *Yes We Can Can* and would go on to score a major country hit with *Fairytale* in 1974, winning a Grammy Award for Best Country Vocal Performance by a Group as well as a nomination for Best Country Song for writers Bonnie and Anita Pointer.

By 1977 however the group was beginning to splinter, with June wanting to take a complete break from the music scene and Bonnie looking to pursue a solo career. Her friend Jeffrey Bowen was responsible for getting Bonnie a contract with Motown, co-producing her debut eponymous album with Berry Gordy. The lead single *Free Me From My Freedom* was to be her biggest R&B hit, peaking at #10 and also making #58 pop following its October 1978 release.

However, it was a cover version of *Heaven Must Have Sent You* that proved to be the bigger hit, making #11 on the pop listings and a lowly #52 R&B. Aided by the single success, the first Bonnie Pointer album would reach #96 pop and #34 R&B. Bowen retained much the same formula for her second album, also entitled **Bonnie Pointer**, with cover versions of six Holland-Dozier-Holland songs, headed by a dance remake of *I Can't Help Myself*. This would become the only hit single lifted from the album, peaking at #40 pop and #42 R&B, with the parent album making #63 pop. Bonnie left Motown soon after owing to a contract dispute and would resume her career with Private I Records in 1984.

ALBUMS: BONNIE POINTER (1978), BONNIE POINTER (1979)

POOR BOYS

A vocal and songwriting trio who recorded one album produced by Mike Valvano, Poor Boys comprised Robert Fazio, Thomas Corio and Edwin Corliss. Their only album, **Ain't Nothin' In Our Pockets But Love** was recorded in July 1970 and released in September on Rare Earth, one of seven albums released on the label that month (out of a total of 26 albums released by the company in September). Aimed at the bubblegum market, it was some two years out of date at the time of release, although *Mary Mary* from the album would later draw a cover version from The Maccabees.

ALBUM: AIN'T NOTHIN' IN OUR POCKET BUT LOVE (1970)

POSSE

Managed and mentored by Eddie Kendricks, Posse opened several live shows for The Temptations and also had a brief recording career of their own, initially with Janus before Eddie brought them into the Motown fold. Featuring Rick Langston, Reggie Thomas, Reggie Carr, Roosevelt Albreight and Dallas Bush, the group recorded *Feel Like Givin' Up*, which was written by Eddie with Ronn Matlock and produced by Eddie. The single was the last release on the V.I.P. imprint in February 1972 but suffered from a lack of promotion, resulting in it doing little. Eddie would revisit the song nearly eighteen months later as a planned single release by former Temptations member Paul Williams, but following his suicide this was subsequently scrapped. Posse meanwhile later had releases on E.J.K., Eddie's own label imprint.

MAXINE POWELL

Taught etiquette and refinement by her aunt, Maxine Powell would in turn teach those qualities to scores of artists who passed through the doors of Hitsville. Born Maxine Blair in Texarcana, Texas on 30 May 1915, she was raised in Chicago by her aunt and moved to Detroit in 1945.

By 1951 she had opened the Maxine Powell Finishing & Modelling School and later opened a banqueting centre on Ferry Street (where Smokey Robinson and Claudette Rogers held their wedding reception) as well as running an agency which would be the first to place black models with several of the local car manufacturers. One such model, Gwen Gordy Fuqua, convinced her brother that Maxine Powell was the woman to coax and school Motown's talent off stage when Berry Gordy set up the Artist Development Department in 1964.

Just about every artist who received instruction during the five years Maxine was associated with Motown reaped the benefit, including Marvin Gaye, who was taught to sing with his eyes open as Maxine thought he looked asleep when he sang with them shut!

And it was not always easy, for Maxine often found some of the artists, "Rude and crude. They were twenty years old, and all they wanted was a hit record. I told them, I'm teaching you skills for life. I taught positive change through body language and word power. I told these young artists that they were not the best singers and dancers in the world, that our race has always had great performers. My job was to keep them from going on an ego trip – to remind them that each performance was a dress rehearsal."

Maxine's involvement with Motown came to an abrupt end in 1969 (she never revealed the reasons why), although she later taught a course in personal development at Wayne Community College. She died at the age of 98 on 14 October 2013 after a lengthy illness.

POWER OF ZEUS

Formed in Detroit, Michigan by guitarist and singer Joe Periano soon after his discharge from the US Marines in 1968, the group also featured Bill Jones (bass and vocals), Dennie Webber (keyboards) and Bob Michalski (drums). Initially gigging under the name Gangrene, they took their musical inspiration from the likes of Black Sabbath and Led Zeppelin and attracted the attention of Motown, looking to beef up the Rare Earth roster. They were signed on condition they change their name, subsequently adopting Power Of Zeus and recording their only album **The Gospel According To Zeus** with producers Russ and Ralph Terrana.

Released in September 1970 it was largely ignored at the time, due in part to Motown not really knowing how to market the only hard rock act they had under their wing. A single, *Hard Working Man* backed with *Realization* was released in Germany but failed to make an impact, resulting in the album remaining unreleased in Europe. This did not stop the album becoming an in demand item over the years, with several artists sampling from the original and the album finally being issued on CD in 2011. The group disbanded in 1971, with Joe Periano remaining at Motown for a short period, later producing an album on Luther Allison.

ALBUM: THE GOSPEL ACCORDING TO ZEUS (1970)

BILLY PRESTON

A supremely talented keyboard player, Billy Preston's chief claim to fame was that he was the only musician to be credited on an official Beatles record, surely the ultimate accolade.

Born William Everett Preston in Houston, Texas on 2 September 1946, Billy spent much of his childhood growing up in Los Angeles, where he and his half-sister Rodena learned to play the piano together. Whilst Rodena was talented, Billy's abilities were on a different plane altogether, resulting in him playing in his local church choir at the age of seven, performing with a symphony orchestra at ten, accompanying Mahalia Jackson soon after and making his film debut at twelve in the role of a young W.C. Handy in 'St Louis Blues' alongside Nat King Cole, Eartha Kitt and Cab Calloway. Adept at both the piano and organ, Billy soon learned to play both at the same time.

"I had been inspired by an organ player named Earl Grant, who played organ and piano together. My mom took me to see him. So I went home, put my piano and organ together too."

Word of his talent soon spread, resulting in a regular position in Little Richard's touring band in 1962.

"We met in church and he was getting ready to go to England to do a gospel tour. Or so we thought. We got over there and it turned out to be a rock and roll tour. That was the first time that I ever played rock and roll because until then I had been strictly gospel. I learned a great deal but the thing I remember most was Little Richard leaving me in London stranded. He was going through some enormous mental changes at the time. He had given up rock and roll for gospel and now he was being forced back."

Despite being left in the lurch, Billy had made some useful contacts, for also on that tour were Sam Cooke and two Liverpool groups in Gerry & The Pacemakers and The Beatles, with Billy forming a close friendship with the latter.

"One night they even asked me to join them on stage but I had to say no because Richard would get mad."

Sam Cooke meanwhile was impressed enough to hand Billy his first recording contract, signing him to his SAR label which released his debut album **Sixteen Year Old Soul**. Following SAR's demise Billy picked up a deal with Vee-Jay where he would record two albums before signing for Capitol in 1966 (where he would work with Sly Stone). In between recording his own albums Billy kept busy as a session musician, which led to an introduction to Ray Charles and with it a three year spell touring and recording.

"The first time I met Ray, I was going to school around the corner from his house. One day, he was playing the piano. I eased up on the porch to listen to him. On stage Ray's band and the Raelettes and I would perform the first half with me sitting in Ray's place. He was very gracious to me and would introduce me to the audience by saying that he was counting on me to carry on for him after he's gone."

It was through Ray, at least indirectly, that Billy would hook up with The Beatles once again. Midway through the recording of **Let It Be**, an exasperated George Harrison walked out of the sessions after growing tired of the arguments between Paul and John and went to see Ray Charles in concert. Backstage he sought out Billy and invited him to Abbey Road, where Billy's easy going manner cooled a volatile atmosphere, at least temporarily, as Billy later recalled.

"It was a struggle for them. They were kind of despondent. They had lost the joy of doing it all." Despite their own internal wrangles, the four looked after Billy. "The Beatles did treat me as a member of the group. And that was a great honour, you know?"

Billy played on a number of tracks, most notably *Get Back* (which would be released with the credit The Beatles With Billy Preston) and several others on both **Abbey Road** and **Let It Be** and quickly earned the moniker of The Fifth Beatle. John Lennon even suggested making the appointment official, although Paul blocked it on the grounds that it was bad enough with four. Instead, The Beatles' signed Billy to their Apple label as a solo artist in 1969, resulting in the Top 20 hit *That's The Way God Planned It* (#11 in the UK and #62 in the US), although the album of the same name failed to make an impact. Billy would release one further album on Apple, **Encouraging Words** being issued on both sides of the Atlantic in 1970 (which contained Billy's version of *My Sweet Lord*, released before George's version) but again generated little by way of sales.

As The Beatles and Apple became entangled in legal problems, Billy sought a release from his contract and received it, subsequently signing with A&M in 1972. There he would record **I Wrote A Simple Song** as his label debut, where *Outa Space* enabled him to claim he wrote a successful one too, topping the R&B chart and earning a Grammy Award for Best Pop Instrumental Performance and sell more than a million copies. He followed this success with *Will It Go Round In Circles* and *Nothing From Nothing*, both of which topped the pop chart, although album sales didn't quite match the success he attained with his singles.

After completing his A&M contract in 1975 Billy became something of a guest musician for a number of artists, most notably The Rolling Stones, appearing on several albums and assisting Mick Jagger in writing the international smash *Miss You* (albeit uncredited, since all Rolling Stones material carried the credit of Jagger/Richards). By 1978 his career had come to something of a temporary halt, although a role in the film 'Sgt Pepper's Lonely Heart Club Band' raised his profile, enough for Motown to offer him a contract.

His first project was the soundtrack album to 'Fast Break' with Syreeta, with the two dueting on *Go For It* and *With You I'm Born Again*. The former was chosen as the first single and did little, although in the UK Motown had already decided that the latter was more radio friendly, as was proved when it was released as a single and sailed all the way to #2 on the pop chart. That success was replicated in the US, where it hit #4. The track also appeared on Billy's debut album for Motown, **Late At Night** being issued in 1979, a much more diverse album than anything Billy had released previously.

"The whole thing about this album was that I had some outside help and support, whereas before it was all down to me to do everything. This time I had writers to help and the fact that it was a team effort [made] me feel very satisfied. Dave Blumberg did the arrangements and he's very good. I am an ideas man, so it was very important to me because it all has to be put down on paper. And he put together some great musicians. In the past most of my albums were done with my own band but this time we used James Gadson, Ollie Brown and a lot of guys that I had always wanted to work with."

The effort proved worth it, with the album hitting #49 pop and #73 R&B. Despite utilising much the same pool of musicians and wide variety of writers and producers, **The Way I Am** was nowhere near as successful following its release in November 1981, forcing Motown and Billy back to the drawing board. Since the duet with Syreeta had worked so well previously, it was suggested that an album of duets might prove beneficial to both artists. Produced by Ollie Brown, **Billy Preston & Syreeta** failed to produce anything as immediately catchy as *With You I'm Born Again*, although the album managed to hit #48 R&B and #127 pop. Billy was to record one further album for Motown, **Pressin' On** being released in August 1982, from which *I'm Never Gonna Say Goodbye* proved to be his final hit for the company, peaking at #88 pop and #64 R&B.

Billy left the label soon after, although he returned in October 1986 for the single *Since I Held You Close*. Thereafter Billy concentrated on session work, picking up the occasional recording contract with the likes of Megatone and NuGroove without ever coming close to matching his earlier successes. By the 1990s Billy had other problems to contend with, not least a succession of legal battles for insurance fraud, testing positive for cocaine and assault charges, although he would eventually exorcise these particular demons and return to session work, most notably with Eric Clapton, The Red Hot Chili Peppers and Steve Winwood, among others.

Having appeared on the Johnny Cash album **American IV** Billy appeared on Ray Charles' masterpiece **Genius Loves Company**, effectively coming full circle in his career, as he would subsequently acknowledge.

"When you're doing it you're just trying to do the best you can. You don't know if you're doing something important, and whether it will make history has yet to be seen. Just the fact of being able to do it, and striving to do the best you can, was the accomplishment."

Having battled kidney disease during his later life, Billy entered a drug rehabilitation centre in Malibu in California where he fell into a coma in November 2005. He died on 6 June 2006 of complications of malignant hypertension that brought on kidney failure without having regained consciousness (his half sisters Letti and Rodena subsequently sued the Kindred Hospital of Scottsdale in Arizona where Billy died for wrongful death, negligence and elder abuse). Among the mourners at his funeral two weeks later was Little Richard, who said, "He made that piano walk and talk. There's nobody in this world who could play the piano like Billy Preston."

ALBUMS: FAST BREAK (1979), LATE AT NIGHT (1979), THE WAY I AM (1981), BILLY PRESTON & SYREETA (1981), PRESSIN' ON (1981)

THE PRETTY THINGS

Somewhat unkindly dubbed the uglier cousins of The Rolling Stones, The Pretty Things followed much the same musical career path as their supposedly more handsome rivals. Formed in 1963 by one time Rolling Stones member Dick Taylor (born in Dartford, Kent on 28 January 1943, guitar) with Phil May (born Phillip Kattner in Dartford on 9 November 1944, vocals and harmonica), Brian Pendleton (born in Wolverhampton, West Midlands on 13 April 1944, rhythm guitar), John Stax (born John Fullager in Crayford, Kent on 6 April 1944, bass) and Pete Kitley (drums). Kitley was subsequently replaced by Viv Andrews and then Viv Prince (born in Loughborough, Leicestershire on 9 August 1941) just as The Pretty Things were about to explode on the UK scene.

The group scored some single success over the next two years, most notably with *Don't Bring Me Down*, a #10 pop hit in 1964 and saw their debut, eponymous album also crack the Top Ten, peaking at #6 in 1965. Further success, however, proved elusive and the group underwent a number of changes to their line-up as they struggled to keep pace with the rest of the British music scene.

Despite their lack of success in the US, their earlier albums attracted interest, with the result Barney Ales signed them to the Rare Earth label in 1969. By this time the line-up consisted of May, Taylor, John Pover (keyboards, percussion and vocals), Wally Allen (bass) and John Charles 'Twink' Alder (who replaced Skip Alan on drums midway through the sessions for their next album).

The first fruits of the deal saw the release of the concept album **S.F. Sorrow** in June 1969, with the single *Private Sorrow* being released the following month (it was the first single issued on the Rare Earth label). Neither made much of an impact either side of the Atlantic, prompting a disillusioned Dick Taylor to walk out, being replaced by Victor Unitt from The Edgar Broughton Band. Just as sessions for the next album began, Twink left to be replaced by the returning Skip Alan. **Parachutes** retained the psychedelic feel of its predecessor but still failed to make any headway on the charts, even if it was critically well received and was supposedly rated Album of the Year by 'Rolling Stone' magazine, even if its rating was given some considerable time after the September 1970 release date.

That was it for The Pretty Things as far as new material on Rare Earth was concerned, although both albums were packaged together as **Real Pretty** in 1976 when the group unexpectedly charted with the albums **Silk Torpedo** and **Savage Eye** on Swan Song. Although **Real Pretty** failed to chart, it did form part of a 1990s lawsuit launched by the group against EMI (to whom they were signed for much of the 1960s) claiming non-payment of royalties from any of the Rare Earth releases – the band won the case, an undisclosed cash settlement and their master tapes were returned complete with copyright.

ALBUMS: S.F. SORROW (1969), PARACHUTE (1970)
COMPILATION: REAL PRETTY (1976)

PRIDE AND JOY – MARVIN GAYE [SINGLE]

Two years after signing with Motown, Marvin Gaye registered his first Top Ten hit. In fact, *Pride And Joy* was only his third chart hit, with *Stubborn Kind Of Fellow* and *Hitch Hike* having peaked inside the Top 50 and Top 40 respectively over the previous few months. Written by Marvin with Norman Whitfield and Mickey Stevenson, the backing tracks were recorded in September 1962, with the vocals being added the following April, along with backing vocals from The Vandellas, shortly before the single as released. Written as something of a tribute to Marvin's then girlfriend and later wife Anna Gordy, the single would hit #10 pop and #2 R&B, the first in a long line of Top Ten hits Marvin was to enjoy over the next fourteen years. There are also a number of different versions of *Pride And Joy* in existence, with a much more jazzier version being featured on the album **Stubborn Kind Of Fellow**.

PRIME TIME

A studio project produced by Hal Davis (three tracks), Harold Johnson (two tracks) and Brenda and Michael Sutton (three tracks) featuring television soundtracks given the Motown treatment. The project saw a single, *Good Times Theme* and an album, **Motown Presents Prime Time** (with a sub title of *Performing TV Themes The Way You Like To Hear Them*) released in May and July 1978 respectively.
ALBUM: MOTOWN PRESENTS PRIME TIME (1978)

DAVE PRINCE

Another of the radio personalities who got to record a single (or more) for Motown, Dave started his broadcasting career in 1949 with KELP, based in El Paso in Texas. He first arrived in Michigan five years later, with WPAG in Ann Arbor, but his profile began to rise once he moved to Detroit, billed as Dave 'Sangoo' Prince on WKMH. Two years later he moved to WXYZ (where two other DJ's also got Motown deals, Lee Allan and Joel Sebastian), further enhancing his reputation by forwarding a cassette of Billy Lee & The Riveiras to Bob Crewe, who would sign them and give them a new moniker in Mitch Ryder & The Detroit Wheels.
Dave remained with WXYZ until 1968 when he joined WCAR and it was during his spell with this station that his one single, *The Greatest Man Who Ever Lived* was released on the Rare Earth label in 1971. Aimed at the Christmas market, *The Greatest Man* featured Dave detailing the life of Jesus Christ over a musical backing of the carol *Silent Night*. He would remain in Detroit until 1975 when he was lured to California by KIIS, remaining in Los Angeles for four years before returning 'home' to Detroit in 1980 with WCZY. After a later spell with CKLW, Dave eventually retired in 1993. "I retired after a 45 year career, mainly in the Detroit area. At one point, I was the oldest living major-market radio personality still performing – I thought it was time to hang up. I was 62 years old in my last year."

PROCOL HARUM

Formed in Southend-On-Sea, Essex in 1959 by Gary Brooker (born in London on 29 May 1945, piano and vocals), Robin Trower (born in Catford, London on 9 March 1945, guitar), Chris Copping (born in Middleton, Lancashire on 29 August 1945, bass), Bob Scott (vocals) and Mick Brownlee (drums) as the Paramounts, the group disbanded in 1966 and reformed a year later as Procol Harum with Brooker, Matthew Fisher (born in Croydon, Surrey on 7 March 1946, keyboards), Ray Royer (born on 8 October 1945, guitar), Dave Knights (born in London on 28 June 1945, bass) and Bobby Harrison (born in London on 22 June 1939, drums), although Royer and Harrison were quickly replaced by Trower and Barrie 'BJ' Wilson (born in London on 18 March 1947) respectively.
Their debut single *A White Shade Of Pale* was a British chart topper for six weeks and would hit #5 in the US following its release in 1967, going on to sell more than ten million copies worldwide. The track was included on the soundtrack to 'The Big Chill' and would subsequently be named Best Single (jointly with Queen's *Bohemian Rhapsody*) at the 1977 BRIT Awards. Wilson died on 8 October 1990. Gary Brooker was appointed an M.B.E. in the Queen's Birthday Honours in 2003.

BILLY PROCTOR

The name Billy Proctor may not have appeared on the charts, but under his real name Billy Hill he hit the very top; as a member of The Essex he scored an R&B and pop number one with *Easier Said Than Done*. Billy was still in the US Marines when he helped form The Essex, who would go on to sign with Roulette and record three albums, also scoring hits with *A Walkin' Miracle*, *She's Got Everything* and *Out Of Sight, Out Of Mind*. With the group still serving in the forces and being posted overseas, promotional work was difficult to undertake.

When Billy left the marines, therefore, it was to work in a music store and then a steel mill before becoming a proctor at Princeton University. Adopting the name Billy Proctor, he recorded for a number of labels in the 1970s, including the Soul label, who issued *What Is Black* and *I Can Take It All* in July 1972, and Epic. He also fronted The Courtship, whose only outing on Tamla also appeared in 1972. Billy later spent 25 years as a correctional officer at Trenton State Prison, where he briefly led a music programme for inmates.

PRODIGAL RECORDS

Formed in Detroit, Michigan in 1974 by former Motown executive Barney Ales with Gordon Prince, Prodigal Records was intended to have an eclectic roster of artists, covering many different musical styles. This it undoubtedly did, signing the likes of Gary U.S. Bonds, Shirley Alston, Ronnie McNeir and even former heavyweight boxer Joe Frazier. The company had been up and running for a little over a year when Berry Gordy approached Barney about returning to Motown and overseeing the company's sales operation. According to industry sources, a succession of distribution deals with European rock labels (Gull and Manticore) had proved ill-advised, with Motown's own rock label Rare Earth also failing to deliver, resulting in Berry needing to bring Barney Ales back into the fold.

He brought the Prodigal Records roster with him (including Rare Earth!), with several of the artists subsequently releasing records on the main Motown label when Prodigal itself was dissolved in 1979. By far the biggest hit artist and record Prodigal enjoyed was Charlene and *I've Never Been To Me*, which topped the charts in the UK and hit #3 pop in the US.

PSYCHEDELIC SHACK – THE TEMPTATIONS [SINGLE]

The very last single release by any of the Motown associated labels in 1969, *Psychedelic Shack* is perhaps the perfect track with which to bring the curtain down on the company's unprecedented success of the 1960s. Whilst the label had exploded in the middle of the decade with its own, almost formulaic sound, by the end of the decade the likes of Norman Whitfield had taken that sound and pushed it ever further forward.

Psychedelic Shack was inspired by a visit to the nightclub Maverick's Flat in Los Angeles, a venue where Norman was heard to tell the owner, 'Man, what you've got here is a psychedelic shack' in honour of the flamboyant decor. Taking the phrase and handing it over to lyricist Barrett Strong, Norman set about putting together an ever expanding musical background, complete with wah wah guitars and multi-tracked drums, mixing rock and soul influences in much the same style of Sly Stone.

In another rare move, all five of The Temptations share lead vocals, with the vocals often shifting from one speaker to the other to create a distinct sound. It found favour in the US, where it would go on to become a #2 R&B and #7 pop hit, although in the UK, where audiences perhaps weren't quite ready for psychedelic soul from traditional R&B artists it had to settle for a rather more modest #33 peak.

PSYCHEDELIC SHACK – THE TEMPTATIONS [ALBUM]

Ever the innovator, Norman Whitfield used the March 1970 album **Psychedelic Shack** to showcase just how far ahead of the game he really was. The album opens with a knock on a door, followed by footsteps and then a record being played on a turntable; it is The Temptations' *I Can't Get Next To You*, perhaps the earliest example of sampling and a good fifteen or twenty years before it became the staple diet of the hip hop movement. Just as *I Can't Get Next To You* gets to the distinctive Dennis Edwards' exaltation to 'hold on, everybody, hold it, hold on, listen', the album then segues into *Psychedelic Shack*. Originally recorded as something of a near on eight minute jam session, *Psychedelic Shack* would ultimately be heavily edited to under four minutes for both the album and single, becoming the only single lifted.

Yet there is plenty of material on **Psychedelic Shack** that could have made it as a single, most notably *War*. It was this track that Norman wanted released as the follow-up, only to be over-ruled by the hierarchy of Motown on the grounds that *War* was a step too far, even for The Temptations; Norman would instead record the song on Edwin Starr (for whom there were no such considerations) and come up with *Ball Of Confusion* for The Temptations instead.

You Make Your Own Heaven And Hell Right Here On Earth would also provide another of Norman's protégés with a hit, in this case The Undisputed Truth, whilst both *You Need Love Like I Do* and *Friendship Train* would ultimately become more closely associated with Gladys Knight & The Pips. While the title track remained the only single lifted as far as The Temptations were concerned, the album still retained enough interest to become another major success, topping the R&B chart and hitting #9 on the pop listings, although it struggled to reach #56 in the UK, the lowest chart placing for any Temptations album up to that point.

PURE MAGIC FEATURING MARILYN McLEOD

Although best known as a songwriter during her time connected with Motown, Marilyn McLeod undertook at least two attempts at a recording career whilst at the company, being a member of Nu Page in 1973 and then fronting Pure Magic in 1979. Their one single was *Perfect Timing (On Valentine's Day)*, written by Marilyn and her usual songwriting partner Pam Sawyer, with Melton Bolton (who had also been a member of Nu Page) on guitar and Gil Askey handling all horn and string arrangements. Housed in an attractive and romantic sleeve and with an instrumental version on the flip, the single was only available as a promotional 7" single, which perhaps indicated it was serviced to radio in order to gauge reaction and, as it failed to make much of an impact was not given a full release.

PUZZLE

Singer and drummer John LiVigni formed Puzzle in Chicago, Illinois with Bobby Villalobos (guitar), Ralf Richert (rhythm guitar, trumpet and flugelhorn), Anthony Siciliano (bass), Larry Klimas (saxophone and flute), Bob Williams (trumpet) and Joseph Spinazola (keyboards). Their brand of pop and jazz, reminiscent of Chicago, made them a popular live act in venues between Detroit and Chicago and eventually led to them being signed by Motown in 1972.

Originally intended for the Rare Earth imprint, they were switched to the main Motown label for their debut album **Puzzle** in April 1973. A second album was released the following February, imaginatively entitled **Second Album**. A third album, **How Do We Get Out Of The Business Alive** was to have been released later in 1974 but was subsequently cancelled. John LiVigni later changed his name to John Valenti and went solo, recording for Ariola America.

ALBUMS: PUZZLE (1973), SECOND ALBUM (1974)

PUZZLE PEOPLE – THE TEMPTATIONS [ALBUM]

Continuing down the same musical path that **Cloud Nine** had trod, **Puzzle People** was another excursion in psychedelic soul material. There were one or two surprises too, with cover versions of *Little Green Apples* (originally a country hit for Roger Miller but first given an R&B feel thanks to O.C. Smith), *Hey Jude* (originally by The Beatles) and *It's Your Thing,* the first major post-Motown hit scored by The Isley Brothers. Yet it is the original material, which covers much the same socially conscious areas as its predecessor that stand out, in particular *Don't Let The Joneses Get You Down* (inspired by *Runaway Child Running Wild*), *Message From A Black Man* and *Slave*.

Message From A Black Man, coming at a time when there was civil unrest in many areas of America, was a popular track on certain radio stations, but The Temptations, who thought the sentiments of the track a little too much for their fanbase, never performed the track live. *I Can't Get Next To You,* however, the major smash hit single featured on the album, was and is a popular inclusion.

Released in the US in October 1969, **Puzzle People** would go on to top the R&B chart and hit #5 on the pop chart. Its release in the UK was delayed until February 1970 (when it finally appeared, The Temptations next album **Psychedelic Shack** was barely a month away from release stateside) but this did not prevent it becoming a major hit, peaking at #20.

QUALITY CONTROL DEPARTMENT

Although Berry Gordy had been pleased to leave behind the regimented work structure of the Ford Motor Company when he set up Motown Records, he did borrow one or two business practices from his erstwhile employers, of which the Quality Control Department was the most important.

"The Friday morning product evaluation meetings were *my* meetings. They were exciting, the lifeblood of our operation. That was when we picked the records we would release. Careers depended on the choices made those Friday mornings. Everybody wanted to be there. The producers, whether or not they got their product on Billie Jean's 'approved' list, wanted to be there to protect their own interests and to challenge each other and me. Some of the employees who came to the meetings weren't creative people, but I felt their reactions to the songs would be like those of the average record buyer. A noncreative person's vote counted just as much as a creative person's."

Berry imposed three rules on the Quality Control meeting; no producer could vote on his own record, only he had the right to overrule a majority verdict, and anyone who was more than five minutes late would be locked out of the meeting; the only time he bent this rule was for Smokey Robinson.

"Another thing I was very serious about was people having the freedom to express their honest opinions openly at these meetings – without fear of reprisal. To me that was critical to the process. Everybody knew that if I got a hint of a reprisal for something coming out of these meetings, the 'reprisalor' would be in serious trouble. This was the one place where everyone was not only free to speak their minds, they were expected to. They tested that freedom. Sometimes they jumped on me just because they could. That always bugged me, but I had to go along with it to make sure that everybody understood that they could say anything in any way. These product evaluation meetings became one of the key elements in our overall growth. Each time a record made it through one of these meetings and became a hit, we grew a little bit bigger."

Berry's own way of testing whether they really believed in the records they were voting for was by asking those present whether they would spend their last $1 on a sandwich or a copy of the relevant record; as Motown's chart history would confirm, they made the right choice on most occasions.

MICHAEL QUATRO

The son of jazz musician Art Quatro and elder brother of fellow singers Suzi, Patti and Arlene Quatro (who would form their own Detroit group, The Pleasure Seekers), Michael Quatro was born in Detroit, Michigan in 1943. He learned to play the piano at an early age and appeared on the Lawrence Welk Show at the age of twelve, but his initial career in music was as a promoter, booking live dates throughout Michigan for a host of different artists. In the early 1970s he turned his attentions to his own career again, signing with the Evolution label in 1972 for his debut album **Paintings**.

He later signed with United Artists, releasing two albums, although the second of these, 1976's **Dancers Romancers Dreamers And Schemers** was subsequently picked up by Prodigal and reissued the same year by the Motown distributed label. A follow-up album **Gettin' Ready** followed in 1977, but whilst both albums were critically acclaimed, sales proved somewhat disappointing. Michael would later record for Rak (where his sister Suzi had enjoyed considerable British success), Lotus and Spector, with worldwide sales estimated at over five million before setting up his own video production company.

ALBUMS: DANCERS, ROMANCERS, DREAMERS AND SCHEMERS (1976), GETTIN' READY (1977)

QUICKSAND – MARTHA & THE VANDELLAS [SINGLE]

Written and produced by the same team that had given Martha & The Vandellas their Top Ten breakthrough *Heat Wave*, *Quicksand* was another gospel influenced outing done in a slightly higher tempo than its predecessor. Recorded in October 1963, the single was released on 4 November, although a couple of days after initial copies hit the streets, Berry Gordy ordered a new, much sharper mix to be released. It proved to be another inspired decision, for the mix of Holland-Dozier-Holland song, a stunning vocal performance from both The Vandellas and The Andantes would go on to hit #8 pop and #7 R&B. Whilst *Heat Wave* and *Quicksand* are something of signature songs for Martha Reeves & The Vandellas, neither made any impression whatsoever in the UK!

QUIET STORM

Formed by Smokey Robinson and named after his 1975 single and album, Quiet Storm became the backing group for Smokey during the early 1980s. He also produced three singles on the group, which was fronted by female singers Ivory Davis (a former member of Third Creation) and Patricia Henley Talbert and male singer James 'Alibe' Sledge and featured assorted musicians, including Marv Tarplin and Sonny Burke. The group debuted in February 1980 with the

Ron Rancifer song *Only You*, following this with *Heartbreak Graffiti* (August 1980) and *When You Came* (July 1981).

MELVIN 'WAH-WAH WATSON' RAGIN

One of the mainstays of the recording studio at Hitsville between 1968 and 1972, Melvin Ragin became best known for his pioneering work with the wah wah pedal, eventually earning the moniker Wah Wah Watson. Born in Detroit, Michigan in 1951, Melvin began working at Motown in 1968, with Edwin Starr's *Stop The War Now* claimed to be his first recording session. He would also accompany several Motown acts out on the road, but it was in the studio that his reputation was made, most notably on such recordings as *Papa Was A Rollin' Stone*.

Although not initially invited to Los Angeles when the label relocated westward in 1972, he eventually moved to California at the invitation of Norman Whitfield, always a staunch champion of Melvin's work. Whilst in California Melvin would add to his Motown credentials on such recordings as Marvin Gaye's **Let's Get It On** before becoming one of the key studio musicians in Los Angeles, working with Quincy Jones, Rose Royce, Bobbi Humphrey and The Pointer Sisters.

His best known work during this period was with Herbie Hancock, both as a performer and co-writer on the album **Man-Child** and **Secrets**, eventually leading to Melvin recording his own album for Columbia, **Elementary** being released in 1976. Whilst his solo album was not a success, he remained in demand as a musician, being utilised by the likes of Alicia Keys, Janet Jackson, Michael Jackson and Stevie Wonder over the next three decades.

THE RAMONES

American rock group The Ramones formed in New York in 1974 with Johnny (born John Cummings in Long Island, New York on 8 October 1951, guitar), Joey (born Jeffrey Hyman in Forest Hills, New York on 19 May 1952, vocals) and Ritchie Ramone. Ritchie was soon replaced by Dee Dee (born Douglas Colvin in Fort Lee, Virginia on 18 September 1952, bass) and Tommy (born Thomas Erdelyi in Budapest, Hungary on 29 January 1952, drums) was added. They signed with Sire in 1975 and released their debut album the following year. Tommy left the group in 1978 (but remained their producer) and was replaced by Marc Bell (born in New York on 15 July 1956 and adopted the name Marky Ramone). In 1986 the group appeared on the soundtrack to 'Get Crazy' performing *Chop Suey*. Joey Ramone died from cancer on 16 April 2001. Dee Dee Ramone was found dead from a drug overdose on 5 June 2002. Johnny Ramone died from prostate cancer on 15 September 2004.

BARBARA RANDOLPH

A former child actress, Barbara Randolph was born in Detroit, Michigan on 5 May 1942 and adopted by Lillian Randolph, herself an actress who appeared in 'It's A Wonderful Life', among other films. Barbara's own show business career began at the age of eight, when billed as Barbara Ann Sanders (taking the name of Lillian's second husband) she appeared in 'Bright Road' with Harry Belafonte. Her singing career started in 1957 when she linked with her mother as a member of The Red Caps, subsequently signing a solo contract with RCA Records in 1960.

"It was a nothing deal. I had a really brief situation with them. They sent a representative out from New York to California, and he signed up a few artists. Then he moved his whole family out and within a month they fired him and dropped all the artists! However, before that happened I recorded something called *Malaguena Salarosa*. I don't know how I got to do it, let alone who chose it! I was sixteen or seventeen at the time. So that was the end of my RCA career!"

Four years later she replaced Zola Taylor in The Platters but remained with the group for only one album before striking out solo once again. In 1967 she appeared in the film 'Guess Who's Coming To Dinner' and combined her acting career with performances at prestigious nightclubs, which indirectly led to a deal with Motown.

"San Juan is like Vegas in as much as the hotels have a main room and a lounge. I was working in the lounge and The Supremes were performing in the main room in this very fancy hotel. The group was just moving then, they were still little girls, but were big stars, even though they hadn't been around the world at the time. They finished their show then came to watch mine, and I think it was Berry Gordy's sister Esther who suggested I go to Detroit to record for Motown."

Signed to the Soul imprint, Barbara released *I Got A Feeling* in August 1967 and *Can I Get A Witness* a year later, with the same track (*You Got Me Hurtin' All Over*) appearing on both flip sides. Despite having been championed at Motown by Esther Gordy Edwards and being briefly considered as a replacement for Florence Ballard in The Supremes, Barbara Randolph was never a major priority for Motown. That did not stop her making a veritable name for herself during her brief sojourn at the label, touring with Marvin Gaye in place of Tammi Terrell following her illness and with The Four Tops and Gladys Knight & The Pips.

"It was difficult working when I went out with Marvin because these were his troubled years. I was Tammi Terrell's on-stage replacement. This venue had booked Marvin and Tammi based on the popularity of their recordings, but Tammi was in hospital, so I was sent in. The club didn't want Marvin as a solo artist, and I think I was chosen because I was capable of singing her part, and came the closest to her stature. Working with him was hectic and nerve-racking. However, he was extremely likeable, easy going, with a very mellow personality. I personally never heard him raise his voice, or get into any type of loud situation with anyone. I had the greatest admiration for him. I admired him before I ever worked with him. But he was like that, everyone loved him."

It was through Marvin Gaye and Motown that Barbara effectively met her later husband Eddie Singleton (the former husband of Berry's former wife Raynoma), and when it became apparent her solo career was not heading in the right direction, Barbara opted to get out of the business and set up a production company with Eddie. She was coaxed back into the studio in 1989, recording a number of tracks for Ian Levine's Nightmare label. Barbara died from cancer in South Africa on 15 July 2002.

JIMMY RANDOLPH

Born in Brewton, Alabama on 21 February 1934, Jimmy made his first recordings for Wing Records (part of the Mercury stable) in 1956, later going on to record for the main Mercury label, Decca, London and Harmon Records. His first Motown involvement came in 1973, with the Shelley Fisher song *Plainsville U.S.A.*, backed with *High Road* released in September of that year, after which he recorded for Honey Bee and subsequently Allgem Records.

Jimmy also made a name for himself as an actor, appearing in several TV series and on Broadway under the names James Randolph and Sir James Randolph. It was under the guise of James Randolph that he appeared in the 1976 revival of 'Guys And Dolls' as Sky Masterson, also featuring on the cast recording album released by Motown in December 1976.

RARE EARTH

Motown had several attempts at breaking into the rock music scene and whilst the general consensus is that they missed the mark more often than not, they did come mightily close with Rare Earth, a group who has sold some 30 million records worldwide.

Initially formed as The Sunliners in Detroit in 1960, the two constants that linked The Sunliners to Rare Earth were saxophonist Gil Bridges (it was his car, a 1956 Ford Sunliner that gave the group their name) and drummer and singer Pete Rivera (born Peter Hoorelbeke in Detroit, Michigan in 1945). Over the years members would come and go, including bass player John Persh (who would become better known by his stage name John Parrish), who joined in 1962, guitar player Rod Richards (born Rod Cox) and keyboard player Kenny James (born Ken Folcik), who both joined in 1966, twin brothers Ralph (keyboards) and Russ Terrana (guitar), who were present at the beginning but exited in 1965, with both eventually gravitating to Motown as engineers and producers, and saxophonist Fred Saxon (born Fred Kotenko), the first to leave the group.

The Sunliners recorded three singles for Hercules, a one-off single for Scepter (under the moniker The Hi-Riders for *Stamp Out The Beatles*, recorded at the time the British Invasion was in full swing) and similar one single deals with Golden World and MGM, where they recorded their Sunliners finale *Land Of Nod* in 1968. *Land Of Nod* would be re-recorded by the group when they became Rare Earth, the moniker first appearing on their debut album for the Verve label in 1968, **Dreams/Answers**, which was produced by Detroit doyens Mike Theodore and Dennis Coffey. That album also contained an early, truncated version of *Get Ready*, the old Temptations number that had been a feature of The Sunliners' live repertoire for a good couple of years.

It was the strength of their live performances that got Rare Earth a contract with Motown, with Barney Ales in particular an early champion of the group when they arrived at Hitsville. It was he who suggested they re-record *Get Ready* for their Motown debut, although the initial version the band recorded was not felt strong enough for inclusion on either the album or release as a single. In an attempt to recapture the magic the group displayed performing live, it was suggested they recreate their live show in the studio, being given a two o'clock in the morning slot at the studio. Therefore, after performing live at a city venue, the group hauled their equipment over to Hitsville, set up and played throughout the morning. *Get Ready* was elongated into a twenty minute plus jam session and would also become the title track to their debut album, which in order to appear as close to their live set as possible had audience applause dubbed in.

During the course of negotiations, it was announced that Motown intended placing Rare Earth onto a specialist rock imprint, although they did not yet have a name for it. Rare Earth then helpfully suggested Rare Earth Records, perhaps more in hope than in expectation, but Motown liked the name enough to give it the go ahead. The label was already three months old when Rare Earth released their debut album for the label, **Get Ready** appearing in September 1969, with the group themselves credited as the producers. Sales on the album were initially slow, although there was a buzz about the band, especially as they had been chosen to perform the soundtrack to the film 'Generation', releasing the theme song *Generation (Light Up The Sky)* in November 1969.

Unfortunately, advance previews on the film were disastrous, killing both the single and quashing the album (although much of the material the group had written would surface in their second album) almost immediately. However, the album did make an early appearance on the album chart in December 1969, with much of the feedback concerning the title track. A hastily arranged edit was issued as a single in February 1970 and would become a major pop hit, sailing up to #4 on the pop chart (it was a rather more modest #20 R&B hit, but Rare Earth weren't necessarily targeting the R&B market), at the same time helping shift copies of the album, which would make #12 pop (and perform even better on the R&B chart, where it reached #4) and sell more than a million copies domestically.

Whilst *Get Ready* was marching up the charts, the group was busy recording their second album **Ecology**. Much of the material had already been written, the group opting to utilise some of the material that had originally been intended for the 'Generation' soundtrack as well as another old Temptations number, *(I Know) I'm Losing You*. The initial sessions for the album were produced by Tom Baird, but midway through recording, Motown planted Norman Whitfield into the proceedings, as Pete Rivera later recalled.

"We did Tom Baird songs, which were great, *Born To Wander* and some of that, and then Norman Whitfield was brought in because they [Motown] thought the **Ecology** album wasn't going to be that strong, and Whitfield came in and did *(I Know) I'm Losing You*. Between *I'm Losing You* and *Born To Wander* there were two producers."

There were also two hits, with *(I Know) I'm Losing You* returning the group to the Top Ten of the pop chart (at #7) and a repeat #20 R&B, and *Born To Wander* making #17 pop and #48 R&B. Motown needn't have worried about the album; it would sell more than half a million copies and make #15 pop and #4 R&B during the course of near on a year on the chart. After **Ecology** hit the streets, Rare Earth underwent something of a line-up change; percussionist Ed Guzman had joined the group in time for **Ecology**, but both Rod Richards and Kenny James exited the group after its release (Rod Richards would return to the Rare Earth label as a member of Road), being replaced by Ray Monette and Mark Olson respectively. They arrived in time to find the group demanding a bit more control of their destiny, opting to record more of their own material, something they'd been pushing for some time.

"Motown was always trying to find us writers," said Pete Rivera. "Tony Clarke was the producer of The Moody Blues and Motown brought him in to do an album on us. Tony came in with his ideas from England and all that, and Motown just didn't understand it, but we were diggin' it. So we were in the studio and started writing. Everyone in the band started writing ideas down and I did *If I Die* and *The Seed*. Tony was axed from the project and they handed it over to Tom Baird. And Tom really liked the songs, so we went in and completed them and it came out on the **One World** album."

Although the group's own material was strong, it was another outside composition that returned them to the charts, Dino Fekaris and Nick Zesses contributing *I Just Want To Celebrate*, another solid pop and R&B hit at #7 and #30 respectively, although even with that rock anthem on display, it was not enough to lift the album beyond #28 pop and #12 R&B in 1971 (the other single extracted was a cover of Ray Charles' *What I'd Say*, which stalled at #61 pop). Perhaps another missed opportunity was that of having Roger Dean work on the artwork and feature it across the inside of the fold out sleeve rather than on the cover.

In between albums the group scored their final Top 20 pop hit, *Hey Big Brother* being released in November 1971 and making #19 pop and #40 R&B. The year closed with a rather grand double album live set, recorded in Jacksonville, Miami, New York and Detroit (as well as one studio track) and featuring extended versions of *Get Ready*, *Thoughts* and *(I Know) I'm Losing You*. Although it slipped down the chart compared with earlier albums (it stalled at #29 pop and #19 R&B) it still sold sufficiently and earned the group another gold disc award, although John Persh left the group at about this time, being replaced by Mike Urso. Emboldened by their success so far, the group held out for even more control of the follow-up **Willie Remembers**, eventually released in October 1972.

"We got in to do **Willie Remembers** with Tom Baird and I remember the day we finished that album, we were loving it because we had some songs on there [six of the eight tracks]. We were diggin' the album and Suzanne De Passe, who was Berry Gordy's right hand man walked in, just looked at us and said, 'Now that you've got that out of your system, we ought to go and do a real album.' When **Willie Remembers** came out it didn't get any promotion at all, and that's when they said the only way to save a dying ship was to bring Norman Whitfield in."

Motown might not have believed in the album but it still managed to haul itself to #90 on the pop chart. The mix of Motown imposing a producer on the group, coupled with internal wrangles between several members made the recording of the next album **Ma** a somewhat fraught time for all involved, as Pete explained.

"Motown thought the only redemption to our career was Norman Whitfield because he had *Papa Was A Rollin' Stone*, *Ball Of Confusion*, *Just My Imagination* and he was Norman Whitfield of Motown. Norman was a great guy, a great producer, and rest his soul, but the political side of it back then was they just didn't trust anybody except in their own stable of people. So Norman came in and we did the **Ma** album. I always called it the Norman Whitfield album played by Rare Earth. And you didn't get the essence of Rare Earth. As a result, **Ma** got just a little bit of attention but nothing serious, and we didn't have the hits, so things just started getting worse."

Like other groups who worked with Norman, there were disagreements with the producer over the material they would and wouldn't record, with Rare Earth rejecting *War* but finding themselves saddled with material that had or would become better known by Norman's other protégés, including *Smiling Faces Sometimes* (The Undisputed Truth), *Ma* (The Temptations) and *Hum Along And Dance* (The Temptations), as well as having their producer's photograph feature prominently on the album's back cover. Despite the undoubted problems the recording had faced, **Ma** still appealed to the group's fanbase, enough for it to hit #65 on the chart (and #12 R&B), itself something of an improvement over their previous album.

Unfortunately, the problems proved insurmountable for Pete Rivera and Mike Urso, who left and linked with Tom Baird in an outfit called HUB (based on their respective initials, Pete opting to utilise his original surname of Hoorelbeke) for two albums on Capitol. Rare Earth meanwhile were kept busy, even if nothing actually appeared; a series of sessions with Frank Wilson remained in the can, whilst a proposed second live album recorded in Chicago was also shelved (the group themselves couldn't recall capturing any of their Chicago dates). When the group eventually reconvened under the production of Stewart Levine (perhaps best known for his jazz funk work with The Crusaders), the line-up of Rare Earth had settled upon Gil Bridges (saxophone, flute and vocals), Reggie McBride (bass and vocals), Ray Monette (guitar), Paul Warren (guitar and vocals), Gabriel Katona (keyboards), Jerry La Croix (lead vocals, saxophone and flute), Ed Guzman (percussion) and Barry Eugene Frost (drums and percussion).

An altogether more pleasurable experience than their previous recording sessions, **Back To Earth** restored the group to the chart, its #59 placing their best in three years. Singles wise the group found the going a little more difficult, with *It Makes You Happy (But It Ain't Gonna Last Too Long)* being written by new recruits Paul Warren and Gabriel Katona and bubbling under at #106. The group's final album on the Rare Earth label reunited them with Norman Whitfield, although both Warren and Katona had departed for pastures new and Frank Westbrook come into the fold. Norman proved unable to halt the decline (although since he was soon to leave Motown and set up his own operation one can but wonder how committed he was to Rare Earth's cause), with **Midnight Lady** becoming the only Rare Earth album released by Motown that failed to chart; even their fanbase, perhaps mystified by the comings and goings, paid little attention to this latest release (and even the cover invoked images of The Undisputed Truth!). With Motown shutting down the Rare Earth label following the release of **Midnight Lady**, the group left the company.

They weren't without a home for long, for long time champion Barney Ales had set up the Prodigal label, featuring an eclectic mix of artists and offered Rare Earth a new contract. Several of the old group members joined up for the ride too, with Rare Earth at this point featuring Gil Bridges, Mike Urso, Pete Rivera and Ed Guzman along with newer recruits Ron Fransen (keyboards) and Daniel Ferguson (guitar). Cal Harris and James Anthony Carmichael handled production, and whilst the resulting **Rarearth** album was hardly a shattering success, at least charting (albeit at #187) proved that they still had an audience. By this time Barney Ales had returned to the Motown fold, taking with him his roster of Prodigal artists. Also back together was perhaps the best known line-up of Rare Earth; Gil Bridges, Pete Rivera, Ray Monette, Mark Olson, Mike Urso and Ed Guzman. The group worked with producer John Ryan, recording two albums worth of material that would be released as **Band Together** (their final chart album, hitting #156) in April 1978, which would also give rise to the minor hit single *Warm Ride* (a cover of a Bee Gees number that peaked at #39) and **Grand Slam** which appeared in November 1978.

Rare Earth would move over to RCA following their release from Motown, but continuing internal problems saw the resulting album only available in Canada. A lengthy hiatus coupled with a number of legal issues prevented anybody from utilising the Rare Earth name for the best part of a decade, although another live album appeared in 1989. Today Gil Bridges tours with his version of Rare Earth (which also features Ray Monette), whilst Pete Rivera tours under his own name. Pete summed up Rare Earth's time at Motown as an enjoyable experience, for the most part, although he offered his explanation for what went wrong.

"I think where Motown made a mistake was when they panicked and they brought in Norman Whitfield, and once you're not selling records with the company, it's like nobody wants you anymore. And then we were having internal problems with jealousy and there were drugs involved and stuff like that, and everybody was acting crazy and it just kind of went away. I believe the management should have taken us all to some house somewhere and said, okay look guys, here's what's happening, you need to put all this stuff aside, almost sequestered us somewhere. Then leave us alone with Tom Baird in the studio and give us a month to see what we can come up with, as well as listen to some songs from other writers. Because it got to a point where the writers didn't want to give you anything from drawer A, they'll give you the drawer B stuff, but once you get a hit, here comes all the stuff out of drawer A, once you stop selling records that drawer is closed again, they're looking around to give other people those songs to because other people are happening and relative to what's going on. So it was harder for us to get songs."

John Persh died from a staph virus in January 1981 (he entered hospital for a routine operation but contracted the infection that led to his death). Mark Olson died from alcohol related complications in 1982. Eddie Guzman died on 29 September 1993.

ALBUMS: GET READY (1969), ECOLOGY (1970), ONE WORLD (1971), IN CONCERT (1971), WILLIE REMEMBERS (1972), MA (1973), BACK TO EARTH (1975), MIDNIGHT LADY (1976), RAREARTH (1977), BAND TOGETHER (1978), GRAND SLAM (1978)

RARE EARTH RECORDS

When Berry Gordy set up the Tamla and then Motown labels, he had very distinct ideas as to what kind of music and artists would appear on each. The lines between one and the other became blurred over the years, with Gordy, Soul and V.I.P. further adding to the musical confusion; there was no such thing as a typical Gordy artist or an obvious Soul single, since they were all bound to the one company entity. When, however, Motown decided to launch a rock label in 1969, it was plain that a new name would be required; the radio stations that leapt enthusiastically on all things Motown weren't going to be best pleased to suddenly discover an out and out rock record blaring out across the airwaves. The eventual name for the new label was suggested by one of the artists that were going to be on it, Rare Earth, as lead singer Pete Rivera later explained.

"Motown wanted to do this white rock FM label and they didn't have a name for it. So we suggested, 'Why don't you call it Rare Earth Records', and a friend of ours actually drew the picture (the distinctive tree image) on the record label. Nobody knew what they were doing back then; there was Gordy Records, Motown Records, and there was Tamla Records, and they've been in existence for years doing things a certain way and all of a sudden we were coming out saying things like posters and artwork on our album covers and they didn't know from all this. So they bought a lot of our suggestions and when we said Rare Earth Records, they said we like that."

Thanks to Motown's international distribution deal with EMI Records in England, the company also picked up the American rights to artists such as The Pretty Things, Love Sculpture, Sounds Nice, The Easybeats (actually an Australian band but licensed to Rare Earth by EMI) and The Cats (a Dutch group acquired as part of the same deal), who joined homegrown artists Stoney & Meatloaf, Rustix, The Impact Of Brass and XIT, among others. Rare Earth Records made its bow in June 1969, with albums from The Pretty Things and Love Sculpture and a single from The Pretty Things, with the group who gave the label its name entering the fray in July. In the UK, the label didn't appear until September 1971.

Some of the artists who appeared on Rare Earth might have been better served allocated to other labels; R. Dean Taylor was not rock by any stretch of the imagination, neither were Impact Of Brass or Sounds Nice, but perhaps the reasoning was they would have sounded even more out of place on other Motown imprints.

Motown also set up something of an independent Rare Earth company in the UK, where local A&R representatives signed the likes of Slowbone, Dan The Banjo Man and Friendly Persuasion, although few of these were granted an American release.

In the event Rare Earth Records was not the success the company hoped it would be, with the label being shut down in March 1976, with Rare Earth, fittingly, being the last album release (in the UK, Rare Earth brought the curtain down on the label in May 1976). When Rare Earth the group later returned to Motown as part of the Prodigal roster, subsequent releases continued to appear on the Prodigal label, although in 1988 it was strongly rumoured that Rare Earth Records was being considered for resurrection. Apart from a single demo disc, nothing came of the plan.

RCA RECORDS

In December 1980 EMI announced that they had sold a total of three million Motown singles and one and a half million albums during the course of the year in the UK. The figures, whilst hardly earth-shattering, were still in keeping with industry expectations, especially as there was a dearth of blockbuster releases on the Motown label during the year. Soon after the announcement, Motown began re-negotiating the British distribution deal, using the EMI sales figures as something of a bargaining tool.

If EMI had been the only serious tender in previous years when the distribution deal had come up for re-negotiation, then that was not the case in 1981. This time around, EMI faced competition from RCA Records, a company that was not so much a sleeping giant as virtually comatose. Indeed, in 1979 there had been some doubts as to whether RCA would even exist in the UK, at least in its current state, with the American owners putting out feelers for an amalgamation with another British company that had fallen on hard times, Pye Records. The proposed deal to combine RCA and Pye floundered soon after they were first muted, leaving RCA with a tough decision to make; they either went for broke or went broke.

In the end, RCA opted to go for broke, submitting a distribution proposal that topped EMI's valuation of the Motown business, resulting in an October 1981 announcement that Motown had signed a new British distribution deal with RCA. Announcing the deal was Motown International's vice-president Peter Prince (ironically, his previous appointment prior to taking up his Motown role had been as Head of Artist & Repertoire for Pye Records!), who said, "We are looking forward to a new partnership with RCA, who have impressed us by the way they have become a major force in today's record market. For the past eighteen years we have enjoyed a highly successful relationship with EMI who have helped Motown maintain their position as one of the leading independent record companies in the world."

The change in distributor caused some initial hardship and confusion, with five EMI staffers losing their jobs and product returns being effectively refused by EMI and RCA, although this latter problem was eventually resolved, if not entirely satisfactorily. For the next five or six years, RCA maintained the numbering system that had served EMI so well across two decades. Then, in 1987, RCA itself was bought out by BMG, who also picked up the Motown distribution deal for much of Europe and switched to a pan-European numbering format. BMG would remain Motown's European distributors for the rest of Motown's time as an independent company.

CHRIS REA

Whilst his American success has been somewhat limited, in Europe Chris Rea is acknowledged as one of the best selling singer-songwriters of his age, having sold more than thirty million albums during the course of his career. Born Christopher Anton Rea in Middlesbrough, Teesside on 4 March 1951 he was a member of local band Magdalene (he replaced David Coverdale in this group) and then Beautiful Losers before obtaining a solo deal with Magnet Records in 1977. His debut album **Whatever Happened To Benny Santini?** was a #49 chart hit and attained gold status in the US, helped by the Grammy nominated single *Fool (If You Think It's Over)*.

Whilst he would have to wait more than ten years to make his next appearance on the US album charts, his appeal in Europe continued to prosper, fuelled by the platinum success of **On The Beach**. In 1987 he released one of his best known singles in *Let's Dance*, which whilst it only peaked at #12 became something of a signature tune for him.

Picked up by Motown at much the same time as fellow Magnet act Gung Ho, *Let's Dance* was released in August 1987, the same month Motown released the parent album **Dancing With Strangers**. Neither made an impact stateside, although Motown's interest did ensure subsequent albums got released in the US on Magnet's parent label, WEA.

Let's Dance meanwhile enjoyed a second lease of life when it was used as the official song for Middlesbrough FC's losing appearance in the 1997 F.A. Cup Final.

ALBUM: DANCING WITH STRANGERS (1987)

REACH OUT - FOUR TOPS [ALBUM]

What would effectively be the last Four Tops album produced by Brian Holland, Lamont Dozier and Eddie Holland at least ensured they bowed out on a high, for **Reach Out** went on to become the group's biggest hit domestically as well as performing extremely well overseas. Containing no fewer than six Top 20 hits, **Reach Out** reads like a mini greatest hits package, offering further proof that Motown would be hard pressed to replace the departing HDH.

Built around the success of the chart topping *Reach Out I'll Be There*, it also contained the hits *Standing In The Shadows Of Love*, *7 Rooms Of Gloom*, *Bernadette*, *Walk Away Renee* and *If I Were A Carpenter*. These latter two tracks were cover versions (of The Left Banke and Tim Hardin respectively), and there were also covers of The Monkees' *Last Train To Clarksville* and *I'm A Believer* and The Association's *Cherish*. The album was completed by three songs from the Jobete catalogue. Released domestically in July 1967, **Reach Out** would hit #3 R&B and #11 pop, but performed even better in the UK, where it would eventually come to rest at #4.

REACH OUT I'LL BE THERE – THE FOUR TOPS [SINGLE]

Written by Holland-Dozier-Holland, partly inspired by Burt Bacharach and Hal David as well as Bob Dylan, featuring an interesting array of instruments and one of the finest vocals ever captured within the Hitsville Studio; *Reach Out I'll Be There* had all the ingredients necessary to make it a sure-fire smash, yet its eventual release seems to have hinged on a casting vote from Berry Gordy! The Four Tops had suffered a slight tailing off after the massive success of *I Can't Help Myself*, with the Ivy Jo Hunter and Stevie Wonder penned *Loving You Is Sweeter Than Ever* barely scraping the Top 50 in May 1966.

Influenced by the classical music Lamont Dozier had listened to as a youngster and largely crafted by Lamont and Brian Holland, *Reach Out* may well have followed the tried and trusted HDH formula in utilising bits and pieces of earlier work but stands out on its own thanks to the distinct feel. This was achieved by utilising a variety of instruments not previously heard, such as the flute (played on the session by the thirteen year old Dayna Hartwick, who had to be carried into the studio as she had a broken leg at the time; she would later appear on Marvin Gaye's **What's Going On**) and a unique percussive effect achieved by tapping hands on a wooden chair.

The end result was unlike anything HDH had produced before, a sound that some thought too much of a departure, including a couple of The Four Tops and many of those present at the Quality Control meeting when the single was first played. Whilst Smokey Robinson was against releasing it, Berry Gordy had the final say and ordered it released in August 1966. It turned out to be The Four Tops biggest ever hit, topping the R&B charts and pop charts on both sides of the Atlantic, helped in the UK by the presence of the group on a nationwide tour. Later cover versions came from Gloria Gaynor (#60 in the US and #14 in the UK in 1975) and Michael Bolton (#73 in the US and #37 in the UK in 1993).

READY STEADY GO – THE SOUND OF MOTOWN (TV SPECIAL)

'Ready Steady Go!' (popularly known as 'RSG!') first aired in August 1963, one of the earliest popular music shows on British national television. It had been the idea of Rediffusion TV's head Elkan Allan, ably assisted by producer and manager Vicki Wickham and, with its tag line 'The Weekend Starts Here' quickly became popular with the youth of the country. Less reliant on the chart as opposed to its BBC rival 'Top Of The Pops', 'RSG!' claimed a number of notable shows, in particular its Motown special. It was Dusty Springfield who suggested to ITV that 'RSG!' should do a Motown special around the Motortown Revue of 1965, a suggestion ITV eventually accepted on the proviso that Dusty herself host the show.

Recorded at Rediffusion's studio at Wembley on 18 March 1965, the show was eventually aired on 28 April – the general consensus held that had the special aired whilst the Motortown Revue was still underway, there would have been an upsurge in ticket sales. The special featured The Supremes, Stevie Wonder, The Temptations, Marvin Gaye, Smokey Robinson & The Miracles and Martha Reeves & The Vandellas, all backed by the Earl Van Dyke Sextet and is also notable for The Supremes' debuting their trademark dance routine for *Stop In The Name Of Love*. Whilst the impact was somewhat muted at the time of airing, the relevance of the show was felt many years later when a compilation album drawn from the recording, entitled **Ready Steady Go! – Sixites Motown Sound** hit #5 on the UK compilation chart when released on CD.

The full line-up for the show was:

The Supremes – *Baby Love*
Smokey Robinson & The Miracles – *You Really Got A Hold On Me*
Stevie Wonder – *I Call It Pretty Music*
The Temptations – *The Way You Do The Things You Do*
Martha Reeves & The Vandellas – *Heat Wave*
Dusty Springfield – *You Lost The Sweetest Boy*
Smokey Robinson & The Miracles – *Ohh Baby Baby*
Martha Reeves & Dusty Springfield – *Wishin' And Hopin'*
The Temptations – *It's Growing*
The Supremes – *Shake*
Martha Reeves & The Vandellas – *Nowhere To Run*
Stevie Wonder – *Kiss Me Baby*
Marvin Gaye – *How Sweet It Is To Be Loved By You*
Marvin Gaye – *Can I Get A Witness*
Dusty Springfield – *Can't Hear You No More*
The Supremes – *Stop! In The Name Of Love*
The Temptations – *My Girl*
Martha Reeves & The Vandellas – *Dancing In The Street*
Smokey Robinson & The Miracles – *Shop Around*
The Supremes – *Where Did Our Love Go*
Smokey Robinson & Ensemble – *Mickey's Monkey*

RECORDED LIVE! THE 12 YEAR OLD GENIUS – LITTLE STEVIE WONDER [ALBUM]

Two albums and three singles into his Tamla career, Little Stevie Wonder had still to make any kind of impact outside of Hitsville. Indeed, there were those who thought of him as little more than a company mascot and Berry Gordy's folly and wondered how long it would be before time was called on his career. As it happened, it was his youthful exuberance that eventually got him his big break and enabled the company to finally get an album to the top of the chart. Stevie was at his most animated whilst actually performing, something that would not have been apparent on his recordings but which was evident to anyone who saw him play live.

His involvement in the 1963 Motortown Revue therefore managed to put him right in the limelight, with the *Fingertips* recording from the Regal Theatre in Chicago considered the perfect showcase of what he was all about. As noted earlier, *Fingertips Part 2* would quickly assail the charts and hit the top of both pop and R&B for three and six weeks respectively. There was more to come, for even as *Fingertips* was climbing, Tamla rush-released the album **Recorded Live! The 12 Year Old Genius**. The title utilised poetic licence, for by the time the album (recorded at the Regal in Chicago and Apollo in Harlem) was released he had enjoyed his thirteenth birthday! What was not in doubt, however, was that *Fingertips* was not a flash in the pan, for the seven tracks on display found Stevie performing on the piano, harmonica, bongos and drums as well as singing on material ranging from *(I'm Afraid) The Masquerade Is Over,* the Ray Charles penned *Hallelujah I Love Her So* and *Don't You Know* and four from the Jobete portfolio.

Whilst a novelty single may sometimes make the top of the chart, the chances of an album doing so are very slim, so **Recorded Live!** topped the pop and R&B charts on its own merits. It would take Stevie more than a decade to achieve the feat again, but the success the single and album enjoyed removed any doubt or question about what Stevie Wonder was doing at Hitsville; he was there on merit.

JIMMY REED

One of the leading blues artists of his age, Mathis James Reed was born in Dunleith, Mississippi on 6 September 1925. He learnt to play the guitar and harmonica from friend Eddie Taylor and busked for a number of years locally before making his way to

Chicago in 1943. Drafted into the US Navy, Jimmy was discharged at the end of the Second World War and returned home to Mississippi for a short period, where he married Mary 'Mama' Reed. By the end of the decade he had moved to Gary, Indiana and was working at a meat packing factory during the day and singing in the evening, eventually getting the opportunity of recording. It was not until the middle of the 1950s that his reputation began to soar, helped by a number of hit singles on Vee-Jay.

Unfortunately, alcohol problems plagued him throughout his career, preventing him from assuming his rightful place in musical folklore. That did not stop him being regarded as influential, with the likes of The Rolling Stones, The Yardbirds and The Grateful Dead either citing him as an influence and/or recording his songs.

After Vee-Jay closed its doors Jimmy signed a brief contract with ABC-Bluesway, but his hit recording days were behind him. Continuing personal problems, including epilepsy and alcoholism hindered his career and he died from respiratory failure on 29 August 1976 at the age of 50. He did not record for Motown, although the company acquired some eighteen tracks that were released as **Compact Command Performances** in August 1986 as part of a major reissue campaign undertaken by Motown. That same year, two of his much earlier Vee-Jay recordings appeared on the compilation CD **Hits From The Legendary Vee-Jay Records**, *Big Boss Man* and *Bright Lights Big City*.

ALBUM: COMPACT COMMAND PERFORMANCES (1986)

LOU REED

Born Louis Firbank in Freeport, Long Island, New York on 2 March 1943 Lou Reed was a founder member of Velvet Underground in 1965, leaving for a solo career in 1970 and releasing his debut in 1972. In 1983 he appeared in the film 'Get Crazy', playing the role of Auden and contributing the track *Little Sister* to the subsequent soundtrack album.

MARTHA REEVES & THE VANDELLAS

Like many of their contemporaries at Motown, Martha Reeves and The Vandellas' route into Hitsville wasn't straight forward, nor was there a contract waiting to be signed when they did arrive; it turned out to be more a case of being in the right place at the right time.

Martha was born in Eufaula, Alabama on 18 July 1941, one of eleven children born to a Methodist father in Elijah and his wife Ruby. The family moved to Detroit when Martha was just one year old, and at the age of six Martha sang in the church with two of her brothers, Benny and Thomas (aged nine and seven respectively). As a teenager Martha had to undertake shift work to help the family out financially, although there was still the opportunity to sing at a local club in Flint, Michigan, where Martha had to sing blues material as it was all the house band knew!

Soon after graduating from Northeastern High School in 1959, Martha linked with Shirley Walker, Bernadine Boswell, Joanne Levell and Fern Bledsoe in a group called The Sabre-Ettes, who got regular work at the Broadway Sportsman Club. The Sabre-Ettes subsequently evolved into The Fascinations but Martha exited the group (who would go on to enjoy their own hit-making career, guided by Curtis Mayfield), accepting an invitation from Rosalind Ashford to replace a departed member and join The Del-Phis.

Joining Martha and Rosalind (born in Detroit, Michigan on 2 September 1943) were Annette Sterling (born in Detroit on 4 July 1943) and lead singer Gloria Jean Williamson (born in Detroit in 1942), with the quartet performing at local parties and benefit shows around the city, also backing the likes of J.J. Barnes, Leon Peterson and Mike Hanks on live dates. It was through Hanks that The Del-Phis made their recording debut, backing him on *When True Love Comes To Be* backed with *The Hawk*, released on the local Mah's label in 1960. Not long after, The Del-Phis got their own, one off single contract, recording *I'll Let You Know* and *It Takes Two* for Billy Roquel Davis' Chess affiliated Check-Mate label. The single wasn't a success, and for a while the individual members did other jobs in order to pay the rent.

In Martha's case this meant entering talent contests, and after winning one of these landed an engagement at the 20 Grand in Detroit, performing under the name Martha LaVaille. During one of her solo spots, she was noticed by Motown A&R head Mickey Stevenson, who handed Martha a business card and told her to come down to Hitsville for an audition. Martha must have misconstrued the invitation, for she turned up at Hitsville at 9.00 am the very next morning, having ditched her full time cleaning job, and duly presented herself to a bemused Mickey Stevenson.

"When I approached him, he said, 'What are you doing here?' after being buzzed in. And I said, 'What do you mean, what am I doing here? Don't you remember giving me your card last night? You asked me to come here.' He said, 'Yeah, you're supposed to take that card and call for an audition. We have auditions the third Thursday of every month.' And I'm going, 'Oh God, what am I gonna do?' And then he said, 'Answer the phone. I'll be right back.' And he left me there. Three hours. These people started coming in. I didn't know none of those guys. Hummin' and mumblin' and bangin' on the piano, asking me who I am. So I assumed that I was the A&R secretary."

That assumption was to last for some eight months, although initially it was unpaid work; Martha would later recall that her father told her to ask for a wage from Berry Gordy and if one wasn't forthcoming, she was to leave the company. In between answering the phone there were a number of opportunities to provide backing vocals, which also added to the income, earning Martha the princely sum of $5 per session. One of these sessions, in June 1962, proved to be rather more valuable.

With The Andantes, Motown's usual female backing group, out of town, Mickey Stevenson instructed Martha to find a suitable group of girls who could provide backing for a planned session. Martha got on the phone and called Rosalind Ashford, Annette Beard and Gloria Jean Williamson and, along with herself, booked them for the session for Marvin Gaye's *Stubborn Kind Of Fellow*. The session went well, with Marvin and Mickey impressed with the way the girls had handled the recording and jotting down the names of the four singers for future reference.

In July all four girls were back in the studio, this time accompanying Saundra Mallett on *Camel Walk,* which whilst it wasn't a hit did at least become the first credited appearance of The Vandellas. Originally the single was to be released with the credit Saundra Mallet & The Dominettes, as Berry Gordy didn't like the name The Del-Phis and there may have been legal issues had they insisted on using the name. Martha was given ten minutes to come up with something more suitable and utilised Van Dyke Street in Detroit, near to where she lived, and the name of her favourite singer Della Reese to create The Vandellas (although for several years after the event Motown's publicity machine put out the story that Marvin Gaye had bestowed the name on the group in deference to the way they had been vocal vandals in the studio; an interesting story that got plenty of coverage but which was way off the truth).

Later the same month (July) the singers were required en masse again. Owing to a recent musician union directive, a singer had to be present when the musicians were recording backing tracks, and on the day The Funk Brothers were scheduled to record *I'll Have To Let Him Go* Mary Wells could not be found. In desperation, Mickey instructed Martha to make her way to the studio, bringing along the rest of The Del-Phis with her. Martha sang lead on *I'll Have To Let Him Go*, produced by Mickey Stevenson, whilst later the same day Berry Gordy himself supervised the session for *You'll Never Cherish A Love So True ('Til You Lose It)* with Gloria on lead vocals. Both tracks sounded good enough to release, but rather than issue them by the same group, utilised two different group names and two different labels. *I'll Have To Let Him Go* was credited to Martha & The Vandellas, with the flip side *My Baby Won't Come Back*, which had been written by Mickey and Martha and recorded back in May 1962. Martha & The Vandellas single was released on the Gordy label on 27 September, followed four days later by the Gloria-led *You'll Never Cherish A Love So True* on the Mel-O-dy label and credited to The Vells.

With Gloria Jean Williamson already discussing plans to leave the music business in order to take up a full-time job with the Detroit City Council, The Vells single was seen as giving her the chance to change her mind and rejoin Motown should the single take off, possibly as leader of a separate group. In the event neither single did much sales wise, with Gloria subsequently becoming a civil servant and Martha, Rosalind and Annette continuing as The Vandellas (the group's original backing vocals for *Camel Walk* were bolted on to a new lead vocal version by LaBrenda Ben, which was subsequently released on both Motown and Gordy credited to LaBrenda Ben & The Beljeans). It didn't take long for The Vandellas to get a hit, and it proved to be something of a landmark recording into the bargain; one of Brian and Eddie Holland and Lamont Dozier's first compositions.

"I saw them write that," Martha said as she recalled *Come And Get These Memories*. "I was with them when they became a team. I was the secretary, sitting there taking notes. I knew it was my song! That was a special moment. That was the first song that they wrote together. And it was ours. They wrote it for us, not The Supremes."

Martha's competitive streak notwithstanding (HDH hadn't started working with The Supremes at this point), *Come And Get These Memories* was not only a hit (#6 R&B and #29 pop) but a song that Berry Gordy would later state as defining the Motown Sound. For Martha, even more than Rosalind and Annette, it was justification for everything that came afterwards.

"I was a musical junkie after that. I just couldn't get enough music out of me. I was hooked on the business and knew I wasn't getting out, I'm sure that if I had wanted to be a secretary, I'd have been the best secretary in my particular office. Being the best, doing my best, is important to me."

Come And Get These Memories would become the title track to the group's first album released in June 1963, something of a mixed bag collection of songs from HDH, Smokey Robinson and assorted covers, all housed in a bizarrely blue tinted sleeve containing a picture of a teddy bear! Not surprisingly, the album did little, but by the time it was released, the group was back in the studio working on what would become their next single and an even bigger hit. Recorded at a time when California was hit by a freak heat wave, the single *Heat Wave* was a topical reminder of the tropical weather. It struck a chord across the country too, finally coming to rest at the top of the R&B chart (although it was the Cashbox R&B chart, Billboard halting publication of their R&B listings, at least until January 1965) and #4 pop. It sold more than a million copies and also became the first Motown associated record to earn a Grammy Award nomination, being selected in the Best R&B Vocal Performance by a Group category, although Martha and The Vandellas lost out on the prize to Ray Charles.

The group ended the year with chart activity on both the singles and album chart. **Heat Wave** was another potpourri of cover versions and the title track hit, although the group did at least get their image on the cover, albeit viewed from the back, and hit #125 on the pop listings. No sooner had *Heat Wave* left the chart than another HDH song replaced it, *Quicksand* becoming a Top Ten hit on both the pop and R&B chart, the fuller sound on the single being achieved by having The Andantes augment The Vandellas in the studio, a ploy that HDH began to use more and more on their productions, including The Supremes and The Marvelettes. Whilst records were still released with the credit Martha & The Vandellas, as far as Marthas was concerned The Vandellas were dispensable.

"The greatest misconception about The Vandellas was that we were a group like, say, The Supremes. My decision to have vocal back-up was a result of my need for companionship on the road, as opposed to a need for serious background singers. I've had more background singers do sessions for me and have their names be Vandellas than the world would know."

The first of the original Vandellas to leave was Annette, who had gotten married (she'd become Annette Beard) and was pregnant with her first child when she exited the group in December 1963, with Betty Kelley (born in Attalla, Alabama on 16 September 1944) brought in from fellow Motown group The Velvelettes as her replacement. Betty was pitched straight into a recording session, with the group back in the studio for their follow-up *Live Wire* barely a week before Christmas. Whilst not as big a hit as the group's two previous singles, *Live Wire* did at least get them back on the chart, hitting #42 pop and #11 R&B, at a time when The Supremes were still struggling to achieve their breakout.

The Vandellas meanwhile kept the hits rolling, with *In My Lonely Room* not only hitting #44 pop and #6 R&B on the chart but instigating a brief dance craze in Philadelphia that went by the name 'The 81', prompting Jerry Ross and Kenny Gamble to build a song around the craze!

After two relatively minor hits, it was back to the virtual top of the charts with The Vandellas next outing. With HDH distracted with trying to find a hit for The Supremes, The Vandellas got a brief switch of producer in William 'Mickey' Stevenson. Along with Marvin Gaye and Ivy Jo Hunter Hunter, he had come up with *Dancing In The Street*, a song that was supposedly intended for Mickey's wife Kim Weston but eventually to become something of an anthem not just for The Vandellas but for the Motown Sound as a whole. A sure-fire smash, *Dancing In The Street* would hit #8 R&B and #2 pop and become the group's first British hit single where it reached #26.

The success of *Dancing In The Street* guaranteed Mickey the opportunity of coming up with the follow-up, with he and Ivy providing *Wild One*, a Top Twenty R&B and Top Forty pop success (at #11 and #34 respectively), something of a slip compared with earlier successes but still better than several of their Motown contemporaries were managing. Fortunately, the creative juices of HDH had become a torrent by the end of 1964, and aside from their work with The Supremes and The Four Tops, still found time to return to The Vandellas' cause.

In September 1964, work began on what would be The Vandellas return to the Top Ten, *Nowhere To Run*. Providing ample proof that Martha and The Vandellas were worthy of a place in Motown's top flight, it showed HDH could adapt their sound to come up with hits for just about everybody they worked with. Not surprisingly, the continued success they enjoyed ensured that virtually every act within Hitsville was keen to get to work with them. Logistics alone ensured that not everyone could, of course, but The Vandellas were still part of the HDH roster, with the hit-making team providing *Love (Makes Me Do Foolish Things)*, released on single in July 1965. However, *Love* was merely the flip side to *You've Been In Love Too Long*, written by Mickey Stevenson, Ivy Jo Hunter and Clarence Paul. Both sides were strong and could possibly have done well on their own, but the effect of the two combined was to split the radio play, resulting in *You've Been In Love* peaking at #25 pop and #36 pop and *Love* making #22 R&B and #70 pop. The Vandellas also released their third album, **Dance Party** in April 1965, an album that featured the hits *Dancing In The Streets, Wild One* and *Nowhere To Run* but, once again, no picture of Martha or The Vandellas anywhere on the sleeve!

Mickey and Ivy linked with lyricist Sylvia Moy on The Vandellas' next single, *My Baby Loves Me*. Another song that had originally been intended for Kim Weston, Martha went into the studio a month after Kim and laid down *her* version over the same backing tracks. The end result was a song that Martha would claim to be among her favourites that the group recorded whilst at Motown.

"My dream was always to be a jazz singer and I was always hoping to record more jazz songs. *My Baby Loves Me* is real close to jazz."

Helping out on the backing vocals were The Four Tops and The Andantes; aside from Martha, there is no Vandella to be heard. It was still released as a Martha & The Vandellas single, soaring to #3 R&B and #22 pop, a fair result but somewhat off the chart positions The Supremes were by now achieving, a fact that rankled several at Hitsville, none more so than Martha and Rosalind.

"We were always told that we had to wait until The Supremes opened the door and then when that door was opened they'd let us through too," Rosalind later claimed. "That was fine and good because Diana Ross opened up a lot of doors for our group and other groups. But the question we always asked was 'why can't we open some doors?' We felt we were a pretty strong act and had a lot of untapped potential and we were at Motown before The Supremes."

It was a question that Martha in particular asked Berry Gordy directly on more than one occasion, leading to a somewhat strained relationship between the two. With The Vandellas' work with HDH becoming sporadic, the group was back in the studio with Mickey Stevenson, who again provided something with a jazz flavour for their next single. *What Am I Going To Do Without Your Love* was released in May 1966 and became one of the group's lowest charting singles, barely scraping in at #71 pop and missing the R&B listing altogether. Perhaps even Motown had their doubts about the song; the **Greatest Hits** package released at much the same time omitted the track from the twelve tracks on display (although the album cover did feature a picture of the girls, facing front, although it was on the reverse of the sleeve!). Despite the omission there were enough hits on the career retrospective to turn the album into a success, hitting #50 pop and #6 R&B. After the disappointment of *What Am I*, The Vandellas ended the year on a high, restored to working with HDH for *I'm Ready For Love*, a song crafted for The Vandellas rather than something intended for someone else. The Vandellas made the most of the new material, sending the single to the Top Ten of both the R&B and pop charts (#2 and #9 respectively), as well as returning them to the Top Thirty in the UK (#22).

Released the same month (October 1966) was a new album, **Watchout!**, another twelve track effort that saw the girls with assorted writers and producers, although the three HDH compositions stood out ahead of their rivals. The album was also the first time the three (Martha, Rosalind and Betty) were featured on the *front* cover, in colour and facing the camera! Sitting on the album was what would become another major hit, *Jimmy Mack*, something the group had originally recorded in 1964 as a possible follow-up to *In My Lonely Room*, although the emergence of *Dancing In The Street* quickly altered The Vandellas release schedule. By 1966, however, Martha was haranguing Berry constantly about the lack of good material The Vandellas was being offered, and in an attempt to placate Martha, ordered all recorded but unreleased Vandellas tracks to be brought to a meeting. According to reports, when he heard *Jimmy Mack* and discovered it had not been utilised, he was beside himself.

It was initially added to **Watchout!**, where the radio stations took over, playing the track constantly and prompting its release as a single in February 1967. Martha could have had no complaints about the promotional effort Motown put behind *Jimmy Mack* once it was released, with the single topping the R&B chart and hitting #10 pop as well as reaching #21 in the UK (the flip side, *Third Finger Left Hand*, another two year old track also got extensive play in the UK, eventually prompting a cover version by The Pearls). Aided by the success of the single, **Watchout!** enjoyed a chart run of its own, peaking at #14 R&B and #116 pop. Whilst *Jimmy Mack* was very much an HDH hallmarked song, Martha and The Vandellas would never work with the hit trio again.

Instead, they found themselves handed over to new writers and producers, commencing with Richard Morris and Sylvia Moy for *Love Bug Leave My Heart Alone*. Sylvia had worked with the group previously, and according to her own recollections specifically asked to work with the group again, despite the fact that everyone else at Hitsville was clamouring to work with The Supremes. The arrangement worked well, with *Love Bug* becoming a sizeable hit (#14 R&B and #25 pop), although it was to mark the last recording by the Mark II Vandellas. Growing friction between Martha and Betty saw the pair bicker and fight (sometimes on stage), resulting in Betty being handed her cards in June 1967, although the pair would later patch up their differences.

Martha didn't have far to look for a replacement, for accompanying The Vandellas on their numerous tours for the last eighteen months or so was Martha's younger sister Sandra Delores Reeves (born in Detroit on 12 April 1948), better known as Lois or Pee Wee (on account of her diminutive size). For much of that time, Lois had stood offstage and moved along to the well rehearsed dance routines Martha, Rosalind and Betty performed centre stage. There was little or no rehearsal needed, for Lois already had the moves down to perfection. Betty's parting shot was to be a live album, recording at the 20 Grand in Detroit during the group's three night engagement on 6 June to 8 June, with the album subsequently released in August 1967 (and would make it to #140 on the chart).

Betty's departure wasn't the only thing to impact on the group, for Mickey Stevenson would also leave Motown for a lucrative job with MGM and HDH were on a go-slow as a result of their own issues with Berry Gordy. Fortunately, Richard Morris and Sylvia Moy were still coming up with the goods, with *Honey Chile* another that performed well on the chart.

"When I first met Sylvia, she decided to write a song that was tailored for me. She caught wind of the fact that I was born in Alabama, the product of a southern upbringing. She wrote *Honey Chile* and filled it full of Southern anecdotes."

Honey Chile also saw a change in artist credit, with the single eventually released in October 1967 as Martha Reeves & The Vandellas, pushing Martha even further out front of the group in much the same way Smokey Robinson and Diana Ross were being projected in The Miracles and The Supremes respectively. *Honey Chile* did even better than its predecessor, going as a far as #5 R&B and #11 pop and a respectable #30 in the UK.

I Promise To Wait My Love saw Martha working with Hank Cosby and Billie Jean Brown, done as something of a favour to Berry Gordy. Billie Jean Brown was the person responsible for bringing the assorted tracks to the weekly Quality Control meeting, although such was her power those songs that she didn't like never quite made it to the meetings; one of her original dislikes had been *Jimmy Mack*! Billie Jean also co-wrote the song and performed backing vocals on the session (once again Martha was the only Vandella that appeared on the recording), with the finished single becoming a small hit, #62 pop and #36 R&B following its release in April 1968. The track would also be the lead track on the album released the same month, **Ridin' High**, which gathered together recent hits in *Love Bug* and *Honey Chile* and assorted cover versions.

The album was a solid seller in R&B markets, peaking at #13 on the chart but struggled to crossover, stalling at #167.

The recording of the next single was mired in problems, with the end result featuring even less of The Vandellas than any previous recording. Martha had been allocated producer and writer Deke Richards, who along with Debbie Dean wrote *I Can't Dance To That Music You're Playin'*, a song Martha would later claim she was unhappy with the storyline, which detailed a love affair with a married musician.

"I didn't like the lyrics. I'm supposed to be a true artist. Anything I ever sang, I had to live up to it."

Motown didn't like the structure, telling Deke to re-edit it so that the chorus appeared as the lead to the song. The initial edit was done and submitted to the Quality Control meeting, who decided they liked the original version better, so instructed Deke to revert back to the first version that had been cut. The only problem was that during the re-edit, parts of Martha's vocal were lost, requiring a re-recording of several bits and pieces. Martha and The Vandellas were by then on tour, with no spare time whatsoever for Martha to journey back to Detroit to undertake the recording session. Motown also refused permission for Deke to journey out to wherever Martha might be performing, and in desperate need of a new Martha Reeves & The Vandellas single, eventually convinced Deke to bring Rita Wright (later better known as Syreeta) into the studio to undertake something of a Martha Reeves impersonation to finish the song!

The end result was, to say the least, something of a mash-up, with Martha complaining, "Instead of sounding like me, she sounded like Diana Ross! That really pissed me off!"

Quite how aware of the subterfuge the public were remains a matter of doubt, but *I Can't Dance* did at least hit the chart if not the spot, peaking at #24 R&B and #42 pop. It was back to Richard Morris for the next single, *Sweet Darlin'* being issued in October 1968, but the result was a minor hit (#80 pop, #45 R&B), although the flip side *Without You* (co-written and produced by Deke Richards) gained some considerable radio action.

After this single was released, original member Rosalind Ashford departed the group, with another former Velvelette in Sandra Tilley (born in Cleveland, Ohio on 6 May 1943) her replacement. In January 1969 The Vandellas became the latest beneficiaries of the upsurge in interest in Britain of all things Tamla Motown, with *Dancing In The Street* being re-released and powering its way to #4 on the chart, becoming the biggest British hit Martha and The Vandellas were to enjoy (in the coming months, *Nowhere To Run* and

Jimmy Mack would also be revived, peaking at #42 and #21 respectively). The British success proved to be a welcome diversion from matters at home, where singles were slipping down the charts as the months progressed; *(We've Got) Honey Love* stalled at #56 pop and #27 R&B, *Taking My Love (And Leaving Me)* did even worse, barely making Top 50 R&B (#44) and bubbling under at #102 on the pop chart.

The album chart offered no respite, with **Sugar N' Spice** missing the charts altogether. So too did the single *I Should Be So Proud*, issued as a single in February 1970, but its failure was not down to public indifference. Martha herself remains convinced the single, with its strong anti-Vietnam War sentiment, was pulled off the playlist of any and all radio stations by forces outside of Motown's control, and with no radio play Berry Gordy eventually called the single back. It did appear on the group's album **Natural Resources**, released in September 1970, but this failed to sell either. Martha Reeves & The Vandellas' only appearance on the chart was with the single *I Gotta Let You Go*, written and produced by Norman Whitfield. This was not a new song, Norman having written it in 1964 for The Temptations, then re-assigned it to Jimmy Ruffin, and subsequently shelving the song for six years until it was dusted down for Martha. The haphazard way it got given to The Vandellas probably contributed to its lacklustre chart performance, creeping into the Hot 100 at #93 and #43 on the R&B chart.

Fortunately, there was still Britain to keep Martha's name in lights, with an old forgotten flip side getting the group back into the Top Twenty; *Forget Me Not* had originally been released in April 1968 as the flip to *I Promise To Wait My Love*, which hadn't exactly raised much of a stir on either side of the Atlantic. But *Forget Me Not* had attracted attention in the UK, where the Northern Soul market had taken to the track enough to justify Tamla Motown releasing it as the top side, with *I Gotta Let You Go* carried along for the ride. The result was a #11 hit, The Vandella's best chart performance since *Dancing In The Street* had been reissued.

Back at home, further changes were in the pipeline, with Motown itself preparing to vacate Detroit for the warmer climes of California. Martha and The Vandellas would complete their Motown tenure with a handful of singles and an album that made the chart, but *Bless You, In And Out Of My Life* and *Tear It Down* couldn't break into the Top Twenty R&B and finished way down the listings on the pop chart. A similar fate befell **Black Magic**, the group's final Motown album released in March 1972 which peaked at #30 R&B and #146 pop.

Since The Vandellas were not to make the journey west with the rest of the Motown roster, Martha couldn't see any point in continuing with the group, so on 21 December 1972, at the Cobo Hall in Detroit, the group performed for the last time as a Motown act. Martha would eventually announce plans for a solo career, negotiating her way out of her Motown contract and eventually signing with MCA, but whilst her work was well received critically, it lacked the same sparkle that had accompanied her body of Motown work, a trait that continued on subsequent recordings with Arista and Fantasy.

Sister Lois would become a member of Quiet Elegance and sing back up for Al Green, whilst Sandra Tilley developed a brain tumour and died following surgery on 9 September 1981. Thus when Martha had to reconvene The Vandellas for an appearance on the 'Motown 25' television spectacular, it was sisters Lois and Delphine that joined her for her performance. Whilst Martha has continued to tour since then and there have been occasional reunions for the original members, today there are two groups out working the circuit, The Original Vandellas fronted by Rosalind Ashord and Annette Beard, and Martha Reeves & The Vandellas. Martha still looks back at her time at Motown with affection, as she told author Bill Dahl.

"I feel good about any accomplishments and all accomplishments that Motown allowed me to achieve. Berry wanted his music to make you feel young, and I feel young every time I sing it. Even when I'm at the end of a song, my heart is racing so fast – and it's beating with joy, knowing I'm part of the Motown sound."

Martha and The Vandellas were inducted into the Rock & Roll Hall of Fame in 1995.

ALBUMS: COME AND GET THESE MEMORIES (1963), HEAT WAVE (1963), DANCE PARTY (1965), WATCHOUT (1966), LIVE (1967), RIDIN' HIGH (1968), SUGAR 'N' SPICE (1969), NATURAL RESOURCES (1970), BLACK MAGIC (1972)

COMPILATIONS: GREATEST HITS (1966), ANTHOLOGY (1974), 26 GREATEST HITS (1986)

FURTHER READING: DANCING IN THE STREET: CONFESSIONS OF A MOTOWN DIVA (1994)

THE REFLECTIONS

Detroit-based vocal group The Reflections was formed by Tony Micale (born in The Bronx, New York on 23 August 1942), Phil Castrodale (born in Detroit, Michigan on 2 April 1940), Dan Bennie (born in Johnstone, Scotland on 13 March 1940), Ray Steinberg (born in Washington, Pennsylvania on 29 October 1942) and John Dean (born in Detroit on 9 November 1941).

After releasing singles on Kay-Ko (*Helpless*, released in 1963) and Tigre (a remake of *In The Still Of The Nite*), the group signed with Ed Wingate and his Golden World label. They scored first time out, with Bob Hamilton and Freddie Gorman penning and Rob Reeco producing *(Just Like) Romeo And Juliet*, which went on to become a major hit, reaching #3 R&B and #6 pop in April 1964. The single was also released in the UK on the Stateside label, albeit without success. The group would never chart as high again, but *Like Columbus Did* (#96), *(I'm Just A) Henpecked Guy* (#123), *Shabby Little Hut* (#121) and *Poor Man's Son* (#55) at least kept them in the limelight.

After a total of seven Golden World singles the group hit problems with the label, disagreeing over the direction they should pursue as well as a royalty dispute, with the result the group left and signed with ABC. They subsequently changed their name to High & The Mighty but never again charted. That might have been the end of their story, but in 1974 Tamla Motown in the UK re-released a number of Ric-Tic and Golden World singles in order to satisfy the burgeoning Northern Soul market. The Reflections' *(Just Like) Romeo And Juliet* was one of those reissued, alongside Edwin Starr's *Stop Her On Sight*, although neither charted the second time around.

REFLECTIONS – DIANA ROSS & THE SUPREMES [SINGLE]

Reflections marked both a beginning and an end for The Supremes, for it was the first single to be issued under the new moniker of Diana Ross & The Supremes and one of the last recordings Florence Ballard would make whilst still a member of the group. The elevation of Diana Ross had long been expected, since Berry Gordy's desire to turn her into a multi-faceted entertainer had indicated that at some point she would be undertaking a solo career.

The song's writers, Brian Holland, Lamont Dozier and Eddie Holland, had also expanded their horizons, listening to the various effects other artists were achieving with their recordings, and not just within the R&B field. If there is a hint of rock in *Reflections*, then that was deliberate, for HDH set out to replicate the psychedelic rock of The Beatles and The Beach Boys. To achieve this they used a variety of new instruments and equipment, including a signal generator designed by in-house engineer Russ Terrana. The end result was something of a different sound for Diana Ross & The Supremes, one that caught the imagination of the record buying public, peaking at #2 pop and #4 R&B and hitting #5 in the UK.

REGAL FUNKHARMONIC ORCHESTRA

A studio project assembled by producers Gil Askey and Russ Terrana, with six symphonic medleys of well known Motown material. Aside from individual tributes to The Supremes, Temptations, Four Tops, Commodores and Rick James, there was a more generic Motown track in *Strung Out On Motown* which was released as a single (backed with *Strung Out On The Commodores*) in August 1982, a month after the **Strung Out On Motown** album had been released.

ALBUM: STRUNG OUT ON MOTOWN (1982)

REMEMBER ME – DIANA ROSS [SINGLE]

Penned by Nickolas Ashford and Valerie Simpson, *Remember Me* had originally been planned as one of the tracks on Valerie's solo album, which would duly appear in May 1971. The pair recorded the backing tracks at Hitsville in August 1970, adding a guide vocal some two weeks later at Golden World after which the song was allocated to Diana Ross, who had launched her own solo career on the back of two hits penned by Ashford and Simpson.

Remember Me turned out to be the perfect song for Diana, at least lyrically, for her relationship with Berry Gordy was beginning to cool, so a song from a spurned woman requesting that her former boyfriend should remember all of the good things that they shared held a certain degree of poignancy. Whilst not a major hit in the US, where it stalled at #10 R&B and #16 pop following its release in December 1970, it struck a chord in the UK, where it would become her second Top Ten hit, peaking at #7. In 1981 The Boystown Gang took two of Diana's major hits, *Ain't No Mountain High Enough* and *Remember Me* and produced a hi-energy medley that hit #46 in the UK.

EUGENE REMUS

Eugene Remus hung around Motown long enough to record one single, which would subsequently get released in a variety of different versions as Berry Gordy tried to find a way of making a hit. Next to nothing is known of Eugene himself, other than he turned up at some point looking for a deal and found himself in the studio recording *You Never Miss A Good Thing*, *Hold Me Tight* and *Gotta Have Your Lovin'*. The October 1959 release paired the first two tracks as a single, with Motown subsequently reissuing *You Never Miss* with *Gotta Have Your Lovin'* as the B side, and then reissued again with the top side having had strings added for additional flavour.

No matter what Motown tried, the single wouldn't shift and Eugene Remus' brief Motown career (indeed, quite possibly his entire musical career, since nothing can be found about him post-Motown) came to an abrupt end. What makes this somewhat surprising is that the one person who did remember him at Motown, songwriter Janie Bradford, claimed Eugene was a more than capable writer himself, even though he was not given the opportunity of proving it at Hitsville.

REPAIRS

The band Repairs was the brain-child of singer and songwriter Peter McCann. The band began as a duo with Peter performing with guitarist Jim Honeycutt at Fairfield University in and around 1968. As time passed, more members joined the duo. Another Fairfield University student, Mike Foley joined as a bassist. Then Jim's future wife Sukie (percussion and vocals) began singing harmony. By the spring of 1970, guitarist extraordinaire Larry Treadwell joined the group during Jim and Peter's senior year of college. After graduating from Villanova University in 1970, Timothy 'Ace' Holleran (drums) rounded out the band's personnel.

In 1971, Repairs was performing on Jesup's Green in Westport where they were spotted by Rolling Stones' manager Andrew Loog Oldham, who helped them get a deal with Rare Earth Records, even producing their debut album for the label. Entitled **Already A Household Word,** it didn't quite live up to its title following its November 1971 release, and neither did the follow-up **The Repairs** issued in October the following year, despite the accompanying release of the single *Songwriter*.

After one further album, a live recording issued by a small European label, Cuckold, in 1973 the group regrouped after both Jim and Sukie Honeycutt's departure. The band remained together for another year or so relocating to the West Coast where they eventually disbanded. Peter McCann continued as a successful songwriter. Larry Treadwell continues to play guitar with many Los Angeles bands as well as at the Groundlings Comedy Club. Ace Holleran continued playing for many artists including Bette Midler and others. Mike Foley continues to play bass. Jim Honeycutt is a high school media teacher in Westport, Connecticut. Sukie Honeycutt lives in Naples, Florida and owns several restaurants there.

ALBUMS: ALREADY A HOUSEHOLD WORD (1971), THE REPAIRS (1972)

RESPECT YOURSELF – BRUCE WILLIS [SINGLE]

Written by Luther Ingram and Mack Rice, *Respect Yourself* had been a huge crossover hit for The Staple Singers in 1971, making the Top Ten of both the pop and R&B charts. Fifteen years later it would become the lead track of Bruce Willis' **The Return Of Bruno** album, being released in December 1986. The track features the uncredited vocal contribution of Bonnie Pointer and became a sizeable pop hit on both sides of the Atlantic, hitting #5 in the US and #7 in the UK. It also made #20 on the R&B chart for good measure, but its true worth was helping publicise the availability of the album, which also sold well in the UK. The song meanwhile has gone on to attract further cover versions, most notably by The Kane Gang and Robert Palmer.

RETURN OF BRUNO – BRUCE WILLIS [ALBUM]

Bruce Willis was in the early flushes of success thanks to the popularity of the television series 'Moonlighting' when he was chosen to be the spokesman for Seagram's wine coolers, with the commercial showcasing his singing talents. Watching Motown executives were impressed enough to offer him a recording contract, one which Bruce was happy to sign. The resulting album relied heavily on cover versions of well known R&B and pop hits, with a smattering of original material to round out the ten tracks.

Produced by Robert Kraft and featuring vocal and musical backing by Booker T Jones, Siedah Garrett, Jeff Lorber and The Temptations, **The Return Of Bruno** was released in December 1986, accompanied by an HBO one hour television special, in which Bruce Willis performs as his fictitious alter ego Bruno Radolini. Although probably not intended as a serious contender for chart honours, **The Return Of Bruno** still sold well, peaking at #14 pop and #27 R&B in the US, aided by the success of the lead single *Respect Yourself*, a #5 pop and #20 R&B hit.

It was in the UK, however, that the album exploded, hitting #4 and earning a gold disc, even though the television special (which featured cameo appearances by Elton John, Phil Collins and Ringo Starr) barely aired. A total of four chart singles were lifted in the UK; *Respect Yourself* (#7), *Under The Boardwalk* (#2), *Secret Agent Man-James Bond Is Back* (#43) and *Comin' Right Up* (#73).

THE RHYTHM & BLUES MUSIC HALL OF FAME

Founded in 2010 by sports entertainer and entrepreneur LaMont Robinson, the Rhythm& Blues Hall of Fame began as a mobile museum displaying the countless items of memorabilia that he had collected following his passion for R&B music. The second phase was the creation of an actual Hall of Fame, with the inaugural ceremony being held in Cleveland, Ohio (LaMont's hometown as well as being the location for the Rock & Roll Hall of Fame) on 17 August 2013. The Motown inductees were as follows:

The Four Tops
The Marvelettes
David Ruffin
Sly, Slick & Wicked
Edwin Starr
The Supremes
The Temptations
The Vandellas
Kim Weston

RHYTHM OF THE NIGHT - DeBARGE [SINGLE]

Rhythm Of The Night marked a departure from the norm for DeBarge, the group having previously made their name and reputation with ballad material. It also represented something of a rare excursion into up-tempo material for Diane Warren, the song's writer who would later become one of the best ballad writers of the age.

The hook up between the two came with the film 'The Last Dragon', ultimately to become the very last feature film for Motown Productions, with producer Berry Gordy bringing in a host of Motown artists to contribute to the accompanying soundtrack. Diane Warren's demo version of *Rhythm Of The Night* was one of the tracks chosen for selection, with veteran producer and record company executive Richard Perry personally chosen by Suzanne De Passe to handle production on the DeBarge single. Fortunately, the group and the producer developed a rapport in the studio, even though Richard was aware that the up-tempo song was outside their normal comfort zone.

"This was very different for them, being up-tempo. But I loved the song. I immediately heard it as a potential hit and felt it would be great for them."

To add to the song's flavour, Richard utilised the same kind of party atmosphere Lionel Richie had achieved on *All Night Long* and, just as he had done with most of his recordings, got a spontaneous feel by recording the single 'live'. The end result was everything producer, writer, artist and record company would have wished, going on to top the R&B chart and hit #3 pop in the US and #4 in the UK.

DEKE RICHARDS

The son of screenwriter Dane Lussier, Deke was born in Los Angeles, California on 8 April 1944 and was widely expected to follow the same career path as his father. Instead, after hearing Elvis Presley's hit *Heartbreak Hotel* Deke became interested in music, picking up a guitar at the age of twelve and mastering the instrument soon after.

At fourteen he had written his first song, a pop ditty called *Bubblegum*, and by his later teenage years had formed his own band, Deke & The Deacons. The R&B influenced group played many of the clubs on Sunset Strip in Los Angeles and quickly established a good reputation, enough to see them fill in for the likes of Ike & Tina Turner and tour with the likes of Dobie Gray, even performing as far afield as Hawaii. By 1965, however, the band (which had also briefly gone by the name of The Four Sounds) had reached a crisis, with the rest of the group wanting to add a brass section but Deke adamant they didn't need one.

He left and quickly assembled a new band, which in time would become the backing band for Debbie Dean. Debbie had her own place in Motown history, having been the first white solo artist signed to the label at the start of the 1960s, but when she started out, Motown had little or no idea how to promote a pop artist. By 1966 her act had changed, with Deke having written a song that the pair thought might be good enough to get them into Motown. Managing to raise some $300 after borrowing from friends, Deke and Debbie secured a reduced rate session at Richard

Podolor's American Recording Studio at which they intended recording that song to demo level. Unfortunately the funds ran out before they had got a chance to record Debbie's vocals, but the backing track alone was good enough to convince the pair that it was still worth a shot at Motown. Fortunately, Debbie still had a few contacts, which she used to get an appointment with Berry Gordy when he was in Los Angeles to see The Supremes perform live. With Deke's backing tracks playing in the background, Debbie sang the song for Berry, who was impressed enough to offer Debbie a recording contract and Deke a writing contract.

Debbie would record one further single (for the V.I.P. label, which was produced by Deke under the name Dennis Lussier) and pen a number of songs with Deke before exiting the company. Deke meanwhile quickly proved his worth around the Los Angeles office and studio, usually working with Frank Wilson. After a year during which Deke (and Frank) had done little of note for Motown, the pair wrote a letter to Berry Gordy expressing their disappointment with the way things were going for them and indicating that they would leave the company for another unless they were better utilised. Quite how serious the pair were remained to be seen, but the mild threat had the desired effect, for they were both summonsed to Detroit and told they could have a song on the next Diana Ross & The Supremes album, with Deke writing *I'm Gonna Make It (I Will Wait For You)* with Debbie Dean that subsequently appeared on the **Reflections** album.

The departure of Holland-Dozier-Holland, coupled with sliding sales on subsequent Diana Ross & The Supremes albums and singles prompted Berry Gordy to rethink his strategy in 1968. Requiring a major hit with which to resurrect their career, he brought in some of the best songwriters from around the company, including Hank Cosby, Frank Wilson, Pam Sawyer, R. Dean Taylor and Deke Richards. Working out of a hotel suite in Detroit, the five came up with *Love Child*, a single that would eventually carry the writing and production credit The Clan (so as to avoid creating a similar personality cult that had surrounded HDH). The single returned the group to the top of the pop charts, with Deke also co-writing *Honey Bee (Keep On Stinging Me)* with Debbie and Janie Bradford that appeared on the subsequent album.

After The Clan was quietly put to rest, Deke became a key member of another songwriting partnership, this time The Corporation, with Freddie Perren, Fonce Mizell and Berry Gordy himself. Charged with launching The Jackson 5 on an unsuspecting public, The Corporation created some of the best pop music to come out of Motown at the turn of the decade, including *I Want You Back*, *ABC*, *The Love You Save*, *Mama's Pearl*, *Maybe Tomorrow* and *Goin' Back To Indiana*.

Whilst working inside The Corporation was time consuming, Deke still found time for other projects aside from The Jackson 5, with varying degrees of success. He was largely responsible, for example, for creating Diana Ross' **Everything Is Everything** album, from which the British chart topper *I'm Still Waiting* was extracted, but it was a matter of some regret to Deke that the song failed to grab the attention of the American record buying public. So too was the failure of Chris Clark's **CC Rides Again** album, which got lost promotionally as Motown concentrated on similar rock releases on the Rare Earth label rather than Deke's own creation, Weed.

Deke's Motown contract ran out in 1973 and he left the company, initially writing and producing for a variety of other artists, including Bonnie Bramlett, Black Oak Arkansas and Dorothy Norwood. Deke eventually tired of both the record business and Los Angeles, relocating to Washington State where he also switched entertainment industries, finally following his father into the film world by setting up the Poster Palace, a company dealing in film posters and memorabilia. Deke died from esophageal cancer on 24 March 2013.

LIONEL RICHIE

During the course of some fifteen years, Lionel Richie became acknowledged as one of the best songwriters of his generation, penning a succession of sweet soul hits that resonated around the world. Unfortunately for The Commodores, their competitive spirit effectively dictated that Lionel would have to leave for a solo career; it was the only way he'd get all of the songs that were welling up inside him out to the market.

"I never wanted to leave The Commodores in the first place. It was stifling in the group, particularly when it got to the point where all of us wanted to write and produce. It was very competitive. I'd been a member of that group for fifteen years or so, and to leave wasn't the easiest of things for me to do."

Born Lionel Brockman Richie Jr. in Tuskegee, Alabama on 20 June 1949, he helped form his first group The Mystics whilst studying at Tuskegee Institute, linking up with future Commodores Thomas McClary and William King. In 1968 The Mystics linked up with another local group, The Jays, which brought into the fold Walter 'Clyde' Orange, Milan Williams and Ronald LaPread, and after agonising for some time over a new name for the group, eventually found it by plucking a name out of a dictionary.

The newly christened Commodores quickly established a healthy reputation around Alabama and the following year journeyed up to New York during the summer vacation, gaining both a short residency at a local club and the opportunity of recording for the first time. A single produced by Jerry 'Swamp Dog' Williams was released on Atlantic Records (*Rise Up* backed with *Keep On Dancin'*), but a planned album was scrapped when the single failed to set the world alight. Fortunately for the group, their live performances continued to attract attention, resulting in an offer from Motown Records to accompany new recruits The Jackson 5 on a prestigious tour that would stretch from New York to Hawaii.

The Commodores would eventually join The Jackson 5 at Motown, being signed by the MoWest label in 1972, where their initial recording sessions were undertaken by in-house writers and producers Gloria Jones and Pam Sawyer. It would take two years for the group to finally release their debut album (by which time MoWest had been closed down and The Commodores switched to the main Motown label), time enough for the group to have developed their own song-writing abilities. The group's initial success came with a driving funk based sound, exemplified by the hit single *Machine Gun*, written by Milan Williams. It was Milan who held sway during the group's early days at Motown, although the rest of the group also contributed to the material on display. Even then, in 1974, the group established a democratic system whereby each member would submit songs to the rest of the group for consideration, with those that received the most votes being those that were recorded.

For that debut album, entitled **Machine Gun** after the hit single, Lionel contributed two numbers in *There's A Song In My Heart* and *Superman* (which was released as a single in the UK in February 1975), but like the majority of the material on the album, these were upbeat songs, in keeping with the rest of the material. The first noticeable swing towards the more mellow sound with which Lionel would make his reputation came on the second album **Caught In The Act**, where *This Is Your Life* would be released as the second single from the album and hit #13 on the R&B chart (Lionel also wrote *Let's Do It Right* and co-wrote *You Don't Know What I Know*).

The group's third album **Movin' On** would feature only one extracted single, but it was Lionel's composition *Sweet Love* that enabled The Commodores to break into the Top Ten of both the pop and R&B charts. That run was maintained on the next album, from where *Just To Be Close To You* emerged as an R&B chart topper and pop Top Ten hit, as well as being the track that enabled The Commodores to move up from being a support act on tour (they had recently supported The O'Jays) to headliners. Following the success of *Just To Be Close To You*, each Commodores album became something of an event, with much anticipation surrounding each successive release, waiting to see what was the latest hit to roll effortlessly off the conveyor belt.

Lionel didn't disappoint either, with *Easy* being the stand out track from the group's **The Commodores** album (which would be released as **Zoom** in the UK), although Lionel also contributed to a further four of the tracks from the million plus selling album. As good as *Easy* was, it was to be surpassed by Lionel's contribution to the next album **Natural High**, with *Three Times A Lady* becoming an international smash and chart topper, coming at a time when he was virtually unrivalled as a writer of sublime love songs. Indeed, even as **Natural High** and *Three Times A Lady* were ascending the charts, manager Benny Ashburn was telling all who would listen that the next album **Midnight Magic**, then in the process of being recorded, contained not one but two tracks that were of at least the same musical value of *Three Times*. Benny's insider knowledge proved to be almost right, for both *Sail On* and *Still* would power up the chart, further improving The Commodores career but, perhaps most importantly, leading to an increase in the number of enquiries from outside artists looking to work with Lionel Richie.

At that particular time Lionel was quite content to continue as a member of The Commodores, the group being more than capable of fulfilling all of his aspirations, so the likes of Kenny Rogers received polite but firm refusals to any and all requests for outside projects. A motorcycle accident suffered by Clyde Orange was to change all of that, with his incapacity for some three weeks enabling Lionel to agree to writing a song for Kenny Rogers. Musically, the song submitted, *Lady*, was little or no different from those Lionel had been writing for The Commodores, but in giving the song to someone outside of The Commodores, Lionel had set in motion his own eventual departure from the group. He had also given away one of his better songs of the era, for neither of the songs contributed to The Commodores' album **Heroes** was in the same league, with *Heroes* failing to break into the Top 50 pop or Top Twenty R&B and *Jesus Is Love* only making something of a fleeting appearance on the R&B chart.

Lionel returned to form with his next two compositions, *Endless Love* and *Oh No,* but unfortunately only one of these (*Oh No*) was given to The Commodores; *Endless Love* was a major hit for Lionel and Diana Ross and Oscar-nominated theme to the film starring Brooke Shields. Publicly at least Lionel Richie and The Commodores denied there was an impending split, even though it was well known that Lionel was working on an eponymous solo album for release in September 1982.

"It was a strange feeling doing this album and it was only when we were finishing it off that I realised there was only me on it because my picture was on the cover! It was different for me for, you see, I was only used to submitting one song for a Commodores' album and when we thought about cutting something on me I realised I'd have to have nine or ten songs ready. Over the years, I've written eighty to a hundred songs and I still had those, so we had to decide which ones were the best. It was such a hard task that I decided to ask James Carmichael to help me. He's one of The Commodores really anyway. He writes and produces with us. I also felt he was the right person, and he really wanted to give it a go. The whole experience was fun. I really enjoyed myself."

So too did the public when the album was released, buying up more than four million copies of the album and turning three singles into Top Ten pop and R&B hits; *Truly, You Are* and *My Love*. Having also taken James Anthony Carmichael it was obvious that a parting of the ways was inevitable, although even as the album was enjoying its success and there was promotional work to undertake, Lionel was still undecided as to whether he should make a clean break.

"The Commodores are a package that took masterminding and as soon as I've finished here, I'm returning to Tuskegee to see the rest of the guys to decide what to do. I suppose, I do feel responsible for The Commodores. We're like six crazy brothers; we've been too close for too long and the group is based on a lot of love. Nothing will change that. We have to make decisions together and make them work because it affects their lives and mine. Even with my work outside the group I'm more concerned that I don't disrupt The Commodores organisation. It must remain intact. I've always been a Commodore and we must keep our heritage alive above all else."

In the end it appeared as though the decision was made for Lionel, with the rest of The Commodores also opting to cut production ties with James Anthony Carmichael for their album **13**. Whilst The Commodores' effort proved to be something of a disjointed affair, Lionel and James crafted one of the best selling Motown albums of all time. He may have made his reputation with his sublime ballads, but there was a diversity and richness about **Can't Slow Down**, his second solo album released in October 1983. He revisited many of those eighty to a hundred songs he had written previously too, although the initial line-up for the album omitted both *Running With The Night, Hello* and *All Night Long*, three tracks that would all go on to become major pop smashes. They were joined in the Top Ten by a further two tracks, whilst the album would top the charts the world over on its way to selling more than twenty million copies, including more than ten million domestically, which earned Lionel a Diamond Disc award from the American trade organisation R.I.A.A. The album also won the Grammy Award for Album of the Year, the fourth Motown album to achieve the feat, whilst Lionel and James were jointly named Producers of the Year at the same ceremony.

Three years would pass before the third album arrived, Lionel wetting the public's appetite with another film theme, *Say You Say Me* from 'White Nights. The single would enable Lionel to fill another spot on his mantelpiece with an award, this time the Oscar for Best Film Song, but his pursuit of aural excellence meant that the album, initially planned to be named after the single, arrived so late it had to change title to **Dancing On the Ceiling**. It was still a diverse collection of songs, with the country flavour even more pronounced on *Deep River Woman*, and a total of four singles would go on to become Top Ten hits. Whilst sales of **Dancing On The Ceiling** were less than half of those of its predecessor, total American sales of more than four million copies were still well in excess those of his contemporaries.

Lionel would release one further album on Motown, the career retrospective **Back To Front** (which also featured three new tracks) appearing in 1992 and going on to become another platinum seller. Thereafter Lionel was switched to the Mercury label, owned by Universal (the same conglomerate who now owned the Motown catalogue), but subsequent albums have so far been commercial and, to an extent, critical disappointments. However, it would be fair to say that with his body of work with The Commodores and his first three solo albums, Lionel set the bar so high even he would struggle to maintain that consistency throughout the rest of his career. Besides, when he started out at college, a career as a musician was the furthest thing from his mind.

"After a while I had to say 'what have I gotten myself into?' I'm the guy who wanted to be a lawyer until the music bug hit me in about seventeen different places. I'm the shy guy who just wanted to sit in the corner.

You've gotten me out here, God. What in the world is going on?"
ALBUMS: LIONEL RICHIE (1982), CAN'T SLOW DOWN (1983), DANCING ON THE CEILING (1986)
FURTHER READING: LIONEL RICHIE: HELLO (2009)

RIGHT CHOICE

Vocal trio The Right Choice formed in Memphis, Tennessee with Archie Love, Eric Shotell and Tony Black (who also doubled as a keyboard player), scoring a #13 R&B hit on Motown in 1988 with a remake of Al Green's *Tired Of Being Alone*. Producer Wayne Douglass also helmed their only album, released the following year, by which time Motown had been sold. Archie Love later recorded solo, releasing a couple of albums on the JEA label.

RICK, ROBIN & HIM

Despite the implication in the name, Rick, Robin & Him was a duo formed by folk rock songwriter and producer Richard Witte and Sally Furman. Richard also produced under the name Richie Sherman, but his only Motown productions of note were *Three Choruses Of Despair* by Rick, Robin & Him (which was originally scheduled with *Copper Kettle* as the flip side, only to be changed to *Cause You Know Me* on the actual single release), released on V.I.P. in June 1966 and The Velvelettes *Ain't No Place Like Motown*. Rick would later be a member of Back To Nature, La Esperanza, Rex and United Zero's; Sally Furman doesn't appear to have remained in the industry.

RICKENSTEIN

In August 1974 Billboard announced that Rickenstein (in reality former Sly & The Family Stone musician Rick Holly) was in the studio with Winston Monseque producing his debut album for Motown. Later reports had Mandre producing, but whoever was in charge, the album eventually got pulled from the schedule, even if a complete track listing was published. Rick subsequently retired from the music business, although he later formed the I.C. Music label based in Tallahassee.

RIOT

Latin rock group Riot was formed by John De Luna (drums and bells), Hungria Carmelo Garcia (various percussion instruments), Hector Andrades (various percussion instruments) and Gabriel Garcia (vocals) and signed to the Rare Earth label in 1973. The group was then paired with writers and producers Nick Zesses and Dino Fekaris for their only album, **Welcome To The World Of Riot**, despite the fact the individual group members had signed three contracts with Motown; as artists, writers and producers! After the album stalled, the group negotiated their way out of Motown and were fixing up a move to Capitol when they decided to disband. John De Luna rejoined his previous group El Chicano after Riot folded.
ALBUM: WELCOME TO THE WORLD OF RIOT (1974)

PAUL RISER

Whilst Paul Riser was introduced to Motown as a more than competent trombonist and played on countless sessions, his true vocation within Hitsville was as an arranger, most notably on many of Norman Whitfield's sessions. Born in Detroit, Michigan on 15 August 1936, Paul was another graduate from the Cass Technical High School in Detroit having studied classical and jazz trombone.

A friend who was already working for Motown suggested Paul join the company since there was regular work to be had as a musician, performing on hundreds of recordings. After three years as a musician, Paul switched to arranging at the instigation of Norman Whitfield.

"Once Norman opened that door, the rest is history. Arranging was more lucrative and less work, so I weaned myself off playing. We were paupers compared to the arrangers in L.A. and New York, but it was good steady money for Detroit."

Indeed, Paul soon showed he could improve the quality of just about any song with well crafted arrangements; he would later claim The Temptations' were not particularly enamoured with *My Girl*, until they heard the string arrangement. His best known work was with Norman Whitfield on *Papa Was A Rollin' Stone* (for which he won a Grammy Award) and *Masterpiece*, and following Motown's move to Los Angeles Paul became in demand across the entire industry. He has since gone on to work with artists as diverse as Phil Collins, Cliff Richard, Aretha Franklin, R Kelly, Stevie Wonder, Carly Simon, Tom Jones and Michael McDonald, among others.

ROAD

Former Jimi Hendrix Experience and Fat Mattress guitarist Noel Redding (born in Folkestone, Kent on 25 December 1945) assembled Road with Rod Richards (formerly of Rare Earth, on guitar and vocals) and Leslie Sampson (drums and vocals) in Los Angeles in 1970. Two years later the band released their only album, **Road** on Motown's Natural Resources label in July 1972. Road disbanded after this album, with Redding and Sampson becoming members of The Noel Redding Band and Richards pursuing a solo career (Sampson also became a member of Stray Dog, who released an album on Manticore in 1974). Redding died on 11 May 2003.
ALBUM: ROAD (1972)

ROBERT & JOHNNY

Vocal duo Robert Carr and Johnny Mitchell first got together in The Bronx and signed with Old Town Records in 1956. They scored their biggest hit with *We Belong Together*, a #12 R&B and #32 pop hit in 1958, with only one other single making the chart (*I Believe In You* hit #93 pop later the same year), despite releasing some 17 singles on Old Town (including reissues) and one apiece on Sue and Barry. *We Belong Together* appeared on the soundtrack to 'Christine' in November 1983. Robert Carr died on 18 May 1993.

MATT ROBINSON

Born in Philadelphia, Pennsylvania on 1 January 1937, Matt Robinson first made his name as an actor, portraying the character Gordon Robinson on the children's programme 'Sesame Street'. He later found equal success as a producer, with 1973's 'Save The Children' among his credits. Matt provides the narration on the accompanying soundtrack album released by Motown in 1974. After suffering from Parkinsons Disease for more than twenty years, Matt died on 5 August 2002.

SMOKEY ROBINSON

Hitsville may have had Berry Gordy's name up above the door, but the subsequent success of the operation owed just as much to Smokey Robinson, as a writer, confidant, recording artist and inspiration. Berry recognised Smokey's talent right from the off, "He reminded me of me – so excited and passionate about his music."

William Robinson Jr. was born in Detroit, Michigan on 19 February 1940, in the same hospital on the same day as future Miracles member Bobby Rogers, although the pair didn't meet up for some fifteen years. He was brought up in Detroit's North End district (where Diana Ross was a neighbour) and given the nickname 'Smokey Joe' at the age of eight by an uncle. Smokey assumed the name was because of his love of cowboy and western films, only to discover later that it was intended to remind the light-skinned Smokey of his heritage, 'smokey' being a pejorative term for dark-skinned Blacks.

As a youngster he attended Dwyer Elementary, Hutchins Intermediate and Northern High schools, and claimed to have written his first song at the age of six. As he grew up so did his interest in music, as he later revealed.

"I used to buy a lot of songbooks with people like Snooky Lansen and Dean Martin on the covers, because I wanted to know the words of the current tunes that were popular. I would buy those rather than candy."

As well as keeping up to date with what was happening on the pop chart, Smokey took an active interest in R&B, with Billy Ward & The Dominoes and Nolan Strong& The Diablos early influences. Eventually, he gathered a number of like-minded school friends to form a group, initially as The Five Chimes and then The Matadors.

"We started singing in Junior High and performed around Detroit at house parties, record hops, talent shows and school functions. Of course, there were groups all over the place; everyone was in one."

Despite the lure of music, when Smokey graduated from Northern High School in June 1957, his initial intention was to attend college the following January and undertake an electrical engineering course. With a few months to kill, music seemed as good as anything to pass the time. In August 1957 Smokey and his group, which by now consisted of Ronald White, Warren 'Pete' Moore, Bobby Rogers and his cousin Claudette Rogers, heard that local manager Nat Tarnapol was holding auditions and was on the lookout for new talent with potential. The Matadors duly auditioned, singing four or five numbers that did little to impress Nat Tarnapol, who sent them off with the advice they should fashion their look and sound less on The Platters and find something unique.

However, someone present in the office that day had been impressed and as The Matadors made their way out of the building, he introduced himself as Berry Gordy. Smokey recognised the name straight away as the writer of Jackie Wilson's hits *To Be Loved* and *Reet Petite*, and after the introductions, the two struck up a conversation about songwriting. Smokey pulled out his songbook and proceeded to sing his way through the first song. Berry critiqued the structure, but unperturbed, Smokey merely turned the page and started singing the second song in the book.

"We finally got through his whole notebook and I had turned down every single song. But at the end I assured him that he had a wonderful talent for expressing his feelings with poetic, catchy lyrics. As for the songs, I told him that some had clever concepts but missed the point; others had good hooks, but no real story. And when there were good stories, they weren't unique enough."

Despite effectively receiving two rejections in one day, Smokey quickly realised he had found something of a kindred spirit and potential mentor in Berry Gordy; the two swapped addresses and Smokey would become regular visitor in the days to come with a fresh set of lyrics and song ideas. In January 1958, when Smokey should have been planning for college, he burst excitedly in to an office at Pearl Music, where Berry was working, and proceeded to sing his latest song attempt, *Got A Job*. This time the only thing Berry felt a need to change was the length of the song (Smokey had written enough verses to stretch the song out to ten minutes), but was confident enough to book a session at United Sound Studios, where *Got A Job* and *My Mama Done Told Me* (one of the songs The Matadors had auditioned in Nat Tarnapol's office) were recorded for eventual release on George Goldner's End label, albeit with the group name changing to The Miracles. The single was released on 19 February 1958; Smokey gave up any idea of pursuing a career as an electrical engineer.

Success did not come immediately, with *I Need Some Money* (End) and *I Need A Change* (Chess, through a deal with Berry's sister Gwen) all going largely unnoticed by the record buying public, but both Berry and Smokey felt they were getting closer with each successive release, enough for Smokey to eventually convince Berry that their best chance of success in the future would be to start their own record company, advice Berry eventually took with the creation of Tamla.

It was still early days and recordings would be leased to other companies as soon as they showed any sign of becoming major sellers, although *It*, which was credited to Ron (Ronald White) and Bill (Smokey Robinson) and leased to Argo not long after release never looked likely to make much of an impact. *Bad Girl* initially appeared on the Motown label before being licensed out to Chess and resulted in a #93 pop hit; The Miracles were getting closer.

Whilst virtually all of the early recordings were co-written by Smokey and Berry (Berry's involvement was becoming minimal, but Smokey insisted on sharing composer credit) and produced by Berry, gradually Smokey was beginning to rely less on Berry and more on his own instincts. When the group came off one road tour, Smokey hurried into Hitsville to lay down tracks for the next Miracles attempt at scaling the charts, *Way Over There*. It sold well locally, shifting a reported 60,000 copies, but the later presence of a version with strings failed to lift the single to national prominence. Yet despite the local sales, real success would only be achieved if Tamla and Motown went national, and it was Smokey's constant encouragement of such a notion that finally persuaded Berry that they had nothing to lose and everything to gain by taking control of their own destiny.

As luck would have it, it was a Smokey song that shifted the balance, *Shop Around*, which Smokey wrote with Barrett Strong in mind but which, with a number of structural amendments, Berry persuaded The Miracles to record. He managed to persuade them to record it twice too, taking the group back into the studio at three o'clock one morning to record a more 'pop' sounding version that would go on to top the R&B chart and hit #2 pop. The eventual success of *Shop Around* was a key element in the development of Smokey Robinson; he already had the writing ability, and few within Hitsville now doubted that he was at least the equal of Berry Gordy when it came to crafting three minutes of musical magic, but if he could combine that with Berry's attention to detail and quest for perfection, then the sky was the limit.

Over the coming years Smokey's abilities would surpass Berry's, with many around Hitsville reaping the benefits, not only The Miracles. Before Holland-Dozier-Holland became fixtures around Hitsville, it was to Smokey Robinson that many of the artists looked for their material, with Smokey writing or assisting on material that would be recorded by Eugene Remus, Popcorn & The Mohawks, Sherri Taylor & Sammy Ward, Henry Lumpkin, Debbie Dean, Barrett Strong, The Contours, Gino Parks and The Supremes during Motown's formative years. Initially at least, all of the really good songs that Smokey came up with were retained and recorded by The Miracles, but as time passed, the quality all around improved, so by December 1961, when Smokey took control of Mary Wells for the first time, few had any doubts that something special was about to be unleashed. That something was *The One Who Really Loves You*, a Top Ten R&B and pop hit.

"I would say that she was the real starter for me, because I got the chance to do exactly as I pleased, you know, the songs any way I wanted them. It really put me in a new frame of mind as far as the business went."

Mary Wells and Smokey Robinson proved an irresistible partnership over the next couple of years, scoring with *You Beat Me To The Punch, Two Lovers, Laughing Boy, Your Old Stand By, What's So Easy For Two Is Hard For One* and *You Lost The Sweetest Guy*. Smokey also played a major part in getting The Supremes to Motown, auditioning the then four girl group and producing three of the first half a dozen outings. Whilst the group's early lack of success earned them the moniker of The No-Hit Supremes around the Hitsville lot, Smokey came closer than anyone at breaking that unenviable run, with *Your Heart Belongs To Me* (#95) and *A Breath Taking Guy* (#75) at least enabling them to shake off the 'no-hit' tag.

The Supremes eventually switched over to Holland-Dozier-Holland, but Smokey, by now vice-president of Motown, found another all female group to champion, providing The Marvelettes with the modest hits *As Long As I Know He's Mine, He's A Good Guy* and *You're Me Remedy* during the course of 1963 and 1964. If the initial lack of major success on The Supremes was a matter of some concern around Motown by 1963, then the same was true for their male counterparts The Temptations. All that was to change with *The Way You Do The Things You Do*, a song written by Smokey with Miracles' member Bobby Rogers (Smokey would write with the other members Pete Moore and Ronnie White or even guitarist Marv Tarplin periodically during the course of the decade), merely the first in a line of hits he was to craft. Ultimately, his crowning glories on Mary Wells and The Temptations were to be the complimentary songs *My Guy* and *My Girl* respectively, both of which topped the R&B and pop charts, and whilst it was something of a swansong for Mary (who was to leave the company upon reaching her twenty first birthday), for The Temptations the hits kept coming a little longer.

As if leading The Miracles and guiding The Temptations wasn't enough, Smokey turned provider for a host of other names at Motown, including Marvin Gaye (*I'll Be Doggone, Ain't That Peculiar, One More Heartache* and *Take This Heart Of Mine*), Brenda Holloway (*When I'm Gone* and *Operator*), The Contours (*First I Look At The Purse*) and The Marvelettes (*Don't Mess With Bill, You're The One* and *The Hunter Gets Captured By The Game*). Even those that weren't necessarily hits still displayed a degree of craftsmanship and guile unrivalled at Hitsville, as material on Jimmy Ruffin and Barbara McNair would confirm; don't mess with Bill, indeed.

Although the songs were seemingly spread around, there was considerable thought behind each and every one.

"I always had people in mind and I tried to tailor the songs to what I thought they would sound like, and all that. I used to even pick words that they would sing well."

With The Temptations, Smokey was spoilt for choice, for everyone in the group could sing well, and whilst Smokey's early efforts brought Eddie Kendricks to the fore, he had an ear on the others too, as he would prove with *My Girl*.

"That song was written specifically with David Ruffin in mind to sing it. Because I had recorded them, and the first hit they had was *The Way You Do The Things You Do* and that was with Eddie Kendricks' voice. So all the producers and writers at Motown jumped on the Eddie Kendricks' bandwagon. And when we recorded The Temps, everybody was using Eddie Kendricks' voice, because he had the first hit with them. But I knew that David was in there, man. He was like a sleeping giant. So if I could get a hit on him, they would be multi-faceted."

Smokey got his hit on David with *My Girl* and continued to churn out a succession of major smashes, all the way to *Get Ready*, something of a rare departure into uptempo territory for Smokey after all the success he had with more traditional love songs.

"I think more people identify with those type of songs. I guess my mind is just orientated towards that type of thought. You can start singing a happy song and it strikes a groove, it gets people happy. But the sad songs, they get the reaction."

When *Get Ready* didn't get the reaction that was anticipated, Norman Whitfield was waiting in the wings to take over control of The Temptations, but Smokey had more than enough to keep him occupied in the ensuing years, not least ensuring The Miracles remained at the pinnacle, as well as his other functions as a vice-president of the company.

"It was part of my life. In the beginning of Motown, when he [Berry Gordy] very first started Motown, there were only five people there. And we did everything. We packaged records, we called disc jockeys, we took records to record stores, to radio stations. We did everything."

As the company had grown, there were other people brought in to package the records, take them to stores and radio stations, but Smokey was still needed on hand to write and then go out on tour, which eventually became something of a chore for him.

"I enjoyed the fact that I was with The Miracles. I had known them since I was very young, and so we had a brotherly love, a brotherly relationship. And I enjoyed being on stage performing. But I was becoming bored with life on the road; the packing and unpacking, the hotels and the restaurants, the airports and the bus stations."

More than anything, Smokey yearned for a settled family life. He and Claudette had married in 1959 and were eager to start a family right away, but suffered a series of misfortunes and miscarriages along the way. Claudette had been 'retired' from the group but still miscarried, seven times in all, before finally giving birth to a son in 1968, who they named Berry Robinson. A year later came a daughter, Tamla Robinson. With two young children to dote on, Smokey wanted more than anything to be a part of their life.

"What really started those wheels to turn was Berry's birth. He was born in 1968, and I was so in love with him. I was so attached to him. I would put him in a baby seat and sit him on the table while I ate. Watch him, and just look at him, everything he did when he moved his hand. And then when he started to grow up, I just hated leaving him. I got to the point where I hated leaving him more and more. Then Tamla was born, and I didn't want to be away from my children all the time, I didn't want them to know me only as a celebrity."

In 1967, Berry Gordy made the decision to change the group's billing to Smokey Robinson & The Miracles (he did much the same thing with Diana Ross and The Supremes), but as attractive as the lure of top billing was, the subsequent birth of his children changed all of his priorities. He would leave the group, probably for a solo career, but he knew that timing was going to be everything.

"We were always gone. We were gone 90 percent of the time. In fact, we were gone so much at one point, by me being the vice-president – see I never really had a rest, 'cause I was always working with some other artists. When I came home, I had to go to the office. And then I was on the road 90 percent of the time. So at one point, I had gotten those guys some jobs at Motown. And when we were off, they could work at Motown, because the road, basically, and semi-annual record royalties were their only source of income. So I had gotten them some jobs at Motown, but of course, they didn't like that, 'cause they made as much money in one night as they did for two weeks at Motown. Just so they could have some money coming in when we weren't working."

Smokey made his mind up to leave the group at the end of 1968, although quite when he would make his exit was still to be decided; twelve to eighteen months hence seemed likeliest as it would give the group time to adapt to the impending change, find a replacement and still have Smokey onboard to train whoever might be the new recruit. Then *Tears Of A Clown*, a track written with Stevie Wonder back in 1967 became an international smash in 1970 and scuppered those plans, for Smokey quickly realised that leaving the group according to the original timetable would put The Miracles at a severe disadvantage; the success of *Tears Of A Clown* resulted in even greater clamour for the group to go out on the road on tour. Eventually, in January 1972, Smokey announced that the forthcoming series of dates for that summer would constitute a farewell tour, with the final bow taking place in Washington D.C.

"It was just a sad event, because I had been with those guys all my life. It wasn't that I regretted leaving. I've never regretted leaving."

Smokey had little time for regrets anyway, for whilst he was no longer out on the road, there was more than enough to keep him occupied. With Motown having switched the centre of its operations from Detroit to California, Smokey moved the Robinson family out west, where he would continue his day to day job as vice-president of Motown as well as watching his two young children grow up.

His recording career would eventually resume in 1973, but whereas much of his work with The Miracles was usually accompanied by full blown promotional campaigns, his solo career enjoyed a much lower profile. Anything he released, certainly initially, would have to stand and fall on the quality of the music alone; Smokey was no longer a slave to the road. His early albums certainly maintained his abilities as a songwriter, with **Smokey**, released in June 1973 and co-produced with Willie Hutch containing his first solo hit in *Baby Come Close* (#7 R&B and #27 pop), a tribute to The Miracles in *Sweet Harmony* (#31 R&B and #48 pop) and a rare excursion into social commentary with *Just My Soul Responding* (which would become a #35 hit in Britain in 1974). The album was a major R&B hit, peaking at #10, although it had to settle for #80 pop.

Whilst **Pure Smokey** a year later didn't fare quite as well (#12 R&B and #99 pop), it did reunite him with Marv Tarplin, who had remained with The Miracles for a year before moving out to California to resume his musical partnership with Smokey. Whilst the album may have struggled for pop acceptance, the resulting singles still struck a chord with the R&B market, with both *Virgin Man* and *I Am I Am* hitting the Top Twenty.

Smokey's third album, **Quiet Storm**, created something of a quiet storm at the time of release but has since gone on to become acknowledged as one of his finest solo albums, even launching something of its own musical genre. The standout hit single was *Baby That's Backatcha*, an R&B chart topper and later joined in the Top Ten by *The Agony And The Ecstasy*, although the title track (its relevance to Smokey can be gauged that when he did return to touring duties, his assembled backing group was given the name Quiet Storm) stalled at #25 R&B. Pop acceptance for the singles was less than expected, but two Top 40 hits for an artist no longer out promoting his own material was still a good return.

Despite the growing clamour for more product and a return to the road, Smokey maintained his leisurely pace and lifestyle, delivering an album a year and no more, including **Smokey's Family Robinson** in 1976 and **Deep In My Soul** a year later. There were plans for a stage show 'Cotillion', which also involved fellow Motown producer Willie Hutch, but this was subsequently abandoned before it came to fruition. Smokey did undertake a number of small acting roles, appearing in a couple of television series 'Police Story' and 'Police Woman' and was the other side of the camera for the film project 'Big Time'. Although Smokey wrote the accompanying soundtrack which made it no further than #39 on the R&B chart, of greater significance was the fact that Smokey had sunk a sizeable amount of money into the project (half a million dollars), all of which was lost when the film failed at the box office.

After the financial failure of 'Big Time', **Love Breeze** would represent a return to former glories, with the album returning him to the Top Twenty and the single *Daylight & Darkness* the Top Ten of the R&B chart. Smokey released two albums in 1979, a live album in **Smokin'** and then **Where There's Smoke**, with the latter album an across the board success (Top Twenty pop and Top Ten R&B), fuelled by the success of the smash hit single *Cruisin'*. Inexplicably, an update of *Get Ready* was originally released as the lead single from **Where There's Smoke**, but after that had stalled at #82 commonsense prevailed and Motown released the single all the radio stations had craved in *Cruisin'*. The single would peak at #4 on both R&B and pop chart, Smokey's biggest hit on the former since *Baby That's Backatcha* and biggest hit period on the latter as well as collecting a Grammy Award nomination for Best Male R&B Vocal Performance.

Warm Thoughts maintained his hot streak in 1980, inching him higher up the chart at #14 pop and #4 R&B, featuring the radio hit *Wine Women And Song*, on which Smokey performed a duet with wife Claudette. The renewed success Smokey enjoyed as a solo performer enabled him to continue to offer songs to other artists, and after Kim Carnes had enjoyed a hit with an old Miracles number in *More Love*, Smokey contacted her producer George Tobin with the offer of a new song, unaware that the relationship between Tobin and Carnes had come to an abrupt end. Still, George reasoned there was little to be lost listening to what Smokey had to offer, and when he was played *Being With You* (Smokey turned up at George's office and actually sang the song for him 'live') suggested to Smokey that he produce it. It proved to be a fortuitous meeting for both of them, for *Being With You* would go on to become the biggest hit of Smokey's solo career, topping the R&B and British chart and hitting #2 pop. The resulting album, which George also produced, did extremely well, again topping the R&B chart, hitting #10 pop and becoming his only solo charting album in Britain where it hit #17.

By now a more than twenty year veteran of the music business, it served as a timely reminder that Smokey had lost none of his sharpness or ability to craft a radio friendly three minutes or so, having worked his way through a period of writer's block and emerged the other side still at the top of his game. In the coming years, he would continue to feature on the pop and R&B charts, although never quite as high as *Being With You*.

He and George Tobin renewed their acquaintance on **Yes It's You Lady** in 1982, which hit #33 pop and #6 R&B, from which *Tell Me Tomorrow* was the standout single release, going agonisingly close to topping the R&B chart (it stalled at #3) and making a respectable #33 pop and #51 in the UK. **Touch The Sky** saw Smokey handling production chores with Sonny Burke on an album that had obvious R&B appeal (it would peak at #8, with the two lifted singles in the title track and *I've Made Love To You A Thousand Times* also performing well, with the latter another Top Ten R&B performer), although at the expense of pop acceptability; the album stalled at #50. A solo career retrospective in 1983 did less well at #124 pop and #28 R&B, and the following year's **Essar** was a major disappointment, halting at #184 pop and #35 R&B.

Yet recording represented something of a welcome respite for Smokey, whose personal life had been disintegrating for several years. By his own admission, up until the late 1960s he had been a teetotal, drug free vegetarian who spent whatever spare time he had keeping fit and healthy. As the seventies began he had experimented with marijuana, subsequently moving on to cocaine, which by the following decade had become a virtual addiction.

Following the death of his father and former Motown label mate Marvin Gaye, Smokey's addiction had gravitated to crack, the very same drug that had brought about the demise of David Ruffin. Adding to his woes was the failing of his marriage, originally believed to have been one of the strongest at Motown. He fathered another child, a son Trey in 1984, by another woman, and whilst his marriage had survived troubles in 1974, this time around it could not, with the pair separating soon after Claudette learned of Trey's existence and subsequently divorcing in 1986. At the time that Smokey's woes were at their greatest, he sought professional help, kicking his drug habit following a visit to a church in 1986 (he has stated that he has been drug-free since that event).

That same year also saw his final album release on the Tamla label, with **Smoke Signals** being released in January 1986, a #23 R&B and #104 pop hit. Once free of his turmoil, it was a revived and refreshed Smokey who went into the studio to record **One Heartbeat**, the album that saw Smokey back on the Motown label for the first time in nearly thirty years. It was very much a welcome home too, for the album would go on to sell more than half a million copies, easily his biggest selling album for a considerable while, as well as an R&B chart topper. The album gave rise to another smash hit single, *Just To See Her*, which hit the Top Ten of both the pop and R&B chart, but more impressive than any chart placing was the ultimate accolade the single picked up, the Grammy Award for Best Male R&B Vocal Performance. It was the perfect way for Smokey to celebrate his thirtieth year in the record business, and no more than he deserved after three decades of enthralling audiences the world over. Smokey continued at Motown as vice-president until 1988 when the company was sold to MCA, although he would record a final album for Motown, **Love Smokey** in 1990. He would later record for SBK, Universal, Liquid 8 and his own Robso label, but in truth little has matched the body of work he recorded, wrote or produced during his heyday on Tamla and at Motown. The one endearing quality Smokey retained was his total devotion to the rest of The Miracles; when it was announced he was to be inducted into the Rock & Roll Hall of Fame in 1987, he led the calls for the rest of the group to be similarly inducted, something of an oversight that was finally rectified in 2012. Smokey married his second wife Frances in 2004 and the couple currently live in Los Angeles.

ALBUMS: SMOKEY (1973), PURE SMOKEY (1974), A QUIET STORM (1975), SMOKEY'S FAMILY ROBINSON (1976), DEEP IN MY SOUL (1977), BIG TIME (1977), LOVE BREEZE (1978), SMOKIN' (1978), WHERE THERE'S SMOKE (1979), WARM THOUGHTS (1980), BEING WITH YOU (1981), YES, IT'S YOU LADY (1982), TOUCH THE SKY (1983), ESSAR (1984), SMOKE SIGNALS (1986), ONE HEARTBEAT (1987)
COMPILATION: BLAME IT ON LOVE & ALL THE GREAT HITS (1983)
FURTHER READING: INSIDE MY LIFE (1989)

ROCK AND ROLL HALL OF FAME

The Rock & Roll Hall of Fame was founded in 1986 and the actual hall and museum opened in Cleveland, Ohio on 2 September 1995. There are currently five categories which carry inductions; Performers, Early influences, Lifetime achievement, Non-performers and Sidemen.

The following Motown artists have been inducted, together with the year of induction:

Performers:
Marvin Gaye (1987)
Smokey Robinson (1987)
The Supremes (1988)
The Temptations (1989)
Stevie Wonder (1989)
The Four Seasons (1990)
The Four Tops (1990)
The Isley Brothers (1992)
Martha & The Vandellas (1995)
Gladys Knight & The Pips (1996)
The Jackson 5 (1997)
Michael Jackson (2001)
The Miracles (2012)

Non-performers:
Berry Gordy (1988)
Holland-Dozier-Holland (1990)

Sidemen:
James Jamerson (2000)
Benny Benjamin (2003)

As interesting as the list of inductees is, there is more controversy raging over those who have so far been excluded, in particular the two M's – Mary Wells and The Marvelettes. As far as many are concerned, Mary Wells effectively carried Motown in its early years, earning the moniker 'Queen Of Motown' after *My Guy* hit number one (although Mary was nominated in both 1986 and 1987; only one of the 25 inductees in those two years was female – Aretha Franklin).

The Marvelettes hold a unique place in Motown's history as it was they who registered the label's first number one smash in *Please Mr. Postman*. Finally, equally frustrating for many years was the exclusion of The Miracles, especially since Smokey Robinson had been inducted as a solo performer in 1987. This oversight was finally rectified in 2012.

ROCKIN' ROBIN – MICHAEL JACKSON [SINGLE]

The three cover versions that appeared on Michael Jackson's debut solo album **Got To Be There** were an eclectic bunch, covering straight R&B in *Ain't No Sunshine* (originally by Bill Withers), folk rock in *You've Got A Friend* (written by Carole King about James Taylor) and rock and roll, represented by *Rockin' Robin*. Written by Leon Rene under the pseudonym of Jimmie Thomas, *Rockin' Robin* had provided Bobby Day with his only chart hit, peaking at #2 in the US and #29 in the UK in 1958.

Michael's version, recorded in November 1971, stayed faithful to Day's original, but producers Mel Larson and Jerry Marcellino ensured Michael's youthful exuberance shone through the single. Released as the second single from the album (after the title track), *Rockin Robin* performed better than its predecessor, and became an across the board hit, peaking at #2 on both the R&B and pop chart in the US and only one position lower in the UK. The song was taken back into the British Top Ten in 1999 when female singer Lolly recorded a cover version that peaked at #10.

THE ROCKITS

British duo John Wilson (guitar and vocals) and Dave Powell (drums) had previously recorded as Nimbo but became The Rockits after they signed with MoWest in the UK in 1973. They released two singles, *Living Without You* in November 1973 and *Gimme True Love* in July 1974 (producer Peter Anders would later state that the demos John and Dave submitted were of such high quality it proved impossible to better them on the actual recordings) and would later form The Dodgers with former Badfinger members Tom Evans and Bob Jackson.

ROCKWELL

Whilst he had dreams of becoming a recording artist, Kennedy William Gordy faced something of an uphill struggle getting a deal, not least because his father was Berry Gordy, the founder of Motown.

Born in Detroit, Michigan on 15 March 1964 to Berry and his then mistress Margaret Norton, he had been named in honour of slain President John F Kennedy and William 'Smokey Robinson. Estranged from his father for much of his formative years, he was living with Berry's ex-wife Ray Singleton and producing demo tracks that would be played to Berry with a view to him getting a deal. Having received little or no encouragement, Kennedy decided to submit material under a pseudonym, taking the name Rockwell from his high school band.

In 1983, therefore, Ray played another demo for Berry Gordy, this one featuring the distinctive backing and co-lead vocals of Michael Jackson. This time Berry was impressed, enough to agree to an initial single deal for *Somebody's Watching Me*. This was followed by a similarly titled album, with **Somebody's Watching Me** going on to make #5 R&B and #15 pop, earning a gold disc along the way. The album would also become Rockwell's only charting album in the UK, where it peaked at #52 in the aftermath of the success of the single. The album also gave rise to another hit single in *Obscene Phone Caller*, a #35 pop and #9 R&B hit following its release in March 1984. The single missed out the chart altogether in the UK, as did a third extraction from the album in *Taxman* (a cover of the George Harrison song).

Work meanwhile continued on his follow-up album, which would be released in January 1985 as **Captured**, similarly produced by Curtis Anthony Nolen and executive produced by Ray Singleton. The album was preceeded by the single *He's A Cobra* in December 1984, which would go on to make #65 R&B and bubble under the Hot 100 at #108, the last of Rockwell's singles to make any kind of impression on the pop charts. With a third single in *Peeping Tom* failing to make any impression whatsoever, the album itself had to settle for a rather lacklustre peak of #52 R&B and #120 pop. A final Motown outing, **The Genie** stalled at #59 on the R&B chart, with the single *Carme* peaking at #46 in 1986.

ALBUMS: SOMEBODY'S WATCHING ME (1984), CAPTURED (1985), THE GENIE (1986)

RON & BILL

Ron and Bill released one single under this moniker, with *It* backed with *Don't Say Bye Bye* appearing on the Tamla label in June 1959 but doing little, even though it was picked up for national distribution by

Chess Records' imprint Argo, who re-released the single in October. The top side was supposedly inspired by Sheb Wooley's *Purple People Eater* but after it again sank without trace, Ron and Bill went back to their day jobs as Ronnie White and William 'Smokey' Robinson of The Miracles.

ROQ-IN' ZOO

Effectively a studio creation, Roq-In' Zoo featured Steve Norris, Charlie Sullivan, Joe Collins, Al Trivette and David Floyd along with producers John Morales and Sergio Munzibai. Their only single, issued in December 1985, was a tribute to Chicago Bears American footballer William Perry, who was known as either The Refrigerator or The Fridge, in honour of his enormous size. The single *Frig-O-Rator* featured sound bites taken from Chicago Bears game plays.

ARTHUR 'T-BOY' ROSS

Given the nickname 'T-Boy' because of his childhood love of T-bone steak, Arthur Ross (born in Detroit, Michigan on 28 February 1948) was the younger brother of Diana Ross. He was introduced to Motown by Diana in 1972 and taken on as a staff writer for Jobete, linking up with Leon Ware and writing *I Wanna Be Where You Are*, a #2 R&B and #16 pop hit for Michael Jackson.

Ware and Ross would also write much of the material that was intended for a Leon Ware album for Motown in 1975 (his first, eponymous album had been released by United Artists in 1972), but when Berry Gordy heard the demos, he reasoned the material might be better suited for Marvin Gaye – the resulting album became **I Want You**, a multi-platinum success in 1976 which returned Marvin to the top of the R&B charts and Top Ten pop. Unfortunately, T-Boy tried to give Marvin too much direction in the studio, leading him to be effectively fired from the project.

He would later link with The Crusaders' keyboardist Joe Sample and Billy Brown to craft his own album **Changes**, which was released in 1979, but sales of just 12,000 copies brought a halt to his musical career.

He effectively retired to Detroit, content to live off his song-writing royalties, although much of this was seemingly spent on drugs. On 26 June 1996 he was due in court to face drug and gun charges after being caught carrying bags of heroin, cocaine and marijuana and a loaded semi-automatic pistol, but a few days before his scheduled appearance his decomposing body was found, alongside that of his wife of ten months Patricia, in the basement of a house in Detroit's Oak Park area. An autopsy revealed the bodies had been there for at least three weeks (resulting in the date of death being given as 30 May 1996) and that the cause of death was murder by suffocation. Although police arrested and charged two men, they were subsequently released and the case remains unsolved.
ALBUM: CHANGES (1979)

DIANA ROSS

Her tally of twelve numbers ones as lead singer of The Supremes, five as a solo singer and one as half a duo with Lionel Richie gives Diana Ross a total of eighteen US number one pop hits, a figure bettered only by The Beatles. Add to this seven American Music Awards, a Golden Globe, a Special Tony Award and an Academy Award nomination and it is easy to see why Diana Ross assumed the mantle of Queen of Motown so readily from Mary Wells.

She was born Diane Ernestine Earle Ross to Fred and Ernestine Ross at the Hutzel Women's Hospital in Detroit, Michigan on 26 March 1944, although there was an error made when filling in her birth certificate, with the name 'Diana' being entered instead. Thus while for the first twenty years or so of her life she was Diane to all and sundry, when she took the name 'Diana' on a more professional basis, it was simply a case of her adopting a name she and her mother Ernestine had used for some considerable time, although many of her close friends still referred to her as Diane.

As a young teenager Diana held dreams of becoming a fashion designer and studied design, millinery, pattern-making and seamstress skills at the Cass Technical High School. In time, however, Diana's aspirations switched to music. When not studying at high school or working a part-time job at Hudson's Department Store, Diana became something of a regular on the local talent contest circuit, even going so far as to make a veritable name for herself.

That reputation proved useful when local impresario Milton Jenkins was looking to assemble a female version of his male act The Primes, with either Paul Williams or Eddie Kendricks suggesting Diana's name as a possible member for The Primettes. Milton made his way to the Brewster-Douglass Projects, where Diana lived (as did future Primettes Flo Ballard and Mary Ross), and convinced Ernestine that Diana would be in good hands and stood a chance of making an even bigger name for herself under his charge, so much so that Ernestine signed a personal service contract there and then. When father Fred came home and learned of the binding agreement, he was at first adamant that Diana should concentrate on her schooling and put any thoughts of show business behind her, only to discover that Milton Jenkins had weaved his magic so well that even Ernestine was a firm believer that all manner of wonderful things would materialise; Ernestine convinced Fred that Diana would be well taken care of.

A few days later, Diana, Mary and Flo, along with Paul Williams' then girlfriend Betty McGlown got together in Milton's room at a hotel and sang for the first time as The Primettes. Diana's talents with a needle and thread also proved useful, at least in The Primettes and then The Supremes' early days, with Diana being utilised as the group's hair stylist, make-up artist and costume designer. As it turned out, Milton Jenkins might have been able to spin a yarn or two but didn't have quite the right connections to turn The Primettes (or The Primes for that matter) into anything more than a success on the live circuit. When he disappeared off the scene both groups were left to their own devices, which in the case of The Primettes meant going back on the talent contest route.

Jenkins' sudden unavailability had other consequences too, for the fact that the group hadn't amounted to much despite the hype convinced Fred Ross that he had been right to insist Diana concentrate on her education, to the extent he refused her permission to go to compete at the Detroit & Windsor International Festival in June 1960. He refused even when Mary and Flo tried to intercede on her behalf, and still refused when Ernestine and Diana virtually pleaded with him to change his mind. Just when it seemed as though the unthinkable was going to happen, that Diana would defy her father and go anyway, he relented, signing the entry form as the only way to stop the moaning that was being aimed in his direction.

The Primettes performed well on the day, with their five song set earning them top spot and a prize of $15, although this was subsequently lost before the day was out, possibly to a pickpocket (although that explanation didn't satisfy Diana, who accused Mary, the group's unofficial treasurer, of wanting to keep the money for herself). It is also claimed that after their performance, Motown executive Robert Bateman approached Flo Ballard and handed her a business card and told her to get in touch for an audition, but Flo opted to keep the information to herself and didn't mention it for some considerable time.

By then the girls had got themselves along to Motown to audition for Berry Gordy, but that was largely at Diana's instigation. Something of a passing acquaintance of Smokey Robinson, Diana badgered him into giving her group a listen, with a view to getting them a proper audition at Motown. When Smokey mentioned that he and the rest of The Miracles were due to go out on tour in a few days, Diana insisted that she would bring The Primettes round the next night! Smokey was impressed with their impromptu audition that evening but was even more impressed with their guitarist, Marv Tarplin and offered something of a compromise; if The Miracles could borrow Marv for a while, Smokey would arrange a proper audition once they returned to Detroit. Smokey was as good as his word (at least as far as the audition was concerned; Marv Tarplin was never returned to The Primettes, becoming a key figure for The Miracles and then Smokey Robinson for more than forty years) and The Primettes did audition for Berry Gordy in the late summer of 1960.

He too was impressed but told them to come back when they had finished school, perhaps as subtle and soft a let-down as he could muster. As they were leaving the building, Robert Bateman approached them a second time and, along with fellow Motown producer Richard Morris, offered to help get them a deal with another record label in the city, LuPine. After undertaking backing vocal duties for a number of other artists signed to LuPine (including Wilson Pickett and Eddie Floyd), The Primettes got their own sessions on *Tears Of Sorrow* and *Pretty Baby*. Although Flo had emerged as the group's early lead singer, with Mary invariably taking over on the slower, softer material, Diana was insistent that she should sing lead, resulting in *Tears Of Sorrow* being assigned to her, although the final mix also features the obvious vocal of Flo, possibly done deliberately by producer Richard Morris as a payback to Diana (Mary has the lead on *Pretty Baby*).

The single got some local airplay but went no further, and that point neither did Betty McGlown who instead announced she was leaving the group in order to get married (although not to Paul Williams, that relationship having coming to an end). The departure of Betty not only left the group a member short, it also robbed The Primettes of the only one who could exert a degree of control over Diana and her ambitions. The episode over insisting on having the lead on the *Tears Of Sorrow* single wasn't the only example of Diana's single-mindedness that at times threatened to beguile the group; on several occasions the group would decide to wear matching outfits for their live performances, only to arrive at the venue and find

Diana was wearing something different and more upmarket, thus appearing on stage to all intents and purposes as the lead singer with Flo, Mary and Betty relegated to *her* backing group. Diana's influence also held sway when it came to selecting Betty's replacement. Mary suggested a friend of hers, Jackie Burkes (so keen was Mary to get Jackie into the group, she suggested the same Jackie Burkes when it appeared The Primettes might lose Flo after she had been raped), only for Diana to be cold and distant when Jackie arrived for rehearsals. Jackie sensed the hostility and decided against joining the group, with the only possible reason for such hostility being that Diana didn't want to have Mary and Jackie in the same camp if it came to future disagreements.

The group eventually found someone who was acceptable to all of them in Barbara Martin (not least Diana, who found Barbara much more pliant than Betty), who brought her own attributes to the group, not least her dancing abilities. Bringing the group back up to full compliment didn't solve all of their problems, however, for now they couldn't find Richard Morris, their ad hoc manager. By the time they learned of his whereabouts, in prison for a supposed parole violation, they had decided to take control of their own destiny, which meant returning to Motown and Berry Gordy, irrespective of what he had said previously about waiting until they graduated from school.

As if to sweeten the deal (or potential deal), Diana brought along a present she had made in her school crafts class, a pair of cuff links which bore his initials. Either Berry Gordy forgot about his earlier instruction to finish school or chose to overlook it, but instead of being shown the door The Primettes were positively encouraged by their second visit to Hitsville.

"Everything was very personal" Diana would later recall. "Walking into Motown was like walking into a corner store where you know everybody, instead of walking into a big cold supermarket. It's like going into a restaurant where the owner works himself. It's personalised. You know the food will be good and fresh. It was a lot of fun. It gave us something to do in the afternoons; we had a purpose in our lives."

Within the next couple of months they were frequently allowed inside the inner sanctum, the studio, providing backing vocals for the likes of Mary Wells, Mable John, Marvin Gaye and Sammy Ward. Singing backing vocals for others was better than nothing, but The Primettes in general and Diana in particular was keen to get their own sessions, with Diana pestering Berry at every opportunity to give the group their chance.

Berry eventually relented with a song he had written with Freddie Gorman and Brian Holland, *I Want A Guy*. That first session obviously made an impression on Diana, as she later remembered.

"I vividly remember this session. It felt so important. With my eyes closed and my arms outstretched, I poured my heart into this song. When I listen to it now, I feel nostalgic; I can hear that teenage yearning."

Berry was also impressed, enough to countenance further sessions, including some that featured the other girls on lead vocals, with *After All* being somewhat unique in that all four were heavily featured. In January 1961, Berry decided *I Want A Guy* was the right song but The Primettes was the wrong name, so instructed Janie Bradford to come up with a number of alternatives. It was Flo Ballard who picked out The Supremes from the assorted monikers, the new name being put into the fourteen page contracts all four girls duly signed (or rather their parents signed on their behalf as Diana, Mary and Flo were still under eighteen years of age; only Barbara Martin was over the threshold but still had her mother sign the document).

Whilst the contracts covered their proposed obligations as far as their recording futures were concerned, it wasn't long before Berry found another role for Diana, appointing her his secretary, even though she was totally unqualified for the job, as she would later admit.

"When I needed to make some extra money, I asked Berry if I could work for him. He actually hired me as a secretary, probably because I was cute and persistent, but I wasn't really a secretary. All I remember doing was clearing off his desk several times a day, awed by the important-looking papers that he handled and so wishing to have my name on some of them."

Yet even then, Berry had spotted something in Diana. "Diane had an innocent manner that let her get away with most anything. Long before she was a star, there was a drive in her that could not be denied. Nor could her appeal – which she used to full advantage."

Indeed, over the next decade, Diane would use that appeal and drive on her single-minded march to the very top. Among the first to spot that side was Mary.

"Even at that young age, I could see that Diane was trying to build up her own self-confidence. She craved attention, and in her attempts to get it, she could seem almost ruthless. Sometimes she would throw a childish tantrum, then moments later pretend it was all a big joke, that she was just being silly. Her bluntness could be disconcerting and feelings were hurt, but we saw Diane's actions as the product of thoughtlessness, not malice."

No doubt that was an opinion Mary was herself forced to change when Diana decided to try and ingratiate herself into the company of Ronnie Hammers, who happened to be Mary's fiancé! When Mary's interest in Ronnie ended, so too did Diana's but by then another target was in her sights, one that should have been even further off limits. Smokey Robinson had been of interest previously because he had the wherewithal to get the then Primettes into Hitsville; now he was of interest because he had the potential to give The Supremes hit material. Everyone around Motown knew Smokey was married to Claudette Rogers, a fellow member of The Miracles, but such formalities cut no ice with Diana. And once she snared her man, Diana couldn't wait to tell Flo and Mary all about their trysts, the flowers he would send and where they had eaten dinner. Word would eventually get back to Claudette, who confronted Smokey about the rumours that were sweeping through Hitsville, after which the relationship reverted back to being purely professional.

As far as Diana was concerned, it was still mission accomplished, with Smokey's *Your Heart Belongs To Me* becoming the first Supremes single to make the chart, albeit at a lowly #95. Whilst Diana appeared to make instant friends with the men of Motown, platonic or otherwise, the same could not be said among the womenfolk. Irrespective of whether it was her competitive nature or a basic streak of jealousy, Diana seemed to make it her mission to upset any and all of them. Even when thrown together, such as during the first Motortown Revue in 1962 (by which time The Supremes had been reduced to three members following Barbara Martin's departure), Diana would invite their wrath, pinching their dance routines, their clothing ideas and engaging in one feud after another.

The person usually at the centre of her loathing was Gladys Horton, lead singer of The Marvelettes, who had the temerity to enjoy a number one pop hit before The Supremes recording career had fully got off the ground. Her actions during that tour even managed to alienate some of the men too, for Diana took it upon herself to act as more than Berry Gordy's secretary whilst on the road; she became his eyes and ears too, reporting back on a regular basis all of the going's on such as who was making out with who, which was in complete disregard to his instructions before they set out on the road. But making small talk so that everyone liked her wasn't Diana's game plan at all; making hit records was, so her next step was to ingratiate herself into the company of someone that she felt was certain to provide the musical goods.

Brian Holland had begun establishing a worthwhile reputation around Hitsville as a writer and producer, initially with Lamont Dozier and Robert Bateman, with Brian's brother Eddie eventually taking Bateman's position in what became the most creative and eventually successful writing trio in the industry. Brian was married, just like Smokey, but Diana's pursuit would eventually mirror that of her earlier conquest. As far as anyone was concerned, in particular Brian's wife Sharon, Brian and Diana were frequently busy in the studio, although once again Diana made little or no secret of what they might be up to, leaving notes around the office addressed to Brian and once again taking Flo and Mary in to her confidence.

Once again Diana's ruse worked, at least as far as getting Brian, his brother Eddie and Lamont Dozier working with the group, for Brian approached Berry Gordy and specifically requested the opportunity of working with The 'No-Hit Supremes', as they had unkindly been christened around Hitsville. The first two recordings were *Run Run Run* and *When The Lovelight Starts Shining Through His Eyes,* which were actually released in reverse order, with *Lovelight* looking as though it signalled The Supremes' major chart breakthrough when it hit #23 pop and #2 R&B. In light of this partial success, there was something of a downturn when *Run Run Run* stopped running at #93 pop and #22 R&B.

As bad as the chart performance was, there was a far more worrying development that same month, February 1964. Whilst Claudette had chosen to confront her husband Smokey when rumours of a liaison with Diana were at their height (which had the desired effect of ending any nefarious activities), Brian Holland's wife Sharon opted to take the matter directly to Diana. Sharon already had her suspicions and had reportedly marched into the studio and warned, "I know Diane Ross is messing with my husband, and if I catch her, I'm going to kick her butt!" Whether the warning reached Diana is not known, but at a Motown event at the 20 Grand in Detroit, Sharon marched up to Diana and told her to her face, along with a few profanities, exactly what the outcome would be if she didn't stay away from her husband. According to those there (which included a somewhat embarrassed Brian), Diana stood her ground and seemed perfectly willing to take on the bigger woman in a physical battle, at least until common sense prevailed and Diana was ushered out of the club. Word of the amazing outburst quickly circulated around Hitsville, with Diana and Brian subsequently deciding their relationship would be strictly professional from there on in. Brian didn't dwell too long on this premature ending with Diana, for he had already begun another romantic liaison, this time with Martha Reeves (which would see Martha join Gladys Horton on Diana's hit list around Motown); not surprisingly Brian's marriage to Sharon came to an end soon after. Diana herself would erase all recollection of the affair from her mind, if her memoirs are to be believed.

"I didn't know much about HDH as people, what they might have been experiencing in their personal lives and where they eventually ended up. Beyond the brilliant music they created, I have to admit I didn't pay much attention to them. But then, I had little attention or energy to put out toward anyone then."

The incident proved beyond doubt that Diana was willing to fight her corner, irrespective of whether she was right or wrong, but fortunately the next battle she fought ended in personal defeat but collective glory. Like several who heard the rudiments of the song *Where Did Our Love Go*, Diana was less than impressed, even going as far as to threaten calling Berry Gordy during the recording in an attempt to get out of the session. Eddie listened to her complaints and made a threat of his own; if Diana made the call, he, his brother and Lamont would never work with The Supremes again. The session was duly completed, the record released and a few weeks later, the No-Hit Supremes were confined to the history books, replaced by the act that would become Motown's flagship for the rest of the decade, and if it was a defeat for Diana, then it would be a very rare one in the years to come.

Diana had been at times difficult to tolerate when The Supremes were struggling for hits and success did not make her magnanimous; if anything her attitude to all and sundry became even more confrontational, and not just towards those within Hitsville. Even when the group was on the brink of their breakthrough during the Dick Clark Caravan of Stars tour, Diana couldn't resist telling in a voice loud enough so that everyone within earshot could hear exactly how their single was progressing.

Around the Hitsville lot, Diana appeared to reserve her most potent venom for Gladys Horton whilst outside her attitude soon saw her at loggerheads with Dolores 'Lala' Brooks of The Crystals (as well as fellow Motown artist Brenda Holloway). It was something of an eye opener for those not used to her tantrums, but Mary Wilson had seen it all before.

"Diane always had a temper, and while some people might have seen her actions as the result of conniving, her behaviour was actually more like that of a spoiled brat. Once she made up her mind about something, there was no reasoning with her, and even being her best friend didn't ensure that what you said would be taken as it was meant. In Diane's mind, anything that wasn't a compliment was a criticism, which hurt her deeply. Diane would fight with anyone, and often she would take a minor issue and keep on until you reacted. Knowing Diane as Flo and I did, we understood the best way to deal with her in these situations was to ignore her. Diane was like a child testing a parent. Over time, her tantrums and shows of temper became like bad habits, and Flo's and my responses became reflexes. When we saw it coming, we just tuned out."

As it happened, Mary and Flo had to do a lot of tuning out over the next few years. It did not help that Berry Gordy picked Diana out for preferential treatment, such as the decision to appoint Diana as lead singer for every recording. Whilst Diana had most of the early leads, there was still a possibility that Flo or Mary would get the occasional lead, a possibility that was dashed when Berry announced Diana as the group's official lead singer to HDH and The Supremes.

"Look, Diana had magic" said Berry later. "She had feeling. Exuberance. Florence had a good voice, sure. Florence was fine. She did what she did, but she wasn't unique. Mary was fine. She did what she did. It was fine. No one ever said those two couldn't sing. They wouldn't have been in the group if they couldn't sing. But, Diana? She was more than fine. Her voice was totally unique, totally something you never heard before. It wasn't just a big voice, you know, a loud voice. Just because a person sings louder than another person doesn't make that person a better singer. Also, Diana put everything into it, her shoulders, her body...all of it."

Of course, Mary and Flo would have put everything into it, had they been given the chance, but by picking Diana as the undisputed lead singer, Berry set in motion her eventual departure from the group. From that point on, in early 1964, Diana was on borrowed time as far as The Supremes was concerned. It helped that out of the group's next twelve official singles (not including the customary Christmas offering or various publicity and interview records that were issued), all but three hit the very top of the pop chart, a run that was virtually without parallel. Indeed, the only group who came anywhere close to matching it was The Beatles, whose own run of hits during the same period of time was a virtual mirror image of the success The Supremes enjoyed.

"The rewards of our realised dream were fabulous," Diana would later recall. "I loved the entire process, and I was so happy to be able to sing, just to be able to perform, to be able to travel, and to have my singing be a serious profession, not just a hobby. Getting my passport to Europe and knowing that I was about to see the world was such a thrill. I was always grateful. The highs were high, but the tension that accompanied them and the work that was required to maintain our performance quality during the recording and extensive touring was overwhelming and debilitating. I continued anyway; I've never been afraid of hard work."

That hard work quickly began to pay dividends, with The Supremes ruling the roost at home and becoming the flag bearer for Motown's international success. Once Berry realised he had a star of even greater potential than Mary Wells in his midst, even more effort was put in making Diana Ross the focal point of not just everything The Supremes were doing but Motown itself. It was to be The Supremes that would enable him to break into such lucrative clubs and live spots such as The Copacabana, with Diana the centre of the entire act (although Flo could usually be relied upon to throw an ad lib spanner into the works) and, from there, take the battle to Hollywood, with Berry already on the lookout for the right movie vehicle for Diana. Here again Flo unwittingly interjected, for her performance at the Copa attracted several reported movie offers, although none of these were ever relayed to her and were quite possibly quashed by Motown.

In 1965 the already close relationship between Berry and Diana moved on from professional to personal, with the pair enjoying a romantic interlude in Paris at the end of the Motortown Revue tour of Britain. Infatuated with Diana from almost the first day she had walked through the door at Hitsville, Berry would now lavish virtually all of his time and attention on her, also directing every department within Motown to expend all of their energy on making The Supremes an even bigger success. Or rather, make Diana an even bigger success; the other two Supremes were to become almost superfluous, eventually not even appearing on the group's records.

Whilst it was designed to propel The Supremes to even greater heights, it had the effect of fracturing the group, with Flo and Mary growing ever more resentful at Berry's obsession with Diana. Despite the obvious friction, Diana believed everything that happened was almost pre-ordained.

"Changes are organic to life experience, so when I look back, it is no surprise that changes occurred with The Supremes. All things considered, it is a human characteristic to resist that change and to wonder what went wrong. Really, nothing went wrong. The shifting was all in the natural scheme of things. Under normal circumstances, change is viewed as inevitable and for the good of progress. The circumstances of our lives were far from normal. When the momentum of our success really got moving, it blew in like a wild hurricane. In our attempt to keep grounded, we lost perspective."

From Diana's lofty position it might have appeared that Flo Ballard lost perspective, but in reality her demons had begun to surface the very moment Berry Gordy had effectively cut her and Mary out of any decision making regarding The Supremes. Berry had set out to make Diana Ross a star, but in the process rendered Flo and Mary largely redundant.

Flo was the first to buckle and was eventually dismissed from The Supremes in July 1967, with Cindy Birdsong brought in as her replacement. Berry used the change to further Diana's credentials within the group, initially toying with the idea of re-christening them The Supremes With Diana Ross and eventually settling on Diana Ross & The Supremes.

"This was not my idea. It came from Berry. He discussed it in detail with Mary and me. It seemed inevitable. He explained to us that it would also be easier to demand more salary if we were a lead singer and a group. Instead of the pressure lifting, it only increased. Something had to give."

That something turned out to be the departure of Holland-Dozier-Holland, who were at loggerheads with Berry over pay and rewards, although Berry was initially unaware of quite how disgruntled his top writing and production team had become, largely because he spent so much time escorting Diana and The Supremes around the world. When the realisation of HDH's departure hit home Berry trawled through the vaults looking for new material, only to discover the cupboard was effectively bare. In desperation, a new writing team (The Clan) was assembled with instructions to return The Supremes to the top of the chart, eventually emerging from the Ponchetrain Hotel in Detroit with *Love Child*, something of a radical departure for the group. It did return the group to the top, but Diana appeared less than impressed.

"*Love Child*, a song about a child born out of wedlock, was the first controversial topic with which we ever dealt. *I'm Livin' In Shame* was supposed to be a girl singing about her mother ('cookin' bread with a dirty raggedy scarf hangin' 'round her head'). The lyrics were good, but those sweet romantic love songs like *Come See About Me* were more real to me. It was the sixties. Life was moving, and everything had to change, our music included."

Berry had already begun his own westward haul, buying a house in California, with Diana, Mary and Cindy soon following. Diana rented a house just down the hill from Berry's whilst her own mansion was being refurbished and when she did move in acquired a houseguest in Michael Jackson. The newly signed family group The Jackson 5 had quickly become the new darlings of Motown, with Berry putting in place a comprehensive plan to catapult the group to stardom as quickly as possible. Apart from assembling a team of writers from the very best at the Jobete stable, Berry also had in mind using the publicity such a group would generate as an opportunity to hoist Diana even further into the public eye.

A backstory was concocted whereby it was Diana who had first spotted the group and alerted Motown to their talents, with Diana introducing the group on the television programme 'Hollywood Palace' as well as writing the sleevenotes for The Jackson 5's debut album. Whilst Diana busied herself assisting The Jackson 5 on their launch for stardom, work continued preparing the ground for the launch of her solo career. Mary and Cindy were equally busy rehearsing with Jean Terrell, the intended replacement for Diana in The Supremes, but whilst Diana was about to embark on the next stage in her career, she could not fathom why Mary and Cindy were keeping their distance.

"The girls treated me very badly. They had gone against me with a vengeance. They were so blinded by jealousy. I had been tormented, treated as if I were invisible, talked about behind my back when my back wasn't even turned. And yet I had tried to continue, I had tried to perform and pretend that all was well."

As far as Berry Gordy was concerned, the only way for things to end well was for Diana's parting gift to The Supremes to be final number one hit, something that was proving to be a difficult task. There was nothing in the can that sounded like a potential number one and the material that Diana had already begun working on was equally unlikely to yield a smash, leaving all concerned with the real prospect of having to delay Diana's solo breakout until such time as the right song could be found. Fate took a hand, sidetracking a song intended for Junior Walker into the hands of Diana Ross, with *Someday We'll Be Together* sounding the perfect candidate. Although billed as the farewell single by Diana Ross & The Supremes, only Diana actually appeared on the recording (at least as the only Supreme, for the single did feature vocal accompaniment from song writer Johnny Bristol and female backing by The Andantes), just as Diana had been the only member of The Supremes to feature on many of the group's recordings over the previous few years or so.

The timing proved fortuitous, with *Someday We'll Be Together* quickly shaping up to become a major hit following its release in October 1969, prompting an official announcement on 3 November that Diana would be launching a solo career once The Supremes had completed a series of dates at the Frontier Hotel in Las Vegas in January 1970. The show was recorded and eventually released as **Farewell**, with Diana also introducing Jean Terrell to the audience just before the curtain came down on this particular chapter in her career.

It would not take long for the solo Diana to appear to the world since much of the preparatory work had already been done, including working with an abundance of producers and writers on material. And not just standard Motown material either, for among the early recordings were cover versions of Laura Nyro's *Time And Love* and *Stoney End*, with the latter seriously considered at one point as a potential single, although when it didn't appear on the schedule (or indeed on Diana's debut solo album), Richard Perry recorded a version on Barbra Streisand that hit the Top Ten.

Time and consideration (as well as a considerable amount of money, said to be $100,000) had gone into presenting a brand new stage show, one that included a band, three female backing singers and two male dancers and a warm up opening act in ventriloquist Willie Tyler and his dummy Lester. After rehearsing the show at Monticello's in Framingham, Massachusetts during the course of an eleven date residency, Diana prepared to return to the Frontier Hotel in Las Vegas in May 1970. Just ahead of the dates came the release of her first solo single, the Nickolas Ashford and Valerie Simpson penned and produced *Reach Out And Touch (Somebody's Hand)*, which would go on to hit #20 pop and #7 R&B (it would hit #33 in the UK when released in June).

Motown had gone to town promoting the launch of Diana Ross' solo career, engaging an outside publicity company, renting billboards and undertaking an extensive commercial campaign, but for some reason ticket sales for the Frontier Hotel opening night were sluggish. In fact, they were disastrous; five hours before the show opened, only some thirty seats out of a six hundred capacity had been pre-booked. In desperation, Berry Gordy and Motown executive Mike Roshkind walked up and down the Las Vegas strip, talking to everyone they met and offering them half a twenty dollar bill; if they turned up at the Frontier Hotel to see Diana Ross perform live, they were to be given the other half. By the time Berry and Mike finished their task and arrived at the hotel, a large crowd had already gathered, demanding their half of the agreement. After attempting to match the serial numbers on a few and finding it an impossible task, Berry used his credit at the hotel and obtained $10,000 in $20 notes from the cashier's cage and dispensed new and crisp notes to those who came.

Diana was unaware of the lengths Motown had undertaken to ensure a packed opening house, after which word of mouth resulted in healthy turn outs for the rest of her residency. Whilst Berry was prepared to go to any length for Diana's career, he stopped short of making the ultimate commitment personally.

"For the past five years she and I had been intensely involved both professionally and romantically. They were interchangeable. One fed off the other. We had had success after success together. I don't think there was a question in either of our minds that we would always be together. I felt certain that our dream was within reach. And I wanted to go for it all the way. So did she. But as in any long-term relationship the question of marriage had come up. Could our romantic relationship continue without it or would marriage destroy our dream, everything we worked for? We both knew that the conflict between our personal relationship as lovers and the roles we played professionally was taking its toll. I was her mentor, her manager, her boss. She was my protégé, my artist, my star. We both recognised that my role had become too defined, too demanding and too unyielding to exist in a loving marriage. And in order to take the dream all the way my role would have to become even more intense. Emotionally, we were on a collision course. We ended our personal relationship sadly and by mutual agreement so we could focus completely on the professional one."

Of course, Berry's statement (made in his autobiography nearly twenty five years after the event) made no mention of several of the bones of contention between the two, of which Berry's involvement with a number of other women, in particular Motown singer Chris Clark was a major stumbling block. So too was Berry's breath-taking decision to appoint a new road manager for Diana, handing the position to his ex-wife Raynoma!

If personally Diana was being pulled from pillar to post, at least her professional life was beginning to settle, with the early mishaps at the Frontier Hotel quickly becoming a distant memory. Her second single was another Ashford and Simpson composition, this time a revisit of *Ain't No Mountain High Enough*. One of the first songs Ashford and Simpson had written when they became staff writers for Jobete, the song had provided Marvin Gaye and Tammi Terrell with a hit in 1967, near enough in the past for Diana to express her doubts about doing an update, but Nick and Val convinced her that the arrangement they had in mind was so significantly different it was virtually a different song. Still not entirely convinced Diana agreed to record it and was pleasantly surprised with the outcome; *Ain't No Mountain High Enough* did sound different. The public were equally enamoured with the new rendition, resulting in the first chart topper of her solo career, spending one week at the top of the R&B chart and three weeks at the pop summit (and hitting the Top Ten in the UK, where it peaked at #6) as well as picking up a Grammy Award nomination for Best Female Pop Vocal Performance and shifting more than a million copies domestically.

Both singles would appear on Diana's eponymous album debut, with the cover another radical departure from what the public had come to expect from Diana. The cover photograph features a waif-like Diana in a t-shirt and cropped jeans, sitting on the floor and eating an apple, far removed from the sophisticated image she had presented whilst a member of The Supremes. Photographer Harry Langdon (the son of the famed silent screen star) would later reveal the shot used was taken at the end of a session, during which Diana had worn many of the costumes and outfits more usually associated with her image. Once the session was done, Harry took a couple of candid shots and, for a joke, had one of these made up into a billboard he submitted to Berry Gordy. A short while later, Harry was summonsed to a meeting at Berry's mansion and arrived to find the entire Motown hierarchy also in attendance. When Berry brought out the poster and asked what he thought he was doing, Harry was faced with a quandary. Since he could hardly announce to all and sundry that it was just a joke that had backfired, he decided to turn the tables.

"Well, Mr Gordy, Diana Ross has been so successful with all of the extremely fortunate people in the world, I wondered what it would be like to appeal to her own people? The black people in the projects and the people who don't have the money to see her perform? The people who can only buy her records? Here, in my photo of her, she looks like one of the masses. She's one of them. So that's why I think we should use this picture not only on the billboard but also on the cover of the first album."

Harry's quick thinking not only got him out of a hole it got him the cover of Diana's debut album, which would duly go on to top the R&B chart and hit #19 pop as well as making #14 in the UK. This success prompted the rush release in October 1970 of her second album, **Everything Is Everything**, which was produced by Deke Richards and Hal Davis and featured a much more sophisticated image on the cover. The lack of a stand out single, at least as far as the US was concerned hampered the album, which would stall at #42 on the pop chart and #5 R&B, also failing to crack the Top 30 in Britain, where it peaked at #41. This despite one track, her version of Aretha Franklin's *I Love You (Call Me)* collecting a Grammy nomination for Best R&B Vocal Performance, Female, although Aretha Franklin won on the night for her version of *Bridge Over Troubled Water*!

Just as the album was reaching its peak in America, Diana confounded everyone by eloping to Las Vegas and marrying Bob Silberstein on 20 January 1971. A music business manager, Bob was the virtual opposite of Berry and no one but close friends were even aware that the pair had become an item. The witness was Motown executive Suzanne De Passe, who was sworn to secrecy and under instructions not to let Berry know until after the event. A day later, Diana returned to Los Angeles where she was working on a forthcoming television special for ABC and Suzanne returned to Motown where she had the unenviable task of informing Berry that long time paramour Diana Ross had got married.

Berry, like just about everyone else, was surprised at this turn of events. Surprise turned to shock some two weeks later when Diana revealed that she was pregnant (the revelation that the father was Berry Gordy wouldn't follow until many years later), with her first daughter Rhonda Suzanne Silberstein being born on 14 August 1971.

The television special 'Diana' was duly aired on 18 April 1971, with Diana being joined on the special by The Jackson 5, Danny Thomas and Bill Cosby. As well the hits in *Reach Out And Touch* and *Ain't No Mountain High Enough*, Diana performed her then recent single *Remember Me* (written by Ashford and Simpson and which peaked at #16 pop and #10 R&B), a number of medleys and more than passable impersonations of Charlie Chaplin, Harpo Marx and W.C. Fields! It was those impersonations as much as her singing ability that impressed a massive television audience, with the special going on to earn several Emmy nominations. The soundtrack album was issued ahead of the airing and would become a #46 hit on the pop chart (it went to #3 R&B) and #43 in the UK, where the special wasn't aired.

However, among the viewers was film producer Jay Weston, who was in the middle of an ambitious plan to bring the story of Billie Holiday to the big screen and after spotting her abilities were not confined to singing began negotiations with Berry Gordy to contract Diana Ross for the lead role. Those negotiations proved lengthy, due for the most part to Berry Gordy testing Weston to prove how much he wanted Diana for the role before he agreed.

Whilst Diana would begin preparing for the role by listening to countless Billie Holiday recordings, her career across the Atlantic in Britain was enjoying something of an upswing. When released as a single, *Remember Me* had become her second Top Ten success in a row, hitting #7 in May 1971. For the follow-up, Tamla Motown opted for *I'm Still Waiting*, a track from the previously discarded album **Everything Is Everything** that had been receiving extensive radio play on Radio 1's 'Breakfast Show', where DJ Tony Blackburn had been playing the track incessantly since it had first appeared, virtually daring release as a single. It was finally issued in July and was given the accolade of Record of the Week by Blackburn, which helped propel the single up the chart, hitting the top on 21 August for the first of four weeks and becoming her first British chart topper since the heady days of The Supremes seven years previously.

Back home, her latest album **Surrender** had been released in July and despite reuniting Diana with Ashford and Simpson had struggled on the charts, peaking at a disappointing #56 whilst the extracted title track stalled at #38 on the singles chart. In Britain, the single did much better in hitting #10, whilst the album would be re-packaged for the British market, with *I'm Still Waiting* being added to the track listing and the album being christened **I'm Still Waiting** and resulted in a #10 hit. *I'm Still Waiting* would be released as a single stateside but failed to crack the Top 40, halting at a lowly #63 in November.

The following month Diana began filming her movie debut alongside Billy Dee Williams, combining filming with recording the soundtrack album. In the absence of any new material, Tamla Motown in Britain kept Diana's name in vogue, scoring a #12 hit single with *Doobedood'ndoobe Doobedood'ndoobe*, another Deke Richards composition, and a **Greatest Hits** package that would enter the chart at its #34 peak in November.

'Lady Sings The Blues' opened with a star-studded premier in New York in October 1972, although Diana was forced to miss the opening as she was at home in California pregnant with her second child, born Tracee Joy Silberstein on 29 October 1972. Whilst 'Lady Sings The Blues' would go on to become a critical and commercial success, aided by the chart topping soundtrack album (a double album), disappointment came at the Academy Awards; nominated for Best Actress for her portrayal, Diana was beaten on the night by Liza Minnelli.

The anti-climax of the Oscars notwithstanding, everything else connected to 'Lady Sings The Blues' had been a success for Diana. So much so, she now saw herself not as a singer who had been steered into films but an actress who was obliged to churn out a regular supply of albums, all of which would keep her name in vogue until her next major film portrayal. To that end, the period between 'Lady Sings The Blues' and 'Mahogany' would be effectively dismissed in her later autobiography with the comment, 'I continued to do concerts and release albums between my films.'

That attitude would also become prevalent on the occasions when Diana was coaxed back into the studio. In order to maintain the momentum created by 'Lady Sings The Blues', Berry Gordy assembled the best songwriters possible for her next solo album, charging Ron Miller personally with coming up with something as memorable as *Ain't No Mountain High Enough*. Ron had a title, *Touch Me In The Morning*, and an idea he wished to pursue, although the song wouldn't be completed until he got with Michael Masser, who had been brought into the project by Suzanne De Passe. Diana didn't think much of the song, viewing it as no more than an album track, and thought even less of the key, instructing Ron Miller to change it before they ventured into the studio. Which he did, although not to the key Diana had spent much of her time rehearsing! The end result, however, was more than a mere album track, it was the album title track. With a major hit single as the perfect publicity (*Touch Me In The Morning* would top the US chart, selling more than a million copies in the process, as well as becoming a Top Ten success in the UK), the album would enter the Top Ten on both sides of the Atlantic and pick up Diana's third Grammy nomination, for Best Female Pop Vocal Performance, although she was again passed over.

If the sessions for **Touch Me In The Morning** had at times been fractious, then those that kick-started the duets album with Marvin Gaye quickly plummeted, leaving the recording studio looking like a war-zone. It was Marvin who was at fault this time around, his insistence of smoking marijuana almost constantly causing Diana considerable discomfort.

"During this album [Diana] was on pins and needles. She was pregnant and her marriage seemed shaky. I could have been a little more understanding. But I'm afraid I went the other way."

Since Marvin wouldn't temper his behaviour around Diana, the only way to get the necessary sessions recorded was to conduct them separately, then weld the two vocals together to create the required duets. The end result was an album that fell way short of expectations in the US, peaking at #26 pop and #7 R&B, although the album appealed to both Diana Ross and Marvin Gaye fans in Europe and became a #6 hit in Britain, with one single, *You Are Everything* also hitting the Top Ten.

Diana reunited with Michael Masser for her next solo album, with Michael linking with new songwriting partner Pam Sawyer on the title track *The Last Time I Saw Him*, which stalled at #14 pop and #15 R&B, although it did better on the Record World and Cashbox charts, making the Top Ten on both. The lack of a major hit single counted against the album in the long run, with **Last Time I Saw Him** running out of steam at #52 pop, and even languishing at a distant #41 in the UK. Indeed, the failure of the album resulted in a host of singles being culled from her back catalogue, at least as far as the UK was concerned, with *All Of My Life* being lifted off **Touch Me In The Morning** and making the Top Ten, alongside a couple more single releases from her album with Marvin Gaye.

As if to prove that Diana had become an actress who sang in between films, it would take a further three years before another solo album of new recordings appeared on the market, although a live recording **Live! At The Caesar's Palace** was released in May 1974 and would hit #64 pop and #15 R&B as well as #21 in the UK.

The next eighteen months or so was spent worrying little about producers or writers, at least of the musical variety, for after much pondering and thought, Motown had finally come up with what was felt to be the best film vehicle for Diana, 'Mahogany'. If 'Lady Sings The Blues' had at times been a rough ride, then 'Mahogany' turned out to be something of a road crash. Although the film would reunite Diana with Billy Dee Williams the chemistry the two had projected on screen on the first occasion was missing in the second. Berry would clash with his original chosen director Tony Richardson and end up directing the film himself, and ultimately would end up clashing with Diana after she refused to reshoot the final scene. The filming of 'Mahogany' had been an unpleasant experience almost from the start, and the eventual mauling the film received from the critics seemed to bring it full circle.

As far as many were concerned, the only good thing to come out of the film was the theme song, *Do You Know Where You're Going To* (and even that had been the subject of tug of war between Michael Masser and Berry Gordy, with Michael preferring one mix and Berry the other, with Michael Masser settling the matter to his advantage by destroying parts of the other mix!), which would go on to become a US pop chart topper and sell more than a million copies in the process (it would also make the Top Ten in the UK). The soundtrack, however, performed little more than adequately, hitting #19 pop and #15 R&B and missed out on the chart altogether in the UK.

The reception to 'Mahogany' hit Diana hard, and there was only one person she blamed for all the negative publicity the film generated; Berry Gordy. He had been the one to select the film, he had been the one had picked most of the supporting cast, and he was the one who had directed what had turned out to be something of a fiasco. If the opportunity arose to do films in the future, then Diana would take a much more hands on approach.

If her professional career had taken a bit of a battering, then her personal life was still seemingly tranquil, with a third daughter Chudney Lane Silberstein being born on 4 November 1975.

In the meantime, Diana was effectively forced to go back to her musical career, the one area where she had a considerable degree of influence. Released in February 1976, **Diana Ross** was an album that a bit of something for everyone, including the 'Mahogany' theme, the track chosen as the second single in *I Thought It Took A Little Time (But Today I Fell In Love)* and even a cover of Charlie Chaplin's song *Smile*. The real killer cut, however, was to be found third track in on the first side; *Love Hangover*, written by Marilyn McLeod and Pam Sawyer. It attracted heavy radio play almost the day the album was serviced, but when it also started picking up extensive club play, topping the Billboard Disco chart into the bargain, *Love Hangover* was earmarked for future release. It hit the stores quicker than expected, Motown learning that Fifth Dimension had recorded a virtual note for note copy that was being similarly readied for release. Diana's version won the day, topping both the pop and R&B charts as well as collecting a further two Grammy nominations. A fourth single would also hit the charts, *One Love In My Lifetime* hitting #32 before the year was out. With no fewer than four major hits on display, **Diana Ross** couldn't help but be a success, but its final resting place inside the Top Five on both sides of the Atlantic was better than anyone had dared to hope.

All four hits would make a return appearance on **Diana Ross' Greatest Hits** (entitled **Greatest Hits 2** for Europe), alongside her earlier entries onto the pop charts and would peak at #13 in the US. A re-assembled package for Europe was an even bigger success, hitting #2. Further success was achieved with both a live show and its subsequent album, **An Evening With Diana Ross**, with the album making #29 in the US and #52 in the UK.

Unfortunately, her marriage to Bob Silberstein had been unravelling for some time, due it was said to the continued presence of Berry Gordy in almost every aspect of Diana's career (Bob was reported to have said that he felt there were three people in their marriage). And whilst it was Diana who instigated the divorce proceedings, she found little or no objection from Bob in bringing the curtain down on their relationship, although Diana would later state that she might have made a mistake.

The sentiment could just as easily have applied to her decision to lobby for the starring role in 'The Wiz'. The Broadway show had been a huge success, making a star out of Stephanie Mills, who Motown had signed to a recording contract. They had also picked up the option on the show, with every indication that Stephanie would reprise her role in the movie and thus kick-start her solo career with a blockbuster. Both Motown and Stephanie reckoned without Diana's powers of persuasion, which were enough to get Rob Cohen behind her placement as Dorothy, not least because Cohen was convinced Universal would be prepared to pay $1 million for Diana's signature. Once Berry Gordy learned of the upfront fee, any reluctance he had regarding Diana quickly evaporated.

Diana Ross may have given the film its major star but it also ended up giving it a major headache. Few could come to terms with a woman who was then thirty three playing the part designed for someone still in their teenage years (Judy Garland had been sixteen when she played Dorothy in the 1939 film, Stephanie Mills eighteen when she landed the role on Broadway), even if a partial re-write had Diana playing a twenty four year old woman. The film would hit other problems before it finally hit the streets, not least of which was spiralling costs (which in fairness were not down to Diana), but the odds were stacked against the film even breaking even, let alone making a profit. Indeed, 'The Wiz' became regarded as such a disaster it was many years before Diana would be given another film role, major or minor. Had 'The Wiz' turned out a success then who knows what the future may have held; Diana and Ryan O'Neal had a brief romance in 1979, during which time he tried to persuade her to get involved in a film project he'd been offered, but since his interpretation of the film would have required some minor nudity, she balked at the proposal. When their relationship ended, so seemingly did O'Neal's interest in the film, which would eventually hit the big screen in 1992 as 'The Bodyguard' with Kevin Costner and Whitney Houston. And no nudity to be seen anywhere.

Even her recording career wasn't hitting the heights of earlier successes. Paired with producer Richard Perry for **Baby It's Me**, all concerned had high hopes the album would be another major success, especially as Perry had been churning out one hit album after another on artists as diverse as Barbra Streisand, Harry Nilsson, Ringo Starr, Carly Simon, Art Garfunkel and Leo Sayer, with a follow-up album success on Carly Simon largely responsible for Motown targeting him to helm Diana's album. **Baby It's Me** was well received critically but wasn't quite able to translate positive reviews into positive sales, the lack of a major hit single the root of the problem. Three tracks were lifted as singles, but not one of *Gettin' Ready For Love, Your Love Is So Good For Me* or *You Got It* made it any further than #27 pop (although *Your Love Is So Good For Me* collected Diana's fifth Grammy Award nomination for Best R&B Vocal Performance, Female; she again ended the evening empty handed); the latter two singles barely troubling the Top 50. With no single with which to propel sales, the album stalled at #18 pop and #7 R&B. The album sold well in Britain, where it was awarded a silver disc for sales in excess of 60,000 units barely two months after release, yet for some reason it failed to make any appearance on the chart. This was all the more surprising considering Diana spent seven weeks on top of the British album listings with a compilation of twenty of her greatest moments with The Supremes.

Her next official album was something a mixed bag package, with the top side featuring four new tracks and the reverse remixes of five of her previous glories. Of the new tracks, *Lovin' Livin' And Givin'* had appeared on the soundtrack to 'Thank God It's Friday', but that film had been another disappointment and Diana's single only made it as far as #54 in the UK (it was scheduled for release in the US but subsequently cancelled). The track extracted for consumption in the US fared even worse, *What You Gave Me* barely scraped into the R&B chart at #86. With no further singles released the album was left to sink or swim; it sank at #49 pop and #32 R&B and again missed out in the UK.

The failure of **Baby It's Me** and **Ross** to make a significant impact, alongside the fiasco that was 'The Wiz' and a deteriorating of her relationship with Berry Gordy caused Diana to have a major rethink on many aspects of her career come 1979. Having been tied to Motown in general and Berry Gordy in particular for the best part of two decades, Diana was keen to strike out on her own. She did not seek total autonomy, just a degree of control that had hitherto been denied her. To this end Diana opened her own office in January 1979, even though she didn't venture too far away from her former home; her suite of offices was in the same building as Motown!

At the same time as preparing for her future, Diana delved into her past for her next album, with Nickolas Ashford and Valerie Simpson brought on board to produce **The Boss**. Since Diana had begun to pull herself away from Motown, she had much more influence on the album, meeting on a regular basis with Nick and Val and giving them some direction on what the album was to say and what it was to achieve. The result was one of her strongest albums in many a year, with virtually every cut a delight. Not for nothing did the album top the Billboard dance chart (carrying the legend that 'all cuts' where being reported as being played by DJ's the length and breadth of the country), with *It's My House* and *The Boss* being singled out for special praise. Motown released both tracks as singles, but that would appear to be virtually all they did – *The Boss* hit #19 pop and #12 R&B whilst *It's My House* made only a fleeting appearance on the R&B listings at #27. In the UK *The Boss* made #40 and *It's My House* #32, with a further single in *No One Gets The Prize* also peaking at #59. The album however made a respectable #14 pop as well as returning Diana to the Top Ten on the R&B chart, also picking up a gold disc award.

If there was disappointment that the album could only make #52 in the UK it was somewhat balanced by the appearance of **20 Golden Greats**, another career retrospective similar in style to the package that had showcased her earlier hits with The Supremes; it would go on to hit #2 and sell more than 300,000 units, thanks to an extensive television marketing campaign. It was proof, as if it was needed, that Diana Ross was still current and could still be a force to be reckoned with. All she needed was the right material, supplied by the right producers. Which is exactly what she got on her next album **diana**, although not without some major disagreements along the way.

Her daughters had become fans of Chic and Sister Sledge, two groups then at the forefront of the disco movement. Or rather, the two men behind both entities, Nile Rodgers and Bernard Edwards were at the forefront, writing and producing everything they released at the time. They also undertook a number of outside projects, including Norma Jean and Sheila B Devotion, and whilst there was undoubtedly a certain degree of sameness about their productions, the fact that they were still flying to the top of the charts was the only criteria that truly mattered. As a treat, Diana took the daughters to see Chic perform live and after the show arranged to meet with Nile and Bernard to discuss working with them on her next album.

The eventual union benefitted both parties, although it looked as though it would all unravel shortly before the album was due to hit the streets. Whilst the initial meetings and song discussions went well, with Nile and Bernard writing an album based around Diana and her life experiences, there were clashes in the studio when the relatively novice producers tried to tell the vastly experienced singer that she was singing flat! That contretemps was eventually resolved and the recording sessions duly completed. The next problem arose when Nile and Bernard delivered the finished album, with Diana and her camp of the opinion that the album was too much Chic and too little Diana

Ross. A remix conducted by Russ Terrana and Diana soon solved that, although there was a flurry of vocal vitriol between the two camps as they tried to state their respective cases. According to Bernard Edwards and Nile Rodgers, the end result was so far from their creation, they would prefer if their names were left off the album!

Even with a remix done to her specifications, Diana was still unsure that the project would be a success, her fears hardly allayed by Motown's own promotional staff expressing their doubts. The album eventually hit the streets in May 1980 and the following month in Britain, with Diana crossing the Atlantic to lend her support to the initial campaign. It was something of a strange reception she received; a press conference held at a central London hotel quickly dissolved into two factions, with the music journalists trying to get Diana's side of the ongoing spat with Chic and the tabloid journalists wanting to discuss her relationship with Gene Simmons, the flamboyant lead singer with rock group Kiss!

Ultimately singer and record label needn't have worried about the prospects for **diana**, for by the middle of June it had begun to made headway on the album charts in both major territories, going on to peak at #2 in the US and #12 in the UK. The campaign was aided by considerable single success, with *Upside Down* and *I'm Coming Out* making the Top Ten stateside and *Upside Down* and *My Old Piano* achieving the feat in Britain. *Upside Down* also garnered a Grammy Award nomination for Best R&B Vocal Performance, Female and won Favourite Soul/R&B Single at the American Music Awards, with Diana also being named Favourite Soul/R&B Female Artist (as if to prove the disparity between the Grammy Awards, voted for by record industry bigwigs, and the American Music Awards, voted for by the public, Diana had received six nominations for a Grammy and won none, but in the same time frame had collected four AMA's). Add to this total worldwide sales in excess of ten million copies of **diana** and the inescapable conclusion was that all of the uncertainty was unfounded; the album was an unqualified success.

It would turn out to be Diana's last complete album for Motown (at least during her first spell with the company), though few would have been aware of it at the time. There were still one or two more major hits to come, with 1980 ending on another high as *It's My Turn,* another Michael Masser composition, this time in conjunction with Carole Bayer Sager and the theme to the film of the same name would become another Top Ten hit.

In December 1980 it became apparent that Diana was not merely planning for the coming year but several years in advance. During the course of her relationship with Gene Simmons she had confided in him some of her doubts about her business dealings with Motown. Diana had felt for some time that the company (or more specifically Berry Gordy) had taken her for granted, expecting her to re-sign her contract almost irrespective of the offer they put in front of her. She had already made discreet enquiries of a number of companies to see what kind of value they would put on having Diana Ross on their roster and had been astonished when one, RCA, had verbally agreed to a $20 million guarantee. Armed with that knowledge, Gene Simmons sent one of his management representatives to meet Berry Gordy to ascertain whether Motown was prepared to match it. Berry took on board the information but stated he couldn't comment or make a counter offer until he had spoken directly to Diana. A couple of weeks later Diana and the manager returned to Berry's office; he was representing her, although much of the direct discussions were between Berry and Diana, with Berry ending the meeting hopeful that Diana would be re-signing with Motown. A short while later Diana visited Berry at his home to deliver the coup de grace; after twenty one years at Motown, she was taking her leave of the label. Berry was disappointed, but financially it was not a deal he could match, let alone better.

"Money is only part of the value," he reminded her. "Value is everything you have – your team, people who know you – love you. If RCA is willing to pay you that kind of money, I guess you should take it."

Before Diana could take her leave there were one or two contractual obligations to be met, resulting in another compilation album **To Love Again**. A gathering together of much of the material written by Michael Masser, it included the major hits *It's My Turn* and *Do You Know Where You're Going To* as well as three new recordings in *Stay With Me, One More Chance* and *Cryin' My Heart Out For You*, with *One More Chance* becoming the only hit single from the package, at #49 pop and #54 R&B, also repeating its pop performance in the UK. The album itself ran out of steam at #32 pop and #16 R&B, although it would eventually pass the platinum sales mark (it was a rather more modest success in Britain, peaking at #26).

Diana's parting shot to Motown proved to be one of her biggest single successes, a duet with Lionel Richie for the theme to the film 'Endless Love'. A double chart topper in the US and a Top Ten hit around the world it would garner nominations for two Grammy Awards and an Oscar, although Diana's jinx ensured it won none.

Whilst Diana busied herself putting the finishing touches to her first album for RCA in **Why Do Fools Fall In Love**, Motown readied yet another compilation, **All The Great Hits**, designed to hang on to the coattails of the attendant publicity her RCA debut would foster as well as a planned world tour in its support. The album did well domestically although without ever getting close to the peaks achieved by **Why Do Fools**, hitting #37 pop and #14 R&B on its way to earning a gold disc (**Why Do Fools** would go platinum). In Europe the roles were reversed. The deal Diana had signed with RCA was for North America alone, leaving her free to sign another, equally lucrative deal with EMI for the rest of the world. EMI had been Motown's licensee since 1963, first through Stateside and then with the creation of the Tamla Motown imprint. EMI's contract came to an end in October 1981 when Motown signed a new deal with RCA, resulting in Diana's old recordings being marketed and promoted by RCA, her new company in the US, and her new ones by EMI, her old company in Europe! **Why Do Fools** would perform better on the chart but only gain a gold disc, whilst **All The Great Hits** would attain platinum status.

Her initial album for RCA would prove to be her best selling. Whilst she would gain gold awards for **Silk Electric** and **Swept Away**, the peaks she had achieved during her time with Motown proved almost impossible for RCA to scale. There were sporadic single successes, most notably with *Muscles*, written and produced by Michael Jackson (Diana got another Grammy Award nomination for Best R&B Vocal Performance, Female), and *Missing You*, a tribute to Marvin Gaye that was written and produced by Lionel Richie, with both singles hitting the Top Ten.

Motown meanwhile would continue to churn out a veritable catalogue of compilations, issued both under its own brand and a host licensed out elsewhere, with Pickwick, K-Tel (**Love Songs** went platinum) and Telstar (**Portrait** hit gold) among those labels carrying Diana Ross repertoire during the 1980s.

Diana would make her first return to Motown in 1983 when she gathered with several of her former label mates for the taping of the television special 'Motown 25'. What should have been a nostalgia-packed celebratory evening, culminating in an eagerly anticipated reunion of The Supremes, was nearly derailed by some very un-Diana like behaviour. As if gatecrashing Adam Ant's performance of *Where Did Our Love Go* wasn't enough, a push and shoving match with Mary Wilson brought a halt to The Supremes reunion midway through the first of a planned four song segment.

In 1985 Diana met billionaire shipping magnate Arne Naess, five years her senior, whilst on holiday in the Bahamas. Both were with their three children from earlier marriages; Diana was taking a break from recording her new album **Eaten Alive** whilst Naess had recently successfully led a Norwegian mountaineering team to the summit of Mount Everest! Diana and Arne were married in a civil ceremony in New York in October 1986. The following February they held a more formal ceremony at the Swiss Reformed church in Romainmotier in Switzerland, with Stevie Wonder singing *I Just Called To Say I Love You* (although *Ain't No Mountain High Enough* might have been more appropriate) at the reception held near Lausanne. This marriage would result in two children, sons Ross Arne Naess (born on 7 October 1987) and Evan Olav Naess (born on 26 August 1988). The marriage would end in divorce in 2000, although Diana would claim that Arne had been the love of her life.

When her RCA contract expired in 1988, Diana decided to shop around for a new deal, including entertaining overtures from Berry Gordy and Motown. Although Diana was aware that Berry was himself in negotiations with MCA for the sale of the company and tried to convince him against it, she still inked a new deal with her spiritual home (including, it was said, taking shares in the company). Whilst her new repertoire has been moderately successful, it does not have the allure of her old. In 1994, the retrospective compilation **One Woman** topped the UK charts and sold over 1.2 million copies. The package was so successful it prompted similar compilations that proved to be a hit around the globe. Unfortunately for Diana, a miss of a different sort was also seen around the world; invited to sing at the opening ceremony for the FIFA World Cup Finals being held in America, Diana was supposed to kick a ball into the goal from the penalty spot at the end of her song performance. The goal would then split into two as part of a carefully orchestrated stunt, but Diana's penalty went wide! The goal still fell apart anyway, the organisers having left absolutely nothing to chance!

Diana would also return to making films, although both roles were in made for television movies, 'Out Of Darkness' and 'Double Platinum' (the latter also starring fellow singer Brandy). Her plans to bring the Josephine Baker story to the big screen also floundered, with Diana having been unable to get financial backing, something she describes as her lost dream. She did however finally get to lift a Grammy Award, being given a Lifetime Achievement statuette in 2012. That award was the pinnacle in a career that has seen her sell more than 100 million records worldwide, collect a Kennedy Center Honor and have two stars on the Hollywood Walk of Fame, one for her contributions to The Supremes and another for her solo career. Ultimately, it's the culmination of a lifetime of hard work.

"You can't just sit there and wait for people to give you that golden dream. You've got to get out there and make it happen for yourself."

ALBUMS: DIANA ROSS (1970), EVERYTHING IS EVERYTHING (1970), DIANA! TV SPECIAL (1971), SURRENDER (1971), LADY SINGS THE BLUES (1972), TOUCH ME IN THE MORNING (1973), DIANA AND MARVIN (1973), LAST TIME I SAW HIM (1973), LIVE! AT THE CAESAR'S PALACE (1974), MAHOGANY FILM SOUNDTRACK (1975), DIANA ROSS (1976), AN EVENING WITH DIANA ROSS (1977), BABY IT'S ME (1977), ROSS (1978), THE BOSS (1979), DIANA (1980)

COMPILATIONS: GREATEST HITS (1976), 20 GOLDEN GREATS (1979), TO LOVE AGAIN (1981), ALL THE GREAT HITS (1981), ANTHOLOGY (1983), 14 GREATEST HITS (1984), ALL THE GREAT LOVE SONGS (1984), ANTHOLOGY (1986)

FURTHER READING: SECRETS OF A SPARROW (1993), DIANA ROSS: GOING BACK (2002)

JERRY ROSS SYMPOSIUM

Born in Philadelphia, Pennsylvania on 1 May 1933, Jerry Ross began his career as a DJ and radio and television announcer in his hometown during the 1950s. By the end of the decade he had become a record promoter, later taking the natural progression into composing and producing.

He was an early collaborator of Kenny Gamble and later introduced Leon Huff into the partnership, with Gamble and Huff eventually breaking off to form a songwriting partnership and record label, Philadelphia International. Before that, however, Jerry, Kenny and Leon had written *I'm Gonna Make You Love Me*, which was originally recorded by Dee Dee Warwick (the sister of Dionne Warwick), produced by Jerry and featured Nickolas Ashford and Valerie Simpson on backing vocals.

Jerry would produce some ten versions of the song, recording it on Jerry Butler and Jay & The Techniques, with both these versions also featuring Ashford and Simpson on backing vocals. It was when Ashford and Simpson introduced the song to Motown, with Frank Wilson and Nickolas Ashford producing a version of the song themselves, on Diana Ross, The Supremes and The Temptations, that Jerry Ross was brought to the company's attention. After the track had been recorded, Berry Gordy called Jerry Ross to let him know Motown was considering releasing the track as a single, a fact Jerry was already aware off thanks to considerable radio play in Philadelphia from an advance copy of the album.

During the course of the telephone conversation, Berry Gordy asked Jerry what he was up to musically, learning that Jerry had formed his own label (Colossus, named after his pet poodle), which was releasing records by a number of Dutch rock acts (Shocking Blue, The Tee Set and The George Baker Selection among them) as well as recording middle of the road versions of hit songs by artists on his labels under the name Jerry Ross Symposium. Intrigued by the concept, Berry Gordy asked Jerry to record a similar album for Motown and signed his Jerry Ross Productions company in order to give the label more of a presence in the New York area.

Jerry brought a number of artists to Motown, including The Courtships, Crystal Mansion and The Festivals, although with little or no chart success. Although his own album for the label, **The Jerry Ross Symposium Volume 2** bore his name prominently on the cover, the material was arranged by Claus Ogerman and featured middle of the road versions of recent chart material, including Stevie Wonder's *Superwoman*. The album was released in August 1972, with the single *It Happened On A Sunday Morning* (originally recorded by The Tree People) and *Duck You Sucker* (by Ennio Morricone) being issued a month later.

ALBUM: JERRY ROSS SYMPOSIUM, VOLUME 2 (1972)

JOHN RUBINSTEIN

Born in Los Angeles, California on 8 December 1946, John Arthur Rubinstein has made his name as an actor, composer and director. He made his Broadway debut in 1972 in the lead role in 'Pippin' for which he would go on to win a Theater World Award. Later Broadway appearances saw him win the Tony Award for 'Children Of A Lesser God' and he has also appeared in numerous films and television series. Among his composer credits are the music for 'The Candidate' and 'Jeremiah Johnson'.

DAVID RUFFIN

David Ruffin had talent in abundance and a voice that still ranks as one of the finest to have graced any Motown record. Unfortunately, he had an ego that was his talent's equal in size, setting him on a path to alienation and eventual self-destruction.

Born Davis Eli Ruffin in Whynot, near Meridian, Mississippi on 18 January 1941, the son of Baptist minister Eli and Ophelia Ruffin, his mother died soon after he was born and Davis was brought up by his stepmother, schoolteacher Earline. His early days were somewhat troubled, with Davis suffering from a heart condition, asthma and rheumatic fever as a child, coupled with a strict and often violent upbringing imposed by his father.

He found solace singing, joining with siblings Quincy, Jimmy and Rita Mae in a family gospel group alongside his father and stepmother, opening for the likes of Mahalia Jackson and The Five Blind Boys of Mississippi. The call of singing gospel music proved strong enough for Davis to contemplate going into a ministry himself, leaving home in 1955 and travelling to Memphis under the guardianship of a minister. The following year, however, he upped sticks and went with jazz musician Phineas Newborn Sr. to Hot Springs in Arkansas, where he would sing in local clubs and ballrooms, eventually linking up with The Dixie Nightingales, The Swan Silvertones and briefly The Soul Stirrers. Along the way, Davis crossed paths with numerous artists who had turned their backs on gospel and gone secular, prompting a similar switch.

He journeyed to Detroit, initially under the guardianship of Eddie Bush and Dorothy Helen, a husband and wife couple who helped get him a couple of bookings in and around the city. According to later claims, Eddie Bush' efforts were designed to benefit him personally, taking a large percentage of Davis' income and dallying with the rebounded women who threw themselves at Davis. He is also the likely source of a change in name, from Davis Ruffin to David Ruffin, which occurred in 1957 soon after the death of his father, something of a new start after the closing of one chapter in his life. It is also claimed that Eddie Bush and his wife made plans to adopt the still sixteen year old David (and David would refer to Eddie as his stepfather), although nothing legal was ever signed to this effect.

Eddie did manage to get David his first recording deal, encouraging the local Vega label to record a couple of tracks on his protégé. The single, featuring *You And I* and *Believe Me* was reportedly released early in 1958 with the credit Little David Bush, but no known copies have ever surfaced and there is some speculation that the record, if it exists, does not feature David Ruffin as the vocalist. Similar confusion surrounds what was said to be his follow-up, *Statue Of A Fool,* written by David but carrying the artist credit of Eddie Bush (the song at least would be revisited, with David re-recording it in 1975).

Whilst the circumstances of his recordings with Vega are mired in confusion, by the end of 1959, David had a new group of acquaintances, having been introduced to Berry Gordy and subsequently ingratiating himself into the Gordy clan, helping Pops Gordy out at his print shop, helping stack records at Gwen Gordy's Anna Records and even undertaking some of the carpentry at the rapidly evolving Hitsville complex. Whilst Pops was impressed with David's construction skills, Berry and Gwen were impressed with his vocal abilities, with Gwen finding a place for him in The Voice Masters.

"He was very much a gentleman," said Gwen, "yes ma'am and no ma'am, but the thing that really impressed me about David was that he was one of the only artists I've seen who rehearsed like he was on stage."

David rehearsed enough to not only feature as one of The Voice Masters, he soon became lead singer and got top billing on *I'm In Love,* released in February 1961. When Gwen shut down Anna in order to open up again as Check-Mate, David was one of the artists brought over for the ride, releasing *You Can Get What I Got* (July 1961) and *Mr Bus Driver* (March 1962) before Check-Mate closed its doors too. His reputation was already made around Detroit, so when Check-Mate closed there was an offer of something at Motown, although initially it didn't look as though a solo deal was that something.

David had been joined in Detroit by his elder brother Jimmy and the pair discussed plans to resurrect their Ruffin Brothers act (the pair would get to record together, but not until 1970), but Motown didn't seem in any particular hurry to get them into the studio, collectively or individually. Whilst Jimmy found work at the Ford car plant, David continued doing odd jobs around Hitsville, waiting his chance. When it eventually came, it was through a mixture of luck and constructed circumstances. David was friendly with several of The Temptations, most notably Otis Williams and Melvin Franklin. Melvin even claimed that he and David were second cousins, a claim Otis has consistently refuted.

"Listen, I love Melvin, but Melvin claimed everybody was his cousin at one time or another. He said Richard Street (later a member of The Temptations) was his cousin. Later on he said Rick James was his cousin. He probably said I was his cousin. When Melvin liked you, he'd want you to be a family member. And he and David hit it off right away. He knew David before he knew the rest of us guys."

Whilst Melvin and David's family ties might have been tenuous, their friendly ones were significant, with David taking to hanging around the group and showing up wherever they might be playing on a regular basis. He was therefore aware of the growing discord between Al Bryant and the rest of the group, a situation David exploited to his advantage one night at a show at Chappy's Lounge in Detroit in October 1963. As the group prepared to sing their encore *Shout*, David leapt onto the stage and joined in, not just with the singing but performing his own devised set of dance steps, a routine that knocked out everyone present, including the five Temptations who found they had temporarily gained an additional member. After the show, a disagreement between Al Bryant and Paul Williams escalated to such an extent that Al smashed a beer bottle into the face of Paul, an action that convinced the rest of The Temptations that Al's days as one of their member were coming to an end; it was just a case of when.

When Bryant was finally given his marching orders, it was obvious that Ruffin would come into the group as his replacement. The only problem was that there were two Ruffin's lining up for the role, although how serious Jimmy was in wanting the role or how serious the group was in offering it to him is still the subject of some debate.

"Jimmy was not in David's league as a singer," Otis Williams would later state, "but he thought he was in line for the job. So that was a little delicate situation. I had to let him down easy. I told him, 'Jimmy, love to have you, but you can't dance, you got flat feet,' which was true. And he said, 'Yeah, Otis, you're right.'"

This chain of events would later be refuted by Jimmy, who said, "No, I was never in The Temptations. I don't recall if I was ever asked, but you gotta understand something. I was moving up on my own. Why would I have given up on that to be part of a group? But people don't know that I had an effect on them by showing them what to do, how to sing, how to look onstage. I made a lot of suggestions that I saw put in place onstage. This was something all of us did at Motown, we all helped each other get ahead, and I happened to have a better sense of stagemanship than they did. What David did with them was part of that; he didn't learn that shit from them. He learned it from me."

If The Temptations were certain that they didn't necessarily want or need Jimmy Ruffin, they weren't entirely sure about taking David either, believing that the same solo motivation that propelled Jimmy was present in David too, with David perhaps seeing The Temptations as little more than a staging post to greater stardom. Eventually, David was able to convince them of his sincerity and was taken on as a singer within the group, just in time to join them in the studio for their breakthrough hit *The Way You Do The Things You Do*, an R&B chart topper and #11 pop hit following its release in January 1964. *The Way You Do The Things You Do* featured Eddie Kendricks on lead vocal, and whilst the hits kept coming Smokey Robinson, who wrote most of the group's material at that point, saw little reason to offer the lead to anyone else.

So the hits continued for the rest of the year, although without hitting the same heights as they had in January. It was after witnessing a live performance that Smokey came up with the idea of crafting something for David to front, playing the group the basics of the song backstage at a show at the Apollo Theater. Whilst it sounded just like another song to the rest of The Temptations, David saw it as his chance to shine, with the resulting single *My Girl* taking The Temptations to the top of the R&B and pop charts soon after its release at the tail-end of 1964.

David did much the same with the follow-up, with *It's Growing* as much a statement about The Temptations fortunes as it was a hugely popular single (although not as popular as *My Girl*). Equally growing was David's ego, fuelled by both the success and the actions of those around him, as The Temptation road manager Don Foster would later recall.

"It was unbelievable the change that took place with David. I think it was mainly because he started listening to people, so-called friends who kept kissing his ass, telling him he was it, he was bad, he was The Temptations. They used to travel with him. They'd call him 'Poppa' – they'd say, 'Man, Poppa, you was *bad* tonight!' They were leeching off him but it was like a salve for him. He needed it. And he started to believe it."

It didn't take too long for David to start creating his own entity, separate from the group and what they were trying to achieve collectively, appointing his own personal manager in Royce Moore and hiring a bodyguard. The problems came when he wanted to continue that separate entity on stage and in the studio.

"He didn't think of them [The Temptations] as family. It wasn't all for one, it was all for David," continued Foster. "He saw them as his backup group. He hated to sing backup on a song when Eddie was on lead. And he'd say so. He'd get into situations where they'd have to restrain him before he got physical with one of them."

As well as problems with the male members of The Temptations, his libido would cause a different set of physical problems with an ever-growing number of females. David had married Sandra prior to joining The Temptations, with the union resulting in two children (Cheryl and Nedra). During a live date in Atlantic City he met Genna Sapia and persuaded her to move to Detroit, avoiding questions as to his marital state by claiming that his wife had died during childbirth! Genna would give birth to a son, David Jr, but even before the birth David had left her in order to return to the still very much alive Sandra (with whom he would have another daughter, Kimberley) only to depart once again for another relationship, one that was to resonate around Hitsville; twenty four year old David Ruffin took up with the newly signed twenty year old artist Tammi Terrell.

David got with Tammi soon after she arrived at Motown and as a couple were soon inseparable, with David buying matching mink coats and jewellery, including at one point an engagement ring. Unfortunately, David forgot to mention or merely overlooked that fact that not only was he still married but he had three children by two women still very much on the scene. Whilst Tammi was known to be distressed by the news, it did not bring about an end to their relationship, although their disagreements and arguments took on a much more violent nature. Others around the Motown lot saw the numerous bruises that Tammi sported but for the most part ignored them, as Otis later observed.

"David could be kinda rough on a lady at times. When you're out on the road like we were, you hear and see things. We knew all about Tammi and James Brown. We knew how James Brown was about women, that he would flip a woman's ass. And back then, you wouldn't ever get the woman's side so people would assume, fairly or not, he flipped her ass because she provoked him to."

Quite how much Tammi provoked David is not known, but the beatings were certainly severe, culminating in an incident when David smashed his motorcycle helmet into the side of Tammi's head (which did have the effect of ending the relationship in 1967). Whilst there is no proof that David's actions directly resulted in Tammi's brain tumour and eventual death, the mental anguish of being involved with David, who hid the true extent of his other female companions and the growing number of children, cannot have helped matters.

David was also causing mental anguish to the other members of The Temptations, who found his growing aloofness from the group difficult to fathom and accept. Whilst the hits kept coming, albeit with a switch of writer and producer to Norman Whitfield after *Get Ready* (one of Eddie's last lead vocals for some considerable time) had failed to become the major hit everyone anticipated, the rest of the group managed to keep a lid on their feelings. David led the group through a succession of hits, with *Ain't Too Proud To Beg, Beauty Is Only Skin Deep, (I Know) I'm Losing You* and *All I Need* keeping the group at the top of the charts and enabling them to get bigger and better live venues at which to perform.

With bigger and better venues came more and more money, funds to be spent or wasted as the individual saw fit. And David had plenty of things he wanted to spend *his* money on, including a stretch El Dorado with all the extras money could buy, including a chauffeur. When he wasn't spending his money as quickly as he was making it, David was, well, no one seemed to know exactly what David was doing since he didn't take any of the other Temptations into his confidence. He would disappear at the end of one concert and, if they were lucky, they might see him at the next venue into which they were booked. He certainly didn't see the need to rehearse on what would ordinarily be their days off, so these had to be conducted in his absence.

The other problem was that no one knew for sure exactly where David lived; he'd spend his money so quickly that he seldom had enough left over to pay for an apartment, flitting from wife (Sandra) to girlfriend (Genna) to other girlfriend (Tammi) with regularity. It soon became apparent where the bulk of David's money was going; up his nose. The more he spent, the more he believed The Temptations in general and he in particular were being short-changed by Berry Gordy, telling Eddie Kendricks that they should confront the Motown boss and get a detailed set of accounting figures, one which would show beyond all doubt that they were owed even more money than was rolling into the coffers.

Paul Williams, who whilst not necessarily siding with Otis Williams and Melvin Franklin on all matters relating to The Temptations, usually managed to dissuade Eddie from taking such direct action. When he wasn't questioning the group's finances, David was directing his attention to the group's billing. When Diana Ross was elevated out of The Supremes and got top billing in Diana Ross & The Supremes, David decided such an event should visit The Temptations and even alluded to it during a live performance, announcing from the stage, "I'm David Ruffin, and these are The Temptations."

"That was all just David playing his head games," Otis would later explain. "There was no chance he'd get his way, and I don't think it was about getting his way. He just wanted to rock the boat. But he didn't want to get off that boat. Look at it like this; David never was a success, never could act like he did, until we brought him into The Temptations. He talked a lot of shit like that, but deep down I think he was scared of being out there alone, on his own, with no support. But he had to be David, so he'd push it. And when he did, we had to push back."

The major problem for all concerned was assessing what would happen if David were to leave the group, either of his own accord or kicked out by the rest. As far as David was concerned, he was the focal point of the group, the lead singer on more of their hit singles than any of the other members and they would amount to little or nothing without him. As far as they were concerned, David was the problem and they'd be better off without him and his ego. Any doubts The Temptations might have had about their future with or without David Ruffin were dispelled by Berry Gordy, who in a rare show of interest in what they were doing, pointed out that the group was unlikely to survive with him, so problematic had he become. And it wasn't only rehearsals he was skipping, for on a number of occasions, his disappearance act had resulted in him failing to turn up for shows.

Matters between The Temptations and David Ruffin reached crisis point on 22 June 1968, midway through a residency at the Versailles Hotel in Cleveland. After a show one night, David left with another girlfriend Barbara Gail Martin (the daughter of singer Dean Martin), a singer who had her own dates that David wanted to attend. So David left Cleveland, bound for Buffalo.

"He never told us, he just thought he'd make it back in time for our next show, but there was a big storm and he got stuck there," said Don Foster. "Everybody was furious and they went on that night as four. Then in the middle of the show David got here and came onstage, and of course he got a big ovation, and he loved that. He would love to come on late and bask in the applause while the others stood there, steaming. Well, this time it was just too much – it was like he was getting an ovation for being irresponsible. He thought it was funny, but that ripped it. When they finished the show, Otis called Gordy and told him, 'We're gonna fire David.' They set up a meeting when they got back. They didn't wanna tell him he was out till then because they didn't want to be swayed, charmed by David, which he was very good at. They wanted the papers to be drawn up, signed, and ready to shove at him."

The coup de grace was delivered five days later at the Hitsville building, David arriving characteristically late to be handed a legal document that spelt out his ejection from the group. It took a short while for the severity of the situation to sink in, after which David bade his farewells, wished the group good luck and waltzed out of Hitsville again. Although his time as a Temptation was at an end, David would still make his presence felt over the coming months. It was he who told Dennis Edwards, long considered a potential replacement in The Temptations and who was involved in a relationship with David's estranged wife Sandra (with David's consent!), that he (David) had left the group and Dennis should get himself in a position to be taken on as the new member. Dennis eventually got the role and quickly rehearsed with his new groupmates, learning the ropes, both vocally and dance-wise, ready to go back out on the road. Whilst Motown issued a press release stating David Ruffin had left the group, they did not go into any further detail, leaving the question as to how and why and even the finality of it unanswered.

On 9 July 1968, Dennis took the stage for his first official date as a member of the five Temptations. Midway through the evening, just as Dennis got to the introduction to *Ain't Too Proud To Beg* and sang 'I know you wanna leave me', David Ruffin leapt onto the stage, grabbed the microphone and sang 'But I refuse to let you go.' Dennis and the rest of the Temptations were caught unaware by this sudden intrusion but quickly recovered their composure and sang the rest of song, invoking memories of the occasion some five years previously when David Ruffin had joined the five Temptations on stage. Much the same thing happened on a further two occasions, despite security guards in place to prevent him getting to the stage. The fact that the 'stunt' was repeated led Dennis to believe that it was all part of the act, and when he saw David in the audience at a show, he began to fear the worst.

"What happened was, we had two shows in Gaithersburg and David was there for the first. He was in the audience, but he wasn't there to jump on the stage, though. I guess they'd come to some sort of agreement for him to come back. Afterward, they told me, 'Look, we know you been with us for a while but we're gonna take David back.' He was gonna make his comeback at the second show later that night. Well, I was just floored by that. Here was I just starting out with them, trying to fit in, and they hit me with that ton of bricks. But what could I do? If David was coming back, who was I? So I went back to the hotel and started packing. But then David did his usual shit and didn't show up for the second show, so they called me and said, 'Get down here right away.'"

Otis Williams and others close to The Temptations didn't remember it quite that way, stating that they never intended to offer David his place back, adding that once the legal papers were served, that was it, no possibility of a reprieve or parole. Once he accepted his time as a Temptation was at an end, David served his own legal papers on Motown, asking for a release from the label and a full accounting of royalties for his time as a member of the group. Motown countersued, intending to hold him to the full term of his contract (due to expire in 1970), with the matter eventually settled with the announcement that David Ruffin would be joining the ranks of solo artists on the Motown label.

David spent the rest of the year in the studio working with a variety of producers on what would be his debut album, with the title track being released as a single in February 1969. The poignantly title *My Whole Life Ended (The Moment You Left Me)* got his career off to the perfect start, hitting the Top Ten pop and R&B (peaking at #9 pop and #2 R&B), with the accompanying album also a success, topping the R&B chart and making #31 pop.

For a while everyone was happy; The Temptations had embarked on their psychedelic soul phase and would enjoy hits that surpassed anything they had accomplished previously, proof that they could prosper without David Ruffin, whilst David was scoring his own hits and proving that he could prosper without The Temptations. David would score with another single culled from his debut, *I've Lost Everything I've Ever Loved,* another apt title and a #58 pop and #11 R&B success. Motown and David wasted little time in getting more music out, with **Feelin' Good** (originally titled **Doin' His Thing**) being issued in November 1969 which returned him to the Top Ten of the R&B chart (at #9) but stalled much lower down the pop listings at #148, also giving rise to the hit single *I'm So Glad I Fell For You* (#18 R&B and #53 pop).

David's next project reunited him with Jimmy, with **I Am My Brother's Keeper** appearing in September 1970. Aside from the obvious *He Ain't Heavy He's My Brother*, the album also contained what would be the only hit single lifted, an update of Ben King's *Stand By Me,* which would hit #61 pop and #24 R&B following its release in October 1970. Equally important as what David was singing in 1970 was what he was signing; his original Motown contract expired that year and he was free to leave the company if he so wished. Given his earlier disagreements with the company, most of which he lay at Berry Gordy's door, it would have been no surprise if David had up and left, for with his recent hits he was undoubtedly a bankable commodity for someone. Add to this the death of Tammi Terrell in March 1970 and he could have been forgiven for wanting to sever all ties with the label and whatever memories Hitsville held for him. Instead he signed a new and extended Motown contract.

That didn't stop him continually beefing about Motown, the slave nature of the contracts, the lack of promotion, the lack of respect he felt Berry Gordy displayed towards him and, most of all, the fact that too much of the money *his* talents had generated had found its way into other pockets. Such tales invariably got into the ear of Eddie Kendricks, with whom David shared a penchant for snorting cocaine, resulting in one embittered Motown employee feeding another the ammunition that would lead to his own departure from The Temptations. Eventually Eddie started down the same route as David, missing rehearsals and even a televised appearance, although he would eventually leave The Temptations of his own accord rather than be fired the way David had.

Whilst David was relatively quiet on the recording front, he still had plenty to say about his erstwhile band-mates, even going so far as to announce that he planned to team up with Eddie Kendricks, lure Dennis Edwards out of The Temptations and bring in Paul Williams (another former Temptation who'd exited the group through illness) whenever he was fit and ready. That flurry of words would result in The Temptations bringing out the single *Superstar (Remember How You Got Where You Are)* as a retort, but David never got anywhere with his plan, at least not for another decade or so. Besides, David would have been better served paying more attention to *his* career rather than that of The Temptations, for after his initial burst of chart activity, he had become something of a forgotten man around Motown. After limited success with Jimmy, it had taken nearly three years for anything new to appear, with the eponymous album in February 1973 containing a variety of songs that had been recorded over a longer period of time, although the album did make a minor dent on the charts, at #160 pop and #34 R&B. *Common Man* was equally a minor hit single, barely scraping into the R&B chart at #84 and bypassing the pop listings altogether (a planned 1971 release entitled **David** was pulled off the schedule and finally appeared in 2004).

In August that year David made an appearance at Paul Williams' funeral, serving as a pallbearer and half singing and half crying his way through Paul's signature tune *The Impossible Dream,* his distress at Paul's death continuing for some considerable time after the event. David was never short of an opinion about Motown and chose to believe that Paul's death was not the suicide it was ruled but something far more sinister. To add weight to his beliefs, the fact that he, Eddie and Cornelius Grant had been mugged the day before the funeral, which had resulted in the theft of his phone book, was a sure sign Motown was prepared to scare him into submission. Or so David believed.

"They'll find a way to get you. They'll fire you and hold you to your contract; and if your contract says you got to do two albums a year, they'll take you to the studio and record you two times a year, and then not release the albums."

If that was the case, then David was at a loss to explain why he was put into the studio with former Temptations mastermind Norman Whitfield for **Me And Rock 'N Roll Are Here To Stay**, recorded over more than a year and finally issued in December 1974. There was an irony in some of the material chosen, including a cover of *Superstar*, the song that had been originally aimed fairly and squarely at him (and Eddie Kendricks) some three or four years previously. Equally, *Smiling Faces Sometimes*, originally recorded by The Temptations and best known for the version by The Undisputed Truth, takes on a slightly different meaning when David Ruffin is the singer! None of the lifted singles made an impression, but the fact the album had the legs to make it to #37 on the R&B chart was proof David still had appeal.

Despite the relative success of the album, there were no plans for a further Norman Whitfield reunion, with David being put into the pending column at Motown. Sometime later Vice President Suzanne De Passe took one of her regular phone calls from Charles Kipps, a songwriter and producer based in New York and a musical partner of Van McCoy. McCoy was well known in R&B circles, having written for and produced the likes of Gladys Knight & The Pips, Jackie Wilson, Betty Everett and The Stylistics during his long and impressive career. He was also seen as one of the vanguards of the burgeoning disco scene, having crafted a number of well appreciated songs on The Choice Four and was enjoying a major hit under his own name, with *The Hustle* on its way to topping the charts around the world. When David's name came into the conversation as a possible act Van might be interested in working with, Charles gleefully accepted.

Although Charles and Van would have been well aware of David's reputation, especially his unreliability, the three quickly set about putting together an album of which all could be proud. Several of the tracks that Van and Charles selected had already been road tested by The Choice Four, with *Walk Away From Love* and *Finger Pointers* having appeared on the Washington D.C. group's recent album on RCA, but with David's vocals layered on top of masterful music from the likes of Eric Gale, John Tropea, Steve Gadd, Richard Tee and Hugh McCracken, those songs took on a whole new life; the difference, said one review, between a demo version and the finished article. *Walk Away From Love* was released as the lead single, appearing in October 1975, just ahead of the resulting album **Who I Am**. Both would turn out to be a return to former glories, with the single topping the R&B chart and hitting the Top Ten in both the US and UK (at #9 and #10 respectively) and the album becoming a #5 R&B and #31 pop hit, both the biggest successes of his solo career. The follow-up single, the Joe Cobb and Van McCoy composition *Heavy Love* was also successful, becoming a Top Ten R&B hit (#8) and Top 50 pop (at #48).

The success of **Who I Am** prompted a return visit to New York a year later to work with Van McCoy again, with much the same bank of top class musicians appearing on **Everything's Coming Up Love**. Whilst similar in style to its predecessor, the album suffered from the lack of a stand out single, with nothing as magical as *Walk Away From Love* on display. Whilst the title track would return David to the Top Ten of the R&B chart (it hit #8), it could barely make #49 on the pop listings. The second single, *On And Off* was as much a statement of David's career as a potential hit single, and it could only limp into #48 R&B. Not surprisingly, the album also slipped, peaking at #16 R&B and #51 pop. Motown, David and Van gave it one final shot, **In My Stride** being released in June 1977, but there was to be no pop acceptance for the album or its singles, with the long player peaking at #36 R&B and *Just Let Me Hold You For A Night* and *You're My Peace Of Mind* stalling at #18 and #71 respectively (*Just Let Me Hold You For A Night* did bubble under at #108, the closest anything came to troubling the pop chart).

David's Motown contract then ran out and he opted to leave the company, eventually to sign for Warner Brothers, where his two albums in two years continued the downward spiral, although *Break My Heart* offered a temporary respite in 1979, hitting the R&B Top Ten. Whilst David was no longer a regular on the chart, he was seldom out of the news, although all too often for entirely the wrong reasons.

His personal life was just as muddled as ever, with a second marriage to Joy Hamilton in 1976 also ending after he had physically beaten her. Talk of a possible Temptations reunion had never been far from the surface however, with Kenny Gamble and Leon Huff proposing the idea when The Temptations were without a contract or label, but the timing wasn't right then, with much of the bitterness still simmering. By 1981, however, circumstances had changed. Eddie and David had their own financial reasons for wanting a reunion to take place, but until Otis Williams and whoever then constituted The Temptations agreed, the idea would remain just that, an idea.

After an unsuccessful stint with Atlantic Records, The Temptations returned to Motown, where Rick James was being lined up to produce a new album. When it was floated that the five man group be expanded to seven, with David and Eddie taking their place alongside Otis, Melvin Franklin, Dennis Edwards, Richard Street and Glenn Leonard, there were few dissenting voices. For Motown it was a publicity dream, ensuring interest in the album even before recording sessions had begun, and should the group go out on the road to promote the album, well, the possibilities were endless.

The subsequent album, **Reunion** lived up to expectations, resulting in a #37 pop and #2 R&B hit and a Top Ten R&B single in *Standing On The Top*. A week before the album was released the seven man group went out on the road, quickly drawing rave reviews, which in turn added extra dates to the tour. As the single and album moved up the charts, even more dates were added, proof that The Temptations had not lost any of their magic. It did not take long for the wheels to come off and, once again, it was David who was the most problematic.

The shows had been a financial success, giving all seven more money than they had expected, but whilst most were content to put some away for the rainy days that were sure to come, David spent his as quickly as was possible, almost all of it on drugs. He began by missing a show, then two and then disappearing virtually for good. Whilst six Temptations were better than five, most of the contracts that had been signed for the reunion tour had stipulated that all seven had to be present for the group to earn their full entitlement; David's constant no-shows hit them all in the pocket. Eventually Otis realised that the reunion in reality wasn't as good as the reunion in theory and told Eddie to tell David, if he could locate him, that once the scheduled tour was finished, so were they.

Eddie obviously managed to locate David, for they then came up with their own plans for a touring group, revisiting David's idea from years before whereby they would hit the road as The Former Lead Singers of The Temptations, with Dennis Edwards as part of the revue. Those plans were to be put on hold for a while as David had rather more pressing matters to attend to; the IRS had been after him for some time and finally caught up with him in 1982, handing him a $5,000 fine and a six month prison sentence in a low security prison in Terre Haute in Indiana. In the end he served four, being released early for good behaviour and went to live with his latest girlfriend in a mobile home in Michigan.

David, Eddie and Dennis would hit the road, often being supported by another former Motown great in Martha Reeves, although playing smaller venues than they might have expected when they had been members of The Temptations. In May 1985 David and Eddie received an offer from blue eyed soul duo Hall & Oates, who had never made a secret of their admiration for the pair, inviting them to join them at the Apollo Theater for a show that was to be recorded as **Live At The Apollo**. The album was a success, as was an extracted medley single (*A Nite At the Apollo Live,* which blended *The Way You Do The Things You Do* and *My Girl*), culminating in David and Eddie joining Hall & Oates for their performance at the Philadelphia leg of the Live Aid concert.

Thanks to Hall & Oates, David and Eddie also got their own deal with RCA, resulting in the album **Ruffin & Kendrick** in September 1987. The following year, Hall & Oates would again play a part in the ongoing Temptations story, for it was announced they were to induct the group into the Rock & Roll Hall of Fame, an event that filled some with trepidation since it meant all members of the group would be in attendance at the Waldorf-Astoria to receive their mementos. The evening passed without incident, with amicable hugs and handshakes all round. Immediately after the show, David and Eddie put the finishing touches to their planned tour with Dennis Edwards, drafting in David Shea and Nate Evans to round out a vocal group that was intended to spend some three years or so out on the road, often dovetailing with the other Temptations.

There were still legal battles to contend with, with David falling foul of the law for violating his parole, possession of a fire arm and being caught with drugs, resulting in him appearing in court almost as regularly as he appeared on stage. Yet when he was off drugs, he was looking forward to touring, as he would tell journalist Spencer Leigh.

"We have a nine-piece band that is travelling with us. We have three background singers and we dance as well as ever. We all have our solo spots where we do our own songs. If I can get up there and I can make someone forget about his troubles, then that makes me feel great, that I have accomplished something. I am sure that we will all get together one time as The Temptations before it is all over and done with, one more time again. It will not be for making money, but just for singing and harmonising together."

Unfortunately, David would not get together with The Temptations for one last time. Instead, the money he made touring with Eddie and Dennis went the way of all previous money he had earned, buying ever increasing amounts of drugs. Wary promoters had guaranteed there were enough clauses in any and all contracts to ensure that if David was a no-show at any of the concerts, the others wouldn't get paid. Sure enough, David would do his disappearing act, failing to turn up at a venue on time and leave Eddie and Dennis to perform for free.

If David wasn't earning he found other ways to raise money for drugs, once selling a Lincoln Continental he had borrowed from his latest girlfriend for just $20. Somehow, the three former singers of the Temptations kept their professional relationship going into 1991, securing a number of dates throughout Europe. Surprisingly, Eddie and Dennis agreed to David acting as manager for the tour, with the added responsibility of collecting the money that was due at the end of each performance. Not surprisingly, none of the money found its way into Eddie or Dennis' pockets, with David putting them off by telling them he didn't have it on him and he would settle later when an advance for an album and book came through.

Eddie and Dennis returned to the United States penniless, whilst David remained in Europe for a while. He returned to Philadelphia in May 1991 with, it was said, some $40,000 of traveller's cheques in his briefcase. A few days later, on 1 June, David got into a stretch limo that had been lent by a friend and was driven to a well-known crack house in West Philadelphia. How long he remained there and how many vials he smoked has been the subject of considerable speculation (partly due, of course, since those who were present that evening did not want to get involved in the subsequent police enquiry), but shortly before three in the morning, the limo pulled up at the University of Pennsylvania Hospital, where the driver helped the orderlies carry David's unconscious body into the emergency room. Since the body carried no identification and only $53 in the pockets, the only clue as to his identity was the driver's shouted observation that it was 'David Ruffin of The Temptations.'

Despite three hours of treatment in the emergency room, David Ruffin never regained consciousness, with a subsequent autopsy giving the cause of death as 'an adverse reaction to drugs', namely cocaine. Since there was no identification, it took some time to confirm that the body lying in the hospital was that of David Ruffin; the briefcase, along with the traveller's cheques, was never found. The funeral and burial were delayed because no one in the Ruffin family had the money, but Michael Jackson stepped in and agreed to cover the entire $7,000 bill; Davis Eli Ruffin was finally laid to rest on 11 June 1991.

ALBUMS: MY WHOLE WORLD ENDED (1969), FEELIN' GOOD (1969), I AM MY BROTHER'S KEEPER (1970), DAVID RUFFIN (1973), ME & ROCK 'N' ROLL ARE HERE TO STAY (1974), WHO I AM (1975), EVERYTHING'S COMING UP LOVE (1976), IN MY STRIDE (1976)
COMPILATION: AT HIS BEST (1978)

JIMMY RUFFIN

If David Ruffin had talent and for the most part wasted it, then sibling Jimmy had talent but it was under exploited, at least whilst at Motown, due in his words to, "I think that they just didn't like me personally. I'm outspoken, I wasn't part of the clique."

Born in Collinsville, Mississippi on 7 May 1939 to Eli and Ophelia Ruffin, Jimmy helped set up a family gospel group with his siblings Quincy, Rita Mae and, eventually youngest brother Davis (who would later become better known as David Ruffin) by the name The Spiritual Trying Four. Like his brother David, the call of gospel music was strong, although not necessarily strong enough to prompt Jimmy to want to continue with it in his later years.

"I never wanted to be a professional singer. I wasn't ambitious - it was just that I loved singing. My father sang in a gospel group and I would hear him and my older brother and these teenage guys practicing at our house when I was seven or eight and I decided I wanted to do that. Then later I heard Mahalia Jackson. We had no electricity in our home so I would hear records at other people's houses and at the local juke joint - a bar where you'd have gospel music on the juke box but also blues, and rhythm and blues."

Both Jimmy and David flew the family nest around 1955, with David heading for Detroit via Memphis and Hot Springs and Jimmy enlisting into the military, although this did not mean an end to his musical career.

"I joined the military and I was still singing gospel and R&B. When I was about twenty I started singing with a group touring the US service clubs in Europe. At that time I was going to make a career of the army and was about to re-enlist, when the woman who booked the acts said I should turn professional. We had little plastic recorders in the military so that you could send a message back home. I recorded myself playing guitar and singing Sam Cooke's *She Was Only Sixteen*. I played it back and darn if I didn't sound better than Sam! We had a guy in our group used to play with a professional outfit called The Spaniards, and he couldn't sing worth a damn - I knew I sang better than him. So I began to think maybe I could do it."

It took some time for Jimmy to do anything about his singing career, for following his exit from the army he returned home to Mississippi for some eight to ten months, although he spoke regularly to David, who was beginning to make a bit of a name for himself up in Detroit and encouraged Jimmy to follow him, especially with a new record label also beginning to make a few worthwhile noises.

"He convinced me to come up to Detroit, and I finally went, because I had family there."

Jimmy didn't find a deal immediately, but he did find work singing at the local Ebony Club in Muskegon, something of a residency that only increased his reputation around the state. Everyone he met thought he had a talent, one that he should take down to Berry Gordy at Motown, although there were other offers supposedly in the pipeline.

"My brother kept insisting that I audition. So after I auditioned for the record companies and everybody wanted to sign me, finally I ended up going down to Motown after some encouragement from certain people like Mary Wells and Marv Johnson. Well, I didn't necessarily want to be discovered but I went and sang for Ronnie White of Smokey Robinson and The Miracles. He called in Ray Gordy, the wife of Berry Gordy. She heard me and she called up Berry and he came over. He rushed into the room, I sang and he was beaming and said, 'We'll sign him up and record everything he's got.'"

Although Jimmy's vocal style was reminiscent of Jackie Wilson, one thing Jimmy had that Jackie didn't was the ability to write his own songs, beginning with both sides of what would be his first single for the company, *Don't Feel Sorry For Me* backed with *Heart*. Issued as the very first release on the newly inaugurated Miracle label and produced by Raynoma Liles (the very first Motown connected record that hadn't been produced by Berry Gordy), the single did little, and despite Berry's earlier claim that they would record everything Jimmy had, it would be another two and a half years before he had anything else released.

"I recorded bits and pieces, but I didn't have any releases. I was working for Ford Motor Company and playing in Detroit on weekends. At one period I was playing guitar with my brother before The Temptations. I was like his musical director. Sometimes I had to take a leave of absence from Ford for a week to play theatres like the Apollo, and tour with the Motortown Revue."

Jimmy also continued writing, penning a number of songs that would be recorded by the Four Hollidays on Master and Markie (some sources state that Jimmy was a member of the group for those recordings but this is highly unlikely – he may have helped out in the studio on the actual recordings, but no known picture of the group from the period in question features Jimmy Ruffin in the line-up). Whilst he couldn't get a release under his own name, he did get to appear on a number of other sessions at Hitsville.

"All the time I spent with Motown the nearest I came to making records was helping on other people's sessions. The studio men hired me to snap my fingers, clap my hands and stomp feet, so I used to go along and get a couple of dollars for an hour's work."

Jimmy finally got a little bit longer in the studio in June 1964, working with Norman Whitfield on *Since I've Lost You* and *I Want Her Love*, which would be released the following month as only the second single release on another new label, Soul Records. Although Norman got the writer and production credit for the top side, Jimmy did more than just sing on the recording.

"We wrote that, actually, I didn't get credited for it. The song was originally called 'They Call Me Mr Blue'. I'm the one that changed [a line] to 'My life is so blue'. It wasn't a big record, but it let me know I had a commercial sound."

Of course, Jimmy was still trying to juggle a full time job at Ford with a singing career, although fate was about to lend a hand and decide the matter one way or another once and for all.

"I had a back injury that kept me off work (at Ford). So I thought I'd use that year to see if I could make it as a singer."

Whilst Jimmy pondered whether he would make it as a singer, others were convinced he had what it took, even if he might have to join a group in order to fulfil all of his ambitions. There is some confusion as to whether or not he was ever offered a place in The Temptations as a replacement for Al Bryant; Jimmy says the position was offered to him but he turned it down, Otis Williams says the role was never offered to Jimmy, only David.

Jimmy had his own reasons for declining any offer from The Temptations, much the same reason he would give when it was suggested that he join The Contours; if he was going to make it, it would be as a solo performer, not as a member of a group. As it turned out, Jimmy made the right decision, for his solo career was about to take off.

"*As Long As There's L-O-V-E Love* was a smash in Detroit. *Brokenhearted* came out [next] and that was it. I didn't go back to the motor company, I can tell you that!"

Penned by Smokey Robinson, *As Long As There Is L-O-V-E Love* deserved to be a smash outside of Detroit too, having to be content with hitting #120 pop, but everyone at Motown felt they were getting closer with Jimmy, himself included. There was still a while to wait, for *What Becomes Of The Brokenhearted* was originally written with The Spinners in mind, subsequently assigned to Ivy Hunter and then purloined by Jimmy. He recorded his lead vocal in November 1965, strings were added the following February and then Motown left it in the can, even going so far as to severely truncate a spoken intro and replace it with a musical one. It was finally released in June 1966, after thirteen different mixes were tried out, but the one that was issued hit all the right spots, peaking at #6 R&B, #7 pop and sailing into the British Top Ten for good measure. The success of *Brokenhearted* not only enabled Jimmy to permanently pack in his job at Ford, it made him into something of a star, a daunting prospect.

"The pressure is incredible. Suddenly you're moving up in society, going to places you're not really prepared for – beyond your own race, culture and class, your own country. I was pretty well grounded, I'd got a philosophy of life from my grandmother. I'm an observer, not a joiner, so I didn't participate in the drugs except in a minor way – I don't like being out of my mind. So I survived. I may not have had as much celebrity as people like Marvin Gaye but I'm still here."

The same team who had provided *Brokenhearted* put together the follow-up *I've Passed This Way Before*, utilising many of the same ingredients that had made its predecessor so successful, including the spoken intro, although this time around Jimmy was unhappy about that part of the song.

"I'll never feel comfortable with that, 'cause they took the talking part off *What Becomes Of The Brokenhearted*. Now with *I've Passed This Way Before*, I thought, 'What am I doing this for? They're going to take it off.' So I did it with no conviction."

Except they kept it on, allowing the single to go nearly as far as its predecessor, peaking at #10 R&B, #17 pop and #29 in the UK. Despite the success, Jimmy would later claim those two hits were too similar.

"The problem was that everyone then expected my records to all sound the same. The next couple were just extensions of *Brokenhearted*, and I had become typecast."

Jimmy's recollections don't quite tally with what was to come, for there was to be a switch of writer and producer for his next single, with *Gonna Give Her All The Love I've Got* hooking Jimmy up with Norman Whitfield, a long time friend. Also joining them in the studio was Barrett Strong, who had returned to Motown after a spell recording elsewhere. Both the top and flip side, *World So Wide, Nowhere To Hide (From Your Heart)* (which was written by James Dean and William Weatherspoon) featured on Jimmy's long time coming debut album, **Jimmy Ruffin Sings Top Ten** finally appearing in January 1967, a month before the extracted single (the album would be released in the UK under the title **The Jimmy Ruffin Way** and hit #32 on the chart).

Whilst the album made a fleeting chart appearance (#133 on the pop chart), the single continued his rich streak of form, hitting #14 R&B, #29 pop and #26 in the UK. With success came continued requests for live performances, with Jimmy out on the road for much of the time.

"The only enjoyment was in the performing. There was a lot of learning the business, learning how to perform - Marvin Gaye never thought he was any good. I'd done it in the military so it was okay for me. In the early days with The Temptations you'd go by station wagon with your bags tied on top. There'd be six of us and we'd drive up to Baltimore then on to Washington and New York and Chicago and on and on. I could drive but I said I couldn't - man, I didn't want that responsibility. By the time I toured with The Supremes we'd progressed to going by coach. Well, Mary and Florence and I went by coach - Diana never took the bus. The problem there was that I was too good. They were headlining but I got the standing ovations - so they took me off the tour."

Jimmy may have been off the tour but he was still on the chart, with Norman and Barrett bringing in Roger Penzabene to help craft *Don't You Miss Me A Little Baby*, a smaller hit when it reached #27 R&B and #68 pop. Jimmy was back working with James and William (along with Stephen Bowden) for his next outing but somehow *I'll Say Forever My Love* missed the mark, stopping at #77 pop when it seemed destined to go further. *Don't Let Him Take Your Love From Me* slipped even further down the listings, stalling at #113, a mark that proved beyond *Gonna Keep On Tryin' Till I Win Your Love*, released in October 1968. Despite the relative failure of his recent singles, Motown issued a second album in February 1969, with **Ruff 'N' Ready** sneaking into the pop chart at #196 and hitting #50 R&B.

Jimmy also got to record an album with David, **I Am My Brother's Keeper**, although the idea behind the album and the sessions for it were somewhat stressful, at least for Jimmy.

"Just something I wanted to do as an ode to my family. That's why there's a picture of my mother and father on the back. I got those pictures together. David, that's the time when he was into the cocaine, and I had to twist his arm to get him to do that. I had to first convince the company to do it, and then try and convince him."

Aside from *He Ain't Heavy He's My Brother*, the album also included a revival of Ben E King's *Stand By Me*.

"I had to do most of the singing on the end of it, 'cause he never showed up for the session. He wasn't that crazy about doing it. He didn't show up for the session, and Frank [Wilson] had me doing all the singing at the end that David was supposed to be doing."

Despite the presence of two star names, the album and single struggled for wider acceptance, with the album reaching no further than #15 R&B and #178 pop and the *Stand By Me* single #25 R&B and #61 pop. Yet in among the disappointments, Jimmy's career was about to take off quite spectacularly, only it was on the other side of the Atlantic, in Britain, that he was to enjoy the biggest hits of his career.

It began with a reissue of *I've Passed This Way Before*, a single that had already been a minor Top Thirty hit in the UK but which almost matched its performance the second time around when it peaked at #33. Whilst Motown in the US concentrated on promoting Jimmy and his brother David's **I Am My Brother's Keeper** album, their counterparts in Britain pulled *Farewell Is A Lonely Sound* off as a single. It had been a minor US hit when released, peaking at #104, so no one held out much hope that it would do much better in the UK. Instead, it heralded something of an annus mirabilis as far as Jimmy Ruffin in Britain was concerned, peaking at #8 and prompting Tamla Motown to line-up *I'll Say Forever My Love*, which had missed out on chart honours the first time around as a follow-up. This time it hit the Top Ten, peaking at #7.

Emboldened with the success they were enjoying selecting their own singles, Tamla Motown kept the run going. Despite the presence of a new Jimmy Ruffin album in America (**The Groove Governor**), in Britain Tamla Motown hadn't quite finished mining **Ruff 'N' Ready** for singles, resulting in *It's Wonderful (To Be Loved By You)* becoming his third Top Ten hit in a row, peaking at #6. Ignored domestically, Jimmy was revered internationally, prompting something of an upheaval.

"I just came to England because there was work. I moved because I was very popular in England and I'd benched my record company. I was too aware of the game and sometimes I didn't agree and I would say no so we didn't always see eye to eye. Plus I'm an ex-soldier, trained since the age of 16 to react aggressively in certain situations. In America those situations arise quite often. London is much more laid back."

There was plenty of work for Jimmy, who became a regular performer across the country at all manner of venues, adding to his already legendary status. A couple of old singles slipped out on both sides of the Atlantic (including the aptly titled *On The Way Out* in the UK), but nothing set the chart alight, at least until 1974. Jimmy was still touring on a regular basis when Tamla Motown decided the time was right for a career retrospective, with **Greatest Hits** going on to hit #41 on the chart. Needing a single to help promote the album, the company re-released *What Becomes Of The Brokenhearted*, which became an even bigger smash the second time around and hit #4. Even *Farewell Is A Lonely Sound* hit again, peaking at #30.

All the activity on his old Motown material enabled Jimmy to get a new deal, signing with Polydor in the UK and scoring a Top 40 hit with his own composition *Tell Me What You Want*. Six years later, Jimmy would return to the British chart with his collaboration with The Bee Gees and *Hold On To My Love*. Over the ensuing years he would continue to work in Britain, linking with Paul Weller and The Style Council on a benefit single and also with Heaven 17 and also hosted his own radio show for the BBC.

ALBUMS: SINGS TOP TEN (1967), RUFF 'N' READY (1969), I AM MY BROTHER'S KEEPER (1970), THE GROOVE GOVERNOR (1970), JIMMY RUFFIN...FOREVER (1973)

COMPILATIONS: GREATEST HITS (1974), 20 GOLDEN CLASSICS (1980)

RUNAWAY CHILD, RUNNING WILD – THE TEMPTATIONS [SINGLE]

Norman Whitfield had taken The Temptations on a completely new direction with *Cloud Nine* and was keen to continue the experimentation with their future material. The second such venture was *Runaway Child, Running Wild*, a song that began life with the working title *Don't Let The Joneses Get You Down*. Whilst Barrett Strong busied himself with the song's lyrics, which dealt with the problem of runaways, Norman was in the studio with his ever-expanding crew of musicians laying down the music. It was to be something of a turning point for The Temptations, with the track eventually clocking in at 9.38 minutes (the resulting **Cloud Nine** album would feature only three tracks on the first side), with even the single edit amounting to 4.30 minutes, the longest Motown single to date.

There are some who have noticed some barbed comments in the song aimed towards David Ruffin, whose acrimonious departure from The Temptations was supposedly the inspiration for the sentiments expressed in his *My Whole World Ended (The Moment You Left Me)* and *I've Lost Everything I Ever Loved* (this theme would later be revisited when Eddie Kendricks left the group, with The Temptations' *Superstar* being a much more direct attack on Eddie and David), but whilst Norman Whitfield is often held as the instigator of these subtle attacks, it was Barrett Strong who wrote most of the lyrics.

Irrespective of whether it was an attack or not, *Runaway Child Running Wild* was released in January 1969 and two months later hit the top of the R&B chart. It would also sail into the Top Ten of the pop listing, finally coming to rest at #6. A short while later, Earl Van Dyke recorded an instrumental version (unlike earlier Earl Van Dyke singles, this was not an overdubbed version of the original but a specially recorded version with Norman Whitfield still in the producer's chair) which would go on to reach #114 on the pop chart. Neither version, however, made an impression in the UK, where The Temptations' original was held back until October 1969 and Earl Van Dyke's version passed over for release. Never one to let anything go to waste, Norman Whitfield would later revive the title *Don't Let The Joneses Get You Down* for The Temptations.

RUNNING WITH THE NIGHT – LIONEL RICHIE [SINGLE]

The second single to be lifted from Lionel Richie's Grammy Award winning album **Can't Slow Down**, *Running With The Night* was co-written by Lionel with Cynthia Weil, best known for her compositions with her husband Barry Mann. Lionel and his co-producer James Anthony Carmichael assembled a veritable who's who of session musicians to help out on the track, including famed percussionist Paulinho Da Costa and two members of Toto, Jeff Porcaro on drums and Steve Lukather on guitar.

When Steve arrived at the Oceanway Recording Studios, he was played the basic backing tracks in order to get a feel of the song and plan what he was going to play. As the music played, he jammed along on guitar, effectively making it up as he went along. When the track finished he told James Anthony Carmichael that he was ready to record a take, only to discover that the tape had been running all a long and what they had recorded was perfect for the song!

Timed at just over six minutes for the album version, the track was edited for single release (losing much of Steve Lukather's guitar solo) and released in November 1983 in both the UK and US. It would power its way into the Top Ten on both sides of the Atlantic, hitting #7 in the US (and also peaking at #6 on the R&B and Adult Contemporary chart) and #9 in the UK.

RUSTIX

Rock group Rustix was formed in Rochester, New York in 1966 by Al Galich (vocals), Chuck Brucato (vocals), Bob D'Andrea (guitar), Kit Nelson (bass), Vinnie Strenk (keyboards) and Bobby Blando (drums) and recorded a couple of singles for Columbia and Cadet in 1968 with little more than local success. Then in 1969 word got out that Motown was launching a rock label and was on the lookout for bands, with Rustix' management submitting a tape and getting a deal with Rare Earth in short order.

By this time the group consisted of Galich, Brucato, D'Andrea, Strenk, Ron Collins (bass) and David Colon (drums). Produced by R. Dean Taylor, their 1969 debut **Bedlam** featured a mix of Chuck Brucato songs with both rock and Jobete standards, including the now obligatory *I Heard It Through The Grapevine,* although the band was unhappy that the label added strings to several tracks without their knowledge, thus altering their overall sound. **Bedlam** did spend two weeks at the lowest possible chart placing, #200 on the main pop listings, although none of the singles shifted.

A second album, again produced by R. Dean Taylor followed in 1970, although **Come On People** failed to chart even though the overall sound was more to Rustix' liking. A third album was recorded in 1971 but left on the shelf, although two singles both of which featured Brucato and Galich backed with the Funk Brothers were scheduled; *My Piece Of Heaven* being unreleased and *We All End Up In Boxes*, produced by Mike Valvano, being issued in September 1971. After that the group disbanded, reforming for a one-off concert in 1979.

ALBUMS: BEDLAM (1969), COME ON PEOPLE (1970)

IRENE RYAN

Born Jessie Irene Noblitt in El Paso, Texas on 17 October 1902, Irene made her name in vaudeville and on radio with her first husband Tim Ryan, developing an act that proved popular between the wars. After divorcing Tim, Irene toured with Bob Hope and made regular appearances on radio and in films. Her television break came in 1955 when she appeared in several long running shows, but it was winning the role of Daisy 'Granny' Moses in 1962, the matriarch of the Clampett family in 'The Beverly Hillbillies', that ensured her lasting fame and popularity and earned her two Emmy nominations for Best Series Actress.

When the series eventually came to an end in 1971, even though it was still a rating's winner, Irene helped to create and star in the Broadway musical 'Pippin' as Berthe, picking up a Tony Award nomination for Best Performance by a Featured Actress. It was also this role that led to her Motown involvement, with the cast recording album being released in December 1972 and Motown also releasing two singles by Irene, *No Time At All* and *I See Your Name Up In Lights* in April 1973. These were effectively released as something of a tribute to Irene, for at the beginning of April she suffered a stroke during a performance, flew home to California to undergo an operation for a brain tumour and died on 26 April 1973.

S

SAIL ON – THE COMMODORES [SINGLE]

Lionel Richie had drawn inspiration from his parents' wedding anniversary for *Three Times A Lady*, the stand out hit from The Commodores' **Natural High** album. By the time he and the rest of the group gathered to discuss material for the follow-up album **Midnight Magic**, it was the break-up of two marriages that had inspired him to write *Sail On* and *Still,* which in turn would be the major hits from the resulting album.

The first of these, *Sail On*, was the result of listening at length as long time friend Walter 'Smitty' Smith detailed the breakdown of his marriage and the effect it had had on him. They talked long and hard throughout the night before parting company the following morning. Some six months later, before the album hit the streets, Lionel sent Smitty a copy of the song, which included the phrase 'Sail On', something the pair had discussed at length.

The inspiration proved irresistible when committed to record, with Motown releasing the single in May 1979, two months before the album was issued. Once again it proved Lionel to be the master of the soul ballad, powering its way to #4 R&B and #8 pop, matching that chart placing when it was issued in the UK in August 1979.

PHYLLIS ST JAMES

A talented songwriter whose work has been recorded by artists as diverse as Norman Connors, Jean Carn, Rodney Franklin and The Jones Girls, Phyllis' own solo career at Motown went no further than a lone album and single release. Born Phyllis Yvonne Williams, she began her career as a backing singer, appearing on countless sessions before getting a very brief recording deal with Playboy Records, who issued her single with La Mancha *Get Happy* and *Peace In Mind* (both co-produced by former Motown staffer Mickey Stevenson with Don Mancha) in 1975.

Phyllis resumed her career as a backing singing and writing until her next deal, signing with Motown in 1984. The label released the album **Ain't No Turning Back** in August 1984, also issuing Phyllis' compositions *Candlelight Afternoon* backed with *Back In The Race* as a single. When both failed to sell, Phyllis returned to doing backing work and becoming an actress on several television series.

ALBUM: AIN'T NO TURNIN' BACK (1984)

SALVATION RECORDS

A subsidiary label of Creed Taylor's CTI organisation, Salvation was originally conceived as a gospel label and issued a little known album by the B.C. & M. Choir in 1972 that also featured the participation of CTI regulars Hank Crawford and Don Sebesky. Two years later Taylor revived the label but switched musical styles to the same kind of jazz that CTI and Kudu were releasing, the only difference being that Creed Taylor did not have a hand in the production of any of the albums.

Johnny Hammond's **Gambler's Life** album, for instance, was largely written and produced by the Mizell brothers Larry and Fonce and Freddie Perren and thus similar in style to the material they recorded with Donald Byrd, whilst other artists who recorded for the revived label were Airto, the New York Jazz Quartet and Gabor Szabo. The Salvation label disappeared with the dissolution of CTI's distribution deal at Motown, but was revived briefly in the 1990s for one album by gospel singer Faith Howard.

THE SAN REMO GOLDEN STRINGS

Teenager Bob Wilson spent countless hours hanging around Hitsville in 1964, initially with his own group and then after they had disbanded on his own. A talented pianist, Bob was well liked around the studio, with Mickey Stevenson in particular letting him loose on the studio piano in between sessions. Unfortunately, however, there wasn't a particular opening for a white teenage pianist at Motown at that time, so although some material was demoed there was little or no prospect of a recording deal.

Eventually Bob's friend Pat Lewis told him he might have better luck at one of the rival Detroit studios, in particular Ed Wingate's Golden World label. Bob duly presented himself to Ed, who was impressed enough with his piano playing to christen him 'the white Ramsey Lewis' and set him to work as a session musician, also letting him record material for his own album.

Utilising an old friend in Richie Ries on drums, Bob Babbitt on bass and Wild Bill Emerson on guitar, with the arrangements handled by Sonny Sanders (of The Satintones), the initial recordings were rounded out by Charlie Gabriel on saxophone on a track they called *Hungry For Love*. The track was credited to Bob Wilson & The San Remo Quartet (the inspiration for San Remo came from the holiday resort on the Italian Riviera where Ed and JoAnne Bratton had holidayed in 1965) and was originally pressed as the flip side to Barbara Mercer's Golden World single *The Things We Do Together*.

The intention had been to ensure that half of the royalties remained in-house, but when radio stations began picking up on the instrumental by Bob Wilson and ignoring the vocal top-side, Ed recalled the single and decided to release *Hungry For Love* in its own right on Ric-Tic in August 1965. The group for the top side was re-christened The San Remo Golden Strings, with Bob getting a name-check on the flip side *All Turned On*, another track that was due for release on Bob's forthcoming album. The single became a Top 30 pop hit (it peaked at #27), but before Ed could capitalise on its success, Bob Wilson had departed for Sound 7 Stage Records (with Ed's blessing).

In his place came assorted members of the Detroit Symphony Orchestra and moonlighting Funk Brothers, who duly recorded a follow-up hit in *I'm Satisfied* (#89 pop) and the album **Hungry For Love** which was released in 1966. The 'group' also created something of a stir with *Festival Time*, released in April 1966, but before long Berry Gordy had acted to remove the thorn in the side that was Golden World and Ric-Tic and snapped up both labels and their respective rosters.

Hungry For Love would be re-issued on the Gordy label (with a different sleeve but the same track listing) in August 1967, and a year later came a new album by the San Remo Golden Strings, **San Remo Swings** produced by Gil Askey and Larry Maxwell, although the album was a mix of both old and new tracks.

There the San Remo Golden Strings story might have ended, but in 1971 Tamla Motown in the UK released *Festival Time* after repeated requests from the Northern Soul fraternity and were rewarded with a #39 pop hit in November 1971 (credited to the truncated San Remo Strings). The success of that single prompted the release of their version of *Reach Out (I'll Be There)* on single in March 1972 and the **San Remo Strings Swing** album in January 1973.

ALBUMS: HUNGRY FOR LOVE (1967), SAN REMO STRINGS SWING (1968)

THE SATINTONES

Collectively and individually, The Satintones appear frequently in the early Motown history, being the first male vocal group signed and having released the first single on the Motown label. For the most part, however, their early contribution has been largely overlooked, not least because they failed to register a hit and the one single that might have given them a presence became the subject of one of Motown's first legal challenges.

Initially formed in Detroit, Michigan in 1957 by James Ellis, William 'Sonny' Sanders (born in Chicago, Illinois on 6 August 1939), Charles 'Chico' Leverett and Robert Bateman, all four would eventually end up at Hitsville, with Robert Bateman also doubling as a member of The Rayber Voices and Chico recording solo. Chico's debut single *Solid Sender* appeared on the Tamla label in April 1959, followed three months later by The Satintones debut *Going To The Hop*, co-written by Berry and Chico. Berry and Chico were joined by Robert Bateman for the group's next single, the very first released on the Motown label, although *My Beloved* was initially released in a version without strings in October 1959. The success enjoyed by The Drifters and *There Goes My Baby*, which did feature a string section, prompted Berry to revisit several Motown and Tamla recordings, with *My Beloved* being reissued in April 1960 with a string section, although neither version made any real impression.

Chico Leverett left the group at this point, with Vernon Williams and Sammy Mack being drafted in his place. The Satintones' next single, *Tomorrow And Always* was also issued in two versions, with and without strings, but it was also the single that attracted Motown's first writ. Initial copies that were released (without strings) claimed the song was written by Robert Bateman, Janie Bradford, Carole King and Gerry Goffin, the latter two names being added in recognition that *Tomorrow And Always* was intended as an answer record to The Shirelles' *Will You Love Me Tomorrow*. Originally released in April 1961, a version with strings was released the following month, but less than a week later Motown received a writ from Aldon Music, the publishing company responsible for Goffin and King's original work. Claiming that *Tomorrow And Always* was not so much an answer record as a blatant copy of *Will You Love Me Tomorrow*, the Motown single was hastily withdrawn, although a month later the same catalogue number was reused for The Satintones new single, *Angel*.

One month on and Motown tried again, this time with *I Know How It Feels* which featured Vernon Williams on lead vocals. There was to be one further Satintones single, *Zing Went The Strings Of My Heart* being a cover version (and properly credited as such as well) that also failed, resulting in the album **The Satintones Sing** being pulled from the release schedule.

The group disbanded soon after, with Robert Bateman initially working in and around Hitsville as a writer and producer (he helped The Marvelettes hit #1 with *Please Mr. Postman*) before heading off to New York. Sonny Sanders meanwhile worked with Carl Davis at Brunswick/Dakar in Chicago as both a writer and arranger, helping craft hits for the likes of The Chi-Lites, Barbara Acklin, Jackie Wilson and The Impressions. The group reformed in 1990 to re-record some of their tracks for Ian Levine and his group of labels.

SAVE THE CHILDREN (SOUNDTRACK)

The brainchild of The Reverend Jesse Jackson, Operation PUSH (originally People United to Save Humanity but subsequently amended to People United to Serve Humanity) was launched on 25 December 1971, with a Black Exposition at Chicago's Amphitheater being staged the following year. Alongside arts, crafts and commerce (all of which would be featured in the resulting documentary film) a welter of top musical stars lent their support to the Exposition, culminating in more than 30 artists from across several musical genres performing live.

Both the documentary film and the accompanying soundtrack took their name from Marvin Gaye's *Save The Children*, a track featured on his landmark album **What's Going On** (also released as a single in the UK, with some success), with the film being written and produced by Matt Robinson, directed by Stan Lathan and executive produced by Clarence Avant. The film was screened in 1973, with the double album soundtrack being released on Motown in April 1974.

Featuring The Reverend Jess Jackson and Matt Jackson on narration and dialogue, the album also featured Marvin Gaye, The Temptations, Gladys Knight & The Pips and The Jackson 5 from within the Motown family and The Main Ingredient, The O'Jays, Zulema, Cannonball Adderley, The Reverend James Cleveland, Bill Withers, Curtis Mayfield, Sammy Davis Jr., Roberta Flack and Quincy Jones, Jerry Butler and Brenda Lee Eager, The Ramsey Lewis Trio, Nancy Wilson and Jackie Verdell from without. The album achieved a modicum of success, hitting #38 on the R&B chart.

PAM SAWYER

Ordinarily, there would be little or nothing to connect Romford in Essex with Detroit, although the close proximity of Dagenham and the Ford car assembly part is a somewhat tenuous link. However, Romford did supply one of the chief Motown songwriters of the late 1960s and early 1970s in Pam Sawyer.

Pam married visiting American musician and producer Bob Mersey and moved to New York in the early 1960s where she made her home and started a family. When the marriage ended in divorce, Pam opted to remain in the United States and turned to songwriting, initially with Helen Miller for Patty Michaels. Pam then linked with Lori Burton and created the Whyte Boots project, with Lori singing the material she and Pam wrote. It was their writing, however, that established their names, with Lulu scoring a UK hit with *Try To Understand* and Patti LaBelle & The Bluebelles and the Young Rascals scoring in the US with *All Or Nothing* and *I Ain't Gonna Eat Out My Heart Anymore* respectively.

Having achieved success within the R&B field, Pam and Lori collared Berry Gordy at a BMI awards event and asked for an audition; he arranged for Holland-Dozier-Holland to fly into New York to listen to their work and they were signed almost immediately. Initially they would submit their songs to Jobete via mail and make the occasional appearance in Detroit, but this process proved too slow for Lori who eventually handed back her contract.

Pam would be teamed with a variety of other writers, most notably Leon Ware (*If I Ever Lose This Heaven* and *Just Seven Numbers*), Gloria Jones (*If I Was Your Woman* and *The Zoo*), Michael Masser (*Last Time I Saw Him* and *Sorry Doesn't Always Make It Right*) and Marilyn McLeod (*Love Hangover*). Pam was also a member of The Clan and the lyricist who came up with the basic idea for *Love Child* and would follow it with *I'm Living In Shame*. Twice nominated for a Grammy Award (Best R&B Song for *If You Were My Woman* and *Love Hangover*), Pam remained with Motown until 1981 upon which she formed her own Pam Sawyer Productions and Barley Lane Music companies.

SAY YOU, SAY ME – LIONEL RICHIE [SINGLE]

Motown had won the Academy Award for Best Original Song in 1984 with Stevie Wonder's *I Just Called To Say I Love You* from 'Woman In Red'. Twelve months later another Motown song, *Say You Say Me* by Lionel Richie ensured a second consecutive win.

Lionel was approached by film director Taylor Hackford to write the theme song to 'White Nights', a drama that was to star Mikhail Baryshnikov as a Russian dancer who has defected but whose plane from Tokyo makes a forced landing in Siberia. Having seen an early print of the film Lionel was keen to get involved, but several weeks into the process sent word via his manager that he was having problems writing a song around the title 'White Nights' but that he had another song that he thought might fit better into the film. When Taylor Hackford heard the song *Say You, Say Me* he agreed, although an over enthusiastic marketing executive at the film company included the demo version on a promotional package that was sent out to various radio stations. *Say You Say Me* was aired on a couple of these, even featuring on the charts thanks to the airplay that was generated in Chicago and the Midwest!

The second problem proved insurmountable. The soundtrack to 'White Nights' was to be issued on Atlantic, but permission for *Say You, Say Me* to be included was refused, Motown reluctant to allow Lionel's first solo single since his successful **Can't Slow Down** album appear on another label. To compensate Motown agreed to release the track as a single at the best possible time to promote the film, issuing it in November 1985 and seeing it become a pop and R&B chart topper in the US and a huge multi-national hit, topping the chart in several Scandinavian countries and reaching at the least the Top Ten across much of the rest of Europe. The single also gave Lionel something of an American chart record – he was the only songwriter (at that time) to have penned a number one hit in as many as nine consecutive years, stretching back to 1978's *Three Times A Lady*.

Unfortunately, whilst the single was an unqualified success, Lionel's own album was delayed and switched title from **Say You Say Me** to **Dancing On The Ceiling**, by which time the film had been and gone, with Columbia Pictures (the studio responsible for 'White Nights') stating that the delay coupled with the absence of the track from the soundtrack may not have hampered the film itself but did harm overall sales of the album.

More than adequate compensation was received at the Academy Awards, with *Say You Say Me* seeing off a strong field (including another song from 'White Nights' in *Separate Lives*) and winning the Oscar for Best Original Song. In 2012 the song enjoyed something of a revival of interest in the UK, with Lionel recording a parody version to accompany a television commercial for Walkers crisps, appearing in the commercial alongside former England footballer and Walkers long-standing frontman Gary Lineker.

SCHERRIE & SUSAYE

The last original Supremes member Mary Wilson made her exit from the group in December 1977, after which, to all intents and purposes, The Supremes officially came to an end. A few short months later, the two remaining members Susaye Greene (born in Houston, Texas on 13 September 1949) and Scherrie Payne (born in Detroit, Michigan on 14 November 1944) announced that the search was on for a replacement third member, with Joyce Vincent-Watson, a session singer best known for her work as a member of Tony Orlando & Dawn the likeliest candidate.

Eventually those plans floundered, due in part to Mary Wilson launching a lawsuit against Motown as she owned at least 50% of the rights to the name The Supremes. With the lawsuit likely to take some time to settle or contest, Motown decided not to proceed with a new Supremes line-up. Instead, Susaye and Scherrie were offered a one-off album deal, which would give them the same degree of control (allowing them to write and act as associate producers) as had been promised for a new Supremes album.

Joyce Vincent-Watson did get to appear on the new album, but it was as a backing singer rather than as a

fully fledged partner. **Partners** was produced by Eugene McDaniels and featured a guest appearance by Ray Charles on the track *Love Bug,* with *Leaving Me Was The Best Thing You've Ever Done* released as the lead single in September 1979. A month later came the album, but Motown extended little promotional activity behind either, something of a disappointment as the album was critically well received as one of the precursors of the quiet storm genre. With the album contract duly completed, Scherrie and Susaye went their separate ways, with both also leaving Motown.
ALBUM: PARTNERS (1979)

LLOYD SCHOONMAKER

Born in Seattle, Washington in 1940, singing baritone for the Seattle Civic Opera Company fuelled a desire to pursue a musical career, with Lloyd moving to Oxnard in California in 1963 in order to get closer to where he thought it was happening musically. It happened slowly for him, with his first hit not coming until 1971 when *Fresno Blues* made it to #90 on the country charts, although he did have a degree of success as a writer.

It was in conjunction with Morton Downey Jr. that his career took something of an upward turn, with the pair writing a number of patriotic songs for a then forth-coming American Bicentennial record. Two years later Lloyd got a brief deal with Hitsville, releasing the single *She Gives Me Love*. By the end of the year Lloyd had switched labels to the MC imprint, where he would record an album with Rick Tucker, an eponymous effort due to be released in November 1977 but which is unlikely to have made it beyond the promotional pressing stage.

Lloyd then turned his back on music, becoming a teacher of mathematics at Haydock Junior High School, although he still carried traces of his earlier career into his lessons, wearing cowboy boots and long hair and peppering his algebra lessons with tales of the recording industry! After twenty five years Lloyd took a leave of absence to work again with Morton Downey, by then a successful television presenter.
ALBUM: TUCKER AND SCHOONMAKER (1977)

CHRISTINE SCHUMACHER

In 1966 Detroit radio station WKNR ran a talent competition on DJ Scott Regan's show entitled 'Record A Record With The Supremes'. The winner of the competiton was local blind high school girl Christine Schumacher, who was aged sixteen at the time of the contest. Christine was taken to the Golden World studios where she recorded her vocal to *Mother You, Smother You,* written by Holland-Dozier-Holland and R. Dean Taylor (the song was originally intended for Chris Clark). Although never intended for commercial release, Motown did press up copies for Christine to keep a permanent memento of her recording session with The Supremes as well as for the radio station to distribute as part of the promotion.

SCOTT JOPLIN (1977 FILM)

The 1977 biographical feature film on Scott Joplin reunited several actors who had almost become stock company with Motown Productions, most notably Billy Dee Williams. A star of 'Lady Sings The Blues', 'Mahogany' and 'Bingo Long', Billy was to take the lead role in 'Scott Joplin', originally a made for television film that also featured The Commodores in a cameo role as The Minstrel Singers. Produced as a joint venture between Universal Pictures and Motown Productions, the finished feature was considered good enough to release to film theatres ahead of its planned television airing. Although the film has a number of factual errors (or maybe someone took artistic licence), the film was considered a critical success. The accompanying soundtrack album, featuring Dick Hyman, was released by MCA.

JOEL SEBASTIAN

Radio DJ Joel Sebastian spent much of his career in Chicago, but it was his time in Detroit on WXYZ that was responsible for getting him a one-off record deal with the Miracle label. According to legend, Berry Gordy offered him the deal in return for playing Motown records on air, with *Angel In Blue* being released in 1961. His recording career duly over, Joel went back to his radio work, working at stations in Dallas, New Haven and Los Angeles before moving to Chicago in 1966. He had a lengthy spell at WCFL, hosting the morning show and later becoming programme director. After a brief spell in New York he returned to Chicago in 1983 and joined WJMX before he died on 17 January 1986.

DON SEBESKY

Multi-instrumentalist Donald John Sebesky was born in Perth Amboy, New Jersey on 10 December 1937 and first came to prominence as a trombonist with Kai Winding, Maynard Ferguson, Stan Kenton and Tommy Dorsey. By the mid 1960s he had become equally well known as an arranger and conductor, working with Wes Montgomery, Jack Sheldon and Paul Desmond as well as George Benson and Herbie Mann. After recording two albums of jazz fusion in the late 1960s for Verve, Don became the house arranger for CTI Records, scoring albums for Hubert Laws, Jackie & Roy and Freddie Hubbard's Grammy Award winning **First Light** and recorded two albums under his own name, with his 1975 album **The Rape Of El Morro** being distributed by Motown.

ALBUM: THE RAPE OF EL MORRO (1975)

SEND ONE YOUR LOVE – STEVIE WONDER [SINGLE]

Stevie Wonder's **Secret Life Of Plants** might have been eagerly anticipated, not least because it was his first album of new material for some three years, but early indications following its release in October 1979 were not looking good. It did not help that the film for which it was the soundtrack never materialised, leaving the material to stand or fall on its own merits. Whilst the album was largely panned, there were still moments when the Stevie of old shone through, none more so than *Send One Your Love*. The lead single culled from the album, *Send One Your Love* did return Stevie to the upper echelons of the chart, at least in America, where it would peak at #4 pop and #5 R&B. In the UK, however, the single struggled for acceptance, failing to break into the Top 50 (it stalled at #52, as did the second single *Outside My Window*, with a third release, *Black Orchid* limping in even further behind at #63), his first major failure since *Superwoman* and *Keep On Running* had failed to chart at all.

KENNY SERATT

The son of a travelling minister, Kenny Seratt was born in Manila, Arkansas on 20 October 1934 and was raised in nearby Dyess. Thanks to his father, Kenny learned to sing in church, also accompanying himself on the guitar and dreamed early on of a career in music. He left home in 1951 at the age of 17 and settled in Hemet, California where his first job was as far away from music as it possibly could get, joining the Howard Rose Company as a horticulturist!

However, during the evenings Kenny became a regular at the country music nightspots and established a veritable reputation for himself, eventually leading to guest appearances on several radio stations. That in turn led to an opportunity to go professional, with Merle Haggard in particular offering him both encouragement and opportunity, with Kenny frequently touring with the elder statesman. It was Merle who produced Kenny's first chart hit, *Goodbye's Come Hard For Me* in 1972, along with two equally successful follow-ups.

In 1975 he signed with Motown, eventually releasing singles across all three of the country outlets the label controlled, Melodyland, Hitsville and MC and his only album, **Kenny Seratt,** released on MC in October 1977 (although there is some doubt as to whether the album was commercially available since only promotional copies have ever been located). Although his time with Motown wasn't as successful as his earlier efforts, he resumed his hit career upon leaving the label.

ALBUM: KENNY SERATT (1977)

THE SERENADERS

It is a still something of a mystery as to how The Serenaders missed out on major success, even more so during their time at Motown, for whilst many of their contemporaries had to wait for material from staff writers, The Serenaders were their own in-house writing team.

Originally formed in 1956, the main members of the group were George Kerr, Sidney Barnes and Timothy 'Andre' Wilson and made their first recordings for Chock Full of Hits in 1957, with *Never Let Me Go* getting picked up by MGM for national distribution. That and another MGM release went nowhere, with the group eventually recording for Cross Country and Rae-Cox before the decade was out.

In 1963 the group (Kerr, Barnes, Wilson and bass singer Howard Curry) auditioned for Raynoma Gordy at Jobete's New York office, who signed Barnes and Kerr as writers and sent the group down to Detroit to audition personally for Berry Gordy. Although they were duly signed and recorded some five tracks, only one single ever appeared, and that after a false start.

If Your Heart Says Yes was originally slated for release on Motown in July 1963 but subsequently got transferred over to the V.I.P. label and appeared in

January 1964. Despite featuring Elbridge Bryant and Eddie Kendricks of The Temptations as guest vocalists on both the top and flip side (*I'll Cry Tomorrow*), lack of promotion doomed the single right from the start. George Kerr and Sidney Barnes would remain signed as writers, although their greatest triumphs came with material placed outside of Motown before they eventually left and attempted to revive their careers elsewhere. Wilson, who married Raynoma's sister Alice in 1965, recorded as a solo artist for United Artists, George Kerr became a successful producer, most notably on Linda Jones, whilst Sidney Barnes made his name with Rotary Connection, Minnie Riperton and several of the acts associated with the Casablanca label, especially George Clinton's Parliament.

SHADEE

Composer, guitarist and producer Shadee Hasan was born in Mississippi and raised in Detroit. He joined Motown as a writer and arranger in the late 1960s and under the moniker Allen Story worked with Diana Ross & The Supremes, Martha Reeves, Marvin Gaye and Stevie Wonder, among others. Following Motown out to Hollywood the following decade, he finally got the chance to record an album under his own truncated name of Shadee, with Anna Gordy producing **I Just Need More Money**. Although not a hit, both the title track and *Disco Hall Of Fame* attracted interested from the burgeoning dance crowd.
ALBUM: I JUST NEED MORE MONEY (1979)

THE SHANGRI-LAS

American vocal group The Shangri-Las formed in New York in 1963 with two pairs of sisters: Mary (born in 1949) and Betty Weiss (born in 1947) and twins Mary Ann and Marge Ganser (born on 4 February 1948). They were discovered by George 'Shadow' Morton and first recorded for Spokane as The Bon Bons, issuing two singles before changing their name and signing with Red Bird. There they recorded a succession of hits, including *Remember (Walking In The Sand)*, *Leader Of The Pack* (which was banned by the BBC when first released because of the lyrical content of the record; it is basically the best example of what became known as 'the death disc' genre) and *Give Him A Big Kiss*. These three tracks found their way onto the soundtrack album to 'Girl Groups: The Story Of A Sound' released by Motown in 1983. Marge Ganser left the group in 1966. Mary Ann died from encephalitis on 14 March 1970, Marge died from breast cancer on 28 July 1996.

RALPH SHARON

Having made his professional debut in 1946, pianist Ralph Sharon has enjoyed the longest career of any Motown associated act. Born in London on 17 September 1923, Ralph began his career with Ted Heath's band before moving on to link up with Frank Weir and then form his own sextet. He emigrated to American in 1953 where he initially worked with Chris Connor and then in 1957 became musical director and pianist for Tony Bennett.
Whilst his work with Tony was undoubtedly a full time affair, Ralph (who became an American citizen in 1959) also recorded a number of albums under his own name, including his 1963 Gordy release **Modern Innovations On Country And Western Themes**, no doubt inspired by Ray Charles' experimentations in the same musical genre. Ralph would go on to enjoy a forty year working relationship with Tony Bennett (they parted company in 1965 but revived their relationship in 1979) and was responsible for crafting many Grammy award winning albums. Ralph continues to perform with the Ralph Sharon Trio in Denver, Colorado.
ALBUM: MODERN INNOVATIONS ON COUNTRY AND WESTERN THEMES (1963)

T.G. SHEPPARD

Whilst Motown made numerous attempts at breaking the country music market over the years, most notably with the Mel-ody, Hitsville, Melodyland and MC imprints, most were destined for failure. The company may have had significant success selling black music to white buyers on their Motown, Soul, Gordy and Tamla labels but selling white music to white buyers, especially country music, was often a bridge too far. There were one or two exceptions, of course, and none more so than T.G. Sheppard.
Born William Neal Browder in Humboldt, Tennessee on 20 July 1944 he ran away from home at the age of 15 looking to break into the music business in Memphis, adopting the name Brian Stacy for his first, unsuccessful attempt at a recording career. In 1974 he signed with Melodyland as T.G. Sheppard and released

his debut single in November 1974, *Devil In The Bottle*, written by Bobby David. By March the following year, the single had topped the country chart for one week and made #54 on the main pop chart. Just as the single reached its peak, the follow-up *Tryin' To Beat The Morning Home* was on its way up the chart, also topping the country chart but finishing a rather more modest #94 on the pop listing.

His eponymous debut album was also well received and provided some evidence that Motown was able to break an artist into the country market, hitting #12 on the listings. Unfortunately, *Tryin'* would prove to be the last of T.G. Sheppard's country chart topper's whilst at Motown, although he would return to the Top Ten with *Motel And Memories* (#7) and *Show Me A Man* (#8) and every one of his seven singles made the Top 20 at least. He would have one further pop hit too, with *Solitary Man* making #100 pop and #14 country in 1976, whilst the parent album **Motels And Memories** would hit #28 on the chart.

Shifted to the Hitsville label in 1976 after Motown had relinquished the rights to the Melodyland brand he saw something of a compilation album **Solitary Man** hit #16 on the chart and an extracted single *Another Woman* peak at #14. Sheppard bowed out of the company with *Lovin' On* in February 1977, a #20 country hit, subsequently signing with Warner Brothers and later Columbia, enjoying even greater success and eventually racking up 42 country hits between 1977 and 1991.

ALBUMS: T.G. SHEPPARD (1975), MOTELS AND MEMORIES (1976), SOLITARY MAN (1976)
COMPILATION: NASHVILLE HITMAKER (1977)

SU SHIFRIN

Sue Linda Shifrin was born in Miami, Florida on 16 April 1949 and quickly came to prominence as a songwriter, with the likes of Cher, Meatloaf, Cliff Richard, Tina Turner, Al Jarreau and Teddy Pendergrass having recorded her material.

Her own recording career commenced in 1971 with a single on London Records (credited to Susan Shifrin) and a later release on Bell. By 1975 she was working in England and had a contract with EMI, with Bruce Welch (formerly of The Shadows) producing both of her compositions *All I Wanna Do* backed with *For You*. The single was subsequently picked up by Motown and released in March 1975, although they presumably passed on the option of a follow-up, which was released in Britain as *Somewhere Over The Rainbow/When You Wish Upon A Star* backed with *Secrets*. All four tracks eventually appeared on Su's debut album, released in Sweden only in 1978. By then Su was recording for United Artists.

Since 1991 Sue has been perhaps better known as Sue Cassidy, the third wife of former teen heart-throb David Cassidy. The pair separated in February 2014 with Sue subsequently filing for divorce.

THE SHIRELLES

R&B vocal group The Shirelles was formed in Passiac, New Jersey in 1957 by school friends Shirley Owens Alston (born in New Jersey on 10 June 1941), Addi 'Micki' Harris (born in New Jersey on 22 January 1940), Doris Coley Kenner (born in New Jersey on 2 August 1941) and Beverley Lee (born in New Jersey on 3 August 1941) as The Poquellos. They signed to Florence Greenberg's Tiara Records in 1957 who suggested a name-change to the Shirelles. The success of their first single *I Met Him On A Sunday* led to Tiara leasing the record to Decca for national distribution and Florence Greenberg later setting up the Scepter label and scoring a number one hit with *Will You Love Me Tomorrow* (although after it became apparent that the trust fund supposedly set up by Scepter was never going to materialise, the group left the label). *Will You Love Me Tomorrow* featured on the soundtrack album 'Girl Groups: The Story Of A Sound' released by Motown in 1983. Harris died from a heart attack on 10 June 1982. Doris Kenner died from breast cancer on 4 February 2000.

SHOO-BE-DOO-BE-DOO-DA-DAY – STEVIE WONDER [SINGLE]

After the success of *Uptight*, Stevie Wonder, Sylvia Moy and Hank Cosby developed something of a routine for writing new material. Stevie would invariably come up with the initial riff, title and part of the lyric, with Sylvia taking care of the vocal melody and the rest of the lyrics and Hank handling the arrangements and instrumental tracks.

Probably inspired by an old Moonglows track, *Shoo Doo Be Doo*, Stevie came up with the initial riff and title that would become *Shoo-Be-Doo-Be-Doo-Da-Dey* (although this was reportedly a mistake at the pressing stage, since Stevie's original title was *Shoo-Be-Doo-Be-Doo-Don-Dey*), with the backing tracks recorded in November 1967 and Stevie's vocal a month later, although there were to be a further two sessions for the lead vocal the following February. Recording the vocals was never an easy task, as Sylvia would later explain.

"I would be in the control room with a microphone and he'd be out in the studio with his earphones on. We'd put on a track and I would sing the song. Stevie would listen to the line I was singing, then he would sing that line listening to the next line, and he would never miss a beat. It was absolutely amazing."

The end result was amazing too, with *Shoo-Be-Doo-Be-Doo-Da-Dey* being released in March 1968 and going on to top the R&B chart and hit #9 on the pop listings. In the UK it was released in April and faltered outside the Top 40, finally peaking at #46.

SHOP AROUND – THE MIRACLES FEATURING BILL 'SMOKEY' ROBINSON [SINGLE]

When Barrett Strong's *Money* became a hit, virtually everyone at Motown turned their attentions to coming up with a suitable follow-up. Smokey Robinson thought he had the best composition, *Shop Around*, which he duly presented to Berry Gordy for consideration. Berry liked the song but felt it might be better recorded on The Miracles, subsequently producing the first, blues-tinged version which was pressed and sent out to local radio stations towards the end of September 1960.

A couple of weeks later Berry rang Smokey at three o'clock in the morning and begged him to grab the rest of the group and get themselves down to Hitsville; there was something about the first version of *Shop Around* that didn't sound right and if all concerned wanted a major hit, they would have to redo the song. Bleary eyed but inquisitive, Smokey and The Miracles re-assembled at the studio where Berry ran them through their paces, eventually coming up with an altogether more pop-sounding version of *Shop Around*.

Fortunately, the second version was ready for release by 15 October 1960, before too many copies of the original had circulated, and the new, tighter version found instant support from radio and subsequently retail. It was to prove something of a masterstroke, with *Shop Around* becoming Motown's first million selling single, an R&B chart topper and hitting #2 on Billboard's pop chart (it went one better on the rival trade magazine Cashbox' chart, hitting #1), with the success of the single also aided by the group's appearance on Dick Clark's 'American Bandstand' before the year was out.

Whilst the single made no impression whatsoever in the UK, where it was the third single issued on the London American label, *Shop Around* has since gone on to become one of Motown's best loved songs, attracting successful cover versions from the likes of Mary Wells, Johnnie Ray and Captain & Tennille, with Captain & Tennille changing the gender of the song and taking it to #4 on the pop charts in 1976.

Shop Around would also attract two answer records (one by Smokey himself, who recorded *It's Time To Stop Shopping Around* in 1987), whilst the single's flip side *Who's Lovin' You* has also being heavily covered, most notably by Michael Jackson, who recorded what many believe to be the definitive version. Smokey did get to contribute to Barrett Strong's follow-up too, co-writing *Money And Me* with Berry Gordy, Janie Bradford and Robert Bateman.

SHOTGUN – JUNIOR WALKER & THE ALL STARS [SINGLE]

Junior Walker didn't mean to be slack about turning up at the studio, it just invariably happened that shortly before heading off to Hitsville for a scheduled session he'd get a call from a promoter somewhere across the country looking for a major act to fill a gap for that evening or the next. Junior would drop *anything* to do a live date, since gigs usually meant cash in hand, and Junior could count his money all the way back to Detroit, whereas he'd have to wait six months or so for a royalty cheque, that is if there was anything left after deductions. Even if it meant Junior missed more sessions than he made, he was usually guaranteed his money.

One of his biggest hits came about because someone else let him down; always a reluctant singer on his own recordings, Junior had arranged for Fred Paton of the Jumping Jacks to undertake the vocal duties on *Shotgun*, only for Fred to be a no show on 15 December 1964. Instead, Junior was forced to virtually mumble his way through the song, accompanied by various members of the Funk Brothers; Junior's own All Stars were considered perfect for his out on the road show, but in the studio a little more musical sophistication was required.

The song itself had been written by Junior after being inspired by the dance craze The Shotgun, and a rough version of the song had been played to Berry Gordy, who would produce the recorded version along with engineer Lawrence Horn. Released a month later, *Shotgun* powered its way up the US charts, hitting #4 pop and #1 R&B, the first major success on the Soul label.

In the UK, the infectious but gritty number was held over until the establishment of the Tamla Motown label and finally issued on 2 April 1965 but missed out on the chart, as it also did when subsequently released on the EP *Shake And Fingerpop* in February 1966. *Shotgun* was one of two Motown songs (the other being *My Girl* by The Temptations) that was nominated for a Grammy Award for Best Rhythm & Blues Recording in 1966, both missing out to James Brown's *Papa's Got A Brand New Bag*.

SIMPLE GAME – THE FOUR TOPS [SINGLE]

Success in America might have diminished since the departure of Holland-Dozier- Success in America might have diminished since the departure of Holland-Dozier-Holland from Motown in 1968, but in Britain The Four Tops remained as popular as ever. Singles that struggled to make headway in the US found a receptive market in the UK, with The Four Tops also a popular live draw.

They were on tour on Britain in the spring of 1970, buoyed by the success of *It's All In The Game*, which had become a Top Five hit in the UK even though it would fail to crack the Top Twenty in their homeland. Stepping off stage one night, they were approached by Tony Clarke, a producer who had made his name with The Moody Blues but had also helmed the likes of The Equals and Pinkerton's Assorted Colours, although The Four Tops and their entourage had little or no idea who he was!

He handed a demo disc to the group, which contained a song he thought might be ideal for them, *A Simple Game*, which had been written by Mike Pinder and which had appeared as the flip side to The Moody Blues single *Ride Me See-Saw* in October 1968. Impressed with the demo, The Four Tops agreed to record the song the very next day, with Clarke booking time at the Wessex Studios in Highbury for the session. Fortunately, he had already gone to the trouble of preparing the backing tracks and it in the correct key, the result of guesswork on the part of him and his team.

Simple Game (the title was shortened) was duly completed on 5 May 1970, along with a couple of other tracks, with The Four Tops being given a copy of the rough mix on cassette and the master tapes subsequently sent over to Motown in America. Although *Simple Game* would have made the perfect follow-up to *It's All In The Game*, Motown sat on the track for the best part of a year, with the single finally appearing in September 1971 after Tamla Motown had rejected releasing *Macarthur Park*. It turned out to be the correct decision, with *Simple Game* becoming the group's biggest British hit after *Reach Out I'll Be There* and on par with *Walk Away Renee*, peaking at #3. Perhaps it was the 'Britishness' of the record that appealed to British record buyers and alienated American ones, for when subsequently issued in the US in January 1972, it could make only #34 R&B and #90 pop.

SIGNED, SEALED, DELIVERED I'M YOURS – STEVIE WONDER [SINGLE]

Stevie Wonder and Lee Garrett first met at the Michigan School for the Blind, where both attended as students during the 1960s. After leaving the school, Lee has pursued a career as a disc jockey, with the pair renewing their friendship when Lee returned to Detroit to take up a job at WGPR after a spell working in Philadelphia. Also joining the new Stevie Wonder inner circle was Rita Wright, a secretary at Motown with aspirations of having a recording career of her own, a dream that would come to fruition in 1968, although she would not achieve any real success until she resorted to her full name Syreeta and Stevie got more directly involved.

In 1968 Stevie, Lee and Rita were in the Golden World studio working on a number of projects, including writing and producing for The Spinners and a few solo tracks for Stevie. One song had the working title 'Nothing For Nothing', although it would ultimately become better known as *Signed Sealed Delivered*, the title reportedly being suggested by Stevie's mother Lula Hardaway. The lyrics were effectively written by all three (Stevie, Rita and Lee), with each bouncing ideas of the others as they went along.

The song was finally ready for recording in August 1969, with the horn section being added the following February. Two months later Stevie returned to the song (it was to be his very first solo production) and recorded his lead vocal over two sessions, finally sending a copy of the tape by messenger to Berry Gordy in Los Angeles. His reaction was that it sounded like a hit and should be released immediately as it was (although there would later be a remix that elongated the fade out at the end), with the single appearing on the release schedule for 3 June 1970. Something of a stylistic departure for Stevie, the change was deliberate.

"If Stax Records had done something with the kind of groove I liked, well...I did *We Can Work It Out* with a Stax kind of groove. I had the desire to move out of the one little thing that the musicians were in, and that Motown was in. And I wanted to do it, hey, because I liked the groove."

The public liked the groove too, sending *Signed Sealed Delivered I'm Yours* all the way to the top of the R&B chart and to #3 pop. The single was released in the UK three weeks after its American appearance and hit #15 the first time around. At the end of the year Stevie, Lee, Rita and Lula, the song's writers, picked up a Grammy Award nomination for Best Rhythm & Blues Song, whilst there was also a separate nomination for Stevie in the Best R&B Vocal Performance, Male category. The song lost out to General Johnson and Ron Dunbar for *Patches*, whilst Stevie's efforts were topped by BB King and *The Thrill Is Gone*.

The song has gone on to attract numerous cover versions (including one by Elton John dating back to his days playing and performing under his given name of Reg Dwight), with The Boystown Gang enjoying a #50 UK hit in 1982. In 2003, Stevie and Angie Stone lent their support to an updated version by British boy band Blue, which hit #11 on the UK chart.

ALFIE SILAS

Born Alphanet Silas in Los Angeles, California on 10 June 1956, Alfie was a member of the church choir and would eventually become lead vocalist of contemporary gospel group Geary Lanier & We. After touring Canada with Martha Reeves and performing on several television shows, Alfie enjoyed several hits on RCA before linking with Motown in 1984. A guest spot on Bobby King's single *Close To Me* saw her make her chart debut for her new home.

Alfie also performed *Star* on the soundtrack to 'The Last Dragon', which made #68 R&B in 1985 and was followed by *Just Gets Better With Time*, which hit #71 a year later. Unfortunately her album **That Look**, produced by heavyweights Norman Whitfield and Willie Hutch did little in the US and was not scheduled internationally.

ALBUM: THAT LOOK (1986)

THE SILHOUETTES

Formed in Philadelphia, Pennsylvania in 1956 as The Thunderbirds, the group comprised Rick Lewis (born on 2 September 1933), Bill Horton (born on 25 December 1929), Earl Beal (born on 18 July 1924) and Raymond Edwards (born on 22 September 1922). Their best known song, *Get A Job*, which featured a sax solo by Rollee McGill was originally released on manager Kaw Williams own Junior Records label before being snapped up for national distribution by Ember, who took the record to the top of the R&B chart (for six weeks) and the pop chart for two, going on to sell more than a million copies (it also attracted an answer record from The Miracles entitled *Got A Job*). *Get A Job* was featured on the soundtrack to the 1984 film 'The Flamingo Kid' issued by Motown. The Silhouettes disbanded in 1968 but reformed to perform on the nostalgia circuit during the 1980s and continued working until 1993. Horton died on 23 January 1995. Edwards died from cancer on 4 March 1997. Beal died on 22 March 2001. Lewis died on 19 April 2005.

SIR DUKE – STEVIE WONDER [SINGLE]

"With *Sir Duke*, I knew the title from the beginning but wanted it to be about the musicians who did something for us. So soon they are forgotten. I wanted to show my appreciation. They gave us something that is supposed to be forever. That's the basic idea of what we do and how we hook it up."

The second single to be lifted from **Songs In the Key Of Life**, *Sir Duke* name checked Duke Ellington in the title and Count Basie, Glenn Miller, Louis Armstrong and Ella Fitzgerald during the course of the lyrics, making this something of an homage to the great American musicians and composers.

Featuring Stevie on the Yamaha GX10 synthesizer, an instrument he would call his 'dream machine', *Sir Duke* also had contributions from Mike Sembello (guitar), Ben Bridges (rhythm guitar), Nathan Watts (bass), Hank Redd (alto saxophone), Trevor Lawrence (tenor saxophone) and Ray Maldonado and Steve Madaio (trumpet). Released as a single in March 1977, it matched its predecessor (*I Wish*) in topping the pop and R&B chart for three weeks and one week respectively. The single also peaked at #2 in the UK (former Wonderlove singer Deniece Williams and *Free* prevented Stevie from hitting the top), earning a silver disc for sales in excess of 250,000 copies.

SISTERS LOVE

One of several Motown groups where achievements did not match expectations, Sisters Love were already seasoned professionals by the time they arrived at the company. Consisting of Lillie Fort, Vermettya Boyster, Gwendolyn Berry and Jeannie Long, the foursome was initially brought together as members of The Raelettes in 1956. After ten years out on the road with Ray Charles and the Ray Charles Revue, the four left to sign with Man-Child where they released their debut single *I Know You Love Me*.

They then toured under the name Sisters Love for a couple of years, appearing at US Air Force bases around the world before returning home and signing with A&M in 1968. That deal would see them release three singles, with the Gene Chandler production *Are You Lonely?* becoming their only hit, peaking at #20 R&B and bubbling under the Hot 100 in 1971.

The following year they were signed by MoWest, with *Mr Fix It Man* their debut single for the imprint appearing in March 1972. They were to release a further two singles on MoWest before getting switched to the main Motown label in 1973 for *My Love Is Yours (Till The End Of Time)* as well as appearing in the film and on the soundtrack to 'The Mack' and providing the vocals to the Motown Disco Machine.

They also created a considerable stir in the UK, touring with The Jackson 5 in 1973 and receiving rave reviews, although neither *Mr Fix It Man* nor *I'm Learning To Trust My Man* could crack the charts. A planned album **With Love** was dropped from the schedule, and there the Sisters Love story might have come to an end, but in 1980 DJ Danny Krivit took the flip side to their final MoWest single, a cover version of Curtis Mayfield's *Give Me Your Love* and put together a near eight minute remix that has been a huge in demand item ever since.

SLOWBONE THE WONDER BOYS

Formed by Barry Hart (guitar and vocals), Jeff Peters (bass), Jim Hunter (keyboards) and Keith Shepherd (drums), British group Slowbone evolved from the 1960s psychedelic group Turquoise and would release two singles on Rare Earth, *Happy Birthday Sweet Sixteen* in May 1974 (under the full name) and *Oh Man* that same October (as Slowbone). Their manager Peter Meaden, who also managed The Who suggested a name change to something more exotic, and although they refused they did record as Rough Riders for the same label (*Hot California Beach,* released in September 1974) and provided the musical accompaniment to Sonny & The Sovereigns release in July 1974. Whilst none of their efforts saw the light of day in the US, they did record one further single for Polydor in 1977.

SLY, SLICK & WICKED

Formed in Cleveland, Ohio in 1970, Sly, Slick & Wicked consisted of John 'Sly' Wilson, Charles 'Slick' Still and Mark 'Wicked' Saxton. They originally recorded for Paramount and scored a regional hit with *Stay My Love* in 1970, but despite Paramount's promotional efforts they could not achieve a national breakout. Saxton left in 1972 and was replaced by Terry Stubbs and it was this new line-up that recorded an eponymous album for Ju-Par in 1977 (in fact the very first album issued by the label). A second album was supposedly recorded but never issued, with the group going on to sign with Epic Records in 1979.

ALBUM: SLY, SLICK & WICKED (1977)

SMILING FACES SOMETIMES – THE UNDISPUTED TRUTH [SINGLE]

Originally recorded by The Temptations for their **Sky's The Limit** album, *Smiling Faces Sometimes* was conceived as the centrepiece of that album, a twelve and a half minute epic that followed the Norman Whitfield blueprint for The Temptations to perfection, with extended instrumental passages dovetailing with the vocals, led by Eddie Kendricks and Dennis Edwards. Unfortunately for Norman, matters out of his control conspired to prevent *Smiling Faces Sometimes* becoming the massive hit he predicted, first by the success of *Just My Imagination*, which proved it was not only the group that preferred The Temptations recording ballads, and secondly by the departure of Eddie Kendricks from the group before *Smiling Faces Sometimes* could be extracted as a single.

Perhaps Norman had seen the writing on the wall, for in March 1971 he was back in the studio, working with much the same musicians who had performed so admirably on The Temptations' version, recording a new version for his latest discovery The Undisputed Truth. They had kicked off their hit career with *Save My Love For A Rainy Day*, another song that had originally been recorded by The Temptations, but rather than complain about recording other group's cast-offs, The Undisputed Truth knuckled down to some serious work.

"I was really scared of *Smiling Faces*, because everybody was talking about it as a hit record, and I'd never had one," lead singer Joe Harris would later explain. "My feeling was, I'm with the number one writer and producer in the world, and he is giving me some special attention. I can't fail."

That special attention resulted in take after take before Norman was finally confident that Joe, together with female singers Billie Rae Calvin and Brenda Joyce had nailed the song to perfection. Significantly different from The Temptations' original, The Undisputed Truth's version was released on the Gordy label in May 1971 and became a major hit, peaking at #2 R&B and #3 pop (it actually topped the R&B chart in Cashbox magazine), subsequently earning a Grammy Award nomination for Best Rhythm & Blues Song.

In the UK The Truth's single was released in October 1971 but failed to chart, resulting in an edited Temptations version being issued a year later (Eddie Kendricks' departure from The Temptations was not viewed as detrimental to the single's chances of success). This too missed out on chart honours, as did a version by David Ruffin as the flip side to his *Discover Me* single in 1976. Norman would produce another version of *Smiling Faces Sometimes* for rock group Rare Earth, whilst the song has attracted covers by flautist Bobbi Humphrey and female singer Joan Osbourne.

O.C. SMITH

Although he graduated from Southern University in Baton Rouge with a degree in psychology, music had always been O.C. Smith's preferred pursuit. Born Ocie Lee Smith in Mansfield, Louisiana on 21 June 1932 he grew up in Little Rock, Arkansas and then Los Angeles following his parent's divorce. After graduating from university he entered the US Air Force, although such was his interest in music he entered countless talent contests whilst still serving.

Discharged in 1955, he linked with Sy Oliver and appeared on 'Arthur Godfrey's Talent Scouts', the result of which was a recording contract with Cadence and later MGM. Whilst nothing made the charts his singles did establish his name, resulting in an offer to join Count Basie's band as a singer in 1961. He would remain with the band until 1965, still releasing the occasional solo single for a variety of labels without success.

By 1968 he was with Columbia and about to be dropped by the label when *The Son Of Hickory Holler's Tramp* crept into the chart, finally reaching #40 and #2 in the UK. The follow-up, a version of Bobby Russell's *Little Green Apples* became a smash, selling more than a million copies on its way to hitting #2 and winning Russell a Grammy Award for Song of the Year. Whilst O.C. Smith's subsequent singles never came anywhere near replicating that level of success, his hit run on the pop charts continued through to 1974.

After hitting the R&B charts with releases on Caribou, Shady Brook and Family, O.C. joined Motown in 1982. He would have one album and two singles released on the label, with title track *Love Changes* making #68 on the R&B chart, although the follow-up *Betcha* failed to make a showing. After further singles on Rendezvous, he became pastor and founder of The City of Angels Church in Los Angeles. He died from a heart attack on 23 November 2001.

ALBUM: LOVE CHANGES (1982)

SOFTOUCH

Female vocal quartet Softouch were discovered and managed by Billy Henderson of The Spinners, who got the girls a deal with Prodigal in 1975, where they released one single, *After You Give Your All (What Else Is There To Give)* in July of that year. After it flopped, the foursome, comprising Candice Ghant, Alicia Ingram, Opal Jones and Paula Denson left the label and eventually resurfaced at Fantasy, where their eponymous album was produced by Hank Cosby and Dale Warren in 1978. Candice later became a member Of The Mary Jane Girls.

SOMEBODY'S WATCHING ME – ROCKWELL [SINGLE]

Kennedy Gordy had struggled to get anyone to listen to his rough demo for *Somebody's Watching Me*, with many at the publishing company uncertain of the song's potential. It didn't help that the demo was in an extremely rough form, with a simple backing track that Kennedy would sign the lyrics over. It also didn't help that Kennedy Gordy's father was none other than Berry Gordy, which would undoubtedly result in charges of nepotism should Kennedy be successful in securing a contract.

About the only person at Jobete who believed the song might have some potential was producer and songwriter Curtis Anthony Nolen, who invited Kennedy to his home where he had built his own recording studio. Curtis stripped the song back and decided to re-arrange it, putting together an altogether more professional demo that might at least lead to an offer from Motown to record the track more professionally.

The revised demo did the job, with Motown funding subsequent sessions, where Jim Felber on bass synthesizer, Curtis on all other synthesizers and Kennedy on drum programming and vocals recorded on the initial version of the single. Once it was complete, Curtis realised they needed an additional vocal for the chorus, and preferably a famous and distinctive one.

The biggest star of the time was undoubtedly Michael Jackson, with whom Kenedy was tenuously linked as Kennedy's step-sister Hazel was married to Michael's brother Jermaine. Armed with the 24 track tape, Curtis and Kennedy journeyed to Michael's home at Encino and performed the song for Michael, with Curtis singing the vocal part he wished Michael to perform. Michael loved the song and agreed to take part, although he was a no-show at the first scheduled session (he was out visiting an amusement park with Donny Osmond). In order to prevent a second no-show, Curtis and Kennedy picked Michael up from home and drove him directly to the studio, where after a little over an hour, he nailed the vocal. After final mixing and over-dubs, Curtis and Kennedy were convinced they had a sure-fire smash on their hands, but there was still the little matter of convincing none other than Berry Gordy of the potential of the track.

They visited Berry at his home one weekend and left him the tape, retiring from the room so Berry could listen to it without interruption. Suitably impressed, Berry sanctioned its release, although in order to remove some of the pressure from Kennedy, it was decided to release it under an pseudonym, opting for Rockwell, the name of the high school band Kennedy had played with (the name was also suggested as a good fit since Kennedy knew how to 'rock well').

Whilst the presence of Michael Jackson (uncredited, but so distinctive was his vocal it soon became public knowledge) undoubtedly helped the track, the song about paranoia had its own appeal that converted into healthy record sales. Berry Gordy had expected the track to do well on the pop chart but struggle on the R&B listings; it would hit #2 pop but also topped the R&B chart for five weeks. The single also proved an international success too, hitting #6 in the UK.

The song itself has been covered on a number of occasions since its January 1984 release, most notably by DJ Bobo, who sampled it heavily for his 1992 single *Somebody Dance With Me* and Beatfreakz in 2006, who sampled the chorus but not the verses on their single that hit #3 in the UK (and actually topped the Spanish chart).

SOMEDAY WE'LL BE TOGETHER – DIANA ROSS & THE SUPREMES [SINGLE]

Officially the very last single by Diana Ross & The Supremes, *Someday We'll Be Together* has gone on to achieve something of legendary status. Much of it is deserved; their twelfth and final #1 pop hit (still a record for a female group), it enabled both Diana and The Supremes to part company at the very top of the tree, whilst the song has become somewhat iconic, being sung by virtually all of those present at the finale of 'Motown 25'.

Yet in other ways both the title and the recording only go to highlight the chasm that had grown between Diana and The Supremes. Johnny Bristol and Jackey Beavers had begun work on the song whilst they were looking for a deal in the late 1950s, finally being able to present it to Harvey Fuqua when they signed with his Tri-Phi label. Their version was recorded and released in 1961 and achieved some local notoriety and success without ever troubling the national listings.

Some eight years later Johnny thought the song might be ideal for Junior Walker and recorded the instrumental tracks as well as some of the backing vocals with Maxine and Julia Waters. When Junior announced himself not interested in the song, Johnny sought out Berry Gordy for advice. If he expected Berry to order Junior to record it he was to be pleasantly surprised, for Berry thought the song and its sentiments would be ideal as the final single for The Supremes before Diana Ross took her leave for a solo career.

The initial sessions with Diana (the other Supremes, who at the time featured Mary Wilson and Cindy Birdsong, had been intentionally left off group recordings ever since the departure of Holland-Dozier-Holland, making The Supremes less a recording act and more a brand name from 1968 onwards) didn't go particularly well, with Diana's general mood restricting her ability to nail the song.

"We had been working on it for hours and Diana was getting tired and a little irritable," Johnny later explained, "so I suggested to Berry that maybe if I went into another booth and sang in her ear, y'know...two people singing back and forth to each other, it could just take her mind off her tiredness long enough to make her finish it. So we did it and I did the things that you hear."

Whether by accident or design, both booth's were fully miked up and both Diana and Johnny's vocals were captured onto tape, with Berry deciding the interplay between the two was part of the magic that was eventually created. The single was duly released on 21 October 1969 and would provide the group with their final bow. An R&B and pop chart topper (for three and one week respectively, as well as peaking at #13 in the UK), it was the final song performed by Diana and The Supremes on their final television appearance, 'The Ed Sullivan Show' on 21 December 1969 and was featured as the last song during the group's three week farewell tour thereafter, culminating in their final appearance at the Frontier Hotel in Las Vegas on 14 January 1970.

In 1976 the song was played at the funeral of former Supreme Florence Ballard, even though she had been an ex-Supreme at the time of the original recording, and similarly, the song's selection as the tune a reunited Supremes should sing at the 'Motown 25' television special was hardly relevant to the contribution Mary in particular had made to The Supremes heritage.

SONGS IN THE KEY OF LIFE - STEVIE WONDER [ALBUM]

Not long after the release of **Fulfillingness First Finale**, Stevie Wonder dropped a bombshell; he was retiring from music and moving to Ghana, where he intended working with handicapped children. Berry Gordy and his advisors knew better than trying to convince Stevie and *his* advisors that this was the height of folly; they could only hope that common sense would prevail and Stevie would come to realise that he could better serve the handicapped children of the world by maintaining his musical career and bringing attention to the plight of the disadvantaged through the power of song.

For a while it seemed as though Stevie was serious, announcing plans for a farewell concert, but fortunately nothing came of it and eventually Stevie and Johanan Vigoda entered into negotiations with Motown on a new and improved contract. The deal that was eventually signed was the biggest in the record industry at the time, a seven year, seven album deal worth a guaranteed $13 million, also granting him full artistic control (although he already had that clause in his earlier contract) and the power of veto should Gordy ever decide to sell Motown or the publishing arm Jobete.

Once the ink was dry on the contract, Stevie announced that the first fruits of this new deal were to be the album **Let's See Life The Way It Is**, scheduled for release in October 1975. Recorded at the Record Plant in Hollywood, Crystal Industries in Los Angeles, Sausalito Music Factory in California and the Hit Factory in New York (where Stevie was the first official customer, initially booking three days that stretched into three months) the initial sessions went well, so well in fact that Stevie announced the album would be a double album package, with new songs literally flowing out of him at a phenomenal rate.

The release date slipped back, with Stevie telling an expectant media that he wanted to remix numerous tracks and took to wearing a t-shirt that bore the legend 'We're almost finished'. Not to be outdone, Motown distributed their own 'Stevie's nearly ready' t-shirts. As the months passed, word on the pending album continued to trickle out; it was now entitled **Songs In The Key Of Life** and had grown in size to become a double album with a free four track EP thrown in for good measure.

Finally, the release date was given, 28 September 1976, with Motown gearing its full pressing capacity to meet the expected heavy demand. A few weeks beforehand, on 7 September, Stevie held an extravagant $30,000 listening party for some two hundred media and invited guests, flying and bussing them from a champagne breakfast at the Essex House hotel in Manhattan to the 145 acre Long View Farm in North Brookfield in Massachusetts.

There they were greeted by Stevie wearing a cowboy's outfit, although the holster didn't carry guns but copies of his impending album! What they heard was an extensive and varied album, one that covered just about every musical base imaginable; the driving funk of *I Wish*, the baroque-styled *Village Ghetto Land*, the extended musical history lesson on *Black Man*, the joyous *Sir Duke*; there was something for everyone. Although largely the work of just one man, with Stevie writing, arranging and producing everything on display (only four tracks were co-written) as well as performing on every track, usually accompanied by his latest toy, the Yamaha GX1 synthesizer, there was a supporting cast of the musical great and good, including Herbie Hancock, George Benson, Minnie Riperton, Deniece Williams, Syreeta, Ronnie Foster and Bobbi Humphrey, among countless others.

Media reaction was favourable despite the tape breaking down midway through the playback (although there was some criticism over the price of the album and the seeming over-indulgence of delivering a double album plus – some thought that had the material been trimmed to a single album it would have been the greatest album of all time), ensuring the album flew out of the stores when it was finally released.

It would enter the Billboard Top 200 chart at #1, the first double album to achieve the feat (and Stevie was only the second artist to have entered the album chart at pole position, behind Elton John and **Captain Fantastic** and **Rock Of the Westies**), going on to spend thirteen consecutive weeks at the summit, returning to the top for a fourteenth and final week at the end of January 1977. It also spent a total of twenty weeks at the top of the R&B chart, its progress aided by two chart topping singles in *I Wish* and *Sir Duke*. In the UK the album entered at #18 and hit its peak of #2 two weeks later, held off the top by the K-Tel compilation album **Soul Motion**, although the generally held opinion was that the album could have eased its way to the top if *Isn't She Lovely* had been released as a single.

Something of a tribute to his daughter Aisha, *Isn't She Lovely* was the most played track from the album, for a time surpassing the popularity of *I Wish* and *Sir Duke*, but despite requests to edit the 6:34 album track, Stevie refused. Instead, a virtual note for note cover version was recorded by British singer David Parton and produced by Tony Hatch; issued on Pye it sailed all the way to #4 on the UK chart.

Yet for all that **Songs In The Key Of Life** didn't achieve (at least as far as the UK was concerned), what it *did* achieve surpassed all expectations; it spent a total of 80 weeks on the Billboard chart, would eventually earn a Diamond Disc Award from the R.I.A.A. on 29 March 2005 (this denotes domestic US sales in excess of 10 million copies, but it should be noted that for the purposes of American certification, each disc in a double album is counted separately, so total US sales exceed 5 million copies) and would earn Stevie a total of seven Grammy Award nominations. Four of these were won; Album of The Year, Producer of the Year, Best Male Pop Vocal Performance and Best Male R&B Vocal Performance for *I Wish*, but even the categories for which he was merely nominated highlight the sheer diversity of the entire album, with *Contusion* nominated for Best Pop Instrumental and Best Instrumental Composition and *Have A Talk With God* Best Inspirational Performance.

On the night of show, Stevie was absent from the ceremony, having travelled to Africa, where he was in Nigeria reportedly exploring his musical heritage. A satellite link was organised so an immediate reaction to his victories could be transmitted to the audience in the Hollywood Palladium in Los Angeles as well as the millions watching at home. The link was poor, breaking up either visually or audibly throughout the evening, with at one point a perplexed and exasperated host Andy Williams asking, "Stevie, can you see us?"

Other celebrities have not been so tongue tied about Stevie Wonder or **Songs In The Key Of Life**, with Elton John a confirmed fan.

"Let me put it this way: wherever I go in the world, I always take a copy of **Songs In The Key Of Life**. For me, it's the best album ever made, and I'm always left in awe after I listen to it. When people in decades and centuries to come talk about the history of music, they will talk about Louis Armstrong, Duke Ellington, Ray Charles and Stevie Wonder. He evolved into an amazing songwriter and a genuine musical force of nature."

Songs In The Key Of Life has retained that musical force in the ensuing decades, just as Elton John predicted.

THE SONGWRITERS HALL OF FAME

Founded in 1969 by songwriter Johnny Mercer and publishers Abe Olman and Howie Richmond, the Songwriters Hall of Fame is a division of the National Academy of Popular Music. In 1980 the hall was expanded with the creation of the Johnny Mercer Award (for artists who had already been inducted into the Hall of Fame and who had composed a number of exceptional works) and the Sammy Cahn Lifetime Achievement Award, subsequently adding the Pioneer Award in 2012 to recognise the careers of historic creators of music.

The inductees and other awards bestowed on Motown personnel, together with the year of each award are as follows:

INDUCTEES
Nickolas Ashford (2002)
Henry Cosby (2006)
Lamont Dozier (1988)
Brian Holland (1988)
Eddie Holland (1988)
Michael Jackson (2002)
Sylvia Moy (2006)
Lionel Richie (1994)
Smokey Robinson (1990)
Valerie Simpson (2002)

Barrett Strong (2004)
Norman Whitfield (2004)
Stevie Wonder (1983)

JOHNNY MERCER AWARD
Michael Jackson (2002)
Stevie Wonder (2004)
Smokey Robinson (2005)
Holland-Dozier-Holland (2009)

SAMMY CAHN LIFETIME ACHIEVEMENT AWARD
Berry Gordy (1998)
Stevie Wonder (2002)

PIONEER AWARD
Berry Gordy (2013)

SONNY & THE SOVEREIGNS

Songwriters and producers Peter Anders, Kenny Laguna and Paul Naumann worked on a number of demos in a studio in Walm Lane, Willesden in London with Slowbone members Barry Hart, Jeff Peters, Jim Hunter and Keith Shepherd. Whilst the songs were intended for other artists on the Rare Earth label, a cover of Gary U.S. Bonds' *School Is Out* was considered good enough for release as it was, resulting in the band name Sonny & The Sovereigns being created for the purpose. The single was released in the UK only in July 1974.

THE S.O.S. BAND

Formed in Atlanta, Georgia by Mary Davis (vocals), Jason Bryant (keyboards), Abdul Raoof (trumpet), Billy Ellis (saxophone), John Simpson (bass), Bruno Speight (guitar), Jerome 'JT' Thomas (drums) and Willie 'Sonny' Killebrew (saxophone) as Santa Monica, they changed their name in 1980 (SOS stands for 'Sounds Of Success') upon signing with Tabu. The group appeared on the soundtrack to 'Police Academy 4: Citizens On Patrol' in 1987 performing *It's Time To Move*.

ISELA SOTELO

Female balladeer Isela Sotelo (born in Los Angeles, California on 21 April 1956) was one of several artists signed by the newly established Motown Latino label in the late summer of 1982. Her only single, *Angelito (Angel Baby)*, was recorded in Spanish and scheduled for August only to be pulled and eventually released on Motown itself in October 1982! She would later provide backing vocals for a host of fellow Latin acts as well as dubbing the voice of Ariel in Disney's Spanish version of 'The Little Mermaid', 'La Sirenita'.

SOUL RECORDS

Berry Gordy's stated mission may have been to only release Top Ten records, but even he realised that some of his artists operated outside of normal pop music. Whilst he had labels that catered for jazz (Workshop Jazz), gospel (Divinity) and country (Mel-O-dy), finding a label home for all that passed through the door of Hitsville didn't present a problem, but one by one the minor labels were shuttered and their rosters dispersed across the remaining labels.

Even that presented something of a problem for the likes of Earl Van Dyke and Junior Walker, who didn't really sit comfortably on Tamla, Motown or Gordy and were too earthy for V.I.P. So in 1964 Berry started a new label, Soul Records, one whose very name gave some indication as to what to expect musically, although over the course of the fourteen years the label was operative, there would be one or two anomalies.

The label was launched in March 1964 with the release of Shorty Long's *Devil With The Blue Dress*, and over the ensuing years the label was the home of Junior Walker & The All Stars, The Originals and Gladys Knight & The Pips, among others. Jimmy Ruffin was also a Soul Records artist, even though his brother David called Motown home. Edwin Starr began his career on Gordy but also released records on Motown and Soul; the supposedly well defined boundaries were subject to change, even at Motown.

Soul Records remained one of the company's most active labels for the best part of twelve years, the output slowing down considerably in 1976. Soul Records released a number of recordings over the next two years before being shut down in 1978, with Major Lance's *I Never Thought I'd Be Losing You* the last release in April 1978.

SOUNDS NICE

In 1968 French songwriter and producer Serge Gainsbourg convinced his then girlfriend Brigitte Bardot to record a song he had written entitled *Je T'aime...Moi Non Plus* (French for 'I love you...me neither'), with Brigitte's 'vocals' amounting to little more than simulating a female orgasm. When she heard the finished recording, she begged Serge to scrap it lest it ruin her reputation, which he reportedly did, although this version eventually appeared in 1986.

However, a year later and by now embroiled in a relationship with British actress Jane Birkin (previously the wife of composer John Barry), he resurrected the song and saw it quickly become a European monster, despite being banned in Iceland, Italy, Poland, Spain, Sweden and Yugoslavia and publicly denounced in a statement issued by the Vatican.

In the UK the rights were picked up by Fontana and it quickly raced to #2 on the chart before being deleted; apparently the wife of Fontana's chief executive had found the record distasteful. Fortunately an immediate deal with Major Minor saw sales on the record continue without a hitch and it would go on to top the chart.

The record, of course, had been banned by radio in the UK, who instead played an instrumental cover version by organist Tim Mycroft with arranger and producer Paul Buckmaster under the name Sounds Nice and titled *Love At First Sight*. Released by Parlophone, this version made #18 on the chart and prompted a follow-up album of easy listening material, including *I Heard It Through The Grapevine*. When Motown asked EMI for their help in putting together a release schedule for the Rare Earth label, Sounds Nice was one of the artists included, although the music has little to do with either Motown or rock.

Both single and album were released in the US to almost total indifference, just like Serge and Jane's original (although Donna Summer and *Love To Love You Baby* was along similar lines in 1975, with Donna also recording a version of *Je T'aime* for the soundtrack to 'Thank God It's Friday'). Mycroft, who hadn't had a hit before *Love At First Sight* and wouldn't have one after either, died on 1 January 2010.

ALBUM: LOVE AT FIRST SIGHT (1970)

SOUPY SALES

In 1953 struggling comic Milton Supman moved from Cleveland to Detroit on the recommendation of a friend, looking to switch career from late night comic to television presenter.

Born in Franklinton, North Carolina on 8 January 1926, Milton had acquired the nickname Soupy as a child and originally worked under the moniker Soupy Hines, but later switched to Soupy Sales as his original choice was too close to the Heinz brand name. As luck would have it he got a job with WXYZ-TV presenting the children's show that would eventually become 'The Soupy Sales Show'.

Whilst the show in its various forms was aimed at children, with puppets and slapstick that invariably ended with Soupy getting a pie in his face, it also appealed to an adult audience, helped by guest appearances by artists such as The Supremes, Martha Reeves & The Vandellas, The Ronettes and a host of jazz names, including Miles Davis on no fewer than six occasions.

Already popular, Soupy's stock soared after a stunt went wrong; asked to host the normal show on New Year's Day, he asked his younger viewers to creep into their parents room and remove from their belongings 'those little pieces of green paper with pictures of men with beards; put them in an envelope and send them to me at Soupy Sales, Channel 5, New York. And you know what I'm going to send you? A postcard from Puerto Rico!' The prank did result in several envelopes containing money arriving at Channel 5 (it was claimed to be as much as $80,000, but Soupy said much of what was sent was actually Monopoly money) and a two week suspension from the air, but he returned to even greater viewing figures.

An early champion of the show was Frank Sinatra, who signed Soupy to a two album deal in 1961 when he launched his Reprise label, but it was with ABC in the middle of the decade that he enjoyed any success, charting two albums and the single *The Mouse*.

In 1969 he was signed by Motown and released the album **A Bag Of Soup** and the single *Muck-Arty Park*, a play on *MacArthur Park*. Soupy also starred in several films and worked as a radio DJ during a lengthy career, but is probably best known for having received some 20,000 pies in the face during his television career. When Soupy died from cancer on 22 October 2009, comedian Tim Powers left a cream pie on his star on the Hollywood Walk of Fame.

ALBUM: A BAG OF SOUP (1969)

SOUTHERN PACIFIC

Country rock group Southern Pacific was formed in 1983 by former Doobie Brothers members Keith Knudsen (born in Le Mars, Iowa on 18 February 1948), John McFee (born in Santa Cruz, California on 9 September 1950) and Jerry Scheff (born in San Francisco, California on 31 January 1941), subsequently adding Tim Goodman and Glen Hardin (born in Wellington, Texas on 18 April 1939). Signed to Warner Brothers in 1984 they released their debut album the following year.

In 1987 they contributed to the film 'Police Academy 4: Citizens On Patrol', by which time the group comprised Knudsen, McFee, Stu Cook, Kurt Howell and David Jenkins, with *Shooting For The Top* appearing on the album soundtrack. The group disbanded in 1991 and Knudsen died from pneumonia on 8 February 2005.

THE SPANIELS

Formed in Roosevelt High School in Gary, Indiana in 1952 as Pookie Hudson & The Hudsonaires, the group comprised Thornton James 'Pookie' Hudson (born in Des Moines, Iowa on 11 June 1934), Ernest Warren, Gerald Gregory, Opal Courtney (born on 22 November 1936) and Willie Jackson. They soon ditched their original name and settled on The Spaniels, picking up a recording contract with Vee-Jay in April 1953, one of the first groups to sign with the Chicago based label.

They scored their first hit later the same year with *Baby It's You*, a single that was leased to the Chance label but registered a much bigger hit on Vee-Jay with *Goodnite Sweetheart, Goodnite* that hit #5 R&B; any chance The Spaniels had of registering a pop hit was halted by a competing cover version by The McGuire Sisters. Warren, Courtney and Jackson left the group in 1957, being replaced by James Cochran, Don Porter and Carl Rainge, although Warren would return to expand the group to a six piece in time for their 1958 recording *Stormy Weather*.

Both *Goodnite Sweetheart Goodnite* and *Stormy Weather* were featured on the CD compilation **Hits From The Legendary Vee-Jay Records** issued by Motown in November 1986. Gerald Gregory died on 12 February 1999. Pookie Hudson died on 16 January 2007. Opal Courtney died on 18 September 2008. Ernest Warren died on 7 May 2012.

SPARKS

Brothers Ron (born in Culver City, California on 12 August 1948) and Russell Mael (born in Santa Monica, California on 5 October 1953) formed their first group Halfnelson in 1968 and recorded their debut album in 1971 on Bearsville. They name changed to Sparks soon after but would not find success until they relocated to England in 1973. There they achieved their breakthrough with the hit *This Town Ain't Big Enough For The Both Us* and album **Kimono My House**.

Their brief appearance on a Motown single came with *Get Crazy*, the title track to the 1983 film 'Get Crazy', with the single being issued on Morocco with Malcolm McDowell's *Hot Shot* on the flip.

C.P. SPENCER

The lead tenor who helped propel *Baby I'm For Real* to glory, C.P. Spencer had begun singing not with The Originals but with an early incarnation of another group who would grace Motown, The Spinners.

Born Cratham Plato Spencer in Detroit, Michigan on 13 January 1938, C.P. sang doo wop on street corners and linked up with Billy Henderson, Henry Fambrough, Pervis Jackson and James Edwards, the group calling themselves The Domingoes (later becoming The Spinners). When C.P. left soon after their formation it was to hook up with long term friend Walter Gaines, with the pair joining another local group, The 5 Jets.

The 5 Jets would later become The 5 Stars and record a one-off single for Mark X in 1958, but for Walter and C.P. things would take a turn for the better when they teamed up with Ty Hunter, Lamont Dozier and David Ruffin as The Voice Masters, releasing four singles for Anna Records. When Anna Records threw in their lot with Berry Gordy at Motown, all but Ty Hunter effectively went with them.

It was Lamont who introduced Walter and C.P. and another friend Hank Dixon to Freddie Gorman, with the four becoming the Originals. Just as The Spinners were to find, getting into Motown was only half the battle, for getting writers and producers assigned and records out to market were not guaranteed. It was only when Marvin Gaye championed The Originals' cause that they got anywhere near the material their talents required, with *The Bells* and *Baby I'm For Real* two shining beacons in an otherwise time of darkness spent at Hitsville.

C.P. left the group for a solo career in 1972, issuing the single *Still Holding On* in 1973 (being replaced in The Originals by Ty Hunter) but found sustained success still elusive. He returned to The Originals fold in 1978, by which time they had left Motown for Fantasy, recording two albums before switching to the independent label Phase II. The death of Ty Hunter in 1981 brought the group to a halt, although they would regroup towards the end of the decade and record for Ian Levine's labels. C.P. Spencer died in Oak Park, Michigan from a heart attack on 20 October 2004.

THE SPINNERS

Like several other artists signed to Motown, The Spinners had a frustrating time at Hitsville, much of it spent kicking their heels waiting for the right song and the right producer to give them some attention. Just as The Originals would enjoy renewed success when Marvin Gaye took an interest, so The Spinners saw their profile raised when Stevie Wonder got hold of the group.

The group could trace its roots back to 1954, when a group of friends from Ferndale near Detroit got together to form a vocal group. The original line-up featured tenor Billy Henderson (born in Detroit, Michigan on 9 August 1939), baritone Henry Fambrough (born in Detroit on 10 May 1938, although some sources state he was born in 1935), bassist Pervis Kackson (born on 17 May 1938), tenor Cratham Plato 'C.P.' Spencer (born in Detroit on 13 January 1938) and James Edwards as The Domingoes, although Edwards only lasted a couple of weeks before being replaced by lead tenor Bobbie Smith (born in Detroit on 10 April 1936). C.P. Spencer didn't last long either, leaving The Domingoes but taking his own route to Motown via The Five Jets, The Voice Masters and then The Originals, with his place in the group being taken by Edgar 'Chico' Edwards (James' brother).

The Domingoes got a number of live dates locally, but there was always a sense of confusion about them, with one or two venues announcing them as The Flamingoes (an extremely popular R&B group of the same time), so the group opted to go by a different name, utilising the hubcaps on Bobbie's Cadillac and renaming themselves The Spinners.

Their growing reputation locally soon had a number of companies interested in signing them, with Harvey Fuqua, of The Moonglows fame, offering them a deal with his newly inaugurated Tri-Phi label. Before the group went into the studio, however, Chico Edwards left, unwilling then to give up a lucrative full time job for the uncertainty of a recording career. In his place the group drafted in George Dixon, and it was this five who went to Chicago to record their debut for Tri-Phi,

That's What Girls Are Made For. Written by Harvey with Gwen Gordy (and, according to some sources, also featuring Harvey on lead vocals, although most sources state the lead is by Bobbie Smith), *That's What Girls Are Made For* was the debut release for both the group and the label but got both off to the perfect start, hitting #5 R&B and #27 pop.

Both Harvey and Bobbie got to sing lead on subsequent releases (Bobbie even being specially credited on *She Don't Love*, which was released as Bobby Smith & The Spinners in December 1962), but nothing came anywhere close to matching the success of the first single. Given the financial implications having a hit entailed, this was probably just as well, but eventually George Dixon decided the music business wasn't for him, leaving the group and going into a ministry, with Chico Edwards coming back into the group in his place.

Harvey meanwhile was in the process of selling his label and roster to Berry Gordy's growing empire, and so in early 1963, The Spinners found themselves newly signed to the Motown label. It would take some time for the group to get into the studio, record and get singles and albums out to the market, something that would be a recurring theme in the years to come. In order to ingratiate themselves into the Motown family, the five members of The Spinners undertook other duties around Hitsville, more often than not driving some of the other artists to and from live performances.

Eventually, in April 1964, The Spinners got their turn in the studio, working with Mickey Stevenson and Ivy Jo Hunter on *Sweet Thing*, which was released in October 1964. Despite the fact it was not too long since The Spinners had enjoyed a major hit, Motown was unable to get *Sweet Thing* into the chart. It would be another eight months before they tried again, with *I'll Always Love You* again being produced by Mickey and Ivy. This time the group got a hit, with *I'll Always Love You* soaring to #8 R&B and #35 pop, but rather than kick-start a successful Motown career for The Spinners, the group found themselves once again left on the sidelines, as Bobbie Smith would later reveal.

"We did have some hits at Motown, but what always happened is that we'd have to wait a year or so to get another record out. Once you get a hit, you have to follow it up. With us, by the time we could get a song out it was always like we were starting over."

Ten months after *I'll Always Love You*, the follow-up *Truly Yours* hit the street, the group's third recording with Mickey and Ivy.

"Ivy Hunter was really the only producer that took a real interest in The Spinners," said Bobbie, something Ivy himself felt was down to their respective stature at

Motown. "Neither one of us was on the A-list, so that put us in the same ballpark, didn't it? It's like the minor leagues – you don't have to go far to find out the teams you're gonna be playing with are in the minor leagues too. But they were a great act. Bobbie had a very commercial, pop voice. I guess they were a little difficult to funnel into that so-called Motown Sound."

The Spinners might have felt like a minor league outfit, but their performances were anything but, with *Truly Yours* deserving better than its final peak of #16 R&B and bubbling under at #111 on the pop chart. If single releases by The Spinners were haphazard, then their debut album was virtually invisible. There is evidence that **The Original Spinners** was released as a mono album in May 1966, but any promotion, if indeed there was any, was withheld until a stereo version was made available the following August (in the UK, both stereo and mono versions were made available in January 1968, with the album slightly changing its title to **The Detroit Spinners**).

Whilst it had taken a good few years for the album to emerge, the material covered virtually their entire career to date, including their first hit *That's What Girls Are Made For* through to *Truly Yours*. The uncertainty of where their recording career was heading was enough to see Chico Edwards leave the group again, exiting the music business to go and work for a roofing company. In his place the group drafted in George Curtis Cameron (born in McCalls Creek, Mississippi on 21 September 1945), better known as G.C. Cameron, fresh from his stint serving with the US Marines in Vietnam.

By then another single had slipped through the net, with *For All We Know,* the well-known standard given a doo-wop style treatment having been released in April 1967. G.C. joined the group on the road in time to appear at the Apollo Theater in November 1967, opening for Marvin Gaye, and the following June joined them in the studio for the first time, with *Bad, Bad Weather (Till You Come Home)* the first fruits of the new line-up. It did little, as did what would be their final single on the Motown label, *In My Diary* being a cover of The Moonglows 1955 outing and an attempt to cash in on the doo wop revival that was sweeping the country. Unfortunately, The Spinners version went the way of the Moonglows' original, leaving the group without a hit of any sort for the previous three years.

Following a switch of labels, The Spinners' found themselves on the V.I.P. imprint, seen as something of a graveyard label by many within Motown and indicative of how far down the pecking order The Spinners had slumped. Yet there were many within Hitsville who believed the group had talent and were worth a shot, with no shortage of potential producers lining up to take their shot.

Next in the firing line was Johnny Bristol, their old colleague from Tri-Phi, who revived The Temptations' *Message From A Blackman* for single release in February 1970. The message was somewhat outspoken for many, enough for the group to refrain from including it in their live show, although the group would claim it received more than its fair share of airplay, even if it wasn't enough to turn it into a hit. Fortunately, even as *Message From A Blackman* was struggling for acceptance, The Spinners were working on what would become their best known Motown release, thanks to a friendship between G.C. Cameron and Stevie Wonder.

"Stevie and I became very tight, so we were like inseparable for a period of time. One night we went out to a club and came back, and he had been working on this song for us called *It's A Shame*. I went down in the basement at his house when I brought him back home that night and listened to it, and that was it. I think the next day we went in and recorded it."

Stevie wrote the song with Lee Garrett and Syreeta Wright, the same team that were also busy crafting *Signed Sealed Delivered* at much the same time. Ready for release in June 1970, *It's A Shame* returned The Spinners to the chart with a vengeance, hitting #4 R&B and #14 pop, as well as becoming the group's chart debut in the UK when it hit #20. In Britain, the presence of a Liverpool based folk group by the name of The Spinners had resulted in the Detroit group's releases being issued with the credit The Detroit Spinners (the name under which all of their later Atlantic releases would be credited) or The Motown Spinners to differentiate one from the other, although the switch between Detroit Spinners and Motown Spinnners caused its own confusion!

Not surprisingly, when the group issued their second album in October the same year, it carried the title **The Second Time Around**, and made it into the chart, reaching #46 R&B and a lowly #199 pop. Stevie and Syreeta would also co-pen The Spinners follow-up and, as it turned out, their swansong in *We'll Have It Made*. Whilst a small hit (it would hit #20 R&B and #89 pop), it was not as big as those involved thought it should have been, although by the end of 1970 the group was already in the throes of exiting Motown.

The seeds of doubt over the direction their career was headed had been evident for some time, but whilst out on the road they had discussed the matter at some length with other artists they encountered, with Aretha Franklin telling the group to come and join her at Atlantic. Reasoning they had little to lose and everything to gain, the group decided that they would let their Motown contracts lapse and then leave the company.

Which was fine for Bobbie Smith, Henry Fambrough, Pervis Jackson and Billy Henderson, who were free to leave en masse, but later arrival G.C. Cameron had a contract that ran for longer than his band-mates. Thus when The Spinners left, G.C. stayed behind at Motown, with Philip Walker being recommended to the group as G.C.'s replacement.

The group duly signed with Atlantic where according to legend they were personally selected by hit songwriter and producer Thom Bell from a list of artists he might wish to work with. For the rest of the decade, The Spinners and Thom Bell crafted some of the finest music of the era, topping both the R&B and pop charts with an array of singles. They were equally regular visitors to the upper echelons of the album chart, proof that the group had the abilities to reach the top, they just needed the right guidance and material, something lacking for much of their time at Hitsville.

Motown would continue to mine The Spinners back catalogue in an attempt to wring out extra sales as their star rose at Atlantic, even getting the compilation album **The Best Of The Spinners** onto the chart at #37 R&B and #124 pop. It was, however, too little and too late for a group who rank among the finest to have passed through the company. Bobbie Smith, however, doesn't regret his time at Motown.

"Motown had a lot of groups of the same calibre as The Spinners, so we felt like we were always getting lost in the shuffle. But it was a good learning experience. To me, it was like going to college and coming out an A student. The Spinners happens to be a group that is very loyal. Sometimes you can be too loyal for your own good. At Motown, we never envied anybody or got angry. When we got to Atlantic and got with Thom, we were ready. When things do happen for you, like they did for us at Atlantic, it just seems like it's your time and everything falls into place."

Philip Walker, who became better known as Philippe Wynne, died from a heart attack on 14 July 1984. C.P. Spencer died from a heart attack on 20 October 2004. George Dixon died in 2005. Bill Henderson died from diabetes on 2 February 2007. Pervis Jackson died from cancer on 18 August 2008. Chico Edwards died on 3 December 2011. Bobbie Smith died from complications from pneumonia and influenza on 16 March 2013.

ALBUMS: THE ORIGINAL SPINNERS (1966), THE SECOND TIME AROUND (1970)
COMPILATION: THE BEST OF THE SPINNERS (1973)

TERRY STAFFORD

Elvis Presley's 1962 album **Pot Luck With Elvis** was not considered to be one of his better efforts, but one track that did stand out was Doc Pomus and Mort Shuman's *Suspicion*. It would eventually get released as a single in 1976, but by then it had already been a US #3 hit thanks to a cover version by Terry Stafford.

Born in Hollis, Oklahoma on 22 November 1941, Terry was raised in Amarillo and began his career singing at high school dances doing impersonations of Elvis Presley and Buddy Holly. He moved to Los Angeles after graduating from Palo Duro high school and was eventually signed by Crusader Records in 1964. His version of *Suspicion*, which would also become his only UK hit at #31, was the record that broke The Beatles stranglehold on the top of the charts, but Terry never got a hit that big again.

By the 1970s he was recording country music and was signed to Melodyland for *Darling Think It Over* in April 1975. A further single, *Reba* was scheduled for September the same year but was not released, with Terry subsequently recording for Casino and Player. Having made an appearance in the film 'Wild Wheels' in 1969, Terry died from liver failure on 17 March 1996.

STANDING IN THE SHADOWS OF LOVE – THE FOUR TOPS [SINGLE]

When it looked likely that *Reach Out I'll Be There* by The Four Tops was going to top the chart (which it ultimately did on 15 October 1966), Berry Gordy virtually demanded a suitable follow-up be ready for release ahead of Christmas. Further squeezing the schedule was the group's forthcoming visit of Britain, where they were booked to appear at the Saville Theatre in London 13 November, returning to Britain again in January for a nine date, twice-nightly tour. Time, therefore, was very much of the essence, with Holland-Dozier-Holland recording the track on 10 October.

Although HDH invariably re-used parts of their own songs in creating new ones, *Standing In The Shadows Of Love* was not a direct descendant of The Supremes' *Standing At The Crossroads Of Love* but rather was constructed by re-using the chord patterns that had featured on *Stop! In The Name Of Love*.

The song may well have been intended for The Supremes, but somewhere along the way 'My Search Has Ended' (the working title of the song) became *Standing In The Shadows Of Love* and was recorded by

The Four Tops. The actual vocal sessions took place on 19 October at Golden World, the first Motown session at the studio Berry Gordy had taken over after buying out Ed Wingate a month previously and which was re-christened Studio B (Hitsville, of course, was Studio A). Further recording and over-dubbing work took place on two occasions, but by 7 November, the single was ready to go.

Released on 28 November 1966, the single would continue both The Four Tops and HDH's hot streak peaking at #2 R&B and #6 pop. In the UK the single was delayed until 6 January 1967, bring released just as the group was due to start their tour, with the result it peaked at #6 the very same week their tour commenced on 28 January.

The song has since been much covered, most notably by The Jackson 5 on their debut album, Barry White on *his* debut album, France Joli, Hall & Oates and Phil Collins, whilst it has also been sampled by Craig David and Flesh-N-Bone.

STANDING IN THE SHADOWS OF MOTOWN (FILM)

In June 1987 Allan Slutsky began writing a book on James Jamerson, entitled 'Standing In The Shadows Of Motown: The Life And Music Of The Legendary Bassist James Jamerson', which alongside the biographical information was intended as a bass guitar instruction book, complete with an accompanying CD. Published in 1989, with some 49 transcribed musical scores, it became a hugely popular book, winning the 'Rolling Stone/BMI Ralph J Gleason Music Book Award' that same year. Over the ensuing years, the book served to remind the public not only of the contribution James Jamerson had made to Motown and its legacy but also visited interest in other members of The Funk Brothers.

In 2002 therefore, the book became the documentary film 'Standing In The Shadows Of Motown', featuring interviews with the surviving members, archive material, still photographs and re-enactments as well as performances of classic Motown material by the likes of Gerald Levert, Chaka Khan, Bootsy Collins, Montell Jordan, Joan Osborne, Ben Harper and Me'shell Ndegeocello. Directed by Paul Justman and opening on 15 November 2002, the film was also a major success, winning the Best Non-Fiction Film award from both the National Society of Film Critics and the New York Film Critics Circle and the Audience Award for Best Documentary Showcase Film at the Austin Film Festival. The accompanying soundtrack also won the Grammy Awards for Best Soundtrack Album and Best Traditional R&B Vocal Performance for Chaka Khan's *What's Going On*. The film was subsequently released on DVD in January 2004 and is required viewing for any Motown aficionado.

GORDON STAPLES

Violinist and concertmaster for the Detroit Symphony Orchestra, Gordon Staples was responsible for organising the string section accompaniment to countless Motown tracks during the 1960s and early 70s. Gordon (born in Los Angeles, California in 1929) graduated from the Philadelphia Academy of Music and was a soloist with the New York Little Symphony, the New Orleans Philharmonic and the Vancouver Symphony before joining the Detroit Symphony Orchestra, becoming concertmaster in 1968.

In 1970 he recorded a whole album for Motown, **Strung Out** which was credited to Gordon Staples & The String Thing, with the title track being released as a single in April 1971 and credited to Gordon Staples & The Motown Strings. With Paul Riser handling production and the Funk Brothers laying down the groove, the rest of the players were Italo Babini, Edward Korkigian, Marcy Schweickhardt and Thaddeus Markiewicz (cello), Carole Crosby and Pat Terry (harp), Anne Mischakoff, David Ireland, Edouard Kesner, Meyer Shaprio and Nathan Gordon (viola) and Alvin Score, Beatrice Budinzky (Gordon's wife), Felix Resnick, James Waring, Lilian Downs, Linda Snedden Smith, Richard Margitza, Virginia Halfmann and Zinovi Bistritzky (violin). Much of the album subsequently turned up in the soundtrack to the Fred Williamson film 'Mean Johnny Barrows'. Gordon died in 1990, although his widow and son Greg continue to perform with the Detroit Symphony Orchestra.

ALBUM: STRUNG OUT (1970)

EDWIN STARR

One of the select few artists to have enjoyed success before, during and after their stint at Motown, Edwin's chief talent appears to have been the ability to reinvent himself musically throughout his entire career.

Born in Nashville, Tennessee on 21 January 1942 Charles Edwin Hatcher grew up in Cleveland, Ohio and joined his first vocal group, The Future Tones whilst still a teenager. Joining Edwin in the group were John Berry, Parnell Burks, Richard Isom and Roosevelt

Harris, with the group recording briefly in 1957 for Reserve (*Please Come Back*) and Tress (*I Know*) before Edwin was forced to call a halt to his musical career after being drafted into the armed forces. After serving in the United States and Germany, Edwin briefly revived The Future Tones and then found full time employment with the Bill Doggett Combo as a vocalist.

"His manager, a guy by the name of Don Briggs, saw me performing with The Future Tones. And he liked very much what I was doing, and he asked me, would I be interested in joining the Bill Doggett organisation. And I said to him, 'Yes I would, definitely,' even though it was less money than I was actually making. But it was a lot more experience. So I got the chance to get my road experience by travelling with Bill for two and a half years."

It was also Don Briggs who gave Edwin the stage name by which he would become world renowned; so convinced was he that Edwin was on his way to the top, he persuaded him to change his name to Edwin Starr. At first Edwin was more than happy to sing whatever it was that Bill Doggett wanted, but in 1965 Edwin came up with an idea for a song.

"We had like three or four days off in New York. I went to the movie while I was there, and the movie just happened to be 'Agent 007' [more than likely to have been either 'Goldfinger' or 'Thunderball'], you know, the James Bond movie. And James Bond, that whole ideology behind the James Bond films, happened to be the flavour of the month. So I watched the movie like three times, and then I went back to my hotel room, and was sitting there contemplating on the idea of what the movie was all about, and trying to figure out how to incorporate that into a song. And I came up with *Agent Double-O-Soul*. So I went to Bill, and I said to him, 'I'd like to record this.' And he said to me, 'Well, maybe in a year's time, we might be ready for you to record.' And I said to him, 'I can't wait a year. This is a current topic now, and if I do wait, by the time I get the chance to actually go in and record it, it'll be old hat.'"

Of course, Edwin wasn't to know that James Bond would go on to become the longest running franchise in film history, but convinced he needed to record it sooner rather than later, Edwin handed in his notice to Bill Doggett, with fate then stepping in to give him a helping hand.

"It was during the same week that I had left Bill Doggett. I had given my notice, looking for some avenue to record the song. LeBaron Taylor [a deejay in Detroit] introduced me to Ed Wingate, and from there they signed me to Golden World and created the label Ric-Tic."

Edwin was put into the studio almost immediately to record *Agent Double-O-Soul*, with Richard Parker producing the track that was arranged by Edwin and Sonny Sanders, formerly of The Satintones (LeBaron Taylor also received a name-check, for the song's composition credit was given to Charles Hatcher and Bill Sharpley, the latter LeBaron's real name). *Agent Double-O-Soul* proved that Edwin's sense of timing was spot on, with the single going on to become a #8 R&B hit and came close to cracking into the pop Top Twenty, stalling at #21. There are claims, albeit unsubstantiated, that as the single was taking off Edwin met up with Sean Connery, the actor who portrayed James Bond at the time, and the pair made a short promotional film, although it is more likely that the actor and singer met on a film set. Although not as big a hit, the follow up *Back Street* also appeared on the chart at #33 R&B and #95 pop, and Edwin made it three in a row with *S.O.S.*

"When I wrote the next song, the initial thought of the song was 'S.O.S. – sending out soul. But then when I realised what I had written, I had written a prelude of *Agent Double-O-Soul*. So I changed it. I got with a guy named Richard Morris, and Richard and I changed it to *Stop Her On Sight* to make it like a girl/guy song. But the whole idea of the song came from the television programme '20,000 Leagues Under The Sea', 'cause I was laying watching that, and they did the Morse code thing on the TV show. And that's where I got the intro for the record."

As instantly appealing as his debut hit, *Stop Her On Sight (S.O.S.)* restored Edwin to the upper echelons of the R&B chart, peaking at #9 and becoming a #48 pop hit. It also started a love affair between Edwin and British audiences, where it was released by Polydor and became a #35 hit the first time around. Edwin meanwhile was back in the Golden World studios working with the same team on his next hit, *Headline News* as well as a couple of other tracks that would eventually surface credited to The Holidays. *Headline News* did nothing on the R&B chart but managed to crossover to #86 pop and crack the Top Forty in Britain, where it peaked at #39 in August 1966. Back in the USA, Edwin had been heard if not seen on the charts with *I'll Love You Forever*, the track that was credited to The Holidays.

"There was no such group as The Holidays. What happened was that Don Davis asked me to do a demo recording. And he, unbeknownst to me, put the record out using my voice on the lead, and calling it The Holidays. Which everyone knew was me, and that there was no such group as The Holidays. But the record got so big that they had to create a group to perform. I just walked in the studio. He said to me, 'Do me a demo of this song.' Handed me the lyrics, and that was it. What you hear on the record is that demo that I did that night."

I'll Love You Forever, which reportedly featured fellow singers J.J. Barnes and Steve Mancha on background vocals, did better than any demo record might normally be expected to do, hitting #7 R&B and #63 pop. Edwin also enjoyed some success as a writer, penning *Oh How Happy* for Shades Of Blue, also producing the session and managing to get a one off deal with Detroit music entrepreneur Harry Balk and the Impact label, with the single going on to become a #12 pop hit. All of this musical activity emanating from Detroit was galling for the main music entrepreneur Berry Gordy, who was convinced he had the city's major talent locked down at Hitsville, so in an effort to remove the competition he bought Ed Wingate's operation, including all of the artist contracts, resulting in Edwin being moved over to Motown.

"I didn't know it at all. It was a done deal by the time I got back to the United States. I was in England performing at the time, and I went back to the United States to go to the Apollo Theater to co-star with The Temptations. And one of The Temptations told me I was a Motown artist. It was a shock to the system, to say the least – and then it took two years before they actually recorded me, 'cause they didn't know what to do with me as an artist."

Edwin, of course, wasn't the only former Ric-Ric or Golden World artist caught up in the confusion, with J.J. Barnes and The Fantastic Four among the bigger names who found their careers effectively stalled after being picked up by Motown and eventually heading off for pastures new. Edwin meanwhile could do little other than wait his time between recording sessions and continue adding to his growing reputation as a live performer.

"There are two ways to do this job. You either say OK, make no waves and thank the Lord you're still getting your cheque every week. Or you make waves, knowing the only way is out after that."

For a time Edwin took the first option, but it must have been frustrating for someone who had enjoyed as many hits as he had prior to joining the company being left unfulfilled and unrecorded.

"I had a hand in my work before I joined Motown, but there I wasn't looked upon as anything other than a singer. I was part of the assembly line and had to take the songs that were offered to me."

Some of the initial songs Edwin did get to record were good, with *I Want My Baby Back* backed with *Gonna Keep On Tryin' Till I Win Your Love* his initial Gordy single in November 1967.

"I liked it very much," he would later remark of the flipside. "But that was one of the reasons why most of the artists left the company, too – because we were all doing the same songs, over and over again. So consequently, as writers, we were losing out a hundred percent all the way around, 'cause we couldn't get a chance to get our foot in the door as a writer. Because they were using only a handful of writers at the company, they were using their material."

The same small band of writers that Edwin got to work with were also handling Jimmy Ruffin, with James Dean and William Weatherspoon combining on *I Am The Man For You Baby*, Edwin's first chart hit on Gordy that hit #45 R&B and bubbled under the Top 100 at #112. In August 1968 Edwin released his debut album, **Soul Master**, but the passage of time since his Ric-Tic hits and the lack of a major hit for Motown prevented **Soul Master** from achieving much action of its own.

Then, finally, things began happening for Edwin at Motown, with a television appearance on '20 Grand Live' leading to an avalanche of telephone calls demanding the closing song Edwin had performed, *25 Miles*. Hastily sent into the studio to get it recorded and then out to the market, it burst on to the chart, hitting #6 R&B and pop, one of Motown's biggest hits of the year. Whilst the British arm held back to see how well it would eventually do before committing a Tamla Motown release, Polydor gathered his two earlier hits in *Stop Her On Sight (S.O.S.)* and *Headline News* and saw their single sail all the way to #11, further confirming the empathy that existed between Edwin and his British fan-base.

"I feel blessed to have a British following. Going back to the fifties/sixties, when I returned to the States after touring here, I told artists like Jimmy Ruffin and J.J. Barnes where I'd been and the reception I'd received, how I'd been treated. They didn't have a clue what I was talking about! I told them to get over here 'cause there's a whole new world here, new fans, people who know us. But they wouldn't. Subsequently, they never built up a solid British following, except maybe Jimmy Ruffin."

When eventually released in Britain, *25 Miles* would become a #36 hit and provide Edwin with plenty of opportunities to continue touring throughout the country. Despite the success of *25 Miles*, Motown still wouldn't allow Edwin to record all his own material, with the resulting album the same varied collection of old and new material, produced by the likes of Norman Whitfield, Smokey Robinson and Dean & Weatherspoon, although the appeal of the single was perhaps sufficient to propel the album into the chart, peaking at #9 R&B and #73. Something else Motown borrowed from the old way of doing things was an album of duets with Sondra 'Blinky' Edwards, an attempt to replicate the success Marvin Gaye had enjoyed with Mary Wells, Kim Weston and Tammi Terrell.

"What they were trying to do was, they had a policy of piggybacking different artists together to try to focus more attention on the lesser of the two artists. But in our particular instance, we were both on a par with each other. Neither one of use was more popular than the other. Blinky and I were orphans because we weren't true Motown artists, weren't the flavour of the month. It was a blazing album and was a potential chart-topping album but we weren't Diana Ross and Marvin Gaye, so we didn't have the support needed for a hit."

Thus **Just We Two** took its place in the ranks of the great and the good Motown albums that didn't get the reception they deserved, at much the same time as it stalled Blinky's career before it had even got off the ground. For Edwin however, a major hit was just around the corner.

War had begun attracting attention whilst it sat as a Temptations' album track, but such was their fan-base, Motown didn't want to run the risk of alienating the customers at the Copa with the anti-war sentiments of the song by releasing it as a single. Writer and producer Norman Whitfield's original intention had been to have Rare Earth record the song, but the rock combo were too interested in performing their own material to bother with *War*, resulting in Norman drafting in Edwin to record what would ultimately become the definitive version. The backing tracks may well have been in place, but what really catapulted the song was Edwin's powerful vocal, one which positively screamed out the message.

"I got a little heat from it. While the song was #1, I never did any work at all. I mean, there was very few places where you could go and sing 'War, what is it good for?' in the political atmosphere of the United States."

Whilst live performances of *War* were somewhat limited, it did not hinder the record's performance on the charts, going on to top the pop chart for three weeks, reach #3 R&B and repeat that position in Britain, where Edwin could perform it without fear. Edwin not only got to sing *War* his way, he was afforded the opportunity of producing at least a third of the resulting album **War And Peace**, with the album going on to hit #9 R&B and #52 pop, despite there being no further hit singles lifted. Norman Whitfield and Barrett Strong, the writers of *War*, offered more of the same on *Stop The War Now*, a song Edwin in particular felt was too much of the same.

"I always felt that the statement 'War, what is it good for?' was strong enough. There was no need to say 'Stop The War', because it was inevitable that it was going to be stopped."

Despite Edwin's feelings, *Stop The War Now* did continue getting the message across, enough for it to reach the R&B Top Ten (at #5) and #23 pop as well as #33 in the UK. Fortunately, Whitfield/Strong avoided the anti-war sentiment for the next song chosen as a single, *Funky Music Sho' Nuff Turns Me On*, which would go on to become Edwin's last R&B Top Ten hit when it peaked at #6, although it stalled a long way off on the pop listings at #64. The resulting album **Involved** struggled for acceptance, barely making #45 R&B and #178 pop, and for the next two years or so Edwin struggled to get back to winning ways.

With Motown having switched operations to the West Coast and revamped their numerous labels, Edwin found himself with releases on Soul and Motown, scoring minor R&B hits on both with *There You Go* on Soul (#12 R&B and #80 pop) and *You Got My Soul On Fire* on Motown *(#40 R&B)*, but as with many of his contemporaries left behind in Detroit, Motown's switch had seen him become something of a forgotten figure, at least in America.

He briefly returned to the spotlight after linking up with Freddie Perren and Fonce Mizell for the soundtrack album to 'Hell Up In Harlem', one of the perennial blaxploitation films that were released during the mid-1970s or thereabouts, with Edwin's album deserving much more than it actually achieved.

In 1975 he left Motown, bound first for Granite and then 20th Century, the latter label benefitting when Edwin made the move towards the burgeoning disco and club scene. Whilst minor chart hits in the US, both *Contact* and *H.A.P.P.Y. Radio* were major club hits and, most importantly, both became Top Ten hits in Britain. Such was Edwin's appeal in Britain, he decided to settle in the country, recording for a number of small labels, enjoying the occasional hit but spending more than two decades exciting audiences the length and breadth of the country, as he would later acknowledge.

"I've spent more time in the UK than the States. America is such a vast area to travel. For example, I can be popular on the West Coast, and then be nothing on the South Coast. Working in this country [Britain] is easier in terms of distance and, of course, Europe is nearby. I had the opportunity to stay in the States – I wasn't chased out or anything like that – but I'm here out of choice and I prefer to live in this environment. Europe and the UK have been good to me, and others, like Frankie Beverly and Maze. They don't sell great quantities of records here, yet their shows are sold out. British loyalty is amazing. It's the love of the British people that keeps me going. You can't fool the British people. You're true to your beliefs and causes. Sure, some Americans say you're stand-offish but that's because they don't know you, which is a shame. If they've not got the patience to find your qualities then that's their problem. I came to this country because I was tired of looking over my shoulder. The more I got out there, the more people wanted to take it away from me. The British don't treat us like stars, which means when the time comes for the comedown it's not so far to fall!"

Yet Edwin was treated as a star, albeit an approachable one. He eschewed the normal trappings of stardom, making himself readily available to pose for pictures, sign autographs and talk with the people who continued to flock to his shows.

"Look, you don't need bodyguards, minders and all that razzmatazz over here. Maybe in America, sure, but not here. Fans respect us because they respect the music, and this is what some of these guys – those with the 'American music attitude', which should be left at Heathrow – don't understand. How can I walk down a street, they say, be so vulnerable? Well, why not? Why not go into an audience? People contact, that's what it's all about. I'm a people person, and it's certainly something that doesn't bother me and never has. That's the respect I'm shown, and I am so thankful. And I've never been threatened or hurt either!"

Edwin continued his love affair with British' audiences right to the end before dying from a heart attack at his Nottingham home on 2 April 2003. He was buried at Southern Cemetery & Wilford Hill Crematorium in Nottinghamshire, where his epitaph reads, 'In Loving Memory of Charles Edwin Hatcher...Our Agent 00 Soul...Edwin Starr. Keep The Faith...Always Loved, Never Forgotten.'

ALBUMS: SOUL MASTER (1968), 25 MILES (1969), JUST WE TWO (1969), WAR AND PEACE (1970), INVOLVED (1971), HELL UP IN HARLEM (1974)
COMPILATION: THE HITS OF EDWIN STARR (1972)

STATESIDE RECORDS

Shortly after the Top Rank label folded in 1962, EMI hired former label head Fred Oxon to front a new imprint named Stateside. Having noted the success Decca (through London American) and Pye Records (with Pye International) had enjoyed with American recordings in Britain, Oxon's brief was to find similar recordings that might find favour in the United Kingdom.

The new imprint was launched in June 1962 and scored a hit first time out with Freddy Cannon's *Palisades Park*, licensed from Swan, subsequently acquiring the Wand, SPQR, Diamond, Pyramid, Sar, Gone, A&M, Legrand, Vee-Jay, Scepter, Rendezvous, Rust and Laurie labels and their respective artists.

In September 1963 Stateside acquired the rights to the Motown label and their imprints from Oriole and kicked off with Martha & The Vandellas' *(Love Is Like A) Heat Wave*, released in October 1963. In May 1964 Stateside released its fifteenth single, Mary Wells' *My Guy*, which would become the first Motown single to break in to the British charts, peaking at #5. Stateside would enjoy further chart success with Mary Wells & Marvin Gaye (*Once Upon A Time*), The Supremes (*Where Did Our Love Go*) and Martha & The Vandellas (*Dancing In the Street*) before registering its first number one with The Supremes' *Baby Love* in October 1964.

In all, Stateside released 45 Motown singles in the UK (as well as five EPs and nine albums), with eight making the charts, before in March 1965 Dave Godin convinced both Berry Gordy and EMI that Motown deserved its own dedicated British imprint, Tamla Motown. Stateside continued through the rest of the decade and beyond, licensing such labels as Crimson, Bell, Tangerine, Musicor, ABC and Brother before being shut down in April 1974. The label name was revived in 2003 as a reissue label.

MAUREEN STEELE

Born in Worcester, Massachusetts on 22 July, Maureen Sandstrom Steele dropped out of college in 1977 in order to join her brother Bobby in the band The Second Chance. Both Bobby and Maureen moved to Los Angeles in 1979 in order to further pursue musical careers, with Bobby becoming keyboard player for Paul Sabu. Through this connection Maureen got an audition with Motown and was signed in 1984.

Her debut single *Save The Night For Me* made #77 on the chart in April 1985, with the flip side *Boys Will Be Boys* also turning up in the soundtrack to 'The Flamingo Kid.' Her album debut came with **Nature Of The Beast** which was also released in April 1985. After leaving Motown Maureen did backing vocals for Appollonia before retiring from music in order to start a family. In 1989 and under the name Maureen Steele-

Volante, she went into the real estate business with her husband Mike Volante.
ALBUM: NATURE OF THE BEAST (1985)

TENNYSON STEPHENS

Singer and pianist Tennyson Stephens was born in the Bay Area but eventually moved to Hawaii, occasionally being tempted back to the American mainland for a number of live and recording appearances. Having recorded sporadically during the 1960s (for Chess and Aries Records as Tenison Stephens and for Columbia with Rheta Hughes) and been a member of Jerry Butler's backing band, he joined Phil Upchurch's band in 1973.

Two years later Phil Upchurch opted to record an R&B influenced album, with Tennyson brought to the fore to such an extent he was given dual billing on the sleeve. Issued on Kudu in 1975, **Upchurch/Tennyson** was a highly regarded album, even if it failed to make a dent on the charts. Whilst Phil Upchurch continued to make musical inroads over the following decades, Tennyson Stephens battled several health problems, most notably gout, but making the occasional performance appearance.
ALBUM: UPCHURCH/TENNYSON (1975)

STEPIN FETCHIT

A hugely successful comic and actor in the 1930s and 40s, Stepin Fetchit was born Lincoln Theodore Monroe Andrew Perry in Key West, Florida on 30 May 1902 (although more recent research claims he may have been born as early as 1896). He adopted the stage name Stepin Fetchit and created a lazy and slow-witted persona. Whilst it was all an act, Perry would use the character for his own benefit during the course of his career; if he found some of the lines in films offensive, he would skip or mumble them, giving the impression that he was too stupid to understand.

Whilst the Stepin Fetchit character was controversial, it was also successful, making Perry the first African American actor to become a millionaire. Unfortunately the money ran out soon after his film career came to an end and he was declared bankrupt in 1947. By the early 1960s he was dependent on charity, which may have been part of the reason why Motown recorded an album on him. Whilst sleeves were printed and at least eight tracks are known to have been completed, **My Son The Sit-In** was shelved, possibly because the character of Stepin Fetchit was not one Motown wished to be associated with. Lincoln died on 19 November 1985.

STERLING

Once described as 'the best soul singer you never heard of', Sterling Harrison was born in Richmond, Virginia on 19 July 1941. A member of The Harrison Family Four that won several local talent competitions, it was after winning another contest that Sterling recorded his first single for VIM in 1960. Thereafter his recordings were somewhat sporadic, with singles appearing on Smash and All Platinum.

Towards the end of the 1970s he was signed by Holland Group Productions, resulting in his only Motown outing *Roll-Her, Skater* released in October 1979. Sterling's debut album was produced by Holland Group Productions and was released by Real World Records in 1980. He died from cancer on 21 August 2005.

KAYE STEVENS

Born Catherine Louise Stephens in Pittsburgh, Pennsylvannia on 21 July 1932, Kaye Stevens began her career as a singer in Las Vegas hotels before graduating to bigger venues and later television game shows. Kaye appeared as a special guest on 'The Temptations Show' in 1969 along with George Kirby and performed with The Temptations on For Once In Your Life, which subsequently appeared on the soundtrack album (although Kaye's name was correctly spelt on the front cover, it was misspelt as 'Kay' everywhere else!). She died from breast cancer on 28 December 2011.

WILLIAM 'MICKEY' STEVENSON

"William 'Mickey' Stevenson showed up at Hitsville for an audition one day with an official looking briefcase and a big, easy grin. Sharply dressed, hip, fast-talking, Mickey was street, much more street than I was. I could see he was definitely an Eastside graduate while I was still sort of that Westside boy at heart. I liked him a lot. Then he sang a song. I liked him less."

Berry Gordy didn't think much of Mickey Stevenson as a singer, but he still liked him enough to find him a role within his organisation, that of A&R director. The only problem was that neither Mickey nor Berry actually knew what an A&R man was or what he did, effectively enabling Mickey to create his own job description at Hitsville.

In time, Mickey would have his own doubts about some of the singers who turned up looking for a recording contract (most notably Morris Broadnax, who Mickey rejected as a singer but employed as a writer), but his initial duties involved gathering together a core of musicians that would be the mainstay of the Motown sound for the rest of the decade.

With Ivy Joe Hunter the ad hoc group's original leader, Mickey recruited the cream of Detroit's musicians, including Benny Benjamin, James Jamerson, Earl Van Dyke, Robert White and Joe Messina. Subsequently known as The Funk Brothers, they provided the musical accompaniment to the singers signed to the label, many of whom auditioned for Mickey before they got to meet with Berry and sign their contracts.

Mickey was also a more than capable writer, producer and arranger himself, linking with Barrett Strong in 1961 to pen Eddie Holland's hit *Jamie* and would go on to co-write early hits such as *Beechwood 4-5789* (The Marvelettes), *Stubborn Kind Of Fellow* (Marvin Gaye) and *Dancing In The Street* (Martha Reeves), among others. Mickey was also responsible for selecting which artists would record which songs, and even when there was a case of a no show, still managed to come up trumps; when Mary Wells failed to turn up for a session, Mickey sent his then secretary Martha Reeves into the studio rather than waste the allocated time, with the result Martha & The Vandellas kicked off their career with *I'll Have To Let Him Go*.

His last major hit at the company was *It Takes Two*, a duet between Marvin Gaye and Mickey's then wife Kim Weston (romance bloomed almost as much as music around Hitsville in those days) that was a Top Twenty hit in 1966. Not long after, Mickey received a lucrative job offer.

"That day he called to see me I could hear something was up in his voice. Heavy confidence was attached to his lower tones. But when he came into my office he was a little more humble, as he told me about a major offer he had received from MGM to set up and run a record division for them on the West Coast. 'I think it's a big shot for me, BG. What do you think?' What could I say? He was only asking my permission out of deep respect. I knew we'd miss him but I wished him luck. I would always remember Mickey Stevenson for his loyalty and dedication. He was one of the greatest creative forces during our formative years."

Unfortunately for Mickey, the grass wasn't particularly greener on the West Coast, despite a reported million dollar deal and the chance to take Kim Weston with him. Denied access to the same musicians and songwriters that had made his job at Hitsville relatively easy, the Venture label he ran on behalf of MGM failed to make an impact.

He would later launch his own label, People Records, assist on the soundtrack to the film 'Changes', record his own, overlooked album for Ember (**Here I Am**, released in 1972) and write numerous musicals, but nothing ever quite matched the period when he had the Midas touch at Motown. Today Mickey runs his own music company, helping today's crop of would be stars in much the same way he did fifty or so years ago.

STILL – THE COMMODORES [SINGLE]

Sail On was still a feature in the upper reaches of the chart when Motown rush-released *Still* as the follow-up single, reacting to both public and radio demand to the track when it had first appeared on the album **Midnight Magic**. Just like its predecessor, *Still* was based on the break-up of a marriage, one where Lionel was on good terms with both parties in the split.

"I admired their strength. They decided their marriage was not the thing for them and they were probably destroying what they had in the first place, which was friendship. They both sat down and said, 'Listen, we want to be friends, we said some things wrong. Let's get a divorce and that way still be in love and still love as friends.'"

Containing something of a country flavour (which Lionel would return to with future compositions), *Still* struck a chord with all sections of the record buying public, topping both the R&B and pop chart and also made a respectable showing on both the Adult Contemporary and Country charts. In the UK it peaked at #4, the group's fourth Top Ten hit of their career. Two years after its release, *Still* would be covered by country artist John Schneider and receive considerable airplay as the flip side to his hit *Them Good Ol' Boys Are Bad*.

STILL WATER (LOVE) – THE FOUR TOPS [SINGLE]

After the heady days of hit after hit from Holland-Dozier-Holland, The Four Tops chart career took a nosedive, at least as far as America was concerned. Struggling to find any real direction with their new material, they recorded covers which, whilst they still kept hitting the big time in the UK, did little to convince that the group could survive without HDH, let alone prosper.

Just as Frank Wilson had been the man to revive The Supremes when they made their first recordings without Diana Ross, so he would guide The Tops back to their best. Having gotten the group to record a cover version of The Beatles' *Got To Get You Into My Life* for one of their earlier albums, Frank was not afraid to look at rock music as an inspiration for his own compositions.

One such was *Still Water*, which was somewhat inspired by Iron Butterfly's *In-A-Gadda-Da-Vida*, an extended jam that was something of a hybrid of psychedelic music and heavy metal. The tune Frank came up with was anything but, being the same kind of melodic material that the group had already experimented with on *It's All In The Game*, but the song really began to take shape when Frank turned the tune over to Smokey Robinson for him to add lyrics.

In its original form, *Still Water (Love)* segued almost effortlessly into *Still Water (Peace)*, the two parts forming one tune in two movements of nearly six minutes in length. The versions that were released, however, separated them altogether, with *Love* opening their album **Still Waters Run Deep** and *Peace* closing it. *Still Water (Love)* was duly issued as single stateside in August 1970 and hit #4 R&B and #11 pop (effectively their biggest hit since *Bernadette* in 1967), whilst in the UK the single was released a month later and hit #10, once again aided by the group being on tour in Britain. The oversight with the extended version was finally rectified in 2002 with the release of the compilation **Fourever**, which contained the full 5:53 version.

THE STONE CITY BAND

Originally formed as a backing back for Rick James, both in the studio and on the road, The Stone City Band were given their own recording career, just like virtually every other act that passed through Rick James' hands. The original line-up consisted of Levi Ruffin Jr (keyboards), Daniel LeMelle (saxophone), Tom McDermott (guitar) Erskine Williams (keyboards), Oscar Alston (bass) and Lanise Hughes (drums), although the band was fluid in so much as Rick employed numerous other musicians to round out the sound.

The group got their first credit on Rick's album **Come And Get It** in 1978, subsequently recording their own album two years later with **In 'N' Out** (by which time keyboardist LaMorris Payne had joined the line-up). Although it was credited as a Stone City Band album, the presence of Rick James was everywhere, writing and producing virtually everything on the album. However, The Stone City Band had made something of a name for themselves during the course of the two previous years thanks to touring with their mentor, and the combined reputations of Rick and the band were enough to lift the album to #30 on the R&B chart (it was a rather more modest #122 on the pop listings). The album also gave rise to two minor hit singles in *Strut Your Stuff* (#48 R&B) and *Little Runaway* (#66 R&B).

The Stone City Band was more directly involved in their follow-up album **The Boys Are Back**, with Rick writing only three of the songs and the assorted members penning the rest. As such the album was much more diverse than their first effort, although that did not necessarily convert to a rise in sales, with the album only making #53 on the R&B chart.

What would be the group's final album, **Out Of The Shadows** in 1983, was supposed to showcase the group emerging from the shadow of Rick James, but his touch is omnipresent as he produced the album. Whilst the album made little or no impact, there were two further hit singles in *Bad Lady* (#76 R&B) and *Ladies Choice* (#53). Unfortunately, Rick's own growing problems with Motown affected all the acts in his stable, bringing about an end to The Stone City Band's recording career after **Out Of The Shadows**. The band continues to tour to this day, with at least three members of the original line-up still present.

ALBUMS: RICK JAMES PRESENTS THE STONE CITY BAND IN 'N' OUT (1980), THE BOYS ARE BACK (1981), OUT OF THE SHADOWS: MEET THE STONE CITY BAND (1983)

DENNIS STONER

Originally a member of a college group called The Metropolitans, Dennis Stoner had a brief spell with another group after graduating from Temple University and then launched a solo career. With a mixture of folk, rock and blues, Dennis had an eponymous album released on Vantage in January 1971 that was subsequently picked up by Rare Earth and reissued in November 1971.

Backed by Loren Peck (bass), Doug Hess (drums), Cliff Seidle (organ) and backing vocalists Diana Sunday and Sandy Simpson and with Dennis performing on guitar, bass and harpsichord, this was probably his only release; he doesn't appear to have recorded anything else.
ALBUM: DENNIS STONER (1971)

STONEY & MEATLOAF

The hit musical show of the late 1960s was 'Hair', written by James Rado, Gerome Ragni and Galt MacDermot. Barely a year after it had began its residency on Broadway, some nine productions opened in major cities around the United States (as well as in London's West End), including one in Detroit.

Motown producer and engineer Russ Terrana visited the Detroit show and, impressed with two of the performers he had seen, invited his brother Ralph to see the show with a view to signing the pair to Motown's Rare Earth imprint.

The two performers in question were Stoney, a powerful female singer who was born Cheryl Murphy (but was also known as Shaun Murphy) in Omaha, Nebraska, and the larger than life male singer Meat Loaf. Meat, as his name is sometimes shortened, was born Marvin Lee Aday in Dallas, Texas on 27 September 1947 (he would claim for many years that he was born in 1951) and was given what would become his professional name by his high school football coach on account of his huge size and ungainly manner.

Ralph put together a deal to get Stoney and Meat Loaf on to the Rare Earth label, with Russ and Mike Valvano also brought on board to produce the duo's debut album, originally slated for release in 1970. With the album still being completed as the New Year commenced, the decision was taken to release a single as something of an advance action, with *What You See Is What You Get* being released in April 1971 (October 1971 in the UK). It proved to be a minor hit, peaking at #71 pop and #36 R&B (its progress being somewhat hampered by the presence of a different song with the same title by The Dramatics also getting heavy airplay).

Three months later the label tried again, this time with *It Takes All Kind Of People*, but the single did little, as did **Stoney & Meatloaf** when it was finally released in September 1971 (in the UK the album finally appeared more than a year later, in October 1972).

The failure of the project saw Stoney and Meat Loaf go their separate ways, with Stoney being retained by Motown (she would release *Let Me Down Easy* on Motown in May 1973 after the single had been pulled from MoWest in January) whilst Meat Loaf would continue to tour with 'Hair' before landing a leading role in another musical, 'More Than You Deserve', which was written by Jim Steinman.

When Steinman subsequently wrote the hugely successful album **Bat Out Of Hell** for Meat Loaf (the album has sold more than 40 million copies since its release in 1978), Motown repackaged their album with a number of track substitutions as **Meat Loaf Featuring Stoney & Meatloaf** and released it on the Prodigal label in October 1978. The album was also reissued in the UK on the Prodigal label in March 1979, albeit with little or no success, despite Meat Loaf's growing popularity.

Stoney meanwhile would go on to do studio work and later tour with Bob Seger as well as recording with Eric Clapton and become a member of Little Feat before resuming a solo career in 2009.
ALBUM: STONEY AND MEATLOAF (1971)

STONED LOVE – THE SUPREMES [SINGLE]

Teenager Kenny Thomas submitted a number of songs to the talent contest being hosted by 'Frantic' Ernie Durham on radio station WJLB in Detroit, with Motown producer Frank Wilson an eager listener. After contacting Kenny via the station, Frank invited him down to Hitsville in order to take a closer look at the material he had written. After running through the songs that had been featured on WJLB, Frank asked if he had anything else.

There was one song, still uncompleted, that Kenny had which he duly presented, which went by the name 'Running Free'. Spotting its obvious appeal, Frank asked Kenny back to Hitsville, where the pair worked the song up, changing the title to 'Hello Sunshine', then 'Stone Love' and finally *Stoned Love*.

Frank recorded the backing tracks in March 1970 and allocated the song to the new look Supremes, who duly arrived at the studio in New York a few weeks later and were bemused at the youthfulness of the song's co-writer (Kenny was barely 17 years of age at the time). However, they soon saw that what he lacked in experience he more than made up for with ability, with *Stoned Love* sounding as much a potential hit to them as it had to Frank Wilson.

Not everyone at Motown shared that opinion, with Berry Gordy reportedly hating the record and refusing to release it. It may well have been the title, which invoked images of drugs, an avenue Motown had already trod somewhat hesitatingly with *Cloud Nine*, but Mary Wilson was in no doubt what the subject matter was about.

"Just one listen to *Stoned Love* and you knew that it was about love, peace and faith in God. Not getting stoned on drugs."

Gordy's reluctance to release the track was eventually overcome by Barney Ales promising a slew of radio stations that would get behind the track if issued as a single, *Stoned Love* finally appearing in October 1970. Regarded as one of the better post-Diana Ross singles by The Supremes, the single bore the writing credit of Frank Wilson and Yennek Samoht, the latter name being Kenny Thomas spelt backwards with the addition of an extra 'e' in order to make it pronounceable. This was Kenny's attempt at paying homage to Stevie Wonder (who had recorded an album as Eivets Rednow, his name spelt backwards) and Nina Simone.

Released in the US on 7 October 1970, it picked up all of the RKO radio stations that Barney Ales had promised, which converted into sales and a #7 pop placing and topped the R&B charts for one week. In the UK it would become the biggest hit of The Supremes' career (without Diana Ross, that is), peaking at #3.

Kenny would see one further composition issued by Motown, *Sing A Song Of Yesterday* being recorded by The Four Tops and carrying the composing credit of Yennik Samoht!

STOP! IN THE NAME OF LOVE – DIANA ROSS & THE SUPREMES [SINGLE]

Caught out cheating by his girlfriend, Lamont Dozier became embroiled in a bitter argument, with the betrayed woman venting all her anger towards Lamont. In a jokey attempt to calm her down, Lamont asked her to 'stop, in the name of love', and quickly realising the importance of the phrase jotted it down so as to show it to Brian Holland when they were next in the studio.

Brian was as taken with the phrase as Lamont and the pair soon had the melody and lyrics ready for recording. The backing track was recorded on 5 January 1965, with The Supremes coming by two days later for their vocal session and completing the task four days later. There were two mixes of the record done, one for radio disc jockeys and another that would appear on the retail single, but in a change from the norm, these mixes were done by Berry Gordy rather than Brian Holland. Berry did not let his producers down, coming up with two equally stunning versions of the track.

Issued on 8 February 1965, The Supremes went back out on the road to support their latest release, armed not only with a sure-fire hit song but a unique dance routine to go with it; Melvin Franklin and Paul Williams of The Temptations came up with the distinctive hand movements that brought to mind a traffic policeman, with Paul drilling the three Supremes until they had the routine down to perfection.

Stop! In The Name Of Love went on to become the group's fourth consecutive #1 hit, knocking The Beatles' *Eight Days A Week* off the top of the chart and spending two weeks at the summit. It had to be content with a #2 placing on the R&B chart but picked up a Grammy Award nomination for Best Contemporary Rock & Roll Group Performance, although it lost out to The Statler Brothers *Flowers On The Wall*.

In the UK *Stop! In The Name Of Love* was the flagship release from the newly created Tamla Motown label, carrying the catalogue number TMG 501 and becoming the biggest hit out of the six singles released on the same day, 19 March 1965. It would peak at #7, ahead of rivals Martha & The Vandellas' *Nowhere To Run* and The Temptations' *It's Growing*.

STRAY DOG

Originally formed in Texas as Aphrodite, Stray Dog effectively reformed in London in the early 1970s, with William Garrett Walden, better known as W.G. Snuffy Walden (guitar and lead vocals) linking with Alan Roberts (bass and keyboards), Tim Dulaine (guitar and vocals), Luis Cabaza (keyboards and vocals), Randy Reader (drums and vocals) and Leslie Sampson (a former member of Road, who had an album released on Rare Earth in 1972, drums) and getting a deal through Greg Lake with Manticore Records.

After their 1973 eponymous debut, the group recorded two further albums, with **While You're Down There** becoming the first album issued in the US under the deal between Manticore and Motown. Despite touring with Emerson, Lake & Palmer on numerous occasions, Stray Dog disbanded in 1975.

ALBUM: WHILE YOU'RE DOWN THERE (1974)

STREET SONGS – RICK JAMES [ALBUM]

After his first three albums had been huge R&B successes, the relative failure of **Garden Of Love** caused Rick James to re-evaluate his musical career. The first three albums had succeeded because his brand of funk had hit a nerve, whilst the pop and R&B hybrid that dominated **Garden Of Love** had failed because it couldn't find an audience to relate to. So it was back to basics, doing what he did best for **Street Songs**.

All but one of the tracks on display was entirely written by Rick, and the one that wasn't was co-composed with Alonzo Miller. Whilst ballads weren't given a complete wide berth, those that were present, including a duet with his former protégé Teena Marie on *Fire And Desire* were top quality. It was the up-tempo material, however, on which he truly excelled, with *Super Freak*, *Give It To Me Baby* and *Ghetto Life* leading the charge.

Released in April 1981, the album would go on to become the biggest smash of his career, topping the R&B charts for five weeks and peaking at #3 pop, selling over three million copies in the process. Whilst it did not do anywhere near as well internationally, failing to chart at all in the UK, additional worldwide sales saw the album top the four million mark in total by 1983.

The album would be named Favourite Soul/R&B Album at the American Music Awards and be nominated for a Grammy Award for Best Rhythm & Blues Vocal Performance, Male, and whilst it did not win (beaten by James Ingram and *One Hundred Ways*), has still become hugely influential, having been heavily sampled by the likes of Busta Rhymes (*Ghetto Life* forming the backdrop for *In The Ghetto*), MC Hammer (*Super Freak* becoming *U Can't Touch This*) and DJ Jazzy Jeff & The Fresh Prince (*Give It To Me Baby* spawning *I'm All That*).

BARRETT STRONG

Ultimately to achieve greater recognition around Hitsville as a songwriter, Barrett Strong enjoyed a very brief recording career whilst with the company, with some degree of success.

Born in West Point, Mississippi on 5 February 1941, he moved to Detroit with the rest of his family when he was aged just five. He learned to play the piano whilst still a teenager and often accompanied his elder sisters in a family gospel group they put together. One of the regular visitors to the Strong household was R&B singer Jackie Wilson, who had attended school with one of Barrett's four sisters. On one occasion Jackie arrived at the house and heard Barrett playing piano and singing, and impressed with his abilities, told him he had a friend in the music business that might be interested in meeting him.

That friend turned out to be Berry Gordy (writer of several of Jackie Wilson's hits at the time), who later came by and was equally impressed. That in turn led to a recording contract with the fledgling Tamla label and a hastily arranged recording session in a small basement studio belonging to WJLB DJ Bristol Bryant. Berry, along with Billy Roquel Davis and Gwen Gordy wrote both sides of Barrett's debut single, *Let's Rock* backed with *Do The Very Best You Can*, which was released in April 1959, although very few copies were actually pressed and the single did not sell much outside of Detroit.

A few months later, Barrett was present when his next single came into being. Berry had recently acquired 2648 West Grand Boulevard, a house that would eventually be converted into a recording studio and offices, but on this particular evening there were just three people present in Berry, Barrett and songwriter Janie Bradford. Berry had come up with a particular piano riff that he was playing over and over again, encouraging the others to think of suitable lyrics.

"He said, 'Come on! Think of something everybody wants!' I said, 'Well, money! That's what I want!'" was Janie's later recollection. "We stood there and just kept writing and throwing out lyrics and improving on the melody, and the whole thing. It just came together. I'm not a spontaneous writer, but *Money* was a spontaneous-type thing. It was a moment-type thing. Barrett Strong was there. He plays piano a little better than Mr. Gordy. So he said, 'Well, let me play it for you.' Naturally, by him singing it – he just kept singing it as we were writing it – so it went on him. He became the artist."

The recording appears to have been almost as spontaneous as the writing, for when *Money* came to be laid down, a white guitarist and bassist walked up to the studio and asked if they could help out.

"Just walked up and asked if they could be on the session. We said yes, and they played on the session. Never saw them again in life. Two young kids on their way home from high school," Barrett said, although a Eugene Grew did come forward nearly fifty years later and indentified himself as the guitarist, also claiming to have worked on subsequent Motown sessions.

When *Money (That's What I Want)* was released, Berry received a flood of orders from retailers in and around Detroit and eventually from further afield. Berry was aware that the record was a hit but that it also stood the chance of burying his still young company, so to remove the threat of over-stretching leased the master to his sister Gwen's label Anna.

With access to Chess' national distribution system, *Money* became the first major hit Berry and his labels enjoyed, forging its way to #2 on the R&B chart and #23 pop. Whilst *Money* became a major hit and influence (later attracting a cover version by The Beatles), Barrett's follow-up *Yes, No, Maybe So* went nowhere, despite also being leased to Anna. By the time Barrett's third single hit the streets, *Whirlwind* in August 1960, Motown had put into place its own distribution set-up to handle orders from around the country, but *Whirlwind* didn't receive many from outside of Detroit.

Neither too did the next single, issued in February 1961, with *Money And Me* a blatant attempt to try and cash in on the success of his debut, although too much time had passed between that hit and his latest effort. Barrett's final Tamla outing came in June 1961 with *Misery*, a single that also failed to generate much action and resulted in a planned album, **Money And Other Big Hits** getting pulled off the schedule. He came close to having another hit, however, working on a song with Mickey Stevenson entitled *Jamie* that was due to be recorded.

"I wrote it for myself, but I left the company. The track was still there, so Eddie Holland just overdubbed his vocal on it. He did a great job. By him singing it, it was my hit too."

Barrett meanwhile left Motown and headed to New York where he teamed up with legendary writers and producers Doc Pomus and Mort Shuman.

"I was in New York, hanging around the Brill Building all the time. I would see Elvis Presley and all the guys coming in and out of there. And I ran into Doc Pomus there. I met him there, and then he introduced me to Mort Shuman. They decided to be my managers. They signed me to Atlantic."

It proved to be a short lived relationship, both with management and label, with only *Seven Sins* backed with *What Went Wrong* appearing on the Atco subsidiary label. From New York Barrett went to Philadelphia for a while, returned home to Detroit and moved on to Chicago. In the Windy City he signed with Vee-Jay Records, which would result in a lone single for the Tollie label, with *Make Up Your Mind* backed with *Better Run* appearing in 1964. This also failed to sell, so Barrett gave up his singing career and turned to writing, penning The Dells' hit *Stay In My Corner* with Wade Flemons and Bobby Miller before leaving Vee-Jay and turning up at Okeh Records.

His compositions were widely covered; Dee Dee Sharp recorded *It's A Funny Situation* on Cameo, Barbara Green did *I Should Have Treated You Right* on Vivid, The Artistics had *This Heart Of Mine* on Okeh and Mary Wells (post-Motown) recorded *Use Your Head* for 20th Century. With his reputation as a writer therefore established, Barrett went back to Hitsville and Motown.

"They were doing something a little different when I left, but they were doing the more soulful, R&B-style stuff, so I thought I had a place there. So I had an idea I thought I could take back and see if they could do something with it. I had 'Grapevine'. I took it back, and they did something with it."

Barrett had known Norman Whitfield from his earlier time at Motown, so teaming up with him seemed like a natural thing.

"We used to hang around together, parties and things during the school days. When I came back over to the company, he was there, so we just hooked up."

Over the course of the next seven years or so, Barrett helped Norman create some of the company's finest moments, including *I Heard It Through The Grapevine* (the 'something they did with it' resulted in two chart-topping smashes for Gladys Knight & The Pips and then Marvin Gaye), *Smiling Faces Sometimes* (The Undisputed Truth), *War* (Edwin Starr), *Friendship Train* (Gladys Knight & The Pips). *Too Busy Thinking About My Baby* (Marvin Gaye), as well as a slew of hits on The Temptations, including *Cloud Nine, I Can't Get Next To You, Runaway Child Running Wild, Just My Imagination, Psychedelic Shack, Papa Was A Rollin' Stone, Ball Of Confusion* and many more. Along the way Barrett would garner three Grammy Award nominations for Best Rhythm & Blues Song, for *I Wish It Would Rain* (1969), *Smiling Faces Sometimes* (1972) and *Papa Was A Rollin' Stone* (1973), finally winning the coveted award on the third occasion.

That was also the year Barrett bade his final farewells to Motown, not long after the company had left Detroit for California. Opting to try something different, Barrett looked to revive his own singing career, signing with Epic and later Capitol (where he enjoyed some success with his 1975 album **Stronghold**) as well as recording for small independent labels. Barrett would eventually settle in Southfield in Michigan where he established his own Blarritt label, with **Stronghold II** in 2001 among the releases.

"I thought it was time to do this again. So I mustered up the energy, and here we are. I miss the energy level we had back in the day. Now it's sort of down. People aren't as focused or true to themselves as we were. It seems to take a little more for them to get motivated. And to me, writers today don't think about how their

songs relate to someone else. They think about how it relates to them. That's not what we did."
Everyone could relate to Barrett's songs, resulting in him being inducted into the Songwriters Hall of Fame in 2004.

JUD STRUNK

Although widely known for his humorous songs, with *The Biggest Parakeets In Town* his most notable, Jud Strunk actually had a very good voice, one which was used to full effect on the biggest hit of his career, *A Daisy A Day* in 1973.

Born Justin Strunk in Jamestown, New York on 11 June 1936 he was raised in Farmington in Maine. After learning to play the banjo he went on to appear on several television shows, most notably Rowan & Martin's Laugh-In where he first premiered *A Daisy A Day*. Spurred by the success of the song on television, Jud recorded a version with the Mike Curb Congregation and released it on MGM (where Curb was head) and saw it hit #14 on the pop chart in 1973. Jud would next make the chart the following year with *My Country*, produced by Glen Campbell, which hit #59, before linking up with Mike Curb again at Motown and the Melodyland label. *The Biggest Parakeets In Town* would be his only hit for the label, making #50 pop and #51 country, the somewhat risqué nature of the song accounting for the disparity of chart positions. A keen pilot, Jud suffered a heart attack whilst taking off from Carrabassett Valley Airport on 5 October 1981 and crashed, killing himself and his passenger.

STUCK ON YOU – LIONEL RICHIE [SINGLE]

Motown had already released three singles from Lionel Richie's multi-platinum album **Can't Slow Down**, with all three hitting the Top Ten of the charts. There was still mileage to be gained, however, with *Stuck On You* being lifted as the fourth single. Something of a radical departure from the earlier singles, *Stuck On You* was much more country influenced than any of its predecessors (although Lionel was no stranger to country, having written for Kenny Rogers), something Motown and Lionel noted by having him wear a cowboy hat for the single's picture sleeve.

Stuck On You was as easily accessible as earlier singles, as evidenced by its final chart positions of #3 and #12 on the pop charts in America and Britain respectively; in the UK the singles progress was hampered by a rival cover version by reggae singer Trevor Walter who took his version to #9. For good measure, *Stuck On You* would also climb to #8 R&B *and* #24 on the country charts, as well as topping the Adult Contemporary listings, offering further proof of Lionel's all round popularity.

THE STYLERS

Formed in Brooklyn, New York by Harry Boorosa and Tony and his brother Lewis Colombo, The Stylers had a very brief glimpse of fame in the mid 1950s when their single for Jubilee, *Confessions Of A Sinner* made #72 on the pop chart. Their sound, very much in the doo-wop genre, was therefore dated by the time they pitched up at Motown for *Going Steady Anniversary* backed with *Pushing Up Daisies*, two self-written songs that were released on Gordy in 1963. Produced by Al Klein, it proved to be their only single for the label.

THE STYLISTS

The Stylists were a Detroit group formed by fast food restaurant manager John Barnett, drafting in guitarist and singer Edward Arrington Jr. (born on 18 July 1947) as the group's band leader. They were spotted performing live by Warren Moore of The Miracles, who not only helped them get a contract with Motown, but also co-wrote and produced both sides of their only release.

What Is Love backed with *Where Did The Children Go* was issued on the V.I.P. label in June 1971 and did little, and with The Stylistics emerging out of Philadelphia at much the same time, The Stylists disappeared in 1972. They resurfaced a year later with a new name, The Naturals, on the main Motown label.

STYLUS

One of few Australian acts to have passed through Motown, Stylus was formed by Peter Cupples (rhythm guitar and vocals), Ron Peers (guitar and vocals), Ashley Henderson (bass and vocals), Sam McNally (keyboards) and Peter Lee (drums). Largely influenced by Motown music, Stylus toured Australia both on their own and as support to visiting acts, including George Benson, The Average White Band and Ike & Tina Turner and recorded two albums for the domestic market.

Their manager took the albums to Midem (the annual music show held in Cannes, France) looking to pitch a deal and found Barney Ales of Prodigal receptive. Thus their next album, **Stylus** was released in October 1978, although in order to keep their ethnicity secret, their image did not appear on the cover.

Indeed, no one knew who the band was or where they came from until they arrived in the US for a series of live dates some time after. Barney Ales' exit in 1979 robbed Stylus of their keenest supporter at Motown, with the result a second album **Part Of It All** got pulled off the schedule.

ALBUM: STYLUS (1978)

SUGAR DADDY – THE JACKSON 5 [SINGLE]

Each successive hit single and album enjoyed by The Jackson 5 only served to add to the pressure being felt by those directly involved at Motown. Keen to capitalise whilst the group was hot, the company scheduled no fewer than three albums in both 1970 and 1971, with each album expected to house at least two hit singles. Quality and quantity therefore become the buzzwords where The Jackson 5 was concerned.

Yet even with the four heads that made up The Corporation, the demanding schedule meant that sometimes singles or tracks intended for one project wouldn't be completed in time and therefore had to be re-allocated for a later or different project.

One such was *Sugar Daddy*, originally meant to have been completed in time to be included on **Maybe Tomorrow**, but other issues meant the song wasn't quite ready when the album went to bed. Instead it was decided to include the track on the group's forthcoming **Greatest Hits** album, even though the track hadn't yet been released as a single.

When *Maybe Tomorrow* stalled at #20, the first Jackson 5 single to fail to crack the Top Ten, *Sugar Daddy* was hastily added to the schedule, being released in November 1971. It restored the group to the Top Ten, peaking at #10 on the pop chart and hitting #3 R&B. In the UK, however, *Sugar Daddy* followed its predecessor *Maybe Tomorrow* in failing to chart at all, a worrying state of affairs after the four consecutive Top Ten hits of barely twelve months previous.

THE SUNDAY FUNNIES

The same Hideout label that had given The Underdogs their break in the mid 1960s also proved to be the launch pad for The Sunday Funnies. Formed in Detroit by Richard Fidge (vocals), Ronald Aitken (bass and vocals), Richard Kosinski (keyboards) and Richard Mitchell (drums), pop/rock group The Sunday Funnies released *Heavy Music* in 1970 and came to the attention of Motown soon after.

They were signed to the Rare Earth label and assigned Andrew Loog Oldham (The Rolling Stones manager) as producer, a role he also fulfilled for The Repairs, for their debut album **The Sunday Funnies** released in May 1971 with the single *Walk Down The Path Of Freedom* being released in September to try and stimulate sales in the album, albeit without success, and a British release in November similarly went nowhere.

In May 1972 the group released their second album **Benediction**, with Aitken and Kosinski who had been responsible for most of their material on their debut also penning the bulk of the group's second Rare Earth album. Although these albums represent the only recordings by The Sunday Funnies, the group continued for a further three years, with a slightly modified line-up of Fidge, Aitken, Kosinski and Gary Quackenbush (guitar) and Ross 'Roscoe' Helco (drums). Gary Quackenbush had previously been a member of SRC/Blue Scepter, who also recorded a single for Rare Earth. The Sunday Funnies disbanded in January 1975.

ALBUMS: THE SUNDAY FUNNIES (1971), BENEDICTION (1972)

SUNSET BOULEVARD

Motown first established a presence on the West Coast in 1963, with Hal Davis and Marc Gordon renting two floors of suites in the Sunset & Vine Tower. When Berry moved the entire operation westward in 1972, he moved into the newly built Sunset Media Tower at 6255 Sunset Boulevard, which had opened a year previously. The studio, meanwhile, was established at Romaine Street, not too far from the office block. He explained his reasoning for the move in a 1974 interview.

"Motown moved west to get into the action, to be closer to the scene, because we feel that the West is certainly the entertainment capital of the future, if it's not the entertainment capital now. And I think that in a growing operation such as ours, we just had to either come to New York or to California. And because I personally like the movie industry and the charisma of California, I chose California. I like the weather."

The office block on Sunset Boulevard would remain Motown's home for the remainder of its creative life, with Jobete remaining in the block long after Motown had effectively closed its doors.

THE SUPERIORS

Step By Step has so far sold over 6.5 million copies worldwide, topped the US charts for three weeks and peaked at number two in the UK. Unfortunately for The Superiors, it was not their version that generated all these sales but a later re-recording by New Kids On the Block.

Formed by Dwight Burgess, Sean Miranda, Travis Fountain, Jay Greer and Delin Green, The Superiors linked up with Maurice Starr for their only Motown single, *Step By Step* being released in June 1987. It wasn't a hit and Starr moved the group to Columbia for **Perfect Timing**, from which came *Temptation* which made #66 on the R&B chart in 1990. Thereafter Maurice Starr devoted all of his energies to New Kids On The Block, with The Superiors eventually returning home to Boston and renaming themselves Ambient.

SUPERSTITION – STEVIE WONDER [SINGLE]

When Stevie Wonder and his co-producers Bob Marghouleff and Malcolm Cecil sat down to analyse the performance of **Music Of My Mind**, they noted that it had been the most successful chart album of Stevie's career since **Recorded Live** in 1963, but whilst **Music Of My Mind** had been successful, it had lacked that vital ingredient of a couple of major hit singles, the kind of hit that would turn a gold selling album into a platinum one. It was an omission that they would ensure would not happen again.

In 1972 therefore the three linked up again at Electric Lady Studio in New York and began working on recording and selecting material that would make up **Talking Book**. Also in the studio with them was British guitarist Jeff Beck, who had come to New York to lend his talents to Stevie's *Lookin' For Another Pure Love* as well as record his own album for Columbia, which was to be produced by Margouleff and Cecil.

Stevie had promised Jeff Beck a song to go on his album, with Jeff keen on *Maybe Your Baby*, a song Stevie had played him in London some time previously. However, Stevie changed his mind when he heard his own version of *Maybe Your Baby*, and so offered him another, incomplete song. Containing little more than a drum pattern (reportedly created by Jeff Beck in the studio) and the clavinet tracks, Stevie had the basics of a title, singing 'very superstitious' over the accompanying instrumental. Cecil and Margouleff needed the song to be completed almost immediately if it was to be recorded in time for Jeff's album, so sent Stevie into another room and told him to emerge only when the full lyrics to *Superstition* were complete.

When that was done, Jeff recorded his version of the song, which Stevie duly asked to hear, only to discover that the song he had handed over might well be the missing major hit from his own project. For the second time, therefore, Stevie pulled the song back and offered to write yet another for Jeff.

Beck refused the offer and, so it is said, relations between the two performers were somewhat strained for a while (although to what extent is open to interpretation, since Jeff Beck would record Stevie Wonder compositions on his next three albums, *I Got To Have A Song* on **Jeff Beck Group** in 1972, *Superstition* on **Beck, Bogart & Appice** in 1973 and *Cause We Ended As Lovers* and *Thelonius* on **Blow By Blow** in 1975, with Stevie also playing clavinet on *Thelonius*).

Stevie intended releasing *Big Brother* as the lead single from **Talking Book** but reportedly Motown executives felt that *Superstition* was stronger and scheduled it for release instead, with Stevie trying to prevent its release in an attempt to prevent further friction between himself and Jeff Beck. However, since Stevie's contract, signed after he turned 21, gave him alone the right to select which tracks were released as singles, this is unlikely; Motown would have had no wish to incur the wrath of their most promising artist barely twelve months into their agreement.

Irrespective of who chose the single, it proved to be the correct choice, topping both the R&B and pop chart (his first pop chart topper since *Fingertips Part 2* in 1963) and making #11 in the UK. *Superstition* would go on to earn two Grammy Awards for Best Rhythm & Blues Song and Best R&B Vocal Performance, Male in 1974 and remains one of Stevie's best known works.

In the UK the track has returned to the charts on four separate occasions and was also a hit in a medley with *Good Times* (originally by Chic) for Clubhouse in 1983. Among the artists to have covered the song are Jeff Beck, Quincy Jones (with Stevie also appearing on this version from the **You've Got It Bad Girl** album, with the title track another Stevie song first featured on **Talking Book**), Jaki Graham and even Mel Torme.

THE SUPREMES

The most successful girl group to come out of America, The Supremes was the act that elevated Motown from a small independent record label operating out of Detroit into a musical powerhouse, revered and admired the world over. Yet the catalyst to their formation was not Motown founder Berry Gordy but rather Alabama-born manager Milton Jenkins.

Jenkins had arrived in Detroit in 1958, hot-footing it from Cleveland with three male singers in tow in Eddie Kendricks, Paul Williams and Kell Osbourne, ultimately better known as The Primes. Milton Jenkins was something of a mystery man, someone who wanted to be involved in the music business, seemingly had all the right contacts, dressed the part and with a pocket that seemed to be always full, with more than enough money with which to pay for outfits for his acts and funding dance lessons so that they may appear more professional. The source of this money was equally clouded in mystery since he had no job to speak of, leading many to believe he was little more than a pimp. There was no evidence to prove this, although the abundance of pretty women that always seemed to be at his constant beck and call, none of whom displayed any musical prowess whatsoever, was indicative of a man whose operations were somewhat shady.

Irrespective of his background, his intentions, at least as far as music was concerned, were honourable. Having established The Primes as one of the leading live acts to be found performing throughout Detroit, Milton was convinced that a female sister group would prove equally beneficial. The seed of that thought may well have been planted by Paul Williams, who would suggest his then girlfriend Betty McGlown (born in Detroit, Michigan on 30 June 1941) as a member, as well as accompanying Milton (along with Eddie and Kell) on his drive through the Brewster-Douglass housing project looking for girls to join the group.

They pulled up alongside a couple of likely candidates in sisters Maxine and Florence Ballard (born in Detroit on 30 June 1943), with Milton making a bee-line for Maxine, the older of the two. In the end it was Flo who agreed to join the group, signing a contract pretty much there and then that was counter-signed by her mother Lurlee. Since she also seemed to know of other girls around the same age that might be interested in joining The Primettes, as the group was to be christened, it was agreed that Flo would bring along another likely singer later the same week.

At school Flo told Mary Wilson (born in Greenville, Mississippi on 6 March 1944) of this opportunity, with the pair arriving at Milton's room at a hotel to find various members of The Primes, Betty McGlown and another girl they knew from around the projects, Diane Ross (born in Detroit on 26 March 1944).

Diane was seemingly well known around the area, with several people suggesting her name to Milton prior to the establishment of The Primettes; he had reportedly gone out to find her based on those recommendations. With the four girls now in place, The Primettes began rehearsing a basic stage act, comprising versions of whatever hit was high on the R&B chart at that time. Milton sent them out to get kitted up, buying each a pleated skirt and a white blouse emblazoned with a big letter 'P' across the chest. It was a look that was very much in vogue at the time, thanks to the success Frankie Lymon & The Teenagers were enjoying, although a million miles away from the sophisticated look The Supremes would later endorse.

Early dates found them performing a mixture of talent contests and illegal performances at clubs (they were underage, although many officials could be persuaded or bribed to look the other way), with Flo invariably the lead singer on numbers such as Ray Charles' *Night And Day*. Diane (as she was still known at that time) had her moment in the spotlight too, although it was accepted that her voice wasn't as strong as Flo's, with even Mary and a reluctant Betty taking the occasional lead.

Their stage act was also becoming much more polished, thanks to the girls having come across a guitarist who would become an integral part of their early history. Marvin Tarplin (born in Atlanta in Georgia on 13 June 1941) had been on his way to the Flame Show Bar when he was accosted by the four girls, who had observed him rehearsing and thought he might be the perfect accompanist. Not only was he the perfect accompanist, Marv was able to work out the arrangements for their repertoire and help them with the harmonies on new material.

Just as soon as The Primettes had everything in place to make a concerted effort at stardom, fate dealt them something of a blow. Milton Jenkins had broken his arm in a car accident, with his distrust of doctor's resulting in him not having the injury attended to properly, reasoning that it would mend itself. That proved to be an almost fatal error, for the bone did not set properly and gangrene set in. When Milton was finally persuaded to get himself along to hospital it was almost too late, for the doctor's feared he might lose his arm at best and his life at worst. Whilst he lay in hospital and then at home recovering, there was no one around to book dates for either The Primes or The Primettes. Milton Jenkins had also sworn to secrecy the only person fully aware of his predicament, Maxine Ballard, resulting in first The Primes and then The Primettes falling out of his orbit of control.

Whilst The Primes would eventually hook up with the various personnel that would go on to form The Temptations, their sister group The Primettes had more pressing things to attend to, such as continuing their education; music was once again on the back burner, although that did not stop them rehearsing at every given opportunity.

In late June 1960 the girls decided to enter a talent contest at the Detroit & Windsor International Freedom Festival (although Diana's involvement was in doubt until the very last moment, her father refusing to sign permission for her to attend), for which top prize was $15. Although the girls won Mary lost the money, possibly to a pickpocket, before it could be shared out.

There was one small consolation, however, for their performance had been observed by Robert Bateman, then working for Motown, who handed Flo his business card and invited The Primettes along for an audition. For some reason, Flo kept the possible introduction into Motown quiet, although some time later the girls did arrive at Hitsville, but that was largely Diana's doing.

A casual acquaintance of Smokey Robinson, Diana badgered him into giving The Primettes a listen, which was duly arranged at the home of Claudette Rogers (Smokey's then girlfriend and later wife), where The Miracles were rehearsing before setting out on tour. Whilst Smokey was quite taken with The Primettes, he especially liked the talents of guitarist Marv Tarplin and offered the girls a deal; if they would allow him to 'borrow' Marv for a while, he would arrange a further meeting with Berry Gordy himself once The Miracles were back into town. That 'while' would eventually be for some four decades, but Smokey did at least keep to the other part of the bargain and arranged for The Primettes to audition for Berry.

Whilst Berry thought they had potential, he advised them to finish school and come back once they'd graduated. Whilst they were somewhat crushed at the let down, they did get something out of their first trip to Hitsville, with Robert Bateman making almost immediate contact and offering his services to help them get a deal elsewhere. With the aid of Richard Morris, another Motown producer (it should be noted that Motown then was not the 'all for one and one for all' family affair it would become in a couple of years; most of the personnel active at Motown at the time did outside deals and production to supplement their income), Robert Bateman got them a deal with manager Bob West's Lupine Records, a label that had been created for West's main artist The Falcons.

The Primettes did backing vocals for a number of releases on Lupine, including those by Wilson Pickett and Eddie Floyd, two other artists in Bob West's stable. In August 1960 however The Primettes got their own session, adding their vocals to *Tears Of Sorrow* and *Pretty Baby* at West's Flick-Contour Studio (the instrumental tracks for the top side were actually recorded at Hitsville!), with Diana doing the lead on *Tears Of Sorrow* and Mary on *Pretty Baby*. The single was released later the same month but did little even locally (a factor Mary would later put down to West's label becoming embroiled in a payola scandal), although the girls soon had another problem to contend with; Betty announced she was leaving the group in order to get married, despite having only recently finished with Paul Williams.

After briefly toying with the idea of bringing in Jackie Burkes, a friend of Mary's, the three remaining Primettes agreed on Barbara Diane Martin (born in Detroit in June 1943), who aside from being a capable singer was a more than competent dancer, one who would lift their somewhat staid live performances.

Richard Morris was impressed with their choice of new recruit and promised to sort out a number of live dates, but then he, just like Milton Jenkins previously, went missing in action. When the girls finally managed to learn of his whereabouts, they were shocked to discover he was in prison for violating parole! With nothing to lose, The Primettes decided to try their luck at Motown once again, even if they hadn't yet graduated from school.

This time around they found Berry much more receptive, and whilst an actual contract took some time to materialise, the girls were kept busy providing the backing vocals for the likes of Mary Wells, Mable John, Marvin Gaye and Sammy Ward as well as running errands and making themselves useful around the office. When not engaged in Motown activity, the four Primettes could usually be found hanging around Hitsville, badgering the writers and producers for their own opportunity to record.

Their persistence paid off, for in December 1960 they were taken into the studio to record *I Want A Guy*, a song written by Freddie Gorman (who was also Mary Wilson's postman!) and Brian Holland with assistance from Berry Gordy, who produced the resulting session. Berry alone provided the flip side, *Never Again*, which was recorded at the start of the following year. Berry liked the two sides the girls had recorded, enough to think about scheduling them for release, but he did not like their name. He instructed songwriter Janie

Bradford to come up with something better, with Janie scribbling a number of names down on paper and then putting them into a hat. Flo Ballard was in the office at the time and pulled out the resulting moniker which was duly added to the four individual contracts that were drawn up, ready for signature on 15 January 1961.

"We weren't exactly crazy about the name; I had my heart set on something that ended in 'ettes'," recalled Mary. "But we were anxious to sign the recording contracts, so even though we didn't all like the name, we were now The Supremes."

The name itself had been used previously, although not by Motown; a five piece vocal group out of Columbus, Ohio had formed as The Fabulous Supremes in 1954, based on a bottle of Bourbon Supreme the group had been drinking, and shortened the name to The Supremes for the first of three recordings they made for Ace that eventually surfaced in 1957.

The contracts were standard Motown contracts for the time, giving Motown the right to hire and fire members of the group as they saw fit, with the four girls being actually signed to Berry Gordy Enterprises and Tamla Records.

"Berry made sure that we got all the right guidance," Diana would later recall. "Artists in this business, especially when they're young can be taken advantage of so easily, trying to figure out how the money comes from the records, and what's legal and what's illegal. I feel that we were all lucky in the beginning with being helped in all these areas."

Thus it was on Tamla that The Supremes first record was issued in March 1961 (although promotional copies appeared on the Motown label, making this one of the rarest of all Motown singles), but even with Berry trying to call in favours of disc jockeys and distributors, the single died a quick death.

Unperturbed, the girls were soon back in the studio, this time recording something of a pop ditty co-written by Berry with sales head Barney Ales entitled *Buttered Popcorn*. A gritty, double entendre laden novelty item, *Buttered Popcorn* featured Flo on lead vocal, with Diana heading up the flip side *Who's Loving You*, written by Smokey Robinson. *Buttered Popcorn* was duly released in July 1961 and quickly withdrawn, Barney Ales preferring to get a crisper pop version out to market, but neither version caused much of a stir, over and above queries about the lyrical content. Berry claimed to be unaware of the controversy and reportedly ordered a switch in focus to the safer sound of *Who's Loving You* (prompting a series of furious arguments with Barney Ales), but neither side made much of an impact, leaving *Buttered Popcorn* little more than a dent in musical history; it was the only Supremes single released with Flo handling lead vocals.

Berry and Barney had other things to preoccupy themselves at the time anyway, with The Marvelettes suddenly taking off thanks to the success of *Please Mr Postman*, a song they helped write and which would become Motown's first pop chart topper. In an instant, The Supremes had been superseded by another girl group at Motown, but whilst the bulk of the group followed the company line that success for one was success for all, Diana Ross took it as virtually a personal insult, as Marvelette Katherine Anderson would later state.

"Diane was so jealous, you could smell the jealousy. Florence and Mary were happy for us, so it wasn't like it was them against us. When we first met them, Florence took to us right away. And Mary was, well, Mary, she was always very nice. But Diane was standoffish. She felt we were a threat. And they were nobodies like us, but Diane felt like they were the first girl-group at Motown so they deserved to have the first hit. To her, The Marvelettes were like dirt, little ninnies from Inkster, and she was Miss Sophistication, and she was from the projects!"

If that was Diana's attitude and battle lines were being drawn, then Flo could be relied upon to calm the troubled waters. According to several sources, it was Flo who offered advice to the various Marvelettes shortly before they went into the studio to record *Please Mr. Postman*, and when the group was scheduled to go on tour and found themselves a member short (Wanda Young was on maternity leave), it was Flo to whom The Marvelettes turned to help them out. The short term deal was agreed by Berry Gordy, with Flo actually looking forward to the opportunity of going out on a major tour, even if it wasn't for her or her group.

"Flo did what we asked and Lord, that girl could sing. But it was obvious she wasn't that good a dancer" said Katherine. "She had problems with the routines. That was the difference between them and us. The Marvelettes were very high-energy and we were known for our dancing. The Supremes never really were dancers. They didn't have any moves, they just sort of stood there and swayed back and forth."

Flo did as best she could with the routines on stage but developed lasting friendships with The Marvelettes off it, even taking lead singer Gladys Horton into her confidence regarding the rape she suffered a year previously. Devoid of one member to become a temporary Marvelette, The Supremes soon found they were to lose another in Barbara Martin. Married during the course of 1961 and now Barbara

Richardson, she originally intended continuing with her singing career, a decision supported by her husband, but when she fell pregnant Barbara decided in the spring of 1962 to leave. After turning down a suggestion to bring aboard Diane Watson, this time there was to be no new member, irrespective of Motown's wishes (who, of course, retained the right to hire and fire); The Supremes would continue as a trio.

Regardless of how many members constituted the group, the one inescapable fact was that they had still to register on the chart (any chart, in fact), which had earned them the rather unwanted moniker of the 'No-hit Supremes' around Hitsville. The latest writer to chance his arm was Smokey Robinson (said to be embroiled in a relationship with Diana Ross), who penned and produced *Your Heart Belongs To Me*, with the flip being *(He's) Seventeen* written by Marv Johnson and Mrs Berry Gordy, Raynoma Liles. With the group switched over to the main Motown label, *Your Heart* at least broke The Supremes' duck where getting a chart placing was concerned, spending three weeks on the Billboard Hot 100 but getting no higher than #95. *(He's) Seventeen* is also worthy of mention, for it was to be the only Supremes single on which Barbara Martin (who'd left the group by the time the record hit the streets) has something of a lead, albeit spoken vocal.

In the late summer of 1962 the girls were back in the studio, recording *Let Me Go The Right Way*, which was written and produced by Mr Berry Gordy, and *Time Changes Things,* written by two thirds of the team that would prove so crucial to their later success in Brian Holland and Lamont Dozier. *Time Changes Things*, which was co-written by Janie Bradford, was originally intended as the plug side but got switched when Berry finally got a mix on *Let Me Go The Right Way* that he was happy with after spending some fourteen straight hours in the control booth. His perseverance paid off too, for *Let Me Go The Right Way* did head the right way, hitting #26 R&B and #90 pop following its release in November 1962, the group's appearance on the first Motortown Revue helping the company's promotion efforts.

Despite the relative success, the Revue only served to highlight The Supremes shortcomings. There were other acts on the tour more successful, such as Mary Wells, The Marvelettes and The Miracles. Most of the other acts had proper dance routines, well beyond The Supremes' simple back and forth swaying. Whilst The Supremes in general and Diana in particular could only bide their time until they were as successful as the other acts with regard to their recording career, Diana was not prepared to be so patient when it came to developing something akin to a proper stage presence. It all began so innocently, as Mary would later recall.

"Whenever we were on tour, we would do our set, then we'd change into our street clothes so we could watch the rest of the show. Every night we'd watch to see if The Contours got a bigger response than The Temptations, or if the crowd favoured Martha & The Vandellas over The Marvelettes. The line-up was determined by whoever had the biggest hit record out, and the order was arranged so that one act would leave the stage hot for the next one. When you hit the stage, you really had to go for blood, because everyone on the tour was so good. The polish and pose Motown acts were famous for came not only from practice but from watching other acts."

Diana Ross was a more than interested observer in all of this and nearly every night she would gather Flo and Mary together and talk about a new dance routine she had come up with, which they would rehearse and introduce into their performance at the next possible opportunity. The only problem with this was that virtually all of the moves were cribbed from other Motown acts, who in turn had to change *their* routines to avoid looking ridiculous.

Whilst the Motortown Revue did pull the majority of the acts together in a bond of brotherhood, having all experienced the hardships of life on the road and the prejudice they encountered whilst touring the Southern states, there was one other unifying trait they all shared, one which even Berry Gordy would later acknowledge; when it came to Diana Ross, "they all hated her guts."

Yet Diana Ross wasn't interested in coming top of any Hitsville popularity poll, only in getting The Supremes to the top of the chart and to achieve that goal, anything and everything was within limits. Despite the lack of single success, Motown issued the group's debut album **Meet The Supremes** towards the end of the 1962, containing much of the material the girls (including Barbara Martin) had recorded over the course of a year between the autumn of 1960 and 1961. Not surprisingly, the album did little more than become something of a curio (in Britain the album would not be released until December 1964, when it was re-packaged to include their then current hit *Where Did Our Love* Go and would hit #13 on the chart).

The next writer to try and get a hit on The Supremes was Clarence Paul, who used the success of Ray Charles' **Modern Sounds In Country And Western Music** as something of a template for a whole album's worth of material he recorded on The Supremes, most of which remained unreleased for the next two years.

The initial release was *My Heart Can't Take It No More*, complete with a steel guitar effect, which was combined with Smokey's *You Bring Back Memories* and released in February 1963; it bubbled under the chart at #129 and was quickly forgotten.

It was back to Smokey Robinson (a decision that reportedly rankled Smokey's wife Claudette, aware of rumours concerning her husband and Diana Ross) for the absurdly titled *A Breath Taking, First Sight Soul Shaking, One Night Love Making, Next Day Heart Breaking Guy*, which fortunately was truncated to the more manageable *A Breath Taking Guy* when commercial copies were delivered to store. Released in June 1963, the single would go further than any previous Supremes single, hitting #75, but much to Claudette's relief, it was decided Holland-Dozier-Holland would take over from here on in.

The trio had quickly established themselves as a power within Hitsville, churning out hits on The Marvelettes, The Vandellas, The Miracles and Marvin Gaye, among others, a ratio of hits that had not gone unnoticed by Diana Ross. Just as she had ingratiated her way into Smokey's line of vision in order to further The Supremes recording career, so she targeted Brian Holland, much to the chagrin of Brian's wife Sharon! In time, the countless hours she had spent in the studio with Smokey, which set tongues wagging around Hitsville, would be swapped with equal time spent in Brian's company.

Irrespective of the nature of their relationship it was not long before Brian requested of Berry Gordy that The Supremes be handed over to Holland-Dozier-Holland for future productions. The first fruits of that request were *Run Run Run*, recorded in May 1963, but Berry felt it wasn't quite good enough to release as a single, not then anyway. Instead, in October the same year, the group was back in the studio laying down *When The Lovelight Starts Shining Through His Eyes*, a song that sounded more like the HDH trademark and which featured The Four Tops on additional backing vocal duties. Released at the end of the same month, with *Standing At the Crossroads Of Love* (another HDH tune), *Lovelight* became the group's first significant hit, peaking at #23 pop and #2 R&B. Now reasoned nearly everyone at Motown, there was little to stop The Supremes' march to the top.

In February *Run Run Run* was released as the follow-up single to great expectation, especially as the group had recently completed a successful series of dates as part of the latest Motortown Revue, even being elevated to third on the roster, behind Martha Reeves & The Vandellas and The Contours. It was, therefore, something of a disappointment that *Run Run Run* didn't maintain the progress. If anything, it was a step backwards, with the single stalling at #22 R&B and #93 pop, well below expectations.

The lack of sustained success was beginning to concern all and sundry, not least Berry Gordy. As he had already proved in ditching some of the early acts, sentiment counted for little and, if Motown was to continue to grow, then all of the acts had to pull their weight. He believed The Supremes in general and Diana Ross in particular had potential, but that had to be converted into success and quickly. Fate, not for the last time, took a hand.

First there was the sudden walkout of Mary Wells, eventually destined for a big contract but small returns with 20th Century Records. The loss of his most bankable star showed Motown was vulnerable, enough for other labels to come circling around Hitsville looking to prise away other talent, with Smokey Robinson reportedly receiving a mega bucks offer from Scepter Records. Berry and Motown needed another major act to take Mary's place as soon as was possible if they were to fend off predators.

Meanwhile, Diana, Flo and Mary were back in the studio working with HDH on a new song, one which was originally intended for The Marvelettes (the backing tracks were recorded with Gladys Horton's vocal key in mind) but which they had turned down in preference for *Too Many Fish In The Sea*. The song had subsequently been handed over to The Supremes, who were equally less than enamoured with *Where Did Our Love Go* but, lacking any kind of veto, had to record pretty much what they were asked, not what they liked. And Diana certainly didn't like it, as Eddie Holland would later relay.

"So finally we got Diana into the vocal booth, and she still hated the fact that she had to do this song. She was not in a good mood, and when Diana wasn't in a good mood it meant one thing – she was gonna call Berry. She said, 'Where's the phone?' and everyone, you know, rolled their eyes. I said, 'Diana, listen, you can go ahead and call Berry. But if he comes down here, me and my brother and Lamont ain't comin' back in here for you girls, ever.'"

Diana recorded her lead vocal, with Flo and Mary being coaxed through the backing vocals (which were subsequently amended so as to remove any difficult phrasing), with the song being topped and tailed with a somewhat unique sound effect of foot stomping (achieved by studio hand Mike Valvano stomping on two boards suspended above the floor). The end result sounded like a Top Ten hit to Berry Gordy and a potential number one to Barney Ales, who would say as much to Billboard magazine in an article designed to allay distributors' fears about Motown following the Mary Wells walkout.

The final piece of the jigsaw that helped catapult *Where Did Our Love Go* into a major hit was Dick Clark, whose 'Caravan Of Stars' was about to hit the road in June 1964. Dick Clark's touring shows always featured a healthy smattering of R&B performers, even when the tour would crisscross the southern states, and for this latest venture out onto the road, he had requested Brenda Holloway as part of the revue that was to be headlined by Gene Pitney. Sensing an opening, Berry Gordy instructed Esther Edwards to speak directly to Dick Clark's people and offer a deal; they could have Brenda Holloway if they would add The Supremes to the line-up. It took extensive negotiation on Motown's part to get The Supremes onto the tour (although contrary to the story Motown told repeatedly in their early history, whereby Dick Clark agreed to take The Supremes on the proviso Berry Gordy paid all of their expenses, Clark actually paid them $600 a week on the tour's early dates), although they were initially placed much in keeping with their status at the time, near the foot of the bill.

The Supremes, with Ernestine Ross (Diana's mother) in the role of chaperone, were driven to Cleveland on 8 June 1964, where they linked up with the likes of Gene Pitney, The Dixie Cups, The Rip Chords, Major Lance, The Shirelles, Brenda Holloway, Mike Clifford, Round Robin, The Crystals, The Reflections and Dean & Jean. Two buses, in an even worse state than the bus that had been an integral part of the previous Motortown Revue, would ferry the artists from city to city, venue to venue. On the tour's early dates, The Supremes received the same kind of reaction that had greeted them on previous tours; muted but polite applause from audiences that were largely unfamiliar with the group's material, comprising as it did a collection of minor hits and misses.

Back at Hitsville, meanwhile, Motown's marketing machine was beginning to work its magic, cajoling radio stations to play *Where Did Our Love Go*, with Barney Ales and his sales department then capitalising on those plays with extra orders to stock the single. On 11 July 1964, *Where Did Our Love Go* made its first appearance on the Billboard chart at #77. As the tour progressed, so did the single, rising up the chart so that by the end of the month, it was inside the Top Twenty. The effect on The Supremes was equally beneficial, with audiences beginning to instantly recognise the song from the group's meagre playlist but giving it a more enthusiastic response at each successive venue. On 1 August, the single leaped into the Top Ten, hitting #5, then up to #2 and two weeks later swapped positions with Dean Martin's *Everybody Loves Somebody* to assume pole position, where it would remain for a further two weeks. The exposure received from being part of Dick Clark's Caravan Of Stars had undoubtedly played its part, and the success of the single also helped drive audiences to see the Caravan, which Dick Clark subsequently repaid by upping the girl's weekly wage to $800 and moving them up the roster.

Where Did Our Love Go would also become The Supremes' international breakthrough, hitting #3 on the British charts following its release on the Stateside label. Also available was the group's second album, **Where Did Our Love Go**, which had been recorded shortly before the group headed off on tour. Whilst the album gathered together the previous near hits and misses, it was the two new tracks that quickly attracted immediate attention, *Baby Love* and *Come See About Me*, tracks that sounded in much the same vein as *Where Did Our Love Go.* This was done deliberately, as Eddie would later confirm.

"Basically what we were trying to do was to keep them in the same ballpark. It stands to reason that you keep the same elements that worked before. You'd be stupid to divert from what worked so well; that's just part of the marketing. That's what people like."

And people certainly did like The Supremes and their new found sound, enough to send **Where Did Our Love Go** to the top of the R&B chart and to #2 pop, where it spent four weeks behind **The Beatles '65**. The extracted singles, *Baby Love* and *Come See About Me* continued the trend, with both topping the pop chart before the year was out and making The Supremes the first act in US chart history to have three number one hit singles lifted from the same album. *Baby Love* would also become a chart topper in Britain, aided by the group headlining the first Motortown Revue to tour the country, even if the attendance figures weren't quite as good as anticipated.

"The high point of my career was The Supremes first trip to Europe," Diana later said. "*Baby Love* was a hit over there before it was here [America]. At that time we hadn't done ant of the TV shows over yet, we had only done the Dick Clark tours and the Motown Revue shows, where we weren't the headliner. We hadn't done the 'Shindig' shows yet. But going to Europe was the most amazing culture shock. Berry and Berry's sister went with us and everyone was so excited to see us, it was a great moment for everyone. It was something we had dreamed of since we were kids. We drove through England, and saw all the things we had read about in school but never imagined to be real."

If singles continued to follow a set pattern, the same could not be said for their albums, which tended to veer towards whatever fad or fashion was in vogue at the time. Thus The Supremes (and Motown) acknowledged the arrival and success of the likes of The Beatles and Gerry & The Pacemakers with the release of **A Bit Of Liverpool** (released in Britain as **With Love From Us To You**), which contained *World Without Love, Can't Buy My Love, I Want To Hold Your Hand, A Hard Day's Night* and *How Do You Do It* as well as taking some poetic licence with the inclusion of *House Of The Rising Sun* (originally by The Animals, from Newcastle-Upon-Tyne), *Bits And Pieces* and *Because* (Dave Clark Five, London). The album was rounded out with two songs from the Jobete catalogue in *You've Really Got A Hold On Me* and *Do You Love Me* (both of which had been covered by British groups) and was something of a success, hitting #21 on the pop chart and #5 R&B.

This would be followed by the release of **The Supremes Sing Country Western & Pop**, the album originally recorded under the supervision of Clarence Paul which finally appeared in February 1965 and stalled at #79 pop. A tribute album to Sam Cooke appeared two months later, but **We Remember Sam Cooke** struggled to get beyond #75, even if it did hit #5 R&B.

It was the singles, however, that set The Supremes head and shoulders above their contemporaries, with the run of three consecutive number ones being stretched to five thanks to *Stop! In The Name Of Love* and *Back In My Arms Again*, all achieved inside a six month period. Both of these hits were part of the next Supremes album to hit the market, **More Hits By The Supremes**, which despite its title was not a compilation album but a collection of twelve all new HDH songs; the result was a welcome return to the upper echelons of the chart, hitting #6 pop and #2 R&B.

Whilst such chart success was undoubtedly pleasing and rewarding, it was only part of Berry Gordy's grand scheme for The Supremes. Not only did he want the group to appear on the chart, he wanted them on radio, television and in the press. Every record release had to be treated as though it was an event (even those albums that were merely cashing in on the group's new found stardom, such as **A Bit Of Liverpool**), with all three girls primed as to what to say and, thanks to their time spent working with Maxine Powell, how to say it. The Supremes were to be elevated from a mere recording group to an industry phenomenon, Motown's equivalent of The Beatles.

It was not enough that the group be invited to appear on such shows as 'The Steve Allan Show' or 'The Ed Sullivan Show', where they would perform whatever single was being plugged at the time, they had to host their own specials or make acting cameos, such as appearing as three nuns in the 'Tarzan' series. It was not enough to fill the Twenty Grand or The Apollo, they had to aim for the prestigious venues, of which the Copacabana in New York City was the undoubted ultimate.

Run by Jules Podell, The Copacabana had opened in 1940 and had played host to just about every major recording and performing star, although even by 1965, very few African Americans and certainly no Motown artist had managed to secure a residency. Berry Gordy made it his mission to have The Supremes open the door for Motown, even if it meant agreeing a punitive deal.

"Nearing the summer of '65 – when club business was slow – General Artists Corporation, the New York talent agency that was booking The Supremes, convinced the Copa's powerful owner to give the girls a shot. That was about all that he was willing to give. Knowing what a major launching pad his club was, Jules made us pay for everything. Nobody got breaks at the Copa. No discounts on food or drinks; you paid full price no matter who you were – manager, husband, musician or star. On top of that we had to sign what many considered a 'slave contract' for three years. We would appear for two or three week periods, seven days a week, two shows a night for less than $3,000 a week. The second year (if he wanted us back) it would go to $10,000, and the third $15,000. *His* option. But I was willing to lose money if it meant building stars."

Diana, Flo and Mary rehearsed extensively before the opening night, even playing small clubs at which every song and every line was worked on so that the three knew the act inside and out. The opening night of 29 July 1965 attracted New York's glitterati, assorted scribes and other V.I.P. guests, with Berry spending some $10,000 making sure those that mattered were well fed and watered. The Supremes performed exceptionally well on the night, as was evidenced by the glowing reviews they received from key media over the next few days. Indeed, they performed exceptionally throughout the entire three week residency, attracting sell out crowds to each and every night.

Their only respite was an appearance on the television show 'What's My Line', offering further proof that The Supremes had left behind the limited R&B circuit and were now being fast-tracked to super-stardom. Or at least one of them was, for ever since Diana Ross had been supplanted as the group's lead singer, virtually every decision that was supposed to impact on the group as a whole was designed to benefit Diana Ross individually.

Flo and Mary had long felt they were something of a sideshow for the main act, with Diana having all of the leads on record and the best lines during live shows, and in a short time would be the only Supreme who actually appeared on the group's records (HDH utilised The Andantes on virtually every Supremes record and subsequently decided that it didn't matter who was doing the 'oohs' and 'aahs' in the background). Flo and Mary were rapidly becoming Supremes in name only, and whilst Mary may have been disgruntled at being sidelined from the group she had helped form, she wasn't about to upset the apple cart by complaining publicly (and perhaps not even privately, if her autobiography is a real indicator).

Not so Flo, however, who would complain bitterly at seeing her role within the group diminished. Nor was she afraid to deviate from the script during performances, if the opportunity arose, and her ad-libs were as much a part of The Supremes show as anything that had been written and approved for Diana. It was felt by Berry however, that Flo's ad-libs were a distraction, and that if Flo had one perhaps they should create something similar for Mary to utter during the course of a performance. Despite being ordered to stick to the script, Flo dropped in ad-libs throughout the engagement, much to Berry's fury. In retaliation, Berry initially ordered the dropping of *People*, a number from the Broadway show 'Funny People' on which Flo did the lead, only to reinstate it later but with Diana up front.

The show would eventually be released on record, **The Supremes At The Copa** being issued in November 1965 and peaking at #11 pop and #6 R&B. By then The Supremes' extraordinary run of number one hit singles had come to an end, *Nothing But Heartaches* failing to even break into the Top Ten, halting at #11 (and failing to make it on to the British chart altogether). In view of the record's failure, Berry sent out a memo to department heads at Hitsville, stating 'We will release nothing less than Top Ten product on any artist; and because the Supremes' world-wide acceptance is greater than the other artists, on them we will only release number one records.'

HDH responded to the challenge by writing *I Hear A Symphony*, something of a classically influenced number that did indeed return the group to the top of the chart, spending two weeks at the summit (and hitting #2 R&B as well as #39 in the UK).

Whilst HDH were busy crafting the group's subsequent assaults on the pop chart, there was an abundance of Supremes material out on the market, with **Merry Christmas** making #6 on the Billboard Christmas chart, whilst the extracted single *Twinkle Twinkle Little Me* backed with *Children's Christmas Song* also charted, with the top side peaking at #5 and the flip #7 on the Christmas singles chart. Two other albums, **Tribute To The Girls** and **There's A Place For Us** were supposedly recorded but subsequently shelved, Motown opting to wait until **I Hear A Symphony** was ready for release and put all their marketing muscle behind what had quickly become a much anticipated long player.

Aside from the title track, which had already been a chart topper, there was what was planned as the group's next single *My World Is Empty Without You*, but long standing fans expecting the album to offer up an abundance of HDH classics were going to be disappointed. Perhaps as a result of the group's acceptance at the Copa, **I Hear A Symphony** contained much of the kind of material they would perform at concerts the world over; one or two hits, a couple of current cover versions and an assortment of revivals. **I Hear A Symphony** therefore contained The Supremes' take on Paul McCartney's *Yesterday* and The Toys' *A Lover' Concerto* (similar in style to *I Hear A Symphony*) and revivals of *Unchained Melody* and *With A Song In My Heart*. Despite the disjointed nature of the album it still proved a sales success, hitting #8 pop and topping the R&B chart. *My World Is Empty Without You* didn't quite meet the target's previously set by Berry Gordy, although it still managed to make #5 pop (its R&B performance was somewhat poorer, peaking at #10). Neither too did the follow-up *Love Is Like An Itching In My Heart*, which slipped down to #9 pop and #7 R&B, although Eddie Holland would later offer his view on why the records weren't performing as well as expected.

"Listen, we didn't need no orders to write #1 songs. We wanted every song we ever wrote to be #1. Like I say, we didn't write songs; we wrote *hits*. But I'll say this; making a hit is a collaborative process. And by that time The Supremes were hardly ever there. They were always out on the road, doing this club, that TV show, this hotel. The only time they saw Detroit was when they flew over it. We'd have to grab them for a few hours at a time every two, three months. And they'd be tired and really didn't want to come in. It wasn't just The Supremes. It was happening with The [Four] Tops, too. I mean, those guys were never around. You had to catch lightning in a bottle with them, all of them. I'd have, like, an hour to rehearse with Levi and then go right in and have him lay down the vocal. Thank God he could get it right on the first take. Diana needed more work, but she got it, too. Me, I personally didn't think any of those records suffered. But, shit, you can always make a record better, if you had time. Since we never had that, we had to get it right the first time, every time."

The demands on the group's time got even greater, too, with The Supremes recording a commercial for Coke Cola and undertaking publicity for the launch of Supremes Special Formula White Bread (the wrappers featured caricatures of the three girls, even though they looked nothing like the real thing!), with further ventures into mass marketing being lined up on a regular basis.

It was soon decided that Motown in general and The Supremes in particular needed additional help to filter the requests and get acts onto the top television shows, eventually recruiting Shelly Berger from the West Coast and supplanting him into Detroit. He quickly proved his usefulness to both Motown and The Supremes, getting the act on the Ed Sullivan show four times a year, obtaining an increase from Jules Podell in the weekly fee The Supremes would receive for performing at the Copa and putting together a Supremes and Temptations television special that was submitted to the major networks for consideration; by the end of the year, Shelly Burger was named The Supremes new manager, later adding The Temptations to his portfolio. He could not have taken over at a better time, for The Supremes were about to embark on their second domination of the singles chart, one that was almost as fulfilling and rewarding as their first spell in 1964.

The group was spoilt for choice over what to release as their next single, for both *You Can't Hurry Love* and *You Keep Me Hangin' On* were completed at much the same time and were ready to go at a moment's notice. In the end Motown opted for *You Can't Hurry Love*, a decision that was vindicated when it raced to the top of both the pop and R&B chart (and also a return to form in the UK, where it came to rest at #3).

The resulting album appeared in August 1966, **Supremes A Go-Go** featuring two Top Ten hits and would become a major success in its own right, topping both the pop and R&B chart (and hit #15 in the UK) on its way to selling more than a million copies domestically and some 3.5 million worldwide. Two months later *You Keep Me Hangin' On* made its bow, going on top the pop chart for two weeks and the R&B listings for double that (and would return The Supremes to the Top Ten in the UK, where it reached #8), followed in January 1967 by the double chart topping single *Love Is Here And Now You're Gone* and the album **The Supremes Sing Holland-Dozier-Holland** (re-titled **The Supremes Sing Motown** in the UK), which would hit #6 pop and #2 R&B (#15 in the UK).

The sustained success opened other doors for The Supremes too, with HDH being asked to provide a couple of tracks to the soundtrack to 'The Happening' a comedy film starring Anthony Quinn. The songs proved more memorable than the film, with the title track becoming The Supremes' tenth pop chart topper and a #6 hit in Britain (although it featured much lower down on the R&B chart, where it stalled at #12). Though they weren't to know it at the time, the release of **The Supremes Sing Holland-Dozier-Holland** marked the end of an era for both the producers and various elements within The Supremes. Flo Ballard had grown ever more resentful of the attention being lavished on Diana Ross, usually by Berry Gordy, whose romantic relationship with his leading lady was now an open secret around Hitsville. Both Flo and Mary felt, with some justification, that everything the group was undertaking was for the benefit of Diana; if there was a dance routine that she didn't feel was right for her, she would complain directly to Berry and the routine would be amended to suit. The stage repertoire had already been altered to showcase Diana even further at the expense of her erstwhile band mates (Mary would later diplomatically ask, "How much more of the spotlight did Diane need?"), with the 'group', such as it was, now effectively two camps both on and off the stage.

Flo began drinking more and more, which led to missed rehearsals and even missed dates, with Diana and Mary going on stage as a duo at one show and performing well enough for few in the audience bothering to mention the missing Supreme. As Flo became more and more unreliable, Berry began casting for a long-term Supreme, with Marlene Barrow (of The Andantes) and Barbara Randolph brought up to speed with The Supremes' routines just in case a replacement was needed in an emergency (it should be noted that Berry had originally intended pulling Diana Ross out of The Supremes for a solo career as early as 1966, with Barbara Randolph slated to be her replacement, but reportedly changed his mind when The Copa reacted angrily to his intention of replacing the unreliable Flo with Marlene Barrow for The Supremes' second residency at the club – they threatened to tear up the entire agreement as they felt Flo was an integral part of the show).

He eventually selected Cindy Birdsong (born in Mount Holly Township, New Jersey on 15 December 1939), a member of Patti Labelle's Blue Belles and a singer who bore more than a passing resemblance to Flo, so much so that during Cindy's early dates as a Supreme few in the audience were even aware that a switch had been made. Whilst Berry wanted to make the change as soon as possible, a fully booked diary meant it was not feasible, with Shelly Berger in particular keen to retain Flo in the group. But Flo's behaviour deteriorated with each passing show, her open defiance towards Berry and Diana also being highlighted on stage, deviating from the script on more than one occasion.

In April 1967, Flo and Mary were summoned to a meeting at Berry's mansion, with Flo arriving with her mother and being somewhat surprised by the presence of Cindy Birdsong, who sat waiting in an ante room. There was little indication of the bombshell that was about to explode during the early part of the conversation, which appeared to revolve around Berry's plan to push Diana even further into the spotlight, if that were possible, with the group now to be christened Diana Ross & The Supremes (thus setting in motion plans for an eventual solo career, which was likened at the time as a 'two for one stock option', whereby two recording entities would be created). Then the devastating news regarding Flo was delivered, with Berry reciting a seemingly endless list of misdeeds, ranging from excessive drinking, weight issues and general conduct unbecoming of a Supreme. Even then he didn't deliver the fatal blow, not least because Cindy was still under contract to The Blue Belles and The Supremes had a significant number of lucrative dates to fulfil. Whether a change in attitude and behaviour on Flo's part might have delayed the inevitable is open to debate, but even with the axe hanging over her, Flo couldn't resist the temptation to push Berry to breaking point and beyond. At The Flamingo Hotel in Las Vegas in July 1967, Flo pushed too hard once too often; criticised off stage that she had put on too much weight, she made a point of thrusting her ample stomach in Berry's direction midway through a performance. Enraged, he raced back stage and told her that she was fired, sending a now contractually free Cindy on stage with Diana and Mary for the second show of the evening. An interested viewer of the second show was Shelly Berger, blissfully unaware of the drama that had unfolded earlier.

"Nobody told me what had happened when I got to the Flamingo. Everyone was acting matter-of-factly, like everything was routine. So I sat down at my table with Berry; the lights come up, the orchestra starts playing and there was Cindy, not Florence. I thought, 'Couldn't somebody have told me this? I'm only the manager of this group.'"

Officially, Flo left The Supremes suffering from exhaustion, which was partly true; she no longer had the energy to fight Berry (or Diana), wanting only to pick up the money she felt she was owed and negotiate her way out of the company. Those funds were considerably less than anticipated; having been repeatedly told they would all be millionaires during the heady hit days, it must have come as some surprise to Flo to find her final settlement amounted to just $139,804 - a sum she would later try unsuccessfully to increase through a series of legal manoeuvres - and that quickly disappeared thanks to the avarice of her soon-to-be-husband Tommy Chapman and her lawyer Leonard Baun.

And it was not only Florence Ballard who crashed and burned during that tumultuous month, with Detroit being hit by the worst rioting in the city's history that left 43 dead, 7,200 arrested and more than 2,000 buildings destroyed (although Hitsville was spared). Amidst the mayhem, Diana Ross & The Supremes released their debut single, *Reflections* being the first carry the new moniker, even though it was recorded by the old guard. Something of a radical musical departure for the group (even more so when placed alongside what was their then current album, **The Supremes Sing Rodgers & Hart**, another collection of old show tunes such as *My Funny Valentine, The Lady Is A Tramp* and *Blue Moon*, with the album, which had originally been planned as a double eventually being trimmed down to a single album and peaking at #20 on the pop chart), it still carried enough of The Supremes' magic to become a major hit, peaking at #2 pop (although it did top the Cashbox chart) and #4 R&B, also crossing over in the UK to rest at #5.

If *Reflections* represented something of a change, utilising the same kind of psychedelic imagery that The Beatles and The Beach Boys were taking to the top of the chart, then the follow-up *In And Out Of Love* was a retrospective step, with something of a country feel. Some of the magic had obviously worn off, for *In And Out Of Love* ran out of steam at #9 pop and a distant #16 R&B as well as failing to crack the Top Ten in the UK, where it stalled at #13. Ordinarily, Berry Gordy would not have worried, for despite his earlier memo regarding The Supremes single releases, he had every faith that HDH would soon come up with something special that would restore the status quo.

Besides, HDH's stock had never been higher, with the double album release **Diana Ross & The Supremes Greatest Hits**, a career retrospective that featured ten number ones among the twenty tracks, topping the charts for five weeks (in Britain the album was truncated to a single disc and still reached the summit for three weeks), selling more than five million copies worldwide in the process. However, it is indicative of how out of touch Berry Gordy had become about *his* record company he was unaware Holland-Dozier-Holland had effectively downed pens. Indeed, he had spent so much time mollycoddling Diana Ross and gallivanting with whoever else constituted The Supremes it came as a major surprise that HDH hadn't been anywhere near Hitsville for some considerable time.

Not only had he lost their writing talents, other crucial areas of his business had been neglected too, including A&R and Quality Control, both of which were under the direct control of HDH. With HDH nowhere to be seen, Berry was forced to take a more hands-on approach, ordering a sweep of the Hitsville vault to find as much previously unreleased material as possible in an attempt to put together something of a holding album in **Reflections**. There wasn't that much new material that could be located, resulting in **Reflections** being cobbled together from whatever was left over from a variety of recording sessions. Of the twelve tracks that made up the platter, only five came from HDH (including the two already released on single in *Reflections* and *In And Out Of Love*), with the rest a mix of cover versions (*What The World Needs Now Is Love, Ode To Billie Joe* and *Up Up And Away*) and usual Jobete filler material. With little or nothing by way of a prepared single, Motown was forced to ready *Forever Came Today* for release. The backing tracks were originally recorded in April 1967 and, according to Flo Ballard's later recollections, she and Mary appear on the version that is featured on the album (although Mary denied it).

The version that was released as a single, however, was a reworked version that had Diana and The Andantes recording their vocals in December and the following January. With HDH absent from these later proceedings, *Forever Came Today* was not as strong as anything previously recorded, resulting in the single barely scraping the Top Thirty (it peaked at #28 pop in both the US and UK and #17 R&B), and devoid of a major hit, the album also struggled, peaking at #18 in the US and #30 in the UK. A plan to release *What The World Needs Now Is Love* as a follow-up was rescinded, perhaps fortunately, with Berry Gordy scouring the Hitsville lot to find a team capable of stepping into the shoes of Holland-Dozier-Holland.

The assignment eventually fell to Nickolas Ashford and Valerie Simpson, then about to get hot with their writing and production on Marvin Gaye and Tammi Terrell. The task for The Supremes unfortunately came with guidelines, not least of which was the need to come up with something that had the feel of an HDH song, which was not necessarily their forte. And so it proved, with *Some Things You Never Get Used To* slipping even further down the listings, stalling at #30 pop and #43 R&B (and performed equally poorly in the UK, where it limped to #34).

Needing time to contemplate what the next move would be for the company's cash cow, Motown released a couple of throw away albums (at least as far as American audiences were concerned), **Live At London's Talk Of The Town** and **Funny Girl**. The group's residency at The Talk Of The Town had given British audiences their first glimpse of Flo's replacement Cindy Birdsong, enough to draw London's glitterati out in force for the series of engagements and turn the album into a success in that territory, where it would become another Top Ten success, peaking at #6 as The Supremes' fans retained their loyalty. Curiosity value alone wasn't enough for their American counterparts, who given a choice between take it or leave largely left it, resulting in a #57 peak (conversely, the mixture of medleys, show tunes and standards *did* find favour with the R&B market, where it repeated the #6 placing). Nobody, fans or otherwise appeared interested in **Funny Girl**, a collection of songs from the Barbara Streisand headlined film, which despite appearing before the official soundtrack came and went without too much fanfare, crawling in at #150 pop and #45 R&B.

Meanwhile, Berry Gordy had decided on a new strategy for the group; since placing them with an established Hitsville writing team hadn't worked, he would create a new one in The Clan. To this end, Frank Wilson, R. Dean Taylor, Deke Richards, Hank Cosby and Pam Sawyer were holed up in a hotel room with orders not to emerge until they had something tangible for their efforts. With Berry Gordy cast in the role of overseer, the new collective eventually surfaced with *Love Child*, as far removed from The Supremes' previous entreaties about love as was possible. Four days later, Diana went into the studio to lay down the lead, with The Andantes again providing the backing vocals; according to Berry, he *had* wanted Mary and Cindy to appear on the track but Mary refused as she wanted to enjoy a brief holiday, and with Mary absent he felt he could not feature Cindy either. According to Mary, every time she enquired about new recordings, she was told the material wasn't yet ready and that the recording session effectively came and went without her being any the wiser.

Showcased on the 'Ed Sullivan Show', *Love Child* proved to be a return to form, so much so that when Eddie Holland first heard it, he wondered aloud whether it was a Holland-Dozier-Holland song! Powering its way up the chart, *Love Child* would elbow The Beatles' *Hey Jude* off the top and remain there for two weeks, although it had to settle for peaking at #2 R&B and #15 in the UK. The same team would continue the theme for the follow-up single *I'm Livin' In Shame*, a somewhat muted success that peaked at #10 pop and #8 R&B. By the time *I'm Livin' In Shame* had run its course, the focus had already switched.

In between their two excursions into social commentary, The Supremes linked up with the group that would make that particular genre their own exclusive property in the years to come, The Temptations. Shelly Berger's connections were beginning to pay dividends, with George Schlatter and Ed Friendly having convinced the NBC network that a television special featuring the two groups could be a ratings winner. Whilst Motown waited on NBC to sign off on the deal, both groups were sent into the studio to record an album of likely material, which would follow the usual Motown template of a mix of well known covers and songs plucked from the ever-expanding Jobete catalogue.

Sessions for **Diana Ross & The Supremes Join The Temptations** commenced in May 1968, with the resulting album being released in November the same year, after the special had been recorded but before it was aired. The stratagem worked to perfection, with the album vaulting the charts to reach #2 pop (it did even better R&B and in the UK, where it spent four weeks surveying the rest of the respective charts), aided by the crossover success of an extracted single. Originally intended to be a cover version of *The Impossible Dream*, the track that was eventually lifted was another cover in *I'm Gonna Make You Love Me*, on which Diana Ross and Eddie Kendricks shared the lead vocal. Soon after promotional copies of the album had been delivered to radio stations, Motown noticed many reported heavy airplay on *I'm Gonna Make You Love Me*, resulting in the single getting switched, even if it was to a track that was not part of the forthcoming television special. The decision was vindicated by the single's performance, surging up the chart to come to rest at #2 pop and R&B as well as hitting #3 in the UK. A hugely successful single and album only served to increase expectation on the forthcoming special, with 'T.C.B.' more than living up to expectations. NCB were reportedly extremely happy with the final viewing figures, whilst Motown made sure they milked the opportunity for all it was worth, releasing the **T.C.B.** soundtrack a day after the airing and being rewarded when it sailed to the top of the pop and R&B chart (despite the popularity of both acts in Britain at the time, the album could get no further than #11, although the fact that the television special wasn't aired may have something to do with its relatively lowly position).

The success of the album and television special may have elevated the fortunes of The Supremes and The Temptations as complete entities, but the inescapable conclusion was that they were all designed to raise the profile of Diana Ross as a soloist. If his original concept of launching Diana solo in 1966 had been thwarted by Jules Podell, Berry wasn't going to be dictated to by outside sources ever again. Thus almost everything Motown did over the next eighteen months or so was a vehicle of one sort or another for the impending solo career of Diana Ross.

With The Clan having served its purpose and been dissolved (with one of their number being co-opted into another conglomerate, The Corporation), writing and production duties on The Supremes were spread around the Motown lot, too widely if **Let The Sunshine In** was anything to go by. Although hosting the previous hit *Livin' In Shame*, there was little on the album to write home about, the extracted singles *The Composer* barely scraping into the Top Thirty at #27 and *No Matter What Sign You Are* faring even worse at #31. And whilst ratings for further television appearances by The Supremes and The Temptations were healthy, they couldn't convert into similar album or single sales, with **Together** and **On Broadway** barely troubling the chart either side of the Atlantic and the extracted singles making even less of a splash. Had *No Matter What Sign You Are* been a major hit, it is likely that Diana would have been lifted out of the group there and then, but the single's failure only delayed the inevitable for a few months. Instead, it focused thoughts on creating the perfect scenario whereby Diana would leave The Supremes where she had taken them; at the top, with the search now on for a final parting gift of another number one record.

There was also the problem of what do with the two remaining Supremes members, with consideration being given at least in some quarters that this might be the an opportunity of bringing Flo Ballard back into the fold, although how serious these thoughts were is open to debate, given the level of animosity that existed between Flo and Berry.

There was an air of change all around Motown during 1969, with much of the hierarchy of the company having relocated to California, where work was well underway grooming and recording the latest group to come through Motown's doors, The Jackson 5. Although the family group had been brought to the company by Bobby Taylor of The Vancouvers, his role would be airbrushed out of Motown's history by switching the emphasis on to Diana Ross; she was the one who spotted them performing at a benefit concert and told Berry he had to sign them. A new history was created, with Michael Jackson a willing student, going so far as claim he thought he'd never get discovered until Diana Ross entered the scene. Whilst The Jackson 5 were busy putting the finishing touches to what would be their debut album in **Diana Ross Presents The Jackson 5**, Diana was busy recording tracks for her planned solo career whilst Mary and Cindy were equally busy training up her eventual replacement Jean Terrell (born in Belzoni, Mississippi on 26 November 1944).

Internally at least the plan was to announce Diana's departure from the group in October, with the curtain coming down on this particular incarnation of The Supremes at the Frontier Hotel in Las Vegas in January 1970. However, for the plan to work smoothly, whereby Diana and The Supremes exited on a high, the final single had to be a successful one. What there was in the can didn't sound right. Neither did anything Diana had already recorded for her solo career, whilst there was insufficient time to commission anything for the occasion, leaving those concerned with the possibility of having to postpone the news until such time as all the elements were in place.

One thing that had served Berry well during his decade long march had been luck, which once again shone on him at a time he needed it most. Johnny Bristol was busy preparing a follow-up single to Junior Walker's *What Does It Take (To Win Your Love)* and had selected a song he, his former singing partner Jackey Beavers and producer Harvey Fuqua had written back in 1959 in *Someday We'll Be Together* (Junior was reportedly not that interested in *Someday*, just as he hadn't been too enamoured with *What Does It Take*). The song hadn't been a hit when Johnny & Jackey had originally recorded it, but the new arrangement Johnny had created for Junior sounded good.

So good, in fact, that the song was immediately handed over to Diana Ross for her to lay her vocal on, with Maxine and Julia Waters original backing vocals left in place. Add to the mix Johnny Bristol's own guiding vocal and as far as Berry was concerned, *Someday We'll Be Together* was the perfect song with which to bring down the career on Diana Ross as a member of The Supremes (whilst the sentiments of the song were perfect as a swansong for The Supremes, the irony of *not* having any Supreme other than Diana on the recording was obviously lost).

The single was released in October 1969 and hit the top of the chart before the year was done, sometime after the official announcement of Diana leaving for a solo career had hit the headlines in all of the music papers as well as many other sections of the media. Capitalising on the increased publicity, Motown made sure there was plenty of material out and available; there was the album **Cream Of The Crop**, which featured the latest hit single but not much else of interest, over and above appearances by Flo Ballard (on *Blowin' In The Wind*) and Syreeta, Berry's preferred replacement for Diana, on *The Beginning Of The End*, with the album making #33 in the US and #34 in the UK as well as #3 R&B, a third package of greatest hits in **Diana Ross & The Supremes Greatest Hits Volume 3** (which would peak at #31 pop) and, once the farewell tour had reached its conclusion, **Farewell**, which was recorded at the final concert and would hit #46 pop.

There was added publicity too when Cindy Birdsong was the target of a kidnap attempt in December, making it all but impossible to avoid hearing or reading about The Supremes as they headed towards the end of their first chapter. Diana duly bade her farewells and embarked on her solo career, whilst the two remaining Supremes (Mary and Cindy) found they had to battle with one last intrusion from Berry Gordy before they could get on with their career. Having initially suggested Syreeta Wright as Diana's replacement, only to select Jean Terrell after watching her perform live with her brother's group, he seemingly did an about turn and decided his original choice was the better bet and tried to coerce Mary into agreeing to the switch. This time Mary stuck to her guns, especially with The Supremes shortly to launch their own recording career; it was too late to make the change, even if they had wanted to. In exasperation, Berry announced he was washing his hands of the group, which was in many ways was music to Mary's ears since it meant they were clear to make their own decisions, without Berry or anyone else at Motown dictating.

Such independence came at a cost, most notably in the corporate funds that were made available for, well, pretty much everything. Whereas The Supremes with Diana had access to the best of everything, from writers, producers, couturiers and chaperones, stayed in the best rooms of the best hotels and were finely dined around the world, this version of The Supremes were pretty much left to make to and mend. Dresses had to be recycled and the travelling staff reduced, as were the size of the hotel rooms, but overall it was a price worth paying.

It helped their cause that their first single beat Diana's into the chart and became a bigger hit too, and whilst their clothes might have been hand me down, their material wasn't. Frank Wilson had come across a singer and songwriter in Vincent DiMirco, whose *Up The Ladder To The Roof* sounded an ideal fit for the new look Supremes. For the first time in a long time all three were present at the recording session for their new single, enabling the lead vocal duties to be shared around for the first time in an even longer time.

The magic of The Supremes name (with or without Diana) could also be guaranteed to get them prestigious live venues in which to perform and the occasional television appearance, all of which dovetailed neatly with whatever promotional activity

Motown was able to rustle up. *Up The Ladder To The Roof* therefore returned the group to the upper echelons of the chart, and whilst never likely to add to their unprecedented tally of twelve number one hits, still did better than many had expected. A #10 pop and #5 R&B hit (Diana's debut *Reach Out And Touch* stalled at #20 and #7 respectively) in the US, the single did even better in Britain, where it powered its way to #5 (and Diana's offering barely crept into the Top 40 at #33).

The resulting album, **Right On** was also helmed by Frank Wilson and proved the group's single success was no fluke, registering a more than healthy #25 pop and #4 R&B, as well as giving rise to a further Top 40 single in *Everybody's Got A Right To Love*. **Right On** was both a critical and commercial success, which certainly pleased Mary Wilson.

"With Jean and **Right On** we expanded The Supremes' image, keeping the sequins but reviving the soulfulness some people thought we'd lost since the early records. What excited the fans was that the formula of our act had changed. Instead of there being only one lead singer, Jean and I now shared leads. Why shouldn't a group have more than one lead singer? Over the years there had been many groups that did, such as The Temptations, The Pointer Sisters and The O'Jays."

The new look certainly impressed the critics, with one writing, 'The Supremes with Diana Ross were great; without her they're just as good, sometimes better.' Frank was on board to produce the follow-up album, with the stand out single *Stoned Love*, which would go on to become the group's biggest post-Diana success, topping the R&B chart and hitting #7 pop in the US and #3 in the UK. The success of the single should have been a launch pad to propel The Supremes back into the big time, but for a number of reasons, Motown missed the opportunity. Plans for the accompanying album were changed, and, as far as Mary was concerned, not for the better.

"Cindy, Jean and I posed for a group portrait in naturals, scant make-up and black turtleneck sweaters. It was simple, classy and the shot that I strongly believed should have been the album's front cover. What Motown put out instead was a hodgepodge of little round pictures of us in various stage costumes. Even worse, Motown decided the LP couldn't be titled **Stoned Love**. I still maintain this album should have been the record to put The Supremes back on top. I think that through neglect and carelessness, Motown squandered our big chance. **New Ways But Love Stays** settled at a very disappointing #68 [as well as #12 R&B], a poor showing for an album bearing a gold single."

Equally disappointing was the reception (at least stateside) to the album The Supremes recorded with fellow labelmates The Four Tops. With the hugely successful series of albums recorded with The Temptations still fresh in the memory, the decision to link The Supremes with The Four Tops was a natural one, with Levi Stubbs and Jean Terrell's lead vocals a dynamic combination. On the evidence of the extracted single, a remake of *River Deep Mountain High* the project had every opportunity of proving just as successful as the earlier combination, sailing to #14 pop and #7 R&B as well as hitting #11 in the UK. Unfortunately, Motown proved unable to convert single success into album sales, with **The Magnificent 7** barely registering at all, stalling at a distant #113.

Consolation, of sorts, was received from the R&B market, where the album at least made the Top 20 (at #18), and, not for the last time, in Britain, where the magic of the combined unit was enough to see the album hit #6. If it was British success that prompted further albums, with **The Return Of The Magnificent Seven** (#154 pop and #18 R&B) and **Dynamite** (#160 pop and #21 R&B) then the exercise failed, with neither album making a showing across the Atlantic. By 1971, however, The Supremes were busy working on their latest album, this time built around the success of the single *Nathan Jones*.

"In February we began work on our last album with Frank Wilson, **Touch**, probably our most rock-orientated work and, I think, our best," was Mary's opinion. "We recorded it all over the country, wherever we happened to be performing. For reasons I could only guess at then, Motown simply didn't push the LP or the follow-up single *Touch*. The latter was different for us, because while I was singing some leads on each album and in our shows, this was the first 45 we'd released with Jean and me sharing leads. The lyrics were very sexy; this was a real soul love ballad. Still, nothing. It was our first flop, stalling outside the Top 40."

The single peaked at #71, failing to make any impression whatsoever on the R&B chart or in Britain, whilst the album could not get beyond #85 pop, even if a #6 R&B placing and #40 in the UK hinted the album could have done better if it had been promoted.

"Not long after **Touch** we stopped seeing Frank Wilson around. He was deservedly proud of the three albums he'd made with The Supremes but understandably disappointed with how poorly they charted. Jean, Cindy and I felt the same way. The unfortunate thing about Frank's not working with us again after **Touch** was that our new sound was finally beginning to evolve."

Whilst Frank would prove his Midas touch had not deserted him with a succession of hits with Eddie Kendricks, The Supremes were handed over to an abundance of producers and writers for a planned December 1971 release **Promises Kept**. This was subsequently scrapped, with Smokey Robinson being assigned the group for what would ultimately become the **Floy Joy** album.

"Everything about **Floy Joy** gave me hope. These tracks were the realisation of what I'd felt The Supremes should be. Smokey achieved a beautiful blend of our voices, especially on *Automatically Sunshine*. Again I was sure that we'd found a match as perfect for The Supremes as Holland-Dozier-Holland were in the sixties. And after losing Frank Wilson, having Smokey now was the best thing that could happen to us, and I wanted him to be our producer forever."

The combination certainly created magic in the studio, with *Floy Joy* and *Automatically Sunshine* becoming successful singles (#16 pop and #5 R&B, #37 pop and #21 R&B respectively), with the album hitting #54 pop and #12 R&B, with a third in *Your Wonderful Sweet Sweet Love* also making a dent at #59 pop and #22 R&B. It was in Britain that the singles found their mark, with both *Floy Joy* and *Automatically Sunshine* making the Top Ten (#9 and #10 respectively), thus continuing a love affair between the group and their British fans that remained constant.

"Ever since the first transatlantic Motown Revue hit England in 1965, it's been one of my favourite places in the world" Mary would reveal. "I've always appreciated that the British respect performers for what they have to offer, with or without current hits. That's why countless performers move or spend large parts of each year there and in Europe. Our stateside lack of the elusive big hit did not diminish our British fans' love for us. In fact, as many British writers pointed out, Diana's leaving mattered very little over there, and our records always charted higher and did much better in the UK than they did in the US."

British audiences had taken to Jean Terrell as Diana's replacement and they would also take to Lynda Laurence (born Lynda Tucker in Philadelphia, Pennsylvania on 20 February 1949), who came into the group when Cindy left in order raise a family. A former member of The Third Generation, Stevie Wonder's vocal backing group who would evolve into Wonderlove, Lynda was already being ushered into The Supremes, appearing on the cover of **Floy Joy** even though she did not appear on any of the recordings (the reason being that Cindy was heavily pregnant at the time of recording and didn't want to appear on the cover in that condition).

Having worked with many of Motown's best producers during the course of the last ten years, The Supremes next album saw them go outside of the company for the first time, with Jimmy Webb being brought on board for **The Supremes** (its full title was **The Supremes Produced And Arranged By Jimmy Webb**, which itself was amended from the original title **Beyond Myself**). The resulting album received many complimentary reviews but failed to set the tills ablaze, much to Mary's disappointment.

"As much as I loved this album, several things about it were not in The Supremes' best interest. For example, Jimmy brought in additional background vocalists. After Smokey's having achieved that perfect vocal blend, I saw this as another big step backward. Except for Jean, the group on **Floy Joy** and the group on **The Supremes** might have been two different entities."

As good as the album was, it struggled to make any impact whatsoever, with the extracted single *I Guess I'll Miss The Man* (a song that featured in the Broadway show 'Pippin') limping to #85 and the album becoming only the second Supremes album to miss the Top 100, stalling at #129 pop and #27 R&B. After this latest disappointment, Lynda suggested to the others that she approach Stevie Wonder and see if he was interested in working with the group. The sessions went well, resulting in the uplifting single *Bad Weather*, but whilst Motown invariably put their entire promotional force behind a Stevie solo record, the same degree of effort was lacking on The Supremes single, which hit #87 pop and #74 R&B and got no further, although it did manage to break into the Top 40 in Britain, where it reached #37.

The failure of the single was a disappointment to all, including Stevie, who tried to get the company behind the project. With the single dead before its time, any plans for a subsequent album were shelved. Indeed, it would be more than two years before The Supremes would record another album for Motown, although there was some doubt as to whether the group would record for the company ever again. Intergroup tensions were beginning to take their toll, with Jean Terrell eventually opting to leave The Supremes and pursue a solo career elsewhere.

In her place came Scherrie Payne (born in Detroit on 14 November 1944), the younger sister of fellow singer Freda, on the advice of Lamont Dozier. Scherrie had experience of singing in a group, having begun her career with Glass House before becoming a backing singer for Charo. Whilst she was more than that when she joined The Supremes, there were no recording sessions, just a seemingly endless list of tour dates which, without a hit single, were beginning to diminish in credibility.

Mary Wilson began taking greater control of The Supremes future, as befitted the last surviving original member, which put her on something of a collision course with Motown, especially when she queried Motown's rights to the group name. Mary's husband Pedro Ferrer took over management of the group and, when Lynda announced her impending departure through pregnancy, Cindy Birdsong returned to the fold.

Still Motown showed little or no interest in getting the group into the studio, with the only material that found its way onto the market being a compilation album, **Anthology (1962-1969)**, which obviously focused on the Diana Ross led era. The album proved The Supremes was still a bankable act, hitting #66 pop and earning the group a gold disc for sales in excess of half a million copies, but still no new material, even though Mary sounded out both Smokey Robinson and Marvin Gaye about working with the group.

Whilst contract negotiations with Motown dragged on (largely over the rights to the name The Supremes), Mary instructed the group's attorney to make tentative enquiries of other record companies, especially ABC, who had briefly had Flo Ballard on their books. In the end The Supremes re-signed with Motown and went into the studio in December 1974 to begin work on their new album, imaginatively entitled **The Supremes**. The initial sessions were produced by Terry Woodford and Clayton Ivy, with later assistance from Brian Holland, Greg Wright, Mark Davis, Michael Lloyd and Hal Davis.

"The industry treated **The Supremes** as a comeback album. Working with so many different producers kept the LP from achieving the kind of cohesiveness our albums with Frank and Smokey had, but maybe that wasn't so bad. There was a little something for everybody, as they say."

Originally, Motown planned on releasing *It's All Been Said Before* as the lead single, only to scrap that plan and release *He's My Man*, a more club orientated song that featured Scherrie and Mary on lead vocals. The track made a small showing on the R&B chart, hitting #69, with a second single in *Where Do I Go From Here* peaking at #93 (although both would feature in the Top Ten of the Dance/Disco Singles chart), with the album making #152 pop and #25 R&B. Although the records received considerable radio play in the UK, nothing made much of an impact on the chart, although The Supremes did come over on tour in support of the album.

The tour nearly ended in disaster, for in September 1975 the hotel in which they were resident, the Hilton Hotel in London, was hit by a bomb planted by the IRA, which killed two people and injured sixty three.

Fortunately, the girls escaped unhurt, although they had been due to congregate in the lobby at the time the bomb exploded. A later tour of South Africa also attracted the wrong kind of headlines, with numerous celebrities requesting the group reconsider their decision, but the tour went ahead, even though it was not the success all had hoped.

By the time the group came to record their next album there were further personnel changes afoot, with Cindy Birdsong again leaving the group and being replaced by Susaye Greene (born in Houston, Texas on 13 September 1949). In the middle of the sessions, The Supremes were rocked by the tragic news that Flo Ballard had died from a blood clot. Temporarily, at least, two of the original Supremes were reunited for Flo's funeral, with Diana Ross and Mary Wilson joining for a silent prayer.

Meanwhile, both Cindy and Susaye appeared vocally on the resulting album **High Energy**, released in April 1976, an album that reunited The Supremes with the architects of their greatest successes, Brian and Eddie Holland. Rolling back the years, **High Energy** proved to be a return to form, with the album hitting #42 pop (and #24 R&B), the best showing by a Supremes album for some six years. There was also single success to savour, with *I'm Gonna Let My Heart Do The Walking* hitting #40 pop and #25 R&B and again making a healthy showing on the dance chart, alongside the title track, hitting the Top Ten. The reunion worked well enough for Brian and Eddie to link with The Supremes on their next album which would ultimately turn out to be their last.

The project started encouragingly, with the single *You're My Driving Wheel* making progress on the club, R&B and pop chart, only to stall at #29, #50 and #85 respectively. With the single having stalled, the album **Mary, Scherrie & Susaye** didn't even get off the ground, although *Let Yourself Go* and *Love I Never Knew* also attracted considerable club play. Perhaps sensing the writing was on the wall, Mary Wilson announced she intended leaving the group once their European tour commitments were done and dusted. The final curtain came down on The Supremes on 12 June 1977 at the Drury Lane Theatre in London, a performance in the city in the country that had always taken well to The Supremes.

So it proved for the finale, with the show, as much a media event as any during the group's heyday, being broadcast live on the BBC. The various members of the group had their own plans once this version of The Supremes were finished, with Mary heading for a solo career and Susaye and Scherrie initially planning on retaining The Supremes moniker and drafting in a third member in Karen Jackson; in the end they recorded as a duo. And it wasn't quite the end for Mary Wilson either, for the discovery of several outstanding dates in South America meant drafting in an assortment of other singers (but most usually Karen Jackson and Karen Ragland) in order to fulfil those obligations, usually under the moniker Mary Wilson of The Supremes.

That The Supremes was (and still is) a magical name in the recording world can be gauged by the continued success compilations of their recordings have enjoyed over the years, with 1977's British package **Diana Ross & The Supremes 20 Golden Greats** topping the British chart.

There have been assorted attempts to bring about a reunion over the years, although the debacle that was the 'Motown 25' performance left the subject off the negotiating table for nearly two decades. In 1986 Scherrie Payne, Jean Terrell and Lynda Laurence formed FLOS (Former Ladies of The Supremes), but the reunion most clamoured for was one that involved Diana Ross and Mary Wilson. The closest those plans came to fruition was in 2000, when the Diana Ross & The Supremes Return To Love tour was muted, but disagreements over money (Diana was offered $15 million, Mary $4 million and Cindy Birdsong just $1 million) brought that line-up to a halt. Diana did go out on the tour with Scherrie Payne and Lynda Laurence, but after a promising start in larger venues attracted negative publicity and was eventually cancelled halfway through, an inglorious end for one of the greatest and most successful groups in history.

They were inducted into the Rock & Roll Hall of fame in 1988. Florence Ballard died from coronary artery thrombosis on 22 February 1976. Betty McGlown-Travis died from diabetes on 12 January 2008. Former guitarist Marv Tarplin died on 30 September 2011.

ALBUMS: MEET THE SUPREMES (1962), WHERE DID OUR LOVE GO? (1964), A BIT OF LIVERPOOL (1964), THE SUPREMES SING COUNTRY AND WESTERN AND POP (1965), WE REMEMBER SAM COOKE (1965), MORE HITS BY THE SUPREMES (1965), THE SUPREMES AT THE COPA (1965), MERRY CHRISTMAS (1965), I HEAR A SYMPHONY (1966), SUPREMES A' GO-GO (1966), SING HOLLAND, DOZIER, HOLLAND (1967), SING RODGERS AND HART (1967), REFLECTIONS (1968), SING AND PERFORM FUNNY GIRL (1968), LIVE AT LONDON'S TALK OF THE TOWN (1968), LOVE CHILD (1968), DIANA ROSS & THE SUPREMES & THE TEMPTATIONS (1968), T.C.B. (1968), LET THE SUNSHINE IN (1969), TOGETHER (1969), CREAM OF THE CROP (1969), ON BROADWAY (1969), FAREWELL (1970), RIGHT ON (1970), NEW WAYS BUT LOVE STAYS (1970), MAGNIFICENT SEVEN (1971), TOUCH (1971), RETURN OF THE MAGNIFICENT SEVEN (1971), DYNAMITE (1971), FLOY JOY (1972), PRODUCED AND ARRANGED BY JIMMY WEBB (1972), THE SUPREMES (1975), HIGH ENERGY (1976), MARY, SCHERRIE AND SUSAYE (1976)

COMPILATIONS: GREATEST HITS (1967), GREATEST HITS VOLUME 3 (1969), ANTHOLOGY (1974), 20 GOLDEN GREATS (1977), AT THEIR BEST (1978), 20 GREATEST HITS – COMPACT COMMAND PERFORMANCES (1984), 25TH ANNIVERSARY COLLECTION (1985), ANTHOLOGY (1987), LOVE SUPREME (1988)

FURTHER READING: THE SUPREMES: A SAGA OF MOTOWN DREAMS, SUCCESS AND BEYOND (2009)

SUPREMES A' GO-GO – THE SUPREMES [ALBUM]

One of the great fallacies about Motown throughout the 1960s was that the company didn't really sell albums, preferring to concentrate on singles success. The facts would tend to disprove this, for during the course of the decade, Motown and its imprints would rack up nearly fifty albums that cracked the Top Twenty of the Billboard charts.

What is not in dispute, however, is the often jumbled make-up of the albums that were released, with a couple of hit singles being coupled with throwaway tracks to make a ten or twelve track long player. However, there is no way a song like *Get Ready* could be described as a throwaway, regardless of who within Motown was doing the recording.

Every track on **Supremes A' Go-Go** was recognisable by title alone, even if it wasn't always The Supremes who had made the song famous. *You Can't Hurry Love* and *Love Is Like An Itching In My Heart* were or would be hit singles in their own right, with Diana, Florence and Mary also borrowing heavily from the HDH songbook to offer their versions of The Four Tops' perennial favourites *Baby I Need Your Loving* and *I Can't Help Myself*. Add to this *Put Yourself In My Place*, *This Old Heart Of Mine* and even *Money* and **Supremes A'Go-Go** does not suffer from the apparent lack of a concept. Instead, the album would become one of the group's earliest successes, going on top the pop and R&B charts in October 1966, knocking The Beatles and **Revolver** off the summit in the process.

THE SUPREMES HITS – THE SUPREMES [EP]

One of three EPs released by Tamla Motown in May 1965, **The Supremes Hits** contained *Where Did Our Love Go, Baby Love, Come See About Me* and *When The Lovelight Starts Shining Thru' His Eyes*. At the time there was a separate EP chart complied by Record Retailer, resulting in The Supremes' issue making #6 in June 1965 and spending a total of twelve weeks on the listings.

THE SUPREMES SING HOLLAND-DOZIER-HOLLAND – THE SUPREMES [ALBUM]

Built around the success of the singles *You Keep Me Hangin' On* and *Love Is Here And Now You're Gone*, the resulting album **The Supremes Sing Holland-Dozier-Holland** would mark the very last complete album HDH would write and helm for the group, even if none of the parties knew it at the time. Whilst HDH invariably wrote material for The Supremes pretty much as required, several of the songs on display here were written as much as two years before they were finally recorded for inclusion on the album. The material was further padded out by getting The Supremes to record versions of songs that had been hits for other Motown artists, such as The Isley Brothers (*I Guess I'll Always Love You*), The Four Tops (*It's The Same Old Song*) and Martha Reeves & The Vandellas (*Heatwave*).

And whilst Motown had been careful to hide the identity of virtually all of their writers, producers and musicians in the past, the selection of the title **The Supremes Sing Holland-Dozier-Holland** can be seen as an attempt to elevate HDH into the exalted company of the likes of George and Ira Gershwin and Richard Rodgers and Lorenz Hart (whose material The Supremes would tackle next on **The Supremes Sing Rodgers & Hart**), although in the UK the title was amended to **The Supremes Sing Motown**. Irrespective of what title in what territory, the album was another major success, topping the R&B chart and hitting #6 as well as peaking at #15 in the UK.

SURRENDER – DIANA ROSS [SINGLE]

Whilst her career stateside had faltered since *Ain't No Mountain High Enough* hit #1 in 1970, in the UK Diana's stock had never been higher. The extraction of *I'm Still Waiting* as a single had proved to be a masterly decision, resulting in the first number one hit of her career (she would not return for fifteen years, when *Chain Reaction* hit the top).

In September 1971, the BBC aired her television special 'Diana!', an hour long programme featuring guest appearances from Bill Cosby and The Jackson 5 that had originally been screened in America in April. When Tamla Motown issued the follow-up single in October, therefore, pretty much anything that was released could reliably be expected to do well.

The track chosen was *Surrender*, written by Nickolas Ashford and Valerie Simpson that had already been released in America and stalled at a lowly #16 R&B and #38 pop. In Britain, however, the single continued Diana's hot streak, hitting #10 towards the end of November and stretching her consecutive Top Ten hits tally to four. This would turn out to be the last Ashford and Simpson composition to be released as a single, with Valerie now beginning to concentrate on her own singing career.

SWEET LOVE – THE COMMODORES [SINGLE]

The Commodores had kicked off their chart career with three funk-influenced hits in *Machine Gun, I Feel Sanctified* and *Slippery When Wet* before slowing the tempo right down with the sublime ballad *This Is Your Life*. Written by Lionel Richie, *This Is Your Life* would serve as something of a template for later Richie compositions, with his ballads often in stark contrast to the upbeat material the other members provided.

By the time of the group's third album **Movin' On**, Lionel's ballads were the key tracks, with *Sweet Love* eventually being the only track issued as a single. Coupled with *Better Never Than Forever*, *Sweet Love* was released stateside in December 1975, two months after the album had made its bow. Although the gospel-tinged track continued the group's success on the R&B chart, peaking at #2, the fact that it should crossover and hit #5 on the pop chart was not only an added bonus but a sign of things to come.

In the UK the track did little following its release in January 1976, although in September 1977 Motown tried again, coupling *Sweet Love* with the group's then massive American hit *Brick House* and saw the double A sided single peak at #32 on the pop chart; better late than never.

THE SWINGING TIGERS

The first name by which The Funk Brothers released their own single on Tamla, with their June 1959 release *Snake Walk Part 1* (the flipside containing Part 2) also showcasing Smokey Robinson as a writer for the very first time. Quite how serious Berry Gordy was about promoting the single remains a matter of some doubt, since the record was pressed with the wrong catalogue number (Tamla 54024 had been used two months previously on a single by Chico Leverett) and whatever copies were pressed were only available in the immediate Detroit area. Two years later The Funk Brothers would get another outing, this time credited to The Twistin' Kings and release an album and two singles.

SWITCH

Formed around brothers Tommy (bass) and Bobby DeBarge (keyboards, drums and vocals), Switch was formed in Mansfield, Ohio in 1974 and also consisted of Gregory Williams (keyboards and trumpet), Phillip Ingram (keyboards), Eddie Fleullen (keyboards and Jody Sims (drums). Initially known as First Class, this multi-talented line-up recorded as White Heat for RCA in 1975 under the supervision of Barry White.

When this project failed, the group re-assembled as Hot Ice and recorded **Pall Mall Groove** for Polydor in 1977, although the album was only released in Germany. They then settled on the name Switch, in deference to their ability to switch instruments, and sent Greg and Jody to Hollywood, armed with a demo tape, with instructions to get it to Jermaine Jackson. As it happened they bumped into him in the elevator at the Motown office and were able to hand it over personally. The very next day, Jermaine called back to offer a deal, the agreement being finalised in the hospital where Jermaine's wife Hazel was about to give birth to their first son!

Signed in May 1977, the group and Jackson spent almost a year working on their debut album, eventually releasing **Switch** in July 1978. From the album came the hit single *There'll Never Be*, which would make #6 R&B and #36 pop, with a second single in *I Wanna Be Closer* also making #22 R&B. Fuelled by this success the album did healthy business and would also make a showing on the charts, reaching #6 R&B and #37 pop.

The success of the album and its singles was a good barometer of Switch; whilst they were readily accepted by the R&B audience, who obviously bought into Jermaine Jackson's comparison of the group with Earth, Wind & Fire, they struggled to achieve major crossover success. Still, whilst their albums and singles were selling in good quantities, few were too concerned.

Their second album, entitled **Switch II** was released in April 1979 and matched the sales and chart position of its predecessor, slipping two places down the R&B listing to #8. There were two successful singles lifted, *Best Beat In Town* returning them to the R&B Top 20 (#16 and #69 pop) and *I Call Your Name* making #10 and becoming their last single to make the pop chart, at #83.

The first two albums would be as good as it got for Switch, with subsequent albums **Reaching For Tomorrow**, **This Is My Dream** and **Switch V** producing diminishing returns, peaking at #23, #21 and #48 on the R&B album chart respectively. There was only one further appearance in the R&B Top Ten on the singles chart too, with *Love Over And Over Again* from **This Is My Dream** peaking at #9 in November 1980.

By the following year and the release of **Switch V**, Tommy and Bobby were looking at other projects to get involved with, most notably a group that had been assembled by their younger siblings. With Tommy and Bobby opting to remain with Motown and Phillip Ingram about to launch a solo career, the rest of the band recruited Gonzales Ozen and Renard Gallo and took the group over to Total Experience for one further album in 1984, **Am I Still Your Boyfriend**. The group disbanded soon after this release.

ALBUMS: SWITCH (1978), SWITCH II (1979), REACHING FOR TOMORROW (1980), THIS IS MY DREAM (1980), SWITCH V (1985)

SYREETA

Just as Martha Reeves began her career at Motown as a secretary for Mickey Stevenson, so Syreeta spent time working in the typing pool before getting her chance at stardom. Born Syreeta Wright in Pittsburgh, Pennsylvania on 3 August 1946, she began singing at the age of four.

"I used to sing 'The Lord's Prayer' and my mother would hold her breath until I made the high notes. I always started about eight notes higher than everyone else and I still have that range," she would later recall.

Syreeta was still a young child when her father was killed in the Korean War, with her mother Essie and grandmother left to bring up Syreeta and her two sisters (Kim and Yvonne). The family moved to Detroit when Syreeta was 11, although she would later move to South Carolina to attend a private school.

"I didn't stay too long! I quit to start work and my family were really upset. I originally wanted to be a ballet dancer but my grandparents said it would cost too much so I had to quit that idea. So I decided to write and sing."

Yet although Syreeta got an introduction to Motown soon after deciding upon her new vocation, the recording career would have to wait for a couple of years, with Syreeta set to work as a receptionist in 1965 before becoming Mickey Stevenson's secretary inside a year. It was not all typing and answering the telephone, with Syreeta later explaining how she got some insider knowledge of Motown.

"I learned all the way up, and now have experience in a little bit of the business side because I used to sit in on Mr Gordy's meetings sometimes and learned how he manoeuvred things. Not to be an executive at Motown but just to know and understand the business side, and that was really thrilling. I was very fortunate that he would allow me to do that from time to time."

As enlightening an experience sitting in on meetings was, it did not beat the thrill of working in the studio, and Syreeta had begun pestering the assorted producers with whom she was in regular contact in order to try and obtain a session for herself, most notably Brian Holland.

"I bothered him every day for over a month to see if he had a song for me. One day he actually said he had and that was when I met Valerie Simpson and Nickolas Ashford for the first time. They wrote my first single."

In fact they wrote *I Can't Give Back The Love I Feel For You* with Brian Holland, who produced the session with Lamont Dozier, with the song apparently intended for Diana Ross & The Supremes (they would record the song more than twelve months later but it was never considered as a possible single release). Syreeta was assigned to the Gordy label, but Motown felt her name was somewhat unwieldy and shortened it to Rita Wright, with the single being released in January 1968 and a month later in the UK.

The single did little at the time of release (although over the next three years it became something of a favourite on the Northern Soul scene, prompting a Tamla Motown reissue in October 1971) and Syreeta went back to her secretarial duties, although there was still the occasional opportunity of doing backing vocal work and, on one occasion, filling in for Martha Reeves on the single *I Can't Dance To That Music You're Playing*.

Syreeta was also kept busy doing demo vocal work for Diana Ross & The Supremes and did well enough for Berry Gordy to at one point consider replacing the solo bound Diana with Syreeta, only to offer the position to Jean Terrell. When he changed his mind and wanted to drop Jean and slot Syreeta in once again, Mary Wilson used her veto to scotch the plan.

By 1970, however, Syreeta's career had started to gather its own momentum, thanks to a flourishing relationship with Stevie Wonder. The two had met in 1968 and began dating the following year, with Stevie encouraging Syreeta in her songwriting. Along with Lee Garrett, the pair would write *It's A Shame*, a hit for The Spinners and Stevie's own smash *Signed Sealed Delivered* (which would garner a Grammy Award nomination for Best R&B Song), a song that changed Syreeta's perception of songwriting.

"It was simple for me but I was amazed that lyrics like that could sell over two million copies. The music told me what to write about, instead of me trying to get someone to write a tune around my lyrics. Once I had written something I liked, I'd tell Steve. If he didn't like it, I'd go back and work on it again. Or he'd give the song to someone else to work on."

Following a four month engagement, Stevie and Syreeta were signed, sealed and delivered in a marriage ceremony in Detroit on 14 September 1970, followed by a honeymoon in Bermuda. Although Syreeta had initially been wary of Stevie's intentions, she quickly fell in love with him.

"Steve's a remarkable person and that's outside the fact that I'm in love with him. He never shows he's sad to anyone. To me he'll show his grievances but when he steps out he never shows it if he's angry or depressed. He feels life is too short to upset other people."

Despite their stated intention of having at least twelve children together, the personal relationship quickly unravelled (they were divorced inside eighteen months), although the pair did retain their professional relationship for a good deal longer. Syreeta co-wrote all of the songs on Stevie's album **Where I'm Coming From** and one on the follow-up **Music Of My Mind** (this latter album also featured two co-writes for sister Yvonne Wright), whilst Stevie was also took control of his ex-wife's solo career, producing **Syreeta** which was released on the MoWest label in June 1972.

The album did reasonable business, hitting #38 R&B and #185 pop, but the lack of a big hit single held the album back – even the presence of *To Know You Is To Love You*, a duet between Syreeta and Stevie failed to set the chart alight. The pair worked together again on the follow-up album, with Stevie nailing his colours firmly to the mast of **Stevie Wonder Presents Syreeta**, even though he was also busy with producing Minnie Riperton and recording his own **Fulfillingness First Finale** album at much the same time.

Presents Syreeta also lacked a major hit single, at least as far as the US was concerned, but the album did make some headway, hitting #116 pop, even if its R&B placing slipped a little to #53. It was in the UK that the album found its true home, with two hit singles in *Spinnin' And Spinnin'* and *Your Kiss Is Sweet* (#49 and #12 respectively), whilst her duet with G.C. Cameron, *I Wanna Be By Your Side* also received some considerable airplay. Stevie would write Syreeta's next hit, *Harmour Love*, a #75 R&B and #32 British pop hit in 1975, although it would take a further two years before the album finally appeared.

By the time **One To One** was released in January 1977, Syreeta had married bass player Curtis Robertson Jr., who helped produce the album with Leon Ware, but it was too late after the success of *Harmour Love* to capitalise on that single's popularity. With her solo career somewhat stalled, Syreeta embarked on a duets album with G.C. Cameron, with **Rich Love Poor Love** being released in August 1977, but neither the album nor the extracted single *Let's Make A Deal* saw much action. As the decade neared its end, there was every likelihood that Syreeta would be leaving Motown, her lack of any tangible and consistent success, both personally and professionally (her second marriage was also short-lived; Syreeta would marry a third time to Torrence Mathis), meant it was unlikely her contract would be renewed when it expired in 1980.

A chance meeting with the newly signed Billy Preston changed both artist's fortunes at Motown, with a song the pair recorded for the film 'Fast Break', a delightful ballad entitled *With You I'm Born Again*, becoming a major hit in the UK (it would peak at #2) being repeated by a #4 placing in the US (the single might have been a major pop hit but R&B acceptance was negligible; it stalled at #86), followed by the duet hits *One More Time* (#52 pop and #72 R&B in the US) and *It Will Come In Time* (#47 in the UK) saw Syreeta given a contract extension at Motown.

Unfortunately, that brief spell of success was as good as it got, with another workout with Billy Preston (*Searchin'*) peaking at #106 and the solo effort *Quick Slick* failing to break into the Top 40 of the R&B chart. Her second eponymous album, released in April 1980 was only a minor hit at #73 pop, and whilst **Set My Love In Motion** hit #40 R&B and #189 pop, **The Spell** failed to make any headway whatsoever. Syreeta's only other chart action was with an album with Billy Preston, which would hit #48 R&B and #127 pop. Changing priorities at Motown saw Syreeta leave the label soon after working with Smokey Robinson on the soundtrack to 'The Last Dragon'.

"When Berry Gordy sold Motown the new regime did not want the likes of *With You I'm Born Again* or that type of format. They went for a younger market. I'm not that old by any means, but I'm not your teenybopper. So when he sold the company, we looked at each other and we knew it just wasn't a thing that would work. In retrospect it wasn't a bad thing because I don't want to be moulded into something that I'm not. I mean, I fought for my own identity and freedom for a number of years so I certainly don't want to be anywhere where they're going to put me in clothes that are slit from my toes up to my neck and where I'm wearing underclothes because it's fashionable, that's not me."

Berry Gordy was equally sorry to see her leave. "I will always love Syreeta Wright - a great woman who co-wrote and sang on some of his records [Stevie Wonder] and whom he married in September of 1970. She is not only one of my favourite singers of all time, but favourite people as well. Versatile, with a rich, interpretative voice, she was one of those artists who really should have made it but didn't. The timing and material didn't come together the right way to do her justice. Yet whenever her voice was on a record, even in the background, it could steal the show."

There was no deal waiting for her when she left Motown, although Syreeta was briefly lured out of semi-retirement in order to record for Ian Levine's Motorcity Records before leaving show business for good in the mid 1990s, eventually settling down in California with her four children. After being diagnosed with breast and bone cancer in 2003, Syreeta underwent extensive chemotherapy and radiation treatment but sadly lost her battle on 6 July 2004.

ALBUMS: SYREETA (1972), STEVIE WONDER PRESENTS SYREETA (1974), ONE TO ONE (1977), RICH LOVE, POOR LOVE (1977), FAST BREAK (1979), SYREETA (1980), SET MY LOVE IN MOTION (1981), BILLY PRESTON & SYREETA (1981), THE SPELL (1983)

GABOR SZABO

Jazz guitarist Gabor Szabo was born in Budapest, Hungary on 8 March 1936 and grew up listening to jazz music on the 'Voice of America' radio broadcasts. He escaped from the communist regime in Hungary in 1956, enrolling in the Berklee School of Music in Boston. After a performance at the Newport Jazz Festival in 1958 he linked up with Chico Hamilton, becoming a member of Chico's quintet between 1961 and 1965. He would then sign with Impulse, recording a series of highly acclaimed albums for the label before forming his own Skye label in 1968, where he recorded with Lena Horne, Gary McFarland and Cal Tjader.

After closing Skye Gabor would sign with Blue Note and then CTI, recording two albums for the latter label. However, his music had never sat comfortably within the jazz idiom, due in part to his throwing pop and rock and traditional Hungarian music into the mix. Thus Creed Taylor took the decision to move him over to the Salvation label for **Macho**, released in 1975. Gabor later moved on to Mercury but died from liver and kidney disease in Budapest on 26 February 1982 whilst on a visit home trying to find treatment for his drug problems.

ALBUM: MACHO (1975)

T

TALKING BOOK – STEVIE WONDER [ALBUM]

His first album after securing artistic freedom (**Music Of My Mind**) had merely hinted at the creativity of Stevie Wonder at the start of the 1970s. He and his producers, Robert Margouleff and Malcolm Cecil, had been busy recording hundreds of tracks, many of which were completed to the point of being ready for release.

The only problem was there was so much material covering a wide range of topics and styles, the three ended up having differing ideas on what songs to select for album release. **Music Of My Mind** also suffered slightly from having only one major hit single in *If You Really Love Me*, although it was later revealed that several of Stevie's later blockbusters had been completed during the early creative rush but held back for reasons known only to Stevie himself.

By the time the three gathered to begin what would become the **Talking Book** album, both Robert and Malcolm were confident enough in their relationship with Stevie to press strongly for specific tracks to be included (Stevie, of course, retained the right of veto!). Fortunately, Stevie had also begun to appreciate the importance of his work, offering *Maybe Your Baby* and then *Superstition* to Jeff Beck and then withdrawing the offer once he realised the value of both songs. Whilst this may have temporarily affected his relationship with Jeff, it gave **Talking Book** two of the key tracks that turned it into such a success.

Helping him out with the songs themselves were his onetime wife Syreeta (on two tracks) and her sister Yvonne (also two tracks), whilst the accompanying musicians included the crème de la crème, from master guitarists Ray Parker Jr. and Jeff Beck (at the time still on talking terms with Stevie) to legendary saxophonist David Sanborn. The backing vocalists were also of the highest calibre, with both Deniece Williams and Jim Gilstrap later to enjoy successful solo careers. Virtually everything else was created by Stevie, who would play drums, keyboards, moog bass and provide lead and background vocals; on two tracks he is the only musician featured.

The cover featured Stevie without his trademark sunglasses, whilst early editions of the album featured a Braille message that read, 'Here is my music. It is all I have to tell you how I feel. Know that your love keeps my love strong – Stevie.'

The two major single releases from the album were *You Are The Sunshine Of My Life* and *Superstition*, widely differing songs that showed Stevie was rapidly becoming an artist that was almost impossible to categorise. Both found huge favour on the pop charts (both were chart toppers) and the R&B equivalent (*Superstition* topped that particular chart), but Motown had long enjoyed success on the singles chart. What really mattered was how well the album performed, and **Talking Book** did not disappoint, topping the R&B chart and hitting #3 pop, also performing well internationally with a #16 peak in the UK.

At the end of the year, **Talking Book** and its attendant singles found themselves nominated for some five Grammy Awards (Stevie's follow-up album **Innervisions** was also nominated the same year) and won three; *Superstition* was named Best R&B Song and Best R&B Vocal Performance whilst *You Are The Sunshine Of My Life* won Best Pop Vocal Performance.

TAMLA RECORDS

But for a measly producer's royalty cheque, Berry Gordy might never have started his own record company. By his own admission, songwriting was his first love, with his affair resulting in numerous hits on Jackie Wilson and later The Miracles. Whilst he had little or no input into how Jackie's singles turned out, he did get heavily involved with Smokey Robinson and The Miracles and their efforts, most notably *Got A Job*, which was leased to George Goldner's End Records.

The record sold well locally and both Smokey and Berry anticipated a healthy royalty cheque would soon be heading their way. Both were crestfallen when the cheque arrived, with the sum of just $3.19 made out to Berry.

"You might as well start your own record label," Smokey said. "I don't think you could do any worse than this."

Berry subsequently borrowed $800 from his family's loan fund and used it to finance both the recording of the first single (*Come To Me* by Marv Johnson) and set up a label on which to release the track.

"The name for my label, Tamla, came by chance. One day looking through an old Cashbox magazine I noticed that *Tammy* by Debbie Reynolds had been the #1 pop record in the country. I knew millions of people were already familiar with that name. I decided to use it. But when I sent it to Washington to be registered, I found somebody had beaten me to it. By that time I had gotten so used to the name I wanted to at least keep the sound of it. So I dropped the last two letters of Tammy and added 'la' – Tamla."

Tammy had indeed been already taken, with Larry Greene, a record shop owner and a former member of The Edsels having set up his Tammy label in Youngstown in Ohio, but ultimately it was to be Tamla that achieved the greater success.

Come To Me was duly issued as the first single on the label (catalogue number Tamla 101) in January 1959, although Berry changed the numbering system in April with the release of Barrett Strong's *Let's Rock* (Tamla 54021/2) to make punters think the label had been established for longer than just a few months (Berry would later claim this change was incorporated onto Barrett's follow-up *Money*).

In September 1959, Berry launched his second label in Motown, initially intending to have solo artists record for the Tamla label and groups on Motown (which is why The Miracles' *Bad Girl* appeared on the Motown label) but soon abandoned that plan, with Tamla ultimately becoming as diverse as Motown.

Whilst Tamla would effectively make its name as home to the likes of Marvin Gaye, Stevie Wonder, The Miracles (with and without Smokey Robinson), The Isley Brothers, Eddie Kendricks and The Marvelettes, it was also the first label The Supremes recorded for prior to their switch to Motown.

The Tamla label remained a vital component of the Motown set-up for the next 27 years, with its last stand alone single being issued in September 1981 Syreeta's *Quick Slick*. After that Tamla, Gordy and Motown releases (alongside other minor imprints Latino and Morocco) were amalgamated into a new numbering system. The final appearance of the Tamla label therefore was in October 1986 with Smokey Robinson's solo outing *Love Will Set You Free*.

Thereafter the label lay dormant for ten or so years until being very briefly revived by Universal as a reggae label, releasing one 12" single by Cocoa Tea.

TAMLA MOTOWN RECORDS

Berry Gordy might have set up Motown and its various offshoots with America foremost in his mind, eventually adopting the slogan 'The Sound of Young America', but overseas sales were very much a part of his long term plan.

At much the same time he signed a national distribution deal with United Artists for Marv Johnson and his breaking hit *Come To Me*, he also inked an international deal with the Decca company for his first batch of releases. *Come To Me* holds its own place in history, for it would go on to be the only Motown or associated single to be released as a 78RPM, appearing in May 1959 on Decca's London American imprint.

As the name might imply, London American was designed as a British outlet for American records and over the next two years London American would release *Money* (Barrett Strong), *Shop Around* and *Ain't It Baby* (The Miracles) and *The Hunch* (Paul Guyten), to little or no impact on the charts, although in fairness to London American (and Decca), the UK charts at this time featured a Top 30 only, making a chart breakthrough virtually impossible for new artists, especially those who were not in the country to undertake promotional work.

Add to this the fact that there wasn't a national radio station, with the music that was played seemingly having to conform to certain standards and it's easy to see why the energetic and frantic *Money* might have missed the boat. It did get some plays on the pirate radio stations, of course, for how else would musicians who would go on to form The Beatles and The Rolling Stones be so aware of what was happening at

Motown? In truth, Tamla and Motown were then too small and Decca too large for the relationship to have flourished and Gordy's interests were still firmly fixed on domestic survival and prosperity.

A short-lived deal with Philips' Fontana imprint followed, with four releases in four months before a longer term deal with the then independent Oriole Records was signed in September 1962. A total of 19 singles were released over the next twelve months, all of which failed to chart, despite including such key tracks as *Do You Love Me* by The Contours (although the song itself provided Brian Poole & The Tremeloes with a #1 hit), *Fingertips* by Stevie Wonder and *Stubborn Kind Of Fellow* by Marvin Gaye.

Having firmly established Tamla and Motown (and subsidiary labels such as Soul, Gordy and V.I.P.) in the minds of American record buyers, Berry Gordy was finally able to sign a deal that would achieve the same kind of impact in the UK in September 1963, licensing his labels to EMI. Suddenly hot thanks to the worldwide success of The Beatles and Gerry & The Pacemakers, EMI certainly had the ability to market and sell singles in the UK market and would eventually prove able to do much the same for the Motown stable. However, the initial deal that was signed between Berry Gordy and Joseph (later Sir Joseph) Lockwood was no more than a straight licensing deal, with Motown's repertoire being issued on the Stateside label. Here it would compete for priority among Stateside's other licensed repertoire, including The Shirelles, Freddy Cannon, Dionne Warwick, Jerry Butler and Dion. There was therefore a further fourteen misses released before Motown finally achieved a hit, with *My Guy* by Mary Wells peaking at #5 in June 1964, no doubt aided by touring with and receiving public endorsement from The Beatles. A further four hits appeared on the Stateside label, with three coming from The Supremes and one by Martha & The Vandellas.

This slow build concerned Berry Gordy, even if one of The Supremes' hits (*Baby Love*) had topped the chart, and so he invited Tamla-Motown Appreciation Society founder and journalist Dave Godin to Detroit in order to discuss how to best proceed with making further inroads into the British market. It is well known that whilst Berry Gordy had envisaged the discussions amounting to little more than a priority list of artists to promote (a list, it has to be said, that did *not* initially include The Supremes; Godin had to specifically request meeting the girls since they had not been invited to the reception Motown held in Dave's honour), Dave Godin convinced him to push for the establishment of a label brand, one which would act as something of a trademark for the quality of repertoire that the label was releasing.

Whilst Tamla, Motown, Gordy and Soul, among others, existed as separate entities in the US, Godin's plan was to have just one for the UK – Tamla Motown. Berry Gordy liked the idea and, perhaps more importantly, so did EMI, who announced the launch of the Tamla Motown label with six 7" singles, six 7" EP's and six 12" LPs in March 1965, with The Supremes' *Stop! In The Name Of Love* the very first single.

Coinciding with the launch was a visit of the Motown Revue, taking in 21 dates over three weeks the length and breadth of the country. The relative success of three of the singles and two EPs, together with critical acclaim for the Revue and a television special helped establish Tamla Motown in the public psyche, whilst the distinctive black label (which would remain constant for eleven years), housed in equally distinctive orange, then full colour and finally brown/olive sleeves for the same period, created an emotional bond between the public and the label that was as vital in Britain as the map of Detroit logo was in America.

Motown's deal with EMI remained in place until June 1975 when Berry Gordy terminated it, intending at the time to launch Motown as an independent company in September the same year. When the due date came and went with Motown having made little or no effort to establish their own company, a new deal was signed with EMI, which in turn resurrected the Tamla Motown label. The very last single released on the famous black label was Jermaine Jackson's *Let's Be Young Tonight* in October 1976, after which the main label became the bright blue Motown, later augmented by Gordy, although Tamla Motown would be sporadically revived for important and historic reissues, by both EMI (who retained distribution rights to Motown until 1981) and RCA (who took over distribution thereafter).

Eventually, four years into the RCA deal, the Tamla Motown label and the TMG numbering system, which had debuted back in March 1965, was sidelined and a European wide numbering system introduced.

TATTOO

Guitarist and vocalist Wally Bryson (born in Gastonia, North Carolina on 18 July 1949) was a founder member of The Raspberries in Cleveland in 1970, a group which also included Eric Carmen. When The Raspberries folded in 1975, Wally headed out west to Los Angeles. Originally he put together a group called

Flyer, but before the year was out had contacted several other Cleveland musicians and invited them to Los Angles to be part of a new group called Tattoo.

Those who answered the call were Jeff Hutton (keyboards), Dan Klawon (bass), Dave Thomas (born in St. Catherines, Ontario on 20 May 1949, guitar) and Thom Mooney (drums).

Produced by Ray Ruffin, Tattoo's eponymous debut album was released in November 1976 to almost universal scorn on Prodigal, with the initial reviews so bad Motown withdrew all promotional activity. Despite the negative feedback Prodigal offered the group another album deal, but this was turned down and the group went their separate ways.

ALBUM: TATTOO (1976)

MARV TARPLIN

Just as guitarist Cornelius Grant was something of a secret weapon for The Temptations, so Marv Tarplin served a similar function with The Miracles. Born Marvin Tarplin in Atlanta, Georgia on 13 June 1941, he moved to Detroit with his family whilst he was still a child. His mother paid for piano lessons, his preferred instrument until he picked up a guitar for the first time, and as he made his way through his teenage years, he became more and more proficient.

In 1959 he was on his way to the Flame Show Bar in Detroit when he was accosted by four girls, two of whom attended the same high school. They had seen him from the window of their rehearsal room across the street and wondered if he would accompany them musically. Marv duly became the resident musician of The Primettes, who subsequently secured an audition with Smokey Robinson at Motown Records. Impressed with the girls, Smokey would get them a later audition for Berry Gordy, who signed the group that would later become The Supremes and achieve worldwide success. Smokey, meanwhile, was in need of a guitarist after the success of his group The Miracles' single *Got A Job* and asked Marv to fill in for a couple of dates. That assignment would end up lasting for 49 years as well as covering more than just a couple of dates!

It was Marv's role to produce the chord charts for whichever house band The Miracles were working with, a role that proved to be extremely vital if the group was to avoid the same kind of embarrassment that had greeted their first appearance at The Apollo Theatre.

Marv would become a fully fledged member of The Miracles, appearing in all their early publicity photographs as well as the cover of their first three albums before slipping into the background, heard but not seen. Yet he was as vital to The Miracles later success as any member of the group, including Smokey, for he helped write such classics as *The Tracks Of My Tears, The Love I Saw In You Was Just A Mirage, Doggone Right, Going To A Go-Go, Come On Do The Jerk* and *I Like It Like That* as well as songs that were hits for others, including *Ain't That Peculiar* and *I'll Be Doggone* by Marvin Gaye.

When Smokey Robinson left the group for a solo career in 1973 and relocated to Los Angeles, he invited Marv Tarplin along. At first Marv was content to remain in Detroit with the reformed Miracles, but eventually he followed Smokey to California and resumed his career as Smokey's musical right hand. The pair continued to craft great music, scoring hits with *Cruisin'* and *I Was Made To Love You A Thousand Times*, with Marv continuing to record and tour with Smokey up until 2008. He died in Las Vegas on 30 September 2011, just a few short months before he was finally and belatedly inducted into the Rock & Roll Hall of Fame.

BOBBY TAYLOR & THE VANCOUVERS

Originating from Vancouver in Canada, Little Daddy & The Bachelors was a multi-racial group formed in 1963 that attracted strong local interest, enough to get them a brief recording contract with RCA, who issued *Too Much Monkey Business* backed with *Junior's Jerk* in 1964.

Based around vocalist Tommy 'Little Daddy' Melton, the group also featured guitarist Tommy Chong (born in Edmonton, Alberta on 24 May 1938), Wes Henderson (born in Edmonton on 11 May 1942) on bass, Ted Lewis (also known as Duris Maxwell and born in East York, Ontario on 15 June 1946) or Don Mallory on drums, Bernie Sneed on keyboards and his brother Floyd, also an occasional drummer.

The group later moved down to San Francisco where they went through a number of name and personnel changes, although their attempts to come up with a moniker that reflected their mixed ethnicity had a detrimental effect; promoters were happy to book Little Daddy & The Bachelors but positively bristled at Four Niggers And A Chink, The Calgary Shades, Four Coloured Fellows And An Oriental Lad and The Four N's And A C.

Whilst in San Francisco, however, they met up with Bobby Taylor (born in Washington D.C. on 18 February 1934), a singer who had started his career with The

Four Pharaohs in 1957. When Taylor and The Bachelors got together, a wholly more acceptable name was agreed upon; Bobby Taylor & The Vancouvers.

The group headed back to Canada, with a somewhat settled line-up of Taylor, Chong, Henderson (who switched instruments to guitar), Lewis/Maxwell (he was born Ted Lewis but legally changed his name to Duris Maxwell in 1970), guitarist Edward Patterson and keyboard player Robbie King (born in Quebec in 1947).

The group soon landed something of a residency at the Elegant Parlor, a late night club in Vancouver where Bobby and the boys kept the punters happy with their mix of Motown covers injected with a rock influence. The Parlor attracted a varied crowd, including one evening members of The Supremes, who subsequently alerted Berry Gordy, resulting in the offer of a recording contract on the Gordy imprint in July 1967.

Whilst Bobby Taylor was the undoubted focus of the group, it was Tommy Chong who provided the group with their first single, writing the lyrics to *Does Your Mother Know About Me*, to which Tom Baird added the music and Berry himself produced the session. Subsequently released in February 1968, the single got the group off to a positive start, hitting #5 R&B and #29 pop. Whilst the group as a whole were recording tracks for a projected album, lead singer Bobby Taylor was also hard at work on a planned solo album, with the Nickolas Ashford and Valerie Simpson penned *I Am Your Man* being produced by Frank Wilson and scheduled to appear on that album.

Whether the need for a quick follow-up single detracted *I Am Your Man* or not is open to debate, but it was released with the full group credit in June 1968 and became their second hit, although it peaked at #40 R&B and #85 pop. Not long after *I Am Your Man* was released, Bobby and The Vancouvers were sent out on the road and landed a date in Chicago, where they caught the act of another group trying to make it, The Jackson 5.

Bobby was impressed with the youngsters and personally arranged for them to travel down to Detroit to audition for Motown, even putting the youngsters up at his apartment for a spell. Bobby would spend some considerable time producing tracks on The Jackson 5 (most of which were shelved once Berry decided he needed a bigger name in charge of writing and production), of which a small handful would eventually appear on the group's albums over the next few years. The dual effect of Bobby concentrating on The Jackson 5 and singles being issued under The Vancouvers name when they were little more than Bobby's solo efforts was having something of a detrimental effect on the group.

Both Tommy Chong and Wes Henderson were sacked from the group by Bobby and producer Johnny Bristol when they went absent without leave (it transpired they had gone to apply for their Green Cards, the permanent residency papers they would need to remain in the United States). Soon after his firing Tommy Chong tried legal action to have the group's contract split into two, where he, Henderson and Bobby Taylor would own the group's name and Robbie King, Eddie Patterson and Ted Lewis would merely be hired musicians. When that failed the group disbanded, with Tommy Chong going on to be one half of the hugely popular comedy duo Cheech & Chong and Wes Henderson eventually returned to Motown where he recorded one single for the Rare Earth label.

Bobby Taylor, meanwhile, was still kept busy with what was now a solo career and production work on The Jackson 5. In August 1968 Motown released the **Bobby Taylor & The Vancouvers** album, which featured the two already successful singles, the Smokey Robinson penned and produced *Malinda* (which was recorded as a solo Bobby track but which would also be released on single as a group effort) and their interpretation of *I Heard It Through The Grapevine*, the diversity enough to enable the album to hit a #20 peak on the R&B chart.

Malinda was to be the final official single released by Bobby Taylor & The Vancouvers, even though The Vancouvers didn't appear on it. That didn't matter to the records' chances of success, hitting #16 R&B and #48 pop. With The Vancouvers having departed Motown, Bobby could record solo material openly, working with a variety of producers on what would be his only solo album **Taylor Made Soul**. The campaign for the album could have got off to a good start, with *Oh I've Been Bless'd* lined up as the first single in July 1969, only to switch the top side to *My Girl Has Gone*. The single, however, did little, making the promotion of the album all the more difficult. Although Motown would release *Oh How I've Been Bless'd* in January 1970, it was put out on the V.I.P. imprint and any momentum Bobby had created with his initial burst of success had been lost. Motown made one final attempt at getting a hit record, releasing *Hey Lordy* on the MoWest imprint in November 1971.

His time at Motown ended somewhat acrimoniously, with his disappointment at being left out of The Jackson 5's rise to stardom, coupled with tax issues relating to the few tracks he did produce on the group the root of the problems. Bobby would go on to enjoy one final hit, recording *Why Play Games* for Playboy in 1975, and after surviving throat cancer eventually settled in Hong Kong. Robbie King died from cancer on 17 September 2003 at the age of 56.

ALBUMS: BOBBY TAYLOR & THE VANCOUVERS (1968), TAYLOR MADE SOUL (1969)

R. DEAN TAYLOR

Richard Dean Taylor was born in Toronto, Canada on 11 May 1939 and began his singing career at the age of twelve, performing at numerous country and western shows in and around the Toronto area. He made his first recording for the Audiomaster label in 1961, *At The High School Dance*, which attracted some local radio play and was subsequently re-issued on the Barry label a year later.

After scoring a number of regional hits on Barry and Mala he was contacted by a friend based in Detroit and told to submit some of his work to Motown, then perceived as an up and coming label. Auditioned by Brian and Eddie Holland and Lamont Dozier, who were impressed with his portfolio of songs, Richard was signed to the V.I.P. label as a singer and Jobete as a writer. Although he contributed to numerous Holland-Dozier-Holland compositions during his early days at Motown, he was seldom credited, although he used the experience as something of a learning curve.

"Eddie was a fantastic writer, he could write from a woman's point of view as well as a man's, and I really learned a lot from working with him. I wanted to learn everything I could about producing and started playing tambourine on the Holland-Dozier-Holland sessions. Seeing the innovative way Brian and Lamont used new sounds in their productions, such as footstomps on an old board as the intro to *Where Did Our Love Go* and many other gimmick sounds, was an inspiration. Watching HDH produce, and playing with those great musicians now referred to as The Funk Brothers, was more than I could have ever hoped for."

Yet Richard still yearned for a recording career of his own, although his debut single *My Lady Bug (Stay Away From That Beatle)*, an attempt to cash in on popularity of the British group, was scheduled but then pulled from release. Richard finally got a single out to the market in November 1965, *Let's Go Somewhere* being released on the V.I.P. label (with the artist credit R. Dean Taylor, the moniker under which all of his later singles would be issued) and attracting some attention north of the border in Canada and several other major cities without crossing over on to the chart.

His next single, *There's A Ghost In My House*, wasn't released until April 1967 but failed to chart (at the time), as did *Gotta See Jane* when originally released on V.I.P. a year later, although it did become a a surprise British hit, peaking at #17 on the Tamla Motown label.

With the departure of HDH, Richard's value as a writer increased, becoming a key member of The Clan who penned Diana Ross & The Supremes' major hits *Love Child* and *I'm Livin' In Shame*. Despite continued success as a writer, Richard still hankered for a successful recording career of his own, a notion that led to some of the groups that worked with him to complain that he was holding back some of his better material, preferring to record it on himself rather than offer it to others.

However, as he would prove on *Indiana Wants Me,* his across the board smash hit single in April 1970, he was invariably the best outlet for his compositions. Richard would enjoy three further minor hits in America, all released on Rare Earth, his label home since 1970 (his album **I Think Therefore I Am** would also make a brief chart showing, peaking at #198 on the album chart), but the closest he got to repeating the success of *Indiana Wants Me* came with a revival of *Gotta See Jane*, which hit #67 in 1971.

Gotta See Jane would also be re-issued and become a hit all over again in Britain in 1974, chosen as a follow-up after *There's A Ghost In My House* had broken onto the chart after heavy exposure from the Northern Soul crowd and hit #3 on the pop chart. By then Richard had left Motown altogether, setting up his own Jane label in 1973 and leasing other tracks to Polydor, for whom he scored the Top Forty hit *Window Shopping* in 1974. Thereafter he effectively went into semi-retirement, although he attempted something of a comeback in the 1980s, albeit without success.

ALBUMS: I THINK THEREFORE I AM (1970), INDIANA WANTS ME (1971)

SHEILA TAYLOR

Country singer Sheila Taylor had one single released on the Melodyland imprint, with both sides of her release *She Satisfies* and *How Important Can It Be* being recorded in sessions in Los Angeles in February 1975, with Steve Stone the producer. The single was released in May the same year but failed to sell, with Sheila seemingly leaving the industry soon after.

SHERRI TAYLOR

Gospel singer and songwriter Sherri Taylor had first come to Motown's attention as a member of The Taylor Tones, a vocal group that also featured Sherri's mother Clara. Sherri had written their local hit *Too Young To Love* that appeared on the LuPine label (also notable for having been the first home of The Primettes). Sherri had a strong and powerful voice and could certainly carry a song, yet for some reason her only Motown outing saw her paired with 'Singin'' Sammy Ward.

It has been suggested that as Motown had pretty much all other bases covered by 1960, a male and female duet might be worthwhile pursuing, and it would certainly pay dividends later in the decade with Marvin Gaye and his assorted musical partners. Sammy and Sherri's only single, *Oh Lover* backed with *That's Why I Love You So Much* was issued in November 1960 and received some local airplay but nothing by way of sales. Sammy remained at Motown for a further four years whilst Sherri moved on.

She resurfaced the following year at PG, releasing *He's The One Who Rings My Bell* in conjunction with George Martin & The Cruisers, with the single subsequently being re-released in 1962 by Gloreco, another Detroit label. Sherri later rejoined her mother Clara in the Taylor Tones, recording singles for Starmaker and C&T. She then seemingly left the industry, only to re-appear on Ian Levine's Motorcity label in 1991.

T.C.B. (TV SPECIAL)

The success of the **Diana Ross & The Supremes & The Temptations** album and a subsequent appearance on 'The Ed Sullivan Show' by the two groups had planted a thought in manager Shelly Berger's mind. Since The Supremes and The Temptations were undoubtedly the two most successful groups on the Motown roster, what could be better than a television special featuring the pair?

Initially it appeared to be little more than a fanciful notion, since none of the television networks gave much airtime to rock and roll and even less to soul artists. However, after pointing out the combined success the groups had enjoyed, not just within the R&B market but also on the crossover chart, Shelly managed to ink a deal with George Schlatter-Ed Friendly Productions (producers of 'Laugh-In') for an hour long special to be aired on NBC TV, with the show to be co-produced by Motown.

Whilst the financial rewards were minimal (both groups were paid $15,000 apiece, much less than they could have expected to earn for a prestigious live date), the chance to perform a show that would be witnessed by millions of viewers was too good an opportunity to pass up.

The show was to be taped on 23 August for broadcast on 9 December 1968, with both groups performing a week long engagement at the Carousel Theater in Framingham, Massachusetts at which they worked out a routine for the show before heading off to Los Angeles for a further week's rehearsals ahead of taping. Whilst the engagement had been a breeze, nothing could have prepared Cindy Birdsong, Mary Wilson and The Temptations for the reality of rehearsing and taping what was effectively the Diana Ross show with special guests.

It was not enough that of the fifteen songs that were to be performed, Diana would feature in nine, including a solo spot, even though officially she was still a member (albeit leader) of The Supremes. Cindy, Mary and The Temptations did get to perform together, without Diana, on the Brazilian number *Mas Que Nada*, a performance that received a loud audience reception.

"We did a good job, but then one of the production people came over and told us that it might not be in the show," Mary later explained. "And, no surprise, it wasn't. Why put us through all the work, then? The whole situation was a mess, and it seemed to get worse every day."

It did not help matters that whilst the two groups had effectively grown and evolved together during Motown's early days, Diana's desire to be the star of the show meant that she insisted on being addressed as 'Miss Ross' by everyone. Whilst somewhat flabbergasted at the request, behind her back the various other singers enjoyed their own joke, insiting that if she was 'Miss Ross', then everyone should address *them* as Mr Franklin, or Mr Williams.

For those involved, however, it was no joke when Diana Ross slapped Eddie Kendricks. The pair had known each other for a long time (Mary would diplomatically state they 'had been buddies from way back' whilst Otis Williams recalled Eddie 'had a brief fling with Diana a few years before'), but this did not stop Diana marching up to Eddie as he sat alone eating some food and demanding sarcastically 'How'd you rate that' before slapping him on the cheek.

Mary Wilson said, "It was absolutely absurd; we couldn't believe our eyes. Ever the gentleman, he did nothing. Having an attitude was one thing, but this had gone too far."

The Supremes and The Temptations would both blame Diana personally for the removal of their number, although Otis Williams of The Temptations would later try to analyse what was taped and what was screened. "I think a lot of the tension on that show was because there was so much pressure to get it done, and get it done in ten days. But to me, the pressure was all on Diana, because it was all about her. We were there as supporting players, so it didn't mean as much. Although I got to say it hurt that after the show was all done, Berry gave The Supremes these expensive gifts for doing such a great job, while we didn't even get a simple thank you. But that's how it was. We just took the cheques and moved on."

For Mary, the experience had its own value. "Amazingly, the show was great. When we were all singing together it was just like old times. When it aired in early December, we got rave reviews, and an album we cut with The Temptations was on its way to the top of the charts. Despite all the tension and unhappiness, the special was a great boost to all of us."

'T.C.B.' did indeed win rave views, along with a huge audience and would pick up a number of Emmy nominations, including Best Costume, Best Television Variety Special and, just to further alienate The Supremes and The Temptations, Best Performance by a Female for Diana Ross!

T.C.B. – DIANA ROSS & THE SUPREMES & THE TEMPTATIONS [ALBUM]

A week ahead of the screening of the 'T.C.B.' on NBC, Motown released the soundtrack album **T.C.B.** Featuring the entire show as it was to be aired (and thus omitting *Mas Que Nada*, which The Supremes and The Temptations had performed but which would be cut from the finished programme), the soundtrack proved equally successful.

Following the screening the album shot up the charts, going on to top both the R&B and pop listings, replacing **Diana Ross & The Supremes Join The Temptations** from the former (where it had been resident for four weeks) and The Beatles' **White Album** on the latter, where it stayed a solitary week before The Beatles returned to the top for a further three weeks. In the UK, where the earlier collaboration between the two supergroups had also been a chart topper, **T.C.B.** could only peak at #11, the relatively low position being a result of the television special not being aired at the time.

TEARS OF A CLOWN – SMOKEY ROBINSON & THE MIRACLES [SINGLE]

What would become Smokey Robinson & The Miracles' biggest single success started life as a planned Stevie Wonder single. Stevie and Hank Cosby had been working on a tune that, for some reason, was not submitted to their usual writing partner Sylvia Moy for lyrical input. Instead, Stevie approached Smokey Robinson at a Motown office party in 1966 (possibly in October or November; claims that it was at the Motown Christmas party of that year are clearly wrong since the track was completed by mid-November 1966) and handed him a tape of what he had so far.

"Guys who did great music who didn't necessarily write songs would give their music to someone who did. Guys who wrote lyrics who didn't do music would give their lyrics to guys who did music. He wanted me to write some lyrics. The music was awesome. The opening, that's a circus thing. I just wanted to write something that would be profound about the circus, and touch people's hearts, I guess. And the only thing I could think of was Pagliacci, the clown who made everybody happy while he was sad because he had nobody to love him."

The completed track was included as the final track on The Miracles' July 1967 album **Make It Happen**, from which *The Love I Saw In You Was Just A Mirage* and *More Love* were extracted as singles, *Tears Of A Clown* being initially overlooked. Three years later, Smokey Robinson and The Miracles enjoyed something of a surprise and belated hit in Britain, where *The Tracks Of My Tears* (which pursued much the same lyrical path as *Tears Of A Clown*) sailed into the Top Ten having been completely overlooked when originally released in 1965.

Searching for a follow-up, the product managers at EMI's Tamla Motown office asked for assistance from Karen Spreadbury, a secretary in the office who also ran the Motown fan club Ad Astra (under the name Sharon Davis, under which moniker she would write a Motown column for 'Blues & Soul' magazine). Handed a pile of Miracles albums, she was asked to pick out a potential single that might have otherwise been overlooked.

Karen selected *Tears Of A Clown*, which was duly released as a single in the UK in July 1970 and entered the chart on 1 August. Seven weeks later, on 12 September, it ended the six week reign of *The Wonder Of You* by Elvis Presley at the top of the chart. Although it spent only a solitary week at the summit (it was dethroned by Freda Payne's *Band Of Gold*), it was present in the Top Ten for seven weeks, going on to earn a silver disc from 'Disc' magazine for sales in excess of 250,000 copies. The British success of *Tears Of A Clown* surprised Smokey, as he later noted.

"I'm really happy with the success but I can't make out what happened because all the singles we've been having success with are from old albums. It's got me thinking that I should re-service all our old stuff and do nothing new. Seriously though, it's given me a good idea of what people want from us, and the success has certainly shown me what direction we need to take because until now I wasn't sure what to do."

The single's success was duly noted in Detroit, with Tamla issuing the track as a single in September 1970 (albeit with a slightly different version, the American release being mono whereas the British issue had been stereo) and seeing much the same kind of public acceptance. On 5 December, *Tears Of A Clown* knocked James Brown's *Super Bad* off the top of the R&B chart, where it would remain for three weeks, and a week later pushed *I Think I Love You* by The Partridge Family off the top of the pop chart, spending two weeks at the summit.

There were consequences of this revived hit, with the **Make It Happen** album being repackaged as **Tears Of A Clown** and became a hit all over again. More importantly, it delayed Smokey Robinson's planned departure from The Miracles by at least two years, since in the wake of the hit, increased concert bookings for the group kept him out on the road for much of the time.

Tears Of A Clown was coupled with *Tracks Of My Tears* in 1976 and became a British hit all over again, hitting #34. Three years later, ska band The Beat (known in the US as The English Beat) recorded their take on *Tears Of A Clown* and scored a #6 hit in their homeland.

THE TEMPTATIONS

Since their formation in 1960, a total of twenty two singers have at one time or another called themselves members of The Temptations, and whilst for many the classic line-up is that which sung together between 1964 and 1968, the fact that the group endured and survived so many changes in both personnel and musical tastes either side of that very brief period in their history is testament to their longevity and popularity. If many of the groups who signed with Motown have a direct lineage, undergoing a subtle name change here and a member swap there, the five men who eventually signed with the company in 1961 as The Temptations came from two distinct sources, either of which could have made it into Motown under their own steam.

Eddie Kendricks (born Edward James Kendrick in Union Springs, Alabama on 17 December 1939) and Paul Williams (born in Birmingham, Alabama on 2 July 1939) met when they were both in their teens, subsequently singing together in church choirs and forming their first group The Cavaliers in 1955. Originally a five piece vocal outfit, four of the group (Eddie, Paul, Kell Osbourne and Wiley Waller) left Birmingham bound for stardom but had only sufficient funds to get themselves as far as Cleveland. They found lodgings with Wiley's grandmother, obtained jobs at a local hotel and supplemented their income by singing together in the evening. Following Wiley's departure the remaining three started to make some headway, attracting local press interest (which dubbed them The Dishwashing Trio in the accompanying article) and acquiring something of a manager and mentor in Milton Jenkins. When Jenkins upped sticks and headed off to Detroit, he persuaded the three to follow, with their arrival in the Motor City seeing them bestowed with a new name, The Primes.

Another recent arrival in Detroit was Otis Williams (born Otis Miles Jr. in Texarkana, Texas on 30 October 1941), who had been raised by his grandmothers in Texas before joining his mother when aged ten in Detroit, where she had got married and settled some years previously. Otis too developed an interest in music during his teenage years and formed several groups, including El Domingos in 1957 with Elbridge 'Al' Bryant, Arthur Walton and Donald Michelhenny. The group quickly expanded with the addition of James 'Pee-Wee' Crawford and swapped Michelhenny with Vernard Plain and also changed name to Otis Williams & The Siberians.

Whilst much of the material they performed around local clubs was interpretations of the hits of the day, The Siberians had one or two of their own songs, including Otis' composition *Pecos Kid* (Crawford remembered it as *Have Gun Will Travel*, which was certainly part of the song's lyrics), which got a sufficient enough reception when performed live for The Siberians to be invited along to radio station WCHB to record it, along with another Otis song in *All Of My Life*.

Never commercially released, *Pecos Kid* did get considerable airplay on WCHB and the offer of management but did not seemingly lead to the real prize of a recording contract with an established label. The initial management deal also turned sour, with the group opting to take control of their own destiny for a spell thereafter.

It was at rehearsals that The Siberians and The Primes first met, with the groups sharing the same rehearsal room for a spell, which in turn led to Milton Jenkins offering to look after The Siberians interests in much the same way he was guiding The Primes and their sister group The Primettes (later, of course to evolve into The Supremes). Jenkins subsequent disappearance from the scene when his fractured arm turned sceptic left all three groups high and dry, and whilst Paul and Eddie returned home to Alabama to lick their wounds (Kell headed out west to Los Angeles to try his luck as a solo performer), The Siberians found their reputation around the city was still enough to open a few doors, resulting in a brief deal but no recordings with Chess Records.

They were then approached by one of the music entrepreneur's operative in Detroit who offered them a recording contract, where they would join up with the likes of Mary Wells and Popcorn Wylie & The Mohawks. Yet this wasn't Berry Gordy and Motown but rather Johnnie Mae Matthews and her Northern Recording Company, an operation that would serve as something of a template for Berry's later efforts.

Eager to record The Siberians, Johnnie instructed them to come up with some fresh material, the result of which was Otis's latest song *Come On*. Before the song could be recorded, two of the group opted to leave in order to concentrate on their school work, requiring immediate replacements be found for Arthur Walton and Vernard Plain. In need of a bass and lead singer, Otis used his connections and knowledge to track down David Melvin English (born in Montgomery, Alabama on 23 October 1942 and professionally known throughout his career as Melvin Franklin as well as by his nickname 'Blue'), whose bass vocal had adorned The Voice Masters' *Needed* on Gwen Gordy's Anna label (Melvin wasn't a member of the group but was utilised as a voice for hire on the session). When Otis located Melvin and persuaded him to join his group, he also acquired Melvin's friend and constant companion Richard Allen Street (born in Detroit, Michigan on 5 October 1942), a more than capable lead singer into the bargain.

With the group now back to its full compliment, albeit with a new name, The Distants returned to Johnnie Mae Matthews and readied themselves for their first recording session, held at Specialty Studios in May 1959. The musicians and singers who gathered to proved accompaniment were known as stock players for Northern and included Popcorn Wylie (piano), Eddie Willis (guitar), Andrew 'Mike' Terry (saxophone), Hank Cosby (trombone), Robert Finch (drums), Norman Whitfield (tambourine) and James Jamerson (bass), along with Marlene Barrow, Jackie Hicks and Louvain Demps, better known as The Andantes on backing vocals.

The single, with Vernard Plain having penned the ballad flip *Always,* attracted some considerable local action and, thanks to the efforts of local producer Harry Balk was leased to Warwick Records in New York (where the credit was amended to The Distants, Vocal by Richard Strick). The single sold well enough to prompt Johnnie Mae Matthews to schedule a second session, which resulted in *Alright* and *Open Your Heart*, recorded with Albert 'Mooch' Harrell as a replacement for Pee-Wee Crawford, who left the group after he got married.

Alright may also have sold well, at least enough for Johnnie Mae Matthews to suddenly display several signs of opulence, such as emblazoning her Buick with the name Otis Williams & The Distants, but the chance of any money filtering down to Otis and the group was distant. When Otis broached the subject of royalties or even their fees from live dates with Johnnie, she flew into a rage and reminded him that she owned the name and had no need for five ungrateful vocalists; she would just get a new set in to take their place. Rather than back down, Otis told her she could do what she liked since they were all quitting with immediate effect.

What he meant was that Otis Williams & The Distants were quitting Northern, but soon Otis would learn that Richard Street and Mooch Harrell were also quitting The Distants, or whatever they were going to call themselves. Their departure came at an inopportune time, for sitting in Otis' pocket was a business card for Berry Gordy, who had seen The Distants perform live and impressed enough to have invited them to Motown whenever they were free of Johnnie Mae Matthews.

Whilst Otis pondered his next move, fate took a hand. Both Eddie Kendricks and Paul Williams had returned to Detroit, determined to give it one last shot at stardom and were making a few telephone calls to old acquaintances to try and generate some action. Eddie's call to Otis when Otis was in need of a tenor singer was fortunate; to also have Paul Williams in tow, a more than capable lead singer, was almost divine intervention. Barely hours later, Eddie and Paul made their way to Otis' house, along with Al and Melvin and the new five piece worked out harmonies on The Distants repertoire and various other songs.

In March 1961 Otis called Berry and informed him his group (which had opted to call themselves The Elgins as Johnnie Mae Matthews claimed to own the name The Distants) was now free of any contractual obligations and available for audition, which was duly arranged for 10 March. The audition was actually undertaken by Mickey Stevenson, Motown's Artist & Repertoire head, who was as impressed with their abilities as Berry had been earlier, although as would have been obvious, the five piece group Mickey auditioned was a different five piece that Berry had observed. If anything, the new line-up was better, with Mickey noting that all five could sing, and sing well, something of a rarity in groups of that time. He liked them and their sound enough to promise a deal, but one thing he did not like was their name; that had to go. So the five retired from the studio, sat on the lawn outside Hitsville and bandied names back and forth, as Otis would later recall.

"I remember it was a beautiful day and we sat there kicking around names, I don't even know what they were. And then a guy named Bill Mitchell, who worked in the office there, came out for a smoke or something and saw what we were doing. He said, 'Hey, what about Temptations?' Just like that. And I loved it, I wanted that one. I asked the guys and they liked it, too. Paul was more neutral. He said, 'Otis, a name is what we make it,' which was Paul in a nutshell. He always kept our heads straight, pounding it into us that nothing would matter but the work we put in."

The newly christened Temptations duly signed their seven year contracts and were ushered back into the studio in May 1961 with Mickey Stevenson to record *Oh Mother Of Mine*, an Otis Williams penned song that the group had performed at their audition. A later session took care of Eddie Kendricks' *Romance Without Finance* (both sides would carry an additional composer credit for Mickey Stevenson) and the pairing was issued in July 1961.

Whilst both the Tamla and Motown labels were beginning to make a mark, The Temptations debut was banished to the Miracle label. As far as Berry Gordy was concerned, Miracle was supposed to be the home of the more R&B influenced artists, but despite the presence of Jimmy Ruffin on the only single thus far released, Miracle was already considered something of an outpost. *Oh Mother Of Mine* was one of several records that was not so much released as escaped, attracting little local attention and nothing nationally.

Absent up until now in The Temptations tale, Berry Gordy stepped in to mentor their second single, helping knock Otis, Al and Melvin's song *Check Yourself* into shape and writing the flip *Your Wonderful Love*. Released in November the single did little but the song at least made an impression, with Gene Chandler recording a cover version some two years later. In the New Year, Berry took The Temptations back into the studio to record another of his compositions, *(You're My) Dream Come True*, with Eddie on lead vocals and with Berry's wife Raynoma Liles playing an Ondioline, an early type of synthesizer that was used to create what sounded like a string section. Backed with *Isn't She Pretty*, the single was scheduled for release in March 1962, although it would appear not on Miracle, which had been shut down but on the newly launched Gordy label. It would also provide The Temptations with their chart debut, hitting #22 on the R&B listings without ever looking likely to crossover pop.

The next song meant for the group might have resolved that predicament, but on the day Berry intended getting The Temptations into the studio to record *Do You Love Me*, they were attending a gospel concert elsewhere, resulting in The Contours getting the opening in their stead and go on to top the R&B chart and hit #3 pop. Missing out on *Do You Love Me* was the result of bad luck, but the company's next move was a near disaster.

The Temptations were sent back into the studio in September to record a cover version of Nolan Strong & The Diablos' *Mind Over Matter (I'm Gonna Make You Mine)*, a song that was supposedly attracting attention but not sales as The Diablos' label Fortune Records had hit distribution problems. By the time the cover version was ready to hit the market, Fortune's problems had been resolved and The Diablos' single was selling well locally, effectively burying the cover version. Which was just as well, as for some inexplicable reason Berry Gordy had opted to re-brand the group as The Pirates and released the single on the Mel-O-dy label, even more of a graveyard than Miracle had been.

Mightily relieved that The Pirates concept had been consigned to history, The Temptations returned to the studio to resume their own career in August and recorded *Paradise*, another Berry composition and production that was aimed more at the pop market than the R&B base they had already established, resulting in the single stalling at #122 on the pop listings and making no headway at all on the R&B one.

Despite the lack of success on the chart, it was not all doom and gloom around The Temptations. Extensive work and rehearsal with Cholly Atkins had seen their stage act become a much more polished event, whilst their abilities as singers were invariably required on other projects, such as providing the male vocal parts for Mary Wells on tour that had been supplied by The Love-Tones in the studio although, perhaps a portent of what was to come, Al Bryant was invariably left off stage during the Mary Wells performances since the backing vocals only required four of the five Temptations.

Even though the reason for sidelining Al had been genuine, it only served to drive a wedge between him and the rest of the group, further exacerbated by Al's almost constant moaning to and from dates around the country. Whilst the other four Temptations were intent of putting their all into making the group a success, for Al singing had become little more than a pastime, something he did in the evenings after a day spent working at a local dairy. The last thing he needed before an early start in the morning was an evening spent driving home from some sweaty venue miles from anywhere.

Even prestigious venues such as The Apollo did little to raise Al's enthusiasm, although on one occasion Al stepped up to the plate and rescued a potentially disastrous live performance in front of the notoriously fickle and hostile Apollo crowd by launching in to something of a comic routine that raised the group's spirits and delighted the crowd. That was to be a brief respite in the growing resentment Al felt about The Temptations and where their career was headed, with recording success offering little or no consolation.

As disgruntled as the rest of The Temptations were with Al's attitude, there was little or no intention of forcing a change; that came about as a result of incidents and coincidences. The group had established a small but loyal core of followers, with David Ruffin (born Davis Eli Ruffin in Whynot, Mississippi on 18 January 1941) among their number, but David wasn't following the group around because of fandom; rather he had either sensed or been advised of growing friction between Al and the others and sought to use it to his own advantage.

David was in attendance when The Temptations performed at Chappy's Lounge in October 1963 and, as the group was about to launch into their encore number *Shout*, jumped on stage, grabbed a microphone and executed an exuberant performance alongside the bemused Temptations, even throwing his own dance routines into the mix. The crowd went wild, with the newly inflated six man group having to perform two further encores to satisfy demand. When the curtain finally came down, David slipped off into the crowd and The Temptations retired to their dressing room, where Al tried to goad them into returning for a further encore. The other four declined, effectively spent from their exertions, which prompted a furious argument between Al and Paul Williams, with Al suddenly smashing a beer bottle into Paul's face. Paul was rushed off to hospital to be stitched up, and whilst Otis, Melvin and Eddie were adamant that Al should be immediately fired from the group, Paul spoke up for his attacker and convinced them that with the group on the verge of greatness, they all deserved to be a part of it.

The reprieve lasted barely a couple more months, with Al's general attitude during the group's performance at the Motown Christmas Party at the Fox Theater a step too far for Otis to accept and when he broached the subject of sending Al on his way, there were no objections this time around, with all in agreement, including Paul.

Despite the synergy the group had experienced with David Ruffin it was not a given that he was going to be accepted into the group, at least if the various stories and myths are to be believed. It has been suggested that at one point it was Jimmy Ruffin that was considered as a possible replacement for Al Bryant, although Otis says that Jimmy was never seriously considered and Jimmy states that he never asked for nor was ever offered the position. The group also had reasons for not necessarily wanting David either, not least of which was the fact that up to that point he had worked almost exclusively as a solo artist. Indeed, there were those within The Temptations who believed that David wanted in only to further his own personal ambitions and that joining the group would give him a better vehicle to that particular destination. Whatever he said in his own defence obviously had the desired effect, with David in place just as the real rollercoaster ride was about to start.

The group gathered at Hitsville in early January 1964, waiting to hear the latest song Smokey Robinson had written on their behalf. Otis was not particularly impressed the first time he heard it.

"I told Smokey, 'What kind of shit is this?' I mean, Smokey had given us these great soulful songs like *Slow Down Heart*. And now we get 'You got a smile so bright you coulda been a candle'? I said, Smoke, I don't know about this.' But once we started rehearsing it, it grew on us. We 'got it.' The lines were a parody of the things guys say, 'cause this guy's so taken with this chick he doesn't know what to say. In the end, he chucks the bad lines and just says, 'You make my life so bright, you make me feel all right.'"

The song The Temptations finally 'got' was *The Way You Do The Things You Do,* with Eddie Kendricks at his exquisite best on lead. The public obviously thought so, turning *The Way You Do* into The Temptations first, bona fide success, topping the R&B chart (albeit the Cashbox variety, Billboard having discontinued theirs at the end of 1963, only to reinstate it some two years later) and #11 pop.

With the group having finally achieved a toehold on the chart, Motown pushed out the group's debut album, **Meet The Temptations**, something of a companion volume to **Meet The Supremes** and similarly compiled from the numerous misses (although omitting both sides of their debut *Oh Mother Of Mine* and the efforts released as The Pirates) recorded over the previous few years. Despite being as uneven a collection of songs as could be imagined (David appeared on only one track, the then current single, whilst Al featured on the remaining eleven), it still found favour critically and commercially, hitting #95 on the pop chart.

It was the success of the single, however, that would dictate the route The Temptations were to undertake for the foreseeable future, with Smokey again utilising Eddie's voice for the follow-up single *I'll Be In Trouble*, which would hit #22 R&B and #33 pop. It then enjoyed a new burst of life as enterprising DJ's flipped the single and began giving airplay to *The Girl's Alright With Me*, written by Eddie Kendricks, Eddie Holland and Norman Whtfield, which would attain #39 R&B and #102 pop in its own right. The success of *The Girl's Alright* got Eddie Holland and Norman Whitfield an opening for the next Temptations single, offering up *Girl (Why You Wanna Make Me So Blue)*, which returned them to the upper reaches of the chart, hitting #11 R&B and #26 pop.

Whilst the Temptations were enjoying sustained success on the chart, their live performances had moved up to a completely different level, with David as much the reason as the hit material they were now recording. Always an energetic performer, some of his moves defied belief, with even his band mates uncertain how some of the more outlandish spins, turns and drops were executed. However they were done they could be guaranteed to send an audience into a frenzy, with his equally robust vocal style (at the time limited to songs which the group had not recorded, such as a version of The Isley Brothers' *Shout*) raising the temperature at a live show to virtual boiling point.

After witnessing the reaction David got whilst performing live, Smokey decided that the next Temptations single would feature David on lead vocal, and he already had one in mind. Smokey had already written *My Guy* and produced a major hit on it for Mary Wells. Just as Holland-Dozier-Holland were doing with The Supremes in taking bits of one song to create another, so Smokey decided to write the other half of the story in *My Girl*.

Originally intended as a Miracles release, Smokey saw it as the perfect song with which to project David Ruffin. The result was an across the board smash, topping the R&B chart for six weeks and the pop listings for one (as well as becoming The Temptations chart debut in the UK, where it reached #43), by which time Smokey already had the follow-up safely recorded and ready to be unleashed. Whilst not as big a hit as its predecessor, *It's Growing* still performed healthily and would become a Top Twenty pop (#18) and Top Ten R&B (#3) hit.

Following the single up the charts was the group's second album, **The Temptations Sing Smokey**, which would go on to hit #35 pop and top the R&B charts for eighteen non-consecutive weeks (since the material on the album was also culled from existing repertoire, Al Bryant makes an appearance here too, on *Baby, Baby I Need You*). That The Temptations had effectively broken through in their American homeland was now not in doubt and they went some way towards achieving similar status in Britain, journeying across the Atlantic with several label mates to contribute to the television special 'Ready Steady Go – The Sound of Motown', on which they performed three numbers (*The Way You Do The Things You*, *It's Growing* and *My Girl*).

Once filming had been completed, The Temptations bade their farewells to the rest of the touring party and flew back across the Atlantic, bound for Bermuda and a weeklong residency at the Forty Thieves, one of the island's most prestigious hotels. Sunny and idyllic the setting might have been but it did not take long for the atmosphere to turn distinctly frosty, the result of a brawl between David Ruffin and Eddie Kendricks over who knows what that began in their shared room and escalated into the hallway. Extensive damage to pieces of furniture and holes knocked into walls saw them all sent packing, with the government even imposing a lifelong ban on the group ever returning to Bermuda, although Berry Gordy would use all of his powers of persuasion to get that rescinded, if only in order to ensure The Supremes would later be able to perform on the island.

At the very least the fracas should have lit warning signs that all was not well within The Temptations camp, with David invariably at the centre of the fragmentation. Perhaps as suspected, David was conspiring to use The Temptations as a stepping stone to solo greatness, but in the process was driving a wedge between the remainder of the group, who seemed to fracture into distinctive camps.

In effect, something of an uneasy truce was established whilst the group went about their business of recording and touring, but the problems were never far from the surface and liable to blow up again and again over the next three years or so. Still with Smokey in harness, The Temptations scored another Top Twenty hit before the year was out, *Since I Lost My Baby*, again featuring David on lead vocals, vaulted up to #17 pop and #4 R&B, with the flip side *You've*

Got To Earn It also making a showing, hitting #22 R&B and #123.

The year came to a close with another double sided hit in *My Baby* (#13 pop and #4 R&B) and *Don't Look Back* (which features a rare Paul Williams lead and which hit #83 pop and #15 R&B), along with a third long player in **Temptin' Temptations**, an album that gathered together a number of singles that had not been included on the previous platter such as *Girl (Why You Wanna Make Me Blue)* and *I'll Be In Trouble*. Whilst David and Eddie handle lead vocals on the bulk of the material, Paul was out front on two; the aforementioned *Don't Look Back* and *Just Another Lonely Night*. **Temptin' Temptations** would go on to become the group's most successful album up to that point, hitting #11 pop and topping the R&B chart, spending a total of fifteen weeks at the R&B summit (again non-consecutively).

Even as Smokey readied himself for the next Temptations single, he was facing stiff competition within Motown. Company policy at the time was that the producer who scored the biggest hit on an artist had something of an exclusive hold over that artist until such time as they failed to deliver the goods. That alone put Smokey in the driving seat when he presented the next Temptations single to Quality Control, with *Get Ready* his offering. It went up against *Ain't Too Proud To Beg*, written by Norman Whitfield and Eddie Holland and produced by Norman alone. Quality Control opted to release *Get Ready*, a decision that was said to have infuriated Norman, although he was able to extract a compromise that if *Get Ready* failed to make Top Ten pop, Norman's production would be released next. *Get Ready* was a more uptempo number than previous efforts, although whether this departure from the norm (at least as far as The Temptations was concerned) lay behind the single's apparent demise is not known, but instead of continuing a blistering chart run, *Get Ready* ran out of steam at #29 pop, even if it did power its way to the top of the R&B chart for one week.

That relative failure brought mixed emotions within Hitsville, but it also gave Norman Whitfield the opportunity he had been waiting for. *Ain't Too Proud To Beg* was duly released in May 1966 and powered its way to #13 on the pop chart as well as returning the group to the top of the R&B listings (and would become the group's first Top Thirty hit in Britain, where it reached #21), although many within the Temptations camp were convinced the single should have done even better.

"To us it *felt* like a number one, more so than *My Girl*" Otis would later claim. "We were told that record was played *everywhere*, and wherever we went, they kept telling us it was number one. So don't ask me how a record like that only gets to number 13."

Ain't Too Proud To Beg did get a little higher on the album chart, with parent album **Gettin' Ready** hitting #12 pop and once again topping the R&B chart (and also made #40 in the &UK, The Temptations' first chart album in that territory). More than any previous Temptations album, **Gettin' Ready** was something of a mixed bag collection, with Smokey producing seven tracks, Norman three, Mickey Stevenson and Ivy Jo Hunter one track and Robert Staunton and Robert Walker the remaining track. There was another link to the past too, with Al Bryant appearing on *Not Now (I'll Tell You Later)*, a song that was co-written by Otis Williams with Smokey Robinson. Aside from the singles, the stand out track was *Too Busy Thinking About My Baby*, which would be revisited by Marvin Gaye some three years later.

Not on the album was Norman and Eddie's follow-up single, *Beauty Is Only Skin Deep,* although it did feature on a greatest hits package released at much the same time, Motown's faith being rewarded when the single hit #3 pop and #1 R&B, enabling the parent album to power its way to #5 pop and also top the R&B chart. If getting to the top had been a long and hard slog for The Temptations, then remaining there would be equally fraught. Whilst the group was seemingly engaged in an endless succession of tours (at their peak, The Temptations would perform a minimum of 300 dates a year), producer Norman Whitfield was cocooned in Detroit, laying down track after track, ready and waiting for their return to the studio.

Recording was pretty much done on the run, just as with The Supremes and The Four Tops, with multiple sessions being undertaken whenever the group breezed through Detroit. Quality, however, was just as vital as quantity, and here The Temptations could count themselves blessed to be attached to Norman Whitfield, himself an acknowledged workaholic.

The Temptations' resident guitarist Cornelius Grant kicked off the session that would lead to their next major hit, *(I Know) I'm Losing You*, with Norman and Eddie Holland licking the song into shape, with the single going on to become a major smash, topping the R&B chart and hitting #8 pop (as well as #19 in the UK). In between studio releases, Motown kept the group hot with a live album recorded at the Roostertail in Detroit and another cross the board hit that again topped the R&B chart, hit #10 pop and #20 in the UK.

And it wasn't only Norman Whitfield who could come up with the goods, for his protégé Frank Wilson was given an opportunity of stepping into his master's shoes on *All I Need*, a song Frank had written with R. Dean Taylor and had polished up by Eddie Holland. The end result was still the same; another pop and R&B Top Ten hit. That put the ball back into Norman's court to try and come up with the goods, a challenge he rose to with *You're My Everything*, a song co-written with Cornelius Grant and Roger Penzabene. As if to prove Frank still had some way to go before he could topple the master, *You're My Everything* was a Top Ten pop and R&B hit and Top Thirty British success.

At much the same time the single was ascending the chart, so the latest album launched its own assault, with **The Temptations With A Lot O' Soul** also hitting the upper reaches despite featuring material drawn from a wide variety of sources, including a rare workout with Holland-Dozier-Holland on *Just One Last Look*. Mainstream success had not only been achieved, it was sustained throughout 1967, culminating in The Temptations following The Supremes in getting a two week stint at the Copacabana club.

With the two acts effectively the spearhead of everything that Motown was undertaking at the time, Berry Gordy made an important executive decision, handing management of The Temptations to the same Shelly Berger who was opening doors for The Supremes. For a while, The Temptations would follow almost exactly the same path that The Supremes had already trodden, including recording of an album of standards.

It was not a decision that was universally popular with The Temptations themselves, especially Paul, who felt the group was in danger of alienating its R&B fan base with such an album, although Shelly Berger successfully argued that their popularity at that time was such that they could afford to take a chance here or there. In the end Berger proved right, with the album topping the R&B chart and reaching #13 pop, a more than healthy performance, especially when compared with The Supremes' offering **Sing Rodgers And Hart**. Indeed, several of the songs would become a staple of The Temptations' live shows for several years after, including *For Once In My Life*, which became Paul Williams' solo showcase. Besides, standards and Broadway songs had become such a staple of their live shows it made sense to have at least one or two recordings of similar material available for purchase; their fan base would still be more than adequately compensated with a succession of hard hitting singles.

Some things remained the same, however, and having had to deal with the blow out of Florence Ballard from The Supremes, Shelly Berger found he had similar problems looming with The Temptations. Whilst David Ruffin had knuckled down to some serious work when he first joined the group, each step on the road to success and stardom made him more disagreeable. Although all five members of the group were making money (big money too, the rewards for hit singles and albums and a full diary of live dates at ever more prestigious venues), the concept of saving some for a rainy day seemed to be alien to David.

It was not just the ostentatious cars and clothes, there was an abundance of jewellery, both for him and a succession of girlfriends, including fellow Motown singer Tammi Terrell, a retinue of managers, gofers and chauffeurs and, most worryingly of all, an increasing drug habit. The solidarity displayed in 1963 and the promise that he was not using the group as a stepping stone to a solo career had quickly dissipated and by 1967 he was a Temptation in name only. At one concert, he introduced the group with the observation 'I'm David Ruffin', paused for a short while and then pointed to the other four and added 'And they are The Temptations'. When admonished backstage after the show, David swore it was all a joke, but it was one he took great care not to repeat. Instead, he pushed for a rebranding of the group, similar to that which had been attached to The Supremes, who were now Diana Ross & The Supremes.

The difference between the two, obviously lost on David, was that Diana *was* the lead singer of The Supremes; David merely one of five capable of handling a song for The Temptations (even bass vocalist Melvin had the occasional moment in the spotlight). By the time the group's next album **Wish It Would Rain** hit the stores (in amongst the bickering, the album performed well, topping the R&B chart and hitting #13 pop), there was virtual open warfare between David and the rest, although Eddie too was beginning to resent what he saw as Otis and Melvin's influence on all group matters. Uncertainty over the group's prospects should David Ruffin be given his marching orders kept the fateful decision on the back-burner for a considerable time.

Whilst Berry Gordy had acted quickly to quell any dissent within The Supremes and sacked Florence Ballard (as might have been expected, since he had effectively hung Motown's future prospects on Diana Ross), he kept a hands off approach with The Temptations, although he did reportedly offer the observation that the group was unlikely to survive with him, so troublesome had David become, never mind their future without him.

Matters finally reached a head in June 1968 when David did something of a disappearing act, skipping

Cleveland in order to accompany his then girlfriend Barbara Martin (the daughter of Dean Martin) to a performance in Buffalo, getting caught in a storm and being unable to make it back in time for the next show. The Temptations took to the stage as a foursome, seething with rage at David's unprofessionalism, with his re-appearance midway through the show and receiving applause from the audience when he bounded onto stage doing nothing to placate them. There and then it was decided to kick David out of the group, irrespective of the consequences, with the necessary legal papers being served on David when the group returned to Detroit.

In as his replacement came Dennis Edwards (born in Birmingham, Alabama on 3 February 1943), who had been singing with The Contours and came into The Temptations highly recommended, with none other than David Ruffin among those who sang his praises. Yet initially it appeared as though David couldn't let go, turning up unannounced at the first few concerts after his sacking and suddenly leaping on stage in order to sing along. There were those who thought the intrusions were stage managed, with David to return to the group once he had served some sort of exile sentence (Dennis Edwards would later claim he was effectively told by the group that David was to return, leaving Dennis the one out in the cold, only for the plan to backfire when David did another of his disappearing acts).

Irrespective of the truth of those stories, Dennis quickly assimilated into the group, a more than capable replacement for the material David had seemingly made his own over the previous few years. Dennis would get an early opportunity of showing exactly how good a vocalist when The Temptations joined with The Supremes for the recording of two albums, **Diana Ross & The Supremes Join the Temptations** and **T.C.B.**, the latter a soundtrack recording of a television special. Filming for the special took place in August 1968, around sessions for the recording of the two albums, all of which were effectively designed as a showcase for Diana Ross; on the collaboration album, she performs lead on every track with various members of The Temptations, including Dennis on *Ain't No Mountain High Enough* and *Funky Broadway*. The television special was more of the same, with Diana being highlighted in more than two thirds of the resulting programme, but the strength of both brand names was enough to take **Diana Ross & The Supremes Join the Temptations** to #2 pop in the US and to the top of the UK chart, whilst **T.C.B.**, released just prior to the December airing, would also go on to top the US chart.

A third album, **Live At The Copa** also appealed to the middle of the road crowd that The Temptations were busy cultivating, hitting #15 pop and #2 R&B (the first Temptations album to fail to reach the top of the R&B chart after ten consecutive albums had achieved the feat). As the year drew to a close, however, The Temptations had unleashed a new sound, one which made Dennis Edwards' a somewhat fortuitous choice of lead singer.

One of the major hits of the year had been Sly & The Family Stone's *Dance To The Music*, a slice of psychedelic soul that had captivated not just the record buying public but Otis Williams of The Temptations, who in one of the frequent meetings between the group and their writer/producer Norman Whitfield, had brought the single and resulting album to his attention. Norman initially viewed *Dance To The Music* as little more than a passing fad, but was still intrigued enough to conduct one or two musical experiments with the Motown Producers Workshop, most notably with guitarist Dennis Coffey. Along with new writing partner Barrett Strong, Norman would create a whole new sound for the group, commencing with the blistering *Cloud Nine*. As adventurous as the single and sound was, there were those within Motown opposed to its release, not least because it represented such a radical departure from the blueprint laid down earlier in the decade. Ultimately both sensibilities would be satisfied, with *Cloud Nine* going on to become a #6 pop and #2 R&B hit (as well as #15 in the UK), winning Motown's first Grammy Award along the way, at much the same time the group was well represented on the mainstream pop charts with their work with The Supremes.

Cloud Nine was just a foretaste for what Norman Whitfield had in mind, which was little short of a musical revolution as far as Motown was concerned. The resulting album, also entitled **Cloud Nine**, was a further departure from the norm, with *Runaway Child Running Wild* an elongated music tour de force of near on ten minutes, although much of the rest of the material was more traditional fare. The mix of the two certainly found favour, with the album going on to become the group's most successful album (without The Supremes, that is) in hitting #4 pop and returning them go the top of the R&B chart (although it made a rather more modest mark in the UK, where it peaked at #32). Edited for single release, *Runaway Child Running Wild* was another major smash, hitting the Top Ten of both pop and R&B charts, even if British audiences gave it a wide berth.

As the year progressed, it could justifiably be claimed there were two variations of The Temptations being offered to the public. One, specifically designed to appeal to the mainstream audience (for which read white audience), would record an assortment of Broadway tunes, middle of the road standards and perform at upper class supper clubs. The other, aimed at The Temptations traditional R&B fan base (for which read black market), would record a succession of harder hitting, socially aware message songs, covering a wide spectrum of topics.

The fact that the Broadway material and standards proved successful on the R&B chart, whilst the progressive soul did well on the pop listings only went to show that The Temptations, then more than anyone at Motown, had the ability to break down musical boundaries; their popularity was across the board. And it would only get better. In July 1969 the group was granted their own hour long television special, 'The Temptations Show' with special guests George Kirby and Kaye Stevens, with the resulting album **The Temptations Show** becoming a Top Thirty success, hitting #24 pop and #2 R&B.

September saw two albums released on the same day, **Together**, which reunited them with Diana Ross & The Supremes, and **Puzzle People**, which continued their psychedelic soul experiment. **Together** was a rather modest #28 pop and #6 R&B hit, its progress hampered by the lack of a major single, with *The Weight* (a cover of The Band's minor hit) failing to crack the Top 40 and *Why (Must We Fall In Love)*, which was released exclusively in the UK hitting #31. **Puzzle People** had no such shackles, giving rise to the across the board smash *I Can't Get Next To You*, a pop and R&B chart topper as well as making #13 UK. Equally hard-hitting was *Don't Let The Joneses Get You Down*, another Top Twenty success, resulting the album sailing to the top of the R&B chart and #5 pop and #20 across the Atlantic.

By the year's end another album had hit the streets, **On Broadway** again being derived from a television special with The Supremes, which would barely crack the Top 40 at #38, even if it did hit #4 R&B. For all the financial success such albums generated, not everyone within Motown viewed them in a positive light, least of all Norman Whitfield. As far as he was concerned such albums were a nuisance, something that deviated from their true calling, which was acting as the mouthpiece for Norman and Barrett Strong's socially conscious material.

There was plenty of that to be found on the group's next album **Psychedelic Shack**, with the title track being released as a single and hitting the Top Ten pop and R&B. This would remain the only single culled from the album, although there were numerous requests for Motown to issue *War* as a 45; the company and group felt the song's message was too politically charged for The Temptations, resulting in a cover version (actually even more hard-hitting) being commissioned on Edwin Starr. Despite the lack of further singles, **Psychedelic Shack** performed well, hitting Top Ten pop and topping the R&B chart, perhaps further convincing Norman Whitfield that The Temptations were now regarded as an important album act as well as a successful singles unit. Having been denied the opportunity of releasing *War* as a single, Norman created *Ball Of Confusion* in a similar vein and saw that race up the chart, perhaps vindicating his belief that The Temptations *could* record politically influenced material.

He would return to similar themes in the ensuing months, but Motown kept The Temptations firmly in the middle of the road with a series of album issues, ranging from **Live At London's Talk Of The Town**, **The Temptations' Greatest Hits II** (the only contemporary album to feature *Ball Of Confusion*) and **Christmas Card**, all of which sold well and maintained the group's undoubted popularity.

When they reported back for duty at Hitsville to begin work on their next official album, cracks were once again beginning to show within the group. Although David Ruffin had been unceremoniously kicked out of the group in 1968, he had maintained his friendship with Eddie Kendricks. The relationship did not bode well for The Temptations, not least because David had issues with Motown in general and The Temptations in particular and used every opportunity to drive a wedge between Eddie and his erstwhile group mates. David argued that they (The Temptations collectively and the singers individually) were being ripped off by Berry Gordy and Motown, with the group being short-changed on their royalties whilst others within the organisation grew rich.

Eventually the message began to sink in and Eddie would question Otis and Melvin, who he saw as the self-appointed leaders of the group. As far as Eddie was concerned, what the group needed to do was show a united front and demand accurate accounting or they would effectively go on strike, refusing to tour or record and thus hit the company where it mattered. The argument fell on deaf ears, not least because Otis and Melvin believed the group was not in a strong enough position to directly confront Berry or anyone else. They had seen Flo Ballard kicked out of The Supremes and had quickly realised that at Motown, no one singer was bigger than the act and no one act was bigger than Motown, with the possible exception, of course, of Diana Ross.

When Paul Williams and Dennis Edwards opted to follow Otis and Melvin, Eddie felt even more estranged from the group, to the extent he became unreliable (just as David had done a couple of years earlier), missing rehearsals and, more importantly, even dates. One date he did make, however, was a meeting with Berry Gordy, charging into his office to question the whereabouts of the vast sums of money The Temptations were generating, using for special leverage a diary that listed all of the group's live performances, most of which had sold out and none of which had resulted in any extra income for the group. Fortunately, Paul Williams attended the meeting with Eddie and promised Berry he would quieten Eddie down, enough for Berry to overlook the outburst. That Paul had seemingly taken the company's side infuriated Eddie even more and, once again, a Temptation was effectively living on borrowed time within the group.

Eddie was at least persuaded not to carry out his threat of a strike, joining Otis, Melvin, Dennis and Paul in the studio for the sessions that would result in the album **Sky's The Limit**. The first track released was *Ungena Za Ulimwengu (Unite The World)* which peaked at #33, the first Temptations single not to break into the Top 30 since 1964. The relative failure of the single prompted something of a rethink on Norman's part and for once he listened to the group, most of whom wished to return to the soul ballads they had made their mark with a few years previously. They got their wish with *Just My Imagination*, a song Norman had written some time previously but left unrecorded as it didn't fit with his plans for the group at the time, but when finally committed to tape, *Just My Imagination* proved to be a welcome return to former glories for all concerned. Eddie Kendricks delivered one of his greatest ever vocal performances, the rest of The Temptations were equally on form and the musical accompaniment was simple yet devastatingly effective. Undoubtedly the standout track to be found on **Sky's The Limit** (which would rise to #16 pop and #2 R&B), *Just My Imagination* was the second single lifted and returned the group to the top of the pop and R&B chart.

Though they weren't to know it, there were some other pointers for the future to be found on the album, not least the elongated tracks *Smiling Faces Sometimes* (later successfully covered by another of Norman Whitfield's protégés Undisputed Truth) and *Love Can Be Anything*. In the end, **Sky's The Limit** proved to be the swansong for not only Eddie who left for a solo career, but also for Paul Williams, who would also depart the group.

Paul's health had been a matter of some concern for a considerable time, with the group noticing that he was drinking far more than was good for him, itself something of surprise since when the group set out on their journey Paul was teetotal. He too became unreliable, resulting in the group taking the precaution of having former Distant member Richard Street (born in Detroit, Michigan on 5 October 1942) positioned off stage with a microphone singing Paul's parts during concerts (although not on Paul's solos; all the group could do was hope that Paul was sufficiently well enough to sing his way through *For Once In My Life* and *The Impossible Dream*).

When finally persuaded to seek medical advice on his failing health, it was revealed Paul suffering from sickle-cell anaemia. Paul was effectively side-lined by the group and thereafter given a brief to get himself better, with his return to the group left as a possible option for the future. The Temptations where therefore faced with the prospect of having to find two replacements, although Richard Street ended one search before it had even begun.

Replacing Eddie, however, was a different proposition altogether. Initially, the group contracted Richard 'Ricky' Owens (born in St. Louis, Missouri on 24 April 1939), a high tenor who had sung with the recently disbanded Vibrations, but his initial performances with The Temptations were so error strewn and nervous Otis quickly took the decision to let him go rather than hope he could grow into the role - there could be no passengers with The Temptations; everyone had to hit the ground running.

Rather than rush the search for a permanent replacement, The Temptations spent the rest of the summer in 1971 performing as a quartet, but the impending sessions for their forthcoming album **Solid Rock** meant a decision would have to be taken sooner rather than later. Of all the personnel Otis and Melvin looked at, the likeliest candidate was Otis Robert Harris Jr. (born in Baltimore, Maryland on 17 July 1950), a twenty year old singer with a Temptations tribute group called The Young Tempts until Motown forced them to change their name under the threat of a lawsuit, eventually settling on The Young Vandals. Given the name Damon Harris and a four year contract with the group, he joined in time to contribute to the bulk of **Solid Rock** (one track *It's Summer* still featured Paul Williams but failed when released as a single, barely making #51 pop and #29 R&B), with Norman using the new Temptations line-up as an opportunity to fire a shot at the departed David Ruffin and Eddie Kendricks on *Superstar (Remember How You Got Where You Are)*, which at least returned the group to the Top Twenty pop (at #18) and Top Ten R&B (at #8), as well as hitting #32 in the UK.

The rest of the album continued Norman's exploits in psychedelic soul in *Take A Look Around* (a Top Thirty pop and Top Ten R&B hit, as well as making the Top

Twenty in the UK), *What It Is?* and *Smooth Sailing* as well as seeing a number of revivals of his own material, including *Stop The War Now* (which had already served as the follow-up to *War* for Edwin Starr), but the lack of a single as endearing as *Just My Imagination* prevented the album from faring any better than #24 pop, even if it did top the R&B chart and make #34 in the UK.

By the summer of 1972 it looked as though The Temptations' bubble might have burst, the abject failure of *Mother Nature* (a rare outing for a song *not* written by Norman Whitfield, this having been penned by Dino Fekaris and Nick Zesses), which limped to #92 pop and only made #27 on the R&B chart when DJ's began flipping the single and playing *Funky Music Sho' Nuff Turns Me On*, itself another cover of a song more readily associated with Edwin Starr.

There was no doubt The Temptations were in need of a fillip, but nothing the group heard when they gathered for their album sessions for **All Directons** filled them with much confidence, especially since Norman appeared to have dispensed with the services of lyric writer Barrett Strong (in reality Barrett had left of his own accord to resume his recording career with CBS); the two tracks that carried his credit were old songs recorded by others around the Hitsville lot, including the afore-mentioned *Funky Music* and *Papa Was A Rollin' Stone*, originally a minor hit for Undisputed Truth. Everything else on the album was a cover version, leading the group to believe that Norman had run out of creative ideas and was merely revisiting former glories. The eventual success of *Papa Was A Rollin' Stone* and **All Directions** proved he had not lost the Midas touch, merely switched focus from song writing to production and instrumentation, to the long-term detriment of The Temptations.

Papa Was A Rollin' Stone was a major success (perhaps the last the group was to enjoy), going on to collect no fewer than three Grammy Awards, topping the pop chart (although it halted at #5 R&B) and shifting more than two million copies domestically, easily the best selling single of their entire career, whilst the album topped the R&B chart and hit #2 pop (and returned the group to the Top Twenty in the UK, where it reached #19).

This success, however, would prove to be something of a poisoned chalice since Norman Whitfield would follow the same musical path time and again over the next few years, even though the group wanted to explore new horizons. Equally as galling was Norman's decision to not look for a writing partner, opting to take complete responsibility for every aspect of the group's recording career. Since he did much the same for others within Motown, most notably Undisputed Truth, what material he did come up with had to be spread around his roster. Which of course Norman solved by having all his acts record much the same repertoire, even if there were subtle (and sometimes not so subtle) differences in the finished sound. Even The Temptations were beginning to grow tired of Norman and his dictatorial attitude in the studio, as Otis late revealed.

"At one point we met with Berry and expressed our opinion that we'd probably gone about as far as we could with Norman, and that the public's boredom with the same old sound was keeping the singles down on the charts. No one else took our complaints seriously or made any moves to fix things, so we continued with Norman for another couple of years, growing less and less happy about it all the time."

If The Temptations were riled about **All Directions**, they were positively livid about **Masterpiece**, which followed its predecessor almost to the letter.

"Norman's picture on the back cover was bigger than ours. On some tracks our singing seemed to function as ornamentation for Norman's instrumental excursions. When we started reading articles where writers referred to The Temptations as 'the Norman Whitfield Choral Singers', we got really mad. Of course, no interviewer who valued his health would call us that to our faces, but the way they talked sometimes, we knew it was what people were starting to think. If there was ever any thought given to us trying something new, *Papa*'s success nipped it."

Much the same could be said for **Masterpiece**, which saw the album and title track soar to #7 pop and top the R&B chart, even if subsequent single culls *The Plastic Man* (#40 pop and #8 R&B), *Hey Girl (I Like Your Style)* (#35 pop and #2 R&B) and *Law Of The Land* (released exclusively in the UK, where it reached #41) failed to match previous efforts.

Denied the opportunity of working with anyone other than Norman Whitfield, Otis and Melvin decided to take matters into their own hands. Along with Temptations' guitarist Cornelius Grant they formed an independent production company called D.O.C., discovered Detroit vocal group Swiss Movement (comprising Ronald Williams, Herbert Clifton, John Hodges and Arthur Booker Jr.) and secured a deal with RCA. Otis, Melvin and Cornelius would write and produce their debut album **It's Time For The Swiss Movement**, although midway through the sessions, they received a visitor in Paul Williams, still kicking his heels since he had been advised to quit The Temptations.

When he heard the material they had come up with for Swiss Movement, in particular the potential single *Take A Chance On A Sure Thing*, he pleaded to be given the opportunity of recording the song himself. Unfortunately, D.O.C.'s deal with RCA was watertight so the three had to let Paul down gently, although Otis later revealed that in the aftermath Paul expressed that the way his life was on a downward spiral he was contemplating suicide. Otis managed to pick Paul up after that outburst, telling him to pull himself together and get his health back and then things would turn around for him. To an extent the advice worked, for Paul did recover sufficiently enough to record a couple of tracks with Eddie Kendricks as producer, but Motown chose not to release them and Paul slipped back into depression almost as quickly as he had emerged. In the early hours of 17 August 1973, he was found slumped in his car, reportedly having taken his own life with a gunshot to the head, not far from the Hitsville complex, the scene of his greatest triumphs.

The tragic end of one of their former band mates reunited The Temptations, with David Ruffin and Eddie Kendricks joining Dennis Edwards, Melvin Franklin, Otis Williams and Cornelius Grant as pallbearers at Paul's funeral a week after his untimely death. And the low points were to keep coming, The Temptations despair at the stalling of their own recording career not helped by Eddie Kendricks' sudden elevation to the top tier thanks to *Keep On Truckin'* and later *Boogie Down*, exactly the radical departure in sound they had hankered after.

Instead, Norman gave them more of the same in **1990**, another album that was low on songs and, more worryingly, even lower on potential hits. Neither was group happy that the lead single, *Let Your Hair Down* featured not only The Temptations but Norman's own in house group who would later emerge as Rose Royce in their own right. *Let Your Hair Down* stalled just inside the Top Thirty at #27 pop, even if it did return them to the top of the R&B chart.

With **1990** on general release and second single *Heavenly* having been serviced to radio, things appeared as though they were on the way up again, that is until a faux pas on the part of Ewart Abner lost virtually every radio station overnight (at least as far as The Temptations were concerned). The Temptations were once again out on tour at the start of 1974 and unable to attend the inaugural American Music Awards ceremony in Los Angeles, where the group had been named Favourite Soul/R&B Group. Ewart Abner accepted the award on their behalf and whilst lavish in his praise of Dick Clark (who had created the AMAs as a rival to the Grammy Awards) omitted any mention of the numerous disc jockeys whose support was vital to The Temptations. In retaliation for the slight, those same disc jockeys dumped *Heavenly,* which came to a grinding halt at #43 pop and #8 R&B.

The third and final single lifted *You've Got My Soul On Fire* fared even worse (#74 pop and #8 R&B), although the album was a minor success that cracked the Top Twenty pop (at #19) and Top Ten R&B (at #2). No one, least of all The Temptations, however, was deluding themselves that **1990** had been a success.

"We were hitting one of those slumps nobody can avoid if you stick around long enough. It seemed as though we could do no right. Not to say everything was miserable; it wasn't, but those songs weren't moving like they would have a year or two earlier. It was obvious to us that people had had enough of hearing the sound Norman was noted for. Travelling the world, we heard people's reactions and opinions. We had a tighter grasp of the situation than the people at Motown who were sitting at their desks. The time for a change was long overdue as far as we were concerned, so we met with Berry about it again. 'You all know what's happening,' I said. 'Our records are dropping off. People are tired of hearing us sing about the world's woes. We need to get back to the ballads.' There was no arguing with the numbers, so Berry decided to team us with James Carmichael, who had produced The Commodores."

Whether Norman's planned exit from Motown to set up his own eponymous label (which would happen at the end of the year, with Norman taking The Undisputed Truth and Rose Royce with him) played any part in Berry's decision to accede to a change in producer is not known, but at least **A Song For You** had the promise to be a much more pleasant experience for The Temptations. That it should end up even more tense and fraught than their time with Norman Whitfield was down to one man, Jeffrey Bowen, who ended up handling the bulk of production instead of James Carmichael.

"Norman became kind of a monster, but like when we kibitzed and shit, he knew us, he grew up with us. We could give each other hell, then it'd fade and we'd go to work. Our disagreements with Norman were strictly professional," said Otis. "But with Jeff, when we worked with him before he was a nice young man who was just happy to be there and treated us like royalty. But now he was really dislikeable. He didn't know how to handle people. He would just act like an asshole and a bully, constantly tearing into us – 'You ain't doin' it! That ain't no good.' How the hell was that gonna help things? Those were some of the most miserable moments of my career."

Matters reached an almost explosive end when Jeffrey Bowen made some inadvisable comments in the control booth, unaware that the microphone link to the studio floor was still on and his utterances had been heard by the group. Another meeting with Berry Gordy was called, resulting in Bowen being told to back off, as much for his own personal safety as for the album.

An uneasy truce was called, resulting in **A Song For You** being completed without further mishap and the results showing little or no sign of the antagonism that had gone into its making. Indeed, **A Song For You** was a remarkably articulate and polished album, featuring five uptempo tracks on side one and four killer ballads on the flip. Despite the wish to return to ballads, it was three uptempo tracks that were issued as singles, *Happy People,* which combined The Temptations with The Commodores, *Shakey Ground* and *Glasshouse*, all of which perhaps deserved to fare better than their peaks of #40, #26 and #37 pop respectively (*Happy People* and *Shakey Ground* would at least top the R&B chart, whilst *Glasshouse* also made the Top Ten at #9). Of special note, however, was *I'm A Bachelor*, one of the ballads which was written by The Temptations and a rare outing for the group's own writing talents, which had lain dormant for the best part of a decade. **A Song For You** was never likely to return the group to the very top of the pop charts, but its final resting place of #13 was a significant improvement on their later days with Norman Whitfield at the helm and proof that the group was still as relevant and successful in 1975 as they had been in ten years previously.

The Temptations barely had time to bask in the glow of this success before the next problem arose, one that had been simmering since the middle of the **A Song For You** sessions. Damon Harris had begun his tenure with The Temptations as a benign and respectful member, courteous to the elder statesmen within the group. As time wore on his attitude diminished, culminating in an episode whilst recording with Berry Gordy, during which Damon effectively refused to add more gusto to his vocal on the grounds he was tired. A furious Gordy was all for having Harris sacked on the spot, but impending tour dates earned him at least a second chance. It was to be a short reprieve, for during the same tour, Damon chose to thank the Harlem crowd at the Apollo Theater, on behalf of The Temptations "for making it all possible for us to buy these fine mink coats and beautiful cars and homes and diamonds." Damon was given his marching orders when the group returned home to Los Angeles (the group had migrated westward, along with the rest of Motown) and, thanks to a suggestion from former Main Ingredient member Tony Silvester recruited Glenn Leonard (born in Washington D.C. on 11 June 1947) as his replacement.

Glenn quickly learned the steps and vocal parts and took his place when the group went back out on the road for the latest in a long string of tours. It was during that tour that Motown dropped the latest Temptations album, but in so doing dropped a clanger. The new album was neither complete nor coherent, being made up from a number of recently completed songs for a proposed album alongside a number of old tracks that had been shelved, as Otis would later state. "While we were on tour in Europe, Motown issued what I consider a totally bogus album, **House Party**. The only decent tracks on it were *Keep Holding On*, which the Hollands wrote and produced, and two of our compositions *Darling, Stand By Me (Song For My Woman)* and *What You Need Most (I Do Best Of All)*. When I received a telex in Holland listing the **House Party** tracks, I was furious. Here we were coming off one of our best records, and Motown was slinging out a mismatched collection of, pardon my French, shit. It seemed in character with Motown's philosophy that some people will buy anything. Not to say that we were happy when the record flopped [#40 pop and #11 R&B, whilst the only single extract *Keep Holding On* peaked at #54 pop and #3 RB], but we were secretly hoping that Motown had learned a lesson; the public expects The Temptations to uphold a certain standard of quality."

The Temptations set about creating a proper follow-up to **A Song For You**, which was to be entitled **Wings Of Love**, an album that would follow much the same pattern as its official predecessor, at least in having one side uptempo and the other mellow. However, the final album was more a Dennis Edwards solo album than a Temptations collective effort, with outside backing vocalists brought in to accompany Dennis on all but one track. That decision was down to producer Jeffrey Bowen (perhaps gaining his revenge for his loss of face over the **A Song For You** sessions), who claimed the album was running late and he therefore only had time to work with lead vocalist Dennis, not with the rest of the group. That that argument was little more than a statement of convenience was revealed when Otis overheard Jeffrey telling Dennis that he no longer needed the rest of The Temptations, he could be a bigger artist on his own and Jeffrey could make things happen for him. Whilst Motown were reportedly happy with the finished album, Otis and the rest of The Temptations were not and were vindicated when the album made barely #29 pop and #3 R&B following its March 1976, whilst the only single lifted, *Up The Creek (Without A Paddle)* (which was co-written by Sly Stone, although his involvement was kept hidden owing to issues with the I.R.S.) halted at a distant #94 pop and #21 R&B.

That left Jeffrey Bowen up the creek, with Berry finally agreeing to allow The Temptations their long desired ambition to write and produce their own material.

The glow from winning independence didn't take long to diminish, with negotiations with Motown over a new contract soon collapsing. To handle discussions on their behalf The Temptations hired Abe Somers, a lawyer who had already locked horns with Motown in the past over unpaid royalties and who quickly discovered a $300,000 discrepancy in the money owed to The Temptations. Barney Ales, who was representing Motown, instructed Otis to fire Somers, only to be met with a rebuke; Abe Somers had obviously ruffled a few Motown feathers, which was exactly why he had been hired in the first place. With Abe Somers and Barney Ales at loggerheads right from the start, there was no way a deal would ever be agreed, and even Berry Gordy's late intervention to try and placate Otis and the rest of the group proved unsuccessful; Berry may have agreed with Otis that Barney Ales had been out of line and owed the group an apology at the very least, the fact that one wasn't forthcoming told The Temptations everything they needed to know about what Motown thought of them.

Although their current deal stated that they still owed Motown two albums, both parties agreed to sever the deal after one. More importantly, at least as far as the future was concerned, when Otis learned that Motown had registered the name The Temptations, he spoke to Berry personally and eventually obtained back the rights (it has been suggested Berry proved amenable to the request, possibly on the grounds that if he ceded those rights, The Temptations might overlook the outstanding $300,000 the group was owed; they didn't, although the matter was eventually settled after The Temptations left the label). Although negotiations had broken down, the group still had the pressing matter of actually putting together their final album.

"Producing ourselves was quite a challenge, but we enjoyed having the chance to prove we were more than just singers. We worked with our friend Benjamin Wright, a producer who also writes and does a lot of work with Gladys Knight & The Pips. Having to wear so many hats – writers, producers, singers – was exhausting but ultimately rewarding. **The Temptations Do The Temptations** remains one of our favourite albums, and it got some wonderful reviews."

Unfortunately that was about all it got, for with the group soon to be out of the door, Motown felt little or no compulsion to put much in the way of promotional support behind the project. **Do The Temptations** thus suffered the ignominy of becoming the group's first album not to make at least the pop Top 40 since their debut album twelve years previously, stalling at #53, even if it did manage to hit #10 R&B. Only one single was lifted, Who Are You also coming to a halt at #22 R&B.

Their deal now done The Temptations began shopping for a new one, although no sooner had they departed from Motown than internal problems once again arose, this time with Dennis Edwards. Perhaps taking Jeffrey Bowen's whispers too much to heart, Dennis had begun speaking with Motown about a solo deal before The Temptations had cut their ties, even going so far as to record a whole album's worth of material in the process. That made him less and less agreeable to The Temptations, but so certain was he that a deal was in the pipeline Dennis wasn't too bothered, even though he was fined more for his unreliability than David Ruffin at his peak! Eventually Otis and Melvin tired of his attitude and told him he was out, drafting in Louis Bernhardt Price (born in Chicago, Illinois on 29 March 1953) almost overnight.

Then it was back to analysing the various offers that were on the table, including a couple from major companies. The deal that appealed the most was one from Philadelphia International founders Kenny Gamble and Leon Huff, who offered to produce the group as an outside project and secure distribution from Columbia. Although a deal was supposedly agreed verbally and seemed a mirror image to that which had lured The Jackson 5 away from Motown, it eventually fell apart when Gamble and Huff decided to concentrate more on their own roster of artists and less on moonlighting projects. When Gamble and Huff's interest waned, so too did Columbia's.

Instead, The Temptations inked a three album deal with Atlantic Records, itself no slouch in the R&B stakes over the previous decade or so. On paper the deal looked appetising, with Atlantic sparing little expense in feting their latest acquisition, hosting a welcoming party at New York's infamous Studio 54 nightclub. Unlike Berry Gordy and Motown, Ahmet Ertegun and Atlantic had no problem with the group wanting to administer their own publishing interests, which would be handled by Tall 'T' Temptations Music. The group also acquired a new manager in Sidney A Seidenberg (who had B.B. King and Gladys Knight & The Pips in his stable) after Shelly Berger opted to remain at Motown.

Kenny Gamble and Leon Huff may have decided not to work with The Temptations but their protégés did, the group being linked with Ron Baker, Norman Harris and Earl Young. The three had been mainstays of MFSB, Philadelphia International's powerhouse backing band who performed much the same role The Funk

Brothers did at Hitsville. Unlike The Funk Brothers, however, Baker, Harris and Young had outside recording interests that had proved especially lucrative. They also brought with them another songwriter in Ron Tyson, who would co-write the bulk of The Temptations' Atlantic debut **Hear To Tempt You**, but the heavily percussive production was perhaps too much at odds with The Temptations' ordinarily smooth vocals, resulting in a distant #113 pop and #38 R&B listing following its release in the autumn of 1977.

With Baker-Harris-Young going off to help set up the Gold Mind label, The Temptations went back to their roots for their second Atlantic album, being linked with Brian and Eddie Holland for **Bare Back**. Whilst an enjoyable reunion, at least as far as the atmosphere in the studio was concerned, the resulting album struggled to combat the barrage of disco-influenced material flooding onto the charts, with **Bare Back** making a fleeting appearance on the R&B chart at #46, alongside two minor single extractions. A third album was recorded, this time with Ron Kersey, but with the deal having not panned out as everyone had hoped both The Temptations and Atlantic Records agreed to an amicable divorce, with the album (which Otis feels was the strongest of the three they recorded for the label) filed away in the vaults.

Their future may have been uncertain (even more so when Melvin Franklin was the victim of a shooting, the result of trying to prevent a thief from driving away in his car that ended with him being shot in the hand and leg but subsequently recovering) but their past had a habit of constantly catching up with them. Although Kenny Gamble had distanced himself from recording The Temptations in 1977, he was interested in recording the group if they could find a way of accommodating Eddie Kendricks, David Ruffin and Dennis Edwards. Otis and Melvin flew to Philadelphia for a meeting with Kenny, expecting it to be about the current Temptations roster, not the old one, but listened to Kenny's plans anyway, with Eddie, David and Dennis also in attendance.

Whilst the proposal seemed fine in theory the reality was entirely different, with Otis pointing out that a reunion with three of the old guard would mean that three of the new (Glenn, Richard and Louis) would be surplus to requirements. Kenny Gamble eventually proved unable to make the deal work, so both old and current Temptations headed their respective ways. In the case of The Temptations, that ultimately meant returning to their spiritual home, just one of several of the previously departed artists, writers and producers who had found the grass was not particularly greener away from Motown and so went cap in hand to Berry Gordy.

Equally beneficial was the decision to re-admit Dennis Edwards to the group, his planned solo career having failed to materialise, at least the first time around, whilst The Temptations had missed his distinct and powerful lead vocal. Louis was the one who paid the price for Dennis' return, but few outside of the group's most diehard fans would ever have been aware he had been a one-time Temptation. For their first project back at their old stomping ground, Berry Gordy elected to produce The Temptations himself, fashioning a spirited and hard-hitting single in *Power* (originally intended for DeBarge) which would go on to hit #43 pop and #11 R&B and might have done better had it not been pulled from numerous radio playlists in the wake of the Miami race riots in 1980, programmers and disc jockeys feeling the sentiments of the song too inflammatory. The resulting **Power** album performed equally well (or miserably, depending on your viewpoint) in hitting #45 pop and #13 R&B, infinitely better than either of the two Atlantic albums had fared. Subsequent single releases *Struck By Lightning Twice* and *Take Me Away* barely made the R&B chart, the latter's lowly position of #69 all the more surprising since it supposedly benefitted from being featured on the soundtrack to 'Loving Couples'.

In 1981 Motown took the decision to pair the group with another of Philadelphia's leading lights, in this case Thom Bell, but he too had had his moment in the sun a good few years previously; having superbly marshalled albums on The Stylistics and Spinners to the upper echelons during the 1970s, by 1981 some of the magic had worn off and **The Temptations** ground to a halt at #119 pop and #36 R&B.

After nearly two decades at the top of the tree, The Temptations had seemingly hit a wall, undone as much by changing musical tastes as by their own legacy. Yet just when it seemed as though the group would have to content themselves with settling for the nostalgia circuit, that legacy became their gateway to a promising future, at least on a temporary basis.

Although Kenny Gamble tried and failed to bring about a Temptations reunion in 1978, others had picked up the chalice and made concerted efforts to bring it to reality, none more so than promoter and disc jockey Jimmy Bishop. Towards the end of 1981, he had managed to secure agreement from both David Ruffin and Eddie Kendricks (in itself not that much of a difficulty, since both had seen their solo careers stall over the previous few years, and the financial implications of a reunion were certainly enough to have David Ruffin chomping at the bit) and made his customary call to Otis and Melvin to ascertain their thoughts.

After sounding out the views of Berry Gordy and Shelly Berger (who had resumed managing the group when they returned to Motown), Otis and Melvin announced they were receptive to the idea, the presence of two of the former greats guaranteed to put bums on seats and shift records if the hype that accompanied the news story was anything to go by. It was arranged for David and Eddie to join their erstwhile band mates at Lake Tahoe where The Temptations were performing at Caesar's, with the pair being introduced to the audience towards the end of the show, as Otis fondly remembered.

"There we stood together for the first time in over fourteen years, and it was like someone had cast a magic spell over the crowd. Even in our peak, at our prime, we'd never gotten a reaction like this one. People were so excited, and it wasn't like they were on some nostalgic trip. They really loved us. And I have to admit that for a few minutes I felt myself falling back in time to those old days. I was very happy to see that, and thought everyone sounded good together."

The finer points of a deal, whereby David and Eddie would join with The Temptations for an album and national tour were quickly worked out, with the expanded seven man group being put into the studio to begin work on recording and Rick James handling production on *Standing On The Top* (which would become a minor pop hit at #66 and major R&B success at #6, also hitting #53 in the UK), the first fruits of those sessions.

The rest of the resulting album **Reunion** was shared around the Motown lot, with a total of six different producers or production teams handling the various songs, seven on the original album release, expanded to nine on CD reissue. In between the sessions came hour upon hour of rehearsal, going over the old steps and learning new ones, all designed to have the group ready for the tour to hit the road in mid March in Los Angeles, a week before the **Reunion** album hit the streets (it would also become a Top 40 pop success at #37 and stall just one place off the top of the R&B chart). The album's cover featured all seven Temptations resplendent in tuxedos gathered around a yellow taxicab. According to Otis it would have been more appropriate to have them surrounding a Rolls Royce, but no matter which vehicle was featured, it did not take too long before the wheels started to come off the bandwagon, with David again at the root of the trouble.

Everyone was on their best behaviour at the start, friendships being rekindled and the show proving to be a major success. They sold out virtually everywhere, fans old and new eager to catch a glimpse of this mix of Temptations old and new. Unfortunately as the money started cascading in, it brought out all of the old temptations. The hangers-on and gofers that had blighted David's life for much of his career crept back out of the woodwork. Matters got worse when the show hit Detroit, where David used his insider knowledge of the best crack houses in the city to miss the first three shows at the Premier Center. Perhaps wary of David's reputation almost all of the promoters had insisted on clauses in the contract that stipulated the group only got paid if all seven of them made the show, resulting in The Temptations letting down their fans and losing money. Knowing Eddie was still tight with him, Otis instructed him to pass on a message whenever he managed to locate David; once the tour was finished, so were they. Otis and Melvin had no wish to prolong the agony any longer than they were contracted, although had they known that Eddie and Dennis Edwards were doing almost as many drugs as David, they might have wrapped up the tour earlier in the day. Somehow, the tour managed to limp on until November, finishing at the Westbury Music Fair shortly before David made himself officially unavailable after getting sentenced to six months in jail for tax-evasion. Soon after the coup de grace was delivered to Eddie; the reunion was over forever.

Perhaps having seen the writing on the wall long before, Eddie and David would announce plans for their own tour (once David had served his time), but they would have to do so without any kind of record company support, Motown having also severed all ties with Eddie Kendricks and David Ruffin at much the same time The Temptations dispensed with their services.

With the tour and album having served its purpose, it was back into the studio and something of a change in direction for **Surface Thrills**, released in February 1983. Produced by Dennis Lambert and Steve Barri, it was an attempt to fuse The Temptations' soul harmonies with a rock sound, but the end result was perhaps too radical a departure from their signature sound to find full acceptance, with the album barely making #159 pop and #19 R&B, whilst the only single success came from *Love On My Mind Tonight* that peaked at #88 pop and #17 R&B.

Glenn Leonard was the next member of the group to depart, developing the same kind of attitude problem that had plagued David Ruffin and missing shows and rehearsals before he too was given his permanent marching orders. Word that the group was looking for a new first tenor soon reached Ron Tyson (born in Philadelphia, Pennsylvania on 8 February 1948), the same Ron Tyson who had earlier crossed The Temptations' path as a songwriter. Ron joined the group just in time to take part in the 'Motown 25' television special, at which The Temptations undertook a rather more pleasant reunion, joining The Four Tops on stage for a 'battle of the bands' segment that revisited both group's heyday of the 1960s.

The slot was so well received both groups agreed that they should consider taking it out on the road for a few dates, with the eventual tour taking both acts around the world for near on three years! Another face from The Temptations' past also came into view in 1983, with Norman Whitfield having returned to Motown after the failure of his eponymous record label and brought in to produce **Back To Basics**.

Midway through the sessions The Temptations were forced into another change of personnel, Dennis Edwards being dismissed when his drug taking proved too problematic for the group to tolerate any longer, with former Drifter Ali-Ollie Woodson (born Ollie Creggett in Detroit on 12 September 1951) his eventual replacement. **Back To Basics** meanwhile promised much but delivered little, slipping down the pop chart to come to rest at a lowly #152 pop and barely troubling the R&B chart at #30. There was some brief respite on the singles chart; after *Miss Busy Body (Get Your Body Busy)* had barely limped to #67 on the R&B listings, the follow-up *Sail Away* berthed at #13 R&B and sailed over to the pop chart, eventually hitting #54. However, one could not help but wonder how well *The Battle Song (I'm The One)* might have fared, especially as it also featured The Four Tops.

With the relative failure of the reunion with Norman Whitfield, The Temptations once again cast their net outside of Motown for the producers of their next album **Truly For You**. There was no musical act hotter than Earth, Wind & Fire at the time, so the chance of working with Al McKay and Ralph Johnson from that group proved somewhat inspirational, along with several members also helping out on musical accompaniment. It helped that the group had written what sounded like a sure fire smash, penned by Otis Williams and new recruit Ollie Woodson, as he'd become known.

"Ollie was a songwriter, so when Melvin's interest in writing with me declined, I paired up with Ollie. His strong suit was melodies; he played several instruments in addition to being a fantastic, flexible singer. Unlike Ron [Tyson], Ollie hadn't gotten that many breaks, and he expressed his frustration over the fact that no one would listen to his stuff. It's hard to say why, because when we heard his songs, we thought they were very good."

They were in fact better than very good, as *Treat Her Like A Lady* would confirm. Issued as a single in October 1984 (and a month later in the UK), *Treat Her Like A Lady* was a more than welcome return to the upper reaches of the chart, hitting #2 R&B. For some reason the single barely scraped into the Top 50 of the pop chart, halting at #48. In the UK however it had sufficiently more legs to venture as far as #12, the group's first Top Twenty hit for more than twelve years. **Truly For You** reaped the benefits of the single's success and would power its way to #3 on the R&B listings, although it would perform rather more modestly on the pop charts, at #55 in the US and #75 in the UK.

Unfortunately, the bar set by **Truly For You** proved to be insurmountable by subsequent releases. The lack of a radio friendly single along the lines of *Treat Her Like A Lady* led to both **Touch Me** and **To Be Continued**, issued in 1985 and 1986 respectively, falling way short of their predecessor, with **Touch Me** finishing a distant #146 pop and #20 R&B. Whilst **To Be Continued**, as apt a title for a Temptations album as any, did at least return the group to the Top Ten of the R&B chart, at #4, it peaked at #74 pop. There was a brief respite for the extracted single, *Lady Soul* becoming a major R&B hit at #4 but was unable to transfer that popularity over to the pop listings, stalling at #47. Yet another compilation, **25th Anniversary** was released in 1986, the nostalgia packed anthology also making a brief showing on the chart, at #55 R&B and #140 pop.

If The Temptations' own recordings had hit a wall, they were still much in demand elsewhere. Former members David Ruffin and Eddie Kendricks had assisted blue-eyed soul duo Daryl Hall and John Oates on their hugely successful **Live At the Apollo** outing in 1985 (and both would perform at the Live Aid benefit in Philadelphia), and not to be outdone, the then current Temptations would perform alongside actor Bruce Willis on his update of *Under The Boardwalk*, a major UK hit that peaked at #2. The group also got to make cameo appearances in the television series 'Moonlighting', which starred Willis, 'The Fall Guy' and 'Love Boat', thus further cementing their position as icons of American popular music.

In 1987 The Temptations renewed their contract with Motown, at much the same time as having another line-up change forced upon them. Ollie Woodson had proved his worth as a songwriter when he originally joined the group, helping compose numerous songs on the three albums recorded during his time. Eventually however, relations between him and the rest of the group began to break down, initially restricted to late time-keeping that had him at loggerheads with Otis. Matters reached a head when the group learned that Ollie had been bad-mouthing the various members whilst they all took a month off. Ollie was eventually given his marching orders in January 1987, at much the same time Ron Tyson reported to Otis Williams that he had recently caught Dennis Edwards' live show and that the former Temptations singer had looked and sounded good. Although initially hesitant about wanting to bring Dennis back into the fold, Otis at least agreed to meet with the errant singer, alongside the rest of the group and management. Dennis convinced those present that he needed the group more than they needed him and something of a truce was declared; Dennis Edwards became a member of The Temptations for a third time.

Produced by Peter Bunetta and Rick Chudacoff, the resulting **Together Again** was the group's first release on the main Motown label, the Gordy imprint having been side-lined. The album would give rise to three R&B hits in *I Wonder Who She's Seeing Now* (which featured a guest harmonica from Stevie Wonder), *Look What You Started* and *Do You Wanna Go With Me*, which would peak at #3, #8 and #53 respectively. The album itself would also hit the R&B Top Twenty, at #12, as well as #112 pop.

By the time the group delivered their next album, **Special** in August 1989, Motown had been sold to MCA. The group had also been inducted into the Rock & Roll Hall of Fame, with Daryl Hall and John Oates handing the statuettes to members both past (David Ruffin and Eddie Kendricks) and present (Otis Williams, Melvin Franklin, Ron Tyson, Richard Street and Dennis Edwards), although the feel-good factor the induction generated didn't last long, with Dennis Edwards deciding to hook his future to David Ruffin and Eddie Kendricks, leaving The Temptations for a third and final time. In his place the group brought Ollie Woodson back!

The ensuing twenty five years or so since that induction has brought a mix of emotions and success for the group. There have been further Grammy Awards victories, a Best Traditional R&B Vocal Performance for the album **Ear-Resistible** in 2000 and a Lifetime Achievement Award in 2013, and further million selling albums, including **Phoenix Rising** in 1998. That same year NBC aired a four hour television miniseries across two nights that told the story of group, based on Otis Williams' 1988 autobiography. The series would top the ratings on both nights it was aired and go on to win five Emmy Awards. The success of the television series would see an upsurge in record sales, enabling **All The Million Sellers** and **The Ultimate Collection** attain platinum and gold status respectively.

The group (the current line up features Otis Williams, the only surviving original member, Ron Tyson, Terry Weeks, Joe Herndon and Bruce Williamson) continues to tour worldwide, still managing some 300 dates a year. Over the years there have been several splinter groups, working much the same venues and criss-crossing dates with the official group. These have included the trio David Ruffin, Eddie Kendricks and Dennis Edwards, Damon Harris & The Temptations Revue (which featured future Temptations member Joe Herndon), Dennis Edwards & The Temptations Revue, Ali-Ollie Woodson & The Emperors of Soul, Glenn Leonard's Temptations Revue, Richard Street's Temptations and Legendary Lead Singers of The Temptations (this group featured Glenn Leonard, Ollie Woodson and Barrington 'Bo' Henderson). The use of the name 'Temptations' in several of these has prompted a number of legal challenges from Otis Williams, who protects the Temptations legacy today as vehemently as he did back in 1960.

"Look, I put my whole damn life into this group. I sweated a lot sweat, bled a lot of blood, buried a lot of friends in this group. I have nothing against Damon Harris or Richard or any of those guys. But they can't be taking food from my plate, you understand? I didn't come all this way to share my baby."

Paul Williams reportedly committed suicide on 17 August 1973. Al Bryant died from liver cirrhosis on 26 October 1975. David Ruffin died from a drug overdose on 1 June 1991. Eddie Kendricks died from cancer on 5 October 1992. Melvin Franklin died on 23 February 1995. Ricky Owens died in Los Angeles on 6 December 1999. Ali-Ollie Woodson died from cancer on 30 May 2010. Damon Harris died from cancer on 18 February 2013. Richard Street died after a lengthy illness on 26 February 2013.

ALBUMS: MEET THE TEMPTATIONS (1964), SING SMOKEY (1965), TEMPTIN' TEMPTATIONS (1965), GETTIN' READY (1966), LIVE! (1967), WITH A LOT OF SOUL (1967), IN A MELLOW MOOD (1967), WISH IT WOULD RAIN (1968), DIANA ROSS & THE SUPREMES JOIN THE TEMPTATIONS (1968), LIVE AT THE COPA (1968), T.C.B. (1968), CLOUD NINE (1969), THE TEMPTATIONS SHOW (1969), PUZZLE PEOPLE (1969), TOGETHER (1969), G.I.T. ON BROADWAY (1969), PSYCHEDELIC SHACK (1970), LIVE AT LONDON'S TALK OF THE TOWN (1970), CHRISTMAS CARD (1970), SKY'S THE LIMIT (1971), SOLID ROCK (1972), ALL DIRECTIONS (1972), MASTERPIECE (1973), 1990 (1973), A SONG FOR YOU (1975), HOUSE PARTY (1975), WINGS OF LOVE (1976), THE TEMPTATIONS DO THE TEMPTATIONS (1976), POWER (1980), GIVE LOVE AT

CHRISTMAS (1980), THE TEMPTATIONS (1981), REUNION (1982), SURFACE THRILLS (1983), BACK TO BASICS (1983), TRULY FOR YOU (1984), TOUCH ME 1985), TO BE CONTINUED... (1986), TOGETHER AGAIN (1987)
COMPILATIONS: GREATEST HITS (1966), GREATEST HITS VOLUME 2 (1970), ANTHOLOGY - 10TH ANNIVERSARY SPECIAL (1973), 17 GREATEST HITS (1985), ANTHOLOGY (1986), 25TH ANNIVERSARY (1986)
FURTHER READING: TEMPTATIONS (1988), THE TEMPTATIONS: AIN'T TOO PROUD TO BEG (2010)

THE TEMPTATIONS GREATEST HITS – THE TEMPTATIONS [ALBUM]

By November 1966, The Temptations had scored no fewer than seven R&B Top Ten hits, including three that sailed all the way to the top of the chart. With several other tracks having also made a more than healthy showing, now was felt to be the right time for a career retrospective, one that would be further augmented by the inclusion of the group's latest single release, *Beauty Is Only Skin Deep*.

With the single becoming a major success, there was little to stop the album following in its wake, but even Motown must have been surprised by the sales **The Temptations Greatest Hits** achieved, enabling the album to become the group's first pop Top Ten success, where it peaked at #3 as well as topping the R&B chart for nine, non-consecutive weeks. The album also proved resilient enough to feature on the British charts, where it would hit #26 in March 1967.

TEMPTATIONS LIVE! – THE TEMPTATIONS [ALBUM]

Something of a triumphant homecoming for The Temptations, who recorded this album in front of effectively their own crowd at the Roostertail Club's Upper Deck in Detroit on 3 October 1966. Featuring the classic Temptations line-up of David Ruffin, Eddie Kendricks, Paul Williams, Melvin Frankin and Otis Williams and their regular live routine, the show was recorded for possible release as an album.

It duly appeared in March 1967 and, following the success of a greatest hits package in 1966, returned the group to the Top Ten of the pop chart for the second time in their career, even if the album was effectively a live version of the same greatest hits album! **Temptations Live!** would also go on to top the R&B chart, hit #10 pop and carry its success overseas, where it would reach #20 in the UK.

RALPH TERRANA

The slightly older twin brother of Russ Terrana, Ralph was born in Detroit, Michigan on 6 July 1942 and joined his first band, also featuring Russ, at the age of eleven when they linked with Fred Saxon in a group eventually called The Glo-Worms. The group would evolve through several names, including The Rebels and The Five Beaus before eventually settling on The Sunliners.

Ralph switched to working the other side of the industry in 1966, linking with Al Sherman in a deal that saw them take over a small Detroit recording studio that they renamed Tera Shirma. The studio would remain in operation for the rest of the decade before closing its doors, although when Ralph sent out a sale prospectus to a number of potential companies he thought might be interested in purchasing the premises, including Motown, he received an offer to go over to Hitsville as studio manager!

He was also signed on as a writer and producer, going on to assist the Rare Earth label, where he produced the likes of Stoney & Meatloaf, My Friends, Matrix and numerous other artists. When Motown departed Detroit and relocated in Los Angeles, Ralph remained in Detroit, eventually leaving the company when the whole Michigan operation was shut down in September 1974.

He then pursued a wide variety of professions and occupations, including piano tuner, freelance musician and producer. He still retains a connection to Motown, serving as Moderator on the website Soulfuldetroit.com.

FURTHER READING: THE ROAD THROUGH MOTOWN (2006)

RUSS TERRANA

The younger twin brother of Ralph Terrana, Russ was born in Detroit, Michigan on 6 July 1942 and linked with his brother in his first band, The Glo-Worms at the age of eleven. The group would go through a number of name changes before finally settling on The Sunliners, enjoying a healthy reputation in and around the Detroit area without ever really troubling the charts.

Like his brother, when his performing career came to an end he went into studio work, landing a job as an engineer at Golden World (the same company that had The Sunliners under a recording contract). He would go on to work at his brother's Tera Shirma studio, where his growing reputation soon had him working for Motown, initially on occasional sessions but subsequently on a full time basis.

Whilst he would also produce a number of acts on the Rare Earth label, it is as a mixer and remixer that he made his name, being responsible for some 89 #1 hits on the various charts during the course of his career. Most notably, he was brought in to remix the Diana Ross album that had been originally mixed by producers Nile Rodgers and Bernard Edwards and later mixed the 'Motown 25' television special. Russ would continue working for Motown long after the company was sold to MCA and was still mixing and remixing Motown material into the 2000s.

FURTHER READING: RUSS TERRANA'S MOTOWN (2010)

JEAN TERRELL

Although much of Berry Gordy's time during 1969 was spent formulating the plans for Diana Ross' solo career, he still cared enough about The Supremes (Mary Wilson and Cindy Birdsong) to give some consideration as to who would replace Diana in the group. He and Mary discussed the matter at some length, especially since what they were looking for was not just a singer but a potential lead singer. The newspapers and magazines were already running polls to offer up their suggestions, with Tammi Terrell apparently well in front. Unfortunately, Tammi was by this time suffering from a brain tumour and was never seriously considered as a possible replacement, at least by Mary. In the event, it was Berry who found the ideal singer, performing in a club in Miami.

Velma Jean Terrell (no relation to Tammi, incidentally) was born in Belzoni, Mississippi on 26 November 1944 and moved with her family to Chicago at an early age. There she pursued an interest in singing and would eventually become a member of her brother's group Ernie Terrell & The Heavyweights. The name was something of a play on Ernie's other occupation, that of a professional boxer, good enough to win the WBA heavyweight boxing title in 1965.

Ernie Terrell & The Heavyweights were performing at a club in Miami Beach when Berry Gordy first spotted Ernie and Jean, with Berry being taken enough by Jean's vocal abilities to sign her to Motown as a solo artist. Even before anything had been released, Berry had a change of mind, telling Mary that he had found someone for the role in The Supremes and introduced Jean to Mary.

"Though it was obvious from the beginning that Jean had a mind of her own and wasn't nearly as much a team player as Cindy and I were, I overlooked it. Things would be worked out, and I was just happy to know that The Supremes would go on."

Although Diana hadn't left the group at this point, Jean was thrown in to a round of rehearsals and subsequently recording, taking her first lead on what would be the new group's 1970 release *Up The Ladder To The Roof*. The old group made their exit in January 1970 with a performance at the Frontier Hotel in Las Vegas, with Diana Ross introducing Jean to the crowd at the end of the performance. Later that night, however, Berry called Mary and told her he didn't like Jean Terrell and he'd changed his mind about The Supremes; he now wanted Syreeta to take over. Mary was adamant that Jean was staying, resulting in Berry saying, "All right. Then I wash my hands of the group."

Over the next few years, a succession of hits, including *Up The Ladder To The Roof, Stone Love, Nathan Jones* and *Floy Joy*, along with recordings with The Four Tops, proved Mary had made the right decision in sticking with Jean. Mary and Jean would be joined by Lynda Laurence when Cindy left through pregnancy in April 1972, but by the following year all three Supremes felt that Motown's promotional efforts on their behalf had begun to slack. Both Jean and Lynda felt the group should leave Motown and look for a deal elsewhere, but the realisation that Motown owned the rights to the name The Supremes meant another deal would never materialise.

Instead, both dissenting members left, with Jean eventually landing a solo deal with A&M Records. Produced by Bobby Martin and featuring material that was in the then very much in vogue disco style, the album **I Had To Fall In Love** in 1978 did little, its progress hampered by Jean's refusal to undertake some promotional activity because it conflicted with her religious beliefs.

Instead Jean went into semi-retirement, eventually being coaxed back out on to the road with a one woman show and then, in 1985, linking with former Supremes' members Cindy Birdsong and Scherrie Payne in FLOS – Former Ladies of The Supremes. Cindy left the following year and was replaced by Lynda Laurence (just as Lynda had replaced Cindy in the original Supremes), with the new line-up touring and then resuming their recording career in 1989 for Ian Levine's Motorcity label. Jean remained in the group until 1992 and went back into semi-retirement.

TAMMI TERRELL

Her body of work with Marvin Gaye in particular is indicative of a musical marriage made in heaven, but too much of her severely shortened life was hell on earth; the contrast between one and the other is nowhere better exemplified than with Tammi Terrell.

Born Thomasina Winifred Montgomery in Philadelphia, Pennsylvania on 29 April 1945, she was the first child born to Thomas and Jennie Montgomery and would later be joined by a sister, Ludie. So certain were her parents that their first born was to be a boy they had already selected a name, affecting a slight change when that child turned out to be a girl. As a child Tommie, as she became known to family and friends, showed an aptitude towards music and dancing, prompting her father to arrange for piano and ballet lessons for his prodigious daughter.

Having sung in the church choir at an early age, Tommie's route to stardom seemed set, appearing on the long running local television talent show 'The Children's Hour' where she was the only black female performer, singing a wide range of pop and even jazz standards on the programme.

Yet despite this success, Tommie endured something of a complicated and troublesome childhood, punctuated by her poet and actress mother undergoing several periods of hospitalisation owing to clinical depression. This however was nothing compared to the horror that visited Tommy one evening in 1956; coming home from a rehearsal at the Wissahickon Boys & Girls Club, Tommy was gang raped and beaten by three much older boys, an event that many would later claim changed Tommy's outlook on life in general and men in particular.

A year after this brutal event, Tommie Montgomery became Tammy, taking the name from the same Debbie Reynolds film and hit single that Berry Gordy had so admired when he looked for a name for his newly created record company. Still only twelve years of age, Tammy performed in high school productions, entered local talent contests on a regular basis and got to perform as an opening act for several major names, including Gary U.S. Bonds and Patti Labelle & The Bluebells, and it was whilst performing locally that she was eventually spotted by songwriter and producer Luther Dixon, who got her a contract with Scepter Records in New York in 1961.

Whilst her initial duties consisted of little more than recording demos for the label's main stars The Shirelles, in time Tammy got her own chance at recording and releasing a single, with *If You See Bill* being released on the Scepter label in November 1961. The following year saw Tammy switched to subsidiary label Wand, which issued *Voice Of Experience*, on which The Shirelles provided backing vocals. In all Tammy completed some seven tracks (these would be reissued in 1967 as part of an album package with Chuck Jackson in an attempt to cash in on Tammy's then high profile) but didn't get anywhere near the charts.

That summer the Montgomery family moved to Wildwood in New Jersey, where Tammy would successfully audition for Steve Gibson & The Red Caps, a group who had been performing, touring and recording since 1939. Their better days may have been well behind them, but for Tammy, the opportunity to work closely with the group and assorted other star names who passed through the city was a musical education too good to pass up.

One of the artists who came through was James Brown and his Famous Flames, with James being taken by both the beauty and talent of Tammy, enough to offer her a place as part of his Revue. Musically her time with James Brown was beneficial, with James writing and producing the single *I Cried* backed with *If You Don't Think* which was released on his Try Me label in July 1963 and crept into the Hot 100 at #99 for a single week. Far more worryingly, however, was the later revelation that Tammy was involved in a relationship with her mentor, one that was at best volatile and at worst violent. Several of Tammy's friends either witnessed or were taken into her confidence regarding the repeated beatings she suffered at his hand, but no one did anything about them, least of all Tammy. Matters reportedly reached a head one evening after a show when James spotted that Tammy had not watched from the sidelines as instructed and, at the end of the performance stormed off stage and administered a particularly savage beating that was witnessed by fellow singer Gene Chandler. Tammy asked Gene for a lift to the local bus stop; Gene called her mother and arranged for her to come and collect her daughter.

Out of the clutches of James Brown, Tammy settled back into life in Wildwood and got another recording deal with Checker, an imprint of Chess Records thanks to producer Bert Berns (she also reportedly married and divorced during this period back at home, although her husband was never identified). Tammy and Bert co-wrote what would be her only single for the label, *If I Would Marry You* being released in 1964, with several other tracks recorded but unreleased. For a while Tammy put her show business aspirations behind her, studying Pre-Med at the University of Pennsylvania for some two years.

Tammy was still a student when she got her next chance at stardom, Jerry Butler offering her the opportunity of touring with his show and continuing with her schooling. It was during a performance at Detroit's 20 Grand that Berry Gordy spotted her act and offered a new recording contract, one that Tammy gleefully accepted, putting pen to paper on 29 April 1965, on her 20th birthday.

It was not only a contract that Berry put on the table; reasoning that Tammy Montgomery was a cumbersome name for a potential star, he came up with moniker Tammi Terrell (the creation of the name led to unfounded rumours that she was married to boxer Ernie Terrell). Tammi was initially assigned to veteran producer and writer Harvey Fuqua, who brought his one-time Tri-Phi artist Johnny Bristol into the studio for what was his first Motown session too. The pair wrote *I Can't Believe You Love Me*, on which The Spinners (another of Harvey's former artists) provided backing vocals. Released as a single in November 1965, *I Can't Believe* would become her first hit under her name and for her new label, hitting #72 pop and #27 R&B.

The same team was responsible for Tammi's follow-up *Come On And See Me*, issued in April 1966 and another minor hit, peaking at #80 pop and #25 R&B. By the time Tammi had new material out on sale, Motown had decided upon a change in focus, one which was to make her reputation and name in the years to come. Marvin Gaye had enjoyed a handful of hits in conjunction with Mary Wells in 1964 and had then gone on to record with Kim Weston when Mary had departed Motown. Whilst the duets with Kim were successful, with *It Takes Two* becoming a major smash, they were somewhat perfunctory, and if the duet recordings were to be consistently successful, then a new recording partner had to be found.

It was Berry Gordy himself who suggested Tammi might be the ideal partner, figuring that the joint project would raise her profile considerably and benefit her future solo recording career. Eager to please her new boss Tammi agreed, with Marvin also happy to enter into a new musical union.

"I had no idea Tammi was as good a singer as she, of course, turned out to be. But some people were on their toes dug her sound and perhaps realised that we may possibly make a good duet. And, wanting to try something new all of my life, it was a challenge and something groovy to do. Tammi was nice, she was pretty, and she was soft and warm and sweet – and misunderstood. I enjoyed working with her and that, coupled with a new team, Ashford & Simpson, made it so marvellous."

To begin with the pair didn't actually record together. *Ain't No Mountain High Enough* was brought to Motown by Nickolas Ashford and Valerie Simpson and was originally envisaged as a solo recording for Tammi, but somewhere along the way Harvey Fuqua and Johnny Bristol wiped some of her lead vocals off the tape and dropped Marvin in instead. Despite the almost random way the recording came together, it doesn't sound disjointed at all; the pair were able to create musical magic when they recorded separately, which would only bode well for the future when they recorded together.

Ain't No Mountain High Enough got the new pairing off to a perfect start, hitting #19 pop and #3 R&B, with the seamless recording also picking up a Grammy nomination for Best R&B Performance by a Duo (it lost out to Sam & Dave's *Soul Man*). The same writing and production pairings were responsible for the next slice of perfection, with *Your Precious Love* becoming an even bigger hit than its predecessor, hitting #5 pop and #2 R&B following release in August 1967.

That same month saw a whole album released, **United** becoming a minor pop hit (at #69) but a major R&B success at #7. There were several reasons why the various singles and album were successful, not least of which was the quality of material Tammi and Marvin were being given to record, but equally, there was a musical chemistry between the two whereby one complimented the other to perfection. It was proof, said many, that the two were not only getting it together in the studio.

Rumours swirled around the industry, with even Marvin's wife Anna said to have believed there might be an element of truth to them. In reality, Marvin and Tammi shared nothing more than a platonic, almost brotherly and sisterly relationship. The secret, if there was one, was that when Marvin and Tammi entered the recording studio together, they took on new persona, that of lovers, and remained in character for the duration of the song. When the recording was finished, so was the special relationship. Besides, both singers had other relationships to contend with, Marvin being married to Anna Gordy and Tammi being involved with David Ruffin.

Tammi had met David when she had toured with The Temptations as their opening act during her early days signed to Motown. Her new choice of paramour was no better than those previously, with the pair fighting and bickering in private and in public. The relationship did get serious however, with David surprising Tammi with a marriage proposal in 1966, although he omitted to tell Tammi that he was already married with three children *and* had another girlfriend living in Detroit!

Tammi was devastated and the pair's fighting got worse, culminating in David hitting her on the side of her face with his motorcycle helmet, an action that brought an end to their relationship. Whilst her personal life was collapsing, her professional career seemed destined to continue its upward momentum.

The success of her duets with Marvin had increased her profile, so much so that Motown readied a new solo single for release, Smokey Robinson and Al Cleveland's *What A Good Man He Is* being scheduled for release on 5 October 1967. A little over a week later, tragedy struck. Marvin and Tammi were performing a series of live dates around the country, and on 14 October were booked to perform at Hampton-Sydney College in Virginia. The Saturday night show, in front of an audience of some 800 students and their dates, was a college home-coming, with Bill Deal & The Rhondells on the same bill. The pair arrived early for the show, although Tammi complained of feeling unwell, having suffered migraines and intense headaches for much of her adult life, and sat alone in the darkened room that served as a dressing room.

Tammi made it out for the show and performed some two or three numbers before collapsing onstage midway through the next song (accounts vary as to whether it was *Ain't No Mountain High Enough* or *Your Precious Love*), with Marvin catching her as she slid to the floor. Marvin continued the rest of the show alone, although the audience didn't complain, with one later commenting, "It was a great concert. Marvin Gaye covered for her very well when she collapsed, to my knowledge she just passed out – no one knew she had headaches or had been abused. At the time we just thought she collapsed from exhaustion or too much of something. She slipped down onto the bleacher seats; eventually she was helped down, and Marvin continued singing, ending the concert with the entire audience happy as clams. The concert was great, she was great, and they made a great duo!"

Taken to hospital and subsequently flown home to Philadelphia, extensive tests revealed Tammi was suffering from a malignant tumour on the right side of her brain, although Motown initially played down the seriousness of her situation, sending Marvin back out on the road with a succession of female singers, including Brenda Holloway, Barbara Randolph and Ann Bogan. With Tammi facing a series of operations, chemotherapy and further tests, her touring days were behind her (Motown also recalled the *What A Good Man He Is* single, with the result it became her only solo single not to chart), but Tammi was convinced she could still do a job in the studio.

In place of the recalled single Motown rushed out another duet with Marvin, initially scheduling *Two Can Have A Party* (which had originally been recorded as a Tammi solo single) and then replacing it with the double header *If I Could Build My Whole World Around You* and *If This World Were Mine*. Both sides made the chart, with the top side hitting #2 R&B and #10 pop (and would hit #41 in the UK for good measure) and the flip #27 R&B and #68 pop, vindication of Motown's policy to try and keep Tammi's name in vogue whilst she underwent a series of lengthy and dangerous operations.

In March 1968 came the next single release, one on which the pair sang at the same microphone at the same time back in September 1967; the vocal interplay between the two was obvious. The version of *Ain't Nothing Like Real Thing* that was released was the version produced by writers Nickolas Ashford and Valerie Simpson, although Motown had a back-up version in the can produced by Harvey Fuqua and Johnny Bristol, just in case. They needn't have worried, for all involved in the single were happy with the end result, especially Marvin.

"We were really enjoying challenging each other with our riffs and our little note changes, and the rises and the falls. That's how it came off that way. We really had fun recording that."

The single would become the first of the duet's singles to top the R&B chart, spending a week at the summit and also sailing up to #8 pop as well as breaking into the Top 40 in the UK (#34). Soon after *Ain't Nothing Like The Real Thing* was released, Tammi and Marvin were back in the studio working on fresh material. For Marvin, it was a welcome break from the non-stop touring; for Tammi a respite from the endless operations and tests. *You're All I Need To Get By* was another smash hit single, again topping the R&B chart for five weeks and returning Tammi and Marvin to the pop Top Ten at #7, also cracking the Top Twenty in the UK (#19).

Tammi was also able to complete a whole album's worth of material, with **You're All I Need** being released in August 1968 and becoming a major R&B hit (it would peak at #4) and minor pop hit (#60). As the year drew to a close, Tammi returned to the chart as a solo performer, with her version of *This Old Heart Of Mine (Is Weak For You)* being the first release from her forthcoming album. The single did relatively well, hitting #31 R&B and #67 pop, although the subsequent album **Irresistible**, a mixed bag collection of previously discarded material released in January 1969 peaked at a much lower #39 R&B. That same month Tammi was to find herself on the charts on both sides of the Atlantic, with *You Ain't Livin' 'Till You're Lovin'* making #21 in the UK and *Good Lovin' Ain't Easy To Come By* making #30 pop and #11 R&B (for good measure, it would hit #26 when subsequently released in the UK in May).

Despite the chart success, Tammi's health was beginning to falter, with the succession of operations (there were to be eight in total) only adding to the pain and suffering. On those occasions when she could make the studio for recording dates, she would invariably have to be wheeled in sitting in a wheelchair, with dark glasses hiding whatever torment was going through her mind.

Considerable controversy has grown around those final sessions, with some believing Tammi's involvement was minimal and others choosing to hold on to the notion that Tammi continued recording right until the very end. Aside from the obvious desire to keep a hit recording career going for as long as possible, Motown had other considerations, not least of which were the growing medical bills that they had continued to pick up ever since she had collapsed back in October 1967. The upshot of the controversy was that many are convinced that Marvin's partner on several of the later recordings was not Tammi Terrell but Valerie Simpson, with even Marvin entering the fray.

"At first I refused to go along with the plan. I saw it as another money-making scheme on BG's part. I said it was cynical and wrong. I didn't want to deceive the public like that. Then Motown convinced me that it'd be a way for Tammi's family to have additional income. [Valerie] amazed me with how faithfully she captured Tammi. I felt strange...I suppose I felt guilty."

Yet despite Marvin's assertions, Valerie herself would later state that all she ever recorded was a guide vocal for Tammi, something for the stricken singer to follow and that the vocal that appeared on the subsequent record releases was indeed Tammi Terrell.

The controversy, which Tammi's sister Ludi would later claim was blown out of all proportion, concerns three tracks in particular, *Good Lovin' Ain't Easy To Come By*, *What You Gave Me* and *The Onion Song*. The last two of these tracks appeared on the final Marvin and Tammi album **Easy**, released in September 1969 and which barely made #184 on the album chart. *The Onion Song* would be released as a single in Britain first and would become the biggest hit the pairing ever enjoyed, gliding all the way to #9 on the chart. Its British success prompted a subsequent American release in November 1969, but for some reason it didn't set the pulses racing in the same way, finally coming to a halt at #18 R&B and #50 pop.

Tammi was to make one final appearance on the pop chart, *California Soul* hitting #56 following its release in March 1970. Tammi had made her final public appearance towards the end of 1969 at the Apollo Theater where Marvin was headlining, but soon after she was confined to a wheelchair on a permanent basis, suffered from blindness and hair loss and her weight had plummeted to just 93 pounds.

After one final operation on 25 January 1970, Tammi fell into a coma (her final words before succumbing were reportedly 'Take care of David [Ruffin]') and finally died on 16 March. The girl who seemed to have her whole career ahead of her and who was engaged to be married to doctor Ernest Garrett (who was a doctor at the hospital where Tammi had been treated) died six weeks short of her 25th birthday. A grief stricken Marvin read the eulogy at her funeral whilst *You're All I Need To Get By* played in the background, with the rest of his Motown colleagues effectively barred from the service on the instructions of Tammi's mother Jennie, still furious at what she believed was Motown's lack of assistance during her daughter's illness, for covering up her worsening condition and for releasing records without her permission. Motown would release another album, a greatest hits package appearing in May 1970 and which hit #171 pop and #17 R&B as well as making #60 in the UK.

ALBUMS: UNITED (1967), YOU'RE ALL I NEED (1968), IRRESISTIBLE (1969), EASY (1969)
COMPILATION: GREATEST HITS (1970)
FURTHER READING: MY SISTER TOMMIE – THE REAL TAMMI TERRELL (2005)

THANK GOD IT'S FRIDAY (1978 FILM)

The success of 'Saturday Night Fever' inspired a veritable rush of similar disco films, with Motown Productions linking with Casablanca FilmWorks for their contribution, 'Thank God It's Friday'. On paper at least, 'Thank God It's Friday' stood every chance of succeeding, with the involvement of Neil Bogart as executive producer (Neil was head of Casablanca, a record label that had cornered a considerable part of the disco market), an adventurous cast that included Donna Summer in her debut starring role, a cameo from The Commodores and early film appearances for Jeff Goldblum and Debra Winger and a musical score from Giorgio Moroder, with key songs from Paul Jabara.

All of the action takes place in Hollywood nightclub The Zoo (filmed at Osko's on La Cienega Boulevard, with the owner Osko Karaghassian given a role as a bouncer in the film) on a Friday evening, culminating in a dance contest. Accompanying the film was a three disc soundtrack album featuring tracks by Donna Summer, Love & Kisses, Pattie Brooks, Paul Jabara, Cameo, Wright Bros Flying Machine, Marathon, Sunshine, Santa Esmeralda, D.C. LaRue and Natural

Juices, all Casablanca recording artists, and The Commodores, Diana Ross and Thelma Houston from Motown.

The film proved less than popular, perhaps not helped by the radio-led disco backlash that was gathering pace in the US. The soundtrack, however, was successful, hitting #6 R&B and #10 pop and winning an Academy Award in the Best Song category for *Last Dance*, performed by Donna Summer. Unfortunately, it was Casablanca that held the rights to the soundtrack, even if The Commodores would score an R&B chart topper with their contribution *Too Hot Ta Trot*.

THAT GIRL – STEVIE WONDER [SINGLE]

The ink on the contract that allowed Motown to release something of a greatest hits package on Stevie Wonder, along with four new tracks, was barely dry when the first of the required tapes arrived at Motown's offices on Sunset Boulevard in December 1981. Inside was a brand new track in *That Girl*, a song Stevie had recorded at his own Wonderland Studios in Los Angeles and which featured him on vocals, drums, harmonica, Fender Rhodes, piano and synthesizers.

It was his first new recording in more than a year, since he had delivered the return to form album **Hotter Than July** in September 1980, and initial reaction to *That Girl* was that the creative juices were still flowing freely. Released in January 1982, *That Girl* was supposed to be a single supporting the greatest hits package **Original Musiquarium 1**, but Stevie continued working on the remaining three new tracks for so long *That Girl* ended up flying the flag on its own.

It still did the business, topping the R&B chart and hitting #4 pop (although in the UK it barely made the Top 40, peaking at #39) and, alongside *Do I Do* when it finally appeared on the album, would earn Stevie two nominations for the Best R&B Song Grammy Award. In the event neither entrant won on the evening, the award going to *Turn Turn Your Love Around*.

THAT'S THE WAY LOVE IS – MARVIN GAYE [SINGLE]

On the charts, the relationship between artist Marvin Gaye and producer Norman Whitfield was paying dividends as hit seemingly followed hit. In the studio, however, the atmosphere was notoriously tense.

"Norman and I came within a fraction of an inch of fighting. He thought I was a prick because I wasn't about to be intimidated by him. We clashed. He made me sing in keys much higher than I was used to. He had me reaching for notes that caused my throat veins to bulge."

Yet that was exactly how Norman Whitfield conducted all his sessions, pushing whichever singer happened to be in the booth to the very limits of their capabilities and patience, just to ensure he got a real and emotional performance out of them. He had treated Gladys Knight, David Ruffin and Eddie Kendricks like that in the past and he wasn't about to change his style for Marvin Gaye now or in the future.

Yet they managed to declare an uneasy truce, and in so doing the hits continued to flow out of Hitsville. *That's The Way Love Is* had originally been recorded and issued as a single by The Isley Brothers in 1967 and failed to make much of an impact, reaching a lowly #125. A year later it was recorded by Gladys Knight & The Pips as an album track, appearing on **Feelin' Bluesy**, with Marvin entering the studio to record his version before the year was out.

The third time around, Norman borrowed much of the overall feel of *I Heard It Through The Grapevine*, making Marvin's version of *That's The Way Love Is* virtually unrecognisable from The Isley Brothers original. Initially featured as a cut on the **MPG** album, the track was released as a single in August 1969 and continued Marvin's rich vein of success, hitting #2 R&B and #7 pop. So successful, in fact, that the single became the lead track on a subsequent album as Motown tried to plug the gap between new Marvin Gaye recordings with repackages of old ones.

THEE IMAGE

Former Blues Image, Iron Butterfly and Cactus guitarist and singer Mike Pinera (born in Tampa, Florida on 29 September 1948) formed Thee Image in 1974 with Duane Hitchings (keyboards, bass and vocals) and Donny Vosburgh (drums), taking the group name from the Miami concert venue that Blues Image had co-founded. The trio recorded two albums for Manticore (something of a boutique label for British rock band Emerson Lake & Palmer), with the eponymous debut being released in the US in February 1975 and **Inside the Triangle** appearing in November the same year.

Despite the two albums and three singles, Thee Image failed to make a lasting impression and disbanded in early 1976. Mike Pinera later recorded solo whilst

Duane Hitchings became a successful session musician and songwriter, including co-penning *Don't Look Any Further*, a major hit for Dennis Edwards.
ALBUMS: THEE IMAGE (1975), INSIDE THE TRIANGLE (1975)

THEME FROM MAHOGANY (DO YOU KNOW WHERE YOU'RE GOING TO) – DIANA ROSS [SINGLE]

Whilst the reviews for 'Mahogany' had been disappointing, the film itself was something of a success, grossing some $7 million during the course of its North American run. Added to this was the relative success of the film's music, which saw the soundtrack album hit the Top Twenty (it would peak at #19 on the pop chart and #15 R&B), although 'Mahogany' would always have to stand comparison with Diana's earlier film vehicle, 'Lady Sings The Blues'.

There was one area where 'Mahogany' scored over its predecessor, however, and that was the major success of the film's title song. Michael Masser had worked with Diana Ross on the singles *Touch Me In The Morning* and *Last Time I Saw Him* before moving on to other projects within Motown, including a planned track for Thelma. Then he was switched over to the soundtrack for 'Mahogany', much of which was incidental music to accompany the action, although there was an opening for a theme song.

For this Michael requisitioned the tune he had originally intended for Thelma Houston, with friend and songwriting legend Gerry Goffin contributing to some of the lyrics in order to make them more relevant to the film. Michael produced two separate mixes of the track, something of a power ballad with a message, but before submitting them to Motown took the precaution of erasing the one he didn't like so as to ensure the one he did favour was the one that got released!

Issued in September 1975 in the US, the single did little on its initial release, leading many to conclude that it had flopped. It fared no better when released in the UK in October, and when the film was almost universally panned upon its release the same month, *Do You Know Where You're Going To* appeared to have sunk without trace. Whilst the reviews might have been derisory, public reaction was altogether different, with the film playing to sell out theatres across America, which in turn led to renewed interest in both the soundtrack album and theme.

Word of mouth alone turned the single around, and by the end of January 1976, it had replaced Barry Manilow's *I Write The Songs* at the top of the Billboard Hot 100 (although it barely made #14 on the R&B listings). This American success resulted in a change in fortunes in the UK, with radio stations beginning to give their support behind *Do You Know Where I'm Coming From*, despite the sudden arrival of Diana's upbeat single *Love Hangover*. The theme from 'Mahogany' crashed into the chart on 3 April and a week later reached the Top Ten, hitting its peak of #5 in the very week *Love Hangover* joined it on the chart. After initially looking likely to miss the charts both sides of the Atlantic altogether, *Do You Know Where You're Going To* became one of the biggest singles of Diana's career, even collecting a nomination for an Academy Award for Best Film Song, although it was apparently overlooked initially on the grounds 'the song wasn't acceptable because of quality standards.'

"Needless to say, Berry went through the roof, and I followed him not long after" said Motown executive Michael Roshkind. "So Berry huddled with the Academy directors, and laid out his objections to their position. And the Academy, somewhat to our surprise, agreed almost immediately."

The directors put forward a proposal to change the rules for the following year's balloting, so as to amend the obstacles Berry had encountered.

"Berry wasn't satisfied, though. This was the year 'Mahogany' was out, not next year."

Berry again lobbied the Academy and succeeded in getting the voting amendments changed in time for the 'Mahogany' theme to be included in that year's nominations. Diana performed the song live at the ceremony via a satellite link from Holland but still lost out to *I'm Easy* from 'Nashville'.

THERE'S A GHOST IN MY HOUSE – R. DEAN TAYLOR [SINGLE]

Brought to Motown in 1963, R. Dean Taylor was a frustrated performer who spent much of his time helping Brian and Eddie Holland and Lamont Dozier with their compositions, although much of the time Taylor's contribution was uncredited. Having seen his first solo recording in 1964 unreleased, it was eighteen months later that he finally got a single on the release schedule, even if *Let's Go Somewhere* failed to register on the V.I.P. label.

Two years later he got another chance, with a song he and HDH had been working on, originally titled 'The End Was Destined To Come' and intended for The Four Tops was re-worked into *There's A Ghost In My House* (The Four Tops' meanwhile were busy recording *7 Rooms Of Gloom*, a song very much similar in style and feel to *Ghost*), which was recorded in October 1966 and issued in March 1967, again on the V.I.P. label.

This too failed to make its mark, missing the chart in the US and not even being afforded a release in the UK, at least as a single. *There's A Ghost In My House* got its first British release in 1973, appearing on the budget album **Gotta See Jane/Indiana Wants Me** that was issued on the Sounds Superb label, something of a compilation album that drew its title from the two hits R. Dean Taylor had previously enjoyed in the UK (in 1968 and 1971 respectively). Copies of the album were picked up by several enterprising Northern Soul DJ's, with Russ Winstanley of the Wigan Casino earmarking the third track on side one as worthy of extended plays at the club (although the track was misspelt as *Ther's A Ghost In My House*).

Spotting the growing popularity of *There's A Ghost In My House*, Tamla Motown finally issued it as a single in May 1974 and saw it forge its way up the chart, finally hitting #3 in June 1974, going on to sell over 250,000 copies and earn a silver disc award from the BPI. By the time *Ghost* belatedly became a hit, R. Dean Taylor had already departed Motown, with his subsequent hit *Window Shopping* appearing on the Polydor label. In 1987 British group The Fall took a rock version to #30 on the UK chart.

THIRD ALBUM – THE JACKSON 5 [ALBUM]

Hardly the most imaginative of album titles, **Third Album** would go on to become the group's most successful album during their time with Motown, with sales exceeding the six million mark. It helped that the group's hit singles had turned them into a teen sensation, regularly trading pop blows with the likes of The Osmonds, but whilst The Osmonds may have been selling vast quantities of their singles, their albums had not yet taken off to the same degree The Jackson 5 were enjoying.

Produced by The Corporation and Hal Davis, **Third Album** would play host to the massive hit singles *I'll Be There* (a chart topper) and *Mama's Pearl* (a #2 hit) and sail to #4 pop as well as the summit of the R&B chart. However, although both singles did well internationally **Third Album** failed to make an impact in the UK, missing the chart altogether. Indeed, despite continued success domestically, The Jackson 5 would not return to the UK's album chart until a greatest hits package was released in 1971.

THIRD CREATION

An obscure female vocal group fronted by Ivory Davis, Third Creation recorded the original version of *Rolling Down The Mountainside*, written by Leon Ware and Jackie Hilliard. The single was arranged and produced by Mark Davis (Ivory's then husband), scheduled for release on Tamla and then switched to Motown, where it was issued in July 1973. The single did little, but the song was recorded by Isaac Hayes later the same year and released as the flip side to *(If Loving You Is Wrong) I Don't Want To Be Right*. Main Ingredient's 1975 version retained much of the arrangement and feel of Third Creation's original and became a deserved hit.

Third Creation meanwhile released one further single, *Where Do I Belong* being similarly issued without fanfare in October 1974. Ivory Davis later became a member of Quiet Storm, Smokey Robinson's backing group.

THIS OLD HEART OF MINE (IS WEAK FOR YOU) – THE ISLEY BROTHERS [SINGLE]

Berry Gordy succeeded in luring The Isley Brothers to Motown in 1965 and handed them over to Brian and Eddie Holland and Lamont Dozier in order to get the group off the mark right from the start. Yet it was not all plain sailing, with The Isley Brothers spending a considerable time begging HDH for material to record, having to join a lengthy queue of artists who were also relying on them for hit material.

HDH had one song (which also had contributions from lyricist Sylvia Moy), a tune that had started life as 'Don't Throw My Love Away' and originally intended for Kim Weston. It subsequently became *This Old Heart Of Mine*, with The Four Tops slated for the session once they finished their then current touring schedule. The backing tracks had already been recorded, but HDH eventually allocated the song to The Isley Brothers, ostensibly to stop the group from continually hassling them for material!

The only problem was that the backing track had been recorded in a key above that which Ronald Isley would normally sing with comfort, requiring some extra exertion on his part (several artists would later claim that Motown often pitched backing tracks intentionally high, forcing the vocalists to stretch themselves vocally). The pitching and Ronald's vocal had the desired effect, however, resulting in *This Old Heart Of Mine* sounding like it had been written specifically for The Isley's rather than The Four Tops.

Released in late January 1966 with a Brian Holland mix, the initial pressings were replaced a couple of weeks later by a mix from Lawrence Horn, the new version being a much more radio friendly version than the original. *This Old Heart Of Mine* did get The Isley Brothers' Motown career off to a winning start, hitting #6 R&B and #12 pop, also spending a solitary week at #47 in the UK.

Two years later, after The Isley Brothers had refused to renew their Motown contract and departed the label, the group enjoyed something of a resurgence of interest in Britain, resulting in a re-promoted *This Old Heart Of Mine* surging up the chart and coming to rest at #3 in November 1968.

The following month Motown in the US released Tammi Terrell's take on the song, a single that was her final solo single and hit, peaking at #67 pop and #31 R&B. *This Old Heart Of Mine* has also made numerous returns to the British chart, with Rod Stewart enjoying a #4 hit in 1975 with a cover version (it was the debut release on Riva, the label formed by Rod's manager Billy Gaff) and re-recording the song with Ronald Isley (who got dual billing) in 1989 that hit #51.

GEORGE THOROGOOD & THE DESTROYERS

Guitarist and singer George Thorogood was born in Wilmington, Deleware on 24 December 1952 and formed The Destroyers in 1973 with Michael Lenn (bass) and Jeff Simon (drums), with Ron 'Roadblock' Smith (guitar) an infrequent member. The group contributed to the 1983 soundtrack 'Christine', with *Bad To The Bone*, the title track to their best known album.

THREE BROTHERS RECORDS

A subsidiary of Creed Taylor's CTI record company, Three Brothers was set up to release popular material, but issued only one album and a handful of singles by Lou Christie and a single by The Clams during its brief life.

The only other artist that appears to have been signed to Three Brothers was Cassandra Morgan, whose only outing *Isn't It Hard To Tell The Truth* was also only released as a promotional single, although she did record an unreleased album for the label.

THREE DOG NIGHT

Taking their name from an Aborigine term relating to how cold it was, with a 'three dog night' the coldest, rock group Three Dog Night was formed in Los Angeles, California in 1968 by Danny Hutton (born in Buncrana, Ireland on 10 September 1946, vocals), Cory Wells (born in New York on 5 February 1944, vocals), Chuck Negron (born in New York on 8 June 1942, vocals), Jimmy Greenspoon (born in Los Angeles on 7 February 1948, organ), Floyd Sneed (born in Calgary, Canada on 22 November 1943, drums), Mike Allsup (born in Modesto, California on 8 March 1947, guitar) and Joe Schermie (born in Madison, Wisconsin on 12 February 1945, bass). The group's 1971 chart topper *Joy To The World* was featured on the soundtrack to 'The Big Chill' in 1983. Schermie died from a heart attack on 25 March 2002.

THREE OUNCES OF LOVE

Detroit born sisters Ann, Elaine and Regina Alexander formed Three Ounces Of Love and first recorded for the Pameline label in the early 1970s. They caused something of a local stir with *Disco Man* on IX Chain Records in 1976, eventually leading to a Motown contract in 1977.

They were also assigned Benny Ashburn as manager, whose involvement with The Commodores ensured Three Ounces Of Love were at least considered something of a priority, with Brian Holland producing several of their tracks. In the event they were to release one eponymous album, issued on the Motown label in April 1978. Two singles were lifted from the album, *Star Love* (which would be their only hit, peaking at #87 on the R&B chart) and *Give Me Some Feeling*, following which the group was dropped from the roster.

After a lengthy hiatus, Three Ounces Of Love returned to the recording studio at the beginning of the 1990s for Ian Levine's Motorcity label.

ALBUM: THREE OUNCES OF LOVE (1978)

THREE TIMES A LADY – THE COMMODORES [SINGLE]

Alberta and Lionel Brockman Richie were celebrating their 37th wedding anniversary, with all of their family in attendance. During the course of the celebrations, Lionel Senior stood to give a speech, during which he reminded those assembled that during all of their time together, through the ups and downs, he had never really taken the time to say thank you to his wife.

That sentiment touched a nerve with Lionel Junior, who was duly inspired to write *Three Times A Lady* in the aftermath and submit the song for consideration when he and the rest of The Commodores gathered to consider material for the **Natural High** album. Whilst it was a definite choice for inclusion on the album, its release as a single was not quite so straightforward, as Lionel would later explain.

"Right in the middle of disco, we came out with *Three Times A Lady*, which people wondered about. The time to make a statement is when everyone is looking at you. I've seen some artists try to make a statement when their careers were over. As a group, we've never been satisfied in one category and being on one level."

Indeed, having made their name with explosive funk cuts like *Machine Gun* and *Slippery When Wet*, the group had begun to make significant strides with their ballad material, much of which was written by Lionel. As sure-fire a smash as anything they released, it powered to the top of the R&B and pop chart, spending two weeks at the top of both.

In order to generate extra sales in the UK for the album, *Three Times A Lady* was released as the second single, a move which might have resulted in a few extra sales but did not ultimately harm *Three Times A Lady*, which eventually hit #1 in August 1978 and stayed there for five weeks. The song was nominated for the Grammy Award for Song of the Year but lost out to another ballad in Billy Joel's *Just The Way You Are* – so much for disco that year!

TIGGI CLAY

New Wave trio Tiggi Clay was formed in the early 1980s by Debravon Lewis (born in Solano County, California on 9 February 1953), Hilary Leon Thompson and DeWayne Sweet, with the three adopting the stage names Fizzy Qwick, Billy Peaches and Romeo 'Breath' McCall.

They signed with Motown's rock label Morocco in 1983 and released their self-written and produced debut album the following year, with the cover showing the three in silhouette so as to hide the real identities. Neither the album nor its only single, *Flashes* made an impact and Motown shut down the Morocco label soon after.

Fizzy Qwick resurfaced two years later with a solo project that resulted in an album, **Fizzy Qwick** and two singles in *Hangin' Out* and *You Want It Your Way*, *Always*, all of which were written and produced by her previous partners in Tiggi Clay.

ALBUM: TIGGI CLAY (1984)

TOE FAT

Another of the acts signed by EMI in the UK that became part of an arrangement deal with Motown, with their material being issued on the Rare Earth label in the US. Toe Fat were formed in 1969 shortly after former Rebel Rouser singer Cliff Bennett (born in Slough, Berkshire on 4 June 1940) dissolved his own band and invited Ken Hensley (born in London on 24 August 1945, guitar and keyboards), John Konas (bass) and Lee Kerslake (born in Bournemouth, Dorset on 16 April 1947, drums) on board, with the group coming up with the name Toe Fat over a dinner as the most distasteful name they could think of!

Signed to the Parlophone label in the UK, their eponymous debut album appeared on Rare Earth in July 1970. Hensley and Kerslake left soon after (and would subsequently emerge in Uriah Heep) to be replaced by Alan Kendall and Brian Glasscock respectively, with John Glasscock replacing Konas by the time the group recorded their second album **Two**, which was released in March 1971.

With neither Regal Zonophone (the UK label that issued the second album) nor Rare Earth prepared to further fund the group they disbanded soon after a US tour in support of their second album.

ALBUMS: TOE FAT (1970), TOE FAT TWO (1971)

TONY & CAROLYN

Tony and Carolyn Rinaldi shared many similarities with The Carpenters, although they were husband and wife rather than brother and sister. The pair had first met in Atlanta when they were both appearing on a cabaret show for Irwin 'Sonny' Block, subsequently getting married whilst Tony undertook basic army training in South Carolina.

Eventually they broke away from Block and developed their own stage act, subsequently getting spotted by Barney Ales, who got them a single deal with Motown's V.I.P. label. Having featured several Carpenters songs in their stage repertoire, it was only fitting that the top side to their only single should be a medley of *We've Only Just Begun* and *I'll Be There*, the latter of course a huge hit for The Jackson 5 (and thus

Motown's way of ensuring at least some of the royalties should the single take off!).

Released in November 1971 the single failed to score, with the result several other tracks they recorded during their brief time at Hitsville remain unreleased. Tony and Carolyn continued to perform together for a further couple of years before their professional and personal relationship came to an end.

TOO BUSY THINKING ABOUT MY BABY – MARVIN GAYE [SINGLE]

When *I Heard It Through The Grapevine* finally became the monster hit Norman Whitfield knew it to be, attention quickly turned to what would be the follow-up. Rather than come up with something similar, Norman went back into his ever-expanding songbook and plucked out an oldie. In fact, he went right back to 1964 for a song he had originally written as *Stop Leading Me On (I Know How To Love Her)* with Janie Bradford and Barrett Strong for Jimmy Ruffin (this version can be found on the first volume of **Cellarful Of Motown**), with two different sets of lyrics.

It was subsequently recorded by The Temptations in 1966 as *Too Busy Thinking About My Baby* and appeared on their **Gettin' Ready** album. Marvin's version was recorded at the beginning of 1969, with additional overdubs and mixing being completed barely three weeks before the single was finally released on 2 April 1969.

The flip side had an even older heritage, *Where I Lay My Hat (That's My Home)* being recorded in 1962 and appeared on the **That Stubborn Kinda' Fellow** album. *Too Busy Thinking About My Baby* may not have quite matched the success of *Grapevine*, but it still managed to top the R&B chart and hit #4 pop as well as reaching #5 in the UK.

Too Busy Thinking About My Baby would make two return appearances on the British chart; in 1972 New York based rock and roll group Mardi Gras took it to #19 whilst in 2001 British pop group Steps took it all the way to #2. Even the flip side served well, with Paul Young slowing the tempo right down and hitting the very top of the UK chart in 1983 with a blue-eyed soul version.

TOUCH ME IN THE MORNING – DIANA ROSS [SINGLE]

It was three years between 'Lady Sings The Blues' and 'Mahogany', a period Diana Ross would later dismiss with the statement 'I continued to do concerts and release albums between my films' in her own autobiography. If she was a reluctant singer on record, then it had much to do with her belief that the success of 'Lady Sings The Blues' had turned her into a serious actress and what she should have been pursuing post 1972 were more film vehicles rather than maintaining a recording career.

Yet on the evidence of those post 1972 recordings, Diana's popularity increased because of her records; the films were merely a bonus. Nowhere is this more evident than on *Touch Me In The Morning*, a song Diana did not want to record at all, only relenting after Berry Gordy had persisted with the claim that it would be a smash hit. The song had been started by Motown's in-house writer Ron Miller, who had title and a clear vision as to the line the song should take.

"I didn't have the vaguest idea what it meant. It was just this great song title without a great song. So, I analyzed Diana as person and realised that she was a contemporary woman who was probably liberal about expressing her sexual values, like most 'Cosmo' women in 1970s society. Once upon a time, it was the man who might give a woman the brush-off after a one-nighter telling her 'nothing good's gonna last forever', now it could be the other way round."

Whilst Ron envisioned the song as a somewhat risqué interpretation of a one night stand from a female point of view, the end message was somewhat toned down.

This was largely due to the song being rounded out by Michael Masser, a former lawyer and stockbroker who had joined the staff at Jobete. Finally convinced to record the track, Diana turned up at the studio in the early hours of the morning (all of her recordings during this period were so recorded in order that Diana could put her children to bed and be there when they awoke in the morning), where Gene Page and Tom Baird had worked out the arrangements and Michael and Tom would produce (although Ron Miller was possibly in the studio as it was later reported that Diana had complained about the key of the song), with Sherlie Matthews, Clydie King and Venetta Fields (otherwise known as The Blackberries) providing backing vocals.

Just as Berry Gordy had predicted, the single became a smash following its release in May 1973, becoming her second pop chart topper since launching her solo career and a #5 hit on the R&B chart.

In the UK, where the single was released in July, the promotion benefitted from Diana's appearance in the country on tour and would hit #9, her first Top Ten hit since *I'm Still Waiting* had topped the chart in 1971. The single would go on to be nominated for the

Grammy Award for Best Female Pop Vocal Performance, ultimately won by Roberta Flack and *Killing Me Softly With His Song*.

TOUCH ME IN THE MORNING - DIANA ROSS [ALBUM]

In 1972 Diana Ross began work on what was planned to be her fourth solo album since departing The Supremes two years previously. As a celebration of her then pregnancy with her daughter Tracee Joy (her child by her then husband Robert Silverstein), the album was intended to have songs appropriate to motherhood, with *Little Girl Blue, My Baby (My Baby My Own)* and a medley of *Brown Baby* and *Save The Children*. Other tracks recorded for this project included *Got To Be There, Young Mothers, The First Time Ever I Saw Your Face* and *Turn Around,* with the album slated to be called **To The Baby**.

The themed album was subsequently scrapped, although three of the tracks survived the cull and found their way onto the renamed **Touch Me In The Morning**, the album gaining its title from the single lifted in May 1973 and which became a #1 hit on the pop chart. Similar in style was *All Of My Life,* penned by Michael Randall, whilst the album was also notable for featuring the very first track that Diana produced herself, the *Brown Baby/Save The Children* medley. Although the title track was the only track released as a single stateside, its success in topping the chart helped sales of the album, which would go on to become a hit in its own right, topping the R&B chart and hitting #5 pop. In the UK the subsequent success of *All Of My Life* also aided the album, which would peak at #7.

THE TRACKS OF MY TEARS – SMOKEY ROBINSON & THE MIRACLES [SINGLE]

Perhaps *the* song with which Smokey Robinson earned the accolade of one of the finest lyricists of all time, *The Tracks Of My Tears* is one of The Miracles' best known songs, even though it was not their biggest hit. The roots of the song began with Miracles' guitarist Marv Tarplin, who was at home tinkering on his guitar. "I got the original idea from the *Banana Boat Song*, sung by Harry Belafonte. I was strumming around with the guitar, playing to Harry's record. I didn't realise the record was playing at the wrong speed...and the riff came to me."

Marv took the riff to Smokey Robinson, reportedly the first tune he had handed over, but it took Smokey some time to come up with the lyrics to fit.

"I had it for about two weeks, and the first thing that I was thinking about on it was the music, which is the chorus. Finally, I came up with this thing one day, 'Take a good look at my face, if you look closer it's easy to trace.' And then I didn't know what 'trace' was! It took me about two more days to think about somebody crying enough so that their tears left tracks in their face – if you look close enough to them, you can see these little ridges, these little tracks that have been left by these tears."

The recording sessions were equally stretched out, with the initial sessions taking place in January 1965, strings being added at the end of the same month and the final sessions being held in mid May. The single was finally released in June 1965 and would become a #2 R&B and #16 pop hit in the US, although the song's status belies the relatively lowly chart placings.

In the UK the single was issued in July 1965 and failed to reach the chart, although it did make a significant impression; Pete Townshend was so inspired by Smokey's delivery of the word 'substitute' in the song he wrote what would become The Who's fourth consecutive Top Ten hit.

Two years after its initial release, *Tracks Of My Tears* was covered by Johnny Rivers, with the rock and roll singer enjoying a major hit as it peaked at #10 in the US. In 1969, Tamla Motown in the UK revived several old singles for a renewed assault on the charts, with *The Tracks Of My Tears* being coupled with a Northern Soul favourite in *Come On Do The Jerk* for release in April 1969. This time around it became the hit it thoroughly deserved to be, peaking at #9 on the 'Record Retailer' chart.

Over the ensuing years, *The Tracks Of My Tears* would become a much covered song, being taken back into the charts by Linda Ronstadt in 1976, who scored a #25 US and #42 UK hit, Colin Blunstone in 1982 (#60) and Go West in 1993 (#16). *The Tracks Of My Tears* has also been covered by Aretha Franklin, Gladys Knight & The Pips and Dean Martin, among others.

Its importance to Smokey Robinson & The Miracles, however, is without question, for it was the success of the revived single in the UK that sent Tamla Motown off in search of a suitable follow-up, finally selecting *Tears Of A Clown*.

TONY TRAVALINI

Singer and songwriter Tony Travalini had one Motown outing, linking with famed writer/producer Teddy Randazzo for *This Is It (This Is Love)* which appeared on the soundtrack to 'It's My Turn' in 1980. Tony later worked with another noted producer in Tony Camillo, performing several tracks with Janice Jarreau on the soundtrack to 'Stitches' in 1985.

TRI-PHI RECORDS

The second of the two label imprints formed by Harvey Fuqua following his arrival in Detroit, Tri-Phi proved to be infinitely more successful than his other label Harvey, but success came with a high price tag. With a roster that included The Spinners, Shorty Long, Johnny (Bristol) and Jackey (Beavers), Merced Blue Notes, The Ervin Sisters, The Challengers, Lorri Rudolph (who also recorded for Harvey with Joe Charles), The Davenport Sisters and Harvey Fuqua himself, Tri-Phi was the only label of the two to register meaningful sales.

However, the success of these singles overstretched Harvey financially, with the result that he was unable to fully capitalise on any success. A total of 24 singles were released between May 1961 and May 1963 before the label was closed, with several of the artists (most notably The Spinners, Shortly Long and Johnny Bristol) following their mentor in to Motown.

JAMAL TRICE

Jamal Trice may not have made much of an impact at Motown, but the quality of his demos was sufficient to get both him and producer Kent Washburn contracts with the company. Kent was working in his studio in St Louis in early 1976 when Jamal first contacted him, asking if Kent would produce a couple of tracks that Jamal could take to Motown with a view to getting a deal.

Jamal paid for the session and took the demos to Los Angeles where he got to play them to Berry Gordy's sister Gwen, who had a production deal with Motown. Suitably impressed Gwen located Kent and invited him down to California to record further tracks on Jamal, although only two of these would ever be released, *If Love Is Not The Answer* backed with *Nothing Is Too Good (For You Baby)* being issued on the Soul label in November 1976.

With the single barely causing a stir, Motown decided to drop Jamal from the roster, although the backing tracks to several of the cuts Kent recorded would later resurface on Major Lance's Motown album. Jamal was reportedly killed in a car accident on his way to Las Vegas in the early 1980s, although there were posthumous singles released on Kon-Kord (*Don't Let Nobody Make A Fool Of You*) and Sabre (*Treat You Right*), again without success.

TROUBLE MAN – MARVIN GAYE [SINGLE]

At the start of the 1970s, a whole new film genre sprung to prominence; blaxploitation. Aimed primarily at black audiences with black casts and for the most part black crews, blaxploitation films had exploded on to the market with 'Shaft' and 'Superfly'. Whilst both films had been commercial successes, proof that the black market could be drawn to the cinema to see their own breed of heroes, it was the soundtracks by Isaac Hayes and Curtis Mayfield respectively that had garnered the most attention. Following the success of these films virtually every major studio green lit its own blaxploitation title, with 20th Century Fox entry being 'Trouble Man'.

Marvin Gaye was at this time hot with his hugely successful **What's Going On** album, a fact duly noted by film producers John DF Black and Joel D Freeman. Offered the opportunity to score the film, Marvin jumped at the chance, opting to write much of the material from the viewpoint of the film's hero, Mister T.

As with many entries to the blaxploitation genre, the music was infinitely better than the film, testament to the excellent score Marvin Gaye wrote and produced. Only one track, the main theme was released as a single, but as with much else that Marvin touched at the time, it still scored big.

Issued in November 1972, a month ahead of the album, the single would become another major chart success, hitting #7 pop and #4 R&B. The theme also proved popular enough for Marvin to feature it regularly in his live set for a good many years after, proof of its endearing qualities. The album also sold well, enough to take it to #14 on the Billboard Top 200 and #3 on the R&B listings.

TRULY – LIONEL RICHIE [SINGLE]

The first single lifted from Lionel Richie's eponymous debut solo album, *Truly* continued in the same vein as his most recent compositions for The Commodores. The undoubted master of the ballad genre from the mid 1970s onwards, his writing was of such quality he would continue to set the bench mark for much of the following decade too.

Released in September 1982 at much the same time the album shipped, *Truly* would become a major hit single, topping the pop and Adult Contemporary charts, peaking at #2 R&B and also cracking the UK Top Ten, where it reached #6. The single would earn a gold disc for American sales (in excess of a million copies) and a silver for UK sales (in excess of 250,000 copies), as well as winning the Grammy Award for Best Male Pop Vocal Performance. Lionel Richie's solo career was off to a flyer, just as many had predicted.

The song meanwhile has attracted several cover versions, with British actor Steven Houghton featuring the song in the television series 'London's Burning' and then enjoying a #23 hit when it was released as a single in 1998.

RICK TUCKER

Rhythm guitarist and singer Rick Tucker was already a twenty year music veteran when he landed a brief recording deal with Motown. His professional career had commenced in 1956 with a recording session at Norman Petty's studio in Clovis in New Mexico, with Roy Orbison and his band backing Rick on the tracks *Patty Baby* and *Don't Do Me This Way* (many years later Rick learned that a couple of days after the initial recording session, Buddy Holly was one of several singers utilised on overdubbed backing vocals). These early tracks were in the then growing in popularity rock and roll idiom, although Rick would later switch to country and western, the style he was pursuing when he joined Hitsville in 1976.

His only single for the label, *I Heard A Song* backed with *Plans That We Made* was released in June 1976, although a lack of airplay meant there was to be no follow-up. Along with most of the other Hitsville artists, Rick was switched to the MC imprint in 1977, where he would record an album with fellow labelmate Lloyd Schoonmaker, with their eponymous effort being scheduled for release in November 1977; promotional copies were produced but it is not known if commercial copies ever made it to market. Rick continues to work professionally from his hometown base in El Paso, Texas.

ALBUM: TUCKER AND SCHOONMAKER (1977)

SAMMY TURNER

An accounting clerk by day and club singer by night, Sammy Turner was discovered by agent Herb Lutz, fortunately whilst he was moonlighting at night! Born Samuel Black in Paterson, New Jersey on 2 June 1932, Sammy served in the US Air Force before undertaking his dual role in the late 1950s. Lutz got him a deal with Big Top Records, where he was initially used to front The Twisters, scoring a minor hit with *Sweet Annie Laurie* in 1959.

He then launched a solo career and was handed over to Jerry Leiber and Mike Stoller, featuring at the top end of the charts with *Lavender Blue* (an old Sammy Kaye number that Sammy Turner took to #3 pop and #14 R&B) and *Always* (most notably recorded by Vince Lopez and Guy Lombardo that reached #19 pop and #2 R&B as well as #26 in the UK). After two further small hits, Sammy found his career in freefall, although in 1963 he turned up at Jobete's New York office and was signed to a contract.

It proved to be an extremely short contract, for only one single *Only You*, produced by George Kerr and Sidney Barnes and an update of The Platters' hit, appeared on the Motown label in February 1964. It is believed Sammy recorded several other tracks in Detroit, but some of these would turn up on 20th Century rather than Motown. He later recorded for Verve but was unable to revive his career.

STANLEY TURRENTINE

A legendary tenor saxophonist, Stanley William Turrentine was born in Pittsburgh on 5 April 1934 into a musical family (his father was a saxophonist with Al Cooper's Savoy Sultans, his mother played piano and his brother Tommy would later become a professional trumpet player). Despite this abundance of music around him, the only formal training Stanley received was during his military service in the 1950s. He had already proved his worth playing with the likes of Lowell Fulson and Earl Bostic and upon leaving the military enrolled into Max Roach' band.

He left Roach in 1960, newly married to organist Shirley Scott, and pursued a solo career with Blue Note Records, also making a number of recordings with Jimmy Smith. In 1970 he split from both his wife and Blue Note, signing with CTI and scoring a major hit with **Sugar**, a #3 jazz, #29 R&B and #162 pop success.

By the time CTI signed a distribution deal with Motown, Stanley Turrentine was virtually out of the door, signing with Fantasy Records in 1974, but CTI still had enough material in the can to continue releasing records for a while yet, including the compilation album **The Baddest Turrentine** (a #11 jazz and #18 R&B hit) and the 1975 issue **The Sugar Man**, comprising material originally recorded in 1971, which would make #8 jazz, #21 R&B and #110 pop. There were also two live albums recorded with Freddie Hubbard, with **In Concert** hitting #12 on the jazz chart, **Volume** 2 #28.

Stanley left Fantasy, where he had enjoyed some success with jazz funk recordings, at the end of the decade and recorded for a number of other labels, most notably Elektra and Concord. His one regret throughout his career was the way he had been unfairly categorised.

"One day, my stepson and I were alphabetising my albums over the years, and I noticed that they categorised me as a rock and roll player on certain albums, a be-bop player on other albums, a pop player, a fusion player. And I'm just saying, I'm just playing with different settings, but I'm still playing the same way."

Stanley continued playing that same way throughout his entire career, suffering a massive stroke just a few hours before he was due to end a week long engagement at the Blue Note jazz club in New York City. He died two days later on 12 September 2000.

ALBUMS: FREDDIE HUBBARD & STANLEY TURRENTINE IN CONCERT VOLUME ONE (1974), IN CONCERT VOLUME TWO (1975), THE BADDEST TURRENTINE (1975), THE SUGAR MAN (1975)

21ST CREATION

A vocal group formed in Chicago as 21st Century they recorded for RCA and scored two minor hits in 1975 with *Remember The Rain?* and *Child*. Fred Williams, Alphonso Smith, Pierre Johnson, Tyrone Moores and Alonzo Martin switched to the Gordy label in 1977 and changed name to 21st Creation, releasing an album **Break Thru** and two singles in *Tailgate* and *Girls Let's Keep Dancing Close*, with the album and *Tailgate* single also being released in the UK, without success. A second, eponymous album was scrapped after which the group disbanded.

ALBUM: BREAK THRU (1978)

25 MILES – EDWIN STARR [SINGLE]

Always a dynamic live performer, Edwin Starr had featured *25 Miles* as the closing number to his show for some five years before getting around to record it. "I wrote that five years before it was ever released. I used to perform at Mickey's Hideaway in Lansing, Michigan, a college student-type club owned by my friend Mickey Shapiro, and I needed a closing number. I knew how powerful it was. It just got bigger and bigger and bigger every time. I wanted to record it but Motown turned it down, saying it was too rock and roll; it had no crossover potential."

Then in July 1968 he was invited to appear on the local television show '20 Grand Live' where he performed the song to a rapturous reception. It was not only in the studio that the audience took to the number, for at Hitsville the phones were ringing off the hook with people demanding to know who was singing and where to get the record. Barney Ales saw the potential and ordered Edwin into the studio to get a version down on tape, with Edwin being joined by The Originals (and possibly members of The Spinners) on backing vocals.

In the studio producers Johnny Bristol and Harvey Fuqua fleshed out the song (although in later years *25 Miles'* similarity to *Mojo Mama* by Wilson Pickett would result in Jerry Wexler and Bert Berns also being added to the list of composers), with the track subsequently being issued as a single in January 1969.

The demand since his appearance on '20 Grand Live' was enough to carry it into the chart, after which it surged to reach #6 pop and R&B. In the UK, where Edwin was confirming his status as one of the leading exponents of Northern Soul by undertaking his ninth tour, the single reached #36, his fourth Top 40 hit in the territory. *25 Miles* would go on to become the title of his second Motown album and, some twenty years later, would be heavily sampled on The Cookie Crew's *Got To Keep On*, a #17 UK hit in 1989. Edwin lent the project some additional credibility by appearing in the accompanying promotional video.

20 GOLDEN GREATS - DIANA ROSS [ALBUM]

After the success of the **20 Golden Greats** compilation album by Diana Ross & The Supremes, a UK chart topper following its release in 1977, Motown's European licensors requested permission to turn their attentions to Diana's solo recordings. Thus **Twenty Golden Greats** was released in the UK in November 1979 (it appears to have been issued in Portugal some time during 1978 with the same cover and tracklisting), specifically released so as to capitalise on the Christmas market, and benefitting from an extensive television advertising campaign.

In order to get to the necessary twenty tracks the running times of some of the original material was edited, but all the major hits were present, including her #1 hit single *I'm Still Waiting* and two of her duets with Marvin Gaye, *Stop Look Listen* and *You Are Everything*. The album would earn a platinum disc for sales in excess of 300,000 copies and peak at #2 on the chart, kept off the top by Abba's **Greatest Hits Volume 2**.

THE TWISTIN' KINGS

The Funk Brothers under a different name, recording an album intended to capitalize on the twist craze that was sweeping the country in 1961. The vocalists are unidentified, but the titles of the album **Twistin' The World Around** and the singles *Xmas Twist* and *Congo Twist* should give you an idea of where the music was aimed. The Funk Brothers had previously recorded and released a single as The Swinging Tigers; they never released a thing as The Funk Brothers.
ALBUM: TWISTIN' THE WORLD AROUND (1961)

TWO FRIENDS

The two friends in question were Chip Carpenter (rhythm guitar) and Bob Weiner (acoustic guitar), a soft rock duo who recorded one album for the Natural Resources label in 1972. Helmed by legendary producer Tom Wilson, the backing musicians included Michael Rubini (piano), Ray Neopolitan (bass), Joe Osborne (bass) and drummers Jim Keltner, Non Morin and John Raines.

The Two Friends had first met through attending church on Sunset Boulevard and began singing and writing together, eventually landing a publishing and management deal. That in turn led to a one album deal with Motown, with the bulk of the album recorded at the Record Plant and the album cover photographed in Death Valley. Their eponymous album was released in May 1972.
ALBUM: TWO FRIENDS (1972)

TWO LOVERS – MARY WELLS [SINGLE]

By the autumn of 1962, Motown's biggest star was undoubtedly Mary Wells, who had already scored two Top Ten hits earlier in the year and was about to release her latest effort, *Two Lovers*. Again written and produced by Smokey Robinson, it was something of a lyrical departure for Smokey, but Mary's commanding vocal performance again carried the day. Promotion for the single was aided by the very first of the Motor Town Revues, with Mary the headlining star thanks to her succession of hits. *Two Lovers* would go on to top the R&B chart (her second R&B chart topper) and peak at #7 on the pop chart, although once again success in the UK proved elusive. Whilst Mary would enjoy a further four major R&B hits, she did not return to the pop Top Ten for some two years, finally scoring with *My Guy* in 1964.

WILLIE TYLER & LESTER

Born in Red Level, Alabama on 8 September 1940, Willie was inspired by ventriloquists such as Paul Winchell and started performing in Detroit at the age of ten. He undertook a ventriloquist correspondence course whilst at still school and appeared at numerous variety shows and talent contests. After four years in the US Air Force, Willie returned to Detroit and, along with his sidekick Lester, eventually got almost permanent employment with Motown Records, appearing on the Motortown Revue as something of a warm-up act for the likes of The Temptations, Gladys Knight & The Pips, Stevie Wonder and Bobby Taylor.

Willie and Lester also got to release an album, with **Hello Dummy** being released on the Tamla label in November 1965. In all Willie (and Lester) would tour with various Motown acts for some eight years before branching out on to television and appearances in numerous commercials. Willie and Lester continue to tour across the United States.
ALBUM: HELLO DUMMY (1965)

TYPICALLY TROPICAL

Studio musician Jeffrey Calvert often used any spare time at his father's Morgan Studio recording his own material, including on one session in October 1974 a couple of songs he had written with Geraint Wyn Hughes, *The Ghost Song*, written with the Christmas market in mind and *Barbados*, a song inspired by a holiday Calvert had on the island. *The Ghost Song* was actually recorded too late for the Christmas market, so Calvert and Hughes (who was often billed and known as Max West) decided to hawk *Barbados* around the industry.

Recorded with fellow session musicians Chris Spedding (guitar), Vic Flick (guitar) and Clem Cattini (drums), *Barbados* was a faux reggae track that featured mock vocals from Captain Tobias Wilcox of Coconut Airways and was initially offered for British release to Trojan Records. Little known Gull Records came up with a better offer (reported to be a £1,500 advance) and released it as a single the following summer, crediting the artist as Typically Tropical.

Although the group was not typically tropical nor reggae, the single caught the British imagination and made it to #1 on the chart, prompting Motown to acquire the American rights. Released in August 1975 and with Gull Records given their own label identity, the single did little business.

Typically Tropical released an album in the UK that similarly did little, relegating the group to the ranks of 'one-hit wonders', although Calvert and Hughes did later write Sarah Brightman's debut hit *I Lost My Heart To A Starship Trooper*.

U

UFO

Originally formed in London in 1969 as Hocus Pocus, Phil Mogg (born in London on 15 April 1948, vocals), Mick Bolton (guitar), Pete Way (born in Enfield, London on 7 August 1951, bass) and Andy Parker (born in Cheshunt, Hertfordshire on 21 March 1952, drums) became UFO a couple of months later after being discovered playing at the London club of the same name.

Noel Moore signed them to Beacon Records, which was to be their home for the next two years, at least in the UK. Their debut album **UFO1**, released in 1970 introduced their brand of hard rock, including a cover version of *C'mon Everybody*, although much of the material was written by the band. The album was picked up for release in the US by Rare Earth and was issued in April 1971, albeit with little success. The group meanwhile would switch to Chrysalis following Beacon's closure in 1972 and by the end of the decade had established themselves as hard rock and heavy metal pioneers.

ALBUM: UFO 1 (1971)

LESLIE UGGAMS

Along with the likes of Diahann Carroll and Mira Waters, Leslie Uggams made a bigger name for herself as an actress. Born in New York on 25 May 1943 into a showbiz family, Leslie made her professional bow at the age of six, appearing on the television series 'Beulah'. The following year she began appearing regularly at the Apollo Theatre, opening for the likes of Louis Washington, Dinah Washington and Ella Fitzgerald.

Enrolled into the Professional Children's School of New York, Leslie combined her schoolwork with guest appearances on numerous television variety programmes, although she announced her retirement at the age of twelve! Leslie was eventually coaxed back into the spotlight and won $12,500 towards her college education on the television quiz show 'Name That Tune'.

Leslie was a student at the Juilliard School when she accepted an invitation to join the cast of 'Sing Along With Mitch', becoming the first African-American member of the cast. After making her film debut in 1962 in 'Two Weeks In Another Town', Leslie pursued her career on two fronts; as an actress in films and on television and Broadway and as a singer, signing a recording contract with Columbia, for whom she would record ten albums.

Her star was also in the ascendency on Broadway; after appearing in 'The Boyfriend', Leslie won the key role in 'Hallelujah, Baby!', replacing Lena Horne in the lead role. This would result in a Tony Award, the highest accolade the theatre world can bestow. Leslie also got her own variety series on CBS in 1970, making her the first African-American in ten years to be afforded such an honour. Unfortunately, 'The Leslie Uggams Show' proved unable to shift 'Bonanza' from the top of the ratings and so was ultimately cancelled.

A switch in recording labels to Atlantic in 1972 did not bring about a change in fortunes, with the result the acting roles she was offered were not of the same quality as previously.

Leslie signed with Motown in 1975, working with producer Don Davis on her eponymous album for the label, which was issued in August 1975 on the Motown label. The only single released, *I Want To Make It Easy For You* was originally scheduled for Motown in April 1975 but was switched to the Gordy label. It failed to make an impact and Leslie was dropped by the label shortly after.

In 1977 she bounced back into the spotlight after landing the role of Kizzy Reynolds in the ratings smash 'Roots', going on to gain an Emmy nomination. That success led to several other highly acclaimed acting roles, both on stage and screen, and Leslie continues to tour with her musical concert across the country.

ALBUM: LESLIE UGGAMS (1975)

UNDER THE BOARDWALK – BRUCE WILLIS [SINGLE]

Written in 1964 by Kenny Young and Arthur Resnick, *Under The Boardwalk* provided The Drifters with a major hit as well as quickly becoming a much recorded song by a host of other artists, including The Undertones, Tom Tom Club, Bette Midler and The Rolling Stones. The song was also chosen for inclusion on Bruce Willis' album **The Return Of Bruno** and subsequently selected for single release after *Respect Yourself* had proven to be a transatlantic Top Ten success.

Featuring the uncredited vocal contribution of The Temptations, *Under The Boardwalk* would become a minor chart hit in the US following release in May 1987 (it peaked at #59 pop and #72 R&B) but stormed up the charts in the UK, spending seven weeks in the Top Ten and two weeks at its peak of #2. Although unable to knock The Pet Shop Boys and *It's A Sin* off the summit, *Under The Boardwalk* would earn Bruce a silver disc for sales in excess of 250,000 copies.

THE UNDERDOGS

The success of the so-called British Invasion prompted scores of copycat bands around the world, with The Underdogs forming at high school in Grosse Point, Michigan in 1964. Initially formed as a six man group by Chuck Schimento (guitar), Chris Lena (rhythm guitar and vocals), Steve Perrin (guitar), Dave Whitehouse (bass and lead vocals), Jack Louisell (keyboards) and Michael Morgan (drums and vocals), The Underdogs played local clubs and recorded their first single in 1965, *Man In The Glass,* for a label started by one of the clubs, the Hideout.

By then The Underdogs had trimmed down to a foursome of Tony Roumell (guitar), Lena, Morgan and Whitehouse. Hideout later issued a sampler that featured four Underdogs tracks, and this, coupled with a growing local reputation attracted the interest of Motown. Assigned to the V.I.P. label, the band issued one single, a remake of HDH's *Love's Gone Bad* (originally done by Chris Clark), which bubbled under at #122 without managing to crack the Hot 100.

They recorded several other tracks whilst at Motown, most of which remain on the shelves with the very occasional track turning up on compilations. Most of the group would later form Nickel Plate Express, a power pop trio.

THE UNDISPUTED TRUTH

Norman Whitfield created so much music there was sometimes a shortage of artists around the Motown lot able or willing to record it. Although the bulk of his activities centred on The Temptations, there were times he would try to expand his musical horizons by trying a different style with a different act, such as rock on Rare Earth or a much funkier vein with Edwin Starr. Sometimes, however, even these outlets weren't enough, so Norman set about creating a group that would be able to fill the gap. As he created them their ability to veto any product would be limited; he would select their material, much as he would select the group members.

The very first incarnation of The Undisputed Truth came together in 1970, with Joe Harris, Billie Rae Calvin and Brenda Joyce Evans plucked from relative obscurity to form the group. Joe (born in Detroit, Michigan on 18 June 1944) had previously been a member of The Fabulous Peps, a Detroit based vocal trio that had recorded for D-Town and Wheelsville. Billie Rae Calvin (born in Los Angeles, California on 12 May 1949) and Brenda Joyce Evans had started their careers with The Delicates, initially a trio (along with a third girl called Michelle) that had recorded for a number of small labels without success. Billie and Brenda had eventually been spotted by Bobby Taylor (of The Vancouvers), who was impressed with their abilities and offered them a chance to go to Motown, as Billie would later recall.

"Bobby recommended that we go back to Detroit. Well, we thought about it, talked it over with our families and decided to go. Bobby took us back to do a show in Detroit with him and people seemed to like it. We started doing background work for Motown acts, like The Four Tops, Stevie Wonder, The Supremes and Smokey Robinson. But Michelle didn't get on too well there and the company dismissed her. Brenda and I carried on and one day Norman Whitfield told us of his plan for a group. Naturally, we liked what he said and immediately agreed to go along with it."

Whilst Norman's initial plan was to have the group road test new material he was working on, it was with an old song from his own catalogue that The Undisputed Truth made their bow. *Save My Love For A Rainy Day* had been a Temptations number, appearing on their 1967 album **With A Lot O' Soul** and then, briefly, been considered as a possible single for Marvin Gaye as the follow-up to *Too Busy Thinking About My Baby*. The backing tracks for *Save My Love For A Rainy Day* had actually been recorded for Marvin, but at the last minute Norman had a change of mind and took The Undisputed Truth into the studio to record it instead.

What was chosen as the flip side was another Norman hand me down, although *Since I've Lost You* had considerably more previous owners, including Jimmy Ruffin, The Velvelettes, Gladys Knight & The Pips and The Temptations. The group's debut single was released in February 1971 and became a minor R&B hit, peaking at #43, but even as it was scaling the chart, the group and Norman were back in the studio, busy recording tracks for their forthcoming debut album and, ultimately, their biggest hit single.

Smiling Faces Sometimes was another former Temptations number, one which had been introduced via a twelve and a half minute epic version on their album **Sky's The Limit**. Norman had intended releasing an edited version as a Temptations single, but the huge success of *Just My Imagination* and the subsequent departure of Eddie Kendricks from the group scotched that plan. Instead, Norman started from scratch and re-assembled the song, providing a much more hypnotic and haunting production for The Undisputed Truth to lay down their vocals. This proved to be a major breakthrough for the group, going on to hit #3 pop, #2 R&B and earning a gold disc for sales in excess of a million copies and a Grammy Award nomination for Best Rhythm & Blues Song.

When The Undisputed Truth's eponymous album appeared in July 1971, it too became a major hit, reaching #47 pop and #7 R&B, although there were one or two somewhat critical reviews pointing out the assorted tracks that had already appeared elsewhere, albeit recorded by other acts (including the obligatory cover of *I Heard It Through The Grapevine* and *Ball Of Confusion*). That formula was retained for the group's second album, **Face To Face With The Truth**, which again contained covers of songs associated with Marvin Gaye (*What's Going On*) and The Temptations (*You Make Your Own Heaven And Hell Right On Earth* and *Superstar*).

The singles lifted (the afore-mentioned *You Make Your Own Heaven And Hell Right On Earth* and *What It Is*) failed to scale the same heights as *Smiling Faces Sometimes*, but in peaking at #72 pop and #24 R&B (*You Make Your Own Heaven And Hell Right On Earth*) and #71 and #35 R&B (*What It Is*) at least kept the group's name in vogue, enough to take the accompanying album to #16 R&B, even if its pop placing of #114 was a disappointment. Equally disappointing was constantly fielding criticism of their mentor's frequent use of his own material, as Billie would confirm.

"People do say that. Every time anyone says it, it hurts me inside a little. I never say anything but it does hurt. I'm hurt as a person rather than as an entertainer, though. You see, Norman Whitfield writes for both The Temptations and us. I think he recuts his songs because he can see them in so many different ways and he wants to record them in different ways, too. But the important thing is that our next album is full of completely new songs. Our next single is from the album and will be *Papa Was A Rollin' Stone*. I hope that now we can forget about comparisons with The Temptations and any other groups."

Unfortunately, whilst *Papa Was A Rollin' Stone* did become a small hit for The Undisputed Truth (it would peak at #63 pop and #24), Norman would return to the song on The Temptations and score one of the biggest hits of his and their career. That third album, entitled **Law Of The Land**, would also feature The Truth's take on *Just My Imagination* and *Law Of The Land*, with the latter becoming a moderate R&B hit (#40), although in Britain it was The Temptations who took the song into the chart (at #41). The lack of a major single hit affected sales of the album, which could barely make #191 on the pop listings and #52 R&B. The album also featured an extensive list of the musicians who had helped craft the sound but made no mention whatsoever of the vocalists, who had effectively become almost surplus to requirements.

In 1973 therefore, Brenda left, initially to be replaced by Diana Evans, but this new trio quickly became redundant with Diana's departure soon after, and with the opportunity to pretty much recreate the group, Norman decided to expand. In came Tyrone Douglas, Tyrone Barkley and Virginia McDonald, who joined Joe and Billie on the album (if not the cover) for **Down To Earth**, which would become the group's first album not to make the pop chart, although it would hit #35 R&B. This was largely down to the success of two hit singles, *Help Yourself* (#19 R&B, also making #63 pop for good measure) and *I'm A Fool For You* (#39 R&B), but the diminishing returns prompted Norman to have something of a rethink for the group's next album.

Whilst the album did at least carry a picture of the group, they were now heavily made up, wearing giant white Afro wigs and heavy face-paint, something of a funky looking Kiss. The new look also meant new monikers, with the group lining up with Joe, Virginia 'V' McDonald, Tyrone 'Big Ty' Douglas, Tyrone 'Lil' Ty' Barkley and Calvin 'Dhaak' Stephenson. The music changed too, with George Clinton's success with Parliament providing the inspiration for Norman's space influenced collection of tracks for **Cosmic Truth**. The album returned them to the pop and R&B charts, #186 and #42 respectively, whilst the extracted singles found different markets, with *Lil' Red Riding Hood* bubbling under at #106 on the pop chart and *UFO's* #62 on the R&B equivalent.

What was destined to be the group's final Gordy outing, **Higher Than High**, featured the same kind of inspiration and exactly the same formula as their previous label outings. The cover this time around was *Ma*, but of the new material, the title track (a minor R&B hit when released as a single, peaking at #77) along with *Boogie Bump Boogie* and *Poontang* attracted some club interest, resulting in the album hitting #173 pop and #52 R&B. Once again the assorted musicians received credit, including several who would become core members of Norman Whitfield's soon to be opened boutique label via Warner Brothers.

The Undisputed Truth followed Norman out of the Motown door, along with members of Total Concept Unlimited, a group that would subsequently evolve into Rose Royce and receive much of Norman's time and attention for the next few years. The Undisputed Truth were not entirely ignored, scoring hits with *You + Me = Love* and *Let's Go Down To The Disco* as well as undergoing numerous personnel changes along the way, most notably acquiring Chaka Khan's sister Taka Boom as a joint lead singer.

The one constant throughout it all was Joe Harris, who remained a member throughout the group's entire career; when he called it a day in 1979 the group effectively came to a halt. Billie Rae Calvin would also pop back into the public eye after penning *Wishing On A Star*, a massive hit for Rose Royce in 1978 and later being successfully covered by The Fresh 4, The Cover Girls, 88.3 Featuring Lisa May, Jay-Z Featuring Gwen Dickey (Gwen having been lead singer on the Rose Royce original), Paul Weller and the 2001 X Factor Finalists collective. Billie Rae died from heart disease in Mureitta in California on 23 June 2007, whilst Joe has survived prostate cancer (reportedly thanks to cannabis!).

ALBUMS: THE UNDISPUTED TRUTH (1971), FACE TO FACE WITH THE TRUTH (1972), LAW OF THE LAND (1973), DOWN TO EARTH (1974), COSMIC TRUTH (1974), HIGHER THAN HIGH (1975)

COMPILATION: THE BEST OF THE UNDISPUTED TRUTH (1977)

UNITED ARTISTS RECORDS

Founded in 1957 as the record arm of the well established film studio, United Artists made its initial mark releasing soundtrack albums of its own film output. In 1958 it began expanding its horizons and issuing records that were not linked to films, either by signing artists direct or picking up finished master deals.

In January 1959 it did a deal with the fledgling Tamla label of Detroit for the master to Marv Johnson's *Come To Me*, which had begun attracting considerable radio play locally and which label owner Berry Gordy was unable to fully capitalise upon financially. United Artists duly reissued the single in February and saw it become a minor pop hit, also agreeing a deal to take another master in Eddie Holland's *Merry Go Round*, although this did not chart.

Undeterred, United Artists did subsequent deals with Berry Gordy, with Marv Johnson holding a United Artists contract for five years and Eddie Holland for two. In addition to continued work for United Artists on Marv and Eddie, Berry undertook outside writing and production work for the label, including Eileen Barton and Wyatt 'Big Boy' Shepherd, who was reportedly signed to Motown but 'loaned' to United Artists for his only single release.

Eventually Berry no longer required the distribution capabilities of the likes of United Artists and could handle everything in house. Both Eddie and Marv eventually returned to the Motown fold, where they were to enjoy further success.

UP THE LADDER TO THE ROOF – THE SUPREMES [SINGLE]

Berry Gordy had a clear vision for Diana Ross when she exited The Supremes, handing her over to Nickolas Ashford and Valerie Simpson for what would become her debut solo album in May 1970. The Supremes, however, was a different story.

Having initially approved the selection of Jean Terrell as the new lead singer, he subsequently changed his mind and requested the group bring in Rita Wright (later to become better known as Syreeta), his original choice. When Mary Wilson and Cindy Birdsong refused to back down and ditch Jean, Berry told them he had effectively washed his hands of the group.

Whilst Berry may have turned his back on the group, there was no shortage of producers and writers willing to pick up the baton, with Johnny Bristol widely expected to assume responsibility for maintaining The Supremes' chart credentials. Johnny did get to work with the group, producing them on *Bill, When Are You Coming Back* which he wrote with Pam Sawyer, but the Vietnam based storyline worried some at Hitsville. Fortunately, Frank Wilson stepped in at the right time with the right song, with *Up The Ladder To The Roof* becoming an obvious single the moment it was played at the Quality Control meeting. The song had been brought to Motown by would-be singer and guitarist Vincent DiMirco, but the moment Frank heard it, he reasoned it would be a better bet for The Supremes. With Frank working up the song on the piano and Vincent playing guitar on the session, The Supremes were able to do something they hadn't done for a long time; perform on their own single.

Showcased on 'The Ed Sullivan Show' shortly before release, *Up The Ladder To The Roof* heralded a triumphant arrival for Jean Terrell and a return to former glories for The Supremes. The single was released stateside on 16 February 1970 and would glide to #5 R&B and #10 pop, subsequently being released in the UK in April and hitting #5, proof that The Supremes intended being a force to be reckoned with for some considerable time yet.

PHIL UPCHURCH

Born in Chicago, Illinois on 19 July 1941, guitarist Phil Upchurch began his career playing with numerous R&B backing bands, including the likes of The Dells, The Kool Gents and The Spaniels as well as performing with Dee Clark.

His own career kicked off in 1961 with the Phil Upchurch Combo and *You Can't Sit Down* on the Boyd label, which would eventually become a British hit in 1966 when reissued on Sue. Switching almost effortlessly between R&B and jazz, Phil would record for United Artists, Milestone, Cadet Concept and Blue Thumb before signing with CTI's Kudu label in 1974.

His band at the time also included singer Tennyson Stephens, who would receive joint top billing on the album the pair made as Phil's Kudu debut in 1975. Critically acclaimed on release, the album did little chartwise even if it enhanced the reputation of both singer and guitarist. This was to be Phil's only release on Kudu, although he borrowed the R&B blueprint for a later album for Marlin in 1978 and scored a #32 jazz hit. He later recorded for Palladin, Ichiban and Ridgetop and continues to appear as a session musician.

ALBUM: UPCHURCH/TENNYSON (1975)

UPSIDE DOWN – DIANA ROSS [SINGLE]

The working relationship between Diana Ross and the Chic Organisation had ended abruptly amid much rancour, with Diana complaining that her vocals were mixed too much into the background and Chic unhappy with the remix that Diana had ordered be done by Russ Terrana.

In between the complaints and accusations that flew between the two camps, there was the little matter of getting what had been recorded out to the market. The album had shipped in May 1980 and was quickly shaping up to be Diana's biggest seller for many a year, proof that Diana may have been unduly worried as to the effect the album would have on her career. Whilst her traditional soul and pop fan base had remained loyal and were taking to **diana** in their droves, an audience that Diana had not much troubled for some four years had also re-awakened; the dance crowd.

Love Hangover in 1976 had been her first major across the board hit (in so much as it proved popular on the R&B, pop and dance charts), and DJs the country over had leapt upon both *I'm Coming Out* and *Upside Down* from the latest offering. It had been claimed that several of the songs on the album had originally been offered to Aretha Franklin and rejected, but Nile Rodgers' explanation of their usual working methods would seem to disprove this.

"We went to visit her [Diana Ross] and told what we always tell people. 'We'll just sit down and talk with you for a couple of hours, then go home and write the album.'" He would later add, "Diana Ross was the first big star we ever worked with and we took it very seriously. This was the first time in her life somebody cared about who she was, what she was, everyone previously had treated her the way we had treated Sister Sledge – they got her in and said 'Sing this.' We took a more personal approach."

Whether *Upside Down* was a rehash of an Aretha Franklin song or specially crafted for Diana Ross will never be known for certain one way or another, but it has certainly become a song most firmly associated with Diana Ross. Whilst the remix did bring Diana back to the fore, there was enough in the accompaniment to remind the listener Chic was responsible for the music.

The combination proved irresistible, with *Upside Down* becoming Diana's first chart topper for four years, hitting the summit of the R&B, pop and dance chart soon after its release in June 1980. In the UK it peaked at #2, denied its place at the top by Abba and *The Winner Takes It All*. The single would also earn a Grammy Award nomination for Best Rhythm & Blues Vocal Performance, Female (it was beaten by Stephanie Mills' *Never Knew Love Like This Before*), perhaps vindicating both parties.

UPTIGHT (EVERYTHING'S ALRIGHT) – STEVIE WONDER [SINGLE]

After bursting onto the musical scene in 1963, Stevie Wonder's career had gone into decline, for whilst the innocence of *Fingertips* and Little Stevie Wonder might have been enough to earn a number one hit in 1963, audiences had moved on, even if Stevie hadn't. There has been speculation that Berry might have considered letting the youngster go after a succession of flops, especially as Berry would not allow his company to carry non-hit making passengers. Although no one from Motown has ever confirmed or denied the suggestion, there was certainly concern that Stevie's career was going nowhere, prompting the placement of the young singer with a number of experienced writers and producers.

These included in house musician Hank Cosby and lyricist Sylvia Moy, with the latter sitting with Stevie for a time and asking him to go through any material he had been working on that they might fashion into a hit single. According to Sylvia, by the time he finished there was nothing that suggested it could become a hit, meaning they would have to concoct something from scratch. Sylvia asked one more time if there was anything else and Stevie, perhaps reluctantly, sang a basic phrase he had come up with, 'Everything is alright, uptight.' It was enough to at least build in to a full-blown song, so the three worked on it some more, with Stevie putting together the chords, Sylvia the lyrics and Hank creating the arrangement.

The recording session was produced with Hank and Mickey Stevenson, and whilst the main instrumentation is by the Funk Brothers, Stevie himself may well have played the drums. One thing he did *not* play was the harmonica, his trademark instrument being left off the recording after discussion with Clarence Paul.

Irrespective of what he did or didn't play, Stevie sang the song to perfection, resulting in a #1 R&B and #3 pop hit in the US, banishing memories of the cute little kid with his harmonica in the process. In the UK *Uptight* would become his UK chart debut, peaking at #14. Stevie's performance was recognised later in the year, picking up his first nomination for a Grammy Award in the Best R&B Vocal Performance, Male category (which was ultimately won by James Brown and *Crying Time*). Stevie would be back again and again in the years to come.

MICHAL URBANIAK

Multi-instrumentalist Michal Urbaniak was born in Warsaw, Poland on 22 January 1943 and learned to play violin, lyricon and saxophone at high school. After touring with Andrzej Trzaskowski and Krzysztof Komeda he formed his own group in 1969, recording their debut album the following year and performing at the Montreux Jazz Festival. He emigrated to the US in 1973 and recorded for Columbia and Arista before landing at Motown in 1980. He would record one album for the label, **Serenade For The City**, with Marcus Miller, Doc Powell and Kenny Kirkland as backing musicians. He would later play with the likes of Joe Zawinul, Quincy Jones and Miles Davis.

ALBUM: SERENADE FOR THE CITY (1980)

THE UTOPIANS

An extremely obscure group, The Utopians were most likely from Brooklyn and recorded *Erlene* for the Cee-Jay label in 1958, the single credited to Mike (Lasman) & The Utopians. They recorded very briefly for Motown ten years later when Al Cleveland and Arthur Crier produced their version of *Whole Lot Of Shakin' In My Heart (Since I Met You)*, a song written by Frank Wilson that had previously been recorded by The Miracles and Barbara McNair, without success. The Utopians version never saw the light of day when originally recorded; it finally got an outing on **A Cellarful Of Motown Volume 4** in 2010.

THE VALADIERS

The very first Valadiers line-up that auditioned for Berry Gordy was turned down, not because of any problem with their sound but supposedly because of their colour. Initially an integrated band The Valadiers had both black and white members but Berry noted The Del Vikings had recently disbanded, proof that the musical world wasn't quite ready for another integrated band. However, he offered them a chance to come back and try again, with either an all white or all black line-up.

The five that made the return journey were all white (thus becoming the very first white group signed to Motown), with Stuart Avig (lead vocals) being joined by Marty Coleman (lead, bass and baritone), Art Glasser (second tenor) and Jerry Light (bass and baritone), along with Gary Frankel, who would subsequently drop out of the group after his father refused to sign the recording contract on his behalf.

Inspired by the likes of The Impressions, The Dells, Jackie Wilson and The Flamingos, The Valadiers had already cultivated a healthy local following and, presenting themselves at Hitsville one afternoon after school, they impressed Berry enough for him to sign them to a three year contract. The initial recording sessions produced two tracks, *Nothing Is Going To Change It* and *Somebody Help Me Find My Baby*, but these were shelved as Berry sought something a little punchier with which to launch their recording career.

That eventually came with *Greetings (This Is Uncle Sam)*, a title that Avig and Light came up with after spotting a newspaper headline, taking the idea down to the studio where Robert Bateman, Brian Holland and Ronald Dunbar worked up into a full blown song. Coupled with *Take A Chance*, *Greetings* was issued on the Miracle label and would become the only hit issued on the label, reaching the less than dizzy heights of #89 following its October 1961 release. With the Miracle label being shuttered soon after, The Valadiers were drafted to Gordy, where their follow-up single *While I'm Away* was released in May 1962, but lacking the same kind of appeal of *Greetings* did little. Neither did the group's third and final single release, *I Found A Girl*, issued in January 1963.

With the group's contract up at the beginning of 1964 and Motown unlikely to offer an extension, The Valadiers decided to call it a day. Stuart Avig went off for a solo career, although Marty Coleman remained at Motown, adopting the name Martin Cohen and joining the team of in-house writers. *Greetings* also made a return appearance, providing The Monitors with a hit in 1966.

VALENTINO

In 1974, twenty-two year singer and performer Charles Harris was appearing in Westbury, Long Island, playing at the Music Fair revival of the musical 'Hair'. After the show, he was approached by label executive and songwriter Bunny Jones.

"Bunny saw me and said, 'You've got more talent than you know. If I can't help you, I won't hurt you.' We became close. She told me she had written a song everyone was afraid to do because of the lyrics, the content of the song, and I said, 'Well, let me see it.' So she showed it to me, and we went into a studio."

The song was *I Was Born This Way*, now acknowledged as the first time a performer had come out as gay on a single. Charles became Valentino for the purposes of the single, with Bunny also establishing the Gaiee Record label for the release, which appeared in January 1975 and became an instant club smash, enabling Bunny to sell some 15,000 copies out of the back of her car.

"New York went up! It was really great! My mother would turn on the radio and go around the apartment singing it. Oh God! It was really incredible," said Charles.

Word of the single spread across the country, with Motown among the labels interested in picking up the single nationwide.

"Berry Gordy kissed me on both sides of my cheeks and said, 'You've got a hit record,' and I felt like a million dollars" said Bunny. "No major company has ever had to deal with a gay protest record before. No one ever stood up and said, 'I'm gay.' Monti Rock said his chiffon was wet, but that didn't say he was gay."

I Was Born This Way was reissued by Motown in April 1975 and in the UK in June 1975 (both territories retained the Gaiee imprint), but whilst the record made significant progress on the club charts, hitting the very top, it was unable to get a toehold on the chart, although that did little to diminish Charles's pride at what the single achieved.

"It was my first time in the record business, and what it's done to me personally has been very heavy, very weird. It's been a trip! I go in as a recording artist who did a record that had a statement that did not put anyone down. I've gotta be me, and I don't know what people are expecting after they've heard the record, but I can't be anyone but me."

Although the single failed to set the charts alight, Motown would revive the song in 1977 on Carl Bean. Charles meanwhile continued his acting and performing career, usually under the name Charles Valentino, and appeared in the revival of 'The Wiz' that toured across the United States in 1984.

FRANKIE VALLI & THE FOUR SEASONS

When The Four Seasons joined Motown in 1971, they were already seasoned veterans of the industry and had registered a significant tally of hits, including no fewer than four chart toppers. Although it had been some seven years since their last number one (*Rag Doll* in 1964) and the group had never been seen as strong sellers in the album market, their acquisition was still a marquee signing, with high hopes held for their immediate Motown future.

The key member of the group was Francis Castelluccio, who had been born in Newark, New Jersey on 3 May 1934 and upon being discovered by singer Texas Jean Valley had adopted the stage name Frankie Valley in her honour (although he would vary the name for a number of years before finally settling on the accepted moniker of Frankie Valli). After recording a number of unsuccessful singles, Frankie linked with brothers Nick and Tommy DeVito (born in New Jersey on 19 June 1928) and Hank Majewski in 1956 as The Variatones. This was to be the first of some eighteen names they would adopt in search of success. Frankie left in 1958 for a solo career masterminded by Bob Crewe, with The Four Lovers, as they had become, drafting in Nick Massi (born in Newark on 19 September 1935) and Bob Guadio (born in The Bronx, New York on 17 December 1942) to replace the departed Nick DeVito and Hank Majewiski. Eventually, Frankie reconvened with Tommy DeVito, Nick Massi and Bob Guadio and the group became The 4 Seasons and brought Bob Crewe into the fold as writer and producer.

It was this classic line-up that got the group off the ground with such hits as *Sherry, Big Girls Don't Cry* and *Walk Like A Man*, with the group one of the few American groups that were able to trade hits with The Beatles. As the decade progressed the group underwent a number of changes, both on stage and in the studio, with Bob Guadio taking over the mantle of producer and chief writer.

It proved to be to no avail however, as the group's harmony sound began to sound dated when compared with the heavier rock others were producing. By 1969 the group was without a contract, reduced to signing brief deals with whoever might be interested in an attempt to restore their reputation. There was no shortage of takers, with Warner Brothers in England signing them to a one-off single in 1970 before Berry Gordy picked them up and assigned them to the MoWest label.

The first fruits of the new deal saw Frankie Valli release a solo single, *Love Isn't Here (Like It Used To Be)* in February 1972, although it failed to make an impact. The whole group was credited on **Chameleon**, released in May 1972, but it was another Frankie Valli solo outing *The Night* that was scheduled next for release. Although promotional copies were mailed out in the US, the single was subsequently withdrawn. It got a little further in the UK, where it was credited as Frankie Valli & The Four Seasons, albeit without success following its October 1972 release.

Subsequently switched to the main Motown label in May 1973 (such was the hesitancy about which market to promote The Four Seasons, in Germany their releases were issued on Rare Earth), the releases kept on coming but success continued to elude them; *Walk On Don't Look Back, How Come* and *Hickory* all sank without trace, severely threatening the group's future prospects with the company.

Busy recording what was planned to be a follow-up album in **Inside Out** as well as a solo album for Frankie, the group was dismayed to learn that Motown would not be releasing anything further, although if they wished to take the tapes with them, the two parties would have to come to a financial agreement. Lacking sufficient funds to buy back either album, the group rescued one song, *My Eyes Adored You*, which they subsequently took to Larry Uttal at Private Stock. He agreed to release the track but only as a Frankie Valli solo effort, leaving the group to eventually secure a separate deal with Warner Brothers.

The Four Seasons' subsequent return to chart glories, at least as far as Europe was concerned, came with an old MoWest single. *The Night* may not have made much of an impact when originally released, but copies had found their way to the numerous Northern Soul venues, where it soon found an appreciative audience. Over the next three years the track became something of an underground hit, prompting Tamla Motown to reissue it; it would go on to become a Top Ten hit, the only such hit on the MoWest label, and heralded something of a resurgence of interest in The Four Seasons, who would go on to enjoy major hits such as *Who Loves You*, *December '63* and *Silver Star* in rapid succession.

Whilst the group's recorded popularity waned and revived over the next three decades, their constant touring made them a hugely successful live draw. Then, in 2005, they were the subject of the immensely popular Broadway show 'Jersey Boys', bringing their multitude of hits to a whole new audience. The show also successfully transferred to Europe, Canada, Australia and Singapore, winning a slew of awards in each territory.

ALBUM: CHAMELEON (1972)

GENE VAN BUREN

Gene Van Buren is something of a mystery man, even though he recorded a solo album for Motown and lent his vocals to a considerable number of outside projects, usually under the name Eugene Van Buren. He first surfaced at Motown in 1982, where he released his debut (and so far only) album **What's Your Pleasure** in December. With Berry Gordy listed as Executive Producer and support from heavyweight names such as Michael Boddicker, James Jamerson and Leon 'Ndugu' Chancler, the album appeared to have been something of a priority for the company. *You've Got Me Where I Want You* was issued as a single in January 1983, followed six months later by *When It's My Turn*, but neither single nor the album made an impression.

Gene meanwhile added to his list of credits by working for Stevie Wonder on 'The Woman In Red' soundtrack as well as recording what was planned to be his second solo album, **Love Never Dies**. Although a single was released in July 1984, *You Excite Me*, when it failed to chart the album was cancelled. Gene would later work with Bob Sinclair and Bustafunk and lend his vocal talents to albums by Luther Vandross, Bette Midler, Donna Summer and Gregory Hines and was last heard of as a member of one of the four groups touring as The Platters. **What's Your Pleasure** was reissued on the Funky Town Grooves label in 2009.

ALBUM: WHAT'S YOUR PLEASURE (1982)

DAVID VAN DePITTE

The in-house arranger at Motown between 1968 and 1972, David Van DePitte was responsible for crafting some of popular music's most memorable moments, earning a Grammy nomination for Best Arranger for his work on Marvin Gaye's **What's Going On** in 1971.

David was born in Detroit, Michigan on 28 October 1941 and studied music at the Westlake College of Music in Los Angeles, becoming proficient in classical, jazz and popular music as well as a more than capable bass player, among several instruments. After graduating from college he returned to Detroit and played trombone with Johnny Trudell's orchestra, subsequently switching to upright bass. It was as a bass player that he got his introduction to Motown, for he became acquainted with James Jamerson, who got him a growing number of recording sessions at Hitsville (James would also play bass with Johnny Trudell on occasions when David was unavailable).

Gradually, the various producers at Motown came to realise that whilst David was a talented bass player, he was a phenomenal arranger, proving his worth on such recordings as *Still Waters (Run Deep), Ball Of Confusion, Psychedelic Shack, I Hear The Bells, Keep On Truckin', Indiana Wants Me* and scores more. A staff member for four years, David would freelance from 1972 onwards but invariably gravitated back to Motown and its artists, working with Marvin Gaye on his **Let's Get It On** project as well as serving as musical director for live performances by Marvin Gaye, Diana Ross, Paul Anka and The Four Tops.

He later served as adjunct professor of Jazz Studies at Wayne State University between 1979 and 1983. He died from cancer in Southfield, Michigan on 9 August 2009.

CHARLIE VAN DYKE

Born Charles Leo Steinle in Dallas, Texas on 19 December 1947, Charlie Van Dyke was a former DJ on Top 40 radio, initially working in the Dallas area with KLIF. Later appointments included CKLW in Windsor and Detroit and KFRC in San Francisco. In 1971 he provided the narration to the five disc box set entitled **The Motown Story: The First Decade** issued in March.

CONNIE VAN DYKE

Born in Nassawadox, Virginia on 28 September 1945, Connie won the Miss Teen USA contest organised by Teen Magazine in 1960 and used the notoriety of that win to gain a Motown contract the following year. Whilst Connie recorded a couple of sides that were eventually released some two years later, *Oh Freddy* backed with *It Hurt Me Too* being issued in March 1963, it would appear that Connie's contract was cancelled by mutual agreement three weeks after it was signed. Connie would later become an actress, appearing in 'Hell's Angels '69' and 'Framed' as well as making sporadic recordings for Wheelsville, Epic and Barnaby Records.

EARL VAN DYKE

One of the very few members of The Funk Brothers to been granted the honour of releasing singles or albums under their own name, Earl Van Dyke was effectively the erstwhile leader of that supremely talented bunch of musicians.

Born in Detroit, Michigan on 8 July 1930, Earl learned to play the piano at the age of five and subsequently studied at the Detroit Conservatory of Music. As a teenager he played professionally with the likes of Kenny Burrell, Hank Jones and Yusef Lateef, but he would eventually drift into combining music with spells working in a factory and two spells in the armed services. After catching tuberculosis Earl was laid low for two and a half years, recuperating in a veterans' administration hospital before finally emerging in 1956 and getting a gig with jazz guitarist Emmett Sleigh.

Having re-established his credentials as a keyboard player, Earl toured with Chris Columbo and Lloyd Price, striking up a friendship with bass player James Jamerson in the process. Jamerson told Earl about the work he had been doing for a new Detroit based label and that there was money to be made doing sessions for Motown Records. Earl quickly returned to Detroit and joined the ranks of freelance musicians, officially joining the label in 1962 on a salary of $150 a week.

At first Earl was one of three pianists at Motown, rotating with Joe Hunter and Johnny Griffith on sessions, although A&R manager Mickey Stevenson came to rely on Earl more and more. When Joe Hunter left Motown in 1963, Mickey moved quickly to appoint Earl Van Dyke as bandleader, assembling a tight core of musicians around Earl's abilities. Recording sessions increased to such an extent Earl and the rest of the Funk Brothers were on call twenty four hours a day, where even if they got some spare time and tried to keep their hands in with impromptu performances by playing jazz at any of Detroit's numerous live venues, these could be brought to an abrupt end by a call to return to Hitsville.

Earl did get to perform elsewhere, leading the band that accompanied various Motown stars on their first official visit overseas in 1965, although Earl caused some friction between the band and their paymasters when he threatened to call a strike if the band weren't paid for performing on a live television show. Not surprisingly, his reputation went up with the rest of The Funk Brothers after that little episode, with the rest of The Funk Brothers granting him the nickname 'Chunk Of Funk'.

Just as he had done with the likes of Earl Washington and George Bohanon, Berry Gordy gave Earl Van Dyke the opportunity of recording under his own name, with *Soul Stomp* being issued on the Soul label in September 1964. A follow-up single appeared in January 1965, *All For You* being credited to Earl Van Dyke & The Soul Brothers as Berry Gordy objected to the use of the word 'funk'. The same moniker was retained for the subsequent album **That Motown Sound**, on which Earl played organ over existing backing tracks.

It would be a further three years before a second album was released, **Earl Of Funk** showing Berry had lost his opposition to the word 'funk', although both this album and its predecessor were more jazz inclined. By then Earl had got as close to a hit as he would do during his career, with *Runaway Child Running Wild* having bubbled under at #114 following its release in March 1969. Unlike the first album, *Runaway Child* and its flip *Gonna Give Her All The Love I've Got* were recorded at separate sessions, produced by Norman Whitfield, although neither track made it on to the **Earl Of Funk** album.

Whilst Berry had been keen to hide the names of the musicians behind his mountain of hits, the names of several of them were common knowledge around the industry, resulting in Earl, Benny, James and assorted others being much in demand for outside session work, appearing on sessions for other labels in Detroit as well as further afield in New York and Chicago.

As Motown began its move westward, Earl remained in Detroit, backing up a variety of artists that performed in the city at its various music venues, including Sammy Davis Jr., Mel Torme and Vic Damone and eventually becoming musical director for Freda Payne. In between Earl would sometimes visit the Hitsville studios to lay down keyboard licks as and when required on numerous recordings, eventually following the rest of his former label-mates to California later in the 1970s.

Unable to adapt to the Californian lifestyle, Earl returned home to Detroit after a couple of years, getting a job with the Detroit Board of Education at Osborne High School. His musical prowess was kept up to speed by performing local dates and the occasional studio booking, most notably appearing on two of The Four Tops' albums for ABC. He stopped playing professionally in 1991, a year before his death from prostate cancer on 18 September 1992. Whilst his keyboard playing is widely heard, thanks to the multitude of hits he performed on during the heady days of the 1960s, his own recordings are often overlooked.

"The opportunities were there to do more and I didn't take advantage of them. I just got locked into the fact that I was playing music and making a living. It was not what I wanted to play but it was good."

ALBUMS: THAT MOTOWN SOUND (1965), THE EARL OF FUNK (1970)

VANITY

Born Denise Katrina Matthews in Niagara Falls, Ontario in Canada on 4 January 1959, her first attempt at making a name was as a model and actress, appearing in several B movies under the stage name DD Winters.

In 1982 she met with Prince at the American Music Awards, at a time when Prince was considering putting together an all female trio to go by the name of The Hookers. After discovering Denise could sing, he lined her up for the role of lead singer with the group, also wanting to rename her Vagina since he reasoned it would be unforgettable. Fortunately, Denise was able to convince him that Vanity would be equally memorable, with Prince subsequently deciding to call the group Vanity 6, the six referring to the number of breasts in the group.

Scantily clad in lingerie and with a provocative stage routine, Vanity 6 was launched later in 1982 with an eponymous album and a hit single with *Nasty Girl*, a Top Ten R&B hit. When the romantic liaison between her and Prince came to an end, Vanity began negotiating a move away from the Prince camp, eventually signing with Motown in 1984.

Vanity would release two albums for Motown, **Wild Animal** in 1984 and **Skin On Skin** two years later, with both making a modest showing on the pop (#62 and #66 respectively) and R&B (#14 and #18) charts. A total of three singles charted, of which *Under The Influence* was the biggest, peaking at #56 pop and #9 on the R&B chart in 1986.

Vanity lived up to her reputation during her time on Motown, posing naked for 'Playboy' magazine, appearing in the May 1985 issue (she would also appear in the April 1988 edition), although she wore considerably more in her numerous film appearances around this time, including the Motown vehicle 'The Last Dragon'.

Vanity left Motown in 1986 and subsequently signed with A&M, although her hit days were behind her. After a lengthy battle with drug abuse, during which time she suffered a heart attack and abandoned her Vanity name, she turned her back on the entertainment industry and became a born again Christian.

ALBUMS: WILD ANIMAL (1984), SKIN ON SKIN (1983)
FURTHER READING: BLAME IT ON VANITY (2000)

VEE-JAY RECORDS

As important and vital an R&B label in the 1950s as Motown would become the following decade, Vee-Jay was formed in Gary, Indiana in 1953. It took its name from the initials of the two primary owners, Vivian Carter and James Bracken (the pair would marry later the same year) and, after borrowing $500 to produce their first record, scored major hits with Jimmy Reed and The Spaniels, although these were leased to Chance Records (where Ewart Abner was an executive) as Vee-Jay lacked any kind of national distribution channels.

Eventually the label relocated to Chicago and made several key appointments, including Vivian's brother Calvin Carter as A&R man and Ewart Abner as manager, later to become vice-president and subsequently president. Success came with an assortment of artists, mainly in the R&B field, but in the 1960s Vee-Jay achieved notoriety thanks to a licensing deal they picked up that gave them access to two acts recording for EMI Records in England, Frank Ifield and The Beatles.

Unfortunately, the label's success led to major problems, with a royalty dispute with The Four Seasons eventually resulting in EMI withdrawing the rights to The Beatles, although Vee-Jay still managed to sell some 2.6 million Beatles records in a single month before their rights were withdrawn.

The ill-fated opening of an office in California further stretched Vee-Jay's finances, and despite closing the west coast office and bringing Ewart Abner back into the fold to try and rescue the company, by August 1966 it had no choice but to file for bankruptcy.

Vee-Jay International emerged in 1967 but was somewhat limited to selling off stock that had been on hand at the time of bankruptcy, and most of the artists had similarly departed for pastures new. It's rich catalogue, however, has been extensively licensed over the years, with Motown issuing a CD compilation entitled **Hits From The Legendary Vee-Jay Records** in November 1986, featuring some twenty six major hits from the 50s and 60s, including Gene Chandler, The Spaniels, Jerry Butler, John Lee Hooker, Betty Everett, The Dells, Dee Clark and Bob & Earl, among others.

TATA VEGA

Signed by Motown in 1976, Tata Vega would record some four albums for the label, registering four minor hit singles and one charted album, something of a poor return for her talents.

Born Carmen Rose Vega in Queens, New York City on 7 October 1951, she was given the nickname 'Tata' by her father as it was reportedly the first word she ever uttered. With her father serving in the US Air Force, the family was often required to move around the world, setting up base in Panama and Puerto Rico and various states across America.

Tata left the family home in Miami in 1968 and headed to Los Angeles, where after a year spent working as a street musician she landed a role in a local production of 'Hair'. Among the cast was another would-be singer in Dobie Gray, and when he left to form his own group, Pollution, Tata followed.

"At the time all I wanted to do was sing my music, but I couldn't avoid the entanglement in management and recording contracts. I wasn't comfortable with that side of the business and I never felt I could trust anyone. I really enjoyed singing with Pollution, but the name seemed like a negative connotation during the time when people and myself were searching for something more positive."

After her spell with Pollution, Tata considered going solo but subsequently accepted an invitation to join Earthquire, along with Brie Brandt, Laurie Anne Ball and Mike Gorlaine. The group would record one album for the Natural Resources label in 1973 that was produced by Tom Wilson, but after the album flopped the group left the label and disbanded.

Tata chose to pursue a solo career, working on a number of demos that subsequently got taken into Motown, where Winston Monseque and Iris Gordy were keen enough to offer her a contract, with Winston also becoming her manager and producer. Her second sojourn at Motown proved much more successful than the first, with the title track from her debut album **Full Speed Ahead** becoming a #90 R&B hit in 1976. Her second album, **Totally Tata** found her appealing to a different audience, with *You'll Never Rock Alone* bubbling under the main Billboard chart at #108. In the end it was the disco market that returned the greatest success, with *Get It Up For Love* peaking at #17 on the dance chart and also becoming her only single to chart overseas, making #52 on the Music Week listings in the UK.

The success of *Get It Up For Love*, alongside *I Just Keep Thinking About You Baby* helped propel the album too, making #63 R&B and #170 pop, but instead of capitalising on this modicum of acceptance, Tata struggled to repeat the success, with her final Motown album, 1980's **Givin' All My Love** failing to chart.

After leaving Motown Tata would forge a career as a backing vocalist, working with the likes of Stevie Wonder, Andre Crouch (with whom she would pick up a Grammy Award nomination for Best Soul Female Gospel Performance in 1985 for *Oh It Is Jesus*), Lou Rawls, Chaka Khan, Michael Jackson, Madonna and Ray Charles. Tata would launch something of a gospel career towards the end of the century, recording for Qwest Records in 1998 and Do Rite Records in 2009.

ALBUMS: FULL SPEED AHEAD (1976), TOTALLY TATA (1977), TRY MY LOVE (1979), GIVIN' ALL MY LOVE (1980)

THE VELLS

Whilst the Motown history books show The Vells released only one single, *You'll Never Cherish A Love So True ('Til You Lose It)* backed with *There He Is (At My Door)*, issued on Mel-O-dy in October 1962, it was not the only recording the various members made, for this is in fact The Vandellas under a different name.

You'll Never Cherish featured the soon to depart Gloria Jean Williamson (born in Detroit, Michigan in 1942) on one of her rare leads. Gloria, with a young family at home and the offer of a job in the civil service with Detroit City Council on the table, opted to leave the music business soon after the recording was completed. With the Gordy label having only just released a Martha & The Vandellas single (*I'll Have To Let Him Go*) that featured Martha Reeves on lead, it was felt branding this as another Vandellas single might confuse the public.

It has also been speculated that Berry Gordy's reasoning for branding this as The Vells was that should it prove successful, it would give Gloria the opportunity of returning to Motown, either as a member of her old group The Vandellas or as a founding member of The Vells. The fact that *You'll Never Cherish* flopped ended all speculation and The Vells in one swoop. Gloria Jean Williamson died in 1999.

THE VELVELETTES

Despite being signed to Motown for more than five years and releasing several hit singles, The Velvelettes were one of the few groups that never released an album during their heyday, a situation that was finally resolved during the CD era.

They were formed in 1961 on the campus at Western Michigan State University by sisters Mildred (born on 15 October 1947 and better known as Millie) and Carolyn (born on 10 August 1949 and better known as Cal) Gill with friends Bertha Barbee, her cousin Norma Barbee and Betty Kelley (born in Attalla, Alabama on 16 September 1944), with Cal quickly becoming recognised as the lead singer of the group.

After performing at local fraternity events and sock hops, a friend Robert Bullock (who was a nephew of Berry Gordy) suggested they should go to Detroit to audition for Motown. In Kalamazoo, Reverend and Mrs Willie Gill loaded four members of the group into their car for the drive to Detroit (the remaining member, Norma, took the bus from Flint) and undertook a difficult journey that took some five hours through a severe snowstorm. They arrived at Hitsville and presented themselves at reception, only to be told Motown didn't audition on a Saturday! Just as they were about to leave the building, producer William 'Mickey' Stevenson stepped out of the studio and immediately recognised cousins Bertha and Norma having previously recorded them as The Barbees. After discovering the reason for their visit, Mickey ensured they got their audition, at which the girls sang *Money* (the Barrett Strong number) and *There He Goes*, which was originally written by Norma (upon release the writing credit would be given to Mickey Stevenson) and a subsequent recording session.

Although Quality Control rejected *There He Goes* (which features Stevie Wonder on harmonica) as a single, Mickey got permission to do a deal with the I.P.G. (Independent Producers Group) label to ensure the record at least got an outing, being released in July 1963.

With all five girls concentrating on their school work, their appearances at Motown were sporadic over the next year or so, although they gathered some considerable studio experience during that time. It should be noted that they were not used for backing vocal work, rather they recorded demo discs for various producers that were then handed out to the artists who were to record the proper versions.

The Velvelettes got their own break in 1964, with Norman Whitfield and Mickey Stevenson penning *Needle In A Haystack* for the group, who were now reduced to a trio after Betty left to join The Vandellas and with Millie absent on maternity leave. Released in September 1964 on the V.I.P. label, *Needle* would go on to become a #31 R&B and #45 pop hit, even though the group later claimed they weren't particularly keen on it!

They did, however, like the follow-up *He Was Really Saying Somethin'*, again written by Norman and Mickey with Eddie Holland but which performed as well as its predecessor, peaking at #21 R&B and #64 pop. A third hit, *These Things Will Keep Me From You* came in August 1966 following a change of label to Soul and a change of producers to Harvey Fuqua and Johnny Bristol. The single peaked at #43 R&B and #102 pop, which might have been the reason why the group's eponymous album appeared briefly on the V.I.P. schedule but never got out of the door.

Although The Velvelettes continued to record for another year or so, the original girls were beginning to head off to pastures new, with Millie, Norma and Barbie deciding to leave music in order to raise their respective families. At times the line-up fluctuated between three and four members, with Cal being joined by former Vandella Sandra Tilley and Annette Rogers-McMillan before she too left the group following her marriage to former Monitor and future Temptation member Richard Street.

The Velvelettes effectively came to an end in 1969 and that, seemingly, was the end of the story. Then in 1971 The Velvelettes made a surprise appearance in the UK charts, with a reissued *These Things Will Keep Me From You* hitting #34 at a time when many old Tamla Motown singes were getting a revived airing on UK radio. Despite the clamour for a reunion (which The Elgins undertook), The Velvelettes resisted the temptation, although in 1984 Cal, Millie, Bertha and Norma got together for a one-off concert appearance that eventually saw them back out on the road.

They would be one of many former Motown acts who recorded for Ian Levine's Motorcity label, releasing the album **One Door Closes**. They also finally got something of an official album release on Motown, with the 2005 **The Velvelettes: The Motown Anthology** gathering all of their Motown recordings, including a number of tracks sung in French.

BILLY VERA & THE BEATERS

William McCord was born in Riverside, California on 28 May 1944 and began his singing career in 1962 as a member of The Resolutions. Although he enjoyed some success as a performer and writer, it was the decision to form a 1950s revival group Billy Vera & The Beaters with Chuck Fiore that made his name and reputation. Their track *Slow Down* featured on the soundtrack to 'A Fine Mess' in 1986.

JACKIE VERDELL

Born in Philadelphia, Pennsylvania in 1937, gospel singer Jackie Verdell was considered one of the most under-rated female singers of all, with none other than Aretha Franklin constantly extolling her virtues. Despite this, Jackie's secular career seldom hit the heights many anticipated, due in part to her struggles to get paid for her work on a regular basis. A one-time member of The Davis Sisters, Jackie was also a member of the PUSH Expo Choir and headlined the group on *I'm Too Close To Heaven To Turn Around* on the 'Save The Children' soundtrack. Jackie died during 2002.

BEN VEREEN

A legendary actor, dancer and singer, he was born Benjamin Augustus Middleton in Miami, Florida on 10 October 1946 and subsequently adopted by James and Pauline Vereen, a fact he did not discover until he was 25 and applied for a passport.

Whilst his successes, of which there have been many, have come from all sectors of the entertainment industry, his involvement with Motown came when he played the Leading Player in 'Pippin' for which he won a Tony Award for Best Actor, having been nominated a year previously for his portrayal of Judas in 'Jesus Christ Superstar'.

THE VERSATONES

The Versatones was a very obscure doo wop group formed in New Jersey by serving members of the US Army who first came to the attention of Dickie Goodman some time in 1957. Goodman had fallen out with the distributor of his Luniverse Records label and decided to go independent, setting up the All Star Record Corporation, penning *Tight Skirt Tight Sweater* for The Versatones as one of the company's early releases. For the flip side the group provided their own song *Bila* (written by C Worrell and S Tindall, the closest we have come to identifying any members of the group), but it was *Tight Skirt Tight Sweater* that attracted the initial radio play before the song was banned by numerous stations, chiefly because of the lyrical content. With radio play diminishing, sales went the same way and eventually the record, The Versatones and All Star Records disappeared.

The record was revived some three years later, although it was the flip side *Bila* that attracted all the attention, prompting Fenway Records of Pittsburgh to reissue it, although it still failed to sell. A further three years on, a Philadelphia radio station again jumped on *Bila*, with Atlantic picking it up for national distribution, although even with their superior network were unable to make the single sell in sufficient quantities for it to chart, subsequently leasing the track for yet another reissue, this time by Lost Nite.

All the while *Bila* was attracting attention if not sales, The Versatones turned up at Motown looking for a deal. Handed over to Robert Gordy they recorded something of a novelty item in *It's Company Time*, although it was not released at the time and the group slipped back into obscurity. *It's Company Time* eventually appeared on Volume 4 of **A Cellarful Of Motown** in 2010.

V.I.P. RECORDS

By 1963 Berry Gordy had begun streamlining his various labels, shutting down Divinity, Miracle and Workshop Jazz but opening up another in V.I.P. Records. The label was originally intended to be an outlet for the company's expanding West Coast output, much of which was produced by Hal Davis and Marc Gordon. This pairing was responsible for the very first release on the label, Patrice Holloway's *Stevie*, a tribute to Little Stevie Wonder that was pulled soon after promotional copies had been circulated.

Thus the first official release was The Serenaders' *If Your Heart Says Yes*, which had been recorded in Detroit and originally scheduled for release on the Motown label in the summer of 1963 but was held back for V.I.P. in late January 1964. Having abandoned the West Coast angle right from the off, the V.I.P. label would become host to an eclectic roster over the nine years or so that it was active, including The Velvelettes, R. Dean Taylor, The Elgins, Chris Clark, The Abbey Tavern Singers and The Spinners.

The very last release came in February 1972, with Posse issuing *Feel Like Givin' Up* (the song would later be recorded by former Temptation Paul Williams) before the label was closed and those artists that were retained assigned new homes.

VIRGIL BROTHERS

Inspired by The Walker Brothers and The Righteous Brothers, The Virgil Brothers was formed in Australia in 1968 by Malcolm McGhee, Peter Doyle (born in Melbourne on 28 July 1949) and Rob Lovett. Lovett and McGhee had both been members of Wild Cherries, and when McGhee left The Virgil Brothers in 1969 before their brief brush with fame, he was replaced by another ex-Wild Cherry in Danny Robinson.

For their debut single they picked *Temptation 'Bout To Get Me*, originally a minor Australian hit for The Knight Brothers but which became a bigger hit for the Virgil Brothers. In fact, it was big enough to win them a trip to England and a reissue of the single on the Parlophone label.

This in turn was picked up by Motown and released on the Rare Earth label in the US and Canada in August 1969. The Virgil Brothers were to record only three singles before disbanding, with Doyle later becoming a member of the hugely successful New Seekers.

THE VISCOUNTS

Formed in New Jersey in 1958, The Viscounts was a rock and roll instrumental group comprising Harry Haller (saxophone), brothers Bobby Spievak (guitar) and Joe Spievak (bass), Larry Vecchiop (organ) and Clark Smith (drums). Their major hit was *Harlem Nocturne*, originally released on the Madison label in 1959 and which hit #17 R&B and #52 pop, subsequently being re-released in 1965 on Amy and hitting #39 the second time around. It was also featured on the soundtrack to 'Christine' released by Motown in 1983.

VOICES OF TABERNACLE

Detroit gospel group Voices Of Tabernacle was formed in 1958 and made a number of religious recordings with The Reverend James Cleveland. They also performed *Steal Away* on the Motown album **In Loving Memory** in 1968, issued following the early death of Loucye Gordy Wakefield.

THE VOLUMES

Formed in Detroit, Michigan in 1960 by Eddie Union (lead vocals), Elijah Davis (first tenor), Joe Travillion (baritone), Ernest Newson (bass) and Larry Wright (second tenor), The Volumes performed at local functions before being discovered by manager Henry Reed.

Reed was able to get them dates at venues outside Detroit, including several over the border in Canada, leading to an introduction to local songwriter and label head Willie Ewing. Ewing and Newson were credited with writing the group's only hit, *I Love You* on Chex Records in 1962 (Eddie Union would later claim to have written the song, but Newson was the only group member over the age of 18 at the time the record came out and was therefore the only member able to sign contracts), which would rise to #22 on the pop chart and #6 R&B.

Unfortunately, the group was unable to capitalise on the breakthrough, with a succession of follow-up singles missing the chart and leading to a breakdown in their relationship with Ewing and Chex Records. The Volumes would go on to record for Jubilee, American Arts and Twirl before landing at Harry Balk's Inferno label in 1967.

By this time The Volumes comprised Newson, Davis, Travillion, Bobby Peterson and Jimmy Burger and released their debut for Inferno in April 1967, *A Way To Love You*. This was followed by *My Road Is The Right Road* in October, shortly before Balk sold the label to Motown.

The Volumes only Motown associated release came in May 1968, with *Ain't That Lovin' You*, at much the same time Jimmy Berger left to become a minister, with a returning Eddie Union his replacement. With Harry Balk concentrating on getting the Rare Earth label up and running, there was no one at Motown to champion The Volumes' cause, with the result they recorded little and released nothing further, eventually leaving the label in 1970 and recording one single for the Karen label.

THE VOWS

The Vows was formed in Los Angeles, California in 1960, with James Moore (born in Belaire, Ohio), Jerome Evans, Robert Washington and Helen Simpson in the first incarnation. The group recorded one single with producer George Motola (his wife Rickie Page would later record for Motown as Joanne & The

Triangles) for the Markay label in 1962, *I Wanna Chance* backed with *Have You Heard*.

Two years later The Vows, by then consisting of Moore, Bobby Solomon and Joe Lawson, found themselves being utilised by Hal Davis and Marc Gordon at Motown's west coast studio, usually doing backing vocals on sessions with Brenda Holloway and Stevie Wonder. They also got to record their own single, with Hal and Marc dusting off Berry Gordy's composition *Buttered Popcorn*, which had been the only Supremes single release that had featured Florence Ballard on lead vocals.

Issued on the V.I.P. label in May 1965, The Vows version did little, although the flip side, *Tell Me* became a favourite on the Northern Soul circuit. The lyrics to *Buttered Popcorn* meanwhile have sparked an ongoing debate ever since it was released; is it about oral sex or popcorn? Berry Gordy insists it's the latter.

VOYAGE

Lead vocalist Donna Taylor fronted five piece funk group Voyage, who were based in Bloomington, Indiana. The group, which also comprised Gregg Pagani and Rodney Thomas alongside Kat and Kelvin, recorded the single *Strange Situation* at Seagrape Studios in Chicago for the local Beet label that attracted enough interest locally to get snapped up by Motown in 1987. A planned reissue on 12" in May 1987 never materialised and following the label's sale to MCA, Voyage was one of the bands subsequently dropped.

JOHN WAGNER COALITION

Producer, studio and record label owner John Wagner had long been a feature of the New Mexico music scene, running the Delta Records label out of Albuquerque throughout the 1960s. Having first come to Motown's attention when he produced both Heart and Corliss albums released on Natural Resources in 1972, he leased a one-off single to Rare Earth the following January, *The Battle Is Over* (written by James Siegling and Frank Larrabee, a duo who also recorded for Albuquerque's Look Records label).

He might have been better licensing an album made in 1976, **Shades Of Brown**, which was something of a private press of 1,000 copies of an album of James Brown covers and which became a much sought after item for the next thirty or so years. John continues to run his own studio in Albuquerque, these days specialising in music for the advertising fraternity.

KATHY WAKEFIELD

One of the many successful female songwriters to pass through Motown Kathy Wakefield had ambitions of becoming a dancer or a singer, moving to Los Angeles as an eighteen year old looking to pursue her dream. She auditioned for Lionel Newman, a successful conductor and musical director for both the film and television divisions of 20th Century, subsequently getting a part in several television shows including The Monkees without setting the world on fire.

Kathy then linked with Dotty Harmony, another dancer and singer, recording the local hit *Prince Of My Dreams* (written by future Bread frontman David Gates) and a number of other singles under the names Dottie & Kathy and The Beverly Sisters. However, it was eventually songwriting that caught Kathy's attention, working with Annette Tucker on *Feelin' Kinda Sunday* which was recorded by Frank and Nancy Sinatra.

The exposure of having such luminaries record their material eventually secured Kathy a contract with Jobette, where she would write with the likes of Leonard Caston, Ron Miller and James Carmichael (the three were billed as Charlemagne), penning hits for the Temptations, Diana Ross, The Supremes, Eddie Kendricks, Thelma Houston, Smokey Robinson and The Four Tops.

After leaving Motown Kathy would continue her writing career, returning to film and television work, although this time around on the other side of the camera, writing the themes and incidental songs to several productions. She also wrote a novel 'Snaketown' and numerous short stories.

WALK AWAY FROM LOVE – DAVID RUFFIN [SINGLE]

No one doubted that David Ruffin had talent in abundance, but every ounce of craft was matched by an ego that was uncontrollable. He had scored a major hit with his first single after he had walked away from The Temptations, but thereafter it was a downward spiral, fuelled by a growing drug problem and continuing battles with the Motown hierarchy. According to David, the only thing that prevented him from becoming a major solo star was Motown and Berry Gordy's refusal to give him access to the better songs, writers and producers. He may well have had a point, for his body of work as a solo performer stands scrutiny with his peers.

In 1975 it had been over six years since he had graced the upper echelons of the pop and R&B charts, with few within Motown prepared to take on the temperamental and at times troublesome singer and it looked to all intents and purposes as though his contract was being allowed to run its course. Then Suzanne De Passe took a phone call from Charles Kipps, a business associate and writing partner of Van McCoy, who would call from time to time to see if there were any projects that Motown might like to throw their way.

After a few pleasantries, it was agreed that David Ruffin might benefit from the talents of Van McCoy, who was then hot on the charts himself with *The Hustle*, one of the disco movement's biggest hits. As it happened, Charles had something that he felt might be ideal for David entitled *Walk Away From Love*, a song that Van had already produced on The Choice Four with little success.

Van assembled a first class musical crew in Richard Tee and Paul Griffin on keyboards, Eric Gale, John Tropea and Hugh McCracken on guitar, Gordon Edwards on bass, Steve Gadd on drums and additional keyboards from Ken Bichel and Van McCoy himself. Backing vocals would be provided by another of Van McCoy's pet groups, Faith Hope & Charity, whilst the string and horn arrangements were handled by Gene Orloff.

Whilst the experience of those within Motown was that the singer was difficult to handle, it was a different David Ruffin that walked through the door of New York's Mediasound Studio, nailing *Walk Away From Love* at the very first attempt.

"Everyone was so knocked out, especially when David went up to the high note. He did it so effortlessly," said Charles later. "What was funny was that we were all saying, 'That's it, that's it,' and David was saying, 'No, I can do better.' So he did another seven or eight takes, and then finally came out and said, 'You're right, that's it.'"

Released as a single in October 1975 (in the UK the single was released two months later in December), it would become the biggest single of his career, hitting #9 pop and topping the R&B chart as well as becoming his only solo hit in the UK where it reached #10.

WALK AWAY RENEE – THE FOUR TOPS [SINGLE]

Renee Fladen-Kamm was a student at the High School of Music and Art and a girlfriend of Tom Finn, a bass player with the baroque pop band Left Banke. Finn wasn't the only member of the group enamoured with Renee, however, for the group's keyboard player Michael Brown (real name Michael Lookofsky) also had feelings for her, enough to have begun composing the song *Walk Away Renee*, which was duly rounded out by Tony Sansone and Bob Calilli.

Released in July 1966 and a Top Five pop hit, the song was good enough for The Four Tops to have recorded a cover version in October the same year, although the track was not considered strong enough for a single release and was slotted onto the **Reach Out** album released in July 1967. When Holland-Dozier-Holland underwent a work to rule and subsequently departed Motown, the company was faced with little or no new product from The Four Tops (although the group and their mentors were believed to have stockpiled possibly hundreds of recordings, much of the material was in fact cover versions intended to pad out original material on albums) for the foreseeable future.

Keen to maintain the momentum that had been built by hits such as *Reach Out I'll Be There, Bernadette* and *7 Rooms Of Gloom*, Tamla Motown in the UK opted to release *Walk Away Renee* as a single in December 1967. Their plan was further helped by the fact that Left Banke's original, whilst a major American hit, had failed to chart at all after being released on the Philips label in October 1966. Widely held to be a better version than the original, The Four Tops' *Walk Away Renee* returned the group to the Top Ten in the UK, peaking at #3 in mid January 1968.

The success of the British release prompted an American response, with *Walk Away Renee* being issued stateside in January and hitting #15 R&B and #14 pop. The Four Tops would later record an Italian version, entitled *L'Arcobaleno* (which translates as 'The Rainbow'), which can be found on the album **Motown Around The World**.

JUNIOR WALKER & THE ALL STARS

Much of the background information on Junior Walker is muddled or contradictory, due largely to Junior's willingness to agree with whatever back-story Motown created for him. Take for example the year of his birth, which has variously been listed as 1931, 1938, 1940 or 1942, or the origins of his nickname, which was attributed to his walking everywhere as a child or in deference to his stepfather, or even a combination of both. Even when pressed he could offer no logical explanation, often just shrugging his shoulders.

As far as is best known, therefore, he was likely born Oscar Mixon in Blythesville, Arkansas on 14 June 1931 and changed name to Autry DeWalt Jr. as a child, possibly as a result of his mother remarrying. As for the Junior Walker tag, this was acquired during his early teenage years.

"They gave me that, walkin' to school. I just walked, and they just gave me that name. And my stepfather was Walker."

When not walking around, Junior was taking an active interest in music and in particular the likes of Louis Jordan, Earl Bostic, Gene Ammons and Charlie Parker, all of whom would unknowingly contribute something to the musical education of Junior Walker.

"There's quite a few guys that were blowin' saxophone when I picked up. Boots Randolph, Stan Getz, and there was Charlie Parker. I used to listen to him a lot. I used to practice after all those different guys. I used to sit down and listen to them, practice by them. That's how I used to get down."

Having long since left Blythesville, Junior moved to South Bend, Indiana where he would assemble his first group.

"I came out of high school like any other kid, and we started trying to put a little band together, that's all. At first, we called ourselves The Jumpin' Jacks, and then we played little clubs for two or three dollars, five dollars, whatever we could pick up. We played for little school proms and stuff like that. Willie Woods (who joined The Jacks as a guitarist) was from South Bend, I was from South Bend for a while. I moved to Battle Creek, Michigan. And Victor Thomas, who played the organ, he was from South Bend. Jimmy Graves was from Cleveland, Ohio. He played the drums. We didn't have a bass player. He played the bass on the organ. That's the way we run it down then. It was pretty strong."

In fact The Jumpin' Jacks appears to have been a short-lived group, with Junior then joining a trio led by Billy 'Stix' Nicks (drums) with Fred Patton (organ), subsequently adding Willie Woods (born on 5 September 1936) on guitar and becoming a quartet. Junior took over control of the group when Nicks left to join the US Army and brought in Tony Washington (drums), replaced Fred Patton with Victor Thomas, Washington with Jack Douglas and then James Graves (born in 1938) and also oversaw a change of name; their ability to play almost anything that was requested of them whilst on the road earned them the moniker of The All-Stars, and it wasn't long before the group's billing became Junior Walker & The All-Stars. That ability saw them backing a number of acts as well as playing their own sets, with a chance meeting at the El Grotto, a small club in Battle Creek resulting in an eventual move to Detroit.

"Johnny Bristol came and got me out of the club and took me to Detroit. He said, 'You wanna cut records?' I said, 'If there's some money in it, yeah!'"

Junior and his All-Stars journeyed to Detroit and were introduced to Harvey Fuqua, then running his own Tri-Phi label, who had them backing Johnny & Jackie as well as offering them their own recording contract, with *Twist Lackawanna* backed with *Willie's Blues* his label debut in January 1962. Seven months later came the follow-up *Cleo's Mood*, a song Junior wrote with Willie Woods.

"Willie Woods was writing that tune one night. We was at a club, and we was playing it. This was before we was famous. And we was fiddlin' around with it, and he looked at me, and he said, 'What about this tune?' I said, 'Boy, that's a bad tune!' And this chick walked across, and I said, 'Mmhmm! Ol' Cleo's back!' Just like that, I didn't know if the girl was named Cleo, but we always called her Cleo."

Tri-Phi lacked the marketing and promotional wherewithal to turn *Cleo's Mood* into a hit in August 1962, but old *Cleo* would be back some three years or so later. Junior Walker & The All-Stars released their final Tri-Phi single in February 1963, *Good Rockin'* being accompanied by *Brainwasher Part 2* (the first instalment had been the flip to *Cleo's Mood*), after which Harvey Fuqua sold his interests in Tri-Phi and Harvey to Berry Gordy at Motown.

"The record company kinda broke up then," was Junior's take on events. "They couldn't really hang on to it, 'cause they didn't have enough money to handle it. We cut a few other tunes, but then they merged with Motown. And I walked over to Motown and talked with Mr Gordy. He said, 'So you want a contract?' I said, 'Yeah, I wanna contract.' He said, 'So you want to record?' 'Yes sir, I wanna record,' said I. 'Give that boy a contract,' says Mr Gordy. When I got the contract I asked what exactly I was signing. 'Can you read?' Mr Gordy asked. 'I can read some stuff but not everything,' I replied. And he told me, 'Go ahead and sign, we won't mess you around.' I trusted him. I signed."

Berry himself took control of Junior Walker on his first sessions, resulting in the single *Satan's Blues* backed with *Monkey Jump* appearing on the Soul label in August 1964. Whilst Junior was happy to sign his Motown contract and record as and when required, much of his and the rest of the All-Stars time was spent out on the road, from where originated their major chart breakthrough.

"I was watching 'em when they came out with this new dance," he said, recalling that night at El Grotto. "They was doing the Karate too, but this dance kind of got to me. They was goin' across the floor like they was shootin'. So I called a couple of 'em. I said, 'What are you doin' now? What kind of junk is this?' The girl looked at me and said, 'Man, that's the Shotgun!' I said, 'The Shotgun?!' They said, 'You better write a tune to that! That's what's happenin'!' So I said okay, and went on to write the thing. I called Mr Gordy up – at that point you could call him and talk to him. So I called him up. And he said, 'Yeah, what's happening?' I said, 'Well, I've got a tune called *Shotgun*!' And he fell out and went to laughing, and said, 'Come on in and record it.' And we went on in and did it, and it come to be a great tune."

Not just a great tune but a successful one too. Junior Walker and his All-Stars turned up at Hitsville in December 1964 to record the tune, with Berry Gordy and Lawrence Horn producing the session, but unfortunately, not all the All-Stars turned up and not all of those who did had the musical ability to satisfy Berry Gordy, with the result *Shotgun* features Benny Benjamin on drums. Also missing was Fred Patton, the former Jumpin' Jacks member that Junior wanted to sing on *Shotgun*, but when he failed to show up at the session, Berry Gordy instructed Junior to sing it instead.

"That was the first song I ever sung. We had a guy gonna come in to sing it, and man, that guy didn't show up. We went on, and Berry Gordy said, 'You guys come here and set this thing up! I can't waste no time with you. Go in there and record it.' I said, 'Well, we need a singer!' He said, 'You sing it then!' Everybody else said, 'You sing it! Get up there and do something!' So we went in there, and I got up there and sung it. I just hollered it, you know. Just went on through it like it should be. And I told the guy when we got through, 'We'll get somebody else, we'll bring somebody in.' He said, 'Man, I got what I want!'"

Whilst the song honoured a number of other dance routines (Junior calls out 'Twine Time' during the song, which Berry thought sounded more like 'Cryin' Time'), it brought prominence to The Shotgun, with the single becoming an R&B chart topper (for four weeks) and a #4 pop hit, setting something of a template Junior Walker & The All-Stars would follow for several years to come. Even as he was back out on the road supporting *Shotgun* (which would go on to garner a Grammy nomination for Best R&B Recording), Junior was putting together the follow-up *Do The Boomerang*, another song based on a dance craze.

Released in May 1965, it would become a Top Ten R&B hit and reach #36 pop. At the same time, he had his debut album out, **Shotgun** going on to top the R&B chart but, perhaps indicative of his appeal at the time, finish a lowly #108 on the pop listings. **Shotgun** was crammed full of hits and potential hits, with *Shotgun* and *Do The Boomerang* being joined by *Shake And Fingerpop*, an updated version of *Cleo's Mood* and *Road Runner*. *Shake And Fingerpop* was combined with *Cleo's Back* for release as a single in July 1965 and became a #7 R&B and #29 pop hit (*Cleo's Back* would peak at #43 pop in its own right), and just in case the public weren't sure which Cleo it was who had returned, Soul released the update of *Cleo's Mood* as a single in December 1965, which hit #14 R&B and #50 pop. It was however *Road Runner* that stood out from the crowd, a song written for Junior by the prolific Holland-Dozier-Holland team.

"I always run in and out of the studio, so Brian Holland and Dozier, they was kinda the ones that wrote the tune, they called me when I was comin' in. He says, 'Hey man, where's your horn?' I said, 'Well, I left it in the car, I left it at home, I think.' He said, 'From now on, when you come to the studio, always bring your horn!' I said, 'Alright, sir.' And then he told me, 'Look, I got a tune for you.' I said, 'What's the name of it?' 'He said, 'The same thing you're doing, 'Road Runner'. So I said, 'The next time I come in, I'll record it.' So we went on a road trip, and when we came back in, I came in the door runnin' again. And he said, 'You ready?' I said, 'Yeah, I'm ready,' and we went right in the studio and cut it."

Road Runner was something of a departure from the norm for HDH, with the resulting single as energetic and frantic as anything Junior had previously recorded and as far removed from HDH's almost sophisticated productions on The Four Tops and The Supremes. Whilst The All-Stars were more than capable of re-producing the required sound out on the road, several within Motown felt the various musicians who made up the group lacked the sophistication needed for recording sessions, with the result the bulk of Junior Walker's recordings feature him being backed with The Funk Brothers. *Road Runner* would prove to be another smash, hitting #4 R&B and #20 pop and would be revisited as the title track of an August 1966 album, but by then Motown had already released **Soul Session** some five months previously.

If the material on **Soul Session** sounded dated then that is because it most likely was, a collection of songs written by Junior and the various All-Stars prior to his arrival at Motown and all produced by Harvey Fuqua (since the album is devoid of any real recording information, the suspicion remains that not only the material but the recordings themselves originate back to Junior's Tri-Phi days). That did not halt the album's progress, with a #7 R&B and #130 pop placing keeping Junior's name in vogue.

There were some old tunes present on **Road Runner** too (most notably *Twist Lackawanna*), which in addition to the title track offered Junior's treatments on a number of old Motown classics, including Marvin Gaye's *How Sweet It Is (To Be Loved By You)* and Barrett Strong's *Money (That's What I Want)*. The success of *Road Runner* and *How Sweet It Is*, which would become an R&B #3 hit and #18 pop (and hit #22 in the UK) helped the album sail to #6 R&B and #64 pop. As successful a chart performer as he was, the only way to fully enjoy the Junior Walker experience was to see him and The All-Stars live, a fact that had been noted by Motown when they had released both *How Sweet It Is* and *Money* by adding the sound of a crowd after the event, although Junior himself was unsure as to how the effect was created.

"When I heard it, then I heard all them people on it. It was like a party thing. They wasn't there when I recorded it." Later, however, he would change tack. "It was kinda live. When I did it, they was there. They was cuttin' it, and I said, 'Cut it to my arrangements.' And we was doin' it to my arrangements, and everybody said, 'This is a party! This ain't no cuttin' no record,' so they went to doin' it like a party. And it turned out to be a big smash. Sometimes you pick up on those things. They just don't come all the time."

In the absence of any new material, Motown raided Junior's albums for singles in 1967, taking *Pucker Up Buttercup* from the **Road Runner** album, which would stall agonisingly short of the Top Thirty pop (at #31) and the Top Ten R&B (at #11). *Shoot Your Shot* dated back even further, having appeared on his debut album **Shotgun**, but that still did not hinder its chart performance, culminating in a #33 R&B and #44 pop hit. In the wake of these successes, minor though they may have been, Motown reasoned that any product on Junior Walker was better than none and captured one of his live shows and released the album **Junior Walker And The All Stars Live** in September 1967.

Motown's hunch proved correct, with the album hitting #119 pop and #22 R&B (the album was also the first chance Junior's fans had to witness new drummer Billy 'Stix' Nicks, who rejoined his old group mate following the departure of Jimmy Graves in 1966 (Graves was tragically killed in a car crash in 1967), being topped and tailed by The Velvelettes and Earl Van Dyke respectively. Junior finally got new studio material out in November 1967, an updated version of The Supremes' hit *Come See About Me* which thrilled his fan-base as much as the original did The Supremes' and became another Top Ten R&B hit at #8 as well as hitting #24 pop in January 1968. His only other hit for 1968 was a new title, *Hip City*, a two part entity that was written by Junior and Eddie Hollis (Part 1) and Junior with Janie Bradford (Part 2). It was to be Part 2 that was plugged to radio, resulting in another R&B Top Ten hit (#7) and #31 pop.

The rest of the year was spent out on the road, although even when Junior was able to go into Hitsville, he spent much of the time trying to avoid Johnny Bristol, who had a song he wanted Junior to record, *What Does It Take (To Win Your Love)*.

"Johnny Bristol was tryin' to get me to do the tune, and I turned it down. I said, 'Oh man, I don't want to cut that tune.' So he said, 'okay.' He didn't say nothin'. So I didn't cut the tune. And it was a year later, I came back in at the time we was cuttin' *Hip City*. So I came in the door, and he was standin' up there lookin' at me just as funny, silly, you know. I said, 'What's happenin', Brits?' He said, 'Nothin' to it. What's goin' on?' I said, 'Oh, everything's mellow. What're you doin' here?' He said, 'I'm waitin' on you to cut this tune!' I said, 'What tune?' He said, *What Does It Take To Win Your Love*. If you turn me down, I'll be here next year.' I said, 'Come on, man.' So we went on in and cut that tune. And that was a big one. I said, 'I'm glad I cut it.' I didn't think I could do it. I really didn't. But he pushed it on me, so I did it."

It was not the first release, however, for Motown inexplicably released the title track from the **Home Cookin'** album, a single that stalled at #19 R&B and #42 pop at much the same time the album was being released. *What Does It Take* had been turned down as a possible single by the Quality Control Department meeting, those present believing the song was too mellow to be a Junior Walker release, but radio play on it whilst it remained an album track convinced all and sundry that it might be worth taking a chance on. The decision proved correct, with the single topping the R&B chart for two weeks and hitting #4 pop.

In the UK Junior Walker was enjoying something of a revival of fortunes, with a reissued *Road Runner* hitting #12 and *What Does It Take* being lined up as the follow-up; it hit #13. Despite his initial reluctance at a mellower sound, Junior soon realised it was for his own benefit.

"After I got into it, I just went on and went to doin' 'em. I stopped sayin' what I couldn't do. I said I couldn't do those slow songs. I really didn't want to do 'em. Johnny said 'This is all I got.' So we did it, and it was a big hit. I turned down *Someday We'll Be Together*. I should have cut that record!"

Motown had released an accompanying album, **Gotta Hold On To This Feeling**, but in the aftermath of the single success, hastily repackaged it as **What Does It Take To Win Your Love**. The material was diverse, including a cover version of The Guess Who's *These Eyes*, with Junior's version being released as a single barely six months after the original, but Junior's outing was well received, hitting #3 R&B and #16 pop. Junior effectively had two albums out at the time, a greatest hits package (which would hit #19 R&B and #43 pop) and the retitled **What Does It Take To Win Your Love**, which would peak at #12 R&B and #92 pop in 1970.

That year also produced two further smash hit R&B singles in *Gotta Hold On To This Feeling* (#2 as well as #21 pop) and *Do You See Me Love (For You Growing)*, an update of an old Johnny & Jackey track that became a #3 R&B and #32 pop hit. Not nearly as successful was a version of Neil Diamond's *Holly Holy*, which slipped down the chart somewhat to #33 R&B and #75 pop, its' presence somewhat diluting the appeal of the flip *Carry Your Own Load*, another song with a Johnny & Jackey heritage.

There was no shortage of Junior Walker material that year, with a further two albums hitting the streets before 1970 was finished, a second live album appearing in May and **A Gasssssssssss**, which appeared four months later. Whilst not a major seller, **A Gassssssssss** did at least keep Junior active on the chart, hitting #28 R&B and #110 pop, the proliferation of cover versions perhaps hindering its chance of greater success. There was more of the same on **Rainbow Funk**, released in July 1971, but the original material was at least stronger, with *Take Me Girl, I'm Ready* deserving a much better fate than to stall at #18 R&B and #50 pop, whilst Junior's rendition of The Crusaders' *Way Back Home* should also have progressed beyond #24 and #52 on the R&B and pop charts respectively. With no major hit single, the album had to content itself with peaking at #91 pop, although its final placing of #12 proved his R&B fan-base hadn't deserted him (although quite what *they* made of his rendition of George Harrison and The Beatles' *Something* is anyone's guess!).

Junior was to make something of a triumphant return to the R&B Top Ten in 1972 with *Walk In The Night*, a #10 R&B and #46 pop hit following its release in February 1972. Whilst the song sounded as though it was a blaxploitation theme looking for a film to which to attach itself, the single became a sizeable hit in the UK, making #16, which in turn enabled *Take Me Girl, I'm Ready* to take its place on the chart, also peaking at #16. Tamla Motown were able to make it three in a row when a revived *Way Back Home* crept into the Top 40, peaking at #35 and becoming the last of Junior Walker's singles to make it on to the British chart.

Way back home, Junior had to deal with diminishing returns on his albums and singles, with **Moody Jr.**, from which *Walk In The Night* was extracted, stalling at a lowly #142 pop and #22 R&B, his final appearance on the album chart. After the heady days of the 1960s, the 1970s finished in some disappointment, with only three further hits singles over the course of the next four years. None of these matched the heights of even his recent success, indeed none even broke into the Top 40 of the R&B chart, but Junior Walker kept busy for much of the rest of the decade by doing what he did best; playing live. The lack of a major hit did little to dim his popularity as a live performer, even if his audience had little time for material drawn from his albums **Peace And Understanding Is Hard To Find, Hot Shot, Sax Appeal, Whopper Bopper Show Stopper** and **Smooth**.

Junior left Motown soon after the release of **Smooth**, linking up with Norman Whitfield at his eponymous label where he recorded one album, **Back Street Boogie**, from which was extracted his final hit single under his own name, a version of Rose Royce's *Wishing On A Star* that peaked at #89 R&B in 1979. Two years later Junior was back on the chart, providing Foreigner's *Urgent* with his distinctive, almost trademarked saxophone solo that enabled the single to gallop to #4 pop.

In 1983, with his son Autry Walt III in tow as the All-Stars drummer, Junior returned to Motown for one final album, **Blow The House Down.** He continued touring, blowing the house down around the country until his death from cancer on 23 November 1995. Willie Woods died from lung cancer on 27 May 1997. Victor Thomas died on 28 November 2010.

ALBUMS: SHOTGUN (1965), SOUL SESSION (1966), ROAD RUNNER (1966), LIVE! (1967), HOME COOKIN' (1969), WHAT DOES IT TAKE TO WIN YOUR LOVE (GOTTA HOLD ON TO THIS FEELING) (1969), LIVE! (1970), A GASSSSSS (1970), RAINBOW FUNK (1971), MOODY JR (1971), PEACE AND UNDERSTANDING IS HARD TO FIND (1973), HOT SHOT (1976), SAX APPEAL (1976), WHOPPER, BOPPER SHOW STOPPER (1976), SMOOTH (1978)

COMPILATIONS: GREATEST HITS (1969), ANTHOLOGY (1974), 19 GREATEST HITS (1986)

EMMETT 'BABE' WALLACE

Born in Brooklyn on 24 June 1909, Emmett Babe Wallace was a bouncer at Harlem's Savoy Ballroom at the age of 19 but would eventually get to perform at the venue as a singer. He would ultimately go on to make his name as a songwriter, actor (indeed he is considered one of the pioneers of black cinema) and singer, equally at home and at ease with all. Having made his Broadway debut in 1946 in 'Lysistrata', he returned in 1976 in the role of Arvide Abernathy in the revival of 'Guys And Dolls'. He died on 3 December 2006.

WAR – EDWIN STARR [SINGLE]

Norman Whitfield and Barrett Strong were never afraid to use music as a way and means of getting across political and social commentary, with The Temptations their usual mouthpiece. In 1970 Barrett wrote *War*, a lyrical exercise in the futility of war in general and the then still raging Vietnam War in particular. With Norman adding a funk fuelled musical accompaniment, The Temptations recorded the track for inclusion on their forthcoming album **Psychedelic Shack**, with Paul Williams and Dennis Edwards handling lead vocal duties alongside Melvin Franklin calling out a recruit training chant in 'hup, two, three, four' in the background.

The album was released amid some of the worst rioting in American history, with students at the Ohio State University staging a campaign of direct action, which in turn led to a clash between the students and the Ohio National Guard that left four dead. The following day, the US military invaded Cambodia to both international outcry and domestic anger. Set against this, *War* was as good a statement against the growing situation as any, with some 4,000 students from across the country writing to Motown and demanding that the track be released as a single.

This was easier said than done, for Berry Gordy believed releasing the track on The Temptations might alienate their more conservative fanbase and have a long term, detrimental effect on the group. Norman Whitfield believed he had the answer; if releasing the track on The Temptations was too risqué, he would merely revisit the song with another act from Motown's stable. The first act chosen was Rare Earth, the rock group who had recently scored a major hit with their take on The Temptations' *Get Ready*. However, it was one thing covering The Temptations' love songs and a completely different thing altogether tackling political commentary. Besides, when they heard the backing tracks Norman had produced they were further convinced that their future would be better served recording their own compositions; they turned the song down.

Instead, Norman called in Edwin Starr, an artist whose only Motown Top Ten hit has been *25 Miles* a year earlier. Edwin would record the song, but he wanted to record it *his* way, which meant numerous vocal ad-libs during the course of the recording. The version of *War* that emerged at the end of the session is a much tighter and harder version than that recorded by The Temptations; Edwin's version invokes exactly the impact Barrett Strong was looking for when he first wrote the song.

Released on 9 June 1970 on the Gordy label, *War* proved to be something of a rallying cry for the whole world, with the single going on to top the pop charts for three weeks and hit #3 on both the R&B and British charts. Whilst the single did have some initial repercussions for Edwin, who found his domestic bookings taking a bit of a blow, internationally it re-affirmed his growing reputation.

War was deemed vital enough to appear on two consecutive Edwin albums, just to ensure the message really hit the spot, whilst the song would later be covered by Bruce Springsteen (his live version was released as a single in 1985 and hit #8 in the US and #19 in the UK), The Jam and Frankie Goes To Hollywood.

Edwin himself would revisit the song in 1993, recording a version with Shadow of the television combat show 'The Gladiators', but this version is a mere shadow of the original, as evidenced by its lowly chart position of #69.

SINGIN' SAMMY WARD

Born James Woodley in Birmingham, Alabama, blues and gospel singer Sammy Ward moved to Detroit in the 1950s and secured regular work as a club singer before the decade was out. He joined Tamla in 1960, issuing *What Makes You Love Him* backed with *That Child Is Really Wild* in September the same year, the single being attributed to Singin' Sammy Ward (a moniker bestowed on him by Berry's wife Raynoma). Before the top side had even registered with record buyers, Berry changed tack, replacing it with *Who's The Fool*, a song written by Berry and Smokey. The switch worked, for *Who's The Fool* would go on to become the only single of Sammy's that made the chart, peaking at #23 R&B.

Two months later Sammy helped establish what would become a hugely successful ploy in the future, recording a duet with Sherri Taylor in *Oh Lover*, although the single did little and would be Sherri's only outing for the company. Sammy meanwhile hung around Hitsville for a few more years, although his recorded output was quite meagre, amounting to a re-recording of *What Makes You Love Him* in October 1961, *Big Joe Moe* backed by *Everybody Knew It But Me* issued in March 1962 and, following a switch to the Soul label, *Bread Winner* in March 1964. None sold particularly well, not least because Sammy's blues vocal style was out of step with the rest of the material being released.

Sammy left Motown in the middle of the 1960s, briefly re-surfacing at the Groove City label in 1968 where, as Sam Ward, he recorded *Stone Broke* and *Sister Lee*. He then left the music business altogether, although he was re-discovered some twenty or so years later and recorded for Ian Levine's Motorcity label before dying some time during the 1990s.

LEON WARE

His credentials as a writer have never been questioned, but it is interesting to imagine what might have happened to Leon Ware as a performer had Motown given his **Musical Massage** a modicum of promotional support. There is no doubt Berry Gordy was impressed with the album, enough to try and convince Leon to hand the songs over the Marvin Gaye!

Born in Black Bottom in Detroit, Michigan on 16 February 1940, the youngest of eleven children and the seventh son, Leon suffered a serious accident with a slingshot whilst still a youth and tore the retina in his right eye, the trauma of which left him totally blind for two years and resulted in him being sent to the Fitzgerald School for the Blind (a school that Stevie Wonder would later attend).

Although he had written his first song at the age of nine, it was as a singer that he first pursed a musical career, singing in a jazz club at the age of 14 and a year later becoming a member of Detroit group The Romeos, which also included Lamont Dozier, Tyrone Hunter, Gene Dyer and Kenny Johnson. When the group disbanded Lamont Dozier headed off on a career that would eventually lead to Motown whilst Leon resorted back to being a jazz singer and writer.

He would eventually move to New York in 1960 where he landed a recording contract with ABC/Paramount and wrote the material for half an album that never materialised before returning to Detroit to concentrate on songwriting. Briefly connected with Motown and Jobete, Leon scored some success with one of his first compositions, *Got To Have You Back* providing The Isley Brothers with a minor pop and R&B hit, before he headed out west to California.

After a spell working at Bell Records as an in-house writer Leon was connected with United Artists, co-writing six songs for Ike & Tina Turner's **Nuff Said** album and eventually getting his own recording contract, which would result in the eponymous debut album in 1972.

By then Leon was again associated with Motown, co-writing *I Wanna Be Where You Are* with T-Boy Ross which would become a hit for Michael Jackson and *Just Seven Numbers* with Pam Sawyer for The Four Tops. The deal with Motown was not exclusive, enabling Leon to work with a string of artists outside of the company, including Quincy Jones (writing and performing on *If I Ever Lose This Heaven*) and Minnie Riperton (co-writing *Inside My Love*). Among his best known songs of the time was *Rolling Down The Mountainside*, a major hit for The Main Ingredient but which was originally recorded by Motown act Third Creation without success.

By 1975 Leon had secured a recording contract with Motown and was working on his planned label debut **I Want You**. Rough mixes of the album were played to Berry Gordy who in turn played them to Marvin Gaye. What had begun as a Leon Ware album was subsequently converted in a Marvin Gaye album, with Leon co-producing (it had originally been planned that Leon's songwriting partner Arthur 'T-Boy' Ross would also co-produce, but after making some ill-advised comments to Marvin found himself barred from the studio) with Marvin and co-writing every track on the album. **I Want You** became a major success, revitalising Marvin's career and sending Leon back into the studio to begin work on his delayed solo album.

Co-produced with Hal Davis, **Musical Massage** was another tour de force, one that Motown felt would again be ideal for Marvin Gaye, but this time Leon stuck to his guns and insisted that it be released as a Leon Ware solo album. Motown duly released the album but did little or nothing else, resulting in the album becoming one of the many lost Motown masterpieces.

Leon would leave the label and whilst continuing to write exceptional songs that provided others with major hits found his own solo career a little more difficult to orchestrate. After recording for Fabulous Records in 1979 Leon signed with Elektra, recording two critically if not commercially received albums in

Rockin' With You Eternally and **Leon Ware**. Whilst he has continued to add to his tally of hits as a composer, his own recording career has been somewhat overlooked, although he remains an immensely popular figure in the UK, where his albums received something of a reissue programme from Expansion Records, including an expanded edition of **Musical Massage**.
ALBUM: MUSICAL MASSAGE (1976)

WARP 9

Originally formed as an electro funk trio by Milton 'Boe' Brown (previously of The Strikers), Chuck Wansley and female singer Alda Dyer, Warp 9 were initially a studio group on Prism Records out of New York. After enjoying a couple of minor hits the group underwent a number of changes, with Alda heading off for a solo career (she would eventually pitch up at Motown), being replaced by Carolyn Harding and then Katherine Joyce. When Brown left, Chuck and Katherine continued as a duo and signed with Motown, releasing the single *Skips A Beat* in December 1985 and their debut album **Fade In, Fade Out** in January 1986.
ALBUM: FADE IN, FADE OUT (1985)

DIONNE WARWICK

Born Marie Dionne Warrick in East Orange, New Jersey on 12 December 1940, she formed the Gospelaires with her sister Dee Dee, cousin Cissy Houston and Doris Troy and worked as backing singers in New York. She was heard by Burt Bacharach on a Drifters session in 1961 and signed by Scepter in 1962, although her name was misspelled on the contract, hence her stage name of Dionne Warwick (she also briefly went by the name Dionne Warwicke, adding the extra 'e' after a visit to a psychic). Dionne recorded a succession of major international hits during the course of the next six years or so, becoming one of the most popular female singers around. In 1984, Dionne was largely responsible for getting Stevie Wonder attached to the film project 'The Woman In Red', with Stevie writing the soundtrack, which featured two duets with Dionne in *It's You* and *Weakness* and also penning a solo song in *Moments Are Moments*.

EARL WASHINGTON ALL STARS

Born in Chicago, Illinois on 3 April 1921, Earl Edward Washington wanted to play jazz as a youngster, even though his mother insisted he study classical piano and organised lessons with the Professor of Music at the Chicago Academy of Music. Dr Walter Dellers was impressed with Earl's hand co-ordination, as were those who had come up against the youngster when he won a Chicago Golden Glove boxing title!

After graduating from Morgan Park High School Earl attended the Chicago and Boston conservatories of music, eventually earning both a Bachelor of Arts and Masters Degree. With the outbreak of the Second World War Earl served in the US Navy and joined Red Saunders' band a couple of years after being demobbed in November 1945.

It was whilst with Red Saunders that Earl earned the nickname The Ghost; a visiting musician spotted Earl playing in the corner of a club and observed that with Earl's light skin complexion he looked just like a ghost. After featuring on sessions in Chicago, New York and Detroit, Earl linked with the Theron label, providing piano accompaniment to the likes of Leon Washington (no relation), The Ebony Moods, Laura Lynn and The Sheppards before releasing his first single under his own name, *Remainder* backed with *Baia* in 1955.

With the demise of Theron Earl recorded a number of tracks for Federal/King that were subsequently sold on to Checker, who released *Miserlou* in 1958. Thereafter Earl returned to session work before signing with Formal, working with several former members of Count Basie's band, including Frank Foster (saxophone), Ed Jones (bass), Thad Jones (trumpet), Ben Powell (trombone), Frank Wess (flute) and Sonny Payne (drums). Formal would also run into problems, with several of the tracks Earl recorded subsequently being picked up by Motown's Workshop Jazz label, beginning with the single *Opus No 3*, released in May 1962.

That November came the album, **All Star Jazz**, which would also feature musical contributions from John Avant (trombone), Herb Brown (bass), John Neely (saxophone) and Walter Perkins (drums). Whilst promotion on the album was minimal, Earl returned to Motown to record a second album, with **Reflections** being released in April 1964 in the US and issued in Belgium by Disques Artone Fonoplatten as part of their five Motown jazz releases.

Earl continued to work and tour around Chicago, gave private jazz piano lessons and lectured on the history of jazz at Indiana University until his death from a heart attack on 16 January 1975.
ALBUMS: ALL STAR JAZZ (1962), REFLECTIONS (1964)

GROVER WASHINGTON JR.

Ultimately to become the biggest selling artist on Creed Taylor's Kudu imprint (and the best selling across any of his labels), Grover Washington Jr. owed his initial breakthrough to the non-appearance of another artist.

Born in Buffalo, New York on 12 December 1943, Grover learned to play the saxophone from his own father at the age of ten and worked his way through a succession of instruments before returning to the saxophone, proficient enough to be playing local clubs some two years later.

"My early lessons were on the saxophone, then it was the piano, the drum and percussion family, and the bass guitar. It was basically what I wanted to do at a very early age, so I had the time. I could really get into all of them on the basic level."

Fortunately, he soon concentrated on just the saxophone (although he managed to master the alto, soprano, baritone and tenor saxophone) and in 1959 joined The Four Clefs and toured with the R&B outfit for some four years before freelancing and then undergoing a stint in the US Army. When he was demobbed he settled in New York but subsequently moved to Philadelphia in 1967, working with the likes of Charles Earland and Johnny Hammond Smith as well as undertaking session work for the Prestige label. He then followed Johnny Hammond into Creed Taylor's CTI and Kudu set up, initially as a session musician.

His big break occurred in 1971 when Hank Crawford was unable to make a recording date for Kudu, with Creed Taylor picking Grover as a late replacement.

"Grover's sound made the sax a less obvious thing" Creed would later state. "Everything was the same as it would have been with Hank, except Grover was Grover. Hank was a blues master alto player and Grover had a more lyrical, romantic thing going. He had a sound that worked in contrast to what we were doing. I think that made the date quite different."

That fortuitous break led to the album **Inner City Blues**, an album that made strong and healthy performances on the jazz, R&B and pop chart (it would also enable him to become a full-time musician, for prior to this success, he was working part-time at a Philadelphia record wholesaler, resulting in Grover "unloading boxes of records with my name on them."). Seizing the initiative, Grover recorded an ever-more successful catalogue of albums for Kudu, with **All The King's Horses** and **Soul Box** topping the jazz charts.

When Motown picked up the CTI group of labels for distribution in 1974, it was the acquisition of Grover Washington Jr. that undoubtedly lay behind the deal, with Grover repaying that confidence by scoring the biggest album of his career with **Mister Magic** in 1975, topping the jazz and R&B charts and hitting Top Ten pop. Outside of George Benson (another former CTI artist), jazz music had never been so popular, with Grover widely seen as the originator of the smooth jazz movement. Whilst Creed Taylor's deal eventually turned sour, resulting in an end to the agreement in 1976, part of the settlement deal was that Grover remained at Motown.

"I signed a mutual agreement with CTI and Kudu and then a separate contract with Motown. That meant I have to supply Motown with two completely new albums, and they also acquired the back catalogue of Kudu which gives them the right to package a 'Best Of' album. It broke my heart that they got the old material because I tried to buy it myself. I did ask Motown and they simply said 'no' and there was no negotiation on the subject."

His subsequent albums utilised much the same musical formula as **Mister Magic** and were equally as successful; **Feels So Good** topped the jazz and R&B charts and hit #10 pop, whilst **A Secret Place**, **Live At The Bijou**, **Reed Seed** and **Skylarkin'** all topped the jazz listings and made the Top Ten on the R&B chart, and whilst their pop placing slipped down a peg or two, they all cracked the Top Forty. The first direct album under the Motown deal was **Reed Seed**, an album Grover was especially pleased with.

"They won't get a better chance to prove themselves in that market. **Reed Seed** is, in my opinion, my best album to date, and I want to thank the people at Motown for giving me total creative freedom. They gave me the opportunity to present the album in the form I believed was best."

Grover would score another hit single with *Do Dat* lifted from the album, which peaked at #75 R&B. By the time **Skylarkin'** was released in February 1980, Grover had already left the company, bound for Elektra Records and continued success, including the Top Ten single *Just The Two Of Us*, recorded with Bill Withers.

He left behind him his entire Kudu recorded output, with Motown subsequently reissuing **Inner City Blues** and **All The King's Horses**. Grover would later record for Columbia as well as making numerous guest appearances on pop and jazz recordings, his status as one of the greatest saxophonists of his age undiminished. Eager to expand his horizons and get into composing film music, Grover applied for a doctoral programme in music composition at Temple University in Philadelphia. He was informed that he would have to audition.

"The next day I came back with a stack of my albums and told them to listen and let me know if they thought I could play."

Not surprisingly, they called back and told him he had been admitted. On 17 December 1999 he was recording a performance for CBS' television show 'The Saturday Early Show' when he suffered a sudden heart attack and was pronounced dead on arrival at a local hospital.

ALBUMS: MISTER MAGIC (1974), FEELS SO GOOD (1975), A SECRET PLACE (1976), LIVE AT THE BIJOU (1976), REED SEED (1978), SKYLARKIN' (1980),

COMPILATIONS: BADDEST (1980), ANTHOLOGY (1981), GREATEST PERFORMANCES (1983), AT HIS BEST (1985)

MIRA WATERS

Although better known as an actress, Mira Laverne Waters recorded two singles for Motown, perhaps owing her recording contract to her long term companionship with Berry Gordy. Born in Philadelphia, Pennsylvania in 1945, Mira first came to prominence in Gordon Parks' 1969 film 'The Learning Tree', appearing in one of the lead roles of Arcella Jefferson. After several television appearances Mira won her best known role in 'The Greatest', the biopic of boxer Muhammad Ali.

In 1979 Mira signed with the Gordy label, releasing in June 1979 the self-written and Hal Davis produced *You Have Inspired Me* which received some action in the clubs. The following September Mira linked with producer and arranger McKinley Jackson and released her follow-up *Rock And Roll Me*. This received little attention, with the result Mira's recording career came to an end and she took a job within the administrative department at Motown.

WILLIAM WEATHERSPOON

A onetime member of The Tornadoes with Stanley Mitchell, Charles Sutton and Ben Knight, William achieved greater success as a writer. Born William Henry Weatherspoon in Detroit, Michigan on 11 February 1936 he had joined The Tornadoes as a tenor vocalist in 1956, appearing on a number of their recordings for Chess and Bumble Bee, also writing *Geni In The Jug* that appeared on the flip side to their single *Love In Your Life*.

When The Tornadoes disbanded in 1960, William joined Correc-tone Records based at 8912 Grand River in Detroit, where many former and future Motown employees were also resident, including Mickey Stevenson, who was head of A&R for the label. Mickey soon got William writing and producing at Correc-tone, most notably for The Pacesetters. Eventually William followed Mickey over to West Grand Boulevard, where Motown was located, linking with fellow writer James Dean.

The pair would write a number of hits for Jimmy Ruffin (*What Becomes Of The Brokenhearted, Farewell Is A Lonely Sound* and *I've Passed This Way Before*) as well as for Edwin Starr (*I'm The Man For You Baby*), Marv Johnson (*I'll Pick A Rose*) and The Contours (*It's So Hard Being A Loser*), but despite their success, William and James never got the chance to work with the cream of Motown's talent.

When Holland-Dozier-Holland left the company to set up their own Invictus/Hot Wax operation, William opted to follow (bizarrely, although James Dean was a first cousin of Brian and Eddie Holland, he decided against throwing his lot in with his relatives and linked instead with Don Davis) and would form a new writing partnership with Angelo Bond.

They would score hits with Laura Lee and The Flaming Embers, although none matched the success James Dean enjoyed, and when Invictus and Hot Wax were closed down, William returned to Motown, taking Angelo with him.

His second sojourn at Motown wasn't as successful as his first, although he did get to work with The Temptations this time around, as well as with some of Motown's newer recruits such as High Inergy. He died from a suspected heart attack at his home in Detroit on 17 July 2005.

WEED RECORDS

Invited by Berry Gordy to produce an album on Chris Clark, Deke Richards imposed a number of conditions before accepting the task, one of which was the creation of a label imprint that would have no outward connection to Motown. Deke's idea was to call the label Weed, giving it the tag line 'Your Favourite Artists Are On Weed' and a logo that was a parody the Stax Records logo, with Weed's two fingers displaying the peace sign. The label only ever released one record, Chris Clark's album **CC Rides Again**, but with the company also creating the Rare Earth label at much the same time, promotional activity focused on the Rare Earth imprint to the detriment of Weed.

MARY WELLS

The company's first bona fide superstar, Mary Wells earned the sobriquet 'The Queen Of Motown', only to leave the label at the height of her fame and endure a lengthy downward spiral.

Born Mary Esther Wells in Detroit, Michigan on 13 May 1943 as one of three children, she contracted spinal meningitis as a young child and had to overcome partial blindness, deafness in one ear and temporary paralysis. By the time she was twelve Mary was out working, helping her mother clean houses in and around Detroit, although she took an active interest in singing, partly to offset the pain and discomfort caused by her earlier illnesses.

Having been a member of the church choir Mary began performing in local clubs from the age of ten, no doubt combining her night time singing with day time cleaning duties. When she graduated from Northwestern High School at the age of 17, Mary had aspirations of becoming a scientist, but the call of music proved too strong to resist.

Always keen on writing, Mary had written a song entitled *Bye Bye Baby* that she thought might be ideal for Jackie Wilson, another local Detroit singer who was enjoying a run of success. Unable to get to Jackie direct, Mary targeted his chief songwriter and producer Berry Gordy, cornering him in the 20 Grand night club to try and get him interested in the song. In an effort to extricate himself from Mary's attentions, Berry asked her to sing the song a capella. Both the song and singer were better than he anticipated, so Berry invited Mary over to Detroit United Sound Studios to record it as a single. Although Mary had not thought of pushing herself as a singer, she listened to Berry's arguments that she was the best interpreter of *Bye Bye Baby*.

According to legend it took some 22 takes before Berry was satisfied with what he had on tape, subsequently taking the still seventeen year old Mary, escorted by her mother, to his office in order to sign her to a contract. Released in December 1960 as only the third record on the newly instituted Motown label, *Bye Bye Baby* got the label off to the perfect start, hitting #45 pop and #8 R&B in the early part of 1961.

Berry got together with Mickey Stevenson to pen Mary's follow-up, *I Don't Want To Take A Chance* being released in July 1961 and performing better on the pop chart, where it hit #33, than its predecessor. It also returned Mary to the Top Ten of the R&B chart when it reached #9, although it still wasn't a given that everything released on Mary was destined for the chart, as the September released *Strange Love* would prove.

By the time the year came to an end, Motown also issued Mary's first album (indeed, it was Motown's first album too), with **Bye Bye Baby/I Don't Want To Take A Chance** featuring both her hit singles alongside eight other tracks from the growing Jobete catalogue, including cover versions of The Miracles' *Shop Around* and Marv Johnson's *Come To Me*.

Mary was then handed over to Smokey Robinson for both writing and production, resulting in a significant change in vocal style. Gone was the almost strained sound that Berry had favoured and in its place a much more cultured and composed style, augmented by a male backing group in The Love-Tones. The new sound got its first airing with *The One Who Really Loves You*, a single that scored big on both the R&B (#2) and pop chart (#8), not surprising since Smokey had gone out of his way to craft the perfect musical vehicle for Mary. The similarly calypso styled follow-up *You Beat Me To The Punch* did even better, at least on the R&B chart, where it knocked *Green Onions* by Booker T & The M.G.'s off the top spot, on its way to hitting #9 on the pop chart (it failed to make an impact in the UK, where it was Mary's first British release when issued on the Oriole label).

In September 1962 Mary released her second album, **The One Who Really Loves You**, built around her two recent hits and drawing material from a variety of in-house sources. The singles success had made Mary a star, as Berry Gordy would later observe.

"It didn't take Mary long to become a star. On stage, her attitude commanded attention. She wore long, glamorous gowns and stylish, trendy wigs – from black bouffant to blonde ponytails. It looked like Mary would be that big female star I had always wanted."

It was not only Berry Gordy who observed Mary's rise with interest, for her star quality made her the perfect headliner for the Motortown Revue, helped by a third consecutive Top Ten hit when *Two Lovers* powered its way to #7 pop and became her second R&B chart topper, spending four weeks at the summit and selling more than a million copies (although it again missed out in the UK). Her next hit also made the R&B Top Ten, with *Laughing Boy* peaking at #6 and reaching #15 on the pop chart (the flip side *Two Wrongs Don't Make A Right* also charted, hitting #100 on the pop chart) prompting the release of a compilation album in **Two Lovers And Other Great Hits** which would register on the album chart at #49 following its March 1963 release.

And still the hits rolled in, with *Your Old Standby* making #40 pop and #8 R&B followed by both sides of her next single, *What's Easy For Two Is So Hard For One* (#8 R&B and #29 pop) and *You Lost The Sweetest Boy* (#10 R&B and #22 pop), with the latter side enabling Mary to work with Holland-Dozier-Holland for the first time.

The following year would see Mary at the very peak of her career, guided there by one of Smokey Robinson's most memorable songs in *My Guy*. A smash on just about every chart, *My Guy* spent seven weeks looking down on all contenders on the R&B chart and two weeks atop the pop chart. In the UK it hit #5, her first British hit at the sixth time of asking (indeed, it was Motown's first chart single, achieved after the previous forty or so had gone by the wayside), its success helping establish Mary as one of The Beatles' favourite singer's, so much so that she was invited to appear on their brief British tour between 9 October and 10 November 1964 alongside The Rustiks, Michael Haslam, Bob Bain, Sounds Incorporated, The Remo Four, Bob Bain and Tommy Quickly.

Prior to that Mary had been back in the studio, recording a series of duets with Marvin Gaye, the fruits of which were to see the singles *What's The Matter With You Baby* and *Once Upon A Time* hit the charts (*What's The Matter* making #17 pop and #2 R&B, whilst *Once Upon A Time* would reach #19 pop, #3 R&B and hit #50 in the UK).

Despite all of this success and her undoubted position as the leading female at Motown, all was not well within the Wells camp. Many of the problems could be traced back to her husband Herman Griffin, a former Motown singer himself (he had recorded for both Tamla and Motown at the beginning of the decade) who had married Mary in 1960. The marriage was volatile, not helped by the young age of the respective parties, but Herman had eventually manoeuvred himself into a position of both husband and manager.

Encouraged by Griffin, Mary informed Berry Gordy that as soon as she reached the age of twenty one (the age of majority), she intended disassociating herself from Motown and that as she had signed the original Motown contract whilst only seventeen and therefore a minor, her contract was effectively null and void. For good measure, Mary intended suing Motown for a greater share in royalties that she felt she was owed (part of her claim was that money generated by *My Guy* was being used to shore up the promotional campaigns for several other Motown acts, most notably The Supremes). The lawsuit was sufficient enough to keep her out of the studio for a considerable time, and not only Hitsville; until the dispute was resolved, Mary could not sign with any other company, although there were plenty of suitors for The Queen Of Motown.

Whilst Mary Wells would win the legal battle, ultimately she lost the war. The negotiated settlement with Motown gave her a lump sum but no rights to any future royalties on anything she had written or recorded. At first that didn't appear to matter, since there were plenty of labels with big ideas and big advances willing to sign Mary to a new contract. She would eventually sign with 20th Century Records, lured in part by the huge signing on fee (believed to be as much as $500,000) but more by the promise of movie roles that 20th Century could offer. Ultimately the movie roles never materialised; Morty Craft, the 20th Century executive who handled negotiations, would later admit that the offer of potential film roles was only ever stated in vague terms and that nothing concrete was put into the contract. Since it wasn't stipulated in the contract, 20th Century was under no obligation to offer Mary anything other than a recording deal.

And even that contract was in danger of becoming more of a burden than a benefit. What Mary lacked was top class writers, producers and musicians, what Motown had but 20th Century didn't. Hot on the album charts when she took her leave of Motown thanks to **Mary Wells Sings My Guy**, a #6 chart album, her eponymous 20th Century debut barely scraped in at #145, despite the songwriting presence of Ron Miller, Sydney Barnes, Van McCoy and Rudy Clark and production from former Motown luminaries Andre Williams and Robert Bateman. The extracted singles fared just as badly, with *Use Your Head,* at #34 pop and #13 R&B her highest placed chart single. Even the new found patronage of The Beatles couldn't revive Mary's career as **Love Songs To The Beatles** failed to chart at all.

In 1966 it was all change, with a new label (Atlantic/Atco) and husband (Cecil Womack of The Valentinos and brother of Bobby Womack), but these new relationships were also brought to an untimely end, with her tenure with Atlantic resulting in just one minor hit single.

Thereafter Mary underwent a nomadic, label-hopping career, recording for Warner Brothers, Jubilee and Reprise, but the closest she came to a hit record was when Tamla Motown in the UK revived *My Guy* in 1972; it would hit #14 and serve to show what might have been.

In 1987 Mary teamed up with Ian Levine and released a number of recordings on both Nightmare and Motor City, shortly before learning that she had cancer of the larynx. Unable to sing, with no health insurance and having to sell her house, Mary was both physically and financially devastated, but several old friends, including many from her Motown days rallied around with financial assistance. Mary also became active in raising awareness and funding for cancer research, stating to the Congressional Committee, "I'm here today to urge you to keep the faith. I can't cheer you on with all my voice, but I can encourage, and I pray to motivate you with all my heart and soul and whispers."

That voice, one of the finest to pass through the doors of Hitsville, was silenced on 26 July 1992.

ALBUMS: BYE, BYE BABY/I DON'T WANT TO TAKE A CHANCE (1961), THE ONE WHO REALLY LOVES YOU (1962), RECORDED LIVE ON STAGE (1963), TOGETHER (1964), MARY WELLS SINGS MY GUY (1964)

COMPILATIONS: TWO LOVERS AND OTHER GREAT HITS (1963), MARY WELLS' GREATEST HITS (1964), VINTAGE STOCK (1966), GREATEST HITS (1983), 22 GREATEST HITS (1986)

FURTHER READING: MARY WELLS: THE TUMULTUOUS LIFE OF MOTOWN'S FIRST SUPERSTAR (2012)

KIM WESTON

Kim Weston made her name thanks to a series of duets with Marvin Gaye, but there was always more to her abilities than just being one half of a partnership; had she remained at Motown there is no doubt her career would have turned out for the better.

Born Agatha Nathalia Weston in Detroit on 20 December 1939, Kim was singing in her local church choir at the age of three. By the time she had become a teenager, she had joined the touring gospel group The Wright Specials, who would later record for Motown's Divinity imprint (although Kim does not appear on these recordings). A few years later Kim had to decide on a career as an actress or singer, but on the recommendation of Johnny Thornton (a cousin of Eddie and Brian Holland) Kim chose music, subsequently signing with Motown in 1961.

Assigned to the Tamla label, Kim would score first time out with *Love Me All The Way*, a #24 R&B and #88 pop hit following its June 1963 release, although it is worth considering how well the flip side, *It Should Have Been Me* might have done since it would later provide Gladys Knight and Yvonne Fair with hits in the US and UK respectively. The company wasted little time before issuing Kim's next single, with *Just Loving You* being issued barely two months later, without success. However, Kim was already out on the road, working with the Marvin Gaye revue and thus beginning a partnership that was to reap benefits for both artists in the long run. In between tours Marvin and Kim were back at Hitsville, with Kim recording *Looking For The Right Guy* for release in July 1964, although looking for the right song might have been more appropriate; according to legend, Kim was offered a song co-written by Mickey Stevenson (her then husband) and Marvin Gaye, *Dancing In The Street* but turned it down, paving the way for Martha Reeves to score her signature hit.

In fairness, Kim would later state that she was unaware until many years after the event that she had first option on the song, but Kim was in the right place at the right time to take over from Mary Wells as the latest Motown female artist to partner Marvin Gaye on record. *What Good Am I Without You* was released in September '64 and reached #28 R&B and #61 pop, prompting the scheduling of the album **Side By Side** for release early the following year. This was subsequently scrapped and Kim also proved unable to fully capitalise on her new found fame, with *A Little More Love* (released in October '64) and *I'm Still Loving You* (January '65) eluding the charts.

Kim's next single, *Thrill A Minute* was originally scheduled for release on Tamla in May 1965, but following a reshuffle of the artists and labels, Kim found herself on the Gordy imprint. The change did not alter her fortunes, but her next single, *Take Me In Your Arms (Rock Me A Little While)* found her working with Holland-Dozier-Holland and returning to the chart, peaking at #4 R&B and #50 (the song was originally recorded by Eddie Holland, and ten years after Kim's chart exploits The Doobie Brothers would score an even bigger hit).

The same writing and production team kept Kim on the chart for her next release, *Helpless*, a #13 R&B and #56 pop hit following its March 1966 release. Later that year the Tamla label released **Take Two**, an album of duets with Marvin Gaye that had been recorded a year previously but allowed to sit on the shelf. Whilst the album made little or no headway on the chart, one track stood head and shoulders above the rest; *It Takes Two*. Issued as a single in December 1966, it would become a major international hit, making #4 R&B and #14 pop as well as hitting #16 in the UK. The success of *It Takes Two* should have enabled Kim Weston to take her place at Motown's top table, but a mixture of mishaps (Kim was slated to record *This Old Heart Of Mine* before it was given to The Isley Brothers) and wrong decisions saw her career hit a slump.

By far the most damaging decision was the one that saw Kim follow her husband Mickey Stevenson out of the door at Motown and into the arms of MGM where Mickey had been offered a lucrative deal to become A&R head. Whilst both of her albums for her new home, **For The First Time** and **This Is America** were well received critically, they proved to be commercial failures, the lack of access to material even halfway as decent as that provided by Motown proving their undoing.

Kim would later record for People, Volt and Johnny Nash's Banyan Tree labels, without ever reaching the same heights as previously. By the 1970s Kim had effectively retired from the mainstream music business, although she became active in community groups and art groups and recorded a series of jazz standards. In 1987 Kim became the first former Motown artist to link up with Ian Levine's Nightmare and Motor City labels, recording two albums that were issued in the 1990s.

ALBUM: TAKE TWO (1966)

WHAT BECOMES OF THE BROKENHEARTED – JIMMY RUFFIN [SINGLE]

Competition for material at Motown was always fierce, even more so for artists who had yet to achieve a major breakthrough. By 1966, both The Spinners and Jimmy Ruffin fell into that category, with the former having had only two Top Ten R&B hits, four years apart, and the latter one single that had bubbled under at #120, *As Long As There Is L-O-V-E.* Whilst David Ruffin enjoyed the highlife as befitted a member of The Temptations, his brother Jimmy supplemented his meagre recording income by working at the local Ford motor factory.

"One day I got home from Fords and I went to Motown to try and canvas some material. I heard this tune being sung by the writer James Dean. When I asked him who the song was for he told me The Spinners were going to cut it. But I told him to give it to me instead. He liked my version enough to let me have it."

That song was *What Becomes Of The Brokenhearted*, co-written with William Weatherspoon and Paul Riser, with Weatherspoon collaborating with Mickey Stevenson on the production. Featuring The Originals and The Andantes on backing vocals, the initial version Jimmy recorded featured an extended spoken introduction, which was subsequently removed from the final mix, leaving a long instrumental in its place. What was left, however, was a captivating song, one which would catapult up the charts, with Jimmy initially unsure as to whether he should quit his job at Ford and concentrate on his singing.

"This started moving real fast for me, too fast. I wasn't sure what was happening to me. The song had the kind of words one can feel and it was a beautiful, melodic song. At the time my career wasn't going too well and I was getting kicked around quite a bit

financially and I really was like a person lost, looking for some kind of hope, needing someone or something to believe in."

The single was released on the Soul label in July 1966 and went on to become a #6 R&B and #7 pop hit, subsequently being issued on the Tamla Motown label in the UK in September the same year and becoming a #10 hit. The success proved to Jimmy that he had made the right decision after all.

"Everything I'd worked for paid off. All my doubts about turning the group down were dissipated and I was no longer shackled by my brother's success."

Over the years, *What Becomes Of The Brokenhearted* cemented its reputation as one of Motown's finest as well as Jimmy's best. In 1974, the single was re-released in the UK and became an even bigger hit the second time around, peaking at #4.

In 1981 British keyboard player Dave Stewart linked with former Zombies lead singer Colin Blunstone on a version that hit #13 in the UK, whilst in 1996 former actors Robson Green and Jerome Flynn topped the British chart with their version. Other versions have been recorded by Paul Young, (it would hit #22 on the US chart), Westlife, Joan Osborne and Vonda Shepard. Even Jimmy Ruffin re-recorded the song, an Italian version entitled *Se Decidi Cosi* being released in Europe in December 1966 (it can be found on the album **Motown Around The World**).

WHAT DOES IT TAKE (TO WIN YOUR LOVE) – JUNIOR WALKER & THE ALL STARS [SINGLE]

Johnny Bristol and Vernon Bullock had come up with the initial concept for *What Does It Take (To Win Your Love)*, with Junior Walker very mind in their minds as they created the song. The only problem was Junior wasn't that impressed with it when he first heard it, feeling it was too drastic a change in musical direction for him. He refused to record it, although a version with a demo vocal was committed to tape in March 1967.

Johnny Bristol persisted with his requests for Junior to record a finished version, Junior maintained his reluctance and a stalemate ensued for the best part of a year. Then, while Junior was recording what would become the **Home Cookin'** album, *What Does It Take* was put back onto the itinerary. Even then it took some time before Johnny and fellow producer Harvey Fuqua had got onto tape exactly what they had in mind, with Junior Walker still unsure about the track. Additional backing vocals (by The Spinners, making this very much a revival of the Tri-Phi team), mixing and overdubs finally saw the track completed by January 1969, with Johnny and Harvey presenting the track as a possible Junior Walker single to the weekly Quality Control Department.

There the antipathy continued, with even Berry Gordy telling the team that the song was too pretty to be considered a Junior Walker single; the company would go with *Home Cookin'* instead and *What Does It Take* would have to content itself with appearing on the album. Whilst *Home Cookin'* did relatively well (it would peak at #19 R&B and #42 pop), radio DJs around the country had already picked up on *What Does It Take*, playing it virtually to death whilst it was still an album cut.

Eventually common sense prevailed, with *What Does It Take* being scheduled for release as a single in April 1969. Just as Johnny Bristol had predicted, it became a million selling hit, topping the R&B chart and peaking at #4 pop as well as reaching #13 in the UK. The track would also pick up a nomination for the Grammy Award for Best R&B Instrumental Performance which was ultimately won by King Curtis for *Games People Play*. In 1986 the song provided Kenny G with a minor hit, reaching #64 in the UK.

WHAT THE WORLD NEEDS NOW IS LOVE/ABRAHAM, MARTIN & JOHN – TOM CLAY [SINGLE]

Marvin Gaye wasn't the only Motown artist writing and releasing songs with a message in 1971, with notorious DJ Tom Clay entering the fray with *What The World Needs Now Is Love/Abraham, Martin & John* later the same year. Tom, of course, had been involved with Motown at the very start, having been instrumental in helping break Marv Johnson and having had a single written by Berry Gordy released on the Chant label in 1958.

After a number of brushes with the payola scandal, Tom had relocated to Los Angeles and was a temporary DJ for KGBS when he came up with the idea for the single. An unconventional single to say the least, it was based around Dick Holler's *Abraham, Martin & John* (a musical tribute to Abraham Lincoln, John F Kennedy and Martin Luther King and a major hit for Dion as well as later being covered by Motown luminaries Smokey Robinson & The Miracles and Marvin Gaye), interspersed with the chorus from *What The World Needs Now Is Love* as performed by the Burt Bacharach Orchestra and the spoken dialogue of Tom and a young (un-named) girl who attempts to describe segregation.

Tom had spared little expense in assembling the single, hiring top arranger Gene Page and the vocal accompaniment of The Blackberries (who were also no strangers to Motown) and played the resulting montage to his audience at KGBS. Listener reaction was favourable, so much so that Motown began taking an interest in the single and quickly moved to snap it up for their MoWest imprint, with *The Victors* (effectively Tom reading a list of the fallen from numerous wars accompanied by a synthesised version of *The Last Post*, the bugle led song traditionally played at military funerals) as the flip side.

A special pressing of some 12,000 copies was readied for mailing to KGBS listeners, but the single exploded across all radio stations and became a surprise hit, peaking at #32 R&B and #8 pop following its release in June 1971. Whilst the sentiment alone should have ensured international attention, the single did little in the UK, despite being released on the Tamla Motown label in January 1972 and again on the MoWest label in December 1973.

WHAT'S GOING ON – MARVIN GAYE [SINGLE]

Over the years, *What's Going On* has acquired the mantle as one of the greatest singles ever recorded, if not something of a turning point for soul music as a whole. Its success revitalised the career of Marvin Gaye and, with the later success of the similarly titled album, changed the public perception of Motown as a company that made great records to a company that made great records with a message. Yet, whilst much if not all of the adulation and praise has been heaped on Marvin, the initial creation owes much to Four Tops member Renaldo 'Obie' Benson and Motown staff writer Al Cleveland.

In May 1969 The Four Tops were on tour and due to play at Berkeley in California. When the tour bus arrived in the city, Obie witnessed the local police deal brutally with an anti-war protest.

"I saw this and started wondering 'what the f**k was going on, what is happening here?' One question led to another. Why are they sending kids so far away from their families overseas? Why are they attacking their own children in the streets?"

He discussed the matter with Al Cleveland and together the pair crafted the rudiments of a song, one which Obie eventually submitted to the rest of The Four Tops for consideration, only for it to be turned down.

"My partners told me it was a protest song. I said, 'no man, it's a love song, about love and understanding. I'm not protesting, I want to know what's going on.'"

So if it wasn't right for The Four Tops, who was it right for? After initially thinking of Joan Baez, Al and Obie thought of approaching Marvin Gaye, whose own career had been inactive since the death of Tammi Terrell, although he had done a few production and writing chores for The Originals. Marvin thought the song might work on them, but Al and Obie convinced him that the message that the song contained could only be properly conveyed by Marvin.

After much pestering, Marvin finally agreed, although he reworked the lyrics and a new melody and "added some things that were more ghetto, more natural, which made it seem like a story than a song…we measured him for the suit and he tailored the hell out of it."

The bits that were added to make more of a story resonated with Marvin and his life at the time, listening to his brother Frankie's tales of fighting in Vietnam, the turmoil in Marvin's life following the loss of Tammi and his ongoing battles with both his surrogate and real father (Berry Gordy and Marvin Senior respectively).

It has been questioned how serious Marvin was about the song when the recording session was booked (the backing tracks were done with The Originals still in the frame for the song), for in addition to the various Funk Brothers who would perform the music, the backing vocalists included Mel Farr and Lem Barney of the Detroit Lions football team (at the time, Marvin harboured dreams of becoming a professional footballer and was working with Mel and Lem on getting into physical shape) as well as Bobby Rogers of The Miracles, songwriter Elgie Stover and The Andantes.

Even when the recording was complete, Marvin, who produced the session wasn't sure which lead vocal he preferred so got engineer Kenneth Sands to put one version on the right channel and one on the left and eventually decided the mixed version with both in harmony was exactly the kind of feel he was looking for. Even the saxophone that kicks off the song came almost by accident; Eli Fontaine played a riff or two that was captured on tape, after which Marvin told Eli he was free to go home. When Eli protested that he was just 'goofing around', Marvin told him, "You goof off exquisitely, thank you."

In the end it was the spontaneity of the recording that lay behind the eventual success of the song, a fact even Marvin came to realise when he attempted to record a more serious version, with proper backing rather than 'goofing around', only to ditch these halfway through and revert back to the original version.

As pleased as Marvin was with the finished recording, not everyone at Hitsville shared his enthusiasm, most notably Berry Gordy. According to several accounts, Berry thought *What's Going On* was the worst record he'd ever heard (not that Berry remembered it that way in his own autobiography) and he turned down a request to release it. He similarly rejected it a further ten times it was submitted to the Quality Control Department meeting, with Harry Balk and Barney Ales eventually going behind Berry's back and scheduling the single for release in January 1971, so desperate were they for new Marvin Gaye product.

In the end, of course, their faith was rewarded when *What's Going On* was sent to radio stations around the country and the sales telephone rang off the hook, with stores ordering 100,000 copies in a single day (quite what would have happened to Barney and Harry if the single had flopped doesn't bear thinking about!).

It soon vaulted the charts, hitting #1 R&B and #2 pop on the Billboard listings (although it topped the Cashbox pop chart), shifting more than two million copies in the process. The single would also garner two Grammy Award nominations, for Best Male R&B Performance and Best Arrangement Accompanying Vocalists (for David Van DePitte), although it won neither.

Equally baffling was the single's lack of success in the UK, where it was released in May 1971 to almost total apathy. Subsequent reissues have also failed to earn the single its' just rewards, although the song was taken into the Top Ten (to #6, to be precise) via a cover version by Artists Against AIDS Worldwide in 2001, Cyndi Lauper hit #57 in 1987 (and #12 in the US) and another collective, Music Relief '94 peaked at #70 in 1994.

WHAT'S GOING ON – MARVIN GAYE [ALBUM]

Berry Gordy was quick to acknowledge his mistake in trying to block the release of *What's Going On*, driving over to Marvin's house soon after the single had started exploding sales wise to encourage him to complete an album. It was imperative that Marvin have the album ready almost immediately if Motown were to fully capitalise on the success of the single. During the course of the discussion, Berry told Marvin he could record whatever he wanted, but it needed to be done inside 30 days. The timeframe aside, Berry's words were music to Marvin's ears.

"In 1969 or 1970, I began to re-evaluate my whole concept of what I wanted my music to say... I was very much affected by letters my brother was sending me from Vietnam, as well as the social situation here at home. I realized that I had to put my own fantasies behind me if I wanted to write songs that would reach the souls of people. I wanted them to take a look at what was happening in the world."

Marvin intended doing a protest album, which wasn't what Berry wanted to hear.

"Protest about what?" "Vietnam, police brutality, social conditions, a lot of stuff," was Marvin's retort. "Marvin, this is crazy. Stick to what you do. Stick to what's happening. Stick to what works!"

But Marvin wouldn't be swayed, seeing this as an opportunity to strike out musically. According to Berry, Marvin wanted to awaken the minds of mankind. Seeing that he wasn't going to be able to persuade Marvin away from his concept, Berry gave his grudging approval, although marked with a word of caution.

"'Marvin, we learn from everything. That's what life's all about. I don't think you're right, but if you really want to do it, do it. And if it doesn't work you'll learn something; and if it does I'll learn something.' The album was called **What's Going On**. I learned something."

Given Berry's blessing to record what he wanted, Marvin eventually assembled many of the musicians who had helped turn *What's Going On* into a tour de force (all of whom, in another radical departure from the norm at Motown, were credited on the album sleeve), including arranger David Van DePitte, who was reportedly given something of a short straw when it came to working with Marvin.

"I thought he was pretty terrific, but I had never worked with him or for him prior to this project. Somebody said to me, 'Guess what, you're elected.' After taking a quick poll around the room, I came to find out that nobody else wanted to do it. They had all worked with Marvin before and found him to be such a pain."

After the success of the single, Marvin didn't want to work with anyone else, bringing David into the album project and telling him he had everything ready to record.

"Then as we sat down and started working on these tunes, not only did he not have a concept, but I thought it bizarre that all this material was finished but he didn't have lyrics for all of it. When James Nyx and I would sit there hour after hour staring at each other, waiting for Marvin to show up from his basketball game or whatever the hell he was doing...then it dawned on me that there were more people involved than he had led me to believe."

Yet despite the haphazard start, the sessions for the album soon came together, aided by David Van DePitte's constructive use of musical bridges from one song to the next, thus creating a seamless whole.

"The way the tunes were laying, they were little stories, and it just kind of felt that one should flow into the next," he would later state.

Marvin linked with Al Cleveland and Obie Benson on two additional tracks on the album, *Save The Children* (which would become a hit single in the UK) and *Wholy Holy*, with James Nyx on two, *What's Happening Brother* and *Inner City Blues (Make Me Wanna Holler)* and assorted co-writers on the remaining four, including his wife Anna. The actual recording sessions took place over the course of ten days in March 1971, with an initial mix being done in Detroit in April but, unhappy with the result, re-worked at The Sound Factory in Hollywood the following month.

The album was finally ready for release on 21 May 1971, with Motown having pressing plants working around the clock in order to have sufficient stock ready to hit the stores. The critical acceptance of the album surpassed that of the single, and whilst Berry Gordy may have been reluctant to have Marvin record a protest or concept album, even he was forced to admit **What's Going On** was something special.

"The songs were laced together in fluid motion producing a sound quality on Marvin I'd never heard before. What an artist Marvin was! His voice on lead vocal, backed up with other colours and tones of himself on background. It was Marvin on top of Marvin on top of Marvin. I was surprised to find out that even with this departure in subject matter, he came off just as sexy as when he sang his 'You' songs directly to women. As Marvin promised, he protested everything. He protested pollution and bought attention to the environment in *Mercy Mercy Me (The Ecology)*, he sang of the pain of ghetto life in *Inner City Blues (Make Me Wanna Holler)*. He pleaded for the future with *Save The Children*. He touched the spirit with *God Is Love* and *Wholy Holy*. Inspired by his own brother, in *What's Happening Brother* he told of the frustration of a veteran returning from the Vietnam War."

Berry Gordy wasn't the only one impressed, with the album topping the R&B chart for nine weeks and hitting #6 on the pop listings, with Motown's plants eventually pressing up more than two million copies as well as three Top Ten singles from this landmark album.

Just like the single, however, the album failed to make a mark in the UK, at least at the time of release, eventually making #56 when it was featured in a classic album television special in 1999 (and has gone on to earn a platinum disc for sales in excess of 300,000 units since 1994). Like much of Marvin's material, it enjoyed a domestic upsurge in sales following his untimely death in 1984, re-charting all over again at #154. In 1994 it appealed to a whole new generation, shifting more than a half a million copies when it was issued on CD for the first time. The album has continued to transcend the generations, aided by the issuing of a deluxe edition (in 2001), a re-master (2002) and a super deluxe edition (2011). In almost every poll of the greatest albums ever, **What's Going On** figures at or near the top, proof of the album's true worth more than forty years after it was first released.

WHERE DID OUR LOVE GO – DIANA ROSS & THE SUPREMES [SINGLE]

By April 1964, The Supremes were still struggling to make a major breakthrough into the charts, both at home and domestically. Only one single, *When The Lovelight Starts Shining Through His Eyes* had cracked the Top 40, albeit at a lowly #23, whilst their four other charts hits had barely troubled the Top 75. Meanwhile, the songwriting and production trio Holland-Dozier-Holland were just beginning to hit their stride, crafting songs with specific artists in mind. One such song was *Where Did Our Love Go*, written with The Marvelettes in mind. Indeed, the instrumentation had already been completed when The Marvelettes first heard the song, but led by Gladys Horton, the group rejected it as being too childish, preferring another HDH composition in *Too Many Fish In The Sea*. Despite the fact that The Marvelettes were still struggling to replicate their own earlier success, Holland-Dozier-Holland swiftly searched within the Motown camp for another act to record the song, finally settling on The Supremes.

The Supremes were as unimpressed with *Where Did Our Love Go* as The Marvelettes, with the result there was something of a frosty atmosphere in Motown's Studio A when HDH and The Supremes gathered on 8 April 1964 to record the vocals. Much of the instrumentation and backing was already in place, the distinctive foot stomping, which sounds like a crowd, was achieved by just one man, teenager Mike Valvano, stomping on two wooden boards suspended by strings.

However, since the song had been written and the instrumentation recorded with The Marvelettes in mind, the key was lower than Diana Ross' natural register. Yet Diana wasn't Lamont Dozier or Eddie Holland's first choice to sing the song either, as Eddie later explained.

"I wanted Mary because at the time Mary had a softer sound and I knew the song required a soft sound. And I had never heard Diana sing soft before. So my natural instinct was to try Mary on it. I felt anybody that could sing the song soft and sensuous would have a hit on it. But they said, no, that Diana could sing softer, just drop her keys. Most of the songs that Diana was doing were in a somewhat higher register. So Brian and Lamont just dropped the keys and she sounded good."

In fact it was Berry Gordy, who had officially declared Diana the group's lead singer, who dictated that she sing the song. Lamont also had to redo the vocal backing, removing any complex vocals with the much more simplistic 'baby baby'. Reluctant though they may have been to record the song when it was first offered, the finished mix was agreed by all to be an outstanding pop single with a good chance of making a significant impact on the charts.

Coupled with *He Means The World To Me*, *Where Did Our Love Go* was released in the US on 17 June 1964 and quickly won the backing of radio, entering the chart on 11 July. On 22 August the single removed Dean Martin's *Everybody Loves Somebody* from the top of the Billboard Hot 100, spending two weeks in pole position. By then the single had also been released in the UK and almost emulated its success across the Atlantic in peaking at #3 and spending three weeks tantalisingly close to the top (this despite the presence of a rival cover version by Peter Jay & The Jaywalkers on the Piccadilly label).

However, the single's success in the two major markets proved to be a defining moment for all concerned – Holland-Dozier-Holland had chanced upon a way of crafting songs that would be continued for much of the rest of their career and The Supremes had forced their way to the top of the priority list at Motown. More importantly, the success of *Where Did Our Love Go*, especially in the British market, was a good indicator that there was plenty more good things to come out of the Detroit hit factory. Whilst *Where Did Our Love Go* would be somewhat overshadowed by *Baby Love*, especially in the UK, the record remains popular on both sides of the Atlantic. It was able to prove its worth in 1972 when Donnie Elbert, a New Orleans singer who recorded for Vee-Jay and All Platinum, took it back into the chart, hitting #6 R&B and #15 pop and #8 in the UK. Later cover versions that became hits in Britain include Manhattan Transfer (#40 in 1978) and Tricia Penrose (#71 in 1996).

WHERE DID OUR LOVE GO - THE SUPREMES [ALBUM]

With *Where Did Our Love Go* finally providing The Supremes with a major hit, Motown wasted little time in getting an album, the group's second long player, out on the market. Indeed, the timing for **Where Did Our Love Go** couldn't have been better, hitting the streets in August 1964 just as the single was sliding into the top spot of the pop charts.

If the first album **Meet The Supremes** had been a mixed bag collection of recordings, then **Where Did Our Love Go** more than made up for it, eventually playing host to no fewer than three pop chart toppers (The Supremes became the first act in Billboard's history to have three number one hits lifted from the same album), with *Baby Love* and *Come See About Me* later to join the album title track at the chart summit.

The rest of the material on display was also top quality, with *When The Lovelight Starts Shining Through His Eyes*, *Run Run Run* and *A Breath Taking Guy* also featuring on the singles charts, with varying degrees of success. Whilst it is the Holland-Dozier-Holland material that propelled The Supremes to the very top, other Motown writers were also represented on the album, including Smokey Robinson (*Long Gone Lover* and the afore-mentioned *A Breath Taking Guy*), Norman Whitfield (who penned *He Means The World To Me* specifically for the group), and Harvey Fuqua and Robert Gordy, who provided *Your Kiss Of Fire*.

At a time when much of America was embracing the so-called British invasion of The Beatles and The Rolling Stones, The Supremes ensured there was a domestic presence near the top of the charts, with **Where Did Our Love Go** topping the R&B chart and peaking at #2 for four weeks, just behind **The Beatles '65**, and would sell over four million copies stateside, one of Motown's best sellers of the decade. In 2004, to mark the fortieth anniversary of **Where Did Our Love Go**, Hip-O Select released an expanded edition on the album on CD, containing both stereo and mono versions of the original album together with various outtakes, alternate versions and a live show recorded in 1964.

NORMAN WHITFIELD

During his decade plus career at Motown, Norman Whitfield managed to upset just about anyone and everyone of any note around Hitsville, from key executives such as Berry Gordy, artists such as The Temptations and Marvin Gaye and most of the musicians. Not one of his contretemps was planned or lasted for long, but such was his pursuit of excellence, 'no' was not a word he liked hearing too often.

Norman Jesse Whitfield was born in Harlem, New York on 12 May 1940 (although there is some confusion as to the actual year; it has been listed as 1940, 1941 and 1943, was confirmed as 1940 by family members following his death but the New York voter registration records state 1941) and spent much of his early teenage years wielding a pool cue, a talent that would come in handy and sustain him a few years later.

When Norman was fourteen, he and his family drove out to California to attend a grandmother's funeral, with the car breaking down somewhere near Detroit on the way back. Rather than continue the journey the Whitfield clan settled in Detroit where they also had family, with Norman's father going to work at a relative's drug store. Norman had no intention of taking a normal nine to five job, instead relying on his pool playing abilities wherever possible (he was known as The Silver Fox around pool halls) and working in a service station to make up any shortfall. In between pool and petrol, Norman developed an interest in music, both playing instruments himself and observing others at work.

"I played congas and bongos. Percussion, mostly. And I just did it at my own leisure time. It wasn't a serious effort. I was around sixteen or seventeen then. A lot of my friends played jazz, but they were on an absolute elite level. These people went on to become very big in the jazz industry. But they were just my friends and they would allow me to come by and listen. Because I don't have any formal musical training. It was done basically by desire, and then I worked at it."

In Detroit at that time there were plenty of places to go and listen, and Norman soon became a regular at Thelma Records, the label owned by Don Davis and Hazel Coleman (and named after Berry Gordy's former wife Thelma). There he played bongos and congas on a number of tracks before being given an opportunity of writing some material, with Richard Street & The Distants' *Answer Me* his first such outing. Over the next few months further Norman compositions would hit the street, including Roger Wade's *Little Girl* and The Sonnettes' *I've Gotten Over You* and *Teardrops* (both of which appeared on the K.O. label).

Compared with what was happening elsewhere in Detroit the action at Thelma was small fry, so Norman decided to try his luck at Motown, turning up on a regular basis and hanging around Hitsville. At first Norman seemed content to just sit on the steps outside the building waiting for an invite into the inner sanctum. His presence was not always welcome, with Berry throwing him out of the control room in the studio on more than one occasion, but Norman was nothing if not tenacious, and after word of his local success with *I've Gotten Over You* spread, Berry relented and offered him a job at Motown.

"I worked in Quality Control. Because Berry discovered, when I first got there, that I have an absolutely perfect ear in terms of picking hits. So he gave me the job in Quality Control which would justify the fifteen dollars. But I enjoyed the work. It was an evaluating experience for me. In a small room with a desk and turntables. We'd have the discs made from the tapes, have the discs sent upstairs, they'd pile up on the desk and I'd sit there and evaluate them. I enjoyed it because I *felt* something. And when I felt something, I was always right. An alarm would go off inside me emotionally when I would hear something special. [The job] consisted of being totally honest about what you were listening to. You couldn't be influenced by who the producer was. After you'd awarded the demos a score, they went to the monthly meeting where the creative people would attend, and Berry would bring in some kids from outside, too. Releases were decided by majority rule."

It wasn't only records Norman was listening too, for like a sponge, he observed and retained everything that was going on around him, eventually deciding that music was definitely a better career pursuit than pool.

"When I saw Smokey Robinson driving in a Cadillac, to be absolutely point-blank, that's what inspired me. And I actually ran up to him one day. I scared him a little bit, I ran up behind him and asked him, after he was half-way frightened by then, 'How do you get started?' And he gave me the most ridiculous answer I've ever heard in my entire life. He said, 'Make your own bed, brother, because you've got to sleep in it.'"

Whilst Norman didn't think much of Smokey Robinson as a career guidance officer, he was impressed with the money he was making.

"Of course, I was only making fifteen dollars a week then when I went with Berry Gordy. And another fifteen dollars a week he'd pay me for any royalties. Which I didn't mind, because I knew in order to make money, you needed to be around a situation where there was some real money being made. And it was an opportunity. The absolute opportunity of a lifetime."

So Norman bided his time in Quality Control, asking questions of the other writers and producers, until eventually he was given the real opportunity of a lifetime, linking with Mickey Stevenson to write *It Should Have Been Me*, which he produced on Mickey's wife Kim Weston and released on Tamla in February 1963. It was the flip side *Love Me All The Way* (written by Mickey with Barney Ales) that became the hit (#24 R&B and #88 pop), but royalties on the disc were split between the top and flip side, so earning Norman some additional money. His second release, issued on the Gordy label in March the same year, brought about his first workings with a group that was to loam large in the future; The Temptations.

Smokey and Norman collaborated on the song, *The Further You Look, The Less You See*, which Norman produced, but it was Smokey's *I Want A Love I Can See* that was promoted as the top side; Norman would have to wait a while before he got his hands on the group permanently. In April Norman scored his first major hit, co-writing *Pride And Joy* with Mickey Stevenson and Marvin Gaye, which would become a #2 R&B and #10 pop hit for Marvin, another act with which Norman would take to greater glories. Whilst Norman was still learning the ropes so to speak around Hitsville he was happy to work with an assortment of other writers and producers, linking with Eddie Holland or Janie Bradford or whoever else might be around. For *The Girl's Alright With Me*, he worked with Eddie Holland and Eddie Kendricks on the song but handled the production on The Temptations himself.

Although tucked away as the flip side to *I'll Be In Trouble* (written and produced by Smokey), *The Girl's Alright With Me* charted at #39 R&B in its own right and could have possibly done better if it had been the lead cut. At this juncture, however, Norman couldn't quite compete with Smokey, but his time would come. Also about to arrive was money, and quite a bit of it. *He Means The World To Me* was one of his earliest Motown compositions and productions, being recorded in January 1963 on The Supremes. Eighteen months later, it was released as the flip side to *Where Did Our Love Go*, the group's breakout hit and an R&B and pop chart topper as well as hitting #3 in the UK.

"Norman made more money than Holland-Dozier-Holland," said Janie Bradford. "He had it a hundred per cent, and they had to split it three ways."

Slowly but surely Norman was making his presence felt at Hitsville, with the company's confidence in him by June 1964 sufficient to get him a shot at both Jimmy Ruffin (*Since I've Lost You*) and The Temptations in the space of a few weeks. His outing on The Temptations, *Girl (Why You Wanna Make Me*

Blue), co-written with Eddie Holland, was a major hit on both the R&B and pop chart, but not quite big enough to permanently dislodge Smokey Robinson from the producer's chair. Instead his education continued, with The Velvelettes, The Majestics (which reunited Norman with Richard Street), The Marvelettes and The Downbeats among the pupils who benefitted. By the end of 1965 however, Norman was ready for a shot at the real big time, with Eddie Holland helping provide him with the ammunition.

"Smokey would always produce The Temptations, but Norman just loved those Temptations. He had a track he felt was so dynamite that he figured if I wrote the lyric and taught the artist how to sing it, then he would have a great record. He brought me the lyrics he wanted me to work with; change this, write this, he said. I didn't really see much there. But I liked one line in the second or third verse, 'ain't too proud to beg'. Norman said, 'Well, I don't care how you do it – just do it!' So I wrote the whole concept around that."

Getting the song together was not even half of the story, for Norman now had get to the sound he wanted as well. Quality Control and Berry Gordy sent him back into the studio twice before they achieved the sound that everyone was comfortable with, although Norman was just as demanding.

"Norman wouldn't ever be satisfied," said Otis Williams. "He always had another take in him. He had to hear something that he wanted, and if he didn't we could forget about getting out of there, sometimes until the sun went down and came up again."

He got what he wanted on *Ain't Too Proud To Beg*, but even though Quality Control was impressed, Smokey still had first option on The Temptations, with his offering *Get Ready* lined up as their next single. Perhaps as a way of appeasing the fuming Norman Whitfield, Berry Gordy promised that should *Get Ready* fail to make the pop Top Ten, *Ain't Too Proud To Beg* would be their next single. *Get Ready* stalled someway off the Top Ten, giving Norman his shot with *Ain't Too Proud To Beg*, which whilst also failing to crack into the Top Ten, did well enough at peaking at #13.

Given the opportunity of replacing Smokey Robinson as The Temptations' producer, Norman made the most of the break and in turn would not relinquish the role for the next seven years. Initially he continued working with lyricist Eddie Holland, crafting the hits *Beauty Is Only Skin Deep* and *(I Know) I'm Losing You*, but Eddie's growing value to the Holland-Dozier-Holland team made it desirous that Norman should find his own regular partner. He found one in Barrett Strong, who had returned to Hitsville after pursuing his own recording career elsewhere.

"I knew him before I ever got in the business," Norman would later recall. "I was like anybody else. I was very young and I had seen him perform. And we got to know each other, because I was hanging around Motown long before they let me participate, writing and producing. And we had some run-ins with some girls. We kind of got together on our own. I was down in one of the Motown rehearsal rooms one day, and Barrett came in and we started talking. We talked about some old times, girls, you know. We were never really very fond of each other. There was a subtle rivalry there because of the girls. We liked similar girls. The only difference was that I had the girls and he was always trying to get to them."

Once the pair had got beyond talking of girls, Norman steered the conversation towards his true intent, that of forming a songwriting partnership, and whilst many of the teams that had sprung up around Hitsville comprised like-minded writers, Norman was quite direct in what he wanted to accomplish.

"I said, 'Look, I've got quite a few hit records.' I played him a few things, I said, 'If you are interested, I can at least guarantee you a hundred thousand dollars a year. To write together.' He said, 'Well, yeah. Sounds pretty good.' I said, 'I can only guarantee you verbally, I can't put it on paper because it would have a lot to do with how much we would put into it.' So it worked out pretty well. From that point on, we were writing."

The first song that pair wrote together was *I Heard It Through The Grapevine*, perhaps their signature song that would be recorded by numerous artists at Motown but enjoy greatest success thanks to first Gladys Knight & The Pips and then Marvin Gaye. The first song to carry the Whitfield/Strong credit, however, was Jimmy Ruffin's *Gonna Give Her All The Love I've Got*, after which the team added to their growing portfolio with hits on Gladys Knight & The Pips, Marvin Gaye, Rare Earth and, most importantly, The Temptations. Right from the start, there was a distinct division of labour, as Norman would later confirm when asked where the pair had written those early classics.

"At home, or in the office, or at his house. And Barrett is a very good piano player and a lot of the time, from being a percussionist, I can figure the rhythm out, and he'd be struggling with a little piano lick and trying to keep the intensity up. When you go over it so many times, it gets hard, especially when you're writing uptempo songs. I shared in the writing but I always produced alone. Kind of like a solo. I'm such a loner when it comes to music. I think it would be a strain for somebody to produce with me because there are so many things that I envision."

For the first couple of years, Norman Whitfield and Barrett Strong's repertoire fitted in perfectly with the kind of music others around Motown were producing, but the departure of HDH occurred almost concurrently with Norman wanting to stretch himself musically, with The Temptations becoming the major beneficiaries. Just as he had done when he first headed to Motown, Norman started the move with a period of observation.

"When we first did a song called *Cloud Nine*, on The Temptations, I started studying African rhythms on my own, and I wanted to know how to make a song have as much impact without using a regular 2/4 or 4/4 backbeat. And it turned out to be very successful."

Indeed it was, earning Motown a Grammy Award for Best R&B Performance By a Group, its first such award after seven near misses. Rather than bask in the glory of that award, Norman kept raising the bar, trying out new techniques and even revisiting his own songs in order to come up with fresher versions.

"With all due respect for Berry, because he is the head honcho, but I've always been very much outspoken. I'm a person of real conviction. When I make records I make records to please me and I cut what I feel inside as opposed to cutting trendy things that you hear on the radio. I can absolutely envision a song before I cut it. I can hear the instruments."

Norman's ability was such that he often envisioned a song and heard the instruments over and over again, turning out a traditional soul and R&B version of a song on The Temptations, then a harder funk version on Edwin Starr or a more rock influenced number on Rare Earth. Sometimes, as in the case of *War*, originally recorded by The Temptations, the song would be offered to Rare Earth, presumably for a rock update and then be transformed into the funk version that became a major hit for Edwin.

"I had fun doing Rare Earth. They were the first white group I ever did. They were very soulful. They had a lot of fire. Tremendous people chemistry. They respected me and I enjoyed what they did. I had offered the song [*War*] to Rare Earth. You know I did it on The Temptations first. It was a much different version. The college polls showed that this song was the most popular song around. And it wasn't in single form. Then I cut the track that was strong enough to be a single, and I tried to give it to Rare Earth. And they refused it. They said, 'We want to play on our own records.' And Edwin was walking down the hall and I said, 'Edwin, I got a song for you.' When we got ready to dub it in, I got a couple of classes of school kids to share the experience with him, of them coming to Motown. They were between nine and eleven. I did that from time to time because I realise there was no vision there, because of the poverty."

As Norman's roster of artists grew, the flow of material sometimes went the other way, as in the case of *Papa Was A Rollin' Stone*.

"The Temptations didn't do the first version of it. The Undisputed Truth did. And it did about three hundred thousand. And I thought there was more to the song. So I went and cut it a whole different way, because I wanted to stay away from the original version. And The Temptations were a little reluctant because they felt it was a used tune. Eventually we saw eye to eye and we worked on it very hard and got excellent results on it."

That is something of an understatement, for it would go on to earn three Grammy Awards, including two for Norman himself, for Best R&B Instrumental Performance (collected by Norman and arranger Paul Riser) and Best Rhythm & Blues Song (for Norman and Barrett Strong). *Papa Was A Rollin' Stone* also marked the curtain coming down on the Norman Whitfield and Barrett Strong partnership, although Norman was initially unaware that their relationship had come to an end.

"He had an attorney that felt Barrett could be doing more and getting more money. Even though many times I offered to get him a producer's contract. Like I say, I don't produce with anybody. He had never shown any sign of being discontented in any way. He disappeared, I didn't know. I was still putting his name on records. Then I saw the announcement that he had gone to CBS and took on a writing, producing and singing career. CBS called me and asked if I was interested in coming over. Meanwhile, I had turned in the new album on The Temptations, **Masterpiece**. I wrote every song on that. But I have a tremendous amount of respect for Barrett. He has good judgement and good tastebuds. I enjoyed working with him. We both made a lot of money and we made a lot of people happy. But the inevitable is that nothing lasts forever. But it didn't end on a sour note."

With Barrett Strong pursuing his own career at CBS, Norman carried on writing and producing alone. Whilst the hits kept coming, they were not nearly as big as they had been in the previous years (although, as Norman often liked to say, they did pretty good in the dollars and cents category), his career at Motown having peaked with the success of *Papa Was A Rollin' Stone*. It would have been almost impossible to maintain that degree of success, but devoid of a sounding board for some of his more outlandish musical experiments, including **Masterpiece**, his roster of artists began looking elsewhere.

Soon too did Norman, who left Motown in 1975 in order to set up his own eponymous label, with the label's emblem being reminiscent of Motown's, with a W replacing the M and a different colour scheme. With funding provided by Warner Brothers, Norman opened offices at 901 Westbound Avenue in Los Angeles (Norman had joined Motown's drift westwards at the start of the decade) and eventually a studio, Fort Knox Recording Studio at 8425 Melrose Avenue. Joining him in the switch from Motown to Whitfield were The Undisputed Truth and the former backing band for Edwin Starr, who had originally worked under the name Total Concept Unlimited and then Magic Wand before eventually settling on Rose Royce. It was the latter group that became the banner act for Whitfield, scoring major hits with the soundtrack to 'Car Wash' (which won Norman the Grammy Award for Best Soundtrack Album) and their own albums **In Full Bloom** and **Strikes Again**.

Not nearly as successful were some of the other new acts that Norman uncovered, including Nytro, Sadane and Mammatapee or former Motown acts that also found themselves recording for Whitfield, including Junior Walker and Willie Hutch. By the start of the 1980s, musical trends had changed but Norman hadn't and his hit ratio was reduced to a mere trickle of his earlier rate. By 1982 he was involved in a financial dispute with Warner Brothers over missed payments relating to the establishment of his studio. Whitfield Records eventually closed its doors and Norman undertook a number of production chores for Motown again, including a reunion with The Temptations, but nothing he touched in the 1980s came anywhere close to matching the magic of a decade and a half previously. There again, how could it?

Largely ignored and forgotten by the industry for the next twenty or so years, Norman appeared in the news if not the charts when word of a settlement of a tax evasion case resulted in him being sentenced to a spell under house arrest. His later years were spent battling diabetes and other major health issues before his death in Los Angeles on 16 September 2008. His legacy, however, lives on. The man who claimed to live by the code 'what my mind can conceive, I can achieve' proved that time and time again.

ROBERT WHITE

Another of the original Funk Brothers, guitarist Robert White was born in Billmyre, Pennsylvania on 19 November 1936 and arrived in Detroit as part of The Moonglows backing band. This led to a number of sessions for Harvey Fuqua and Anna Records which in turn led to an invitation to perform on Motown's sessions. One of the first through the door in 1959, Robert quickly linked with fellow guitarists Joe Messina and Eddie Willis, with the three often discussing ahead of a session which part each would play. Robert's role was usually that of rhythm guitarist, with his best performances to be found on *My Girl* (The Temptations), *My Cherie Amour* (Stevie Wonder) and *You Keep Me Hanging On* (The Supremes).

In order to unwind after the gruelling recording sessions, Robert would often join his fellow musicians performing at local night clubs and according to Eddie Willis, at many of these dates The Funk Brothers would actually play whatever material they had been recording earlier, giving the lucky patrons of whichever club they were in something of a sneak preview of an upcoming hit! When Motown headed west to California Robert retired for a period before 'always in search of some higher meaning for his life, Robert moved to Los Angeles in the mid-70s hoping to continue his musical career and continue his spiritual quest.' Robert died from complications brought about by heart surgery in Los Angeles on 27 October 1994.

WHO'S HOLDING DONNA NOW? – DeBARGE [SINGLE]

Hot on the heels of the worldwide smash *Rhythm Of The Night*, DeBarge opted to return to the more familiar surroundings of a ballad for the follow up single, released in May 1985. Written by David Foster, Jay Graydon and Randy Goodrum and featuring El DeBarge on lead vocals, *Who's Holding Donna Now?* was another Top Ten hit, reaching #6 pop and #2 R&B as well as topping the Adult Contemporary chart. This was to prove something of a peak for DeBarge, with El DeBarge gaining top billing on subsequent releases before heading off for a solo career, followed by siblings Bunny and Chico.

WHO'S JOHNNY – EL DeBARGE [SINGLE]

Motown may have ceased making films by 1986 but they still retained an interest in several others, most notably through providing repertoire for soundtracks. Any film based around the 1960s or 70s would have a Motown track or two to lend the film authenticity, reaching its pinnacle with the success of The Contours' *Do You Love Me* which became a massive hit all over again when it was included in the film 'Dirty Dancing' some 26 years after it was originally released.

However, for major success, getting a new song in a film was seen as a sure-fire way of gaining exposure and the possibility of serious sales. Peter Wolf had a brief recording career with Motown, releasing **Wolf & Wolf** with his wife Ina on the Morocco imprint in 1984 but achieved better success as a writer and producer. One of his writing successes came with *Playing With The Boys*, recorded by Kenny Loggins and featured in the film 'Top Gun', which resulted in the producers of 'Short Circuit' seeking him out to write a song or two for their forthcoming film.

A comedy science fiction film about a robot that goes haywire, the music for the film was largely incidental music written by David Shire (who had co-written Billy Preston & Syreeta's smash hit *With You I'm Born Again*, a track that originally featured in the film 'Fast Break'), but the producers decided they wanted a more traditional song for use in the film at some point. Peter and Ina wrote *Who's Johnny*, even coming up with the name for the robot themselves (the robot was merely known as SAINT Number 5 in the film, with SAINT standing for Strategic Artificially Intelligent Nuclear Transport), recording the track on a reluctant El DeBarge.

"I thought it was a bit different from where I was at musically. But it was for a movie. They had convinced me that it would open a whole lot of ears to El DeBarge. Well, I said, that's a good thing."

Equally impressed were the film's producers, who upon hearing the song decided to rename the robot Johnny 5! The track became a major success for El Debarge, topping the R&B chart and hitting #3 on the pop chart, although it didn't convert quite so well in the UK where it peaked at #60.

WHY I OPPOSE THE WAR IN VIETNAM – DR MARTIN LUTHER KING, JR. [ALBUM]

On 15 April 1967, some 130,000 people marched through New York City in protest against American involvement in the Vietnam War. Later that day, some 70,000 held a similar protest on the West Coast, marching through San Francisco in what was up to that point the largest organised protest against the war. The following day Dr Martin Luther King shared the pulpit at Atlanta's Ebenezer Baptist Church with his father, Martin Luther King Senior, and delivered an address entitled 'Why I Oppose The War In Vietnam'. Dr King had first spoken out against the ongoing war in 1965 and returned to the theme for the forty minute plus sermon in Atlanta.

"The time has come for America to hear the truth about this tragic war," Dr King said. "There comes a time when silence is betrayal. I could never again raise my voice against violence of the oppressed in the ghettoes without having first spoken to the greatest purveyor of violence in the world today - my own government."

Motown had released two albums of Dr King's speeches during his lifetime and would release a further two posthumously, with **Why I Oppose The War In Vietnam** becoming one of the first issues on the Black Forum imprint in October 1970. Produced by Junius Griffin, the sermon's message was even more poignant in 1970 than it had been when originally given some three years previously, and whilst the record did little in terms of sales action, the album would go on to win the 1970 Grammy Award for Best Spoken Recording.

ANDRE WILLIAMS

Born in Bessemer, Alabama on 1 November 1936, Andre was just six years of age when his mother died, with a succession of aunts raising him until he was sixteen. It was in Chicago that he got his start in the record business, singing with The Cavaliers, The Five Thrills and The Five Echoes before heading on to Detroit. There he joined The Five Dollars, a group who had a recording contract with Fortune Records.

After a couple of singles Andre linked with The Don Juans, a group that also featured future Motown artist Gino Parks. In 1957 Andre scored his first hit, *Bacon Fat* credited to Andre 'Mr Rhythm' Williams & His New Group selling well locally and getting picked up for national distribution by Epic, who took it to #9 R&B. Subsequent singles such as *Jail Bait* and *The Greasy Chicken* again did local business without ever troubling the national charts but did serve to spread Andre's name and reputation around Detroit.

A chance meeting with Berry Gordy in a barbershop in 1959 would prove beneficial to both; Berry got the name and number of Art Talmadge at United Artists, who would pick up Marv Johnson for national distribution, and Andre would get a call to join what was happening at Motown once his Fortune contract expired. Andre went to Hitsville as a writer, producer and artist, although the only single he recorded, *Rosa Lee (Stay Off The Bell)* was never released.

He did produce The Temptations first record for the company and wrote Little Stevie Wonder's debut too, but his abrasive character often had him at loggerheads with Berry Gordy; according to Andre, he was hired and fired some six or seven times! After a 1963 firing he relocated to Chicago and worked for One-derful! and Mar-V-Lus Records, scoring a number of hits for the labels.

"Every time I'd get a hit at One-derful!, Berry would send for me. He was that type. He wanted to keep everybody under his roof. He didn't want to release nothing on me, but when I would leave and catch a hit, he would send for me. I would go back. I would mess-up. He'd fire me. I'd go back and get a hit, and he'd send for me again."

During the times he was in favour he produced Mary Wells and The Contours, and whilst he was out of favour he launched Blue Rock for Mercury and had a spell recording for Motown's big Detroit rivals Golden World and Ric-Tic. It was after his link with Ed Wingate that Andre reckoned he could go head to head with Berry Gordy in Detroit, setting up Sport Records and getting a hit on The Dramatics. Sport ran out of steam in 1967, with Andre returning to Chicago and working for Chess, scoring a final hit under his own name with *Cadillac Jack* on the Checker imprint in 1968.

HERBIE WILLIAMS

Jazz trumpeter Herbie Williams was one of the core musicians at Hitsville, appearing on numerous recordings during the early 1960s. He also had his own album scheduled for release on the Workshop Jazz label in 1963, **The Soul And Sound Of Herbie Williams**. Although a total of eleven tracks were recorded (nine at the Hitsville studio between 16 March and 17 April and a further two live at the Graystone Ballroom in Detroit in September), a cover was publicised on several other Motown releases and the album has been given a star rating at allmusic.com and a guide price valuation in Goldmine, it is unlikely to have ever been released! Herbie, who had previously played with Charlie Parker, later became a member of The Decoys that performed in and around the Detroit era into the 1970s. He was also involved in teaching jazz at a number of universities and colleges.

LARRY WILLIAMS

Lawrence Eugene Williams was born in New Orleans, Louisiana on 10 May 1935 and formed his own band The Lemon Drops at the age of 18 before becoming pianist for Lloyd Price and scoring with energetic rocking numbers. He was to enjoy barely three years at the top of his profession, with *Bony Moronie* among his biggest hits and subsequently being featured on the soundtrack to 'Christine' in 1983.

He was sent to prison in 1960 for narcotics dealing, effectively ending his recording career, although he earned considerable royalties for the rest of his life after his compositions were recorded by the likes of The Beatles and John Lennon. During the 1960s it was rumoured he was a successful burglar and pimp! He was found shot through the head on 2 January 1980 and believed to have committed suicide, although friends remain convinced he was murdered by organised crime.

LENNY WILLIAMS

Although Lenny Williams would go on to enjoy a successful solo career, he is best remembered for his three year stint as lead vocalist of Tower Of Power, a role that raised his profile enough for him to resume a solo career.

Born Leonard Charles Williams in Little Rock, Arkansas on 16 February 1945, Lenny moved to Oakland in California at a very young age and began his interest in music whilst still at school, learning to play the trumpet at elementary school. He also sang in gospel choirs in and around the Bay Area, often rubbing shoulders with the likes of Sly Stone, Andre Crouch and Billy Preston, among others, and took to gospel music so much he held dreams of becoming a Christian minister. However, after entering and winning several talent contests, Lenny opted to pursue secular music, ultimately landing a contract with Fantasy Records in 1969.

His debut single, *Lisa's Gone*, received considerable local airplay, even if this did not convert into sales, whilst his second release, *I'd Cry Every Minute Of The Day* also failed to make an impact. After a one off single for the Galaxy label in 1970 (*How Can I Forget You* backed with the John Fogerty of Creedence Clearwater Revival penned *Feelin' Blue*) Lenny was coaxed over to Atlantic by Jerry Wexler.

He seemed set to score his first hit with *People Make The World Go Round*, the Thom Bell and Linda Creed song that was produced by Brad Shapiro and Dave Crawford, but before Atlantic could get the single out to the market, Avco released The Stylistics' original and scored a major hit, nullifying the impact of Lenny's version. In 1972 he put his solo career on hold after he learned Tower Of Power were looking for a lead singer to replace Rick Stevens (who had a number of drug problems that would eventually lead to his conviction for double murder and manslaughter); it would prove to be a fortuitous and timely switch as Tower Of Power were about to enter their most successful phase.

Lenny contributed (both as a vocalist and writer) to three albums, including the gold selling **Tower Of Power**, as well as proving an adroit frontman during the group's coast to coast tours. After recording **Urban Renewal** in 1974 Lenny returned to his solo career, signing with Warner Brothers for **Pray For The Lion**, produced by Eugene McDaniels.

The following year he signed with Motown, but the stay was short-lived, resulting in the album **Rise Sleeping Beauty** and the minor hit single *Since I Met You*, which peaked at #94 on the R&B chart following its October 1975 release.

Lenny would enjoy much greater success following his switch to ABC in 1977, where **Choosing You** would eventually hit gold and *Shoo Doo Fu Fu Ooh* became a major hit single. With ABC being bought by MCA, Lenny recorded a couple of albums for the parent label before moving on to Rocshire, although the label eventually went to the wall still owing Lenny his advance. Whilst his career since has seen him record for a number of independent labels, most notably Volt and Bellmark, he has yet to recapture his former chart storming days.

ALBUM: RISE SLEEPING BEAUTY (1975)

PATRICK WILLIAMS

Composer and musical director Patrick Moody Williams was born in Bonne Terre, Missouri on 23 April 1939 and has gone on to score more than 150 films during the course of his career, picking up 21 Emmy nominations, twelve Grammy nominations and nominations for an Academy Award and Pulitzer Prize (he has won four Emmys and two Grammys). In 1980 he scored the film 'It's My Turn' starring Michael Douglas and Jill Clayburgh, with Motown releasing the soundtrack album from which the title track was a major hit for Diana Ross.

PAUL WILLIAMS

A member of The Temptations' classic line-up of the 1960s, Paul Williams has become something of a forgotten man in the years that have passed, most probably because he did not to make a go of it with a solo career.

Born in Birmingham, Alabama on 2 July 1939 he met up with Eddie Kendricks whilst still a teenager, the pair going on to become life-long friends. They sang together in church choirs before forming their first group in 1955, The Cavaliers, along with Kell Osborne, Jerome Averette and Wiley Waller, with their doo-wop act causing something of a stir in and around Birmingham.

Four of the group (Eddie, Paul, Kell and Wiley) left Birmingham in order to seek their fame and fortune in the music business, although they had sufficient funds to only get as far as Cleveland, where they stayed with Wiley's grandmother and secured jobs in local hotels during the day and singing in the evening. With Wiley also leaving the group, the remaining three were dubbed The Dishwashing Trio in a local press article until they were fortunate enough to get spotted by would-be manager Milton Jenkins, who invited them to follow him to Detroit where he too had plans at making a musical impact.

When they arrived in Detroit Jenkins gave them a new name, The Primes, and also created something of a female equivalent group in The Primettes, who featured Paul's then girlfriend Betty McGlown in their line-up and would attain greater success as The Supremes. The Primes also established a good name for themselves, as much for their stunning dance routines (devised by Paul) and the sharpness of their dress (the responsibility of Eddie), but aside from a healthy live diary no one seemed interested in signing the group to a record contract.

The three decided to part company, with Paul and Eddie returning home to Birmingham and Kell heading out west to California in order to become a solo performer. A short while later Paul managed to convince Eddie that their prospects would be better served in Detroit and persuaded him to go back to the Motor City. Fortunately for the pair, another local group had also undergone something of an upheaval and line-up change, resulting in there being an opening for the pair with Otis Williams, Melvin Franklin and Al Bryant in a group that would become The Elgins.

The five successfully auditioned for Motown, who whilst more than happy with the potential of the group as singers was less than enamoured with their name. With a recording contract on the table, the five spent a considerable time contemplating a new name before finally settling on The Temptations. The change in name did not bring about an immediate change in fortunes however, with the group scoring a minor R&B

hit with *Dream Come True* (#22 in May 1962) with their third release.

Despite being passed on to most of Motown's major songwriting and production teams, including label head Berry Gordy, Mickey Stevenson, Norman Whitfield and Brian and Eddie Holland and even a temporary try at recording under a different name (The Pirates, whose recordings were supervised by Clarence Paul), nothing managed to make much of an impact.

Their lack of success heightened the tension within the group, with Paul's growing dispute with Al Bryant growing more and more volatile as the weeks progressed. Convinced the group was not going to make it, Al had taken a full time job as a milkman, requiring him to be at the local dairy early each morning; the last thing he needed was endless hours spent rehearsing or travelling long distances in order to undertake live shows.

However, it was the group's growing live reputation that was keeping them all going, and one night in particular in 1963 found them having wowed the crowd, who refused to leave the venue until the group had come out and performed another encore. A heated argument between Al and Paul ensued that resulted with Paul receiving a bottle to the face that required hospital treatment. Although the rest of the group was inclined to sack Al on the spot, it was Paul who argued most strongly for his continued presence. However, when Al again upset the group by refusing to go back on stage at the Motortown Christmas show, even Paul lost faith in keeping a disinterested Al in the group. He was fired from The Temptations with immediate effect, with David Ruffin stepping into the breach to restore the group to five members.

David's arrival coincided with a Motown decision to hand the group over to Smokey Robinson in search of that elusive hit, with Eddie Kendricks also initially picked as lead singer. *The Way You Do The Things You Do* became their first major hit, topping the R&B chart and hitting #11 pop, whilst follow-ups *I'll Be In Trouble*, *The Girl's Alright With Me* and *Girl (Why You Wanna Make Me Blue)* maintained the momentum. At that point everyone in The Temptations had their own responsibilities, with Paul devising the ever more intricate dance routines (and also lending a hand to some of the other groups within the Motown stable; it was he who helped come up with the now legendary hand dance that The Supremes introduced on *Stop! In The Name Of Love*), but it would not be long before divisions began to appear within the group.

When Norman Whitfield singled out David Ruffin as the new lead singer he set in motion an ego that quickly became too big for the group to contain. Eddie was beginning to resent Otis' control on the group (although that control was also being threatened by David Ruffin), and Paul had his own issues, not least of which was the decision, possibly imposed by Berry Gordy, that Cholly Atkins take over the choreography for the group, perhaps with a view to the group being able to perform at more up market venues.

Whatever the reason, Paul reacted badly to being effectively sidelined within the group, beginning to drink more than was healthy, especially given the physical demands of non-stop touring and recording and made all the more surprising by the fact he was originally teetotal. The divisions within the group saw the end of the Classic 5 line-up in 1968, with David Ruffin pushing for top billing a little too strongly for the rest of the group to tolerate; they voted him out in June 1968.

At first he refused to accept the democratic decision, even turning up and joining his former group on stage, snatching the microphone from his replacement Dennis Edwards in the process. The friction between David and The Temptations continued for some time after his official departure, with David keeping in contact with Eddie Kendricks and feeding him information (right or wrong) that served only to alienate Eddie from the group. With all of these problems going on, it is no wonder that Paul's growing issues were overlooked.

Whilst the group couldn't help but notice his failing health, which saw him weak and listless and sometimes having to sit and breathe in oxygen from a tank, there appeared to be no attempt to get to the root of the problem. It was down to drink they surmised (and he was drinking ever more copious amounts) or drugs, both of which he undoubtedly did more than was good for him. Yet Paul had problems both within and without The Temptations.

He was estranged from his wife Mary Agnes, with whom he had five children (Sarita, Paula, Mary, Kenneth and Paul Junior) and had commenced an affair with Winnie Brown, a hair stylist for The Supremes, with whom he would later go into business by opening a celebrity fashion boutique. Money was tight, even though The Temptations were a hugely successful recording and touring act, a matter that caused Eddie in particular much bitterness. Where was all the money going, because all too little of it was finding its way to The Temptations? In between dealing with his own issues, Paul found himself dragged into Eddie's too, with David Ruffin in the background fuelling the flames of resentment.

Matters reach a head at some point, with Eddie bursting into Berry Gordy's office to question where all the money they were generating was going, with

Paul having to try and calm the muddy waters in the immediate aftermath. Whilst Paul undoubtedly calmed the situation enough for Eddie to remain a member of the group (at least for a couple more years), he also effectively lost the respect of Eddie because of his preparedness to toe the company line. Eddie could see that Paul's health was declining but he no longer had the will to fight Paul's battles when he had his own with which to contend.

Those battles would eventually result to Eddie departing the group in 1970 after an escalation of the rows between Eddie and Otis. Eddie failed to turn up one night for the second show at the Copacabana, leaving the auditorium during the break and never returning. He did, however, leave a masterful legacy, with his performance on *Just My Imagination* widely held to be his finest performance as a member of The Temptations. Equally contributing to the performance was Paul, who had an all too brief chance to shine on the song, which would eventually become something of his swansong in the group too.

It was when the group was out on the road that the real problems lay, for as Paul's health declined so did his vocal ability. In desperation the group took to employing Richard Street as a back-up singer; he would be positioned behind the stage curtain and effectively sing all of Paul's parts in the performance. Whether Paul was aware of the steps they were undertaking in order to maintain the subterfuge is not known, but at least the one or two solo spots Paul had in the show, most notably with *For Once In My Life* and *The Impossible Dream,* were sung by Paul.

Perhaps if Paul had taken the advice of the rest of the group earlier matters might have turned out better, for when he did finally visit a doctor and learn the true extent of his problems, that he was suffering from sickle cell anaemia, there was at least a cause if not a solution for his problems. His health continued to decline, he continued to drink and eventually even The Temptations could stand it no more, informing him shortly after the recording sessions for **Solid Rock** had commenced that his time in the group was at an end.

According to Otis, they left it open that he might be able to return to the group if and when his health was restored, but if that is the case such news was not relayed to Eddie Kendricks, who upon learning that his life-long friend had been unceremoniously turned out of the group launched a bitter and highly public series of critical interviews, which brought a retaliation from Otis.

"Eddie didn't think I had Paul's interests in mind, but it wasn't my choice to pull him off the road. It was Paul's doctor. We'd finally convinced him to see one, and after he did the doctor told Don Foster [The Temptations' road manager] that Paul had to come off the road, no ifs, ands, or buts, he was just too sick. His respiratory system was shot, he had no lungs left, basically, and he may have had a spot on his liver."

What Eddie may not have known was that out of loyalty to Paul, the group kept him on the payroll as an advisor and choreographer but without The Temptations, Paul Williams had little or nothing. His relationship with Winnie Brown was on and off, largely because she had been cheating on him, but somehow she managed to convince him to sink his savings into a fashion boutique, The Celebrity House. It may have been one of the first boutiques that combined fashion, beauty and hairdressing, along with a restaurant, but it quickly became a financial drain on Paul and would eventually go bankrupt, with Paul reportedly owing some $80,000 in taxes on the venture.

He would eventually cut down on his drinking and smoking, which at least helped his long term health. Whilst his romantic relationships were still in turmoil, with his estranged wife becoming pregnant again during a period of reconciliation, his platonic relationship with Eddie was repaired, enough for the two to start writing songs together. Two of the songs the pair wrote, *Feel Like Givin' Up* and *Once You Had A Heart* seemingly had enough potential for the pair to go into Hitsville and record, although being back at the scene of his previous triumphs filled Paul with dread and he was unable to sing. Undaunted they moved on to another studio, where Paul recorded both tracks, if not to perfection then at least to a standard that warranted release.

Yet for some reason, when presented to Motown they refused to release them, sitting on both tracks (which would remain unissued for many a year until finally being given an airing on CD in 1996). Worse still, Motown wouldn't release Paul either, holding him to a contract he had signed as a member of The Temptations (Paul's reaction to Motown's refusal to release the single or him from his contract was to demand full accounting, in much the same way Eddie Kendricks had previously). With The Temptations not requiring Paul either, the only people taking an interest appeared to be the IRS and his wife, who was demanding a divorce.

By August 1973 Paul's life and prospects appeared to be slipping backwards. He had moved back into his family home following the birth of their sixth child Mary Agnes (there would be at least two further children in Paul Williams Lucas and Derrick Vinyard by other women), but this proved short-lived and he moved in with a former girlfriend Ronnie, having bought her a house in Detroit and moving his belongings in over a number of weeks.

He had finished moving all of his stuff by 16 August, but in the early hours of the following morning, he was found dead sitting in his car. Whilst his death has been declared a suicide, there are many who question the official verdict. Paul was found slumped inside his Ford Maverick, wearing only his swimming trunks (other sources claim it was his underpants), with a bullet hole on the left hand side of his head and a half drunk bottle of alcohol lying near his left side as though it had been dropped the moment he had been shot.

The full autopsy report was never released in full, which in itself is questionable, but the revelation that the right handed Paul had shot himself in the head through his left temple was also queried by those who refused to believe Paul would have taken his own life. Besides, they claim, he had just bought a house and finished moving into it the night before, which didn't add up to a man proposing to take his own life.

Irrespective of the circumstances, which continue to be hotly debated forty years later, one short-term effect of Paul's death was that it reunited The Temptations, at least for his funeral. David Ruffin had asked to sing Paul's trademark song *The Impossible Dream* at the wake, but midway through the song was sobbing so much he was unable to continue. As he began falling to his knees, Eddie Kendricks rushed up to steady him, with the rest of the group joining them to continue and complete the song.

In light of the suicide verdict, Motown felt even less like releasing *Feel Like Givin' Up* since it seemed more like a farewell statement than a comeback single. The only Paul Williams track to have emerged is *I Need You More Than Ever*, which was released on the **Cellarful Of Motown 4** album in 2010.

BRUCE WILLIS

The son of an American soldier and his German wife, Walter Bruce Willis was born in Idar-Oberstein on 19 March 1955 in what was then West Germany and was the oldest of four children. When his father was discharged from the US Army, the family returned to the United States and settled in Carney's Point in New Jersey.

Bruce became interested in acting whilst still at school and joined the drama club, but after graduating he worked as a security guard at a nuclear power plant and private investigator before enrolling in the drama programme at Montclair State University. After auditioning unsuccessfully for a number of television series, he won the part of David Addison Junior in 'Moonlighting' alongside Cybill Shepherd in 1985.

The show was an instant hit, resulting in numerous commercial and acting openings for Bruce, including becoming the spokesman for Seagram and their Golden Wine Cooler products. It was this role that effectively led to a recording deal, for one of the commercial's featured him singing. The success of the commercial led to a joint recording and acting contract, with 'The Return Of Bruno' being a mockumentary featuring Bruce as singer Bruno Radolini who recorded the accompanying soundtrack album for Motown in 1987.

Whilst the television special was well received in the US and aided sales of the album, it was in Europe that his singing career took off, with the album hitting #4 in the UK and earning a gold disc as well as giving rise to two Top Ten hits in *Respect Yourself* and *Under The Boardwalk* and a further two charted singles in *Secret Agent Man-James Bond Is Back* and *Comin' Right Up*. As successful a venture as **The Return Of Bruno** was, it is as an actor that his reputation has been enhanced, with his numerous films having grossed over $2.5 billion, including the 'Die Hard' franchise, 'Look Who's Talking', 'Sin City' and 'The Sixth Sense'.

Bruce recorded a follow-up album for Motown in 1989, although **If It Don't Kill You, It Just Makes You Stronger** was not nearly as successful as its predecessor.

ALBUM: THE RETURN OF BRUNO (1986)

EDDIE WILLIS

One of the original recognised Funk Brothers, Eddie 'Chank' Willis was born in Grenada, Mississippi on 3 June 1936. He left Mississippi in 1953 to rejoin his mother, who was then living in Detroit, and after leaving high school joined a group called The Playboys as guitarist. The group was effectively a vocal group and also included Marv Johnson, who subsequently left for a solo career but invited Eddie along to the recording session for *Come To Me*. It was the first record Eddie had ever played on but wouldn't be the last; two weeks after the session, Berry Gordy invited Eddie back for further work. Soon Eddie was one of the three house guitarists with Joe Messina and Robert White, sometimes with all three playing on the same session.

"We took our time and worked out what the three guitars were going to do, especially in the beginning. I did quite a bit of adlib, because I had more of a blues feel, and my head was full of everything. Robert was a good rhythm guy and Joe often went note-for-note with the bass. I would adlib in and out, never covering up anybody. We had to play according to the record, you know—you didn't want to jam it up with a bunch of crap."

Eddie also spent a considerable time out on the road during his early Motown days, touring with The Marvelettes. When Motown shut down its Detroit operation and moved to Los Angeles, Eddie opted out and became a member of the Four Tops road band, spending some two decades touring around the world. The release of 'Standing In The Shadows Of Motown' brought renewed interest and with it a chance to tour all over again, with Eddie linking with Bob Babbitt, Uriel Jones, Jack Ashford and Joe Messina (effectively the then last surviving Funk Brothers) to perform live.

BRIAN WILSON

Keyboard player, bassist and singer Brian Douglas Wilson was born in Hawthorne, California on 20 June 1942 and a founding member of The Beach Boys, although he stopped touring with the group in 1964 in order to concentrate on songwriting, with Glen Campbell being his replacement. He made his first solo recording in 1966 with the single *Caroline No*, finally issuing an album in 1988 with **Love And Mercy**. In 1987 his track *Let's Go To Heaven In My Car* was featured on the soundtrack to Police Academy 4: Citizens On Patrol'.

FRANK WILSON

Initially brought into the Motown fold in 1963 as a writer, Frank Wilson would go on to become one of its most successful producers, stepping into the void left by the departure of Holland-Dozier-Holland.

Born Frank Edward Wilson in Houston, Texas on 5 December 1940 he moved to Los Angeles whilst still in his teens and began his career as a gospel singer with The Angelaires. However, soon after Hal Davis and Marc Gordon were asked to st up a Motown office in the city, Frank joined the team as a writer, penning *Stevie*, a tribute to Little Stevie Wonder for Patrice Holloway.

A contractual problem that arose between Patrice and Motown resulted in the single being pulled, and whilst Frank continued to write for a number of other artists on the label, he maintained his own career with a succession of releases although usually under pseudonyms on Power (as Sonny Daye), A&M (as Chester St Anthony) and Vee-Jay's Tollie imprint (as Eddie Wilson).

He eventually got to record under his own name, with his composition *Do I Love You (Indeed I Do)* being produced by Hal and Marc in Los Angeles and scheduled for released on the Soul label in November 1965. This time it was Berry Gordy who pulled the plug on the single, shortly before it was due for release.

"I went to Detroit and I hadn't been in town more than a week. We were standing backstage at the Fox Theatre, they were having a Motown Revue. Berry said, 'Frank, now you know I'm getting ready to release this record on you. We're excited about it. But I want to ask you a question. Do you really want to be an artist, or do you want to be a writer and a producer?' And it was right then and there I told him I wanted to be a writer and a producer. And it was decided that he would not release that record on me."

Officially every known copy of the record was destroyed, although the backing tracks were subsequently overdubbed by Chris Clark for release as a single the following April. However, at least two copies of Frank's original survived, with one turning up at auction many years later in Britain and selling for £25,742, confirming the record's place as the most expensive single in history.

Frank meanwhile went back to writing and producing, two things he did exceptionally well for Motown, and relocated to Detroit in 1966. He worked with artists such as Martha & The Vandellas, The Miracles, The Four Tops, The Marvelettes, The Isley Brothers and Marvin Gaye, scoring his biggest hits with The Supremes both before and after the departure of Diana Ross for a solo career. By the early 1970s the hits had begun to slow down on The Supremes, but Frank had assembled a hit writing team with Leonard Caston and Anita Poree that would score a number of major hits on Eddie Kendricks, most notably his chart topper *Keep On Truckin'*.

Frank left Motown in 1976 and set up as an independent producer, helming albums by Lenny Williams, Lakeside, New Birth and Alton McLain & Destiny before turning his back on secular music towards the end of the decade and becoming a born again Christian. Along with his wife Bunny he was a regular on the speaking circuit as well as writing a number of books and producing gospel music. Frank died after a lengthy battle with prostate cancer on 27 September 2012.

JACKIE WILSON

Jackie Wilson never actually recorded for Motown, although it is quite conceivable that but for Jackie, Motown Records would not have existed. In his early career Berry Gordy had no greater aspirations than being a songwriter, putting together a portfolio that he would show to managers and artists he thought might be ideal for his songs. In 1957 Jackie Wilson (born Jack Leroy Wilson Jr. in Detroit, Michigan on 9 June 1934) left The Dominoes for a solo career, signing a management deal with Al Green, the erstwhile owner of Detroit's Flame Show Bar, who got Jackie a recording deal with Brunswick Records.

It was at this point that Berry Gordy entered into the story, offering Jackie first option on a song he had written with his sister Gwen (who held the photographic concession at the Flame Bar) and Billy Roquel Davis (who wrote under the pseudonym Tyran Carlo) entitled *Reet Petite (The Finest Girl You Ever Want To Meet)*. *Reet Petite* would become Jackie's debut hit, peaking at #62 on the pop chart (it found greater favour in the UK, where it would reach #6 first time out, but subsequently hit #1 in 1986 following its use in a claymation video that prompted a reissue), but with Al Green's sudden death, management of Jackie Wilson passed on to Nat Tarnopol.

He was more than happy to continue the working relationship with Berry Gordy and his assorted writers, but there were one or two changes to the agreement. Whilst Berry, Roquel and Gwen continued churning out hits on Jackie Wilson, including *To Be Loved* (#22 pop, #7 R&B and #23 in the UK), *We Have Love* (#93 pop), *Lonely Teardrops* (#7 pop and #1 R&B), *That's Why (I Love You So)* (#13 pop and #2 R&B) and *I'll Be Satisfied* (#20 pop and #6 R&B), the songwriting team only ever received half of the royalties their hits had generated. This was because Nat Tarnopol refused to include their songs on the flip side, which owing to the complexities of the recording business received half of the income from sales, irrespective of the fact that it was the top side that drove demand. In fact, Nat went further than that; he would often buy a song outright for a small sum, get Jackie to record it for the B side of a Berry Gordy penned single and assign the writing credits to either Jackie or a member of Nat's own family, thus ensuring the royalties stayed within the Wilson camp.

By 1959, Berry Gordy had grown tired of battling Nat Tarnopol over the issue and opted to launch his own recording company, one which he could control what went on any side of a record. Since Berry's argument had undoubtedly been with Nat Tarnopol, he and Jackie Wilson retained a more than amicable relationship, so much so that Jackie recommended The Contours to Motown (although Jackie's involvement would no doubt have been influenced by the presence of his cousin Hubert Johnson in the line-up) and recommended Berry sign them up.

Jackie's career after his early days involved with Berry Gordy saw him attain greater heights, slip down the pecking order and then enjoy something a revival. And whilst he still never recorded for Motown, there were those at Motown who recorded with him; the musical prowess of The Funk Brothers was such that they were much in demand for other recording sessions, conducting virtually all of them in a clandestine fashion. Chief among these sessions were a number for Chicago based producer Carl Davis.

"They used to come over on the weekends. They'd load up in the van and come over and I would pay them double scale, and I'd pay them in cash."

Also picking up extra money were The Andantes, whose backing vocals grace *(You're Love Keeps Lifting Me) Higher And Higher* and *I Get The Sweetest Feeling*, two of the most obvious Motown derivatives imaginable.

Jackie suffered a heart attack whilst performing on 29 September 1975 and slipped into a coma, remaining hospitalised for the rest of his life. Many Motown artists contributed to his continued hospital fees until his death on 21 January 1984, with Michael Jackson dedicating to Jackie his Album of the Year Grammy Award for **Thriller** a month later.

MARY WILSON

The longest serving of any of The Supremes, Mary Wilson spent some sixteen years providing the 'oohs' and 'aahs' for Diana Ross, Jean Terrell and Scherrie Payne before finally calling it a day as a background singer and launching her own solo career. Unfortunately, her solo efforts never quite matched the successes achieved as a member of The Supremes, but a tally of twelve pop chart toppers was always going to be difficult to emulate.

Born in Greenville, Mississippi on 6 March 1944 to Sam and Johnnie Mae Wilson, Mary endured a confusing childhood, moving to St Louis and then Chicago with her parents and then being sent to live with her aunt and uncle. For three year old Mary, living with Ivory (Johnnie Mae's sister) and John Pippin in Detroit provided the first period of stability, so much so that in time Mary came to call I.V. (as Ivory was known) and John 'Mom' and 'Daddy'. That stability was somewhat crushed when Johnnie Mae reappeared three years later, along with Mary's brother Roosevelt and sister Cat, moving in with the Pippin's who also had a daughter Pat of their own.

After a spell living with another aunt, Monever, Mary eventually moved to the Brewster-Douglass Housing Projects in 1956 with her mother and siblings. Two years later Mary met Florence Ballard when both entered a talent show, forming a friendship that would last nearly two decades. It was through her friendship with Flo, as everyone knew her, that Mary was invited to help form a vocal group in 1959; local manager Milton Jenkins had The Primes on his books and wanted to create a female equivalent in The Primettes.

Joining Flo and Mary was Betty McGlown, who was dating The Primes' Paul Williams, and another young girl from the projects in Diane Ross. The Primettes rehearsed endlessly over the ensuing months before performing at local dances and hops, dovetailing their musical experiences with school work. Flo, Diana and Mary all graduated from the eighth grade in the spring of 1959, with Mary initially heading off to Commerce in order to study business and then changing her mind and enrolling at Northeastern.

The group continued rehearsing and performing whilst continuing with their school studies, and even auditioned for Berry Gordy at Motown in 1960. Whilst he was impressed with their abilities, he had no real desire to take on such a young group and told them to come back after they had graduated from high school. The Primettes therefore made their recording debut for another local label, LuPine Records, who issued *Tears Of Sorrow* and *Pretty Baby* in August 1960. Betty left the group in order to get married soon after, being replaced by Barbara Martin, but with the LuPine Records release having garnered little by way of sales, The Primettes decided to try their luck at Motown once again.

This time around they found Berry Gordy more receptive, giving them a recording contract in January 1961, although he did not particularly like their name and instructed them to come up with something new; Flo selected The Supremes from the list that was provided. It would take some two years before The Supremes achieved their major breakthrough, by which time Barbara Martin had left and Diana Ross elevated to the focal point of a group that opted to remain a trio.

Despite appearing close to the outside world, there were divisions within the camp even in those days, as Mary would reveal in her autobiography.

"Most of the time it was easy to ignore Diane's behaviour, but things took a different turn when she decided that she could borrow my boyfriend as easily as she borrowed my clothes. Diane was one to covet anything that belonged to someone else, and, as we got older, those things could include men. Diane liked a challenge – whether it was to get into a sorority, make a team, or get a guy – and she never walked away, no matter what the odds or who would get hurt."

Mary got engaged in late 1961 to Ronnie Hammers, something of a high-school sweetheart, but even the official status of Mary and Ronnie cut no ice with Diana.

"After Ronnie and I announced our engagement, Diane began dropping hints that she wanted Ronnie for herself. Fluttering her eyelashes at him, she tried to charm him. If we were all out together, she would act as though he were her boyfriend. Ronnie and I would be dancing, and she would cut in. But all I could do was shrug my shoulders. I could never have said what I thought without looking bad, and, more than anything, I wanted Ronnie to see me as a nice girl, a mature young lady. When Diane made disparaging remarks about my thin legs or flat behind in front of Ronnie, I'd be torn between rage and fear that any rocking of the boat might destroy the group. Of course The Supremes were important, but standing up for myself was even more so. I was just too young to know how."

Mary was also probably too young to contemplate marriage, but when Mary and Ronnie called off their engagement, Diana's interest in Ronnie cooled as well. The internal battles with men aside, the remaining three Supremes did begin to all pull in the same direction once they achieved their major chart breakthrough with *When The Lovelight Starts Shining Through His Eyes* and *Where Did Our Love Go*, although the latter song set the benchmark for everything that was to come for the rest of the decade.

"One day in late March 1964 Eddie Holland wanted us to record *Where Did Our Love Go*, which needed a subtle lead," remembered Mary. "Since that was my forte and I'd been doing the ballads for as long as we'd been singing together, I was certain it would be given to me. As was the usual procedure, he'd played the song for Berry, the Quality Control people, and a few other singers to get an idea of who might be best for it. Berry suggested that he try The Supremes on it. It had childish, repetitive lyrics, a limited melody, and no drive. It was too smooth, and I couldn't imagine anyone liking it. Still, this was probably going to be my lead, so I decided to make the best of it. But it was soon clear just what Berry had meant by his announcement. I later learned that Eddie wanted me to sing it, but that his partners had convinced him that

Diana had the more commercial sound and, besides, wasn't she the lead singer?"

Indeed, Diana would be lead singer on each and every Supremes single from there on in, irrespective of whether the song would have been a better fit vocally for Flo or Mary. The hits came one after another, with The Supremes racking up runs of five and four consecutive number ones as well as three other chart toppers, a more than impressive tally of twelve pop number ones in the space of five years. Unfortunately, the more success the group achieved, the greater the divisions between the members, with Mary and Flo eventually being virtually relegated into the background, both officially and unofficially.

"Our good fortune was the answer to all our prayers, and I believed that this would bring us closer together. Instead, our personal differences were suddenly cast in a new light. The higher we ascended, the more Diane wanted for herself. Around this time, she began dating Berry, and whenever she was unhappy about something, she would let him know. It had been hard enough dealing with her when all we had to face was her temper; knowing that even the most personal argument or discussion – even if it had absolutely nothing to do with our work – would be relayed to Berry fostered an atmosphere of distrust."

The first to buckle was Flo, unceremoniously booted out of The Supremes in July 1967, to be replaced by Cindy Birdsong. Although upset at Flo's departure, Mary had seen the writing on the wall and prepared to welcome new recruit Cindy.

"I was pleased that things were going so well for Cindy, but as time passed, I realised that she had come to the group believing – as did the public – that Diane was the leader. Nonetheless, Cindy and I gradually became good friends, and in her I had a confidante and buddy, which I needed very badly."

If being a member of The Supremes was not all she had hoped it would be, due to Diana's involvement with Berry Gordy and the special privileges that gave her, Mary would find solace with her friendship with Cindy and a blossoming relationship with fellow singer Tom Jones. Reportedly unaware that Tom was married with a child when they first met, Mary resolved to break off the relationship before it got too involved, only to find that point had already been passed. The pair, who often dined in public, irrespective of whether the paparazzi were in attendance, would remain an item well into the following decade.

Besides, Mary had seemingly long since given up caring what the media or paparazzi thought, even being captured on camera during the filming of the 'Tarzan' television show with her nun's habit rolled up to her knees, a cigarette in one hand and a beer can in the other. It was hardly appropriate behaviour for a Supreme (even less a nun), but by then, Mary and Cindy were effectively Supremes in name only. Virtually everything recorded and released by The Supremes was effectively created in the studio by Diana Ross with vocal accompaniment of The Andantes, with Mary and Cindy basically required to perform on stage, not in the studio.

If there was any consolation for Mary, then it surely came with the realisation that Diana was being groomed for a solo career, meaning Mary and Cindy would get the chance to sing on record, and possibly lead too, once Diana had exited The Supremes. That eventually came to fruition in 1970, although Berry Gordy still retained enough interest in The Supremes to recommend Diana's replacement. It was initially believed that Rita Wright (later better known as Syreeta) would get the role, only for Berry to recommend another female singer he had recently discovered, Jean Terrell. After watching her perform with Mary and Cindy, Berry reportedly had a change of heart and recommended The Supremes co-opt Syreeta. Mary stuck to her guns and insisted Jean Terrell was the perfect fit, with the result Berry announced that he was washing his hands of the group. To an extent, that might have worked in The Supremes' favour, for with Diana Ross now out of the picture and Berry having no direct involvement, The Supremes could develop as they wished.

Whilst Jean was brought into The Supremes in order to take over as lead singer, the three women were now a proper group once again, with all three being present in the studio recording their material. There were increased roles for both Mary and Cindy (Cindy would leave The Supremes in 1972 after falling pregnant), along with Cindy's eventual replacement Lynda Laurence. Whilst the hits were never going to be as big as they had been the previous decade, The Supremes in general and Mary in particular were much more content.

It was not just on record either, for on 11 May 1974 Mary married Puerto Rican businessman Pedro Ferrer, with whom she would have three children (although her son Rafael was killed in a freak car accident in 1994). The line-up of The Supremes underwent several changes during the course of the 1970s, although the one constant was Mary Wilson, with Pedro Ferrer eventually taking over the group's management, even though he had little or no experience of the record industry. Eventually, even Mary tired of the revolving door policy of members, along with Motown's lack of interest (despite a brief sojourn when they were handed over to Brian and Eddie Holland for production) in the group and decided to call a halt to The Supremes after a farewell concert in 1977.

A protracted legal battle with Motown then ensued, concerning everything from Motown acting illegally as both manager and agent to the rights to the name The Supremes. The lawsuits were eventually dropped, with Mary picking up a solo recording contract and Marvin Gaye and then Hal Davis slated to produce. Hal had made his reputation with The Jackson 5 and, more recently, taken both Diana Ross and Thelma Houston to the upper echelons of the chart with disco-influenced tracks.

Although Mary's preference was for ballads, much of the material that appeared on her eponymous album in 1979 was uptempo material with the extracted single *Red Hot* hitting #95 on the R&B chart and #85 on Billboard's Hot Dance chart. Mary began work on a second album, taking the first four songs she had recorded with British producer Gus Dudgeon into Motown for their approval. Since Mary had chosen to eschew uptempo material, Motown showed no interest and handed her back the songs and tore up her contract.

The following year Mary divorced Pedro and, with her recording ambitions seemingly blocked, maintained her career with a succession of world tours and the occasional acting assignment. A second album, **Walk The Line** did appear briefly in 1992, although the label (CEO) filed for bankruptcy a day after the album was released.

Whilst her singing and recording career may have stalled, Mary was to enjoy international success with two instalments of her autobiography, 'Dreamgirl: My Life As A Supreme' in 1986 and 'Supreme Faith: Someday We'll Be Together' in 1990, with a combined edition of both books appearing in 1999. Mary continues to tour around the world, still making the occasional record.

ALBUM: MARY WILSON (1979)
FURTHER READING: DREAMGIRL: MY LIFE AS A SUPREME (1986), SUPREME FAITH: SOMEDAY WE'LL BE TOGETHER (1990)

NANCY WILSON

The first of six children born to a foundry worker father and domestic working mother, Nancy Wilson was born in Chillicothe, Ohio on 20 February 1937 and began singing in church choirs whilst still a young child. After winning a talent contest at the age of 15, Nancy made her television debut and performed in clubs, thus starting in motion a career that would stretch across six decades.

Nancy was one of the performers on the 'Save The Children' film and soundtrack, where she sang the appropriately named *The Greatest Performance Of My Life*. This was released on Motown in April 1974. A three time Grammy Award winner, Nancy announced her retirement from live performance in May 2011.

TOM WILSON

Best known for his pioneering production on Bob Dylan, Simon & Garfunkel and Frank Zappa, among others, Tom produced several of Motown's rock orientated albums of the late 1960s and early 1970s. Born in Waco, Texas on 25 March 1931 he formed his own Transition Records label in the 1950s, releasing albums by Sun Ra and Cecil Taylor, but it was as a staff producer at United Artists, Savoy and Columbia that he made his reputation.

He would later join Verve and produce Mothers Of Invention, Lou Reed and Velvet Underground for the label. Later becoming a freelance producer, he would work with Earthquire and Two Friends among his several Motown credits. Tom died from a heart attack on 6 September 1978.

ED WINGATE

Along with Harry Balk, Ed Wingate (along with his future wife JoAnne Bratton) represented the biggest threat to Berry Gordy's domination of the musical scene in Detroit. And just like Harry Balk, when Ed Wingate and his various labels became too much of a thorn Berry bought out the competition and folded the labels into Motown.

Born in Detroit, Michigan in 1925, Ed had become a hugely successful businessman by the end of the 1950s, with interests in hotels, restaurants and even taxi companies in and around Detroit. By the turn of the decade, Ed was looking to diversify, with music a more than passing interest owing to the success Berry Gordy was beginning to enjoy right on his doorstep.

Helping him in his many ventures was JoAnne Bratton, the wife of champion boxer Johnny Braxton, who arranged a meeting between Ed and Berry early in 1961. Whilst Ed went into the meeting with the intention of fishing for information on how to start up a record label, Berry was looking for a financial partner, since the regional success of The Miracles' *Shop Around* had left him financially stretched.

Indeed, at the end of the meeting Berry offered Ed a partnership in Motown, but Ed took the advice of JoAnne and turned him down, looking to start up his own recording venture based on the information he had gleaned.

The first of these, Golden World launched in January 1962 with Sue Perrin's *I Wonder*, followed a month later by Ric-Tic, the name being a tribute to JoAnne's son Derek who was killed in an accident in January 1962. Over the next six years Ed and JoAnne set about making the Golden World group of labels a viable alternative to Motown, locating and kitting out their own studio complex at 3246 West Davison Avenue. In a short space of time this facility would earn a reputation for being every bit as good as the facilities at Hitsville, and the Golden World studios became a magnet for other Detroit based artists and labels.

Indeed, Berry Gordy was said to be so concerned at the quality of material emanating from Golden World he hired private detectives to sit outside and make a note of the artists and musicians who were recording there. If any Motown personnel were discovered to have recorded at Golden World (and there were plenty, including virtually all of The Funk Brothers and The Andantes), then the culprits would be hit with $1,000 fines! Ed Wingate found the whole matter so amusing he invariably reimbursed those fined out of his own pocket!

By 1966 Berry had had enough of the local competition and paid a reported $1 million for the entire Golden World set-up, apparently buying the studio, the recording catalogue, options on artists' contracts and inserting a non-compete clause that prevented Ed Wingate from operating another record company in Michigan. Instead Ed revived Ric-Tic, registering the company in Illinois and enjoyed a further two years involved in recording before Berry came back again, purchasing Ric-Tic and its roster, thus removing the biggest threat to Motown within Detroit once and for all!

Whereas Berry found former rival Harry Balk (he had owned the Impact and Inferno labels until bought out) a position within his newly expanded organisation, there was no such job offer put to Ed Wingate or JoAnne Bratton. Instead Ed and JoAnne (who were later married) left the record business and retired to Las Vegas where Ed died on 5 May 2006.

MICHAEL WINSLOW

Born in Spokane, Washington on 6 September 1958, Michael is best known for his portrayal of the character Sergeant Larvelle Jones in the 'Police Academy' series of films. Known as the 'Man of 10,000 Sound Effects', he recorded a one-off 12" single for Island in 1985 and contributed *Citizens On Patrol* to the 1987 film of the same name, being backed by the L.A. Dream Team.

WITH A LOT O' SOUL – THE TEMPTATIONS [ALBUM]

The fourth Temptations album to top the R&B chart, **With A Lot O' Soul** was also their first studio album to break into the Top Ten of the pop chart, having previously peaked just outside with both **Temptin' Temptations** and **Gettin' Ready**. Although largely produced by Norman Whitfield, he had not yet received an exclusive on the group, resulting in productions from Smokey Robinson, Frank Wilson, Brian Holland and Lamont Dozier and Ivy Jo Hunter. However, Norman was responsible for three of the album's four Top Twenty hits in *(I Know) I'm Losing You*, *You're My Everything* and *(Loneliness Made Me Realise) It's You That I Need*, with Frank Wilson weighing in with *All I Need*.

David Ruffin singes lead on most of the tracks, with Eddie Kendricks heading two and sharing lead vocals with David on *You're My Everything*. The one controversy surrounding the album was the track *Just One Last Look*, written and produced by HDH, which the hit making team had to fight to get included on the album and found Norman Whitfield blocking its potential release as a single. The track, therefore, is the only HDH production on The Temptations that actually made it as far as an album, Norman Whitfield's eventual solid lock on the group just about to take effect. Released in July 1967, **With A Lot O' Soul** would hit #7 on the pop chart and top the R&B listings for a single week, also going on to make #19 in the UK.

WITH YOU I'M BORN AGAIN – BILLY PRESTON & SYREETA [SINGLE]

A duet by Billy Preston and Syreeta, *With You I'm Born Again* was written by noted film composer David Shire (whose previous credits include 'The Taking Of Pelham One Two Three' and contributions to 'Saturday Night

Fever', most notably *Night On Bald Mountain*) and Carol Connors (a former vocalist with The Teddy Bears who also earned a Grammy nomination for co-writing *Gonna Fly Now*, the theme to 'Rocky').

Featured in the film 'Fast Break', the track first appeared on the soundtrack album released in the US in March 1979. However, the first single released was *Go For It*, another duet between Billy and Syreeta, which struggled for acceptance and barely made #108 on the Billboard chart.

In Britain several enterprising DJ's had already latched onto the ballad *With You I'm Born Again*, forcing Motown in the UK to schedule it for release as a single in August 1979. It took almost three months to hit the charts, finally appearing at #75 two weeks before Christmas, but once it had got a toehold there was little to stop it rising up the listings, finally coming to rest at #2, held off the top by The Pretenders and *Brass In Pocket*, with Syreeta excited about the single's success.

"I didn't expect *With You I'm Born Again* stood a chance of success because everyone is into disco and not love songs. The people in England worked super hard to break it and we owe our success in America to that British breakthrough. It's been a funny song all the way through because in Los Angeles my managers always believed in it and it's one of the songs that I liked best myself. And now it's ended up being my biggest success so far and I certainly don't mind sharing it with Billy because he's such a nice guy to work with."

This success would indeed be replicated in America, where it was released in November and became a major hit, reaching #4 pop and #2 on the Adult Contemporary chart. However, for some reason it failed to appeal to the R&B crowd, barely making #86.

BILL WITHERS

Born William Harrison Withers Jr. in Slab Fork, West Virginia on 4 July 1938, Bill was making toilet seats for Lockheed Aircraft during the day and recording self-financed demos in the evening, which he eventually hawked around the music industry looking for a deal. He was signed by Clarence Avant and Sussex Records in 1970 and scored virtually first time out with *Ain't No Sunshine* (later a major UK hit for Michael Jackson), which earned a gold disc and a Grammy Award. His first chart topper came with the largely autobiographical *Lean On Me*, a song based on his experiences growing up in Slab Fork and which Bill would perform in the film and on the soundtrack to 'Save The Children', released by Motown in April 1974.

THE WIZ (1978 FILM)

A Broadway show that had won seven Tony awards (the theatre world equivalent of the Oscar), made a star out of its leading performer, already had memorable songs and had attracted some of the biggest names in Hollywood all eager to get aboard 'The Wiz' – it sounded like a project that could not fail. That it did, and spectacularly so, was effectively down to Diana Ross' insistence at being cast in the leading role.

Frank Baum's 'The Wonderful Wizard Of Oz' had made a star out of Judy Garland when made into a film in 1939. 'The Wiz' was ostensibly an update of this, but done as an all-black contemporary version. Trialled in Baltimore in 1974, it had moved to Broadway the following year and, after a shaky start, gone on to become a major success. It would eventually run for four years and more than 1,600 performances, with Stephanie Mills in the leading role reckoned to be destined for stardom.

Motown obviously thought so, signing her to a contract in 1976 after Jermaine Jackson and his wife Hazel had seen her perform in the musical and sang her praises to Berry Gordy. Motown also picked up the option for the film rights to 'The Wiz', initially in conjunction with 20th Century, although Universal would later partner Motown in getting the film to the market.

It was widely assumed that Stephanie Mills would reprise her role as Dorothy, news that was enough to get John Badham, who had recently worked with Motown on 'Bingo Long', on board as director. Others keen to commit in one capacity or another were Quincy Jones, Richard Pryor, another actor who had worked with Motown previously (in his case in 'Lady Sings The Blues') and several other key personnel.

Then along came Diana Ross, who initially spoke to Berry Gordy to try and convince him to let her play the part of Dorothy. He refused, but Diana was not prepared to accept this as the final decision, contacting Rob Cohen at Motown Productions and persuading him that she could make the part work. He agreed and must also have convinced Berry (not least because Cohen promised Berry that Universal would be prepared to pay $1 million to have Diana attached to the film), for it was then announced that Diana Ross would play the role of Dorothy, even if this meant a major re-write of the script.

Diana would later claim that having read the original Frank Blaum book, Dorothy's age is never revealed, but in every production, both in film and on stage, the role of Dorothy had gone to a young girl, making the whole story as she is transported into the wonderful world of Oz believable. As a result of the re-write, Diana Ross would be a thirty three year old woman playing twenty four year old schoolteacher Dorothy, a role that had most notably been played by Judy Garland at sixteen and Stephanie Mills at eighteen. This change was enough to have Badham resign as director.

"I wouldn't know how to make the film with a mature lady as much as I respect Diana's talents. I didn't want to quit but I didn't understand what concept they had in mind."

Indeed, Diana Ross' character re-alignment wasn't the only element of the show that had undergone a radical change, with Joel Schumacher's script also deviating from the original storyline. New director Sidney Lumet obviously understood the script, fielding questions as to how close to the 1939 Judy Garland film 'The Wiz' remake was going to be with something of a retort.

"There was nothing to be gained from 'The Wizard Of Oz' other than to make certain we didn't use anything from it. They made a brilliant movie, and even though our concept is different – they're Kansas, we're New York, they're white, we're black, and the score and the books are totally different – we wanted to make sure that we never overlapped in any area."

There were a couple of bright spots, with Diana Ross' insistence on Michael Jackson for the role of the Scarecrow, and Quincy Jones came on board as a favour to Lumet to handle the soundtrack. Several of the sets were little short of breathtaking, with nothing spared in trying to make the whole thing workable – it was said $237,000 was spent on twenty miles of yellow vinyl to make the infamous yellow brick road.

And therein lay another problem; everyone was so convinced they had a hit on their hands no one bothered to set a budget, with costs racking up to such an extent the total expenditure was said to have hit $35 million and a further $10 million committed on promotional publicity thereafter. In short, to recoup the film would have to take some $60 million in receipts just to break even. Whilst these figures may seem small by comparison with the cost of making a film today, it is worth considering that when 'The Wiz' was released, only one film in history had achieved the kind of box office receipts it would now have to chase – 'Star Wars'.

Released in October 1978 'The Wiz' was universally panned, drawing headlines in the UK that read 'Wiz That Never Woz' (The Daily Mirror) and 'The Wiz In Blunderland' (Financial Times). Somehow, most probably by behind the scenes lobbying, 'The Wiz' garnered Oscar nominations for Best Art Direction, Best Costume Design, Best Cinematography and Best Original Music Score, although it won none. More tellingly, domestic rentals amounted to only $13.6 million, way below expectations, and no amount of behind the scenes lobbying could ever hide that.

The only people connected with the film who came out of it virtually unscathed were Michael Jackson, whose acting debut received many complimentary reviews, Richard Pryor, who proved his worth as an actor and comedian in one film, and Quincy Jones, whose work on the soundtrack did at least return one hit single in *Ease On Down The Road* and mark the first occasion he worked closely with Michael Jackson – that particular relationship was to change musical history over the next few years.

E.D. WOFFORD

An obscure country singer from Tennessee, E.D. Wofford released a cover version of The Four Tops *Baby I Need Your Lovin'* backed with *Why Not Try Lovin' Me* on the MC label in May 1978 which would eventually hit #77 on the country chart when the label was re-launched as MC/Curb. This was to be Wofford's only chart hit and possibly his only single, as research has thus far revealed no further releases on any label.

WOLF & WOLF

Austrian songwriter, producer and arranger Peter Wolf (born in Vienna on 26 August 1952) studied classical piano for ten years before switching to jazz, subsequently joining the Art Farmer Quartet. Fellow Austrian Ina Ganahl's roots were in folk music and opera before she too switched to jazz, recording two solo albums as Christina. The pair met in 1975 and travelled to the United States together the following year, with Peter initially playing with Frank Zappa before linking more permanently with Ina, first as man and wife in 1979 and then forming the new wave pop duo Wolf & Wolf.

Signed to the Morocco label in 1984, they released an eponymous album and two singles, *Don't Take The Candy* and *Talk Of The Town*, but even with an opening slot for The Rolling Stones could attract no interest in their records. However, they would go on

to make a considerable impact as writers, penning the R&B #1 hit *Who's Johnny* for El DeBarge. Peter would also become a successful producer, helming albums for Go West, The Commodores and Starship, among others.
ALBUM: WOLF & WOLF (1984)

WOLFE

John Pantry trained as a recording engineer and would go on to work with the likes of The Bee Gees, The Who, The Kinks and The Small Faces during the 1960s. He also wrote songs and played keyboards and would eventually link with John Richmond (who played guitar, banjo and piano) and Nick Ryan (bass) and release singles under the monikers Norman Conquest, The Bunch, The Factory, Sounds Around and Peter & The Wolves. They were subsequently joined by Robin Slater (guitar and vocals) and Mike Wade (drums) and adopted the name Wolfe, recording an album at IBC Studios in London where John Pantry regularly engineered.

Comprising material largely written by Pantry and Ryan, the group's album was picked up for the US by the Rare Earth label, which released Wolfe's eponymous album in July 1972. A single, *Ballad Of The Unloved* (written by Scott English and Larry Weiss) was to have been released as a single but was pulled from the schedule. Although Wolfe was technically part of the same EMI deal that saw numerous albums released stateside on Rare Earth, all that was released in Britain was the single *Dancing In The Moonlight* backed with *Snarlin' Mama Lion*, which was released as something of an afterthought in February 1973 after the song had become a major American hit for King Harvest. Neither Wolfe's version nor the original (or indeed a further cover by Young Generation) managed to dent the chart, although the song remained well known but something of a lost hit until Toploader took a version into the Top Ten in 2000.

Wolfe, meanwhile, went their separate ways after the release of their album, with Pantry later converting to Christianity and being ordained an Anglican minister in Kent in 1993.
ALBUM: WOLFE (1972)

BOBBY WOMACK

Born in Cleveland, Ohio on 4 March 1944, Robert Dwayne Womack was the third of five sons born to Friendly and Naomi Womack. With the mother playing organ in the church where the father was minister (he also played guitar), the five siblings were raised by a musical family, with Bobby joining brothers Cecil, Curtis, Harry and Friendly Jr. in the gospel quintet The Womack Brothers. After opening for The Soul Stirrers in 1953 Bobby befriended Sam Cooke, and when the singer formed his own SAR label towards the end of the 1950s recruited The Womack Brothers as one of his first signed acts.

The move to secular music resulted in Friendly Sr. throwing the brothers of out the house, with Sam Cooke wiring over enough money for them to journey to Los Angeles to begin recording. Renamed The Valentinos, they enjoyed a number of successes, but it was Bobby's growing reputation as a writer and guitarist that attracted most attention, with his 1964 composition *It's All Over Now* being covered by The Rolling Stones and taken to the #1 spot in the UK.

With Sam Cooke's tragic death in December 1964 The Valentinos lost more than just a record label boss, they lost their mentor, with Bobby's marriage to Sam's widow Barbara less than three months after his death causing considerable controversy among R&B circles (the marriage lasted some five years before the couple divorced in 1970).

With his own solo career blocked as a result of the supposed marriage scandal, Bobby became a touring musician, working with Ray Charles, Aretha Franklin, Joe Tex and most notably Wilson Pickett. The relationship with Wilson Pickett was especially close, with Bobby giving Wilson several songs that had originally been intended for Bobby's own solo album on Minit, resulting in Bobby recording R&B versions of numerous pop and standard classics, including his first hit single *Fly Me To The Moon*.

From Minit Bobby moved to United Artists, where he was given the opportunity of expanding as an artist; in addition to the R&B material that had made his reputation, Bobby scored the film 'Across 110th Street' and recorded a country album that was well received but not a commercial success, resulting in the end of his tenure with UA. From there he moved to Columbia, but a mix of growing drug problems and family tragedies (his brother Harry was murdered by a girlfriend in Bobby's home) derailed his career for a while.

His career began to pick up again in the 1980s, working with Wilton Felder of The Crusaders and signing a new solo contract with entrepreneur Otis Smith's Beverly Glen label. His debut album for the label, **The Poet** was released in 1981 to critical and commercial acclaim, seemingly restoring Bobby to the mainstream of the music world, but not long after its release Bobby became embroiled in a legal battle with Smith over unpaid royalties and advances. The resulting court case was something of a disaster for Bobby, who at one point attacked Smith in court, delaying the follow-up album by three years. Both albums were released in Europe on the Motown label, an astute piece of business that saw **Poet II** hit the UK chart at #31, his first charting album in Britain.

Bobby meanwhile severed his ties with Beverly Glen and signed directly to MCA, going on to record three albums for the label. His career since those heady days has seen him recording only sporadically, although he made a welcome return to the charts in 2012 with **The Bravest Man In The Universe** on XL Recordings. Inducted into the Rock & Roll Hall of Fame in 2009, he died on 27 June 2014.

ALBUMS: THE POET (1982), THE POET II (1984)

THE WOMAN IN RED (OST) - STEVIE WONDER & FEATURING DIONNE WARWICK [ALBUM]

After the failure of **The Secret Life Of Plants** album, Motown must have viewed the news that Stevie Wonder's main project for 1984 was another film soundtrack with some trepidation. However, that was the year that numerous R&B artists crossed over with their contributions to successful films, including Ray Parker Junior with *Ghostbusters* and Deniece Williams with her hit from 'Footloose', *Let's Hear It For The Boy*. Starring Gene Wilder and Kelly LeBrock, 'The Woman In Red' actually got released at the cinema, which at least helped the initial promotion for Stevie's soundtrack.

In the final analysis, however, what *really* helped the album was the presence of Stevie's most commercial single of his career, *I Just Called To Say I Love You*. Having been brought into the film project by legendary singer Dionne Warwick, Stevie would repay her faith by recording two duets (*It's You* and *Weakness*), writing a solo song for Dionne (*Moments Aren't Moments*) and recording five new tracks, with *I Just Called To Say I Love You* topping the charts around the world and *Love Light In Flight* making #17 pop and #4 R&B. A third single, *Don't Drive Drunk* was also released in the UK (where it hit #62) but achieved greater notoriety after it was part of a campaign by the US Department of Transportation, the Ad Council and Chrysler against drunk driving.

The film was something of a box office disappointment, grossing some $25 million, but the soundtrack album was a big success, topping the R&B chart and hitting #4 on the pop listings. It would also garner a Grammy Award nomination for Best R&B Vocal Performance, Male, although Billy Ocean and *Caribbean Queen* won the honour. *I Just Called To Say I Love You*, however, would win an Academy Award and Golden Globe. In the UK the album stalled at #2, the third time Stevie had been denied a chart topping album, this time by the compilation **Now That's What I Call Music 3** and David Bowie's **Tonight**.

STEVIE WONDER

Of all the stars at Motown, none shone brighter nor for longer than Stevie Wonder, who made his debut in 1962 and is still releasing albums more than fifty years later.

He was born in Saginaw, Michigan on 13 May 1950 as Steveland Morris, although his father's name was Calvin Judkins and his mother's Lula Mae Hardaway. Even his first name has been variously spelt, with Stevland appearing in more than one source, with neither Lula nor Stevie ever confirming for once and for all exactly what his name was (the first passport he acquired was in the name Steveland Morris). What is known, of course, is that the prematurely born boy was placed into an incubator into which oxygen was pumped in order to keep him alive but at the same time he developed retrolental fibroplasias, rendering him blind.

When Stevie was three years of age, he and his family, which also included elder brothers Milton and Calvin left Saginaw, bound for Detroit.

"We lived on Breckinridge Street in Detroit, which is on the west side, and they were very beautiful people around us. It was a very warm atmosphere. We lived in what you would call an upper-lower class area, or more upper class, you know. We had enough to get by and I didn't really know what being poor was, but what we did receive we were always grateful for and appreciative."

Later, when he was feeling more mischievous, Stevie would claim that in fact he and the rest of the family had suffered somewhat during those early days.

"Sometimes we would go without eating – I can prove it to you by the pains I felt in my stomach!"

Such claims would always bring a stern rebuke from Lula.

"I don't know why Stevie says those things, we weren't badly off."

Irrespective of who is right and who is wrong, the family did suffer some financial hardship during Stevie's early days in Detroit, with matters not helped when Calvin Judkins eventually left home, Lula then placed in the unenviable position of having to bring in the money to keep her and her family.

"My mother raised us by herself during that early time...that was until she was fortunate enough to meet my second father [Paul Hardway]. They had two children, Timothy, who's a Libra, and Renee, who's a Cancer. Besides them, I have another young brother, Larry, who's a Capricorn, and two older brothers, Calvin (Aries) and Milton, the eldest, who's a Virgo."

Despite his obvious handicap his mother and brothers tried to treat Stevie exactly as they would a sighted child, allowing him out to explore his neighbourhood and get into the same kind of scrapes as the other children.

"I did what all kids of my age were doing. I played games, rode bikes and climbed trees. I did all the things that, you know, a normal boy did. I mean I just used to go out climbing trees, we used to hop barns – they were places where you'd keep different parts for the car, but it wasn't really large enough for a car."

The decision to allow Stevie to go out and about and make his own way in the world was somewhat inspired, although there would sometimes be occasions when it backfired. Since Stevie couldn't see, he invariably memorised his locale and kept to the areas that were familiar. Unfortunately, there would occasionally be piles of dog droppings that probably weren't there the last time he walked down that particular street, most of which Stevie would then traipse into the house, much to Lula's horror! Yet she couldn't remain angry at him for long, as Stevie would fondly recall.

"I had a very beautiful youth, and even though I know it wasn't yesterday, it isn't too many years ago. I can see it in front of me, crystal clear, as being a very special part of my life, one which even if I could live it over again I wouldn't want it to be any other way."

Fortunately, plenty of others in the Breckenridge neighbourhood kept a watch over Stevie, ensuring he didn't get into too much trouble, and it wasn't long before Stevie had found a regular friend in John Glover.

"You see, I owe a lot to the neighbours that we had, and John's mother Ruth, who was responsible for us actually getting to Motown and for helping us to deal with the many things that we were not aware of, things that sometimes even my mother was not aware of. You see I used to go around the neighbourhood on my own a lot, and just about every day John and I would meet and we'd go off to play and sing."

Stevie had developed an interest in music at a very early age, initially as something of a percussionist, banging spoons and whatever else was to hand on pots and pans, eventually being given his own set of small drums one Christmas. By Boxing Day they had been smashed to bits and the pots and pans were brought back out to take their place! Then Stevie took up the harmonica, learning to play the instrument quickly and competently. Indeed, Stevie would later prove adept at quickly learning any instrument he tried his hand to, including the gift of a piano from a local boys club.

That interest in music was fuelled by listening avidly to the radio, tuning in to a wide range of stations and music styles.

"Detroit had the best cross section of music, different cultures. I listened to stations like WJZZ, now WCHD, WJBL, WGPR, CXYZ and WJBK. Like I was the only black kid on the bus, and I would always turn the radio down, because I felt ashamed to let them hear me listening to B.B. King. But I loved B.B. King. Yet I felt ashamed because – because I was different enough to want to hear him and because I had never heard him anywhere else."

Stevie and John would eventually form an impromptu duo, hosting informal music sessions on the steps of their houses, playing their versions of the hits of the day as well as one or two of their own, rudimentary compositions. Word of their abilities soon spread, and whilst a small handful of kids had gathered round the steps to listen in their early days, the size of the crowd soon grew. Fortunately, John Glover had the wherewithal to turn that growing popularity into something a little more positive, for his cousin was none other than Ronnie White, a member of The Miracles. In June 1961, John contacted Ronnie and asked whether he and his friend Stevie could come over and play some songs for him. A date was duly arranged, with John taking Stevie over to Ronnie's house, where fellow Miracle Bobby Rogers was also in attendance. With John playing acoustic guitar and Stevie singing and playing harmonica, the pair performed several original numbers, in between which Stevie told Bobby and Ronnie how much he admired The Miracles but how their various hits could have been better, vocally demonstrating for them exactly what he had in mind! Impressed with both his ability and his gall, Bobby and Ronnie arranged to take Stevie (and John) into Motown for a more formal audition.

That occurred on 23 September 1961, with Stevie having to perform for Brian Holland and then Mickey Stevenson before finally getting in front of Berry Gordy. Brian and Mickey were as knocked out with Stevie's abilities as Bobby and Roger had been earlier and put in an urgent call to Berry; he had to stop whatever he was doing and come and listen.

"Singing for me was fun and I didn't realise that I was going through all the auditions. I was just having fun singing. When Berry Gordy got a call to come and hear me sing, he was eating a steak dinner. I often wonder which was more worthy, the steak dinner or myself!"

Berry obviously thought that Stevie was more worthy, readying a contract once he had cleared the necessary approval from the state department responsible for dealing with minors (it should be noted that John Glover was also signed at the same time, with the eventual contract naming the act 'Steven and John', although John would eventually get side-tracked into a writing and production role at Hitsville).

"I signed with Motown in '61, and as you may know Motown was like a studio out of nowhere; no one ever thought there would be music coming out of Detroit, and I think it caught everyone by surprise."

Although Motown had got their hands on Stevie they were initially unsure what exactly it was they were going to do with him. He could sing (although Berry Gordy would late state that he was not particularly knocked out by his voice, thinking it no more than adequate) and play a variety of instruments, each more than adequately, but if he was going to become a star, then he would have to trained and drilled, a task that fell to several within the Motown building.

"Everyone over the age of eleven was my parent. Clarence Paul loved me like his own son, Esther Edwards, Berry's sister, and Ardena Johnston, all the musicians and artists watched over me. Wanda, of the Marvelettes, would always tell me when she thought I was eating too much candy. I wish kids today could have the same kind of caring expressed and shown to them. Today, there is a lack of concern for others and for oneself."

Equally beneficial to Stevie's musical education was Benny Benjamin, the Funk Brothers' master drummer who took a particular shine to the youngster and would spend much time teaching new tricks and new licks on the drums. The first producer assigned to Stevie was Clarence Paul, who, as Stevie would later acknowledge, became something of a father figure. Stevie would spend his time outside school either at the Hitsville complex or at Clarence's apartment, working on potential material and further practice on a variety on instruments. It was these abilities that would eventually earn Stevie the moniker by which he became world-renowned; someone remarked that he was a wonder, someone else that he was a little wonder, and eventually the name Little Stevie Wonder became permanently attached to the precocious youngster who was running around Hitsville, sometimes into the studio right in the middle of a session!

"If they had waited a while longer they might have called me Knuckle Head or something. I used to get into a lot of trouble then. I loved to play jokes on people. I knew the com-line numbers of everyone at Motown, and could change my voice and say, for example, 'This is Berry Gordy and I want you to get Stevie that tape recorder right away. He's a great new artist, so it's okay to get him the tape recorder. He'll have it back in a few days.' After they fell for this about three times and never got the recorder back, they gave it to me as a belated birthday present. I had turned eleven that May and received the tape recorder that September."

Whilst Motown might initially have been amused and willing to accommodate Stevie, soon the reality bit that little or nothing came for free; Stevie would have to pay his own his way, much like everybody else on the roster. Berry Gordy's original plan was to focus more on Stevie's abilities as a performer than as a singer, reasoning that R&B wouldn't allow him room enough to display that talent, but jazz would. So Berry decided Little Stevie should record a jazz number, or at least an approximation of jazz, since the material was going to be written in-house. Such a notion alarmed Clarence Paul, although he was unable to get Berry to change his mind. He was, however, able to extract something of a concession in getting Motown to agree to a whole album of such material.

The very idea of Stevie recording an album, even before he'd released a single was something of an anomaly within Motown. Virtually every artist had started their career by releasing a succession of singles and then albums, only as and when there was sufficient demand to justify the extra expense. Most albums issued were little more than a couple of hit singles and an abundance of filler, since it was through singles that Motown earned its corn. Now here was a new artist, albeit a talented one, and he was getting the full long player right from the off!

"I found that when you're a new singer, the first time you go into a studio, or the first time you're in front of a mike, you really don't have any technique – you only have what you feel. As far as getting a large ego is concerned, many people felt that I was getting too much too soon, but I didn't realise that it was all happening. I just enjoyed singing. Sometimes when it was time for an interview or rehearsal, I asked for candy. I just wanted to go play or have a few cookies or candy. I didn't care about interviews. I wanted to do other things. That might have made some feel that I was a brat, but not true. I was just a normal kid."

In the long run, Clarence Paul was right to stick to his guns about getting an album out. A lone jazz influenced single, with Stevie's vocal hidden deep in the mix, would not have allowed any of his talents to come to the fore. **The Jazz Soul Of Little Stevie Wonder** eventually featured nine tracks, with Clarence having a hand in eight tracks in total, five with Hank Cosby, two with Stevie and one with Marvin Gaye (another artist Stevie had become tight with around Motown) and the final, closing number a Berry Gordy composition. Berry himself might have had second thoughts when he first heard the album, putting **Jazz Soul** on the shelf and Stevie back in to the studio. This time the brief was to come up with a musical homage to Ray Charles, with Clarence pulling six numbers from the Ray Charles songbook, a traditional folk song here, a standard there and one or two new numbers. One of these was *Sunset*, written by Clarence and Stevie, a song that was subsequently presented to the weekly Quality Control meeting, only to be rejected. So to was the resulting album, **Tribute To Uncle Ray**, at least for the time being, as Berry began to have third thoughts about what to do with his child protégé.

It was not that Stevie lacked talent – he had that in abundance, but nothing Berry had heard so far on record captured the essence or appeal of the youngster. In short, there was nothing particularly wonderful about either album. So Clarence was sent back into the studio a third time, this time with a brief to try and get something that was again different but marketable. Clarence and Hank put together an elongated song, opting to record it in two differing styles, which would duly appear on either side of what was to become Stevie's first release.

I Call It Pretty Music (But The Old Folks Call It The Blues) was not out and out blues nor necessarily pretty, thanks to some particularly exuberant vocal work on Stevie's part, but it was certainly a step in the right direction. This time the single made it through Quality Control and was released as a single on Tamla in August 1962, picking up a few radio playlists here and the odd sale there, enough to get the single tantalisingly close to making it on to the charts, stalling at #101 on the Billboard pop chart, bubbling under without every reaching boiling point. That limited success (which, it has to be said, was better than The Supremes and The Temptations managed with their debut releases) was enough for Berry to authorise the release of **Jazz Soul** and **A Tribute** in September and October 1962 respectively. Neither album made an impact, although over the years they have become critically well received, their curiosity appeal notwithstanding.

If Little Stevie Wonder had attracted any kind of following with the near success of *I Call It Pretty Music*, then Motown wasted little time in ensuring there was a regular supply of material to keep the punters happy. *Little Water Boy* and *Contract On Love* were rushed out before the year was out, although neither made an impact, despite *Contract On Love* having been written by Brian Holland and Lamont Dozier with Janie Bradford and featuring *Sunset* on the flip.

Even as those singles and albums were failing to hit the mark, fate was waiting to deliver the perfect remedy. In October 1962, Berry had sent out most of his roster out on the road, including Stevie, although unaware of the problems he caused himself by including the youngster on a two month trek around the country.

"The Motown Revues – they were also known as the Motown Specials – featured the biggest acts back then, like nearly everyone had a record riding high on the charts, but when I started on them I wasn't the headliner, I was just Little Stevie Wonder and *Fingertips* wasn't even out. So the response I was getting was I guess because I was little, and 'Stevie's shaking his head fifty thousand revolutions a second'."

Stevie certainly appealed to the audiences that saw the shows, although his popularity at Motown took something of a battering during the course of the tour. On the bus, his inability to differentiate between day and night meant he would often be practising the harmonica or bongos whilst all around him were trying to sleep! On stage, his natural exuberance often resulted in him playing to the audience; the more they cheered, the more excited he became and less likely to want to call a halt to his brief set. Often, he would have to be physically manhandled off stage by Clarence Paul, which would bring a chorus of boos from the audience and bickering between singer and mentor when they exited stage left.

Following the near success of *I Call It Pretty Music* Berry Gordy had sent Clarence and Stevie back into the studio, but nothing they recorded sounded much like a hit. So Berry dug out some tapes of early Motown live shows, listening to Stevie's brief set at the Chicago Regal Theater. Actually it wasn't that brief, for Stevie had again supposedly outstayed his welcome, at least as far as the Motown stage hands and personnel were concerned and had again been led off stage by Clarence Paul. However, what Berry heard in the ten minutes or so prior to then was little short of exciting, as his live version of *Fingertips* (originally the lead track from **Jazz Soul**) burst out of its jazz origins and into a joyous explosion of music. A simple edit produced parts one and two, with the second part being deemed the more effervescent and likely to appeal.

Released in May 1963, the single added radio station after radio station and picked up sale after sale, hitting the Top 40 of the Billboard chart in July and hit the top of the chart the following month. And that was just the pop chart, for the single did much the same on the R&B listings. By then the album, **Recorded Live! The 12 Year Old Genius** was similarly vaulting the charts, also going on to achieve double top. The success of both ensured that when the Motown Revue next rolled out, Little Stevie Wonder would be considered one of the bigger names, further up the line-up and unlikely to be hauled off stage before he was good and ready to end his set. For all the success, Stevie tried to keep his feet firmly on the ground, refuting suggestions that he had now been elevated to the same ranks as his peers.

"I said, what is a genius? I was not able to compare anything to anything. I was having fun. I felt that I was only having fun really and that the Ray Charles's were the professionals."

As successful as the single and album undoubtedly were, they also presented Stevie and Motown with something of a conundrum; how on earth were they going to follow them? Berry's normal reaction with his other artists had been to churn out more of the same, often only vaguely different from the major hit, but *Fingertips* had been something of novelty. There would have to be a subtle difference in whatever Motown came up with as a follow-up, with *Workout Stevie, Stevie* being a studio recording designed to sound as though it was recorded live. The glow from *Fingertips* was enough to help *Workout* make it into the Top 40 of the pop chart at #33, but for some reason the single failed to make any impact on the R&B chart.

Not everyone was delighted with the success Stevie was enjoying. His mother Lula had become concerned at the amount of time he was spending in the studio or on the road rather than attend to his school studies. That concern turned to alarm when the state education authorities threatened to step in and put an end to his recording career.

"Because of this, my teachers told me I should stop pursuing music and continue my education until I was nineteen years old. They informed me that legally they could keep me in school until that time. I just went in the bathroom and cried and prayed that God would allow me to remain in the industry."

Lula had made her fears known to Berry Gordy, who spoke with the same authorities to try and find a solution that would satisfy. The eventual proposal was for a tutor to accompany Stevie at all times, giving him schooling in between those visits to the studio and out on the road. After brief spell with Helen Traub, who resigned the position because she felt it inappropriate for a grown woman to undertake the task of schooling a pubescent boy, the role fell to Ted Hull. He proved to be the perfect choice; partially sighted but legally blind, he could fully comprehend the problems Stevie was facing. For the next couple of years, the pair was inseparable, with Ted also now responsible for ensuring Stevie was where he needed to be at any given time, be it in the studio, on stage or in the classroom.

"Ted could see well enough to not be considered blind and was considered partially sighted. By Ted having experience of travelling around the world, he helped me a great deal from the standpoint of understanding what blindness is about, how to deal and communicate with people. A person who had not had experience of travelling the world may not have been able to so readily understand the things that should be checked out by a person with the opportunities. If Ted had been a different person he might have felt that as long as we got the studies done and toured a little that would be enough. But he explained the foreign currencies to me, taught me about the electric currents and their differences. He connected the blind world with the sighted world."

Whilst Ted took care of Stevie's standard education, Clarence Paul was still responsible for ensuring his musical education continued unabated. After the relative failure of *Workout Stevie, Workout*, it was decided that a change of musical direction might be beneficial, although the change was not subtle but drastic.

Several others at Motown had tried to do albums of standards, most notably Marvin Gaye, with little or no success, and there is no reason to suppose that Stevie's attempts at staying in the middle of the road would be any different. Despite this he recorded an entire album of such material, featuring such songs as *Put On A Happy Face, On The Sunny Side Of The Street, Smile* and the album's title track *With A Song In My Heart*. The recording sessions were conducted in Detroit, Chicago and Los Angeles, although they dragged on to such an extent the album wasn't ready for release when Stevie headed back out on the road for the second Motown Revue, but compared with the exhilarating experiences of twelve months previously the 1963 Revue was a chore, made all the worse by the assassination of President Kennedy midway through the tour. Few felt like going to see a show in the aftermath of that event, and even fewer felt like performing for them.

With A Song In My Heart (his first album to drop the 'Little' moniker from his name) was eventually completed in time for release after Christmas 1963 but since it lacked an obvious single was effectively finished the moment it hit the streets. It barely found an audience, even if it did hit #78 on the R&B chart.

Despite the failure of the album, Stevie's name still had enough allure to land him cameo roles in a couple of films. Berry Gordy had been approached by producers Samuel Z Arkoff and James H Nicholson of American International Pictures, who were working on a couple of muscle beach movies starring former idols Frankie Avalon and Annette Funicello. Stevie was sent to Hollywood where he would work with Hal Davis and Marc Gordon on the songs to be featured in 'Muscle Beach Party' and 'Bikini Beach' and would later lip-synch *Happy Street* and *Dance And Shout* in the two films. He was also kept out on the west coast long enough to record more material, supposedly in the same vein, resulting in the eventual album **Stevie At The Beach** and extracted single *Castle In The Sand* (the last single issued as Little Stevie Wonder in the US).

Yet *Castle In The Sand* wasn't in the same vein at all, which would probably explain why it would do relatively well when released as a single, hitting #6 R&B and #52 pop. The album was promoted during the summer, at much the same time the first of the films was released, with Motown also able to land Stevie a guest spot on the Ed Sullivan Show (although he performed *Fingertips*). Eager to capitalise on this burst of activity, a follow-up single was issued, *Hey Harmonica Man*, which would at least return him to the Top 30 pop, peaking at #29 and #5 R&B for good measure. The album meanwhile would halt at a lowly #68 R&B.

The whole concept was not viewed with the same degree of enthusiasm in Britain, with *Hey Harmonica Man* being issued as a single in August 1964 (still with artist credit to Little Stevie Wonder) and the album subsequently titled **Hey Harmonica Man** when it finally appeared on the Stateside label in January 1965. Not surprisingly both failed to make an impression, leaving Stevie still hitless in that territory, despite having made several visits to the country in order to appear on a number of television shows, including 'Ready Steady Go' and 'Thank Your Lucky Stars'.

Steve would return to Britain in March 1965, alongside several of his label mates for both a tour (the first Mototown Revue outside of America) and for the filming of a Tamla Motown special on ITV's 'Ready Steady Go'. That was just part of a planned European assault that would also see the Revue swing into the Netherlands, France and Germany, other areas where Motown had begun to weave its magic. Stevie performed two numbers on the special, *Fingertips*, which was already more than two years old, alongside his most recent solo outing *Kiss Me Baby*, which had missed the chart altogether on both sides of the Atlantic.

The trip to Europe proved to be the highlight of the year. There was little or no recording done, with those tracks that were completed sounding as though they had little chance of changing Stevie's fortunes on the charts.

What was changing, however, was Stevie's voice. It was something Motown privately feared; when his voice broke, would he emerge on the other side a better singer, or had they already reached the pinnacle?

There were other considerations too. Whilst the label had not gone out of its way to actively encourage Stevie in his writing (Smokey Robinson and to a lesser extent Marvin Gaye were the only artists on the Hitsville lot entrusted with writing their own material), his natural instinct right from day one had been to involve himself in everything connected with his career, and that most definitely included writing. His initial attempts, which dated back to his debut album, had been in conjunction with producer Clarence Paul, whilst later he would write with an assortment of personnel, including Ted Hull and Lula Mae Hardaway. Or rather, they would be credited on numerous songs, although quite how much they contributed could be open to debate; composer credits were already something of a thorny issue at Motown, with names being added to songs as part of a financial favour. As were production credits, with several artists claiming that they did more than just sing on their records, irrespective of what the actual record said.

As Stevie contemplated what would happen to his voice, he had other issues that needed addressing. His professional relationship with Clarence Paul had cooled somewhat, at least as far as working together in the studio was concerned (Paul would continue to work with his young charge as conductor and musical director for some considerable time), which required replacement writers and producers sign up for Team Stevie. There wasn't much of a queue, with only staff writer Sylvia Moy volunteering for the task. That in turn would bring Hank Cosby into the fold, since Sylvia was seen around Motown as Hank's apprentice, although given their later success, it proved to be fortuitous to the extreme.

It has been claimed that Stevie was almost out of the door at Hitsville when Sylvia and Hank signed up to guide his future, the dropping off of hits after *Fingertips* leading to many to think of him as one hit wonder rather than Stevie Wonder. The key players at Motown at the time, label head Berry Gordy and A&R chief Mickey Stevenson have consistently denied that Stevie was close to the end, although they were undoubtedly concerned that his career had cooled. Rather, they were desperate to ensure that he be channelled in the right direction in the future.

Sometime after Sylvia and Hank began working with Stevie, the three sat down to sift through the various bits and pieces of songs that he might have sitting around. According to Sylvia there wasn't much (certainly nothing that sounded as though it could be a hit), other than a couple of simple phrases and refrain that he had, built around 'uptight' and 'outta sight'. The threesome set about crafting a song out of those, resulting in *Uptight (Everything's Alright)*, produced by Hank but overseen by Mickey Stevenson for backup.

Released in November 1965 (January 1966 in the UK), *Uptight* did all it set out to achieve, returning Stevie to the top of the R&B chart for five weeks, hitting #3 pop and proving to be his breakthrough in Britain where it would reach #14. Even as *Uptight* was powering its way up the chart, the trio were back in the studio writing a follow-up, the similarly styled *Nothing's Too Good For My Baby*, although *Uptight* had gone too far outta sight for *Nothing's Too Good* to get anywhere close, eventually stalling at #4 R&B and #20 pop, even after DJ's had flipped the record and begun playing *With A Child's Heart* (that would halt at #8 R&B and a distant #131 pop). Neither side made an impression in Britain, although Stevie wasn't unduly concerned about that. What he was concerned with was Motown's continued insistence that he follow a hit with something that sounded almost identical; he would not allow himself to get dragged into that line of thinking in the future.

Irrespective of the relative failure of *Nothing's Too Good*, it did mean the resulting album **Uptight** already had two hit singles going in its favour when it was released in May 1966. That tally would be expanded to three when a cover of Bob Dylan's *Blowin' In The Wind* was released, another single that attained pole position on the R&B chart and made Top Ten pop (but still missed out on charting in the UK), resulting in the album also becoming a major success, hitting #2 R&B and #33 pop.

Both single and album were still current when Stevie went back into the studio, this time recording a composition by new Jobete recruit Ron Miller (Stevie's arrangement with Sylvia Moy and Hank Cosby was not exclusive), *A Place In The Sun*, which was produced by Clarence Paul. This too would make the Top Ten on both the R&B and pop charts (and hit #20 in Britain for good measure), and before the year was out Tamla released a follow-up album in **Down To Earth**. Something of a ragbag collection, featuring eight songs from the Jobete catalogue, with the covers including Bob Dylan's *Mr Tambourine Man*, Sonny & Cher's *Bang Bang* and *Sixteen Tons*, the latter perhaps best known thanks to a country version by Tennessee Ernie Ford! The end result was too eclectic for most palates, stalling at a distant #72 on the pop charts, even if it did hit #8 R&B.

The year ended positively for Stevie, for having supposedly been on his way out of the company barely twelve months previously, a new five year deal was agreed with Motown. Although many of the conditions, including the right to decide what tracks would be recorded and what would be released, remained heavily weighted in Motown's favour, there was the realisation that this was the last contract that Stevie would sign on somebody else's terms; when this contract expired, he would be twenty one and able to dictate what he wanted. It was therefore the last contract Stevie Wonder signed that allowed Berry Gordy to have a wry smile on his face.

Ron Miller meanwhile provided Stevie with his first stab at a Christmas song, penning *Some Day At Christmas* which would go on to limp into the Christmas chart at #24. Despite the relative failure of the single, Berry Gordy was encouraged enough to commission a whole album's worth of similar Yuletide fare, which would be released the following year.

Still working with Ron Miller, Stevie recorded *Travelin' Man* for release in February 1967 (issued a month later in the UK), but this didn't travel far, halting at #31 R&B and #32 pop, and even an attempt to get some action on the flip side *Hey Love* backfired, peaking at #90 pop even if it did make the Top Ten of the R&B chart.

Perhaps reasoning that ballad material wasn't what the public wanted, Berry Gordy vetoed a planned release on a song composed by Stevie, Clarence Paul and Morris Broadnax, with *Until You Come Back To Me (That's What I'm Going To Do)* remaining unissued for the next seven years, although it was obviously pushed by Jobete, which would account for Aretha Franklin enjoying an R&B chart topper and Top Five pop hit with it in 1973. Even more worryingly, Berry didn't think *My Cherie Amour* was an ideal candidate for a single either and put that back on the shelf, although fortunately that would make a re-appearance sooner rather than later.

Instead, Stevie was put back into the care of Sylvia Moy and Hank Cosby and instructed to come up with material similar in style and feel to *Uptight*. The sessions were somewhat pained, not least because Stevie seemed to have so many song ideas whirling around. According to Hank, Stevie was writing five or six songs a day (although to what degree they were finished remains a matter of some doubt) and presenting some 25 songs a week to the team (and some he gave to others around Motown, including bits and pieces that would become *Tears Of A Clown* for Smokey Robinson & The Miracles).

"If you keep your life happening then there's no problem with writing on the road," said Stevie. "It only is a problem when you look at it as a problem. But even when you're touring you can keep your life in order and do the things that you want to do."

It usually fell to Sylvia to select those that were the most coherent and put an actual song around the idea, then for Hank to get that down on tape. By the time the recording session came around, Stevie had already tired of the song and was working on yet another idea or segment. Somehow, the three managed to get enough of one idea down, with *I Was Made To Love Her* (which also had a co-writing credit for Lula Mae Hardaway) sounding much more like a Stevie Wonder single. Released in May 1967 (and a month later in the UK), *I Was Made* stormed the charts, taking pole position on the R&B listings and hitting #2 pop, behind Aretha Franklin's *R.E.S.P.E.C.T.* It also became a major breakout internationally, peaking at #5 in the UK.

The resulting album, rush released whilst the single was still sitting on top of the R&B chart, was something of a departure for Stevie, being very blues influenced and complete with his attempts at sounding like Ray Charles, James Brown and Otis Redding. Whatever the reasoning behind such a ploy, it didn't meet with universal acclaim, halting at a lowly #45 pop, even if it did hit #7 on the R&B chart.

With his next album project slated as a Christmas offering, Tamla kept his fans happy with another single in *I'm Wondering,* which would hit #4 R&B and #12 pop (it would be bolted onto the forthcoming greatest hits package). Unfortunately, it did not keep Stevie happy, already beginning to bristle at having to record what Motown wanted him to, rather than what he wanted to do. Indeed, it wasn't only recording matters that Motown dictated; when Martin Luther King and later Robert Kennedy were slain, Stevie wanted to attend both funerals and record something of a tribute song but found Motown had other ideas, with Berry Gordy and The Supremes leading Motown's contingent at King's funeral.

One area where Stevie was allowed to expand, however, was experimenting with new instruments, with *Shoo Be Doo Be Doo Da Day* becoming one of his first to feature the clavinet. Heralding much the same sound he would make his own some three or so years later, *Shoo Be Doo* would become a major hit, peaking at #9 pop and topping the R&B chart for a week (although it barely made the Top 50 in the UK, hovering at #46). In the wake of that success, a greatest hits package was rushed out in March 1968, so rushed in fact that little or no thought was given to the cover design (when it appeared in Europe in August, virtually every territory did their own design), but despite this oversight it still proved a success, hitting #36 R&B and #6 pop. The UK edition made #25, all the more impressive when the fact he had only had five hit singles was taken into consideration.

Then came *You Met Your Match*, which represented another first, for it was the first single on which Stevie was given a production credit (albeit shared with Motown staffer Don Hunter), although the single stalled at #35 pop even if it did hit #2 R&B.

The relative success of *You Met Your Match*, at least as far as the production was concerned, inspired other ideas in Stevie. Having become tight with legendary guitarist Wes Montgomery, Steve presented him with a song he had written entitled *Bye Bye World*. The pair discussed working together, with Stevie to produce an album, although whether Motown would have agreed to him producing an artist outside of the company (Wes was signed to A&M at the time) is a question left unanswered; Wes died from a heart attack on 15 June 1968 without ever recording Stevie's song. Instead, Stevie accepted an invitation to record an album of instrumentals, with *Alfie*, a cover of Burt Bacharach's theme to the Michael Caine film the first track to appear. The not too subtle artist credit was to Eivets Rednow, Stevie's own name spelt backwards (and to further distance the project was released on the Gordy imprint), although even this proved beyond the understanding of some people.

"There was this cat in the airport that came up and said 'Hey man, these whites are taking over everything. I heard a kid today, man, played *Alfie* just like you, man!' 'Oh,' I said. 'This cat named Rednow?' 'Yeah, that's it,' he said. 'Oh, man,' I grinned, 'that cat is – well, don't worry about him...'"

Stevie, or rather Eivets took *Alfie* to #66 on the pop chart, although the resulting album, which featured *Bye Bye World* and three other Stevie Wonder compositions as well as two from Bacharach and David, failed to make much of an impression, peaking at #37 R&B and missing the pop chart altogether. Just in case anyone was unsure where the nine tracks originated from, a small legend in one corner asked the pertinent question 'How do you spell Stevie Wonder backwards?' As a musical experiment, however, it did at least enable Stevie to get out some of the music that was bubbling up inside him.

Barely weeks after the Eivets Rednow experiment had been put to bed Tamla readied a more mainstream single for release. *For Once In My Life* had been recorded by Stevie in the summer of 1967 but was not universally liked around the Hitsville lot, with writer Ron Miller said to be particularly unhappy with the change of tempo Stevie had inflicted on the song. Billie Jean Brown, the head of the Quality Control Department however was convinced the version had the ability to do well and finally convinced Berry to release it in October 1968. Billie Jean's persistence paid off, with the single becoming one of the best selling of Stevie's career, peaking at #2 on both the pop and R&B chart and #3 in the UK. It would also pick up a Grammy Award nomination for Best R&B Vocal Performance, the first of his career.

The success of For Once In My Life, belatedly and despite opposition within the company, elevated Stevie into the top rank at Motown, with each successive single being eagerly awaited. Motown still seemed unsure of where to position him with his albums, assembling each release with the same formula as before; a hit or two, a couple of Jobete covers and a couple of fillers. Yet, the inescapable conclusion was that with a certain degree of care and attention, Stevie could have been a serious competitor even at the tail end of the 1960s. **For Once In My Life** featured no fewer than eight of his compositions, including the track that would be chosen as his next single in I Don't Know Why. The album was a major seller on the R&B chart where it made #4, although its pop performance was rather more modest at #50.

I Don't Know Why was released in January 1969 as the top side and struggled for acceptance, barely making the Top 40 pop and Top 20 R&B. It was equally sluggish in the UK, although to would hit #14 on the Record Retailer chart. Then the single got flipped, with My Cherie Amour proving considerably more radio friendly, powering up to #4 on the R&B and pop charts on both sides of the Atlantic (the record's turnaround in the UK was aided by Stevie being in the country on tour).

Once again Tamla hurried out an accompanying album, **My Cherie Amour** also playing host to later hit Yester-Me, Yester-You, Yesterday (another song written by Ron Miller and Bryan Wells that had been recorded by several other artists around the Hitsville lot), with the album inching further up the chart and becoming a #3 R&B and #34 pop hit. It also became his first album to break into the Top 20 in the UK, hitting #17.

Gradually, Stevie was coming to rely less and less on Ron Miller (although there would still be further releases penned by Miller) and more on his own songwriting team. That too had undergone something a change, with Hank Cosby and Sylvia Moy eventually being superseded by new recruits, initially producer Don Hunter and then Lee Garrett. Like Stevie, Lee had been born blind and was treated with some suspicion when he first met up with Stevie, at least by Lula Mae Hardaway.

"At this time I was a disc jockey for a Detroit radio station and before I found a flat, Stevie had invited me to live with him and his family. The first few weeks were a bit weird, because Lula knew me as a friend of Stevie's but at the same time she was very suspicious of me. She thought that I was a singer who hadn't made it; that I had now taken a job in Detroit to be close to Stevie and try to take advantage of him. There were so many people who tried to get things out of Stevie. Especially when we started writing together Lula freaked a little. Up to then he had mostly stuck with Hank and Sylvia. Now he and I would sit there and make music. Only when Lula joined us, she realised that I had no intentions of clinging on to Stevie's fame and then Lula accepted me."

There was soon another writer joining the trio, a would be singer who had released one single on the Gordy label (as Rita Wright) and had at one point been considered a possible candidate for The Supremes. She would, of course, become better known under her birth name, Syreeta.

"I met her when Don Hunter and I were working together. After hearing her voice, I thought she could do a particular song. She was working in the arranging department of Motown. Brian Holland had discovered her also. We became very good friends – in love at first sight. She was older than I, but I was determined to get her."

Whilst it was obvious (at least to Lee Garrett) that Stevie had an ulterior motive in inviting Syreeta into their songwriting partnership, the new team quickly hit gold, penning Signed, Sealed Delivered (I'm Yours) that would become a major hit for Stevie (and collect a Grammy Award nomination for Best R&B Song, as well as a separate nomination for Stevie in the Best R&B Male Vocal Performance category; it won neither) and It's A Shame, which Stevie produced on The Spinners. Whilst Stevie had been taking more control on his own productions, The Spinners was the first outside production, although there are apparently many more still sitting in the vaults at Motown, including a number of tracks on Rare Earth artists (Magic for one), Martha Reeves and David Ruffin.

Busy as he was in the studio, Motown would push out a live album in March 1970 to keep his name in vogue, with **Stevie Wonder Live** hitting #81 pop and #16 R&B, although it made no impression whatsoever in the UK. Instead, Tamla Motown waited until October in order to release the more British influenced track selection to be found on **Live At The Talk Of The Town**, but the album also failed to make an impression, despite the fact it was following in the wake of two major hit singles in *Signed Sealed Delivered* and *Heaven Help Us All*. Struggling though he may have been to maintain his album success in the UK, there was still his homeland to keep the hits turning over, with **Signed Sealed Delivered** making the Top Thirty pop (at #27) and Top Ten R&B (at #7), even if it again missed the chart in Britain. Motown tried to extract extra sales from the album by releasing a cover version of The Beatles' *We Can Work It Out*, which would hit #13 pop and #3 R&B (and #27 in Britain for good measure), as well as earning Stevie another unsuccessful Grammy Award nomination, again for Best R&B Vocal Performance, Male.

The professional relationship between Stevie and Syreeta had quickly become a more personal one in May 1970 when they announced their engagement, tying the knot four months later, on 14 September 1970 at the Burnette Baptist Church in Detroit, although not without a mishap or two before the event, including *Stevie* being late when he suffered a serious nosebleed that took nearly an hour to get under control! After the three hundred guests had been treated to a sumptuous reception at the Mauna Loa Hawaiian restaurant, the newlyweds headed off to Bermuda for their honeymoon.

When they returned it was to a new home in Inkster, where Stevie had a rudimentary recording studio installed, all the better to get down on to tape the torrent of musical ideas that were swirling around. Those ideas manifested themselves into an album Stevie planned on calling **Steve Wonder The Man**, although that title was quickly discarded in favour of **Where I'm Coming From**, which was scheduled for release in April 1971.

Berry Gordy already had one artist bucking the traditional Motown system, Marvin Gaye having blown almost everyone away with his epic **What's Going On**. As successful as that album was (and it was, becoming Motown's best seller up to that time), he did not necessarily need another musical maverick, but equally, if he refused Stevie his artistic freedom, the chances are Stevie would look elsewhere when his contract came up for renewal in May 1971.

When Berry listened to **Where I'm Coming From** for the first time, he could have been forgiven for thinking that he had been right all along; it was a good album, but not an exceptional album. There were good tunes and good songs but no obvious single (at least to Berry's ears), and whilst Marvin Gaye's opus had a message from start to finish, **Where I'm Coming From** was ambitious but lacked coherency. Promotional copies of the album were sent out to radio stations and selected press with postcards, designed to give the recipients an insight into the thought process that had gone into making the album. That was the sum total of Motown's promotional activity behind an album that meant a lot to Stevie Wonder.

"If it had been pushed there wouldn't have been all the fuss about **Music Of My Mind** later. Because people would have been prepared for it. Motown felt uneasy to touch social and political themes. People are not interested in 'Baby, Baby' songs any more. There is more to life than that, I also think that singles are very important but I don't want to rely on singles only. There are some rock artists who don't want to do singles at all. I don't mind – as long as they come off an album but for me they are generally only one page in the book."

The book **Music Of My Mind** would halt at #62 pop and #7 R&B and failed to chart at all in the UK. The page, however, turned out to be *If You Really Love Me*, which rescued the project somewhat by becoming at Top Ten hit on both the pop and R&B listings, at #8 and #4 respectively, as well as making the Top Twenty in Britain. Motown's failure to use that success as a tool to aid the album infuriated Stevie, which would not bode well for the forthcoming contract negotiations.

If Berry thought he could easily persuade Stevie into signing a new, extended contract when he reached the age of twenty one, he was to be very much surprised. A grand birthday celebration was held at Berry's mansion in the Boston-Edison neighbourhood, at which Berry told the assembled throng how much he had enjoyed working with Stevie in the past and how much he was looking forward to working with him in the future. That Stevie had prospered under the tutelage of Motown and that the best was yet to come.

In the run up to the party, Stevie had been taking legal advice on his options as and when his contract expired. Considered opinion, based on the figures Motown had quoted during the course of his career, was that his records had sold some 35 million copies worldwide. According to the lawyers and accountants Stevie had retained, his royalty income should have amounted to approximately $3.5 million (based on a basic ten cents per record), less whatever expenses Motown deemed deductable. It was Stevie's camp who fired the first bullet, with the lawyer sending a letter to Berry informing him that as Stevie was no longer a minor, he was disaffirming every contract he held with the company, as a performer, writer and producer. Berry did not react well to the contents of the letter, eventually reaching Stevie and laying into him about the way the matter was being handled, especially in light of the party the night before. Instead of referring Berry back to the lawyer (who was subsequently let go), Stevie apologised, explaining that it was not the way he wanted to conduct contract negotiations. Eventually, without a lawyer, Stevie explained the terms he was looking for in order to re-sign with Motown; an increase in record royalty to twenty percent, total artistic and creative freedom on all recordings, which meant only he could decide what was released, both singles and albums, and he wanted to create his own publishing company, separate from Jobete, meaning he would receive all publishing income. In the meantime, the only thing he would sign was a receipt for the money that Motown held for him, which was rather less than he anticipated; depending on sources it was $100,000 and according to others $1 million. Whatever the true figure, it was a paltry return on ten years of hits that had played their part in helping Motown grow.

Whilst Berry Gordy and his lieutenants prepared to move Motown out west, Stevie and Syreeta headed east, taking up residence at the Howard Johnson Motor Inn in New York. There Stevie could concentrate on making music, experimenting with both sounds and equipment, especially a new generation of keyboards, including the Moog and ARP synthesizers.

"Even though I had done more or less my own thing with **Where I'm Coming From** it didn't look like I was getting a chance like this again. Admittedly the album didn't do too well but I didn't feel like going through all this hassle with other producers again. Because I knew that I just wasn't produced right. It came to a thing where I was going 'dit-dit-dit-dun-da-dun' for three minutes until they shouted cut and 'That's enough, fade it out, fade it out, fade it out, fade it out' and I couldn't deal with that. I wanted to do an album with the money I had accumulated. But this time it wasn't so much a question of where I was coming from but rather where I was going to. I had to find out what my direction and my destiny was. And there was no way that I could just go on from where I had stopped with Motown. It was a completely different thing that was in my head."

Much of what was going on inside Stevie's head was influenced by other sounds he had heard, most notably Walter Carlos' 1968 album **Switched On Bach** and an album by the hitherto unknown Tonto's Expanding Head Band. An acronym for The Original New Timbral Orchestra, Tonto was in effect a duo formed by Malcolm Cecil and Robert Margouleff, two strangely matched electronic musicians. Their album **Zero Time** was critically acclaimed but an unspectacular seller, although of greater interest to Stevie Wonder was the possibilities the synthesizer offered. He eventually tracked down Malcolm Cecil and turned up at his apartment with a copy of the album tucked under his arm and asked to see Tonto. Taken into the studio and guided to the equipment, Stevie sat down at a piano and began playing, with Cecil switching on a tape recorder by instinct. By the time Robert Margouleff arrived a few hours later, several songs had already been recorded (Malcolm Cecil would later claim they record 35 songs in the first week!). The same process continued on virtually every day for the next couple of months, Stevie enjoying both the creativity and freedom Tonto gave him.

"By using the synthesizer you get rid of all the people standing between the artist and his music," said Malcolm. "Like without it Stevie had to have someone who arranged his songs for him. So Stevie told him what he wanted and the arranger put down what *he* thought that Stevie had played. When the music came back from the copyist the musicians who played it interpreted what *they* thought the arranger had written down. This way it was really hard for Stevie to get the sound that *he* had wanted originally."

Recording of the album that eventually became **Where I'm Coming From** took months, with sessions being conducted at Cecil and Margouleff's own Media Sound studio as well as Electric Lady in New York and Crystal Industries in Los Angeles. Officially, the album was produced by Stevie Wonder, with Malcolm and Robert credited as Associate Producers and Programmers, but unofficially the whole album was overseen by all three, working in unison. Stevie was responsible for writing virtually all of the songs, with a co-credit for Syreeta on one track and her sister Yvonne on two. He was also largely responsible for performing all of the music, aside from a trombone solo by Art Baron on one track and electric guitar by Buzz Feiten on another.

When the album was all but done, Stevie turned his attentions to getting a deal to release it. To avoid a repetition of the embarrassing telephone conversation with Berry Gordy, Stevie decided to hire another lawyer and, more importantly, leave him to deal with the negotiating with whichever record company Stevie wanted to conclude a deal. As it happened, he was already in touch with a likely candidate, one who was handling Malcolm Cecil and Robert Margouleff.

"I met an attorney who I thought was a jerk, but who I came to love as a human being during the time of freedom from my Motown contract. Johanan set up appointments for me with many people at the major record companies. We talked, the vibe was good, but I felt that I still wanted to be with Motown. Johanan would ask me if I was sure that I wanted to pursue other labels and I said I was sure, but deep inside I wanted to stay with Motown."

That lawyer was Johanan Vigoda, who had negotiated the first Beatles album deal in the US with Vee-Jay Records, had represented Atlantic Records, Jimi Hendrix and Ritchie Havens. Known as a tough negotiator, he proved more than a match for Berry Gordy, finally extracting an unprecedented deal with Motown that ran for a reported 120 pages. Most of the key elements went in Stevie's favour, including a massive hike in royalty terms, the establishment of his own publishing company Black Bull, although this was administered through Jobete, his own production company in Taurus Productions, an advance of $1 million against future earnings and almost total artistic control. That deal would eventually be signed *after* **Music Of My Mind** was released, meaning the album was released under a verbal agreement to a continuation of the old Motown deal!

The album Stevie had spent six months putting together did not overly impress Motown when they finally got their hands on it, with Ewart Abner, who had taken over the running of the record company following Berry Gordy's elevation to head of Motown Industries, somewhat dismissive of the album, stating it lacked an obvious single. Released in March 1972 without fanfare or much in the way of promotion, **Music Of My Mind** still managed to creep up to #21 pop and #6 R&B. In the end there would be two singles extracted too, with *Superwoman (Where Where You When I Needed You)* hitting #33 pop and #13 R&B, although the more uptempo *Keep On Running* ran out of steam at #90 pop and #36. Both the album and *Superwoman* were released in Britain but neither made any impression whatsoever, despite the recent success a compilation album **Greatest Hits Volume 2** had achieved in reaching the Top Thirty (it would hit #69 pop and #10 R&B in the US).

"I've been trying to see why it didn't do very good in the States," Stevie would later say. "I think maybe because **Music Of My Mind** didn't have a really fantastic single on it. It was more of an album than something you could take a single off. I didn't feel with **Music Of My Mind** that here was a good chance to give out with some craziness. I just felt that the doors were open to me to play."

By the time the album came out, Stevie's marriage to his own superwoman had all but ended, Syreeta relocating to Los Angeles whilst Stevie remained ensconced in New York, although the split was amicable, enough for the pair to maintain their professional relationship for many a year, both as a writing partnership and Stevie trying to aid Syreeta's own recording ambitions, eventually producing two albums on his former wife. The first album appeared soon after the divorce, with **Syreeta** being released in June 1972, another album that was a critical success but commercial disappointment; Stevie would blame Motown for their lack of promotion, whilst Motown would claim it was the lack of potential singles that hindered their efforts.

The issue over potential singles was one that had concerned Stevie. Aware that Motown had now used it to effectively curtail promotion on three albums, he would ensure they could have no such qualms about any of his future work. Malcolm Cecil would claim that Stevie's main problem was that he didn't so much make albums as create songs, with seldom any real coherency to whichever album they happened to appear on. When the three sat down to discuss the next project, there were some thirty songs that Stevie felt might work, with Stevie wanting to release them all as singles! Restricted as they were to some eighteen minutes a side on a vinyl album, a compromise of ten tracks was reached.

Even those ten tracks caused their own problems, with two of them resulting in a temporary falling out between Stevie and British guitarist Jeff Beck. Stevie had offered to write a song for Jeff (who was also working with Robert Margouleff and Malcolm Cecil, in the same studio at much the same time) and offered him *Maybe Your Baby*, only to change his mind and offer him another song as compensation. The song wasn't quite finished, but Stevie offered to work it up right away, only to change his mind about giving it away when he completed *Superstition* and realised what a strong number it was!

Stevie and Jeff would eventually repair their relationship, enough for them to work together in the future, but the two key tracks were kept by Stevie for his next album, which by now had a title attached to it in **Talking Book**. Before the album was released, Stevie and Johanan discussed how they might force Motown's hand when it came to promotion, with the idea of getting a major tour slot one possibility. Not a headlining tour, which Stevie could possibly have undertaken, but rather a supporting slot on another major tour. And the biggest of tours about to head off across North America was undoubtedly The Rolling Stones, which would kick off in Vancouver in June 1972.

Malcolm Cecil used his contacts to get a message through to the Stones' management that Stevie Wonder would be interested in supporting them on their forthcoming tour (something of a turnaround, since in 1965 The Rolling Stones had opened for Stevie Wonder!). Financially the tour made little sense, at least for Stevie, since he was paid no more than

$1,000 a date, and out of that he had to pay all his own expenses, including his full touring band.

"It was not even meant to be a money-making thing. What I needed was exposure. I wanted to reach people. I feel there is so much through music that can be said. And I felt that the Stones' audiences were the kind of people that we could get to so I thought we should do it. My biggest aim was to introduce the new Stevie Wonder."

The two month tour was a mixed success. For the Stones' it was a case of business as usual, with riots, forged tickets, a bomb going off under their equipment truck, stormed gates and bad publicity following the arrest of Mick Jagger and Keith Richard in Rhode Island after a fight with a photographer pretty much par for the course. Stevie had his own negative aspects to deal with, including the possibility of having to cancel one of his shows when his drummer quit midway through the tour, verbal battles from time to time with Keith Richard and, perhaps most importantly, stories being bandied around that Stevie was performing so well (certainly much better than a warm up act might be otherwise expected) he was showing up the headlining act! One or two promoters advised The Stones' to drop Stevie from the bill (Martha Reeves, who was on the early dates as a warm up act for Stevie, had quit midway through the tour), although by all accounts it was Mick Jagger who stood up for Stevie and insisted he be retained, even joining him on stage most nights for an encore on *Uptight* and *Satisfaction*.

The real benefit for Stevie would come when he released his next new product, the single *Superstition* being issued in October 1972. Universally popular when it had been performed on the Rolling Stones tour, it shot up the chart and hit the top of the pop and R&B chart, his first double topper since *Fingertips* nine years previously. And this time Motown could have no complaints about potential singles, since *Superstition* was doing much of their promotional work for them. When **Talking Book** was released in the wake of *Superstition*, it too bounded every chart possible, hitting #3 pop and topping the R&B chart, retaining its popularity when *You Are The Sunshine Of My Life* was lifted as the second single, another pop chart topper (it would have to settle for only reaching #3 on the R&B listings). *Superstition* proved popular enough to garner two nominations for a Grammy Award (Best R&B Song and Best Male R&B Vocal Performance), both which were won, whilst *Sunshine* would get three nominations, for Record of the Year, Song of the Year and Best Male Pop Vocal Performance, winning the latter. Since the awards were not dished out until 1974, Stevie was also nominated in another category, Album of the Year, for his *next* album, giving him an almost unprecedented clean sweep of nominations in all the major categories. And it would only get better.

That album was **Innervisions**, which Stevie, Robert and Malcolm began work on, even as Motown's presses were knocking out thousands of copies of **Talking Book**. In truth, many of the songs were already complete, with Stevie having stockpiled so many songs during the two years or so that he had been working with Tonto. Then an incident, event or headline would inspire another new song and it would be filed away for future use.

"It always seemed that the things I wanted to do musically were somewhat ahead of the things that were being released at the time. And I think that's good because you are always looking forward to doing something and progressing. I think that after you sing a song or whatever, after you've done it, it's done; the most important thing is to look forward to doing something that is another time, another place."

Stevie had two songs in particular that were of another time and place, *Living For The City* and *Higher Ground*, which would become the focal points of the next album **Innervisions**. *Living For The City* was a near on seven and a half minute musical extravaganza, telling the story of a boy moving from Mississippi to New York and getting framed for drug running. Partly inspired by the death of ten year old child Cloephus Glover by the police in New York, *Living For City* featured cameo roles for a number of local policemen, Johanan Vigoda and Stevie's brother Calvin. *Higher Ground* came out of nowhere.

"I wrote it on 11 May 1973. The song just came to me, the words, the music, it all happened within a few hours and I recorded it at once. I didn't know what it was all about, but it was almost as if I had to get it done. As if something was going to happen, some change would come up."

Stevie had often said that he had premonitions about death, most notably Benny Benjamin, and now he was talking about visions of his own demise. *Higher Ground* was released as a single on 31 July 1973, followed a few days later by the **Innervisions** album. Radio reception to both was immediate, increasing the demand on Stevie to make himself available for promotional work. On 6 August, he was on his way to perform at a benefit concert on Durham, South Carolina. He was sat asleep in the passenger seat of a car being driven by John Harris along Highway 85, midway between Greenville and Raleigh, following a truck loaded with logs. Accounts as to what happened next vary; either Harris attempted to overtake the truck or the truck suddenly braked, but either way the two vehicles collided, resulting in one of the logs crashing through the windscreen of the car and smashing Stevie in the forehead.

He was rushed to the Rowan Memorial Hospital in Salisbury, North Carolina, in a coma, being transferred to the North Carolina Baptist Hospital in Winston-Salem later the same day. As rumours and counter-rumours swirled, the hospital issued a press release.

'Stevie Wonder was listed in a satisfactory condition at North Carolina Baptist Hospital. He was hospitalised in the intensive care unit of Baptist Hospital soon after arriving at the hospital at 8.55 pm on 6 August. He remains in the intensive care unit today. He is being attended by a team of physicians as having a brain contusion, which is a bruise on the brain. He is making satisfactory progress and is slowly regaining consciousness, the doctor added.'

'Stevie Wonder was transferred here from Rowan Memorial Hospital in Salisbury, North Carolina, where he was first taken after being in an auto accident near Salisbury. The transfer was desirable because of the presence of a Department of Neurosurgery at Baptist Hospital. No surgery, however, is indicated or contemplated.'

Which meant that all anyone could do was wait and see. Whilst he remained in a coma, only close friends and relatives were permitted to visit him, with close aide Ira Tucker reportedly whispering the lyrics to *Higher Ground* into his ear. He eventually came out of the coma after a few days and, a couple of days later, Ira brought a Clavinet into the hospital room. At first the instrument just sat on the bed, Stevie hardly able to bring himself to pick it up.

"I was frightened that I might not be able to play again. To create again. But then I just tried playing a few tunes on the clavinet - and I knew that it would be all right again."

After two weeks he was well enough to be transferred to Los Angeles, being taken to the UCLA Medical Center where his treatment continued. Whilst he had seemingly not lost his musical abilities, his sense of taste and smell were affected, although how badly and for how long no one was quite sure. The only real outward sign of the mishap was a big lump on his forehead, the scar of which remains to this day.

His general well being would no doubt have been bolstered by the news that *Higher Ground* had gone on to top the R&B chart and reach #4 pop (as well as #29 in the UK), whilst in less than four weeks **Innervisions** had shifted more than a million copies on its way to similar chart placings of #4 pop and #1 R&B (and became his first Top Ten album in Britain, peaking at #8). The album would go on to collect two Grammy Awards, for Album of the Year alongside a Best Engineered Recording, Non-Classical for Robert Margouleff and Malcolm Cecil.

As a result of the accident, his tour schedule was effectively torn up, although if the plan had been for Stevie to fully rest and recuperate during his enforced layoff then he could find plenty of other things to keep himself occupied. Disappointed with the reception his former wife Syreeta's debut album had received he opted to record a second album, this time making it quite plain who was responsible for the endorsement, calling the album **Stevie Wonder Presents Syreeta**. Motown still put next to no promotion behind the album, resulting in it quickly disappearing without trace in the US, although it found some favour across the Atlantic thanks to the extracted singles *Spinnin' And Spinnin'* and *Your Kiss Is Sweet*. Stevie also worked with another female singer, co-producing Minnie Riperton's smash hit **Perfect Angel** with her husband Richard Rudolph, although under a pseudonym. The album would give rise to an international hit in *Lovin' You*, which topped the US chart and reached #2 in the UK.

Work meanwhile continued on Stevie's own album, **Fulfillingness First Finale**, an album that would mark the end of the association between Stevie, Robert Margouleff and Malcolm Cecil. It was therefore almost pre-ordained that the songs that eventually made it onto the album should span almost the entire creative relationship between the three, with *They Won't Go When I Go* having been one of the first songs they had worked on back in 1971. In all the three had created some 250 songs that were said to be completed (and they would continue to turn up on Stevie's albums over the next few years, even after Cecil and Margouleff had ended their working relationship). At much the same time he severed his links with them and their studio at Media Sound, Stevie set up his own recording studio in Los Angeles, predictably called Wonderland.

Fulfillingness was released in July 1974 and was eagerly anticipated, so much so that advance orders ensured it shipped gold. It came out at a time when it was almost impossible to avoid Stevie Wonder; in addition to his own album, there was the continued success of Minnie Riperton's album as well as Rufus, whose interpretation of Stevie's song *Tell Me Something Good* was also riding high. Both singles released from **Fulfillingness** scored well, *You Haven't Done Nothin'*, a direct attack on the soon to be outgoing president Richard Nixon, topped the pop and R&B chart, whilst the follow up *Boogie On Reggae Woman* peaked at #3 pop but topped the R&B chart, enabling the parent album to top both the R&B and pop chart. For the second year in succession Stevie would go on to be the big winner at the annual Grammy Awards ceremony, collecting Best Male R&B Vocal Performance for *Boogie On Reggae Woman*, Best R&B Song for his earlier *Living For The City* and another Album of the Year (only the second time the Album of the Year Grammy Award had been won in consecutive years, after Frank Sinatra) as well as Best Male Pop Vocal Performance for **Fulfillingness**. For good measure, *Tell Me Something Good* would also nab the award for Best R&B Vocal Performance by a Group.

Stevie's contract with Motown was due to expire in May 1976, but both parties thought it advantageous to begin negotiations on an extension as soon as possible, with Johanan Vigoda sitting down with Motown in early 1975, whilst the success of **Fulfillingness** was still fresh in everyone's memory. Over the years Motown had lost several major acts, including The Isley Brothers, The Four Tops, The Jackson Five and Gladys Knight & The Pips, whilst their two flagships, The Supremes and The Temptations had already reached their peak. Motown's bargaining position was therefore weakened; they needed Stevie Wonder infinitely more than he needed them, even if his continued loyalty was taken almost for granted.

In the midst of the negotiations, Motown was alarmed to see Stevie announce that he was considering quitting the music business altogether. He intended undertaking a Farewell World Tour and then move to Africa, where he would devote his time and energy working with handicapped, blind and under privileged children.

"People ask me why I am going to Africa when there's so much to be done here. Well, America doesn't make a lot of people aware of what's happening in other parts of the world. I hope to bring back an alternative way from Africa. Also I want to do something for blind people over there. Like 40 per cent of the blindness in Ethiopia, for example, is caused by a fly that carries a fungus to the cornea. We have to do something about this disease which is called 'sleeping sickness' and causes blindness, I want to try and set up a foundation to combat this illness."

Motown made frantic noises about how he would be better able to help the world's poor by remaining in America and bringing attention to their plight through the power of song, but one cannot help but wonder how serious he was about such plans, especially as he was about to become a father for the first time. He had met his latest girlfriend, Yolanda Simmons via a telephone conversation.

"She was applying for a job as a secretary at my publishing company Black Bull in New York. Fortunately I was around when she rang up and so I talked to her. I liked the way the lady's voice sounded, so I asked her to come into the office. I was right about my first impression; Yolanda is one of the warmest people I've ever met. We soon became friends and eventually lovers."

Despite the failure of his first marriage to Syreeta, Stevie was not averse to marrying again. He and Yolanda did get engaged and discussed wedding plans, only to shelve them later on.

"When your hearts are joined together it's love with or without a ring. I just think that marriage turns love into a commitment which can make you feel trapped. Marriage can bring about chains and fences that make you feel like you want to get out. It can turn into a very heavy possessive thing. But love is supposed to be freedom. Freedom to be with each other, happy and loving one another and communicating with ideas. I think only as long as you are not married you can be sure that you are with your love because of your own free will – because you want to. And that for me is that love is all about."

In March 1975 Yolanda gave birth to their first child, a daughter that they named Aisha, the name reportedly being African for strength and intelligence. Eventually, Stevie would renounce plans to quit music, although his subsequent announcements that his next album project would probably not be ready until 1976 hardly pleased Motown, not least because they needed the income a Stevie Wonder album would inevitably bring. There was one major beneficiary to the delayed album, however, for when Paul Simon went on to win the Grammy Award for Album of the Year with **Still Crazy After All These Years** at the ceremony in February 1976, he made a point of thanking Stevie Wonder for *not* releasing an album that year!

The delay further benefitted Stevie, for it gave Johanan Vigoda all the aces in his negotiations with Motown. The deal, when it was finally agreed, was unprecedented in the music business.

"I have a policy with my attorney – you do the best you can with the business and handling of the money, and I do the best I can do to give the best product, so whatever you ask for will not be unreasonable. The result was a seven year, thirteen million dollar contract with Motown. I didn't feel that I was being greedy. It really isn't important to me as much as it is for my children, family and loved ones. I want them to be taken care of and to be well off."

The guaranteed advance was some $5 million *more* than the previous mega buck deals that had been granted to the likes of Elton John and Paul McCartney. More important than the money, however, were the other terms and conditions that Stevie made a prerequisite before signing, including full control over what was released in his name (Motown had retained the right to chose single releases in the earlier contract), the right to openly produce other projects, including those outside Motown under his own name. That deal put a temporary hold on a planned anthology Motown wanted to release (the issue would arise again in 1977 when Stevie learned Motown were planning on issuing **Looking Back**, a three disc set that featured all Stevie's recordings prior to 1971, which Motown believed they owned outright; Stevie was able to get that similarly shelved), but with the prospect of what was becoming not so much an album release as an industry event on the horizon, it was a concession Motown was prepared to grant.

The only problem was that horizon didn't seem to be getting any nearer. Planned release dates came and went with no one, especially Motown, any the wiser as to when the album might be ready. All that was known was that it was going to be a double album, **Songs In The Key Of Life** having supplanted 'Let's See Life The Way It Is' as its title. After another enforced delay as Stevie wished to remix several of the cuts, the album was finally ready for release on 28 September 1976. Demand was exceptionally high, with the album debuting on the Billboard pop chart at number one (for only the third time in American chart history, and Stevie became the first American artist to achieve the feat, whilst **Songs In The Key Of Life** was the first double album to do so). The album was equally well received globally, topping the Canadian chart, hitting #2 in the UK and the Top Ten across virtually the whole of Europe. Domestic sales would eventually earn Stevie a Diamond Award from the R.I.A.A. (Recording Industry Association of America), whilst there were assorted platinum, gold and silver hauls from virtually every other nation.

The album was helped by two particularly strong singles in *Sir Duke* and *I Wish* as well as the presence of a track that wasn't released as a single, *Isn't She Lovely*. A tribute to his daughter Aisha, Stevie opted against editing it down for single release, although that didn't stop every radio station the world over from picking that track out as worthy of extra attention. Eventually a cover was issued in the UK, David Parton hitting #4 with his version, which begged the question of how well the original might have done had it been released.

Irrespective of where *Isn't She Lovely* might have finished, the inescapable fact was that **Songs In The Key Of Live** was another unqualified success. This was confirmed the following February, when Stevie won a further four Grammy Awards, for Producer of the Year, Album of the Year and Best Male Pop Vocal Performance, all relating to the album, and Best Male R&B Vocal Performance for *I Wish* as well as being nominated in a further three categories. Stevie was not present at the actual awards ceremony, having finally made good on his earlier promise to visit Africa, spending two weeks exploring his musical heritage.

Professional accolades were followed by the arrival of another child, Yolanda giving birth in April 1977 to a son Keita Sawandi, meaning worshipper and founder. Becoming a father for the second time occupied Stevie for much of the next twelve months, although marriage was still out of the question, with Stevie more than happy to keep his relationship with Yolanda on whatever basis had existed for the previous couple of years.

When finally coaxed back into the studio to begin work on a new album, it was for a project completely divorced from his usual fare. Several film producers and directors had approached Stevie over the years with a view to scoring a film, but none of the vehicles Stevie had been offered had much appeal. Then in 1974 producer Michael Braun came with 'The Secret Life Of Plants' a film based on an earlier book by journalists Peter Tompkins and Christopher Bird. Braun had got Paramount Pictures to commit to a visual documentary based on the book and approached Stevie about composing the score. It was different enough to interest Stevie; scoring any film would have been a challenge for a blind composer, but one which relied on time-lapse photography made it a herculean effort. Yet is was the difficulty of the task in particular that appealed to Stevie, and so he set about the task with his usual vigour, surrounding himself in many musical influences, including African, Indian and Japanese, all of which would find their way on to the eventual album.

Motown had several reservations about the project Stevie had gotten himself tied into. For a start there was the subject matter; whilst they had themselves had only limited success in the film soundtrack market, most of those had been with obvious story and plot lines. An album about plants was something outside their comfort zone and, they suspected well outside Stevie's too. Then there was the fact that Stevie was stretching the music out across two albums (part of this may well have been down to wanting to meet certain contractual obligations, making up for not releasing an album in 1977 or 1978 by effectively releasing two in 1979); the album might have made a good single album, but there were doubts even the best of intentions could stretch the interest across two. There again, there were practical reasons for Stevie wanting to keep the album as long as it was; this wasn't going to be a highlights album but the full film score.

Except there never was a film, at least one that was released at cinemas for a paying audience, as somewhere along the way Paramount got cold feet and never put the film on general release. The problem for Stevie was that the album **Secret Life Of Plants** would now have to be judged not as a soundtrack album but as a new Stevie Wonder album, based on a concept few had seen and even fewer understood. Advance sales alone ensured it charted high following its release in October 1979, but a lot of the stock would find its way back to Motown, giving Stevie his first professional setback of the decade.

"I have to think why it was not successful. Were people unable to get into **Secret Life Of Plants**? The true meaning of an artist is to be expressive and innovative. A lot of things have been afforded me by the people, so I have to share with them the experiences I had had and am having."

If previously he had believed that Motown's lack of promotion behind a project had invariably been its death knell, then Stevie obviously came to a different realisation following the release of **Secret Life Of Plants**. The failure of the album was as much Paramount's fault as it was Motown's, and now the need to get his career back on track was paramount.

That much of the industry thought of **Plants** as no more than a temporary blip was obvious, for Stevie was still very much in demand to provide material and production to several outside projects, gifting Jermaine Jackson *Let's Get Serious*, penning two tracks in *You Are My Heaven* and *Don't Make Me Wait Too Long* for Robert Flack's album with the late Donny Hathaway (who bore more than a passing vocal resemblance to Stevie Wonder) and another for Quincy Jones' **The Dude**, *Betcha Wouldn't Hurt Me*. As good as all of those tracks undoubtedly were (*Let's Get Serious* topped the R&B chart and hit the Top Ten on both sides of the Atlantic, whilst *You Are My Heaven* made the R&B Top Ten), it was his own material that would rescue his reputation.

Thus less than a year after the fiasco that was **Secret Life Of Plants**, Stevie was ready to roll with his next album, **Hotter Than July**. Gone was the idea of a concept, gone too, for the most part, were the social commentary epics. In their place was a collection of more traditional and certainly more accessible songs, resulting in much more favourable reviews. More importantly, there were healthy sales figures for both the album, which would earn platinum status in both the US and UK, and the extracted singles, with all four attaining Top Ten status in the UK. That figure included *Happy Birthday*, a homage to Dr Martin Luther King and a call to make his birthday a public holiday in the United States. It was a call Stevie would pick up and run with for a considerable time, working with King's widow Coretta Scott King and getting congressman John Conyers to sponsor a bill in support of such a holiday. In January 1982 Stevie joined a crowd of some 50,000 souls, including Gladys Knight, Gil Scott-Heron, Diana Ross and Jesse Jackson who gathered in Washington to peacefully protest their support.

"I know you've been standing in the cold for a long time," Stevie addressed the crowd, "but I hope your spirits are warm. Dr King left an unfinished symphony which we must finish."

Stevie would get his wish, with President Ronald Reagan signing into law the creation of Martin Luther King Day in November 1983. Side-tracked as he had been by political considerations, new recordings by Stevie Wonder during 1982 were restricted to guest appearances on other artists albums. Having performed at the 1982 Reggae Sunsplash Festival in Montego Bay with Third World, he renewed his acquaintance by writing and producing two songs on their album **You've Got The Power**, *Try Jah Love* and *You're Playing Us Too Close*. Both tracks were released as singles, albeit with a modicum of success, unlike his other major collaboration, a duet on the Paul McCartney composition *Ebony And Ivory*. Equal part poignant and trite, *Ebony And Ivory* was a massive success, topping the charts on both sides of the Atlantic (for seven weeks in the US and three in the UK), enabling Stevie to take pole position in the UK for the first time in his career.

The fact that *Ebony And Ivory* could only be found on Paul McCartney's album did not harm Stevie, who finally got some new product out to the market in May 1982. Having convinced Motown to pull **Looking Back** some years previously, Stevie finally agreed to a compilation album in **Original Musiquarium,** which mixed twelve old tracks with four new ones. The album was another major success, aided by three of the newer tracks being released as singles, of which two, *That Girl* and *Do I Do* went on to pick up a nomination for Best R&B Song. Stevie lost out, for once, also going empty handed when *Do I Do* was overlooked for Best Male R&B Vocal Performance.

Those four tracks would have to do for the next couple of years, although Stevie still managed to pop up here and there, appearing on Elton John's *I Guess That's Why They Call It The Blues*, The Gap Band's *Someday*, Chaka Khan's *I Feel For You* and later The Eurythmics' *There Must Be Angel (Playing With My Heart)* playing the harmonica, on 'Saturday Night Live' playing the fool as well as showcasing a new song in *Overjoyed* and producing a couple of tracks on Eddie Murphy's debut album as a singer. He also bought his own radio station, KJLH in Los Angeles, set up his own label in Wondirection (with Stevie being heavily involved in the only release, Gary Byrd's *The Crown*) and appeared on Motown's 25th anniversary television special.

When he did venture back into the studio to work on his own material, he soon got distracted from a solo album into a project that contained the word Motown most dreaded hearing; soundtrack.

Although 'Woman In Red' was a more conventional film than his previous involvement with 'Secret Life Of Plants', the early track listing sounded to Motown as though it was be another sales disaster, even with the involvement of Dionne Warwick. That was until Stevie played them another track he intended adding to the album, *I Just Called To Say I Love You*. Apparently conceived some seven years previously but only completed for inclusion in 'Woman In Red', it sounded a sure fire smash, even if it was as far away from his *Superstition* and *Higher Ground* material as it was possible to be. For once, Motown's reluctance proved unfounded; the film might have been a flop, but *I Just Called To Say I Love You* topped the charts and sold a million copies on both sides of the Atlantic (it was his first and so far only solo chart topper in the UK), with the resulting album **Woman In Red** also performing well and going Top Ten in both markets. Add to this an Academy Award (Motown's first) and Golden Globe and nominations for Record of the Year (for the single) and Best Male R&B Vocal Performance (for the album) and the film's failure counted for little.

Eager to capitalise on the success of the single and album, Stevie wasted little time in getting **In Square Circle** ready for release, pushing out *Part Time Lover* as the advance guard in August 1985. A number one hit on both the pop (his last chart topper as a soloist on that particular chart) and R&B chart, the single repeated its success internationally, hitting #3 in the UK and making at least the Top Ten across the rest of Europe. With that fillip, the album couldn't help but be a success, with **In Square Circle** making #5 pop in both the US and UK as well as topping the R&B chart. The album would collect a Grammy Award for Best Male R&B Vocal Performance whilst *Part Time Lover* was nominated in the corresponding pop category.

Stevie's profile also benefitted by his involvement in the USA For Africa single *We Are The World* (written by Michael Jackson and Lionel Richie), with Stevie joining a host of contemporary stars for the recording overseen by Quincy Jones. Similarly, Stevie lent his talents to another charity ensemble, this time assembled by Dionne Warwick for AIDS research, alongside Elton John and Gladys Knight, with the single *That's What Friends Are For* topping the US chart and collecting a Grammy for Best Pop Performance by a Group.

A slight switch in musical styles greeted his next album **Characters** in 1987, with much of the material being aimed at the R&B market. They lapped it up, with the album debuting in pole position, but such acceptance came at the expense of his pop support, with the album only making #17, his lowest charting album since **Music Of My Mind** some fifteen years previously. The album suffered an even worse fate in the UK, barely scraping into the Top Forty at #33. Even three Grammy nominations, for Best R&B Song and Best Male R&B Vocal Performance for the extracted single *Skeletons* and a similar R&B Vocal Performance for the album itself failed to lift it out of the doldrums. Despite Stevie's best efforts, Motown had haemorrhaged money throughout the 1980s. Berry Gordy had considered selling off Jobete in 1986 but realised he needed Stevie's agreement to such a sale, flying into France where Stevie was on tour to discuss the matter in person. It proved a worthless trip, with Stevie unwilling to agree to his songs (albeit a half share) being sold on. Berry tried selling Jobete without Stevie's songs as part of the package, but the potential buyer cut their offer in half, resulting in Berry backing out of the deal. Motown struggled on for a further two years or so, by which time Berry was faced with the alternative of selling the record company or watching it slide into bankruptcy. This time he did the deal, selling the record company (but retaining the publishing) to MCA for $67 million.

Stevie has retained his connection to Motown ever since (or least whatever is left of Motown), releasing albums even more sporadically since 1988 than he did prior; the wait between **Conversation Peace** and **A Time 2 Love** was ten years, from 1995 to 2005. There was another soundtrack in **Jungle Fever**, but again the music was infinitely more memorable than the film, even with Spike Lee attached as a director. There was also a third live album, **Natural Wonder** being recorded in Japan but failing to shift beyond #88 on the R&B chart.

If Stevie Wonder has become largely a forgotten figure at home, at least as far as the charts are concerned, then the same cannot be said for his international fortunes, especially in the UK. **Song Review** may have only crept into the Top Twenty at #19 in the UK but it quickly earned Stevie a platinum disc award. **The Definitive Collection** fared even better; #11 pop and a triple platinum award. Even **Number 1's** went gold when it hit #23 in 2007.

In America, Stevie's appearances have been equally sporadic, although he has still been a regular at the Grammy Awards, collaborating with a host of artists across numerous genres and taking his tally to twenty two statuettes, more than any other male solo artist. The death of his mother Lula Mae Hardaway on 31 May 2006 affected him considerably, with Stevie becoming something of a recluse for the next twelve months, eventually turning the sadness of the event into something of a celebration as he undertook his first US tour in ten years, later taking the show around the world. In 2009 the sudden death of Michael Jackson saw Stevie perform at his memorial service, another sad event.

His private life has been equally turbulent, with a further five children by two women in sons Kailand, Kwame, Mandla Kadjay and Mumtaz and a daughter in Sophia. He was married again in 2001 to Kai Millard, although the pair separated in 2009 and subsequently divorced in 2012. His first wife Syreeta died on 6 July 2004, with Stevie at her side.

Irrespective of his personal troubles, he is still highly regarded around the globe, collecting an assortment of honours and accolades during the course of his career. He has also been feted by kings, queens and presidents throughout his career, performing both in public and private for all of them.

Depending on which side of the Atlantic you reside, it is a matter of debate as to which was the most prestigious event – performing at President Barack Obama's Inauguration Ball in 2009 or for Queen Elizabeth II's Diamond Jubilee in 2012. At the former, he was joined by Usher and Shakira for a rendition of *Higher Ground*, whilst at the latter he performed a ten minute set, including both *Isn't She Lovely* and *Happy Birthday* with the lyrics changed in honour of Queen Elizabeth. It was a fitting tribute to the Queen of the United Kingdom from the undisputed King of Motown. Long may he reign.

ALBUMS: THE JAZZ SOUL OF LITTLE STEVIE WONDER (1962), TRIBUTE TO UNCLE RAY (1962), RECORDED LIVE! - THE 12 YEAR OLD GENIUS (1963), WITH A SONG IN MY HEART (1963), STEVIE AT THE BEACH (1964), HEY HARMONICA MAN (1965), UPTIGHT (1966), DOWN TO EARTH (1966), I WAS MADE TO LOVE HER (1967), SOMEDAY AT CHRISTMAS (1967), FOR ONCE IN MY LIFE (1968), MY CHERIE AMOUR (1969), STEVIE WONDER LIVE! (1970), LIVE! AT THE TALK OF THE TOWN (1970), SIGNED, SEALED & DELIVERED (1970), WHERE I'M COMING FROM (1971), MUSIC OF MY MIND (1972), TALKING BOOK (1972), INNERVISIONS (1973), FULLFILLINGNESS' FIRST FINALE (1974), SONGS IN THE KEY OF LIFE (1976), STEVIE WONDER'S JOURNEY THROUGH THE SECRET LIFE OF PLANTS (1979), HOTTER THAN JULY (1980), STEVIE WONDER'S ORIGINAL MUSIQUARIUM (1982), THE WOMAN IN RED SOUNDTRACK (1984), IN SQUARE CIRCLE (1985), CHARACTERS (1986)

COMPILATIONS: GREATEST HITS (1968), GREATEST HITS VOLUME 2 (1971), ANTHOLOGY/LOOKING BACK (1977), LOVE SONGS: 20 CLASSIC HITS (1985)

FURTHER READING: STEVIE WONDER (1977), RHYTHMS OF WONDER (2003), SIGNED, SEALED, AND DELIVERED (2010)

MICKEY WOODS

Mickey Woods was an unknown white singer when he arrived at Motown in 1961 and after recording two singles that disappeared without trace, he left the company the same unknown white singer. His two singles featured a good pedigree with regards to the writers and producers, with Berry Gordy penning *Poor Sam Jones*, his first single, and co-penning *Please Mr Kennedy*, his second, with Loucye Gordy Wakefield. This latter single also saw a first writing credit for Norman Whitfield on the B-side *They Call Me Cupid*, but no matter which side of which single was played, none garnered any activity.

WORKSHOP JAZZ RECORDS

Berry Gordy had got his start in the music business running a record store that concentrated on jazz, so it was only to be expected that among the labels he formed during Motown's early days would be one similarly devoted. Workshop Jazz was also a way for him to keep the numerous musicians at Motown happy; he would utilise them on hundreds and hundreds of sessions churning out pop and R&B hits but cater for their artistic whims by allowing them to record and release the occasional jazz album.

Among the artists therefore who appeared on Workshop Jazz were Earl Washington All Stars, Paula Greer, Johnny Griffith Trio, Dave Hamilton, George Bohanon and Lefty Edwards. It was also planned at one point to release a Four Tops album on the label, but they were later switched to the more mainstream Motown label. Workshop Jazz was up and walking for some two years, releasing eleven albums and scheduling at least two more. Whilst Berry Gordy may have met his side of the bargain in putting the albums out to market, lack of promotion meant hardly anyone was aware they were available.

THE WRIGHT SPECIALS

One of the small handful of gospel acts who got to record for Motown, The Wright Specials at one time could count Kim Weston as one of their flock, but she does not appear on any of their recordings. Assembled by manager Thomas Wright, the group featured Ernest Fowler on piano, with his brother George working for Motown at the time and was tipped to head up the new gospel imprint Divinity, hence their subsequent signing by Motown in September 1961. The Wright Specials would release two singles on the label, *That's What He Is To Me* appearing in July 1962 and *Ninety-Nine And A Half Won't Do* in June 1963.

RICHARD WYLIE & HIS BAND

Motown's first A&R manager and the musical director of the first live orchestra, Richard 'Popcorn' Wylie had two spells at Motown, even though both appeared to end in some acrimony, resulting in him being another person omitted from Berry Gordy's later autobiography.

Born in Detroit, Michigan on 6 June 1939 into a musical family, Richard learned to play the piano at an early age and was already proficient by the time he entered Northwestern High School. There he acquired both his nickname (he was dubbed Popcorn because of his habit of quickly popping out of the team huddle during football matches) and a band, recruiting James Jamerson on bass and Clifford Mack on drums, both of whom would ultimately follow him into Histville.

Richard recorded his first single for another local Detroit label, Northern, with *Pretty Girl* being issued in 1960. He and his band then got a residency at the local 20 Grand club, where he was spotted by Motown songwriter and engineer Robert Bateman, who recommended Popcorn and his band to Berry Gordy. Whilst Richard, James and Clifford became part of the embryonic Funk Brothers, there were still opportunities for releases under his own name, with *Custer's Last Man* being released in June 1960 and *Real Good Lovin'* in October 1961.

Sandwiched in between these two releases, which were issued under the moniker Popcorn & The Mohawks, was a cover version of *Money (That's What I Want)*, released in April 1961 as Richard Wylie & His Band. Whilst none of these charted, Richard appeared on many of the label's early hits, including The Miracles' *Shop Around* and The Marvelettes' *Please Mr. Postman*, as well as serving as bandleader for the very first Motortown Revue that went out on the road in 1962.

Richard left Motown in 1962 following a falling out with Berry Gordy, subsequently signing with Epic Records before settling on a freelance career as a songwriter, producer and session player. His most notable assignments were for Ed Wingate's Golden World group of labels, handling writing and production chores for the likes of Edwin Starr, The Reflections and J.J. Barnes and scoring a hit with Jamo Thomas' *I Spy (For The F.B.I.)*.

He also launched his own label, named Pameline after his three daughters, scoring a major Northern Soul hit with The Detroit Executives and *The Cool Off* (the label would also discover future Motown act Three Ounces Of Love). When Golden World was sold to Berry Gordy and Motown, Richard resurrected his own career, recording for Karen Records (which would yield another perennial Northern favourite in *Rosemary What Happened*) and then Carla for *Move Over Babe (Here Comes Henry)*.

He resurfaced at Motown in 1971 where he recorded *Funky Rubber Band* for the Soul label (it was not issued in the UK until 1975), resulting in the only hit of his career, peaking at #40 R&B and #109 pop. Despite this Richard moved on from Motown, subsequently recording **Extrasensory Perception** for ABC Records in 1974, his only album release.

Blissfully unaware of his continued popularity in Britain, Richard finally came over to the country in the mid-1980s to do some promotional work, subsequently recording with Ian Levine and the Motorcity label. Richard died on 7 September 2008 from heart problems.

BARBARA WYRICK

Born in Dyersburg, Tennessee, Barbara Wyrick began her professional career as a singer, recording at the age of twelve with the then unknown Muscle Shoals producer Rick Hall. Even at that early age, Barbara was interested in writing.

"I found I couldn't sing the songs I heard on the radio because I just didn't have the range, so I made up my own songs."

While her initial recordings did little, Barbara spent the next five years honing her talents until she felt confident enough to approach Rick again, who by this time had become a well known producer. As a result, Barbara secured a five year contract with Fame Publishing as an artist-writer.

"I came to Muscle Shoals every two or three months to demo my songs and find out what was wrong with them and how I could improve them. Then, Muscle Shoals was predominantly R&B and I'm not an R&B writer, but I stuck it out for the great learning experiences I had."

Her songs would be covered by Liza Minnelli, Donnie Osmond, The Supremes (*Give Out But Don't Give Up*) and Candi Staton, but Barbara was not given a chance to record herself. That changed when Clayton Ivy and Terry Woodford, who were freelancing for Motown, invited her to cut a couple of singles for Melodyland, Motown's country label, with *Baby I Love You Too Much* (later covered by Thelma Houston) and *Pity Little Billy Jo* being released in May and September 1975.

After this all too brief recording career, Barbara went back to what she did best, with two of her compositions, *Tell Me A Lie* and *In My Eyes* topping the country chart (by Sammi Jo and John Conlee respectively). *Tell Me A Lie* also attracted a version by Janie Fricke that peaked at number two, and combined the versions of the song have achieved more than a million plays on radio. Barbara did resurface as a singer, recording an album for the Calliope label in 1977.

XIT

A Native American rock group originally formed in Albuquerque, New Mexico by Tom Bee (a vocalist and writer who had a number of songs published by Jobete, including *Joyful Jukebox Music* recorded by The Jackson 5), A Michael Martinez (guitar and vocals), Lee Herrera (drums), Mac Suazo (bass) and R.C. Gariss (guitar) as Lincoln Street Exit, their new name XIT was an acronym for Crossing of Indian Tribes. They debuted on Rare Earth in 1972 with the concept album **Plight Of The Redman**, from which *I Was Raised* was lifted as a single, with both the album and single appearing on both sides of the Atlantic.

The following year saw **Silent Warrior** issued, together with the single *Reservation Of Education,* although only the single was ever issued in the UK. A third album, **Relocation** was scheduled for release on the main Motown label in the US but was unreleased at the time, subsequently turning up in 1977 on Canyon and 1994 on the Spalax Music label. Tom Bee would later form Sound Of America Records, the first Native American owned record label and was also instrumental in getting a Native American Folk category added to the annual Grammy Awards ceremony.

ALBUMS: PLIGHT OF THE REDMAN (1972), SILENT WARRIOR (1973)

YESTER-ME YESTER-YOU YESTERDAY – STEVIE WONDER [SINGLE]

Written by Ron Miller and Bryan Wells, *Yester-Me Yester-You Yesterday* was first recorded by Chris Clark in 1966, although her version didn't appear in any format until an anthology CD was released in the UK in 2005. Harvey Fuqua and Johnny Bristol then readied a version for Barbara McNair, with the musical arrangement being worked out by Paul Riser and the backing tracks laid down in December 1966. Barbara went into the Hitsville Studio on 14 January 1967 and recorded the song, but a week later the same backing tracks were utilised on a new version by Stevie Wonder, with The Originals providing the backing vocals.

Initially recorded with the intention of being included on his **I Was Made To Love Her** album, it was left off the released album for reasons unknown, although there is speculation that even in 1967 Stevie was keen to record as much of his own material as Berry Gordy would allow. *Yester-Me Yester-You Yesterday* was subsequently dusted down for single release in September 1969, the overall sound of the song having shown little sign of dating in the two years since it was recorded.

Yester-Me Yester-You Yesterday represented a return to the upper reaches of the chart, hitting #7 pop and #5 R&B in the US and making #2 in the UK, his biggest UK hit up to that point. Only The Archies and *Sugar Sugar* prevented Stevie from registering his first UK chart topper; he would have to wait another fifteen years before he finally exorcised that particular ghost. Two other Stevie Wonder versions of the song exist; *Mi Ayer, Tu Ayer El Ayer* (a Spanish version) and *Solo Te, Solo Me, Solo Noi* (Italian) being issued in those respective territories and can be found on the 2010 CD release **Motown Around The World**.

YOU ARE – LIONEL RICHIE [SINGLE]

Written by Lionel with his then wife Brenda, *You Are* represented a subtle departure from the norm where Lionel was concerned; virtually all of his major successes had come with ballads, harking back to his days as a member of The Commodores. Indeed, the first single lifted from his eponymous debut album in 1982 had been *Truly*, but *You Are* is a much more upbeat number than many of its predecessors. The US singles market took to *You Are* immediately, enabling the single to hit #2 R&B and #4 pop. It did not fare anywhere near as well in the UK, only making #43, something of a disappointment after two previous Top Ten hits.

YOU ARE EVERYTHING – DIANA ROSS & MARVIN GAYE [SINGLE]

Thom Bell and Linda Creed were busy trying to write material for The Stylistics, an act that had recently been signed by Avco and in the process of recording their debut album. Midway through the writing sessions, Thom and Linda hit something of a creative brick wall, struggling to get anything out of their writing sessions together. The pair left the office to stretch their legs and get some fresh air when Thom observed a man hurrying after a woman walking on the pavement. The man called out to the woman and apologised profusely when the woman turned around and he saw it wasn't who he thought it to be.

Excited, Thom told Linda they had to hurry back to the office as he had an idea for a song. That song became *You Are Everything*, which would be a million selling Top Ten hit for the Philadelphia group in 1971. For some reason, the single missed out in the UK (at least by The Stylistics; a cover version by The Pearls became a minor #41 hit), leaving a clear playing field for Diana Ross and Marvin Gaye's Hal Davis produced version to be issued in March 1974 as the follow-up to *You're A Special Part Of Me*, which had similarly given the UK charts a wide berth.

The presence of two major Motown names on one single helped propel the single up the charts, peaking at #5, a position The Stylistics original should have attained. As an added bonus, the single would shift over 250,000 copies, earning both Diana and Marvin a silver disc award from the BPI, their first such single awards. More than twenty years later the song was revived again, this time by Melanie Williams and Joe Roberts, who took their version to #28 on the British chart in 1995.

YOU ARE THE SUNSHINE OF MY LIFE – STEVIE WONDER [SINGLE]

One of Stevie Wonder's most endearing songs, *You Are The Sunshine Of My Life* was originally written shortly after Stevie had met future wife Syreeta. It was recorded at much the same time and was considered for inclusion on **Music Of My Mind**, although subsequently omitted and eventually resurrected a year later for **Talking Book**.

The opening vocals were provided by Jim Gilstrap, Lani Groves and Gloria Barley before Stevie came in with an uplifting declaration of love and affection, made all the more poignant by the fact that by the time the song was released as a single in February 1973, he and Syreeta had ended their personal relationship! Radio friendly to the extreme, *You Are The Sunshine Of My Life* went all the way to the top of the pop charts, even though it stalled at #3 on the R&B listings. The song and record would go on to garner three nominations at the Grammy Awards, for Record of the Year, Song of the Year and Best Male Pop Vocal Performance, winning the latter category.

In the UK the single returned Stevie top the Top Ten for the first time in three years (since *Never Had A Dream Come True*), hitting #7. Not surprisingly, *You Are The Sunshine Of My Life* has become one of Stevie's most covered songs, attracting versions by artists as diverse as Frank Sinatra, Tom Jones, Perry Como, Liza Minnelli, Acker Bilk, Andy Williams, Petula Clark and Ella Fitzgerald as well as a couple from Motown artists, including country artist Marty Mitchell who released both a single and album entitled *You Are The Sunshine Of My Life*.

YOU BEAT ME TO THE PUNCH – MARY WELLS [SINGLE]

Having found something of a winning formula for Mary Wells with *The One Who Really Loves You*, Smokey Robinson came up with more of the same for her follow-up single *You Beat Me To The Punch*. The calypso theme was still in evidence, as was the vocal backing of The Love Tones, but Smokey was creative enough to ensure that this wasn't *The One Who Really Loves You Part 2*.

"I always had people in mind, and I tried to tailor the songs to what I thought they would sound and feel like. I used to even pick words that they would sing well."

Fortunately for Smokey and Motown, Mary Wells sang all of the songs on *You Beat Me To The Punch* exceptionally well, turning in a performance that would ultimately become an even bigger hit than its predecessor. *You Beat Me To The Punch* would hit #9 on the pop chart and topped the R& listings, dethroning Booker T & The M.G.'s *Green Onions* in September 1962 in the process.

It also attracted something of an answer record, with Gene Chandler recording the novelty item *You Threw A Lucky Punch* with Cal Carter & Friends and hitting #25 R&B, although it was the flip side *Rainbow* that eventually became a bigger hit at #11. Mary's single was issued in the UK on the Oriole label in September 1962, two months after its American release, but like much of Motown's output at the time, was overlooked by British record buyers.

YOU CAN'T HURRY LOVE – THE SUPREMES [SINGLE]

The Supremes' hectic touring schedule created as many problems as it solved. Every successive hit further fuelled an already full itinerary, with the calibre of venue improving as each single hit its mark. Somehow, however, time had to be found for the girls to return to the studio to keep on recording, meaning they would often come off stage in some far flung place, get driven to the airport to catch a plane back to Detroit, record a couple of tracks and then head back out on the road.

Sometimes there would be just enough time to lay down the vocals for two or three numbers, a situation that occurred in June 1966 when The Supremes recorded both *You Can't Hurry Love* and *You Keep Me Hangin' On* in between engagements in San Francisco and Toronto, with Quality Control being given the final decision on which to release first. In the final analysis it didn't matter which was selected ahead of the other as they both would go on to top the charts, justifying Berry Gordy's clarion call that Motown would only release number one records on the group.

Constructed out of an earlier song Holland-Dozier-Holland had been working on called 'This Is Where I Came In', *You Can't Hurry Love* was a return to form for HDH. A chart topper on both the pop and R&B chart in the US, the song would have a particular resonance in the UK, with many seeing it as the track that heralded the arrival of a golden spell for Tamla Motown. A #3 hit at the time of release in September 1966, it was the first Top Twenty hit the label had enjoyed in some eighteen months; over the remaining three months of the year, a further six would follow.

The actual song also had an impact, with the intro later reworked by Paul Weller of The Jam on their hit *A Town Called Malice* and Hall & Oates would revisit elements on *Maneater*. In 1982 former Genesis drummer Phil Collins recorded a cover version that would make it all the way to the top of the UK charts for two weeks, aided by an accompanying video that saw him portray all three of The Supremes! His version also had enough legs to make the Top Ten in the US, proof of the song's endearing qualities.

YOU HAVEN'T DONE NOTHIN' – STEVIE WONDER [SINGLE]

Social commentary had provided Stevie Wonder with the biggest hits of his career on the **Innervisions** album, but its successor **Fulfillingness First Finale** concentrated more on the spiritual side. The main exception was *You Haven't Done Nothin'*, a statement from Stevie Wonder to then President Richard Nixon. Written when Wonder was at his creative peak and the full background to Richard Nixon's re-election was not in the public domain, *You Haven't Done Nothin'* was musically reminiscent of *Superstition*. By the time the track was extracted for single release, however, the Watergate scandal was dominating the national papers and Richard Nixon was shortly to resign rather than be impeached.

"Everybody promises you everything, but in the end, nothing comes out of it," Stevie said at the time of release. "I don't vote for anybody until after they have really done something that I know about. I want to see them do something first. The only trouble is that you always hear the President or people say that they are doing all they can. And they feed you with hopes for years and years. But that is probably typical of most people in very important positions who have a lot of power. I'm sick and tired of listening to all their lies."

Featuring Reggie McBride on bass and Stevie on virtually everything else, save for the vocal backing that was provided by The Jackson 5, *You Haven't Done Nothin'* (coupled with the equally scathing *Big Brother*) was a timely release, hitting #1 on both the R&B and pop charts in October 1974 as America vented its anger on the disgraced president and the government.

That might account for its lack of success in the UK; it peaked at #30.

YOU KEEP ME HANGIN' ON – THE SUPREMES [SINGLE]

With *You Can't Hurry Love* having restored The Supremes to the top of the pop (and R&B) charts after an absence of two official singles (plus two Christmas singles released at the tail end of 1965), Motown wasted little time in maintaining the momentum with the release of *You Keep Me Hangin' On* barely two months later. Writers Brian and Eddie Holland and Lamont Dozier recorded the backing tracks for several potential hits during the summer of 1966, with *You Keep Me Hangin' On* initially being given the working title of *Pay Back*.

The group recorded their vocals on 30 June, returning to the studio the following day in order to redo the song, with additional overdubs being added at the very start of August, including 'fattening up the rhythm' by making it sound like three or four guitars were playing the song's introduction. Yet for all the instrumentation, what the single revealed most was the growing maturity of the vocals, most notably Diana on lead, which would strike a chord with the record buying public.

Released in October 1966, with *You Can't Hurry Love* still on the listing, *You Keep Me Hangin' On* would emulate its predecessor and top both the pop and R&B charts, spending two weeks at the top of the former and four weeks on the latter, also making #8 in the UK.

In 1967, psychedelic rock group Vanilla Fudge recorded an extended version of the song which ran for nearly seven minutes (reportedly recorded in one take), which was then edited down to three minutes and released as a single – it hit #6 in the US and #18 in UK. Nearly two decades later, British singer Kim Wilde recorded an updated version that would top the US charts for one week in June 1987, having peaked at #2 in the UK behind Berlin's *Take My Breath Away*.

YOUR PRECIOUS LOVE – MARVIN GAYE & TAMMI TERRELL [SINGLE]

One of the songs Nickolas Ashford and Valerie Simpson wrote in New York and presented to their Detroit paymasters in 1967, *Your Precious Love* was earmarked for Marvin Gaye and Tammi Terrell, with Harvey Fuqua and Johnny Bristol assigned to produce. Harvey and Johnny didn't only produce either, for the pair also joined Marvin and Tammi on backing vocals, with Johnny claiming that the four billed themselves the Riff Brothers Plus One for the purposes of the recording session. Yet it was Marvin and Tammi's performances that really stood out, as Marvin would later reveal to biographer David Ritz.

"What we accomplished was to create two characters and let them sing to each other. That's how the Marvin and Tammi characters were born. While we were singing, we were in love, but when the music ended, we kissed each other on the cheek and said goodbye."

For the three minutes plus the single lasts, it is possible to believe they are in love, so effective are their respective vocal performances. Indeed, it was performances like this that convinced everyone outside of Motown (and no doubt one or two inside, most notably Marvin's wife Anna) that the pair were more than just singing partners, that the only way they were able to get that special closeness inside the studio was by maintaining that closeness elsewhere. The scrutiny would only grow too, aided by the success of *Your Precious Love*, which would mark Tammi's first appearance in the Top Ten of the pop chart (where it peaked at #5) and also make #2 on the R&B listings, even if it failed to make much of an impression in the UK. The song itself has also been covered by a slew of artists since its release, most notably by Neil Sedaka and his daughter Dara who enjoyed an Adult Contemporary hit with it in 1984.

YOU'RE ALL I NEED TO GET BY – MARVIN GAYE & TAMMI TERRELL [SINGLE]

The very first batch of songs Nickolas Ashford and Valerie Simpson took to Motown were effectively a collection of songs that could have been recorded by any of the Motown stable, although as it turned out pretty much everything they brought would be assigned to Marvin Gaye and Tammi Terrell. With those songs turning out to be a success, Nickolas and Valerie began writing almost exclusively for Marvin and Tammi and, eventually, were also given the opportunity of producing the sessions themselves.

You're All I Need To Get By also features Valerie on piano, with her and her future husband Nickolas adding their backing vocals to Marvin and Tammi's, creating the same kind of cosy vocal foursome that Marvin, Tammi, Harvey Fuqua and Johnny Bristol had achieved. Yet the recording sessions for the single were somewhat drawn out, with the backing tracks being recorded in mid April 1968 and the strings and horns added by the end of the month. The demo lead vocals (by Valerie and Nickolas; whilst Valerie's vocal style was very similar to Tammi's, Nickolas chose to do the male vocal very straight, reasoning that Marvin would put his own spin on it when it came to record the finished version) were recorded on 21 May, with Marvin and Tammi coming in to lay down their vocals the following day.

Not entirely happy with the session, Marvin returned a day later and Tammi nearly a week later to redo their respective parts, with both coming into the studio on 29 May to finally nail the song. Released in July 1968, the finalised version proved worth the additional effort, hitting the top of the R&B chart and making #7 pop. The single would also become the pair's biggest hit internationally too, making #19 in the UK, although it was later surpassed by *The Onion Song*.

Ten years later Johnny Mathis and Deniece Williams recorded a cover version that also became a hit, peaking at #47 in the US and #45 in the UK.

YOU'RE MY EVERYTHING – THE TEMPTATIONS [SINGLE]

Featuring a rare return to lead vocal duties for Eddie Kendricks, *You're My Everything* was especially crafted for the singer by main writers Cornelius Grant (also the group's resident lead guitarist) and Roger Penzabene. It was Cornelius who had noticed that out on the road, the female audiences were invariably drawn towards Eddie, even if David Ruffin was usually to be found out front. He put a picture of Eddie singing to his girl in Roger's mind, with the lyrics to *You're My Everything* quickly falling into place.

Licked into final shape by Norman Whitfield, the backing tracks were recorded in December 1966, with strings and vocals being added some two months later. To be found on The Temptations album **The Temptations With A Lot 'O Soul**, the track was lifted as a single a month before the album and proved a major success, hitting #6 pop and #3 R&B, also returning to the group to the charts in the UK where it would reach #26. The flip side *I've Been Good To You*, written by Smokey Robinson and originally recorded by The Miracles (who took the single to #103) also made an impact, hitting #124 and bubbling under for several weeks.

YOU'VE REALLY GOT A HOLD ON ME – THE MIRACLES [SINGLE]

You've Really Got A Hold On Me has become one of Smokey Robinson's most covered songs, attracting versions from artists as diverse as The Beatles, Mickey Gilley and countless others. Yet when originally released in November 1962, it languished as a B-side to *Happy Landing*, Motown believing that The Miracles were in need of an up-tempo song as a single. Smokey was in New York on business when he retired to his hotel room and turned on the radio, which played Sam Cooke's *Bring It On Home To Me* as it was then in the charts.

Duly inspired, Smokey wrote *You Really Got A Hold On Me* and, upon returning to Detroit, went into the studio on 16 October 1962 and recorded both tracks, *Happy Landing* and *You Really Got A Hold On Me* on the same day. *Happy Landing* attracted some interest, with regional radio giving it sufficient plays to enable it to appear on a number of charts, but it was the national disc jockeys who flipped it, giving *You Really Got A Hold On Me* a growing number of plays and a subsequent place on the national chart. Despite the group's own promotional efforts being somewhat hampered by Smokey being laid low by a bout of Asian flu and Pete Moore missing from the touring line-up as he had been drafted, the single would go on to hit #8 pop and top the R&B chart, thus becoming one of the group's biggest hits of their early career.

MONALISA YOUNG

Born in Los Angeles, California Monalisa Young came from a musical family, with her father a composer and her mother a classically trained opera singer. Monalisa also undertook opera training as a youngster, although her professional singing career has covered virtually every musical genre *but* opera. She toured with the likes of Bob Dylan, Joe Cocker and Neil Diamond during the 1970s before becoming a part of disco troupe Saint Tropez in time for their third album **Hot And Nasty**, featuring on several dance hits.

That eventually led to a contract with Motown in 1983, working with legendary producer Hal Davis on her debut **Knife**, which saw her doing cover versions of several well-known Motown hits, including *Superstition*, *Don't Mess With Bill* and three Jackson 5 songs. These included *Dancing Machine* which was lifted as a single, along with *Sweet Remedy* which appeared in February 1984. The shortage of new material counted against the album however, and

Monalisa was dropped soon after. She later joined the World Class Wreckin' Cru, who did feature on the charts.
ALBUM: KNIFE (1983)

VAL YOUNG

Although best known as a protégé of Rick James, Val Young's undoubted talents had first been spotted by George Clinton, himself no slouch when it came to unearthing rough diamonds. Born Valaria Young in Detroit, Michigan on 13 June 1958, Val was hired as a backing vocalist by George Clinton for The Brides Of Funkenstein, spending twelve months within the Parliafunkadelicment camp. Val then recorded and toured with Roy Ayers and later The Gap Band before approaching Rick James looking for a solo career.

Rick was impressed enough to recommend her to Gordy Records, also concocting a marketing campaign that saw her presented as the 'Black Marilyn Monroe'. Her debut album **Seduction**, produced by Rick was released in July 1985 and promoted largely on the back of a five month tour with Rick James and his other acts Mary Jane Girls and Process & The Doo Rags. The album would hit #39 on the R&B chart and give rise to two R&B hits in *Seduction* (#17) and *If You Should Ever Be Lonely* (#21).

Even before Val could think about recording a follow-up album, Rick ran into problems with Motown over the status of his growing stable of artists, with a legal wrangle preventing Val from recording, at least for Motown. In 1987 Val signed to Amherst Records in New York, releasing her follow-up later the same year.
ALBUM: SEDUCTION (1985)

THE YOUNG RASCALS

The Young Rascals formed in New York City in 1964 by Felix Cavaliere (born in Pelham, New York on 29 February 1943, keyboards and vocals), Dino Danelli (born in New York on 23 July 1945, drums), Eddie Brigati (born in New York on 22 October 1946, vocals) and Gene Cornish (born in Ottawa, Canada on 14 May 1946, guitar), all of whom with the exception of Daneli having previously been members of Joey Dee's Starlighters. The group recorded as The Rascals from 1968 until they disbanded in 1972 but reformed in 1988. Their 1966 chart topper *Good Lovin'* appeared on the soundtrack to 'The Big Chill', with their cover version of *In The Midnight Hour* (which originally appeared on the same album as *Good Lovin'*, **The Young Rascals**) appearing on the subsequent **More Songs From 'The Big Chill'**.

Z

CAPTAIN ZAP & THE MOTORTOWN CUT-UPS

A second attempt by Motown at a cut-in record, the first having been Bert Haney and Brice Armstrong's 1963 outing. *The Luney Landing* backed with *The Luney Take-Off* was released on 16 July 1969, the very day the Apollo 11 mission set off for the moon, with the single being somewhat unique in that it featured all Motown clips. Background information on the makers of the single is sparse, with the only credit being production by 'David And William In Their Spare Time'.

NICK ZESSES

Nick Zesses first linked with Dino Fekaris in a vocal duo called Nick & Dino, recording a single for Harry Balk's Impact label, *Wish I Was A Kid Again* backed with *Boy*. John Rhys was responsible for producing the single and joined with Nick and Dino in a songwriting partnership that penned *Time Will Pass You By* for Tobi Legend, released on the Mala label in 1968. Nick would also become a member of Motown groups Other People and Matrix with Dino, the latter group also featuring producer Tom Baird.

However, it is as a writer and producer that Nick made his name at Motown, penning numerous hits and handling production for the likes of Rare Earth, Riot and Stoney & Meatloaf. Whilst several of his compositions have subsequently appeared in film, in 1974 Nick and Dino were arrangers and producers of the soundtrack to 'Sugar Hill', something of a zombie blaxploitation film starring Marki Bey and featuring The Originals singing the theme song.

ZULEMA

Born in Tampa, Florida on 3 January 1947, Zulema Cusseaux linked with schoolfriends Brenda Hilliard and

Albert Bailey as The Lovelles, changing their name to Faith, Hope & Charity when signed by Maxwell Records in 1970. Zulema left for a solo career the following year, signing with Sussex Records and releasing her eponymous album in 1972. She also performed at the PUSH Expo in Chicago, with her performance of *This Child Of Mine* featuring in both the film and soundtrack, with the latter released by Motown in April 1974.

BIBLIOGRAPHY

Abbott, Kingsley – *Calling Out Around The World: A Motown Reader*
Betts, Graham – *Complete UK Hit Albums*
Betts, Graham – *Complete UK Hit Singles*
Betts, Graham – *Michael Jackson: A Celebration*
Cadman, Chris & Craig Halstead – *Michael Jackson: The Early Years*
Dahl, Bill – *Motown: The Golden Years*
Dannen, Fredric – *Hit Men*
Davis, Sharon – *Chinwaggin*
Davis, Sharon – *Marvin Gaye: I Heard It Through The Grapevine*
Davis, Sharon – *Motown The History*
Davis, Sharon – *Stevie Wonder: Rhythms Of Wonder*
Elsner, Constance – *Stevie Wonder*
Gaye, Frankie – *Marvin Gaye, My Brother*
George, Nelson – *Where Did Our Love Go*
Gordy, Berry – *To Be Loved*
Jefferson, Margo – *On Michael Jackson*
Knight, Gladys – *Between Each Line Of Pain And Glory: My Life Story*
MacKenzie, Alex – *The Motown Stars*
Posner, Gerald – *Motown: Music, Money, Sex, And Power*
Rees, Dafydd & Luke Crampton – *Encyclopedia Of Rock Stars*
Ribowsky, Mark – *Ain't Too Proud To Beg: The Troubled Lives And Enduring Soul Of The Temptations*
Ribowsky, Mark – *The Supremes: A Saga of Motown Dreams, Success, And Betrayal*
Rodgers, Nile – *Le Freak*
Rosen, Craig – *Number One Albums*
Ross, Diana – *Secrets Of A Sparrow*
Taraborrelli, J Randy – *Diana Ross*
Taraborrelli, J Randy – *Michael Jackson*
Terrana, Ralph – *The Road Through Motown*
Turner, Steve – *Trouble Man: The Life And Death Of Marvin Gaye*
Waller, Don – *The Motown Story*
Whitburn, Joel – *Bubbling Under The Billboard Hot 100 1959-2004*
Whitburn, Joel – *Hot Dance/Disco 1974-2003*
Whitburn, Joel – *The Billboard Albums*
Whitburn, Joel – *The Billboard Hot 100 Annual*
Whitburn, Joel – *Top Pop Singles 1955-2002*
Whitburn, Joel – *Top R&B/Hip Hop Singles*
White, Adam – *The Motown Story*
White, Adam & Fred Bronson – *Number One Rhythm & Blues Hits*
Williams, Otis with Patricia Romanowski - *Temptations*
Wilson, Mary – *Dreamgirl*
Wilson, Mary – *Supreme Faith*
Wilson, Terry – *Tamla Motown: The Stories Behind The UK Singles*

ABOUT THE AUTHOR

Born in London in 1957 Graham began his working career training to be an architect before switching to the music industry in 1978 as a Press Officer with Pye Records. He subsequently went on to work for CBS Records (where he was Head of Press) and a number of budget labels, including Tring, before becoming Artist & Repertoire Manager for the Hallmark label. He is currently A&R Manager for the Pickwick Group. He has written for numerous magazines and publications over the last twenty five years, including Blues & Soul, Record Buyer and The History Of Rock. A contributor to numerous books on music and football, Graham has also had more than thirty published under his own name.

George Michael: Read Without Prejudice (UFO Publishing 1997) ISBN 978-1-873884-92-8
Spurs – A Day To Day Life (Mainstream Publishing 1998) – ISBN 1-84018-040-4
The Villans – A Day To Day Life (Mainstream Publishing 1998) – ISBN 1-84018-033-1
The Gers – A Day To Day Life (Mainstream Publishing 1998) – ISBN 1-84018-032-3
United – A Day To Day Life (Mainstream Publishing 1998) – ISBN 1-84018-038-2
The Toffees – A Day To Day Life (Mainstream Publishing 1998) – ISBN 1-84018-036-6
United Factfile (Parragon 1998) – ISBN 0-75252-550-6
Complete UK Hit Singles 1952-2004 (Harper Collins 2004) – ISBN 0-00-717931-6
Complete British Hit Albums (Harper Collins 2004) – ISBN 0-00-719551-6
Complete UK Hit Singles 1952-2005 (Harper Collins 2005) – ISBN 0-00-720076-5
Complete UK Hit Albums 1956-2005 (Harper Collins 2005) – ISBN 0-00-720532-5
The Little Book Of Chelsea (Green Umbrella 2005) – ISBN 1-905009-24-0
Complete UK Hit Singles 1952-2006 (Harper Collins 2006) – ISBN 0-00-720077-3
History Of The World Cup (Sutton Publishing 2006) – ISBN 0-7509-4490-0
England Player By Player (Green Umbrella 2006) – ISBN 1-905009-63-1
The Little Book Of European Football (Green Umbrella 2006) – ISBN 1-905828-01-2
The Little Book Of Football Legends (Green Umbrella 2006) – ISBN 1-905009-49-6
The Little Book Of Spurs (Green Umbrella 2006) – ISBN 1-905009-69-0
Greatest Moments Of Football (Green Umbrella 2007) – ISBN 978-1-906229-39-9
Legends Of Football (Green Umbrella 2007) – ISBN 978-1-905828-33-3
England Player By Player (Green Umbrella 2007) – ISBN 978-905828-12-8
The DVD Book Of Tottenham Hotspur (Green Umbrella 2007) – ISBN 978-1-906229-13-9
The Little Book Of Celtic (Green Umbrella 2007) – ISBN 978-1-905009-88-6
The Little Book Of Rangers (Green Umbrella 2007) – ISBN 978-1-905009-89-3
Country Legends (Green Umbrella 2008) - ISBN 978-1-905828-73-9
The DVD Book Of England (Green Umbrella 2008) – ISBN 978-1-906229-09-2
The DVD Book Of Tottenham Hotspur (Green Umbrella 2008) – ISBN 978-1-906229-92-4
Michael Jackson 1958-2009 A Celebration (Reynolds & Hearn 2009) ISBN 978-1904674-10-8
Rihanna: Bad Girl (Flame Tree Publishing 2012) – ISBN 978-0-85775-275-8
Michael Jackson A Celebration (G2 Entertainment 2012) ISBN 978-1-909-040-81-6
The Little Book Of Spurs (G2 Entertainment 2012) – ISBN 978-1-907803-08-6
England Player By Player (Demand Media 2013) – ISBN 978-1-909217-40-9

Printed in Germany
by Amazon Distribution
GmbH, Leipzig